CHAMBERS
Book of Facts

Editor

MIN LEE

Chambers

EDINBURGH NEW YORK

Published 1992 by W & R Chambers Ltd
43–45 Annandale Street, Edinburgh EH7 4AZ

British Library Cataloguing in Publication Data

A catalogue record for this book is available from the British Library

ISBN 0 550 17255 6

This book includes information assembled for Chambers *Quick Facts*, extensively revised and updated.

Compilers
Antonia Dodds
Thérèse Duriez
Melanie Hanbury
Jo Hargreaves
Kieran Lee
Mary Lorenz
Hazel Muir
Ruth Thomas
David Whyte

Cover design by Art and Graphics Ltd, Edinburgh

Typeset by Charlesworth & Co Ltd
Printed in England by Clays, St Ives plc

CONTENTS

SPACE

EARTH

NATURAL HISTORY

HUMAN LIFE

HISTORY

HISTORY *continued*

SOCIAL STRUCTURE

COMMUNICATION

SCIENCE, ENGINEERING AND MEASUREMENT

ARTS AND CULTURE

SPORT AND GAMES

THOUGHT AND BELIEF

ALPHABETICAL CONTENTS

ABBREVIATIONS USED IN BOOK OF FACTS

AD Anno Domini
admin administration
AD Before Christ
c century
c. circa
C Celsius (Centigrade)
C central
cc cubic centimetre(s)
Chin Chinese
cm centimetre(s)
Co County
cont. continued
cu cubic
cwt hundredweight(s)
e estimate
E east(ern)
eg for example
Eng English
F Fahrenheit
fl oz fluid ounce(s)
fl flourished (floruit)
Fr French
Ft foot (feet)
g gram(s)
gall gallons
Ger German
Gr Greek
h hour(s)
ha hectare(s)
Hung Hungarian
I(s) Island(s)
ie that is (id est)
in inch(es)
Ir Irish
Ital Italian
Jap Japanese
K Kelvin
kg kilogram(s)
kJ kilojoules
km kilometre(s)
l litre(s)
L Lake
Lat Latin
lb pound(s)
l y light year(s)
m metre(s)
min minute(s)
ml mile(s)
mm millimetre(s)
Mt Mount(ain)
Mts Mountains
N north(ern)
no. number
oz ounce(s)
p(p) page(s)
pop population
Port Portuguese
pt pint(s)
r. reigned
R River
Russ Russian
S South(ern)
sec second(s)
Span Spanish
sq square
St Saint
Sta Santa
Ste Sainte
Swed Swedish
TV Television
UT Unified Team
v. versus
vols. volumes
W west(ern)
yd yard(s)
Z zodiac

Other conventions

Months in parenthesis are abbreviated to the first three letters (3 Jan 1817)

National holiday abbreviations p 264
Currency abbreviations pp 241–263
Chemistry abbreviations p 387
International organizations pp 273, 275

SPACE

PLANETARY DATA

Planet	Distance from sun (million km/ml) Maximum		Minimum		Sidereal period	Axial rotation period (equatorial)	Diameter (equatorial) km	ml
Mercury	69.4	43.0	46.8	29.0	88 d	58 d 16 h	4878	3031
Venus	109.0	67.6	107.6	66.7	224.7 d	243 d	12104	7521
Earth	152.6	94.6	147.4	91.4	365.26 [1]	23 h 56 m	12756	7927
Mars	249.2	154.5	207.3	128.5	687 d	24 h 37 m 23 s	6794	4222
Jupiter	817.4	506.8	741.6	459.8	11.86 y	9 h 50 m 30 s	142800	88700
Saturn	1512	937.6	1346	834.6	29.46 y	10 h 14 m	120000	74600
Uranus	3011	1867	2740	1699	84.01 y	16–28 h [2]	52000	32300
Neptune	4543	2817	4466	2769	164.79 y	18–20 h [2]	48400	30000
Pluto	7364	4566	4461	2766	247.7 y	6 d 9 h	1145	711

[1] 365 d 5 h 48 m 46 s [2] Different latitudes rotate at different speeds.
y: years d: days h: hours m: minutes s: seconds km: kilometres ml: miles

PLANETARY SATELLITES

	Year discovered	Distance from planet km	ml	Diameter km	ml
Earth					
Moon	–	384000	238000	3476	2155
Mars					
Phobos	1877	938000	583000	27	17
Deimos	1877	2346000	1458000	15	9
Jupiter					
Metis	1979	128000	79000	40	25
Adrastea	1979	129000	80000	24	15
Amalthea	1892	181000	112000	270	168
Thebe	1979	222000	138000	100	60
Io	1610	422000	262000	3650	5850
Europa	1610	671000	417000	3400	1925
Ganymede	1610	1070000	665000	5260	3270
Callisto	1610	1883000	1170000	4800	3000
Leda	1974	11110000	6904000	20	12
Himalia	1904	11480000	7134000	180	110
Lysithea	1938	11720000	7283000	40	25
Elara	1905	11740000	7295000	80	50
Ananke	1951	21200000	13174000	30	19
Carme	1938	22600000	14044000	40	25
Pasiphae	1908	23500000	14603000	50	30
Sinope	1914	23700000	14727000	40	25

PLANETARY SATELLITES (cont.)

	Year discovered	Distance from planet km	ml	Diameter km	ml
Saturn					
Atlas	1980	138 000	86 000	40	25
1980 S27	1980	139 000	86 000	100	60
1980 S26	1980	142 000	88 000	100	60
Epimetheus	1980	151 000	94 000	140	90
Janus	1980	151 000	94 000	200	120
Mimas	1789	186 000	116 000	390	240
Enceladus	1789	238 000	148 000	500	310
Calypso	1980	295 000	183 000	30	19
Telesto	1980	295 000	183 000	24	15
Tethys	1684	295 000	183 000	1 050	650
Dione	1684	377 000	234 000	1 120	700
Dione B	1982	378 000	235 000	15	9
Rhea	1672	527 000	327 000	1 530	950
Titan	1655	1 222 000	759 000	5 150	3200
Hyperion	1848	1 481 000	920 000	400	250
Iapetus	1671	3 560 000	2 212 000	1 440	900
Phoebe	1898	12 965 000	8 047 000	160	100
1990S18	1990	~135 000		~10	
Uranus					
Miranda	1948	130 000	81 000	400	250
Ariel	1851	191 000	119 000	1 300	800
Umbriel	1851	266 000	165 000	1 100	700
Titania	1787	436 000	271 000	1 600	1000
Oberon	1787	583 000	362 000	1 600	1000
Cordelia	1986	49 300	31 000	15	9
Ophelia	1986	53 300	33 000	20	12
Bianca	1986	59 100	37 000	50	30
Cressida	1986	61 750	38 000	70	40
Desdemona	1986	62 700	39 000	50	30
Juliet	1986	64 350	40 000	70	40
Portia	1986	66 090	41 000	90	55
Rosalind	1986	69 920	43 000	50	30
Belinda	1986	75 100	47 000	50	30
Puck	1986	85 890	53 000	170	105
Neptune					
Triton	1846	355 000	221 000	3 800	2 400
Nereid	1949	5 510 000	3 424 000	300	190
1989 N6	1989	48 200	30 000	50	30
1989 N5	1989	50 000	31 000	90	55
1989 N3	1989	52 500	33 000	140	90
1989 N4	1989	62 000	39 000	160	100
1989 N2	1989	73 600	46 000	200	125
1989 N1	1989	117 600	73 000	420	260
Pluto					
Charon	1978	20 000 000	12 500 000	1 000	620

ANNUAL METEOR SHOWERS

Meteors appear to radiate from named star region

Name	Dates	Star region	Name	Dates	Star region
Quadrantids	1–6 January	Beta Boötis	Leonids	14–20 November	Zeta Leonis
Lyrids	19–22 April	Nu Herculis	Andromedids	26 November–4 December	Gamma Andromedae
Eta Aquarids	1–8 May	Eta Aquarii			
Delta Aquarids	15 July–10 August	Delta Aquarii	Geminids	9–13 December	Castor
Perseids	27 July–17 August	Eta Persei	Ursids	20–22 December	Kocab
Orionids	15–25 October	Nu Orionis			

TOTAL & ANNULAR SOLAR ECLIPSES 1991–2007

Date	Extent of eclipse	Visible from parts of[1]
15 January 1991	Annular[2]	S Pacific, New Zealand, S Australia
11 July 1991	Total	Mid-Pacific, C & S America
4–5 January 1992	Annular	N American coast, Mid-Pacific
30 June 1992	Total	S American coast, S Atlantic Ocean
10 May 1994	Annular	Mid-Pacific, N America, N Africa
3 November 1994	Total	Indian Ocean, S Atlantic, S America, Mid-Pacific
29 April 1995	Annular	S Pacific, S America
24 October 1995	Total	Middle East, S Asia, S Pacific
9 March 1997	Total	C & N Asia, Arctic
26 February 1998	Total	Mid-Pacific, C America, N Atlantic
22 August 1998	Annular	Indonesia, S Pacific, Indian Ocean
16 February 1999	Annular	Indian Ocean, Australia
11 August 1999	Total	N Atlantic, N Europe, Middle East, N India
21 June 2001	Total	S Atlantic, S Africa, Madagascar
14 December 2001	Annular	Pacific, C America
10 June 2002	Annular	Indonesia, Pacific, Mexico
4 December 2002	Total	S Africa, Indian Ocean, Australia
31 May 2003	Annular	Iceland, Greenland
23 November 2003	Total	Antarctic
8 April 2005	Annular/ Total	Pacific, Panama, Venezuela
3 October 2005	Annular	Atlantic, Spain, Libya, Indian Ocean
29 March 2006	Total	Atlantic, Libya, Turkey, Russia
22 September 2006	Annular	Guyana, Atlantic, Indian Ocean

[1] The eclipse begins in the first country named.
[2] In an annular eclipse a ring-shaped part of the sun remains visible.

LUNAR ECLIPSES 1991–2008

Date	Percentage eclipsed	Time of mid-eclipse	Where visible
21 December 1991	Partial	10.34	Pacific, N America (W Coast), Japan, Australia
15 June 1992	Partial	04.58	N, C and S America, W Africa
9–10 December 1992	Total	23.45	Africa, Europe, Middle East, part of S America
4 June 1993	Total	13.02	Pacific, Australia, SE Asia
29 November 1993	Total	06.26	N and S America
25 May 1994	Partial	03.32	C and S America, part of N America, W Africa
15 April 1995	Partial	12.19	Pacific, Australia, SE Asia
4 April 1996	Total	00.11	Africa, SE Europe, S America
27 September 1996	Total	02.55	C and S America, part of N America, W Africa
24 March 1997	Partial	04.41	C and S America, part of N America, W Africa
16 September 1997	Total	18.47	S Africa, E Africa, Australia
28 July 1999	Partial	11.34	Pacific, Australia, SE Asia
21 January 2000	Total	04.45	N America, part of S America, SW Europe, W Africa
16 July 2000	Total	13.57	Pacific, Australia, SE Asia
9 January 2001	Total	20.22	Europe, Asia, Africa
5 July 2001	Partial	14.57	Asia, Australia, Pacific
16 May 2003	Total	03.41	Americas, Europe, Africa
9 November 2003	Total	01.20	Americas, Europe, Africa, W Asia
4 May 2004	Total	20.32	Europe, Africa, Asia
28 October 2004	Total	03.05	Americas, Europe, Africa
17 October 2005	Partial	12.05	E Asia, Pacific, N America
7 September 2006	Partial	18.53	Australia, Asia, E Africa
3 March 2007	Total	23.22	Europe, Asia, Africa
28 August 2007	Total	10.39	Australia, Pacific, part of N America
21 February 2008	Total	03.27	Americas, Europe, Africa
16 August 2008	Partial	21.12	Europe, Africa, W Asia

THE LUNAR ‘SEAS’

Latin name	English name
Lacus Somniorum	Lake of Dreams
Mare Australe	Southern Sea
Mare Crisium	Sea of Crises
Mare Fecunditatis	Sea of Fertility
Mare Frigoris	Sea of Cold
Mare Humboldtianum	Humboldt's Sea
Mare Humorum	Sea of Humours
Mare Imbrium	Sea of Showers
Mare Ingenii	Sea of Geniuses
Mare Marginis	Marginal Sea
Mare Moscoviense	Moscow Sea
Mare Nectaris	Sea of Nectar
Mare Nubium	Sea of Clouds
Mare Orientale	Eastern Sea
Mare Serenitatis	Sea of Serenity
Mare Smythii	Smyth's Sea
Mare Spumans	Foaming Sea
Mare Tranquillitatis	Sea of Tranquillity
Mare Undarum	Sea of Waves
Mare Vaporum	Sea of Vapours
Oceanus Procellarum	Ocean of Storms
Palus Epidemiarum	Marsh of Epidemics
Palus Putredinis	Marsh of Decay
Palus Somnii	Marsh of Sleep
Sinus Adstuum	Bay of Heats
Sinus Iridum	Bay of Rainbows
Sinus Medii	Central Bay
Sinus Roris	Bay of Dew

THE CONSTELLATIONS

Latin name	English name
Andromeda	Andromeda
Antlia	Air Pump
Apus	Bird of Paradise
Aquarius (Z)	Water Bearer
Aquila	Eagle
Ara	Altar
Aries (Z)	Ram
Auriga	Charioteer
Boötes	Herdsman
Caelum	Chisel
Camelopardalis	Giraffe
Cancer (Z)	Crab
Canes Venatici	Hunting Dogs
Canis Major	Great Dog
Canis Minor	Little Dog
Capricornus (Z)	Sea Goat
Carina	Keel
Cassiopeia	Cassiopeia
Centaurus	Centaur
Cepheus	Cepheus
Cetus	Whale
Chamaeleon	Chameleon
Circinus	Compasses
Columba	Dove
Coma Berenices	Berenice's Hair
Corona Australis	Southern Crown
Corona Borealis	Northern Crown
Corvus	Crow
Crater	Cup
Crux	Southern Cross
Cygnus	Swan
Delphinus	Dolphin
Dorado	Swordfish
Draco	Dragon
Equuleus	Little Horse
Eridanus	River Eridanus
Fornax	Furnace
Gemini (Z)	Twins
Grus	Crane
Hercules	Hercules
Horologium	Clock
Hydra	Sea Serpent
Hydrus	Water Snake
Indus	Indian
Lacerta	Lizard
Leo (Z)	Lion
Leo Minor	Little Lion
Lepus	Hare
Libra (Z)	Scales
Lupus	Wolf
Lynx	Lynx
Lyra	Harp
Mensa	Table
Microscopium	Microscope
Monoceros	Unicorn
Musca	Fly
Norma	Level
Octans	Octant
Ophiuchus	Serpent Bearer
Orion	Orion
Pavo	Peacock
Pegasus	Winged Horse
Perseus	Perseus
Phoenix	Phoenix
Pictor	Easel
Pisces (Z)	Fishes
Piscis Austrinus	Southern Fish
Puppis	Ship's Stern
Pyxis	Mariner's Compass
Reticulum	Net
Sagitta	Arrow
Sagittarius (Z)	Archer
Scorpius (Z)	Scorpion
Sculptor	Sculptor
Scutum	Shield
Serpens	Serpent
Sextans	Sextant
Taurus (Z)	Bull
Telescopium	Telescope
Triangulum	Triangle
Triangulum Australe	Southern Triangle
Tucana	Toucan
Ursa Major	Great Bear
Ursa Minor	Little Bear
Vela	Sails
Virgo (Z)	Virgin
Volans	Flying Fish
Vulpecula	Fox

Z: Found on the Zodiac

LARGEST GROUND-BASED TELESCOPES

Telescope name	Type	Observatory	Site (altitude m/ft)	Mirror/dish size	Founded
Anglo-Australian Telescope (AAT)	optical	Anglo-Australian Observatory	Siding Spring Mountain NSW, Australia (1 165 m/ 3 820 ft)	3.9 m	1974
Arecibo Telescope	radio	National Astronomy and Ionosphere Centre	Puerto Rico 496 m	304.8 m	1963
Australia Telescope	radio	Commonwealth Scientific and Industrial Research Organisation	Throughout NSW, Australia	7 × 22 m, 1 × 64 m	1989 or 1990

LARGEST GROUND-BASED TELESCOPES (cont.)

Telescope name	Type	Observatory	Site (altitude m/ft)	Mirror/dish size	Founded
Bol'shoi Teleskop Azimutal'nyi	optical	Special Astrophysical Observatory	Mt Pastukhov, Zehenshuskaia, Russia (2 100 m/ 6 900 ft)	6.0 m	1976
—	optical	Byurakan Astrophysical Observatory	Mt Aragatz, Armenia (1 500 m/ 5 000 ft)	2.6 m	1976
C Donald Shane Telescope	optical	Lick Observatory	Mt Hamilton California, USA (1 277 m/ 4 190 ft)	3.05 m	1959
California Submillimetre Observatory	submillimetre	California Institute of Technology	Mauna Kea, Hawaii, USA (4 160 m/ 13 650 ft)	10.4 m	1986
Canada-France-Hawaii Telescope (CFHT)	optical	Canada-France-Hawaii Telescope Corporation	Mauna Kea, Hawaii, USA (4 180 m/ 13 720 ft)	3.6 m	1979
—	optical	Cerro Tololo Inter-American Observatory	Cerro Tololo, Chile (2 160 m/ 7 100 ft)	4.0 m	1976
Effelsberg Radio Telescope	radio	Max Planck Institut für Radioastronomie	Effelsberg, nr Bonn, Germany	100 m	1971
ESO New Technology Telescope	optical	European Southern Observatory	Cerro Tololo, Chile (2 160 m/ 7 100 ft)	3.6 m	1990
ESO 3.6 m	optical	European Southern Observatory	Cerro La Silla, Chile (2 400 m/ 7 850 ft)	3.6 m	1976
—	radio	Five College Radio Astronomy	New Salem, Massachusetts,	14 m	1969
George Ellery Hale Telescope	optical	Palomar Observatory	Palomar Mountain, California, USA (1 700 m/ 5 600 ft)	5.08 m	1948
		Observatory	USA		
—	optical	German-Spanish Astronomical Centre	Calar Alto, Spain (2 160 m/ 7 100 ft)	3.5 m	1985
Ire'ne'e du Pont Telescope	optical	Mount Wilson and Las Campanas Observatories	Cerro Las Campanas, Chile (2 510 m/ 8 235 ft)	2.57 m	1977
IRAM Array	millimetre	Institut de Radio Astronomie Millimétrique	Plateau de Bure, France	4 × 15 m	1979

LARGEST GROUND-BASED TELESCOPES (cont.)

Telescope name	Type	Observatory	Site (altitude m/ft)	Mirror/dish size	Founded
Isaac Newton Telescope	optical	Observatory Roque de los Muchachos	La Palma, Canary Islands (2 336 m/ 7 660 ft)	2.54 m	1984
James Clerk Maxwell Telescope (JCMT)	submillimetre	Royal Observatory, Edinburgh, UK	Mauna Kea, Hawaii, USA (4 160 m/ 13 650 ft)	15.0 m	1987
Keck Telescope	optical/ infrared	California Association for Research and Astronomy (CARA)	Mauna Kea, Hawaii, USA (4 160 m/ 13 650 ft)	10.0 m	1990
Lovell Telescope	radio	Nuffield Radio Astronomy Laboratory (Jodrell Bank), University of Manchester	Jodrell Bank, Cheshire, UK	76 m	1957
—	optical	McDonald Observatory	Mt Locke, Texas, USA (2 070 m/ 6 791 ft)	2.7 m	1968
MERLIN (Multi-Element Radio-Linked Interferometer Network)	radio	Nuffield Radio Astronomy Laboratory (Jodrell Bank), University of Manchester	UK (Midlands and Wales)	5 × 25 m, 1 × 32 m, 1 × 76 m	1980
Multiple Mirror Telescope	optical	Whipple Observatory	Mt Hopkins, Arizona, USA (2 606 m/ 8 550 ft)	4.5 m	1979
NASA Infrared Telescope Facility (IRTF)	infrared	NASA	Mauna Kea, Hawaii, USA (4 160 m/ 13 650 ft)	3.0 m	1979
—	millimetre	National Radio Astronomy Observatory (NRAO)	Kitt Peak, Arizona, USA 1920 m	12 m	1982
Nicholas U Mayall Telescope	optical	Kitt Peak National Observatory	Kitt Peak, Arizona, USA (2 100 m/ 6 900 ft)	4 m	1973
Nobeyama Millimetre Array	millimetre	Nobeyama Radio Observatory	Nobeyama, Japan (1300 m)	5 × 10 m	1986
Nobeyama Radio Telescope	radio	Nobeyama Radio Observatory	Nobeyama, Japan (1300 m)	45 m	1970

LARGEST GROUND-BASED TELESCOPES (cont.)

Telescope name	Type	Observatory	Site (altitude m/ft)	Mirror/dish size	Founded
Parkes Radio Telescope	radio	Australian National Radio Observatory	Nr Parkes, NSW, Australia (392 m)	64 m	1961
Shajin Telescope	optical	Crimean Astrophysical Observatory	Simeis, Ukraine (680 m/ 2 230 ft)	2.6 m	1961
Swedish/ European Submillimetre Telescope	submillimetre	European Southern Observatory	Cerro Tololo, Chile (2 160 m/ 7 100 ft)	10 m	1987
United Kingdom Infrared Telescope (UKIRT)	infrared	Royal Observatory, Edinburgh	Mauna Kea, Hawaii, USA (4 180 m/ 13 720 ft)	3.8 m	1979
Very Large Array (VLA)	radio	National Radio Astronomy Observatories	Socorro, New Mexico, USA	27 × 25 m	1980–1
William Herschel Telescope	optical	Observatory Roque de los Muchachos	La Palma, Canary Islands (2 332 m/ 7 650 ft)	4.2 m	1987

MAJOR SPACE 'FIRSTS'

Mission	Nation/ Agency	Launch date	Event date	Event description
Sputnik 1	USSR	4 Oct 57	4 Oct 57	Earth satellite
Sputnik 2	USSR	3 Nov 57	3 Nov 57	Dog Laika
Explorer 1	USA	1 Feb 58	1 Feb 58	Discovered radiation belt (Van Allen)
Luna 1	USSR	2 Jan 59	2 Jan 59	Escaped earth gravity
Vanguard 2	USA	17 Feb 59	17 Feb 59	Earth photo
Luna 2	USSR	12 Sep 59	14 Sep 59	Lunar impact
Luna 3	USSR	4 Oct 59	7 Oct 59	Lunar photo (far side)
TIROS 1	USA	1 Apr 60	1 Apr 60	Weather satellite
Transit 1B	USA	13 Apr 60	13 Apr 60	Navigation satellite
ECHO 1	USA	12 Aug 60	12 Aug 60	Communications satellite
Sputnik 5	USSR	19 Aug 60	20 Aug 60	Two dogs recovered alive
Vostok 1	USSR	12 Apr 61	12 Apr 61	Manned orbital flight
Mariner 2	USA	26 Aug 62	14 Dec 62	Venus flyby
Vostok 6	USSR	16 Jun 63	16 Jun 63	Woman in orbit
Ranger VII	USA	28 Jul 64	31 Jul 64	Close-up television pictures of the moon
Mariner 4	USA	28 Nov 64	15 Jul 65	Mars flyby pictures
Early Bird	USA	6 Apr 65	6 Apr 65	Commercial geostationary communications satellite

MAJOR SPACE 'FIRSTS' (cont.)

Mission	Nation/ Agency	Launch date	Event date	Event description
Venera 3	USSR	16 Nov 65	1 Mar 66	Venus impact
A-1 Asterix	France	26 Nov 65	26 Nov 65	French launched satellite
Gemini 7	USA	4 Dec 65	15 Dec 65	Manned rendevous
Gemini 6	USA	15 Dec 65		
Luna 9	USSR	31 Jan 66	3 Feb 66	Lunar soft landing
Gemini 8	USA	16 Mar 66	16 Mar 66	Manned docking
Luna 10	USSR	31 Mar 66	3 Apr 66	Lunar orbiter
Surveyor 1	USA	30 May 66	2 Jun 66	US soft landing on moon
Lunar orbiter 1	USA	10 Aug 66	29 Oct 66	US lunar orbiter
Cosmos 186/188	USA	22 Oct 67– 28 Oct 67	27 Oct 67– 29 Oct 67	Automatic docking
Zond 5	USSR	14 Sep 68	21 Sep 68	Animals around the moon
Apollo 8	USA	21 Dec 68	24 Dec 68	Manned lunar orbit
Soyuz 4	USSR	14 Jan 69	16 Jan 69	Transfer of crews
Soyuz 5	USSR	15 Jan 69		
Apollo 11	USA	16 Jul 69	20 Jul 69	Manned lunar landing
Oshumi	Japan	11 Feb 70	11 Feb 70	Japanese launched satellite
Long March	China	24 Apr 70	24 Apr 70	Chinese launched satellite
Venera 7	USSR	17 Aug 70	15 Dec 70	Venus soft landing
Luna 16	USSR	12 Sep 70	21 Sep 70	Unmanned sample return
Luna 17	USSR	10 Nov 70	17 Nov 70	Unmanned Moon rover
Mars 2	USSR	19 May 71	27 Nov 71	Mars orbit
Mars 3	USSR	28 May 71	2 Dec 71	Mars soft landing, no data returned
Mariner 9	USA	30 May 71	13 Nov 71	Mars orbit
Prospero	UK	28 Oct 71	28 Oct 71	UK launched satellite
Pioneer 10	USA	3 Mar 72	3 Dec 73	Jupiter flyby
			Apr 83	Crossed Pluto orbit
			14 Jun 83	Escaped solar system
Pioneer 11	USA	6 Apr 73	Apr 74	Jupiter flyby
			Sep 79	Saturn flyby
Mariner 10	USA	3 Nov 73	5 Feb 74	Venus flyby
			Mar 74– Mar 75	Three Mercury flybys
Venera 9	USSR	8 Jun 75	22 Oct 75	Venus orbit
Apollo/Soyuz	USA/ USSR	15 Jul 75	17 Jul 75	Manned international co-operative mission
Viking 1	USA	20 Aug 75	20 Jul 76	Spacecraft operations on Mars surface
Viking 2	USA	9 Sep 75	3 Sep 76	
Voyager 2	USA	20 Aug 77	9 Jul 79	Jupiter flyby
			26 Aug 81	Saturn flyby
			24 Jan 86	Uranus flyby
			24 Aug 89	Neptune flyby
Voyager 1	USA	5 Sep 77	5 Mar 79	Jupiter flyby
			13 Nov 80	Saturn flyby
ISEE-C	USA	12 Aug 78	Sep 85	Comet intercept
Ariane/CAT	ESA	24 Dec 79	24 Dec 79	European launcher
Rohini	India	18 Jul 80	18 Jul 80	Indian launched satellite
STS1	USA	12 Apr 81	12 Apr 81	Space shuttle flight
STS2	USA	12 Nov 81	12 Nov 81	Launch vehicle re-use
Soyuz T9	USSR	27 Jun 83	27 Jun 83	Construction in space

MAJOR SPACE 'FIRSTS' (cont.)

Mission	Nation/ Agency	Launch date	Event date	Event description
STS 51A	USA	8 Nov 84	16 Nov 84	Satellite retrieval
Vega 1	USSR	15 Dec 84	6 Mar 85	Halley flyby
Giotto	ESA	2 Jul 85	13 Mar 86	Close up of comet Halley
Soyuz T15	USSR	13 Mar 86	13 Mar 86	Ferry between space stations
Soyuz TM4/6	USSR	21 Dec 87	21 Dec 88	Year-long flight
Phobos 2	USSR	12 Jan 88	Apr 89	Phobos rendezvous
Buran	USSR	15 Nov 88	15 Nov 88	Unmanned space shuttle
Muses-A	Japan	24 Jan 90	21 Apr 90	Moon orbiter
HST	USA/ ESA	24 Apr 90	25 Apr 90	Large space telescope
Soyuz TM-11	USSR	2 Dec 90	12 Dec 90	Paying passenger flight
Galileo	USA	18 Oct 89	30 Oct 91	Close-up photographs of an asteroid

NASA LAUNCHES (Crew-related)

Mission	Launch	Duration (h:min)	Crew	Comment
Mercury MR3 (Freedom 7)	5 May 61	00:15	Shepard	First US manned suborbital flight
Mercury MR4 (Liberty Bell 7)	21 Jul 61	00:16	Grissom	Suborbital flight
Mercury MA5	29 Nov 61	03:16	Enos	Chimpanzee
Mercury MA6 (Friendship 7)	20 Feb 62	04:55	Glenn	First US manned orbital flight
Mercury MA7 (Aurora 7)	24 May 62	04:56	Carpenter	Orbital flight; manual re-entry
Mercury MA8 (Sigma 7)	3 Oct 62	09:13	Schirra	6 orbits
Mercury MA9 (Faith 7)	15 May 62– 16 May 62	34:20	Cooper	22 orbits; last Mercury flight
Gemini I	8 Apr 64			Test of launch vehicle compatibility
Gemini II	19 Jan 65			Unmanned suborbital test flight
Gemini III	23 Mar 65	04:53	Grissom Young	First manned Gemini flight
Gemini IV	3 Jun 65– 7 Jun 65	97:56	McDivitt White	First spacewalk (by White, 36 min)
Gemini V	21 Aug 65– 29 Aug 65	190:56	Cooper Conrad	Simulated rendezvous manoeuvres
Gemini VI	25 Oct 65			Orbit not achieved
Gemini VII	4 Dec 65– 18 Dec 65	330:35	Borman Lovell	Part of mission with-out spacesuits
Gemini VII-A	15 Dec 65– 16 Dec 65	25:51	Schirra Stafford	First space rendezvous (with Gemini VII)
Gemini VIII	16 Mar 66– 17 Mar 66	10:42	Armstrong Scott	Rendezvous/docking with Agena target vehicle
Gemini IX-A	3 Jun 66– 6 Jun 66	72:21	Stafford Cernan	Docking not achieved
Gemini X	18 Jul 66– 21 Jul 66	70:47	Young Collins	First docked vehicle manoeuvres and spacewalks

NASA LAUNCHES (Crew-related) (cont.)

Mission	Launch	Duration (h:min)	Crew	Comment
Gemini XI	12 Sep 66– 15 Sep 66	71:17	Conrad Gordon	Rendezvous/docking and spacewalks
Gemini XII	11 Nov 66– 15 Nov 66	94:35	Lovell Aldrin	Rendezvous/docking and spacewalks
Apollo I	Jan 67		Grissom White Chaffee	Astronauts killed in command module in fire at launch site
Apollo IV	9 Nov 67			First launch by Saturn V rocket; successful launch of unmanned module
Apollo V	22 Jan 68– 24 Jan 68			Flight test of lunar module in earth orbit
Apollo VII	11 Oct 68– 22 Oct 68	260:09	Schirra Eisele Cunningham	First manned Apollo flight in earth orbit
Apollo VIII	21 Dec 68– 27 Dec 68	147:01	Borman Lovell Anders	First manned orbit of moon (10 orbits)
Apollo IX	3 Mar 69– 13 Mar 69	241:01	McDivitt Scott Schweickart	First manned lunar module flight in earth orbit
Apollo X	18 May 69– 26 May 69	192:03	Stafford Young Cernan	First lunar module orbit of moon
Apollo XI	16 Jul 69– 24 Jul 69	195:18	Armstrong[1] Aldrin[1] Collins	First men on moon 20 Jul, Sea of Tranquillity
Apollo 12	14 Nov 69– 24 Nov 69	244:36	Conrad[1] Bean[1] Gordon	Moon landing, 19 Nov, Ocean of Storms
Apollo 13	11 Apr 70– 17 Apr 70	142:54	Lovell Swigert Haise	Mission aborted, ruptured oxygen tank
Apollo 14	31 Jan 71– 9 Feb 71 9 Feb 71	216:02	Shepard[1] Mitchell[1] Roosa	Moon landing 5 Feb, Fra Mauro area
Apollo 15	26 Jul 71– 7 Aug 71	295:12	Scott[1] Irwin[1] Worden	Moon landing, 30 Jul, Hadley Rille; Lunar Roving Vehicle used
Apollo 16	16 Apr 72– 27 Apr 72	265:51	Young[1] Duke[1] Mattingly	Moon landing, 20 Apr, Descartes
Apollo 17	7 Dec 72– 19 Dec 72	301:52	Cernan[1] Schmitt[1] Evans	Longest Apollo mission, 11 Dec, Taurus-Littrow
Skylab 1	14 May 73		Unmanned space station	Launched unmanned, uncontrolled re-entry 1979
Skylab 2	25 May 73	672:50	Conrad Kerwin Weitz	Repairs in orbit, duration record (28 days)

Skylab 3	28 Jul 73	1427:09	Bean Garriott Lousma	New duration record (59 days)
Skylab 4	16 Nov 73	2017:15	Carr Gibson Pogue	Final visit (84 days)
Apollo-Soyuz Test project	15 Jul 75– 24 Jul 75	217:28	Stafford Brand Slayton	Rendezvous/docking with Soyuz 19 (see facing page)

[1]Astronauts who landed on the moon; the remaining astronaut was the pilot of the command module.

SHUTTLE FLIGHTS 1981–92

Flight/ Name	Launch	Landing	Commander/Pilot/Number of other crew	Payload
STS-1 (C)	12 Apr 81	14 Apr 81	Young/Crippen/none	Test flight
STS-2 (C)	12 Nov 81	14 Nov 81	Engle/Truly/none	Test flight
STS-3 (C)	22 Mar 82	30 Mar 82	Lousma/Fullerton/none	OSS 1[1] (PDP[1])
STS-4 (C)	27 Jun 82	4 Jul 82	Mattingly/Hartsfield/none	CIRRIS 1[1]
STS-5 (C)	11 Nov 82	16 Nov 82	Brand/Overmyer/2	SBS 3, Telesat 6
STS-6 (Ch)	4 Apr 83	9 Apr 83	Weitz/Bobko/2	TDRS 1
STS-7 (Ch)	18 Jun 83	24 Jun 83	Crippen/Hauck/3	Telesat 7, Palapa 3
STS-8 (Ch)	30 Aug 83	5 Sep 83	Truly/Brandenstein/3	Insat 1B
STS-9 (C)	28 Nov 83	8 Dec 83	Young/Shaw/4	Spacelab 1[1]
STS 41-B (Ch)	3 Feb 84	11 Feb 84	Brand/Gibson/3	Westar 6, IRT, Palapa 4, MMU1
STS 41-C (Ch)	6 Apr 84	13 Apr 84	Crippen/Scobee/3	LDEF 1, MMU 2
STS 41-D (D)	30 Aug 84	5 Sept 84	Hartsfield/Coats/4	SBS 4, Leasat 2, Telstar 3C
STS 41-G (Ch)	5 Oct 84	13 Oct 84	Crippen/McBride/5	ERBS
STS 51-A (D)	8 Nov 84	16 Nov 84	Hauck/Walker/3	Telesat 8, Leasat 1
STS 51-C (D)	24 Jan 85	27 Jan 85	Mattingly/Shriver/3	USA 8
STS 51-D (D)	12 Apr 85	19 Apr 85	Bobko/Williams/5	Telesat 9, Leasat 3
STS 51-B (Ch)	29 Apr 85	6 May 85	Overmyer/Gregory/5	Nusat, Spacelab 3[1]
STS 51-G (D)	17 Jun 85	24 Jun 85	Brandenstein/Creighton/5	Morelos 1, Arabsat 1B, Telstar 3D, Spartan 1
STS 51-F (Ch)	29 Jul 85	6 Aug 85	Fullerton/Bridges/5	PDP
STS 51-I (D)	27 Aug 85	3 Sep 85	Engle/Covey/3	Aussat 1, ASC 1, Leasat 4
STS 51-J (A)	3 Oct 85	7 Oct 85	Bobko/Grabe/3	USA 11, USA 12
STS 61-A (Ch)	30 Oct 85	6 Nov 85	Hartsfield/Nagel/6	GLOMR, Spacelab D1[1]
STS 61-B (A)	26 Nov 85	3 Dec 85	Shaw/O'Connor/5	Morelos 2, Aussat 2, OEX, RCA Satcom K2
STS 61-C (C)	12 Jan 86	18 Jan 86	Gibson/Bolden/5	RCA Satcom K1, Hitchhiker G1[1]
STS 51-L (Ch)	28 Jan 86	exploded	Scobee/Smith/5	TDRS
STS 26 (D)	29 Sept 88	3 Oct 88	Hauck/Covey/3	TDRS 3
STS 27 (A)	2 Dec 88	6 Dec 88	Gibson/Gardner/3	USA 34 (Lacrosse 1)
STS 29 (D)	13 Mar 89	18 Mar 89	Coates/Blaha/3	TDRS
STS 30 (A)	4 May 89	8 May 89	Walker/Grabe/3	Magellan
STS 28 (C)	8 Aug 89	13 Aug 89	Shaw/Richards/3	Dept of Defense
STS 34 (A)	18 Oct 89	23 Oct 89	Williams/McCulley/3	Galileo
STS 33 (D)	23 Nov 89	28 Nov 89	Gregory/Blaha/3	Dept of Defense
STS 32 (C)	9 Jan 90	20 Jan 90	Brandenstein/Wetherbee/3	LDEF
STS 36 (A)	28 Feb 90	4 Mar 90	Creighton/Casper/3	Dept of Defense
STS 31 (D)	25 Apr 90	29 Apr 90	Shriver/Bolden/3	HST
STS 41 (D)	6 Oct 90	10 Oct 90	Richards/Cabana/3	Ulysses
STS 38 (A)	16 Nov 90	20 Nov 90	Covey/Culbertson/3	Dept of Defense
STS 35 (C)	3 Dec 90	10 Dec 90	Brand/Gardner/3	Astro-1

STS 37 (A)	5 Apr 91	11 Apr 91	Nagel/Cameron/3	GRO
STS 40 (C)	5 Jun 91	14 Jun 91	O'Conner/Gutierrez/5	Spacelab Life Sciences 1
STS 43 (A)	2 Aug 91	11 Aug 91	Blaha/Baker/3	TDRS-E
STS 48 (D)	13 Sep 91	18 Sep 91	Creighton/Reightler/3	UARS
STS 44 (A)	24 Nov 91	1 Dec 91	Gregory/Henricks/4	Dept of Defense
STS 42 (D)	22 Jan 92	30 Jan 92	Grabe/Oswald/5	International microgravity laboratory[1]
STS 45 (A)	24 Mar 92	2 Apr 92	Bolden/Duffy/5	ATLAS[1] (earth observation)
STS 49 (E)	7 May 92	16 May 92	Brandenstein/Chilton/5	satellite reorientation

A: Atlantis Ch: Challenger C: Columbia D: Discovery E: Endeavour

[1]Not separated from shuttle

MAJOR USSR LAUNCHES (Crew-related)

Mission	Launch	Duration (h:min)	Crew	Comment
Vostok 1	12 Apr 61	01:48	Gagarin	First space flight (1 orbit)
Vostok 2	6 Aug 61	25:18	Titov	Day-long mission
Vostok 3	11 Aug 62	94:22	Nikolayev	First dual mission
Vostok 4	12 Aug 62	71:00	Popovich	First dual mission
Vostok 6	16 Jun 63	70:50	Tereshkova	First woman in space
Voshkod 1	12 Oct 64	24:17	Komarov/Feoktistov/Yegorov	Three man flight
Voshkod 2	18 Mar 65	26:02	Belyayev/Leonov	First spacewalk (EVA)
Soyuz 1	23 Apr 67	27:00	Komarov	Cosmonaut killed on re-entry
Soyuz 4	14 Jan 69	71:14	Shatalov	Khrunov and Yeliseyev transferred from Soyuz 5
Soyuz 5	15 Jan 69	72:46	Volynov/Khrunov/Yeliseyev	Docked with Soyuz 4
Soyuz 10	22 Apr 71	48:00	Shatalov/Yeliseyev/Rukavishnikov	Docked with Salyut 1 space station but did not enter for undisclosed reason.
Soyuz 11	6 Jun 71	552:00	Dobrovolsky/Volkov/Patsayev	Docked with Salyut 1; crew killed on re-entry
Salyut 3	25 Jun 74	214 days	Soyuz 14	Operational military space station
Soyuz 14	4 Jul 74	16 days	Popovich/Artyukhin	Docked with Salyut 3
Salyut 4	26 Dec 74	769 days	Soyuz 17/Soyuz 18/Soyuz 20	Space station; re-entered 2 Feb 1977
Soyuz 17	9 Jan 75	30 days	Gubarev/Grechko	Docked with Salyut 4
Soyuz 19 (Apollo-Soyuz Test Project)	15 Jul 75	6 days	Kubasov/Leonov	First international space mission with USA; crew transfer
Salyut 5	22 Jun 76	412 days	Soyuz 21/Soyuz 24	Space station; re-entered 8 Aug 1977
Soyuz 21	6 Jul 76	49 days	Volynov/Zholobov	Docked with Salyut 5
Soyuz 23	14 Oct 76	2 days	Zudov/Rozhdestivensky	Attempted docking with Salyut 5
Soyuz 24	7 Feb 77	18 days	Gorbatko/Glazkov	Docked with Salyut 5
Salyut 6	29 Sep 77	1764 days	Soyuz 25 through Soyuz 40	Space station; re-entered 29 July 82
Soyuz 26	10 Dec 77	96 days	Romanenko/Grechko	First prime crew Salyut 6; broke endurance record
Soyuz 27	10 Jan 78	65 days	Dzhanibekov/Makarov	First visiting crew to Salyut 6
Soyuz 28	2 Mar 78	8 days	Gubarev/Remek	Second visiting crew to Salyut 6
Soyuz 29	15 Jun 78	140 days	Kovalenok/Ivanchenko	Second prime crew of Salyut 6

MAJOR USSR LAUNCHES (Crew-related) (cont.)

Mission	Launch	Duration	Crew	Comment
Soyuz 32	25 Feb 79	108 days	Lyakhov/Ryumin	Third prime crew of Salyut 6, broke endurance record
Soyuz T1	16 Dec 79	100 days		Redesigned Soyuz craft
Soyuz T4	12 Mar 81	75 days	Kovalenok/Savinykh	Last prime crew of Salyut 6
Soyuz 39	22 Mar 81	8 days	Dzhanibekov/Gurragcha	Mongolian cosmonaut
Soyuz 40	14 May 81	8 days	Popov/Prunariu	Last visiting crew to Salyut 6
Salyut 7	19 Apr 82	9 years	Soyuz T5 through Soyuz T15	Space station; re-entered 7 Feb 91
Soyuz T5	14 May 82	106 days	Berezovoy/Ledebev	Crew broke endurance record
Soyuz T7	19 Aug 82	113 days	Popov/Serebrov/Savitskaya	Savitskaya, second woman in space
Soyuz T9	27 Jun 83	149 days	Lyakhov/Alexandrov	Docked with Salyut 7
Soyuz T10-1	27 Sep 83		Titov/Strekalov	Exploded on launch-pad; crew safe
Soyuz T10	8 Feb 84	263 days	Kizim/Solovyev/Atkov	Crew broke endurance record
Soyuz T12	17 Jul 84	12 days	Dzhanibekov/Savitskaya/Volk	Docked with Salyut 7; first female EVA
Soyuz T14	17 Sep 85	65 days	Vasyutin/Volkov/Grechko	Docked with Salyut 7; mission terminated when Vasyutin fell ill
MIR 1	19 Feb 86	Projected orbit 10 years	Soyuz T15 onwards	Space station; designed for modular construction
Soyuz T15	13 Mar 86	125 days	Kizim/Solovyov	Docked with both MIR 1 and Salyut 7
Soyuz TMI	21 May 86	9 days		Redesigned Soyuz T craft
Kvant 1	31 Mar 87	in orbit		Astrophysical module attached to MIR 1
Soyuz TM3	22 Jul 87	160 days	Viktorenko/Alexandrov/Faris	Docked with MIR 1
Soyuz TM4	21 Dec 87	179 days	Titov/Manarov/Levchenko	Docked with MIR 1; Titov and Manarov completed 365-day flight
Kvant 2	26 Nov 89	in orbit		Module added to MIR 1 station on 6 Dec 89
Kristall	31 May 90	in orbit		Material processing module added to MIR 1
Soyuz TM11	2 Dec 90	175 days	Afanasyev/Manarov/Akiyama	Docked with MIR 1; Japanese journalist on board
Soyuz TM12	18 May 91		Artsebarsky/Krikalev/Sharman	Docked with MIR 1; first British cosmonaut
Soyuz TM13	2 Oct 91		Volkov/Aubakirov/ Vietiboeck (Austria)	Docked with MIR; partial crew rotation (Artsebarsky down)
Soyuz TM14	17 Mar 92		Viktorenko/Kaleri/ Flade (Germany)	Docked with MIR; crew rotation (Volkov, Krikalev down)

SOME SATELLITES IN GEOSTATIONARY ORBIT

Communications

Business

SBS 1	1980
SBS 2	1981
SBS 3	1982
SBS 4	1984
SBS 5	1988
SBS 6	1990

International

Intelsat 2 F-2	1967
Intelsat 2 F-3	1967
Intelsat 2 F-4	1967
Intelsat 3 F-2	1968
Intelsat 3 F-3	1969
Intelsat 3 F-4	1969
Intelsat 3 F-6	1970
Intelsat 3 F-7	1970
Intelsat 4 F-1	1975
Intelsat 4 F-2	1971
Intelsat 4 F-3	1971
Intelsat 4 F-4	1972
Intelsat 4 F-5	1972
Intelsat 4 F-7	1973
Intelsat 4 F-8	1974
Intelsat 4A F-1	1975
Intelsat 4A F-2	1976
Intelsat 4A F-3	1978
Intelsat 4A F-4	1977
Intelsat 4A F-6	1978
Intelsat 5 F-1	1981
Intelsat 5 F-2	1980
Intelsat 5 F-3	1981
Intelsat 5 F-4	1982
Intelsat 5 F-5	1982
Intelsat 5 F-6	1983
Intelsat 5 F-7	1983
Intelsat 5 F-8	1984
Intelsat 5 F-9	1984
Intelsat 5A F-10	1985
Intelsat 5A F-11	1985
Intelsat 5A F-12	1985
Intelsat 5A F-13	1988
Intelsat 5A F-15	1989
Intelsat 6 F-2	1989
Intelsat 6 F-4	1990
Intelsat 6F-5	1991

Arabian

Arabsat 1A	1985
Arabsat 1B	1985

Asian

Asiasat 1	1990

Australian

Aussat 1	1985
Aussat 2	1985
Aussat 3	1987

Brazilian

Brasilsat 1	1985
Brasilsat 2	1986

Canadian

Anik 1	1972
Anik 2	1973
Anik 3	1975
Anik C1	1985
Anik C2	1983
Anik C3	1982
Anik D1	1982
Anik D2	1984
Anik E2	1991
Anik E1	1991
Telesat 1	1972
Telesat 2	1973
Telesat 3	1975
Telesat 4	1978
Telesat 5	1982
Telesat 6	1982
Telesat 7	1983
Telesat 8	1984
Telesat 9	1985

Chinese

China 15	1984
China 18	1986
China 22	1988
China 25	1988
China 26	1990

European

Astra 1A	1988
Astra 1B	1991
ECS 1	1983
ECS 2	1984
ECS 4	1987
ECS 5	1988
Marcopolo 1	1989
Olympus	1989
Eutelsat 2	1990
Eutelsat 2	1991
Astra 1B	1991

French

TDF 1	1988
Telecom 1A	1984
Telecom 1B	1985
Telecom 1C	1988
TDF 2	1990

French/German

Symphonie 1	1974
Symphonie 2	1975

German

DFS-Kopernicus 1	1989
TV-Sat 1	1987
TV-Sat 2	1989
DFS Copernicus 2	1990

Indian

Apple	1981
Insat 1A	1982
Insat 1B	1983
Insat 1C	1988
Insat 1D	1990

Indonesian

Palapa 1	1976
Palapa 2	1977
Palapa 3	1983
Palapa 5	1987
Palapa B-2R	1990

Italian

Sirio 1	1977
Italsat	1991

Japanese

Ayama 1	1979
Ayama 2	1980
CS-2A	1983
CS-2B	1983
CS-3A	1988
CS-3B	1988
ECS 1	1979
ECS 2	1980
ETS 2	1977
ETS 3	1982
ETS 5	1987
JCSat 1	1989
JCSat 2	1990
Sakura 2A	1983
Sakura 2B	1983
Sakura 3A	1988
Sakura 3B	1988
Superbird 1	1989
Yuri 3A	1990

Mexican

Morelos 1	1985
Morelos 2	1985

Pan-American

Panamsat (PAS 1)	1988

Soviet

Cosmos 1888	1987

SOME SATELLITES IN GEOSTATIONARY ORBIT (cont.)

Cosmos 1894	1987
Cosmos 1897	1987
Cosmos 1940	1988
Cosmos 1961	1988
Cosmos 2054	1989
Cosmos 2085	1990
Ekran 1	1976
Ekran 2	1977
Ekran 3	1979
Ekran 4	1979
Ekran 5	1980
Ekran 6	1980
Ekran 7	1981
Ekran 8	1982
Ekran 9	1982
Ekran 10	1983
Ekran 11	1983
Ekran 12	1984
Ekran 13	1984
Ekran 14	1985
Ekran 15	1986
Ekran 16	1987
Ekran 17	1987
Ekran 18	1988
Ekran 19	1988
Gorizont 1	1978
Gorizont 2	1979
Gorizont 3	1979
Gorizont 4	1980
Gorizont 5	1982
Gorizont 6	1982
Gorizont 7	1983
Gorizont 8	1983
Gorizont 9	1984
Gorizont 10	1984
Gorizont 11	1985
Gorizont 12	1986
Gorizont 13	1986
Gorizont 14	1987
Gorizont 15	1988
Gorizont 16	1988
Gorizont 17	1989
Gorizont 18	1989
Gorizont 19	1989
Gorizont 20	1990
Gorizont 21	1990
Gorizont 22	1990
Gorizont 23	1991
Raduga 1	1975
Raduga 2	1976
Raduga 3	1977
Raduga 4	1978
Raduga 5	1979
Raduga 6	1980
Raduga 7	1980
Raduga 8	1981
Raduga 9	1981
Raduga 10	1981
Raduga 11	1982
Raduga 12	1983
Raduga 13	1983
Raduga 14	1984
Raduga 15	1984
Raduga 16	1985
Raduga 17	1985
Raduga 18	1986
Raduga 19	1986
Raduga 20	1987
Raduga 21	1987
Raduga 22	1988
Raduga 23	1989
Raduga 24	1989
Raduga 25	1989
Raduga 26	1990
Raduga 27	1991

Swedish

Tele-X	1989

US

ASC 1	1985
Aurora 2	1991
Comstar 1A	1976
Comstar 1B	1976
Comstar 1C	1978
Comstar 1D	1981
Early Bird	1965
Galaxy 1	1983
Galaxy 2	1983
Galaxy 3	1984
Galaxy 6	1990
Gstar 1	1985
Gstar 2	1986
Gstar 3	1988
Gstar 4	1990
Intelsat 1 F-1	1965
Leasat 1	1984
Leasat 2	1984
Leasat 3	1985
Leasat 4	1985
Leasat 5	1990
LES 6	1968
LES 8	1976
LES 9	1976
RCA Satcom 1	1975
RCA Satcom 2	1976
RCA Satcom 3	1979
RCA Satcom 3R	1981
RCA Satcom 4	1982
RCA Satcom 5	1982
RCA Satcom 6	1983
RCA Satcom 7	1983
RCA Satcom K1	1986
RCA Satcom K2	1985
RCA Satcom C1	1990
TDRS 1	1983
TDRS 3	1988
TDRS 4	1989
TDRS 5	1991
Telstar 3A	1983
Telstar 3C	1983
Telstar 3D	1985
Westar 1	1974
Westar 2	1974
Westar 3	1979
Westar 4	1982
Westar 5	1982

Maritime Communications

Marecs 1	1981
Marecs 2	1984
Marisat 1	1976
Marisat 2	1976
Marisat 3	1976
Inmarsat 2	1990
Inmarsat 2	1991

Meteorology

Japanese

GMS 1	1977
GMS 2	1981
GMS 3	1984
GMS 4	1989
Himawari 1	1977
Himawari 2	1981
Himawari 3	1984

European

Meteosat 1	1977
Meteosat 2	1981
Meteosat P2	1988
MOP 1	1989
MOP 2	1991

US

GOES 1	1975

SOME SATELLITES IN GEOSTATIONARY ORBIT (cont.)

GOES 2	1977
GOES 3	1978
GOES 4	1980
GOES 5	1981
GOES 6	1983
GOES 7	1987
SMS 1	1974
SMS 2	1975
SMS 3	1975

Military Communications

NATO 1	1970
NATO 2	1971
NATO 3A	1976
NATO 3B	1977
NATO 3C	1978
NATO 3D	1984
NATO 4A	1991

Soviet

Cosmos 2133	1991

UK

Skynet 1A	1969
Skynet 2A	1974
Skynet 2B	1974
Skynet 4A	1990
Skynet 4B	1988
Skynet 4C	1990

US

DSCS 1	1971
DSCS 2	1971
DSCS 3	1973
DSCS 4	1973
DSCS 5	1975
DSCS 6	1975
DSCS 7	1977
DSCS 8	1977
DSCS 11	1978
DSCS 12	1978
DSCS 13	1979
DSCS 14	1979
DSCS 15	1982
DSCS 16	1982
DSCS TYPE 3	1985
Fleetsatcom 1	1978
Fleetsatcom 2	1979
Fleetsatcom 3	1980
Fleetsatcom 4	1980
Fleetsatcom 5	1981
Fleetsatcom 7	1986
Fleetsatcom 8	1989
IMEWS	1987
IMEWS 1	1970
IMEWS 2	1971
IMEWS 3	1972
IMEWS 4	1973
IMEWS 5	1975
IMEWS 6	1976
IMEWS 7	1977
IMEWS 8	1978
IMEWS 9	1979
IMEWS 10	1979
IMEWS 11	1981
IMEWS 12	1981
IMEWS 13	1982
Tactical comsat	1969
USA 7	1984
USA 11	1985
USA 12	1985
USA 20	1986
USA 28	1987
USA 48	1989
DSP	1990
DSP 16	1992

Research

ESA GEOS 2	1978
IUE Ultra-violet Obs	1978

EARTH

There are no universally agreed estimates of the natural phenomena given in this section. Surveys make use of different criteria for identifying natural boundaries, and use different techniques of measurement. The sizes of continents, oceans, seas, deserts, and rivers are particularly subject to variation.

Age 4500000000 years (accurate to within a very small percentage of possible error)
Area 509600000 sq km/197000000 sq ml
Mass 5976×10^{27} grams
Land surface 148000000 sq km/57000000 sq ml (c.29% of total area)
Water surface 361600000 sq km/140000000 sq ml (c.71% of total area)
Circumference at equator 40076 km/24902 ml
Circumference of meridian 40000 km/24860 ml

CONTINENTS

Name	Area sq km	sq ml	Lowest point below sea level	m	ft	Highest elevation	m	ft
Africa	30293000	11696000 (20.2%)	Lake Assal, Djibouti	156	512	Mt Kilimanjaro, Tanzania	5895	19340
Antarctica	13975000	5396000 (9.3%)	Bently subglacial trench	2538	8327	Vinson Massif	5140	16864
Asia	44493000	17179000 (29.6%)	Dead Sea, Israel/Jordan	400	1312	Mt Everest, China-Nepal	8848	29028
Oceania	8945000	3454000 (6%)	Lake Eyre, S Australia	15	49	Puncak Jaya (Ngga Pulu)	5030	16500
Europe[1]	10245000	3956000 (6.8%)	Caspian Sea, SW Asia	29	94	Mt El'brus, Russia	5642	18510
North America	24454000	9442000 (16.3%)	Death Valley, California	86	282	Mt McKinley, Alaska	6194	20320
South America	17838000	6887000 (11.9%)	Peninsular Valdez, Argentina	40	131	Aconcagua, Argentina	6960	22831

[1] Including the former western USSR.

MAJOR ISLAND GROUPS

Name	Country	Sea/Ocean	Constituent islands
Aeolian	Italy	Mediterranean	Stromboli, Lipari, Vulcano, Salina
Åland	Finland	Gulf of Bothnia	Ahvenanmaa, Eckero, Lemland, Lumparland, Vardo
Aleutian	Alaska	Pacific	Andreanof, Adak, Atka, Fox, Umnak, Unalaska, Unimak, Near, Attu, Rat, Kiska, Amchitka
Alexander	Canada	Pacific	Baranof, Prince of Wales
Antilles, Greater	–	Caribbean	Cuba, Jamaica, Haiti and the Dominican Republic, Puerto Rico
Antilles, Lesser	–	Caribbean	Windward, Leeward, Netherlands Antilles

MAJOR ISLAND GROUPS (cont.)

Name	Country	Sea/Ocean	Constituent islands
Andaman	India	Bay of Bengal	over 300 islands including N Andaman, S Andaman, Middle Andaman, Little Andaman
Azores	Portugal	Atiantic	nine main islands: Flores, Corvo, Terceira, Graciosa, São Jorge, Faial, Pico, Santa Maria, Formigar, São Miguel
Bahamas	UK	Atlantic	700 islands including Great Abaco, Acklins, Andros, Berry, Cay, Cat Crooked, Exuma, Grand Bahama, Inagua, Long, Mayaguana, New Providence, Ragged
Balearic	Spain	Mediterranean	Ibiza, Mallorca, Menorca, Formentera, Cabrera
Bay Islands	Honduras	Caribbean	Utila, Roatan, Guanja
Bismarck Archipelago	Papua New Guinea	Pacific	c.200 islands including New Britain, New Ireland, Admiralty, Lavonga, New Hanover
Bissagos	Guinea-Bissau	Atlantic	15 islands including Orango, Formosa, Caravela, Roxa
Canadian Arctic Archipelago	Canada	Arctic	main islands: Baffin, Victoria, Queen Elizabeth, Banks
Canaries	Spain	Atlantic	Tenerife, Gomera, Las Palmas, Hierro, Lanzarote, Fuerteventura, Gran Canaria
Cape Verde	Cape Verde	Atlantic	10 islands divided into 1. Barlavento (windward) group: Santo Antão, São Vicente, Santa Luzia, Sao Nicolau, Boa Vista, Sal and 2. Sotavento (leeward) group: São Tiago, Maio Fogo, Brava
Caroline	USA	Pacific	c.680 islands including Yop, Ponape, Truk, Kusac, Belau
Chagos	UK	Indian	Diego Garcia, Peros, Banhos, Salomon
Channel	UK	English	Jersey, Guernsey, Alderney, Sark
Chonos Archipelago	Chile	Pacific	main islands: Chaffers, Benjamin, James, Melchior, Victoria, Luz
Commander	Russia	Bering Sea	main islands: Bering, Medny
Comoros	Republic of the Comoros (excluding French Mayotte)	Mozambique Channel	Grande Comore, Anjouan, Moheli, Mayotte
Cook	New Zealand	Pacific	main islands: Rarotonga, Palmerston, Mangaia
Cyclades	Greece	Aegean	c.220 islands including Andros, Mikonos, Milos, Naxos, Paros, Kithnos, Sérifos, Tinos, Siros
Denmark	Denmark	Baltic	main islands: Zealand, Fyn, Lolland, Falster, Bornholm

MAJOR ISLAND GROUPS (cont.)

Name	Country	Sea/Ocean	Constituent islands
Desolation	France	Indian	Kerguélen, Grande Terre, and 300 islets
Dodecanese	Greece	Aegean	12 islands including Kásos, Kárpathos, Rhodes, Sámos, Khalki, Tilos, Simi, Astipalaia, Kós, Kálimnos, Léros, Pátmos
Ellice	Tuvalu	Pacific	main islands: Funafuti, Nukefetau, Nukulailai, Nanumea
Falkland	UK	Atlantic	over 200 islands including W Falkland, E Falkland, S Georgia, S Sandwich
Faroe	Denmark	Atlantic	22 islands including Stromo, Ostero
Fiji	Fiji	Pacific	main islands: Viti Levu, Vanua Levu
Frisian, North	Germany and Denmark	North Sea	main islands: (German) Sylt, Föhr, Nordstrand, Pellworm, Amrum; (Danish) Rømø, Fanø, Mandø
Frisian, East	Germany and Denmark	North Sea	main islands: Borkum, Juist, Norderney, Langeoog, Spiekeroog, Wangerooge
Frisian, West	Germany and Denmark	North Sea	main islands: Texel, Vlieland, Terschelling, Ameland, Schiermonnikoog
Galapagos	Ecuador	Pacific	main islands: San Cristobal, Santa Cruz, Isabela, Floreana, Santiago, Fernandina
Gilbert	Kiribati	Pacific	main islands: Tarawa, Makin, Abaiang, Abemama, Tabiteuea, Nonouti, Beru
Gotland	Sweden	Baltic	main islands: Gotland, Fårö, Karlsö
Greenland	Denmark	N Atlantic/Arctic	main islands: Greenland, Disko
Hawaiian	USA	Pacific	8 main islands: Hawaii, Oahu, Maui, Lanai, Kauai, Molokai, Kahoolawe, Niihau
Hebrides, Inner	UK	Atlantic	main islands: Skye, Eigg, Coll, Tiree, Mull, Iona, Staffa, Jura, Islay
Hebrides, Outer	UK	Atlantic	Lewis, N and S Uist, Benbecula, Barra
Indonesia	Republic of Indonesia	Pacific	13 677 islets and islands including Java, Sumatra, Kalimantau, Celebes, Lesser Sundas, Moluccas, Irian Jaya
Ionian	Greece	Aegean	Kerkira, Kefalliniá, Zakinthos, Levkas
Japan	Japan	Pacific	main islands: Hokkaido, Honshu, Shikoku, Kyushu, Ryuku
Juan Fernandez	Chile	Pacific	Más a Tierra, Más Afuera, Santa Clara
Kuril	Russia	Pacific	56 islands including Shumsu, Iturup, Urup, Paramushir, Onekotan, Shiaskhotan, Shikotan-to, Kunashir, Shimushir

MAJOR ISLAND GROUPS (cont.)

Name	Country	Sea/Ocean	Constituent islands
Laccadive	India	Arabian Sea	27 islands including Amindivi, Laccadive, Minicoy, Androth, Kavaratti
Line	Kiribati	Pacific	main islands: Christmas, Fanning, Washington
Lofoton	Norway	Norwegian Sea	main islands: Hinnøy, Austvågøy, Vestvågøy, Moskenes
Madeira	Portugal	Atlantic	Madeira, Ilha do Porto Santo, Ilhas Desertas, Ilhas Selvagens
Malay Archipelago	Federation of Malay	Pacific/Indian	main islands: Borneo, Celebes, Java, Luzon, Mindanao, New Guinea, Sumatra
Maldives	Republic of Maldives	Indian	19 clusters, main island: Male
Malta	Republic of Malta	Mediterranean	main islands: Malta, Gozo, Comino
Mariana	Commonwealth of the Northern Mariana Islands	Pacific	14 islands including Saipan, Tinian, Rota, Pagan, Guguan
Marquesas	France	Pacific	10 islands including Nukultiva, Ua Pu, Ua Huka, Hiva Oa, Tahuata, Fatu Hiva, Eĩao, Hatutu
Marshall	Marshall Islands	Pacific	main islands: Bikini, Wotha, Kwajalein, Eniwetok, Maiura, Jalut, Rogelap
Mascarenes	France	Indian	main islands: Réunion, Mauritius, Rodrigues
Melanesia	–	Pacific	main groups of islands: Solomon Islands, Bismarck Archipelago, New Caledonia,Papua New Guinea, Fiji, Vanuatu
Micronesia	–	Pacific	main groups of islands: Caroline, Gilberts, Marianas, Marshalls, Guam, Kiribati, Nauru
New Hebrides	Republic of Vanuatu	Pacific	main islands: Espíritu Santo, Malekula, Efate, Ambrim, Eromanga, Tanna, Epi, Pentecost, Aurora
New Siberian	Russia	Arctic	main islands: Kotelny, Faddeyevski
Newfoundland	Canada	Atlantic	Prince Edward, Anticosti
Nicobar	India	Bay of Bengal	main islands: Great Nicobar, Camorta with Nancowry, Car Nicobar, Teressa, Little Nicobar
Northern Land	Russia	Arctic	main islands: Komsomolets, Bolshevik, October Revolution
Novaya Zemlya	Russia	Arctic	2 main islands: North, South
Orkney	UK	North Sea	main islands: Mainland, South and North Ronaldsay, Sanday, Westray, Hoy, Stronsay, Shapinsay, Rousay
Pelagian	Italy	Mediterranean	Lampedusa, Linosa, Lampione

MAJOR ISLAND GROUPS (cont.)

Name	Country	Sea/Ocean	Constituent islands
Philippines	Republic of the Philippines	Pacific	over 7100 islands and islets including Luzon, Mindanao, Samar, Palawan, Mindoro, Panay, Negros, Cebu, Leyte, Masbate, Bohol
Polynesia	–	Pacific	main groups of islands: New Zealand, French Polynesia, Phoenix islands, Hawaii, Line, Cook islands, Pitcairn, Tokelau, Tonga, Society, Easter, Samoa, Kiribati, Ellice
Queen Charlotte	Canada	Pacific	150 islands including Prince Rupert, Graham, Moresby, Louise, Lyell, Kunghit
São Tomé and Príncipe	Republic of São Tomé and Príncipe	Atlantic	main islands: São Tomé, Príncipe
Scilly	UK	English Channel	c.150 islands including St Mary's, St Martin's, Tresco, St Agnes, Bryher
Seychelles	Republic of Seychelles	Indian	115 islands including Praslin, La Digue, Silhouette, Mahé, Bird
Shetland	UK	North Sea	100 islands including Mainland, Unst, Yell, Fetlar, Whalsay
Society	France	Pacific	island groups: Windward, Leeward; main island: Tahiti.
Solomon	Solomon Islands	Pacific	main islands: Choiseul, Guadalcanal, Malaita, New Georgia, San Cristobal, Santa Isabel
South Orkney	UK	Atlantic	main islands: Coronation, Signy, Laurie, Inaccessible
South Shetland	UK	Atlantic	main islands: King George, Elephant, Clarence, Gibbs, Nelson, Livingstone, Greenwich, Snow, Deception, Smith
Sri Lanka	Republic of Sri Lanka	Indian	main islands: Sri Lanka, Mannar
Taiwan	Republic of China	China Sea/Pacific	main islands: Taiwan, Lan Hsü, Lü Tao, Quemoy, the Pescadores
Tasmania	Australia	Tasman Sea	main islands: Tasmania, King, Flinders, Bruny
Tierra del Fuego	Argentina/Chile	Pacific	main islands: Tierra del Fuego, Isla de los Estados, Hoste, Navarino, Wallaston, Diego Ramirez, Desolacion, Santa Ines, Clarence, Dawson
Tres Marias	Mexico	Pacific	Maria Madre, Maria Magdalena, Maria Cleofas, San Juanito
Tristan da Cunha	UK	Atlantic	5 islands including Tristan da Cunha, Gough, Inaccessible, Nightingale

MAJOR ISLAND GROUPS (cont.)

Name	Country	Sea/Ocean	Constituent islands
Tuamotu Archipelago	France	Pacific	c.80 islands including Makatea, Fakarava, Rangiroa, Anaa, Hao, Reao, Gambiev, Duke of Gloucester
Vesterålen	Norway	Norwegian Sea	main islands: Hinnøy, Langøya, Andøya, Hadseløy
Virgin	USA	Caribbean	over 50 islands including St Croix, St Thomas, St John
Virgin	UK	Caribbean	main islands: Tortola, Virgin Gorda, Anegada, Jost Van Dyke.
Zanzibar	Tanzania	Indian	main islands: Zanzibar, Tumbatu, Kwale
Zemlya Frantsa-Iosifa	Russia	Arctic	c.167 islands, including Graham Bell, Wilczekland, Georgeland, Hooker, Zemlya Alexsandry, Ostrov Rudol'fa

OCEANS

Name	Area sq km	sq ml		Greatest depth	m	ft	Average depth	m	ft
Arctic	13 986 000	5 400 000	(3%)	Eurasia Basin	5 122	16 804	Arctic	1 330	4 300
Atlantic	82 217 000	31 700 000	(24%)	Puerto Rico Trench	8 648	28 372	Atlantic	3 700	12 100
Indian	73 426 000	28 350 000	(20%)	Java Trench	7 725	25 344	Indian	3 900	12 800
Pacific	181 300 000	70 000 000	(46%)	Mariana Trench	11 040	36 220	Pacific	4 300	14 100

LARGEST SEAS

Name	Area[1] sq km	sq ml	Name	Area[1] sq km	sq ml
Coral Sea	4 791 000	1 850 200	Arafura Sea	1 037 000	400 000
Arabian Sea	3 863 000	1 492 000	Philippine Sea	1 036 000	400 000
S China (Nan) Sea	3 685 000	1 423 000	Sea of Japan	978 000	378 000
Mediterranean Sea	2 516 000	971 000	E Siberian Sea	901 000	348 000
Bering Sea	2 304 000	890 000	Kara Sea	883 000	341 000
Bay of Bengal	2 172 000	839 000	E China Sea	664 000	256 000
Sea of Okhotsk	1 590 000	614 000	Andaman Sea	565 000	218 000
Gulf of Mexico	1 543 000	596 000	North Sea	520 000	201 000
Gulf of Guinea	1 533 000	592 000	Black Sea	508 000	196 000
Barents Sea	1 405 000	542 000	Red Sea	453 000	175 000
Norwegian Sea	1 383 000	534 000	Baltic Sea	414 000	160 000
Gulf of Alaska	1 327 000	512 000	Arabian Gulf	238 000	92 200
Hudson Bay	1 232 000	476 000	St Lawrence Gulf	238 300	92 000
Greenland Sea	1 205 000	465 000			

Oceans are excluded.

[1]Areas are rounded to the nearest 1 000 sq km/sq ml.

LARGEST ISLANDS

Name	Area[1] sq km	sq ml
Australia	7892300	3046500
Greenland	2131600	823800
New Guinea	790000	305000
Borneo	737000	285000
Madagascar	587000	227600
Baffin	507000	196000
Sumatra	425000	164900
Honshu (Hondo)	228000	88000
Great Britain	219000	84400
Victoria, Canada	217300	83900
Ellesmere, Canada	196000	75800
Celebes	174000	67400
South I, New Zealand	151000	58200
Java	129000	50000
North I, New Zealand	114000	44200
Newfoundland	109000	42000
Cuba	105000	40500
Luzon	105000	40400
Iceland	103000	39700
Mindanao	94600	36500
Novaya Zemlya (two islands)	90600	35000
Ireland	84100	32500
Hokkaido	78500	30300
Hispaniola	77200	29800
Sakhalin	75100	29000
Tierra del Fuego	71200	27500
Tasmania	67900	26200

[1]Areas are rounded to the nearest 100 sq km/sq ml.

LARGEST LAKES

Name/Location	Area[1] sq km	sq ml
Caspian Sea, Iran/Russia/ Turkmenistan/Kazakhstan/ Azerbaijan	371000	143240[2]
Superior, USA/Canada	82260	31760[3]
Aral Sea, Uzbekistan/ Kazakhstan	64500	24900[2]
Victoria, E Africa	62940	24300
Huron, USA/Canada	59580	23000[3]
Michigan, USA	58020	22400
Tanganyika, E Africa	32000	12350
Baikal, Russia	31500	12160
Great Bear, Canada	31330	12100
Great Slave, Canada	28570	11030
Erie, USA/Canada	25710	9920[3]
Winnipeg, Canada	24390	9420
Malawi/Nyasa, E Africa	22490	8680
Balkhash, Kazakhstan	17000–22000	6500–8500[2]
Ontario, Canada	19270	7440[3]
Ladoga, Russia	18130	7000
Chad, W Africa	10000–26000	4000–10000
Maracaibo, Venezuela	13010	5020[4]
Patos, Brazil	10140	3920[4]
Onega, Russia	9800	3800
Rudolf, E Africa	9100	3500
Eyre, Australia	8800	3400[4]
Titicaca, Peru	8300	3200

The Caspian and Aral Seas, being entirely surrounded by land, are classified as lakes.
[1]Areas are rounded to the nearest 10 sq km/sq ml.
[2]Salt lakes
[3]Average of areas given by Canada and USA
[4]Salt lagoons

HIGHEST MOUNTAINS

Name	Height[1] m	ft	Location
Everest	8850	29030	China-Nepal
K2	8610	28250	Kashmir-Jammu
Kangchenjunga	8590	28170	India-Nepal
Lhotse	8500	27890	China-Nepal
Kangchenjunga S Peak	8470	27800	India-Nepal
Makalu I	8470	27800	China-Nepal

HIGHEST MOUNTAINS (cont.)

Name	Height[1] m	ft	Location
Kangchenjunga W Peak	8420	27620	India-Nepal
Llotse E Peak	8380	27500	China-Nepal
Dhaulagiri	8170	26810	Nepal
Cho Oyu	8150	26750	China-Nepal
Manaslu	8130	26660	Nepal
Nanga Parbat	8130	26660	Kashmir-Jammu
Annapurna I	8080	26500	Nepal
Gasherbrum I	8070	26470	Kashmir-Jammu
Broad-highest	8050	26400	Kashmir-Jammu
Gasherbrum II	8030	26360	Kashmir-Jammu
Gosainthan	8010	26290	China
Broad-middle	8000	26250	Kashmir-Jammu
Gasherbrum III	7950	26090	Kashmir-Jammu
Annapurna II	7940	26040	Nepal
Nanda Devi	7820	25660	India
Rakaposhi	7790	25560	Kashmir
Kamet	7760	25450	India
Ulugh Muztagh	7720	25340	Tibet
Tirich Mir	7690	25230	Pakistan
Muz Tag Ata	7550	24760	China
Communism Peak	7490	24590	Tadzhikistan
Pobedy Peak	7440	24410	China-Kirgiziya
Aconcagua	6960	22830	Argentina
Ojos del Salado	6910	22660	Argentina-Chile

[1]Heights are given to the nearest 10 m/ft.

LARGEST DESERTS

Name/Location	Area[1] sq km	sq ml
Sahara, N Africa	8600000	3320000
Arabian, SW Asia	2330000	900000
Gobi, Mongolia and NE China	1166000	450000
Patagonian, Argentina	673000	260000
Great Victoria, SW Australia	647000	250000
Great Basin, SW USA	492000	190000
Chihuahuan, Mexico	450000	175000
Great Sandy, NW Australia	400000	150000
Sonoran, SW USA	310000	120000
Kyzyl Kum, Kazakhskan	300000	115000
Takla Makan, N China	270000	105000
Kalahari, SW Africa	260000	100000
Kara Kum, Turkmenistan	260000	100000
Kavir, Iran	260000	100000
Syrian, Saudi Arabia/Jordan/Syria/Iraq	260000	100000
Nubian, Sudan	260000	100000
Thar, India/Pakistan	200000	77000
Ust'-Urt, Kazakhstan	160000	62000

LARGEST DESERTS (cont.)

Name/Location	Area[1] sq km	sq ml
Bet-Pak-Dala, S Kazakhstan	155 000	60 000
Simpson, C Australia	145 000	56 000
Dzungaria, China	142 000	55 000
Atacama, Chile	140 000	54 000
Namib, SE Africa	134 000	52 000
Sturt, SE Australia	130 000	50 000
Bolson de Mapimi, Mexico	130 000	50 000
Ordos, China	130 000	50 000
Alashan, China	116 000	45 000

[1]Desert areas are very approximate, because clear physical boundaries may not occur.

LONGEST RIVERS

Name	Outflow	Length[1] km	ml
Nile-Kagera-Ruvuvu-Ruvusu-Luvironza	Mediterranean Sea (Egypt)	6 690	4 160
Amazon-Ucayali-Tambo-Ene-Apurimac	Atlantic Ocean (Brazil)	6 570	4 080
Mississippi-Missouri-Jefferson-Beaverhead-Red Rock	Gulf of Mexico (USA)	6 020	3 740
Chang Jiang (Yangtze)	E China Sea (China)	5 980	3 720
Yenisey-Angara-Selenga-Ider	Kara Sea (Russia)	5 870	3 650
Amur-Argun-Kerulen	Tartar Strait (Russia)	5 780	3 590
Ob-Irtysh	Gulf of Ob, Kara Sea (Russia)	5 410	3 360
Plata-Parana-Grande	Atlantic Ocean (Argentina/Uruguay)	4 880	3 030
Huang Ho (Yellow)	Yellow Sea (China)	4 840	3 010
Congo (Zaire)-Lualaba	Atlantic Ocean (Angola-Zaire)	4 630	2 880
Lena	Laptev Sea (Russia)	4 400	2 730
Mackenzie-Slave-Peace-Finlay	Beaufort Sea (Canada)	4 240	2 630
Mekong	S China Sea (Vietnam)	4 180	2 600
Niger	Gulf of Guinea (Nigeria)	4 100	2 550

[1]Lengths are given to the nearest 10 km/ml, and include the river plus tributaries comprising the longest watercourse.

HIGHEST WATERFALLS

Name	Height[1] m	ft
Angel (upper fall), Venezuela	807	2 648
Itatinga, Brazil	628	2 060
Cuquenan, Guyana-Venezuela	610	2 000
Ormeli, Norway	563	1 847
Tysse, Norway	533	1 749
Pilao, Brazil	524	1 719
Ribbon, USA	491	1 612
Vestre Mardola, Norway	468	1 535
Roraima, Guyana	457?	1 500?
Cleve-Garth, New Zealand	450?	1 476?

[1]Height denotes individual leaps.

DEEPEST CAVES

Name/Location	Depth m	ft	Name/Location	Depth m	ft
Jean Bernard, France	1 494	4 900	Dachstein-Mammuthöhle, Austria	1 174	3 852
Snezhnaya, Caucasus	1 340	4 397	Zitu, Spain	1 139	3 737
Puertas de Illamina, Spain	1 338	4 390	Badalona, Spain	1 130	3 707
Pierre-Saint-Martin, France	1 321	4 334	Batmanhöhle, Austria	1 105	3 626
Sistema Huautla, Mexico	1 240	4 067	Schneeloch, Austria	1 101	3 612
Berger, France	1 198	3 930	G E S Malaga, Spain	1 070	3 510
Vqerdi, Spain	1 195	3 921	Lamprechtsofen, Austria	1 024	3 360

MAJOR VOLCANOES

Name	Height m	ft	Major eruptions (years)	Last eruption (year)
Aconcagua (Argentina)	6 960	22 831	extinct	
Ararat (Turkey)	5 198	18 350	extinct	Holocene
Awu (Sangihe Is)	1 327	4 355	1711, 1856, 1892	1968
Bezymianny (USSR)	2 800	9 186	1955–6	1984
Coseguina (Nicaragua)	847	1 598	1835	1835
El Chichón (Mexico)	1 349	4 430	1982	1982
Erebus (Antarctica)	4 023	13 200	1947, 1972	1986
Etna (Italy)	3 236	10 625	122, 1169, 1329, 1536, 1669, 1928, 1964, 1971	1986
Fuji (Japan)	3 776	12 388	1707	1707
Galunggung (Java)	2 180	7 155	1822, 1918	1982
Hekla (Iceland)	1 491	4 920	1693, 1845, 1947–8, 1970	1981
Helgafell (Iceland)	215	706	1973	1973
Hudson (Chile)	1 740	5742	1971, 1973	1991
Jurullo (Mexico)	1 330	4 255	1759–74	1774
Katmai (Alaska)	2 298	7 540	1912, 1920, 1921	1931
Kilauea (Hawaii)	1 247	4 100	1823–1924, 1952, 1955, 1960, 1967–8, 1968–74, 1983–7	1991
Kilimanjaro (Tanzania)	5 930	19 450	extinct	Pleistocene
Klyuchevskoy (Russia)	4 850	15 910	1700–1966, 1984	1985
Krakatoa (Sumatra)	818	2 685	1680, 1883, 1927, 1952–3, 1969	1980
La Soufrière (St Vincent)	1 232	4 048	1718, 1812, 1902, 1971–2	1979
Laki (Iceland)	500	1 642	1783	1784
Lamington (Papua New Guinea)	1 780	5 844	1951	1956
Lassen Peak (USA)	3 186	10 453	1914–5	1921
Mauna Loa (Hawaii)	4 172	13 685	1859, 1880, 1887, 1919, 1950	1984
Mayon (Philippines)	2 462	8 084	1616, 1766, 1814, 1897, 1968	1978
Nyamuragira (Zaire)	3 056	10 026	1921–38, 1971, 1980	1984
Paricutin (Mexico)	3 188	10 460	1943–52	1952
Pelée, Mont (Martinique)	1 397	4 584	1902, 1929–32	1932
Pinatubo, Mt (Philippines)	1 462	4 795	1391, 1991	1991
Popocatepetl (Mexico)	5 483	17 990	1920	1943
Rainier, Mt (USA)	4 392	14 416	1st-c BC, 1820	1882
Ruapehu (New Zealand)	2 796	9 175	1945, 1953, 1969, 1975	1986
St Helens, Mt (USA)	2 549	8 364	1800, 1831, 1835, 1842–3, 1857, 1980–	1987
Santorini/Thira (Greece)	1 315?	4 316?	1470 BC, 197 BC, AD 46, 1570–3, 1707–11, 1866–70	1950
Stromboli (Italy)	931	3 055	1768, 1882, 1889, 1907, 1930, 1936, 1941, 1950, 1952	1986
Surtsey (Iceland)	174	570	1963–7	1967

MAJOR VOLCANOES (cont.)

Name	Height m	ft	Major eruptions (years)	Last eruption (year)
Taal (Philippines)	1 448	4 752	1911, 1965, 1969	1977
Tambora (Sumbawa)	2 868	9 410	1815	1880
Tarawera (New Zealand)	1 149	3 770	1886	1973
Unzen (Japan)	1 360	4 461	1360, 1791	1991
Vesuvius (Italy)	1 289	4 230	79, 472, 1036, 1631, 1779, 1906	1944
Vulcano (Italy)	502	1 650	antiquity, 1444, 1730–40, 1786, 1873, 1888–90	1890

MAJOR EARTHQUAKES

All magnitudes on the Richter scale.

The energy released by earthquakes is measured on the logarithmic Richter scale. Thus

2 Barely perceptible
5 Rather strong
7+ Very strong

Location	Year	Magnitude	Deaths
Erzincum (Turkey)	1992	6.7	2000
Uttar Pradesh (India)	1991	6.1	1000
Costa Rica/Panama	1991	7.5	80
Georgia	1991	7.2	100
Afghanistan	1991	6.8	1000
Pakistan	1991	6.8	300
Cabanatuan City	1990	7.7	1653
NW Iran	1990	7.5	40 000
N Peru	1990	5.8	200
Romania	1990	6.6	70
Philippines	1990	7.7	1600
San Francisco	1989	6.9	100
Armenia	1988	7.0	25 000
SW China	1988	7.6	1000
Nepal/India	1988	6.9	900
Mexico City	1985	8.1	7 200
N Yemen	1982	6.0	2 800
S Italy	1980	7.2	4 500
El Asnam (Algeria)	1980	7.3	5 000
NE Iran	1978	7.7	25 000
Tangshan (China)	1976	8.2	242 000
Guatemala City	1976	7.5	22 778
Kashmir	1974	6.3	5 200
Managua (Nicaragua)	1972	6.2	5 000
S Iran	1972	6.9	5 000
Chimbote (Peru)	1970	7.7	66 000
NE Iran	1968	7.4	11 600

Location	Year	Magnitude	Deaths
Anchorage (USA)	1964	8.5	131
NW Iran	1962	7.1	12 000
Agadir (Morocco)	1960	5.8	12 000
Erzincan (Turkey)	1939	7.9	23 000
Chillan (Chile)	1939	7.8	30 000
Quetta (India)	1935	7.5	60 000
Gansu (China)	1932	7.6	70 000
Nan-shan (China)	1927	8.3	200 000
Kwanto (Japan)	1923	8.3	143 000
Gansu (China)	1920	8.6	180 000
Avezzano (Italy)	1915	7.5	30 000
Messina (Italy)	1908	7.5	120 000
Valparaiso (Chile)	1906	8.6	20 000
San Francisco (USA)	1906	8.3	500
Ecuador/Colombia	1868	*	70 000
Calabria (Italy)	1783	*	50 000
Lisbon (Portugal)	1755	*	70 000
Calcutta (India)	1737	*	300 000
Hokkaido (Japan)	1730	*	137 000
Catania (Italy)	1693	*	60 000
Caucasia (Caucasus)	1667	*	80 000
Shensi (China)	1556	*	830 000
Chihli (China)	1290	*	100 000
Silicia (Asia Minor)	1268	*	60 000
Corinth (Greece)	856	*	45 000
Antioch (Turkey)	526	*	250 000

*Magnitude not available

EARTHQUAKE SEVERITY MEASUREMENT

Modified Mercalli intensity scale (1956 Revision)

Intensity value	Description
I	Not felt; marginal and long-period effects of large earthquakes.
II	Felt by persons at rest, on upper floors or favourably placed.
III	Felt indoors; hanging objects swing; vibration like passing of light trucks; duration estimated; may not be recognized as an earthquake.
IV	Hanging objects swing; vibration like passing of heavy trucks, or sensation of a jolt like a heavy ball striking the walls; standing cars rock; windows, dishes, doors rattle; glasses clink; crockery clashes; in the upper range of IV, wooden walls and frames creak.
V	Felt outdoors; direction estimated; sleepers wakened; liquids disturbed, some spilled; small unstable objects displaced or upset; doors swing, close, open; shutters, pictures move; pendulum clocks stop, start, change rate.
VI	Felt by all; many frightened and run outdoors; persons walk unsteadily; windows, dishes, glassware break; knickknacks, books, etc, fall off shelves; pictures off walls; furniture moves or overturns; weak plaster and masonry D crack; small bells ring (church, school); trees, bushes shake visibly, or heard to rustle.
VII	Difficult to stand; noticed by drivers; hanging objects quiver; furniture breaks; damage to masonry D, including cracks; weak chimneys broken at roof line; fall of plaster, loose bricks, stones, tiles, cornices, also unbraced parapets and architectural ornaments; some cracks in masonry C; waves on ponds, water turbid with mud; small slides and caving in along sand or gravel banks; large bells ring; concrete irrigation ditches damaged.
VIII	Steering of cars affected; damage to masonry C and partial collapse; some damage to masonry B; none to masonry A; fall of stucco and some masonry walls; twisting, fall of chimneys, factory stacks, monuments, towers, elevated tanks; frame houses move on foundations if not bolted down; loose panel walls thrown out; decayed piling broken off; branches broken from trees; changes in flow or temperature of springs and wells; cracks in wet ground and on steep slopes.
IX	General panic; masonry D destroyed; masonry C heavily damaged, sometimes with complete collapse; masonry B seriously damaged; general damage to foundations; frame structures, if not bolted, shift off foundations; frames racked; serious damage to reservoirs; underground pipes break; conspicuous cracks in ground; in alluviated areas sand and mud ejected, earthquake fountains, sand craters.
X	Most masonry and frame structures destroyed with their foundations; some well-built wooden structures and bridges destroyed; serious damage to dams, dikes, embankments; large landslides; water thrown on banks of canals, rivers, lakes, etc; sand and mud shifted horizontally on beaches and flat land; rails bent slightly.
XI	Rails bent greatly; underground pipelines completely out of service.
XII	Damage nearly total; large rock masses displaced; lines of sight and level distorted; objects thrown into the air.

Note

Masonry A. Good workmanship, mortar and design; reinforced, especially laterally, and bound together by using steel, concrete etc; designed to resist lateral forces.

Masonry B. Good workmanship and mortar; reinforced, but not designed in detail to resist lateral forces.

Masonry C. Ordinary workmanship and mortar; no extreme weakness like failing to tie in at corners, but neither reinforced nor designed against horizontal forces.

Masonry D. Weak materials, such as adobe; poor mortar; low standards of workmanship; weak horizontally.

MAJOR TSUNAMIS

Tsunamis are long-period ocean waves associated with earthquakes, volcanic explosions, or landslides. They are also referred to as *seismic sea waves* and popularly, but incorrectly, as *tidal waves*.

Location of source	Year	Height m	Height ft	Location of deaths/damage	Deaths
Sea of Japan	1983	15	49	Japan, Korea	107
Indonesia	1979	10	32	Indonesia	187
Celebes Sea	1976	30	98	Philippine Is	5 000
Alaska	1964	32	105	Alaska, Aleutian Is, California	122
Chile	1960	25	82	Chile, Hawaii, Japan	1 260
Aleutian Is	1957	16	52	Hawaii, Japan	0
Kamchatka	1952	18.4	60	Kamchatka, Kuril Is, Hawaii	many
Aleutian Is	1946	32	105	Aleutian Is, Hawaii, California	165
Nankaido (Japan)	1946	6.1	20	Japan	1 997
Kii (Japan)	1944	7.5	25	Japan	998
Sanriku (Japan)	1933	28.2	93	Japan, Hawaii	3 000
E Kamchatka	1923	20	66	Kamchatka, Hawaii	3
S Kuril Is	1918	12	39	Kuril Is, Russia, Japan, Hawaii	23
Sanriku (Japan)	1896	30	98	Japan	27 122
Sunda Strait	1883	35	115	Java, Sumatra	36 000
Chile	1877	23	75	Chile, Hawaii	many
Chile	1868	21	69	Chile, Hawaii	25 000
Hawaii Is	1868	20	66	Hawaii Is	81
Japan	1854	6	20	Japan	3 000
Flores Sea	1800	24	79	Indonesia	4–500
Ariake Sea	1792	9	30	Japan	9 745
Italy	1783	?	?	Italy	30 000
Ryukyu Is	1771	12	39	Ryukyu Is	11 941
Portugal	1775	16	52	W Europe, Morocco, W Indies	60 000
Peru	1746	24	79	Peru	5 000
Japan	1741	9	30	Japan	1 000+
SE Kamchatka	1737	30	98	Kamchatka, Kuril Is	?
Peru	1724	24	79	Peru	?
Japan	1707	11.5	38	Japan	30 000
W Indies	1692	?	?	Jamaica	2 000
Banda Is	1629	15	49	Indonesia	?
Sanriku (Japan)	1611	25	82	Japan	5 000
Japan	1605	?	?	Japan	4 000
Kii (Japan)	1498	?	?	Japan	5 000

WIND FORCE AND SEA DISTURBANCE

Beaufort number	m/sec	Wind speed kph	Wind speed mph	Wind name	Observable wind characteristics	Sea disturbance number	Average wave ht. m	Average wave ht. ft	Observable sea characteristics
0	1	<1	<1	Calm	Smoke rises vertically	0	0	0	Sea like a mirror
1	1	1–5	1–3	Light air	Wind direction shown by smoke drift, but not by wind vanes	0	0	0	Ripples like scales, without foam crests
2	2	6–11	4–7	Light breeze	Wind felt on face; leaves rustle; vanes moved by wind	1	0.3	0–1	More definite wavelets, but crests do not break
3	4	12–19	8–12	Gentle breeze	Leaves and small twigs in constant motion; wind extends light flag	2	0.3–0.6	1–2	Large wavelets; crests beginning to break; scattered white horses
4	7	20–28	13–18	Moderate	Raises dust, loose paper; small branches moved	3	0.6–1.2	2–4	Small waves becoming longer; fairly frequent white horses
5	10	29–38	19–24	Fresh	Small trees in leaf begin to sway; crested wavelets on inland waters	4	1.2–2.4	4–8	Moderate waves with a more definite long form; many white horses; some spray possible
6	12	39–49	25–31	Strong	Large branches in motion; difficult to use umbrellas; whistling heard in telegraph wires	5	2.4–4	8–13	Large waves forming; more extensive white foam crests; some spray probable
7	15	50–61	32–38	Near gale	Whole trees in motion; inconvenience walking against wind	6	4–6	13–20	Sea heaps up; streaks of white foam blown along
8	18	62–74	39–46	Gale	Breaks twigs off trees; impedes progress	6	4–6	13–20	Moderately high waves of greater length; well-marked streaks of foam
9	20	75–88	47–54	Strong gale	Slight structural damage occurs	6	4–6	13–20	High waves; dense streaks of foam; sea begins to roll; spray affects visibility
10	26	89–102	55–63	Storm	Trees uprooted; considerable damage occurs	7	6–9	20–30	Very high waves with long overhanging crests; dense streaks of foam blown along; generally white appearance of surface; heavy rolling
11	30	103–17	64–72	Violent storm	Widespread damage	8	9–14	30–45	Exceptionally high waves; long white patches of foam; poor visibility; ships lost to view behind waves
12–17	⩾33	⩾118	⩾73	Hurricane		9	14	>45	Air filled with foam and spray; sea completely white; very poor visibility

WINDSTORMS

A **cyclone** is a circulation of winds in the atmosphere which rotates anticlockwise round a depression in the northern hemisphere and clockwise in the southern.

A **hurricane** is a windstorm originating over tropical oceans in the N hemisphere, having winds in excess of 74mph. Hurricanes are named by the National Hurricane Center, USA, in alphabetical sequence as they occur each year. Since 1978 names given have been alternately male/female. In the N Pacific they are known as **typhoons**. Abbrev H. and T.

A **tornado** is a column of air rotating rapidly around a very low pressure centre.

Name	Location	Year	Deaths	Damage in US $ million[1]
H.Bob	NE USA	1991	17	1 500
Cyclone	Bangladesh	1991	200 000	–
H.Hugo	S Carolina	1989	49	7 000
H.Gilbert	Caribbean, Mexico	1988	318	5 000
H.Joan	Caribbean	1988	216	–
Winter Storm	S England, NW France	1987	17	1 700
T.Vera	Korea (Democratic Republic)	1986	–	40
H.Juan	Louisiana	1985	12	1 500
H.Elena	Mississippi, Alabama, NW Florida	1985	2	1 250
H.Gloria	E USA	1985	15	900
H.Kate	Florida (Keys), NW Florida	1985	16	300
Cyclone	Bangladesh	1985	11 000	–
Ts.Ike and June	Philippines (Mindanao)	1984	1 000	220
H.Alicia	N Texas	1983	18	2 000
H.Allen	S Texas	1980	235	300
H.David	Florida, E USA	1979	2400	320
H.Frederic	Alabama, Mississippi	1979	31	2 300
H.Eloise	NW Florida	1975	100	490
H.Carmen	Louisiana	1974	1	150
Tornadoes	C USA	1974	322	1 000
H.Fifi	C America (Honduras)	1974	10 000	1 000
Cyclone Tracy	Australia (Darwin)	1974	65	1 000
H.Agnes	E Coast, USA	1972	122	2 100
Cyclone	Bangladesh	1970	300 000	86
H.Camille	Mississippi, Louisiana	1969	256	1 420.7
H.Beulah	S Texas	1967	15	200
H.Betsy	SE Florida, SE Louisiana, Mississippi	1965	75	1 420.5
T.Louise	Philippines (Mindanao)	1964	58	600
H.Hilda	C Louisiana	1964	38	125
H.Dora	NE Florida	1964	5	250
H.Cleo	SE Florida	1964	154	128.5
H.Flora	Haiti, Cuba, Dominican Republic	1963	7 000	625
H.Carla	Texas	1961	46	408
H.Donna	Florida, E USA	1960	50	387
T.Vera	Ise Bay, Japan	1959	5 098	600
H.Audrey	Louisiana, N Texas	1957	390	150
H.Diane	NE USA	1955	184	831.7
H.Hazel	S Carolina, N Carolina	1954	95	281
H.Carol	NE USA	1954	60	461
Typhoon	Japan (Toyama, N Honshu)	1954	3 000	–
Hurricane	SE Florida, Louisiana, Mississippi	1947	51	110
Typhoon	Japan (Makurazaki)	1945	3 756	400

Phanerozoic	Palaeozoic	Permian	Late Early	258 286	Some sea areas cut off to form lakes. Earth movements form mountains. Glaciation in southern hemisphere.	Some shelled fish become extinct.	Deciduous plants. Reptiles dominant. Many insect varieties.
		Carboniferous	Pennsylvanian Mississippian	320 360	Sea-beds rise to form new land areas. Enormous swamps. Partly-rotted vegetation forms coal.	Amphibians and sharks abundant.	Extensive evergreen forests. Reptiles breed on land. Some insects develop wings.
		Devonian	Late Middle Early	374 387 408	Collision of continents causing mountain formation (Appalachians, Caledonides and Urals). Sea deeper but narrower. Climatic zones forming. Iapetus ocean closed.	Fish abundant. Primitive sharks. First amphibians.	Leafy plants. Some invertebrates adapt to land. First insects.
		Silurian	Pridoli Ludlow Wenlock Llandovery	414 421 428 438	New mountain ranges form. Sea level varies periodically. Extensive shallow sea over the Sahara.	Large vertebrates.	First leafless land plants.
		Ordovician	Ashgill Caradoc Llandeilo Llanvirn Arenig Tremadoc	448 458 468 478 488 505	Shore lines still quite variable. Increasing sedimentation. Europe and N America moving together.	First vertebrates. Coral reefs develop.	None.
		Cambrian	Merioneth St David's Caerfai	525 540 590	Much volcanic activity, and long periods of marine sedimentation.	Shelled invertebrates. Trilobites.	None.
Proterozoic	Precambrian	Vendian		650	Shallow seas advance and retreat over land areas. Atmosphere uniformly warm.	Seaweed. Algae and invertebrates.	None.
		Riphean	Late Middle Early	900 1300	Intense deformation and metamorphism.	Earliest marine life and fossils.	None.
		Early Proterozoic		1600 2500	Shallow shelf seas. Formation of carbonate sediments and 'red beds'.	First appearance of stromatolites.	None.
Archaean		Archaean (Azoic)		4600	Banded iron formations. Formation of the earth's crust and oceans.	None.	None.

CLIMATIC ZONES

The earth may be divided into zones, approximating to zones of latitude, such that each zone possesses a distinct type of climate.

The principal zones are:

Tropical One zone of wet climate near the equator (either constantly wet or monsoonal with wet and dry seasons, tropical savannah with dry winters); the average temperature is not below 18°C;

Amazon forest	Congo Basin
Malaysia	Indonesia
S Vietnam	S E Asia
India	Australia
Africa	

Subtropical Two zones of steppe and desert climate (transition through semi-arid to arid);

Sahara	Australia
Central Asia	Kalahari
Mexico	

Mediterranean Zones of rainy climates with mild winters; coolest month above 0°C but below 18°C;

California	parts of Chile
S Africa	SW Australia
S Europe	

Temperate Rainy climate (includes areas of temperate woodland, mountain forests, and plains with no dry season; influenced by seas – rainfall all year, small temperature changes); average temperature between 3°C and 18°C;

Most of Europe	New Zealand
Eastern Asia	Southern Chile
NW/NE USA	

Boreal Climate with a great range of temperature in the northern hemisphere (in some areas the most humid month is in summer and there is ten times more precipitation than the driest part of winter. In other areas the most humid month is in winter and there is ten times more precipitation than in the driest part of summer); in the coldest period temperatures do not exceed 3°C and in the hottest do not go below 10°C;

Prairies of USA	parts of Russia
parts of S Africa	parts of Australia

Polar caps (2) of arctic snow climate (tundra and ice-cap) with little or no precipitation. There is permafrost in the tundra and vegetation includes lichen and moss all year and grass in the summer; the highest annual temperature in the polar region is below 0°C and in the tundra the average temperature is 10°C

Arctic regions of Russia and N America	Antartica

GREAT ICE AGES

Precambrian era	Early Proterozoic
Precambrian era	Upper Proterozoic
Palaeozoic era	Upper Carboniferous
Cenozoic era	Pleistocene[1] (Last 4 periods of glaciation) Gunz (Nebraskan or Jerseyan) 520 000–490 000 years ago Mindel (Kansan) 430 000–370 000 years ago Riss (Illinoian) 130 000–100 000 years ago Wurm (Wisconsan and Lowan) 40 000–18 000 years ago

[1]The Pleistocene era is synonymous with 'The Ice Age'

YEAR EQUIVALENTS

Jewish[1] (AM)

5752	(9 Sep	1991—27 Sep	1992)
5753	(28 Sep	1992—15 Sep	1993)
5754	(16 Sep	1993— 5 Sep	1994)
5755	(6 Sep	1994—24 Sep	1995)
5756	(25 Sep	1995—13 Sep	1996)
5757	(14 Sep	1996— 1 Oct	1997)
5758	(2 Oct	1997—20 Sep	1998)
5759	(21 Sep	1998—10 Sep	1999)
5760	(11 Sep	1999—29 Sep	2000)

Islamic[2] (H)

1412	(13 Jul	1991— 1 Jul	1992)
1413	(2 Jul	1992—20 Jun	1993)
1414	(21 Jun	1993— 9 Jun	1994)
1415	(10 Jun	1994—30 May	1995)
1416	(31 May	1995—18 May	1996)
1417	(19 May	1996— 8 May	1997)
1418	(9 May	1997—27 Apr	1998)
1419	(28 Apr	1998—16 Apr	1999)
1420	(17 Apr	1999— 5 Apr	2000)

Hindu[3] (SE)

1913	(22 Mar	1991—20 Mar	1992)
1914	(21 Mar	1992—21 Mar	1993)
1915	(22 Mar	1993—21 Mar	1994)
1916	(22 Mar	1994—21 Mar	1995)
1917	(22 Mar	1995—20 Mar	1996)
1918	(21 Mar	1996—21 Mar	1997)
1919	(22 Mar	1997—21 Mar	1998)
1920	(22 Mar	1998—21 Mar	1999)
1921	(22 Mar	1999—21 Mar	2000)

Gregorian equivalents are given in parentheses and are AD (= Anno Domini).

[1] Calculated from 3761 BC, said to be the year of the creation of the world. AM = Anno Mundi.

[2] Calculated from AD 622, the year in which the Prophet went from Mecca to Medina. H = Hegira.

[3] Calculated from AD 78, the beginning of the Saka era (SE), used alongside Gregorian dates in Government of India publications since 22 Mar 1957. Other important Hindu eras include: Vikrama era (58 BC), Kalacuri era (AD 248), Gupta era (AD 320), and Harsa era (AD 606).

MONTH EQUIVALENTS

Gregorian equivalents to other calendars are given in parentheses; the figures refer to the number of solar days in each month.

Gregorian

(Basis: Sun)
January (31)
February (28 or 29)
March (31)
April (30)
May (31)
June (30)
July (31)
August (31)
September (30)
October (31)
November (30)
December (31)

Jewish

(Basis: Moon)
Tishri (Sep–Oct) (30)
Heshvan (Oct–Nov) (29 or 30)
Kislev (Nov–Dec) (29 or 30)
Tevet (Dec–Jan) (29)
Shevat (Jan–Feb) (30)
Adar (Feb–Mar) (29 or 30)
Adar Sheni *leap years only*
Nisan (Mar–Apr) (30)
Iyar (Apr–May) (29)
Sivan (May–Jun) (30)
Tammuz (Jun–Jul) (29)
Av (Jul–Aug) (30)
Elul (Aug–Sep) (29)

Islamic

(Basis: Moon)
Muharram (Sep–Oct) (30)
Safar (Oct–Nov) (29)
Rabi I (Nov–Dec) (30)
Rabi II (Dec–Jan) (29)
Jumada I (Jan–Feb) (30)
Jumada II (Feb–Mar) (29)
Rajab (Mar–Apr) (30)
Shaban (Apr–May) (29)
Ramadan (May–Jun) (30)
Shawwal (Jun–Jul) (29)
Dhu al-Qadah (Jul–Aug) (30)
Dhu al-Hijjah (Aug–Sep) (29 or 30)

Hindu

(Basis: Moon)
Chaitra (Mar–Apr) (29 or 30)
Vaisakha (Apr–May) (29 or 30)
Jyaistha (May–Jun) (29 or 30)
Asadha (Jun–Jul) (29 or 30)
Dvitiya Asadha (*certain leap years*)
Sravana (Jul–Aug) (29 or 30)
Dvitiya Sravana (*certain leap years*)
Bhadrapada (Aug–Sep) (29 or 30)
Asvina (Sep–Oct) (29 or 30)
Karttika (Oct–Nov) (29 or 30)
Margasirsa (Nov–Dec) (29 or 30)
Pausa (Dec–Jan) (29 or 30)
Magha (Jan–Feb) (29 or 30)
Phalguna (Feb–Mar) (29 or 30)

CHINESE ANIMAL YEARS AND TIMES 1984–2007

Chinese	English	Years		Time of day (hours)	Chinese	English	Years		Time of day (hours)
Shu	Rat	1984	1996	2300–0100	Ma	Horse	1990	2002	1100–1300
Niu	Ox	1985	1997	0100–0300	Yang	Sheep	1991	2003	1300–1500
Hu	Tiger	1986	1998	0300–0500	Hou	Monkey	1992	2004	1500–1700
T'u	Hare	1987	1999	0500–0700	Chi	Cock	1993	2005	1700–1900
Lung	Dragon	1988	2000	0700–0900	Kou	Dog	1994	2006	1900–2100
She	Serpent	1989	2001	0900–1100	Chu	Boar	1995	2007	2100–2300

PERPETUAL CALENDAR 1801–2000

The calendar for each year is given under the corresponding letter overpage.

1801	I	1821	C	1841	K	1861	E	1881	M
1802	K	1822	E	1842	M	1862	G	1882	A
1803	M	1823	G	1843	A	1863	I	1883	C
1804	B	1824	J	1844	D	1864	L	1884	F
1805	E	1825	M	1845	G	1865	A	1885	I
1806	G	1826	A	1846	I	1866	C	1886	K
1807	I	1827	C	1847	K	1867	E	1887	M
1808	L	1828	F	1848	N	1868	H	1888	B
1809	A	1829	I	1849	C	1869	K	1889	E
1810	C	1830	K	1850	E	1870	M	1890	G
1811	E	1831	M	1851	G	1871	A	1891	I
1812	H	1832	B	1852	J	1872	D	1892	L
1813	K	1833	E	1853	M	1873	G	1893	A
1814	M	1834	G	1854	A	1874	I	1894	C
1815	A	1835	I	1855	C	1875	K	1895	E
1816	D	1836	L	1856	F	1876	N	1896	H
1817	G	1837	A	1857	I	1877	C	1897	K
1818	I	1838	C	1858	K	1878	E	1898	M
1819	K	1839	E	1859	M	1879	G	1899	A
1820	N	1840	H	1860	B	1880	J	1900	C
1901	E	1921	M	1941	G	1961	A	1981	I
1902	G	1922	A	1942	I	1962	C	1982	*K*
1903	I	1923	C	1943	K	1963	E	1983	M
1904	L	1924	F	1944	N	1964	H	1984	B
1905	A	1925	I	1945	C	1965	K	1985	E
1906	C	1926	K	1946	E	1966	M	1986	G
1907	E	1927	M	1947	G	1967	A	1987	I
1908	H	1928	B	1948	J	1968	D	1988	L
1909	K	1929	E	1949	M	1969	G	1989	A
1910	M	1930	G	1950	A	1970	I	1990	C
1911	A	1931	I	1951	C	1971	K	1991	E
1912	D	1932	L	1952	F	1972	N	1992	H
1913	G	1933	A	1953	I	1973	C	1993	K
1914	I	1934	C	1954	K	1974	E	1994	M
1915	K	1935	E	1955	M	1975	G	1995	A
1916	N	1936	H	1956	B	1976	J	1996	D
1917	C	1937	K	1957	E	1977	M	1997	G
1918	E	1938	M	1958	G	1978	A	1998	I
1919	G	1939	A	1959	I	1979	C	1999	K
1920	J	1940	D	1960	L	1980	F	2000	N

PERPETUAL CALENDAR 1801–2000 (cont.)

A

January

S	M	T	W	T	F	S
1	2	3	4	5	6	7
8	9	10	11	12	13	14
15	16	17	18	19	20	21
22	23	24	25	26	27	28
29	30	31				

February

S	M	T	W	T	F	S
			1	2	3	4
5	6	7	8	9	10	11
12	13	14	15	16	17	18
19	20	21	22	23	24	25
26	27	28				

March

S	M	T	W	T	F	S
			1	2	3	4
5	6	7	8	9	10	11
12	13	14	15	16	17	18
19	20	21	22	23	24	25
26	27	28	29	30	31	

April

S	M	T	W	T	F	S
						1
2	3	4	5	6	7	8
9	10	11	12	13	14	15
16	17	18	19	20	21	22
23	24	25	26	27	28	29
30						

May

S	M	T	W	T	F	S
	1	2	3	4	5	6
7	8	9	10	11	12	13
14	15	16	17	18	19	20
21	22	23	24	25	26	27
28	29	30	31			

June

S	M	T	W	T	F	S
				1	2	3
4	5	6	7	8	9	10
11	12	13	14	15	16	17
18	19	20	21	22	23	24
25	26	27	28	29	30	

July

S	M	T	W	T	F	S
						1
2	3	4	5	6	7	8
9	10	11	12	13	14	15
16	17	18	19	20	21	22
23	24	25	26	27	28	29
30	31					

August

S	M	T	W	T	F	S
		1	2	3	4	5
6	7	8	9	10	11	12
13	14	15	16	17	18	19
20	21	22	23	24	25	26
27	28	29	30	31		

September

S	M	T	W	T	F	S
					1	2
3	4	5	6	7	8	9
10	11	12	13	14	15	16
17	18	19	20	21	22	23
24	25	26	27	28	29	30

October

S	M	T	W	T	F	S
1	2	3	4	5	6	7
8	9	10	11	12	13	14
15	16	17	18	19	20	21
22	23	24	25	26	27	28
29	30	31				

November

S	M	T	W	T	F	S
			1	2	3	4
5	6	7	8	9	10	11
12	13	14	15	16	17	18
19	20	21	22	23	24	25
26	27	28	29	30		

December

S	M	T	W	T	F	S
					1	2
3	4	5	6	7	8	9
10	11	12	13	14	15	16
17	18	19	20	21	22	23
24	25	26	27	28	29	30
31						

B (leap year)

January

S	M	T	W	T	F	S
1	2	3	4	5	6	7
8	9	10	11	12	13	14
15	16	17	18	19	20	21
22	23	24	25	26	27	28
29	30	31				

February

S	M	T	W	T	F	S
			1	2	3	4
5	6	7	8	9	10	11
12	13	14	15	16	17	18
19	20	21	22	23	24	25
26	27	28	29			

March

S	M	T	W	T	F	S
				1	2	3
4	5	6	7	8	9	10
11	12	13	14	15	16	17
18	19	20	21	22	23	24
25	26	27	28	29	30	31

April

S	M	T	W	T	F	S
1	2	3	4	5	6	7
8	9	10	11	12	13	14
15	16	17	18	19	20	21
22	23	24	25	26	27	28
29	30					

May

S	M	T	W	T	F	S
		1	2	3	4	5
6	7	8	9	10	11	12
13	14	15	16	17	18	19
20	21	22	23	24	25	26
27	28	29	30	31		

June

S	M	T	W	T	F	S
					1	2
3	4	5	6	7	8	9
10	11	12	13	14	15	16
17	18	19	20	21	22	23
24	25	26	27	28	29	30

July

S	M	T	W	T	F	S
1	2	3	4	5	6	7
8	9	10	11	12	13	14
15	16	17	18	19	20	21
22	23	24	25	26	27	28
29	30	31				

August

S	M	T	W	T	F	S
			1	2	3	4
5	6	7	8	9	10	11
12	13	14	15	16	17	18
19	20	21	22	23	24	25
26	27	28	29	30	31	

September

S	M	T	W	T	F	S
						1
2	3	4	5	6	7	8
9	10	11	12	13	14	15
16	17	18	19	20	21	22
23	24	25	26	27	28	29
30						

October

S	M	T	W	T	F	S
	1	2	3	4	5	6
7	8	9	10	11	12	13
14	15	16	17	18	19	20
21	22	23	24	25	26	27
28	29	30	31			

November

S	M	T	W	T	F	S
				1	2	3
4	5	6	7	8	9	10
11	12	13	14	15	16	17
18	19	20	21	22	23	24
25	26	27	28	29	30	

December

S	M	T	W	T	F	S
						1
2	3	4	5	6	7	8
9	10	11	12	13	14	15
16	17	18	19	20	21	22
23	24	25	26	27	28	29
30	31					

PERPETUAL CALENDAR 1801–2000 (cont.)

C

January

S	M	T	W	T	F	S
	1	2	3	4	5	6
7	8	9	10	11	12	13
14	15	16	17	18	19	20
21	22	23	24	25	26	27
28	29	30	31			

February

S	M	T	W	T	F	S
				1	2	3
4	5	6	7	8	9	10
11	12	13	14	15	16	17
18	19	20	21	22	23	24
25	26	27	28			

March

S	M	T	W	T	F	S
				1	2	3
4	5	6	7	8	9	10
11	12	13	14	15	16	17
18	19	20	21	22	23	24
25	26	27	28	29	30	31

April

S	M	T	W	T	F	S
1	2	3	4	5	6	7
8	9	10	11	12	13	14
15	16	17	18	19	20	21
22	23	24	25	26	27	28
29	30					

May

		1	2	3	4	5
6	7	8	9	10	11	12
13	14	15	16	17	18	19
20	21	22	23	24	25	26
27	28	29	30	31		

June

					1	2
3	4	5	6	7	8	9
10	11	12	13	14	15	16
17	18	19	20	21	22	23
24	25	26	27	28	29	30

July

1	2	3	4	5	6	7
8	9	10	11	12	13	14
15	16	17	18	19	20	21
22	23	24	25	26	27	28
29	30	31				

August

			1	2	3	4
5	6	7	8	9	10	11
12	13	14	15	16	17	18
19	20	21	22	23	24	25
26	27	28	29	30	31	

September

						1
2	3	4	5	6	7	8
9	10	11	12	13	14	15
16	17	18	19	20	21	22
23	24	25	26	27	28	29
30						

October

	1	2	3	4	5	6
7	8	9	10	11	12	13
14	15	16	17	18	19	20
21	22	23	24	25	26	27
28	29	30	31			

November

				1	2	3
4	5	6	7	8	9	10
11	12	13	14	15	16	17
18	19	20	21	22	23	24
25	26	27	28	29	30	

December

						1
2	3	4	5	6	7	8
9	10	11	12	13	14	15
16	17	18	19	20	21	22
23	24	25	26	27	28	29
30	31					

D (leap year)

January

S	M	T	W	T	F	S
	1	2	3	4	5	6
7	8	9	10	11	12	13
14	15	16	17	18	19	20
21	22	23	24	25	26	27
28	29	30	31			

February

S	M	T	W	T	F	S
				1	2	3
4	5	6	7	8	9	10
11	12	13	14	15	16	17
18	19	20	21	22	23	24
25	26	27	28	29		

March

S	M	T	W	T	F	S
					1	2
3	4	5	6	7	8	9
10	11	12	13	14	15	16
17	18	19	20	21	22	23
24	25	26	27	28	29	30
31						

April

S	M	T	W	T	F	S
	1	2	3	4	5	6
7	8	9	10	11	12	13
14	15	16	17	18	19	20
21	22	23	24	25	26	27
28	29	30				

May

			1	2	3	4
5	6	7	8	9	10	11
12	13	14	15	16	17	18
19	20	21	22	23	24	25
26	27	28	29	30	31	

June

						1
2	3	4	5	6	7	8
9	10	11	12	13	14	15
16	17	18	19	20	21	22
23	24	25	26	27	28	29
30						

July

	1	2	3	4	5	6
7	8	9	10	11	12	13
14	15	16	17	18	19	20
21	22	23	24	25	26	27
28	29	30	31			

August

				1	2	3
4	5	6	7	8	9	10
11	12	13	14	15	16	17
18	19	20	21	22	23	24
25	26	27	28	29	30	31

September

1	2	3	4	5	6	7
8	9	10	11	12	13	14
15	16	17	18	19	20	21
22	23	24	25	26	27	28
29	30					

October

		1	2	3	4	5
6	7	8	9	10	11	12
13	14	15	16	17	18	19
20	21	22	23	24	25	26
27	28	29	30	31		

November

					1	2
3	4	5	6	7	8	9
10	11	12	13	14	15	16
17	18	19	20	21	22	23
24	25	26	27	28	29	30

December

1	2	3	4	5	6	7
8	9	10	11	12	13	14
15	16	17	18	19	20	21
22	23	24	25	26	27	28
29	30	31				

PERPETUAL CALENDAR 1801–2000 (cont.)

E

January

S	M	T	W	T	F	S
		1	2	3	4	5
6	7	8	9	10	11	12
13	14	15	16	17	18	19
20	21	22	23	24	25	26
27	28	29	30	31		

February

S	M	T	W	T	F	S
					1	2
3	4	5	6	7	8	9
10	11	12	13	14	15	16
17	18	19	20	21	22	23
24	25	26	27	28		

March

S	M	T	W	T	F	S
					1	2
3	4	5	6	7	8	9
10	11	12	13	14	15	16
17	18	19	20	21	22	23
24	25	26	27	28	29	30
31						

April

S	M	T	W	T	F	S
	1	2	3	4	5	6
7	8	9	10	11	12	13
14	15	16	17	18	19	20
21	22	23	24	25	26	27
28	29	30				

May

			1	2	3	4
5	6	7	8	9	10	11
12	13	14	15	16	17	18
19	20	21	22	23	24	25
26	27	28	29	30	31	

June

						1
2	3	4	5	6	7	8
9	10	11	12	13	14	15
16	17	18	19	20	21	22
23	24	25	26	27	28	29
30						

July

	1	2	3	4	5	6
7	8	9	10	11	12	13
14	15	16	17	18	19	20
21	22	23	24	25	26	27
28	29	30	31			

August

				1	2	3
4	5	6	7	8	9	10
11	12	13	14	15	16	17
18	19	20	21	22	23	24
25	26	27	28	29	30	31

September

1	2	3	4	5	6	7
8	9	10	11	12	13	14
15	16	17	18	19	20	21
22	23	24	25	26	27	28
29	30					

October

		1	2	3	4	5
6	7	8	9	10	11	12
13	14	15	16	17	18	19
20	21	22	23	24	25	26
27	28	29	30	31		

November

					1	2
3	4	5	6	7	8	9
10	11	12	13	14	15	16
17	18	19	20	21	22	23
24	25	26	27	28	29	30

December

1	2	3	4	5	6	7
8	9	10	11	12	13	14
15	16	17	18	19	20	21
22	23	24	25	26	27	28
29	30	31				

F (leap year)

January

S	M	T	W	T	F	S
		1	2	3	4	5
6	7	8	9	10	11	12
13	14	15	16	17	18	19
20	21	22	23	24	25	26
27	28	29	30	31		

February

S	M	T	W	T	F	S
					1	2
3	4	5	6	7	8	9
10	11	12	13	14	15	16
17	18	19	20	21	22	23
24	25	26	27	28	29	

March

S	M	T	W	T	F	S
						1
2	3	4	5	6	7	8
9	10	11	12	13	14	15
16	17	18	19	20	21	22
23	24	25	26	27	28	29
30	31					

April

S	M	T	W	T	F	S
		1	2	3	4	5
6	7	8	9	10	11	12
13	14	15	16	17	18	19
20	21	22	23	24	25	26
27	28	29	30			

May

				1	2	3
4	5	6	7	8	9	10
11	12	13	14	15	16	17
18	19	20	21	22	23	24
25	26	27	28	29	30	31

June

1	2	3	4	5	6	7
8	9	10	11	12	13	14
15	16	17	18	19	20	21
22	23	24	25	26	27	28
29	30					

July

		1	2	3	4	5
6	7	8	9	10	11	12
13	14	15	16	17	18	19
20	21	22	23	24	25	26
27	28	29	30	31		

August

					1	2
3	4	5	6	7	8	9
10	11	12	13	14	15	16
17	18	19	20	21	22	23
24	25	26	27	28	29	30
31						

September

	1	2	3	4	5	6
7	8	9	10	11	12	13
14	15	16	17	18	19	20
21	22	23	24	25	26	27
28	29	30				

October

			1	2	3	4
5	6	7	8	9	10	11
12	13	14	15	16	17	18
19	20	21	22	23	24	25
26	27	28	29	30	31	

November

						1
2	3	4	5	6	7	8
9	10	11	12	13	14	15
16	17	18	19	20	21	22
23	24	25	26	27	28	29
30						

December

	1	2	3	4	5	6
7	8	9	10	11	12	13
14	15	16	17	18	19	20
21	22	23	24	25	26	27
28	29	30	31			

PERPETUAL CALENDAR 1801–2000 (cont.)

G

January

S	M	T	W	T	F	S
			1	2	3	4
5	6	7	8	9	10	11
12	13	14	15	16	17	18
19	20	21	22	23	24	25
26	27	28	29	30	31	

February

S	M	T	W	T	F	S
						1
2	3	4	5	6	7	8
9	10	11	12	13	14	15
16	17	18	19	20	21	22
23	24	25	26	27	28	

March

S	M	T	W	T	F	S
						1
2	3	4	5	6	7	8
9	10	11	12	13	14	15
16	17	18	19	20	21	22
23	24	25	26	27	28	29
30	31					

April

S	M	T	W	T	F	S
		1	2	3	4	5
6	7	8	9	10	11	12
13	14	15	16	17	18	19
20	21	22	23	24	25	26
27	28	29	30			

May

				1	2	3
4	5	6	7	8	9	10
11	12	13	14	15	16	17
18	19	20	21	22	23	24
25	26	27	28	29	30	31

June

1	2	3	4	5	6	7
8	9	10	11	12	13	14
15	16	17	18	19	20	21
22	23	24	25	26	27	28
29	30					

July

		1	2	3	4	5
6	7	8	9	10	11	12
13	14	15	16	17	18	19
20	21	22	23	24	25	26
27	28	29	30	31		

August

					1	2
3	4	5	6	7	8	9
10	11	12	13	14	15	16
17	18	19	20	21	22	23
24	25	26	27	28	29	30
31						

September

	1	2	3	4	5	6
7	8	9	10	11	12	13
14	15	16	17	18	19	20
21	22	23	24	25	26	27
28	29	30				

October

			1	2	3	4
5	6	7	8	9	10	11
12	13	14	15	16	17	18
19	20	21	22	23	24	25
26	27	28	29	30	31	

November

						1
2	3	4	5	6	7	8
9	10	11	12	13	14	15
16	17	18	19	20	21	22
23	24	25	26	27	28	29
30						

December

	1	2	3	4	5	6
7	8	9	10	11	12	13
14	15	16	17	18	19	20
21	22	23	24	25	26	27
28	29	30	31			

H (leap year)

January

S	M	T	W	T	F	S
			1	2	3	4
5	6	7	8	9	10	11
12	13	14	15	16	17	18
19	20	21	22	23	24	25
26	27	28	29	30	31	

February

S	M	T	W	T	F	S
						1
2	3	4	5	6	7	8
9	10	11	12	13	14	15
16	17	18	19	20	21	22
23	24	25	26	27	28	29

March

S	M	T	W	T	F	S
1	2	3	4	5	6	7
8	9	10	11	12	13	14
15	16	17	18	19	20	21
22	23	24	25	26	27	28
29	30	31				

April

S	M	T	W	T	F	S
			1	2	3	4
5	6	7	8	9	10	11
12	13	14	15	16	17	18
19	20	21	22	23	24	25
26	27	28	29	30		

May

					1	2
3	4	5	6	7	8	9
10	11	12	13	14	15	16
17	18	19	20	21	22	23
24	25	26	27	28	29	30
31						

June

	1	2	3	4	5	6
7	8	9	10	11	12	13
14	15	16	17	18	19	20
21	22	23	24	25	26	27
28	29	30				

July

			1	2	3	4
5	6	7	8	9	10	11
12	13	14	15	16	17	18
19	20	21	22	23	24	25
26	27	28	29	30	31	

August

						1
2	3	4	5	6	7	8
9	10	11	12	13	14	15
16	17	18	19	20	21	22
23	24	25	26	27	28	29
30	31					

September

		1	2	3	4	5
6	7	8	9	10	11	12
13	14	15	16	17	18	19
20	21	22	23	24	25	26
27	28	29	30			

October

				1	2	3
4	5	6	7	8	9	10
11	12	13	14	15	16	17
18	19	20	21	22	23	24
25	26	27	28	29	30	31

November

1	2	3	4	5	6	7
8	9	10	11	12	13	14
15	16	17	18	19	20	21
22	23	24	25	26	27	28
29	30					

December

		1	2	3	4	5
6	7	8	9	10	11	12
13	14	15	16	17	18	19
20	21	22	23	24	25	26
27	28	29	30	31		

PERPETUAL CALENDAR 1801–2000 (cont.)

I

January

S	M	T	W	T	F	S
				1	2	3
4	5	6	7	8	9	10
11	12	13	14	15	16	17
18	19	20	21	22	23	24
25	26	27	28	29	30	31

February

S	M	T	W	T	F	S
1	2	3	4	5	6	7
8	9	10	11	12	13	14
15	16	17	18	19	20	21
22	23	24	25	26	27	28

March

S	M	T	W	T	F	S
1	2	3	4	5	6	7
8	9	10	11	12	13	14
15	16	17	18	19	20	21
22	23	24	25	26	27	28
29	30	31				

April

S	M	T	W	T	F	S
			1	2	3	4
5	6	7	8	9	10	11
12	13	14	15	16	17	18
19	20	21	22	23	24	25
26	27	28	29	30		

May

					1	2
3	4	5	6	7	8	9
10	11	12	13	14	15	16
17	18	19	20	21	22	23
24	25	26	27	28	29	30
31						

June

	1	2	3	4	5	6
7	8	9	10	11	12	13
14	15	16	17	18	19	20
21	22	23	24	25	26	27
28	29	30				

July

			1	2	3	4
5	6	7	8	9	10	11
12	13	14	15	16	17	18
19	20	21	22	23	24	25
26	27	28	29	30	31	

August

						1
2	3	4	5	6	7	8
9	10	11	12	13	14	15
16	17	18	19	20	21	22
23	24	25	26	27	28	29
30	31					

September

		1	2	3	4	5
6	7	8	9	10	11	12
13	14	15	16	17	18	19
20	21	22	23	24	25	26
27	28	29	30			

October

				1	2	3
4	5	6	7	8	9	10
11	12	13	14	15	16	17
18	19	20	21	22	23	24
25	26	27	28	29	30	31

November

1	2	3	4	5	6	7
8	9	10	11	12	13	14
15	16	17	18	19	20	21
22	23	24	25	26	27	28
29	30					

December

		1	2	3	4	5
6	7	8	9	10	11	12
13	14	15	16	17	18	19
20	21	22	23	24	25	26
27	28	29	30	31		

J (leap year)

January

S	M	T	W	T	F	S
				1	2	3
4	5	6	7	8	9	10
11	12	13	14	15	16	17
18	19	20	21	22	23	24
25	26	27	28	29	30	31

February

S	M	T	W	T	F	S
1	2	3	4	5	6	7
8	9	10	11	12	13	14
15	16	17	18	19	20	21
22	23	24	25	26	27	28
29						

March

S	M	T	W	T	F	S
	1	2	3	4	5	6
7	8	9	10	11	12	13
14	15	16	17	18	19	20
21	22	23	24	25	26	27
28	29	30	31			

April

S	M	T	W	T	F	S
				1	2	3
4	5	6	7	8	9	10
11	12	13	14	15	16	17
18	19	20	21	22	23	24
25	26	27	28	29	30	

May

						1
2	3	4	5	6	7	8
9	10	11	12	13	14	15
16	17	18	19	20	21	22
23	24	25	26	27	28	29
30	31					

June

		1	2	3	4	5
6	7	8	9	10	11	12
13	14	15	16	17	18	19
20	21	22	23	24	25	26
27	28	29	30			

July

				1	2	3
4	5	6	7	8	9	10
11	12	13	14	15	16	17
18	19	20	21	22	23	24
25	26	27	28	29	30	31

August

1	2	3	4	5	6	7
8	9	10	11	12	13	14
15	16	17	18	19	20	21
22	23	24	25	26	27	28
29	30	31				

September

			1	2	3	4
5	6	7	8	9	10	11
12	13	14	15	16	17	18
19	20	21	22	23	24	25
26	27	28	29	30		

October

					1	2
3	4	5	6	7	8	9
10	11	12	13	14	15	16
17	18	19	20	21	22	23
24	25	26	27	28	29	30
31						

November

	1	2	3	4	5	6
7	8	9	10	11	12	13
14	15	16	17	18	19	20
21	22	23	24	25	26	27
28	29	30				

December

			1	2	3	4
5	6	7	8	9	10	11
12	13	14	15	16	17	18
19	20	21	22	23	24	25
26	27	28	29	30	31	

PERPETUAL CALENDAR 1801–2000 (cont.)

K

January

S	M	T	W	T	F	S
					1	2
3	4	5	6	7	8	9
10	11	12	13	14	15	16
17	18	19	20	21	22	23
24	25	26	27	28	29	30
31						

February

S	M	T	W	T	F	S
	1	2	3	4	5	6
7	8	9	10	11	12	13
14	15	16	17	18	19	20
21	22	23	24	25	26	27
28						

March

S	M	T	W	T	F	S
	1	2	3	4	5	6
7	8	9	10	11	12	13
14	15	16	17	18	19	20
21	22	23	24	25	26	27
28	29	30	31			

April

S	M	T	W	T	F	S
				1	2	3
4	5	6	7	8	9	10
11	12	13	14	15	16	17
18	19	20	21	22	23	24
25	26	27	28	29	30	

May

						1
2	3	4	5	6	7	8
9	10	11	12	13	14	15
16	17	18	19	20	21	22
23	24	25	26	27	28	29
30	31					

June

		1	2	3	4	5
6	7	8	9	10	11	12
13	14	15	16	17	18	19
20	21	22	23	24	25	26
27	28	29	30			

July

				1	2	3
4	5	6	7	8	9	10
11	12	13	14	15	16	17
18	19	20	21	22	23	24
25	26	27	28	29	30	31

August

1	2	3	4	5	6	7
8	9	10	11	12	13	14
15	16	17	18	19	20	21
22	23	24	25	26	27	28
29	30	31				

September

			1	2	3	4
5	6	7	8	9	10	11
12	13	14	15	16	17	18
19	20	21	22	23	24	25
26	27	28	29	30		

October

					1	2
3	4	5	6	7	8	9
10	11	12	13	14	15	16
17	18	19	20	21	22	23
24	25	26	27	28	29	30
31						

November

	1	2	3	4	5	6
7	8	9	10	11	12	13
14	15	16	17	18	19	20
21	22	23	24	25	26	27
28	29	30				

December

			1	2	3	4
5	6	7	8	9	10	11
12	13	14	15	16	17	18
19	20	21	22	23	24	25
26	27	28	29	30	31	

L (leap year)

January

S	M	T	W	T	F	S
					1	2
3	4	5	6	7	8	9
10	11	12	13	14	15	16
17	18	19	20	21	22	23
24	25	26	27	28	29	30
31						

February

S	M	T	W	T	F	S
	1	2	3	4	5	6
7	8	9	10	11	12	13
14	15	16	17	18	19	20
21	22	23	24	25	26	27
28	29					

March

S	M	T	W	T	F	S
		1	2	3	4	5
6	7	8	9	10	11	12
13	14	15	16	17	18	19
20	21	22	23	24	25	26
27	28	29	30	31		

April

S	M	T	W	T	F	S
					1	2
3	4	5	6	7	8	9
10	11	12	13	14	15	16
17	18	19	20	21	22	23
24	25	26	27	28	29	30

May

1	2	3	4	5	6	7
8	9	10	11	12	13	14
15	16	17	18	19	20	21
22	23	24	25	26	27	28
29	30	31				

June

			1	2	3	4
5	6	7	8	9	10	11
12	13	14	15	16	17	18
19	20	21	22	23	24	25
26	27	28	29	30		

July

					1	2
3	4	5	6	7	8	9
10	11	12	13	14	15	16
17	18	19	20	21	22	23
24	25	26	27	28	29	30
31						

August

	1	2	3	4	5	6
7	8	9	10	11	12	13
14	15	16	17	18	19	20
21	22	23	24	25	26	27
28	29	30	31			

September

				1	2	3
4	5	6	7	8	9	10
11	12	13	14	15	16	17
18	19	20	21	22	23	24
25	26	27	28	29	30	

October

						1
2	3	4	5	6	7	8
9	10	11	12	13	14	15
16	17	18	19	20	21	22
23	24	25	26	27	28	29
30	31					

November

		1	2	3	4	5
6	7	8	9	10	11	12
13	14	15	16	17	18	19
20	21	22	23	24	25	26
27	28	29	30			

December

				1	2	3
4	5	6	7	8	9	10
11	12	13	14	15	16	17
18	19	20	21	22	23	24
25	26	27	28	29	30	31

PERPETUAL CALENDAR 1801–2000 (cont.)

M

January

S	M	T	W	T	F	S
						1
2	3	4	5	6	7	8
9	10	11	12	13	14	15
16	17	18	19	20	21	22
23	24	25	26	27	28	29
30	31					

February

S	M	T	W	T	F	S
		1	2	3	4	5
6	7	8	9	10	11	12
13	14	15	16	17	18	19
20	21	22	23	24	25	26
27	28					

March

S	M	T	W	T	F	S
		1	2	3	4	5
6	7	8	9	10	11	12
13	14	15	16	17	18	19
20	21	22	23	24	25	26
27	28	29	30	31		

April

S	M	T	W	T	F	S
					1	2
3	4	5	6	7	8	9
10	11	12	13	14	15	16
17	18	19	20	21	22	23
24	25	26	27	28	29	30

May

1	2	3	4	5	6	7
8	9	10	11	12	13	14
15	16	17	18	19	20	21
22	23	24	25	26	27	28
29	30	31				

June

			1	2	3	4
5	6	7	8	9	10	11
12	13	14	15	16	17	18
19	20	21	22	23	24	25
26	27	28	29	30		

July

					1	2
3	4	5	6	7	8	9
10	11	12	13	14	15	16
17	18	19	20	21	22	23
24	25	26	27	28	29	30
31						

August

	1	2	3	4	5	6
7	8	9	10	11	12	13
14	15	16	17	18	19	20
21	22	23	24	25	26	27
28	29	30	31			

September

				1	2	3
4	5	6	7	8	9	10
11	12	13	14	15	16	17
18	19	20	21	22	23	24
25	26	27	28	29	30	

October

						1
2	3	4	5	6	7	8
9	10	11	12	13	14	15
16	17	18	19	20	21	22
23	24	25	26	27	28	29
30	31					

November

		1	2	3	4	5
6	7	8	9	10	11	12
13	14	15	16	17	18	19
20	21	22	23	24	25	26
27	28	29	30			

December

				1	2	3
4	5	6	7	8	9	10
11	12	13	14	15	16	17
18	19	20	21	22	23	24
25	26	27	28	29	30	31

N (leap year)

January

S	M	T	W	T	F	S
						1
2	3	4	5	6	7	8
9	10	11	12	13	14	15
16	17	18	19	20	21	22
23	24	25	26	27	28	29
30	31					

February

S	M	T	W	T	F	S
		1	2	3	4	5
6	7	8	9	10	11	12
13	14	15	16	17	18	19
20	21	22	23	24	25	26
27	28	29				

March

S	M	T	W	T	F	S
			1	2	3	4
5	6	7	8	9	10	11
12	13	14	15	16	17	18
19	20	21	22	23	24	25
26	27	28	29	30	31	

April

S	M	T	W	T	F	S
						1
2	3	4	5	6	7	8
9	10	11	12	13	14	15
16	17	18	19	20	21	22
23	24	25	26	27	28	29
30						

May

	1	2	3	4	5	6
7	8	9	10	11	12	13
14	15	16	17	18	19	20
21	22	23	24	25	26	27
28	29	30	31			

June

				1	2	3
4	5	6	7	8	9	10
11	12	13	14	15	16	17
18	19	20	21	22	23	24
25	26	27	28	29	30	

July

						1
2	3	4	5	6	7	8
9	10	11	12	13	14	15
16	17	18	19	20	21	22
23	24	25	26	27	28	29
30	31					

August

		1	2	3	4	5
6	7	8	9	10	11	12
13	14	15	16	17	18	19
20	21	22	23	24	25	26
27	28	29	30	31		

September

					1	2
3	4	5	6	7	8	9
10	11	12	13	14	15	16
17	18	19	20	21	22	23
24	25	26	27	28	29	30

October

1	2	3	4	5	6	7
8	9	10	11	12	13	14
15	16	17	18	19	20	21
22	23	24	25	26	27	28
29	30	31				

November

			1	2	3	4
5	6	7	8	9	10	11
12	13	14	15	16	17	18
19	20	21	22	23	24	25
26	27	28	29	30		

December

					1	2
3	4	5	6	7	8	9
10	11	12	13	14	15	16
17	18	19	20	21	22	23
24	25	26	27	28	29	30
31						

INTERNATIONAL TIME DIFFERENCES

The time zones of the world are conventionally measured from longitude 0 at Greenwich Observatory (Greenwich Mean Time, GMT).

Each 15° of longitude east of this point is one hour ahead of GMT (eg when it is 2pm in London it is 3pm or later in time zones to the east). Hours ahead of GMT are shown by a plus sign, eg +3, +4/8.

Each 15° west of this point is one hour behind GMT (eg 2pm in London would be 1pm or earlier in time zones to the west). Hours behind GMT are shown by a minus sign, eg −3, −4/8.

Some countries adopt time zones that vary from standard time. Also, during the summer, several countries adopt Daylight Saving Time (or Summer Time), which is one hour ahead of the times shown below.

Afghanistan	+4
Albania	+1
Algeria	0
Angola	+1
Antigua	−4
Argentina	−3
Australia	+8/10
Austria	+1
Bahamas	−5
Bahrain	+3
Bangladesh	+6
Barbados	−4
Belgium	+1
Belize	−6
Benin	+1
Bermuda	−4
Bolivia	−4
Botswana	+2
Brazil	−2/5
Brunei	+8
Bulgaria	+2
Burkina Faso	0
Burma	+6
Burundi	+2
Cameroon	+1
Canada	−3 /9
Cape Verde	−1
Central African Republic	+1
Chad	+1
Chile	−4
China	+8
Colombia	−5
Comoros	+3
Congo	+1
Costa Rica	−6
Cuba	−5
Cyprus	+2
Czechoslovakia	+1
Denmark	+1
Djibouti	+3
Dominica	−4
Dominican Republic	−4
Ecuador	−5
Egypt	+2
El Salvador	−6
Equatorial Guinea	+1
Ethiopia	+3
Falkland Is	−3
Fiji	+12
Finland	+2
France	+1
Gabon	+1
Gambia, The	0
Germany	+1
Ghana	0
Gibraltar	+1
Greece	+2
Greenland	−3
Grenada	−4
Guatemala	−6
Guinea	0
Guinea-Bissau	0
Guyana	−3
Haiti	−5
Honduras	−6
Hong Kong	+8
Hungary	+1
Iceland	0
India	+5
Indonesia	+7/9
Iran	+3
Iraq	+3
Ireland	0
Israel	+2
Italy	+1
Ivory Coast	0
Jamaica	−5
Japan	+9
Jordan	+2
Kampuchea	+7
Kenya	+3
Kiribati	+12
Korea, North	+9
Korea, South	+9
Kuwait	+3
Laos	+7
Lebanon	+2
Lesotho	+2
Liberia	0
Libya	+1
Liechtenstein	+1
Luxembourg	+1
Madagascar	+3
Malawi	+2
Malaysia	+8
Maldives	+5
Mali	0
Malta	+1
Mauritania	0
Mauritius	+4
Mexico	−6/8
Monaco	+1
Morocco	0
Mozambique	+2
Nauru	+12
Nepal	+5
Netherlands	+1
New Zealand	+12
Nicaragua	−6
Niger	+1
Nigeria	+1
Norway	+1
Oman	+4
Pakistan	+5
Panama	−5
Papua New Guinea	+10
Paraguay	−3/4
Peru	−5
Philippines	+8
Poland	+1
Portugal	0
Qatar	+3
Romania	+2
Rwanda	+2
St Christopher and Nevis	−4
St Lucia	−4
St Vincent	−4
Samoa	−11
San Marino	+1
Sao Tomé	0
Saudi Arabia	+3
Senegal	0
Seychelles	+4
Sierra Leone	0
Singapore	+8
Solomon Is	+11
Somalia	+3
South Africa	+2
South West Africa	+2
Spain	+1
Sri Lanka	+5
Sudan	+2
Suriname	−3
Swaziland	+2
Sweden	+1
Switzerland	+1
Syria	+2
Taiwan	+8
Tanzania	+3
Thailand	+7
Togo	0
Tonga	+13
Trinidad and Tobago	−4
Tunisia	+1
Turkey	+3
Tuvalu	+12
Uganda	+3
United Arab Emirates	+4
UK	0
Uruguay	−3
USA	−5/11
USSR (former)	+3/13
Vanuatu	+11
Venezuela	−4
Vietnam	+7
Yemen	+3
Yugoslavia	+1
Zaire	+1/2
Zambia	+2
Zimbabwe	+2

INTERNATIONAL TIME ZONES

World times at 12 noon GMT Some countries have adopted half-hour time zones which are indicated on the map as a combination of two coded zones. For example, it is 1730 hours in India at 1200 GMT. The standard times shown are subject to variation in certain countries where Daylight Saving/Summer Time operates for part of the year.

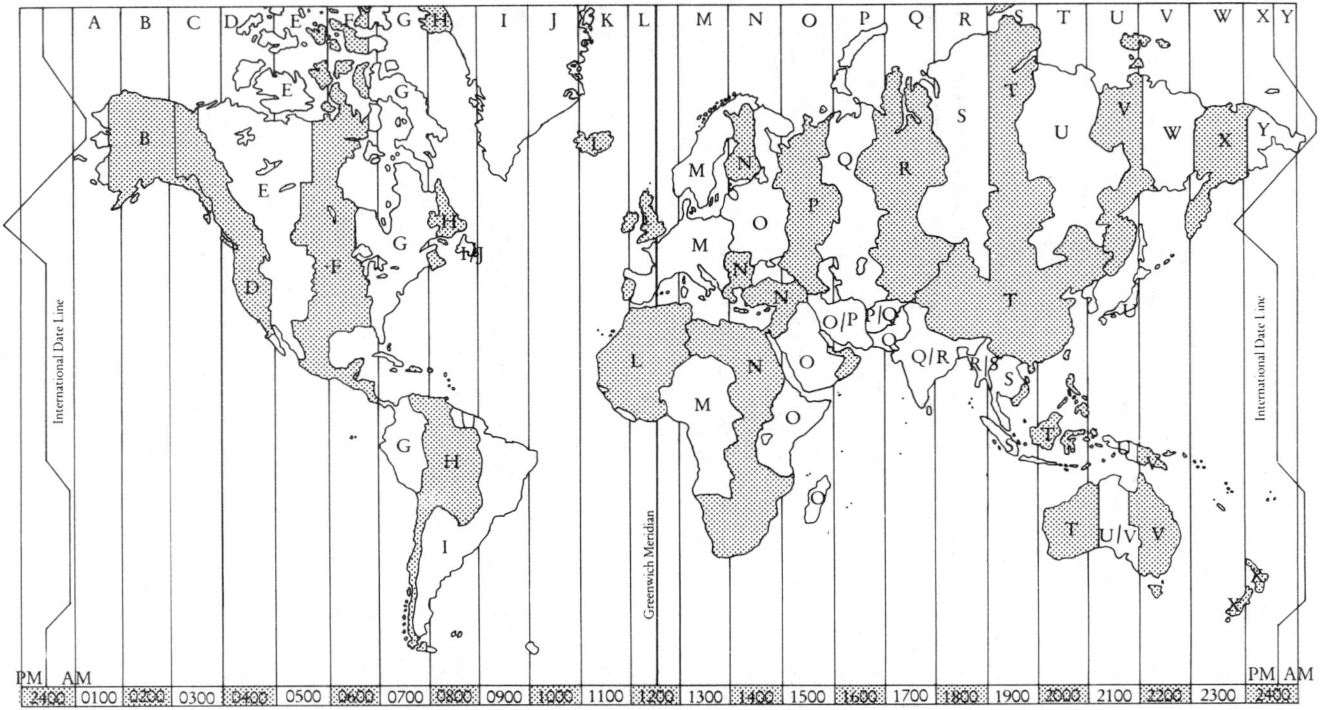

THE SEASONS

N Hemisphere	S Hemisphere	Duration
Spring	Autumn	From vernal/autumnal equinox (c.21 Mar) to summer/winter solstice (c.21 Jun)
Summer	Winter	From summer/winter solstice (c.21 Jun) to autumnal/spring equinox (c.23 Sept)
Autumn	Spring	From autumnal/spring equinox (c.23 Sept) to winter/summer solstice (c.21 Dec)
Winter	Summer	From winter/summer solstice (c.21 Dec) to vernal/autumnal equinox (c.21 Mar)

MONTHS (Associations of gems and flowers)

In many Western countries, the months are traditionally associated with gemstones and flowers. There is considerable variation between countries. The following combinations are widely recognized in North America and the UK.

Month	Gemstone	Flower
January	Garnet	Carnation, Snowdrop
February	Amethyst	Primrose, Violet
March	Aquamarine, Bloodstone	Jonquil, Violet
April	Diamond	Daisy, Sweet Pea
May	Emerald	Hawthorn, Lily of the Valley
June	Alexandrite, Moonstone, Pearl	Honeysuckle, Rose
July	Ruby	Larkspur, Water Lily
August	Peridot, Sardonyx	Gladiolus, Poppy
September	Sapphire	Aster, Morning Glory
October	Opal, Tourmaline	Calendula, Cosmos
November	Topaz	Chrysanthemum
December	Turquoise, Zircon	Holly, Narcissus, Poinsettia

WEDDING ANNIVERSARIES

In many Western countries, different wedding anniversaries have become associated with gifts of different materials. There is some variation between countries.

1st	Cotton	10th	Tin	35th	Coral
2nd	Paper	11th	Steel	40th	Ruby
3rd	Leather	12th	Silk, Linen	45th	Sapphire
4th	Fruit, Flowers	13th	Lace	50th	Gold
5th	Wood	14th	Ivory	55th	Emerald
6th	Sugar	15th	Crystal	60th	Diamond
7th	Copper, Wool	20th	China	70th	Platinum
8th	Bronze, Pottery	25th	Silver		
9th	Pottery, Willow	30th	Pearl		

NATURAL HISTORY

CEREALS

English name	Species	Area of origin
barley	*Hordeum vulgare*	Middle East
maize (or corn, sweet corn, Indian corn)	*Zea mays*	C America
millet, common	*Panicum miliaceum*	tropics, warm temperate regions
millet, foxtail or Italian	*Setaria italica*	as common millet
millet, bulrush	*Pennisetum glaucum*	as common millet
oats	*Avena sativa*	Mediterranean basin
rice	*Oryza sativa*	Asia
rye	*Secale cereale*	Mediterranean, SW Asia
sorghum (or Kaffir corn)	*sorghum vulgare*	Africa, Asia
wheat	Genus *Triticum*, 20 species	Mediterranean, W Asia

VEGETABLES

English name	Species	Part eaten	Colour	Area of origin
artichoke, Chinese	*Stachys affinis*	tuber	white	China
artichoke, globe	*Cynara scolymus*	buds	green, purple	Mediterranean
artichoke, Jerusalem	*Helianthus tuberosus*	tuber	white	N America
asparagus	*Asparagus officinalis*	young shoots	green, white	Europe, Asia
aubergine (or eggplant)	*Solanum melongena*	fruit	purple, white	Asia, Africa
avocado	*Persea americana*	fruit	green, purple	C America
bean sprouts	*Vigna radiata*	shoots	white, pale brown	China
beans, black-eyed	*Vigna sinensis*	seeds	white/black	India, Iran
beans, borlotti (or Boston or pinto)	*Phaseolus vulgaris*	seeds	pink/brown	America
beans, broad	*Vicia faba*	seeds and pods	white	Africa, Europe

VEGETABLES (cont.)

English name	Species	Part eaten	Colour	Area of origin
beans, flageolot	*Phaseolus vulgaris*	seeds	white, pale green	America
beans, French	*Phaseolus vulgaris*	pods	green	America
beans, haricot	*Phaseolus vulgaris*	seeds	white	America
beans, kidney	*Phaseolus vulgaris*	seeds	red	America
beans, runner	*Phaseolus coccineus*	pod	green	America
beans, soya	*Glycine soja*	seeds	green	E Asia
beetroot	*Beta vulgaris*	root	white, dark red	Mediter- ranean
broccoli	*Brassica olearacea*	buds and leaves	green, purple	Europe
Brussels sprout	*Brassica oleracea (gemmifera)*	buds	green	N Europe
cabbage	*Brassica oleracea*	leaves	green, red, white	Europe, W Asia
cardoon	*Cynara cardunculus*	inner stalks and flower heads	white, green	Mediter- ranean
carrot	*Daucus carota*	root	orange	Asia
cauliflower	*Brassica oleracea*	flower buds	white, green	Middle East
celeriac	*Apium graveolens (rapacium)*	root	white	Mediter- ranean
celery	*Apium graveolens*	stalks	white, green	Europe, N Africa, America
chayote (or chocho)	*Sechium edule*	fruit	white, green	America
chick-pea	*Cicer arietinum*	seed	beige, golden, dark brown	W Asia
chicory	*Chicorium intybus*	leaves	red, green	Europe, W Asia
chinese leaf	*Brassica pekinensis*	leaf stalks	white, green	E Asia, China
chives	*Allium schoenoprasum*	leaves	green, white	Europe, N America
courgette (or zucchini)	*Cucurbita pepo*	fruit	green	S America, Africa
cucumber	*Cucumus satius*	fruit	green	S Asia
eggplant *see* aubergine				
endive	*Cichorium endivia*	leaves	yellow, green	S Europe, E Indies, Africa
fennel, Florentine	*Foeniculum dulce*	leaf stalks	white and green	Europe
kale (or borecole)	*Brassica oleracea acephala*	leaves	green	Europe

VEGETABLES (cont.)

English name	Species	Part eaten	Colour	Area of origin
kohlrabi	*Brassica oleracea caulorapa*	stem	white	Europe
laver	*Porphyra leucosticta, Pumbilicalis*	leaves and stems	purple-pink	Europe
leek	*Allium porrum*	stem and leaves	green, white	Europe, N Africa
lentil	*Lens esculenta*	seed	white, green, pink, red	S Asia
lettuce	*Lactuca sativa*	leaves	green, white	Middle East
marrow	*Cucurbita pepo*	fruit	green	America
mooli	*Raphanus sativus*	roots	white	E Africa
mushroom	*Agaricus campestris*	fruiting body	brown, white	worldwide
okra	*Hibiscus esculentus*	pods and seeds	green, white	Africa
onion	*Allium cepa*	bulb	white, pink	Central Asia
parsnip	*Pastinaca sativa*	root	white, yellow	Europe
pea	*Pisum sativum*	pods and seeds	green	Asia, Europe
pepper	*Capsicum annuum*	fruit	red, green, yellow	S America
potato	*Solanum tuberasum*	tuber	white	S America
pumpkin	*Cucurbita pepo*	fruit	yellow, orange	S America
radish	*Raphanus sativus*	root	red, white	China, Japan
salsify	*Trapogon porrifolius*	roots	white	S Europe
sorrel	*Rumex acetosa*	leaves	green	Europe
spinach	*Spinacea oleracea*	leaves	green	Asia
squash, winter	*Cucurbita maxima*	fruit	green, yellow, orange	America
squash, summer	*Cucurbita pepo*	fruit	yellow, orange, green	America
swede	*Brassica napus (napobrassica)*	root	yellow, white	Europe
sweet potato	*Ipomaea batatas*	tuber	white, yellow, red to purple	C America
swiss chard	*Beta vulgaris cicla*	leaves and stems	green and white	Europe
tomato	*Lycopersicum esculentum*	fruit	red	S America
turnip	*Brassica rapa*	root	white	Middle East
watercress	*Nasturtium officinale*	leaves and stems	green	Europe, Asia
yam	Genus *Dioscorea* 60 species	tuber	white, orange	tropics
zucchini *see* courgette				

HERBS

Herbs may be used for medicinal, cosmetic or culinary purposes. Any part of those marked * may be poisonous when ingested.

English name	Species	Origin	Part of plant used
aconite* (or monkswood, winter aconite)	*Aconitum nepellus*	Europe, NW Asia	tuber
agrimony	*Agrimonia officinalis*	Europe	flowers
alecost (or costmary)	*Tanacetum balsimata*	E Mediterranean	leaves, flowers
aloe	*Aloe vera*	Africa	leaves
anise	*Pimpinella anisum*	Egypt	fruits (seed heads)
basil	*Ocimum basilicum*	Middle East	leaves, flowering shoots
borage	*Borago officinalis*	Mediterranean	leaves, flowers
celandine	*Chelidonium majus*	Europe	buds
celery	*Apium graveolens*	Europe	roots, stems, leaves
chamomile	*Chamaemelum nobile*	Europe, Asia	flowers
chervil	*Anthnius cerefolium*	Europe, Asia	leaves
chicory	*Chicoium intybus*	Europe	leaves, roots
chives	*Allium schoenoprasum*	Europe, America	leaves
coriander	*Coriandrum sativum*	N Africa, W Asia	leaves, fruits
dandelion	*Taraxacum officinale*	Europe	leaves, roots
deadly nightshade*	*Atropa belladonna*	Europe, Asia	root
dill	*Anethum graveolens*	S Europe	leaves, fruits (seeds)
elderberry	*Sambucus nigra*	Europe	flowers, fruits
epazote	*Chenopodium ambrosioides*	C and S America	leaves
fennel, Florentine	*Foeniculum dulce*	Mediterranean	leaves, stems, fruits (seeds)
feverfew	*Tanacetum parthenium*	SE Europe, W Asia	leaves, flowers
foxglove*	*Digitalis purpurea*	Europe	leaves
garlic	*Allium sativum*	Asia	bulbs
gentian	*Gentiana lutea*	Europe	rhizomes, roots
ginseng	*Panax ginseng*	China	roots

HERBS (cont.)

English name	Species	Origin	Part of plant used
guaiacum	*Guaiacum officinale*	Caribbean	leaves
heartsease (or wild pansy)	*Viola tricolor*	Europe	flowers
hemlock*	*Conium maculatum*	Europe	all parts
hemp (ganja, cannabis, or marijuana)	*Cannabis sativa*	Asia	leaves, flowers
henbane	*Hyoscyamus niger*	Europe, W Asia, N Africa	leaves, fruits (seeds)
henna	*Lawsonia inermis*	Asia, Africa	leaves
horseradish	*Armoracia rusticana*	SE Europe, W Asia	roots, flowering shoots, leaves
hyssop	*Hyssopus officinalis*	S Europe	leaves, flowers
juniper	*Juniperus communis*	Mediterranean	fruits (berries), wood
lavender	*Lavandula officinalis*	Mediterranean	flowers, stems
leek	*Allium porrum*	Europe	stem, leaves
lemon	*Citrus limon*	Asia	fruits
lemon balm	*Melissa officinalis*	S Europe	leaves
lily of the valley	*Convallaria majalis*	Europe, N America	leaves, flowers
lime	*Tilia cordata*	Europe	flowers
liquorice	*Glycyrrhiza glabra*	Egypt	roots
lovage	*Levisticum officinale*	W Asia	leaves, shoots, stems, roots
mandrake	*Mandragora officina*	Himalayas, SE Europe, W Asia	roots
marjoram	*Majorana hortensis*	Africa, Mediterranean, Asia	leaves, shoots, stems
marsh mallow	*Althaea officinalis*	Europe, Asia	leaves, roots
maté	*Ilex paraguariensis*	S America	leaves
monkswood *see* aconite			
mugwort	*Artemesia vulgaris*	Europe, Asia	leaves
myrrh	*Commiphora molmol*	Arabia, Africa	resin

HERBS (cont.)

English name	Species	Origin	Part of plant used
myrtle	*Myrtus communis*	Asia, Mediterranean	leaves, flower heads, fruits (berries)
nasturtium	*Tropaelom majus*	Peru	leaves, flowers, fruits
onion	*Allium cepa*	Asia	bulbs
oregano	*Origanum vulgare*	Mediterranean	leaves, shoots, stems
parsley	*Petroselinum crispum*	Mediterranean	leaves, stems
peony	*Paeonia officinalis*	Europe, Asia, N America	roots, seeds
peppermint	*Menthaxpiperita*	Europe	leaves
poppy*, opium	*Papaver somniferum*	Asia Minor	fruits, seeds
purslane	*Portulaca oleracea*	Europe	leaves
rosemary	*Rosmarinus officinalis*	Mediterranean	leaves
rue	*Ruta graveolens*	Mediterranean	leaves, stems, flowers
saffron	*Crocus sativus*	Asia Minor	flowers
sage	*Salvia officinalis*	N Mediterranean	leaves
sorrel	*Rumex acetosa*	Europe	leaves
spearmint	*Mentha spicata*	Europe	leaves
tansy	*Tanacetum vulgare*	Asia	leaves, flowers
tarragon, French	*Artemesia dracunculus*	Asia, E Europe	leaves, stems
thyme	*Thymus serpyllum*	Mediterranean	leaves, stems, flowers
valerian	*Valeriana officinalis*	Europe, Asia	rhizomes, roots
vervain	*Verbena officinalis*	Europe, Asia, N Africa	leaves, flowers
watercress	*Nasturtium officinale*	Europe, Asia	leaves, shoots, stems
witch hazel	*Hamamelis virginiana*	N America, E Asia	leaves, shoots, bark
wormwood	*Aretemesia absinthium*	Europe	leaves, flowering shoots
yarrow (or milfoil)	*Achillea millefolium*	Europe, W Asia	flower heads, leaves

SPICES

English name	Species	Origin	Part of plant used
allspice	*Pimenta officinalis*	America, W Indies	fruits
annatto	*Bixa orellana*	S America, W Indies	seeds
asafoetida	*Ferula assa-fetida*	W Asia	sap
bay	*Laurus nobilis*	Mediterranean, Asia Minor	leaves
caraway	*Carum carvi*	Europe, Asia	seeds
cardamom	*Elettaria cardamomum*	SE Asia	seeds
cayenne	*Capsicum frutescens*	America, Africa	fruit pods
chilli pepper	*Capiscum annuum*	America	fruit pods
cinnamon	*Cinnamomum zeylanium*	Ceylon	bark
cloves	*Eugenia caryophyllata*	Moluccas	buds
cocoa	*Theobroma cacoa*	S America	seeds (beans)
coconut	*Cocus nucifera*	Polynesia	fruits
coriander	*Coriandrum sativum*	S Europe	fruits
cumin	*Cuminum cyminum*	Mediterranean	fruits (seed heads)
curry leaf	*Murraya koenigi*	India	leaves
fennel	*Foeniculum vulgare*	S Europe	fruits
fenugreek	*Trigonella foenum-graecum*	India, S Europe	seeds
horseradish	*Armoracia rusticana*	E Europe	roots
ginger	*Zingiber officinale*	SE Asia	rhizomes
mace	*Myristica fragrans*	Moluccas	seeds
mustard, black	*Brassica niger*	Europe, Africa, Asia, America	seeds
mustard, white	*Sinapis alba*	Europe, Asia	seeds
nutmeg	*Myristica fragrans*	Moluccas	seeds
paprika	*Capiscum annuum*	S America	fruit pods
pepper	*Piper nigrum*	India	seeds
sandalwood	*Santalum album*	India, Indonesia, Australia	heartwood, roots
sassafras	*Sassafras albidum*	N America	root bark
sesame	*Sesamum indicum*	tropics	seeds
soya	*Glycine max*	China	fruit (beans)
tamarind	*Tamarindus indica*	Africa	fruits
turmeric	*Curcuma longa*	SE Asia	rhizomes
vanilla	*Vanilla fragrans*	C America	fruit pods

EDIBLE FRUITS (Temperate and Mediterranean)

English name	Species	Colour	Area of origin
apple	*Malus sylvestris*	green, yellow, red	temperate regions
apricot	*Prunus armeniaca*	yellow, orange	Asia
bilberry	*Vaccinium myrtillus*	blue, black	Europe, N Asia
blackberry	*Rubus ulmifolius*	purple, black	N hemisphere
blackcurrant	*Ribes nigrum*	black	Europe, Asia, Africa
blueberry	*Vaccinium vacillans*	blue, purple, black	America, Europe
cherry (sour)	*Prunus cerasus*	red	temperate regions

EDIBLE FRUITS (Temperate and Mediterranean) (cont.)

English name	Species	Colour	Area of origin
cherry (sweet)	*Prunus avium*	purple, red	temperate regions
clementine	*Citrus reticulata* (Cultured clementine)	orange	W Mediterranean
cranberry	*Oxycoccus macrocarpus*	red	N America
damson	*Prunus institia*	purple	temperate regions
date	*Phoenix dactylifera*	yellow, red, brown	Persian Gulf
fig	*Ficus carica*	white, black, purple, green	W Asia
gooseberry	*Ribes grossularia*	green, red	Europe
grape	*Vitis vinefera*	green, purple, black	Asia
grapefruit	*Citrus paradisi*	yellow	W Indies
greengage	*Prunus domestica*	green	temperate regions
kiwi fruit	*Actinidia chinensis*	brown skin, green flesh	China
kumquat	*Fortunella margarita*	orange	China
lemon	*Citrus limon*	yellow	India, S Asia
lime	*Citrus aurantifola*	green	SE Asia
loganberry	*Rubus loganobaccus*	red	America
loquat	*Eriobotrya japonica*	yellow	China, Japan
lychee	*Litchi chinensis*	reddish-brown skin, white flesh	China
mandarin (or tangerine)	*Citrus reticulata*	orange	China
medlar	*Mespilus germanica*	russet brown	SE Europe, Asia
melon	*Cucumis melo*	green, yellow	Egypt
minneola	a type of tangelo	orange	N America
mulberry	*Morus nigra*	purple, red	W Asia
nectarine	*Prunus persica*	orange, red	China
orange	*Citrus sinensis*	orange	China
peach	*Prunus persica*	yellow, red	China
pear	*Pyrus cummunis*	yellow	Middle East, E Europe
persimmon (or date-plum)	*Diospyros kaki*	yellow, orange	E Asia
physalis (or Cape gooseberry)	*Physalis peruviana*	yellow	S America
plum	*Prunus domestica*	red, yellow, purple, orange	temperate regions
pomegranate	*Punica granatum*	red, yellow	Persia
pomelo	*Citrus maxima*	yellow	Malaysia
quince	*Cydonia vulgaris*	golden	Iran
raspberry	*Rubus idaeus*	red, crimson	N hemisphere
redcurrant	*Ribes rubrum*	red	Europe, Asia, Africa
rhubarb	*Rheum rhaponticum*	red, green, pink	Asia
satsuma	*Citrus nobilis*	orange	Japan
strawberry	*Fragaria*	red	Europe, Asia
tangelo	*Citrus paradisi* × *Citrus reticulata*	orange	N America
tangerine *see* mandarin			

EDIBLE FRUITS (Temperate and Mediterranean) (cont.)

English name	Species	Colour	Area of origin
ugli	a type of tangelo	yellow	N America
water melon	*Citrullus vulgaris*	green, yellow	Africa
white currant	*Ribes rubrum*	white	W Europe

EDIBLE FRUITS (Tropical)

English name	Species	Colour	Area of origin
acerola	*Malpighia glabra*	yellow, red	America
avocado	*Persea americana*	green, purple	C America
banana	*Musa sapientum*	yellow	India, S Asia
breadfruit	*Artocarpus incisus*	greenish brown, yellow	Malaysia
carambola	*Averrhoa carambola*	yellow, green	S China
cherimoya	*Annona cherimolia*	green skin, white flesh	Peru
guava	*Psidium guajava*	green, yellow	S America
mango	*Mangifera indica*	green, yellow, orange, red, purple	S Asia
papaya	*Carica papaya*	green, yellow, orange	tropics
passion fruit	*Passiflora edulis*	purple, yellow, brown	S America
pineapple	*Ananas comosus*	green, yellow	S America
sapodilla plum	*Achras zapota*	brown	C America
soursop	*Anona muricata*	green	America
tamarind	*Tamarindus indica*	brown	Africa, S Asia

TREES (Europe and N America)

English name	Species	Deciduous/ evergreen	Continent of origin
alder, common	*Alnus glutinosa*	deciduous	Europe
almond	*Prunus dulcis*	deciduous	W Asia, N Africa
apple	*Malus pumila*	deciduous	Europe, W Africa
apple, crab	*Malus sylvestris*	deciduous	Europe, Asia
ash, common	*Fraxinus exzcelsior*	deciduous	Europe
aspen	*Populus tremula*	deciduous	Europe
bean tree, Red Indian	*Catalpa bignonioides*	deciduous	America, E Asia
beech, common	*Fagus sylvatica*	deciduous	Europe
beech, copper	*Fagus purpurea*	deciduous	Europe
beech, noble	*Nothofagus obliqua*	deciduous	S America
birch, silver	*Betula pendula*	deciduous	Europe, America, Asia
box	*Buxus sempervirens*	evergreen	Europe, N Africa
Brazil nut	*Bertholletia excelsa*	evergreen	S America

TREES (Europe and N America) (cont.)

English name	Species	Deciduous/ evergreen	Continent of origin
camellia, deciduous	*Stewartia pseudocamellia*	deciduous	Asia
castor-oil tree, prickly	*Kalopanax pietus*	deciduous	tropics
cedar of Lebanon	*Cedrus libani*	evergreen	Asia
cedar, smooth Tasmanian	*Athrotaxis cupressiodes*	evergreen	Australia
cedar, white	*Thuja occidentalis*	evergreen	America
cherry, morello (or sour)	*Prunus cerasus*	deciduous	Europe, Asia
cherry, wild (or gean)	*Prunus avium*	deciduous	Europe
chestnut, horse	*Aesculus hippocastanum*	deciduous	Asia, SW Europe
chestnut, sweet (or Spanish)	*Castanea sativa*	deciduous	Europe, Africa, Asia
cypress, Lawson	*Chamaecyparis lawsoniana*	evergreen	America
deodar	*Cedrus deodara*	evergreen	Asia
dogwood, common	*Cornus sanguinea*	deciduous	Europe
elm, Dutch	*Ulmus hollandica*	deciduous	Europe
elm, English	*Ulmus procera*	deciduous	Europe
elm, wych	*Ulmus glabra*	deciduous	Europe
fig	*Ficus carica*	evergreen	Asia
fir, douglas	*Pseudotsuga menziesii*	evergreen	America
fir, red	*Abies magnifica*	evergreen	America
ginkgo	*Ginkgo biloba*	deciduous	Asia
grapefruit	*Citrus paradisi*	evergreen	Asia
gum, blue	*Eucalyptus globulus*	evergreen	Australia
gum, cider	*Eucalyptus gunnii*	evergreen	Australia
gum, snow	*Eucalyptus niphophila*	evergreen	Australia
gutta-percha tree	*Eucommia ulmoides*	deciduous	China
hawthorn	*Crataegus oxyacanthoides*	deciduous	Europe
hazel, common	*Corylus avellana*	deciduous	Europe, W Asia, N Africa
hemlock, Western	*Tsuga heterophylla*	evergreen	America
holly	*Ilex aquifolium*	evergreen	Europe, N Africa, W Asia
hornbeam	*Carpinus betulus*	deciduous	Europe, Asia
Joshua-tree	*Yucca brevifolia*	evergreen	America
Judas-tree	*Cercis siliquastrum*	deciduous	S Europe, Asia
juniper, common	*Juniperus communis*	evergreen	Europe, Asia
laburnum, common	*Laburnum anagyroides*	deciduous	Europe
larch, European	*Larix decidua*	deciduous	Europe
larch, golden	*Pseudolarix amabilis*	deciduous	E Asia
leatherwood	*Eucryphia lucida*	evergreen	Australia
lemon	*Citrus limonia*	evergreen	Asia
lime	*Citrus aurantiifolia*	evergreen	Asia
lime, small-leafed	*Tilia cordata*	deciduous	Europe
locust tree	*Robinia pseudoacacia*	deciduous	America
magnolia (or white laurel)	*Magnolia virginiana*	evergreen	America
maple, field (or common)	*Acer campestre*	deciduous	Europe
maple, sugar	*Acer saccharum*	deciduous	America

TREES (Europe and N America) (cont.)

English name	Species	Deciduous/ evergreen	Continent of origin
medlar	*Mespilus germanica*	deciduous	Europe
mimosa	*Acacia dealbata*	deciduous	Australia, Europe
mockernut	*Carya tomentosa*	deciduous	America
monkey puzzle	*Araucaria araucana*	evergreen	S America
mulberry, common	*Morus nigra*	deciduous	Asia
mulberry, white	*Morus alba*	deciduous	Asia
myrtle, orange bark	*Myrtus apiculata*	evergreen	S America
nutmeg, California	*Torreya californica*	evergreen	America
oak, California live	*Quercus agrifoma*	deciduous	America
oak, cork	*Quercus suber*	evergreen	S Europe, N Africa
oak, English (or common)	*Quercus robur*	deciduous	Europe, Asia, Africa
oak, red	*Quercus borealis*	deciduous	America
olive	*Olea europea*	evergreen	S Europe
orange, sweet	*Citrus sinensis*	evergreen	Asia
pagoda-tree	*Sophora japonica*	deciduous	China, Japan
pear	*Pyrus communis*	deciduous	Europe, W Asia
pine, Austrian	*Pinus nigra*	evergreen	Europe, Asia
pine, Corsican	*Pinus nigra Maritinia*	evergreen	Europe
pine, Monterey	*Pinus radiata*	evergreen	America
pine, Scots	*Pinus sylvestris*	evergreen	Europe
plane, London	*Platanus* x *hispanica*	deciduous	Europe
plane, Oriental	*Platanus orientalis*	deciduous	SE Europe, Asia
plum	*Prunus domestica*	deciduous	Europe, Asia
poplar, balsam	*Populus balsamifera*	deciduous	America, Asia
poplar, black	*Populus nigra*	deciduous	Europe, Asia
poplar, Lombardy	*Populus italica*	deciduous	Europe
poplar, white	*Populus alba*	deciduous	Europe
quince	*Cydonia oblonga*	deciduous	Asia
raoul	*Nothofagus procera*	deciduous	S America
rowan (or mountain ash)	*Sorbus aucuparia*	deciduous	Europe
sassafras, American	*Sassafras albidum*	deciduous	America
service tree, true	*Sorbus domestica*	deciduous	Europe
silver fir, common	*Abies alba*	evergreen	Europe
spruce, Norway	*Picea abies*	evergreen	Europe
spruce, sitka	*Picea sitchensis*	evergreen	America, Europe
strawberry tree	*Arbutus unedo*	evergreen	Europe
sycamore ('plane')	*Acer pseudoplatanus*	deciduous	Europe, W Asia
tamarack	*Larix laricina*	deciduous	N America
tree of heaven	*Ailanthus altissima*	deciduous	China
tulip tree	*Liriodendron tulipifera*	deciduous	America
walnut, black	*Juglans nigra*	deciduous	America
walnut, common	*Juglans regia*	deciduous	Europe, Asia
whitebeam	*Sorbus aria*	deciduous	Europe
willow, pussy, goat or sallow	*Salix caprea*	deciduous	Europe, Asia
willow, weeping	*Salix babylonica*	deciduous	Asia
willow, white	*Salix alba*	deciduous	Europe
yew, common	*Taxus baccata*	evergreen	N temperate regions

TREES (Tropical)

Name	Species	Deciduous/ evergreen	Continent of origin
African tulip tree	*Spathodea campanulata*	evergreen	Africa
almond, tropical	*Terminalia catappa*	deciduous	Asia
angel's trumpet	*Brugmansia × candida*	deciduous	S America
autograph tree	*Clusia rosea*	evergreen	Asia
avocado	*Persea americana*	evergreen	America
bamboo	*Schizostachyum glauchifolium*	deciduous	America
banana	*Musa × paradisiaca*	plant dies after fruiting	Asia
banyan	*Ficus benghalensis*	evergreen	Asia
baobob (or dead rat's tree)	*Adansonia digitata*	deciduous	Africa
beach heliotrope	*Messerschmidia argentea*	evergreen	S America
bo tree	*Ficus religiosa*	deciduous	Asia
bombax	*Bombax ceiba*	deciduous	Asia
bottle brush	*Callistemon citrinus*	evergreen	Australia
breadfruit	*Artocarpus altilis*	evergreen	Asia
brownea	*Brownea macrophylla*	evergreen	C America
calabash	*Crescentia cujete*	evergreen	America
candlenut	*Aleurites moluccana*	evergreen	Asia
cannonball	*Courouptia guianensis*	evergreen	S America
chinaberry (or bead tree)	*Melia azedarach*	deciduous	Asia
Christmas-berry	*Schinus terebinthifolius*	evergreen	America
coconut palm	*Cocus nucifera*	evergreen	Asia
coffee tree	*Coffea liberica*	evergreen	Africa
Cook pine	*Araucaria columnaris*	evergreen	America
coral tree	*Erythrina coralloides*	deciduous	C America
coral shower	*Cassia grandis*	deciduous	Asia
cotton, wild	*Cochlospermum vitifolium*	deciduous	C and S America
crape myrtle	*Lagerstroemia indica*	deciduous	Asia
date palm	*Phoenix dactylifera*	evergreen	Asia and Africa
dragon tree	*Dracaena draco*	evergreen	Africa (Canary Is)
durian	*Durio zibethirius*	evergreen	Asia
ebony	*Diospyros ebenum*	evergreen	Asia
elephant's ear	*Enderolobium cyclocarpum*	deciduous	S America
flame tree	*Delonix regia*	deciduous	Africa (Madagascar)
gold tree	*Cybistax donnell-smithii*	deciduous	Asia
golden rain	*Koelreuteria paniculata*	deciduous	Asia
golden shower	*Cassia fistula*	deciduous	Asia
guava	*Psidium guajeve*	evergreen	S America
ironwood (or casuarina)	*Casuarina equisetifolia*	deciduous	Australia and Asia
jackfruit (or jack)	*Artocarpus heterophyllus*	evergreen	Asia
jacaranda	*Jacaranda mimosifolia*	deciduous	S America
kapok tree	*Ceiba pentandra*	deciduous	Old and New World tropics
koa	*Acacia koa*	evergreen	Oceania (Hawaii)
lipstick tree	*Bixa orllanna*	evergreen	America
lychee	*Litchi chinensis*	evergreen	China
macadamia nut	*Macadamia integrifolia*	evergreen	Australia
mahogany	*Swietenia mahogoni*	evergreen	S America

TREES (Tropical) (cont.)

Name	Species	Deciduous/ evergreen	Continent of origin
mango	*Mangifera idica*	evergreen	Asia
mesquite	*Prosopis pallida*	evergreen	America
monkeypod (or rain tree)	*Samanes saman*	evergreen	S America
Norfolk island pine	*Araucaria heterophylla*	evergreen	Oceania (Norfolk I)
octopus tree	*Brassaia actinophylla*	evergreen	Australia
ohi'a lehua	*Metrosideros collina*	evergreen	Oceania (Hawaii)
pandanus (or screw pine)	*Pandanus tectorius*	evergreen	Oceania
paperbark tree	*Melaleuca leucadendron*	evergreen	Australia
powderpuff	*Calliandra haematocephala*	evergreen	S America
royal palm	*Roystonea regia*	evergreen	America (Cuba)
sandalwood	*Santalum album*	deciduous	Asia
sand-box tree	*Hura crepitans*	deciduous	Americas
sausage tree	*Kigelia pinnata*	evergreen	Africa
scrambled egg tree	*Cassia glauca*	evergreen	Americas
Surinam cherry	*Eugenia uniflora*	evergreen	S America
teak tree	*Tectona grandis*	evergreen	Asia
tiger's claw	*Erythrina idica*	deciduous	Asia
yellow oleander	*Thevetia nereifolia*	evergreen	Americas (W Indies)

FUNGI

English name	Species	Colour	Edibility
base toadstool (or ugly toadstool)	*Lactarius necator*	green, brown	poisonous
beautiful clavaria	*Ramaria formosa*	yellow, ochre, red, purple	poisonous
blusher	*Amanita fubescens*	red, brown	poisonous(raw) or edible (cooked)
brain mushroom	*Gyromitra esculenta*	chestnut, dark brown	poisonous
buckler agaric	*Entoloma clypeatum*	grey, brown	edible
Caesar's mushroom	*Amanita Caesarea*	red, yellow	edible
chantarelle	*Cantharellus cibarius*	yellow, ochre	edible
clean mycena	*Mycena pura*	purple	poisonous
clouded agaric	*Lepista nebularis*	grey, brown	poisonous
common earthball	*Scleroderma aurantium*	ochre, yellow, brown	poisonous
common grisette	*Amanita vaginita*	grey, yellow	edible
common morel	*Morchella esculenta*	light brown, black	edible
common puffball	*Lycoperdon perlatum*	white, cream, brown	edible
common stinkhorn	*Phallus impudicus*	white, green	edible
death cap	*Amanita phalloides*	grey, green, yellow, brown	poisonous
deceiver, common laccaria	*Laccaria laccata*	purple, pink, orange	edible
destroying angel	*Amanita virosa*	white, brown	poisonous

FUNGI (cont.)

English name	Species	Colour	Edibility
dingy agaric	*Tricholoma portentosum*	grey, black, yellow, lilac	edible
fairy ring champignon	*Marasmius oreades*	beige, ochre, red, brown	edible
field mushroom	*Agaricus campestris*	white, brown	edible
firwood agaric	*Tricholoma auratum*	green, yellow, brown	edible
fly agaric	*Amanita muscaria*	red, orange, white	poisonous
garlic marosmius	*Marosmius scorodonius*	red, brown	edible
gypsy mushroom	*Rozites caperata*	yellow, ochre	edible
hedgehog mushroom	*Hydnum repandum*	white, beige, yellow	edible
honey fungus	*Armillariella polymyces*	honey, brown, red	poisonous (raw) or edible (cooked)
horn of plenty (or trumpet of the dead)	*Craterellus cornucopiodes*	brown, black	edible
horse mushroom	*Agaricus arvensis*	white, yellow, ochre	edible
Jew's ear fungus	*Hirneola auricula-judae*	yellow, brown	edible
larch boletus	*Suillus grevillei*	yellow	edible
lurid boletus	*Boletus luridus*	olive, brown, yellow	poisonous (raw) or edible (cooked)
naked mushroom	*Lepista nuda*	purple, brown	edible
old man of the	*Strobilomyces floccopus*	brown, black	edible woods
orange-peel fungus	*Aleuria aurantia*	orange, red	edible
oyster fungus	*Pleurotus ostreatus*	brown, black, grey, blue, purple	edible
panther cap (or false blusher)	*Amanita pantherina*	brown, ochre, grey, white	poisonous
parasol mushroom	*Macrolepiota procera*	beige, ochre, brown	edible
penny-bun boletus	*Boletus edulis*	chestnut brown	edible
perigord truffle	*Tuber melanosporum*	black	edible
Piedmont truffle	*Tuber magnatum*	white	edible
purple blewit	*Tricholomopsis rutilans*	yellow, red	edible
saffron milk cap	*Lactorius delicioses*	orange, red	poisonous (raw) or edible (cooked)
St George's mushroom	*Calocybe gambosa*	white, cream	edible
Satan's boletus	*Boletus satanus*	grey	poisonous (raw) or edible (cooked)
scarlet-stemmed boletus	*Boletus calopus*	grey, brown	poisonous
shaggy cap (or lawyer's wig)	*Coprinus comatus*	white, ochre	edible
sickener (or emetic russala)	*Russala emetica*	pink, red	poisonous
stinking russala	*Russala foetens*	ochre, brown	poisonous

FUNGI (cont.)

English name	Species	Colour	Edibility
stout agaric	*Amanita spissa*	grey, brown	edible
strong scented garlic	*Tricholoma saponaceum*	grey, green, brown	poisonous
sulphur tuft (or clustered woodlover)	*Hypholoma fasciculare*	yellow, red, brown	poisonous
summer truffle	*Tuber aestivum*	dark brown, black	poisonous
white truffle	*Choiromyces meandriformis*	*cream, pale brown*	*edible*
winter fungus (or velvet shank)	*Flammulina velutipes*	yellow, brown, ochre	edible
wood agaric	*Collybia dryophila*	yellow, brown, rust	edible
wood mushroom	*Agaricus sylvaticus*	grey, red, brown	edible
woolly milk-cap (or griping toadstool)	*Lactarius torminosus*	pink, brown	poisonous
yellow stainer	*Agaricus xanthodermus*	white, yellow, grey	poisonous
yellow-brown boletus (or slippery jack)	*Suillus luteus*	yellow, brown	edible

FLOWERS (Shrubs)

English name	Genus	Colour	Country/continent of origin
abelia	*Abelia*	white, rose-purple	Asia, China, Mexico
abutilon	*Abutilon*	lavender-blue	S America
acacia (or mimosa or wattle)	*Acacia*	yellow	Australia, tropical Africa, tropical America
almond, dwarf	*Prunus*	white, crimson, rose-pink	Asia, Europe
ampelopsis	*Ampelopsis*	green (blue-black fruit)	Far East
anthyllis	*Anthyllis*	yellow	Europe
azalea	*Rhododendron*	pink, purple, white, yellow, crimson	N hemisphere
berberis	*Berberis*	yellow, orange	Asia, America, Europe
bottle brush	*Callistemon*	red	Australia
bougainvillea	*Bougainvillea*	lilac, pink, purple, red, orange, white	S America
broom	*Sarothamnus*	yellow	Europe
buckthorn	*Rhamnus*	red, black	N hemisphere
buddleia	*Buddleia*	purple, yellow, white	China, S America
cactus	*Cactaceae*	red, purple, orange, yellow, white	America

FLOWERS (Shrubs) (cont.)

English name	Genus	Colour	Country/continent of origin
calico bush (or mountain laurel)	*Kalmia*	white, pink	China
camellia	*Camellia*	white, pink, red	Asia
caryopteris	*Caryopteris*	blue, violet	Asia
ceanothus	*Ceanothus*	pink, blue, purple	N America
ceratostigma	*Ceratostigma*	purple-blue	China
Chinese lantern	*Physalis*	orange, red	Japan
cistus	*Cistus*	white, pink	Europe
clematis	*Clematis*	white, purple, violet, blue, pink, yellow	N temperate regions
clerodendron	*Clerodendron*	white, purple-red	China
colquhounia	*Colquhounia*	scarlet, yellow	Himalayas
cornelian cherry	*Cornus*	yellow	Europe
coronilla	*Coronilla*	yellow	S Europe
corylopsis	*Corylopsis*	yellow	China, Japan
cotoneaster	*Cotoneaster*	white (red fruit)	Asia
currant, flowering	*Ribes*	red, white, pink	N America
Desfontainia	*Desfontainia*	scarlet-gold	S America
deutzia	*Deutzia*	white, pink	Asia
diplera	*Diplera*	pale pink	China
dogwood	*Cornus*	white	Europe, SW Asia
embothrium	*Embothrium*	scarlet	S America
escallonia	*Escallonia*	white, pink	S America
euchryphia	*Euchryphia*	white	Chile, Australasia
euryops	*Euryops*	yellow	S Africa
fakiana	*Fakiana*	white, mauve	S America
firethorn	*Pyracantha*	white (red, orange, yellow fruits)	China
forsythia	*Forsythia*	yellow	China
frangipani	*Plumeria*	white, pink, yellow	tropical America
fuchsia	*Fuchsia*	red, pink, white	C and S America, New Zealand
gardenia	*Gardenia*	white	tropics
garland flower	*Daphne*	pink, crimson, white, purple	Europe, Asia
garrya	*Garrya*	green	California and Oregon
gorse, furze, whin	*Ulex*	yellow	Europe, Britain
hawthorn	*Crataegus*	white (orange-red berries)	N America, Europe, N Africa
heath, winter-flowering	*Erica*	white, pink, red	Africa, Europe
heather	*Calluna*	pink, purple, white	Europe, W Asia
hebe	*Hebe*	blue-white	New Zealand
helychrysum	*Helychrysum*	yellow	Australia, S Africa

FLOWERS (Shrubs) (cont.)

English name	Genus	Colour	Country/continent of origin
hibiscus	*Hibiscus*	pink, mauve, purple, white, red	China, India
honeysuckle	*Lonicera*	white, yellow, pink, red	temperate regions
hydrangea	*Hydrangea*	white, pink, blue	Asia, America
hyssop	*Hyssopus*	bluish-purple	S Europe, W Asia
indigofera	*Indigofera*	rose-purple	Himalayas
ipomoea (or morning glory)	*Ipomoea*	white, red, blue	tropical America
japonica	*Chaenomeles*	white, pink, orange, red, yellow	N Asia
jasmine	*Jasminum*	white, yellow, red	Asia
Jerusalem sage	*Phlomis*	yellow	Europe
kerria	*Kerria*	yellow	China
kolkwitzia	*Kolk witzia*	pink	China
laburnum	*Laburnum*	yellow	Europe, Asia
lavender	*Lavandula*	purple	Europe
leptospermum	*Leptospermum*	red, white	Australasia
leycerteria	*Leycerteria*	claret	Himalayan
lezpedeza	*Lezpedeza*	rose-purple	China, Japan
lilac (or syringa)	*Syringa*	purple, pink, white	Balkans
lion's tail	*Leonotis*	red	S Africa
magnolia	*Magnolia*	yellow, white, rose, purple	China, Japan
mahonia	*Mahonia*	yellow	Japan
malus	*Malus*	white, pink, red	N America, Asia
menziesa	*Menziesa*	wine-red	Japan
mimosa *see* acacia			
mimulus	*Mimulus*	cream, orange, red	N America
mock orange	*Philadelphus*	white	Europe, Asia, N America
moltkia	*Moltkia*	violet-blue	Greece
morning glory *see* ipomoea			
mother-of-pearl	*Symphoricarpus*	pink, white, red *fruit*	N America
mountain ash *see* rowan			
myrtle	*Myrtus*	pink, white	Europe
oleander	*Nerium oleander*	white, pink, purple, red	Mediterranean
olearia	*Olearia*	white, yellow	New Zealand
oleaster	*Elaeagnus*	yellow	Europe, Asia, N America
osmanthus	*Osmanthus delavayi*	white	China
pearl bush	*Exochorda*	white	China

FLOWERS (Shrubs) (cont.)

English name	Genus	Colour	Country/continent of origin
peony	*Paeonia*	pink, red, white, yellow	Europe, Asia, N America
pieris	*Pieris*	white	China
poinsettia	*Euphorbia*	scarlet	America (Mexico)
potentilla	*Potentilla*	yellow, red, orange	Asia
rhododendron	*Rhododendron*	red, purple, pink, white	S Asia
rhus	*Rhus*	foliage grey, purple, red	Europe, N America
ribbon woods	*Hoheria*	white	New Zealand
robinia	*Robinia*	rose-pink	N America
rock rose (or sun rose)	*Helianthemum*	white, yellow, pink, orange, red	Europe
rose	*Rosa*	pink, red, white, cream, yellow	N temperate regions
rosemary	*Rosmarinus*	violet	Europe, Asia
rowan (or mountain ash)	*Sorbus*	white (red, yellow berries)	Europe, Asia
sage, common	*Salvia*	green, white, yellow, reddish purple	S Europe
St John's wort	*Hypericum*	yellow	Europe, Asia
sea buckthorn	*Hippophae rhamnoides*	silver, orange	SW Europe
senecio	*Senecio*	yellow	New Zealand
skimmia	*Skimmia*	white	Japan, China
snowberry	*Symphoricarpos*	pink, white	N America
spiraea	*Spiraea*	white, pink, crimson	China, Japan
stachyurus	*Stachyurus*	pale yellow	China
staphylea	*Staphylea*	rose-pink	Europe, Asia
sun rose *see* rock rose			
syringa *see* lilac			
tamarix	*Tamarix*	pink, white	Europe
thyme	*Thymus*	purple, white, pink	Europe
veronica	*Veronica*	white, pink, lilac, purple	New Zealand
viburnum	*Viburnum*	white, pink	Europe, Asia, Africa
Virgina creeper	*Parthenocissus*	blue, black	N America
wattle *see* acacia			
weigela	*Weigela*	pink, red	N China
winter sweet	*Chimonanthus*	yellow	China
wisteria	*Wisteria*	mauve, white, pink	China, Japan
witch-hazel	*Hamamelis*	red, yellow	China, Japan

FLOWERS (Herbaceous)

English name	Genus	Colour	Country/continent of origin
acanthus	*Acanthus*	white, rose, purple	Europe
African violet	*Saintpaulia*	violet, white, pink	Africa
alum root	*Heuchera*	rose, pink, red	N America
alyssum	*Alyssum*	white, yellow, pink	S Europe
anchusa	*Anchusa*	blue	Asia, S Europe
anemone	*Hepatica*	white, red-pink, blue	Europe, Caucasus
asphodel	*Asphodelus*	white, yellow	S Europe
aster	*Aster*	white, blue, purple, pink	Europe, Asia, N America
astilbe	*Astilbe*	white, pink, red	Asia
aubrietia	*Aubrietia*	purple	SE Europe
begonia	*Begonia*	pink	S America, the Pacific
bellflower	*Campanula*	blue, white	N temperate regions
bergamot	*Monarda*	white, pink, red, purple	N America
bistort	*Polygonum*	rose-pink	Japan, Himalayas
bleeding heart	*Dicentra*	pink, white, red	China, Japan, N America
bugbane	*Cimicifuga*	white	N America, Japan
busy lizzie	*Impatiens*	crimson, pink, white	tropics
buttercup	*Ranunculus*	yellow	temperate regions
carnation	*Dianthus*	white, pink, red	temperate regions
catmint	*Nepeta*	blue, mauve	Europe, Asia
celandine, giant	*Ranunculus*	white, copper-orange	Europe
Christmas rose	*Helleborus*	white, pink	Europe
chrysanthemum	*Chrysanthemum*	yellow, white	China
cinquefoil	*Potentilla*	orange, red, yellow	Europe, Asia
columbine (or granny's bonnet)	*Aquilegia*	purple, dark blue, pink, yellow	Europe
Cupid's dart	*Catananche*	blue, white	Europe
dahlia	*Dahlia*	red, yellow, white	Mexico
daisy	*Bellis perennis*	white, yellow, pink	Europe
delphinium	*Delphinium*	white, mauve, pink, blue	Europe, N America
echinacea	*Echinacea*	rose-red, purple	N America
edelweiss	*Leontopodium alpinum*	yellow, white	Europe, Asia
evening primrose	*Oenothera*	yellow	N America
everlasting flower (or immortelle)	*Helichrysum bracteatum*	yellow	Australia

FLOWERS (Herbaceous) (cont.)

English name	Genus	Colour	Country/continent of origin
everlasting flower, pearly	*Anaphalis*	white	N America, Himalayas
fleabane	*Erigeron*	white, pink, blue, violet	Australia
forget-me-not	*Myosotis*	blue	Europe
foxglove	*Digitalis*	white, yellow, pink, red	Europe, Asia
fraxinella	*Dictamnus*	white, mauve	Europe, Asia
gentian	*Gentiana*	blue, yellow, white, red	temperate regions
geranium	*Pelargonium*	scarlet, pink, white	temperate regions, subtropics
geum	*Geum*	orange, red, yellow	S Europe, N America
goat's beard	*Aruncus*	white	N Europe
golden rod	*Solidago*	yellow	Europe
granny's bonnet *see* columbine			
gypsophila	*Gypsophila*	white, pink	Europe, Asia
Hattie's pincushion (or the melancholy gentleman)	*Astrantia*	white, pink	Europe
heliopsis	*Heliopsis*	orange-yellow	N America
helleborus	*Helleborus*	plum-purple, white	Asia, Greece
herb Christopher	*Actaea*	white	N America
hollyhock	*Althaea*	white, yellow, pink, red, maroon	Europe, China
horta	*Horta*	violet, white	China, Japan
immortelle *see* everlasting flower			
kaffir lily	*Schizostylis*	red, pink	S Africa
kirengeshoma	*Kirengeshoma*	yellow	Japan
liatris	*Liatris*	heather-purple	N America
lobelia	*Lobelia*	white, red, blue, purple	Africa, N America, Australia
loosestrife	*Lysimachia*	rose-pink, purple	Europe
lotus	*Lotus*	yellow, pink, white	Asia, America
lupin	*Lupinus*	blue, yellow, pink, red	N America
marigold, African, French	*Tagetes*	yellow, orange	America (Mexico)
marigold, pot	*Calendula*	orange, apricot, cream	unknown
meadow rue	*Thalictrum*	yellow-white	Europe, Asia
mullein	*Verbascum*	yellow, white, pink, purple	Europe, Asia
nasturtium	*Tropaeolum*	yellow, red, orange	S America, Mexico

FLOWERS (Herbaceous) (cont.)

English name	Genus	Colour	Country/continent of origin
orchid	*Orchidaea*	red, purple, white violet, green, brown, yellow, pink	tropics
ox-eye daisy	*Buphthalmum*	yellow	Europe
pansy	*Viola tricolor*	white, yellow	temperate regions
peony	*Paeonia*	white, yellow, pink, red	Asia, Europe
Peruvian lily	*Alstroemeria*	cream, pink, yellow, orange, red	S America
petunia	*Petunia*	blue, violet, purple, white, pink	S America
phlox	*Phlox*	blue, white, purple, red	America
poppy	*Papaver*	red, orange, white, yellow, lilac	N temperate regions
primrose	*Primula*	yellow	N temperate regions
primula	*Primula*	white, pink yellow, blue, purple	N temperate regions
red-hot poker	*Kniphofia*	white, yellow, orange, red	S Africa
salvia	*Salvia*	red, yellow, blue	S America, Europe, Asia
sea holly	*Eryngium*	blue, green-grey, white	Europe, S America
sidalcea	*Sidalcea*	lilac, pink, rose	N America
snapdragon	*Antirrhinum*	white, yellow, pink, red, maroon	Europe, Asia, S America
speedwell	*Veronica teucrium*	blue, white	Europe, Asia
spiderwort	*Tradescantia*	white, blue, pink, red, purple	N America
stokeria	*Stokeria*	white, blue, purple	N America
sunflower	*Helianthus*	yellow	N America
sweet pea	*Lathyrus*	purple, pink, white, red	Mediterranean
sweet william	*Dianthus*	white, pink, red, purple	S Europe
thistle, globe	*Echinops*	blue, white-grey	Europe, Asia
thistle, Scotch (or cotton)	*Onopordum*	purple	Europe
violet	*Viola*	mauve, blue	N temperate regions
water chestnut	*Trapa natans*	white, lilac	Asia
water lily	*Nymphaea*	white, blue, red, yellow	worldwide
wolf's bane	*Aconitum*	blue, white, rose, yellow	Europe, Asia
yarrow	*Achillea*	white, cream	Europe, W Asia

FLOWERS (Bulbs, corms, rhizomes and tubers)

English name	Genus	Colour	Country/continent of origin
acidanthera	*Acidanthera*	white	NE Africa
African lily (or lily-of-the-Nile)	*Agapanthus*	white, purple	S Africa
agapanthus	*Agapanthus*	blue, white	S Africa
allium	*Allium*	blue, lilac, white, rose	Asia, Europe
amaryllis (or belladonna lily)	*Amaryllis*	rose-pink	S Africa, tropical America
anemone	*Anemone*	white, lilac, blue	Mediterranean, Asia, Europe
belladonna lily *see* amaryllis			
bluebell	*Endymion nonscriptus*	blue	Europe
camassia	*Camassia*	white, cream, blue, purple	N America
chionodoxa (or glory of the snow)	*Chionodoxa*	blue, white, pink	Greece, Turkey
crinum	*Crinum*	rose-pink, white	S Africa
crocosmia	*Crocosmia*	orange	S Africa
crocus	*Crocus*	purple, rose, yellow, pink, orange	Mediterranean, Asia, Africa
crown imperial	*Fritillaria*	orange	N India
curtonus	*Curtonus*	orange	S Africa
cyclamen	*Cyclamen*	white, pink, red	Asia, Mediterranean
daffodil (or narcissus)	*Narcissus*	white, yellow, orange	Mediterranean, Europe
dog's tooth violet) *see* erythronium			
erythronium (or dog's tooth violet)	*Erythronium*	purple, pink, white, yellow	Europe, Asia
fritillaria	*Fritillaria*	red, yellow	Europe, Asia, N America
galtonia	*Galtonia*	white	S Africa
gladiolus	*Gladiolus*	purple, yellow	Europe, Asia
glory of the snow *see* chionodoxa			
harebell	*Campanula rotundifolium*	blue	N temperate regions
hippeastrum	*Hippeastrum*	pink, white, red	tropical America
hyacinth	*Hyacinthus orientalis*	blue, white, red	S Europe, Asia
hyacinth, grape	*Muscari*	blue	Europe, Mediterranean
hyacinth, wild	*Scilla*	blue, purple, pink, white	Asia, S Europe
iris	*Iris*	purple, white, yellow	N temperate regions
Ithuriel's spear	*Brodiaea*	white, pink, blue	N America
lapeyrousia	*Lapeyrousia*	red	S Africa

FLOWERS (Bulbs, corms, rhizomes and tubers) (cont.)

English name	Genus	Colour	Country/continent of origin
lily	*Lilium*	white, pink, crimson, yellow, orange, red	China, Europe, America
lily-of-the-Nile *see* African lily			
lily-of-the-valley	*Convallaria majalis*	white	Europe, Asia, America
naked ladies	*Colchicum*	white, pink, purple	Asia, Europe
nerine	*Nerine*	pink, salmon	S Africa
ornithogalum	*Ornithogalum*	white, yellow	S Africa
peacock (or tiger flower)	*Tigridia*	white, orange, red, yellow	Asia
rouge, giant	*Tigridia*	white, yellow, red, lilac	Mexico
snake's head	*Fritillaria*	purple, white	Europe
snowdrop	*Galanthus*	white	Europe
snowflake	*Leucojum*	white, green	S Europe
solfaterre	*Montbretia*	orange, red	S Africa
Solomon's seal	*Polygonatum*	white	Europe, Asia
squill	*Scilla*	blue, purple	Europe, Asia, S Africa
sternbergia	*Sternbergia*	yellow	Europe
striped squill	*Puschkinia*	bluish-white	Asia
tiger flower *see* peacock			
tiger lily	*Lilium*	orange	Asia
tulip	*Tulipa*	orange, red, pink, white, crimson, lilac	Europe, Asia
wand flower	*Dierama*	white, pink, mauve, purple	S Africa
winter aconite	*Eranthis*	yellow	Greece, Turkey

RAINFORESTS (Rate of destruction)

The destruction of the world's rainforests has taken place largely as a result of economic pressures for more agricultual land and products. This destruction has led to a huge increase in the amount of carbon-dioxide being released into the atmosphere. It also causes the degradation of top-soil and increases risks of flooding. Rainforests are home to half the world's plant and animal species, many of which are now in imminent danger of extinction. The following data are estimated and subject to continuing work and revision.

Region	Area in sq km[1]	Annual rate of destruction %	Net loss %
Asia			
Burma	245 000	3.3	23.0
Cambodia	67 000	0.75	47.0
India	165 000	2.4	72.0
Indonesia	860 000	1.4	28.0
Laos	68 800	1.5	49.3
Malaysia	157 000	3.1	25.0
Papua N.G.	360 000	1.0	5.3
Philippines	50 000	5.4	49.0
Thailand	74 000	8.4	54.0
Vietnam	60 000	5.8	42.0
Total	2 106 800	4.6	36.5
Africa			
Cameroon	160 000	1.2	2.4
Congo	90 000	0.8	58.0
Gabon	200 000	0.3	2.9
Ivory Coast	16 000	15.6	80.0
Madagascar	24 000	8.3	71.0
Nigeria	28 000	10.0	81.3
Zaire	1 000 000	0.4	44.0
Total	1 518 000	5.6	44.6
Central and South America			
Bolivia	70 000	2.1	89.5
Brazil	3 171 000	2.3	38.8
Colombia	180 000	2.3	65.4
Ecuador	76 000	4.0	48.7
Mexico	166 000	4.2	65.0
Peru	515 000	0.7	27.0
Venezuela	350 000	0.4	–
Total	4 528 000	5.4	43.7
Total	8 152 800	5.3	42.2

[1] 1989 figures. To convert sq km to sq ml, multiply by 0.3861

TROPICAL RAINFOREST DISTRIBUTION

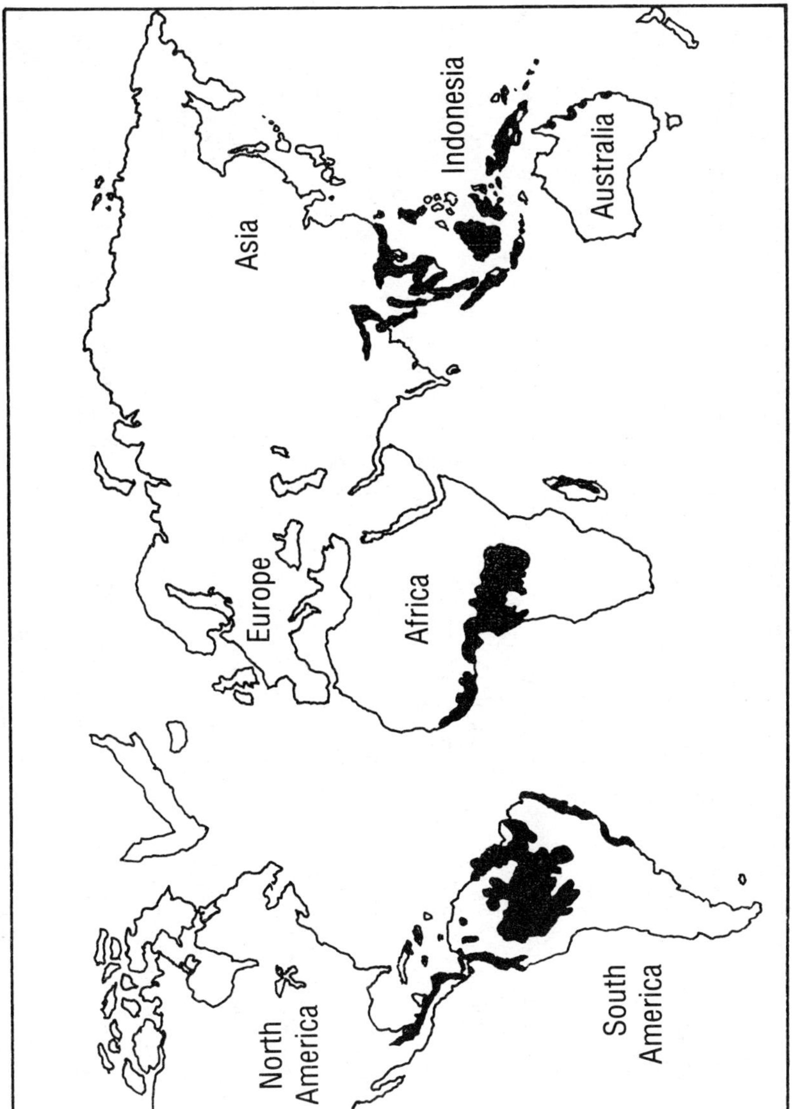

FISH

Name	Family	Size (cm[1])	Habitat	Distribution	Special features
albacore	*Scombridae*	to 130	open waters	tropical, warm temperate	tuna fish with large pectoral fins; prized food and sport fish
anchovy	*Engraulidae*	9–12	surface ocean	temperate	important food fish in S Europe, Black Sea, Peru
angler fish	*Chaunacidae*	5–8	deep ocean	tropical, temperate	large jaws; fishing lure at tip of modified dorsal ray
barracuda	*Sphyraenidae*	30–240	surface ocean	tropical, warm temperate	carnivorous; voracious; large teeth
blenny	*Blennidae*	20–49	sea bed	temperate, tropical	devoid of scales
bonito	*Scombridae*	to 90	open sea surface water	temperate, warm	commercially important; member of tuna family; food fish; sport fish
bream	*Cyprinidae*	41–80	freshwater lakes, rivers	temperate (N Europe)	deep-bodied; food fish
brill	*Scophthalmidae*	to 70	sea bed	temperate	flat fish; eyes on left side; food fish
butterfly fish	*Chaetodontidae*	to 15	reefs	tropical	deep, compressed body; brightly coloured
carp	*Cyprinidae*	51–61	beds of freshwater lakes, rivers	temperate	important food fish; used in aquaculture
catfish	*Ictaluridae*	90–135	sea bed	temperate (N America)	females lay eggs in nest scooped out in mud; important food fish
chub	*Cyprinidae*	30–60	lakes, rivers	temperate (Europe)	popular sport fish
cod	*Gadidae*	to 120	ocean shelf	temperate, N hemisphere	common cod very important food fish
conger eel	*Congridae*	274	sea bed, deep inshore pools	temperate	rounded cylindrical body; upper jaw longer than lower
dab	*Pleuronectidae*	20–40	shallow sea bed	temperate (Europe)	flat fish; eyes on right side; food fish

dace	*Cyprinidae*	15–30	freshwater lakes, rivers	temperate (Europe, former USSR)	sport fish
damsel fish	*Pomacentridae*	5–15	reefs, rocky shores	tropical, temperate	brightly coloured
dogfish	*Scyliorhinidae*	60–100	sea bed	temperate (Europe)	skin very rough; food fish (sold as rock salmon)
dolphin fish (dorado)	*Corypaenidae*	to 200	surface	tropical, warm temperate	predatory; prized sport fish; food fish
dory	*Zeidae*	30–60	mainly shallow ocean	temperate	deep-bodied; food fish
eagle ray	*Myliobatidae*	to 200	mainly inshore sea bed	tropical, temperate	pectoral fins form 'wings'; young born live
eel	*Anguillidae*	to 50 (male), to 100 (female)	rivers, mid-ocean	temperate	elongate cylindrical body form; adults live in rivers but spawn in sea; important food fish
electric eel	*Electrophoridae*	to 240	shallow streams	Orinoco, Amazon basins (S America)	produces powerful electric shocks to stun prey and as defence
electric or torpedo ray	*Torpenidae*	to 180	sea bed	tropical, temperate	produces strong electric shocks to stun prey
file fish	*Monacanthidae*	5–13	reefs, shallow water	tropical, warm temperate	rough skin; food fish
flounder	*Pleuronectidae*	to 51	shallow sea bed, saline estuaries, lakes	temperate (Europe)	flatfish (eyes may be on right or left side); locally important food fish
flying fish	*Exocoetidae*	25–50	surface ocean	tropical, warm temperate	enlarged pelvic and pectoral fins give ability to jump and glide above water surface
goat fish *see* red mullet					
goby	*Gobiidae*	1–27	shallow sea bed, rocky pools	tropical, temperate	pelvic fins joined to form single sucker-like fin
goldfish	*Cyprinidae*	to 30	freshwater ponds, rivers	temperate	popular ornamental fish
grenadier *see* rat-tail					
grey mullet	*Mugilidae*	to 75	coastal sea bed; occasionally tropical freshwaters	tropical, temperate	food fish

FISH (cont.)

Name	Family	Size (cm[1])	Habitat	Distribution	Special features
grouper	*Serranidae*	5–370	deep sea	tropical, warm temperate	common around reefs, wrecks; prized sport and food fish
gurnard (or sea robin)	*Triglidae*	to 75	sea bed	tropical, warm temperate	bony plates on head; many produce audible sounds
hake	*Merlucciidae*	to 180	continental shelf waters	temperate	head and jaws large; food fish
halibut	*Pleuronectidae*	to 250	sea bed	temperate (Atlantic)	flat fish; eyes on right side; prized food fish
herring	*Clupeidae*	to 40	surface ocean	temperate (N Atlantic, Arctic)	important food fish
lamprey	*Petromyzonidae*	to 91	streams, river; parasitic in open sea	temperate (N Atlantic)	primitive jawless fish; mouth sucker-like; food fish
lantern fish	*Myctophidae*	2–15	deep sea, but many migrate to surface at night	tropical, temperate	body has numerous light organs
lemon sole	*Pleuronectidae*	to 66	sea bed	temperate	flat fish; specialized feeder on polychaete worms; food fish
loach	*Cobitidae*	to 15	freshwater lakes, rivers	temperate (Europe, Asia)	popular aquarium fish
mackerel	*Scombridae*	to 66	surface ocean	temperate (N Atlantic)	seasonal migrations; important food fish
manta ray	*Mobulidae*	120–900 (width)	surface ocean	tropical	fleshy 'horns' at side of head; young born, not hatched
minnow	*Cyprinidae*	to 12	fast flowing freshwater lakes, rivers	temperate (N Europe, Asia)	locally abundant
monkfish	*Squatinidae*	to 180	sea bed	temperate (N Atlantic, Mediterranean)	pectoral fins very broad, tail slender, intermediate in shape between shark and ray; food fish
moorish idol	*Zanclidae*	to 22	reefs	tropical (Indo-Pacific)	body deep, tall dorsal and anal fins; bold black/white stripes with some yellow

moray eel	*Muraenidae*	to 130	rocky shores	temperate, tropical	pointed snout; long, sharp teeth; aggressive
parrot fish	*Scaridae*	25–190	reefs	tropical	jaw teeth fused to form parrot-like beak for scraping algal growth from reefs, and for breaking coral
perch	*Percidae*	30–50	freshwater lakes, rivers, Baltic Sea	temperate	food fish; sport fish
pike	*Esocidae*	to 130	freshwater lakes, rivers	temperate	snout pointed; jaws large; predatory; prized by anglers
pilchard (or sardine)	*Clupeidae*	to 25	surface	temperate (N Atlantic, Mediterranean)	important food fish, often canned
pipefish	*Syngnathidae*	15–60	shallow seas	tropical, warm temperate	slender segmented body; males of some species carry eggs in brood pouch
plaice	*Pleuronectidae*	50–90	shallow sea bed	temperate (Europe)	flatfish; eyes on right side; important food fish
puffer	*Tetraodontidae*	3–25	inshore shallow seas, reefs	tropical, warm temperate	body often spiny; some organs and tissues very poisonous, but a food delicacy in Japan
rat-tail (or grenadier)	*Macrouridae*	40–110	close to deep-sea bed	temperate, tropical	large head, tapering body; some species make sounds by resonating swim bladder
ray	*Rajidae*	39–113	sea bed	temperate	skate and ray family; front part of body flattened with large pectoral fins
red muliet (or goat fish)	*Mullidae*	to 40	sea bed	tropical, temperate	food fish
remora	*Echeneidae*	12–46	open sea	tropical, warm temperate	large sucking disc on head, with which it attaches self to other fish, especially sharks
roach	*Cyprinidae*	35–53	freshwater lakes, rivers	temperate (Europe, former USSR)	popular sport fish

FISH (cont.)

Name	Family	Size (cm[1])	Habitat	Distribution	Special features
sailfish	*Istiophoridae*	to 360	open ocean surface	tropical, warm temperate	long tall dorsal fin; prized sport fish
salmon	*Salmonidae*	to 150	surface ocean; rivers	temperate	swims upriver to breed; prized sport and food fish
sandeel	*Ammodytidae*	to 20	inshore sea bed	temperate (N hemisphere)	very important food for seabirds
sardine *see* pilchard					
scorpion-fish	*Scorpaenidae*	to 50	shallow sea bed, reefs	tropical, temperate	distinctive fin and body spines; venom glands
sea bass	*Percichthyidae*	60–100	inshore waters; reefs	tropical, temperate	food fish; popular sport fish
sea robin *see* gurnard					
sea-bream	*Sparidae*	35–51	close to sea bed	tropical, temperate	food fish; sport fish
seahorse	*Syngnathidae*	to 15	surface ocean	tropical, warm temperate	snout extended to form horse-like head; swims upright
shark, basking	*Cetorhinidae*	870–1350	surface ocean	tropical, temperate	feeds on plankton; second largest living fish
shark, great white	*Isuridae*	to 630	surface ocean	tropical	fierce; voracious; young born, not hatched
shark, hammerhead	*Sphyrnidae*	360–600	mainly surface ocean	tropical, warm temperate	head flattened into hammer shape; voracious; young born, not hatched
shark, tiger	*Galeorhinidae*	360–600	surface ocean	tropical, warm temperate	vertical stripes on body; fierce
shark, whale	*Rhinocodontidae*	1020–1800	surface ocean	tropical	largest living fish; feeds on plankton
skate	*Rajidae*	200–285	mid-ocean, sea bed	temperate	food fish
smelt	*Osmeridae*	20–30	freshwater lakes, rivers; inshore seas	temperate	related to salmon and trout; food fish
sole	*Soleidae*	30–60	sea bed	tropical, temperate	flat fish; eyes on right side; food fish

sprat	*Clupeidae*	13–16	surface–mid-ocean	temperate	food fish (white bait when small)
squirrel fish	*Holocentridae*	12–30	reefs	tropical	brightly coloured; nocturnal
stickleback	*Gasterosteidae*	5–10	freshwater lake, rivers; inshore seas	temperate (N hemisphere)	male builds nest, guards eggs
stingray	*Dasyatidae*	106–140	sea bed; tropical freshwaters	tropical, temperate	tail whip-like, armed with poison spine(s)
sturgeon	*Acipenseridae*	100–500	shallow sea bed; rivers	temperate (N hemisphere)	primitive fish; eggs prized as caviar
sunfish	*Molidae*	to 400	surface–mid open ocean	tropical, warm temperate	tail fin absent; body almost circular
surgeon fish (or tang)	*Acanthuridae*	20–45	reefs	tropical, subtropical	brightly coloured; sharp spine on sides of tail can be erected for defence
swordfish	*Xiphiidae*	200–500	surface–mid open ocean	tropical, temperate	upper jaw extended to form flathead 'sword'; food fish; sport fish
tang *see* surgeon fish					
trigger fish	*Balistidae*	10–60	sea bed outside reefs	tropical	colourful; dorsal spine can be erected to wedge fish in crevice as defence; food fish, but can be poisonous
trout	*Salmonidae*	surface ocean; freshwater lakes, rivers	23–140	temperate	brown trout confined to fresh water; sea trout migratory; prized food fish
tuna, skipjack	*Scombridae*	to 100	mid-ocean	tropical, temperate	fast swimmer; important food fish
tuna, yellow fin	*Scombridae*	to 200	surface ocean	tropical, warm temperate	elongated body, long dorsal and anal fins; important food fish
turbot	*Scophthalamidae*	50–100	shallow sea bed	temperate (N Atlantic)	flat fish; eyes on left side of body; prized food fish
wrasse	*Labridae*	7–210	reefs, rocky coasts	tropical, warm temperate	brightly coloured

[1] To convert cm to in, multiply by 0.3937

REPTILES

Reptiles are egg-laying vertebrates of the class Reptilia, having evolved from primitive amphibians; 6547 species divided into Squamata (lizards and snakes), Chelonia (tortoises and turtles), Crocodylia (crocodiles and alligators) and Rhynococephalia (the tuatara).

Most reptiles live on the land, breathe with lungs, and have horny or plated skins. Reptiles require the rays of the sun to maintain their body temperature, ie they are cold-blooded or ectothermic. This confines them to warm, tropical and sub-tropical regions, but does allow some species to exist in particularly hot desert environments in which mammals and birds would find it impossible to sustain life.

Extinct species of reptile include the dinosaur and pterodactyl.

Name	Family	Size (cm^1)	Distribution	Food	Special features
alligator	*Alligatoridae*	200–550	S USA, C and S America and E China	fish, birds, mammals, amphibians, reptiles	able to inflict fatalities on humans but attacks rare; only the American alligator is currently free from being an endangered species, noted for its longevity in protected environments
anguid	*Anguidae*	6–30	N and S America, Europe, Asia and NW Africa	small lizards, mice, birds' eggs, tadpoles, earthworms, spiders, scorpions, grasshoppers, moths, wasps, larvae	distinctive bony-plated scales which reach round the underside giving the creature a rigid appearance
boa	*Boidae*	200–400	West N America, S America, Africa, Madagascar, Asia, Fiji, Solomons and New Guinea	birds, mammals	famous constricting snake, includes within its family species of anaconda
chameleon	*Chamaeleontidae*	2–28	Africa outwith the Sahara, Madagascar, Middle East, S Spain, S Arabian peninsula, Sri Lanka, Crete, India and Pakistan	insects, spiders, scorpions, small birds, mammals	noted for its ability to change colour and blend into its environment

crocodile	*Crocodylidae*	150–750	pantropical and some temperate regions of Africa	vertebrates	distinguished from the alligator by the visible fourth tooth in the lower jaw; famous for its huge jaws, fierce appearance and violent hunting and ambush techniques when capturing prey; populations have been decimated by the demand for luxury leather and several species are endangered
gecko	*Gekkonidae*	1.5–24	N and S America, Africa, S Europe, Asia and Australia	mainly insects	noted for its vocalization and ability to climb; able to shed its tail as a defence mechanism against predators
iguana	*Iguanidae*	to 200	C and S America, Madagascar, Fiji and Tonga	mainly insects	terrestrial and tree-dwelling lizard; active by day, able to survive in exceptionally high temperatures
lizard, beaded	*Helodermatidae*	33–45	SW United States, W Mexico to Guatemala	small mammals, birds, lizards, frogs, birds, eggs insects, earthworms, carrion	possesses a mildy venomous bite
lizard, blind	*Dibamidae*	12–16.5	SE Asia	insects	so-named because the eyes are concealed within the skin
lizard, Bornean earless	*Lanthanotidae*	to 20	Borneo	fish, earthworms, birds' eggs	lacks an external ear opening; partly aquatic and a good swimmer; capable of short, rapid movements on land
lizard, chisel-tooth	*Agamidae*	4–35	Africa, Asia and Australia	insects, fruit, plants, eggs	named after its distinctive teeth; family includes the flying dragon which is able to glide from perch to perch
lizard, girdle-tailed	*Cordylidae*	5–27.5	Africa south of the Sahara, Madagascar	mainly insectivorous and carnivorous	terrestrial; active by day; adapted to arid environments

REPTILES (cont.)

Name	Family	Size (cm[1])	Distribution	Food	Special features
lizard, monitor	*Varanidae*	12–150	Africa, S Asia, Indo-Australian archipelago, Philippines, New Guinea and Australia	carrion, large snails, grasshoppers, beetles, scorpions, crocodiles' and birds' eggs, fish, lizards, snakes, birds, shrews, squirrels	consumes its prey whole in the manner of snakes; includes the Komodo dragon, the largest living lizard which has a prodigious appetite and is capable of killing pigs and small deer
lizard, night	*Xantisiidae*	3.5–12	C America	mainly insects	most species active by night, secretive by day
lizard, snake	*Pygopodidae*	6.5–31	New Guinea and Australia	mainly insects	snake-like appearance; broad but highly extensible tongue
lizard, wall and sand	*Lacertidae*	4–22	Europe, Africa, Asia and Indo-Australian archipelago	mainly insects, snails, worms	highly conspicuous lizard living in open and sandy environments; terrestrial, active by day
lizard, worm	*Amphisbaenidae*	15–35	subtropical regions of N and S America, Africa, Middle East, Asia and Europe	mainly insects, snails, worms	worm-like, burrowing reptile; some of the species have the rare ability to move backwards and forwards
pipesnake	*Aniliidae*	less than 100	S America, SE Asia	snakes, eels	tail has brilliantly coloured red underside; burrows in swampy regions and feeds on other snakes
python	*Pythonidae*	100–1000	tropical and subtropical Africa, SE Asia, Australia, Mexico and C America	birds, mammals	capable of killing humans, especially children, by constriction
skink	*Scincidae*	2.8–35	tropical and temperate regions	crabs, insects, seeds	family of terrestrial, tree-dwelling or burrowing species, including highly adept swimmers and those able to swim through sand

snake, dawn blind	*Anomalepidae*	11–30	C and S America	ants, termites	short tail, indistinct head, one or two teeth in the lower jaw
snake, front fanged	*Elapidae*	38–560	worldwide in warm regions	frogs, snakes, eels, rodents, lizards, and other vertebrates	highly venomous family with short fangs; responsible for numerous human fatalities, includes the mamba, the adder and the cobra with its famous broad, hooded head
snake, harmless	*Colubridae*	13–350	worldwide	wide variety of vertebrates	large family which includes terrestrial, burrowing, arboreal and aquatic species; called harmless because of the inability of most species to inject or produce venomous saliva
snake, shieldtail	*Uropeltidae*	20–50	S India and Sri Lanka	earthworms and insects	small burrowing snake, with tiny eyes, so-called because the tail ends abruptly and forms a rough cylindrical shield
snake, thread	*Leptotyphlopidae*	15–90	C and S America, Africa, Asia	ants and termites	small and exceptionally slender burrowing snake
snake, typical blind	*Typhlopidae*	15–90	C and S America, Africa south of the Sahara, SE Europe, S Asia, Taiwan and Australia	ants, termites, larvae	burrowing snake with tiny, concealed eyes and no teeth on lower jaw
tortoise	*Testudinidae*	10–140	S Europe, Africa, Asia, C and S America	mainly herbivorous	includes smallest species of turtle, the Speckled Cape tortoise (10cm) and one of the longest lived turtles, the spur-thighed tortoise with a possible life span of over a century
tuatara	*Sphenodontidae*	45–61	islands off New Zealand	ground insects, geckos, skinks, birds' eggs	lizard-like reptile with a third eye in the top of its head

REPTILES (cont.)

Name	Family	Size (cm[1])	Distribution	Food	Special features
turtle, Afro-American side-necked	*Pelomedusidae*	12–90	S America, Africa, Madagascar, Seychelles and Mauritius	herbivorous and omnivorous species	bottom-dweller that rarely requires to come to the surface
turtle, American mud and musk	*Kinosternidae*	11–27	N and S America	molluscs, insects, crustaceans, fish, plants	lives permanently or semipermanently in freshwater, glands produce distinctive and evil smelling secretion
turtle, Austro-American side-necked	*Chelidae*	14–48	S America, Australia and New Guinea	omnivorous and carnivorous species	family includes the peculiar looking matamata, the most adept of the ambush-feeders at the gape and suck technique of capturing prey
turtle, big-headed	*Platyssternidae*	20	SE Asia	small invertebrates	distinctive large head which cannot be retracted; active at night; exceptionally good climbers
turtle, C American river	*Dermatemydidae*	to 65	Vera Cruz, Mexico, Honduras	fish, insects, fruit, leaves, plants	freshwater creature with well-developed shell
turtle, Mexican musk	*Staurotypidae*	to 38	Mexico to Honduras	worms, fishes, newts	freshwater creature dwelling in marshes and swamps
turtle, pig-nosed softshell	*Carettochelyidae*	55 or over	New Guinea and N Australia	crustaceans, insects, molluscs, fish, aquatic plants and fruit	specialized swimmer named for its plateless skin and fleshy, pig-like snout
turtle, pond and river	*Emydidae*	11.4–80	N and C America, S Europe, N Africa, Asia and Argentina	insects, molluscs, vertebrates, plants	family ranges from tiny bog turtle (11.4) to the largest of the river turtles, the Malaysian giant turtle; includes box turtle with possible life span of over a century, also species of terrapin

turtle, sea	*Cheloniidae*	75–213	pantropical, and some subtropical and temperate regions	sponges, jellyfish, mussels, crabs, sea urchins, fish	rapid movement through water contrasts with characteristically slow movements of turtles on land
turtle, snapping	*Chelydridae*	47–66	N and C America	carrion, insects, fish, turtles, molluscs, plant food	large-headed, aggressive bottom dweller; includes other turtles in its diet; ambush feeder with rapid snapping movements; alligator snapping turtle has unique worm-like projection on the tongue which fills with blood, turns red, and acts as lure to catch fish
turtle, softshell	*Trionychidae*	30–115	N America, Africa, Asia and Indo-Australian archipelago	insects, crustaceans, fish	named after its leathered, plateless skin; noted for its prominent, pointed snout
viper	*Viperidae*	25–365	N and S America, Africa, Europe and Asia	vertebrates	famous, venomous family of snakes, including the rattlesnake which vibrates its tail when disturbed, and the sidewinder with its distinctive sideways movements
whiptail and racerunner	*Teiidae*	37–45	N and S Asia	small mammals, birds, fish, frogs, tadpoles, lizards, insects, snails and plants	captured and eaten by S American Indians, the fat and flesh also being used in traditional medicines
xenosaur	*Xenosauridae*	10–15	Mexico, Guatemala and S China	insects, tadpoles, fish	terrestrial, sedentary and secretive

[1] To convert cm to in, multiply by 0.3937

BIRDS

Birds are warm-blooded, egg-laying, and, in the case of adults, feathered vertebrates of the class Aves; there are approximately 8600 species classified into 29 Orders and 181 Families. Birds are constructed for flight. The body is streamlined to reduce air resistance, the fore-limbs are modified as feathered wings, and the skeletal structure, heart and wing muscles, centre of gravity, and lung capacity are all designed for the act of flying.

Two exceptions to this are the ratites or flightless birds which have become too large to be capable of sustained flight, eg the ostrich, kiwi and emu, and the penguin which has evolved into a highly aquatic creature.

Birds have evolved from reptiles, their closest living relative being the crocodile.

Flightless birds

Name	Family	Size (cm[1])	Distribution	Food	Special features
cassowary	*Casauriidae*	150	Australia and New Guinea	fruit, plants, insects	claws capable of inflicting fatal wounds on humans
emu	*Dromaiidae*	160–190	Australia	plants, fruit, flowers, insects	highly mobile, nomadic population
kiwi	*Apterygidae*	35–55	New Zealand	earthworms, insects, seeds, berries	smallest of the Ratitae order; nocturnal
ostrich	*Struthonidae*	275	dry areas of Africa	mainly leaves, flowers, seeds of plants	fastest animal on two legs
rhea	*Rheidae*	100–150	grasslands of S America	leaves, roots, seeds, insects, small vertebrates	live in flocks
tinamou	*Tinamidae*	15–49	C and S America	seeds, fruit, insects, small animals	sustains flight over short distances

Birds of prey

Name	Family	Size (cm[1])	Distribution	Food	Special features
barn owl	*Tytonidae*	30–45	worldwide	small vertebrates	feathered legs; nests high above ground
falcon	*Falconidae*	15–60	worldwide	birds, carrion, large insects, small mammals	remarkable powers of flight and sight
buzzard	*Accipitridae*	80	worldwide except Australasia and Malaysia	small mammals	spends much time perching; kills prey on ground

condor	*Cathartidae*	60–100	the Americas	carrion	Andean condor has largest wingspan of any living bird (up to 3m)
eagle, bald	*Accipitridae*	80–100	N America	fish, birds, mammals	name refers to white plumage on head and neck; national symbol of USA
eagle, golden	*Accipitridae*	80–100	N hemishpere	rabbits, hares, carrion	kills with talons; most numerous large eagle
eagle, harpy	*Accipitridae*	90	C America to Argentina	some birds, tree dwelling mammals	the world's largest eagle; black, white and grey; large feet
eagle, sea	*Accipitridae*	70–120	coastline worldwide	fish	breeds on sea cliffs
harrier	*Accipitridae*	50	worldwide	small mammals, birds	hunts by flying low in regular search pattern
kite	*Accipitridae*	52–58	worldwide	insects, snails, small vertebrates, carrion	most varied and diverse group of hawks
sparrowhawk	*Accipitridae*	to 27 (male), to 38 (female)	Eurasia, NW Africa, C and S America	small birds	long tail, small round wings
osprey	*Pandionidae*	55–58	worldwide	fish	feet specially adapted for catching fish
owl	*Strigidae*	12–73	worldwide	mainly small mammals	acute sight and hearing; swallows prey whole; nocturnal
secretary bird	*Sagittaridae*	100	Africa	rodents, reptiles, large beetles, grasshoppers	walks up to 30km/20ml per day
vulture (New World)	*Cathartidae*	60–100	the Americas	carrion, carcasses	lives in colonies; locates food mainly by sight; head often lacking long feathers
vulture (Old World)	*Accipitridae*	150–270 (wingspan)	worldwide except the Americas	carrion	no sense of smell

Songbirds

Name	Family	Size (cm^1)	Distribution	Food	Special features
accentor	*Prunellidae*	14–18	Palaearctic	insects, seeds	complex social organization and mating systems

BIRDS (cont.)

Songbirds

Name	Family	Size (cm^1)	Distribution	Food	Special features
American warbler	*Parulidae*	10–16	N and S America	insects, berries, vegetable matter	well developed and often complex songs
Australian tree-creeper	*Climacteridae*	15	Australia and New Guinea	mainly ants	forages for food on the trunks and limbs of trees
bird of paradise	*Paradisaeidae*	12.5–100	New Guinea, Moluccas and Eastern Australia	frogs, nestling birds, insects, fruit, plants	brilliantly ornate plumage; elaborate courtship displays
bowerbird	*Ptilinorhynchidae*	23–37	Australia and New Guinea	mainly fruit, vegetable matter	male builds bowers to attract female for mating
bulbul	*Pycnonotidae*	13–23	Africa, Madagascar, S Asia and the Philippines	fruits, berries, insects	several species renowned for powerful, beautiful singing voice
bunting	*Emberizidae*	15–20	worldwide	seeds, crustaceans, insects	large family including species of sparrow, finch, and cardinals
butcherbird	*Cracticidae*	26–58	Australia, New Guinea and New Zealand	large insects, crustaceans, reptiles, small mammals, young birds	highly aggressive; sings loudly at dawn; thus has alternative name of 'bushman's clock'
chaffinch	*Fringillidae*	11–19	Europe, N and S America, Africa and Asia	seeds	strong bill; melodious singing voice
cowbird	*Icteridae*	17–54	N and S America	fruit, seeds, crustaceans, insects	forages for food using distinctive gaping movements of the bill
crow	*Corvidae*	20–66	worldwide, except New Zealand	omnivorous	adaptable, intelligent; with complex social systems
cuckoo-shrike	*Campephagidae*	14–40	Africa, S Asia,	mainly insects, caterpillars	peculiar courtship display; family includes colourful minivets
dipper	*Cinclidae*	17–20	Europe, S Asia and W regions of N and S America	water insects, molluscs, crustaceans, worms, tadpoles, small fish	strong legs and toes allow mobility to walk under water
drongo	*Dicruridae*	18–38	S Asia and Africa	insects, lizards, small birds	pugnacious
flowerpecker	*Dicaeidae*	8–20	SE Asia and Australasia	berries, nectar, insects	short tongue specially adapted for feeding on nectar

flycatcher (Old World)	*Muscicapidae*	9–27	worldwide except N and S America	insects	tropical species brightly coloured; feeds on the wing
flycatcher, silky	*Ptilogonidae*	to 14	N and S America	insects	feeds on the wing
Hawaiian honeycreeper	*Drepanididae*	10–20	Hawaiian Islands	nectar, fruit, seeds, insects	widely varying bills between species adapted to different environments
honeyeater	*Meliphagidae*	10–32	Australasia, Pacific Islands, Hawaii and S Africa	nectar, insects, fruits, berries	brush tongue adapted for nectar feeding
lark	*Alaudidae*	11–19	worldwide	seeds, flowers, leaves, insects	ground-dwelling; elaborate singing displays
leafbird	*Irenidae*	12–24	S Asia	insects, fruit	forest dwellers; ability to mimic sounds of other birds
magpie-lark	*Grallinidae*	19–50	Australasia and New Guinea	insects, tadpoles, seeds, fruit	adaptation to urban surroundings makes it amongst the best known birds in Australia
mockingbird	*Mimidae*	20–33	N and S America	invertebrates, fruit	great ability to mimic sounds
nuthatch	*Sittidae*	14–20	worldwide except S America and New Zealand	insects, invertebrates, seeds, nuts	name reflects ability of the European species to break open nuts
oriole	*Oriolidae*	18–30	Europe, Asia, Philippines, Malaysia, New Guinea, and Australia	insects, fruit	melodious singing voice
palmchat	*Dulidae*	18	Hispaniola and W Indies	berries, flowers and plants	communal nesting with individual compartments for each nesting pair
robin	*Turdinae*	13	worldwide except New Zealand	worms, snails, fruit, insects	territorial, uses song to deter intruders
shrike	*Laniidae*	15–35	Africa, N America, Asia and New Guinea	mainly insects	noted for its sharply hooked bill
sparrow	*Ploceidae*	10–20	African tropics in origin, now worldwide	seed, insects, bread, household scraps	some species renowned for having adapted to man's urban environment
starling	*Sturnidae*	16–45	Europe, Asia and Africa	fruit, insects, pollen, nectar, seeds	gregarious; nests in colonies, roosts communally

BIRDS (cont.)

Songbirds

Name	Family	Size (cm^1)	Distribution	Food	Special features
sunbird	*Nectariniidae*	8–16	Africa, SE Asia and Australasia	insects, nectar	named for its bright plumage
swallow	*Hirundinidae*	12–23	worldwide	insects	noted for strong and agile flight
thrush	*Turdinae*	12–26	worldwide, except New Zealand	worms, snails, fruit	loud and varied singing voice
tit	*Paridae*	11–14	N America, Europe, Asia and Africa	insects, seeds, vegetable matter, nuts	nests in holes, wide range of singing voice
tree-creeper	*Certhiidae*	12–15	N hemisphere and S Africa	insects, seeds	forages on trees for food
vanga shrike	*Vangidae*	12–30	Madagascar	insects, frogs, small reptiles	dwindling numbers of population; some endangered species
vireo	*Vireonidae*	10–17	N and S America	insects, fruit	distinctive thick and slightly hooked bill
wagtail	*Motacillidae*	14–17	worldwide, although rare in Australia	insects, seeds	spectacular song in flight
wattle-bird	*Callaeidae*	25–53	New Zealand	insects, fruit, invertebrates	distinctive fleshy fold of skin at base of bill
waxbill	*Estrildidae*	9–13.5	Africa, SE Asia and Australasia	mainly seeds, grain	several species drink by sucking, in the manner of pigeons and doves
waxwing	*Bombycillidae*	18	W hemisphere	fruit, berries, insects	waxlike, red tips on secondary flight feathers
white-eye	*Zosteropidae*	12	Africa, SE Asia and Australasia	insects, spiders, nectar, fruit	distinctive ring of tiny white feathers formed round the eye
wood-swallow	*Artamidae*	15–20	tropical Asia and Australasia	insects	tends to huddle together in small groups on branches of trees; elegant flyer and glider; highly agressive towards other birds
wren	*Troglodytidae*	8–15	N and S America, Europe and Asia	invertebrates	nests play ceremonial role in courtship

Waterfowl

Name	Family	Size (cm[1])	Distribution	Food	Special features
duck	*Anatidae*	wide range	worldwide	vegetation	gregarious; migratory
flamingo	*Phoenicopterides*	90–180	tropics, N America, S Europe	minute organisms	red/pink colour of plumage caused by diet
goose	*Anatidae*	wide range	N hemisphere	grass, underwater plants	migratory
grebe	*Podicipedidae*	22–60	worldwide	insects, crustaceans, fish	highly aquatic, adapted for swimming and diving under water
hammerhead	*Scopidae*	56	Africa S of the Sahara, Madagascar, and S Arabia	mainly frogs and tadpoles, also small fish, shrimps, insects	builds a remarkably elaborate nest with entrance tunnel and internal chamber
heron	*Ardeidae*	30–140	worldwide	carnivorous; aquatic prey	mainly a wading bird
ibis	*Threskiornithidae*	50–100	warmer regions of all continents	crustaceans, insects, larvae, small fish, frogs, small reptiles	family also includes species of spoonbill named for shape of bill
loon	*Gaviidae*	66–95	High latitudes of the N hemisphere, migrating to temperate zones	mainly fish	highly territorial and aggressive; loud warning calls; also known as diver
screamer	*Anhimidae*	69–90	warmer parts of S America	herbivorous	highly vocal, trumpet-like alarm calls give it its name
shoebill	*Balaenicipitidae*	120	E Africa	fish, aquatic prey	also known as the whale-headed stork because it has a large head on a short neck
stork	*Ciconiidae*	60–120	S America, Asia, Africa and Australia	fish, insects, frogs, snakes, mice, lizards	known for its long bill and long neck
swan	*Anatidae*	100–160	worldwide, freshwater, sheltered shores and estuaries	underwater plants	very long neck

Shorebirds

Name	Family	Size (cm[1])	Distribution	Food	Special features
auk	*Alcidae*	16–76	cold waters of the N Hemisphere	fish, plankton	same family as the extinct and flightless Great Auk, species include varieties of puffin and guillemot

BIRDS (cont.)

Shorebirds

Name	Family	Size (cm[1])	Distribution	Food	Special features
avocet	*Recurvirostridae*	29–48	worldwide, except high latitudes	insects, larvae	particulary graceful walk, long slender legs give rise to alternative name of stilt
courser	*Glareolidae*	15–25	Africa, S Europe, Asia and Australia	insects	inhabits dry, flat savanna, grassland and the shores of large rivers
crab plover	*Dromadidae*	38	coasts of E Africa, India, Persian Gulf, Ceylon and Madagascar	crabs	single species with mainly white and black plumage gull
gull	*Laridae*	31–76	worldwide, scarce in the tropics	fish, marine invertebrates	highly gregarious with elaborate systems of communication
jacana	*Jacanidae*	17–53	tropics	insects, frogs, fish, invertebrates	ability to walk on floating vegetation gives alternative name of lily trotters
oystercatcher	*Haematopididae*	40–45	tropical and temperate coastlines, except tropical Africa and S Asia	shellfish, worms, insects	powerful bill for breaking shells; despite the name, they do not eat oysters
painted snipe	*Rostratulidae*	19–24	S America, Africa, S Asia and Australia	molluscs, earthworms, seeds	spectacular female plumage; distinctive running action with lowered head
phalarope	*Phalaropidae*	19–25	high latitudes of N hemishpere	insects, crabs, shrimps	wading bird who also regularly swims
plover	*Charadriidae*	15–40	worldwide	shellfish, insects	swift runner; strong flier
sandpiper	*Scolopacidae*	12–60	worldwide	invertebrates, insects, berries	spectacular flight patterns
seedsnipe	*Thinocoridae*	17–28	W coast of S America	seeds, leaves	named after its diet
sheathbill	*Chionididae*	35–43	sub-Antarctic and E coast of S America	plankton, algae, carcasses, offal	scavenger of a communal and quarrelsome nature
skimmer	*Rhynchopidae*	37–51	tropics and subtropics of N and S America, Africa and S Asia	fish, shrimps	uniquely shaped bill aids capture of prey in shallow waters

skua	*Stercorariidae*	43–61	mainly high latitudes of the N Hemisphere	fish, small sea birds, insects, eggs	known for chasing other seabirds until they disgorge their food
stone-curlew	*Burhinidae*	36–52	Africa, Europe, Asia, Australia and parts of S America	eggs, insects, worms, molluscs, crustaceans, small vertebrates, amphibians	leg joints give alternative name thickknee

Seabirds

Name	Family	Size (cm^1)	Distribution	Food	Special features
albatross	*Diomedidae*	70–140	S Hemisphere	fish	noted for its size and power of flight
cormorant (or shag)	*Phalacrocoracidae*	50–100	worldwide	fish and crustaceans	marine equivalent of falcons, used in fishing
darter	*Anhingidae*	80–100	tropical, sub-tropical, temperate regions	fish, insects	distinctive swimming action occasions name of snake-bird
diving-petrel	*Pelecanoididae*	16–25	S Hemisphere	fish	great resemblance to the auk
frigatebird	*Fregatidae*	70–110	tropical oceans	fish, young birds	enormous wings; adept at flying; forces other birds to disgorge their food
fulmar	*Procellariidae*	to 60	N and S oceans	fish	comes to land only to breed; can eject foul-smelling vomit to deter predators
gannet	*Sulidae*	up to 90	worldwide	fish, squid	complex behaviour during mating
guillemot	*Alcidae*	38–42	N Hemisphere	fish, crustaceans, worms	eggs shaped so they do not roll off cliff ledge
pelican	*Pelecanidae*	140–180	tropics and subtropics	fish, crustaceans	known for its long bill
penguin	*Spheniscidae*	40–115	S Hemisphere	fish, crustaceans, squid	flightless: wings modified as flippers; feathers waterproof; highly social
puffin	*Alcidae*	28–32	N Hemisphere	fish and crustaceans	nests in burrows in very large colonies
shag *see* cormorant					
shearwater	*Procellariidae*	28–91	subantartic and subtropical zones	fish, plankton	many species known for long migrations

BIRDS (cont.)

Seabirds

Name	Family	Size (cm[1])	Distribution	Food	Special features
storm-petrel	*Hydrobatidae*	12–25	high latitudes of N and S Hemispheres	fish, other marine organisms	considerable powers of migration
tropicbird	*Phaethontidae*	25–45	tropical seas	small fish and squid	elongated central tail feathers produce distinctive flight pattern

Arboreal birds

Name	Family	Size (cm[1])	Distribution	Food	Special features
barbet	*Capitonidae*	9–32	tropics, except Australasia	mainly fruits, berries, buds, insects	nests in holes made in rotten timber or sand banks
bee-eater	*Meropidae*	15–38	Africa, Asia and Australia	insects	colourful plumage
cuckoo	*Cuculidae*	15–90	worldwide	insects, especially caterpillars	some species lay eggs in the nests of other birds and rely on foster parents to feed the young
cuckoo-roller	*Leptosomatidae*	38–43	Madagascar and Comoro Islands	large insects, chameleons	diminishing population due to destruction of natural habitat
honeyguide	*Indicatoridae*	10–20	Africa and S Asia	insects, beeswax	named for peculiar habit of eating the wax of honeycombs
hoopoe	*Upupidae*	31	Africa, SE Asia and S Europe	mainly small insects	named after its distinctive 'hoo hoo' call
hornbill	*Bucerotidae*	38–126	tropics of Africa and Australasia	fruit, insects, small animals	noted for its long, heavy bill
jacamar	*Galbulidae*	13–30	tropical America	insects	long, slender bill; attractive, green, metallic plumage
kingfisher	*Alcedinidae*	10–46	worldwide	insects, shrimps, frogs, lizards, crabs, snails, worms	colourful plumage, strong bill; characteristic diving movements to catch prey
motmot	*Momotidae*	20–50	tropical America	insects, frogs, small reptiles, fruit	typically attractive, with distinctive long tail feathers

mousebird	*Coliidae*	30–35	Africa, S of the Sahara	leaves, fruit, seeds, nectar	distinguished by its crest and long tail
parrot	*Psittacidae*	10–100	mainly tropics of S Hemisphere	seeds, nuts, berries, fruit, insects	mainly sedentary; unmelodic voice, not known to mimic sounds outwith captivity
pigeon	*Columbidae*	17–90	worldwide, except high latitudes	seeds, flowers, fruit, berries, leaves, small snails	large family including species of dove, known for its distinctive cooing sound
puffbird	*Bucconidae*	14–32	tropical America	insects, lizards	named after its stout, puffy appearance
roller	*Coraciidae*	27–38	Africa, Europe, Asia, Australia	insects, frogs, fruit	named after its courtship display of diving from great heights in a rolling motion
sandgrouse	*Pteroclididae*	25–48	Africa, S Europe and S Asia	seeds, berries, insects	mainly terrestrial birds
tody	*Todidae*	10–12	Greater Antilles	mainly insects, seeds	captures its insect prey from underside of leaves and twigs
toucan	*Ramphastidae*	34–66	S America	seeds, berries, fruits, insects, small animals	known for its bright plumage and immense bill
trogon	*Trogonidae*	25–35	tropics, except Australasia	mainly insects, fruit	colourful, attractive plumage
turaco	*Musophagidae*	35–76	Africa S of the Sahara	mainly fruit	noted for its loud and resounding call
woodhoopoe	*Phoeniculidae*	21–43	Africa S of the Sahara	insects, fruit	long graduated tail; strongly hooked bill (some species also called scimitar bill)
woodpecker	*Picidae*	10–58	worldwide, except Australasia and Antarctica	insects, fruit, nuts	named after its manner of excavating wood and tree bark for food

Aerial feeders

Name	Family	Size (cm^1)	Distribution	Food	Special features
crested swift	*Hemiprocnidae*	17–33	SE Asia and New Guinea	insects	named after prominent crest on its head

BIRDS (cont.)

Aerial feeders

Name	Family	Size (cm[1])	Distribution	Food	Special features
frogmouth	*Podargidae*	23–53	SE Asia and Australasia	beetles, scorpions, centipedes, frogs, snails, mice, small birds, fruit	distinctively shaped bill with extremely wide gape
hummingbird	*Trochilidae*	6–22	N and S America	nectar, insects	the humming sound is made by the wings when hovering
nightjar	*Caprimulgidae*	19–29	worldwide	mainly insects	nocturnal
oilbird	*Steatornithidae*	53	tropical S America	fruit	the only nocturnal, fruit-eating bird
potoo	*Nyctibiidae*	23–51	tropical C and S America	insects	nocturnal bird, also known as 'tree-nighthawk'
owlet-nightjar	*Aegothelidae*	23–44	Australasia	insects, small vertebrates	perches in upright owl-like way
swift	*Apodidae*	10–25	worldwide	insects	lands only on near-vertical surfaces; spends most of life flying

Passerines[2]

Name	Family	Size (cm[1])	Distribution	Food	Special features
antbird	*Formicariidae*	8–36	parts of S America and W Indies	small insects, spiders, lizards, frogs	named after the habit some species have of following armies of ants to prey
bellbird	*Cotingidae*	9–45	C and S America	fruit	long, metallic sounding display call
broadbill	*Eurylaimidae*	13–28	tropical Africa and Asia, and the Philippines	mainly insects	noted for its colourful broad bill
false sunbird	*Philepittidae*	15	Madagascar	fruit	noted for the bright blue and emerald wattle which develops around the eye of the male during breeding season
flycatcher (New World)	*Tyrannidae*	9–27	N and S America	insects	feed on wing
gnateater	*Conopophagidae*	14	parts of S America	insects	long thin legs; short tail

lyrebird	*Menuridae*	80–90	SE Australia	invertebrates	named after its extravagant tail which resembles a Greek lyre
manakin	*Pipridae*	9–15	C and S America	fruit, insects	highly elaborate courtship display
New Zealand wren	*Xenicidae*	8–10	New Zealand	insects	bird family thought to have colonized the islands in the Tertiary Period[3]
ovenbird	*Furnariidae*	to 25	S America	mainly insects	one species, the true ovenbird, builds substantial nests like mud-ovens
pitta	*Pittidae*	15–28	Africa, SE Asia and Australasia	mainly insects, spiders, worms, snails	long legs; short tail; colourful plumage
plantcutter	*Phytotomidae*	18–19	western S America	buds, shoots, leaves, fruit	bill is ideally adapted for feeding on fruit and plants; regarded as a horticultural and agricultural pest
scrub-bird	*Atrichornithidae*	16–21	E and SW Australia	insects, small lizards, frogs	small terrestrial bird; long graduated tail
tapaculo	*Rhinocryptidae*	8–25	S and C America	insects, larvae, spiders	distinctive moveable flap covers the nostril
tyrant flycatcher	*Tyrannidae*	5–14	N and S America, W Indies and Galapagos	insects, fish, fruit	many species known for spectacular aerial courtship display
woodcreeper	*Dendrocolaptidae*	20–37	S America and W Indies	insects, frogs, lizards	stiff tail feathers used as support in climbing trees, foraging for food

Game-birds and cranes

Name	Family	Size (cm[1])	Distribution	Food	Special features
bustard	*Otitidae*	37–132	Africa, S Europe, Asia and Australia	plants, leaves, seeds, berries, insects, small reptiles and mammals, bird eggs, nestlings	characterized by its frequent pauses during walking to observe its surroundings
button quail	*Turnicidae*	11–19	Africa, S Asia and Australia	insects, seeds, plants	secretive; terrestrial; only three toes, hind toe absent
coot	*Rallidae*	14–51	worldwide	small animals and vegetable food	conspicuous for its loud harsh vocal strains at night
crane	*Gruidae*	80–150	worldwide, except S America and Antartica	omnivorous	characterized by its long legs

BIRDS (cont.)

Game-birds and cranes

Name	Family	Size (cm[1])	Distribution	Food	Special features
currasow	*Cracidae*	75–112	Southern N America and S America	leaves, insects, frogs	noted for agility in running along branches before taking flight
finfoot	*Heliornithidae*	30–62	tropics of America, Africa, and SE Asia	mainly insects	long, slender neck; agile on land and in water
grouse	*Tetraonidae*	30–90	Northern Hemisphere	leaves, buds, berries, fruit, insects	many species threatened by hunting and use of pesticides
guinea fowl	*Numididae*	45–60	Africa	mainly insects, bulbs	virtually unfeathered head and neck; often domesticated
hoatzin	*Opisthocomidae*	60	tropical S America	leaves, fruit and flowers of the White Mangrove, fish, crabs	musky odour; top-heavy, retarded flight; unique digestive system
kagu	*Rhynochetidae*	56	New Caledonia	earthworms	sole species, forest dwelling
limpkin	*Aramidae*	60–70	C and S America	large snails	sole species, noted for its wailing voice
mesite	*Mesoenatidae*	25–27	Madagascar	fruit, insects	highly terrestrial, sedentary; endemic to Madagascar
pheasant	*Phasianidae*	40–235	worldwide	seeds, shoots, berries, insects	elaborate courtship display
plains wanderer	*Pedionomidae*	16	SE Australia	insects, seeds, vegetable substances	male incubates the eggs and raises the young
seriema	*Cariamidae*	75–90	S America	omniverous, especially small snakes	heavily feathered head and crest
sunbittern	*Eurypygidae*	46	forest swamps of C and S America	insects, crustacea, minnows	complex markings
trumpeter	*Psophiidae*	43–53	tropical S America	berries, fruit, insects	named after its trumpeting call of warning or alarm
turkey	*Meleagrididae*	90–110	N America	fruit, seeds, vegetation, invertebrates	characterized by male's distinctive strutting displays during breeding

[1] To convert cm to in, multiply by 0.3937
[2] Any bird of the worldwide order *Passeriformes* ('perching birds'), which comprises more than half the living species of birds; landbirds.
[3] *see* GEOLOGICAL TIME SCALE pp 34–5

MAMMALS

Mammals are the group of animals to which humans belong. They are characterized by the presence of mammary glands in the female which produce milk on which the young can be nourished. They are divided into monotremes or egg-laying mammals; marsupials in which the young are born at an early stage of development and then grow outside the mother's womb, often in a pouch; placental mammals in which the young are nourished in the womb by the mother's blood and are born at a late stage of development. A crucial aspect of mammals is the fact that their hair and skin glands allow them to regulate their temperatures from within, ie they are endothermic (warm-blooded). This confers on them the ability to adapt to more varied environments than the reptiles from which they are descended.

There are over 4000 species of mammals, most of which are terrestrial, the exceptions being species of bat which have developed the ability to fly and the whale which leads an aquatic existence.

Monotremes

Name	Family/Species	Size (cm^1)	Distribution	Food	Special features
echidna, long-beaked	Species *Zaglossus bruijni*	45–90	New Guinea	earthworms	prominent beak; short spines scattered among fur
echidna, short-beaked	Species *Tachyglossidae aculeatus*	30–45	Australia, Tasmania and New Guinea	ants, termites	fur covered in protective spines; known to live up to 50 years in captivity
platypus	Family *Ornithorhynchidae*	45–60	E Australia and Tasmania	invertebrates, larvae	noted for its duck-like snout

Marsupials

Name	Family	Size (cm^1)	Distribution	Food	Special features
bandicoot	Family *Peramelidae*	15–56	Australia and New Guinea	insectivorous and omnivorous	highest reproductive rate of all marsupials
brushtail possum	Family *Phalangeridae*	34–70	Australia, New Guinea, Solomon Is and New Zealand	leaves, fruit, bark, eggs, invertebrates	the most commonly encountered of all Australian mammals
kangaroo	Family *Macropodidae*	to 165	Australia and New Guinea	grasses, plants	most popularly known of Australian mammals, noted for its bounding motion and prominent female pouch; includes all species of wallaby
koala	Family *Phascolarctidae*	78	E Australia	eucalyptus leaves	marsupial with popular reputation; intensive management has significantly revived population numbers which at one time seemed threatened with extinction

MAMMALS (cont.)

Marsupials

Name	Family	Size (cm^1)	Distribution	Food	Special features
marsupial mole	Family *Notoryctidae*	13–15	Australia	insects, larvae	only Australian mammal that has specialized in burrowing
opossum	Family *Didelphidae*	7–55	C and S America	earthworms, fruit, insects, small vertebrates, crustaceans, fish, frogs, reptiles	generally known for its dreadful smell
rat kangaroo	Family *Macropodidae*	28.4–30	Australia and New Guinea	grasses, plants	rabbit-sized version of its larger namesake
wombat	Family *Vombatidae*	870–115	SE Australia and Tasmania	grasses	poor eyesight compensated by keen senses of smell and hearing

Placental mammals

Name	Family etc	Size (cm^1)	Distribution	Food	Special features
aardvark	Family *Orycteropodidae*	105–130	Africa S of the Sahara	ants, termites	secretive, nocturnal creature; characterized by its long, tubular snout
anteater	Family *Myrmecophagidae*	16–22	C and S America	ants and sometimes termites	noted, particulary the Giant ant-eater, for its long, elongated snout
antelope, dwarf	Tribe *Neotragini*	45–55	Africa	leaves, grass, fruit, buds	unusual among hoofed mammals in that the female is larger than the male
armadillo	Family *Dasypodidae*	12.5–100	southern N America, C and S America	vertebrates, insects, fungi, tubers, fruit, carrion	noted, particularly the Giant armadillo, for its protective suit of armour
ass	Subgenus *Asinus*	200–210	Africa and Asia	grass, leaves	renowned as man's reluctant beast of burden
baboon and mandrill	Genus *Papio*	56–80	Africa	fruit, plants, insects, small mammals	able to walk over long distances
badger	Family *Mustelidae*	50–100	Africa, Europe, Asia and N America	vertebrates, invertebrates, fruit, roots, earthworms	mainly nocturnal, European species characterized by its distinctive black and white markings

bat	Order *Chiroptera*	15–200 (wingspan)	worldwide except for the Arctic and Antarctic	insects, vertebrates, fish, fruit	the only vertebrate, outwith birds, capable of sustained flight; famous for its powers of echo location and tendency to cluster in large numbers
bear, black	Species *Ursus americanus*	1.3–1.8m	N America	omniverous	smaller and more secretive than the brown or grizzly bear, its greater ability to adapt has helped it to survive in greater numbers
beaver	Genus *Castor*	80–120	N America, Asia and Europe	plants, wood	renowned for its industry and ability to construct dams and lodges in streams and ponds
bison, American	Species *Bison bison*	to 380	N America	grazing fodder	once numbered in millions in the prairies of N America, now survives only in parks and refuges
bison, European	Species *Bison bonasus*	to 290	former USSR	grazing fodder	became extinct in the wild in 1919, but has now been re-established in parts of the former USSR
boar	Family *Suidae*	58–210	Europe, Africa and Asia	plants, larvae, frogs, mice, earthworms	wild pig; characteristically ugly appearance; intelligent and highly adaptable; includes species of warthog
buffalo, wild water	Species *Bubalus arnee*	240–280	SE Asia	grazing fodder	adept at moving through the muddy areas which they inhabit
bush baby	Subfamily *Galaginae*	12–32	Africa and S Asia	insects, fruit, gum	highly agile, arboreal creature
bushbuck	Species *Tragelaphus scriptus*	110–145	Africa S of the Sahara	grazing fodder	occupies habitats with dense cover; dark brown or chestnut coat with white markings
camel	Species *Camelus bactrianus*	190–230 (height of hump)	Mongolia	plants, vegetation	two humps
capybara	Family *Hydrochoeridae*	106–134	S America	grass	largest living rodent, lives in groups by the edge of water; traditionally hunted for its meat and skin

MAMMALS (cont.)

Placental mammals

Name	Family	Size (cm[1])	Distribution	Food	Special features
capuchin monkey	Family *Cebidae*	25–63	S America	insects, fruit, leaves, seeds, other small mammals	mainly lives in social groupings for the purposes of defence, foraging for food, and rearing young
cat	Family *Felidae*	20–400	worldwide	carnivorous	acute senses of vision and smell
cattle	Family *Bovidae*	180–200	worldwide	grass	agricultural animal existing in both long-horned and polled or hornless breeds
chamois	Species *Rupicapra rupicapra*	125–135	Europe and Asia	grass, leaves, lichen	has adapted to alpine and subalpine conditions and to life on snowy mountains; part of its defence mechanism in fighting is its evasive running and dodging movement
cheetah	Family *Felidae*	112–135	Africa	hoofed animals up to 40kg, such as gazelles, impala, wildebeest calves	the fastest of all land animals, reaching speeds of 96kph/60mph
chimpanzee	Genus *Pan*	70–85	W and C Africa	fruit, leaves, seeds, insects, small mammals	most sophisticated mammal in use of tools as an aid to eg feeding and fighting
chinchilla	Family *Chinchillidae*	25	S America	grazing fodder	widely hunted as food and for its valuable fur
civet	Family *Viverridae*	33–84	Africa and Asia	fruit, small mammals, birds, rodents, insects, small reptiles	cat-like carnivore; nocturnal hunter; economic source of civet oil
colugo	Genus *Cynocephalus*	33–42	SE Asia	leaves, shoots, buds, flowers	also known as flying lemur, a reference to the membrane which stretches from its neck to the tips of its fingers, toes and tail, allowing it to glide from tree to tree

coyote	Species *Canis latrans*	70–97	N America	squirrels, rabbits, mice, antelope, deer, mountain sheep	makes unique howling sound; regarded as agricultural pest for its attacks on farm animals, but also kills off agricultural vermin
coypu	Species *Myocastor coypu*	50	S America	freshwater plants	highly aquatic rodent; burrows into banks; beaver-like qualities
deer	Family *Cervidae*	41–152	N and S America, Europe, and Asia	grass, shoots, twigs, leaves, flowers, fruit	distinguished in the male by the presence of antlers most characteristically used to attack other males during the rutting period; species include red deer, reindeer, waipiti, and the moose or elk
dingo	Species *Canis dingo*	150	Australasia	rabbits, lizards, grasshoppers, wild pigs, kangaroos	history of the dingo in Australia dates back 8000 years; descendant of the wolf; lives in packs
dog	Species *Canis familiaris*	20–75	worldwide	carnivorous	first animal to be domesticated; c.400 domestic breeds
dolphin	Family *Delphinidae*	120–400	worldwide	fish, squid	renowned for grace, agility, intelligence; highly developed social organization and communication systems
dolphin, river	Family *Platanistidae*	210–260	SE Asia and S America	fish, shrimp, squid, octupus	virtually blind, but with highly sensitive system of echo location
dormouse	Family *Gliridae*	6–19	Europe, Africa, Turkey, Asia and Japan	omnivorous	halfway between mouse and squirrel both in form and behaviour
dromedary	Species *Camelus dromedarius*	190–230 height of hump	SW Asia, N Africa and Australia	plants, vegetation	domesticated camel with one hump, important to man as a beast of burden, and source of wool and milk
duiker	Subfamily *Cephalophinae*	55–72	Africa S of the Sahara	leaves, fruit, shoots, buds, seeds, bark, small birds, rodents	named after its habit of diving into cover when disturbed

MAMMALS (cont.)

Placental mammals

Name	Family	Size (cm[1])	Distribution	Food	Special features
eland	Genus *Taurotragus*	250–350	Africa	grazing fodder	elegant and highly mobile spiral horned antelope; experiments in the agricultural domestication of the common eland have taken place in Africa
elephant, African	Species *Loxodonta africana*	600–750	Africa S of the Sahara	grass, plants, leaves, twigs, flowers, fruit	largest living mammal, with distinctive trunk and large tusks and ears; drastically reduced population
elephant-shrew	Order *Macroscelidea*	10.4–29.4	Africa	invertebrates, plants, fruit, seeds	distinctive creature with beady eyes long, pointed snout and short legs
fox	Family *Canidae*	24–100	N and S America, Europe, Asia and Africa	rodents, birds, invertebrates, fruit, fish, rabbits, hares, earthworms	justified reputation for cunning, intelligence and resourcefulness
gazelle	Genus *Gazella*	122–166	Africa	leaves, grass, fruit	birth peaks adapted to coincide with abundance of feeding vegetation during the spring and early rains
gerbil	Subfamily *Gerbillinae*	6–7.5	Africa and Asia	seeds, fruits, leaves, stems, roots, bulbs, insects, snails	defence mechanisms include colour of skin closely allied to the environment for hiding purposes, wide field of vision, and the ability to hear low frequency sounds such as the beating of owls' wings; domesticated form is the Mongolian gerbil often kept as a pet
gerenuk	Genus *Litocranius*	140–160	Africa	leaves, shoots, flowers, fruit	graceful, delicate creature; rises on hind legs in order to extend its reach when feeding on the leaves of tall shrubs and bushes

gibbon	Family *Hylobatidae*	45–65	SE Asia	fruit, leaves, invertebrates	renowned for spectacular ability to move among trees using swinging movements of arms; loud and sophisticated voice
giraffe	Species *Giraffa camelopardalis*	380–470	Africa S of the Sahara	leaves, shoots, herbs, flowers, fruit, seeds	distinguished by its mottled coat and the length of its neck which allows it to feed on foliage which is out of the reach of smaller mammals
gnu	Genus *Connochaetes*	194–209	Africa	grazing fodder	characterized by massive head and mane, bearded throat, tail which reaches almost to the ground
goat, mountain	Species *Oreamnos americanus*	to 175	N America	grazing fodder	large, ponderous rock climber, adapted to living in snowy mountains of N America
goat, wild	Species *Capra aegagrus*	130–140	S Europe, Middle East and Asia	grazing fodder	subspecies includes domestic goat
gopher	Family *Geomyidae*	12–22.5	N America	plant materials	highly adapted to its burrowing and subterranean existence
gorilla	Genus *Gorilla*	150–170	C Africa	leaves and stems	largest living primate; the most intelligent of land animals (after man); unjustified reputation for ferocity, perhaps based on its size, and habit of beating its chest in a show of aggression
grizzly or brown bear	Species *Ursus arctos*	200–280	NW America and former USSR	omnivorous	noted for its size (up to half a ton); much reduced population due to hunting, loss of natural habitat
guinea pig	Genus *Cavia*	28	S America	herbs, grasses	tailless rodent; domesticated form is the *Cavia porcellus*
hamster	Subfamily *Cricetinae*	5.3–10.2	Europe, Middle East, former USSR and China	mainly seeds, shoots, root vegetables	familiar western pet, but aggressive towards own species in the wild

MAMMALS (cont.)

Placental mammals

Name	Family	Size (cm^1)	Distribution	Food	Special features
hare	Genus *Lepus*	40–76	N and S America, Africa, Europe, Asia and Arctic	grass, herbs, plants, bark, twigs	well-developed ability to run from predators; species incude jack-rabbits and the Arctic hare
hare, Patagonian	Genus *Dolichotis*	45	S America	grasses, herbs	unusual characteristic in a mammal of being strictly monogamous
hartebeest	Genus *Alcelaphus*	195–200	Africa	grass, vegetation	distinctive long face, sloping back
hedgehog	Subfamily *Erinaceinae*	10–15	Europe, Asia and Africa	earthworms, beetles, slugs, earwigs, caterpillars	ability to curl up and use prickly, spined back as protection
hippopotamus	Family *Hippopotamidae*	150–345	Africa	terrestrial vegetation	large, heavy and barrel-shaped with short stumpy legs; wallows in water
horse	Subgenus *Equus*	200–210	worldwide in domesticated form; Asia, N and S America and Australia in the wild	grass, leaves	historically useful to man as a beast of burden and means of transport, and for agricultural, military, recreational purposes
hyena	Family *Hyaeninae*	85–140	Africa and Asia	carrion, mammals, insects, small vertebrates, eggs, fruit, vegetables	scavenger and hunter, with highly developed systems of communication; family includes the aardwolf
ibex	Species *Capra ibex*	85–143	C Europe, Asia and Africa	grazing fodder	large horned creature saved from extinction in C Europe
impala	Genus *Aepyceros*	128–142	Africa	grass, leaves, flowers, fruit, seeds	attractive, graceful creature with fawn and mahogany coat; females and young gather in large herds; male has a lyre-shaped horn
jackal	Genus *Canis*	65–106	Africa, SE Europe and Asia	fruit, invertebrates, reptiles, birds, small mammals, carrion	unfair reputation as cowardly scavenger

jaguar	Species *Panthera onca*	112–185	C and S America	deer, monkeys, sloths, birds, turtles, frogs, fish and small rodents	only cat to be found in the Americas
jerboa	Family *Dipodidae*	4–26	N Africa, Turkey, Middle East and C Asia	seeds, vegetation, insects	long hind legs allow movement by hopping and jumping
lemming	Tribe *Lemmini*	10–11	N America and Eurasia	plants, bulbs, roots, mosses	Norway lemming is noted for its mass migration which some-times results in drowning
lemur	Family *Lemuridae*	12–70	Madagascar	flowers, leaves, bamboo shoots	mainly nocturnal and arboreal
leopard	Species *Panthera pardus*	100–190	Africa and Asia	mainly small mammals, birds	opportunistic, nocturnal hunters; adept at climbing trees
lion	Species *Panthera leo*	260–330	Africa	meat of animals which weigh 50–500kg	known as the 'King of Beasts'; the most socially organized of the cat family
llama	Species *Lama glama*	230–400	S America	plants and vegetation	S American beast of burden
lynx	Species *Felis lynx*	67–110	Europe and N America	rodents, small hoofed mammals	lives in cold northern latitudes; well adapted to travelling through deep snow
macaque	Genus *Macaca*	38–70	Asia and N Africa	mainly fruit, insects, leaves, crops, small animals	heavily built and partly terrestrial genus of monkey; includes the Rhesus monkey adapted to life in the Himalayas, and the Barbary apes imported into Gibraltar in the 18th-c
marmoset	Family *Callitrichidae*	17.5–40	S America	fruit, flowers, nectar, gum, frogs, snails, lizards, spiders, insects	small, colourful, squirrel-like monkeys; includes species of tamarins
marten	Genus *Martes*	30–75	N America, Europe and Asia	mice, squirrels, rabbit, grouse, fruit, nuts	one species, the fisher, unique for its ability to penetrate the quilled defences of the porcupine
mole	Family *Talpidae*	2.4–7.5	Europe, Asia and N America	earthworms, insect larvae, slugs	almost exclusively subterranean existence

MAMMALS (cont.)

Placental mammals

Name	Family	Size (cm^1)	Distribution	Food	Special features
mongoose	Family *Viverridae*	24–58	Africa, S Asia and SW Europe	vertebrates, insects, fruit, snakes	some species live in social groups; often seen in the tripod position, ie standing up on hind legs and tail
mountain beaver	Family *Aplondontidae*	30–41	Pacific Coast of Canada and USA	leaves, plant materials	land-dwelling and burrowing animal; causes great damage to forest areas
mouse *see* rat					
narwhal	Species *Monodon monceros*	400–500	former USSR, N America and Greenland	shrimp, cod, flounder	distinctive single tusk in the male can reach lengths of up to 3m
okapi	Species *Okapia johnstoni*	190–200	Zaire	mainly leaves and shoots	secretive and elusive creature; strange-looking mixture of giraffe and zebra
orang-utan	Species *Pongo pygmaeus*	150	forests of N Samutra and Borneo	fruit, leaves, insects	sparse covering of long red-brown hair; adults with large naked fatty folds around face; life span of 35 years in the wild; much diminished population
otter	Subfamily *Lutrinae*	40–123	N and S America, Europe, Asia and Africa	frogs, crabs, fish, aquatic birds	only truly amphibious members of the general weasel family; greatly reduced population due to persecution, loss of natural habitat
panda, giant	Species *Ailuropoda melanoleuca*	70–80	China	bamboo	rare; poor breeder; the success rate of breeding in captivity has been extremely low
polar bear	Species *Ursus maritimus*	250–300	N polar regions	mainly seals, carcasses of large marine animals	unique for its large size, white coat and adaptation to aquatic living
porcupine (New World)	Family *Erethizontidae*	30–86	N and S America	bark, roots, shoots, leaves, berries, seeds, nuts, flowers	arboreal version of Old World porcupine; excellent climber
porcupine (Old World)	Family *Hystricidae*	37–47	Africa and Asia	roots, bulbs, fruit, berries	heavily quilled and spiny body

porpoise	Family *Phocoenidae*	120–150	N temperate zone, W Indo-Pacific, temperate and sub-antarctic waters of S America and Auckland Islands	fish, squid, crustaceans	large range of sounds for the purpose of echo location
puma	Species *Felis concolor*	105–196	N and S America	deer, rodents	wide ranging hunter; includes sub-species cougar
rabbit, European	Genus *Oryctolagus*	38–58	Europe, Africa, Australia, New Zealand and S America	grass, herbs, roots, plants, bark	burrowing creature; opportunistic animal in widespread environment; noted for its breeding capacity; domesticated rabbits descended from this genus
racoon	Genus *Procyon*	55	N, S and C America	frogs, fish, birds, eggs, fruit, nuts, small rodents, insects, corn	black masked face; distinctive ringed tail; reputation for mischief
rat (New World)	Subfamily *Hesperomyinae*	5–8	N and S America	seeds, grain, plants, nuts, fruit, fungi, insects, crustaceans, fish	numerous species adapted to living in all possible forms of different habitat
rat (Old World)	Subfamily *Murinae*	4.5–8.2	Europe, Asia, Africa and Australia	omnivorous	large number of species; one of the most successful mammals at adapting to any form of environment
reedbuck	Genus *Redunca*	110–176	Africa	grass, leaves, crops	graceful, elegant animals; distinctive whistling sounds, leaping movements
rhinoceros	Family *Rhinocerotidae*	250–400	Africa and tropical Asia	plant foliage	name derives from horn growing from snout; man's desire to use the horn for commercial purposes has brought the animal to the verge of extinction
seal	Family *Phocidae*	117–490	mainly polar, subpolar and temperate seas	fish, squid, crustaceans	graceful swimmer and diver; some species have been the object of controversial culling procedures
sheep, American bighorn	Species *Ovis canadensis*	168–186	N America	grazing fodder	large horns and body similar to an ibex; clings to the vicinity of cliffs

MAMMALS (cont.)

Placental mammals

Name	Family	Size (cm[1])	Distribution	Food	Special features
sheep, barbary	Genus *Ammotragus*	155–165	N Africa	grazing fodder	large head and horns up to 84cm in length
sheep, blue	Genus *Pseudois*	91 shoulder height	Asia	grazing fodder	blue coat; curved horns
shrew	Family *Soricidae*	3.5–4.8	Europe, Asia, Africa, N America and northern S America	insects, earthworms	generally poor eyesight compensated for by acute sense of smell and hearing
skunk	Subfamily *Mephitinae*	40–68	N and S America	insects, small mammals, eggs, fruit	evil-smelling defence mechanism; major carrier of rabies
sloth, three-toed	Family *Bradypodidae*	56–60	S America	leaves	smaller version of the two-toed sloth; slightly more active both by day and night
sloth, two-toed	Family *Megalonychidae*	58–70	S America	leaves	arboreal, nocturnal creature noted for the slowness of its movement
springbuck	Genus *Antidorcas*	96–115	S Africa	mainly grass	gregarious creature which migrates together in herds of tens of thousands
springhare	Family *Pedetidae*	36–43	S Africa	grass and soil	burrowing creature like a miniature kangaroo, moves usually by hopping; hunted by man as a source of food and for its skin
squirrel	Family *Sciuridae*	6.6–10	N and S America, Europe, Africa and Asia	nuts, seeds, plants, insects	large number of species living in a variety of environments and including arboreal, burrowing and flying creatures; species include the marmot and chipmunk, grey squirrel noted for its ablility to strip bark and damage young trees

tapir	Genus *Tapirus*	180–250	C and S America and SE Asia	grass, leaves, vegetation, buds, fruit, shoots	strange-looking, nocturnal mammal with distinctive snout; all species exist in vastly reduced numbers
tarsier	Genus *Tarsius*	11–14	islands of SE Asia	insects, lizards, bats, birds, snakes	proportionally large eyes; extra-ordinary ability to rotate neck
tiger	Species *Panthera tigris*	220–310	India, Manchuria, China and Indonesia	hoofed animals eg deer and wild pigs	solitary hunters, stalk for prey
vole	Tribe *Microtini*	10–11	N America, Europe, Asia and the Arctic	grasses, seeds, aquatic plants, insects	population fluctuates in regular patterns or cycles
walrus	Species *Odobenus rosmarus*	250–320	Arctic seas	marine molluscs and invertebrates	characterized by its thick folds of skin, twin tusks
waterbuck	Species *Kobus ellipsiprymnus*	177–235	Africa	grasses, reeds, rushes, aquatic vegetation	shaggy coat and heavy gait; gives off an oily, detectable secretion on its coat
weasel	Subfamily *Mustelinae*	15–55	Arctic, N and S America, Europe, Asia and Africa	rodents, rabbits, birds, insects, lizards, frogs	certain species have been exploited for their fur, eg mink, ermine; includes species of ferret and polecat
whale, beaked	Family *Ziphiidae*	400–1280	worldwide	mainly squid	named after its distinctive, protuberant, dolphin-like beak
whale, blue	Species *Balaenoptera musculus*	to 3000	Arctic and subtropics	krill	largest animal that has ever lived
whale, grey	Species *Eschrichtius robustus*	1190–1520	N Pacific	fish, crustaceans, ocean floor molluscs	long migration to breed, from the Arctic to the subtropics; one of the most heavily barnacled of the whale species
whale, humpback	Species *Megaptera novaeangliae*	1600	worldwide	mainly fish, krill	highly acrobatic, with wide range of sounds; migrates between Arctic and mid-Pacific

MAMMALS (cont.)

Placental mammals

Name	Family	Size (cm[1])	Distribution	Food	Special features
whale, killer	Species *Orcinus orca*	900–1000	worldwide in cool coastal waters	fish, squid, birds, and other marine mammals	toothed whale; dorsal fin narrow and vertical; co-operative and highly co-ordinated hunter, with triangular fins and distinctive white and black colouring, not generally a threat to man
whale, long-finned pilot	Species *Globicephala melaena*	600	temperate waters of the N Atlantic	cuttlefish, squid	best known for mysterious mass strandings on beaches
whale, sperm	Species *Physeter catodon*	to 2070	widespread in temperate and tropical waters	mainly squid	largest of the toothed whales, prodigious deep sea diver
whale, white	Species *Delphinaptems leucas*	300–500	N Russia, N America and Greenland	crustaceans, worms, molluscs	distinctive white skin; wide range of bodily, facial and vocal expressions
wild cat	Species *Felis silvestris*	50–80	Europe, India and Africa	small mammals, birds	domestic cat may be descended from the African wild cat
wolf, grey	Species *Canis lupus*	100–150	N America, Europe, Asia and Middle East	moose, deer, caribou	noted for hunting in packs
wolverine	Species *Gulo gulo*	to 83	Arctic and subarctic regions	small mammals, deer, caribou, birds, plants, carrion	heavily built; long, dark coat of fur; adapted for hunting in soft, deep snow
zebra	Subgenus *Hippotigris*	215–230	Africa	grass, leaves	famous for black and white stripes

[1] To convert cm to in, multiply by 0.3937; generally, size denotes length from head to tip of tail.

ENDANGERED SPECIES (Reptiles, birds, mammals)

Reptiles

Name	Species	Location	Cause of endangerment
alligator, China	*Alligator sinensis*	E China	exploitation for meat, leather; extermination as vermin
anole, giant or Culebra giant	*Anolis roosevelti*	Puerto Rico	loss of habitat, probably already extinct
boa, Puerto Rican or Culebra Grande	*Epicrates inornatus*	Puerto Rico; Virgin Islands	human persecution; predation by the mongoose
boa, Round Island	*Bolyeria multocarinata*	Round Island, near Mauritius	deterioration of palm forest habitat, possibly already extinct
boa, Round Island keel-scaled	*Casarea dussumieri*	Round Island, near Mauritius	deterioration of palm forest habitat
caiman, black	*Melanosuchus niger*	S America	hunting; exploitation for hides; loss of habitat to cattle ranching
caiman, broad-nosed	*Caiman latirostris*	S America	hunting for hides
caiman, Magdalena or C American	*Caiman crocodilus fuscus*	S America	exploitation for hides; animal trade; souvenir trade for stuffed skins
caiman, Paraguay or Yacare	*Caiman crocodilus yacare*	S America	hunting; export of hides
caiman, red apaporis	*Caiman crocodilus apaporiensis*	Columbia	hunting; exploitation for hides; interbreeding with spectacled caiman
caiman, spectacled	*Caiman crocodilus crocodilus*	Venezuela, the Guianas, Amazon, Columbia and Peru	animal trade, hunting for hides; souvenir trade in stuffed skins
cobra, C Asian	*Naja oxiana*	C Asia	loss of natural habitat
crocodile, African slender-snouted	*Crocodylus cataphractus*	W and C Africa	hunting; exploitation for meat, hides, eggs
crocodile, American	*Crocodylus acutus*	Florida, USA	hunting for sport; exploitation for skin; human persecution; loss of habitat
crocodile, Cuban	*Crocodylus rhombifer*	Cuba	exploitation for skins; loss of habitat; hybridization
crocodile, dwarf	*Ostealaemus tetraspis*	Africa	loss of habitat to cultivation; exploitation for hides, meat, eggs
crocodile, marsh or mugger	*Crocodylus palustris palustris*	Pakistan, India, Iran and Sri Lanka	exploitation for skins; hunting; loss of habitat, food resources
crocodile, Morelet's	*Crocodylus moreletii*	Mexico and Honduras	exploitation for hides
crocodile, Orinoco	*Crocodylus intermedius*	Venezuela; Colombia	hunting; exploitation for hides
crocodile, Siamese	*Crocodylus siamensis*	Thailand	hunting; exploitation for hides
gavial, false	*Tomistoma schlegelii*	Malay Peninsula, Sumatra; Borneo	trapping, hunting for its hide

ENDANGERED SPECIES (cont.)

Reptiles

Name	Species	Location	Cause of endangerment
gavial, Indian or gharial	*Gavialis gangeticus*	India, Pakistan; Nepal	hunting for its skin; human disturbance; loss of habitat to cultivation
gecko, Rodriguez day	*Phelsuma edwardnewtonii*	Rodriguez Islands	predation by rats, cats
iguana, Fiji banded	*Brachylophus fasciatus*	Fiji Islands and Tonga	predation by the mongoose
iguana, Anegada ground	*Cyclura pinguis*	Virgin Islands	loss of habitat; human disturbance; predation by pets, wild animals
iguana, Watling Island ground or San Salvador rock	*Cyclura rileyi rileyi*	Bahamas	hunting; poaching; zoo trade
lizard, black or Californian legless	*Anniella pulchra niger*	California, USA	loss of habitat
lizard, blunt-nosed or San Joaquin leopard	*Cryptaphytus wislizenii silus*	USA and Mexico	destruction of habitat by agriculture
lizard, Hierro giant	*Gallotia somonyi*	Hierro, Canary Islands	human disturbance; loss of habitat
lizard, St Croix ground	*Ameiva polops*	Virgin Islands	loss of habitat; predation by the mongoose
rattlesnake, New Mexico ridge-nosed	*Crotalus willardi obscurus*	Mexico and New Mexico, USA	human disturbance; loss of habitat
snake, San Fransico garter	*Thamnophis sirtalis tetrataenia*	California, USA	collecting as specimens; loss of habitat to drainage, housing developments
terrapin, river or tuntong	*Batagur baska*	Malaysia and Burma	water pollution; damage to nesting areas by commercial sand removal, tin mining, flooding, silt deposits
tortoise, Abingdon saddlebacked	*Testudo elephantopus abingdoni*	Galapagos	slaughter by whalers; other fishermen; competition for food with goat population
tortoise, Chatham Island	*Testudo elephantopus chathamensis*	Galapagos	animal trade, exploitation; predation of nests; killing of young by wild dogs
tortoise, Cowley Mountain	*Testudo elephantopus vandenburghi*	Galapagos	poaching for meat; oil, animal trade; competition for food with wild donkeys
tortoise, Duncan saddlebacked	*Testudo elephantopus ephippium*	Galapagos	animal trade, exploitation; predation of young by black rats
tortoise, Hood saddlebacked	*Testudo elephantopus hoodensis*	Galapagos	slaughter by whalers and other fishermen; human settlement; poaching; exploitation for oil; predation by, or competition with, variety of mammals

ENDANGERED SPECIES (cont.)

Reptiles

Name	Species	Location	Cause of endangerment
tortoise, Indefatigable Island	*Testudo elephantopus nigrita*	Galapagos	human settlement; exploitation for oil, meat by farmers and fishermen; animal trade; predation by pigs, cats, rats; competition for food with goats
tortoise, James Island	*Testudo elephantopus darwini*	Galapagos	animal trade, exploitation; predation of nests by wild goats; competition for food with wild goats
tortoise, North Albemarle saddlebacked	*Testudo elephantopus becki*	Galapagos	animal trade; poaching for meat, oil; predation by cats, rats
tortoise, South Albemarle	*Testudo elephantopus elephantopus*	Galapagos	persecution; poaching; predation by cats, dogs, pigs
tortoise, Tagus Cove	*Testudo elephantopus microphyes*	Galapagos	animal trade; illegal export
tortoise, Vilamil Mountain or South West Albemarle	*Testudo elephantopus guentheri*	Galapagos	exploitation for oil; poaching; predation by pigs, dogs, cats, rats; competition for food from goats, donkeys, cattle
turtle, Atlantic Ridley	*Lepidochelys kempi*	Gulf of Mexico, USA and Europe	exploitation of turtles for eggs; leather; killing of turtles by trawlers fishing for shrimps
turtle, green	*Chelonia mydas*	warm waters	exploitation of turtle meat, hides, eggs, shells; killing of turtles in the trawling nets of fishermen; human disturbance; loss of natural habitat; international trade in turtles
turtle, hawksbill	*Eretmochelys imbricata*	Atlantic, Pacific and Indian Oceans, Gulf of Mexico and Caribbean	exploitation for tortoiseshell, skin, stuffed turtles as souvenirs
turtle, leathery, leatherback or luth	*Dermochelys coriacea*	tropics; some temperate regions	exploitation for eggs which are considered a delicacy
turtle, Pacific Ridley or olive	*Lepidochelys olivacea*	Indo-Pacific and Atlantic Oceans	exploitation for eggs, skin, oil
turtle, short-necked or swamp	*Pseudemydura umbrina*	W Australia	drainage and clearance of habitat for agriculture; disruption by wildfires; predation by foxes, wild dogs
turtle, S American red-lined	*Pseudemys ornata callirostris*	Colombia	over-collecting for food and for the pet trade
turtle, S American river or arrau	*Podocnemis expansa*	northern S America	exploitation for meat, eggs, oil; animal trade
viper, Latifi's	*Vipera latifii*	Lar Valley, Teheran	loss of habitat to hydroelectric plant

ENDANGERED SPECIES (cont.)

Birds

Name	Species	Location	Cause of endangerment
'akiapola'au	*Hemignathus wilsoni*	Hawaiian Islands	deterioration of forest habitat; disease; competition with imported birds; predation by rats
'akiola, Kauai	*Hemignathus obscurus*	Hawaiian Islands	disease; overgrazing of forest habitat by livestock; competition with imported birds; predation by rats
albatross, short-tailed	*Diomedea albatrus*	Japan	loss of habitat; exploitation for feathers; low rate of reproduction
antwren, black-hooded	*Myrmotherula erythronotos*	SE Brazil	destruction of tropical forest habitat
barbthroat, black	*Threnetes grzimeki*	SE Brazil	hummingbird threatened by destruction of forest habitat
blackbird, grey-headed	*Turdus poliocephalus poliocephalus*	Norfolk Island, SW Pacific Ocean	destruction of habitat; competition with European blackbird; predation by rats
booby, Abbot's	*Sula abbotti*	Christmas Island, Indian Ocean	destruction of nesting areas by phosphate mining; low rate of reproduction
bristlebird, western rufous	*Dasyornis broadbenti littoralis*	W Australia	clearance, burning of scrubland habitat may have already led to extinction
bullfinch, São Miguel	*Pyrrhula pyrrhula murina*	Azores	shooting to protect budding fruit trees may have already led to extinction
bustard, great Indian	*Choriotis nigriceps*	NW India and Pakistan	hunting for its meat; loss of grassland habitat to cultivation, grazing of domestic livestock
cahow	*Pterodroma cahow*	Bermuda	human persecution; disturbance, predation by rats, wild pigs; competition for nesting sights with tropical birds
capercaillie, Cantabrian	*Tetrao urogallus cantabricus*	Spain	hunting; loss of deciduous forest habitat
condor, Californian	*Gymnogyps californianus*	California	low reproductive potential; shooting, trapping, poisoning, egg-collecting; extinction appears inevitable
crane, Mississipi sandhill	*Grus canadensis pulla*	USA Gulf Coast	hunting, loss of habitat; possible genetic deterioration
crane, Siberian white	*Grus leucogeranus*	Siberia	hunting, disturbance; destruction of nests by domesticated reindeer
crane, whooping	*Grus americanus*	USA	pollution; destruction, disturbance of wetland habitat

ENDANGERED SPECIES (cont.)

Birds

Name	Species	Location	Cause of endangerment
creeper, Molokai	*Paroreomyza maculata flammea*	Hawaiian Islands	disease to which Hawaiian honeycreepers have limited immunity; destruction of rain forest habitat by grazing livestock; competition from imported birds; predation by mammals
crow, Hawaiian	*Corvus tropicus*	Hawaiian Islands	disease; loss of habitat to wild pigs, cattle, goats; predation by black rats
crow, Marianas	*Corvus kubaryi*	Marianas	reasons for decline are unrecorded
cuckoo, south-eastern rufous-vented ground	*Neomorphus geoffroyi dulcis*	SE Brazil	rare bird threatened by the felling of forest habitat
curassow, red-billed	*Crax blumenbachii*	Brazil	hunting; loss of rainforest habitat
curassow, eastern razor-billed	*Crax mitu mitu*	Brazil	seriously threatened with extinction by hunting; loss of rainforest habitat
curlew, Eskimo	*Numenius borealis*	Arctic tundra and S America	shooting; loss of prairie habitat to agriculture; climactic changes possibly altering migratory and reproductive processes
currawong, Lord Howe	*Strepera graculina crissalis*	Lord Howe Island, SW Pacific Ocean	cause of decline unknown
eagle, Madagascar sea	*Haliaeetus vociferoides*	Madagascar	hunting; human persecution
eagle, Madagascar serpent	*Eutriorchis astur*	Madagascar	clearing of forest habitat
eagle, monkey-eating	*Pithecophaga jefferyi*	Philippines	shooting; animal trade; destruction of forest habitat
eagle, southern bald	*Heliaeetus leucocephalus leucocephalus*	US and N Mexico	mortality and breeding failure due to contamination of habitat and prey by pesticides; habitat loss; disturbance
eagle, Spanish imperial	*Aquila heliaca adalberti*	Spain and Portugal	poisoning and contamination by pesticides; shooting; loss of habitat to forest clearance, overgrazing
falcon, American peregrine	*Falco peregrinus anatum*	USA, Canada and Mexico	killing; capture; contamination of birds and eggs by pesticides
falcon, tundra peregrine	*Falco peregrinus tundrius*	Alaska, Canada and Greenland	contamination by chlorinated hydrocarbons in S American wintering grounds

ENDANGERED SPECIES (cont.)

Birds

Name	Species	Location	Cause of endangerment
fernbird, Codfish Island	*Bowdleria punctat wilsoni*	New Zealand	modification of low scrub habitat by brush-tailed possum; predation on birds and eggs by Polynesian rats
fire-eye, fringe-backed	*Pyriglena atra*	E Brazil	loss of tropical forest habitat to human settlement; industrial, agricultural development
flycatcher, Hivoa	*Pomarea mendozae mendozae*	Marquesas Islands, S Pacific Ocean	deterioration of wooded valley habitat by overgrazing of cattle, sheep, pigs, goats
flycatcher, Nukuhiva	*Pomarea mendozae nukuhivae*	Marquesas Islands, S Pacific Ocean	deterioration of wooded valley habitat by overgrazing of cattle, wild goats
flycatcher, Seychelles black paradise	*Terpsiphone corvina*	Seychelles	human disturbance; loss of lowland forest habitat
flycatcher, Tahiti	*Pomarea nigra nigra*	Tahiti	causes of decline are unknown
fody, Mauritius	*Foudia rubra*	Mauritius	destruction of montane evergreen forest habitat; competition from other species of fody; predation of nests by macaque monkeys, black rats
fody, Rodrigues	*Foudia flavicans*	Rodrigues Island, Indian Ocean	destruction of forest habitat; competition from other species of fody
gallinule, Hawaiian	*Gallinula chloropus sandvicensis*	Hawaiian Islands	draining of wetland habitat; predation by rats, cats, mongooses
grebe, Atitlan or giant pied-billed	*Podilymbus gigas*	Guatemala	competition for food, predation on grebe chicks by bass fish; loss of nesting habitat to housing development
grebe, Colombian	*Podiceps andinus*	Colombia	competition for food from trout; possible contamination by pesticides
grebe, Junin	*Podiceps taczanowskii*	Peru	pollution of lake habitat by copper mining
guan, black-fronted piping	*Aburria jacutinga*	Brazil	hunting; loss of tropical forest habitat
guan, Cauca	*Penelope perspicax*	Colombia	almost total loss of forest habitat
guan, horned	*Oreophasis derbianus*	Mexico and Guatemala	hunting; loss of forest habitat to agriculture, coffee plantations, overgrazing
guan, Trinidad piping	*Pipile pipile pipile*	Trinidad	hunting; loss of forest habitat; may already be extinct

ENDANGERED SPECIES (cont.)

Birds

Name	Species	Location	Cause of endangerment
guan, white-winged	*Penelope albipennis*	Peru	hunting; loss of forest habitat to charcoal burning
hermit, hook-billed	*Glaucis dohrnii*	SE Brazil	destruction of forest habitat
honeyeater, helmeted	*Meliphaga melanops cassidix*	Victoria, Australia	alteration of habitat; destruction of habitat by fire; competition with other species
honeyeater, Mukojima Bonin	*Apalopteron familiare familiare*	Bonin Islands, Japan	clearance of subtropical and scrub forest habitat for tourist developments
ibis, hermit	*Geronticus eremita*	Turkey and Morocco	hunting; nest disturbance; poaching for eggs; animal, zoo trade; reproductive failure due to pesticide contamination
ibis, Japanese crested	*Nipponia nippon*	Sado Island, Japan	hunting; loss of forest habitat
kagu	*Rhynochetos jubatus*	New Caledonia	trapping; animal trade; destruction of forest habitat by nickel mining; predation by dogs, cats, pigs, rats
kakapo	*Strigops habroptilus*	New Zealand	human disturbance; loss of forest habitat; competition for food; predation by rats, stoats
kestrel, Mauritius	*Falco punctatus*	Mauritius	destruction of forest habitat; hunting; predation of nests by macaque monkeys
kingfisher, Guam Micronesian	*Halycon cinnamomina cinnamomina*	Guam, Mariana Islands, W Pacific Ocean	human development; loss of forest habitat
kite, Grenada hook-billed	*Chondrohierax uncinatus mirus*	Lesser Antilles, W Indies	hunting; decrease in numbers of snails on which the kite subsists; effects of hurricanes
macaw, glaucous	*Anodorynchus glaucus*	S America	possibly already extinct
macaw, Lear's or indigo	*Anodorhynchus leari*	S America	rare bird in great demand among aviculturists who threaten its continued existence in the wild
mallard, Marianas	*Anas oustaleti*	Mariana Islands, W Pacific Ocean	hunting; draining of wetland habitat
monal, Chinese	*Lophophorus lhuysii*	W China	hunting
nukupu'u	*Hemignathus lucidus*	Fiji, Hawaiian Islands	disease; predation by rats; competition from other birds
'o'u	*Psittirostra psittacea*	Hawaiian Islands	loss of forest habitat due to overgrazing by livestock; competition with imported birds; disease; predation

ENDANGERED SPECIES (cont.)

Birds

Name	Species	Location	Cause of endangerment
owl, Anjouan scops	*Otus rutilus capnodes*	Anjouan Island, W Indian Ocean	over-collecting; destruction of evergreen forest habitat by felling, banana cultivation, cyclones
owl, Lanyu scops	*Otus elegans botelensis*	Taiwan	loss of forest habitat; human disturbance in the form of tourism
owl, Soumagne's	*Tyto soumagnei*	Madagascar	loss of humid forest habitat
oystercatcher, Canarian black	*Haematopus moquini meadewaldoi*	Canary Islands	has always been rare, may no longer be extant
oystercatcher, Chatham Island	*Haematopus chathamensis*	Chatham Islands, off New Zealand	destruction of vegetation by grazing sheep
parakeet, Chatham Island yellow-crowned or Forbe's	*Cyanoramphus auriceps forbesi*	Chatham Islands, off New Zealand	human development; climatic damage to habitat
parakeet, Mauritius	*Psittacula echo*	Mauritius	loss of evergreen forest habitat; competition for nest sites; nest predation by macaque monkeys, rats
parakeet, Norfolk Island	*Cyanoramphus novaeseelandiae cookii*	Norfolk Island, SW Pacific Ocean	competition for nest sites; shooting; loss of rainforest habitat
parakeet, Paradise or beautiful	*Psephotus pulcherrimus*	S Queensland and New South Wales, Australia	drought; expansion of livestock grazing; last confirmed sighting was in 1927, but there have been more recent unconfirmed sightings
parakeet, Uvea horned	*Eunymphicus cornutus uvaeensis*	Uvea, Loyalty Islands, SW Pacific Ocean	animal trade; loss of woodland habitat
parrot, Imperial or sisserou	*Amazona imperialis*	Lesser Antilles, W Indies	hunting for meat, sport
parrot, maroon fronted	*Rhynchopsitta pachyrhyncha terrisi*	NE Mexico	logging of pine forest habitat; animal trade; shooting
parrot, Puerto Rican	*Amazona vittata*	Puerto Rico	clearance of lowland forest habitat; predation of nests by rats
parrot, red-necked or jacquot	*Amazona arausiaca*	Lesser Antilles, W Indies	hunting; competition for nesting ranges, predation of eggs and young by pearly-eyed thrashers
parrot, red-tailed	*Amazona brasiliensis*	SE Brazil	animal trade; loss of forest habitat
parrot, St Lucia	*Amazona versicolor*	St Lucia, W Indies	hunting; loss of forest habitat to agriculture
parrot, St Vincent	*Amazona guildingii*	Lesser Antilles, W Indies	animal trade; hunting

ENDANGERED SPECIES (cont.)

Birds

Name	Species	Location	Cause of endangerment
parrot, Seychelles lesser vasa	*Coracopsis nigra barklyi*	Seychelles	destruction of palm forest habitat by cutting, burning
parrot, Western ground	*Pezoporus wallicus flaviventris*	SW Australia	clearing, burning, draining of grassland and wetland habitat
partridge, Italian grey	*Perdix perdix italica*	C Italy	interbreeding with other grey partridges; contamination by agricultural herbicides, pesticides; competition for food from pheasants
petrel, black	*Procellaria parkinsoni*	New Zealand	predation on breeding adults and fledglings by cats
petrel, Chatham Island	*Pterodroma hypoleuca axillaris*	Chatham Islands off New Zealand	competition from other subspecies
petrel, dark-rumped	*Pterodroma phaeopygia phaeopygia*	Galapagos	destruction of habitat due to agriculture; predation by dogs, pigs, black rats
petrel, Hawaiian dark-rumped	*Pterodroma phaeopygia sandwichensis*	Hawaiian Islands	predation by black rats, cats, mongooses
petrel, magenta	*Pterodroma magentae*	New Zealand	predation by cats, rats; deterioration of forest habitat due to overgrazing of livestock, presence of other herbivores
pheasant, brown-eared	*Crossoptilon mantchuricum*	N China	human persecution; loss of forest habitat
pheasant, cheer	*Catreus wallichii*	India and Nepal	hunting; destruction of forest habitat
pheasant, Elliot's	*Syrmaticus ellioti*	E China	hunting; destruction of forest habitat
pigeon, Chatham Island	*Hemiphaga novaeseelandiae chathamensis*	Chatham Islands, off New Zealand	hunting; predation by cats; destruction of woodland habitat by grazing stock, winds, fire
pigeon, laurel	*Columba junoniae*	Canary Islands	hunting; loss of laurel forest habitat
pigeon, Marquesas	*Ducula galeata*	Marquesas Islands	hunting for its meat; loss of habitat to human disturbance, grazing of cattle, pigs, goats
pigeon, Palau Nicobar	*Caloenas nicobarica pelewensis*	Palau Islands, SW Pacific Ocean	hunting
pigeon, pink	*Nesoenas mayeri*	Mauritius	predation of nests by macaque monkeys, black rats; hunting; loss of forest habitat
pigeon, Puerto Rican plain	*Columba inornata wetmorei*	Puerto Rico	human persecution; plundering of nests; loss of forest habitat to housing development
pigeon, Truk Micronesian	*Ducula oceanica teraokai*	Caroline Islands, W Pacific Ocean	hunting for its meat; loss of forest habitat

ENDANGERED SPECIES (cont.)

Birds

Name	Species	Location	Cause of endangerment
plover, New Zealand shore	*Thinornis novaeseelandiae*	Chatham Islands, off New Zealand	animal trade; destruction of vegetation by grazing sheep
quail, gorgeted wood	*Odontophorus strophium*	Colombia	absence of suitable habitat; current survival is in doubt
quail, masked bobwhite	*Colinus virginianus ridgwayi*	USA and Mexico	deterioration of habitat due to drought, overgrazing by cattle
rail, barred-wing	*Rallus poecilopterus*	Fiji Islands	predation by mongooses, cats, rats
rail, light-footed clapper	*Rallus longirostris levipes*	California, USA and Mexico	loss of saltmarsh habitat
rail, Lord Howe wood	*Tricholimnas sylvestris*	Lord Howe Island, SW Pacific Ocean	damage to vegetation by wild goats, pigs; predation of eggs by rats
rhea, Puna	*Pterocnemia pennata tarapacensis*	Peru, Chile, Bolivia and Argentina	hunting for its feathers and skin; poaching its eggs
robin, Chatham Island black	*Petroica traversi*	Chatham Islands off New Zealand	destruction and deterioration of scrub forest habitat by human disturbance, climatic conditions; nesting of petrels
robin, dappled mountain	*Modulatrix orostruthus*	Mozambique and Tanzania	loss of forest habitat to agriculture
robin, Seychelles magpie	*Copsychus sechellarum*	Seychelles	predation by cats; competition for nest sites; decreased availability of food
robin, Southern Ryukyu	*Erithacus komadori subrufa*	Ryukyu Islands	destruction of forest habitat
scrub-bird, noisy	*Atrichornis clamosus*	SW Australia	clearance of eucalyptus forest habitat; drought; predation by cats
shrike, black-capped bush	*Malaconotus alius*	Tanzania	loss of canopy forest habitat due to felling
shrike, San Clemente loggerhead	*Lanius ludovicianus mearnsi*	California, USA	deterioration of brush vegetation habitat due to overgrazing by goats, sheep, pigs
silver-eye, white-breasted	*Zosterops albogularis*	Norfolk Island, SW Pacific Ocean	almost complete destruction of rainforest habitat
siskin, red	*Spinus cucullatus*	S America	trapping for the cagebird trade
sparrow, Amok song	*Melospiza melodia amaka*	Amak Island off Alaska	predation by Arctic foxes
sparrow, dusky seaside	*Ammodramus maritimus nigrescens*	Florida, USA	destruction of salt marshland habitat by fires; human development; alterations in habitat by mosquito control, waterfowl enhancement, inundation of freshwater

ENDANGERED SPECIES (cont.)

Birds

Name	Species	Location	Cause of endangerment
sparrow, San Clemente sage	*Amphispiza belli clementeae*	S California, USA	deterioration of shrubland and grassland habitat by overgrazing of wild goats, pigs
sparrowhawk, Anjouan	*Accipiter francesii pusillus*	Anjouan Island, Indian Ocean	destruction of forest habitat by human settlement, cyclones, soil erosion; banana plantations
stilt, black	*Himantopus novaesealandiae*	New Zealand	loss of breeding and feeding habitat
starling, Rothschild's	*Leucopsar rothschildi*	Bali, Indonesia	loss of forest habitat to human settlement; competition from other starlings; trapping for the cagebird trade
stork, Oriental white	*Ciconia ciconia boyciana*	Asia	shooting; contamination by mercury causing mortality or reproductive failure; loss of wetland habitat to agriculture, extinct in Europe
takahe	*Notornis mantelli*	New Zealand	competition for food from deer; predation by stoats
tanager, cherry-throated	*Nemosia rourei*	SE Brazil	unrecorded for over a century, probably already extinct
tern, Californian least	*Sterna albifrons browni*	California, USA and Mexico	destruction and deterioration of coastal beach and marshland habitat by pollution, human settlement, development
thrasher, Martinique white-breasted	*Ramphocinclus brachyurus brachyurus*	Martinique	hunting; predation by rats, mongooses
thrasher, St Lucia white-breasted	*Ramphocinclus brachyurus sanctaeluciae*	St Lucia	loss of habitat to human development; predation by rats, mongooses
thrush, Kauai	*Phaeornis obscurus myadestina*	Hawaiian Islands	disease; loss of rainforest habitat
thrush, Molokai	*Phaeornis obscurus rutha*	Hawaiian Islands	disease; loss of rainforest habitat; deterioration of habitat caused by grazing livestock; predation by rats, cats, mongooses
thrush, St Lucia forest	*Cichlherminia lherminieri sanctaeluciae*	St Lucia, W Indies	loss of rainforest habitat
thrush, small Kauai	*Phaeornis palmeri*	Hawaiian Islands	disease; competition with other birds; loss of habitat to grazing; predation by mammals
tinamou, Pernambuco solitary	*Tinamus solitarius pernambucensis*	Brazil	hunting; loss of forest habitat

ENDANGERED SPECIES (cont.)

Birds

Name	Species	Location	Cause of endangerment
tragopan, Cabot's	*Tragopan caboti*	SE China	loss of forest habitat to agricultural cultivation
tragopan, western	*Tragopan melanocephalus*	India and Pakistan	hunting; trapping; disturbance by humans, goats; destruction of forest habitat
trembler, Martinique	*Cinclocerthia ruficauda gutturalis*	Martinique	loss of woodland habitat to sugar cane plantations; predation by rats, mongooses
turtle dove, Seychelles	*Streptopelia picturata rostrata*	Seychelles	virtually eliminated by the introduction of the Madagascar turtle dove and the resultant interbreeding
vanga, Pollen's	*Xenopirostris polleni*	Madagascar	destruction of humid forest habitat
vanga, Van Dam's	*Xenopirostris damii*	Madagascar	clearance of deciduous forest habitat
warbler, Bachman's	*Vermivora bachmanii*	USA	destruction of deciduous swampland forest habitat for timber, agriculture, sugar cane plantation; now N America's rarest songbird
warbler, Barbados yellow	*Dendroica petechia petechia*	Barbados	clearance of mangrove swampland habitat; effects of parasitism by cowbirds
warbler, Eiao Polynesian	*Acrocephalus caffer aquilonis*	Marquesas Islands	destruction of woodland habitat by grazing sheep, swine
warbler, Kirtland's	*Dendroica kirtlandii*	USA	loss of forest habitat; reduced breeding due to invasion by cowbirds who have parasitized nests
warbler, long-legged	*Trichocichla rufa*	Fiji	predation by cats, rats, mongooses
warbler, Moorea Polynesian	*Acrocephalus caffer longirostris*	Society Islands	disease
warbler, Rodrigues brush	*Bebrornis rodericana*	Rodrigues Island, Mascarenes	human disturbance; clearance of thicket habitat
warbler, Semper's	*Leucopeza semperi*	St Lucia	predation by mongooses
white-eye, Gizo	*Zosterops luteirostris luteirostris*	Solomon Islands, SW Pacific Ocean	destruction of lowland forest habitat
white-eye, Truk greater	*Rukia rukia*	Caroline Islands, W Pacific Ocean	occupies limited and unprotected range of mountain forest habitat
woodpecker, American ivory-billed	*Campephilus principalis principalis*	SE USA	bird collection; clearance of swampland habitat; human disturbance

ENDANGERED SPECIES (cont.)

Birds

Name	Species	Location	Cause of endangerment
woodpecker, Cuban ivory-billed	*Campephilus principalis bairdii*	Cuba	shooting; loss of pine forest habitat to timber trade, sugar cane plantation
woodpecker, Imperial	*Campephilus imperialis*	Mexico	shooting; loss of forest habitat due to logging
woodpecker, Okinawa	*Sapheopipo noguchii*	Ryukyu Islands	loss of woodland habitat to woodcutting, fires
woodpecker, Tristram's	*Drycopus javenssis richardsi*	C Korea	destruction of forest habitat by logging, road-building, the effects of war
woodstar, Chilean	*Eulidua yarrellii*	Chile	reasons for decline in population are unknown
wren, Guadeloupe	*Troglodytes aedon guadeloupensis*	Guadeloupe	hunting; predation by rats, cats, mongooses
wren, New Zealand bush	*Xenicus longipes*	New Zealand	predation by black rats
wren, St Lucia	*Troglodytes aedon mesoleucus*	St Lucia	predation by mongooses, rats, boa constrictors; development of scrub forest habitat will render the bird extinct

Mammals

Name	Species	Location	Cause of endangerment
anoa, lowland	*Bubalus depressicornis*	Sulawesi	hunting; destruction of habitat
anoa, mountain	*Bubalus quarlesi*	Sulawesi	hunting; destruction of habitat
antelope, giant sable	*Hippotragus niger variani*	Angola	human settlement; destruction of habitat
ass, African wild	*Equus africanus*	Somalia and Ethiopia	hunting for the medical properties of its meat and fat; poaching; human disturbance in the form of tourism; droughts; competition for pasture and water from domestic livestock
ass, Indian wild	*Equus hemionus khur*	Gujarat and Pakistan border regions	disease; loss of habitat to agriculture, land development; droughts; competition for food from domestic livestock; human disturbance
aye-aye	*Daubentonia madagascariensis*	Madagascar	primate threatened by loss of forest habitat
bandicoot, pig-footed	*Chaeropus ecaudatus*	Australia	possibly already extinct, last seen by aborigines in 1920s
bandicoot, rabbit-eared or bilby	*Macrotis lagotis*	Australia	human settlement; competition with rabbits for habitat; subject to hunting

ENDANGERED SPECIES (cont.)

Mammals

Name	Species	Location	Cause of endangerment
bat, ghost or Australian false vampire	*Macroderma gigas*	N Australia	quarrying of the caves which form their natural habitat
bat, gray	*Myotis grisescens*	SE United States	disturbance of habitat by caving, vandalism
bat, Singapore roundleaf horseshoe	*Hipposideros ridlegi*	Malaysia	logging of its lowland peat forest habitat
bear, Baluchistan	*Selenarctos thibetanus gedrosianus*	Baluchistan and Iran	human persecution; hunting because of its damage to crops and the threat posed by it to domestic stock
bear, Mexican grizzly	*Ursus horribilis nelsoni*	Mexico	may already have been exterminated by hunting, poisoning
cat, Iriomote	*Prionailurus iriomotensis*	Ryukyu Islands	loss of natural habitat to agriculture
cat, Pakistan sand	*Felis margarita scheffeli*	Pakistan	animal trade
cheetah, Asiatic	*Acinonyx jubatus venaticus*	SW Asia	fur trade; decline in population of its natural prey, the gazelle
civet, Malabar large spotted	*Viverra megaspila civettina*	S India	possibly already extinct due to persecution, loss of habitat to agriculture
colobus, black	*Colobus satanas*	Cameroon, Guinea, Gabon and the Congo	hunting; loss of habitat due to logging
colobus, Preuss's red	*Colobus badius preussi*	Cameroon	hunting; loss of forest area due to logging
colobus, Tana River red	*Colobus badius rufomitratus*	Kenya	human settlement; loss of forest area due to shifting cultivation
colobus, Zanzibar red	*Colobus kirkii*	Zanzibar	human disturbance
deer, Bactrian	*Cervus elaphus bactrianus*	SW Asia	loss of habitat to land development, damming, human settlement, stock grazing
deer, Argentinian pampas	*Ozotoceros bezoarticus celer*	Argentina	hunting; disease; loss of habitat to agriculture, domestic livestock
deer, Barbary	*Cervus elaphus barbarus*	Algeria and Tunisia border regions	poaching; loss of forest habitat
deer, Cedros Island	*Odocoileus hemionus cerrosensis*	Cedros Island off California, USA	hunting; disturbance by wild dogs; destruction of habitat by fires
deer, Colombian white-tailed	*Odocoileus virginianus leucurus*	Washington and Oregon, USA	loss of habitat to agriculture

ENDANGERED SPECIES (cont.)

Mammals

Name	Species	Location	Cause of endangerment
deer, Corsican red	*Cervus elaphus corsicanus*	Sardinia	poaching; human disturbance; loss of habitat through burning, domestic livestock grazing, deforestation
deer, northern brow-antlered	*Cervus eldi eldi*	Manipur, India	hunting; loss of habitat to domestic stock grazing, cultivation, logging, burning
deer, Persian fallow	*Dama mesopotamica*	Iran	hunting; loss of forest habitat to irrigation, agriculture, grazing of domestic livestock
deer, swamp	*Cervus duvauceli*	India and Nepal	poaching, human disturbance; competition for grazing from domestic livestock
deer, Thailand brow-antlered	*Cervus eldi siamensis*	Thailand, Laos, Kampuchea and Vietnam	hunting; loss or destruction of habitat by the effects of war, agriculture, land development, shifting cultivation, forest clearance
dog, African wild	*Lycaon pictus*	Africa south of the Sahara	human hunting, persecution
dolphin, Indus	*Platanista indi*	Indus River	withdrawal of water for irrigation; illegal exploitation by fishermen
drill	*Papio leuchopaeus*	Cameroon	hunting; loss of habitat due to clearance of forest, cultivation of land
duiker, Jentink's	*Cephalophus jentinki*	Liberia; Ivory Coast	destruction of natural habitat; almost extinct
eland, Western giant	*Taurotragus derbianus derbianus*	W Africa	hunting; persecution; disease
elephant, Asian	*Elephas maximus*	Asia	severe loss of natural habitat
ferret, black-footed	*Mustela nigripes*	USA	poisoning; loss of grassland habitat
flying fox, Guam	*Pteropus tokudae*	Guam Island	hunting; loss of forest areas
flying fox, Rodrigues	*Pteropus rodricensis*	Rodrigues Island	almost total loss of natural habitat
fox, N Kit	*Vulpes velox hebes*	USA	almost extinct due to trapping, hunting, poisoning
fox, N Simien	*Simenia simensis simensis*	Ethiopia	widespread hunting on false assumption that it is a threat to sheep
fox, Simien or Abyssinian wolf	*Canis simensis*	Ethiopia	hunting; loss of habitat; decreasing availability of rodents as food
gazelle, Arabian	*Gazella gazella arabica*	Saudi Arabia, Yemen and Red Sea	hunting; deterioration of habitat

ENDANGERED SPECIES (cont.)

Mammals

Name	Species	Location	Cause of endangerment
gazelle, Cuvier's	*Gazella cuvieri*	Tunisia, Algeria and Morocco	hunting; loss of habitat to overgrazing by livestock, forest plantation
gazelle, Dorcas	*Gazella dorcas*	N Africa, Middle East and India	hunting; loss of habitat due to overgrazing by domestic livestock
gazelle, Mhorr	*Gazella dama mhorr*	Morocco	human disturbance; occupation of habitat by domestic livestock
gazelle, Rio de Oro dama	*Gazella dama lozanoi*	Sahara	hunting; drought; loss of habitat
gazelle, sand	*Gazella subgutturosa marica*	Jordan and Arabian peninsula	hunting; deterioration of habitat due to overgrazing
gazelle, slender-horned	*Gazella leptoceros*	N Africa	hunting; deterioration of habitat
gibbon, Java or silvery	*Hylobates moloch*	Indonesia	destruction of forest habitat for timber, human settlement
gibbon, pileated, crowned or capped	*Hylobates pileatus*	Asia	loss of forest habitat
gorilla, mountain	*Gorilla gorilla beringei*	Rwanda, Zaire and Uganda	human disturbance, encroachment on natural habitat
hartebeest, Swayne's	*Alcelaphus buselaphus swaynei*	Ethiopia	hunting; destruction of habitat
hartebeest, Tora	*Alcelaphus buselaphus tora*	Ethiopia, Sudan; Egypt	hunting; loss of habitat; disease
hog, pygmy	*Sus salvanius*	N India	destruction of thatchland habitat by settlement, forestry, fires; also hunted for its meat
horse, Przewalski's or takh	*Equus przewalskii*	China and Mongolia	severe competition for natural pasture; water from domestic livestock; possibly already extinct in the wild
hyena, Barbary	*Hyaena hyaena barbara*	N Africa	loss of habitat due to human settlement, agriculture
ibex, Pyrenean	*Capra pyrenaica pyrenaica*	Pyrenees	hunting; now virtually extinct
ibex, Walia	*Capra walia*	Ethiopia	destruction of habitat by agriculture, livestock
impala, black-faced	*Aepyceros melampus petersi*	Angola and SW Africa	hunting; low reproductive rate
indris	*Indri indri*	Madagascar	primate threatened by widespread destruction of forests
jerboa, Eastern marsupial	*Antechinomys laniger*	Victoria, Australia	reasons for decline are unknown

ENDANGERED SPECIES (cont.)

Mammals

Name	Species	Location	Cause of endangerment
kangaroo rat, Morro Bay	*Dipodomys heermanni morroensis*	California, USA	loss or change of natural habitat; urban development; predation by domestic cats
kouprey	*Bos sauveli*	Kampuchea, Laos and Thailand	hunting for meat, horns; effects of warfare; low reproductive rate
langur, pig-tailed	*Simias concolor*	Mentawai Islands off Sumatra	hunting for meat; loss of forest habitat
lemur, black	*Lemur macaco macaco*	Madagascar	lack of protective measures from hunting, poisoning
lemur, red-fronted	*Lemur macaco rufus*	Madagascar	hunting; loss of habitat
lemur, red-tailed sportive	*Lepilemur mustelinus ruficaudatus*	Madagascar	hunting; destruction of forest habitat
lemur, Sandford's	*Lemur macaco sanfordi*	Madagascar	intensive hunting; loss of rain forest
lemur, Sclater's	*Lemur macaco flavifrons*	Madagascar	possibly extinct due to loss of coastal forest lands
lemur, white-footed sportive	*Lepilemur mustelinus leucopus*	Madagascar	destruction of natural environment by bad land use; competition from cattle, goats
leopard, Amur	*Panthera pardus orientalis*	Korea, Russia, China	human persecution; depletion of natural prey
leopard, Anatolian	*Panthera pardus tulliana*	W Asia	hunting, trapping, poisoning as a protection against its predation of livestock; loss of habitat to cultivation
leopard, Barbary	*Panthera pardus panthera*	N Africa	hunting for sport, for its fur; because of the threat it poses to humans, domestic livestock
leopard, Formosan clouded	*Neofelis nebulosa brachyurus*	Taiwan	hunting for its fur
leopard, Sinai	*Panthera pardus jarvisi*	Sinai	human persecution; depletion of natural prey
leopard, snow or ounce	*Panthera uncia*	C Asia	hunting for fur and because of the threat it poses to domestic livestock; loss of natural prey
leopard, S Arabian	*Panthera pardus nimr*	Arabian peninsula	persecution by shepherds protecting their flocks
lion, Asiatic	*Panthera leo persica*	Gujarat State, India	loss of natural habitat and prey
lynx, Spanish or Pardel	*Felis pardina*	Spain and Portugal	loss of habitat due to reforestation; the effects of myxomatosis on its main prey, the rabbit; incidental killing, trapping

ENDANGERED SPECIES (cont.)

Mammals

Name	Species	Location	Cause of endangerment
macaque, lion-tailed	*Macaca silenus*	S India	loss of habitat; hunting for meat; animal trade
manatee, Amazonian	*Trichechus inunguis*	Amazon River	loss of population due to hunting
mangabey, Tana River	*Cercocebus galeritus galeritus*	Kenya	primate threatened by loss of habitat due to agriculture
markhor, straight-horned	*Capra falconeri megaceros*	Pakistan; Afghanistan	hunting; loss of habitat to stock grazing
marmoset, buff-headed	*Callithrix flaviceps*	SE Brazil	destruction of natural habitat
marmot, Vancouver Island	*Marmota vancouverensis*	Vancouver Island, Canada	collection; exploitation; loss of habitat due to logging
mole, giant golden	*Chrysopalax trevelyani*	S Africa	drought; loss of habitat
monkey, C American or red-backed squirrel	*Saimiri oerstedi*	Panama and Costa Rica	animal exportation; loss of forest habitat
monkey, woolly spider	*Brachyteles arachnoides*	São Paulo state, Brazil	hunting; clearance of forest habitat for fuel, agriculture, human settlement
monkey, yellow-tailed woolly	*Lagothrix flavicauda*	Peru	hunting for its skin, meat; destruction of its habitat for human settlement
mouflon, Mediterranean	*Ovis ammon musimon*	Corsica, Sardinia; Cyprus	hunting; predation by wild dogs; hybridization
mouse, salt-marsh harvest	*Reithrodontomys raviventris*	California, USA	water pollution; loss of habitat due to urban, industrial development
muntjac, Fea's	*Muntiacus feae*	Burma and Thailand	hunting for the meat of this small deer which is highly valued
orang-utan	*Pongo pygmaeus*	Borneo and Sumatra	animal trade; felling of forests by timber industry
ocelot, Texas	*Felis pardalis albescens*	Texas and Mexico	bush clearance; hunting for fur; because it is perceived as a threat to agricultural livestock
oryx, Arabian	*Oryx leucoryx*	Oman	hunting for its meat, skin, medical uses
otter, Cameroon clawless	*Aonyx microdon*	Cameroon and Nigeria	fur trade
otter, giant	*Pteronura brasiliensis*	S America	fur trade
otter, La Plata	*Lutra platensis*	S America	hunting for its fur; water pollution affecting stocks of fish on which it depends for food

ENDANGERED SPECIES (cont.)

Mammals

Name	Species	Location	Cause of endangerment
otter, marine	*Lutra felina*	Pacific coast of S America	persecuted; shot because it is perceived as a threat to stocks of freshwater prawns
otter, southern river	*Lutra provocax*	Chile	fur trade; water pollution
panther or Florida cougar	*Felis concolor coryi*	SE USA	loss of habitat; hunting; decreased prey on which to feed
possum, Leadbetter's	*Gymnbelideus leadbeateri*	Victoria, Australia	felling of forest areas has led to loss of habitat
pronghorn, Lower Californian	*Antilocapra americana peninsularis*	California	hunting; competition for fodder from domestic livestock
pronghorn, Sonoran	*Antilocapra americana sonoriensis*	Mexico and Arizona, USA	destruction of habitat; competition for food and water from livestock; hunting
puma, Eastern or Eastern cougar	*Felis concolor cougar*	N America	loss of habitat; hunting; decreased prey on which to feed
rabbit, Ryukyu	*Pentalagus furnessi*	Ryukyu Island	loss of habitat; predation by wild dogs
rabbit, Assam or hispid hare	*Caprolagus hispidus*	N India	loss of habitat due to human settlement; cultivation; forestry; burning of thatchlands, also illegally hunted for food
rabbit, volcano	*Romerolagus diazi*	Mexico	loss of habitat; wanton destruction by shooting
rhinoceros, great Indian	*Rhinoceros unicornis*	India and Nepal	hunting; poaching for rhino horn; loss of habitat to agriculture, stock grazing
rhinoceros, Javan	*Rhinoceros sondaicus*	Java, Laos; Kampuchea	hunting for rhino horn, medical properties of rhino blood; loss of habitat to human settlement
rhinoceros, northern square-lipped	*Caratotherium simum cottoni*	Sudan, Uganda, Zaire and C Africa	hunting for the supposed aphrodisiac qualities of the rhino horn; disturbance by military operations
rhinoceros, Sumatran	*Didermocerus sumatrensis*	SE Asia	hunting for the aphrodisiac and medical qualities of the horn and other parts of the carcass which fetches high prices; loss of forest habitat to timber exploitation, human settlement
sea lion, Japanese	*Zapophus californianus japonicus*	Japanese coastal islands	human disturbance; persecution by fishermen

ENDANGERED SPECIES (cont.)

Mammals

Name	Species	Location	Cause of endangerment
seal, Caribbean monk	*Monachus tropicalis*	Caribbean	slaughtered by 18th-c seal fishermen; natural habitat now increasingly subject to human disturbance; the demands of tourism; possibly already extinct
seal, Hawaiian monk	*Monachus schauinslandi*	Hawaiian Islands	initial decline in population due to 19th-c seal fishermen; present population threatened by attacks by sharks; human disturbance of breeding grounds leading to low rates of reproduction, high rates of juvenile mortality
seal, Mediterranean monk	*Monachus monachus*	N Africa, Lebanon, Cyprus and Turkey	persecution by fishermen; human disturbance; marine pollution
serow, Sumatran	*Capricornis sumatraensis sumatraensis*	Sumatra	hunting; destruction of habitat
sifaka, Verreaux's	*Propithecus verreauxi*	Madagascar	hunting; destruction of forests
sika, Formosan	*Cervus nippon taiouanus*	Taiwan	hunting for meat, antlers; the medical properties of the carcass; loss of habitat to agriculture; probably already extinct in the wild
sika, N China	*Cervus nippon mandarinus*	China	hunting; loss of habitat; possibly already extinct in the wild
sika, Ryukyu or Kerama deer	*Cervus nippon keremae*	Ryukyu Islands	drought; low qualities of feeding vegetation; competition with goats for grazing fodder
sika, Shansi	*Cervus nippon grassianus*	China	hunting for the antler trade; clearance of forest habitat for agriculture
sika, S China	*Cervus nippon kopschi*	China	hunting for the antler trade; trapping; loss of habitat
sloth, maned	*Bradtpus torquatus*	Brazil	loss of forest habitat
solenodon, Haitian	*Solenodon paradoxus*	Dominican Republic and Haiti	land development; deforestation
squirrel, Delmarva Peninsula fox or Bryant's fox	*Sciurus niger cinereus*	Maryland, USA	loss of habitat due to logging
stag, Hangul or Kashmir	*Cervus elaphus hanglu*	India	poaching; human disturbance; deterioration of habitat caused by domestic livestock, particularly grazing sheep

ENDANGERED SPECIES (cont.)

Mammals

Name	Species	Location	Cause of endangerment
suni, Zanzibar	*Neotragus moschatus moschatus*	Zanzibar	hunting; destruction of habitat
tahr, Arabian	*Hemitragus jayakari*	Oman	hunting; competition for food from domestic goats
tamaraw	*Bubalus mindorensis*	Philippines	hunting; loss of forest habitat
tamarin, cotton-top	*Saguinus oedipus oedipus*	NW Colombia	animal trade; loss of habitat to agriculture
tamarin, golden or lion	*Leontopithecus rosalia*	Brazil	loss of forest habitat to agriculture, urban development
tamarin, golden-headed	*Leontopithecus rosalia chrysomelas*	E Brazil	loss of Atlantic rainforest
tamarin, golden-rumped	*Leontopithecus rosalia chrysopygus*	Sao Paulo area of Brazil	loss of forest habitat; possibly careless use of defoliants by farmers
tapir, Central American	*Tapirus bairdii*	C and S America	loss of rainforest habitat; hunting; human settlement
tapir, Malayan	*Tapirus indicus*	Malaysia	human disturbance; loss of forest habitat to logging, oil exploitation, human settlement, mining, agriculture
tapir, mountain	*Tapirus pinchaque*	S America	human disturbance; competition for natural habitat with livestock
tarsier, Philippine	*Tarsius syrichta*	Philippines	primate threatened by capture, exportation; destruction of forest habitat
tiger	*Panthera tigris*	Eurasia	loss of habitat and prey; hunting for sport; because of the threat posed by it to both humans and domestic livestock
tiger, Bengal or Indian	*Panthera tigris tigris*	Indian sub-continent	loss of habitat to agriculture, urban development; depletion of natural prey; hunting for skin; poisoning; current low rate of reproduction
tiger, Bali	*Panthera tigris balica*	S and SE Asia	loss of population due to hunting; possibly already extinct
tiger, Caspian	*Panthera tigris virgata*	SW Asia	loss of habitat to logging, cultivation; loss of natural prey; hunting
tiger, Chinese	*Panthera tigris amoyensis*	China	hunting; clearance of habitat for agricultural development
tiger, Javan	*Panthera tigris sondaica*	Java	hunting; loss of forest habitat; loss of natural prey

ENDANGERED SPECIES (cont.)

Mammals

Name	Species	Location	Cause of endangerment
tiger, Siberian	*Panthera tigris altaica*	Siberia, China and Korea	hunting; loss of habitat and natural prey
uakari, bald	*Cacajao calvus*	S America	primate threatened by hunting; animal trade
uakari, white	*Cacajao calvus calvus*	Brazil	primate threatened by human development of its habitat
wallaby, bridle nail-tailed	*Onychogalea fraenata*	Queensland, Australia	loss of natural habitat to settlement; introduction of livestock; predation from foxes
wallaby, crescent nail-tailed	*Onychogalea lunata*	C Australia	hunting; loss of natural habitat to settlement
whale, black right	*Eubalaena glacialis*	N Atlantic and N Pacific Oceans and S hemisphere	whaling
whale, blue	*Balaenoptera musculus*	Atlantic, Pacific and Indian Oceans	whaling
whale, bowhead or Greenland right	*Balaena mysticetus*	Arctic waters	whaling
whale, humpback	*Megaptera novaeangliae*	N Atlantic and N Pacific Oceans; S hemisphere	whaling
wolf, Northern Rocky Mountain	*Canis lupus irremotus*	USA	poisoning, trapping, hunting by man
wolf, red	*Canis rufus*	Texas and Louisiana, USA	loss of habitat; hunting; trapping; hybridization with coyotes
yak, wild	*Bos grunniens*	Tibet, Kashmir and W China	hunting
zebra, Grevy's	*Equus grevyi*	Kenya and Ethiopia	hunted because of its attractive, highly-prized skin

HUMAN LIFE

COMPOSITION OF SELECTED FOODS

Approximate values given are for 100g of the food named

Food	Calories[1]	Protein (g)	Carbohydrates (g)	Fat (g)	Fibre (g)
almonds	564	19	20	54	15
apples	38	trace	15	trace	2
apricots, dried	182	5	67	1	24
apricots, raw	25	1	13	trace	2
asparagus, cooked	18	2	4	trace	1
aubergine, cooked	14	1	4	trace	2
avocados	221	2	6	16	2
bacon, back, grilled	271	15	2	24	0
bacon, streaky, grilled	308	16	2	27	0
bananas	85	1	22	trace	2
beans, broad, cooked	46	4	66	1	4
beans, dried white, cooked	118	8	21	7	25
beans, green, cooked	25	2	5	trace	4
beef, minced	221	31	0	16	0
beef, rump steak, grilled	218	30	0	12	0
beetroot, cooked	43	1	7	trace	2
biscuit, chocolate digestive	506	6	64	25	4
biscuit, digestive	486	7	62	23	5
blackberries, raw	29	1	13	1	7
blackcurrants	29	2	14	trace	9
brazil nuts, raw	618	14	11	67	9
bread, white	232	10	58	2	3
bread, wholemeal	216	10	55	3	9
broccoli, cooked	26	3	5	trace	4
brussel sprouts, cooked	18	4	6	trace	3
butter, salted	740	1	trace	82	0
cabbage, cooked	11	2	trace	trace	2
cabbage, raw	25	2	5	trace	3
carrots, cooked	20	1	5	trace	3
carrots, raw	25	1	6	trace	3
cauliflower, cooked	22	2	4	trace	2
celery, raw	36	1	2	trace	2
cheese, Brie	314	19	2	23	0
cheese, Cheddar	414	25	2	32	0
cheese, cottage	96	17	2	4	0
cheese, Edam	314	30	trace	23	0
cherries, raw	70	1	17	trace	1
chick peas, dry	320	20	50	6	15
chicken, meat only, roast	142	19	0	4	0

COMPOSITION OF SELECTED FOODS (cont.)

Food	Calories[1]	Protein (g)	Carbohydrates (g)	Fat (g)	Fibre (g)
chocolate bar, plain	510	4	63	29	0
cod, cooked	94	19	0	1	0
corn (on the cob)	91	3	21	1	5
courgettes, cooked	14	1	3	trace	1
crab, cooked	129	18	1	5	0
cream, double	446	2	3	48	0
crisps	517	6	40	37	11
cucumber, raw	15	1	3	trace	trace
dates	214	2	73	1	7
egg, boiled	163	13	1	12	0
eggplant *see* aubergine					
figs, dried	214	4	69	1	19
flour, white	350	9	80	1	4
flour, wholemeal	318	13	56	2	10
grapefruit	41	1	11	trace	trace
grapes, raw	69	1	16	1	1
haddock, cooked	96	19	0	1	0
ham, lean	168	22	0	5	0
honey	289	trace	82	0	0
jam	261	1	79	trace	1
lamb chop, boned, grilled	353	24	0	29	0
leeks, cooked	25	1	7	0	4
lentils, cooked	106	8	19	trace	4
lettuce, raw	12	1	3	trace	1
liver, cooked	254	20	6	13	0
lobster, cooked	119	20	trace	3	0
mackerel, cooked	188	25	0	11	0
margarine	730	trace	1	80	0
melon, honeydew	21	1	5	trace	1
melon, water	21	trace	5	trace	1
milk, cow's, skimmed	36	4	5	trace	0
milk, cow's, whole	65	4	5	4	0
mushrooms, raw	14	3	4	trace	2
mussels, cooked	86	17	0	1	0
nectarines	64	1	17	trace	2
oatmeal, cooked	399	2	10	1	7
oats, porridge	377	10	70	7	7
oil, vegetable	900	0	0	100	0
onions, raw	38	2	9	trace	1
orange juice	45	1	10	trace	0
oranges, peeled, raw	49	1	12	trace	2
parsnip, cooked	50	1	17	trace	4
pasta, dry	353	12	71	2	4
peaches, raw	38	1	8	trace	1
peanuts, fresh	571	26	19	48	8
pears, raw	61	1	15	trace	2
peas, fresh, cooked	54	5	4	trace	5
pepper, green, raw	14	1	5	trace	1
pepper, red, raw	20	1	7	trace	1
pineapple, raw	46	trace	14	trace	1

COMPOSITION OF SELECTED FOODS (cont.)

Food	Calories[1]	Protein (g)	Carbohydrates (g)	Fat (g)	Fibre (g)
pork chop, boned, grilled	328	28	0	24	0
potatoes, baked in skin	86	3	21	trace	2
potatoes, boiled in skin	75	2	17	trace	2
prawns, cooked	107	18	0	1	0
prunes, raw	136	1	77	trace	14
raisins	246	3	77	trace	7
raspberries, raw	25	1	14	1	7
rice, brown, cooked	129	3	26	1	1
rice, white, cooked	121	3	33	trace	1
salmon, cooked	196	20	0	13	0
spinach, cooked	23	3	4	trace	6
strawberries, raw	37	1	8	1	2
sugar	394	0	100	0	0
swede, cooked	18	1	4	trace	3
tomatoes, raw	14	1	5	trace	1
tuna, canned in brine	118	28	0	1	0
turkey, meat only, roast	140	36	0	3	0
turnip, cooked	14	1	5	trace	2
walnuts	525	15	16	64	5
yogurt, skimmed milk	50	3	5	2	0
yogurt, whole milk	62	3	5	3	0

[1] To convert calories into kilojoules multiply by 4.187

MAIN TYPES OF VITAMIN

Fat soluble vitamins

Vitamin	Chemical name	Deficiency symptoms	Source
A	retinol (carotene)	night blindness; rough skin; impaired bone growth	milk, butter, cheese, egg yolk, liver, fatty fish, dark green vegetables, yellow/red fruits and vegetables, especially carrots
D	cholecalciferol	rickets; osteomalacia	egg yolk, liver, fatty fish; made on skin in sunlight
E	tocopherols	multiple diseases produced in laboratory animals; in humans, multiple symptoms follow impaired fat absorption	vegetable oils
K	phytomenadione	haemorrhagic problems	green leafy vegetables, beef, liver

MAIN TYPES OF VITAMIN (cont.)

Water soluble vitamins

Vitamin	Chemical name	Deficiency symptoms	Source
B^1	thiamin	beri-beri, Korsakov's syndrome	germ and bran of seeds, grains, yeast
B^2	riboflavin	skin disorders; failure to thrive	liver, milk, cheese, eggs, green leafy vegetables, pulses, yeast
B^6	pyridoxine	dermatitis; neurological disorders	liver, meats, fruits, cereals, leafy vegetables
	pantothenic acid	dermatitis; neurological disorders	widespread in plants and animals; destroyed in heavily-processed food
	biotin	dermatitis	liver, kidney, yeast extract; made by microorganisms in large intestine
B^{12}	cyanocobalamin	anaemia; neurological disturbance	liver, kidney, milk; none found in plants
	folic acid	anaemia	liver, green leafy vegetables, peanuts; cooking and processing can cause serious losses in food
C	ascorbic acid	scurvy	blackcurrants, citrus fruits, other fruits, green leafy vegetables, potatoes; losses occur during storage and cooking

MAIN TRACE MINERALS

Mineral	Deficiency symptoms	Source
calcium	rickets in children; osteoporosis in adults	milk, butter, cheese, sardines, green leafy vegetables, citrus fruits
chromium	adult-onset diabetes	brewer's yeast, black pepper, liver, wholemeal bread, beer
copper	anaemia; Menkes' syndrome	green vegetables, fish, oysters, liver
fluorine	tooth decay; possibly osteoporosis	fluoridated drinking water, seafood, tea
iodine	goitre; cretinism in new-born children	seafood, salt-water fish, seaweed, iodized salt, table salt
iron	anaemia	liver, kidney, green leafy vegetables, egg yolk, dried fruit, potatoes, molasses
magnesium	irregular heart beat; muscular weakness; insomnia	green leafy vegetables (eaten raw), nuts, whole grains
manganese	not known in man	legumes, cereal grains, green leafy vegetables, tea

MAIN TRACE MINERALS (cont.)

Mineral	Deficiency symptoms	Source
molybdenum	not known in man	legumes, cereal grains, liver, kidney, some dark green vegetables
phosphorus	muscular weakness; bone pain; loss of appetite	meat, poultry, fish, eggs, dried beans and peas, milk products
potassium	irregular heart beat; muscular weakness; fatigue; kidney and lung failure	fresh vegetables, meat, orange juice, bananas, bran
selenium	not known in man	seafood, cereals, meat, egg yolk, garlic
sodium	impaired acid-base balance in body fluids (very rare)	table salt, other naturally occurring salts
zinc	impaired wound healing; loss of appetite; impaired sexual development	meat, whole grains, legumes, oysters, milk

E-NUMBERS

Colours

Number	Name	Source	Function
E100	Curcumin	extract of dried rhizome of turmeric (*Curcuma longa*)	orange-yellow
E101	Riboflavin	liver, kidneys, green vegetables, malted barley, eggs, milk	yellow or orange-yellow
101(a)	Riboflavin-5′-phosphate	chemical Riboflavin	yellow or orange-yellow; vitamin B2
E102	Tartrazine	synthetic, an azo[1] dye	yellow
E104	Quinoline yellow	synthetic 'coal tar' dye	dull yellow to greenish yellow
107	Yellow 2G	synthetic 'coal tar' dye and azo[1] dye	yellow
E110	Sunset Yellow FCF	synthetic 'coal tar' and azo[1] dye	yellow
E120	Cochineal	pregnant scale insects (*Dactilopius coccus*)	red
E122	Carmoisine	synthetic azo[1] dye	red
E123	Amaranth	synthetic 'coal tar' dye and azo[1] dye	purplish red
E124	Poncean 4R	synthetic 'coal tar' dye and azo[1] dye	red
E127	Erythrosine	the di Sodium salt of 2,4,5,7-tetraiodofluorescein; synthetic 'coal tar' dye	cherry pink to red

[1] Azo dyes are derivatives of azobenzene (see footnote p 158)

E-NUMBERS (cont.)

Colours

Number	Name	Source	Function
128	Red 2G	synthetic 'coal tar' dye and azo[1] dye	red
129	Allura red AC	artificial, an azo[1] dye	red (prohibited throughout EC)
E131	Patent blue V	synthetic 'coal tar' dye	dark bluish-violet; diagnostic agent
E132	Indigo carmine	synthetic 'coal tar' dye	blue; diagnostic agent
133	Brilliant blue FCF	synthetic 'coal tar' dye	blue, green hues when used with tartrazine
E140	Chlorophyll	green pigment in leaf cells	olive to dark green
E141	copper complexes of Chlorophyll and Chlorophyllins	from Chlorophyll by substituting the magnesium ion with copper; by processing Chlorophyll extracts and adding copper	olive green; green
E142	Green S	synthetic 'coal tar' dye	green
E150	Caramel colour	sugar	brown to black
E151	Black PN	synthetic 'coal tar' dye and azo[1] dye	black
E153	Carbon black	animal charcoal, furnace black, lampblack, activated charcoal; laboratory preparation	black
154	Brown FK	synthetic mixture of six azo[1] dyes and sodium chloride and/or sodium sulphate	brown
155	Brown HT	synthetic 'coal tar' dye and azo[1] dye	brown
E160(a)	Alpha-carotene, beta-carotene, gamma-carotene	plant pigment, (especially in carrots, green leafy vegetables, tomatoes, apricots, rosehips and oranges)	orange-yellow; becomes vitamin A in the body
E160(b)	Annatto, Bixin, Norbixin	from the pericarp (seed coat) of the tropical Annatto tree (*Bixa orellana*)	yellow to peach or red
E160(c)	Capsanthin	from the fruit pods and seeds of the Red Pepper (*Capsicum annum*)	red to orange
E160(d)	Lycopene	tomatoes	red
E160(e)	beta-apo-8′-carotenal	synthesized pigments	orange to yellowish-red
E160(f)	Ethyl ester of beta-apo-8′-carotenoic acid	synthesized pigments	orange to yellow

[1] Azo dyes are derivatives of azobenzene (see footnote p 158)

E-NUMBERS (cont.)

Colours

Number	Name	Source	Function
E161(a)	Xanthophylls Flavoxanthin	alpha-, beta-, and gamma-carotenes (not commercially available)	yellow
E161(b)	Xanthophylls Lutein	plant pigment related to carotene	yellow to reddish
E161(c)	Xanthophylls Cryptoxanthin	petals and berries of the Bladder Cherry or Cape Gooseberry (*Physalis*) genus; potato and tomato family (*Solanceae*); orange rind; egg yolk; butter (not commercially available)	yellow
E161(d)	Xanthophylls Rubixanthin	plant pigment related to carotene (rosehips) (not commercially available)	yellow
E161(e)	Xanthophylls Violoxanthin	carotene, especially from yellow pansies (*viola tricolor*) (not commercially available)	yellow
E161(f)	Xanthophylls Rhodoxanthin	carotenoid pigment (seeds of yew tree (*Taxus baccata*)) (not commercially available)	yellow
E161(g)	Xanthophylls Canthaxanthin	carotenoid pigment (some mushrooms; various crustacea; fish; flamingo feathers); also synthesized commercially	orange
E162	Beetroot red	beetroot	deep purplish-red
E163	Anthocyanins	plant cell sap (grape skin, red cabbage)	red, blue, violet
E170	Calcium carbonate	naturally occurring white mineral	alkali for deacidification of wine; firming agent; releasing agent; calcium supplements; surface food colour
E171	Titanium dioxide	from naturally occurring mineral ilmenite	white; increases opacity
E172	Iron oxides, iron hydroxides	natural iron pigments	yellow, red, orange, brown, black
E173	Aluminium	naturally occurring, from bauxite	metallic surface colour
E174	Silver	naturally occurring metal	metallic surface colour
E175	Gold	naturally occurring metal	metallic surface colour
E180	Pigment Rubine	synthetic, an azo[1] dye	reddish

[1] Azo dyes are derivatives of azobenzene (see footnote p 158)

E-NUMBERS (cont.)

Preservatives

Number	Name	Source	Function
E200	Sorbic acid	some fruits; berries of mountain ash (*Sorbus aucuparia*); synthetically manufactured from ketene	preservative
E201	Sodium sorbate	neutralization of sorbic acid	preservative
E202	Potassium sorbate	neutralization of sorbic acid with potassium hydroxide	antifungal and antibacterial preservative
E203	Calcium sorbate	neutralization of sorbic acid	antifungal and antibacterial preservative
E210	Benzoic acid	berries, fruits, vegetables; chemical synthesis	antifungal and antibacterial preservative (in an acid medium only)
E211	Sodium benzoate	sodium salt of benzoic acid	antifungal and antibacterial preservative (in a slightly acid medium only)
E212	Potassium benzoate	potassium salt of benzoic acid	antifungal and antibacterial preservative
E213	Calcium benzoate	calcium salt of benzoic acid	antifungal and antibacterial preservative
E214	Ethyl 4-hydroxybenzoate	benzoic acid	antifungal and antibacterial preservative
E215	Ethyl 4-hydroxybenzoate, sodium salt	benzoic acid	antifungal and antibacterial preservative
E216	Propyl 4-hydroxybenzoate	benzoic acid	antimicrobial preservative
E217	Propyl 4-hydroxybenzoate, sodium salt	benzoic acid	antimicrobial preservative
E218	Methyl 4-hydroxybenzoate	synthetic	antimicrobial preservative
E219	Methyl 4-hydroxybenzoate, sodium salt	benzoic acid	preservative, active against fungi and yeasts, less active against bacteria
E220	Sulphur dioxide	natural; chemical production by combustion of sulphur or gypsum	preservative; bleaching agent; improving agent; stabilizer; antioxidant; used in beer and wine making
E221	Sodium sulphite	sodium salt of sulphurous acid	antimicrobial preservative; sterilizer; prevents discoloration
E222	Sodium hydrogen sulphite	sodium salt of sulphurous acid	preservative for alcoholic beverages
E223	Sodium metabisulphite	sodium salt of sulphurous acid (commercially manufactured)	antimicrobial preservative; antioxidant; bleaching agent

E-NUMBERS (cont.)

Preservatives

Number	Name	Source	Function
E224	Potassium metabisulphite	sodium salt of sulphurous acid (commercially manufactured)	antimicrobial preservative; antibrowning agent
E226	Calcium sulphite	calcium salt of sulphurous acid	preservative; firming agent; disinfectant
E227	Calcium hydrogen sulphite	calcium salt of sulphurous acid	preservative; firming agent; used in washing beer casks and to prevent secondary fermentation
E230	Biphenyl	synthetic, from benzene	fungistatic agent; acts against *Penicillium*
E231	2-Hydroxybiphenyl	phenyl ether or dibenzofuran	antibacterial and antifungal preservative
E232	Sodium biphenyl-2-yl oxide	synthetic	antifungal (alternative to E231)
E233	2 (Thiazol-4-yl) benzimidazole	reaction of 4-thiazolecarboxamide with O-phenylenediamine in polyphosphoric acid	fungicide; treatment of nematode worms in man
234	Nisin	produced by growth of bacterium *Streptococcus lactis*	preservative
E236	Formic acid	ants	antibacterial preservative; flavour adjunct (prohibited in UK)
E237	Sodium formate	sodium salt from formic acid	preservative (prohibited in UK)
E238	Calcium formate	calcium salt of formic acid	preservative (prohibited in UK)
E239	Hexamine	formaldehyde and ammonia	antimicrobial preservative
E249	Potassium nitrate	potassium salt of nitrous acid	meat preservative; curing agent; prevents growth of *Clostridium botulinum* (the bacterium responsible for botulism)
E250	Sodium nitrate	chemical or bacterial action on sodium nitrate	food preservative; prevents growth of *Clostridium botulinum*; salt curing agent; red meat colour
E251	Sodium nitrate	naturally occurring mineral	preservative; salt curing agent; colour fixative
E252	Potassium nitrate	naturally occurring mineral	preservative; salt curing agent; colour fixative
E260	Acetic acid	methanol and carbon monoxide; from ethanol by oxidation	antibacterial preservative; food acidity stabilizer; colour diluent; flavouring agent

E-NUMBERS (cont.)

Preservatives

Number	Name	Source	Function
E261	Potassium acetate	potassium salt of acetic acid	preservative of natural colour; neutralizing agent; acidity regulator
E262	Sodium hydrogen diacetate	'bound' compound of sodium acetate and acetic acid	antimicrobial preservative; acidity regulator; sequestrant
262	Sodium acetate	sodium salt of acetic acid	buffer
E263	Calcium acetate	calcium salt of acetic acid	antimould agent; anti rope (development of sticky yellow patches in bread) agent; sequestrant; firming agent; stabilizer; buffer
E270	Lactic acid	naturally occurring in milk, molasses, apples and other fruit, tomato juice, some seeds; produced by the heating and fermenting of carbohydrates (whey, corn-starch, potatoes or molasses)	food preservative; increases antioxidant effect of other substances; acid and flavouring
E280	Propionic acid	naturally occurring fatty acid: foods and dairy products; commercially produced from ethylene, carbon monoxide and steam or by oxidation of proprionaldehyde; natural gas; fermented wood pulp waste liquor	antifungal food preservative
E281	Sodium propionate	sodium salt of propionic acid	antimicrobial preservative
E282	Calcium propionate	naturally occurring in Swiss cheese; propionic acid	antimicrobial preservative
E283	Potassium propionate	potassium salt of propionic acid	antimould preservative (especially of 'rope' micro-organisms in bread)
E290	Carbon dioxide	natural gas; fermentation; action of acid on a carbonate	preservative; coolant; freezant (liquid form); packaging gas; aerator
296	Malic acid	green apples, pears, redcurrants, potatoes; metabolite in all living cells; chemical synthesis	acid, flavouring
297	Fumaric acid	natural organic acid in cells; Common Fumitory (*Fumaria officinalis*), edible toadstool (*Boletus scaber*) and fungus (*Fomes igniarius*); fermentation of glucose	acidifier, raising agent, antioxidant

E-NUMBERS (cont.)

Antioxidants

Number	Name	Source	Function
E300	L-Ascorbic acid	naturally occurring in many fruits and vegetables; biological synthesis, various methods	Vitamin C; antibrowning agent; flour improving agent; meat colour preservative; antioxidant
E301	Sodium L-ascorbate	sodium salt of ascorbic acid (synthetic preparation)	Vitamin C; antioxidant; colour preservative
E302	Calcium L-ascorbate	synthetic preparation	Vitamin C; antioxidant; meat colour preservative
E304	6-0-Palmitoyl-L-ascorbic acid	ascorbic acid ester	same function as Vitamin C; antioxidant; colour preservative; antibrowning agent
E306	Extracts of natural origin rich in tocopherols	soya bean oil, wheat germ, rice germ, cottonseed, maize and green leaves	Vitamin E; antioxidant
E307	Synthetic alpha-tocopherol	synthetic	Vitamin E; antioxidant
E308	Synthetic gamma-tocopherol	synthetic	Vitamin E; antioxidant
E309	Synthetic delta-tocopherol	synthetic	Vitamin E; antioxidant
E310	Propyl gallate	propyl ester of gallic acid	antioxidant in oils and fats
E311	Octyl gallate	ester of gallic acid	antioxidant
E312	Dodecyl gallate	ester of gallic acid	antioxidant
E320	Butylated hydroxyanisole	mixture of 2-and 3-tert-butyl-4-methoxyphenol	antioxidant
E321	Butylated hydroxytoluene	synthetic	antioxidant

Emulsifiers, stabilizers and others

Number	Name	Source	Function
E322	Lecithins	animal and vegetable foodstuffs (soya beans), egg yolk, leguminous seeds	emulsifier
E325	Sodium lactate	sodium salt of lactic acid	humectant; glycerol substitute; increases antioxidant effect of other substances; bodying agent
E326	Potassium lactate	potassium salt of lactic acid	increases antioxidant effect of other substances; buffer
E327	Calcium lactate	calcium salt of lactic acid	antioxidant; buffer; firming agent; fruit and vegetable colour preservative; powdered and condensed milk improver; yeast food; dough conditioner

E-NUMBERS (cont.)

Emulsifiers, stabilizers and others

Number	Name	Source	Function
E330	Citric acid	citrus juices and ripe fruits; fermentation of molasses	enhances effects of antioxidants; fruit colour preservative; retains Vitamin C; acidity stabilizer; sequestrant; flavouring; setting agent
E331(a)	Sodium dihydrogen citrate	*mono* Sodium salt of citric acid in the anhydrous or monohydrate form	enhances effects of antioxidants; acidity-controlling and carbonation-retaining buffer; emulsifying salt; sequestrant; prevents curds forming and cream clotting in aerosols
E331(b)	*di* Sodium citrate	Sodium salt of citric acid	antioxidant; enhances effects of antioxidants; buffer; emulsifying salt
E331(c)	*tri* Sodium citrate	*tri* Sodium salt of citric acid in anhydrous, dihydrate or pentahydrate form	antioxidant; buffer; emulsifying salt; sequestrant; stabilizer; used with polyphosphates and flavours to inject into chickens before freezing
E332	Potassium dihydrogen citrate	anhydrous *mono* Potassium salt of citric acid	buffer; emulsifying salt; yeast food
E332	*tri* Potassium citrate	potassium salt of citric acid	antioxidant; buffer in confectionery and artificially sweetened jellies and preserves; emulsifying salt; sequestrant
E333	*mono*, *di*, and *tri* Calcium citrate	monohydrated *mono* Calcium, trihydrated *di* Calcium and tetrahydrated *tri* Calcium salts of citric acid	buffers to neutralize acids in jams, jellies and confectionery; firming agents; emulsifying salts; sequestrants; flour improvers
E334	L-(+)-Tartaric acid	fruit acid (grapes)	antioxidant; enhances effects of antioxidants; acidity adjuster; sequestrant; food colour diluent; flavouring; acid
E335	*mono* Sodium L-(+)-tartrate and *di* Sodium L-(+)-tartrate	monohydrated *mono* Sodium salt and dihydrated *di* Sodium salt of tartaric acid	antioxidant; enhances effects of antioxidants; buffer; emulsifying salt; sequestrant

E-NUMBERS (cont.)

Emulsifiers, stabilizers and others

Number	Name	Source	Function
E336	*mono* Potassium L-(+)-tartrate (cream of tartar)	anhydrous monopotassium salt of L-(+)-tartaric acid	acid; buffer; emulsifying salt; raising agent for flour, used with sodium bicarbonate; inverting agent for sugar
E336	*di* Potassium L-(+)-tartrate	*di* Potassium salt of L-(+)-tartaric acid	antioxidant; enhances effects of antioxidants; buffer; emulsifying salt
E337	Potassium sodium L-(+)-tartrate	derivative of L-(+)-tartaric acid; commercially available in the form of potassium sodium tartrate	buffer for confectionery and preserves: emulsifying salt; stabilizer; enhances effects of antioxidants
E338	Orthophosphoric acid	from phosphate ore	enhances effects of antioxidants; acidulant; flavouring agent; acidifier in cheese and beer production; sequestrant
E339	Sodium dihydrogen orthophosphate	phosphoric acid	texture improver; speeds brine penetration; enhances effects of antioxidants; buffer; nutrient; gelling agent; stabilizer; sugar clarifying agent
E340(a)	Potassium dihydrogen orthophosphate	phosphoric acid	buffer; sequestrant; emulsifying salt; enhances effects of antioxidants
E340(b)	*di* Potassium hydrogen orthophosphate	*di* Potassium salt of phosphoric acid	buffer; emulsifying salt; enhances effects of antioxidants; yeast food; sequestrant
E340(c)	*tri* Potassium orthophosphate	*tri* Potassium salt of phosphoric acid	emulsifying salt; enhances effects of antioxidants; buffer; sequestrant
E341(a)	Calcium tetrahydrogen diorthophosphate	naturally occurring calcium phosphate; phosphoric acid	bakery improving agent; firming agent; sequestrant; yeast food; aerator-acidulant; enhances effects of antioxidants; texturizer
E341(b)	Calcium hydrogen orthophosphate	phosphoric acid	firming agent; yeast food; nutrient mineral supplement; enhances effects of antioxidants; animal feed supplement; abrasive in toothpaste; dough conditioner

E-NUMBERS (cont.)

Emulsifiers, stabilizers and others

Number	Name	Source	Function
E341(c)	*tri* Calcium *di* orthophosphate	calcium phosphate	anti-caking agent; nutrient yeast food; vegetable extract diluent; clarifying agent
350	Sodium malate	sodium salt of malic acid	buffer; seasoning agent
350	Sodium hydrogen malate	sodium salt of malic acid	buffer
351	Potassium malate	potassium salt of malic acid	buffer
352	Calcium malate	calcium salt of malic acid	buffer; firming agent; seasoning agent
352	Calcium hydrogen malate	calcium salt of malic acid	firming agent
353	Metatartaric acid	tartaric acid	sequestrant (wine)
355	Adipic acid	organic acid in living cells (beet juice); cyclohexanol oxidized with nitric acid (synthetic preparation)	acid buffer; neutralizing agent; flavouring agent; raising agent in baking powders
363	Succinic acid	naturally occurring in fossils, fungi and lichens; acetic acid	acid; buffer; neutralizing agent
370	1,4-Heptonolactone	hydroxycarboxylic acid	acid; sequestrant
375	Nicotinic acid	naturally occurring in yeast, liver, legumes, rice polishings and lean meats; nicotine oxidized with nitric acid	B vitamin; colour protector
380	*tri* Ammonium citrate	salt of citric acid	buffer; emulsifying salt; softening agent
381	Ammonium ferric citrate	citric acid	dietary iron supplement; raises red blood cell level
381	Ammonium ferric citrate, green	citric acid	dietary iron supplement
385	Calcium disodium ethylenediamine-NNN'N' tetra-acetate (EDTA)	synthetic preparation	chelating agent; antioxidant
E400	Alginic acid	brown seaweeds (*Laminaria, Macrocystis, Ascophyllum*)	alginate production
E401	Sodium alginate	sodium salt of alginic acid	stabilizer; suspending agent; thickening agent; gelling agent (with a source of calcium); copper fining agent in brewing

E-NUMBERS (cont.)

Emulsifiers, stabilizers and others

Number	Name	Source	Function
E402	Potassium alginate	potassium salt of alginic acid	emulsifier; stabilizer; boiled water additive; gelling agent
E403	Ammonium alginate	ammonium salt of alginic acid	emulsifier; stabilizer; colour diluent; thickener
E404	Calcium alginate	calcium salt of alginic acid	emulsifier; stabilizer; thickener; gelling agent
E405	Propane-1,2-diol alginate	propylene ester of alginic acid	emulsifier; stabilizer; thickener; solvent; foam stabilizing agent
E406	Agar	red seaweeds (*Gelidium amansii* and Gelidiaceae family)	thickener; stabilizer; gelling agent; humectant; copper fining agent in brewing
E407	Carrageenan	red seaweeds (*Chondrus crispus* and *Gigartina*)	stabilizer; thickener; suspending and gelling agent; texture modifier
E410	Locust or Carob bean gum	Locust or Carob tree (*Ceratonia siliqua*)	gelling agent; stabilizer; emulsifier; thickening agent; texture modifier
E412	Guar gum	*Cyamopsis tetragonolobus* or *C. psoraloides* (members of the pea family)	thickening agent; emulsion stabilizer; suspending agent; dietary bulking agent; helps diabetics control blood sugar levels
E413	Tragacanth	*Astragalus gummifer* (member of the pea family)	emulsifier; stabilizer; thickener; prevents crystallization of sugar; converts royal icing to a paste
E414	Gum arabic	*Acacia senegal* (member of the pea family)	retards sugar crystallization; thickener; converts royal icing to a paste; emulsifier; stabilizer; glazing agent; copper fining agent in brewing
E415	Xanthan gum	carbohydrate fermentation	stabilizer; thickener; emulsifier; 'pseudoplasticizer' to improve pouring; gelling agent (with guar gum)
416	Karaya gum	*Sterculia urens* trees	stabilizer; emulsifier; thickener; binding agent in meat products; prevents formation of ice crystals; filling agent; citrus and spice flavouring agent

E-NUMBERS (cont.)

Emulsifiers, stabilizers and others

Number	Name	Source	Function
E420	Sorbitol syrup	Mountain ash (*Sorbus aucuparia*) fruits, cherries, pears, plums, apples; seaweeds, other algae	sweetening agent; glycerol substitute; retards crystallization; masks taste of saccharin; texturizing agent; humectant; stabilizer
E421	Mannitol	coniferous trees; seaweed; Manna ash (*Fraxinus ornus*); hydrogenation of invert sugar	texturizing agent; dietary supplement; humectant; sweetener; anti-caking agent; anti-sticking agent
E422	Glycerol	naturally occurring in plant cells; sugar fermentation; propylene	solvent; humectant; sweetener; bodying agent (with gelatins and gums); plasticizer
430	Polyoxyethylene (8) stearate	stearate and ethylene oxide mixture	emulsifier; stabilizer
431	Polyoxyethylene (40) stearate	stearate and ethylene oxide mixture	emulsifier; makes bread 'feel fresh'
432	Polyoxyethylene (20) sorbitan monolaurate	sorbitol and ethylene oxide	emulsifier; stabilizer; dispersing agent
433	Polyoxyethylene (20) sorbitan monooleate	sorbitol and ethylene oxide	emulsifier; de-foamer; preserves moistness; prevents oil leaking from artificial whipped cream; solubility improver
434	Polyoxyethylene (20) sorbitan monopalmitate	sorbitol and ethylene oxide	emulsifier; stabilizer; dispersing agent (flavours); defoaming agent; wetting agent
435	Polyoxyethylene (20) sorbitan monostearate	sorbitol and ethylene oxide	emulsifier; stabilizer; prevents leakage of oils; preserves moistness; wetting and dispersing agent; prevents greasy taste; foaming agent
436	Polyoxyethylene (20) sorbitan tristearate	sorbitol and ethylene oxide	emulsifier; prevents leakage of oils and water; preserves moistness; wetting and solution agent; defoaming agent; flavour dispersing agent
E440(a)	Pectin	ripe fruits	emulsifying and gelling agent in acid media; bodying agent; syrups; stabilizer
E440(b)	Amidated pectin	pectin treated with ammonia	emulsifier; stablizer; gelling agent; thickener

E-NUMBERS (cont.)

Emulsifiers, stabilizers and others

Number	Name	Source	Function
442	Ammonium phosphatides	synthetic preparation	stabilizer; emulsifier
E450(a)	*di* Sodium dihydrogen diphosphate	sodium salt of pyrophosphoric acid	buffer; sequestrant; emulsifier; raising agent (with sodium bicarbonate); colour improver; chelating agent
E450(a)	*tri* Sodium diphosphate	sodium salt of pyrophosphoric aid	buffer; sequestrant; emulsifier; colour improver; chelating agent
E450(a)	*tetra* Sodium diphosphate	sodium salt of pyrophosphoric acid	buffer; emulsifying salt; sequestrant; gelling agent; stabilizer; hydration aid
E450(a)	*tetra* Potassium diphosphate	potassium salt of pyrophosphoric acid	emulsifying salt; buffer; sequestrant; stabilizer
E450(b)	*penta* Sodium triphosphate	sodium salt of triphosphoric acid	emulsifying salt; texturizer; buffer; sequestrant; stabilizer; water-binding agent; protein solubilization agent
E450(b)	*penta* Potassium triphosphate	potassium salt of triphosphoric acid	emulsifying salt; texturizer; buffer; sequestrant; stabilizer
E450(c)	Sodium polyphosphates	sodium salts of polyphosphoric acids	emulsifying salts; sequestrants; stabilizers; texturizers
E450(c)	Potassium polyphosphates	potassium salts of polyphosphoric aids	emulsifying salts; stabilizers; sequestrants
E460	Microcrystalline cellulose	plant fibres	bulking agent; binder; anti-caking agent; dietary fibre; hydration aid; emulsion stabilizer; heat stabilizer; alternative ingredient; tablet binder and disintegrant; quickdrying carrier and dispersant; cellulose component; texture modifier
E460	Alpha-cellulose	plant cells	bulking aid; anti-caking agent; binder; dispersant; thickening agent; filter aid; assists isinglass finings in brewing
E461	Methylcellulose	cellulose	emulsifier; stabilizer; thickener; bulking agent; binding agent; film former; water-soluble gum substitute; useful in sugar-and gluten-free diets; fat barrier

E-NUMBERS (cont.)

Emulsifiers, stabilizers and others

Number	Name	Source	Function
E463	Hydroxypropyl-cellulose	cellulose (synthetic preparation)	stabilizer; emulsifier; thickener; suspending agent
E464	Hydroxypropyl-methylcellulose	cellulose	gelling or suspending agent; emulsifier; stabilizer and thickening agent; fat barrier
E465	Ethylmethylcellulose	cellulose	emulsifier; foam stabilizer; thickener; suspending agent
E466	Carboxymethyl-cellulose, sodium salt	cellulose	thickening agent; texture modifier; stabilizer; moisture migration controller; gelling agent; bulking agent; prevents crystal growth and syneresis (drawing together of particles in a gel); decreases fat absorption; foam stabilizer
E470	Sodium, potassium and calcium salts of fatty acids	fatty acids	emulsifiers; stabilizers; anti-caking agents
E471	Mono-and di-glycerides of fatty acids	naturally occurring product of digestion; glycerin and fatty acids	retains foaming power of egg protein in presence of fat (in cakes); emulsifier; stabilizer; thickening agent
E472(a)	Acetic acid esters of mono-and di-glycerides of fatty acids	esters of glycerol and acetic acid	emulsifiers; stabilizers; coating agents; texture modifiers; solvents; lubricants
E472(b)	Lactic acid esters of mono-and di-glycerides of fatty acids	esters of glycerol and lactic acid	emulsifiers; stabilizers
E472(c)	Citric acid esters of mono-and di-glycerides of fatty acids	esters of glycerol and citric acid	emulsifiers; stabilizers
E472(d)	Tartaric acid esters of mono-and di-glycerides of fatty acids	esters of glycerol and tartaric acid	emulsifiers; stabilizers
E472(e)	Mono-and di-acetyltartaric acid esters of mono-and di-glycerides of fatty acids	esters of glycerol and tartaric acid	emulsifiers; stabilizers

E-NUMBERS (cont.)

Emulsifiers, stabilizers and others

Number	Name	Source	Function
E473	Sucrose esters of fatty acids	esters of glycerol and sucrose	emulsifiers; stabilizers
E474	Sucroglycerides	action of sucrose on natural triglycerides (lard, tallow, palm oil, etc)	emulsifiers; stabilizers
E475	Polyglycerol esters of fatty acids	laboratory preparation	emulsifiers; stabilizers
476	Polyglycerol esters of polycondensed fatty acids of castor oil	castor oil and glycerol esters	emulsifiers; stabilizers; improves chocolate fluidity (with lecithin) for coating
E477	Propane-1,2-diol esters of fatty acids	propylene glycol	emulsifiers; stabilizers
478	Lactylated fatty acid esters of glycerol and propane-1,2-diol	esters of glycerol and lactic acid	emulsifiers; stabilizers; whipping agents; plasticizers; surface-active agents
E481	Sodium stearoyl-2-lactylate	lactic acid	emulsifier; stabilizer
E482	Calcium stearoyl-2-lactylate	lactic acid	emulsifier; stabilizer; whipping aid
E483	Stearyl tartrate	tartaric acid	emulsifier; stabilizer; flour improver
491	Sorbitan monostearate	stearic acid and sorbitol (synthetic preparation)	emulsifier; stabilizer; glazing agent
492	Sorbitan tristearate	stearic acid (synthetic preparation)	emulsifier; stabilizer
493	Sorbitan monolaurate	sorbitol and lauric acid	emulsifier; stabilizer; antifoaming agent
494	Sorbitan mono-oleate	sorbitol and oleic acid	emulsifier; stabilizer
495	Sorbitan monopalmitate	sorbitol and palmitic acid	oil-soluble emulsifier; stabilizer
500	Sodium carbonate	naturally occurring; sea or saline lake water	base; removal of testinic acid in brewing
500	Sodium hydrogen carbonate	synthetic preparation	base; aerating agent; diluent
500	Sodium sesquicarbonate	naturally occurring in saline residues; commercial preparation	base
501	Potassium carbonate and potassium hydrogen carbonate	potassium carbonate and carbon dioxide	base; alkali

E-NUMBERS (cont.)

Emulsifiers, stabilizers and others

Number	Name	Source	Function
503	Ammonium carbonate	ammonium sulphate and calcium carbonate	buffer; neutralizing agent; raising agent
503	Ammonium hydrogen carbonate	carbon dioxide passed through ammonia water	alkali; buffer; aerating agent; raising agent
504	Magnesium carbonate	naturally occurring; magnesium sulphate and sodium carbonate	alkali; anti-caking agent; acidity regulator; anti-bleaching agent
507	Hydrochloric acid	naturally occurring in the stomach; sodium chloride and sulphuric acid	acid; for consistent quality in beer
508	Potassium chloride	naturally occurring	gelling agent; salt substitute; dietary supplement
509	Calcium chloride	salt brines; by-product of Solvay process	sequestrant; firming agent; for consistent quality in beer
510	Ammonium chloride	synthetic preparation	yeast food; flavour
513	Sulphuric acid	commercial preparation by 'contact' or 'Chamber' process	acid; for consistent quality in beer
514	Sodium sulphate	naturally occurring as thenardite and mirabilite	diluent; for consistent quality in beer
515	Potassium sulphate	naturally occurring as a triple sulphate of potassium, magnesium and calcium	
516	Calcium sulphate	naturally occurring mineral	firming agent; sequestrant; nutrient; yeast food; inert excipient; for consistent quality in beer
518	Magnesium sulphate	naturally occurring in sea and mineral waters	dietary supplement; firming agent; used in beer-making
524	Sodium hydroxide	brine; sodium carbonate and lime	
525	Potassium hydroxide	potassium chloride	base; oxidizing agent (black olives)
526	Calcium hydroxide	lime	firming agent; neutralizing agent; removes testinic acid and ensures consistent quality in beer making
527	Ammonium hydroxide	ammonia gas	food colouring diluent and solvent; alkali
528	Magnesium hydroxide	naturally occurring mineral (periclase); magnesite ores	alkali
529	Calcium oxide	limestone	alkali; nutrient

E-NUMBERS (cont.)

Emulsifiers, stabilizers and others

Number	Name	Source	Function
530	Magnesium oxide	naturally occurring mineral; magnesite ores	anti-caking agent; alkali
535	Sodium ferrocyanide	synthetic manufacture	anti-caking agent; crystal modifier
536	Potassium ferrocyanide	coal gas purification by-product	anti-caking agent; metals removal in wine making ('blue finings')
540	*di* Calcium diphosphate	naturally occurring mineral (monetite); synthetic preparation	neutralizing agent; dietary supplement; buffering agent; yeast food; mineral supplement (little used in UK)
541	Sodium aluminium phosphate	phosphoric acid	aerator acidulant (raising agent)
541	Sodium aluminium phosphate, basic	phosphoric acid	emulsifying salt
542	Edible bone phosphate	animal bones	anti-caking agent; mineral supplement; tablet filler
544	Calcium polyphosphates	calcium salts of polyphosphoric acids	emulsifying salts; mineral supplements; calcium source; firming agents (not used in UK)
545	Ammonium polyphosphates	ammonium salts of polyphosphoric acids	emulsifiers; emulsifying salts; sequestrants; yeast foods; stabilizers

Anti-caking agents

Number	Name	Source	Function
551	Silicon dioxide	naturally occurring mineral	suspending agent; anti-caking agent; thickener; stabilizer; assists isinglass finings in clearing beer
552	Calcium silicate	naturally occurring as wollastonite; lime and diatomaceous earth	anti-caking agent; antacid (pharmacology); glazing, polishing and release agent (sweets); dusting agent (chewing gum); coating agent (rice); suspending agent
553(a)	Magnesium silicate, synthetic and magnesium trisilicate	magnesium oxide and silicon dioxide (synthetic compound); sodium silicate and magnesium sulphate; magnesium trisilicate is a naturally occurring mineral (meerschaum, parasepiolite, sepiolite)	anti-caking agent; tablet excipient; antacid (pharmacology); glazing, polishing and release agent (sweets); dusting agent (chewing gum); coating agent (rice)

E-NUMBERS (cont.)

Anti-caking agents

Number	Name	Source	Function
553(b)	Talc	naturally occurring mineral	release agent; anti-caking agent; chewing gum component; filtering aid; dusting powder
554	Aluminium sodium silicate	naturally occurring mineral (analcite, natrolite); quartz; gibbsite	anti-caking agent
556	Aluminium calcium silicate	naturally occuring as scolecite and heulandite	anti-caking agent
558	Bentonite	naturally occurring clay deposit	anti-caking agent; clarifying agent; filtration aid; emulsifier; suspending agent
559	Kaolin, heavy; and Kaolin, light	naturally occurring altered mineral in granite	anti-caking agent; clarifying agent
570	Stearic acid	naturally occurring fatty acid (animal fats and vegetable oils); synthetic preparation	anti-caking agent
572	Magnesium stearate	stearic acid (synthetic preparation)	anti-caking agent; emulsifier; release agent
575	D-Glucono-1,5-lactone	glucose	acid; sequestrant; prevents formation of milkstone (magnesium, calcium phosphate deposits) and beerstone
576	Sodium gluconate	sodium salt of gluconic acid (synthetic preparation)	sequestrant; dietary supplement
577	Potassium gluconate	potassium salt of gluconic acid (synthetic preparation)	sequestrant
578	Calcium gluconate	calcium salt from gluconic acid (synthetic preparation)	buffer; firming agent; sequestrant

Flavour enhancers

Number	Name	Source	Function
620	L-Glutamic acid	naturally occurring amino acid; carbohydrate fermentation	dietary supplement flavour enhancer; salt substitute
621	*mono* Sodium glutamate	sodium salt of glutamic acid	flavour enhancer
622	Potassium hydrogen L-glutamate	synthetic preparation	flavour enhancer; salt substitute
623	Calcium dihydrogen di-L-glutamate	synthetic preparation	flavour enhancer; salt substitute

E-NUMBERS (cont.)

Flavour enhancers

Number	Name	Source	Function
627	Guanosine 5′-(*di* Sodium phosphate)	sodium salt of 5′guanylic acid (synthetic preparation)	flavour enhancer
631	Inosine 5′-(*di* Sodium phosphate)	disodium salt of inosinic acid (meat extract and dried sardines)	flavour enhancer
635	Sodium 5′-ribonucleotide	*di* Sodium guanylate and *di* sodium inosinate mixture	flavour enhancer
636	Maltol	naturally occurring (young larch tree bark, pine needles, chicory wood, tars, oils, roasted malt); streptomycin salt (chemical preparation)	flavouring agent ('freshly baked'); synthetic coffee, fruit, maple, nut and vanilla flavours
637	Ethyl maltol	maltol (chemical preparation)	sweet taste flavouring; flavour enhancer
900	Dimethyl-polysiloxane	dimethylpolysiloxane and silicon gel or silicon dioxide	water repellent; anti-foaming agent; chewing gum base; anti-caking agent; used in beer making

Glazing agents

Number	Name	Source	Function
901	Beeswax, white, and beeswax, yellow	naturally occurring (bee honeycomb)	glazing and polishing agent; release agent; fruit and honey flavourings
903	Carnauba wax	Brazilian wax palm (*Copernica cerifera*) leaves	glazing and polishing agent (sugar confectionery); enhances hardness and lustre of other waxes; used in cosmetic materials
904	Shellac	lac insect (*Laccifer lacca*) resin	glazing agent and polish up to 0.4 per cent.
905	Mineral hydrocarbons	petroleum distillates	polishes, glazing agents, sealing agents; chewing gum ingredient; defoaming agent; coating for fresh fruit and vegetables; lubricant and binder for capsules and tablets; lubricant in food-processing equipment and meat-packing plants

E-NUMBERS (cont.)

Glazing agents

Number	Name	Source	Function
907	Refined microcrystalline wax	petroleum	chewing gum ingredient; polishing and release agent; stiffening agent; tablet coating

Improving agents

Number	Name	Source	Function
920	L-cysteine hydrochloride and L-cysteine hydrochloride monohydrate	L-cysteine, a naturally occurring amino acid (animal hair and chicken feathers)	flour improving agent; flavouring (chicken); used in shampoo
924	Potassium bromate	synthetic preparation	flour-maturing or -improving agent; used in beer making
925	Chlorine	naturally occurring gas (earth's crust, seawater)	flour bleaching; drinking water
926	Chlorine dioxide	(synthetic preparation) chlorine and sodium chloride; potassium chlorate and sulphuric acid; nitrogen dioxide passed through sodium chlorate	bleaching agent; improving agent; oxidizing agent; water purifying agent; taste and odour control of water; bactericide and antiseptic
927	Azo dicarbonamide	synthetic preparation	flour-improving or maturing agent

[1] Azo dyes are derivatives of azobenzene, obtained as the reaction products of diazonum salts with tertiary amines or phenols (hydroxy-benzenes). Usually coloured yellow, red, or brown, they have acidic or basic properties.

INFECTIOUS DISEASES AND INFECTIONS

Name	Cause	Transmission	Incubation	Symptoms
AIDS (Acquired Immune Deficiency Syndrome)	Human Immuno Deficiency Virus (HIV)	sexual relations, sharing of syringes, blood tranfusion	several years	fever, lethargy, weight loss, diarrhoea, lymph node enlargement, viral and fungal infections
amoebiasis	*Entamoeba histolytica*	organism in contaminated food	up to several years	fever, diarrhoea, exhaustion, rectal bleeding
anthrax	*Bacillus antracis* bacterium	animal hair	1–3 days	small red pimple on hand or face enlarges and discharges pus

INFECTIOUS DISEASES AND INFECTIONS (cont.)

Name	Cause	Transmission	Incubation	Symptoms
appendicitis	usually *E coli* organism	not transmitted	sudden onset	abdominal pain, which moves from left to right after a few hours, nausea
bilharziasis (schistosomiasis)	*Schistosoma haematobium*, (also called Bilharzia) *S.mansoni* or *S.japonicum*	certain snails living in calm water	varies with lifespan of parasite	fever, muscle aches, abdominal pain, headaches
bronchiolitis (babies only)	respiratory syncytical virus (RSV)	droplet infection	1–3 days	blocked or runny nose, irritability
brucellosis	*Brucella abortus* or *B.meliteusis* bacteria	cattle or goats	3–6 days	fever, drenching sweats, weight loss, muscle and joint pains, confusion and poor memory
bubonic plague	*Yersinia pestis* bacterium	fleas	3–6 days	fever, muscle aches, headaches, exhaustion, enlarged lymph glands ('buboes')
chicken pox (varicella)	varicella-zoster virus	droplet infection	14–21 days	blister-like eruptions, lethargy, headaches, sore throat
cholera	*Vibrio cholerae*	contaminated water	a few hours to 5 days	severe diarrhoea, vomiting
common cold (coryza)	Rhinoviruses	droplet infection	1–3 days	blocked or runny nose, sneezing, sore throat, runny eyes
conjunctivitis	virus, bacterium or allergy	variable	variable	if viral, watery discharge from eyes; if bacterial, sticky yellow discharge from eyes
dengue fever (break-bone fever)	B group of arboviruses	mosquito	5–6 days	fever, severe muscle cramps, enlarged lymph nodes
diptheria	*Cornybacterium diptheriae*	droplet infection	4–6 days	grey exudate across throat; swelling of throat tissues may lead to asphyxiation; toxin secreted by bacteria may seriously damage heart

INFECTIOUS DISEASES AND INFECTIONS (cont.)

Name	Cause	Transmission	Incubation	Symptoms
dysentery	*Shigella* genus of bacteria	contaminated food or water	variable, can cause death within 48 hours	diarrhoea, with or without bleeding
gastro-enteritis	bacteria, viruses and food poisoning	droplet infection or food	variable	varying from nausea to severe fever, vomiting and diarrhoea
german measles (rubella)	togavirus	droplet infection	18 days	1–2 days catarrh and sore throat, then red rash, enlargement of lymph nodes
glandular fever (infectious mononucleosis)	Epstein-Barr virus	saliva of infected person	1–6 weeks	sore throat, fever, enlargement of tonsils and lymph nodes, lethargy, depression
gonorrhorea	*Neisseria gonorrhoreae* bacterium	usually sexually transmitted	2–10 days	in men, burning sensation on urination and discharge from urethra; in women (if any), vaginal discharge
hepatitis	hepatitis A, B or C virus	contaminated food or water (type A); sexual relations, sharing syringes, transfusion (type B)	3–6 weeks (type A); up to a few weeks (type B)	often no symptoms, otherwise similar to 'flu, loss of appetite, tenderness below right ribs, jaundice
influenza ('flu)	influenza A, B or C virus	droplet infection	1–3 days	fever, sweating, muscle aches
kala-azar (leishmaniasis)	parasites genus leishmania	sandfly	usually 1–2 months, can be up to 10 years	lymph gland, spleen and liver enlargement
laryngitis	same viruses that cause colds and 'flu, ie adeno and rhinoviruses	droplet infection	1–3 days	sore throat, coughing, hoarseness
lassa fever	arenavirus	urine	3 weeks	fever, sore throat, muscle aches and pains, haemorrhage into the skin

INFECTIOUS DISEASES AND INFECTIONS (cont.)

Name	Cause	Transmission	Incubation	Symptoms
Legionnaire's disease	*Legionella pneumophila* bacterium	water droplets in infected humidifiers, cooling towers; stagnant water in cisterns and shower heads	1–3 days	'flu and pneumonia-like symtoms, fever, diarrhoea, mental confusion
leprosy	*Mycobacterium leprae* bacterium	droplet infection; minimally contagious	variable	insensitive white patches on skin, nodules, thickening of and damage to nerves
malaria	*Plasmodium falciparium, P.vivax, P.ovale, P.malariae*	anopheline mosquito	several weeks for *P.falciparium*, to several months for *P.vivax*	severe swinging fever, cold sweats, shivers
Marburg (or green monkey) disease	unclassified virus	monkeys, body fluids	5–9 days	fever, diarrhoea, affects brain, kidneys and lungs
measles	paramyxovirus	droplet infection	14 days	fever, severe cold symptoms, bloody red rash
meningitis	various bacteria, viruses or fungi eg *Cryptococcus*	droplet infection	variable	severe headache, stiffness in neck muscles, dislike of the light, nausea, vomiting, confusion
mumps	paramyxovirus	droplet infection	18 days	lethargy, fever, pain at the angle of the jaw; swelling of parotid gland(s)
orchitis	bacterium or virus: if bacterial, urinary infection due to eg gonorrhoea, if viral due to eg mumps	*see* cause	variable	painful red and swollen testis, fever, nausea
osteomyelitis	usually staphylococci organisms	infection spreads from eg boil or impetigo	1–10 days	abrupt onset of fever, and pain at site of infected bone (usually tibia or femur)
parotitis	bacterium or virus	common in mumps (viral), may follow severe febrile illness or abdominal operation	1–10 days	inflammation of one or both parotid glands

INFECTIOUS DISEASES AND INFECTIONS (cont.)

Name	Cause	Transmission	Incubation	Symptoms
pericarditis	bacterium or virus eg *Coxsackie B*	infection follows a chest disease or heart attack	variable	inflamed pericardium (fibrous bag which encloses the heart); tight chest pain
peritonitis	usually *E.coli* organism; sometimes chemical irritation	usually appendicitis; perforation of the gut allows escape of barrel contents into peritoneal cavity	1–10 days	severe abdominal pain, vomiting, rigidity, shock
pharyngitis	bacteria or virus	droplet infection	3–5 days	sore throat, fever, pain on swallowing, enlarged neck glands
pneumonia	*Streptococcus pneumoniae* bacterium, *Legionella pneumophila* etc	droplet infection	1–3 weeks	cough, fever, chest pain
poliomyelitis	three types of polio virus	droplet infection and hand to mouth infection from faeces	7–14 days	affects spinal cord and brain; headache, fever, neck and muscle stiffness; may result in meningitis or paralysis
proctitis	fungal infection possible	contact	variable	inflammation of the rectum and anus resulting from thrush, piles or fissures pain on defecation
psittacosis	*Chlamydis psittaci*	close contact infected birds (parrots)	1–2 weeks	pneumonitis, fever, nausea
puerperal fever	infection within uterine cavity or vagina	follows childbirth	1–10 days	fever; often fatal in past, now rare
pylitis	bacteria	kidney infection	1–10 days	fever, rigors, loin pain, burning on passing urine
rabies	virus	bite or lick by infected animal	2–6 weeks	headache, sickness, excitability, fear of drinking water, convulsions, coma and death
river blindness (or onchocerciasis)	*Onchocerca volvulus* worm	bites of infected flies of genus *Simulium*	worms mature in 2–4 months, may live 12 years	worms inhabit skin, causing nodules and sometimes blindness
salpingitis	infection of the Fallopian tubes	usually gonorrhoea	variable	abdominal pain, fever, irregular periods, vaginal discharge

INFECTIOUS DISEASES AND INFECTIONS (cont.)

Name	Cause	Transmission	Incubation	Symptoms
scarlet fever	*haemolytic streptococcus*	droplet infection or streptococci infected milk or ice-cream	2–4 days	sudden onset; headache, sore throat, fever, vomiting, red skin rash
shingles	*Herpes zoster* virus (also causes chickenpox)	dormant virus in body becomes active following a minor infection	variable	pain, numbness, blisters
sinusitis	virus or bacteria	droplet infection; common with a cold	1–3 days	fever, sinus pain, nasal discharge
sleeping sickness (or African trypanosomiasis)	**1.** *Trypanosoma brucei gambieuse* or **2.** *Tb rhodesieuse*	bites by infected tsetse fly	**1**.weeks-months, **2**.7–14 days	fever, lymph node enlargement, headache, behavioural change, drowsiness, coma, sometimes death
smallpox	variole major or minor virus	now eradicated worldwide	12 days	fever, rash followed by pustules on face and extremities
syphilis	*Treponema pallidum*	sexually transmitted: organism enters bloodstream through a mucous membrane, usually genital skin	ulcer after 2–6 weeks, skin rash after weeks or months	late syphilis damages brain, heart and main blood vessels, and unborn babies
tetanus	*Clostridium tetni*	bacteria from soil infect wounds	2 days–weeks	muscular spasms cause lockjaw and affect breathing, potentially fatal
thrush	*Candida albicans* yeast	the yeast is present on skin of most people and multiplies when resistance to infection is low; during pregnancy or when taking contraceptive pill	variable	white spots on tongue and cheeks; irritant vaginal discharge; rash in genital area or between folds of skin
tonsillitis	usually same viruses responsible for colds; sometimes bacterial (streptococci)	droplet infection	1–3 days	red inflamed tonsils, sore throat

INFECTIOUS DISEASES AND INFECTIONS (cont.)

Name	Cause	Transmission	Incubation	Symptoms
trachoma	*Chlamydia trachomatis* organism	poor hygiene: organism infects eye	5 days	conjuctivitis, swelling and scarring in cornea, often leading to blindness
tuberculosis	*Myobacterium tuberculosis bacterium*	inhalation of bacterium from person with active tuberculosis pneumonia or from infected milk	up to several years	cough with bloodstained sputum, weight loss, chest pain
typhoid	*Salmonella typhi* bacillus	contaminated water or food	10–14 days	slow onset of fever, abdominal discomfort, cough, rash, constipation then diarrhoea, delirium, coma, potentially fatal
typhus	*Rickettsiae* parasites	bite by infected flea, tick, mite or louse	7–14 days	fever, rigors, headache, muscular pain, rash
urethritis	virus or bacteria	may occur with cystitis or venereal infection	variable	bloody stools, abdominal pain, burning on urination
whooping cough	*Bordetella pertussis*	droplet infection	7–14 days	severe coughing followed by 'whoop' of respiration
yellow fever	zoonosis virus	mosquitoes infected by monkeys	3–6 days	rigors, high fever, bone pains, headache, nausea, jaundice, kidney failure, coma, potentially fatal

MAJOR CAUSES OF DEATH

Death from respiratory ailments, infectious diseases and injuries (other than car accidents) is lower in the developed world due to better preventative medicine, safer living conditions and powerful modern drugs; however, people in the developed world are the most likely to die from cancer or heart disease.

The chart shows the percentage likelihood of an individual eventually dying from the causes listed. Percentages have been rounded to the nearest whole number, except where the figure is smaller than 1. AIDS is not included in these statistics. Survey 1988.

Country	Infectious/ parasitic	Cancer	Circulatory (heart; stroke)	Respir-atory	Injuries (car accidents)
OECD[1] member countries					
Australia	0.5	22	52 (35;8)	6	4 (1)
Canada	0.6	24	46 (33;9)	9	5 (1)
Denmark	0.4	24	48 (33;9)	7	6 (0.9)
France	1	24	38 (22;11)	7	8 (1)
West Germany	0.7	24	51 (33;13)	6	4 (0.9)
Italy	0.4	22	48 (25;15)	8	5 (1)
Japan	1	21	43 (22;18)	13	5 (1)
Netherlands	0.6	27	43 (29;10)	8	4 (0.8)
Spain	0.9	19	49 (25;17)	10	4 (1)
Sweden	0.6	20	55 (38;11)	8	5 (0.7)
Switzerland	0.7	25	48 (32;11)	7	7 (1)
UK	0.4	24	48 (31;13)	11	3 (0.6)
US	1	21	49 (37;8)	9	5 (1)
East Europe					
Czechoslovakia	0.3	21	56 (29;17)	6	6 (0.8)
East Germany	0.4	17	58 (24;10)	6	3 (0.8)
Poland	0.7	18	56 (21;7)	4	5 (1)
USSR	1	15	63 (37;22)	7	6 (0.9)
Asia Pacific					
South Korea	2	12	32 (8;15)	5	6 (2)
Singapore	3	20	38 (23;12)	20	4 (0.9)
South Asia					
Sri Lanka	5	4	14 (10;2)	5	7 (0.7)
Sub-Saharan Africa					
Mauritius	2	8	53 (33;15)	10	4 (0.7)
Mid East/North Africa					
Bahrain	2	10	38 (29;4)	7	4 (4)
Israel	2	17	47 (34;11)	7	6 (0.9)
Kuwait	3	11	46 (24;4)	9	5 (3)
Latin America/Caribbean					
Argentina	2	17	33 (35;11)	6	4 (0.7)
Bahamas	3	15	44 (19;14)	10	3 (1)
Chile	3	19	34 (18;11)	13	6 (0.5)
Cuba	1	18	50 (32;11)	11	7 (0)
Guatemala	17	7	17 (12;4)	16	5 (0.1)
Mexico	7	11	28 (17;7)	11	9 (2)
Uruguay	2	22	44 (23;14)	7	5 (0.7)
Venezuela	6	14	45 (28;10)	8	7 (3)

[1] Organization for Economic Co-operation and Development

AN A TO Z OF PHOBIAS

Technical term	Everyday term	Technical term	Everyday term	Technical term	Everyday term
acero-	sourness	entomo-	insects	nepho-	clouds
achulo-	darkness	eoso	dawn	moso- (patho-)	disease
acro-	heights	eremo-	solitude	ocho-	vehicles
aero-	air	erete-	pins	odonto-	teeth
agora-	open spaces	ereuthro-	blushing	oiko-	home
aichuro-	points	ergasio-	work	olfacto-	smell
ailuro-	cats	geno-	sex	ommato-	eyes
akoustico-	sound	geuma-	taste	oneiro-	dreams
algo-	pain	grapho-	writing	ophidio-	snakes
amaka-	carriages	gymno-	nudity	ornitho-	birds
amatho-	dust	gyno-	women	ourano-	heaven
andro-	men	hamartio-	sin	pan- (panto-)	everything
anemo-	wind	haphe-	touch	partheno-	girls
angino-	narrowness	harpaxo-	robbers	patroio-	heredity
anthropo-	man	hedono-	pleasure	penia-	poverty
antlo-	flood	haemoto-	blood	phasmo-	ghosts
apeiro-	infinity	helmintho-	worms	phobo-	fears
arachno-	spiders	hodo-	travel	photo-	light
astheno-	weakness	homichlo-	fog	pnigero-	smothering
astra-	lightning	horme-	shock	poine-	punishment
ate-	ruin	hydro-	water	poly-	many things
aulo-	flute	hypegia-	responsibility	poto-	drink
aurora-	Northern Lights	hypno-	sleep	pterono-	feathers
bacilli-	microbes	ideo-	ideas	pyro-	fire
baro-	gravity	kakorraphia-	failure	rypo-	soiling
baso-	walking	katagelo-	ridicule	Satano-	Satan
batracho-	reptiles	keno-	void	seia-	flash
belone-	needles	kineso-	motion	sidero-	stars
bronto-	thunder	klepto-	stealing	sito-	food
cheimai	cold	kopo-	fatigue	sperma- (spermato-)	germs
chiono-	snow	kristallo-	ice	stasi-	standing
chrometo-	money	lalio-	stuttering	stygio- (hade-)	hell
chrono-	duration	linono-	string	syphilo-	syphilis
chrystallo-	crystals	logo-	words	thaaso-	sitting
claustro-	closed spaces	lysso- (mania)	insanity	thalasso-	sea
cnido-	stings	mastigo-	flogging	thanato-	death
cometo-	comets	mechano-	machinery	theo-	God
cromo-	colour	metallo-	metals	thermo-	heat
cyno-	dogs	meteoro-	meteors	toxi-	poison
demo-	crowds	miso-	contamination	tremo-	trembling
demono-	demons	mono-	one thing	triskaideka-	thirtheen
dermato-	skin	musico-	music	zelo-	jealousy
dike-	injustice	muso-	mice	zoo-	animals
dora-	fur	necro-	corpses	xeno-	strangers
eisoptro-	mirror	nelo	glass		
electro-	electricity	neo-	newness		

AN A TO Z OF PHOBIAS (cont.)

Everyday term	Technical term
air	aero-
animals	zoo-
birds	orthino-
blood	haemato-
blushing	ereutho-
carriages	amaka-
cats	ailuro-
closed spaces	claustro-
clouds	nepho-
cold	cheima-
colour	cromo-
comets	cometo-
contamination	miso-
corpses	necro-
crowds	demo-
crystals	chrystallo-
darkness	achluo-
dawn	eoso-
death	thanato-
demons	demono-
disease	noso- (patho-)
dogs	cyno-
dreams	oneiro-
drinks	poto-
duration	chrono-
dust	amatho-
electricity	electro-
everything	pan- (panto-)
eyes	ommato-
failure	kakoraphia-
fatigue	kopo-
fears	phobo-
feathers	pterono-
fire	pyro-
flash	sela-
flogging	mastigo-
flood	antlo-
flute	aulo-
fog	homichlo-
good	sito-
fur	dora-
germs	sperma- (spermato-)
ghosts	phasmo-
girls	partheno-
glass	nelo-
God	theo-
gravity	baro-
heat	thermo-
heaven	ourano-
heights	acro-
hell	stygio- (hade-)
heredity	patroio-
home	oiko-
ice	kristallo-
ideas	ideo-
infinity	apeiro-
injustice	dike-
insanity	lysso (mania-)
insects	entomo-
jealousy	zelo-
light	photo-
lightning	astra-
machinery	mechano-
man	anthropo-
many things	poly-
men	andro-
metals	metallo-
meteors	meteoro-
mice	muso-
microbes	bacilli-
mirrors	eisoptro-
money	chrometo-
motion	kineso-
music	musico-
narrowness	angino-
needles	belone-
newness	neo-
Northern Lights	aurora-
nudity	gymno-
one thing	mono-
open spaces	agora-
pain	algo-
pins	erete-
pleasure	hedono-
points	aichuro-
poison	toxi-
poverty	penia-
punishment	poine-
reptiles	batracho-
responsibility	hypegia-
ridicule	katagelo-
robberies	harpaxo-
ruin	ate-
Satan	Satano-
sea	thalasso-
sex	geno-
shock	horme-
sin	hamartio-
sitting	thaaso-
skin	dermato-
sleep	hypno-
smell	olfacto-
smothering	pnigero-
snakes	ophidio-
snow	chiono-
soiling	rypo-
solitude	eremo-
sound	akoustico-
sourness	acero-
spiders	arachno-
standing	stasi-
stars	sidero-
stealing	klepto-
stings	cnido-
strangers	xeno-
string	linono-
stuttering	lalio-
syphilis	syphilo-
taste	geuma-
teeth	odonto-
thirteen	triskaideka-
thunder	bronto- (tonitro)
touch	haphe-
travel	hodo-
trembling	tremo-
vehicles	ocho-
void	keno-
walking	baso-
water	hydro-
weakness	stheno-
wind	anemo-
women	gyno-
words	logo-
work	ergasio-
worms	helmintho-
writing	grapho-

IMPORTANT DISCOVERIES IN MEDICINE

Discovery	Date	Discoverer(s)	Nationality
adrenal gland, function of	1856	Vulpian (b.1826)[1]	French
adrenaline	1901	Jokichi Takamine (1854–1922)	Japanese
		based on work by Edward Sharpey-Schafer (1850–1935) and Oliver	UK
AIDS (Acquired Immune Deficiency Syndrome)	1981	scientists in Los Angeles	—
allergenic nature of hayfever	1906	Clemens Peter von Pirquet (b.1874)	Austrian
allergy recognized in skin's reaction to tuberculin	1906	Clemens Peter von Pirquet (b.1874)	Austrian
anaesthetic, epidural	1885	James Leonard Corning (1855–1923)	US
anaesthetic, general	1840s	priority claimed by Crawford Long (1815–78) Gardner Cotton (1814–98) Horace Wells (1815–48) Charles Jackson (1805–80)	all US
anaesthetic, local (mandrake leaves and polenta)	described in *Natural History*	Pliny the Elder (23–79AD)	Roman
anaphylaxis	1902	Charles Robert Richet (1850–1935)	French
		Pierre Portier	French
androsterone	1931	Adolf Friedrich Johann Butenandt (1903–)	German
anthrax bacillus	1850	Casimir Joseph Davaine (1812–82)	French
anthrax bacillus	1876	Louis Pasteur (1822–95)	French
		Robert Koch (1843–1910)	German
anthrax, serum against	1895	Achille Sclavo (b.1861)	Italian
		E Marchoux	French
antihistamine	1937	Bonet	
		Hans Staub (b.1890)	Swiss
antipyretic agent (lowers temperature)	4th–5th century BC	Hippocrates (c.460–c.377 or 359BC)	Greek
antisepsis	1865	Joseph Lister (1827–1912)	UK
asepsis by boiling and by dry heat autoclave	1883	Octave Terrillon	French
		Louis-Félix Terrier (b.1837)	French
atropine (isolated)	1819	Rudolph Brondes	
bacillus *see* diptheria, gangrene, tuberculosis, typhus bacteria	1673	Anton van Leeuwenhoek (1632–1723)	Dutch
benzoadiazepines (tranquillizers) ('the time pill')	1986	Fred W Turck	US
		Susan Losee Olsen	US
blood circulation	1628	William Harvey (1578–1677)	UK
blood groups A, O, B, AB	1901	Karl Landsteiner (1868–1943)	Austrian–US
blood groups M, N and P	1927	Karl Landsteiner (1868–1943)	Austrian–US
		Levine	US
blood pressure greater than atmospheric pressure	1733	Stephen Hales (1677–1761)	UK
brain, electric activity in the (*see* EEG)	1875	Richard Caton	UK
cellular division	1855	Rudolph Virchow (1821–1902)	German

IMPORTANT DISCOVERIES IN MEDICINE (cont.)

Discovery	Date	Discoverer(s)	Nationality
chloroform, anaesthetic properties of	1847	James Young Simpson (1811–70)	UK
cholera vibrion	1883	Robert Koch (1843–1910)	German
chromosome X, heredity linked to sex	1909	Thomas Hunt Morgan (1866–1945)	US
chromosomes	1888	Thomas Hunt Morgan (1866–1945)	US
chromosomes (48) in man	—	Herbert McLean Evans (1882–1971)	US
circadian rhythm of 25 hours	1972	Michel Siffre	—
coagulation, role of fibrin in	1771	William Henson	UK
coagulation (formation of fibrin following dissolution of fibrinogen under influence of thrombin)	1876	Olaf Hammarsten (b.1841)	Swedish
cochlea or inner ear, stimulation mechanism of	1961	Georg von Békésy (1899–1972)	Hungarian–US
corpuscles, red	1675 or 1684	Anton van Leeuwenhoek (1632–1723)	Dutch
cortisone (adrenal cortex hormone) (isolated)	1934	Edward Calvin Kendall (1886–1972)	US
cyclosporin-A, immunosuppressive properties of	1972	J-F Borel	Swiss
digestion system	—	Claude Bernard (1813–78)	French
diptheria bacillus	1882	Theodor Albrecht Edwin Klebs (b.1834)	Swiss–US
diptheria, serum against	1892	Emil Adolf von Behring (1854–1917)	German
		Shibasaburo Kitasato (1852–1931)	Japanese
		Pierre Émile Roux (1853–1933)	French
disinfection of wounds, chemical	1825	Antoine Labarraque	French
DNA, structure of	1953, 1961	Francis Harry Crompton Crick (1916–)	UK
		James D Watson (1928–)	US
Down's Syndrome, cause of ('the extra chromosome')	1958	Turpin	French
		Gautier	French
		Lejeune	French
electro-encephalogram (EEG) (spontaneous activity of the brain)	1929	Hans Berger (1873–1941)	German
electroplating	1786	Luigi Galvani (1737–98)	Italian
endorphins	1975	Hughes	US
		Roger Guillemin	French–US
enzymes	1833	Anselme Payen	French
		Jean-François Persoz	French
enzymes, restriction	1970	Hamilton Smith	US
estrogen produced by ovarian follicle	1924	Courrier	French
estrone	1929	Edward Adelbert Doisy (b.1893)	US
		Adolf Friedrich Johann Butenandt (1903–)	German
ether first used as anaesthetic	1846	William Thomas Morton (1819–68)	US
fertilization	1875	Oskar Hertwig	German
gangrene, gas bacillus of	1878	Louis Pasteur (1822–95)	French
genes, chemical regulation by	1952	Jacques Monod (1910–76)	French
		Edwin Joseph Cohn (1892–1953)	US
gonococcus	1879	Ulric Richard Gustav Neisser (1928–)	German

IMPORTANT DISCOVERIES IN MEDICINE (cont.)

Discovery	Date	Discoverer(s)	Nationality
heparin (anticoagulant secreted by liver cells)	1916	J McLean	US
hepatitis-C virus	1989	Dr Qui-Lim-Choo's research team of the Chiron Corporation	California
heredity	1865	Gregor Johann Mendel (1822–84)	Austrian
HIV virus (isolated)	1983	Luc Montaigner and others	French
HLA (human leuckocyte locus A) system (responsible for transplant rejection)	1950–77	Jean Dausset (1916–)	French
hormone *see* adrenaline, cortisone, estradiol, inhibin, insulin, progesterone, testosterone			
inhibin	1985	Roger Guillemin (1924–)	French–US
insulin (isolated)	1921	Frederick Grant Banting (1891–1941)	Canadian
		Charles Herbert Best (1899–1978)	Canadian
		John James McLeod (1876–1935)	Canadian
insulin	1921	Nicolas Paulesco	Romanian
interferon	1957	Alick Isaacs (1921–67)	UK
		J Lindemann	Swiss
interleukin 2	1985	Steven Rosenberg	US
interleukin 3	1986	Steven Clark	US
		Yu Chang Yang	US
leprosy bacillus	1869	Gerhard Henrik Armauer Hansen (1841–1912)	Norwegian
malaria, plasmodium protozoon as agent of	1880	Charles-Louis-Alphonse Laveran (1845–1922)	French
microbes	1762	M A Plenciz (1705–86)	Austrian
morphine	1805	Friedrich Serturner	German
mosquitoes in infectious diseases, role of	1895	Ronald Ross (1857–1932)	UK
mosquitoes, transmission of filariae by	1883	Patrick Manson (1844–1922)	UK
nervous reaction, chemical transmission of	1936	Otto Loewi (1873–1961)	German–US
		Henry Hallet Dale (1875–1968)	UK
nitrous oxide (laughing gas)	1776	Joseph Priestley (1733–1804)	UK
nitrous oxide, analgesic and laughter-provoking effect of	1799	Humphry Davy (1778–1829)	UK
nucleic acid	1869	Johann Friedrich Miescher (1844–95)	Swiss
oncogenes	1981	Robert Weinberg	US
		Geoffrey Cooper	US
		Michael Wigler	US
ovulation, substances acting against	1921	Haberlandt	German
penicillin	1928	Alexander Fleming (1881–1955)	UK
phagocytes (cells which devour infective organisms)	1882–6	Ilya Ilich Mechnikov (1845–1916)	Russian
phenol, disinfectant properties of	1865	Joseph Lister (1827–1912)	UK
Phenytoin (for treatment of epilepsy)	1939	—	—
pituitary, secretion of growth hormone	1921	Herbert McLean Evans (1882–1971)	US
prion (proteinaceous infectious particles)	1982	Stanley Prusiner	US
progesterone	1929	George Washington Corner (b.1889)	US
		Edgar Allen (1892–1943)	US

IMPORTANT DISCOVERIES IN MEDICINE (cont.)

Discovery	Date	Discoverer(s)	Nationality
protozoa (unicellular organisms)	1675	Anton van Leeuwenhoek (1632–1723)	Dutch
quinoline (later discovered to be antimicrobial agent)	1834	Friedlieb Ferdinand Runge (1795–1867)	German
rabies vaccination	1798	Louis Pasteur (1822–95)	French
relapsing fever, spirochaete of	1873	Obermeier	German
respiration, use of oxygen in	1770–80	Antoine Lavoisier (1743–94)	French
rhesus factor	1939–40	Karl Landsteiner (1868–1943)	Austrian–US
		Levine	US
scurvy, lemon juice treatment for	1740s	James Lind (1716–94)	UK
skin culture	1950	Howard Green	US
sleeping sickness, transmission by tsetse flies	1895	David Bruce (1855–1931)	UK
smallpox vaccination	1796	Edward Jenner (1749–1823)	UK
smallpox innoculation, introduction of	1718	Lady Mary Wortley Montagu (1689–1762)	UK
spermatozoa	1677	Anton van Leeuwenhoek (1632–1723)	Dutch
Staphylococcus and Streptococcus	1880	Louis Pasteur (1822–95)	French
streptomycin (antibiotic against tuberculosis)	1943	Selman Abraham Walksman (1888–1973)	US
sulphonamides (first antibiotics)	1935	Gerhard (Johannes Paul) Domagk (1895–1964)	German
T-lymphocytes	1966	J David	US
		V Blum	US
testosterone (isolated)	1929	—	—
testosterone (synthesized)	1935	Leopold Stephen Ružička (1887–1976)	Swiss
tetanus, serum against	1890	Emil von Behring (1854–1917)	German
		Shibasaburo Kitasato (1852–1931)	Japanese
		Pierre-Paul-Émile Roux (1853–1933)	French
thyroxine (thyroid hormone) (isolated)	1914	Edward Calvin Kendall (1886–1972)	US
tomography	1915	André Bocage	French
tuberculosis bacillus	1882	Robert Koch (1843–1910)	German
tubocarine (muscle relaxant)	1935	Harold King	—
Tumor Necrosis Factor (TNF)	1975	Carswell	US
typhus bacillus	1880	Karl Joseph Eberth (1835–1926)	German
vaccination	c.10th century	—	Turkey and China
vaccination *see* rabies, smallpox virus	1892	Dmitry Ivanovsky	Russian
viruses, cultivation of (on chicken embryos)	1986	Goodpasture	US
vitamin A	1913	Elmer Verner McCollum (b.1870)	US
		M Davis	US
		Thomas Burr Osborne (b.1859)	US
		L B Mendel	US
vitamin B (niacin) (isolated)	1913	Casimir Funk (1884–1967)	Polish–US
vitamin B1 (thiamin)	1897	Christiaan Eijkman (1858–1930)	Dutch
vitamin B2 (riboflavin)	1933	R Kühn	German
		P György	German
		T Wagner-Jauregg	German

IMPORTANT DISCOVERIES IN MEDICINE (cont.)

Discovery	Date	Discoverer(s)	Nationality
vitamin B3	1937	Madden	UK
		Strong	UK
		Woolley	UK
		Elvehjem	UK
vitamin B5	1933	Williams	US
vitamin B6	1936	T W Birch	US
		P György	German
vitamin B9	1938	Day	UK
vitamin B12	1927	Minot	UK
		Murphy	UK
vitamin B12 (isolated)	1948	E L Smith	US
		L F J Parke	US
		E L Rickes	UK
	same date in UK	N G Brink	UK
		F R Koniuszy	UK
		T R Wood	UK
		K Folkers	UK
vitamin C (isolated but not recognized as a vitamin)	1928	Albert von Nagyrapolt Szent Györgyi (1893–1986)	Hungarian–US
vitamin C (isolated)	1932	Glen King	US
vitamin D (role in prevention of rickets)[2]	1918	E Mellenby	UK
vitamin D (isolated)	1924	Steenbock	German
		Hess	German
		Weinstock	German
vitamin E	1923	Herbert McLean Evans (1882–1971)	US
		K S Bishop	US
vitamin K1	1934	K Dam	Danish
		Schönheyder	Danish
vitamins, necessity of	1906	Sir Frederick Gowland Hopkins (1861–1947)	UK
X-rays	1892	Heinrich Hertz (1857–94)	German
X-rays, properties of	1895	Wilhelm Konrad von Röntgen (1845–1923)	German
yellow fever, transmission by *stegmyia* mosquito	1881	Ronald Ross (1857–1932)	UK
		Carlos Juan Finlay (1833–1915)	Cuban

[1] Vulpian = Edmé Félix Alfred Vulpian
[2] not known as Vitamin D at this time

HISTORY

JOURNEYS OF EXPLORATION

Date	Name	Exploration
490 BC	Hanno	Makes voyage round part of the coast of Africa
325 BC	Alexander the Great	Leads fleet along the N Indian coast and up the Persian Gulf
84 AD	Agricola	His fleet circumnavigates Britain
1003	Leif Ericsson	Voyages to N America and discovers 'Vinland' (possibly Nova Scotia)
1418	Henry the Navigator	Sends seamen who discover Madeira
1433	Henry the Navigator	Sails round Cape Bojadar
1446	Denis Fernandez	Discovers Cape Verde and the Senegal
1469	Fernao Gomes	Crosses the equator and reaches Cape Catherine
1488	Bartholomew Diaz	Sails rounds the Cape of Storms (Cape of Good Hope)
1492	Christopher Columbus	Discovers the New World
1493	Christopher Columbus	Discovers Puerto Rico, Antigua and Jamaica
1497	John Cabot	Explores the coast of Newfoundland
1497	Vasco da Gama	Voyages round the Cape of Good Hope
1498	Vasco da Gama	Explores coast of Mozambique and discovers sea route to India
1498	Christopher Columbus	Discovers Trinidad and South America
1499	Amerigo Vespucci	Discovers mouth of the River Amazon
1500	Pedro Alvarez Cabral	Discovers Brazil
1500	Diego Diaz	Discovers Madagascar
1500	Gaspar de Corte Real	Explores east coast of Greenland and Labrador
1501	Amerigo Vespucci	Explores S American coast
1502	Christopher Columbus	Explores Honduras and Panama
1513	Vasco Nunez de Balboa	Crosses the Panama Isthmus to discover the Pacific Ocean
1520	Ferdinand Magellan	Discovers the Straits of Magellan
1521	Ferdinand Magellan	Discovers the Philippines
1524	Giovanni de Verrazano	Discovers New York Bay and the Hudson River
1526	Sebastian Cabot	Explores the Rio de la Plata
1531	Diego de Ordaz	Explores the River Orinoco
1534	Jacques Cartier	Explores the Gulf of St Lawrence
1535	Jacques Cartier	Navigates the St Lawrence River
1536	Pedro de Mendoza	Founds Buenos Aires and explores Parana and Paraguay rivers
1539	Hernando de Soto	Explores Florida
1540	G L de Cardenas	Discovers the Grand Canyon
1580	Francis Drake	Completes circumnavigation of the globe
1585	John Davis	Discovers Davis Strait on expedition to Greenland
1595	Walter Raleigh	Explores the River Orinoco
1610	Henry Hudson	Discovers Hudson's Bay
1616	William Baffin	Discovers Baffin Bay during search for the N W Passage

JOURNEYS OF EXPLORATION (cont.)

Date	Name	Exploration
1617	Walter Raleigh	Begins expedition to Guiana
1642	Abel Janszoon Tasman	Discovers Tasmania and New Zealand
1678	Robert Cavelier de Salle	Explores the Great Lakes of Canada
1692	Ijsbrand Iders	Explores the Gobi Desert
1736	Andreas Celsius	Undertakes expedition to Lapland
1761	C Niebuhr	Undertakes expedition to Arabia
1766	Louis de Bougainville	Voyage of discovery in Pacific, names Navigator Is.
1769	James Cook	Names Society Islands; charts coasts of New Zealand and E Australia
1770	James Cook	Lands at Botany Bay, Australia
1774	James Cook	Discoveries and rediscoveries in the Pacific; discovers and names S Georgia and the S Sandwich Is.
1772	James Bruce	Explores Abyssinia and the confluence of the Blue Nile and White Nile
1778	James Cook	Discovers Hawaiian group; surveys coast of Bering Straits
1787	Horace Saussure	Makes first ascent of Mont Blanc
1790	George Vancouver	Explores the coast of N W America
1795	Mungo Park	Explores the course of the Niger
1818	John Ross	Attempts to discover N W Passage
1819	John Barrow	Enters Barrow Straits in the N Arctic
1823	Walter Oudney	Discovers Lake Chad in C Africa
1841	David Livingstone	Discovers Lake Ngami
1845	John Franklin	Attempts to discover N W Passage
1854	Richard Burton and John Speke	Explore interior of Somaliland
1855	David Livingstone	Discovers the Victoria Falls on the Zambesi River
1858	Richard Burton and John Speke	Discover Lake Tanganyika
1875	Henry Morton Stanley	Traces the Congo to the Atlantic
1888	Fridtjof Nansen	Crosses Greenland
1893	Fridtjof Nansen	Attempts to reach North Pole
1909	Robert Edwin Peary	Reaches North Pole
1911	Roald Amundsen	Reaches South Pole
1912	Robert Falcon Scott	Reaches South Pole
1914	Ernest Shackleton	Leads expedition to the Antarctic
1953	Edmund Hillary and Norgay Tensing	Make first ascent of Mt Everest
1961	Yuri Gagarin	Becomes first man in space
1969	Neil Armstrong and Buzz Aldrin	Make first landing on the moon

This table comprises mainly European explorers; 'discovers' is used to indicate the first recorded visit by a European

MONARCHS

BELGIUM

Belgium became an indpendent kingdom in 1831. A national congress elected Prince Leopold of Saxe–Coburg as king.

Regnal dates	Name
1831–65	Leopold I
1865–1909	Leopold II
1909–34	Albert
1934–51	Leopold III
1951–	Baudouin

DENMARK

Regnal dates	Name
1448–81	Christian I
1481–1513	John
1513–23	Christian II
1523–34	Frederick I
1534–59	Christian III
1559–88	Frederick II
1588–1648	Christian IV
1648–70	Frederick III
1670–99	Christian V
1699–1730	Frederick IV
1730–46	Christian VI
1746–66	Frederick V
1766–1808	Christian VII
1808–39	Frederick VI
1839–48	Christian VIII
1848–63	Frederick VII
1863–1906	Christian IX
1906–12	Frederick VIII
1912–47	Christian X
1947–72	Frederick IX
1972–	Margaret II

ENGLAND

Regnal dates	Name
West Saxon Kings	
0802–39	Egbert
0839–58	Æthelwulf
0858–60	Æthelbald
0860–5	Æthelbert
0866–71	Æthelred
0871–99	Alfred
0899–924	Edward (the Elder)
0924–39	Athelstan
0939–46	Edmund
0946–55	Edred
0955–9	Edwy
0959–75	Edgar
0975–8	Edward (the Martyr)
0978–1016	Æthelred (the Unready)
1016	Edmund (Ironside)
Danish Kings	
1016–35	Cnut (Canute)
1035–7	Harold *Regent*
1037–40	Harold I (Harefoot)
1040–2	Harthacnut
1042–66	Edward (the Confessor)
1066	Harold II
House of Normandy	
1066–87	William I (the Conqueror)
1087–1100	William II (Rufus)
1100–35	Henry I
House of Blois	
1135–54	Stephen
House of Plantagenet	
1154–89	Henry II
1189–99	Richard I (Cœur de Lion)
1199–1216	John
1216–72	Henry III
1272–1307	Edward I
1307–27	Edward II
1327–77	Edward III
1377–99	Richard II
House of Lancaster	
1399–1413	Henry IV
1413–22	Henry V
1422–61	Henry VI
House of York	
1461–70	Edward IV
House of Lancaster	
1470–1	Henry VI
House of York	
1471–83	Edward IV
1483	Edward V
1483–5	Richard III
House of Tudor	
1485–1509	Henry VII
1509–47	Henry VIII
1547–53	Edward VI
1553–8	Mary I
1558–1603	Elizabeth I

FRANCE

France became a republic in 1793 and an empire in 1804 under Napoleon Bonaparte. The monarchy was restored in 1814 and then once more dissolved in 1848.

Regnal dates	Name
987–996	Hugh Capet
996–1031	Robert II
1031–60	Henry I
1060–1108	Philip I
1108–37	Louis VI
1137–80	Louis VII
1180–1223	Philip II Augustus
1223–6	Louis VIII
1226–70	Louis IX
1270–85	Philip III
1285–1314	Philip IV
1314–16	Louis X
1316	John I
1316–22	Philip V
1322–8	Charles IV
1328–50	Philip VI
1350–64	John II
1364–80	Charles V
1380–1422	Charles VI
1422–61	Charles VII
1461–83	Louis XI
1483–98	Charles VIII
1498–1515	Louis XII
1515–47	Francis I

MONARCHS (cont.)

France (cont.)

1547–59	Henry II
1559–60	Francis II
1560–74	Charles IX
1574–89	Henry III
1589–1610	Henry IV (of Navarre)
1610–43	Louis XIII
1643–1715	Louis XIV
1715–74	Louis XV
1774–92	Louis XVI
1814–24	Louis XVIII
1824–30	Charles X
1830–48	Louis-Philippe

GERMANY

Modern Germany was united under Prussia in 1871; it became a republic (1919) after World War I and the abdication of William II in 1918.

Regnal dates	Name
1871–88	William I
1888	Frederick
1888–1918	William II

GREECE

In 1832 the Greek National Assembly elected Otto of Bavaria as King of modern Greece. In 1917 Constantine I abdicated the throne in favour of his son Alexander. In 1920 a plebiscite voted for his return. In 1922 he again abdicated. In 1923 the monarchy was deposed and a republic was proclaimed in 1924. In 1935 a plebiscite restored the monarchy until in 1967 a military junta staged a coup. The monarchy was formally abolished in 1973; Greece became a republic again in 1975.

Regnal dates	Name
1832–62	Otto of Bavaria
1863–1913	George I (of Denmark)
1913–17	Constantine I
1917–20	Alexander
1920–2	Constantine I
1922–3	George I
1935–47	George I
1947–64	Paul
1964–7	Constantine II

ITALY

Modern Italy became a united kingdom in 1861; it voted by referendum to become a republic in 1946.

Regnal dates	Name
1861–78	Victor-Emanuel II
1878–1900	Humbert I
1900–46	Victor Emanuel III
1946	Humbert II

LUXEMBOURG

The Duchy of Luxembourg formally separated from the Netherlands in 1890.

Regnal dates	Name
1890–1905	Adolf of Nassau
1905–12	William
1912–19	Marie-Adelaide
1919–64	Charlotte
1964–	John

NETHERLANDS

Regnal dates	Name
1572–84	William the Silent
1584–1625	Maurice
1625–47	Frederick Henry
1647–50	William II
1672–1702	William III
1747–51	William IV
1751–95	William V
1806–10	Louis Bonaparte
1813–40	William I
1840–9	William II
1849–90	William III
1890–1948	Wilhelmina
1948–80	Juliana
1980–	Beatrix

PORTUGAL

From 1383 to 1385 the Portuguese throne was the subject of a dispute between John of Castile and John of Aviz. In 1826 Peter IV (I of Brazil) renounced his right to the Portuguese throne in order to remain in Brazil. His abdication was contingent upon his successor and daughter, Maria II marrying her uncle, Miguel. In 1828 Miguel usurped the throne on his own behalf. In 1834 Miguel was deposed and Maria II was restored to the throne. In 1910 Manuel II was deposed and Portugal became a republic.

Regnal dates	Name
1095–1112	Henry of Burgandy
1112–85	Alfonso I
1185–1211	Sancho I
1211–23	Alfonso II
1223–45	Sancho II
1245–79	Alfonso III
1279–1325	Diniz
1325–57	Alfonso IV
1357–67	Peter I
1367–83	Ferdinand
1385–1433	John I of Aviz
1433–8	Edward
1438–81	Alfonso V
1481–95	John II
1495–1521	Manuel I
1521–57	John III
1557–78	Sebastian

MONARCHS (cont.)

1578–80	Henry
1580–98	Philip I (II of Spain)
1598–1621	Philip II (III of Spain)
1621–40	Philip III (IV of Spain)
1640–56	John IV of Braganza
1656–83	Alfonso VI
1683–1706	Peter II
1706–50	John V
1750–77	Joseph
1777–1816	Maria I
1777–86	Peter III (King Consort)
1816–26	John VI
1826	Peter IV (I of Brazil)
1826–8	Maria II
1828–34	Miguel
1834–53	Maria II
1853–61	Peter V
1861–89	Luis
1889–1908	Charles
1908–10	Manuel II

SCOTLAND

Regnal dates	Name
1005–34	Malcolm II
1034–40	Duncan I
1040–57	Macbeth
1057–8	Lulach
1058–93	Malcolm III
1093–4	Donald Bane Deposed 1094 Restored 1094–7
1094	Duncan II
1097–1107	Edgar
1107–24	Alexander I
1124–53	David I
1153–65	Malcolm IV
1165–1214	William I
1214–49	Alexander II
1249–86	Alexander III
1286–90	Margaret
1290–2	(Interregnum)
1292–96	John Balliol
1296–1306	(Interregnum)
1306–29	Robert I (the Bruce)
1329–71	David II
1371–90	Robert II
1390–1406	Robert III
1406–37	James I
1437–60	James II
1460–88	James III
1488–1513	James IV
1513–42	James V
1542–67	Mary Queen of Scots
1567–1625	James VI [1]

[1] In 1603, James VI succeeded Elizabeth I to the English throne (Union of the Crowns) and united the thrones of Scotland and England.

SPAIN

Philip V abdicated in favour of Luis in 1724, but returned to the throne in the same year following Luis' death. After the French invasion of Spain in 1808 Napoleon set up Joseph Bonaparte as king. In 1814 Ferdinand was restored to the crown. In 1868 a revolution deposed Isabella II. In 1870 Amadeus of Savoy was elected as king. In 1873 he resigned the throne and a temporary republic was formed. In 1874 Alfonso XII restored the Bourbon dynasty to the throne. In 1931 Alfonso XIII was deposed and a republican constitution was proclaimed. From 1939 Franco ruled Spain under a dictatorship until his death in 1975 and the restoration of King Juan Carlos.

Regnal dates	Name
1516–56	Charles I (Emperor Charles V)
1556–98	Philip II
1598–1621	Philip III
1621–65	Philip IV
1665–1700	Charles II
1700–24	Philip V
1724	Luis
1724–46	Philip V
1746–59	Ferdinand VI
1759–88	Charles III
1788–1808	Charles IV
1808	Ferdinand VII
1808–14	Joseph Bonaparte
1814–33	Ferdinand VII
1833–68	Isabella II
1870–3	Amadeus of Savoy
1874–85	Alfonso XII
1886–1931	Alfonso XIII
1975–	Juan Carlos

UNITED KINGDOM

Regnal dates	Name
House of Stuart	
1603–25	James I (VI of Scotland)
1625–49	Charles I
Commonwealth and Protectorate	
1649–53	*Council of State*
1653–8	Oliver Cromwell *Lord Protector*
1658–9	Richard Cromwell *Lord Protector*
House of Stuart (restored)	
1660–85	Charles II
1685–8	James II
1689–94	William III (*jointly with* Mary II)
1694–1702	William III (*alone*)
1702–14	Anne
House of Hanover	
1714–27	George I
1727–60	George II
1760–1820	George III
1820–30	George IV
1830–7	William IV
1837–1901	Victoria
House of Saxe-Coburg	
1901–10	Edward VII
House of Windsor	
1910–36	George V
1936	Edward VIII
1936–52	George VI
1952–	Elizabeth II

ANCIENT EGYPT: DYNASTIES

Date BC	Dynasty	Period
c.3100–2890	I	**Early Dynastic Period**
c.2890–2686	II	First use of stone in building
c.2686–2613	III	**Old Kingdom**
c.2613–2494	IV	The age of the great
c.2494–2345	V	pyramid builders
c.2345–2181	VI	Longest reign in history: Pepi II, 90 years
c.2181–2173	VII	**First Intermediate Period**
c.2173–2160	VIII	Social order upset; few
c.2160–2130	IX	monuments built
c.2130–2040	X	
c.2133–1991	XI	
1991–1786	XII	**Middle Kingdom**
1786–1633	XIII	Golden age of art and craftsmanship
1786–c.1603	XIV	**Second Intermediate Period**
1674–1567	XV	Country divided into principalities
c.1684–1567	XVI	
c.1660–1567	XVII	
1567–1320	XVIII	**New Kingdom**
1320–1200	XIX	Began with colonial
1200–1085	XX	expansion, ended in divided rule
1085–945	XXI	**Third Intermediate Period**
945–730	XXII	Revival of prosperity and
817?–730	XXIII	restoration of cults
720–715	XXIV	
751–668	XXV	
664–525	XXVI	**Late Period**
525–404	XXVII	Completion of Nile–
404–399	XXVIII	Red Sea canal
399–380	XXIX	
380–343	XXX	
343–332	XXXI	Alexander the Great reached Alexandria in 332 BC

ANCIENT CHINA: DYNASTIES

Regnal dates	Name
22nd–18th-c BC	Hsai Dynasty
18th–12th-c BC	Shang or Yin Dynasty
1111–770 BC	Western (Hsi) Chou Dynasty
770–256 BC	Eastern (Tung) Chou Dynasty
475–221 BC	Warring States Period
221–206 BC	Ch'in Dynasty (Unified Empire)
206 BC–220 AD	Han Dynasty
206 BC–9 AD	Western (Hsi) Han
9–23 AD	Hsin (Wang Mang, usurper)
25–220 AD	Eastern (Tung) Han
220–265 AD	Three Kingdoms (San-kuo)
265–317 AD	Western (Hsi) Chin Dynasty
317–420 AD	Eastern (Tung) Chin Dynasty
420–589 AD	Southern Dynasties
581–618 AD	Sui Dynasty (Unified China)
618–907 AD	Tang Dynasty
907–960 AD	Five Dynasties and Ten Kingdoms Period
960–1279 AD	Sung Dynasty
960–1127 AD	Northern (Pei) Sung
990–1227 AD	Western (Hsi) Sung
1115–1234 AD	Chin or Juchen Dynasty (Tartars)
1206–1368 AD	Yuan or Mongol Dynasty
1368–1644 AD	Ming Dynasty (Capital at Nanking (1368–1421), and Peking (1421–1644)
1644–1911	Ching or Manchu Dynasty

MUGHAL EMPERORS

The 2nd Mughal emperor, Humayun lost his throne in 1540, became a fugitive, and did not regain his title until 1555.

Regnal dates	Name
1526–30	Babur
1530–56	Humayun
1556–1605	Akbar
1605–27	Jahangir
1627–58	Shah Jahan
1658–1707	Aurangzeb (Alamgir)
1707–12	Bahadur Shah I (or Shah Alam I)
1712–13	Jahandar Shah
1713–19	Farruksiyar
1719	Rafid-ud-Darajat
1719	Rafi-ud-Daulat
1719	Nekusiyar
1719	Ibrahim
1719–48	Muhammad Shah
1748–54	Ahmad Shah
1754–9	Alamgir II
1759–1806	Shah Alam II
1806–37	Akbar II
1837–57	Bahadur Shah II

JAPANESE EMPERORS

The first 14 emperors (to Chuai) are regarded as legendary, and the regnal dates for the 15th to the 28th emperor (Senka), taken from the early Japanese chronicle, 'Nihon shoki' are not considered to be authentic.

Regnal dates	Name
660–585 BC	Jimmu
581–549 BC	Suizei
549–511 BC	Annei
510–477 BC	Itoku
475–393 BC	Kosho
392–291 BC	Koan
290–215 BC	Korei
214–158 BC	Kogen
158–98 BC	Kaika
97–30 BC	Sujin
29 BC–70 AD	Suinin
71 AD–130 AD	Keiko
131–190 AD	Selmu
192–200 AD	Chuai
270–310 AD	Ojin
313–399 AD	Nintoku
400–405 AD	Richu
406–410 AD	Hanzel
412–453 AD	Ingyo
453–456 AD	Anko
456–479 AD	Yuryaku
480–484 AD	Seinei
485–487 AD	Kenzo
488–498 AD	Ninken
498–506 AD	Buretsu
507–531 AD	Keitai
531–535 AD	Ankan
535–539 AD	Senka
539–571 AD	Kimmei
572–585 AD	Bidatsu
585–587 AD	Yomei
587–592 AD	Sushun
592–628 AD	Suiko
629–641 AD	Jomei
642–645 AD	Kogyoku
645–654 AD	Kotuko
655–661 AD	Saimei
662–671 AD	Tenji
671–672 AD	Kobun
673–686 AD	Temmu
686–697 AD	Jito
697–707 AD	Mommu
707–715 AD	Gemmei
715–724 AD	Gensho
724–749 AD	Shomu
749–758 AD	Koken
758–764 AD	Junnin
764–770 AD	Shotoku
770–781 AD	Konin
781–806 AD	Kammu
806–809 AD	Heizei
809–823 AD	Saga
823–833 AD	Junna
833–850 AD	Nimmyo
850–858 AD	Montoku
858–876 AD	Seiwa
876–884 AD	Yozei
884–887 AD	Koko
887–897 AD	Uda
897–930 AD	Daigo
930–946 AD	Suzaku
946–967 AD	Murakami
967–969 AD	Reizei
969–984 AD	En'yu
984–986 AD	Kazan
986–1011 AD	Ichijo
1011–16 AD	Sanjo
1016–36	Go-Ichijo
1036–45	Go-Suzako
1045–68	Go-Reizei
1068–72	Go-Sanyo
1072–86	Shirakawa
1086–1107	Horikawa
1107–23	Toba
1123–41	Sutoku
1141–55	Konoe
1155–8	Goshirakawa
1158–65	Nijo
1165–8	Rokujo
1168–80	Takakura
1180–3	Antoku
1183–98	Go-Toba
1198–1210	Tsuchimikado
1210–21	Juntoku
1221	Chukyo
1221–32	Goshirakawa
1232–42	Shijo
1242–6	Go-Saga
1246–59	Go-Fukakusa
1259–74	Kameyama
1274–87	Go-Uda
1287–98	Fushimi
1298–1301	Go-Fushimi
1301–8	Go-Nijo
1308–18	Hanazono
1318–39	Go-Daigo
1339–68	Go-Murakami
1368–83	Chokei
1383–92	Go-Kameyama
Northern Court	
1331–3	Kogon
1336–48	Komyo
1348–51	Suko
1352–71	Go-Kogon
1371–82	Go-Enyu
1382–1412	Go-Komatsu
1412–28	Shoko
1428–64	Go-Hanazono
1464–1500	Go-Tsuchimikado
1500–26	Go-Kashiwabara
1526–57	Go-Nara
1557–86	Ogimachi
1586–1611	Go-Yozei
1611–29	Go-Mizunoo
1629–43	Meisho
1643–54	Go-Komyo
1654–63	Go-Sai
1663–87	Reigen
1687–1709	Higashiyama
1709–35	Nakamikado
1735–47	Sakuramachi
1747–62	Momozono
1762–70	Go-Sakuramachi
1770–9	Go-Momozono
1779–1817	Kokaku
1817–46	Ninko
1846–66	Komei
1867–1912	Meiji
1912–26	Taisho
1926–89	Hirohito
1989–	Akihito

ROMAN KINGS

The founding of Rome by Romulus is a Roman literary tradition.

Regnal dates	Name
753–715 BC	Romulus
715–673 BC	Numa Pompilius
673–642 BC	Tullus Hostilius
642–616 BC	Ancus Marcius
616–578 BC	Tarquinius Priscus
578–534 BC	Servius Tullius
534–509 BC	Tarquinius Superbus

ROMAN EMPERORS

Dates overlap where there are periods of joint rule (e.g. Marcus Aurelius and Lucius Verus) and where the government of the empire divides between east and west.

Regnal dates	Name
27 BC–14 AD	Augustus (Caesar Augustus)
14–37	Tiberius
37–41	Caligula (Gaius Caesar)
41–54	Claudius
54–68	Nero
68–69	Galba
69	Otho
69	Vitellius
69–79	Vespasian
79–81	Titus
81–96	Domitian
96–98	Nerva
98–117	Trajan
117–138	Hadrian
138–161	Antoninus Pius
161–180	Marcus Aurelius
161–169	Lucius Verus
176–192	Commodus
193	Pertinax
193	Didius Julianus
193–211	Septemius Severus
198–217	Caracalla
209–212	Geta
217–218	Macrinus
218–222	Elagabalus
222–235	Alexander Severus
235–238	Maximin
238	Gordian I
238	Gordian II
238	Maximus
238	Balbinus
238–244	Gordian III
244–249	Philip
249–251	Decius
251	Hostilian
251–253	Gallus
253	Aemilian
253–260	Valerian
253–268	Gallienus
268–269	Claudius II (the Goth)
269–270	Quintillus
270–275	Aurelian
275–276	Tacitus
276	Florian
276–282	Probus
282–283	Carus
283–285	Carinus
283–284	Numerian
284–305	Diocletian–(East)
286–305	Maximian–(West)
305–311	Galerius–(East)
305–306	Constantius I
306–307	Severus–(West)
306–312	Maxentius–(West)
306–337	Constantine I
308–324	Licinius–(East)
337–340	Constantine II
337–350	Constans I
337–361	Constantius II
350–351	Magnentius
360–363	Julian
363–364	Jovian
364–375	Valentinian I–(West)
364–378	Valens–(East)
365–366	Procopius–(East)
375–383	Gratian–(West)
375–392	Valentinian II–(West)
379–395	Theodosius I
395–408	Arcadius–(East)
395–423	Honorius–(West)
408–450	Theodosius II–(East)
421–423	Constantius III–(West)
423–455	Valentinian III–(West)
450–457	Marcian–(East)
455	Petronius Maximus–(West)
455–456	Avitus–(West)
457–474	Leo I–(East)
457–461	Majorian–(West)
461–467	Libius Severus–(West)
467–472	Anthemius–(West)
472–473	Olybrius–(West)
474–480	Julius Nepos–(West)
474	Leo II–(East)
474–491	Zeno–(East)
475–476	Romulus Augustus–(West)

HOLY ROMAN EMPERORS

Regnal dates	Name
800–814	Charlemagne (Charles I)
814–840	Louis I (the Pious)
840–843	(Civil War)
843–855	Lothair I
855–875	Louis II
875–877	Charles II (the Bald)
877–881	(Interregnum)
881–887	Charles III (the Fat)
887–891	*Interregnum*
891–894	Guido of Spoleto
892–898	Lambert of Spoleto[1]
896–899	Arnulf[2]
901–905	Louis III
911–918	Conrad I[2]
905–924	Berengar
919–936	Henry I
936–973	Otto I (the Great)
973–983	Otto II
983–1002	Otto III
1002–24	Henry II (the Saint)
1024–39	Conrad II
1039–56	Henry III (the Black)
1056–1106	Henry IV
1077–80	Rudolf[2]
1081–93	Hermann[2]
1093–1101	Conrad[2]
1106–25	Henry V
1125–37	Lothair II
1138–52	Conrad III
1152–90	Frederick I (Barbarossa)
1190–7	Henry VI
1198–1208	Philip[2]
1198–1214	Otto IV
1215–50	Frederick II
1246–7	Henry Raspe[2]
1247–56	William of Holland[2]
1250–4	Conrad IV
1254–73	*Great Interregnum*
1257–72	Richard[2]
1257–75	Alfonso (Alfonso X of Castile)[2]
1273–91	Rudolf I
1292–8	Adolf
1298–1308	Albert I
1308–13	Henry VII
1314–26	Frederick (III)[3]
1314–46	Louis IV
1346–78	Charles IV
1378–1400	Wenceslas
1400–10	Rupert
1410–37	Sigismund
1438–9	Albert II
1440–93	Frederick III
1493–1519	Maximilian I
1519–56	Charles V
1556–64	Ferdinand I
1564–76	Maximilian II
1576–1612	Rudolf II
1612–19	Matthias
1619–37	Ferdinand II
1637–57	Ferdinand III
1658–1705	Leopold I
1705–11	Joseph I
1711–40	Charles VI
1740–42	*Interregnum*
1742–5	Charles VII
1745–65	Francis I
1765–90	Joseph II
1790–2	Leopold II
1792–1806	Francis II

[1]Co-emperor
[2]Rival
[3]Co-regent

RUSSIAN RULERS

In 1610 Vasili Shuisky was deposed as Tsar and the throne remained vacant until the election of Michael Romanov in 1613. In 1682 a condition of the succession was that the two step-brothers, Ivan V and Peter I (the Great) should jointly be proclaimed as Tsars. In 1917 the empire was overthrown and Tsar Nicholas II was forced to abdicate.

Regnal dates	Name
1283–1303	Daniel
1303–25	Yuri
1325–41	Ivan I
1341–53	Semeon
1353–59	Ivan II
1359–89	Dimitri Donskoy
1389–1425	Vasili I
1425–62	Vasili II
1462–1505	Ivan III (the Great)
1505–33	Vasili III
1533–84	Ivan IV (the Terrible)
1584–98	Feodor I
1598–1605	Boris Godunov
1605	Feodor II
1605–6	Dimitri II
1606–10	Vasili IV Shuisky
1613–45	Michael Romanov
1645–76	Alexei
1676–82	Feodor III
1682–96	Ivan V
1682–1725	Peter I (the Great)
1725–7	Catherine I
1727–30	Peter II
1730–40	Anne
1740–1	Ivan VI
1741–62	Elizabeth
1762	Peter III
1762–96	Catherine II (the Great)
1796–1801	Paul
1810–25	Alexander I
1825–55	Nicholas I
1855–81	Alexander II
1881–94	Alexander III
1894–1917	Nicholas II

POPES

Antipopes (who claimed to be pope in opposition to those canonically chosen) are given in parentheses.

until *c*.64	Peter
c.64–*c*.76	Linus
c.76–*c*.90	Anacletus
c.90–*c*.99	Clement I
c.99–*c*.105	Evaristus
c.105–*c*.117	Alexander I
c.117–*c*.127	Sixtus I
c.127–*c*.137	Telesphorus
c.137–*c*.140	Hyginus
c.140–*c*.154	Pius I
c.154–*c*.166	Anicetus
c.166–*c*.175	Soter
175–89	Eleutherius
189–98	Victor I
198–217	Zephyrinus
217–22	Callistus I
[217–*c*.235	Hippolytus]
222–30	Urban I
230–5	Pontian
235–6	Anterus
236–50	Fabian
251–3	Cornelius
[251–*c*.258	Novatian]
253–4	Lucius I
254–7	Stephen I
257–8	Sixtus II
259–68	Dionysius
269–74	Felix I
275–83	Eutychianus
283–96	Caius
296–304	Marcellinus
308–9	Marcellus I
310	Eusebius
311–314	Miltiades
314–35	Sylvester I
336	Mark
337–52	Julius I
352–66	Liberius
[355–65	Felix II]
366–84	Damasus I
[366–7	Ursinus]
384–99	Siricius
399–401	Anastasius I
402–17	Innocent I
417–18	Zosimus
418–22	Boniface I
[418–19	Eulalius]
422–32	Celestine I
432–40	Sixtus III
440–61	Leo I
461–8	Hilarus
468–83	Simplicius
483–92	Felix III (II)
492–6	Gelasius I
496–8	Anastasius II
498–514	Symmachus
[498, 501–5	Laurentius]
514–23	Hormisdas
523–6	John I
526–30	Felix IV (III)
530–2	Boniface II
[530	Dioscorus]
533–5	John II
535–6	Agapetus I
536–7	Silverius
537–55	Vigilius
556–61	Pelagius I
561–74	John III
575–9	Benedict I
579–90	Pelagius II
590–604	Gregory I
604–6	Sabinianus
607	Boniface III
608–15	Boniface IV
615–18	Deusdedit *or* Adeodatus I
619–25	Boniface V
625–38	Honorius I
640	Severinus
640–2	John IV
642–9	Theodore I
649–55	Martin I
654–7	Eugenius I[1]
657–72	Vitalian
672–6	Adeodatus II
676–8	Donus
678–81	Agatho
682–3	Leo II
684–5	Benedict II
685–6	John V
686–7	Cono
[687	Theodore]
[687–92	Paschal]
687–701	Sergius I
701–5	John VI
705–7	John VII
708	Sisinnius
708–15	Constantine
715–31	Gregory II
731–41	Gregory III
741–52	Zacharias
752	Stephen II (*not consecrated*)
752–7	Stephen II (III)
757–67	Paul I
[767–9	Constantine II]
[768	Philip]
768–72	Stephen III (IV)
772–95	Hadrian I
795–816	Leo III
816–17	Stephen IV (V)
817–24	Paschal I
824–7	Eugenius II
827	Valentine
827–44	Gregory IV
[844	John]
844–7	Sergius II
847–55	Leo IV
855–8	Benedict III
[855	Anastasius Bibliothecarius]
858–67	Nicholas I
867–72	Hadrian II
872–82	John VIII
882–4	Marinus I
884–5	Hadrian III
885–91	Stephen V (VI)
891–6	Formosus
896	Boniface VI
896–7	Stephen VI (VII)
897	Romanus
897	Theodore II
898–900	John IX
900–3	Benedict IV
903	Leo V
[903–4	Christopher]
904–11	Sergius III
911–13	Anastasius III
913–14	Lando
914–28	John X
928	Leo VI
928–31	Stephen VII (VIII)
931–5	John XI
936–9	Leo VII
939–42	Stephen IX
942–6	Marinus II
946–55	Agapetus II
955–64	John XII
963–5	Leo VIII
964–6	Benedict V
965–72	John XIII
973–4	Benedict VI
[974, 984–5	Boniface VII]
974–83	Benedict VII

POPES (cont.)

983–4	John XIV
985–96	John XV
996–9	Gregory V
[997–8	John XVI]
999–1003	Sylvester II
1003	John XVII
1004–9	John XVIII
1009–12	Sergius IV
1012–24	Benedict VIII
[1012	Gregory]
1024–32	John XIX
1032–44	Benedict IX
1045	Sylvester III
1045	Benedict IX (*second reign*)
1045–6	Gregory VI
1046–7	Clement II
1047–8	Benedict IX (*third reign*)
1048	Damasus II
1048–54	Leo IX
1055–7	Victor II
1057–8	Stephen IX (X)
[1058–9	Benedict X]
1059–61	Nicholas II
1061–73	Alexander II
[1061–72	Honorius II]
1073–85	Gregory VII
[1080, 1084–1100	Clement III]
1086–7	Victor III
1088–99	Urban II
1099–1118	Paschal II
[1100–2	Theodoric]
[1102	Albert]
[1105–11	Sylvester IV]
1118–19	Gelasius II
[1118–21	Gregory VIII]
1119–24	Callistus II
1124–30	Honorius II
[1124	Celestine II]
1130–43	Innocent II
[1130–8	Anacletus II]
[1138	Victor IV][2]
1143–4	Celestine II
1144–5	Lucius II
1145–53	Eugenius III
1153–4	Anastasius IV
1154–9	Hadrian IV
1159–81	Alexander III
[1159–64	Victor IV][2]
[1164–8	Paschal III]
[1168–78	Callistus III]
[1179–80	Innocent III]
1181–5	Lucius III
1185–7	Urban III
1187	Gregory VIII
1187–91	Clement III
1191–8	Celestine III
1198–1216	Innocent III
1216–27	Honorius III
1227–41	Gregory IX
1241	Celestine IV
1243–54	Innocent IV
1254–61	Alexander IV
1261–4	Urban IV
1265–8	Clement IV
1271–6	Gregory X
1276	Innocent V
1276	Hadrian V
1276–7	John XXI[3]
1277–80	Nicholas III
1281–5	Martin IV
1285–7	Honorius IV
1288–92	Nicholas IV
1294	Celestine V
1294–1303	Boniface VIII
1303–4	Benedict XI
1305–14	Clement V
1316–34	John XXII
[1328–30	Nicholas V]
1334–42	Benedict XII
1342–52	Clement VI
1352–62	Innocent VI
1362–70	Urban V
1370–8	Gregory XI
1378–89	Urban VI
[1378–94	Clement VII]
1389–1404	Boniface IX
[1394–1423	Benedict XIII]
1404–6	Innocent VII
1406–15	Gregory XII
[1409–10	Alexander V]
[1410–15	John XXIII]
1417–31	Martin V
[1423–9	Clement VIII]
[1425–30	Benedict XIV]
1431–47	Eugenius IV
[1439–49	Felix V]
1447–55	Nicholas V
1455–8	Callistus III
1458–64	Pius II
1464–71	Paul II
1471–84	Sixtus IV
1484–92	Innocent VIII
1492–1503	Alexander VI
1503	Pius III
1503–13	Julius II
1513–21	Leo X
1522–3	Hadrian VI
1523–34	Clement VII
1534–49	Paul III
1550–5	Julius III
1555	Marcellus II
1555–9	Paul IV
1559–65	Pius IV
1566–72	Pius V
1572–85	Gregory XIII
1585–90	Sixtus V
1590	Urban VII
1590–1	Gregory XIV
1591	Innocent IX
1592–1605	Clement VIII
1605	Leo XI
1605–21	Paul V
1621–3	Gregory XV
1623–44	Urban VIII
1644–55	Innocent X
1655–67	Alexander VII
1667–9	Clement IX
1670–6	Clement X
1676–89	Innocent XI
1689–91	Alexander VIII
1691–1700	Innocent XII
1700–21	Clement XI
1721–4	Innocent XIII
1724–30	Benedict XIII
1730–40	Clement XII
1740–58	Benedict XIV
1758–69	Clement XIII
1769–74	Clement XIV
1775–99	Pius VI
1800–23	Pius VII
1823–9	Leo XII
1829–30	Pius VIII
1831–46	Gregory XVI
1846–78	Pius IX
1878–1903	Leo XIII
1903–14	Pius X
1914–22	Benedict XV
1922–39	Pius XI
1939–58	Pius XII
1958–63	John XXIII
1963–78	Paul VI
1978	John Paul I
1978–	John Paul II

[1] Elected during the banishment of Martin I [2] Different individuals [3] There was no John XX

POLITICAL LEADERS 1900–1992

Countries and organizations are listed alphabetically. Rulers are named chronologically since 1900 or (for new nations) since independence. For the major English-speaking nations, relevant details are also given of pre-20th-century rulers, along with a note of any political affiliation.

The list does not distinguish successive terms of office by a single ruler.

There is no universally agreed way of transliterating proper names in non-Roman alphabets; variations from the spellings given are therefore to be expected, especially in the case of Arabic rulers.

Minor variations in the titles adopted by Chiefs of State, or in the name of an administration, are not given; these occur most notably in countries under military rule.

Listings complete to June 1992.

AFGHANISTAN

Afghan Empire

Monarch

1881–1901 Abdur Rahman Khan
1901–19 Habibullah Khan
1919–29 Inayatullah Khan
1929 Habibullah Ghazi
1929–33 Nadir Shah
1933–73 Zahir Shah

Republic of Afghanistan

Prime Minister

1973–8 Mohammad Daoud Khan

Democratic Republic of Afghanistan Revolutionary Council

President

1978–9 Nur Mohammad Taraki
1979 Hafizullah Amin

Soviet Invasion

1979–86 Babrak Karmal
1986–7 Haji Mohammad Chamkani *Acting President*
1987–92 Mohammad Najibullah
1992 Sibghatullah Mojaddedi *Acting President*
1992– Burhanuddin Rabbani

General Secretary

1978–86 *As President*
1986–92 Mohammad Najibullah

Prime Minister

1929–46 Sardar Mohammad Hashim Khan
1946–53 Shah Mahmoud Khan Ghazi
1953–63 Mohammad Daoud
1963–5 Mohammad Yousef
1965–7 Mohammad Hashim Maiwandwal
1967–71 Nour Ahmad Etemadi
1972–3 Mohammad Mousa Shafiq
1973–9 *As President*
1979–81 Babrak Karmal
1981–8 Sultan Ali Keshtmand

Republic of Afghanistan from 1987

1988–9 Mohammad Hasan Sharq
1989–90 Sultan Ali Keshtmand
1990–92 Fazal Haq Khaliqyar
1992–

ALBANIA

Monarch

1928–39 Zog I (Ahmed Zogu)
1939–44 *Italian rule*

People's Socialist Republic

President

1944–85 Enver Hoxha
1985–92 Ramiz Alia

Republic of Albania from 1991

1992– Sali Berisha

Prime Minister

1914 Turhan Pashë Permëti
1914 Esad Toptani
1914–18 Abdullah Rushdi
1918–20 Turhan Pashë Permëti
1920 Sulejman Deluina
1920–1 Iljaz Bej Vrioni
1921 Pandeli Evangeli
1921 Xhafer Ypi
1921–2 Omer Vrioni
1922–4 Ahmed Zogu
1924 Iljaz Bej Vrioni
1924–5 Fan Noli

POLITICAL LEADERS 1900–1992 (cont.)

1925–8	Ahmed Zogu
1928–30	Koço Kota
1930–5	Pandeli Evangeli
1935–6	Mehdi Frashëri
1936–9	Koço Kota
1939–41	Shefqet Verlaci
1941–3	Mustafa Merlika-Kruja
1943	Eqrem Libohova
1943	Maliq Bushati
1943	Eqrem Libohova
1943	*Provisional Executive Committee* (Ibrahim Biçakçlu)
1943	*Council of Regents* (Mehdi Frashëri)
1943–4	Rexhep Mitrovica
1944	Fiori Dine
1944–54	Enver Hoxha
1954–81	Mehmed Shehu
1981–91	Adil Carcani
1991–	Fatos Nano

ALGERIA

President

1962–5	Ahmed Ben Bella
1965–78	Houari Boumédienne
1979–92	Bendjedid Chadli
1992	High Commission of State: chair Mohamed Boudiaf

ANGOLA

President

1975–9	Antonio Agostinho Neto
1979–	José Eduardo dos Santos

ANTIGUA AND BARBUDA

Prime Minister

1981–	Cornwall Vere Bird

ARGENTINA

President

1898–1904	Julio Argentino Roca
1904–6	Manuel Quintana
1906–10	José Figueroa Alcorta
1910–14	Roque Sáenz Peña
1914–16	Victorino de la Plaza
1916–22	Hipólito Yrigoyen
1922–8	Marcelo T de Alvear
1928–30	Hipólito Yrigoyen
1930–2	José Félix Uriburu
1932–8	Augustin Pedro Justo
1938–40	Roberto M Ortiz
1940–3	Ramón S Castillo
1943–4	Pedro P Ramírez
1944–6	Edelmiro J Farrell
1946–55	Juan Perón
1955–8	Eduardo Lonardi
1958–62	Arturo Frondizi
1962–3	José María Guido
1963–6	Arturo Illia
1966–70	Juan Carlos Onganía
1970–1	Roberto Marcelo Levingston
1971–3	Alejandro Agustin Lanusse
1973	Héctor J Cámpora
1973–4	Juan Perón
1974–6	Martínez de Perón
1976–81	*Military Junta* (Jorge Rafaél Videla)
1981	*Military Junta* (Roberto Eduardo Viola)
1981–2	*Military Junta* (Leopoldo Galtieri)
1982–3	Reynaldo Bignone
1983–8	Raúl Alfonsín
1988–	Carlos Menem

ARMENIA

President

1991–	Levon Ter-Petrosyan

AUSTRALIA

Chief of State: British monarch, represented by Governor General

Prime Minister

1901–3	Edmund Barton *Prot*
1903–4	Alfred Deakin *Prot*
1904	John Christian Watson *Lab*
1904–5	George Houston Reid *Free*
1905–8	Alfred Deakin *Prot*
1908–9	Andrew Fisher *Lab*
1909–10	Alfred Deakin *Fusion*
1910–13	Andrew Fisher *Lab*

POLITICAL LEADERS 1900–1992 (cont.)

Australia (cont.)

1913–14 Joseph Cook *Lib*
1914–15 Andrew Fisher *Lab*
1915–17 William Morris Hughes *Nat Lab*
1917–23 William Morris Hughes *Nat*
1923–9 Stanley Melbourne Bruce *Nat*
1929–32 James Henry Scullin *Lab*
1932–9 Joseph Aloysius Lyons *Un*
1939 Earle Christmas Page *Co*
1939–41 Robert Gordon Menzies *Un*
1941 Arthur William Fadden *Co*
1941–5 John Joseph Curtin *Lab*
1945 Francis Michael Forde *Lab*
1945–9 Joseph Benedict Chifley *Lab*
1949–66 Robert Gordon Menzies *Lib*
1966–7 Harold Edward Holt *Lib*
1967–8 John McEwen *Co*
1968–71 John Grey Gorton *Lib*
1971–2 William McMahon *Lib*
1972–5 Edward Gough Whitlam *Lab*
1975–83 John Malcolm Fraser *Lib*
1983–91 Robert James Lee Hawke *Lab*
1991– Paul Keating *Lab*

Co *Country*
Free *Free Trade*
Lab *Labor*
Lib *Liberal*
Nat *Nationalist*
Nat Lab *National Labor*
Prot *Protectionist*
Un *United*

AUSTRIA

President

1918–20 Karl Sätz
1920–8 Michael Hainisch
1928–38 Wilhelm Miklas
1938–45 *German rule*
1945–50 Karl Renner
1950–7 Theodor Körner
1957–65 Adolf Schärf
1965–74 Franz Jonas
1974–86 Rudolf Kirchsläger
1986–92 Kurt Waldheim
1992– Thomas Klestil

Chancellor

1918–20 Karl Renner
1920–1 Michael Mayr
1921–2 Johann Schober
1922 Walter Breisky
1922 Johann Schober
1922–4 Ignaz Seipel
1924–6 Rudolph Ramek
1926–9 Ignaz Seipel
1929–30 Ernst Streeruwitz
1930 Johann Schober
1930 Carl Vaugoin
1930–1 Otto Ender
1931–2 Karl Buresch
1932–4 Engelbert Dollfus
1934–8 Kurt von Schuschnigg
1938–45 *German rule*
1945 Karl Renner
1945–53 Leopold Figl
1953–61 Julius Raab
1961–4 Alfons Gorbach
1964–70 Josef Klaus
1970–83 Bruno Kreisky
1983–6 Fred Sinowatz
1986– Franz Vranitzky

AZERBAIJAN

President

1991–2 Ayaz Mutalibov
1992 Yakub Mamedov *Acting President*
1992– Abul Fez Elchibey

THE BAHAMAS

Chief of State: British monarch, represented by Governor General

Prime Minister

1973– Lynden O Pindling

BAHRAIN

Emir

1971– Isa Bin Salman Al-Khalifa

Prime Minister

1971– Khalifa Bin Salman Al-Khalifa

POLITICAL LEADERS 1900–1992 (cont.)

BANGLADESH

President

1971–2	Sayed Nazrul Islam *Acting President*
1972	Mujibur Rahman
1972–3	Abu Saeed Chowdhury
1974–5	Mohammadullah
1975	Mujibur Rahman
1975	Khondaker Mushtaq Ahmad
1975–7	Abu Saadat Mohammad Sayem
1977–81	Zia Ur-Rahman
1981–2	Abdus Sattar
1982–3	Abdul Fazal Mohammad Ahsanuddin Chowdhury
1983–90	Hossain Mohammad Ershad
1990–91	Shehabuddin Ahmed *Acting President*
1991–	Abdur Rahman Biswas

Prime Minister

1971–2	Tajuddin Ahmed
1972–5	Mujibur Rahman
1975	Mohammad Monsur Ali
1975–9	*Martial Law*
1979–82	Mohammad Azizur Rahman
1982–4	*Martial Law*
1984–5	Ataur Rahman Khan
1986–88	Mizanur Rahman Chowdhury
1988–90	Kazi Zafar Ahmed
1991–	Begum Khaleda Zia

BARBADOS

Prime Minister

1966–76	Errol Walton Barrow
1976–85	JMG (Tom) Adams
1985–6	H Bernard St John
1986–7	Errol Walton Barrow
1987–	L Erskine Sandiford

BELGIUM

Monarch

1865–1909	Leopold II
1909–34	Albert I
1934–50	Leopold III
1950–	Baudoin I

Prime Minister

1899–1907	Paul de Smet de Nayer
1907–8	Jules de Trooz
1908–11	Frans Schollaert
1911–18	Charles de Broqueville
1918	Gerhard Cooreman
1918–20	Léon Delacroix
1920–1	Henri Carton de Wiart
1921–5	Georges Theunis
1925	Alois van de Vyvere
1925–6	Prosper Poullet
1926–31	Henri Jaspar
1931–2	Jules Renkin
1932–4	Charles de Broqueville
1934–5	Georges Theunis
1935–7	Paul van Zeeland
1937–8	Paul Émile Janson
1938–9	Paul Henri Spaak
1939–45	Hubert Pierlot
1945–6	Achille van Acker
1946	Paul Spaak
1946	Achille van Acker
1946–7	Camille Huysmans
1947–9	Paul Spaak
1949–50	Gaston Eyskens
1950	Jean Pierre Duvieusart
1950–2	Joseph Pholien
1952–4	Jean van Houtte
1954–8	Achille van Acker
1958–61	Gaston Eyskens
1961–5	Théodore Lefèvre
1965–6	Pierre Harmel
1966–8	Paul Vanden Boeynants
1968–72	Gaston Eyskens
1973–4	Edmond Leburton
1974–8	Léo Tindemans
1978	Paul Vanden Boeynants
1979–81	Wilfried Martens
1981	Marc Eyskens
1981–91	Wilfried Martens
1992–	Luke Dehaene

BELIZE

Chief of State: British Monarch, represented by Governor General

Prime Minister

1981–4	George Cadle Price
1985–9	Manuel Esquivel
1989–	George Cadle Price

POLITICAL LEADERS 1900–1992 (cont.)

BENIN

President

Dahomey

1960–3 Hubert Coutoucou Maga
1963–4 Christophe Soglo
1964–5 Sourou Migan Apithy
1965 Justin Tométin Ahomadegbé
1965 Tairou Congacou
1965–7 Christophe Soglo
1967–8 Alphonse Amadou Alley
1968–9 Émile Derlin Zinsou
1969–70 *Presidential Committee* (Maurice Kouandete)
1970–2 (Hubert Coutoucou Maga)
1972–5 Mathieu Kerekou

People's Republic of Benin

1975–91 Mathieu (*from 1980* Ahmed) Kerekou

Republic of Benin

1991– Nicéphore Soglo

Prime Minister

1958–9 Sourou Migan Apithy
1959–60 Hubert Coutoucou Maga
1960–4 *As President*
1964–5 Justin Tométin Ahomadegbé
1965–7 *As President*
1967–8 Maurice Kouandete
1968–90 *As President*

Republic of Benin

1990– Nicéphore Soglo

BHUTAN

Monarch (Druk Gyalpo)

1907–26 Uggyen Wangchuk
1926–52 Jigme Wangchuk
1952–72 Jigme Dorji Wangchuk
1972– Jigme Singye Wangchuk

BOLIVIA

President

1899–1904 José Manual Pando
1904–9 Ismael Montes
1909–13 Heliodoro Villazón
1913–17 Ismael Montes
1917–20 José N Gutiérrez Guerra
1920–5 Bautista Saavedra
1925–6 José Cabina Villanueva
1926–30 Hernando Siles
1930 Roberto Hinojusa *President of Revolutionaries*
1930–1 Carlos Blanco Galindo
1931–4 Daniel Salamanca
1934–6 José Luis Tejado Sorzano
1936–7 David Toro
1937–9 Germán Busch
1939 Carlos Quintanilla
1940–3 Enrique Peñaranda y del Castillo
1943–6 Gualberto Villaroel
1946 Nestor Guillen
1946–7 Tomas Monje Gutiérrez
1947–9 Enrique Hertzog
1949 Mamerto Urriolagoitía
1951–2 Hugo Ballivián
1952 Hernán Siles Suazo
1952–6 Victor Paz Estenssoro
1956–60 Hernán Siles Suazo
1960–4 Victor Paz Estenssoro
1964–5 René Barrientos Ortuño
1965–6 René Barrientos Ortuño *and* Alfredo Ovando Candía
1966 Alfredo Ovando Candía
1966–9 René Barrientos Ortuño
1969 Luis Adolfo Siles Salinas
1969–70 Alfredo Ovando Candía
1970 Rogelio Mirando
1970–1 Juan José Torres Gonzales
1971–8 Hugo Banzer Suárez
1978 Juan Pereda Asbún
1978–9 *Military Junta* (David Padilla Arericiba)
1979 Walter Guevara Arze
1979–80 Lydia Gueiler Tejada
1980–1 *Military Junta* (Luis García Meza)
1981–2 *Military Junta* (Celso Torrelio Villa)
1982 Guido Vildoso Calderón
1982–5 Hernán Siles Suazo
1985–9 Victor Paz Estenssoro
1989– Jaime Paz Zamora

BOSNIA-HERZEGOVINA

President

1991– Alija Izetbegovic

POLITICAL LEADERS 1900–1992 (cont.)

BOTSWANA

President

1966–80	Seretse Khama
1980–	Quett Masire

BRAZIL

President

1898–1902	Manuel Ferraz de Campos Sales
1902–6	Francisco de Paula Rodrigues Alves
1906–9	Alfonso Pena
1909–10	Nilo Peçanha
1910–14	Hermes Rodrigues da Fonseca
1914–18	Venceslau Brás Pereira Gomes
1918–19	Francisco de Paula Rodrigues Alves
1919–22	Epitácio Pessoa
1922–6	Artur da Silva Bernardes
1926–30	Washington Luís Pereira de Sousa
1930–45	Getúlio Dorneles Vargas
1945–51	Eurico Gaspar Dutra
1951–4	Getúlio Dorneles Vargas
1954–5	João Café Filho
1955	Carlos Coimbra da Luz
1955–6	Nereu de Oliveira Ramos
1956–61	Juscelino Kubitschek de Oliveira
1961	Jănio da Silva Quadros
1961–3	João Belchior Marques Goulart
1963	Pascoal Ranieri Mazilli
1963–4	João Belchior Marques Goulart
1964	Pascoal Ranieri Mazilli
1964–7	Humberto de Alencar Castelo Branco
1967–9	Artur da Costa e Silva
1969–74	Emílio Garrastazu Médici
1974–9	Ernesto Geisel
1979–85	João Baptista de Oliveira Figueiredo
1985–90	José Sarney
1990–	Fernando Collor de Mello

BRUNEI

Monarch (Sultan)

1967–	Muda Hassanal Bolkiah Muizzadin Waddaulah

BULGARIA

Monarch

1887–1908	Ferdinand *Prince*
1908–18	Ferdinand I
1918–43	Boris III
1943–6	Simeon II

President

1946–7	Vasil Kolarov
1947–50	Mincho Naichev
1950–8	Georgi Damianov
1958–64	Dimitro Ganev
1964–71	Georgi Traikov
1971–89	Todor Zhivkov
1989–90	Petar Mladenov
1990–	Zhelyu Zhelev

Premier

1946–9	Georgi Dimitrov
1949–50	Vasil Kolarov
1950–6	Vulko Chervenkov
1956–62	Anton Yugov
1962–71	Todor Zhivkov
1971–81	Stanko Todorov
1981–86	Grisha Filipov
1986–90	Georgy Atanasov
1990	Andrei Lukanov
1990–91	Dimitur Popov

First Secretary

1946–53	Vulko Chervenkov
1953–89	Todor Zhivkov
1989–90	Petar Mladenov
1990–	Alexander Lilov

Prime Minister

1991–	Filip Dimitrov

BURKINA FASO

President

Upper Volta

1960–6	Maurice Yaméogo
1966–80	Sangoulé Lamizana
1980	Saye Zerbo

POLITICAL LEADERS 1900–1992 (cont.)

Burkina Faso (cont.)

People's Salvation Council
1982–3 Jean-Baptiste Ouedraugo *Chairman*

National Revolutionary Council
1983–4 Thomas Sankara *Chairman*

Burkina Faso
1984–7 Thomas Sankara *Chairman*
1987– Blaise Compaoré

BURMA (Union of Myanma)

President

1948–52 Sao Shwe Thaik
1952–7 Agga Maha Thiri Thudhamma Ba U
1957–62 U Wing Maung
1962 Sama Duwa Sinwa Nawng

Revolutionary Council
1962–74 Ne Win

State Council
1974–81 Ne Win
1981–8 U San Yu
1988 U Sein Lwin
1988 Maung Maung
1988– Saw Maung

Prime Minister

1947–56 Thakin Nu
1956–7 U Ba Swe
1957–8 U Nu
1958–60 Ne Win
1960–2 U Nu
1962–74 Ne Win
1974–7 U Sein Win
1977–8 U Maung Maung Ka
1988 U Tun Tin
1988– Saw Maung

BURUNDI

Monarch

1962–6 Mwambutsa IV
1966 Ntare V

President

1966–77 Michel Micombero
1977–87 Jean-Baptiste Bagaza
1987– *Military Junta* (Pierre Buyoya)

BYELORUSSIA

Chair of Supreme Soviet

1991– Stanislav Shushkevich

CAMBODIA (Kampuchea)

Monarch

1941–55 Norodom Sihanouk II
1955–60 Norodom Suramarit

Chief of State

1960–70 Prince Norodom Sihanouk

Khmer Republic
1970–2 Cheng Heng *Acting Chief of State*
1972–5 Lon Nol
1975–6 Prince Norodom Sihanouk
1976–81 Khieu Samphan
1981– Heng Samrin

Government in exile until 1991

President

1970–5 Prince Norodom Sihanouk
1982– Prince Norodom Sihanouk

Prime Minister

1945–6 Son Ngoc Thanh
1946–8 Prince Monireth
1948–9 Son Ngoc Thanh
1949–51 Prince Monipong
1951 Son Ngoc Thanh
1951–2 Huy Kanthoul
1952–3 Norodom Sihanouk II
1953 Samdech Penn Nouth
1953–4 Chan Nak
1954–5 Leng Ngeth
1955–6 Prince Norodom Sihanouk
1956 Oum Chheang Sun
1956 Prince Norodom Sihanouk
1956 Khim Tit
1956 Prince Norodom Sihanouk
1956 Sam Yun
1956–7 Prince Norodom Sihanouk
1957–8 Sim Var

POLITICAL LEADERS 1900–1992 (cont.)

1958	Ek Yi Oun
1958	Samdech Penn Nouth *Acting Prime Minister*
1958	Sim Var
1958–60	Prince Norodom Sihanouk
1960–1	Pho Proung
1961	Samdech Penn Nouth
1961–3	Prince Norodom Sihanouk
1963–6	Prince Norodom Kantol
1966–7	Lon Nol
1967–8	Prince Norodom Sihanouk
1968–9	Samdech Penn Nouth
1969–72	Lon Nol

Khmer Republic (1970)

1972	Sisovath Sivik Matak
1972	Son Ngoc Thanh
1972–3	Hang Thun Hak
1973	In Tam
1973–5	Long Boret
1975–6	Samdech Penn Nouth
1976–9	Pol Pot
1979–81	Khieu Samphan
1981–5	Chan Si
1985–	Hun Sen

Government in exile until 1991

1970–3	Samdech Penn Nouth
1982–	Son Sann

CAMEROON

President

1960–82	Ahmadun Ahidjo
1982–	Paul Biya

CANADA

Chief of State: British monarch, represented by Governor General

Prime Minister

1867–73	John A MacDonald *Con*
1873–8	Alexander Mackenzie *Lib*
1878–91	John A MacDonald *Con*
1891–2	John J C Abbot *Con*
1892–4	John S D Thompson *Con*
1894–6	Mackenzie Bowell *Con*
1896	Charles Tupper *Con*
1896–1911	Wilfrid Laurier *Lib*
1911–17	Robert Borden *Con*
1917–20	Robert Borden *Con*
1920–1	Arthur Meighen *Con*
1921–6	William Lyon Mackenzie King *Lib*
1926	Arthur Meighen *Con*
1926–30	William Lyon Mackenzie King *Lib*
1930–5	Richard Bedford Bennett *Con*
1935–48	William Lyon Mackenzie King *Lib*
1948–57	Louis St Laurent *Lib*
1957–63	John George Diefenbaker *Con*
1963–8	Lester Bowles Pearson *Lib*
1968–79	Pierre Elliott Trudeau *Lib*
1979–80	Joseph Clark *Con*
1980–4	Pierre Elliott Trudeau *Lib*
1984	John Turner *Lib*
1984–	Brian Mulroney *Con*

Con Conservative
Lib Liberal

CAPE VERDE

President

1975–91	Aristides Pereira
1991–	Antonio Monteiro

Prime Minister

1975–91	Pedro Pires
1991–	Carlos Veiga

CENTRAL AFRICAN REPUBLIC

President

1960–6	David Dacko
1966–79	Jean-Bédel Bokassa (*from 1977,* Emperor Bokassa I)
1979–81	David Dacko
1981–	André Kolingba

CHAD

President

1960–75	François Tombalbaye
1975–9	*Supreme Military Council* (Félix Malloum)
1979	Goukouni Oueddi
1979	Mohammed Shawwa
1979–82	Goukouni Oueddi
1982–90	Hissène Habré
1990–	Idriss Déby

POLITICAL LEADERS 1900–1992 (cont.)

CHILE

President

1900–1	Federico Errázuriz Echaurren
1901	Aníbal Zañartu *Vice President*
1901–3	Germán Riesco
1903	Ramón Barros Luco *Vice President*
1903–6	Germán Riesco
1906–10	Pedro Montt
1910	Ismael Tocornal *Vice President*
1910	Elías Fernández Albano *Vice President*
1910	Emiliano Figueroa Larraín *Vice President*
1910–15	Ramón Barros Luco
1915–20	Juan Luis Sanfuentes
1920–4	Arturo Alessandri
1924–5	*Military Juntas*
1925	Arturo Alessandri
1925	Luis Barros Borgoño *Vice President*
1925–27	Emiliano Figueroa
1927–31	Carlos Ibáñez
1931–	Pedro Opaso Letelier *Vice President*
1931–	Juan Esteban Montero *Vice President*
1931– –	Manuel Trucco Franzani *Vice President*
1931–2	Juan Estaban Montero
1932–	*Military Juntas*
1932–	Carlos G Dávila *Provisional President*
1932– –	Bartolomé Blanche *Provisional President*
1932–	Abraham Oyanedel *Vice President*
1932–8	Arturo Alessandri Palma
1938–41	Pedro Aguirre Cerda
1941–2 –	Jerónimo Méndez Arancibia *Vice President*
1942–6	Juan Antonio Ríos Morales
1946–52	Gabriel González Videla
1952–8	Carlos Ibáñez del Campo
1958–64	Jorge Alessandri Rodríguez
1964–70	Eduardo Frei Montalva
1970–3	Salvador Allende Gossens
1973–90	Augusto Pinochet Ugarte
1990–	Patricio Aylwin Azócar

CHINA

Emperor

1875–1908	Kuang-hsü
1908–12	Hsüan-T'ung

President

1912	Sun Yat-sen
1912–16	Yüan Shih-k'ai
1916–17	Li Yuan-hung
1917–18	Feng Kuo-chang
1918–22	Hsü Shih-ch'ang
1921–5	Sun Yat-sen *Canton Administration*
1922–3	Li Yuan-hung
1923–4	Ts'ao K'un
1924–6	Tuan Ch'i-jui
1926–7	*Civil Disorder*
1927–8	Chang Tso-lin
1928–31	Chiang Kai-shek
1931–2	Ch'eng Ming-hsu *Acting President*
1932–43	Lin Sen
1940–4	Wang Ching-wei *in Japanese-occupied territory*
1943–9	Chiang Kai-shek
1945–9	*Civil War*
1949	Li Tsung-jen

People's Republic of China

1949–59	Mao Zedong (Mao Tse-tung)
1959–68	Liu Shaoqi
1968–75	Dong Biwu
1975–6	Zhu De
1976–8	Sung Qingling
1978–83	Ye Jianying
1983–8	Li Xiannian (Li Hsien-nien)
1988–	Yang Shangkun

Prime Minister

1901–3	Jung-lu
1903–11	Prince Ch'ing
1912	Lu Cheng-hsiang
1912–13	Chao Ping-chiin
1913–14	Sun Pao'chi
1914–16	*no Prime Minister*
1916–17	Chang-hsün
1917	Tuan Ch'i-jui
1918–19	Ch'ien Neng-hsün
1919	Kung Hsin-chan
1919–20	Chin Yün-p'eng
1920	Sa Chen-ping
1920–1	Chin Yün-p'eng
1921–2	Liang Shihi
1922	Yen Hui-ching
1922	Chow Tzu-ch'i
1922	Yen Hui-ching
1922	Wang Ch'ung-hui

POLITICAL LEADERS 1900–1992 (cont.)

1922–3	Wang Ta-hsieh
1923	Chang Shao-ts'ĕng
1923–4	Kao Ling-wei
1924	Jun Pao-ch'i
1924	Ku Wei-chiin
1924	Yen Hui-ch'ing
1924–5	Huang Fu
1925	Tuan Ch'i-jui
1925–6	Hsu Shih-ying
1926	Chia Teh-yao
1926	Hu Wei-te
1926	Yen Hui-ch'ing
1926	Tu Hsi-kuei
1926–7	Ku Wei-chün
1927	*Civil Disorder*
1927	*Executive Council*
1927–9	P'an Fu
1929–30	T'an Yen-kai
1930	Sung Tzu-wen *Acting Prime Minister*
1930	Wang Ching-wei
1930–1	Chiang Kai-shek
1931–2	Sun Fo
1932–5	Wang Ching-wei
1935–7	Chiang Kai-shek
1937–8	Wang Ch'ung-hui *Acting Prime Minister*
1938–9	K'ung Hsiang-hsi
1939–44	Chiang Kai-shek
1944–7	Sung Tzu-wen
1945–9	*Civil War*
1947–8	Chang Ch'ün
1948	Wong Wen-hao
1948–9	Sun Fo
1949	Ho Ying-ch'in
1949	Yen Hsi-shan
1949–76	Zhou Enlai (Chou En-lai)
1976–80	Hua Guofeng
1980–7	Zhao Ziyang (Chao Tzu-yang)
1987–	Li Peng

Communist Party

Chairman

1935–76	Mao Zedong (Mao Tse-tung)
1976–81	Hua Guofeng
1981–2	Hu Yaobang

General Secretary

1982–7	Hu Yaobang
1987–9	Zhao Ziyang (Chao Tzu-yang)
1989–	Jiang Zemin

CIS (Commonwealth of Independent States)

see Armenia, Azerbaijan, Byelorussia, Kazakhstan, Kirghizia, Moldavia, Russia, Tadzhikistan, Turkmenistan, Ukraine, Uzbekistan

COLOMBIA

President

1900–4	José Manuel Marroquín *Vice President*
1904–9	Rafael Reyes
1909–10	Ramón González Valencia
1910–14	Carlos E Restrepo
1914–18	José Vicente Concha
1918–21	Marco Fidel Suárez
1921–2	Jorge Holguín *President Designate*
1922–6	Pedro Nel Ospina
1926–30	Miguel Abadía Méndez
1930–4	Enrique Olaya Herrera
1934–8	Alfonso López
1938–42	Eduardo Santos
1942	Alfonso López
1945–6	Alberto Lleras Camargo *President Designate*
1946–50	Mariano Ospina Pérez
1950–3	Laureano Gómez
1953–7	Gustavo Rojas Pinilla
1957	*Military Junta*
1958–62	Alberto Lleras Camargo
1962–6	Guillermo León Valencia
1966–70	Carlos Lleras Restrepo
1970–4	Misael Pastrana Borrero
1974–8	Alfonso López Michelsen
1978–82	Julio César Turbay Ayala
1982–6	Belisario Betancur
1986–90	Virgilio Barco Vargas
1990–	César Gaviria Trujillo

COMMONWEALTH

Secretary General

1965–75	Arnold Smith
1975–90	Shridath S Ramphal
1990–	Emeka Anyaoku

POLITICAL LEADERS 1900–1992 (cont.)

COMOROS

President

1976–78	Ali Soilih
1978–89	Ahmed Abdallah Abderemane
1989–	Said Mohammed Djohar

CONGO

President

1960–3	Abbé Fulbert Youlou
1963–8	Alphonse Massemba-Debat
1968	Marien Ngouabi
1968	Alphonse Massemba-Debat
1968–9	Alfred Raoul
1969–77	Marien Ngouabi
1977–9	Joachim Yhomby Opango
1979–	Denis Sassou-Nguesso

COSTA RICA

President

1894–1902	Rafael Yglesias y Castro
1902–6	Ascención Esquivel Ibarra
1906–10	Cleto González Víquez
1910–12	Ricardo Jiménez Oreamuno
1912–14	Cleto González Víquez
1914–17	Alfredo González Flores
1917–19	Federico Tinoco Granados
1919	Julio Acosta García
1919–20	Juan Bautista Quiros
1920–4	Julio Acosta García
1924–8	Ricardo Jiménez Oreamuno
1928–32	Cleto González Víquez
1932–6	Ricardo Jiménez Oreamuno
1936–40	León Cortés Castro
1940–4	Rafael Ángel Calderón Guardia
1944–8	Teodoro Picado Michalski
1948	Santos Léon Herrera
1948–9	*Civil Junta* (José Figueres Ferrer)
1949–52	Otilio Ulate Blanco
1952–3	Alberto Oreamuno Flores
1953–8	José Figueres Ferrer
1958–62	Mario Echandi Jiménez
1962–6	Francisco José Orlich Bolmarcich
1966–70	José Joaquín Trejos Fernández
1970–4	José Figueres Ferrer
1974–8	Daniel Oduber Quirós
1978–82	Rodrigo Carazo Odio
1982–6	Luis Alberto Monge Álvarez
1986–90	Oscar Arias Sánchez
1990–	Rafael Angel Calderón

CÔTE D'IVOIRE

President

1960–	Félix Houphouët-Boigny

CROATIA

President

1991–	Franjo Tudjman

CUBA

President

1902–6	Tomas Estrada Palma
1906–9	*US rule*
1909–13	José Miguel Gómez
1913–21	Mario García Menocal
1921–5	Alfredo Zayas y Alfonso
1925–33	Gerardo Machado y Morales
1933	Carlos Manuel de Céspedes
1933–4	Ramón Grau San Martín
1934–5	Carlos Mendieta
1935–6	José A Barnet y Vinagres
1936	Miguel Mariano Gómez y Arias
1936–40	Federico Laredo Bru
1940–4	Fulgencio Batista
1944–8	Ramón Grau San Martín
1948–52	Carlos Prío Socarrás
1952–9	Fulgencio Batista
1959	Manuel Urrutia
1959–76	Osvaldo Dorticós Torrado
1959–76	Fidel Castro Ruz *Prime Minister and First Secretary*
1976–	Fidel Castro Ruz *President*

CYPRUS

President

1960–77	Archbishop Makarios
1977–88	Spyros Kyprianou
1988–	Georgios Vassiliou

POLITICAL LEADERS 1900–1992 (cont.)

CZECHOSLOVAKIA

President

1918–35	Tomáš Garrigue Masaryk
1935–8	Edvard Beneš
1938–9	Emil Hácha

Occupation

1938–45	Edvard Beneš *President in Exile*
1939–45	Emil Hácha *State President*
1939–45	Jozef Tiso *Slovak Republic President*

Post-war

1945–8	Edvard Beneš
1948–53	Klement Gottwald
1953–7	Antonín Zápotocký
1957–68	Antonín Novotný
1968–75	Ludvík Svoboda
1975–89	Gustáv Husák
1989–	Vaclav Havel

Prime Minister

1918–19	Karel Kramář
1919–20	Vlastimil Tusar
1920–1	Jan Černý
1921–2	Edvard Beneš
1922–6	Antonin Švehla
1926	Jan Černý
1926–9	Antonin Švehla
1929–32	František Udržal
1932–5	Jan Malypetr
1935–8	Milan Hodža
1938	Jan Syrový
1938–9	Rudolf Beran
1940–5	Jan Šrámek *in exile*
1945–6	Zdeněk Fierlinger
1946–8	Klement Gottwald
1948–53	Antonin Zápotocký
1953–63	Viliam Široký
1963–8	Josef Lenárt
1968–70	Oldřich Černik
1970–88	Lubomír Štrougal
1988–9	Ladislav Adamec
1989–	Marian Calfa

First Secretary

1948–52	Rudolf Slánsky
1953–68	Antonín Novotný
1968–9	Alexander Dubček
1969–87	Gustáv Husák
1987–9	Mílos Jakes
1989	Karel Urbanek
1989–	Ladislav Adamec

DENMARK

Monarch

1863–1906	Christian IX
1906–12	Frederik VIII
1912–47	Christian X
1947–72	Frederik IX
1972–	Margrethe II

Prime Minister

1900–1	H Sehested
1901–5	J H Deuntzer
1905–8	J C Christensen
1908–9	N Neergaard
1909	L Holstein-Ledreborg
1909–10	C Th Zahle
1910–13	Klaus Berntsen
1913–20	C Th Zahle
1920	Otto Liebe
1920	M P Friis
1920–4	N Neergaard
1924–6	Thorvald Stauning
1926–9	Th Madsen-Mygdal
1929–42	Thorvald Stauning
1942	Wilhelm Buhl
1942–3	Erik Scavenius
1943–5	*No government*
1945	Wilhelm Buhl
1945–7	Knud Kristensen
1947–50	Hans Hedtoft
1950–3	Erik Eriksen
1953–5	Hans Hedtoft
1955–60	Hans Christian Hansen
1960–2	Viggo Kampmann
1962–8	Jens Otto Krag
1968–71	Hilmar Baunsgaard
1971–2	Jens Otto Krag
1972–3	Anker Jorgensen
1973–5	Poul Hartling
1975–82	Anker Jorgensen
1982–	Poul Schlüter

DJIBOUTI

President

1977–	Hassan Gouled Aptidon

POLITICAL LEADERS 1900–1992 (cont.)

Djibouti (cont.)

Prime Minister

1977–8	Abdallah Mohammed Kamil
1978–	Barkat Gourad Hamadou

DOMINICA

President

1978–9	Louis Cods-Lartigue *Interim President*
1977	Frederick E Degazon
1979–80	Lenner Armour *Acting President*
1980–4	Aurelius Marie
1984–	Clarence Augustus Seignoret

Prime Minister

1978–9	Patrick Roland John
1979–80	Oliver Seraphine
1980–	Mary Eugenia Charles

DOMINICAN REPUBLIC

President

1899–1902	Juan Isidro Jiménez
1902–3	Horacio Vásquez
1903	Alejandro Wos y Gil
1903–4	Juan Isidro Jiménez
1904–6	Carlos Morales
1906–11	Ramon Cáceres
1911–12	Eladio Victoria
1912–13	Adolfo Nouel y Bobadilla
1913–14	José Bordas y Valdés
1914	Ramon Báez
1914–16	Juan Isidro Jiménez
1916–22	*US occupation* (Francisco Henríquez y Carrajal)
1922–4	(Juan Batista Vicini Burgos)
1924–30	Horacio Vásquez
1930	Rafael Estrella Urena
1930–8	Rafael Leónidas Trujillo y Molina
1938–40	Jacinto Bienvenudo Peynado
1940–2	Manuel de Jesus Troncoso de la Concha
1942–52	Rafael Leónidas Trujillo y Molina
1952–60	Hector Bienvenido Trujillo
1960–2	Joaquín Videla Balaguer
1962	Rafael Bonnelly
1962	*Military Junta* (Huberto Bogaert)
1962–3	Rafael Bonnelly
1963	Juan Bosch Gavino
1963	*Military Junta* (Emilio de los Santos)
1963–5	Donald Reid Cabral
1965	*Civil War*
1965	Elias Wessin y Wessin
1965	Antonio Imbert Barreras
1965	Francisco Caamaño Deñó
1965–6	Héctor García Godoy Cáceres
1966–78	Joaquín Videla Balaguer
1978–82	Antonio Guzmán Fernández
1982–6	Salvador Jorge Blanco
1986–	Joaquín Videla Balaguer

ECUADOR

President

1895–1901	Eloy Alfaro
1901–5	Leónides Plaza Gutiérrez
1905–6	Lizardo García
1906–11	Eloy Alfaro
1911	Emilio Estrada
1911–12	Carlos Freile Zaldumbide
1912–16	Leónides Plaza Gutiérrez
1916–20	Alfredo Baquerizo Moreno
1920–4	José Luis Tamayo
1924–5	Gonzálo S de Córdova
1925–6	*Military Juntas*
1926–31	Isidro Ayora
1931	Luis A Larrea Alba
1932–3	Juan de Dios Martínez Mera
1933–4	Abelardo Montalvo
1934–5	José María Velasco Ibarra
1935	Antonio Pons
1935–7	Federico Páez
1937–8	Alberto Enriquez Gallo
1938	Manuel María Borrero
1938–9	Aurelio Mosquera Narváez
1939–40	Julio Enrique Moreno
1940–4	Carlos Alberto Arroya del Río
1944–7	José María Velasco Ibarra
1947	Carlos Mancheno
1947–8	Carlos Julio Arosemena Tola
1948–52	Galo Plaza Lasso
1952–6	José María Velasco Ibarra
1956–60	Camilo Ponce Enríquez
1960–1	José María Velasco Ibarra
1961–3	Carlos Julio Arosemena Monroy
1963–6	*Military Junta*
1966	Clemente Yerovi Indaburu
1966–8	Otto Arosemena Gómez
1968–72	José María Velasco Ibarra
1972–6	Guillermo Rodríguez Lara
1976–9	*Military Junta*

POLITICAL LEADERS 1900–1992 (cont.)

1979–81	Jaime Roldós Aguilera
1981–4	Oswaldo Hurtado Larrea
1984–8	León Febres Cordero
1988–	Rodrigo Borja Cevallos

EGYPT

Khedive

1895–1914	Abbas Helmi II

Sultan

1914–17	Hussein Kamel
1917–22	Ahmed Fouad

Kingdom of Egypt

Monarch

1922–36	Fouad I
1936–7	Farouk *Trusteeship*
1937–52	Farouk I

Republic of Egypt

President

1952–4	Mohammed Naguib
1954–70	Gamal Abdel Nasser
1970–81	Mohammed Anwar El-Sadat
1981–	Mohammed Hosni Mubarak

Prime Minister

1895–1908	Mustafa Fahmy
1908–10	Butros Ghali
1910–14	Mohammed Said
1914–19	Hussein Rushdi
1919	Mohammed Said
1919–20	Yousuf Wahba
1920–1	Mohammed Tewfiq Nazim
1921	Adli Yegen
1922	Abdel Khaliq Tharwat
1922–3	Mohammed Tewfiq Nazim
1923–4	Yehia Ibrahim
1924	Saad Zaghloul
1924–6	Ahmed Zaywan
1926–7	Adli Yegen
1927–8	Abdel Khaliq Tharwat
1928	Mustafa An-Nahass
1928–9	Mohammed Mahmoud
1929–30	Adli Yegen
1930	Mustafa An-Nahass
1930–3	Ismail Sidqi
1933–4	Abdel Fattah Yahya
1934–6	Mohammed Tewfiq Nazim
1936	Ali Maher
1936–7	Mustafa An-Nahass
1937–9	Mohammed Mahmoud
1939–40	Ali Maher
1940	Hassan Sabri
1940–2	Hussein Sirry
1942–4	Mustafa An-Nahass
1944–5	Ahmed Maher
1945–6	Mahmoud Fahmy El-Nuqrashi
1946	Ismail Sidqi
1946–8	Mahmoud Fahmy El-Nuqrashi
1948–9	Ibrahim Abdel Hadi
1949–50	Hussein Sirry
1950–2	Mustafa An-Nahass
1952	Ali Maher
1952	Najib El-Hilali
1952	Hussein Sirry
1952	Najib El-Hilali
1952	Ali Maher
1952–4	Mohammed Najib
1954	Gamal Abdel Nasser
1954	Mohammed Najib
1954–62	Gamal Abdel Nasser
1958–61	*United Arab Republic*
1962–5	Ali Sabri
1965–6	Zakariya Mohyi Ed-Din
1966–7	Mohammed Sidqi Soliman
1967–70	Gamal Abdel Nasser
1970–2	Mahmoud Fawzi
1972–3	Aziz Sidki
1973–4	Anwar El-Sadat
1974–5	Abdel Aziz Hijazy
1975–8	Mamdouh Salem
1978–80	Mustafa Khalil
1980–1	Anwar El-Sadat
1981–2	Hosni Mubarak
1982–4	Fouad Monyi Ed-Din
1984	Kamal Hassan Ali
1985–6	Ali Lotfi
1986–	Atif Sidqi

EL SALVADOR

President

1899–1903	Tomás Regalado
1903–7	Pedro José Escalon
1907–11	Fernando Figueroa
1911–13	Manuel Enrique Araujo

POLITICAL LEADERS 1900–1992 (cont.)

El Salvador (cont.)

1913–14	Carlos Meléndez *President Designate*
1914–15	Alfonso Quiñónez Molina *President Designate*
1915–18	Carlos Meléndez
1918–19	Alfonso Quiñónez Molina *Vice President*
1919–23	Jorge Meléndez
1923–7	Alfonso Quiñónez Molina
1927–31	Pio Romero Bosque
1931	Arturo Araujo
1931	*Military Administration*
1931–4	Maximiliano H Martinez *Vice President*
1934–5	Andrés I Menéndez *Provisional President*
1935–44	Maximiliano H Martinez
1944	Andrés I Menéndez *Vice President*
1944–5	Osmin Aguirre y Salinas *Provisional President*
1945–8	Salvador Castaneda Castro
1948–50	*Revolutionary Council*
1950–6	Oscar Osorio
1956–60	José María Lemus
1960–1	*Military Junta*
1961–2	*Civil-Military Administration*
1962	Rodolfo Eusebio Cordón *Provisional President*
1962–7	Julio Adalberto Rivera
1967–72	Fidel Sánchez Hernández
1972–7	Arturo Armando Molina
1977–9	Carlos Humberto Romero
1979–82	*Military Juntas*
1982–4	*Government of National Unanimity* (Alvaro Magaña)
1984–9	José Napoleón Duarte
1989–	Alfredo Cristiani

EQUATORIAL GUINEA

President

1968–79	Francisco Macias Nguema
1979–	Teodoro Obiang Nguema Mbasogo

ESTONIA

President

1990–	Arnold Rüütel

ETHIOPIA

Monarch

1889–1911	Menelik II
1911–16	Lij Iyasu (Joshua)
1916–28	Zawditu
1928–74	Haile Selassie *Emperor from 1930*

Provisional Military Administrative Council

Chairman

1974–7	Teferi Benti
1977–87	Mengistu Haile Mariam

People's Democratic Republic

President

1987–91	Mengistu Haile Mariam
1991–	Tesfaye Gebre Kidan *Acting President*

EUROPEAN COMMUNITY (EC) COMMISSION

President

1967–70	Jean Rey
1970–2	Franco M Malfatti
1972–3	Sicco L Mansholt
1973–7	Francois-Xavier Ortoli
1977–81	Roy Jenkins
1981–5	Gaston Thorn
1985–	Jacques Delors

FIJI

Chief of State: British monarch, represented by Governor General

Prime Minister

1970–87	Kamisese Mara
1987	Timoci Bavadra

Interim Administration

Governor General

1987	Penaia Ganilau
1987	*Military administration* (Sitiveni Rabuka)

Republic

Chairman

1987	Sitiveni Rabuka

POLITICAL LEADERS 1900–1992 (cont.)

President

1987–	Penaia Ganilau

Prime Minister

1987–92	Kamisese Mara
1992–	Sitiveni Rabuka

FINLAND

President

1919–25	Kaarlo Juho Ståhlberg
1925–31	Lauri Kristian Relander
1931–7	Pehr Evind Svinhufvud
1937–40	Kyösti Kallio
1940–4	Risto Ryti
1944–6	Carl Gustaf Mannerheim
1946–56	Juho Kusti Paasikivi
1956–81	Urho Kekkonen
1982–	Mauno Koivisto

Prime Minister

1917–18	Pehr Evind Svinhufvud
1918	Juho Kusti Pasaikivi
1918–19	Lauri Johannes Ingman
1919	Kaarlo Castrén
1919–20	Juho Vennola
1920–1	Rafael Erich
1921–2	Juho Vennola
1922	Aino Kaarlo Cajander
1922–4	Kyösti Kallio
1924	Aino Kaarlo Cajander
1924–5	Lauri Johannes Ingman
1925	Antti Agaton Tulenheimo
1925–6	Kyösti Kallio
1926–7	Väinö Tanner
1927–8	Juho Emil Sunila
1928–9	Oskari Mantere
1929–30	Kyösti Kallio
1930–1	Pehr Evind Svinhufvud
1931–2	Juho Emil Sunila
1932–6	Toivo Kivimäki
1936–7	Kyösti Kallio
1937–9	Aino Kaarlo Cajander
1939–41	Risto Ryti
1941–3	Johann Rangell
1943–4	Edwin Linkomies
1944	Andreas Hackzell
1944	Urho Jonas Castrén
1944–5	Juho Kusti Paasikivi
1946–8	Mauno Pekkala
1948–50	Karl August Fagerholm
1950–3	Urho Kekkonen
1953–4	Sakari Tuomioja
1954	Ralf Törngren
1954–6	Urho Kekkonen
1956–7	Karl August Fagerholm
1957	Väinö Johannes Sukselainen
1957–8	Rainer von Fieandt
1958	Reino Iisakki Kuuskoski
1958–9	Karl August Fagerholm
1959–61	Väinö Johannes Sukselainen
1961–2	Martti Miettunen
1962–3	Ahti Karjalainen
1963–4	Reino Ragnar Lehto
1964–6	Johannes Virolainen
1966–8	Rafael Paasio
1968–70	Mauno Koivisto
1970	Teuvo Ensio Aura
1970–1	Ahti Karjalainen
1971–2	Teuvo Ensio Aura
1972	Rafael Paasio
1972–5	Kalevi Sorsa
1975	Keijo Antero Liinamaa
1975–7	Martti Miettunen
1977–9	Kalevi Sorsa
1979–82	Mauno Koivisto
1982–87	Kalevi Sorsa
1987–91	Harri Holkeri
1991–	Esko Aho

FRANCE

President

Third Republic

1899–1906	Emile Loubet
1906–13	Armand Fallières
1913–20	Raymond Poincaré
1920	Paul Deschanel
1920–4	Alexandre Millerand
1924–31	Gaston Doumergue
1931–2	Paul Doumer
1932–40	Albert Lebrun

Fourth Republic

1947–54	Vincent Auriol
1954–8	René Coty

Fifth Republic

1958–69	Charles de Gaulle
1969–74	Georges Pompidou
1974–81	Valéry Giscard d'Estaing
1981–	François Mitterrand

POLITICAL LEADERS 1900–1992 (cont.)

France (cont.)

Prime Minister

Third Republic

1899–1902	Pierre Waldeck-Rousseau
1902–5	Emile Combes
1905–6	Maurice Rouvier
1906	Jean Sarrien
1906–9	Georges Clemenceau
1909–11	Aristide Briand
1911	Ernest Monis
1911–12	Joseph Caillaux
1912–13	Raymond Poincaré
1913	Aristide Briand
1913	Louis Barthou
1913–14	Gaston Doumergue
1914	Alexandre Ribot
1914–15	René Viviani
1915–17	Aristide Briand
1917	Alexandre Ribot
1917	Paul Painlevé
1917–20	Georges Clemenceau
1920	Alexandre Millerand
1920–1	Georges Leygues
1921–2	Aristide Briand
1922–4	Raymond Poincaré
1924	Frédéric François-Marsal
1924–5	Edouard Herriot
1925	Paul Painlevé
1925–6	Aristide Briand
1926	Edouard Herriot
1926–9	Raymond Poincaré
1929	Aristide Briand
1929–30	André Tardieu
1930	Camille Chautemps
1930	André Tardieu
1930–1	Théodore Steeg
1931–2	Pierre Laval
1932	André Tardieu
1932	Edouard Herriot
1932–3	Joseph Paul-Boncour
1933	Edouard Daladier
1933	Albert Sarrault
1933–4	Camille Chautemps
1934	Edouard Daladier
1934	Gaston Doumergue
1934–5	Pierre-Etienne Flandin
1935	Fernand Bouisson
1935–6	Pierre Laval
1936	Albert Sarrault
1936–7	Léon Blum
1937–8	Camille Chautemps
1938	Léon Blum
1938–40	Edouard Daladier
1940	Paul Reynaud
1940	Philippe Pétain

Vichy Government

1940–4	Philippe Pétain

Provisional Government of the French Republic

1944–6	Charles de Gaulle
1946	Félix Gouin
1946	Georges Bidault

Fourth Republic

1946–7	Léon Blum
1947	Paul Ramadier
1947–8	Robert Schuman
1948	André Marie
1948	Robert Schuman
1948–9	Henri Queuille
1949–50	Georges Bidault
1950	Henri Queuille
1950–1	René Pleven
1951	Henri Queuille
1951–2	René Pleven
1952	Edgar Faure
1952–3	Antoine Pinay
1953	René Mayer
1953–4	Joseph Laniel
1954–5	Pierre Mendès-France
1955–6	Edgar Faure
1956–7	Guy Mollet
1957	Maurice Bourgès-Maunoury
1957–8	Félix Gaillard
1958	Pierre Pflimin
1958–9	Charles de Gaulle

Fifth Republic

1959–62	Michel Debré
1962–8	Georges Pompidou
1968–9	Maurice Couve de Murville
1969–72	Jacques Chaban Delmas
1972–4	Pierre Mesmer
1974–6	Jacques Chirac
1976–81	Raymond Barre
1981–4	Pierre Mauroy
1984–6	Laurent Fabius
1986–8	Jacques Chirac
1988–91	Michel Rocard
1991–92	Édith Cresson
1992–	Pierre Bérégovoy

POLITICAL LEADERS 1900–1992 (cont.)

GABON

President

1960–7	Léon M'ba
1967–	Omar (Bernard-Albert, *to 1973*) Bongo

Prime Minister

1960–75	*As President*
1975–90	Léon Mébiame (Mébiane)
1991–	Casimir Oyé Mba

THE GAMBIA

President

1965–	Dawda Kairaba Jawara

GEORGIA

President

1991–2	Zviad Gamsakhurdia (office abolished 1992)

Prime Minister

1992–	Tengiz Sigua *Acting Prime Minister*

State Council

Chair

1992–	Eduard Shevardnaze

GERMANY

German Empire

Emperor

1888–1918	Wilhelm II

Chancellor

1909–17	Theobald von Bethmann-Hollweg
1917	Georg Michaelis
1917–18	Georg Graf von Hertling
1918	Prince Max of Baden
1918	Friedrich Ebert

German Republic

President

1919–25	Friedrich Ebert
1925–34	Paul von Hindenburg

Reich Chancellor

1919	Philipp Scheidemann
1919–20	Gustav Bauer
1920	Hermann Müller
1920–1	Konstantin Fehrenbach
1921–2	Karl Joseph Wirth
1922–3	Wilhelm Cuno
1923	Gustav Stresemann
1923–4	Wilhelm Marx
1925–6	Hans Luther
1926–8	Wilhelm Marx
1928–30	Hermann Müller
1930–2	Heinrich Brüning
1932	Franz von Papen
1932–3	Kurt von Sleicher
1933	Adolf Hitler

Chancellor and Führer

1934–45	Adolf Hitler
1945	Karl Dönitz

German Democratic Republic (East Germany)

President

1949–60	Wilhelm Pieck

Chairman of the Council of State

1960–73	Walter Ernst Karl Ulbricht
1973–6	Willi Stoph
1976–89	Erich Honecker
1989	Egon Krenz
1989–90	Gregor Gysi

General Secretary as Chairman

Premier

1949–64	Otto Grotewohl
1964–73	Willi Stoph
1973–6	Horst Sindermann
1976–89	Willi Stoph
1989–90	Hans Modrow
1990	Lothar de Maizière

POLITICAL LEADERS 1900–1992 (cont.)

Germany (cont.)

German Federal Republic (West Germany)

President

1949–59 Theodor Heuss
1959–69 Heinrich Lübke
1969–74 Gustav Heinemann
1974–9 Walter Scheel
1979–84 Karl Carstens
1984–90 Richard von Weizsäcker

Chancellor

1949–63 Konrad Adenauer
1963–6 Ludwig Erhard
1966–9 Kurt Georg Kiesinger
1969–74 Willy Brandt
1974–82 Helmut Schmidt
1982–90 Helmut Kohl

Germany

President

1990– Richard von Weizsäcker

Chancellor

1990– Helmut Kohl

GHANA

President

1960–6 Kwame Nkrumah

National Liberation Council

Chairman

1966–9 Joseph Arthur Ankrah
1969 Akwasi Amankwa Afrifa
1969–70 *Presidential Committee*

President

1970–2 Edward Akufo-Addo

Chairman

1972–8 *National Redemption Council* (Ignatius Kuti Acheampong)
1978–9 *Supreme Military Council* (Fred W Akuffo)
1979 *Armed Forces Revolutionary Council* (Jerry John Rawlings)

President

1979–81 Hilla Limann

Provisional National Defence Council

Chairman

1981– Jerry John Rawlings

Prime Minister

1960–9 *As President*
1969–72 Kufi Abrefa Busia
1972–8 *As President*
1978– *No Prime Minister*

GREECE

Monarch

1863–1913 George I
1913–17 Constantine I
1917–20 Alexander
1920–2 Constantine I
1922–3 George II
1923–4 Paul Koundouriotis *Regent*

Republic

President

1924–6 Paul Koundouriotis
1926 Theodore Pangalos
1926–9 Paul Koundouriotis
1929–35 Alexander T Zaïmis

Monarch

1935 George Kondylis *Regent*
1935–47 George II
1947–64 Paul
1964–7 Constantine II
1967–73 *Military Junta*
1973 George Papadopoulos *Regent*

Republic

President

1973 George Papadopoulos
1973–4 Phaedon Gizikis
1974–5 Michael Stasinopoulos
1975–80 Constantine Tsatsos
1980–5 Constantine Karamanlis
1985–90 Christos Sartzetakis
1990– Constantine Karamanlis

Prime Minister

1899–1901 George Theotokis
1901–2 Alexander T Zaïmis

POLITICAL LEADERS 1900–1992 (cont.)

1902–3	Theodore Diligiannis
1903	George Theotokis
1903	Demetrius G Rallis
1903–4	George Theotokis
1904–5	Theodore Deligiannis
1905	Demetrius G Rallis
1905–9	George Theotokis
1909	Demetrius G Rallis
1909–10	Kyriakoulis P Mavromichalis
1910	Stephen N Dragoumis
1910–15	Eleftherios K Venizelos
1915	Demetrius P Gounaris
1915	Eleftherios K Venizelos
1915	Alexander T Zaïmis
1915–16	Stephen Skouloudis
1916	Alexander T Zaïmis
1916	Nicholas P Kalogeropoulos
1916–17	Spyridon Lambros
1917	Alexander T Zaïmis
1917–20	Eleftherios K Venizelos
1920–1	Demetrius G Rallis
1921	Nicholas P Kalogeropoulos
1921–2	Demetrius P Gounaris
1922	Nicholas Stratos
1922	Peter E Protopapadakis
1922	Nicholas Triandaphyllakos
1922	Sotirios Krokidas
1922	Alexander T Zaïmis
1922–3	Stylianos Gonatas
1924	Eleftherios Venizelos
1924	George Kaphandaris
1924	Alexander Papanastasiou
1924	Themistocles Sophoulis
1924–5	Andreas Michalakopoulos
1925–6	Alexander N Chatzikyriakos
1926	Theodore Pangalos
1926	Athanasius Eftaxias
1926	George Kondylis
1926–8	Alexander T Zaïmis
1928–32	Eleftherios K Venizelos
1932	Alexander Papanastasiou
1932	Eleftherios K Venizelos
1932–3	Panagiotis Tsaldaris
1933	Eleftherios K Venizelos
1933	Nicholas Plastiras
1933	Alexander Othonaos
1933–5	Panagiotis Tsaldaris
1935	George Kondylis
1935–6	Constantine Demertzis
1936–41	John Metaxas
1941	Alexander Koryzis
1941	*Chairman of Ministers* George II
1941	*German Occupation*
	Emmanuel Tsouderos
1941–2	George Tsolakoglou
1942–3	Constantine Logothetopoulos
1943–4	John Rallis

Government in exile

1941–4	Emmanuel Tsouderos
1944	Sophocles Venizelos
1944–5	George Papandreou

Post-war

1945	Nicholas Plastiras
1945	Peter Voulgaris
1945	Damaskinos, Archbishop of Athens
1945	Panagiotis Kanellopoulos
1945–6	Themistocles Sophoulis
1946	Panagiotis Politzas
1946–7	Constantine Tsaldaris
1947	Demetrius Maximos
1947	Constantine Tsaldaris
1947–9	Themistocles Sophoulis
1949–50	Alexander Diomedes
1950	John Theotokis
1950	Sophocles Venizelos
1950	Nicholas Plastiras
1950–1	Sophocles Venizelos
1951	Nicholas Plastiras
1952	Demetrius Kiusopoulos
1952–5	Alexander Papagos
1955	Stephen C Stefanopoulos
1955–8	Constantine Karamanlis
1958	Constantine Georgakopoulos
1958–61	Constantine Karamanlis
1961	Constantine Dovas
1961–3	Constantine Karamanlis
1963	Panagiotis Pipinellis
1963	Stylianos Mavromichalis
1963	George Papandreou
1963–4	John Paraskevopoulos
1964–5	George Papandreou
1965	George Athanasiadis-Novas
1965	Elias Tsirimokos
1965–6	Stephen C Stefanopoulos
1966–7	John Paraskevopoulos
1967	Panagiotis Kanellopoulos
1967–74	*Military Junta*
1967	Constantine Kollias
1967–73	George Papadopoulos
1973	Spyridon Markezinis

POLITICAL LEADERS 1900–1992 (cont.)

Greece (cont.)

1973–4	Adamantios Androutsopoulos
1974–80	Constantine Karamanlis
1980–1	George Rallis
1981–9	Andreas Papandreou
1989	Tzannis Tzannetakis
1989–	Xenofon Zolotas

GRENADA

Chief of State: British monarch, represented by Governor General

Prime Minister

1974–9	Eric M Gairy
1979–83	Maurice Bishop
1983–4	Nicholas Braithwaite *Chairman of Interim Council*
1984–9	Herbert A Blaize
1989–90	Ben Jones
1990–	Nicholas Braithwaite

GUATEMALA

President

1898–1920	Manuel Estrada Cabrera
1920–2	Carlos Herrera y Luna
1922–6	José María Orellana
1926–30	Lázaro Chacón
1930	Baudillo Palma
1930–1	Manuel María Orellana
1931	José María Reyna Andrade
1931–44	Jorge Ubico Castañeda
1944	Federico Ponce Vaidez
1944–5	Jacobo Arbenz Guzmán
1945–51	Juan José Arévalo
1951–4	Jacobo Arbenz Guzmán
1954	*Military Junta* (Carlos Díaz)
1954	Elfego J Monzón
1954–7	Carlos Castillo Armas
1957	*Military Junta* (Oscar Mendoza Azurdia)
1957	Luis Arturo González López
1957–8	*Military Junta* (Guillermo Flores Avendaño)
1958–63	Miguel Ydígoras Fuentes
1963–6	*Military Junta* (Enrique Peralta Azurdia)
1966–70	Julio César Méndez Montenegro
1970–4	Carlos Araña Osorio
1974–8	Kyell Eugenio Laugerua García
1978–82	Romeo Lucas García
1982	Angel Aníbal Guevara
1982–3	Efraín Rios Montt
1983–6	Oscar Humberto Mejía Victores
1986–91	Marco Vinicio Cerezo Arévalo
1991–	Jonge Serrano Elias

GUINEA

President

1961–84	Ahmed Sékou Touré
1984–	Lansana Conté

Prime Minister

1958–72	Ahmed Sékou Touré
1972–84	Louis Lansana Beavogui
1984–5	Diarra Traore
1985–	*None*

GUINEA-BISSAU

President

1974–80	Luis de Almeida Cabral
1980–4	*Revolutionary Council* (João Bernardo Vieira)
1984–	João Bernardo Vieira

GUYANA

President

1970	Edward A Luckhoo
1970–80	Arthur Chung
1980–5	Linden Forbes Sampson Burnham
1985–	Hugh Desmond Hoyte

Prime Minister

1966–85	Linden Forbes Sampson Burnham
1985–	Hamilton Green

HAITI

President

1896–1902	P A Tirésias Simon Lam
1902	Boisrond Canal

POLITICAL LEADERS 1900–1992 (cont.)

1902–8	Alexis Nord
1908–11	Antoine Simon
1911–12	Michel Cincinnatus Leconte
1912–13	Tancrède Auguste
1913–14	Michael Oreste
1914	Oreste Zamor
1914–15	Joseph Davilmare Théodore
1915	Jean Velbrun-Guillaume
1915–22	Philippe Sudre Dartiguenave
1922–30	Joseph Louis Bornó
1930	Étienne Roy
1930–41	Sténio Joseph Vincent
1941–6	Élie Lescot
1946	*Military Junta* (Frank Lavaud)
1946–50	Dumarsais Estimé
1950	*Military Junta* (Frank Lavaud)
1950–6	Paul E Magloire
1956–7	François Sylvain
1957	*Military Junta*
1957	Léon Cantave
1957	Daniel Fignolé
1957	Antoine Kebreau
1957–71	François Duvalier ('Papa Doc')
1971–86	Jean-Claude Duvalier ('Baby Doc')
1986–8	Henri Namphy
1988	Leslie Manigat
1988	Henri Namphy
1988–90	Prosper Avril
1990–1	Ertha Pascal-Trouillot

Government in exile

1991–	Jean-Bertrand Aristide

HONDURAS

President

1900–3	Terencio Sierra
1903	Juan Angel Arias
1903–7	Manuel Bonilla Chirinos
1907–11	Miguel R Dávila
1912–15	Manuel Bonilla Chirinos
1915–20	Francisco Bertrand
1920–4	Rafael López Gutiérrez
1924–5	Vicente Tosta Carrasco
1925–8	Miguel Paz Barahona
1929–32	Vicente Mejía Clindres
1932–49	Tiburcio Carías Andino
1949–54	Juan Manuel Gálvez

Head of State

1954–6	Julio Lozano Diaz
1956–7	*Military Junta*

President

1958–63	José Ramón Villeda Morales

Head of State

1963–5	Oswaldo López Arellano

President

1965–71	Oswaldo López Arellano
1971–2	Ramón Ernesto Cruz

Head of State

1972–5	Oswaldo López Arellano
	Juan Alberto Melgar Castro
1978–82	Policarpo Paz García

President

1982–6	Roberto Suazo Córdova
1986–9	José Azcona Hoyo
1989–	Rafael Callejas

HUNGARY

Monarch

1900–16	Franz Josef I
1916–18	Charles IV

President

1919	Mihály Károlyi
1919	*Revolutionary Governing Council* (Sándor Garbai)
1920–44	Miklós Horthy *Regent*
1944–5	*Provisional National Assembly*
1946–8	Zoltán Tildy
1948–50	Árpád Szakasits
1950–2	Sándor Rónai
1952–67	István Dobi
1967–87	Pál Losonczi
1987–8	Károly Németh
1988–9	Bruno Ferenc Straub
1989–90	Matyas Szuros
1990–	Arpad Göncz

Premier

1899–1903	Kálmán Széll
1903	Károly Khuen-Héderváry
1903–5	István Tisza

POLITICAL LEADERS 1900–1992 (cont.)

Hungary (cont.)

1905–6	Géza Fejérváry
1906–10	Sándor Wekerle
1910–12	Károly Kuen Héderváry
1912–13	László Lukács
1913–17	István Tisza
1917	Móric Esterházy
1917–18	Sándor Wekerle
1918–19	Mihály Károlyi
1919	Dénes Berinkey
1919	*Revolutionary Governing Council*
1919	Gyula Peidl
1919	István Friedrich
1919–20	Károly Huszár
1920	Sándor Simonyi-Semadam
1920–1	Pál Teleki
1921–31	István Bethlen
1931–2	Gyula Károlyi
1932–6	Gyula Gömbös
1936–8	Kálman Darányi
1938–9	Béla Imrédy
1939–41	Pál Teleki
1941–2	László Bárdossy
1942–4	Miklós Kállay
1944	Döme Sztójay
1944	Géza Lakatos
1944	Ferenc Szálasi
1944–5	*Provisional National Assembly* (Béla Dálnoki Miklós)
1945–6	Zoltán Tildy
1946–7	Ferenc Nagy
1947–8	Lajos Dinnyés
1948–52	István Dobi
1952–3	Mátyás Rákosi
1953–5	Imre Nagy
1955–6	András Hegedüs
1956	Imre Nagy
1956–8	János Kádár
1958–61	Ferenc Münnich
1961–5	János Kádár
1965–7	Gyula Kállai
1967–75	Jenö Fock
1975–87	György Lázár
1987–8	Károly Grosz
1988–90	Miklás Németh
1990–	Jozsef Antall

First Secretary

1949–56	Mátyás Rákosi
1956	Ernö Gerö
1956–88	János Kádár
1988–	Károly Grosz

ICELAND

President

1944–52	Sveinn Björnsson
1952–68	Ásgeir Ásgeirsson
1968–80	Kristján Eldjárn
1980–	Vigdís Finnbogadóttir

Prime Minister

1900–1	C Goos
1901–4	P A Alberti
1904–9	Hannes Hafstein
1909–11	Björn Jónsson
1911–12	Kristján Jónsson
1912–14	Hannes Hafstein
1914–15	Sigurður Eggerz
1915–17	Einar Arnórsson
1917–22	Jón Magnússon
1922–4	Sigurður Eggerz
1924–6	Jón Magnússon
1926–7	Jon Þorláksson
1927–32	Tryggvi Þórhallsson
1932–4	Ásgeir Ásgeirsson
1934–42	Hermann Jónasson
1942	Ólafur Thors
1942–4	Björn Þórðarsson
1944–7	Ólafur Thors
1947–9	Stefán Jóhann Stefánsson
1949–50	Ólafur Thors
1950–3	Steingrímur Steinþórsson
1953–6	Ólafur Thors
1956–8	Hermann Jónasson
1958–9	Emil Jónsson
1959–61	Ólafur Thors
1961	Bjarni Benediktsson
1961–3	Ólafur Thors
1963–70	Bjarni Benediktsson
1970–1	Jóhann Hafstein
1971–4	Ólafur Jóhannesson
1974–8	Geir Hallgrímsson
1978–9	Ólafur Jóhannesson
1979	Benedikt Gröndal
1980–3	Gunnar Thoroddsen
1983–7	Steingrímur Hermannsson
1987–8	Thorsteinn Pálsson
1988–91	Steingrímur Hermannsson
1991–	Davíd Oddsson

POLITICAL LEADERS 1900–1992 (cont.)

INDIA

President

1950–62 Rajendra Prasad
1962–7 Sarvepalli Radhakrishnan
1967–9 Zakir Husain
1969 Varahagiri Venkatagiri *Acting President*
1969 Mohammed Hidayatullah *Acting President*
1969–74 Varahagiri Venkatagiri
1974–7 Fakhruddin Ali Ahmed
1977 B D Jatti *Acting President*
1977–82 Neelam Sanjiva Reddy
1982–7 Giani Zail Singh
1987– Ramaswami Venkataraman

Prime Minister

1947–64 Jawaharlal Nehru
1964 Gulzari Lal Nanda *Acting Prime Minister*
1964–6 Lal Bahadur Shastri
1966 Gulzari Lal Nanda *Acting Prime Minister*
1966–77 Indira Gandhi
1977–9 Morarji Desai
1979–80 Charan Singh
1980–4 Indira Gandhi
1984–9 Rajiv Gandhi
1989–90 Vishwanath Pratap Singh
1990–1 Chandra Shekhar
1991– P V Narasimha Rao

INDONESIA

President

1945–9 Ahmed Sukarno

Republic

1949–66 Ahmed Sukarno
1966– T N J Suharto

Prime Minister

1945 R A A Wiranatakusumah
1945–7 Sutan Sjahrir
1947–8 Amir Sjarifuddin
1948 Mohammed Hatta
1948–9 Sjarifuddin Prawiraranegara
1949 Susanto Tirtoprodjo
1949 Mohammed Hatta
1950 Dr Halim
1950–1 Mohammed Natsir
1951–2 Sukiman Wirjosandjojo
1952–3 Dr Wilopo
1953–5 Ali Sastroamidjojo
1955–6 Burhanuddin Harahap
1956–7 Ali Sastroamidjojo
1957–9 Raden Haji Djuanda Kurtawidjaja
1959–63 Ahmed Sukarno
1963–6 S E Subandrio
1966– *No Prime Minister*

IRAN (Persia)

Shah

1896–1907 Muzaffar Ad-Din
1907–9 Mohammed Ali
1909–25 Ahmad Mirza
1925–41 Mohammed Reza Khan
1941–79 Mohammed Reza Pahlavi

Republic

Leader of the Islamic Revolution

1979–89 Ruhollah Khomeini
1989– Sayed Ali Khamenei

President

1980–1 Abolhassan Bani-Sadr
1981 Mohammed Ali Rajai
1981–9 Sayed Ali Khamenei
1989– Hashemi Rafsanjani

Prime Minister

1979 Shahpur Bakhtiar
1979–80 Mehdi Bazargan
1980–1 Mohammed Ali Rajai
1981 Mohammed Javad Bahonar
1981 Mohammed Reza Mahdavi-Kani
1981–9 Mir Hossein Moussavi

IRAQ

Monarch

1921–33 Faisal I
1933–9 Ghazi I
1939–58 Faisal II
(*Regent, 1939–53,* Abdul Illah)

POLITICAL LEADERS 1900–1992 (cont.)

Iraq (cont.)

Republic

Commander of the National Forces

1958–63 Abdul Karim Qassem

Head of Council of State

1958–63 Mohammed Najib Ar-Rubai

President

1963–6 Abdus Salaam Mohammed Arif
1966–8 Abdur Rahman Mohammed Arif
1968–79 Said Ahmad Hassan Al-Bakr
1979– Saddam Hussein At-Takriti

IRELAND

Governor General

1922–7 Timothy Michael Healy
1927–32 James McNeill
1932–6 Donald Buckley

President

1938–45 Douglas Hyde
1945–59 Sean Thomas O'Kelly
1959–73 Eamon de Valera
1973–4 Erskine H Childers
1974–6 Carroll Daly
1976–90 Patrick J Hillery
1990– Mary Robinson

Prime Minister

1919–21 Eamon de Valera
1922 Arthur Griffiths
1922–32 William Cosgrave
1932–48 Eamon de Valera
1948–51 John Aloysius Costello
1951–4 Eamon de Valera
1954–7 John Aloysius Costello
1957–9 Eamon de Valera
1959–66 Sean Lemass
1966–73 John Lynch
1973–7 Liam Cosgrave
1977–9 John Lynch
1979–82 Charles Haughey
1982–7 Garret FitzGerald
1987–92 Charles Haughey
1992– Albert Reynolds

ISRAEL

President

1948–52 Chaim Weizmann
1952–63 Itzhak Ben-Zvi
1963–73 Zalman Shazar
1973–8 Ephraim Katzair
1978–83 Yitzhak Navon
1983– Chaim Herzog

Prime Minister

1948–53 David Ben Gurion
1954–5 Moshe Sharett
1955–63 David Ben Gurion
1963–9 Levi Eshkol
1969–74 Golda Meir
1974–7 Itzhak Rabin
1977–83 Menachem Begin
1983–4 Yitzhak Shamir
1984–8 Shimon Peres
1988–92 Yitzhak Shamir
1992– Yitzhak Rabin

ITALY

Kingdom of Italy

Monarch

1900–46 Victor Emmanuel III

Italian Republic

President

1946–8 Enrico de Nicola
1948–55 Luigi Einaudi
1955–62 Giovanni Gronchi
1962–4 Antonio Segni
1964–71 Giuseppe Saragat
1971–8 Giovanni Leone
1978–85 Alessandro Pertini
1985– Francesco Cossiga

Kingdom of Italy

Prime Minister

1900–1 Giuseppe Saracco
1901–3 Giuseppe Zanardelli
1903–5 Giovanni Giolitti
1905–6 Alessandro Fortis
1906 Sydney Sonnino
1906–9 Giovanni Giolitti

POLITICAL LEADERS 1900–1992 (cont.)

1909–10 Sydney Sonnino
1910–11 Luigi Luzzatti
1911–14 Giovanni Giolitti
1914–16 Antonio Salandra
1916–17 Paolo Boselli
1917–19 Vittorio Emmanuele Orlando
1919–20 Francesco Saverio Nitti
1920–1 Giovanni Giolitti
1921–2 Ivanoe Bonomi
1922 Luigi Facta
1922–43 Benito Mussolini
1943–4 Pietro Badoglio
1944–5 Ivanoe Bonomi
1945 Ferrucio Parri
1945 Alcide de Gasperi

Italian Republic
1946–53 Alcide De Gasperi
1953–4 Giuseppe Pella
1954 Amintore Fanfani
1954–5 Mario Scelba
1955–7 Antonio Segni
1957–8 Adone Zoli
1958–9 Amintore Fanfani
1959–60 Antonio Segni
1960 Fernando Tambroni
1960–3 Amintore Fanfani
1963 Giovanni Leone
1963–8 Aldo Moro
1968 Giovanni Leone
1968–70 Mariano Rumor
1970–2 Emilio Colombo
1972–4 Giulio Andreotti
1974–6 Aldo Moro
1976–8 Giulio Andreotti
1979–80 Francisco Cossiga
1980–1 Arnaldo Forlani
1981–2 Giovanni Spadolini
1982–3 Amintore Fanfani
1983–7 Bettino Craxi
1987 Amintore Fanfani
1987–8 Giovanni Goria
1988–9 Ciriaco de Mita
1989–92 Giulio Andreotti
1992– Giuliano Amato

JAMAICA

Chief of State: British monarch, represented by Governor General

Prime Minister

1962–7 William Alexander Bustamante
1967 Donald Burns Sangster
1967–72 Hugh Lawson Shearer
1972–80 Michael Norman Manley
1980–9 Edward Phillip George Seaga
1989–92 Michael Norman Manley
1992– Percival James Patterson

JAPAN

Chief of State (Emperor)

1867–1912 Mutsuhito (Meiji)
1912–26 Yoshihito (Taishō)
1926–89 Hirohito (Shōwa)
1989– Akihito (Heisei)

Prime Minister

1900–1 Hirobumi Itō
1901–6 Tarō Katsura
1906–8 Kimmochi Saionji
1908–11 Tarō Katsura
1911–12 Kimmochi Saionji
1912–13 Tarō Katsura
1913–14 Gonnohyōe Yamamoto
1914–16 Shigenobu Ōkuma
1916–18 Masatake Terauchi
1918–21 Takashi Hara
1921–2 Korekiyo Takahashi
1922–3 Tomosaburō Katō
1923–4 Gonnohyōe Yamamoto
1924 Keigo Kiyoura
1924–6 Takaaki Katō
1926–7 Reijirō Wakatsuki
1927–9 Giichi Tanaka
1929–31 Osachi Hamaguchi
1931 Reijirō Wakatsuki
1931–2 Tsuyoshi Inukai
1932–4 Makoto Saitō
1934–6 Keisuke Okada
1936–7 Kōki Hirota
1937 Senjūrō Hayashi
1937–9 Fumimaro Konoe
1939 Kiichirō Hiranuma
1939–40 Nobuyuki Abe
1940 Mitsumasa Yonai
1940–1 Fumimaro Konoe
1941–4 Hideki Tōjō
1944–5 Kuniaki Koiso
1945 Kantarō Suzuki
1945 Naruhiko Higashikuni
1945–6 Kijūrō Shidehara
1946–7 Shigeru Yoshida
1947–8 Tetsu Katayama

POLITICAL LEADERS 1900–1992 (cont.)

Japan (cont.)

1948	Hitoshi Ashida
1948–54	Shigeru Yoshida
1954–6	Ichirō Hatoyama
1956–7	Tanzan Ishibashi
1957–60	Nobusuke Kishi
1960–4	Hayato Ikeda
1964–72	Eisaku Satō
1972–4	Kakuei Tanaka
1974–6	Takeo Miki
1976–8	Takeo Fukuda
1978–80	Masayoshi Ōhira
1980–2	Zenkō Suzuki
1982–7	Yasuhiro Nakasone
1987–9	Noburu Takeshita
1989	Sasuke Uno
1989–91	Toshiki Kaifu
1991–	Kiichi Miyazawa

JORDAN

Monarch

1921–51	Abdallah Bin Hussein
1951–2	Talal I
1952–	Hussein II

Prime Minister

1921	Rashid Tali
1921	Muzhir Ar-Raslan
1921–3	Rida Ar-Riqabi
1923	Muzhir Ar-Raslan
1923–4	Hassan Khalid
1924–33	Rida Ar-Riqabi
1933–8	Ibrahim Hashim
1939–45	Taufiq Abul-Huda
1945–8	Ibrahim Hashim
1948–50	Taufiq Abul-Huda
1950	Said Al-Mufti
1950–1	Samir Ar-Rifai
1951–3	Taufiq Abul-Huda
1953–4	Fauzi Al-Mulqi
1954–5	Taufiq Abul-Huda
1955	Said Al-Mufti
1955	Hazza Al-Majali
1955–6	Ibrahim Hashim
1956	Samir Ar-Rifai
1956	Said Al-Mufti
1956	Ibrahim Hashim
1956–7	Suleiman Nabulsi
1957	Hussein Fakhri Al-Khalidi
1957–8	Ibrahim Hashim
1958	Nuri Pasha Al-Said
1958–9	Samir Ar-Rifai
1959–60	Hazza Al-Majali
1960–2	Bahjat Talhuni
1962–3	Wasfi At-Tall
1963	Samir Ar-Rifai
1963–4	Sharif Hussein Bin Nasir
1964	Bahjat Talhuni
1965–7	Wasfi At-Tall
1967	Sharif Hussein Bin Nasir
1967	Saad Jumaa
1967–9	Bahjat Talhuni
1969	Abdul Munem Rifai
1969–70	Bahjat Talhuni
1970	Abdul Munem Rifai
1970	*Military Junta* (Mohammed Daud)
1970	Mohamed Ahmed Tuqan
1970–1	Wasfi At-Tall
1971–3	Ahmad Lozi
1973–6	Zeid Rifai
1976–9	Mudar Badran
1979–80	Sharif Abdul Hamid Sharaf
1980	Kassem Rimawi
1980–4	Mudar Badran
1984–5	Ahmad Ubayat
1985–9	Zeid Ar-Rifai
1989	Sharif Zaid Ibn Shaker
1989–91	Mudar Badran
1991	Taher al-Masri
1991–	Sharif Zaid Ibn Shaker

KAZAKHSTAN

President

1991–	Nursultan Nazarbayev

KENYA

President

1963–78	Mzee Jomo Kenyatta
1978–	Daniel arap Moi

KIRGHIZIA

President

1991–	Askar Akayev

POLITICAL LEADERS 1900–1992 (cont.)

KIRIBATI

President

1979–91 Ieremia T Tabai
1991– Teatao Teannaki

DEMOCRATIC PEOPLE'S REPUBLIC OF KOREA (North Korea)

President

1948–57 Kim Doo-bong
1957–72 Choi Yong-kun
1972– Kim Il-sung

Prime Minister

1948–76 Kim Il-sung
1976–7 Park Sung-chul
1977–84 Li Jong-ok
1984–6 Kang Song-san
1986–8 Yi Kun-mo
1988– Yon Hyong Muk

REPUBLIC OF KOREA (South Korea)

President

1948–60 Syngman Rhee
1960 Ho Chong *Acting President*
1960 Kwak Sang-hun *Acting President*
1960 Ho Chong *Acting President*
1960–3 Yun Po-sun
1963–79 Park Chung-hee
1979–80 Choi Kyu-hah
1980 Park Choong-hoon *Acting President*
1980–8 Chun Doo-hwan
1988– Roh Tae Woo

Prime Minister

1948–50 Lee Pom-sok
1950 Shin Song-mo *Acting Prime Minister*
1950–1 John M Chang
1951–2 Ho Chong *Acting Prime Minister*
1952 Lee Yun-yong *Acting Prime Minister*
1952 Chang Taek-sang
1952–4 Paik Too-chin
1954–6 Pyon Yong-tae
1956–60 Syngman Rhee
1960 Ho Chong
1960–1 John M Chang
1961 Chang To-yong
1961–2 Song Yo-chan
1962–3 Kim Hyun-chul
1963–4 Choe Tu-son
1964–70 Chung Il-kwon
1970–1 Paik Too-chin
1971–5 Kim Jong-pil
1975–9 Choi Kyu-hah
1979–80 Shin Hyun-hwak
1980 Park Choong-hoon *Acting Prime Minister*
1980–2 Nam Duck-woo
1982 Yoo Chang-soon
1982–3 Kim Sang-hyup
1983–5 Chin Lee-chong
1985–8 Lho Shin-yong
1988 Lee Hyun Jae
1988–90 Kang Young Hoon
1990–1 Ro Jai Bong
1991– Chung Won Shik

KUWAIT

Emir

Family name: Al-Sabah
1896–1915 Mubarak
1915–17 Jaber II
1917–21 Salem Al-Mubarak
1921–50 Ahmed Al-Jaber
1950–65 Abdallah Al-Salem
1965–77 Sabah Al-Salem
1978– Jaber Al-Ahmed Al-Jaber

Prime Minister

1962–3 Abdallah Al-Salem
1963–5 Sabah Al-Salem
1965–78 Jaber Al-Ahmed Al-Jaber
1978– Saad Al-Abdallah Al-Salem

LAOS

Monarch

1904–59 Sisavang Vong
1959–75 Savang Vatthana

POLITICAL LEADERS 1900–1992 (cont.)

Laos (cont.)

Lao People's Republic

President

1975–87 Souphanouvong
1987–91 Phoumi Vongvichit
1991– Kaysone Phomvihane

Prime Minister

1951–4 Souvanna Phouma
1954–5 Katay Don Sasorith
1956–8 Souvanna Phouma
1958–9 Phoui Sahanikone
1959–60 Sunthone Patthamavong
1960 Kou Abhay
1960 Somsanith
1960 Souvana Phouma
1960 Sunthone Patthamavong
1960 Quinim Pholsena
1960–2 Boun Oum Na Champassac
1962–75 Souvanna Phouma

Lao People's Democratic Republic
1975–91 Kaysone Phomvihane
1991– Khantay Siphandon

LATVIA

President

1990– Anatolijs Gorbunovs

LEBANON

President

1943–52 Bishara Al-Khoury
1952–8 Camille Shamoun
1958–64 Fouad Shehab
1964–70 Charle Hilo
1970–6 Suleiman Frenjieh
1976–82 Elias Sarkis
1982 Bashir Gemayel
1982–8 Amin Gemayel
1988–9 *No President*
1989 Rene Muawad
1989– Elias Hrawi

Prime Minister

1943 Riad Solh
1943–4 Henry Pharaon
1944–5 Riad Solh
1945 Abdul Hamid Karame
1945–6 Sami Solh
1946 Saadi Munla
1946–51 Riad Solh
1951 Hussein Oweini
1951–2 Abdullah Yafi
1952 Sami Solh
1952 Nazem Accari
1952 Saeb Salam
1952 Fouad Chehab
1952–3 Khaled Chehab
1953 Saeb Salam
1953–5 Abdullah Yafi
1955 Sami Solh
1955–6 Rashid Karami
1956 Abdullah Yafi
1956–8 Sami Solh
1958–60 Rashid Karami
1960 Ahmad Daouq
1960–1 Saeb Salam
1961–4 Rashid Karami
1964–5 Hussein Oweini
1965–6 Rashid Karami
1966 Abdullah Yafi
1966–8 Rashid Karami
1968–9 Abdullah Yafi
1969–70 Rashid Karami
1970–3 Saeb Salam
1973 Amin al-Hafez
1973–4 Takieddine Solh
1974–5 Rashid Solh
1975 Noureddin Rifai
1975–6 Rashid Karami
1976–80 Selim al-Hoss
1980 Takieddine Solh
1980–4 Chafiq al-Wazan
1984–8 Rashid Karami
1988–90 Michel Aoun/Selim al-Hoss
1990– Umar Karami

LESOTHO

Monarch

1966–90 Moshoeshoe II
1991– Letsie III

Prime Minister

1966–86 Leabua Jonathan

POLITICAL LEADERS 1900–1992 (cont.)

Chairman of Military Council

1986–91 Justin Metsing Lekhanya
1991– Elias Tutsoane Ramaema

LIBERIA

President

1900–4 Garretson Wilmot Gibson
1904–12 Arthur Barclay
1912–20 Daniel Edward Howard
1920–30 Charles Dunbar Burgess King
1930–43 Edwin J Barclay
1943–71 William V S Tubman
1971–80 William Richard Tolbert

People's Redemption Council

Chairman

1980–6 Samuel K Doe

President

1986–90 Samuel K Doe
1991– Amos Sawyer

LIBYA

Monarch

1951–69 Mohammed Idris Al-Mahdi Al-Senussi

Revolutionary Command Council

Chairman

1969–77 Muammar Al-Gadhafi (Qadhafi)

General Secretariat

Secretary General

1977–9 Muammar Al-Gadhafi
1979–84 Abdul Ati Al-Ubaidi
1984–6 Mohammed Az-Zaruq Rajab
1986–90 Omar Al-Muntasir
1990– Abu Zayd 'Umar Durda

Leader of the Revolution

1969– Muammar Al-Gadhafi

LIECHTENSTEIN

Prince

1858–1929 Johann II
1929–38 Franz von Paula
1938–89 Franz Josef II
1989– Hans Adam II

Prime Minister

1928–45 Franz Josef Hoop
1945–62 Alexander Friek
1962–70 Gérard Batliner
1970–4 Alfred J Hilbe
1974–8 Walter Kieber
1978– Hans Brunhart

LITHUANIA

President

1990– Vytautas Landsbergis

LUXEMBOURG

Grand Dukes and Duchesses

1890–1905 Adolf
1905–12 William IV
1912–19 Marie Adelaide
1919–64 Charlotte *in exile 1940–4*
1964– Jean

Prime Minister

1889–1915 Paul Eyschen
1915 Mathias Mongenast
1915–16 Hubert Loutsch
1916–17 Victor Thorn
1917–18 Léon Kaufmann
1918–25 Emil Reuter
1925–6 Pierre Prum
1926–37 Joseph Bech
1937–53 Pierre Dupong *in exile 1940–4*
1953–8 Joseph Bech
1958 Pierre Frieden
1959–69 Pierre Werner
1969–79 Gaston Thorn
1979–84 Pierre Werner
1984– Jacques Santer

POLITICAL LEADERS 1900–1992 (cont.)

MADAGASCAR

President

1960–72	Philibert Tsiranana
1972–5	Gabriel Ramanantsoa
1975	Richard Ratsimandrava
1975	Gilles Andriamahazo
1975–	Didier Ratsiraka

Prime Minister

1960–75	*As President*
1975–6	Joël Rakotomala
1976–7	Justin Rakotoriaina
1977–88	Désiré Rakotoarijaona
1988–91	Victor Ramahatra
1991–	Guy Willy Razanamasy

MALAWI

President

1966–	Hastings Kamuzu Banda

MALAYSIA

Chief of State (Yang di-Pertuan Agong)

1957–63	Abdul Rahman
1963–5	Syed Putra Jamalullah
1965–70	Ismail Nasiruddin Shah
1970–5	Abdul Halim Muadzam Shah
1975–9	Yahya Petra Ibrahim
1979–84	Haji Ahmad Shah Al-Mustain Billah
1984–9	Mahmood Iskandar
1989–	Azlan Muhibuddin Shah

Prime Minister

Malaya

1957–63	Abdul Rahman Putra Al-Haj

Malaysia

1963–70	Abdul Rahman Putra Al-Haj
1970–6	Abdul Razak bin Hussein
1976–9	Haji Hussein bin Onn
1979–	Mahathir bin Mohamad

MALDIVES

Monarch (Sultan)

1954–68	Mohammed Farid Didi

Republic

President

1968–78	Ibrahim Nasir
1978–	Maumoon Abdul Gayoom

MALI

President

1960–8	Modibo Keita
1969–91	Moussa Traoré
1991–92	Amadou Toumani Touré
1992–	Alpha Oumar Konare

Prime Minister

1986–88	Mamadou Dembelé
1988–91	*No Prime Minister*
1991–	Soumana Sacko

MALTA

President

1974–6	Anthony Mamo
1976–81	Anton Buttigieg
1982–7	Agatha Barbara
1987–9	Paul Xuereb *Acting President*
1989–	Vincent Tabone

Prime Minister

1962–71	G Borg Olivier
1971–84	Dom Mintoff
1984–7	Carmelo Mifsud Bonnici
1987–	Edward Fenech-Adami

MARSHALL ISLANDS

President

1990–	Amata Kabua

POLITICAL LEADERS 1900–1992 (cont.)

MAURITANIA

President

1961–78	Mokhtar Ould Daddah
1979	Mustapha Ould Mohammed Salek
1979–80	Mohammed Mahmoud Ould Ahmed Louly
1980–4	Mohammed Khouna Ould Haydalla
1984–	Moaouia Ould Sidi Mohammed Taya

MAURITIUS

Chief of State: British monarch, represented by Governor General

Prime Minister

1968–82	Seewoosagur Ramgoolam
1982–	Aneerood Jugnauth

MEXICO

President

1876–1911	Porfirio Diaz
1911	Francisco León de la Barra
1911–13	Francisco I Madero
1913–14	Victoriano Huerta
1914	Francisco Carvajal
1914	Venustiano Carranza
1914–15	Eulalio Gutiérrez *Provisional President*
1915	Roque González Garza *Provisional President*
1915	Francisco Lagos Chazaro *Provisional President*
1917–20	Venustiano Carranza
1920	Adolfo de la Huerta
1920–4	Alvaro Obregón
1924–8	Plutarco Elías Calles
1928–30	Emilio Portes Gil
1930–2	Pascual Ortíz Rubio
1932–4	Abelardo L. Rodríguez
1934–40	Lazaro Cardenas
1940–6	Manuel Avila Camacho
1946–52	Miguel Alemán
1952–8	Adolfo Ruiz Cortines
1958–64	Adolfo López Mateos
1964–70	Gustavo Díaz Ordaz
1970–6	Luis Echeverría
1976–82	José López Portillo
1982–8	Miguel de la Madrid Hurtado
1988–	Carlos Salinas de Gortari

MOLDAVIA

President

1991–	Mircea Snegur

MONACO

Head of State

1889–1922	Albert
1922–49	Louis II
1949–	Rainier III

MONGOLIA

Prime Minister

1924–8	Tserendorji
1928–32	Amor
1932–6	Gendun
1936–8	Amor
1939–52	Korloghiin Choibalsan
1952–74	Yumsjhagiin Tsedenbal
1990–	Dashiyn Byambasuren

Chairman of the Praesidium

1948–53	Gonchighlin Bumatsende
1954–72	Jamsarangiin Sambu
1972–4	Sonomyn Luvsan
1974–84	Yumsjhagiin Tsedenbal
1984–90	Jambyn Batmunkh

President

1990–	Punsalmaagiyn Ochirbat

Premier

1974–84	Jambyn Batmunkh
1984–90	Dumaagiyn Sodnom

MOROCCO

Monarch

1927–61	Mohammed V
1961–	Hassan II

POLITICAL LEADERS 1900–1992 (cont.)

Morocco (cont.)

Prime Minister

1955–8	Si Mohammed Bekkai
1958	Ahmad Balfrej
1958–60	Abdullah Ibrahim
1960–3	*As Monarch*
1963–5	Ahmad Bahnini
1965–7	*As Monarch*
1967–9	Moulay Ahmed Laraki
1969–71	Mohammed Ben Hima
1971–2	Mohammed Karim Lamrani
1972–9	Ahmed Othman
1979–83	Maati Bouabid
1983–6	Mohammed Karim Lamrani
1986–	Izz Id-Dien Laraki

MOZAMBIQUE

President

1975–86	Samora Moïses Machel
1986–	Joaquim Alberto Chissanó

NAMIBIA

President

1990–	Sam Nujoma

NAURU

President

1968–86	Hammer de Roburt
1986	Kennan Adeang
1986–9	Hammer de Roburt
1989	Kenas Aroi
1989–	Bernard Dowiyogo

NEPAL

Monarch

1881–1911	Prithvi Bir Bikram Shah
1911–50	Tribhuvan Bir Bikram Shah
1950–2	Bir Bikram
1952–5	Tribhuvan Bir Bikram Shah
1956–72	Mahendra Bir Bikram Shah
1972–	Birenda Bir Bikram Shah Deva

Prime Minister

1901–29	Chandra Sham Sher Jang Bahadur Rana
1929–31	Bhim Cham Sham Sher Jang Bahadur Rana
1931–45	Juddha Sham Sher Rana
1945–8	Padma Sham Sher Jang Bahadur Rana
1948–51	Mohan Sham Sher Jang Bahadur Rana
1951–2	Matrika Prasad Koirala
1952–3	Tribhuvan Bir Bikram Shah
1953–5	Matrika Prasad Koirala
1955–6	Mahendra Bir Bikram Shah
1956–7	Tanka Prasad Acharya
1957–9	*King also Prime Minister*
1959–60	Sri Bishawa Prasad Koirala
1960–3	*No Prime Minister*
1963–5	Tulsi Giri
1965–9	Surya Bahadur Thapa
1969–70	Kirti Nidhi Bista
1970–1	*King also Prime Minister*
1971–3	Kirti Nidhi Bista
1973–5	Nagendra Prasad Rijal
1975–7	Tulsi Giri
1977–9	Kirti Nidhi Bista
1979–83	Surya Bahadur Thapa
1983–6	Lokendra Bahadur Chand
1986–91	Marich Man Singh Shrestha
1991–	Girija Prasad Koirala

THE NETHERLANDS

Monarch

1898–1948	Wilhelmina Helena Paulina Maria
1948–80	Juliana Louise Emma Marie Wilhelmina
1980–	Béatrix Wilhelmina Armgard

Prime Minister

1897–1901	Nicholas G Pierson
1901–5	Abraham Kuyper
1905–8	Theodoor H de Meester
1908–13	Theodorus Heemskerk
1913–18	Pieter W A Cort van der Linden

POLITICAL LEADERS 1900–1992 (cont.)

1918–25	Charles J M Ruys de Beerenbrouck
1925–6	Hendrikus Colijn
1926	Dirk J de Geer
1926–33	Charles JM Ruys de Beerenbrouck
1933–9	Hendrikus Colijn
1939–40	Dirk J de Geer
1940–5	Pieter S Gerbrandy *in exile*
1945–6	Willem Schemerhorn/Willem Drees
1946–8	Louis J M Beel
1948–51	Willem Drees/Josephus R H van Schaik
1951–8	Willem Drees
1958–9	Louis J M Beel
1959–63	Jan E de Quay
1963–5	Victor G M Marijnen
1965–6	Joseph M L T Cals
1966–7	Jelle Zijlstra
1967–71	Petrus J S de Jong
1971–3	Barend W Biesheuvel
1973–7	Joop M Den Uyl
1977–82	Andreas A M van Agt
1982–	Ruud F M Lubbers

NEW ZEALAND

Chief of State: British monarch, represented by Governor General

Prime Minister

1856	Henry Sewell
1856	William Fox
1856–61	Edward William Stafford
1861–2	William Fox
1862–3	Alfred Domett
1863–4	Frederick Whitaker
1864–5	Frederick Aloysius Weld
1865–9	Edward William Stafford
1869–72	William Fox
1872	Edward William Stafford
1873	William Fox
1873–5	Julius Vogel
1875–6	Daniel Pollen
1876	Julius Vogel
1876–7	Harry Albert Atkinson
1877–9	George Grey
1879–82	John Hall
1882–3	Frederick Whitaker
1883–4	Harry Albert Atkinson
1884	Robert Stout
1884	Harry Albert Atkinson
1884–7	Robert Stout
1887–91	Harry Albert Atkinson
1891–3	John Ballance
1893–1906	Richard John Seddon *Lib*
1906	William Hall-Jones *Lib*
1906–12	Joseph George Ward *Lib/Nat*
1912	Thomas Mackenzie *Nat*
1912–25	William Ferguson Massey *Ref*
1925	Francis Henry Dillon Bell *Ref*
1925–8	Joseph Gordon Coates *Ref*
1928–30	Joseph George Ward *Lib/Nat*
1930–5	George William Forbes *Un*
1935–40	Michael Joseph Savage *Lab*
1940–9	Peter Fraser *Lab*
1949–57	Sidney George Holland *Nat*
1957	Keith Jacka Holyoake *Nat*
1957–60	Walter Nash *Lab*
1960–72	Keith Jacka Holyoake *Nat*
1972	John Ross Marshall *Nat*
1972–4	Norman Eric Kirk *Lab*
1974–5	Wallace Edward Rowling *Lab*
1975–84	Robert David Muldoon *Nat*
1984–89	David Russell Lange *Lab*
1989–90	Geoffrey Palmer *Lab*
1990	Mike Moore *Lab*
1990–	Jim Bolger *Nat*

Lab *Labour*
Lib *Liberal*
Nat *National*
Ref *Reform*
Un *United*

NICARAGUA

President

1893–1909	José Santos Zelaya
1909–10	José Madriz
1910–11	José Dolores Estrada
1911	Juan José Estrada
1911–17	Adolfo Díaz
1912	Luis Mena *rival President*
1917–21	Emiliano Chamorro Vargas
1921–3	Riego Manuel Chamorro
1923–4	Martínez Bartolo
1925–6	Carlos Solórzano
1926	Emiliano Chamorro Vargas
1926–8	Adolfo Díaz
1926	Juan Bautista Sacasa *rival President*
1928–32	José Marcia Moncada
1933–6	Juan Bautista Sacasa

POLITICAL LEADERS 1900–1992 (cont.)

Nicaragua (cont.)

1936	Carlos Brenes Jarquin
1937–47	Anastasio Somoza García
1947	Leonardo Argüello
1947	Benjamin Lascayo Sacasa
1947–50	Victor Manuel Román y Reyes
1950–6	Anastasio Somoza García
1956–63	Luis Somoza Debayle
1963–6	René Schick Gutiérrez
1966–7	Lorenzo Guerrero Gutiérrez
1967–72	Anastasio Somoza Debayle
1972–4	*Triumvirate*
1974–9	Anastasio Somoza Debayle
1979–84	*Government Junta of National Reconstruction*
1984–90	Daniel Ortega Saavedra
1990–	Violeta Chamorro

NIGER

President

1960–74	Hamani Diori
1974–87	Seyni Kountché
1987–	Ali Saibou

NIGERIA

President

1960–6	Nnamdi Azikiwe

Prime Minister

1960–6	Abubakar Tafawa Balewa

Military Government

1966–	J T U Aguiyi-Ironsi
1966–75	Yakuba Gowon
1975–6	Murtala R Mohamed
1976–9	Olusegun Obasanjo

President

1979–83	Alhaji Shehu Shagari

Military Government

1983–4	Mohammadu Buhari
1985–	Ibrahim B Babangida

NORWAY

Monarch

1872–1905	Oscar II *union with Sweden*
1905–57	Haakon VII
1957–91	Olav V
1991–	Harald V

Prime Minister

1898–1902	Johannes Steen
1902–3	Otto Albert Blehr
1903–5	George Francis Hagerup
1905–7	Christian Michelsen
1907–8	Jørgen Løvland
1908–10	Gunnar Knudsen
1910–12	Wollert Konow
1912–13	Jens Bratlie
1913–20	Gunnar Knudsen
1920–1	Otto Bahr Halvorsen
1921–3	Otto Albert Blehr
1923	Otto Bahr Halvorsen
1923–4	Abraham Berge
1924–6	Johan Ludwig Mowinckel
1926–8	Ivar Lykke
1928	Christopher Hornsrud
1928–31	Johan Ludwig Mowinckel
1931–2	Peder L Kolstad
1932–3	Jens Hundseid
1933–5	Johan Ludwig Mowinckel
1935–45	Johan Nygaardsvold
1945–51	Einar Gerhardsen
1951–5	Oscar Torp
1955–63	Einar Gerhardsen
1963	John Lyng
1963–5	Einar Gerhardsen
1965–71	Per Borten
1971–2	Trygve Bratteli
1972–3	Lars Korvald
1973–6	Trygve Bratteli
1976–81	Odvar Nordli
1981	Gro Harlem Brundtland
1981–6	Kåre Willoch
1986–9	Gro Harlem Brundtland
1989–90	Jan P Syse
1990–	Grottarlem Brundtland

OMAN

Sultan

1888–1913	Faisal Bin Turki
1913–32	Taimur Bin Faisal

POLITICAL LEADERS 1900–1992 (cont.)

1932–70 Said Bin Taimur
1970– Qabous Bin Said

PAKISTAN

President

1956–8 Iskander Mirza
1958–69 Mohammad Ayoub Khan
1969–71 Agha Mohammad Yahya Khan
1971–3 Zulfikar Ali Bhutto
1973–8 Fazal Elahi Chawdry
1978–88 Mohammad Zia Ul-Haq
1988– Ghulam Ishaq Khan

Prime Minister

1947–51 Liaqat Ali Khan
1951–3 Khawaja Nazimuddin
1953–5 Mohammad Ali
1955–6 Chawdry Mohammad Ali
1956–7 Hussein Shahid Suhrawardi
1957 Ismail Chundrigar
1957–8 Malik Feroz Khan Noon
1958 Mohammad Ayoub Khan
1958–73 *No Prime Minister*
1973–7 Zulfikar Ali Bhutto
1977–85 *No Prime Minister*
1985–88 Mohammad Khan Junejo
1988 Mohammad Aslam Khan Khattak
1988–90 Benazir Bhutto
1990 Ghulam Mustafa Jatoi
1990– Mian Nawaz Sharif

PANAMA

President

1904–8 Manuel Amador Guerrero
1908–10 José Domingo de Obaldia
1910 Federico Boyd
1910 Carlos Antonio Mendoza
1910–12 Pablo Arosemena
1912 Rodolfo Chiari
1912–16 Belisario Porras
1916–18 Ramón Maximiliano Valdés
1918 Pedro Antonio Diaz
1918 Cirilo Luis Urriola
1918–20 Belisario Porras
1920 Ernesto T Lefevre
1920–4 Belisario Porras
1924–8 Rodolfo Chiari
1928 Tomás Gabriel Duque
1928–31 Florencio Harmodio Arosemena
1931 Harmodio Arias
1931–2 Ricardo Joaquín Alfaro
1932–6 Harmodio Arias
1936–9 Juan Demóstenes Arosemena
1939 Ezequiel Fernández Jaén
1939–40 Augusto Samuel Boyd
1940–1 Arnulfo Arias Madrid
1941 Ernesto Jaén Guardia
1941 José Pezet
1941–5 Ricardo Adolfo de la Guardia
1945–8 Enrique Adolfo Jiménez Brin
1948–9 Domingo Diaz Arosemena
1949 Daniel Chanis
1949 Roberto Francisco Chiari
1949–51 Arnulfo Arias Madrid
1951–2 Alcibiades Arosemena
1952–5 José Antonio Remón
1955 José Ramón Guizado
1955–6 Ricardo Manuel Arias Espinosa
1956–60 Ernesto de la Guardia
1960–4 Roberto Francisco Chiari
1964–8 Marco A Robles
1968 Arnulfo Arias Madrid
1968 *Military Junta*
1968–9 Omar Torrijos Herrera
1969–78 Demetrio Basilio Lakas
1978–82 Aristides Royo
1982–4 Ricardo de la Esoriella
1984 Jorge Enrique Illueca Sibauste
1984–5 Nicolás Ardito Barletta
1985–8 Eric Arturo Delvalle
1988–9 Manuel Solís Palma
1989– Guillermo Endara Galimany

PAPUA NEW GUINEA

Prime Minister

1975–80 Michael T Somare
1980–2 Julius Chan
1982–5 Michael T Somare
1985–8 Paias Wingti
1988– Rabbie Namaliu

POLITICAL LEADERS 1900–1992 (cont.)

PARAGUAY

President

1898–1902	Emilio Azeval
1902	Hector Carvallo
1902–4	Juan Antonio Escurra
1904–5	Juan Gaona
1905–6	Cecilio Baez
1906–8	Benigno Ferreira
1908–10	Emiliano Gonzáles Navero
1910–11	Manuel Gondra
1911	Albino Jara
1911	Liberato Marcial Rojas
1912	Pedro Peña
1912	Emiliano González Navero
1912–16	Eduardo Schaerer
1916–19	Manuel Franco
1919–20	José P Montero
1920–1	Manuel Gondra
1921	Félix Paiva
1921–3	Eusebio Ayala
1923–4	Eligio Ayala
1924	Luis Alberto Riart
1924–8	Eligio Ayala
1928–31	José Particio Guggiari
1931–2	Emiliano González Navero
1932	José Particio Guggiari
1932–6	Eusebio Ayala
1936–7	Rafael Franco
1937–9	Félix Paiva
1939–40	José Félix Estigarribia
1940–8	Higino Moríñigo
1948	Juan Manuel Frutos
1948–9	Juan Natalicio González
1949	Raimundo Rolón
1949	Felipe Molas López
1949–54	Federico Chaves
1954	Tomás Romero Pareira
1954–89	Alfredo Stroessner
1989–	Andres Rodríguez

PERU

President

1899–1903	Eduardo López de Romaña
1903–4	Manuel Candamo
1904	Serapio Calderón
1904–8	José Pardo y Barreda
1908–12	Augusto B Leguía
1912–14	Guillermo Billinghurst
1914–15	Oscar R Benavides
1915–19	José Pardo y Barreda
1919–30	Augusto B Leguía
1930	Manuel Ponce
1930–1	Luis M Sánchez Cerro
1931	Leoncio Elías
1931	Gustavo A Jiménez
1931	David Samanez Ocampo
1931–3	Luis M Sánchez Cerro
1933–9	Oscar R Benavides
1939–45	Manuel Prado
1945–8	José Luis Bustamante y Rivero
1948–56	Manuel A Odría
1956–62	Manuel Prado
1962–3	*Military Junta*
1963–8	Fernando Belaúnde Terry
1968–75	*Military Junta* (Juan Velasco Alvarado)
1975–80	*Military Junta* (Francisco Morales Bermúdez)
1980–5	Fernando Belaúnde Terry
1985–90	Alan García Pérez
1990–	Alberto Keinya Fujimori

PHILIPPINES

President

Commonwealth
1935–44 Manuel L Quezon

Japanese Occupation
1943–4 José P Laurel

Commonwealth
1944–6 Sergio Osmeña

First Republic
1946–8 Manuel A Roxas
1948–53 Elpidio Quirino
1953–7 Ramon Magsaysay
1957–61 Carlos P Garcia
1961–5 Diosdado Macapagal
1965–72 Ferdinand E Marcos

Martial Law
1972–81 Ferdinand E Marcos

New Republic
1981–6 Ferdinand E Marcos
1986–92 Corazon C Aquino
1992– Fidel Ramos

POLITICAL LEADERS 1900–1992 (cont.)

POLAND

Polish People's Republic

Chief of State

1945–7 Bolesław Bierut *Acting President*
1947–52 Bolesław Bierut
1952–64 Aleksander Zawadzki
1964–8 Edward Ochab
1968–70 Marian Spychalski
1970–2 Józef Cyrankiewicz
1972–85 Henryk Jabłonski
1985–90 Wojciech Jaruzelski *President 1989*
1990– Lech Walesa

Premier

1947–52 Józef Cyrankiewicz
1952–4 Bolesław Bierut
1954–70 Józef Cyrankiewicz
1970–80 Piotr Jecoszewicz
1980 Edward Babiuch
1980–1 Józef Pinkowski
1981–5 Wojciech Jaruzelski
1985–8 Zbigniew Messner
1988–9 Mieczyslaw Rakowski
1989 Czeslaw Kiszczak
1989–90 Tadeusz Mazowiecki
1991 Jan Krzysztof Bielecki
1991–2 Jan Olszewski
1992– Waldemar Pawlak

First Secretary

1945–8 Władysław Gomułka
1948–56 Bolesław Bierut
1956 Edward Ochab
1956–70 Władysław Gomułka
1970–80 Edward Gierek
1980–1 Stanisław Kania
1981–9 Wojciech Jaruzelski
1989– Mieczyslaw Rakowski

PORTUGAL

President

1st Republic
1910–11 Teófilo Braga
1911–15 Manuel José de Arriaga
1915 Teófilo Braga
1915–17 Bernardino Machado
1917–18 Sidónio Pais
1918–19 João do Canto e Castro
1919–23 António José de Almeida
1923–5 Manuel Teixeira Gomes
1925–6 Bernardino Machado

New State
1926 *Military Junta* (José Mendes Cabeçadas)
1926 *Military Junta* (Manuel de Oliveira Gomes da Costa)
1926–51 António Oscar Fragoso Carmona
1951–8 Francisco Craveiro Lopes
1958–74 Américo de Deus Tomás

2nd Republic
1974 *Military Junta* (António Spínola)
1974–6 *Military Junta* (Francisco da Costa Gomes)

3rd Republic
1976–86 António dos Santos Ramalho Eanes
1986– Mario Soares

Prime Minister

1932–68 António de Oliveira Salazar
1968–74 Marcelo Caetano
1974 Adelino da Palma Carlos
1974–5 Vasco Gonçalves
1975–6 José Pinheiro de Azevedo
1976–8 Mário Soares
1978 Alfredo Nobre da Costa
1978–9 Carlos Alberto de Mota Pinto
1979 Maria de Lurdes Pintasilgo
1980–1 Francisco de Sá Carneiro
1981–3 Francisco Pinto Balsemão
1983–5 Mário Soares
1985– Aníbal Cavaço Silva

QATAR

Emir

Family name: Al-Thani
1971–2 Ahmad Bin Ali
1972– Khalifah Bin Hamad

ROMANIA

Monarch

1881 1914 Carol I

POLITICAL LEADERS 1900–1992 (cont.)

Romania (cont.)

1914–27	Ferdinand I
1927–30	Michael *Prince*
1930–40	Carol II
1940–7	Michael I

Republic

President

1947–8	Mihai Sadoveanu *Interim*
1948–52	Constantin I Parhon
1952–8	Petru Groza
1958–61	Ion Georghe Maurer
1961–5	Georghe Gheorghiu-Dej
1965–7	Chivu Stoica
1967–89	Nicolae Ceaușescu
1989–	Ion Iliescu

General Secretary

1955–65	Georghe Gheorghiu-Dej
1965–89	Nicolae Ceaușescu

Prime Minister

1900–1	Petre P Carp
1901–6	Dimitrie A Sturdza
1906–7	Gheorge Grigore Cantacuzino
1907–9	Dimitrie A Sturdza
1909	Ionel Brătianu
1909–10	Mihai Pherekyde
1910–11	Ionel Brătianu
1911–12	Petre P Carp
1912–14	Titu Maiorescu
1914–18	Ionel Brătianu
1918	Alexandru Averescu
1918	Alexandru Marghiloman
1918	Constantin Coandă
1918	Ionel Brătianu
1919	Artur Văitoianu
1919–20	Alexandru Vaida-Voevod
1920–1	Alexandru Averescu
1921–2	Take Ionescu
1922–6	Ionel Brătianu
1926–7	Alexandru Averescu
1927	Ionel Brătianu
1927–8	Vintila I C Brătianu
1928–30	Juliu Maniu
1930	Gheorghe C Mironescu
1930	Juliu Maniu
1930–1	Gheorghe C Mironescu
1931–2	Nicolae Iorga
1932	Alexandru Vaida-Voevod
1932–3	Juliu Maniu
1933	Alexandru Vaida-Voevod
1933	Ion G Duca
1933–4	Constantin Angelescu
1934–7	Gheorghe Tătărescu
1937	Octavian Goga
1937–9	Miron Cristea
1939	Armand Călinescu
1939	Gheorghe Argeșanu
1939	Constantine Argetoianu
1939–40	Gheorghe Tătărescu
1940	Ion Gigurtu
1940–4	Ion Antonescu
1944	Constantin Savbnătescu
1944–5	Nicolas Rădescu
1945–52	Petru Groza
1952–5	Gheorghe Gheorghiu-Dej
1955–61	Chivu Stoica
1961–74	Ion Gheorghe Maurer
1974–80	Manea Mănescu
1980–3	Ilie Verdet
1983–9	Constantin Dăscălescu
1989–91	Petre Roman
1991–	Theodor Stolojan

RUSSIA

President

1991–	Boris Yeltsin

Prime Minister

1991–2	Boris Yeltsin
1992–	Yegor Gaidar *Acting Prime Minister*

RWANDA

President

1962–73	Grégoire Kayibanda
1973–	Juvénal Habvarimana

SAINT CHRISTOPHER AND NEVIS

Chief of State: British monarch, represented by Governor General

Prime Minister

1983–	Kennedy A Simmonds

POLITICAL LEADERS 1900–1992 (cont.)

SAINT LUCIA

Chief of State: British monarch, represented by Governor General

Prime Minister

1979	John Compton
1979–81	Allan Louisy
1981–3	Winston Francis Cenac
1983–	John Compton

SAINT VINCENT AND THE GRENADINES

Chief of State: British monarch, represented by Governor General

Prime Minister

1979–84	Milton Cato
1984–	James Fitz-Allan Mitchell

SAN MARINO

Regent

2 regents appointed every 6 months

SÃO TOMÉ AND PRINCIPE

President

1975–91	Manuel Pinta da Costa
1991–	Miguel Trovoada

SAUDI ARABIA

Monarch

Family name: Al-Saud

1932–53	Abdulaziz Bin Abdur-Rahman
1953–64	Saud Bin Abdulaziz
1964–75	Faisal Bin Abdulaziz
1975–82	Khalid Bin Abdulaziz
1982–	Fahd Bin Abdulaziz

SENEGAL

President

1960–80	Léopold Sédar Senghor
1981–	Abdou Diouf

SEYCHELLES

President

1976–7	James R Mancham
1977–	France-Albert René

SIERRA LEONE

President

1971	Christopher Okero Cole
1971–85	Siaka Stevens
1985–	Joseph Saidu Momoh

Prime Minister

Commonwealth

1961–4	Milton Margai
1964–7	Albert Michael Margai
1967	Siaka Stevens
1967	David Lansana
1967	Ambrose Genda
1967–8	*National Reformation Council* (Andrew Saxon-Smith)
1968	John Bangura
1968–71	Siaka Stevens

Republic

1971–5	Sorie Ibrahim Koroma
1975–8	Christian Alusine Kamara Taylor
1978–	*No Prime Minister*

SINGAPORE

President (Yang di-Pertuan Negara)

1959–70	Yusof bin Ishak
1970–81	Benjamin Henry Sheares
1981–5	Chengara Veetil Devan Nair
1985–	Wee Kim Wee

POLITICAL LEADERS 1900–1992 (cont.)

Singapore (cont.)

Prime Minister

1959–90 Lee Kuan Yew
1990– Goh Chok Tong

SLOVENIA

President

1991– Milan Kucan

SOLOMON ISLANDS

Chief of State: British monarch, represented by Governor General

Prime Minister

1978–82 Peter Kenilorea
1982–4 Solomon Mamaloni
1984–6 Peter Kenilorea
1986–9 Ezekiel Alebua
1989– Solomon Mamaloni

SOMALIA

President

1961–7 Aden Abdallah Osman
1967–9 Abdirashid Ali Shermarke

Supreme Revolutionary Council
1969–80 Mohammed Siad Barre

Republic
1980–91 Mohammed Siad Barre
1991– Ali Mahdi Mohammed

Prime Minister

1961–4 Abdirashid Ali Shermarke
1964–7 Abdirizak Haji Hussein
1967–9 Mohammed Haji Ibrahim Egal
1987–90 Mohammed Ali Samater
1990–91 Mohamed Hawadie Madar
1991– Umar Arteh Ghaleb

SOUTH AFRICA

Governor General

1910–14 Herbert, Viscount Gladstone
1914–20 Sydney, Earl Buxton
1920–4 Arthur, Duke of Connaught
1924–31 Alexander, Earl of Athlone
1931–7 George Herbert Hyde Villiers
1937–43 Patrick Duncan
1943–5 Nicolaas Jacobus de Wet
1945–51 Gideon Brand Van Zyl
1951–9 Ernest George Jansen
1959 Lucas Cornelius Steyn
1959–61 Charles Robberts Swart

Republic

President

1961–7 Charles Robberts Swart
1967 Theophilus Ebenhaezer Dönges
1967–8 Jozua François Nandé
1968–75 Jacobus Johannes Fouché
1975–8 Nicolaas Diederichs
1978–9 Balthasar Johannes Vorster
1979–84 Marais Viljoen
1984–89 Pieter Willem Botha
1989– Frederick Willem de Klerk

Prime Minister

1910–19 Louis Botha *SAf*
1919–24 Jan Christiaan Smuts *SAf*
1924–39 James Barry Munnick Hertzog *Nat*
1939–48 Jan Christiaan Smuts *Un*
1948–54 Daniel François Malan *Nat*
1954–8 Johannes Gerardus Strijdom *Nat*
1958–66 Hendrik Frensch Verwoerd *Nat*
1966–78 Balthasar Johannes Vorster *Nat*
1978–84 Pieter Willem Botha *Nat*
1984– *No Prime Minister*

Nat National
SAf South African Party
Un United

SPAIN

Monarch

1886–1931 Alfonso XIII

Second Republic

President

1931–6 Niceto Alcalá Zamora y Torres

POLITICAL LEADERS 1900–1992 (cont.)

1936 Diego Martínez Barrio *Acting President*

Civil War
1936–9 Manuel Azaña y Díez
1936–9 Miguel Cabanellas Ferrer

Nationalist Government

Chief of State

1936–75 Francisco Franco Bahamonde

Monarch

1975– Juan Carlos I

Prime Minister

1900–1 Marcelo de Azcárraga y Palmero
1901–2 Práxedes Mateo Sagasta
1902–3 Francisco Silvela y Le-Vielleuze
1903 Raimundo Fernández Villaverde
1903–4 Antonio Maura y Montaner
1904–5 Marcelo de Azcárraga y Palmero
1905 Raimundo Fernández Villaverde
1905 Eugenio Montero Ríos
1905–6 Segismundo Moret y Prendergast
1906 José López Domínguez
1906 Segismundo Moret y Prendergast
1906–7 Antonio Aguilar y Correa
1907–9 Antonio Maura y Montaner
1909–10 Segismundo Moret y Prendergast
1910–12 José Canalejas y Méndez
1912 Álvaro Figueroa y Torres
1912–13 Manuel García Prieto
1913–15 Eduardo Dato y Iradier
1915–17 Álvaro Figueroa y Torres
1917 Manuel García Prieto
1917 Eduardo Dato y Iradier
1917–18 Manuel García Prieto
1918 Antonio Maura y Montaner
1918 Manuel García Prieto
1918–19 Álvaro Figueroa y Torres
1919 Antonio Maura y Montaner
1919 Joaquín Sánchez de Toca
1919–20 Manuel Allendesalazar
1920–1 Eduardo Dato y Iradier
1921 Gabino Bugallal Araujo *Acting Prime Minister*
1921 Manuel Allendesalazar
1921–2 Antonio Maura y Montaner
1922 José Sánchez Guerra y Martínez
1922–3 Manuel García Prieto
1923–30 Miguel Primo de Rivera y Oraneja
1930–1 Dámaso Berenguer y Fusté
1931 Juan Bautista Aznar-Cabañas
1931 Niceto Alcalá Zamora y Torres
1931–3 Manuel Azaña y Díez
1933 Alejandro Lerroux y García
1933 Diego Martínez Barrio
1933–4 Alejandro Lerroux y García
1934 Ricardo Samper Ibáñez
1934–5 Alejandro Lerroux y García
1935 Joaquín Chapaprieta y Terragosa
1935–6 Manuel Portela Valladares
1936 Manuel Azaña y Díez
1936 Santiago Casares Quiroga
1936 Diego Martínez Barrio
1936 José Giral y Pereyra
1936–7 Francisco Largo Caballero
1937–9 Juan Negrín

Chairman of the Council of Ministers

1939–73 Francisco Franco Bahamonde

Prime Minister

1973 Torcuato Fernández Miranda y Hevía *Acting Prime Minister*
1973–6 Carlos Arias Navarro
1976–81 Adolfo Suárez
1981–2 Calvo Sotelo
1982 Felipe González

SRI LANKA

President

1972–8 William Gopallawa
1978–89 Junius Richard Jayawardene
1989– Ranasinghe Premadasa

Prime Minister

Ceylon
1947–52 Don Stephen Senanayake
1952–3 Dudley Shelton Senanayake
1953–6 John Kutewala
1956–9 Solomon West Ridgeway Dias Bandaranaike
1960 Dudley Shelton Senanayake
1960–5 Sirimavo Ratwatte Dias Bandaranaike
1965–70 Dudley Shelton Senanayake

Sri Lanka
1970–7 Sirimavo Bandaranaike
1977–89 Ranasinghe Premadasa
1989– D B Wijetunge

POLITICAL LEADERS 1900–1992 (cont.)

THE SUDAN

Chief of State

1956–8 *Council of State*
1958–64 Ibrahim Abboud
1964–5 *Council of Sovereignty*
1965–9 Ismail Al-Azhari
1969–85 Jaafar Mohammed Nimeiri *President from 1971*

Transitional Military Council

Chairman

1985–6 Abd Al-Rahman Siwar Al-Dahab

Supreme Council

Chairman

1986–9 Ahmad Al-Mirghani

Prime Minister

1955–6 Ismail Al-Azhari
1956–8 Abdullah Khalil
1958–64 *As President*
1964–5 Serr Al-Khatim Al-Khalifa
1965–6 Mohammed Ahmed Mahjoub
1966–7 Sadiq Al-Mahdi
1967–9 Mohammed Ahmed Mahjoub
1969 Babiker Awadalla
1969–76 *As President*
1976–7 Rashid Al-Tahir Bakr
1977–85 *As President*
1985–6 *Transitional Millitary Council* (Al-Jazuli Dafallah)
1986–9 Sadiq Al-Mahdi *Military Council, Prime Minister*
1989– Omar Hassan Ahmed al-Bashir

SURINAME

President

1975–80 J H E Ferrier
1980–2 Henk Chin-a-Sen
1982–8 L F Ramdat-Musier *Acting President*
1988–90 Ramsewak Shankar
1990–91 Johan Kraag
1991– Ronald Venetiaan

National Military Council

Chairman

1980–90 Desi Bouterse
1990– Iwan Granoogst

Prime Minister

1975–80 Henk Arron
1980 00 Henk Chin-a-Sen
1980–2 *No Prime Minister*
1982–3 Henry Weyhorst
1983–4 Errol Alibux
1984–6 Wim Udenhout
1986–7 Pretaapnarian Radbakishun
1987– Jules Wijdenbosch

SWAZILAND

Monarch

1967–82 Sobhuza II *Chief since 1921*
1983 Dzeliwe *Queen Regent*
1983–6 Ntombi *Queen Regent*
1986– Mswati III

Prime Minister

1967–78 Prince Makhosini
1978–9 Prince Maphevu Dlamini
1979–83 Prince Mbandla Dlamini
1983–6 Prince Bhekimpi Dlamini
1986–9 Sotsha Dlamini
1989 Obed Dlamini *Acting Prime Minister*

SWEDEN

Monarch

1872–1907 Oskar II
1907–50 Gustav V
1950–73 Gustav VI Adolf
1973– Carl XVI Gustaf

Prime Minister

1900–2 Fredrik von Otter
1902–5 Erik Gustaf Boström
1905 Johan Ramstedt
1905 Christian Lundeberg
1905–6 Karl Staaf

POLITICAL LEADERS 1900–1992 (cont.)

1906–11	Arvid Lindman
1911–14	Karl Staaf
1914–17	Hjalmar Hammarskjöld
1917	Carl Swartz
1917–20	Nils Edén
1920	Hjalmar Branting
1920–1	Louis de Geer
1921	Oscar von Sydow
1921–3	Hjalmar Branting
1923–4	Ernst Trygger
1924–5	Hjalmar Branting
1925–6	Rickard Sandler
1926–8	Carl Gustaf Ekman
1928–30	Arvid Lindman
1930–2	Carl Gustaf Ekman
1932	Felix Hamrin
1932–6	Per Albin Hansson
1936	Axel Pehrsson-Branstorp
1936–46	Per Albin Hansson
1946–69	Tage Erlander
1969–76	Olof Palme
1976–8	Thorbjörn Fälldin
1978–9	Ola Ullsten
1979–82	Thorbjörn Fälldin
1982–6	Olof Palme
1986–91	Ingvar Carlsson
1991–	Carl Bildt

SWITZERLAND

President

1900	Walter Hauser
1901	Ernst Brenner
1902	Joseph Zemp
1903	Adolf Deucher
1904	Robert Comtesse
1905	Marc-Emile Ruchet
1906	Ludwig Forrer
1907	Eduard Müller
1908	Ernst Brenner
1909	Adolf Deucher
1910	Robert Comtesse
1911	Marc-Emile Ruchet
1912	Ludwig Forrer
1913	Eduard Müller
1914	Arthur Hoffmann
1915	Guiseppe Motta
1916	Camille Decoppet
1917	Edmund Schulthess
1918	Felix Calonder
1919	Gustave Ador
1920	Giuseppe Motta
1921	Edmund Schulthess
1922	Robert Haab
1923	Karl Scheurer
1924	Ernest Chuard
1925	Jean-Marie Musy
1926	Heinrich Häberlin
1927	Giuseppe Motta
1928	Edmund Schulthess
1929	Robert Haab
1930	Jean-Marie Musy
1931	Heinrich Häberlin
1932	Giuseppe Motta
1933	Edmund Schulthess
1934	Marcel Pilet-Golaz
1935	Rudolf Minger
1936	Albert Meyer
1937	Giuseppe Motta
1938	Johannes Baumann
1939	Philipp Etter
1940	Marcel Pilet-Golaz
1941	Ernst Wetter
1942	Philipp Etter
1943	Enrico Celio
1944	Walter Stampfli
1945	Eduard von Steiger
1946	Karl Kobelt
1947	Philipp Etter
1948	Enrico Celio
1949	Ernst Nobs
1950	Max Petitpierre
1951	Eduard von Steiger
1952	Karl Kobelt
1953	Philipp Etter
1954	Rodolphe Rubattel
1955	Max Petitpierre
1956	Markus Feldmann
1957	Hans Streuli
1958	Thomas Holenstein
1959	Paul Chaudet
1960	Max Petitpierre
1961	Friedrich Wahlen
1962	Paul Chaudet
1963	Willy Spühler
1964	Ludwig von Moos
1965	Hans Peter Tschudi
1966	Hans Schaffner
1967	Roger Bonvin
1968	Willy Spühler
1969	Ludwig von Moos
1970	Hans Peter Tschudi

POLITICAL LEADERS 1900–1992 (cont.)

Switzerland (cont.)

1971	Rudolf Gnägi
1972	Nello Celio
1973	Roger Bonvin
1974	Ernst Brugger
1975	Pierre Graber
1976	Rudolf Gnägi
1977	Kurt Furgler
1978	Willi Ritschard
1979	Hans Hürlimann
1980	Georges-André Chevallaz
1981	Kurt Furgler
1982	Fritz Honegger
1983	Pierre Aubert
1984	Leon Schlumpf
1985	Kurt Furgler
1986	Alphons Egli
1987	Pierre Aubert
1988	Otto Stich
1989	Jean-Pascal Delamuraz
1990	Arnold Koller
1991	Flavio Cotti
1992	René Felber

SYRIA

President

1943–9	Shukri Al-Quwwatli
1949	Husni Az-Zaim
1949–51	Hashim Al-Atasi
1951–4	Adib Shishaqli
1954–5	Hashim Al-Atasi
1955–8	Shukri Al-Quwwatli
1958–61	*Part of United Arab Republic*
1961–3	Nazim Al-Qudsi
1963	Luai Al-Atassi
1963–6	Amin Al-Hafiz
1966–70	Nureddin Al-Atassi
1970–1	Ahmad Al-Khatib
1971–	Hafez Al Assad

Prime Minister

1946–8	Jamil Mardam Bey
1948–9	Khalid Al-Azm
1949–	Husni Az-Zaim
1949	Muhsi Al-Barazi
1949	Hashim Al-Atassi
1949	Nazim Al-Qudsi
1949–50	Khalid Al-Azm
1950–1	Nazim Al-Qudsi
1951	Khalid Al-Azm
1951	Hassan Al-Hakim
1951	Maruf Ad-Dawalibi
1951–3	Fauzi As-Salu
1953–4	Adib Shishaqli
1954	Shewqet Shuqair
1954	Sabri Al-Asali
1954	Said Al-Ghazzi
1954–5	Faris Al-Khuri
1955	Sabri Al-Asali
1955–6	Said Al-Ghazzi
1956–8	Sabri Al-Asali
1958–61	*Part of United Arab Republic*
1961	Abd Al-Hamid As-Sarraj
1961	Mamun Kuzbari
1961	Izzat An-Nuss
1961–2	Maruf Ad-Dawalibi
1962	Bashir Azmah
1962–3	Khalid Al-Azm
1963	Salah Ad-Din Al-Bitaar
1963	Sami Al-Jundi
1963	Salah Ad-Din Al-Bitaar
1963–4	Amin Al-Hafez
1964	Salah Ad-Din Al-Bitaar
1964–5	Amin Al-Hafez
1965	Yousif Zeayen
1966	Salah Ad-Din Al-Bitaar
1966–8	Yousif Zeayen
1968–70	Nureddin Al-Atassi *Acting Prime Minister*
1970–1	Hafez Al-Assad
1971–2	Abdel Rahman Khleifawi
1972–6	Mahmoud Bin Saleh Al-Ayoubi
1976–8	Abdul Rahman Khleifawi
1978–80	Mohammed Ali Al-Halabi
1980–7	Abdel Rauof Al-Kasm
1987–	Mahmoud Zubi

TADZHIKISTAN

President

1991–	Rakhman Nabiyev

TAIWAN

President

1950–75	Chiang Kai-shek

POLITICAL LEADERS 1900–1992 (cont.)

1975–8 Yen Chia-kan
1978–87 Chiang Ching-kuo
1987– Lee Teng-hui

President of Executive Council

1950–4 Ch'eng Ch'eng
1954–8 O K Yui
1958–63 Ch'eng Ch'eng
1963–72 Yen Chia-ken
1972–8 Chiang Ching-kuo
1978–84 Sun Yun-suan
1984–9 Yu Kuo-hwa
1989–90 Lee Huan
1990– Hau Pei-tsun

TANZANIA

Pesident

1964–85 Julius Kambarage Nyerere
1985– Ali Hassan Mwinyi

Prime Minister

1964–72 Rashid M Kawawa *Vice President*
1972–7 Rashid M Kawawa
1977–80 Edward M Sokoine
1980–3 Cleopa D Msuya
1983–4 Edward M Sokoine
1984–5 Salim A Salim
1985–90 Joseph S Warioba
1990– Iohn Malecela

THAILAND

Monarch

1868–1910 Chulalongkorn, Rama V
1910–25 Rama VI
1925–35 Rama VII
1935–9 Rama VIII (Ananda Mahidol)
1939–46 Nai Pridi Phanomyong *Regent*
1946 Rama IX
1946–50 Rangsit of Chainat *Regent*
1950– Bhumibol Adulyadej

Prime Minister

1932–3 Phraya Manopakom
1933–8 Phraya Phahon Phonphahuyasena
1938–44 Luang Phibun Songgram
1945 Thawi Bunyaket
1945–6 Mom Rachawongse Seni Pramoj
1946 Nai Khuang Aphaiwong
1946 Nai Pridi Phanomyong
1946–7 Luang Thamrong Nawasawat
1947–8 Nai Khuang Aphaiwong
1948–57 Luang Phibun Songgram
1957 Sarit Thanarat
1957 Nai Pote Sarasin
1957–8 Thanom Kittikatchom
1958–63 Sarit Thanarat
1963–73 Thanom Kittikatchom
1973–5 Sanya Dharmasaki
1975–6 Mom Rachawongse Kukrit Pramoj
1976 Seni Pramoj
1976–7 Thanin Kraivichien
1977–80 Kriangsak Chammanard
1980–7 Prem Tinsulanonda
1987–91 Chatichai Choonhaven
1991–2 Anand Panyarachun
1992 Suchinda Kraprayoon
1992– Anand Panyarachun

TOGO

President

1960–3 Sylvanus Olympio
1963–7 Nicolas Grunitzky
1967– Gnassingbe Eyadema

TONGA

Monarch

1893–1918 George Tupou II
1918–65 Salote Tupou III
1965– Taufa'ahau Tupou IV

Prime Minister

1970–91 Fatafehi Tu'ipelehake
1991– Baron Vaea

TRINIDAD AND TOBAGO

President

1976–87 Ellis Emmanuel Clarke
1987– Noor Hassanali

POLITICAL LEADERS 1900–1992 (cont.)

Trinidad and Tobago (cont.)

Premier

1956–62 Eric Williams

Prime Minister

1962–81 Eric Williams
1981–6 George Chambers
1986–91 Arthur Napoleon Raymond Robinson
1991– Patrick Manning

TUNISIA

Bey

1943–57 Muhammad VIII

President

1957–87 Habib Bourguiba
1987– Zine Al-Abidine Bin Ali

Prime Minister

1956–7 Habib Bourguiba
1957–69 *No Prime Minister*
1969–70 Bahi Ladgham
1970–80 Hadi Nouira
1980–6 Mohammed Mezali
1986–7 Rashid Sfar
1987 Zine Al-Abidine Bin Ali
1987–9 Hadi Baccouche
1989– Hamed Karoui

TURKEY

Sultan of the Ottoman Empire

1876–1909 Abdülhamit
1909–18 Mehmet Reşat
1918–22 Mehmet Vahideddin

Turkish Republic

President

1923–38 Mustafa Kemal Atatürk
1938–50 İsmet İnönü
1950–60 Celal Bayar
1961–6 Cemal Gürsel
1966–73 Cevdet Sunay
1973–80 Fahri S Korutürk
1980 Ihsan Çaglayangil *Acting President*
1982–9 Kenan Evren
1989– Turgut Özal

Prime Minister

1923–4 İsmet İnönü
1924–5 Ali Fethi Okyar
1925–37 İsmet İnönü
1937–9 Celal Bayar
1939–42 Dr Refik Saydam
1942–6 Şükrü Saracoğlu
1946–7 Recep Peker
1947–9 Hasan Saka
1949–50 Şemşettin Günaltay
1950–60 Adnan Menderes
1960–1 Cemal Gürsel
1961–5 İsmet İnönü
1965 S Hayri Ürgüplü
1965–71 Süleyman Demirel
1971–2 Nihat Erim
1972–3 Ferit Melen
1973–4 Naim Talu
1974 Bülent Ecevit
1974–5 Sadi Irmak
1975–7 Süleyman Demirel
1977 Bülent Ecevit
1977–8 Süleyman Demirel
1978–9 Bülent Ecevit
1979–80 Süleyman Demirel
1980–3 Bülent Ülüsü
1983–9 Turgut Özal
1989–91 Yildirim Akbulut
1991 Mesut Yilmaz
1991– Süleyman Demirel

TURKMENISTAN

President

1991– Suparmurad Niyazov

TUVALU

Chief of State: British monarch, represented by Governor General

Prime Minister

1978–81 Toalipi Lauti
1981–9 Tomasi Puapua
1989– Bikenibeu Paeniu

POLITICAL LEADERS 1900–1992 (cont.)

UGANDA

President	
1962–6	Edward Muteesa II
1967–71	Apollo Milton Obote
1971–9	Idi Amin
1979	Yusuf Kironde Lule
1979–80	Godfrey Lukongwa Binaisa
1981–5	Apollo Milton Obote
1985–6	*Military Council* (Tito Okello Lutwa)
1986–	Yoweri Kaguta Museveni

Prime Minister	
1962–71	Apollo Milton Obote
1971–81	*No Prime Minister*
1981–5	Eric Otema Alimadi
1985	Paulo Muwanga
1985–6	Abraham N Waliggo
1986–91	Samson B Kisekka
1991–	George Cosmas Adyebo

UKRAINE

President	
1991–	Leonid Kravchuk

UNITED ARAB EMIRATES

President	
1971–	Zayed Bin Sultan Al-Nahyan

Prime Minister	
1971–9	Maktoum Bin Rashid Al-Maktoum
1979–	Rashid Bin Said Al-Maktoum

ABU DHABI

Tribe: Al Bu Falah *or* Al Nahyan (Bani Yas)
Family name: Al-Nahyan

Shaikh	
1855–1909	Zayed
1909–12	Tahnoun
1912–22	Hamdan
1922–6	Sultan
1926–8	Saqr
1928–66	Shakhbout
1966–	Zayed

AJMAN

Tribe: Al Bu Kharayban (Naim)
Family name: Al-Nuaimi

Shaikh	
1900–10	Abdel-Aziz
1910–28	Humaid
1928–81	Rashid
1981–	Humaid

DUBAI

Tribe: Al Bu Flasah (Bani Yas)
Family name: Al-Maktoum

Shaikh	
1894–1906	Maktoum
1906–12	Butti
1912–58	Said
1958–90	Rashid
1990–	Maktoum

FUJAIRAH

Tribe: Sharqiyyin
Family name: Al-Sharqi

Shaikh	
1952–75	Mohammed
1975–	Hamad

RAS AL-KHAIMAH

Tribe: Huwalah
Family name: Al-Qasimi

Shaikh	
1921–48	Sultan
1948	Saqr

SHARJAH

Tribe: Huwalah
Family name: Al-Qasimi

Shaikh	
1883–1914	Saqr
1914–24	Khaled
1924–51	Sultan
1951–65	Saqr
1965–72	Khaled
1972–87	Sultan
1987	Abdel-Aziz
1987–	Sultan

POLITICAL LEADERS 1900–1992 (cont.)

United Arab Emirates (cont.)

UMM AL-QAIWAIN
Tribe: Al-Ali
Family name: Al-Mualla

Shaikh

1873–1904	Ahmad
1904–22	Rashid
1922–3	Abdullah
1923–9	Hamad
1929–81	Ahmad
1981–	Rashid

UNITED KINGDOM

For list of previous monarchs see p 177

Monarch

House of Hanover	
1714–27	George I
1727–60	George II
1760–1820	George III
1820–30	George IV
1830–7	William IV
1837–1901	Victoria
House of Saxe-Coburg	
1901–10	Edward VII
House of Windsor	
1910–36	George V
1936	Edward VIII
1936–52	George VI
1952–	Elizabeth II

Prime Minister

1721–42	Robert Walpole *Whig*
1742–3	Earl of Wilmington (Spencer Compton) *Whig*
1743–54	Henry Pelham *Whig*
1754–6	Duke of Newcastle (Thomas Pelham-Holles) *Whig*
1756–7	Duke of Devonshire (William Cavendish) *Whig*
1757–62	Duke of Newcastle *Whig*
1762–3	Earl of Bute (John Stuart) *Tory*
1763–5	George Grenville *Whig*
1765–6	Marquess of Rockingham (Charles Watson Wentworth) *Whig*
1766–70	Duke of Grafton (Augustus Henry Fitzroy) *Whig*
1770–82	Lord North (Frederick North) *Tory*
1782	Marquess of Rockingham *Whig*
1782–3	Earl of Shelburne (William Petty-Fitzmaurice) *Whig*
1783	Duke of Portland (William Henry Cavendish) *Coal*
1783–1801	William Pitt *Tory*
1801–4	Henry Addington *Tory*
1804–6	William Pitt *Tory*
1806–7	Lord Grenville (William Wyndham) *Whig*
1807–9	Duke of Portland *Tory*
1809–12	Spencer Perceval *Tory*
1812–27	Earl of Liverpool (Robert Banks Jenkinson) *Tory*
1827	George Canning *Tory*
1827–8	Viscount Goderich (Frederick John Robinson) *Tory*
1828–30	Duke of Wellington (Arthur Wellesley) *Tory*
1830–4	Earl Grey (Charles Grey) *Whig*
1834	Viscount Melbourne (William Lamb) *Whig*
1834–5	Robert Peel *Con*
1835–41	Viscount Melbourne *Whig*
1841–6	Robert Peel *Con*
1846–52	Lord John Russell *Lib*
1852	Earl of Derby (Edward George Stanley) *Con*
1852–5	Lord Aberdeen (George Hamilton-Gordon) *Peelite*
1855–8	Viscount Palmerston (Henry John Temple) *Lib*
1858–9	Earl of Derby *Con*
1859–65	Viscount Palmerston *Lib*
1865–6	Lord John Russell *Lib*
1866–8	Earl of Derby *Con*
1868	Benjamin Disraeli *Con*
1868–74	William Ewart Gladstone *Lib*
1874–80	Benjamin Disraeli *Con*
1880–5	William Ewart Gladstone *Lib*
1885–6	Marquess of Salisbury (Robert Gascoyne-Cecil) *Con*
1886	William Ewart Gladstone *Lib*
1886–92	Marquess of Salisbury *Con*
1892–4	William Ewart Gladstone *Lib*
1894–5	Earl of Rosebery (Archibald Philip Primrose) *Lib*
1895–1902	Marquess of Salisbury *Con*
1902–5	Arthur James Balfour *Con*
1905–8	Henry Campbell-Bannerman *Lib*

POLITICAL LEADERS 1900–1992 (cont.)

1908–15	Herbert Henry Asquith *Lib*
1915–16	Herbert Henry Asquith *Coal*
1916–22	David Lloyd George *Coal*
1922–3	Andrew Bonar Law *Con*
1923–4	Stanley Baldwin *Con*
1924	James Ramsay MacDonald *Lab*
1924–9	Stanley Baldwin *Con*
1929–31	James Ramsay MacDonald *Lab*
1931–5	James Ramsay MacDonald *Nat*
1935–7	Stanley Baldwin *Nat*
1937–40	Arthur Neville Chamberlain *Nat*
1940–5	Winston Churchill *Coal*
1945–51	Clement Attlee *Lab*
1951–5	Winston Churchill *Con*
1955–7	Anthony Eden *Con*
1957–63	Harold Macmillan *Con*
1963–4	Alec Douglas-Home *Con*
1964–70	Harold Wilson *Lab*
1970–4	Edward Heath *Con*
1974–6	Harold Wilson *Lab*
1976–9	James Callaghan *Lab*
1979–90	Margaret Thatcher *Con*
1990–	John Major *Con*

Coal *Coalition* *Lib* *Liberal*
Con *Conservative* *Nat* *Nationalist*
Lab *Labour*

UNITED NATIONS

Secretary General

1946–53	Trygve Lie *Norway*
1953–61	Dag Hammarskjöld *Sweden*
1962–71	U Thant *Burma*
1971–81	Kurt Waldheim *Austria*
1982–91	Javier Pérez de Cuéllar *Peru*
1991–	Boutros Boutros-Ghali *Egypt*

UNITED STATES OF AMERICA

President

Vice President in parentheses

1789–97	George Washington (1st) (John Adams)
1797–1801	John Adams (2nd) *Fed* (Thomas Jefferson)
1801–9	Thomas Jefferson (3rd) *Dem-Rep* (Aaron Burr, 1801–5) (George Clinton, 1805–9)
1809–17	James Madison (4th) *Dem-Rep* (George Clinton, 1809–12) *no Vice President 1812–13* (Elbridge Gerry, 1813–14) *no Vice President 1814–17*
1817–25	James Monroe (5th) *Dem-Rep* (Daniel D Tompkins)
1825–9	John Quincy Adams (6th) *Dem-Rep* (John C Calhoun)
1829–37	Andrew Jackson (7th) *Dem* (John C Calhoun, 1829–32) *no Vice President 1832–3* (Martin van Buren, 1833–7)
1837–41	Martin van Buren (8th) *Dem* (Richard M Johnson)
1841	William Henry Harrison (9th) *Whig* (John Tyler)
1841–5	John Tyler (10th) *Whig* *no Vice President*
1845–9	James Knox Polk (11th) *Dem* (George M Dallas)
1849–50	Zachary Taylor (12th) *Whig* (Millard Fillmore)
1850–3	Millard Fillmore (13th) *Whig* *no Vice President*
1853–7	Franklin Pierce (14th) *Dem* (William R King, 1853) *no Vice President 1853–7*
1857–61	James Buchanan (15th) *Dem* (John C Breckinridge)
1861–5	Abraham Lincoln (16th) *Rep* (Hannibal Hamlin, 1861–5) (Andrew Johnson, 1865)
1865–9	Andrew Johnson (17th) *Dem-Nat* *no Vice President*
1869–77	Ulysses Simpson Grant (18th) *Rep* (Schuyler Colfax, 1869–73) (Henry Wilson, 1873–5) *no Vice President 1875–7*
1877–81	Rutherford Birchard Hayes (19th) *Rep* (William A Wheeler)
1881	James Abram Garfield (20th) *Rep* (Chester A Arthur)
1881–5	Chester Alan Arthur (21st) *Rep* *no Vice President*
1885–9	Grover Cleveland (22nd) *Dem* (Thomas A Hendricks, 1885) *no Vice President 1885–9*
1889–93	Benjamine Harrison (23rd) *Rep* (Levi P Morton)
1893–7	Grover Cleveland (24th) *Dem* (Adlai E Stevenson)

POLITICAL LEADERS 1900–1992 (cont.)

United States of America (cont.)

1897–1901	William McKinley (25th) *Rep* (Garret A Hobart, 1897–9) *no Vice President 1899–1901* (Theodore Roosevelt, 1901)
1901–9	Theodore Roosevelt (26th) *Rep* *no Vice President 1901–5* (Charles W Fairbanks, 1905–9)
1909–13	William Howard Taft (27th) *Rep* (James S Sherman, 1909–12) *no Vice President 1912–13*
1913–21	Woodrow Wilson (28th) *Dem* (Thomas R Marshall)
1921–3	Warren Gamaliel Harding (29th) *Rep* (Calvin Coolidge)
1923–9	Calvin Coolidge (30th) *Rep* *no Vice President 1923–5* (Charles G Dawes, 1925–9)
1929–33	Herbert Clark Hoover (31st) *Rep* (Charles Curtis)
1933–45	Franklin Delano Roosevelt (32nd) *Dem* (John N Garner, 1933–41) (Henry A Wallace, 1941–5) (Harry S Truman, 1945)
1945–53	Harry S Truman (33rd) *Dem* *no Vice President 1945–9* (Alben W Barkley, 1949–53)
1953–61	Dwight David Eisenhower (34th) *Rep* (Richard M Nixon)
1961–3	John Fitzgerald Kennedy (35th) *Dem* (Lyndon B Johnson)
1963–9	Lyndon Baines Johnson (36th) *Dem* *no Vice President 1963–5* (Hubert H Humphrey, 1965–9)
1969–74	Richard Milhous Nixon (37th) *Rep* (Spiro T Agnew, 1969–73) *no Vice President 1973, Oct–Dec* (Gerald R Ford, 1973–4)
1974–7	Gerald Rudolph Ford (38th) *Rep* *no Vice President 1974, Aug–Dec* (Nelson A Rockefeller, 1974–7)
1977–81	Jimmy Carter (39th) *Dem* (Walter F Mondale)
1981–9	Ronald Wilson Reagan (40th) *Rep* (George H W Bush)
1989–	George Herbert Walker Bush (41st) *Rep* (J Danforth Quayle)

Dem *Democrat* *Nat* *National Union*
Fed *Federalist* *Rep* *Republican*

URUGUAY

President

1899–1903	Juan Lindolfo Cuestas
1903–7	José Batlle y Ordóñez
1907–11	Claudio Williman
1911–15	José Batlle y Ordóñez
1915–19	Feliciano Viera
1919–23	Baltasar Brum
1923–7	José Serrato
1927–31	Juan Capisteguy
1931–8	Gabriel Terra
1938–43	Alfredo Baldomir
1943–7	Juan José de Amézaga
1947	Tomás Berreta
1947–51	Luis Batlle Berres
1951–5	Andrés Martínez Trueba

National Government Council (1955–67)

1955–6	Luis Batlle Berres
1956–7	Alberto F Zubiría
1957–8	Alberto Lezama
1958–9	Carlos L Fischer
1959–60	Martín R Etchegoyen
1960–1	Benito Nardone
1961–2	Eduardo Víctor Haedo
1962–3	Faustino Harrison
1963–4	Daniel Fernández Crespo
1964–5	Luis Giannattasio
1965–6	Washington Beltrán
1966–7	Alberto Heber Usher
1967	Oscar Daniel Gestido
1967–72	Jorge Pacheco Areco
1972–6	Juan María Bordaberry Arocena
1976–81	Aparicio Méndez
1981–4	Gregorio Conrado Álvarez Armelino
1984–90	Julio María Sanguinetti Cairolo
1990–	Luis Alberto Lacalle Herrera

USSR (Union of Soviet Socialist Republics)

No longer in existence, but included for reference.

President

1917	Leo Borisovich Kamenev
1917–19	Yakov Mikhailovich Sverlov
1919–46	Mikhail Ivanovich Kalinin
1946–53	Nikolai Shvernik

POLITICAL LEADERS 1900–1992 (cont.)

1953–60 Klimentiy Voroshilov
1960–4 Leonid Brezhnev
1964–5 Anastas Mikoyan
1965–77 Nikolai Podgorny
1977–82 Leonid Brezhnev
1982–3 Vasily Kuznetsov *Acting President*
1983–4 Yuri Andropov
1984 Vasily Kuznetsov *Acting President*
1984–5 Konstantin Chernenko
1985 Vasily Kuznetsov *Acting President*
1985–8 Andrei Gromyko
1988–90 Mikhail Gorbachev

Executive President

1990–91 Mikhail Gorbachev
1991 Gennady Yanayev *Acting President*
1991 Mikhail Gorbachev

Chairman (Prime Minister)

Council of Ministers
1917 Georgy Evgenyevich Lvov
1917 Aleksandr Fyodorovich Kerensky

Council of People's Commissars
1917–24 Vladimir Ilyich Lenin
1924–30 Aleksei Ivanovich Rykov
1930–41 Vyacheslav Mikhailovich Molotov
1941–53 Josef Stalin

Council of Ministers
1953–5 Georgiy Malenkov
1955–8 Nikolai Bulganin
1958–64 Nikita Khrushchev
1964–80 Alexei Kosygin
1980–5 Nikolai Tikhonov
1985–91 Nikolai Ryzhkov
1991 Valentin Pavlov
1991 Ivan Silayev *Acting*

General Secretary

1922–53 Josef Stalin
1953 Georgiy Malenkov
1953–64 Nikita Khrushchev
1964–82 Leonid Brezhnev
1982–4 Yuri Andropov
1984–5 Konstantin Chernenko
1985–91 Mikhail Gorbachev

See separate entries for former constituent states of USSR from 1990/91

UZBEKISTAN

President

1991– Islam Karimov

VANUATU

President

1980–9 George Sokomanu (*formerly* Kalkoa)
1989– Fred Timakata

Prime Minister

1980–91 Walter Lini
1991– Donald Kalpokas

VENEZUELA

President

1899–1908 Cipriano Castro
1908–36 Juan Vicente Gomez
1936–41 Eleazar Lopez Contreras
1941–5 Isaias Medina Angarita
1945–7 *Military Junta* (Romulo Betancourt)
1947–8 Romulo Gallegos
1948–50 *Military Junta* (Carlos Delgado Chalbaud)
1950–9 *Military Junta* (Marcos Perez Jimenez)
1959–64 Romulo Betancourt
1964–9 Raul Leoni
1969–74 Rafael Caldera Rodriguez
1974–9 Carlos Andres Perez
1979–84 Luis Herrera Campins
1984–9 Jaime Lusinchi
1989– Carlos Andres Perez

VIETNAM

President

Democratic Republic of Vietnam
1945–69 Ho Chi Minh
1969–76 Ton Duc Thang

State of Vietnam
1949–55 Bao Dai

POLITICAL LEADERS 1900–1992 (cont.)

Vietnam (cont.)

Republic of Vietnam

1955–63 Ngo Dinh Diem
1963–4 Duong Van Minh
1964 Nguyen Khanh
1964–5 Phan Khac Suu
1965–75 Nguyen Van Thieu
1975 Tran Van Huong
1975 Duong Van Minh
1975–6 *Provisional Revolutionary Government* (Huynh Tan Phat)

Socialist Republic of Vietnam

1976–80 Ton Duc Thang
1980–1 Nguyen Hun Tho *Acting President*
1981–7 Truongh Chinh
1987– Vo Chi Cong

Prime Minister

Democratic Republic of Vietnam

1955–76 Pham Van Dong

State of Vietnam

1949–50 Nguyen Van Xuan
1950 Nguyen Phan Long
1950–2 Tran Van Huu
1952 Tran Van Huong
1952–3 Nguyen Van Tam
1953–4 Buu Loc
1954–5 Ngo Dinh Diem

Republic of Vietnam

1955–63 Ngo Dinh Diem
1963–4 Nguyen Ngoc Tho
1964 Nguyen Khan
1964–5 Tran Van Huong
1965 Phan Huy Quat
1965–7 Nguyen Cao Ky
1967–8 Nguyen Van Loc
1968–9 Tran Van Huong
1969–75 Tran Thien Khiem
1975 Nguyen Ba Can
1975–6 Vu Van Mau

Socialist Republic of Vietnam

Premier

1976–87 Pham Van Dong
1987–8 Pham Hung
1988 Vo Van Kiet *Acting Premier*
1988–91 Do Muoi
1991– Vo Van Kiet

General Secretary

1960–80 Le Duan
1986 Truong Chinh
1986– Nguyen Van Linh

WESTERN SAMOA

President

1962–3 Tupua Tamesehe Mea'ole
Mallietoa Tanumafili II
joint Presidents
1963– Malietoa Tanumafili II

Prime Minister

1962–70 Fiame Mata'afa Faumuina Mulinu'u II
1970–6 Tupua Tamasese Leolofi IV
1976–82 Tupuola Tamasese Efi
1982 Va'ai Kolone
1982 Tupuola Taisi Efi
1982–6 Tofilau Eti Alesana
1986–8 Va'ai Kolone
1988– Tofilau Eti Alesana

YEMEN

Yemen Arab Republic (North Yemen)

Monarch (Imam)

1918–48 Yahya Mohammed Bin Mohammed
1948–62 Ahmed Bin Yahya
1962–70 Mohammed Bin Ahmed

1962 Civil War

President

1962–7 Abdullah Al-Sallal
1967–74 Abdur Rahman Al-Iriani
1974–7 *Military Command Council* (Ibrahim Al-Hamadi)
1977–8 Ahmed Bin Hussein Al-Ghashmi
1978–90 Aii Abdullah Saleh

Prime Minister

1964 Hamud Al-Jaifi
1965 Hassan Al-Amri
1965 Ahmed Mohammed Numan
1965 *As President*
1965–6 Hassan Al-Amri
1966–7 *As President*

POLITICAL LEADERS 1900–1992 (cont.)

1967 Muhsin Al-Aini
1967–9 Hassan Al-Amri
1969–70 Abd Allah Kurshumi
1970–1 Muhsin Al-Aini
1971 Abdel Salam Sabra *Acting Prime Minister*
1971 Ahmed Mohammed Numan
1971 Hassan Al-Amri
1971–2 Muhsin Al-Aini
1972–4 Qadi Abdullah Al-Hijri
1974 Hassan Makki
1974–5 Muhsin Al-Aini
1975 Abdel Latif Deifallah *Acting Prime Minister*
1975–90 Abdel-Aziz Abdel-Ghani

People's Democratic Republic of Yemen (South Yemen)

President

1967–9 Qahtan Mohammed Al-Shaabi
1969–78 Salim Ali Rubai
1978 Ali Nasir Mohammed Husani
1978–80 Abdel Fattah Ismail
1980–6 Ali Nasir Mohammed Husani
1986–90 Haidar Abu Bakr Al-Attas

Prime Minister

1969 Faisal Abd Al-Latif Al-Shaabi
1969–71 Mohammed Ali Haithem
1971–85 Ali Nasir Mohammed Husani
1985–6 Haidar Abu Bakr Al-Attas
1986–90 Yasin Said Numan

Republic of Yemen

President

1990– Ali Abdullah Saleh

Prime Minister

1990– Haidar Abu Bakr Al-Attas

YUGOSLAVIA

Monarch

1921–34 Aleksandar II
1934–45 Petar II *in exile, 1941–*

Republic

National Assembly

Chairman

1945–53 Ivan Ribar

President

1953–80 Josip Broz Tito

Collective Presidency
1980 Lazar Koliševski
1980–1 Cvijetin Mijatović
1981–2 Serghei Kraigher
1982–3 Petar Stambolić
1983–4 Mika Spiljak
1984–5 Veselin Đuranović
1985–6 Radovan Vlajković
1986–7 Sinan Hasani
1987–8 Lazar Mojsov
1988–9 Raif Dizdarević
1989–90 Janez Drnovsek
1990–1 Borisav Jovic
1991 Stipe Mesic

Prime Minister

1929–32 Pear Živkovic
1932 Vojislav Marinković
1932–4 Milan Srškić
1934 Nikola Uzunović
1934–5 Bogoljub Jevtić
1935–9 Milan Stojadinović
1939–41 Dragiša Cvetković
1941 Dušan Simović

Government in exile
1942 Slobodan Jovanović
1943 Miloš Trifunović
1943–4 Božidar Purić
1944–5 Ivan Šubašić
1945 Drago Marušić

Home government
1941–4 Milan Nedić
1943–63 Josip Broz Tito
1963–7 Petar Stambolić
1967–9 Mika Špiljak
1969–71 Mitja Ribičič
1971–7 Džemal Bijedić
1977–82 Veselin Đuranović
1982–6 Milka Planinc
1986–9 Branko Mikulić
1989–91 Ante Marković

POLITICAL LEADERS 1900–1992 (cont.)

Yugoslavia (cont.)

Communist Party

First Secretary

1937–52 Josip Broz Tito

League of Communists
1952–80 Josip Broz Tito

League of Communists Central Committee

President

1979–80 Stevan Doronjski *Acting President*
1980–1 Lazar Mojsov
1981–2 Dušan Dragosavac
1982–3 Mitja Ribičič
1983–4 Dragoslav Marković
1984–5 Ali Šukrija
1985–6 Vidoje Žarkovic
1986–7 Milanko Renovica
1987–8 Boško Krunić
1988–9 Stipe Suvar
1989–90 Milan Pancevski
1990– Miomir Grbovic
Civil War since 1991. *See* Bosnia-Herzegovina, Croatia, Slovenia

ZAÏRE

President

1960–5 Joseph Kasavubu
1965 Mobuto Sese Seko
(*formerly* Joseph Mobutu)

Prime Minister

1960 Patrice Lumumba
1960 Joseph Ileo
1960–1 *College of Commissioners*
1961 Joseph Ileo
1961–4 Cyrille Adoula
1964–5 Moïse Tshombe
1965 Evariste Kimba
1965–6 Mulamba Nyungu wa Kadima
1966–77 *As President*
1977–80 Mpinga Kasenga
1980 Bo-Boliko Lokonga Monse Mihambu
1980–1 Nguza Karl I Bond
1981–3 Nsinga Udjuu
1983–6 Kengo wa Dondo
1986–8 *No Prime Minister*
1988 Sambura Pida Nbagui
1988–90 Kengo Wa Dondo
1990–1 Lunda Bululee
1991 Mulumba Lukeji
1991 Etienne Tshisekedi
1991 Bernardin Mungul Diaka

ZAMBIA

President

1964–91 Kenneth Kaunda
1991– Frederik Chiluba

Prime Minister

1964–73 Kenneth Kaunda
1973–5 Mainza Chona
1975–7 Elijah Mudenda
1977–8 Mainza Chona
1978–81 Daniel Lisulu
1981–5 Nalumino Mundia
1985–9 Kebby Musokotwane
1989– Malimba Masheke

ZIMBABWE

President

1980–7 Canaan Sodindo Banana
1987– Robert Gabriel Mugabe

Prime Minister

1980– Robert Gabriel Mugabe

MAJOR BATTLES AND WARS

Date	Event	Explanation
c.1200 BC	Trojan Wars	Greeks v. Trojans
490–479 BC	Persian Wars	Persia v. Greek city states
490 BC	Battle of Marathon	Athens defeat of Persia
460–445 BC	First Peloponnesian War	Sparta v. Athens
431–404 BC	Second Peloponnesian War	Sparta, Corinth, Persia v. Athens
334–323 BC	Conquests of Alexander the Great Battle of Issus (333 BC) Battle of Granicus (334 BC) Battle of Guagmela (331 BC)	v. Persia, Indian states
306 BC	Battle of Ipsus	'Battle of the Kings', warring 'successors' of Alexander the Great
264–241 BC	First Punic War	Rome v. Carthage
218–202 BC	Second Punic War	Rome v. Carthage
149–146 BC	Third Punic War	Destruction of Carthage
112–106 BC	Numidian War	Rome v. Juguertia, King of Numidia
73–71 BC	Revolt of Spartacus	Slaves v. Rome
58–51 BC	Gallic Wars of Caesar	Rome v. Celtic tribes of Gaul (ancient France)
55 BC	Caesar's expedition to Britain	Rome v. British tribes
48 BC	Battle of Pharsalus	Julius Caesar's defeat of Pompei.
31 BC	Battle of Actium	Octavian's defeat of Antony and Cleopatra
70 AD	Siege of Jerusalem	Rome v. Israel (destruction of the Temple)
84 AD	Battle of Mons Graupius	Rome (Agricola) v. Scottish tribes
375–454 AD	Hun raids on the Roman Empire	Attila v. tribes of Gaul and Italy
665 AD	Battle of Basra	Arabs conquered by Muslims
771–814 AD	Conquests of Charlemagne (Charles the Great)	v. Saxons, Lombards, Arabs (in Spain)
800–1016	Viking Raids	v. Britain, Normandy, Russia, Spain, Morocco, Italy
1066	Battle of Hastings and Norman Conquest of England	William (the Conquerer) v. Harold II (king of Anglo Saxons)
1089–94	El Cid's conquest of Valencia	v. the Moors
1095–1272	The Crusades	Christians v. Turks
1190–1227	Conquests of Genghis Khan	v. Naimans, Uigurs, N China, Kara-Chitai empire, Kharezm empire
1211–1227	Genghis Khan's conquest of N China and development of the Mongol empire	
1206–1405	Mongol Conquests	v. China
1208–29	Albigensian Crusade	Inquisition v. Cathars
1220	Fall of Samarkand to Genghis Khan	
1282–1302	War of the Sicilian Vespers	Sicilian rebels v. French rulers
1297–1305	Revolt of William Wallace	Scots v. English
1314	Battle of Bannockburn	Scots (under Robert Bruce) v. English

MAJOR BATTLES AND WARS (cont.)

Date	Event	Explanation
1337–1453	Hundred Years' War	England v. France
	Battle of Sluys (1340)	English defeat of French
	Battle of Crécy (1346)	English defeat of French
	Battle of Poitiers (1356)	English defeat of French
	Battle of Agincourt (1415)	English defeat of French
1360–1405	Conquests of Tamerlane (Timur)	v. Mongols, Persia, Prussia, India
1388	Battle of Otterburn (Chevy Chase)	Scots' defeat of English (under Sir Henry Percy, 'Hotspur')
1403	Battle of Shrewsbury	Glendower and Percies defeated by Henry V
1411	Battle of Harlaw	Highland v. Lowland Scots
1429	Siege of Orleans	Joan of Arc's defeat of English
1453	The Fall of Constantinople	Turkish conquest of Byzantine Empire
1455–85	Wars of the Roses	Series of civil wars in England (House of York v. House of Lancaster)
	Battle of St Albans (1455)	First battle of war: Yorkist victory:
	Battle of Bosworth Field (1485)	Lancastrian victory: death of Richard III, ancession of Henry VII
1491–2	The Siege of Granada	Spanish defeat of Moors
1494–1559	Habsburg-Valois Wars	
1513	Battle of Flodden	English defeat of Scots
1542	Battle of Solway Moss	Scots defeat of English
1546–7	War of the Schmalkaldic League	France v. German Protestant Estates
1562	Massacre at Vassy	Huguenots killed by de Guize
1562–98	French Wars of Religion	Catholics v. Huguenots
1568–1648	Dutch Wars of Independence	Successful revolt of Netherlands v. Phillip II of Spain
1571	Battle of Lepanto	Spanish and Italian defeat of Turkish navy
1572	St Bartholomew's Day Massacre	Slaughter of French Huguenots by Charles IX
1585–9	War of the Three Henries	Henry IV secures succession to French throne
1587	Sack of Cadiz by Drake	Defeat of Philip II's Spanish ships
1588	Defeat of the Spanish Armada	English defeat of Spanish navy
1592–9	Japanese invasion of Korea	
1596–1603	Tyrone's Rebellion in Ireland	Irish v. English
1605	Gunpowder Plot	Catholic conspiracy against James I and the English Parliament
1609–14	War of the Julich Succession	Protestant v. Catholic powers of Europe
1618–48	Thirty Years' War	French king v. Habsburg rulers
1620	Battle of the White Mountain (Prague)	Defeat of Bohemian Protestants
1628–31	War of the Mantuan Succession	France v. Spain
1639	First Bishops' War	Scotland v. England
1640	Second Bishops' War	Scots' defeat of English
1641–9	Great Irish Rebellion	Ireland v. England
1642–6	English Civil War	Royalist forces of Charles I v. Parliamentarians under Cromwell
	Battle of Marston Moor (1644)	Parliamentary defeat of Royalists
1688	The Glorious Revolution	William II and Mary II ascend English throne after flight of James II

MAJOR BATTLES AND WARS (cont.)

Date	Event	Explanation
1688–97	War of the League of Augsburg	European alliance's defeat of Louis XIV
1689	Battle of Killiecrankie	Highland Scots' defeat of government
1690	Battle of the Boyne	Defeat of James II's Catholic forces by Protestant William II
1692	The Glencoe Massacre	Slaughter of McDonalds by Campbells (anti-Jacobite forces)
1701–14	War of the Spanish Succession	Grand Alliance v. Louis XIV of France
1702–13	Queen Anne's War	Britain v. France
1704	Battle of Blenheim	Allied troops' defeat of Louis XIV
1715–16	Jacobite Rebellion	Led by Earl of Mar v. Hanoverians
	Battle of Sherrifmuir (1715)	Hanoverians v. Jacobites, indecisive battle
1739–43	War of Jenkin's Ear	Britain v. Spain
1740–48	War of the Austrian Succession	Prussia v. Austria
1745–6	Jacobite Rebellion	Led by Charles Edward Stuart (Bonnie Prince Charlie)
	Battle of Prestonpans (1745)	Jacobite defeat of Hanoverians
	Battle of Culloden (1746)	Jacobite Highlanders crushed by Hanoverian forces
1756–63	Seven Years' War	Austria, France, Russia, Sweden and Saxony v. Prussia, Britain and Portugal
1759	Battle of Quebec	British defeat of French
1763–6	Pontiac's War	Unsuccessful uprising of American Indians v. British colonists
1775–83	US War of Independence	American settlers v. British government forces
	Battle of Bunker Hill (1775)	First battle of war; heavy British losses
	Battle of Stillwater or Saratoga (1777)	American defeat of British
	Battle of Yorktown (1781)	American defeat of British, decisive campaign of war
1789–92	French Revolution	Popular movement overthrowing *ancien régime* to establish new constitution
1792–1802	French Revolutionary Wars	French campaigns v. various neighbouring states
1792	Battle of Valmy	French defeat of Prussians
1798	Battle of Aboukir Bay or the Nile	Napoleon's French fleet destroyed by Nelson
1800–15	Napoleonic Wars	Fought to preserve new French constitution and influence under Napoleon Bonaparte
	Battle of Austerlitz (1805)	French defeat of Austro-Russian army
	Battle of Trafalgar (1805)	English defeat of Napoleonic fleet
1808–14	Peninsular War	France v. Britain
	Battle of Corunna (1809)	British commander Sir John Moor killed by French
1812	Napoleon's retreat from Moscow	
1814–16	Gurkha War	Gurkhas v. British in India
1815	Battle of Waterloo	Napoleon defeated by Allied forces under Duke of Wellington
1821–32	Greek War of Independence	Greek rebellion v. Turkish rule

MAJOR BATTLES AND WARS (cont.)

Date	Event	Explanation
1836	Texan War of Independence, Battle of the Alamo	Americans v. Mexican rule
1838–9	Boer-Zulu War	
1839–42	First Opium War in China	British defeat of China
1843–51	Siege of Montevideo	Combined Argentine-Uruguayan army v. Montevideo with French and English support
1844–7	First Maori War	Maoris v. British settlers in New Zealand
1846–7	Mexican War	USA v. Mexico
1853–6	Crimean War	Britain v. Russia
	Battle of Balaclava (1856)	Unsuccessful Russian attack on British base; heavy British losses
1856–60	Second Opium War in China	British defeat of China
1857–8	Mormon Utah War	Mormons v. Federal Government of USA
1859	John Brown's raid on Harper Ferry	Abolitionist attack on Federal arsenal
1859–61	Italian War of Unification	Austria v. Italy and France
	Battle of Solferino (1859)	French defeat of Austria
1860–72	Second Maori War	Maoris v. British settlers in New Zealand
1861–5	American Civil War	North (Union) states v. South (Confederate)
	Battle of Shiloh (1862)	Heavy losses to both sides
	Battle of Gettysburg (1863)	Unionist defeat of Confederates
	Battles of Petersburg (1864)	Successful Unionist campaign v. Confederates
1866	Seven Weeks' War	Prussia and Italy's defeat of Austria and allies
1876	Battle of Little Bighorn (Custer's Last Stand)	Defeat of US cavalry under General Custer by Sioux and Cheyenne Indians
1879	Zulu War	Zulu defeat of British
1879–84	War of the Pacific	Chile v. Peru and Bolivia
1880–1	First Boer War	Boers' defeat of British
1885	Fall of Khartoum	Mahdli defeat of British; death of General Gordon
1890	Massacre of Wounded Knee	US defeat of Sioux Indians
1899–1901	Boxer Uprising in China	Unsuccessful anti-foreign uprising
1899–1902	Great Boer War	Boers v. British
	Battle of Ladysmith (1900)	Sieges of the British by the Boers
	Battle of Mafeking (1900)	
1911–12	Chinese Revolution	Overthrow of Manchu dynasty
1914–18	World War 1	Triple Alliance (Britain, France and Russia) v. Triple Entente (Germany, Austria-Hungary and Turkey)
	Battles of Liège, Marne, Ypres and Tannenberg (1914)	Allied v. German forces
	Dardanelles and Gallipoli Campaigns (1915)	Unsuccessful Allied operations
	Battles of Loos and Ypres (1915)	Britain v. Germany
	Battle of Jutland (1916)	British fleet v. German fleet

MAJOR BATTLES AND WARS (cont.)

Date	Event	Explanation
1914–18	World War 1 (cont.)	
	Battle of Verdun (1916)	France v. Germany
	Battle of Passchendaele (1917)	Third battle of Ypres, Britain v. Germany
	Zeebrugge Raid (1918)	Failed British blockade of German fleet
	Battles of Amiens, Antwerp and the Somme (1918)	Allied v. German forces
1916	Easter Rebellion in Dublin	Unsuccessful revolt by Irish nationalists v. British rule
1917	Russian Revolution	Overthrow of monarchy and beginning of Communism
1918	Hungarian Revolution	Communist revolt
1932–7	Communist rebellion in China	
1935–6	Italian invasion of Ethiopia	Mussolini's troops v. Ethiopia under Haile Selassie
1936–9	Spanish Civil War	Republicans v. Nationalists
	Battle of Ebro River (1938)	Nationalist defeat of Republicans
1939–45	World War 2	Allied forces (Britain, France, USA, USSR) v. Germany, Japan, Italy
	Battle of Britain, Battle of Flanders, Evacuation of Dunkirk, Fall of France (1940)	Allied forces v. Germany
	Babi Yar Massacre (1941)	German slaughter of Jews
	Bombing of Pearl Harbour (1941)	Japanese attack on US naval base
	Battle of Stalingrad and Moscow (1941–2)	Soviet defeat of Germany
	Battle of Tobruk (1941–2)	Allied v. German forces
	Battle of Midway Island (1942)	US defeat of Japanese air force
	Battle of El Alamein (1942)	British defeat of Rommel's Afrika Corps
	Battle of Singapore (1942)	Japanese siege and occupation
	Battle of Salerno, Invasion of Sicily (1943)	Allied defeat of Germany and Italy
	Burma Campaigns (1943–5)	British-Indian forces v. Japan
	D-Day allied invasion of Normandy (1944)	Allied defeat of Germany
	Battles of Anzio, Arnhem and Monte Cassino (1944)	Allied forces v. Germany
	Battle of the Bulge in the Ardennes (1944–5)	Eventual Allied defeat of Germany
	Battle of Iwo Jima (1945)	Allied capture of Japanese air-base
	Battle of the Rhine (1945)	Allied defeat of Germany
1945–9	Chinese civil war	Communist v. non-communist forces
1946–54	French War of Indochina	Vietnam v. France
1947–8	Indian Civil War	Pakistan v. India
1950–3	Korean War	Communist v. non-communist forces
1952–6	Mau-Mau uprisings in Kenya	Kikuyu revolt v. white settlers
1956	Suez War	Israel, Britain and France v. Egypt
1956–1975	Vietnam War	North Vietnam (communist) v. South Vietnam (non-communist) and US forces
1960–8	Civil War in the Congo	Military coup created first Marxist state in Africa, 1968
1961	Bay of Pigs Invasion	Cuban defeat of exiles supported by USA

MAJOR BATTLES AND WARS (cont.)

Date	Event	Explanation
1962–74	Mozambique War of Independence	Nationalist revolt against Portuguese rule
1967	Six-Day War	Israel v. Arab states
1967–70	Nigerian-Biafran War	Nigerian defeat of Biafra
1968	Soviet invasion of Czechoslovakia	Defeat of attempt at liberalization from communism
1968	Tet offensive in Vietnam	USA v. North Vietnam
1970–1	Jordanian Civil War	Jordan v. Palestinian guerillas
1970–5	Cambodian War	Cambodia, South Vietnam and USA v. North Vietnam, Viet Cong and Khmer Rouge
1971	Civil war in Pakistan	East v. West Pakistan
1971	My Lai massacre	Slaughter of Vietnamese villagers by US troops
1973	Chilean Revolution	Marxist government overthrown in military coup
1974	Turkish invasion of Cyprus	Turkey v. Greek Cypriots
1975–88	Angolan Civil War	Internal fighting after independence
1978–9	Ugandan Civil War	Ugandan exiles and Tanzanian defeat of Idi Amin Dada's regime
1978	Lebanese Civil War	Israeli invasion of S Lebanon
1979–	Afghan Civil War and Soviet Invasion	Afghan resistance to Soviet invasion and to the Soviet-backed government remaining after their withdrawal in 1988, and subsequent internal disputes between Islamic factions.
1979	Iranian Islamic Revolution	Republic established under Ayatollah Khomeini
1980–8	Iran-Iraq Gulf War	
1982	Falklands War	British defeat of Argentina
1982–90	Nicaraguan Civil War	Contras (supported by USA) v. socialist junta
1983	Invasion of Grenada	US troops on peace-restoring mission
1983–8	Civil War in Sri Lanka	Buddhist v. Hindu groups
1986	Civil War in Haiti	Military coup and new constitution
1990	Iraqi invasion of Kuwait	
1991	Gulf War	Defeat of Iraq by US-led allies (29 countries, including UK)
1991–	Civil War in Yugoslavia	Serbia v. Slovenia, Croatia, Macedonia and Bosnia-Herzegovina

SOCIAL STRUCTURE

MAJOR CITIES OF THE WORLD

Abidjan Ivory Coast	1 850 000 (1984)
Abu Dhabi United Arab Emirates	670 125 (1985)
Acapulco Mexico	409 335 (1980)
Accra Ghana	949 100 (1988)
Adana Turkey	916 150 (1990)
Addis Ababa Ethiopia	1 495 266 (1986e)
Adelaide Australia	1 049 900 (1990e)
Aden Yemen	318 000 (1984)
Agadir Morocco	700 000 (1987e)
Agra India	899 195 (1991)
Ahmdabad India	2 872 865 (1991)
Ahvaz Iran	579 826 (1986)
Ajmer India	401 930 (1991)
Alajuela Costa Rica	147 396 (1988e)
Albuquerque USA	384 801 (1989)
Aligarh India	479 978 (1991)
Aleppo Syria	1 308 000 (1989)
Alexandria Egypt	2 917 327 (1986e)
Algiers Algeria	1 507 241 (1987)
Allahabad India	806 447 (1991)
Alma-Ata Kazakhstan	1 128 000 (1989)
Amagasaki Japan	500 976 (1989)
Amman Jordan	972 000 (1986)
Amritsar India	709 456 (1991)
Amsterdam Netherlands	694 680 (1989)
Ankara Turkey	2 559 471 (1990)
Anshan China	1 172 800 (1989e)
Antananarivo Madagascar	802 390 (1990e)
Antwerp Belgium	476 644 (1987)
Anyang China	388 800 (1989e)
Aracaju Brazil	360 013 (1987e)
Archangel Russia	416 000 (1989)
Arequipa Peru	634 500 (1990e)
Asahikawa Japan	363 704 (1989e)
Ashkhabad Turkmenistan	398 000 (1989)
Astrakhan Russia	509 000 (1989)
Asuncion Paraguay	607 706 (1990e)
Athens Greece	885 737 (1981)
Atlanta USA	426 482 (1989)
Auckland New Zealand	841 700 (1988e)
Austin USA	468 907 (1989)
Baghdad Iraq	3 844 608 (1987)
Bakhtaran Iran	560 514 (1986)
Baku Azerbaijan	1 150 000 (1989)
Baltimore USA	763 138 (1989)
Bamako Mali	646 163 (1987)
Bandung Indonesia	1 566 700 (1983e)
Bangalore India	2 650 659 (1991)
Bangkok Thailand	5 845 152 (1989e)
Bangui Central African Republic	596 776 (1988e)
Banjarmasin Indonesia	423 600 (1983e)
Banjul Gambia	44 188 (1986e)
Baoding China	467 000 (1988e)
Baoji China	301 000 (1988e)
Baotou China	936 000 (1988e)
Barcelona Spain	1 703 744 (1987e)
Barcelona Venezuela	442 677 (1989e)
Bareilly India	583 473 (1991)
Bari Italy	358 906 (1987)
Barnaul Russia	602 000 (1989)
Barquisimeto Venezuela	764 216 (1989e)
Barranquilla Colombia	899 781 (1985)
Basra Iraq	616 700 (1985e)
Beijing (Peking) China	5 468 000 (1988e)
Beirut Lebanon	1 500 000 (1985e)
Belém Brazil	1 116 578 (1987e)
Belfast UK	354 400 (1981)
Belgorod Russia	300 000 (1989)
Belgrade Yugoslavia	1 087 915 (1981)
Belo Horizonte Brazil	2 114 429 (1987e)
Bengpu China	419 000 (1988e)
Benxi China	726 000 (1988e)
Berlin Germany	3 126 072 (1987e)
Berne Switzerland	135 147 (1988e)
Bhavnagar India	400 636 (1991)
Bhilainagar India	389 601 (1991)
Bhopal India	1 063 662 (1991)
Bilbao Spain	382 413 (1987e)
Birmingham UK	992 000 (1989)
Bissau Guinea-Bissau	125 000 (1988e)
Bochum Germany	381 200 (1986e)
Bogota Colombia	3 982 941 (1985)
Bologna Italy	427 240 (1987)
Bombay (Greater) India	9 909 547 (1991)
Bonn Germany	291 400 (1986e)
Boston USA	580 095 (1989)
Brasilia Brazil	1 567 709 (1987e)
Brasov Romania	351 493 (1986e)

MAJOR CITIES OF THE WORLD (cont.)

Bratislava	Czechoslovakia	424 378 (1987e)
Brazzaville	Congo	760 300 (1990e)
Bremen	Germany	522 000 (1986e)
Brisbane	Australia	1 301 700 (1990e)
Bristol	UK	373 000 (1989)
Brno	Czechoslovakia	385 965 (1987e)
Brussels	Belgium	970 346 (1987)
Bryansk	Russia	452 000 (1989)
Bucaramanga	Colombia	352 326 (1985)
Bucharest	Romania	1 989 823 (1986e)
Budapest	Hungary	2 104 700 (1988)
Buenos Aires	Argentina	2 922 829 (1980)
Buffalo	USA	314 284 (1989)
Bulawayo	Zimbabwe	413 800 (1982)
Bursa	Turkey	834 576 (1990)
Bydgoszcz	Poland	377 900 (1988e)
Cairo	Egypt	6 452 000 (1990e)
Calcutta	India	4 388 262 (1991)
Calgary	Canada	671 326 (1986)
Cali	Colombia	1 350 565 (1985)
Calicut	India	394 447 (1981)
Callao	Peru	588 600 (1990e)
Caloocan City	Philippines	746 000 (1990)
Campinas	Brazil	841 016 (1987e)
Campo Grande	Brazil	384 398 (1987e)
Campos	Brazil	366 716 (1987e)
Canberra	Australia	310 000 (1990e)
Canton (Guangzhou)	China	2 718 000 (1988e)
Cape Town	South Africa	1 911 521 (1985)
Caracas	Venezuela	3 373 059 (1989e)
Cartagena	Colombia	531 246 (1985)
Casablanca	Morocco	2 904 000 (1987e)
Catania	Italy	372 212 (1987)
Cebu City	Philippines	610 000 (1990)
Chandigarh	India	552 992 (1991)
Changchun	China	1 557 000 (1988e)
Changsha	China	1 030 000 (1988e)
Changzhou	China	485 000 (1988e)
Charlotte	USA	372 612 (1989)
Cheboksary	Russia	420 000 (1989)
Chelyabinsk	Russia	1 143 000 (1989)
Chengdu	China	1 614 000 (1988e)
Cherepovets	Russia	310 000 (1989)
Chiba	Japan	800 620 (1988)
Chicago	USA	2 988 260 (1989)
Chiclayo	Peru	426 300 (1990e)
Chifeng	China	316 000 (1988e)
Chihuahua	Mexico	385 603 (1980)
Chimkent	Kazakhstan	393 000 (1989)
Chita	Russia	366 000 (1989)
Chittagong	Bangladesh	980 000 (1981)
Chongjin	North Korea	530 000 (1986)
Chongju	South Korea	497 499 (1990)
Chonju	South Korea	517 104 (1990)
Chongqing	China	2 179 000 (1988e)
Christchurch	New Zealand	300 700 (1988e)
Chungho	Taiwan	334 663 (1986)
Cincinnati	USA	372 282 (1989)
Ciudad Guayana	Venezuela	516 596 (1989e)
Ciudad Juárez	Mexico	544 496 (1980)
Cleveland	USA	523 906 (1989)
Cluj-Napoca	Romania	310 017 (1986e)
Cochabamba	Bolivia	360 446 (1987e)
Cochin	India	564 038 (1991)
Coimbatore	India	853 402 (1991)
Cologne	Germany	914 300 (1986e)
Colombo	Sri Lanka	609 000 (1988e)
Columbus	USA	572 341 (1989)
Conakry	Guinea	705 280 (1983)
Constanta	Romania	332 676 (1986e)
Constantine	Algeria	440 842 (1987)
Contagem	Brazil	383 904 (1987e)
Copenhagen	Denmark	1 351 999 (1986)
Córdoba	Argentina	983 969 (1980)
Coventry	UK	322 573 (1981)
Cracow	Poland	743 700 (1988e)
Cucuta	Colombia	379 478 (1985)
Culiacan	Mexico	304 826 (1980)
Curitiba	Brazil	1 279 205 (1983e)
Dakar	Senegal	1 382 000 (1985e)
Dalian	China	1 619 000 (1988e)
Dallas	USA	996 320 (1989)
Damascus	Syria	1 361 000 (1989e)
Da Nang	Vietnam	370 670 (1989)
Dandong	China	491 000 (1988e)
Daqing	China	601 000 (1988e)
Dar es Salaam	Tanzania	1 360 850 (1988)
Datong	China	740 000 (1988e)
Davao City	Philippines	850 000 (1990)
Delhi	India	7 174 755 (1991)
Denver	USA	494 589 (1989)
Detroit	USA	1 039 599 (1989)
Dhaka	Bangladesh	3 430 312 (1981)
Diyarbakir	Turkey	381 144 (1990)
Dnepropetrovsk	Ukraine	1 179 000 (1989)
Doha	Qatar	217 294 (1986)
Donetsk	Russia	1 110 000 (1989)
Dortmund	Germany	568 200 (1986e)
Douala	Cameroon	1 029 731 (1968e)
Dresden	Germany	519 523 (1987e)
Dubai	United Arab Emirates	585 189 (1989e)

MAJOR CITIES OF THE WORLD (cont.)

Dublin Republic of Ireland 920 956 (1986)
Duisburg Germany 514 600 (1986e)
Dukou China 384 000 (1988e)
Duque de Caxias Brazil 664 105 (1987e)
Durban South Africa 982 075 (1985)
Durgapur India 415 986 (1991)
Dushanbe Tadzhikistan 595 000 (1989)
Düsseldorf Germany 560 000 (1986e)
Dzhambul Kazakhstan 307 000 (1989)

Edinburgh UK 433 000 (1989)
Edmonton Canada 785 465 (1986)
El Giza Egypt 2 156 000 (1990e)
El Mahalla el-Koubra Egypt 358 844 (1986)
El Mansoura Egypt 316 870 (1986)
El Paso USA 515 607 (1989)
Eskisehir Turkey 413 082 (1990)
Essen Germany 615 400 (1986e)

Faisalabad Pakistan 1 104 209 (1981)
Faridabad India 613 828 (1991)
Feira de Santana Brazil 355 201 (1987e)
Fez Morocco 933 000 (1987e)
Florence Italy 421 299 (1987)
Fortaleza Brazil 1 582 414 (1987e)
Fort Worth USA 430 481 (1989)
Frankfurt am Main Germany 592 400 (1986e)
Freetown Sierra Leone 469 776 (1985)
Fujisawa Japan 336 892 (1988)
Fukuoka Japan 1 157 111 (1988)
Fukuyama Japan 363 123 (1988)
Funabashi Japan 515 294 (1988)
Fushun China 1 151 000 (1988e)
Fuxin China 608 000 (1988e)
Fuzhou China 832 000 (1988e)

Ganzhou China 356 000 (1988e)
Gaziantep Turkey 603 434 (1990)
Gdańsk Poland 461 500 (1988e)
Genoa Italy 722 026 (1987)
Georgetown Guyana 150 368 (1986e)
Gifu Japan 407 827 (1988)
Glasgow UK 696 000 (1989)
Goiania Brazil 923 333 (1987e)
Gomel Byelorussia 500 000 (1989)
Gorakhpur India 489 850 (1991)
Gorky Russia 1 438 000 (1989)
Gorlovka Ukraine 337 000 (1989)
Gothenburg Sweden 431 840 (1989e)
Grozny Russia 401 000 (1989)
Guadalajara Mexico 1 626 152 (1980)
Guarulhos Brazil 713 582 (1987e)
Guatemala City Guatemala 1 057 210 (1989e)
Guayaquil Ecuador 1 509 108 (1986e)
Guilin China 341 000 (1988e)
Guiyang China 938 000 (1988e)
Gujranwala Pakistan 658 753 (1981)
Guntur India 471 020 (1991)
Gwalior India 692 982 (1991)
Gwangju South Korea 1 144 695 (1990)

Hachioji Japan 432 731 (1988)
The Hague Netherlands 443 845 (1989)
Haiphong Vietnam 456 049 (1989)
Hakodate Japan 311 591 (1988)
Hamamatsu Japan 522 299 (1988)
Hamburg Germany 1 571 300 (1986e)
Hamhumg North Korea 670 000 (1986)
Handan China 778 000 (1988e)
Hangzhou China 1 049 000 (1988e)
Hanoi Vietnam 1 088 862 (1989)
Hamilton Canada 557 029 (1986)
Hanover Germany 505 700 (1986e)
Harare Zimbabwe 681 000 (1983e)
Harbin China 2 328 000 (1988e)
Havana Cuba 2 036 799 (1986e)
Hefei China 669 000 (1988e)
Hegang China 492 000 (1988e)
Helsinki Finland 490 034 (1987e)
Hengyang China 446 000 (1988e)
Hermosillo Mexico 297 175 (1980)
Higashiosaka Japan 502 893 (1989)
Himeji Japan 450 374 (1988)
Hirakata Japan 385 739 (1988)
Hiroshima Japan 1 042 629 (1988)
Ho Chi Minh City Vietnam 3 169 135 (1989)
Hohot China 605 000 (1988e)
Homs Syria 464 000 (1989e)
Hong Kong Hong Kong 5 736 100 (1989e)
Honolulu USA 848 959 (1989)
Houston USA 1 713 499 (1989)
Howrah India 946 732 (1991)
Huaibei China 325 000 (1988e)
Huainan China 655 000 (1988e)
Huangshi China 430 000 (1988e)
Hubli-Dharwar India 647 640 (1991)
Hunjiang China 458 000 (1988e)
Hyderabad India 2 991 884 (1991)
Hyderabad Pakistan 751 529 (1981)

Iasi Romania 313 060 (1986e)
Ibadan Nigeria 1 232 000 (1990e)

MAJOR CITIES OF THE WORLD (cont.)

Icel Turkey	422 357 (1990)
Ichikawa Japan	412 214 (1988)
Inchon South Korea	1 818 293 (1990)
Indianapolis USA	784 056 (1989)
Indore India	1 086 673 (1991)
Irkutsk Russia	626 000 (1989)
Isfahan Iran	1 000 000 (1986)
Istanbul Turkey	6 620 241 (1990)
Ivanovo Russia	481 000 (1989)
Iwaki Japan	357 056 (1988)
Izhevsk Russia	635 000 (1989)
Jabalpur India	739 961 (1991)
Jaboatoa Brazil	409 528 (1987e)
Jacksonville USA	654 737 (1989)
Jaipur India	1 454 678 (1991)
Jakarta Indonesia	7 347 800 (1983e)
Jalandhar India	519 530 (1991)
Jamshedpur India	461 212 (1991)
Jedda Saudi Arabia	1 500 000 (1983e)
Jerusalem Israel	504 100 (1990)
Jiamusi China	449 000 (1988e)
Jiaozuo China	364 000 (1988e)
Jilin China	971 000 (1988e)
Jinan China	1 257 000 (1988e)
Jingdezhen China	315 000 (1988e)
Jinzhou China	641 000 (1988e)
Jixi China	650 000 (1988e)
Joao Pessoa Brazil	396 197 (1987e)
Jodhpur India	648 621 (1991)
Johannesburg South Africa	1 609 408 (1985)
Juiz de Fora Brazil	349 720 (1987e)
Kabul Afghanistan	1 424 400 (1988e)
Kaesong North Korea	310 000 (1986)
Kagoshima Japan	527 979 (1988)
Kaifeng China	473 000 (1988e)
Kalinin Russia	451 000 (1989)
Kaliningrad Russia	401 000 (1989)
Kaluga Russia	312 000 (1989)
Kampala Uganda	1 008 707 (1990e)
Kanazawa Japan	422 751 (1988)
Kano Nigeria	580 200 (1990e)
Kanpur India	1 958 282 (1991)
Kansas City USA	440 435 (1989)
Kaohsiung Taiwan	1 342 797 (1987e)
Karachi Pakistan	5 180 562 (1981)
Karaganda Kazakhstan	614 000 (1989)
Karaj Iran	275 100 (1986)
Karl-Marx-Stadt Germany	313 347 (1987e)
Kathmandu Nepal	235 160 (1981)
Katowice Poland	365 800 (1988e)
Kaunas Lithuania	423 000 (1989)
Kawaguchi Japan	418 880 (1988)
Kawasaki Japan	1 114 173 (1988)
Kayseri Turkey	421 362 (1990)
Kazan Russia	1 094 000 (1989)
Keelung Taiwan	348 541 (1987e)
Kemerovo Russia	520 000 (1989)
Kenitra Morocco	833 000 (1987e)
Khabarovsk Russia	601 000 (1989)
Kharkov Ukraine	1 611 000 (1989)
Khartoum Sudan	476 218 (1983)
Khartoum North Sudan	341 146 (1983)
Kherson Ukraine	355 000 (1989)
Khulna Bangladesh	646 359 (1981)
Kiev Ukraine	2 587 000 (1989)
Kigali Rwanda	363 607 (1990e)
Kingston Jamaica	661 600 (1990e)
Kingston upon Hull UK	325 835 (1981)
Kinshasa Zaire	3 562 122 (1990e)
Kirkuk Iraq	535 000 (1977)
Kirov Russia	441 000 (1989)
Kishinyov Moldavia	665 000 (1989)
Kitakyushu Japan	1 035 053 (1988)
Kitchener Canada	311 195 (1986)
Kitwe Zambia	472 255 (1988e)
Kobe Japan	1 426 838 (1988)
Kochi Japan	311 710 (1988)
Kolhapur India	405 118 (1991)
Komsomolsk Russia	315 000 (1989)
Konya Turkey	513 346 (1990)
Koriyama Japan	303 418 (1988)
Kota India	536 444 (1991)
Krasnodar Russia	620 000 (1989)
Krasnoyarsk Russia	912 000 (1989)
Krivoy Rog Ukraine	713 000 (1989)
Kuala Lumpur Malaysia	919 610 (1980)
Kumamoto Japan	554 904 (1988)
Kumasi Ghana	385 192 (1988e)
Kunming China	1 144 000 (1988e)
Kurashiki Japan	415 780 (1988)
Kurgan Russia	356 000 (1989)
Kursk Russia	424 000 (1989)
Kuwait City Kuwait	44 335 (1985)
Kuybyshev Russia	1 257 000 (1989)
Kyoto Japan	1 419 390 (1988)
Lagos Nigeria	5 600 000 (1992)
Lahore Pakistan	2 952 689 (1981)
Lanzhou China	1 121 000 (1988e)
La Paz Bolivia	1 013 688 (1987e)
La Plata Argentina	564 750 (1980)
Las Palmas Grand Canary	358 272 (1987e)

MAJOR CITIES OF THE WORLD (cont.)

Leeds	UK	712 000 (1989)
Leicester	UK	328 835 (1981)
Leipzig	Germany	549 229 (1987)
Leon	Mexico	593 002 (1980)
Leshan	China	329 000 (1988e)
Lianyungang	China	317 000 (1988e)
Liaoyang	China	461 000 (1988e)
Liaoyuan	China	328 000 (1988e)
Libreville	Gabon	352 000 (1987e)
Lima	Peru	6 404 500 (1990e)
Lipetsk	Russia	450 000 (1989)
Lisbon	Portugal	829 600 (1986e)
Liupanshui	China	328 000 (1988e)
Liuzhou	China	561 000 (1988e)
Liverpool	UK	466 000 (1989)
Ljubljana	Yugoslavia	305 211 (1981)
Lodz	Poland	851 500 (1988e)
Lomé	Togo	366 476 (1983e)
London	Canada	342 302 (1986)
London	UK	6 756 000 (1991)
Londrina	Brazil	346 676 (1987e)
Long Beach	USA	426 025 (1989)
Los Angeles	USA	3 441 449 (1989)
Luanda	Angola	1 544 400 (1990e)
Lublin	Poland	339 500 (1988e)
Lucknow	India	1 592 010 (1991)
Ludhiana	India	1 012 062 (1991)
Luoyang	China	697 000 (1988e)
Lusaka	Zambia	870 030 (1988e)
Luxembourg	Luxembourg	116 987 (1991)
Lyons	France	415 000 (1990)
Maceio	Brazil	482 195 (1987e)
Machida	Japan	335 347 (1988)
Madras	India	3 795 028 (1991)
Madrid	Spain	3 100 507 (1987e)
Madurai	India	951 696 (1991)
Magnitogorsk	Russia	440 000 (1989)
Makassar	Indonesia	840 500 (1983e)
Makeyevka	Ukraine	430 000 (1989)
Makhachkala	Russia	315 000 (1989)
Malaga	Spain	566 330 (1987e)
Malang	Indonesia	547 100 (1983e)
Managua	Nicaragua	682 111 (1985e)
Manaus	Brazil	809 914 (1987e)
Manchester	UK	444 000 (1989)
Mandelay	Burma	532 895 (1983)
Manila	Philippines	7 832 000 (1990)
Maputo	Mozambique	1 006 765 (1987e)
Maracaibo	Venezuela	1 365 308 (1989e)
Maracay	Venezuela	923 673 (1989e)
Mar del Plata	Argentina	414 696 (1980)
Mariupal	Ukraine	517 000 (1989)
Marrakesh	Morocco	1 425 000 (1987e)
Marseilles	France	801 000 (1990)
Masan	South Korea	496 639 (1990)
Matsudo	Japan	439 106 (1988)
Matsuyama	Japan	433 886 (1988)
Mecca	Saudi Arabia	550 000 (1980)
Medan	Indonesia	1 805 500 (1983e)
Medellin	Colombia	1 468 089 (1985)
Meerut	India	752 078 (1991)
Meknes	Morocco	704 000 (1987e)
Melbourne	Australia	3 080 800 (1990e)
Memphis	USA	651 081 (1989)
Mendoza	Argentina	605 623 (1980)
Meshed	Iran	1 500 000 (1986)
Mexicali	Mexico	341 559 (1980)
Mexico City	Mexico	8 236 960 (1990)
Miami	USA	381 206 (1989)
Milan	Italy	1 478 505 (1987)
Milwaukee	USA	600 898 (1989)
Minneapolis	USA	348 384 (1989)
Minsk	Byelorussia	1 589 000 (1989)
Mogadishu	Somalia	700 000 (1985e)
Mogilyov	Byelorussia	356 000 (1989)
Mombasa	Kenya	425 600 (1984e)
Monrovia	Liberia	421 058 (1984)
Monterrey	Mexico	1 090 009 (1980)
Montevideo	Uruguay	1 246 500 (1985)
Montreal	Canada	2 921 357 (1986)
Moradabad	India	416 836 (1991)
Moscow	Russia	8 801 500 (1991)
Mosul	Iraq	570 926 (1985)
Multan	Pakistan	722 070 (1981)
Mudanjiang	China	531 000 (1988e)
Munich	Germany	1 274 700 (1986e)
Murcia	Spain	305 278 (1987e)
Murmansk	Russia	468 000 (1989)
Mysore	India	480 006 (1991)
Naberezhnye Chelny	Russia	501 000 (1989)
Nagano	Japan	341 074 (1988)
Nagasaki	Japan	445 814 (1988)
Nagoya	Japan	2 099 564 (1988)
Nagpur	India	1 622 225 (1991)
Naha	Japan	309 641 (1988)
Nairobi	Kenya	1 103 600 (1984e)
Namangan	Uzbekistan	308 000 (1989)
Nanchang	China	1 003 000 (1988e)
Nanjing	China	1 972 000 (1988e)
Nanning	China	660 000 (1988e)
Nantong	China	306 000 (1988e)

MAJOR CITIES OF THE WORLD (cont.)

Naples Italy	1 200 958 (1987)
Nara Japan	338 842 (1988)
Nashville USA	501 398 (1989)
Nassau Bahamas	168 798 (1990)
Natal Brazil	510 106 (1987e)
N'Djamena Chad	511 700 (1986e)
Ndola Zambia	442 666 (1988e)
Netzahualcoyott Mexico	1 341 230 (1980)
Newark USA	313 839 (1989)
Newcastle Australia	428 800 (1990e)
New Delhi India	294 149 (1991)
New Orleans USA	528 589 (1989)
New York USA	7 369 454 (1989)
Niamey Niger	398 265 (1988)
Nice France	342 000 (1990)
Nicosia Cyprus	168 800 (1990e)
Niigata Japan	469 521 (1988)
Nikolayev Ukraine	503 000 (1989)
Ningbo China	520 000 (1988e)
Nis Yugoslavia	643 470 (1981)
Nishinomiya Japan	412 267 (1988)
Niteroi Brazil	441 684 (1987e)
Nizhny Tagil Russia	440 000 (1989)
Nova Iguacu Brazil	1 319 491 (1987e)
Nouakchott Mauritania	393 325 (1988)
Novokuznetsk Russia	600 000 (1989)
Novosibirsk Russia	1 436 000 (1989)
Nuremberg Germany	467 000 (1986e)
Oakland USA	356 860 (1988e)
Odessa Ukraine	1 115 000 (1989)
Ogbomosho Nigeria	628 000 (1990e)
Oita Japan	392 566 (1988)
Okayama Japan	575 837 (1988)
Oklahoma City USA	431 982 (1989)
Olinda Brazil	334 686 (1987e)
Omaha USA	353 170 (1988e)
Omdurman Sudan	526 287 (1983)
Omiya Japan	383 720 (1988)
Omsk Russia	1 148 000 (1989)
Oporto Portugal	347 300 (1986e)
Oran Algeria	628 558 (1987)
Ordzhonikidze Russia	300 000 1989)
Orenburg Russia	547 000 (1989)
Oryol Russia	337 000 (1989)
Osaka Japan	2 543 520 (1988)
Osasco Brazil	591 568 (1987e)
Osijek Yugoslavia	867 646 (1981)
Oslo Norway	456 124 (1989)
Ostrava Czechoslovakia	328 373 (1987e)
Ottawa Canada	819 263 (1986)
Oujda Morocco	895 000 (1987e)
Padang Indonesia	656 800 (1983e)
Palembang Indonesia	1 205 800 (1983e)
Palermo Italy	728 843 (1987)
Palma Majorca	306 840 (1987e)
Panama City Panama	595 643 (1989e)
Panchiao Taiwan	506 220 (1987e)
Panshan China	308 000 (1988e)
Paris France	2 152 000 (1990)
Patna India	916 980 (1991)
Pavlodar Kazakhstan	331 000 (1989)
Penza Russia	543 000 (1989)
Perm Russia	1 091 000 (1989)
Perth Australia	1 193 100 (1990e)
Peshawar Pakistan	566 248 (1981)
Philadelphia USA	1 652 188 (1989)
Phoenix USA	941 948 (1989)
Pingdingshan China	403 000 (1988e)
Pingxiang China	404 000 (1988e)
Pittsburg USA	376 412 (1989)
Plovdiv Bulgaria	364 162 (1989e)
Poltava Ukraine	315 000 (1989)
Pontianak Indonesia	342 700 (1983e)
Poona India	1 559 558 (1991)
Port-au-Prince Haiti	514 438 (1989e)
Port Elizabeth South Africa	651 993 (1985)
Portland USA	425 788 (1989)
Port Louis Mauritius	141 870 (1990e)
Port Moresby Papua New Guinea	145 300 (1987e)
Porto Alegre Brazil	1 272 121 (1987e)
Port of Spain Trinidad	59 200 (1988)
Port Said Egypt	461 000 (1990e)
Poznan Poland	586 500 (1988e)
Prague Czechoslovakia	1 200 266 (1987e)
Pretoria South Africa	822 925 (1985)
Puebla Mexico	835 759 (1980)
Pusan South Korea	3 797 566 (1990)
Pyongyang North Korea	2 000 000 (1986)
Qinhuangdao China	333 000 (1988e)
Qiqihar China	1 018 000 (1988e)
Quebec Canada	603 267 (1986)
Quezon City Philippines	1 632 000 (1990)
Quito Ecuador	1 093 278 (1986e)
Qom Iran	543 139 (1986)
Rabat Morocco	1 287 000 (1987e)
Raipur India	437 887 (1991)
Rajkot India	556 137 (1991)
Ranchi India	598 498 (1991)
Rangoon Burma	2 458 712 (1983)
Rawalpindi Pakistan	794 843 (1981)

MAJOR CITIES OF THE WORLD (cont.)

Recife Brazil	1 287 623 (1987e)
Reykjavik Iceland	97 569 (1990e)
Ribeirao Preto Brazil	383 125 (1987e)
Riga Latvia	915 000 (1989)
Rio de Janeiro Brazil	5 603 388 (1987e)
Riyadh Saudi Arabia	1 308 000 (1981)
Rome Italy	2 817 227 (1987)
Rosario Argentina	957 301 (1982)
Rostov-na-Duna Russia	1 020 000 (1989)
Rotterdam Netherlands	576 232 (1989)
Sacramento USA	341 172 (1989)
Safi Morocco	793 000 (1987e)
Sagamihara Japan	498 995 (1988)
St Catherines-Niagara Canada	343 258 (1986)
St Louis USA	405 066 (1989)
St Petersburg Russia	4 456 000 (1989)
Sakai Japan	807 680 (1988)
Salem India	363 934 (1991)
Salonika Greece	406 413 (1981)
Salvador Brazil	1 804 538 (1987e)
Samarkand Uzbekistan	566 000 (1989)
San'a Yemen Arab Republic	427 185 (1986)
San Antonio USA	949 691 (1989)
San Cristobal Venezuela	355 895 (1989e)
San Diego USA	1 098 639 (1989)
San Francisco USA	750 964 (1989)
San Juan Puerto Rica	437 745 (1990)
San José USA	757 964 (1989)
San Luis Potosi Mexico	362 371 (1980)
San Miguel de Tucuman Argentina	498 578 (1980)
San Pedro Sula Honduras	429 300 (1987e)
San Salvador El Salvador	462 652 (1985e)
Santa Cruz de la Sierra Bolivia	577 803 (1987e)
Santiago Chile	4 318 305 (1985)
Santiago de Cuba Cuba	364 554 (1986e)
Santo Andre Brazil	635 129 (1987e)
Santo Domingo Dominican Republic	1 600 000 (1986e)
Santos Brazil	460 100 (1987e)
São Bernardo do Campo Brazil	562 485 (1987e)
São Gonçalo Brazil	728 469 (1987e)
São João de Merití Brazil	457 753 (1987e)
São José dos Campos Brazil	372 578 (1987e)
São Luis Brazil	561 859 (1987e)
São Paulo Brazil	10 063 110 (1987)
Sapporo Japan	1 582 073 (1988)
Saragossa Spain	575 317 (1987e)
Sarajevo Yugoslavia	448 519 (1981)
Saransk Russia	312 000 (1989)
Saratov Russia	905 000 (1989)
Seattle USA	514 398 (1989)
Semarang Indonesia	1 805 500 (1983e)
Semipalatinsk Kazakhstan	334 000 (1989)
Sendai Japan	865 630 (1988)
Seoul South Korea	10 627 790 (1990)
Shanchung Taiwan	362 171 (1987e)
Shanghai China	7 112 000 (1988e)
Shantou China	513 000 (1988e)
Shaoguan China	324 000 (1988e)
Sheffield UK	527 000 (1989)
Shenyang China	3 412 000 (1988e)
Shihezi China	301 000 (1988e)
Shijiazhuang China	987 000 (1988e)
Shiraz Iran	848 289 (1986)
Shizuoka Japan	469 782 (1988)
Sholapur India	603 870 (1991)
Shoubra el-Kheima Egypt	811 000 (1990e)
Shuangyashan China	362 000 (1988e)
Sialkot Pakistan	302 009 (1981)
Sian (Xian) China	1 828 000 (1988e)
Simferopol Ukraine	344 000(1989)
Singapore Singapore	2 674 000 (1989e)
Sinuiju North Korea	330 000 (1986)
Skopje Yugoslavia	506 547 (1981)
Smolensk Russia	341 000 (1989)
Smyrna Turkey	1 489 772 (1985)
Sochi Russia	337 000 (1989)
Sofia Bulgaria	1 136 875 (1989e)
Songnam South Korea	540 764 (1990)
Sorocaba Brazil	327 468 (1987e)
Srinagar India	594 775 (1981)
Stavropol Russia	318 000 (1989)
Stockholm Sweden	672 187 (1989e)
Stuttgart Germany	565 500 (1986e)
Suita Japan	341 590 (1988)
Surabaya Indonesia	2 223 600 (1983e)
Surakarta Indonesia	490 900 (1983e)
Surat India	1 496 943 (1991)
Suva Fiji	69 655 (1986)
Suwon South Korea	644 968 (1990)
Suzhou China	649 000 (1988e)
Sverdlovsk Russia	3 391 600 (1985e)
Sydney Australia	3 656 900 (1990)
Szczecin Poland	409 500 (1988e)
Tabriz Iran	971 482 (1986)
Taegu South Korea	2 228 834 (1990)
Taejon South Korea	1 062 084 (1990)
Taichung Taiwan	715 107 (1987e)
Tainan Taiwan	656 927 (1987e)

MAJOR CITIES OF THE WORLD (cont.)

Taipei Taiwan	2 637 100 (1987e)
Taiyuan China	1 480 000 (1988e)
Takamatsu Japan	327 538 (1988)
Takatsuki Japan	353 940 (1988)
Tallinn Estonia	482 000 (1989)
Tambov Russia	305 000 (1989)
Tangier Morocco	509 000 (1987e)
Tangshan China	980 000 (1988e)
Tanta Egypt	334 505 (1986)
Tashkent Uzbekistan	2 073 000 (1989)
Tbilisi Georgia	1 260 000 (1989)
Tegucigalpa Honduras	640 900 (1987e)
Teheran Iran	6 022 029 (1986)
Tel Aviv Israel	321 700 (1990e)
Teresina Brazil	473 901 (1987e)
Tetouan Morocco	800 000 (1987e)
Thane India	796 620 (1991)
Tianjin (Tientsin) China	4 314 000 (1988e)
Tijuana Mexico	429 500 (1980)
Timisoura Romania	325 272 (1986e)
Tirana Albania	225 700 (1987)
Tiruchchirapalli India	386 628 (1991)
Tokyo Japan	8 155 781 (1988)
Toledo USA	342 418 (1989)
Tolyatti Russia	630 000 (1989)
Tomsk Russia	502 000 (1989)
Tonghua China	304 000 (1988e)
Toronto Canada	3 427 168 (1986)
Toulouse France	359 000 (1990)
Toyama Japan	316 061 (1988)
Toyoda Japan	314 996 (1988)
Toyohasi Japan	325 862 (1988)
Toyonaka Japan	405 859 (1988)
Tripoli Libya	591 062 (1988e)
Trivandrum India	523 733 (1991)
Trujillo Peru	532 000 (1990e)
Tucson USA	383 174 (1988)
Tula Russia	540 000 (1989)
Tulsa USA	366 297 (1989)
Tunis Tunisia	596 654 (1984)
Turin Italy	1 025 390 (1987)
Tyumen Russia	477 000 (1989)
Ufa Russia	1 083 000 (1989)
Ulan Bator Mongolia	548 400 (1989)
Ulan-Ude Russia	353 000 (1989)
Ulsan South Korea	682 978 (1990)
Ulyanovsk Russia	625 000 (1989)
Urawa Japan	391 530 (1988)
Urumqi China	986 000 (1988e)
Ust-Kamenogorsk Kazakhstan	324 000 (1989)
Utsunomiya Japan	415 695 (1988)
Vadodara India	1 021 084 (1991)
Valencia Spain	732 491 (1987e)
Valencia Venezuela	1 227 472 (1989e)
Valladolid Spain	329 206 (1987e)
Vancouver Canada	1 380 729 (1986)
Varanasi India	925 962 (1991)
Vargas Venezuela	338 312 (1989e)
Varna Bulgaria	306 300 (1989e)
Venice Italy	327 700 (1987)
Veracruz Mexico	284 822 (1980)
Victoria Seychelles	23 000 (1985e)
Vienna Austria	1 531 346 (1981)
Vientiane Laos	377 409 (1985)
Vijayawada India	701 351 (1991)
Vilnius Lithuania	582 000 (1989)
Vina del Mar Chile	305 303 (1990e)
Vinnitsa Ukraine	374 000 (1989)
Virginia Beach USA	370 316 (1989)
Visakhapatnam India	750 024 (1991)
Vitebsk Byelorussia	350 000 (1989)
Vladimir Russia	350 000 (1989)
Vladivostok Russia	648 000 (1989)
Volgograd Russia	999 000 (1989)
Voronezh Russia	887 000 (1989)
Voroshilovgrad Ukraine	497 000 (1989)
Wakayama Japan	401 194 (1988)
Warangal India	446 760 (1991)
Warsaw Poland	1 651 200 (1988e)
Washington USA	604 000 (1989)
Weifang China	332 000 (1988e)
Wellington New Zealand	325 200 (1988e)
Wenzhou China	383 000 (1988e)
Windhoek Namibia	114 500 (1988e)
Winnipeg Canada	625 304 (1986)
Wroclaw Poland	637 400 (1988e)
Wuhan China	3 107 000 (1988e)
Wuhu China	409 000 (1988e)
Wuppertal Germany	374 200 (1986e)
Wuxi China	752 000 (1988e)
Xiamen China	360 000 (1988e)
Xiangfan China	351 000 (1988e)
Xiangtan China	411 000 (1988e)
Xiangyang China	312 000 (1988e)
Xining China	527 000 (1988e)
Xinxiang China	433 000 (1988e)
Xuzhou China	753 000 (1988e)
Yakeshi China	355 000 (1988e)
Yangquan China	334 000 (1988e)
Yantai China	369 000 (1988e)

MAJOR CITIES OF THE WORLD (cont.)

Yaounde Cameroon	649 000 (1987)
Yaroslavl Russia	633 000 (1989)
Yerevan Armenia	1 199 000 (1989)
Yichang (Ichang) China	353 000 (1988e)
Yichun (Ichun) China	770 000 (1988e)
Yinchuan China	314 000 (1988e)
Yingkou China	391 000 (1988e)
Yogyakarta Indonesia	490 900 (1983e)
Yokohama Japan	3 121 601 (1988)
Yukosuko Japan	430 656 (1988)
Zagreb Yugoslavia	768 700 (1981)
Zamboanga City Philippines	444 000 (1990)
Zaporozhye Ukraine	884 000 (1989)
Zarqa Jordan	392 220 (1986)
Zhangjiakou China	511 000 (1988e)
Zhengzhou China	1 065 000 (1988e)
Zhenjiang China	339 000 (1988e)
Zhuzhou China	371 000 (1988e)
Zibo China	801 000 (1988e)
Zigong China	376 000 (1988e)
Zürich Switzerland	345 159 (1988e)

LARGEST CITIES — World

São Paulo Brazil	10 063 110
Bombay India	9 909 547
Moscow Russia	8 801 500
Mexico City Mexico	8 236 960
Tokyo Japan	8 155 781
New York USA	7 369 454
Shanghai China	7 112 000
London UK	6 756 000
Cairo Egypt	6 452 000
Teheran Iran	6 022 029

LARGEST CITIES — Europe

Moscow Russia	8 801 500
London UK	6 756 000
Istanbul Turkey	6 620 241
St Petersburg Russia	4 456 000
Berlin Germany	3 126 072
Madrid Spain	3 100 507
Rome Italy	2 817 227
Paris France	2 152 000
Budapest Hungary	2 104 700
Bucharest Romania	1 989 823

LARGEST CITIES — USA

New York New York	7 369 454
Los Angeles California	3 441 449
Chicago Illinois	2 988 260
Houston Texas	1 713 499
Philadelphia Pennsylvania	1 652 188
San Diego California	1 098 639
Detroit Michigan	1 039 599
Dallas Texas	996 320
San Antonio Texas	949 691
Phoenix Arizona	941 948

NATIONS OF THE WORLD

In the case of countries that do not use the Roman alphabet (such as the Arabic countries), there is variation in the spelling of names and currencies, depending on the system of transliteration used.

Where more than one language is shown within a country, the status of the languages may not be equal. Some languages have a 'semi-official' status, or are used for a restricted set of purposes, such as trade or tourism.

Population census estimates are for 1989 or later.

English name	Local name	Official name (in English)	Capital (English name in parentheses)	Official language(s)	Currency	Population
Afghanistan	Afghānestān	Republic of Afghanistan	Kābul	Dari, Pushtøu	1 Afghani (Af) = 100 puls	14 825 000
Albania	Shqīpëri	Republic of Albania	Tiranë (Tirana)	Albanian	1 Lek (L) = 100 qindarka	3 197 000
Algeria	Al-Jazā'ir (Arabic) Algérie (French)	Democratic and Popular Republic of Algeria	El Djazair (Algiers)	Arabic	1 Algerian Dinar (AD, DA) = 100 centimes	24 946 000
Andorra	Andorra	Principality of Andorra; the Valleys of Andorra	Andorra La Vella	Catalan, French	French Franc, Spanish Peseta	50 000
Angola	Angola	People's Republic of Angola	Luanda	Portuguese	1 Kwanza (kw, kz) = 100 lweis	9 739 000
Antigua and Barbuda	Antigua and Barbuda	Antigua and Barbuda	St John's	English	1 East Caribbean Dollar (EC$) = 100 cents	78 400
Argentina	Argentina	Argentine Republic	Buenos Aires	Spanish	1 Austral (Arg $, $a) = 100 centavos	32 425 000
Armenia	Haikaka	Republic of Armenia	Yerevan	Armenian	Rouble	3 304 000
Australia	Australia	Commonwealth of Australia	Canberra	English	1 Australian Dollar ($A) = 100 cents	16 804 000
Austria	Österreich	Republic of Austria	Vienna	German	1 Schilling (S, Sch) = 100 groschen	7 603 000
Azerbaijan	Azerbaijan	Republic of Azerbaijan	Baku	Azeri (Azerbaijani)	Rouble	7 020 000
Bahamas	Bahamas	Commonwealth of the Bahamas	Nassau	English	1 Bahamian Dollar (BA$, B$) = 100 cents	249 000
Bahrain	Al-Bahrayn	State of Bahrain	Al-Manāmah (Manama)	Arabic	1 Bahrain Dinar (BD) = 1000 fils	488 500
Bangladesh	Bangladesh	People's Republic of Bangladesh	Dhaka (Dacca)	Bengali	1 Taka (TK) = 100 poisha	114 718 000

Barbados	Barbados	Barbados	Bridgetown	English	1 Barbados Dollar (Bds$) = 100 cents	255 000
Belgium	Belgique (French) België (Flemish)	Kingdom of Belgium	Bruxelles (Brussels)	Flemish, French, German	1 Belgian Franc (BFr) = 100 centimes	9 878 000
Belize	Belize	Belize	Belmopan	English	1 Belize Dollar (Bz$) = 100 cents	185 000
Benin	Bénin	Republic of Benin	Porto-Novo	French	1 CFA Franc (CFAFr) = 100 centimes	4 592 000
Bhutan	Druk-Yul	Kingdom of Bhutan	Thimbu/Thimphu	Dzongkha	1 Ngultrum (N, Nu) = 100 chetrum	1 534 000
Bolivia	Bolivia	Republic of Bolivia	La Paz/Sucre	Spanish	1 Bolivian Peso (B$) = 100 centavos	7 193 000
Bosnia-Herzegovina	Bosnia-Herzegovina	Republic of Bosnia-Herzegovina	Sarajevo	Serbo-Croat	Croatian Dinar	4 124 256
Botswana	Botswana	Republic of Botswana	Gaborone	English, Setswana	1 Pula (P, Pu) = 100 thebes	1 256 000
Brazil	Brasil	Federative Republic of Brazil	Brasília	Portuguese	1 Cruzado (= 1000 old Cruzeiros) (Cr$) = 100 centavos	147 404 000
Brunei	Brunei	State of Brunei, Abode of Peace	Bandar Seri Begawan	Malay, English	1 Brunei Dollar (Br$) = 100 cents	251 000
Bulgaria	Bălgarija	People's Republic of Bulgaria	Sofija (Sofia)	Bulgarian	1 Lev (Lv) = 100 stotinki	8 987 000
Burkina Faso	Burkina Faso	Burkina Faso	Ouagadougou	French	1 CFA Franc (CFAFr) = 100 centimes	8 714 000
Burma	Myanma	Socialist Republic of the Union of Burma	Rangoon	Burmese	1 Kyat (K) = 100 pyas	40 452 000
Burundi	Burundi	Republic of Burundi	Bujumbura	French, (Ki) Rundi	1 Burundi Franc (BuFr, FBu) = 100 centimes	5 450 000
Byelorussia	Byelarus	Republic of Byelorussia	Minsk	Byelorussian, Russian	Rouble	10 149 000
Cambodia	Cambodia	State of Cambodia	Phnum Pénh (Phnom Penh)	Khmer	1 Riel (CRl) = 100 sen	6 838 000
Cameroon	Cameroun	Republic of Cameroon	Yaoundé	English, French	1 CFA Franc (CFAFr) = 100 centimes	11 407 000
Canada	Canada	Canada	Ottawa	English, French	1 Canadian Dollar (C$, Can$) = 100 cents	26 311 000
Cape Verde	Cabo Verde	Republic of Cape Verde	Praia	Portuguese	1 Escudo (CVEsc) = 100 centavos	337 000
Central African Republic	République Centrafricaine	Central African Republic	Bangui	French	1 CFA Franc (CFAFr) = 100 centimes	2 813 000

NATIONS OF THE WORLD (cont.)

English name	Local name	Official name (in English)	Capital (English name in parentheses)	Official language(s)	Currency	Population
Chad	Tchad	Republic of Chad	N'Djamena	French	1 CFA Franc (CFAFr) = 100 centimes	5538000
Chile	Chile	Republic of Chile	Santiago	Spanish	1 Chilean Peso (Ch$) = 100 centavos	12961000
China	Zhonghua	People's Republic of China	Beijing/Peking	Chinese	1 Renminbi Yuan (RMBY, $, Y) = 10 jiao = 100 fen	1133682501
Colombia	Colombia	Republic of Colombia	Bogotá	Spanish	1 Colombian Peso (Col$) = 100 centavos	32317000
Comoros	Comores	Federal Islamic Republic of the Comoros	Moroni	French	1 Comorian Franc (CFr) = 100 centimes	448000
Congo	Congo	People's Republic of the Congo	Brazzaville	French	1 CFA Franc (CFAFr) = 100 centimes	2245000
Costa Rica	Costa Rica	Republic of Costa Rica	San José	Spanish	1 Costa Rican Colón (CR₡) = 100 centavos	2954000
Côte d'Ivoire (Ivory Coast)	Côte d'Ivoire	Republic of Côte d'Ivoire	Abidjan/ Yamoussoukro	French	1 CFA Franc (CFAFr) = 100 centimes	12135000
Croatia	Hrvatska	Republic of Croatia	Zagreb	Serbo-Croat	Croatian Dinar	4601469
Cuba	Cuba	Republic of Cuba	La Habana (Havana)	Spanish	1 Cuban Peso (Cub$) = 100 centavos	10540000
Cyprus	Kipros (Greek) Kibris (Turkish)	Republic of Cyprus	Levkosia (Nicosia)	Greek, Turkish	1 Cyprus Pound (£C) = 100 cents	733000
Czechoslovakia	Československo	Czech and Slovak Federative Republic	Praha (Prague)	Czech, Slovak	1 Koruna (Kčs) = 100 haler	15636000
Denmark	Danmark	Kingdom of Denmark	København (Copenhagen)	Danish	1 Danish Krone (Dkr) = 100 øre	5135000
Djibouti	Djibouti	Republic of Djibouti	Djibouti	Arabic, French	1 Djibouti Franc (DF, DjFr) = 100 centimes	512000
Dominica	Dominica	Commonwealth of Dominica	Roseau	English	1 East Caribbean Dollar (EC$) = 100 cents	82800
Dominican Republic	República Dominicana	Dominican Republic	Santo Domingo	Spanish	1 Dominican Peso (RD$, DR$) = 100 centavos	7012000
Ecuador	Ecuador	Republic of Ecuador	Quito	Spanish	1 Sucre (Su, S/.) = 100 centavos	10490000

Egypt	Misr	Arab Republic of Egypt	Al-Qāhirah (Cairo)	Arabic	1 Egyptian Pound (E£, LE) = 100 piastres	54778000
El Salvador	El Salvador	Republic of El Salvador	San Salvador	Spanish	1 Colón (ES₡) = 100 centavos	5125000
Equatorial Guinea	Guinea Ecuatorial	Republic of Equatorial Guinea	Malabo	Spanish	1 Ekuele (E, Ek) = 100 céntimos	343000
Estonia	Eesti	Republic of Estonia	Tallinn	Estonian	Kroon	1573000
Ethiopia	Ityopiya	Socialist Ethiopia	Adis Abeba (Addis Ababa)	Amharic	1 Ethiopian Birr (Br) = 100 cents	48898000
Fiji	Fiji	Fiji	Suva	English	1 Fiji Dollar (F$) = 100 cents	734000
Finland	Suomi (Finnish) Finland (Swedish)	Republic of Finland	Helsinki Helsingfors (Swedish)	Finnish, Swedish	1 Markka (FMk) = 100 penni	4960000
France	France	French Republic	Paris	French	1 French Franc (Fr) = 100 centimes	56107000
Gabon	Gabon	Gabonese Republic	Libreville	French	1 CFA Franc (CFAFr) = 100 centimes	1077000
Gambia	Gambia	Republic of the Gambia	Banjul	English	1 Dalasi (D, Di) = 100 butut	835000
Georgia	Gruzinskaya	Republic of Georgia	Tbilisi	Georgian, Russian	Rouble	5396000
Germany	Bundesrepublik Deutschland	Federal Republic of Germany	Berlin	German	1 Deutsche Mark (DM) = 100 Pfennige	77744000
Ghana	Ghana	Republic of Ghana	Accra	English	1 Cedi (₵) = 100 pesewas	14566000
Greece	Ellás	Hellenic Republic	Athínai (Athens)	Greek	1 Drachma (Dr) = 100 leptae	10096000
Greenland	Grønland (Danish) Kalaallit Nunaat	Greenland	Godthåb	Danish, Greenlandic	1 Danish Krone (DKr) = 100 øre	55400
Grenada	Grenada	Grenada	St George's	English	1 East Caribbean Dollar (EC$) = 100 cents	96600
Guatemala	Guatemala	Republic of Guatemala	Guatemala City	Spanish	1 Quetzal (Q) = 100 centavos	9117000
Guinea	Guinée	Republic of Guinea	Conakry	French	1 Guinean Franc (GFr) = 100 cauris	6705000
Guinea-Bissau	Guiné-Bissau	Republic of Guinea-Bissau	Bissau	Portuguese	1 Guinea-Bissau Peso (GBP, PG) = 100 centavos	953000
Guyana	Guyana	Co-operative Republic of Guyana	Georgetown	English	1 Guyana Dollar (G$) = 100 cents	754000
Haiti	Haïti	Republic of Haiti	Port-au-Prince	French	1 Gourde (G, Gde) = 100 centimes	5520000
Holland *see* Netherlands, The						
Honduras	Honduras	Republic of Honduras	Tegucigalpa	Spanish	1 Lempira (L, La) = 100 centavos	5104000
Hong Kong	Hsiang Kang (Chinese) Hong Kong (English)	Hong Kong	Hong Kong	English, Chinese	1 Hong Kong Dollar (HK$) = 100 cents	5754000

NATIONS OF THE WORLD (cont.)

English name	Local name	Official name (in English)	Capital (English name in parentheses)	Official language(s)	Currency	Population
Hungary	Magyarország	Hungarian People's Republic	Budapest	Hungarian	1 Forint (Ft) = 100 fillér	10580000
Iceland	Ísland	Republic of Iceland	Reykjavik	Icelandic	1 Króna (IKr, ISK) = 100 aurar	254000
India	Bhārat (Hindi)	Republic of India	New Delhi	Hindi, English	1 Indian Rupee (Re, Rs) = 100 paisa	833422000
Indonesia	Indonesia	Republic of Indonesia	Jakarta	Bahasa Indonesia	1 Rupiah (Rp) = 100 sen	177046000
Iran	Īrān	Islamic Republic of Iran	Tehrān (Tehran)	Farsi	1 Iranian Rial (Rls, Rl) = 100 dinars	54333000
Iraq	Al-'Īrāq	Republic of Iraq	Baghdād (Baghdad)	Arabic	1 Iraqi Dinar (ID) = 1000 fils	17215000
Ireland	Eire (Gaelic) Ireland (English)	Republic of Ireland	Baile Átha Cliath (Dublin)	Irish, English	1 Irish Pound/Punt (I£, IR£) = 100 pighne	3515000
Israel	Yisra'el (Hebrew) Isrā'īl (Arabic)	State of Israel	Yerushalayim (Jerusalem)	Hebrew, Arabic	1 Shekel (IS) = 100 agorot	4563000
Italy	Italia	Italian Republic	Roma (Rome)	Italian	1 Italian Lira (L, Lit) = 100 centesimi	57436000
Ivory Coast *see* Côte d'Ivoire						
Jamaica	Jamaica	Jamaica	Kingston	English	1 Jamaican Dollar (J$) = 100 cents	2376000
Japan	Nihon	Japan	Tōkyō (Tokyo)	Japanese	1 Yen (Y, =Y) = 100 sen	123220000
Jordan	Al 'Urdunn	Hashemite Kingdom of Jordan	'Ammān (Amman)	Arabic	1 Jordan Dinar = 1000 fils	3059000
Jugoslavia *see* Yugoslavia						
Kampuchea *see* Cambodia						
Kazakhstan	Kazakhstan	Republic of Kazakhstan	Almaata	Kazakh	Rouble	16463000
Kenya	Kenya	Republic of Kenya	Nairobi	(Ki) Swahili, English	1 Kenyan shilling (KSh) = 100 cents	23883000
Kirghizia	Kirgizstan	Republic of Kirgizstan	Frunze	Kirghiz	Rouble	4258000
Kiribati	Kiribati	Republic of Kiribati	Bairiki	English	1 Australian Dollar ($A) = 100 cents	69600
Korea, North	Chosōn Minjujuüi In'min Konghwaguk	Democratic People's Republic of Korea	P'yŏngyang (Pyongyang)	Korean	1 Won (NKW) = 100 chon	22521000
Korea, South	Taehan-Min'guk	Republic of Korea	Sŏul (Seoul)	Korean	1 Won (W) = 100 chon	43247000
Kuwait	Al-Kuwayt	State of Kuwait	Al-Kuwayt (Kuwait City)	Arabic	1 Kuwaiti Dinar (KD) = 1000 fils	2048000

Laos	Lao	Lao People's Democratic Republic	Viangchan (Vientiane)	Lao	1 Kip (Kp) = 100 at	3936000
Latvia	Latvija	Republic of Latvia	Riga	Latvian	Lat	2681000
Lebanon	Al-Lubnān	Republic of Lebanon	Bayrūt (Beirut)	Arabic	1 Lebanese Pound/Livre (LL, £L) = 100 piastres	2897000
Lesotho	Lesoto	Kingdom of Lesotho	Maseru	English, (se)Sotho	1 Loti (*plural* Maloti) (M, LSM) = 100 lisente	1715000
Liberia	Liberia	Republic of Liberia	Monrovia	English	1 Liberian Dollar (L$) = 100 cents	2508000
Libya	Lībiyā	Socialist People's Libyan Arab Jamahiriya	Tarābulus (Tripoli)	Arabic	1 Libyan Dinar (LD) = 1000 dirhams	4080000
Liechtenstein	Liechtenstein	Principality of Liechtenstein	Vaduz	German	1 Swiss Franc (SFr, SwF) = 100 centimes	28450
Lithuania	Lietuvo	Republic of Lithuania	Vilnius	Lithuanian	Litas	3690000
Luxembourg	Lëtzebuerg (Letz.) Luxembourg (Fr.) Luxemburg (Ger.)	Grand Duchy of Luxembourg	Luxembourg	French, German, Letzebuergesch	1 Luxembourg Franc (LFr) = 100 centimes	385000
Madagascar	Madagasikara	Democratic Republic of Madagascar	Antananarivo	Malagasy, French	1 Madagascar Franc (FMG, MgFr) = 100 centimes	11602000
Malawi	Malaŵi (Chewa) Malawi (English)	Republic of Malaŵi	Lilongwe	(chi)Chewa, English	1 Kwacha (MK) = 100 tambala	8515000
Malaysia	Malaysia	Malaysia	Kuala Lumpur	Malay	1 Malaysian Dollar/Ringgit (M$) = 100 cents	17421000
Maldives	Maldives Divehi Jumhuriya	Republic of Maldives	Male	Divehi	1 Rufiyaa (MRf, Rf) = 100 laaris	209000
Mali	Mali	Republic of Mali	Bamako	French	1 CFA Franc (CFAFr) = 100 centimes	7911000
Malta	Malta	Republic of Malta	Valletta	English, Maltese	1 Maltese Lira (LM) = 100 cents	349000
Mauritania	Mauritanie (French) Mūrītāniyā (Arabic)	Islamic Republic of Mauritania	Novakchott	Arabic, French	1 Ouguiya (U, UM) = 5 khoums	1946000
Mauritius	Mauritius	Mauritius	Port Louis	English	1 Mauritian Rupee (MR, MauRe) = 100 cents	1061000
Mexico	México	United Mexican States	Ciudad de México (Mexico City)	Spanish	1 Mexican Peso (Mex$) = 100 centavos	86366000
Moldavia	Moldova	Republic of Moldova	Kishinev	Moldavian	Rouble	4332000
Monaco	Monaco	Principality of Monaco	Monaco	French	1 Monaco Franc (MnFr) = 100 centimes	29100
Mongolia	Mongol Ard Uls	Mongolian People's Republic	Ulaanbaatar (Ulan Bator)	Khalka	1 Tugrik (Tug) = 100 möngö	2096000
Morocco	Al-Magrib	Kingdom of Morocco	Rabat	Arabic	1 Dirham (DH) = 100 centimes	25606000

NATIONS OF THE WORLD (cont.)

English name	Local name	Official name (in English)	Capital (English name in parentheses)	Official language(s)	Currency	Population
Mozambique	Moçambique	People's Republic of Mozambique	Maputo	Portuguese	1 Metical (Mt, MZM) = 100 centavos	15293000
Namibia	Namibia	Republic of Namibia	Windhoek	Afrikaans, English	1 South African Rand (R) = 100 cents	1550000
Nauru	Naeoro (Nauruan) Nauru (English)	Republic of Nauru	Yaren District	Nauruan, English	1 Australian Dollar ($A) = 100 cents	8100
Nepal	Nepāl	Kingdom of Nepal	Kathmandu	Nepali	1 Nepalese Rupee (NRp, NRs) = 100 paise/pice	18700000
Netherlands, The	Nederland	Kingdom of the Netherlands	Amsterdam/ 's-Gravenhage (The Hague)	Dutch	1 Dutch Guilder (Gld)/Florin (f) = 100 cents	14846000
New Zealand	New Zealand	New Zealand	Wellington	English	1 New Zealand Dollar ($NZ) = 100 cents	3371000
Nicaragua	Nicaragua	Republic of Nicaragua	Managua	Spanish	1 Córdoba (C$) = 100 centavos	3503000
Niger	Niger	Republic of Niger	Niamey	French	1 CFA Franc (CFAFr) = 100 centimes	7523000
Nigeria	Nigeria	Federal Republic of Nigeria	Lagos	English	1 Naira (N, ₦) = 100 kobo	88500000
Norway	Norge	Kingdom of Norway	Oslo	Norwegian	1 Norwegian Krone (NKr) = 100 øre	4202000
Oman	'Umān	Sultanate of Oman	Masqat (Muscat)	Arabic	1 Rial Omani (RO) = 1000 baizas	1422000
Pakistan	Pākistān	Islamic Republic of Pakistan	Islāmābād (Islamabad)	Urdu, English	1 Pakistan Rupee (PRs, Rp) = 100 paisa	110407000
Panama	Panamá	Republic of Panama	Panamá (Panama City)	Spanish	1 Balboa (B, Ba) = 100 centésimos	2373000
Papua New Guinea	Papua New Guinea	Independent State of Papua New Guinea	Port Moresby	English, Tok Pïsin, Hi-i Motu	1 Kina (K) = 100 toea	3592900
Paraguay	Paraguay	Republic of Paraguay	Asunción	Spanish	1 Guaraní (₲) = 100 céntimos	4157000

Peru	Perú	Republic of Peru	Lima	Spanish	1 Inti (I/.) = 100 centavos	21 792 000
Philippines	Filipinas	Republic of the Philippines	Manila	English, Pilipino	1 Philippine peso (PP, ₱) = 100 centavos	59 906 000
Poland	Polska	Polish People's Republic	Warszawa (Warsaw)	Polish	1 Złoty (Zl) = 100 groszy	37 875 000
Portugal	Portugal	Republic of Portugal	Lisboa (Lisbon)	Portuguese	1 Escudo (Esc) = 100 centavos	10 372 000
Puerto Rico	Puerto Rico	Commonwealth of Puerto Rico	San Juan	Spanish, English	1 US Dollar (US$) = 100 cents	3 308 000
Qatar	Qatar	State of Qatar	Ad-Dawhah (Doha)	Arabic	1 Qatar Riyal (QR) = 100 dirhams	427 000
Romania	Romănia	Romania	București (Bucharest)	Romanian	1 Leu (*plural* lei) = 100 bani	23 168 000
Russia	Rossiya	The Russian Federation	Moskva (Moscow)	Russian	Rouble	147 386 000
Rwanda	Rwanda	Republic of Rwanda	Kigali	(Kinya) Rwanda, French	1 Rwanda Franc (RF, RWFr) = 100 centimes	6 989 000
Saint Christopher and Nevis	Saint Christopher/Kitts and Nevis	Federation of Saint Christopher and Nevis	Basseterre	English	1 East Caribbean Dollar (CD$) = 100 cents	44 100
Saint Lucia	Saint Lucia	Saint Lucia	Castries	English	1 East Caribbean Dollar (EC$) = 100 cents	150 000
Saint Vincent and the Grenadines	Saint Vincent and the Grenadines	Saint Vincent and the Grenadines	Kingstown	English	1 East Caribbean Dollar (EC$) = 100 cents	114 000
San Marino	San Marino	Republic of San Marino	San Marino	Italian	1 San Marino Lira (SML) = 100 centesimi	22 860
São Tomé and Príncipe	São Tomé e Príncipe	Democratic Republic of São Tomé and Príncipe	São Tomé	Portuguese	1 Dobra (Db) = 100 centavos	118 000
Saudi Arabia	Al-'Arabīyah as Sa'ūdīyah	Kingdom of Saudi Arabia	Ar-Riyād (Riyadh)	Arabic	1 Saudi Arabian Riyal (SAR, SRls) = 100 halalah	13 592 000
Senegal	Sénégal	Republic of Senegal	Dakar	French	1 CFA Franc (CFAFr) = 100 centimes	7 400 000
Seychelles	Seychelles	Republic of Seychelles	Victoria	Creole French, English, French	1 Seychelles Rupee (SR) = 100 cents	67 100
Sierra Leone	Sierra Leone	Republic of Sierra Leone	Freetown	English	1 Leone (Le) = 100 cents	3 957 000
Singapore	Singapore	Republic of Singapore	Singapore	Chinese, English, Malay, Tamil	1 Singapore Dollar (S$)/Ringgit = 100 cents	2 674 000
Slovenia	Slovenija	Republic of Slovenia	Ljubluana	Slovene	Slovenian Dinar	1 891 864

NATIONS OF THE WORLD (cont.)

English name	Local name	Official name (in English)	Capital (English name in parentheses)	Official language(s)	Currency	Population
Solomon Islands	Solomon Islands	Solomon Islands	Honiara	English	1 Solomon Islands Dollar (SI$) = 100 cents	308000
Somalia	Somaliya	Somali Democratic Republic	Muqdisho (Mogadishu)	Arabic, Somali	1 Somali Shilling (SoSh) = 100 cents	7339000
South Africa	South Africa (English) Suid-Afrika (Afrikaans)	Republic of South Africa	Pretoria/Cape Town	Afrikaans, English	1 Rand (R) = 100 cents	30224000
Spain	España	Kingdom of Spain	Madrid	Spanish	1 Peseta (Pta, Pa) = 100 céntimos	39159000
Sri Lanka	Sri Lanka	Democratic Socialist Republic of Sri Lanka	Colombo	Sinhala, Tamil	1 Sri Lanka Rupee (SLR, SLRs) = 100 cents	16855000
Sudan	As-Sūdān	Democratic Republic of Sudan	Al-Khartūm (Khartoum)	Arabic	1 Sudanese pound (LSd, £S) = 100 piastres	27268000
Suriname	Suriname	Republic of Suriname	Paramaribo	Dutch	1 Suriname Guilder/Florin (SGld, F) = 100 cents	405000
Swaziland	Swaziland	Kingdom of Swaziland	Mbabane	English, (si)Swati	1 Lilangeni (*plural* Emalangeni) (Li, E) = 100 cents	746000
Sweden	Sverige	Kingdom of Sweden	Stockholm	Swedish	1 Swedish Krona (Skr) = 100 øre	8459000
Switzerland	Schweiz (German) Suisse (French) Svizzera (Italian)	Swiss Confederation	Bern (Berne)	French, German, Italian, Romansch	1 Swiss Franc (SFr, SwF) = 100 centimes	6673000
Syria	As-Sūrīyah	Syrian Arab Republic	Dimashq (Damascus)	Arabic	1 Syrian pound (LS, Syr£) = 100 piastres	11719000
Tadzhikistan	Tadzhikistan	Republic of Tadzhikistan	Dushanbe	Tadzhik	Rouble	5090000
Taiwan	T'aiwan	Republic of China	T'aipei (Taipei)	Chinese	1 New Taiwan Dollar (NT$) = 100 cents	20024000
Tanzania	Tanzania	United Republic of Tanzania	Dar es Salaam	(ki)Swahili, English	1 Tanzanian Shilling (TSh) = 100 cents	23729000
Thailand	Muang Thai	Kingdom of Thailand	Krung Thep (Bangkok)	Thai	1 Baht (B) = 100 satang	55258000
Togo	Togo	Republic of Togo	Lomé	French	1 CFA Franc (CFAFr) = 100 centimes	3622000
Tonga	Tonga	Kingdom of Tonga	Nuku'alofa	English, Tongan	1 Pa'anga/ Tongan Dollar (T$) = 100 seniti	95900

Trinidad and Tobago	Trinidad and Tobago	Republic of Trinidad and Tobago	Port of Spain	English	1 Trinidad and Tobago Dollar (TT$) = 100 cents	1 285 000
Tunisia	Tunis (Arabic) Tunisie (French)	Republic of Tunisia	Tunis	Arabic	1 Tunisian Dinar (TD, D) = 1000 millémes	7 916 000
Turkey	Türkiye	Republic of Turkey	Ankara	Turkish	1 Turkish Lira (TL) = 100 Kurus	55 541 000
Turkmenistan	Turkmenistan	Republic of Turkmenistan	Ashkhabad	Turkmen	Rouble	3 512 000
Tuvalu	Tuvalu	Tuvalu	Fongafale (on Funafuti)	English	1 Tuvalu Dollar = 1 Australian Dollar = 100 cents	8 900
Uganda	Uganda	Republic of Uganda	Kampala	English	1 Uganda Shilling = 100 cents	16 452 000
Ukraine	Ukrainskaya	Republic of Ukraine	Kiev	Ukrainian, Russian	Rouble	51 449 000
United Arab Emirates	Ittihād al-Imārāt al-'Arabīyah	United Arab Emirates	Abū Zaby (Abu Dhabi)	Arabic	1 Dirham (DH) = 100 fils	1 827 000
United Kingdom	United Kingdom	United Kingdom of Great Britain and Northern Ireland	London	English	1 Pound Sterling (£) = 100 new pence	57 218 000
USA	United States of America	United States of America	Washington, DC	English	1 US Dollar ($, US$) = 100 cents	249 231 000
Uruguay	Uruguay	Oriental Republic of Uruguay	Montevideo	Spanish	1 Uruguayan New Peso (NUr$, UrugN$) = 100 centésimos	3 017 000
Uzbekistan	Uzbekistan	Republic of Uzbekistan	Tashkent	Uzbek	Rouble	19 808 000
Vanuata	Vanuatu	Republic of Vanuatu	Port Vila	English, French	1 Vatu (V, VT) = 100 centimes	154 000
Venezuela	Venezuela	Republic of Venezuela	Caracas	Spanish	1 Bolívar (B) = 100 céntimos	19 246 000
Vietnam	Viět-nam	Socialist Republic of Vietnam	Ha-noi (Hanoi)	Vietnamese	1 Dông (D) = 10 hao = 100 xu	66 820 000
Western Samoa	Western Samoa (English) Samoa i Sisifo (Samoan)	Independent State of Western Samoa	Apia	English, Samoan	1 Tala/Western Samoan Dollar (WS$) = 100 cents	163 000
Yemen	Al-Yaman	Republic of Yemen	San 'ā'	Arabic	1 Yemeni Riyal (YR, YRI) = 100 fils 1 Yemeni Dinar (YD) = 1000 fils	11 240 000
Yugoslavia	Jugoslavija	Socialist Federal Republic of Yugoslavia	Beograd (Belgrade)	Macedonian, Serbo-Croat, Slovene	1 Yugoslav Dinar (D, Din) = 100 paras	23 688 000
Zaire	Zaire	Republic of Zaire	Kinshasa	French	1 Zaïre (Z) = 100 makuta (*sing.* likuta)	33 336 000
Zambia	Zambia	Republic of Zambia	Lusaka	English	1 Kwacha (K) = 100 ngwee	8 148 000
Zimbabwe	Zimbabwe	Republic of Zimbabwe	Harare	English	1 Zimbabwe Dollar (Z$) = 100 cents	9 122 000

NATIONAL HOLIDAYS

The first part of each listing gives the holidays that occur on fixed dates (though it should be noted that holidays often vary according to local circumstances and the day of the week on which they fall). Most dates are accompanied by an indication of the purpose of the day eg Independence= Independence Day; dates which have no gloss are either fixed dates within the Christian calendar (for which see below) or bank holidays.

The second part of the listing gives holidays that vary, usually depending on religious factors. The most common of these are given in abbreviated form (see list below).

A number in brackets such as (*Independence*) (*2*) refers to the number of days devoted to the holiday.

The listings do not include holidays that affect only certain parts of a country, half-day holidays, or Sundays.

The following abbreviations are used for variable religious feast-days:

A Ascension Thursday
Ad Id-ul-Adha (also found with other spellings — especially Eid-ul-Adha; various names relating to this occasion are used in different countries, such as Tabaski, Id el-Kebir, Hari Raja Haji)
Ar Arafa
As Ashora (found with various spellings)
C Carnival (immediately before Christian Lent, unless specified)
CC Corpus Christi
D Diwali, Deepavali
EM Easter Monday
ER End of Ramadan (known generally as Id/Eid-ul-Fitr, but various names relating to this occasion are used in different countries, such as Karite, Hari Raja Puasa)
ES Easter Sunday
GF Good Friday
HS Holy Saturday
HT Holy Thursday
NY New Year
PB Prophet's Birthday (known generally as Maul-id-al-Nabi in various forms and spellings)
R First day of Ramadan
WM Whit Monday

The following fixed dates are shown without gloss:

Jan 1 New Year's Day
Jan 6 Epiphany
May 1 Labour Day (often known by a different name, such as Workers' Day)
Aug 15 Assumption of Our Lady
Nov 1 All Saints' Day
Nov 2 All Souls' Day
Dec 8 Immaculate Conception
Dec 24 Christmas Eve
Dec 25 Christmas Day
Dec 26 Boxing Day/St Stephen's Day
Dec 31 New Year's Eve

Afghanistan Apr 27 (Sawr Revolution), May 1, Aug 19 (Independence); Ad(3), Ar, As, ER(3), NY (Hindu), PB, R

Albania Jan 1, 11 (Republic), May 1, Nov 28 (Independence), 29 (Liberation)

Algeria Jan 1, May 1, Jun 19 (Righting), Jul 5 (Independence), Nov 1 (Revolution); Ad, As, ER, NY (Muslim), PB

Andorra Jan 1, 6, Mar 19 (St Joseph), May 1, Jun 24 (St John), Aug 15, Sep 8 (Our Lady of Meritxell), Nov 1, 4 (St Charles), Dec 8, 25, 26; A, C, CC, EM, GF, WM

Angola Jan 1, Feb 4 (Commencement of the Armed Struggle), May 1, Sep 17 (National Hero), Nov 11 (Independence), Dec 10 (MPLA Foundation), 25 (Family)

Argentina Jan 1, May 1, 25 (National), Jun 10 (Malvinas Islands Memorial), 20 (Flag), Jul 9 (Independence), Aug 17 (Death of General San Martin), Oct 12 (Columbus), Dec 8, 25, 31; GF, HT

Australia Jan 1, Apr 25 (Anzac), Dec 25, 26 (*except South Australia*); Australia (Jan), EM, GF, HS; *additional days vary between states*

Austria Jan 1, 6, May 1, Aug 15, Oct 26 (National), Nov 1, Dec 8, 24, 25, 26; A, CC, EM, WM

NATIONAL HOLIDAYS (cont.)

Bahamas Jan 1, Jul 10 (Independence), Dec 25, 26; EM, GF, WM; Labour (Jun), Emancipation (Aug), Discovery (Oct)

Bahrain Jan 1, Dec 16 (National); Ad(3), As(2), ER(3), NY (Muslim), PB

Bangladesh Feb 21 (Shaheed), Mar 26 (Independence), May 1, Jul 1, Nov 7 (National Revolution), Dec 16 (Victory), 25, 31; Ad(3), ER(3), NY (Bengali), NY (Muslim), PB, Jumat-ul-Wida (May), Shab-e-Barat (Apr), Buddah Purnima (Apr/May), Shab-I-Qadr (May), Jumat-ul-Wida (May), Durga Puza (Oct)

Barbados Jan 1, Nov 30 (Independence), Dec 25, 26; EM, GF, WM, Kadooment (Aug), May Holiday, United Nations (Oct)

Belgium Jan 1, May 1, Jul 21 (National), Aug 15, Nov 1, 11 (Armistice), Dec 25; A, EM, WM; May, Aug, Nov Bank Holidays; Regional Holiday (Jul *in N*, Sep *in S*)

Belize Jan 1, Mar 9 (Baron Bliss), May 1, 24 (Commonwealth), Sep 10 (National), 21 (Independence), Oct 12 (Columbus), Nov 19 (Garifuna Settlement), Dec 25, 26; EM, GF, HS

Benin Jan 1, 16 (Martyrs), Apr 1 (Youth), May 1, Oct 26 (Armed Forces), Nov 30 (National), Dec 25, 31 (Feed Yourself); Ad, ER

Bhutan May 2 (Birthday of Jigme Dorji Wangchuk), Jun 2 (Coronation of Fourth Hereditary King), Jul 21 (First Sermon of Lord Buddha, Death of Jigme Dorji Wangchuk), Nov 11–13 (Birthday of HM Jigme Singye Wangchuk), Dec 17 (National)

Bolivia Jan 1, May 1, Aug 6 (Independence), Nov 1, Dec 25; C(2), CC, GF

Botswana Jan 1, 2, Sep 30 (Botswana), Dec 25, 26; A, EM, GF, HS, President's Day (Jul); Jul, Oct Public Holidays

Brazil Jan 1, Apr 21 (Independence Hero Tiradentes), May 1, Sep 7 (Independence), Oct 12, Nov 2 (Memorial), 15 (Proclamation of the Republic), Dec 25; C(2), CC, GF, HS, HT

Brunei Jan 1, Feb 23 (National), May 31 (Royal Brunei Malay Regiment), Jul 15 (Sultan's Birthday), Dec 25; Ad, ER(2), GF, NY (Chinese), NY (Muslim), PB, R, Meraj (Mar–Apr), Revelation of the Koran (May)

Bulgaria Jan 1, May 1(2), 24 (Slav Literature, Bulgarian Education and Culture), Sep 9 (National) (2), Nov 7 (October Revolution)

Burkina Faso Jan 1, 3 (1966 Revolution), May 1, Aug 4, 15, Nov 1, Dec 25; A, Ad, EM, ER, PB, WM

Burma Jan 4 (Independence), Feb 12 (Union), Mar 2 (Peasants), 27 (Resistance), Apr 1, May 1, Jul 19 (Martyrs), Oct 1, Dec 25; NY (Burmese), Thingyan (Apr)(4), End of Buddhist Lent (Oct), Full Moon days

Burundi Jan 1, May 1, Jul 1 (Independence), Aug 15, Sep 18 (Victory of Uprona), Nov 1, Dec 25; A

Cameroon Jan 1, Feb 11 (Youth), May 1, 20 (National), Aug 15, Dec 25; A, Ad, ER, GF

Canada Jan 1, Jul 1 (Canada) (*except Newfoundland*), Nov 11 (Remembrance) Dec 25, 26; EM, GF, Labour (Sep), Thanksgiving (Oct), Victoria (May); *additional days vary between states*

Cape Verde Is Jan 1, 20 (National Heroes), Mar 8 (Women), May 1, Jun 1 (Children), Sep 12 (National), Dec 24, 25; GF

Central African Republic Jan 1, Mar 29 (Death of President Boganda), May 1, Jun 1 (Mothers), Aug 13 (Independence), 15, Sep 1 (Arrival of the Military Committee for National Recovery), Nov 1, Dec 1 (Republic), 25; A, EM, WM

Chad Jan 1, May 1, 25 (Liberation of Africa), Jun 7 (Liberation), Aug 11 (Independence), Nov 1, 28 (Republic), Dec 25; Ad, EM, ER, PB

Chile Jan 1, May 1, 21 (Battle of Iquique), Jun 29 (Sts Peter and Paul), Aug 15, Sep 11 (National Liberation), 18 (Independence), 19 (Armed Forces), Oct 12 (Day of the Race), Nov 1, Dec 8, 25, 31; GF, HS

NATIONAL HOLIDAYS (cont.)

China Jan 1, May 1, Oct 1 (National) (2); Spring Festival (4) (Jan/Feb)

Colombia Jan 1, 6, May 1, Jun 29 (Saints Peter and Paul), Jul 20 (Independence), Aug 7 (National), 15, Oct 12 (Columbus), Nov 1, 15 (Independence of Cartagena), Dec 8, 25, 30, 31; A, CC, GF, HT, St Joseph (Mar), Sacred Heart (Jun)

Congo Jan 1, Mar 18 (Day of the Supreme Sacrifice), May 1, Jul 31 (Revolution), Aug 13–15 (The Three Glorious Days), Nov 1 (Day of the Dead), Dec 25 (Children), 31 (Foundation of the Party and People's Republic)

Costa Rica Jan 1, Mar 19 (St Joseph), Apr 11 (National Heroes), May 1, Jun 29 (Saints Peter and Paul), Jul 25 (Annexation of Guanacaste), Aug 2 (Our Lady of the Angels), 15 (Mothers), Sep 15 (Independence), Oct 12 (Day of the Race), Dec 8, 25; CC, GF, HS, HT

Côte d'Ivoire Jan 1, May 1, Aug 15, Nov 1, Dec 7 (Independence), 24, 25, 31; A, Ad, EM, ER, GF, WM

Cuba Jan 1 (Day of Liberation), May 1, Jul 25 (National Rebellion) (2), Oct 10 (Beginning of the Independence Wars)

Cyprus Jan 1, 6, Mar 25 (Greek Independence), May 1, Oct 28 (Greek National), 29 (Turkish National), Dec 25, 26; Ad, EM, ER, GF, HS, PB

Czechoslovakia Jan 1, 2, May 1, 9 (Anniversary of Liberation), Dec 24, 25, 26, 31; EM

Denmark Jan 1, Jun 5 (Constitution), Dec 24, 25, 26; A, EM, GF, HT, WM, General Prayer (Apr/May)

Djibouti Jan 1, May 1, Jun 27 (Independence)(2), Dec 25; Ad(2), ER(2), NY (Muslim), PB, Al-Isra Wal-Mira'age (Mar–Apr)

Dominica Jan 1, May 1, Nov 3 (Independence), 4 (Community Service), Dec 25, 26; C(2), EM, GF, WM, August Monday

Dominican Republic Jan 1, 6, 21 (Our Lady of Altagracia), 26 (Duarte), Feb 27 (Independence), May 1, Aug 16 (Restoration of the Republic), Sep 24 (Our Lady of Mercy), Dec 25; CC, GF

Ecuador Jan 1, May 1, 24 (Independence Battle), Jun 30, Jul 24 (Bolivar), Aug 10 (Independence), Oct 9 (Independence of Guayaquil), 12 (Columbus), Nov 2, 3 (Independence of Cuenca), Dec 6 (Foundation of Quito), 25, 31; C(2), GF, HT

Egypt Jan 7 (Eastern Orthodox Christmas), Apr 25 (Sinai Liberation), May 1, Jun 18 (Evacuation), Jul 1, 23 (Revolution Anniversary), Oct 6 (Armed Forces); Ad(2), Ar, ER(2), NY (Muslim), PB, Palm Sunday and Easter Sunday (Eastern Orthodox), Sham El-Nessim (Apr–May)

El Salvador Jan 1, May 1, Jun 29, 30, Sep 15 (Independence), Oct 12 (Columbus), Nov 2, 5 (First Cry of Independence), Dec 24, 25, 30, 31; GF, HT, Ash Wednesday, San Salvador(4)

England & Wales Jan 1, Dec 25, 26; EM, GF, Early May, Late May and Summer (Aug) Bank Holidays

Equatorial Guinea Jan 1, May 1, Jun 5 (President's Birthday), Aug 3 (Armed Forces), Oct 12 (Independence), Dec 10 (Human Rights), 25; CC, GF, Constitution (Aug)

Ethiopia Jan 7 (Ethiopian Christmas), 19 (Ethiopian Epiphany), Mar 2 (Victory of Adwa), Apr 6 (Patriots), May 1, Sep 12 (Revolution), 27 (Finding of the True Cross); Ad, ER, NY (Ethiopian, Sep), PB, Ethiopian Good Friday and Easter

Fiji Jan 1, Oct 12 (Fiji), Dec 25, 26; D, EM, GF, HS, PB, August Bank Holiday, Queen's Birthday (Jun), Prince Charles' Birthday (Nov)

Finland Jan 1, May 1, Oct 31 (All Saints Observance), Nov 1, Dec 6 (Independence), 24, 25, 26, 31; A, EM, GF, Midsummer Eve and Day (Jun), Twelfthtide (Jan), Whitsuntide (May–Jun)

France Jan 1, May 1, 8 (Armistice), Jul 14 (Bastille), Aug 14 (Assumption Eve), 15, Oct 31 (All Saints Eve), Nov 1, 11 (Armistice), Dec 24, 25, 31; A, EM, GF, HS, WM, Ascension Eve, Whit Holiday Eve, Law of 20 Dec 1906, Law of 23 Dec 1904

NATIONAL HOLIDAYS (cont.)

Gabon Jan 1, Mar 12 (Anniversary of Renewal), May 1, Aug 17 (Independence), Nov 1, Dec 25; Ad, EM, ER, WM

Gambia Jan 1, Feb 1 (Senegambia), 18 (Independence), May 1, Aug 15 (St Mary), Dec 25; Ad, As, ER(2), GF, PB

German Democratic Republic Jan 1, May 1, Oct 7 (Foundation of GDR), Dec 25, 26; GF, WM

German Federal Republic Jan 1, May 1, Jun 17 (National), Dec 24, 25, 26; A, EM, GF, WM, Day of Penance (Nov)

Ghana Jan 1, Mar 6 (Independence), May 1, Jun 4 (June 4 Revolution), Jul 1 (Republic), Dec 25, 26, 31 (Revolution); EM, GF, HS

Greece Jan 1, 6, Mar 25 (National), May 1, Aug 15, Oct 28 (National), Dec 25, 26; GF, EM, WM, Monday in Lent

Grenada Jan 1–2, Feb 7 (Independence), May 1, Aug 3–4 (Emancipation), Oct 25 (Thanksgiving), Dec 25, 26; CC, EM, GF, WM

Guatemala Jan 1, May 1, Jun 30 (Army Day), Jul 1, Sep 15 (Independence), Oct 12 (Day of the Race), 20 (1944 Revolution), Nov 1, Dec 24, 25, 31; GF, HS, HT

Guinea Jan 1, Apr 3 (Second Republic), May 1, Aug 15, Oct 2 (Independence), Nov 1 (Army), Dec 25; Ad, EM, ER, PB

Guinea-Bissau Jan 1, 20 (National Heroes), Feb 8 (BNG Anniversary and Monetary Reform) Mar 8 (Women), May 1, Aug 3 (Martyrs of Colonialism), Sep 12 (National), 24 (Establishment of the Republic), Nov 14 (Readjustment), Dec 25

Guyana Jan 1, Feb 23 (Republic), May 1, Aug 1 (Freedom), Dec 25, 26; Ad, D, EM, GF, PB, Phagwah (Mar), Caribbean (Jul)

Haiti Jan 1 (Independence), 2 (Ancestry), Apr 14 (Americas), May 1, Aug 15, Oct 17 (Dessalines), 24 (United Nations), Nov 1, 2, 18 (Vertières), Dec 5 (Discovery), 25; A, C, CC, GF

Honduras Jan 1, Apr 14 (Pan American), May 1, Sep 15 (Independence), Oct 3 (Francisco Morazán's Birthday), 12 (America's Discovery), 21 (Armed Forces), Dec 25, 31; GF, HT

Hungary Jan 1, Apr 4 (Liberation Day), May 1, Aug 20 (Constitution), Nov 7 (October Socialist Revolution), Dec 25, 26; EM

Iceland Jan 1, May 1, Jun 17 (Independence), Dec 25, 26; A, EM, GF, HT, WM, First Day of Summer, August Holiday Monday

India Jan 1 (*some states*), 26 (Republic), May 1 (*some states*), Jun 30, Aug 15 (Independence), Oct 2 (Mahatma Ghandi's Birthday), Dec 25, 31; NY (Parsi, Aug, *some states*)

Indonesia Jan 1, Aug 17 (Independence), Dec 25; A, Ad, ER(2), GF, NY (Icaka, Mar), NY (Muslim), PB, Ascension of the Prophet (Mar/Apr), Waisak (May)

Iran Feb 11 (Revolution), Mar 20 (Oil), 21 (Now Rooz)(4), Apr 1 (Islamic Republic), 2 (13th of Farvardin), Jun 5 (15th Khordad Uprising); Ad, As, ER, PB, Prophet's Mission (Apr), Birth of the Twelfth Imam (Apr/May), Martyrdom of Imam Ali (May), Death of Imam Jaffar Sadegh (Jun/Jul), Birth of Imam Reza (Jul), Id-E-Ghadir (Aug), Death of the Prophet and Martyrdom of Imam Hassan (Oct/Nov)

Iraq Jan 1, 6 (Army Day), Feb 8 (8th February Revolution), Mar 21 (Spring Day), May 1, Jul 14 (14th July Revolution), 17 (17th July Revolution); Ad(4), As, ER(3), NY (Muslim), PB

Ireland Jan 1, Mar 17 (St Patrick), Dec 25, 26; EM, GF, June Holiday, August Holiday, October Holiday, Christmas Holiday

NATIONAL HOLIDAYS (cont.)

Israel Jan 1, May 14 (Independence Day); NY (Jewish, Sep/Oct), Purim (Mar), First Day of Passover (Apr), Last Day of Passover (Apr), Pentecost (Jun), Fast of Av (Aug), Day of Atonement (Oct), Feast of Tabernacles (Oct)(2)

Italy Jan 1, 6, Apr 25 (Liberation), May 1, Aug 14 (Mid-August Holiday)(2), Nov 1, Dec 8, 25, 26; EM

Jamaica Jan 1, May 23 (Labour), Aug 5 (Independence), Oct 20 (National Heroes), Dec 25, 26; Ash Wednesday, EM, GF

Japan Jan 1, 2, 3, 15 (Adults), Feb 11 (National Founding), Mar 21 (Vernal Equinox), Apr 29 (Emperor's Birthday), May 3 (Constitution Memorial), 5 (Children), Sep 15 (Respect for the Aged), 23 (Autumn Equinox), Oct 10 (Health-Sports), Nov 3 (Culture), 23 (Labour Thanksgiving)

Jordan Jan 1, May 1, 25 (Independence), Jun 10 (Great Arab Revolt and Army), Aug 11 (Accession of King Hussein), Nov 14 (King Hussein's Birthday), Dec 25; Ad(4), R, ER(4), NY (Muslim), PB

Kenya Jan 1, May 1, Jun 1 (Madaraka), Oct 20 (Kenyatta), Dec 12 (Independence), 25, 26; EM, GF, ER(3)

Kiribati Jan 1, Jul 12 (Independence)(3), Dec 25, 26; GF, HS, EM, Youth (Aug)

Korea, South Jan 1–3, Mar 1 (Independence Movement), 10 (Labour), Apr 5 (Arbor), May 5 (Children), Jun 6 (Memorial), Jul 17 (Constitution), Aug 15 (Liberation), Oct 1 (Armed Forces), 3 (National Foundation), 9 (Korean Alphabet), Dec 25; NY (Chinese, Jan/Feb), Lord Buddha's Birthday (May), Moon Festival (Sep/Oct)

Kuwait Jan 1, Feb 25 (National)(3); Ad(3), ER(3), NY (Muslim), PB, Ascension of the Prophet (Mar/Apr), Standing on Mt Arafat (Aug)

Lebanon Jan 1, Feb 9 (St Maron), May 1, Aug 15, Nov 1, 22 (Independence), Dec 25; Ad(3), As, EM, GF, ER(3), NY (Muslim), PB

Lesotho Jan 1, Mar 12 (Moshoeshoe's Day), 21 (National Tree Planting), May 2 (King's Birthday), Oct 4 (Independence), Dec 25, 26; A, EM, GF, Family (Jul), National Sports (Oct)

Liberia Jan 1, Feb 11 (Armed Forces), Mar 15 (J J Roberts), Apr 12 (Redemption), May 14 (National Unification), Jul 26 (Independence), Aug 24 (National Flag), Nov 29 (President Tubman's Birthday), Dec 25; Decoration (Mar), National Fast and Prayer (Apr), Thanksgiving (Nov)

Libya Mar 2 (Declaration of Establishment of Authority of People), 8 (National), 28 (Evacuation of British troops), Jun 11 (Evacuation of US troops), Jul 23 (National), Sep 1 (National), Oct 7 (Evacuation of Italian Fascists); Ad(4), ER(3), PB

Liechtenstein Jan 1, 6, Feb 2 (Candlemas), Mar 19 (St Joseph), May 1, Aug 15, Nov 1, Dec 8, 24, 25, 26, 31; A, C, CC, EM, GF, WM

Luxembourg Jan 1, May 1, Jun 23 (National), Aug 15, Nov 1, 2, Dec 25, 26, 31; A, EM, WM, Shrove Monday

Madagascar Jan 1, Mar 29 (Memorial), May 1, Jun 26 (Independence), Aug 15, Nov 1, Dec 25, 30 (National); A, EM, GF, WM

Malawi Jan 1, Mar 3 (Martyrs), May 14 (Kamuzu), Jul 6 (Republic), Oct 17 (Mothers), Dec 22 (Tree Planting), 25, 26; EM, GF, HS

Malaysia Jan 1 (*some states*), May 1, Jun 3 (Head of State's Birthday), Aug 31 (National), Dec 25; Ad, D (*most states*), ER(2), NY (Chinese, Jan/Feb, *most states*), NY (Muslim), PB, Wesak (*most states*); *several local festivals*

Maldives Jan 1, Jul 26 (Independence)(2), Nov 11 (Republic) (2); Ad(4), ER(3), NY (Muslim), PB, R(2), Huravee (Feb), Martyrs (Apr), National (Oct/Nov)(2)

Mali Jan 1, 20 (Army), May 1, 25 (Africa), Sep 22 (National), Nov 19 (Liberation), Dec 25; Ad, ER, PB, Prophet's Baptism (Nov)

NATIONAL HOLIDAYS (cont.)

Malta Jan 1, Mar 31 (National), May 1, Aug 15, Dec 13 (Republic), 25; GF

Mauritania Jan 1, May 1, 25 (Africa), Jul 10 (Armed Forces), Nov 28 (Independence); Ad, ER, NY (Muslim), PB

Mauritius Jan 1, 2, Mar 12 (Independence), May 1, Nov 1, Dec 25; Ad, D, ER, PB, Chinese Spring Festival (Feb)

Mexico Jan 1, Feb 5 (Constitution), Mar 21 (Juárez' Birthday), May 1, 5 (Puebla Battle), Sep 1 (Presidential Report), 16 (Independence), Oct 12 (Columbus), Nov 2, 20 (Mexican Revolution), Dec 12 (Our Lady of Guadaloupe), 25, 31; HT, GF

Monaco Jan 1, 27 (St Devote), May 1, 8 (Armistice, 1945), Jul 14 (National), Aug 15, Sep 3 (Liberation), Nov 1, 11 (Armistice, 1918), 19 (Prince of Monaco), Dec 8, 25; EM, WM

Mongolia Jan 1, 2, Mar 8 (International Women), May 1, Jul 10 (People's Revolution)(3), Nov 7 (October Revolution)

Morocco Jan 1, Mar 3 (Throne), May 1, 23 (Fête Nationale), Jul 9 (Youth), Aug 14 (Oued-ed-Dahab), Nov 6 (Al-Massira Day), 18 (Independence); Ad(2), ER(2), NY (Muslim), PB

Mozambique Jan 1, Feb 3 (Heroes), Apr 7 (Mozambican Women), May 1, Jun 25 (Independence), Sep 7 (Victory), 25 (Armed Forces), Dec 25

Nauru Jan 1, 31 (Independence), May 17 (Constitution), Jul 1 (Takeover), Oct 27 (Angam), Dec 25, 26; EM, GF, Easter Tuesday

Nepal Jan 11 (King Prithvi Memorial), Feb 19 (Late King Tribhuvan Memorial and Democracy), Nov 8 (Queen's Birthday), Dec 16 (King Mahendra Memorial and Constitution), 29 (King's Birthday); NY (Sinhala/Tamil, Apr), Maha Shivarata (Feb/Mar)

Netherlands Jan 1, Apr 30 (Queen's Birthday), May 5 (Liberation), Dec 25, 26; A, EM, GF, WM

New Zealand Jan 1, 2, Feb 6 (Waitangi), Apr 25 (Anzac), Dec 25, 26; EM, GF, Queen's Birthday (Jun), Labour (Oct)

Nicaragua Jan 1, May 1, Jul 19 (Sandinista Revolution), Sep 14 (Battle of San Jacinto), 15 (Independence), Dec 8, 25; GF, HT

Niger Jan 1, Apr 15 (Assumption of Power by Supreme Military Council), May 1, Aug 3 (Independence), Dec 18 (National), 25; Ad, ER, PB

Nigeria Jan 1, May 1, Oct 1 (National), Dec 25, 26; Ad(2), EM, ER(2), GF, PB

Northern Ireland Jan 1, Mar 17 (St Patrick, *not general*), Dec 25, 26, 29; GF, EM, Early May, Late May, July Bank Holiday, Summer Bank Holiday (Aug)

Norway Jan 1, May 1, 17 (Constitution), Dec 25, 26; A, EM, GF, HT, WM

Oman Nov 18 (National)(2), Dec 31; Ad(5), ER(4), NY (Muslim), PB, Lailat al-Miraj (Mar/Apr)

Pakistan Mar 23 (Pakistan), May 1, Jul 1, Aug 14 (Independence), Sep 6 (Defence of Pakistan), 11 (Death of Quaid-e-Azam), Nov 9 (Iqbal), Dec 25 (Christmas/Birthday of Quaid-e-Azam), 31; Ad(3), As(2), ER(3), PB, R

Panama Jan 1, 9 (National Mourning), May 1, Oct 11 (Revolution), 12 (Dia de la Hispanidad), Nov 3 (Independence from Colombia), 4 (Flag), 28 (Independence from Spain), Dec 8 (Mothers), 25; C(2), GF

Papua New Guinea Jan 1, Aug 15 (National Constitution), Sep 16 (Independence), Dec 25, 26; EM, GF, HS, Queen's Birthday (Jun), Remembrance (Jul)

Paraguay Jan 1, Feb 3 (St Blás), Mar 1 (Heroes), May 1, 14 (National Flag), 15 (Independence), Jun 12 (Peace with Bolivia), Aug 15, 25 (Constitution), Sep 29 (Battle of Boqueron Day), Oct 12 (Day of the Race), Nov 1, Dec 8, 25, 31; CC, GF, HT

NATIONAL HOLIDAYS (cont.)

Peru Jan 1, May 1, Jun 29 (Sts Peter and Paul), 30, Jul 28 (Independence)(2), Aug 30 (St Rose of Lima), Oct 8 (Combat of Angamos), Nov 1, Dec 8, 25, 31; GF, HT

Philippines Jan 1, May 1, Jun 12 (Independence), Jul 4 (Philippine-American Friendship), Nov 1, 30 (National Heroes), Dec 25, 30 (Rizal), 31; GF, HT

Poland Jan 1, May 1, Jul 22 (National Liberation), Nov 1, Dec 25, 26; CC, EM

Portugal Jan 1, Apr 25 (Liberty), May 1, Jun 10 (Portugal), Aug 15, Oct 5 (Republic), Nov 1, Dec 1 (Independence Restoration), Dec 8, 24, 25; C, CC, GF

Qatar Sep 3 (Independence), Dec 31; Ad(4), ER(4)

Romania Jan 1, 2, May 1(2), Aug 23 (National)

Rwanda Jan 1, 28 (Democracy), May 1, Jul 1 (Independence), 5 (Peace), Aug 1 (Harvest), 15, Sep 25 (Referendum), Oct 26 (Armed Forces), Nov 1, Dec 25; A, EM, WM

Saint Christopher and Nevis Jan 1, Sep 19 (Independence), Dec 25, 26, 31; EM, GF, WM, Labour (May), Queen's Birthday (Jun), August Monday

Saint Lucia Jan 1, 2, Feb 22 (Independence), May 1, Dec 13 (Saint Lucia), Dec 25, 26; C, CC, EM, GF, WM, Emancipation (Aug), Thanksgiving (Oct)

Saint Vincent and the Grenadines Jan 1, 22 (Discovery), Oct 27 (Independence), Dec 25, 26; C (Jul), EM, GF, WM, Labour (May), Caricom (Jul), Emancipation (Aug)

São Tomé and Príncipe Jan 1, Feb 3 (Liberty Heroes), May 1, Jul 12 (National Independence), Sep 6 (Armed Forces), 30 (Agricultural Reform), Dec 21 (Power of the People), 25 (Family)

Saudi Arabia Sep 23 (National); Ad(7), ER(4)

Scotland Jan 1, 2, Dec 25, 26; GF, Early May, Late May, Summer Bank Holiday (Aug)

Senegal Jan 1, Feb 1 (Senegambia), Apr 4 (National), May 1, Aug 15, Nov 1, Dec 25; Ad, EM, ER, NY (Muslim), PB, WM

Seychelles Jan 1, 2, May 1, Jun 5 (Liberation), 29 (Independence), Aug 15, Nov 1, Dec 8, 25; CC, GF, HS

Sierra Leone Jan 1, Apr 19 (Republic), Dec 25, 26; Ad, EM, ER, GF, PB

Singapore Jan 1, May 1, Aug 9 (National), Dec 25; Ad, D, ER, GF, NY (Chinese, Jan/Feb)(2), Vesak

Solomon Islands Jan 1, Jul 7 (Independence), Dec 25, 26; EM, GF, HS, WM, Queen's Birthday (Jun)

Somalia Jan 1, May 1, Jun 26 (Independence), Jul 1 (Union), Oct 21 (Revolution)(2); Ad(2), ER(2), PB

South Africa Jan 1, Apr 6 (Founders), May 31 (Republic), Oct 10 (Kruger), Dec 16 (Vow), 25, 26; A, GF, Family (Mar/Apr)

Spain Jan 1, 6, Mar 19 (*most areas*), May 1, Aug 15, Oct 12 (Hispanity), Nov 1, Dec 6 (Constitution), 8, 25; CC, GF, HS, HT

Sri Lanka Jan 14 (Tamil Thai Pongal), Feb 4 (Independence), May 1, 22 (National Heroes), Jun 30, Dec 25, 31; Ad, D, ER, GF, NY (Sinhala/Tamil, Apr), PB, Maha Sivarathri (Feb/Mar), Full Moon (*monthly*)

Sudan Jan 1 (Independence), Mar 3 (Unity), Apr 6 (Revolution), Dec 25; Ad(5), ER(5), NY (Muslim), PB, Sham al-Naseem (Apr/May)

Suriname Jan 1, Feb 25 (Revolution), May 1, Jul 1 (Freedom), Nov 25 (Independence), Dec 25, 26; EM, ER, GF, Holi (Mar)

Swaziland Jan 1, Apr 25 (National Flag), Jul 22 (King's Birthday), Sep 6 (Independence), Oct 24 (United Nations), Dec 25, 26; A, EM, GF, Commonwealth (Mar)

NATIONAL HOLIDAYS (cont.)

Sweden Jan 1, 6, May 1, Nov 1 (All Saints), Dec 24, 25, 26, 31; A, EM, GF, WM, Midsummer Eve and Day (Jun)

Switzerland Jan 1, Aug 1 (National), Aug 15 (*many cantons*), Nov 1 (*many cantons*), Dec 24, 25, 26; A, CC (*many cantons*), EM, GF, WM; *several local holidays*

Syria Jan 1, Mar 8 (Revolution), Apr 17 (Evacuation) May 1, 6 (Martyrs), Jul 23 (Egyptian Revolution), Sep 1 (Libyan Unity), Oct 6 (Liberation), Dec 25; Ad(3), ER(4), ES, NY (Muslim), PB

Taiwan Jan 1, 2, 3, Mar 29 (Youth), Apr 5 (Ching Ming), Jul 1, Sep 28 (Birthday of Confucius), Oct 10 (National), 25 (Taiwan Restoration), 31 (Birthday of Chiang Kai-Shek), Nov 12 (Birthday of Dr Sun Yat Sen), Dec 25 (Constitution); NY (Chinese, Jan/Feb)(3), Dragon Boat Festival (Jun), Mid-Autumn Festival (Sep/Oct)

Tanzania Jan 1, 12 (Zanzibar Revolution), Feb 5 (Chama Cha Mapinduzi and Arusha Declaration), May 1, Jul 7 (Saba Saba Peasants), Dec 9 (Independence/Republic), 25; Ad, EM, ER(2), GF, PB

Thailand Jan 1, Apr 6 (Chakri), 13 (Songkran), May 1, 5 (Coronation), Jul 1 (Mid-Year), Aug 12 (Queen's Birthday), Oct 23 (King Chulalongkorn), Dec 5 (King's Birthday), 10 (Constitution), 31; ER, Makha Bucha (Feb), Visakha Bucha (May), Buddhist Lent (Jul)

Togo Jan 1, 13 (Liberation), 24 (Economic Liberation), Apr 24 (Victory), 27 (National), May 1, Aug 15, Nov 1, Dec 25; A, Ad, ER

Tonga Jan 1, Apr 25 (Anzac), May 5 (Birthday of Crown Prince Tupouto'a), Jun 4 (Emancipation), Jul 4 (Birthday and Coronation of King Taufa'ahau Tupou IV), Nov 4 (Constitution), Dec 4 (King Tupou I), 25, 26; EM, GF

Trinidad and Tobago Jan 1, Jun 19 (Labour), Aug 1 (Discovery), 31 (Independence), Sep 24 (Republic), Dec 25, 26; CC, EM, GF, WM

Tunisia Jan 1, 18 (Revolution), Mar 20 (Independence), Apr 9 (Martyrs), May 1, Jun 1 (Victory), 2 (Youth), Jul 25 (Republic), Aug 3 (President's Birthday), 13 (Women), Sep 3 (Sep 3 1934), Oct 15 (Evacuation); Ad(2), ER(2), NY (Muslim), PB

Turkey Jan 1, Apr 23 (National Sovereignty and Children), May 19 (Youth and Sports), Aug 30 (Victory), Oct 29 (Republic); Ad(4), ER(3)

Uganda Jan 1, Apr 1 (Liberation), May 1, Oct 9 (Independence), Dec 25, 26; EM, ER, GF, HS

UK *see* **England & Wales; Northern Ireland; Scotland**

United Arab Emirates Jan 1, Aug 6 (Accession of Ruler), Dec 2 (National)(2); Ad(3), ER(4), NY (Muslim), PB, Lailat al-Miraj (Mar/Apr)

USA Jan 1, Jan 21 (Martin Luther King's Birthday) (*not all states*), Jul 4 (Independence), Nov 11 (Veterans), Dec 25; Washington's Birthday (3rd Mon in Feb), Memorial (last Mon in May), Labor (1st Mon in Sep), Discoverers' (2nd Mon in Oct), Thanksgiving (last Thurs of Nov); *much local variation*

Uruguay Jan 1, Apr 19 (Landing of the 33 Orientales), May 1, 18 (Las Piedras Battle), Jun 19 (Artigas), Jul 18 (Constitution), Aug 25 (Independence), Oct 12 (Columbus), Nov 2, Dec 25; C(2), GF, HT, Monday—Wednesday of Holy Week

Vanuatu Jan 1, Mar 5 (Chiefs), May 1, Jul 30 (Independence), Aug 15, Dec 25, 26; A, EM, GF, Constitution (Oct), Unity (Nov)

Venezuela Jan 1, 6, Mar 19 (St Joseph), Apr 19 (Constitution), May 1, Jun 24 (Battle of Carabobo), 29 (Saints Peter and Paul), Jul 5 (Independence), 24 (Bolivar), Aug 15, Oct 12 (Columbus), Nov 1, Dec 8, 25; A, C(2), CC, GF, HT

Vietnam Jan 1, May 1, Sep 2 (Independence)

Western Samoa Jan 1, 2, Apr 25 (Anzac), Jun 1 (Independence) (3), Oct 12 (Lotu-o-Tamai), Dec 25, 26; EM, GF, HS

NATIONAL HOLIDAYS (cont.)

Yemen Arab Republic May 1, Sep 26 (National); Ad(5), ER(4), NY (Muslim), PB

Yemen People's Democratic Republic Jan 1, Mar 8 (Women), May 1, Jun 22 (Corrective Move), Sep 26 (Revolution, *N area*), Oct 14 (Revolution), Nov 30 (Independence); Ad(3), ER(2), NY (Muslim), PB

Yugoslavia Jan 1, 2, May 1(2), Jul 4 (Fighters), Nov 29 (Republic)(3); People's Uprising (Jul)

Zaire Jan 1, 4 (Martyrs of Independence), May 1, 20 (Mouvement Populaire de la Revolution), Jun 24 (Anniversary of Currency, Promulgation, Constitution and Day of Fishers), 30 (Independence), Aug 1 (Parents), Oct 14 (Founder/Youth), 27 (Country's Change of Name), Nov 17 (Armed Forces), 24 (New Regime), Dec 25

Zambia Jan 1, May 1, 25 (Africa Freedom), Oct 24 (Independence), Dec 25; GF, HS, Youth (Mar), Heroes (Jul), Unity (Jul), Farmers (Aug)

Zimbabwe Jan 1, Apr 18 (Independence), 19 (Defence Forces), May 1, 25 (Africa), Aug 11 (Heroes)(2), Dec 25, 26; EM, GF

WORLD POPULATION ESTIMATES

Date (AD)	Millions	Date (AD)	Millions	Date (AD)	Millions
1	200	1900	1625	1970	3700
1000	275	1920	1860	1980	4450
1250	375	1930	2070	1985	4845
1500	420	1940	2295	1990	5246
1700	615	1950	2500	2000	6100
1800	900	1960	3050	2050	11000

Estimates for 2000 and 2050 are United Nations 'medium' estimates. They should be compared with the 'low' estimates for these years of 5400 and 8500, and 'high' estimates of 7000 and 13500, respectively.

UNITED NATIONS MEMBERSHIP

Grouped according to year of entry.

1945 Argentina, Australia, Belgium, Byelorussian SSR, Bolivia, Brazil, Canada, Chile, China (Taiwan) (to 1971), Colombia, Costa Rica, Cuba, Czechoslavakia, Denmark, Dominican Republic, Ecuador, Egypt, El Salvador, Ethiopia, France, Greece, Guatemala, Haiti, Honduras, India, Iran, Iraq, Lebanon, Liberia, Luxembourg, Mexico, Netherlands, New Zealand, Nicaragua, Norway, Panama, Paraguay, Peru, Philippines, Poland, Saudi Arabia, South Africa, Syria, Turkey, Ukranian SSR, USSR, UK, USA, Uruguay, Venezuela, Yugoslavia

1946 Afghanistan, Iceland, Sweden, Thailand

1947 Pakistan, Yemen

1948 Burma

1949 Israel

1950 Indonesia

1955 Albania, Austria, Bulgaria, Kampuchea (formerly Cambodia), Sri Lanka (formerly Ceylon), Finland, Hungary, Ireland, Italy, Jordan, Laos, Libya, Nepal, Portugal, Romania, Spain

1956 Japan, Morocco, Sudan, Tunisia

1957 Ghana, Malaya (Malaysia, 1963)

1958 Guinea

1960 Benin (formerly Dahomey), Burkina Faso (formerly Upper Volta), Cameroon, Central African Republic, Chad, Congo,

UNITED NATIONS MEMBERSHIP (cont.)

1960 (cont.) Ivory Coast (Côte d'Ivoire), Cyprus, Gabon, Madagascar, Mali, Niger, Nigeria, Senegal, Somalia, Togo, Zaïre
1961 Mauritania, Mongolia, Sierra Leone, Tanganyika (within Tanzania, 1964)
1962 Algeria, Burundi, Jamaica, Rwanda, Trinidad and Tobago, Uganda
1963 Kenya, Kuwait, Zanzibar (within Tanzania, 1964)
1964 Malawi, Malta, Zambia, Tanzania
1965 Gambia, Maldives, Singapore
1966 Barbados, Botswana, Guyana, Lesotho
1968 Equatorial Guinea, Mauritius, Swaziland
1970 Fiji
1971 Bahrain, Bhutan, China (Peoples' Republic), Oman, Qatar, United Arab Emirates
1973 Bahamas, German Democratic Republic, German Federal Republic)
1974 Bangladesh, Grenada, Guinea-Bissau
1975 Cape Verde, Comoros, Mozambique, Papua New Guinea, São Tomé and Príncipe, Suriname
1976 Angola, Seychelles, Western Samoa
1977 Djibouti, Vietnam
1978 Dominica, Solomon Islands
1979 St Lucia
1980 St Vincent and the Grenadines, Zimbabwe
1981 Antigua and Barbuda, Belize, Vanuatu
1983 St Christopher and Nevis
1984 Brunei
1990 Namibia, Yemen (formerly N Yemen and S Yemen) (Germany replaced GDR and GFR)
1991 Estonia, Latvia, Lithuania, Marshall Islands, Micronesia, N Korea, Russia, S Korea
1992 Armenia, Azerbaijan, Kazakhstan, Kirgizia, Moldavia, San Marino, Tadzhikistan, Turkmenistan, Uzbekistan

UNITED NATIONS — SPECIALIZED AGENCIES

Abbreviated form	Full title	Area of concern
ILO	International Labour Organization	Social justice
FAO	Food and Agriculture	Improvement of the production and distribution of agricultural products
UNESCO	United Nations Educational, Scientific and Cultural Organization	Stimulation of popular education and the spread of culture
ICAO	International Civil Aviation Organization	Encouragement of safety measures in international flight
IBRD	International Bank for Reconstruction and Development	Aid of development through investment
IMF	International Monetary Fund	Promotion of international monetary co-operation
UPU	Universal Postal Union	Uniting members within a single postal territory
WHO	World Health Organization	Promotion of the highest standards of health for all people
ITU	International Telecommunication Union	Allocation of frequencies and regulation of procedures
WMO	World Meteorological Organization	Standardization and utilization of meteorological observations
IFC	International Finance Corporation	Promotion of the international flow of private capital
IMCO	Inter-governmental Maritime Consultative Organization	The co-ordination of safety at sea
IDA	International Development Association	Credit on special terms to provide assistance for less developed countries
WIPO	World Intellectual Property Organization	Protection of copyright, designs, inventions etc
IFAD	International Fund for Agricultural Development	Increase of food production in developing countries by the generation of grants or loans

COMMONWEALTH MEMBERSHIP

The Commonwealth is an informal association of sovereign states.

Member countries are grouped by year of entry.

1931	Australia, Canada, New Zealand, United Kingdom
1947	India, Pakistan (left 1972, rejoined 1989)
1948	Sri Lanka
1957	Ghana, Malaysia
1960	Nigeria
1961	Cyprus, Sierra Leone, Tanzania
1962	Jamaica, Trinidad and Tobago, Uganda
1963	Kenya, Malawi
1964	Malawi, Malta, Zambia
1965	the Gambia, Singapore
1966	Barbados, Botswana, Guyana, Lesotho
1968	Mauritius, Nauru, Swaziland
1970	Tonga, Western Samoa
1972	Bangladesh
1973	Bahamas
1974	Grenada
1975	Papua New Guinea
1976	Seychelles
1978	Dominica, Solomon Islands, Tuvalu
1979	Kiribati, St Lucia, St Vincent and the Grenadines
1980	Vanuatu, Zimbabwe
1981	Antigua and Barbuda, Belize
1982	Maldives
1983	St Christopher and Nevis
1984	Brunei

Three countries have left the Commonweath: Fiji (1987), Ireland (1949), South Africa (1961)

EUROPEAN COMMUNITY MEMBERSHIP

Member countries are listed by year of entry.

1958	Belgium
1958	France
1958	Germany (Federal Republic of)
1958	Italy
1958	Luxembourg
1958	The Netherlands
1973	Denmark
1973	Republic of Ireland
1973	United Kingdom
1981	Greece
1986	Portugal
1986	Spain

Austria, Cyprus, Malta, Sweden and Turkey have applied for membership

EUROPEAN COMMUNITY ORGANIZATIONS

Abbreviation	Full title	Area of concern
	European Court of Justice	Adjudication of disputes arising from application of the Treaties
CAP	Common Agricultural Policy	Aiming to ensure reasonable standards of living for farmers; its policies have led to surpluses in the past
EMS	European Monetary System	Assistance of trading relations between member countries; all members of the community are in the EMS except Greece, Spain, Portugal
EIB	European Investment Bank	Financing of capital investment projects to assist development of the Community
ECSC	European Coal and Steel Community	Regulation of prices and trade in these commodities
EURATOM	European Atomic Energy Community	Creation of technical and industrial conditions to produce nuclear energy on a large scale

COUNTIES OF ENGLAND

County	Area sq km	sq ml	Population[1]	Admin centre
Avon[2]	1346	520	919800	Bristol
Bedfordshire	1235	477	514200	Bedford
Berkshire	1259	486	716500	Reading
Buckinghamshire	1883	727	619500	Aylesbury
Cambridgeshire	3409	1316	640700	Cambridge
Cheshire	2328	899	937300	Chester
Cleveland[2]	583	225	541100	Middlesbrough
Cornwall	3564	1376	469300	Truro
Cumbria[2]	6810	2629	486900	Carlisle
Derbyshire	2631	1016	915000	Matlock
Devon	6711	2591	1008300	Exeter
Dorset	2654	1025	645200	Dorchester
Durham	2436	941	589800	Durham
Essex	3672	1418	1495600	Chelmsford
Gloucestershire	2643	1020	520600	Gloucester
Greater London[2]	1579	610	6378600	—
Greater Manchester[2]	1287	497	2445200	—
Hampshire	3777	1458	1511900	Winchester
Hereford and Worcester[2]	3926	1516	667800	Worcester
Hertfordshire	1634	631	951500	Hertford
Humberside[2]	3512	1356	845200	Hull

COUNTIES OF ENGLAND (cont.)

County	Area sq km	sq ml	Population[1]	Admin centre
Isle of Wight	381	147	126600	Newport
Kent	3731	1441	1485600	Maidstone
Lancashire	3063	1183	1365100	Preston
Leicestershire	2553	986	860500	Leicester
Lincolnshire	5915	2284	573900	Lincoln
Merseyside[2]	652	252	1376800	Liverpool
Norfolk	5368	2073	736700	Norwich
Northamptonshire	2367	914	568900	Northampton
Northumberland	5032	1943	300600	Newcastle upon Tyne
Nottinghamshire	2164	836	980600	Nottingham
Oxfordshire	2608	1007	553800	Oxford
Shropshire	3490	1347	401600	Shrewsbury
Somerset	3451	1332	459100	Taunton
Staffordshire	2716	1049	1020300	Stafford
Suffolk	3797	1466	629900	Ipswich
Surrey	1679	648	997000	Kingston upon Thames
Sussex, East	1795	693	670600	Lewes
Sussex, West	1989	768	692800	Chichester
Tyne and Wear[2]	540	208	1087000	Newcastle
Warwickshire	1981	765	477000	Warwick
West Midlands[2]	899	347	2500400	Birmingham
Wiltshire	3481	1344	553300	Trowbridge
Yorkshire, North	8309	3208	698800	Northallerton
Yorkshire, South	1560	602	1249300	Barnsley
Yorkshire, West	2039	787	1984700	Wakefield

[1]1991 census, provisional figures
[2]New counties in 1974 were formed as follows:

Avon: parts of Somerset and Gloucestershire
Cleveland: parts of Durham and Yorkshire
Cumbria: Cumberland, Westmoreland, parts of Lancashire and Yorkshire
Greater London: London and most of Middlesex
Greater Manchester: parts of Lancashire, Cheshire and Yorkshire
Hereford and Worcester: Hereford, most of Worcestershire
Humberside: parts of Yorkshire and Lincolnshire
Merseyside: parts of Lancashire and Cheshire
Tyne and Wear: parts of Northumberland and Durham
West Midlands: parts of Staffordshire, Warwickshire and Worcestershire

REGIONS OF SCOTLAND

Region	Area sq km	sq ml	Population[1]	Admin centre	Former counties	New districts
Borders	4672	1804	102649	Newton St Boswells	Berwick, Peebles, Roxburgh, Selkirk, part of Midlothian	Berwickshire, Ettrick & Lauderdale, Roxburgh, Tweeddale
Central	2631	1016	267964	Stirling	Clackmannan, most of Stirling, parts of Perth and W Lothian	Clackmannan, Falkirk, Stirling
Dumfries & Galloway	6370	2459	147064	Dumfries	Dumfries, Kirkcudbright, Wigtown	Annandale & Eskdale, Nithsdale, Stewartry, Wigtown
Fife	1307	505	339284	Glenrothes	Fife	Dunfermline, NE Fife, Kirkcaldy
Grampian	8704	3361	493155	Aberdeen	Aberdeen, Banff, Kincardine, most of Moray	Aberdeen, Banff & Buchan, Gordon, Kincardine & Deeside, Moray
Highland	25391	9804	209419	Inverness	Caithness, Inverness, Nairn, Ross & Cromarty, Sutherland, parts of Argyll and Moray	Badenoch & Strathspey, Caithness, Inverness, Lochaber, Nairn, Ross & Cromarty, Sutherland, Skye & Lochalsh
Lothian	1755	678	723678	Edinburgh	E Lothian, Midlothian, W Lothian	Edinburgh, E Lothian, Midlothian, W Lothian
Strathclyde	13537	5227	2218229	Glasgow	Ayr, Bute, Dunbarton, Lanark, Renfrew, most of Argyll, part of Stirling	Argyll & Bute, Bearsden & Milngavie, Clydebank, Clydesdale, Cumnock & Doon Valley, Cunninghame, Cumbernauld & Kilsyth, Dunbarton, E Kilbride, Eastwood, Glasgow, Hamilton, Inverclyde, Kilmarnock & Loudoun, Kyle & Carrick, Monklands, Motherwell, Renfrew, Strathkelvin
Tayside	7493	2893	385271	Dundee	Angus, Kinross, most of Perth	Angus, Dundee, Kinross, Perth
Orkney Is	976	377	19450	Kirkwall		
Shetland Is	1433	553	22017	Lerwick		
Western Is	2898	1119	29109	Stornoway		

[1] 1991 census, provisional figures

COUNTIES OF WALES

County	Area sq km	sq ml	Population[1]	Admin centre	Former counties	New districts
Clwyd	2426	937	401500	Mold	Flint, most of Denbigh	Alyn & Deeside, Colwyn, Delyn, Glyndwr, Rhuddlan, Wrexham Maelor
Dyfed	5768	2227	341600	Carmarthen	Camarthen, Cardigan, Pembroke	Camarthen, Ceredigion, Dinefwr, Llanelli, Preseli, South Pembrokeshire
Gwent	1376	531	432300	Cwmbrăn	Most of Monmouth, part of Brecon	Blaenau Gwent, Islwyn, Monmouth, Newport, Torfaen
Gwynedd	3869	1494	238600	Caernarvon	Anglesey, Caernarvon, Merioneth, part of Denbigh	Aberconwy, Arfon, Dwyfor, Meirionydd, Ynys Mŏn (Anglesey)
Powys	5077	1960	116500	Llandrindod Wells	Montgomery, Radnor, most of Brecon	Brecknock, Montgomery, Radnor
Mid Glamorgan	1018	393	526500	Cardiff	Parts of Glamorgan, Brecon, and Monmouth	Cynon Valley, Merthyr Tydfil, Ogwen, Rhondda, Rhymney Valley, Taff-Ely
S Glamorgan	416	161	383300	Cardiff	Parts of Glamorgan and Monmouth	Cardiff, Vale of Glamorgan
W Glamorgan	817	315	357800	Swansea	Part of Glamorgan	Afan, Lliw Valley, Neath, Swansea

[1]1991 census, provisional figures

UK ISLANDS

Name	Area sq km	Area sq ml	Population (1986)	Admin centre
Channel Is				
Alderney	8	3	2000	St Anne's
Guernsey	63	24	54380	St Peter Port
Jersey	116	45	80212	St Helier
Sark	4	2	604	
Isle of Man	572	221	64282	Douglas

DISTRICTS OF NORTHERN IRELAND

District	Area sq km	Area sq ml	Population (1991)	Admin centre	Formerly part of
Antrim	563	217	44264	Antrim	Antrim
Ards	369	142	64006	Newtownards	Down
Armagh	672	259	51287	Armagh	Armagh
Ballymena	638	246	55916	Ballymena	Antrim
Ballymoney	419	162	24080	Ballymoney	Antrim
Banbridge	444	171	33144	Banbridge	Down
Belfast	140	54	280972	—	Antrim
Carrickfergus	87	34	32299	Carrickfergus	Antrim
Castlereagh	85	33	60720	Belfast	Down, Antrim
Coleraine	485	187	51060	Coleraine	Antrim
Cookstown	623	240	30883	Cookstown	Tyrone
Craigavon	382	147	74350	Craigavon	Armagh, Down, Antrim,
Down	646	249	57503	Downpatrick	Down
Dungannon	779	301	45408	Dungannon	Tyrone, Armagh
Fermanagh	1876	715	54290	Enniskillen	Fermanagh
Larne	338	131	29280	Larne	Antrim
Limavady	587	227	29144	Limavady	Londonderry
Lisburn	444	171	98826	Lisburn	Antrim, Down
Londonderry	382	147	94721	—	Londonderry
Magherafelt	573	221	35884	Magherafelt	Londonderry
Moyle	495	191	14635	Ballycastle	Antrim
Newry & Mourne	895	346	82237	Newry	Down, Armagh
Newtownabbey	152	59	73718	Newtownabbey	Antrim
North Down	73	28	70065	Bangor	Down
Omagh	1129	436	45568	Omagh	Tyrone
Strabane	870	336	35711	Strabane	Tyrone

EUROPE — ADMINISTRATIVE DIVISIONS

ALBANIA

Province	Area sq km	Area sq ml	Population 1989 est	Capital
Berat	1 027	396	177 246	Berat
Dibër	1 568	605	150 484	Peshkopi
Durrës	848	327	246 865	Durrës
Elbasan	1 481	572	243 211	Elbasan
Fier	1 175	454	246 394	Fier
Gjirokastër	1 137	439	66 626	Gjirokastër
Gramsh	695	268	43 855	Gramsh
Kolonjë	805	311	24 863	Ersekë
Korçë	2 181	842	216 038	Korçë
Krujë	607	234	107 483	Krujë
Kukës	1 330	514	102 040	Kukës
Lezhë	479	185	62 315	Lezhë
Librazhd	1 013	391	72 381	Librazhd

EUROPE — ADMINISTRATIVE DIVISIONS (cont.)

Albania (cont.)

Province	Area sq km	Area sq ml	Population 1989 est	Capital
Lushnjë	712	275	135 138	Lushnjë
Mat	1 028	397	77 102	Burrel
Mirditë	867	335	50 709	Rrëshen
Përmet	929	359	39 920	Përmet
Pogradec	725	280	71 860	Pogradec
Pukë	1 034	399	49 222	Pukë
Sarandë	1 097	424	88 168	Sarandë
Shkodër	2 528	976	237 403	Shkodër
Skrapar	775	299	46 784	Corovoda
Tepelenë	817	315	50 117	Tepelenë
Tiranë	1 238	478	370 262	Tiranë
Tropojë	1 043	403	45 059	Bajram
Vlorë	1 609	621	177 688	Vlorë

AUSTRIA

State	Area sq km	Area sq ml	Population 1989 est	Capital
Burgenland	3 966	1 531	267 200	Eisenstadt
Carinthia (Kärnten)	9 533	3 681	542 300	Klagenfurt
Lower Austria (Niederösterreich)	19 172	7 402	1 430 200	Sankt Pölten
Salzburg	7 154	2 762	468 400	Salzburg
Styria (Steiermark)	16 387	6 327	1 180 400	Graz
Tyrol (Tirol)	12 647	4 883	619 600	Innsbruck
Upper Austria (Oberösterreich)	11 980	4 626	1 306 600	Linz
Vienna (Wien)	415	160	1 487 600	—
Vorarlberg	2 601	1 004	321 400	Bregenz

BELGIUM

Province	Area sq km	Area sq ml	Population 1989 est	Capital
Antwerp	2 867	1 107	1 597 310	Antwerp
Brabant	3 358	1 297	2 243 026	Brussels
E Flanders	2 982	1 151	1 331 608	Ghent
Hainaut	3 787	1 462	2 278 039	Mons
Liège	3 862	1 491	998 213	Liège
Limburg	2 422	935	745 034	Hasselt
Luxembourg	4 441	1 715	230 827	Arlon
Namur	3 665	1 415	421 224	Namur
W Flanders	3 314	1 210	1 102 501	Brugge

BULGARIA

Province	Area sq km	Area sq ml	Population 1987 est	Capital
Blagoevgrad	6 484	2 503	349 546	Blagoevgrad
Burgas	7 702	2 974	450 516	Burgas

EUROPE — ADMINISTRATIVE DIVISIONS (cont.)

Province	Area sq km	Area sq ml	Population 1987 est	Capital
Gabrovo	2 034	785	174 066	Gabrovo
Khaskovo	4 008	1 547	303 064	Khashkovo
Kŭrdzhali	4 027	1 555	303 877	Kŭrdzhali
Kyustendil	3 055	1 180	189 327	Kyustendil
Lovech	4 135	1 597	200 939	Lovech
Mikhaylovgrad	3 623	1 399	222 553	Mikhaylovgrad
Pazardzhik	4 457	1 721	328 755	Pazardzhik
Pernik	2 391	923	175 469	Pernik
Pleven	4 335	1 674	361 218	Pleven
Plovdiv	5 642	2 178	759 114	Plovdiv
Razgrad	2 654	1 025	199 196	Razgrad
Ruse	2 618	1 011	304 965	Ruse
Shumen	3 390	1 309	255 945	Shumen
Silistra	2 854	1 102	174 066	Silistra
Sliven	3 620	1 398	240 012	Sliven
Smolyan	3 487	1 346	165 566	Smolyan
Sofiya	7 091	2 738	304 123	Sofia (Sofiya)
Stara Zagora	5 077	1 960	413 519	Stara Zagora
Tolbukhin	4 707	1 817	257 544	Tolbukhin
Tŭrgovishte	2 717	1 049	170 207	Tŭrgovishte
Varna	3 832	1 480	464 946	Varna
Veliko Tŭrnovo	4 646	1 794	338 073	Veliko Tŭrnovo
Vidin	3 041	1 174	164 848	Vidin
Vratsa	3 943	1 522	286 740	Vratsa
Yambol	4 113	1 588	203 910	Yambol
City commune				
Sofiya	1 311	506	1 203 553	Sofia (Sofiya)

CYPRUS

District	Area sq km	Area sq ml	Population 1989 est	Capital
Famagusta			29 100	Famagusta
Larnaca	1 121	433	91 500	Larnaca
Limassol	1 393	538	158 400	Limassol
Nicosia			234 200	Nicosia
Paphos	1 396	539	49 500	Paphos

CZECHOSLOVAKIA

Region	Area sq km	Area sq ml	Population 1990 est	Capital
Czech Republic				
C Bohemia (Středocesky)	10 994	4 245	1 118 232	Prague
E Bohemia (Východočeský)	11 240	4 340	1 239 726	Hradec Králové
N Bohemia (Severočeský)	7 819	3 019	1 190 442	Ústí nad Labem
N Moravia (Severomoravský)	11 067	4 273	1 972 200	Ostrava
Prague (city)	496	192	1 214 772	—

EUROPE — ADMINISTRATIVE DIVISIONS (cont.)

Czechoslovakia (cont.)

Region	Area sq km	Area sq ml	Population 1990 est	Capital
S Bohemia (Jihočeský)	11 345	4 380	699 564	České Budějovice
S Moravia (Jihomoravský)	15 028	5 802	2 058 156	Brno
W Bohemia (Západočeský)	10 875	4 199	869 461	Plzeň
Slovak Republic				
Bratislava (city)	367	142	440 421	—
C Slovakia (Středoslovenský)	17 986	6 944	1 615 438	Banska Bystrica
E Slovakia (Východoslovenský)	16 191	6 251	1 503 421	Košice
W Slovakia (Západoslovenský)	14 492	5 595	1 727 800	Bratislava

DENMARK

County	Area sq km	Area sq ml	Population 1989 est	Capital
Aarhus (Aerhus)	4 561	1 761	594 184	Acerhus
Bornholm	588	227	46 105	Rønne
Copenhagen (København)	526	203	602 046	—
Frederiksborg	1 347	520	340 513	Hillerød
Fyn	3 486	1 346	458 111	Odense
N Jutland (Nordjylland)	6 173	2 383	483 754	Aalborg (Aelborg)
Ribe	3 131	1 209	218 460	Ribe
Ringkøbing	4 853	1 874	266 834	Ringkøbing
Roskilde	891	344	215 993	Roskilde
S Jutland (Sønderjylland)	3 938	1 520	250 158	Aebeurace
Storstrøm	3 398	1 312	257 007	Nykøbing Falster
Vejle	2 997	1 157	329 847	Vejle
Viborg	4 122	1 592	230 318	Viborg
W Zealand (Vestsjaelland)	2 984	1 152	283 271	Sorø

FINLAND

Province	Area sq km	Area sq ml	Population 1990 est	Capital
Häme	17 010	6 568	687 914	Hämeenlina
Keski-Suomi	16 230	6 266	250 795	Jyväskylä
Kuopio	16 509	6 374	256 411	Kuopio
Kymi	10 783	4 163	335 196	Kouvola
Lappi	93 056	35 929	200 101	Rovaniemi
Mikkeli	16 342	6 310	208 066	Mikkeli
Oulun	56 868	21 957	436 940	Oulu
Pohjois-Karjala	17 782	6 866	176 413	Joensuu
Turku ja Pori	22 170	8 559	716 704	Turku
Uusimaa	9 898	3 882	1 234 489	Helsinki
Vaasa	26 447	10 211	444 695	Vaasa
Autonomous province				
Aeland (Ahvenanmaa)	1 527	590	24 120	Mariehamn (Maarianhamina)

EUROPE — ADMINISTRATIVE DIVISIONS (cont.)

FRANCE

Region	Area sq km	Area sq ml	Population 1990	Admin centre
Alsace	8 280	3 197	1 622 000	Strasbourg
Aquitaine	41 309	15 950	2 793 500	Bordeaux
Auvergne	26 013	10 044	1 318 200	Clermont-Ferrand
Brittany (Bretagne)	27 209	10 505	2 792 800	Rennes
Burgundy (Bourgogne)	31 582	12 194	1 608 500	Dijon
Centre	39 151	15 116	2 369 200	Orléans
Champagne-Ardenne	25 606	9 887	1 345 700	Reims
Corsica (Corse)	8 680	3 351	240 200	Ajaccio
Franche-Comté	16 202	6 256	1 097 100	Besançon
Île de France	12 011	4 637	10 650 600	Paris
Languedoc-Roussillon	27 376	10 570	2 109 800	Montpellier
Limousin	16 962	6 549	723 800	Limoges
Lorraine	23 547	9 092	2 303 700	Nancy
Midi-Pyrénées	45 349	17 509	2 427 400	Toulouse
Nord-Pas-de-Calais	12 413	479	3 960 000	Lille
Normandy, Lower (Basse-Normandie)	17 589	6 791	1 390 500	Caen
Normandy, Upper (Haute-Normandie)	12 318	4 756	1 736 400	Rouen
Pays de la Loire	32 082	1 237	3 058 000	Nantes
Picardy (Picardie)	19 399	7 490	1 809 600	Amiens
Poitou-Charentes	25 809	9 965	1 594 800	Poitiers
Provence Alpes-Côte d'Azur	31 400	12 124	4 260 000	Marseilles
Rhône-Alpes	43 968	16 976	5 344 000	Lyons

GERMANY

District	Area sq km	Area sq ml	Population 1990 est	Capital
Baden-Württemberg	35 751	13 804	9 619 000	Stuttgart
Bayern	70 554	27 241	11 221 000	Munich
Berlin	883	341	3 410 000	Berlin
Brandenburg	29 059	11 220	2 641 000	Potsdam
Bremen	404	156	674 000	Bremen
Hamburg	755	292	1 626 000	Hamburg
Hessen	21 114	8 152	5 661 000	Wiesbaden
Mecklenburg-Vorpommern	23 838	9 204	1 964 000	Schwerin
Niedersachsen	47 344	18 280	7 238 000	Hannover
Nordrhein-Westfalen	34 070	13 155	17 104 000	Düsseldorf
Rheinland-Pfalz	19 849	7 664	3 702 000	Mainz
Saarland	2 570	992	1 065 000	Saarbrücken
Sachsen	18 337	7 080	4 901 000	Dresden
Sachsen-Anhalt	20 445	7 894	2 965 000	Magdeburg
Schleswig-Holstein	15 728	6 073	2 595 000	Kiel
Thüringen	16 251	6 275	2 684 000	Erfurt

EUROPE — ADMINISTRATIVE DIVISIONS (cont.)

GREECE

Region	Area sq km	Area sq ml	Population 1981
Attica (Attikí)	3 808	1 470	3 369 424
C Greece (Stereá Ellás)	15 549	6 004	537 984
C Macedonia (Kedrikí Makedhonía)	19 147	7 393	1 602 892
Crete (Kríti)	8 336	3 218	502 165
E Macedonia and Thrace (Anatolikí Makedhonía kaí Thráki)	14 157	5 466	575 210
Epirus (Ípiros)	9 203	3 553	324 541
Ionian Is (Iónioi Nísoi)	2 307	891	182 651
N Aegean (Vóreion Aiyaíon)	3 836	1 481	195 004
Peleponnese (Pelopónnisos)	15 490	5 981	577 030
S Aegean (Nótion Aiyaíon)	5 286	2 041	233 529
Thessaly (Thessalía)	14 037	5 420	695 654
W Greece (Dhytikí Ellás)	11 350	4 382	655 262
W Macedonia (Dhytikí Makedhonía)	9 451	3 649	289 071

GREENLAND

County/commune	Area sq km	Area sq ml	Population 1990 est
Avanersuaq (Nordgrønland) (county)	106 700	41 200	—
Qaanaaq (Thule)			846
Kitaa (Vestgrønland) (county)	119 100	46 000	—
Aasiaat (Egedesminde)			3 599
Ilulissat (Jakobshavn)			4 568
Ivittuut (Ivigtut)			4
Kangaatsiaq (Kangaetsiaq)			1 347
Maniitsoq (Sukkertoppen)			4 075
Nanortalik			2 672
Narsaq (Narssaq)			2 148
Nuuk (Godthaeb)			12 687
Paamiut (Frederiskhaeb)			2 556
Qaqortoq (Julianehaeb)			3 543
Qasigiannguit (Christianshaeb)			1 712
Qeqertarsuaq (Godhavn)			1 164
Sisimiut (Holsteinsborg)			5 090
Upernavik			2 375
Uummannaq (Umanaq)			2 677
Tunu (Owstgrønland) (county)	115 900	44 700	—
Ittoqqortoormiit (Scoresbysund)			554
Tasiilaq (Angmagssalik)			2 889

HUNGARY

County	Area sq km	Area sq ml	Population 1990	Capital
Baranya	4 487	1 732	430 000	Pécs
Bács-Kiskun	8 362	3 229	545 000	Kecskemét

EUROPE — ADMINISTRATIVE DIVISIONS (cont.)

County	Area sq km	sq ml	Population 1990	Capital
Békés	5 632	2 175	410 000	Bekéscsaba
Borsod-Abaúj-Zemplén	7 247	2 798	770 000	Miskolc
Budapest (capital)[1]	525	203	2 000 000	—
Csongrád	4 263	1 646	450 000	Szeged
Fejér	4 373	1 688	425 000	Székesfehérvár
Györ-Sopron	4 012	1 549	430 000	Györ
Hajdú-Bihar	6 211	2 398	550 000	Debrecen
Heves	3 637	1 404	335 000	Eger
Jász-Nagykun-Szolnok	5 607	2 165	430 000	Szolnok
Komárom-Esztergom	2 251	869	320 000	Tatabánya
Nógrád	2 544	982	230 000	Salgótarján
Pest	6 394	2 469	970 000	Budapest
Somogy	6 036	2 331	350 000	Kaposvár
Szabolcs-Szatmár-Bereg	5 938	2 293	570 000	Nyíregyháza
Tolna	3 704	1 430	260 000	Szekszárd
Vas	3 337	1 288	280 000	Szombathely
Veszprém	4 689	1 810	385 000	Veszprém
Zala	3 784	1 461	310 000	Zalaegerszeg

[1] Budapest has county status

ICELAND

Region	Area sq km	sq ml	Population 1989 est	Admin centre
Austurland	21 991	8 491	13 243	Egilsstadhir
Höfudhborgarsvaedhi	1 982[1]	765	143 864[2]	Reykjavik
Nordhurland eystra	22 368	8 636	26 107	Akureyri
Nordhurland vestra	13 093	5 055	10 450	Saudhárkrókur
Sudhurland	25 214	9 735	20 229	Selfoss
Sudhurnes	—[1]	—[1]	15 082	Keflavik
Vestfirdhir	9 470	3 657	9 840	Ísafjördhur
Vesturland	8 701	3 360	14 685	Borgarnes

[1] Höfudhborgarsvaedhi includes Sudhurnes
[2] 1 Dec 1990 est: 146 141

IRELAND

County	Area sq km	sq ml	Population 1991	Admin centre
Carlow	896	346	40 946	Carlow
Cavan	1 891	730	52 756	Cavan
Clare	3 188	1 231	90 826	Ennis
Cork	7 459	2 880	409 814	Cork
Donegal	4 830	1 865	127 994	Lifford
Dublin	922	356	1 024 429	Dublin
Galway	5 939	2 293	180 304	Galway
Kerry	4 701	1 815	121 719	Tralee

EUROPE — ADMINISTRATIVE DIVISIONS (cont.)

Ireland (cont.)

County	Area sq km	Area sq ml	Population 1991	Admin centre
Kildare	1 694	654	122 516	Naas
Kilkenny	2 062	796	73 613	Kilkenny
Laoighis (Leix)	1 720	664	52 325	Portlaoise
Leitrim	1 526	589	25 297	Carrick
Limerick	2 686	1 037	161 856	Limerick
Longford	1 044	403	30 293	Longford
Louth	821	317	90 707	Dundalk
Mayo	5 398	2 084	110 696	Castlebar
Meath	2 339	903	105 540	Trim
Monaghan	1 290	498	51 262	Monaghan
Offaly	1 997	771	58 448	Tullamore
Roscommon	2 463	951	51 876	Roscommon
Sligo	1 795	693	54 736	Sligo
Tipperary	4 254	1 642	132 620	Clonmel
Waterford	1 839	710	91 608	Waterford
Westmeath	1 764	681	61 882	Mullingar
Wexford	2 352	908	102 045	Wexford
Wicklow	2 025	782	97 293	Wicklow

ITALY

Region	Area sq km	Area sq ml	Population 1989	Capital
Abruzzi	10 794	4 168	1 266 448	L'Aquila
Basilicata	9 992	3 858	523 175	Potenza
Calabria	15 080	5 823	2 152 539	Catanzaro
Campania	13 595	5 249	5 808 705	Naples (Napoli)
Emilia-Romagna	22 123	8 542	3 921 597	Bologna
Friuli-Venezia Giulia	7 845	3 029	1 202 877	Trieste
Lazio	17 203	6 642	5 170 672	Rome (Roma)
Liguria	5 418	2 092	1 727 212	Genoa (Genova)
Lombardy (Lombardia)	23 857	9 211	8 911 995	Milan (Milano)
Marche	9 693	3 743	1 430 726	Ancona
Molise	4 438	1 713	335 348	Campobasso
Piedmont (Piemonte)	25 399	9 807	4 357 559	Turin (Torino)
Puglia	19 348	7 470	4 069 359	Bari
Sardinia (Sardegna)	24 090	9 301	1 657 562	Cagliari
Sicily (Sicilia)	25 709	9 926	5 172 785	Palermo
Tuscany (Toscana)	22 992	8 877	3 560 582	Florence (Firenze)
Trentino-Alto Adige	13 618	5 258	886 679	Bozen (Bolzano)[1], Trent, Trient (Trento)[1]
Umbria	8 456	3 265	820 316	Perugia
Valle d'Aosta	3 262	1 259	115 270	Aosta
Veneto	18 364	7 090	4 385 023	Venice (Venezia)

[1]Joint regional capitals

EUROPE — ADMINISTRATIVE DIVISIONS (cont.)

LIECHTENSTEIN

Commune	Area sq km	Area sq ml	Population 1990 est
Balzers	19.6	7.6	3 668
Eschen	10.3	4.0	2 964
Gamprin	6.1	2.4	944
Mauren	7.5	2.9	2 978
Planken	5.3	2.0	295
Ruggell	7.4	2.9	1 454
Schaan	26.8	10.3	4 930
Schellenberg	3.5	1.4	769
Triesen	26.4	10.2	3 377
Triesenberg	29.8	11.5	2 379
Vaduz	17.3	6.7	4 874

LUXEMBOURG

District/canton	Area sq km	Area sq ml	Population 1989 est
Diekirch (district)	1 157	447	55 910
Clervaux	332	128	10 050
Diekirch	239	92	22 930
Redange	267	103	10 880
Vianden	54	21	2 710
Wiltz	265	102	9 340
Grevenmacher (district)	525	203	41 370
Echternach	186	72	11 300
Grevenmacher	211	82	17 610
Remich	128	49	12 460
Luxembourg (district)	904	349	277 620
Capellen	199	77	30 290
Esch	243	94	113 960
Luxembourg (city)	238	92	114 830
Mersch	224	86	18 540

MALTA

Census region	Area sq km	Area sq ml	Population 1990 est
Gozo and Comino	70	27	25 775
Inner Harbour	15	6	101 429
N Malta	78	30	33 157
Outer Harbour	32	12	101 759
SE Malta	53	20	44 404
W Malta	69	27	45 906

EUROPE — ADMINISTRATIVE DIVISIONS (cont.)

THE NETHERLANDS

Province	Area sq km	sq ml	Population 1989 est	Capital
Drenthe	2 654	1 025	439 100	Assen
Flevoland	1 422	549	202 700	Lelystad
Friesland	3 353	1 295	599 200	Leeuwarden
Gelderland	5 011	1 935	1 794 700	Arnhem
Groningen	2 346	906	555 200	Groningen
Limburg	2 170	838	1 099 600	Maastricht
N Brabant (Noord-Brabant)	4 946	1 910	2 172 600	ś-Hertogenbosch
N Holland (Noord-Holland)	2 665	1 029	2 365 200	Haarlem
Overijssel	3 339	1 289	1 014 900	Zwolle
S Holland (Zuid-Holland)	2 908	1 123	3 200 400	The Hague
Utrecht	1 331	514	1 004 600	Utrecht
Zeeland	1 792	692	355 600	Middelburg

NORWAY

County	Area[1] sq km	sq ml	Population 1990 est	Capital
Akershus	4 917	1 898	414 473	—
Aust-Agder	9 212	3 557	96 953	Arendal
Buskerud	14 927	5 763	224 712	Drammen
Finnmark	48 637	18 779	74 279	Vadsø
Hedmark	27 388	10 575	186 909	Hamar
Hordaland	15 634	6 036	409 167	Bergen
Møre og Romsdal	15 104	5 832	238 438	Molde
Nordland	38 327	14 798	239 571	Bodø
Nord-Trøndelag	22 463	8 673	126 919	Steinkjer
Oppland	25 260	9 753	182 544	Lillehammer
Oslo	454	175	457 818	Oslo
Owstfold	4 183	1 615	238 000	Moss
Rogaland	9 141	3 529	335 727	Stavanger
Sogn og Fjordane	18 634	7 195	106 618	Leikanger
Sør-Trøndelag	18 831	7 271	250 401	Trondheim
Telemark	15 315	5 913	163 066	Skien
Troms	25 954	10 021	146 609	Tromsø
Vest-Agder	7 281	2 811	144 050	Kristiansand
Vestfold	2 216	856	197 232	Tønsberg

[1]Excludes Scalbard and Jay Mayen (63 080 sq km/24 360 sq ml)

POLAND

Province	Area sq km	sq ml	Population 1989 est	Capital
Biała Podlaska	5 348	2 065	304 500	Biała Podlaska
Białystok	10 055	3 882	690 300	Białystok

EUROPE — ADMINISTRATIVE DIVISIONS (cont.)

Province	Area sq km	sq ml	Population 1989 est	Capital
Bielsko	3 704	1 430	895 300	Bielsko Biala
Bydogoszcz	10 349	3 996	1 106 600	Bydgoszcz
Chełm	3 866	1 493	246 200	Chełm
Ciechanów	6 362	2 456	427 000	Ciechanów
Częstochowa	6 182	2 387	776 100	Częstochowa
Elbląg	6 103	2 356	476 600	Elbląg
Gdańsk	7 394	2 855	1 423 300	Gdańsk
Gorzów	8 484	3 276	498 300	Gorzów Wielkopolski
Jelenia Góra	4 378	1 690	517 000	Jelenia Góra
Kalisz	6 512	2 514	708 300	Kalisz
Katowice	6 650	2 568	3 968 300	Katowice
Kielce	9 211	3 556	1 126 000	Kielce
Konin	5 139	1 984	467 600	Konin
Koszalin	8 470	3 270	504 200	Koszalin
Kraków	3 254	1 256	1 227 800	Kraków
Krosno	5 702	2 202	491 800	Krosno
Legnica	4 037	1 559	512 000	Legnica
Leszno	4 154	1 604	384 500	Leszno
Łódź	1 523	588	1 013 400	Łódź
Łomzda	6 684	2 581	345 600	Łomzdoa
Lublin	6 792	2 622	1 142 700	Lublin
Nowy Sącz	5 576	2 153	692 200	Nowy Sącz
Olsztyn	12 327	4 759	748 500	Olsztyn
Opole	8 535	3 295	1 014 900	Opole
Ostrołęka	6 498	2 509	395 000	Ostrołęka
Piła	8 205	3 168	478 000	Piła
Piotrków	6 266	2 419	642 000	Piotrków Trybunalski
Płock	5 117	1 976	515 400	Płock
Poznań	8 151	3 147	1 327 900	Poznań
Przemyśl	4 437	1 713	405 100	Przemyśl
Radom	7 294	2 816	748 300	Radom
Rzeszów	4 397	1 698	714 400	Rzeszów
Siedlce	8 499	3 281	649 300	Siedlce
Sieradz	4 869	1 880	408 000	Sieradz
Skierniewice	3 960	1 529	418 200	Skierniewice
Słupsk	7 453	2 878	410 400	Słupsk
Suwałki	10 490	4 050	466 300	Suwałki
Szczecin	9 981	3 854	967 300	Szczecin
Tarnobrzeg	6 283	2 426	596 400	Tarnobrzeg
Tarnów	4 151	1 603	666 000	Tarnów
Toruń	5 384	2 065	655 700	Toruń
Wałbrzych	4 168	1 609	741 200	Wałbrzych
Warszawa	3 788	1 463	2 419 100	Warszawa
Włocławek	4 402	1 700	428 900	Włocławek
Wrocław	6 287	2 427	1 126 300	Wrocław
Zamość	6 980	2 695	489 800	Zamość
Zielona Góra	8 868	3 424	657 400	Zielona Góra

EUROPE — ADMINISTRATIVE DIVISIONS (cont.)

PORTUGAL

Region	Area sq km	Area sq ml	Population 1989 est	Admin centre
Aveiro	2 808	1 084	670 100	Aveiro
Beja	10 225	3 948	175 400	Beja
Braga	2 673	1 032	778 200	Braga
Bragança	6 608	2 551	183 900	Bragança
Castelo Branco	6 675	2 577	221 200	Castelo Branco
Coimbra	3 947	1 524	446 600	Coimbra
Évora	7 393	2 854	172 800	Évora
Faro	4 960	1 915	342 900	Faro
Guarda	5 518	2 131	194 100	Guarda
Leiria	3 515	1 357	436 200	Leiria
Lisboa	2 761	1 066	2 128 700	Libon (Lisboa)
Portalegre	6 065	2 342	136 200	Portalegre
Porto	2 395	925	1 683 200	Porto
Sautarém	6 747	2 605	459 900	Sautarém
Setúbal	5 064	1 955	798 900	Setúbal
Viana do Castelo	2 255	871	266 700	Viano do Castelo
Vila Real	4 328	1 671	261 500	Vila Real
Viscu	5 007	1 933	421 400	Viscu
Autonomous regions				
The Azores	2 247	868	253 600	Ponta Delgada
Madeira	794	306	273 200	Funchal

ROMANIA

County	Area sq km	Area sq ml	Population 1989 est	Capital
Alba	6 231	2 406	431 722	Alba lulia
Arad	7 652	2 954	493 588	Arad
Arges	6 801	2 626	679 050	Pitești
Bacău	6 606	2 551	760 315	Bacău
Bihor	7 535	2 909	662 761	Oradea
Bistrița-Năsăud	5 305	2 048	333 040	Bistrița
Botoșani	4 965	1 917	502 985	Botoșani
Brăila	4 724	1 824	403 303	Brăila
Brașov	5 351	2 066	646 983	Brașov
Buzău	6 072	2 344	538 998	Buzău
Caraș-Severin	8 503	3 283	398 375	Reșița
Călăriși	5 074	1 959	356 358	Călărași
Cluj	6 650	2 568	736 170	Cluj-Napoka
Constanța	7 055	2 724	707 513	Constanța
Covasna	3 705	1 431	235 765	Sfintu Gheorghe
Dîmbovița	4 036	1 559	576 775	Tirgoviște
Dolj	7 413	2 862	775 189	Craiova
Galați	4 425	1 708	643 186	Galați
Giurgiu	3 636	1 404	332 449	Giurgiu
Gorj	5 641	2 178	386 489	Tirgu Jiu

EUROPE — ADMINISTRATIVE DIVISIONS (cont.)

County	Area sq km	Area sq ml	Population 1989 est	Capital
Harghita	6 610	2 552	362 899	Miercurea-Ciuc
Hunedoara	7 016	2 709	558 012	Deva
Ialomiţa	4 449	1 718	319 730	Slobozia
Iaşi	5 469	2 112	821 453	Iaşi
Maramureş	6 215	2 400	564 955	Baia Mare
Mehedinţi	4 900	1 892	333 235	Drobeta-Turnu-Severin
Mureş	6 696	2 585	628 178	Tirgu Mureş
Neamţ	5 890	2 274	608 836	Piatra Neamţ
Olt	5 507	2 126	549 361	Slatina
Prahova	4 694	1 812	876 053	Ploieşti
Sălaj	3 850	1 486	278 026	Zalăo
Satu Mare	4 405	1 701	421 465	Satu Mare
Sibiu	5 422	2 093	494 965	Sibiu
Suceava	8 555	3 303	716 756	Suceava
Teleorman	5 760	2 224	523 401	Alexandria
Timiş	8 692	3 356	667 925	Timişoara
Tulcea	8 430	3 255	278 301	Tulcea
Vaslui	5 297	2 045	499 240	Vaslui
Vîlcea	5 705	2 203	443 890	Rimnicu Vîlcea
Vrancea	4 863	1 878	409 227	Focşani
Municipality				
Bucharest	1 695	654	2 194 583	Bucharest

SPAIN

Region	Area sq km	Area sq ml	Population 1990 est	Admin centre
Andalucía	87 268	33 694	7 100 060	Seville
Aragón	47 650	18 398	1 201 344	Zaragoza
Asturias	10 565	4 079	1 128 372	Ovieda
Balearic Is (Baleares)	5 014	1 936	767 918	Palma de Mallorca
Basque Provinces (Páis Vasco)	7 261	2 803	2 159 701	Vitoria
Canary Is (Canarias)	7 242	2 796	1 589 403	Santa Cruz de Tenerife-Las Palmas de Gran Canaria
Cantabria	5 289	2 042	534 690	Santander
Castilla-La Mancha	79 230	30 591	1 695 144	Toledo
Castilla-León	94 193	36 368	2 513 011	Valladolid
Catalonia (Cataluña)	31 930	12 328	6 165 638	Barcelona
Extremadura	41 602	16 063	1 102 321	Mérida
Galicia	29 434	11 365	2 914 514	Santiago de Compostela
La Rioja	5 034	1 944	266 286	Logroño
Madrid	7 995	3 087	5 028 120	Madrid
Murcia	11 317	4 370	1 062 066	Murcia
Navarra	10 421	4 023	527 318	Pamplona
Valencia	23 305	8 998	3 902 429	Valencia

EUROPE — ADMINISTRATIVE DIVISIONS (cont.)

SWEDEN

County	Area sq km	sq ml	Population 1990 est	Capital
Älvsborg	11 395	4 400	441 391	Vänersborg
Blekinge	2 941	1 136	150 564	Karlskrona
Gävleborg	18 191	7 024	289 294	Gävle
Gothenburg (Göteborg och Bohus)	5 141	1 985	739 945	Gothenburg
Gotland	3 140	1 212	57 108	Visby
Halland	5 454	2 106	254 725	Halmstad
Jämtland	49 443	19 090	135 726	Östersund
Jönköping	9 944	3 839	308 290	Jönköping
Kalmar	11 170	4 313	241 102	Kalmar
Kopparberg	28 194	10 886	289 067	Falun
Kristianstad	6 087	2 350	289 278	Kristianstad
Kronoberg	8 458	3 266	177 882	Växjö
Malmöhus	4 938	1 907	779 309	Malmö
Norrbotten	98 913	39 191	263 735	Lulece
Örebro	8 519	3 289	272 513	Örebro
Östergötland	10 562	4 078	403 011	Linköping
Skaraborg	7 937	3 065	276 830	Mariestad
Södermanland	6 060	2 340	255 636	Nyköping
Stockholm	6 488	2 505	1 641 669	Stockholm
Uppsala	6 989	2 698	268 835	Uppsala
Värmland	17 584	6 789	283 110	Karlstad
Västerbotten	55 401	21 390	251 968	Umeace
Västernorrland	21 678	8 370	261 155	Härnösand
Västmanland	6 302	2 433	258 487	Västeraces

SWITZERLAND

Canton	Area sq km	sq ml	Population 1989 est	Capital
Aargau	1 405	542	490 412	Aarau
Appenzell Ausser-Rhoden[1]	243	94	50 882	Herisau
Appenzell Inner-Rhoden[1]	172	66	13 504	Appenzell
Basle (Basel-Landschaft)[1]	428	165	229 030	Liestal
Basle (Basel-Stadt)[1]	37	14	190 347	Basel
Berne	6 049	2 335	937 365	Berne
Fribourg	1 670	645	204 328	Fribourg
Geneva (Genève)	282	109	156 505	Geneva
Glarus	684	264	37 253	Glarus
Graubünden (Fr: Grisons)	7 106	2 744	169 005	Chur (Coire)
Jura	837	323	64 942	Delémont
Lucerne (Luzern)	1 492	576	314 837	Lucerne
Neuenberg (Neuchâtel)	797	308	158 569	Neuenberg
Nidwalden[1]	276	107	32 030	Stans
Obwalden[1]	491	189	28 323	Sarnen
St Gall (Sankt Gallen)	2 014	778	414 718	St Gall
Schaffhausen	298	115	70 949	Schaffhausen
Schwyz	908	351	108 063	Schwyz

EUROPE — ADMINISTRATIVE DIVISIONS (cont.)

Switzerland (cont.)

Canton	Area sq km	sq ml	Population 1989 est	Capital
Solothurn	791	305	223 534	Solothurn
Thurgau	1 013	391	201 620	Frauenfeld
Ticino	2 811	1 085	283 023	Bellinzona
Uri	1 076	416	33 511	Altdorf
Valais	5 226	2 018	243 705	Sion
Vaud	3 219	1 243	571 973	Lausanne
Zug	239	92	84 009	Zug
Zürich	1 729	668	1 144 899	Zürich

[1]Demicanton – functions as a full canton

TURKEY

Geographic region	Area sq km	sq ml	Population 1990 est
Black Sea Coast (Karadeniz Kıyısı)	81 295	31 388	6 900 805
C Anatolia (İç Anadolu)	236 347	91 254	13 154 473
E Anatolia (Doğu Anadolu)	176 311	68 074	6 909 594
Marmara and Aegean coasts (Marmara ve Ege kıyıları)	85 560	33 035	11 784 535
Mediterranean Coast (Akdeniz kıyısı)	59 395	22 933	5 497 536
SE Anatolia (Güneydoğu)	39 749	15 347	2 793 894
Thrace (Trakya)	23 764	9 175	6 021 591
W Anatolia (Batı Anadolu)	77 031	29 742	3 906 681

STATES OF THE USA

Population: figures from the 1990 population census

Abbreviations are given after each state name: the first is the common abbreviation, the second the ZIP (postal) code.

Alabama (Ala; AL)
Entry to Union 1819 (22nd)
Pop 4 062 608
Nickname Camellia State, Heart of Dixie
Inhabitant Alabamian
Area 133 911 sq km/51 705 sq ml
Capital Montgomery
Bird Yellowhammer *Fish* Tarpon
Flower Camellia *Tree* Southern Pine

Alaska (Alaska; AK)
Entry to Union 1959 (49th)
Pop 551 947
Nickname Mainland State, The Last Frontier
Inhabitant Alaskan
Area 1 518 748 sq km/586 412 sq ml
Capital Juneau
Bird Willow Ptarmigan *Fish* King Salmon
Flower Forget-me-not
Gemstone Jade *Tree* Sitka Spruce

Arizona (Ariz; AZ)
Entry to Union 1912 (48th)
Pop 3 677 985
Nickname Apache State, Grand Canyon State
Inhabitant Arizonan
Area 295 249 sq km/114 000 sq ml
Capital Phoenix
Bird Cactus Wren *Flower* Giant Cactus
Gemstone Turquoise *Tree* Paloverde

Arkansas (Ark; AR)
Entry to Union 1836 (25th)
Pop 2 362 239
Nickname Bear State, Land of Opportunity
Inhabitant Arkansan

STATES OF THE USA (cont.)

Area 137 403 sq km/53 187 sq ml
Capital Little Rock
Bird Mockingbird *Flower* Apple Blossom
Gemstone Diamond *Tree* Pine

California (Calif; CA)
Entry to Union 1850 (31st)
Pop 29 839 250
Nickname Golden State
Inhabitant Californian
Area 411 033 sq km/158 706 sq ml
Capital Sacramento
Animal California Grizzly Bear
Bird California Valley Quail
Fish South Fork Golden Trout
Flower Golden Poppy
Tree California Redwood

Colorado (Colo; CO)
Entry to Union 1876 (38th)
Pop 3 307 912
Nickname Centennial State
Inhabitant Coloradan
Area 269 585 sq km/104 091 sq ml
Capital Denver
Animal Rocky Mountain Bighorn Sheep
Bird Lark Bunting *Flower* Columbine
Gemstone Aquamarine *Tree* Blue Spruce

Connecticut (Conn; CT)
Entry to Union 1788 (5th)
Pop 3 295 669
Nickname Nutmeg State, Constitution State
Inhabitant Nutmegger
Area 12 996 sq km/5 018 sq ml
Capital Hartford
Bird American Robin *Flower* Mountain Laurel
Gemstone Garnet *Tree* White Oak

Delaware (Del; DE)
Entry to Union 1787 (1st)
Pop 668 696
Nickname Diamond State, First State
Inhabitant Delawarean
Area 5 296 sq km/2 045 sq ml
Capital Dover
Bird Blue Hen Chicken *Flower* Peach Blossom
Tree American Holly

District of Columbia (DC; DC)
Pop 609 909
Inhabitant Washingtonian
Area 173.5 sq km/67 sq ml
Capital Washington
Bird Woodthrush *Flower* American Beauty Rose
Tree Scarlet Oak

Florida (Fla; FL)
Entry to Union 1845 (27th)
Pop 13 003 362
Nickname Everglade State, Sunshine State
Inhabitant Floridian
Area 151 934 sq km/58 664 sq ml
Capital Tallahassee
Bird Mockingbird *Flower* Orange Blossom
Gemstone Agatized Coral *Tree* Sabal Palm

Georgia (Ga; GA)
Entry to Union 1788 (4th)
Pop 6 508 419
Nickname Empire State of the South, Peach State
Inhabitant Georgian
Area 152 571 sq km/58 910 sq ml
Capital Atlanta
Bird Brown Thrasher *Flower* Cherokee Rose
Tree Live Oak

Hawaii (Hawaii; HI)
Entry to Union 1959 (50th)
Pop 1 115 274
Nickname Aloha State
Inhabitant Hawaiian
Area 16 759 sq km/6 471 sq ml
Capital Honolulu
Bird Nene *Flower* Hibiscus *Tree* Kukui

Idaho (Idaho; ID)
Entry to Union 1890 (43rd)
Pop 1 011 986
Nickname Gem State
Inhabitant Idahoan
Area 216 422 sq km/83 564 sq ml
Capital Boise
Bird Mountain Bluebird *Flower* Syringa
Gemstone Idaho Star Garnet
Tree Western White Pine

Illinois (Ill; IL)
Entry to Union 1818 (21st)
Pop 11 466 682
Nickname Prairie State, Land of Lincoln
Inhabitant Illinoisan
Area 145 928 sq km/56 345 sq ml
Capital Springfield
Bird Cardinal *Flower* Butterfly Violet
Tree White Oak

Indiana (Ind; IN)
Entry to Union 1816 (19th)
Pop 5 564 228
Nickname Hoosier State
Inhabitant Hoosier
Area 93 715.5 sq km/36 185 sq ml

STATES OF THE USA (cont.)

Capital Indianapolis
Bird Cardinal *Flower* Peony
Tree Tulip Tree
Iowa (Iowa; IA)
Entry to Union 1846 (29th)
Pop 2 787 424
Nickname Hawkeye State, Corn State
Inhabitant Iowan
Area 145 747 sq km/56 275 sq ml
Capital Des Moines
Bird Eastern Goldfinch *Flower* Wild Rose
Tree Oak
Kansas (Kans; KS)
Entry to Union 1861 (34th)
Pop 2 485 600
Nickname Sunflower State, Jayhawker State
Inhabitant Kansan
Area 213 089 sq km/82 277 sq ml
Capital Topeka
Animal Bison *Bird* Western Meadowlark
Flower Native Sunflower *Tree* Cottonwood
Kentucky (Ky; KY)
Entry to Union 1792 (15th)
Pop 3 698 969
Nickname Bluegrass State
Inhabitant Kentuckian
Area 104 658 sq km/40 410 sq ml
Capital Frankfort
Bird Cardinal *Flower* Goldenrod
Tree Kentucky Coffee Tree
Louisiana (La; LA)
Entry to Union 1812 (18th)
Pop 4 238 216
Nickname Pelican State, Sugar State, Creole State
Inhabitant Louisianian
Area 123 673 sq km/47 752 sq ml
Capital Baton Rouge
Bird Eastern Brown Pelican *Flower* Magnolia
Tree Bald Cypress
Maine (Maine; ME)
Entry to Union 1820 (23rd)
Pop 1 233 223
Nickname Pine Tree State
Inhabitant Downeaster
Area 86 153 sq km/33 265 sq ml
Capital Augusta
Bird Chickadee *Flower* White Pine Cone and Tassel *Gemstone* Tourmaline
Tree Eastern White Pine
Maryland (Md; MD)
Entry to Union 1788 (7th)
Pop 4 798 622
Nickname Old Line State, Free State
Inhabitant Marylander
Area 27 090 sq km/10 460 sq ml
Capital Annapolis
Bird Baltimore Oriole *Fish* Striped Bass
Flower Black-eyed Susan *Tree* White Oak
Massachusetts (Mass; MA)
Entry to Union 1788 (6th)
Pop 6 029 051
Nickname Bay State, Old Colony
Inhabitant Bay Stater
Area 21 455 sq km/8 284 sq ml
Capital Boston
Bird Chickadee *Flower* Mayflower
Tree American Elm
Michigan (Mich; MI)
Entry to Union 1837 (26th)
Pop 9 328 784
Nickname Wolverine State, Great Lake State
Inhabitant Michigander
Area 151 579 sq km/58 527 sq ml
Capital Lansing
Bird Robin *Fish* Trout
Flower Apple Blossom *Gemstone* Chlorastrolik
Tree White Pine
Minnesota (Minn; MN)
Entry to Union 1858 (32nd)
Pop 4 387 029
Nickname Gopher State, North Star State
Inhabitant Minnesotan
Area 218 593 sq km/84 402 sq ml
Capital St. Paul
Bird Loon *Fish* Walleye
Flower Moccasin Flower
Gemstone Lake Superior Agate
Tree Red Pine
Mississippi (Miss; MS)
Entry to Union 1817 (20th)
Pop 2 586 443
Nickname Magnolia State
Inhabitant Mississippian
Area 123 510 sq km/47 689 sq ml
Capital Jackson
Bird Mockingbird *Flower* Magnolia
Tree Magnolia
Missouri (Mo; MO)
Entry to Union 1821 (24th)
Pop 5 137 804
Nickname Bullion State, Show Me State
Inhabitant Missourian
Area 180 508 sq km/69 697 sq ml
Capital Jefferson City

STATES OF THE USA (cont.)

Bird Bluebird *Flower* Hawthorn
Tree Dogwood

Montana (Mont; MT)
Entry to Union 1889 (41st)
Pop 803 655
Nickname Treasure State, Big Sky Country
Inhabitant Montanan
Area 380 834 sq km/147 046 sq ml
Capital Helena
Bird Western Meadowlark *Flower* Bitterroot
Gemstone Sapphire, Agate
Tree Ponderosa Pine

Nebraska (Nebr; NE)
Entry to Union 1867 (37th)
Pop 1 584 617
Nickname Cornhusker State, Beef State
Inhabitant Nebraskan
Area 200 342 sq km/77 355 sq ml
Capital Lincoln
Bird Western Meadowlark *Flower* Goldenrod
Gemstone Blue Agate *Tree* Cottonwood

Nevada (Nev; NV)
Entry to Union 1864 (36th)
Pop 1 206 152
Nickname Silver State, Sagebrush State
Inhabitant Nevadan
Area 286 341 sq km/110 561 sq ml
Capital Carson City
Bird Mountain Bluebird *Flower* Sagebrush
Tree Single-leaf Piñon

New Hampshire (NH; NH)
Entry to Union 1788 (9th)
Pop 1 113 915
Nickname Granite State
Inhabitant New Hampshirite
Area 24 032 sq km/9 279 sq ml
Capital Concord
Bird Purple Finch *Flower* Purple Lilac
Tree White Birch

New Jersey (NJ; NJ)
Entry to Union 1787 (3rd)
Pop 7 748 634
Nickname Garden State
Inhabitant New Jerseyite
Area 20 167 sq km/7 787 sq ml
Capital Trenton
Bird Eastern Goldfinch *Flower* Purple Violet
Tree Red Oak

New Mexico (N Mex; NM)
Entry to Union 1912 (47th)
Pop 1 521 779
Nickname Sunshine State, Land of Enchantment
Inhabitant New Mexican
Area 314 914 sq km/121 593 sq ml
Capital Santa Fe
Animal Black Bear *Bird* Roadrunner
Fish Cutthroat Trout *Flower* Yucca
Gemstone Turquoise *Tree* Piñon

New York (NY; NY)
Entry to Union 1788 (11th)
Pop 18 044 505
Nickname Empire State
Inhabitant New Yorker
Area 127 185 sq km/49 108 sq ml
Capital Albany
Bird Bluebird *Flower* Rose
Gemstone Garnet *Tree* Sugar Maple

North Carolina (NC; NC)
Entry to Union 1789 (12th)
Pop 6 657 630
Nickname Old North State, Tar Heel State
Inhabitant North Carolinian
Area 136 407 sq km/52 699 sq ml
Capital Raleigh
Animal Grey Squirrel *Bird* Cardinal
Fish Channel Bass *Flower* Dogwood
Gemstone Emerald *Tree* Longleaf Pine

North Dakota (N Dak; ND)
Entry to Union 1889 (39th)
Pop 641 364
Nickname Flickertail State, Sioux State
Inhabitant North Dakotan
Area 180 180 sq km/69 567 sq ml
Capital Bismarck
Bird Western Meadowlark *Fish* Northern Pike
Flower Wild Prairie Rose
Gemstone Teredo petrified wood
Tree American Elm

Ohio (Ohio; OH)
Entry to Union 1803 (17th)
Pop 10 887 325
Nickname Buckeye State
Inhabitant Ohioan
Area 107 040 sq km/41 330 sq ml
Capital Columbus
Bird Cardinal *Flower* Scarlet Carnation
Tree Buckeye

Oklahoma (Okla; OK)
Entry to Union 1907 (46th)
Pop 3 157 604
Nickname Sooner State
Inhabitant Oklahoman
Area 181 083 sq km/69 919 sq ml
Capital Oklahoma City

STATES OF THE USA (cont.)

Bird Scissor-tailed Flycatcher
Flower Mistletoe *Tree* Redbud
Oregon (Oreg; OR)
Entry to Union 1859 (33rd)
Pop 2 853 733
Nickname Sunset State, Beaver State
Inhabitant Oregonian
Area 251 409 sq km/97 073 sq ml
Capital Salem
Animal Beaver *Bird* Western Meadowlark
Fish Chinook Salmon *Flower* Oregon Grape
Gemstone Thunder Egg *Tree* Douglas Fir
Pennsylvania (Pa; PA)
Entry to Union 1787 (2nd)
Pop 11 924 710
Nickname Keystone State
Inhabitant Pennsylvanian
Area 117 343 sq km/45 308 sq ml
Capital Harrisburg
Animal Whitetail Deer *Bird* Ruffed Grouse
Flower Mountain Laurel *Tree* Hemlock
Rhode Island (RI; RI)
Entry to Union 1790 (13th)
Pop 1 005 984
Nickname Little Rhody, Plantation State
Inhabitant Rhode Islander
Area 3 139 sq km/1 212 sq ml
Capital Providence
Bird Rhode Island Red *Flower* Violet
Tree Red Maple
South Carolina (SC; SC)
Entry to Union 1788 (8th)
Pop 3 505 707
Nickname Palmetto State
Inhabitant South Carolinian
Area 80 579 sq km/31 113 sq ml
Capital Columbia
Animal Whitetail Deer *Bird* Carolina Wren
Fish Striped Bass *Flower* Yellow Jessamine
Tree Cabbage Palmetto
South Dakota (S Dak; SD)
Entry to Union 1889 (40th)
Pop 699 999
Nickname Sunshine State, Coyote State
Inhabitant South Dakotan
Area 199 723 sq km/77 116 sq ml
Capital Pierre
Animal Coyote *Bird* Ring-necked Pheasant
Flower Pasque *Gemstone* Fairburn Agate
Tree Black Hills Spruce
Tennessee (Tenn; TN)
Entry to Union 1796 (16th)
Pop 4 896 641
Nickname Volunteer State
Inhabitant Tennessean
Area 109 149 sq km/42 144 sq ml
Capital Nashville
Animal Raccoon *Bird* Mockingbird
Flower Iris *Gemstone* Pearl *Tree* Tulip Poplar
Texas (Tex; TX)
Entry to Union 1845 (28th)
Pop 17 059 805
Nickname Lone Star State
Inhabitant Texan
Area 691 003 sq km/266 807 sq ml
Capital Austin
Bird Mockingbird *Flower* Bluebonnet
Gemstone Topaz *Tree* Pecan
Utah (Utah; UT)
Entry to Union 1896 (45th)
Pop 1 727 784
Nickname Mormon State, Beehive State
Inhabitant Utahn
Area 219 880 sq km/84 899 sq ml
Capital Salt Lake City
Bird Sea Gull *Flower* Sego Lily
Gemstone Topaz *Tree* Blue Spruce
Vermont (Vt; VT)
Entry to Union 1791 (14th)
Pop 564 964
Nickname Green Mountain State
Inhabitant Vermonter
Area 24 899 sq km/9 614 sq ml
Capital Montpelier
Animal Morgan Horse *Bird* Hermit Thrush
Flower Red Clover *Tree* Sugar Maple
Virginia (Va; VA)
Entry to Union 1788 (10th)
Pop 6 216 568
Nickname Old Dominion State, Mother of Presidents
Inhabitant Virginian
Area 105 582 sq km/40 767 sq ml
Capital Richmond
Bird Cardinal *Flower* Dogwood
Tree Flowering Dogwood
Washington (Wash; WA)
Entry to Union 1889 (42nd)
Pop 4 887 941
Nickname Evergreen State, Chinook State
Inhabitant Washingtonian
Area 176 473 sq km/68 139 sq ml
Capital Olympia
Bird Willow Goldfinch *Fish* Steelhead Trout

STATES OF THE USA (cont.)

Flower Western Rhododendron
Gemstone Petrified Wood
Tree Western Hemlock

West Virginia (W Va; WV)
Entry to Union 1863 (35th)
Pop 1 861 625
Nickname Panhandle State, Mountain State
Inhabitant West Virginian
Area 62 758 sq km/24 232 sq ml
Capital Charleston
Animal Black Bear *Bird* Cardinal
Flower Big Rhododendron *Tree* Sugar Maple

Wisconsin (Wis; WI)
Entry to Union 1848 (30th)
Pop 4 906 745
Nickname Badger State, America's Dairyland
Inhabitant Wisconsinite
Area 145 431 sq km/56 153 sq ml
Capital Madison
Animal Badger, Whitetail Deer *Bird* Robin
Fish Muskellunge *Flower* Wood Violet
Tree Sugar Maple

Wyoming (Wyo; WY)
Entry to Union 1890 (44th)
Pop 455 975
Nickname Equality State
Inhabitant Wyomingite
Area 253 315 sq km/97 809 sq ml
Capital Cheyenne
Bird Meadowlark *Flower* Indian Paintbrush
Gemstone Jade *Tree* Cottonwood

AUSTRALIAN STATES AND TERRITORIES

Name	Area sq km	sq ml	State Capital
Australian Capital Territory	2 400	930	Canberra
New South Wales	801 400	309 400	Sydney
Northern Territory	1 346 200	519 800	Darwin
Queensland	1 727 200	666 900	Brisbane
South Australia	984 000	379 900	Adelaide
Tasmania	67 800	26 200	Hobart
Victoria	227 600	87 900	Melbourne
Western Australia	2 525 500	975 000	Perth

CANADIAN PROVINCES

Name	Area sq km	sq ml	Provincial Capital
Alberta	661 190	255 285	Edmonton
British Columbia	947 800	365 945	Victoria
Manitoba	649 950	250 945	Winnipeg
New Brunswick	73 440	28 355	Fredericton
Newfoundland	405 720	156 648	St John's
Northwest Territories	3 426 320	1 322 902	Yellowknife
Nova Scotia	55 490	21 424	Halifax
Ontario	1 068 580	412 578	Toronto
Prince Edward Islands	5 660	2 185	Charlottetown
Quebec	1 540 680	594 856	Quebec City
Saskatchewan	652 380	251 883	Regina
Yukon Territory	483 450	186 660	Whitehorse

RANKS OF THE ARISTOCRACY

England	France	Holy Roman Empire (Germany)	Italy	Spain
king	roi	Kaiser	re	rey
prince	prince	Herzog	duca	duque
duke	duc	Pfalzgraf	principe	principe
marquess	marquis	Markgraf	marchese	marques
earl	comte	Landgraf	conde	conde
viscount	vicomte		visconte	vizconde
baronet				

MILITARY RANKS

France

Army	Air Force	Navy
Général d'Armée	Général d'Armée Aérienne	Amiral
Général de Corps d'Armée	Général de Corps Aérien	Vice-Amiral d'Escadre
Général de Division	Général de Division Aérienne	Vice-Amiral
Général de Brigade	Général de Brigade Aérienne	Contre-Amiral
Colonel	Colonel	Capitaine de Vaisseau
Lieutenant-Colonel	Lieutenant-Colonel	Capitaine de Frégate
Commandant	Commandant	Capitaine de Corvette
Capitaine	Capitaine	Lieutenant de Vaisseau
Lieutenant	Lieutenant	Enseigne de Vaisseau de 1 ère classe
Sous-Lieutenant	Sous-Lieutenant	Enseigne de 2 ère classe

Germany

Army	Air Force	Navy
General	General	Admiral
Generalleutnant	Generalleutnant	Vizeadmiral
Generalmajor	Generalmajor	Konteradmiral
Brigadegeneral	Brigadegeneral	Flotillenadmiral
Oberst	Oberst	Kapitan zur See

Germany (cont.)

Army	Air Force	Navy
Oberstleutnant	Oberstleutnant	Fregatten-kapitän
Major	Major	Korvetten-kapitän
Hauptmann	Hauptmann	Kapitän-leutnant
Oberleutnant	Leutnant	Oberleutnant zur See
Leutnant	Oberfahnrich	Leutnant zur See

United Kingdom

Army	Air Force	Navy
Field Marshal	Marshal of the Royal Air Force	Admiral of the Fleet
General	Air Chief Marshal	Admiral
Lieutenant-General	Air Marshal	Vice-Admiral
Major-General	Air Vice-Marshal	Rear-Admiral
Brigadier	Air Commodore	Commodore Admiral
Colonel	Group Captain	Captain RN
Lieutenant-Colonel	Wing Commander	Commander
Major	Squadron Leader	Lieutenant Commander
Captain	Flight Lieutenant	Lieutenant
Lieutenant	Flying Officer	Sub-Lieutenant
Second-Lieutenant	Pilot Officer	Midshipman

MILITARY RANKS (cont.)

USA

Army	Air Force	Navy
General of the Army	General of the Air Force	Fleet Admiral
General	General	Admiral
Lieutenant-General	Lieutenant-General	Vice-Admiral
Major-General	Major-General	Rear-Admiral
Brigadier-General	Brigadier-General	Commodore Admiral
Colonel	Colonel	Captain
Lieutenant-Colonel	Lieutenant-Colonel	Commander
Major	Major	Lieutenant-Commander
Captain	Captain	Lieutenant
First-Lieutenant	First-Lieutenant	Lieutenant Junior Grade

USSR

Army	Air Force	Navy
Marshal of the Soviet Union	Chief Marshal of the Air Force	Admiral of the Fleet of the Soviet Union
Army General	Marshal of the Air Force	Admiral of the Fleet
Colonel-General	Marshal of the Air Force	Admiral
Lieutenant-General	Marshal of the Air Force	Vice-Admiral
Major-General	Marshal of the Air Force	Rear-Admiral
Colonel	Marshal of the Air Force	Captain 1st class
Lieutenant-Colonel	Marshal of the Air Force	Captain 2nd class
Major	Marshal of the Air Force	Captain 3rd class
Captain	Marshal of the Air Force	Captain-Lieutenant

HONOURS: EUROPE

DENMARK

Order of Dannebrog believed to have been founded in 1219 and one of the oldest orders in existence, revived in 1671, with six main classes, Grand Commanders, Knights Grand Cross, Commanders of the First Degree, Commanders, Knights of the First Degree and Knights, and an auxiliary class known as the Badge of Honour.

Order of the Elephant founded in 1462 and revived by King Christian V in 1693, the premier order of Denmark.

FRANCE

Croix du Guerre military award established in 1915 to commemorate individuals mentioned in despatches.

Légion d'Honneur instituted by Napoleon in 1802 to reward distinguished military or civil service, and divided into five classes, Grands Croix, Grands Officiers, Commandeurs, Officiers and Chevaliers.

GERMANY

The Iron Cross established by Frederick William in 1813 as an award for gallantry in action, with various grades of award.

Order of Merit instituted by the Federal German Republic in 1951, and divided into eight classes, Grand Cross (three grades), Large Merit Cross (three grades) and Merit Cross (two grades).

ITALY

Al Merita della Republica Italiana established in 1952, with five classes of award, Grand Cross, Grand Officer, Commander, Officer and Member.

NETHERLANDS

Huisorde van Oranje established in 1905, awarded for outstanding services to the Royal House, corresponds to the Royal Victorian Order in the United Kingdom.

Militaire Willemsorde founded by King William I in 1815, the highest military decoration open to members of the forces of all ranks and to civilians for acts of bravery and devotion to duty.

Nederlandsche Leeuw also founded by King William I in 1815, awarded to those of proven patriotism, outstanding zeal and devotion to civil duty, and to those with extraordinary ability in the arts and sciences, open to civilians, members of the military and foreigners, divided into three

HONOURS: EUROPE (cont.)

classes, Grand Cross, Commander and Knight, with an attached brotherhood whosemembers are nominated for acts of distinction, self-sacrifice and philanthropy.

Orde van Oranje Nassau established in 1892, awarded to Netherlanders and foreigners for distinguished performance to the state or society, open to civilians or members of the forces, divided into five classes, Grand Cross, Grand Officer, Knight Commander, Officer and Knight.

HONOURS: UK

CBE *see* **The Most Excellent Order of the British Empire**

The Distinguished Service Order (DSO) established in 1886, bestowed as a reward for the distinguished service in action of commissioned officers in the Navy, Army and Royal Air Force, extended in 1942 to cover officers of the Merchant Navy.

The George Cross (GC) instituted in 1940 as a reward for gallantry, and conferred upon those responsible for 'acts of the greatest heroism or of the most conspicuous courage in circumstances of extreme danger'.

The Imperial Service Order (ISO) instituted in 1902 to reward members of the Civil Service, with one class of membership, numbers limited to 1,700 in total, 1,100 belonging to the Home Civil Service, and 600 coming from the Overseas Civil Service.

MBE *see* **The Most Excellent Order of the British Empire.**

The Most Ancient and Most Noble Order of the Thistle (KT) an ancient order revived by King James II in 1687, and re-established by Queen Anne in 1703, limited to 16 knights.

The Most Distinguished Order of St Michael and St George founded in 1818 by King George III, conferred upon British subjects for services abroad or in the British Commonwealth, with the motto 'Auspicium melioris aevi' (Token of a better age), and divided into three classes, Knight Grand Cross (GCMG), Knight Commander (KCMG) and Companion (CMG)

The Most Excellent Order of the British Empire an order of knighthood, the first to be granted to both sexes equally, instituted 1917, divided into military and civil divisions in 1918, with five divisions, Knight or Dame Grand Cross (GBE), Knight or Dame Commander (KBE/DBE), Commander (CBE), Officer (OBE) and Member (MBE)

The Most Honourable Order of the Bath founded in 1399, revived by King George in 1725, originally a military order, the civil branch was established in 1847. Women became eligible in 1971. The order has three divisions: Knight or Dame Grand Cross (GCB), Knight or Dame Commander (KCB/DCB), and Companion (CB).

The Most Noble Order of the Garter (KG) instituted in 1348 by Edward III, limited to 24 knights companion only, and with the motto 'Honi soit qui mal y pense' (Shame on him who thinks evil of it).

OBE *see* **The Most Excellent Order of the British Empire**

The Order of Merit (OM) instituted in 1902, with civil and military divisions, and limited to 24 in number.

The Order of the Companions of Honour instituted in 1917 at the same time as the Most Excellent Order of the British Empire. It carries no title or precedence and consists of one class ranking immediately after the first class of the Order of the British Empire. Membership is limited to 65 in number, excluding honorary members.

The Royal Red Cross instituted by Queen Victoria in 1883, the first military order designed solely for women, and conferred upon members of the nursing services for their efforts in the field, and for others undertaking voluntary work on behalf of the sick or wounded or on behalf of the Red Cross.

The Royal Victorian Chain founded in 1902 by King Edward VII, it confers no precedence on the holder, and is largely, although not exclusively, awarded to foreign monarchs.

The Royal Victorian Order established by Queen Victoria in 1896, with no limit to the number of members, conferred for services to the sovereign or Royal Family, bestowed upon foreigners as well as British subjects. Women became eligible in 1936.

The Victoria Cross (VC) instituted by Queen Victoria in 1856 to reward conspicuous bravery, and the most highly coveted of British military decorations.

HONOURS: USA

The Bronze Star established in 1944, awarded to members of the forces for acts of heroism or merit and for services beyond the call of duty, but not sufficiently outstanding to merit the Silver Star or Legion of Merit.

The Congressional Medal of Honor instituted in 1861/1862, and first awarded during the American Civil War, conferred upon members of the forces showing exceptional gallantry and bravery in action.

The Distinguished Service Cross instituted in 1918, confined to the army, and awarded to those showing extraordinary heroism in circumstances which do not justify the Congressional Medal of Honour.

The Legion of Merit instituted in 1942, awarded to members of both the United States and foreign forces for distinguished service and meritorious conduct over a period of time.

The Purple Heart first instituted by George Washington in 1782 and reinstituted by Congress in 1932, awarded to those wounded in military action, and bearing the inscription 'For Military Merit'.

The Medal for Merit established by President Roosevelt in 1942 to award civilians of the United States or her allies for distinguished and meritorious service.

The Silver Star first authorised during World War I, it takes precedence over the Legion of Merit.

CHARITIES (UK)

This chart gives information on the 25 charities in the UK which have the largest income.

Abbreviated name	Full name	Date founded	Voluntary income in £000	Donations received in £000
–	National Trust	1895	55 727	18 055
RNLI	Royal Lifeboat Institution	1824	47 366	6 832
–	Oxfam	1942	45 027	15 815
ICRF	Imperial Cancer Research Fund	1902	42 117	2 596
–	Cancer Research Campaign	1923	40 284	2 465
–	Salvation Army	1865	38 985	23 848
–	Save the Children Fund	1919	38 610	26 158
–	Barnardo's	1866	29 938	10 667
–	Help the Aged	1961	24 508	17 188
–	Guide Dogs for the Blind Association	1934	24 449	4 034
RSPCA	Royal Society for the Prevention of Cruelty to Animals	1824	23 839	6 018
–	British Heart Foundation	1961	23 752	6 266
NSPCC	National Society for the Prevention of Cruelty to Children	–	22 571	15 095
–	British Red Cross Society	1870	21 800	12 783
RNIB	Royal National Institute for the Blind	1868	19 938	999
–	Marie Curie Memorial Foundation	1948	19 686	7 635
–	Spastics Society	1952	19 135	10 365
–	Christian Aid	1949	18 680	14 682
WWFN	World Wide Fund for Nature	1961	17 086	10 991
–	ActionAid	1972	16 169	6 103
–	Jewish Philanthropic Association	–	15 627	11 610
–	Cancer Relief Macmillan Fund	1911	14 820	7 177
RSPB	Royal Society for the Protection of Birds	1889	14 794	7 928
–	Tear Fund	–	13 873	9 054
PDSA	People's Dispensary for Sick Animals	1917	13 421	2 762

CHARITIES (USA)

Abbreviated name	Full name	Date founded	Income in US $000[1]
ALSAC-SJCRH	ALSAC-St Jude Children's Research Hospital	1957	126 782
ACS	American Cancer Society	1913	335 758
AHA	American Heart Association	1924	248 776
–	American National Red Cross	1881	985 175
AF	AmeriCares Foundation	1979	69 373
–	Arthritis Foundation	1948	55 534
BGEA	Billy Graham Evangelistic Association	1950	89 178
–	Boys Town/Father Flanagan's Boys' Home	1917	64 779
–	Campus Crusade for Christ	1951	129 734
–	CARE USA	1945	329 126
CRS	Catholic Relief Services	1943	288 296
CTW	Children's Television Workshop	1969	71 333
CCF	Christian Children's Fund	1938	101 744[2]
–	City of Hope	1913	133 013
CH	Covenant House	1969	88 167
LSA	Leukemia Society of America	1949	54 439
–	March of Dimes Birth Defects Foundation	1938	119 655
MDA	Muscular Dystrophy Association	1950	111 498
NBA	National Benevolant Association of the Christian Church	1887	81 421
NJCIRM	National Jewish Center for Immunology and Respiratory Medicine	1899	62 439
NMSS	National Multiple Schlerosis Society	1946	65 590
NWF	National Wildlife Federation	1936	78 753
–	The Nature Conservancy	1951	168 554
PPHF	People-to-People Health Foundation	1958	53 200
–	Rotary Foundation of Rotary International	1917	106 276
SCF	Save the Children Federation	1932	84 301
–	Shriner's Hospital for Crippled Children	1922	339 266
UJA	United Jewish Appeal	1939	367 863
WV	World Vision	1950	188 735

[1] Data from 1988 or 1989

[2] Includes income from related organizations in Germany and Australia

COMMUNICATION

LANGUAGES: NUMBER OF SPEAKERS

Language families

Estimates of the numbers of speakers in the main language families of the world in the early 1980s. The list includes Japanese and Korean, which are not clearly related to any other languages.

Main language families	
Indo-European	2 000 000 000
Sino-Tibetan	1 040 000 000
Niger-Congo	260 000 000
Afro-Asiatic	230 000 000
Austronesian	200 000 000
Dravidian	140 000 000
Japanese	120 000 000
Altaic	90 000 000
Austro-Asiatic	60 000 000
Korean	60 000 000
Tai	50 000 000
Nilo-Saharan	30 000 000
Amerindian (North, Central, South America)	25 000 000
Uralic	23 000 000
Miao-Yao	7 000 000
Caucasian	6 000 000
Indo-Pacific	3 000 000
Khoisan	50 000
Australian aborigine	50 000
Palaeosiberian	25 000

Specific languages

The first column gives estimates (in millions) for mother-tongue speakers of the 20 most widely used languages. The second column gives estimates of the total population of all countries where the language has official or semi-official status; these totals are often over-estimates, as only a minority of people in countries where a second language is recognized may actually be fluent in it.

Mother-tongue speakers		Official language populations	
1 Chinese	1 000	1 English	1 400
2 English	350	2 Chinese	1 000
3 Spanish	250	3 Hindi	700
4 Hindi	200	4 Spanish	280
5 Arabic	150	5 Russian	270
6 Bengali	150	6 French	220
7 Russian	150	7 Arabic	170
8 Portuguese	135	8 Portuguese	160
9 Japanese	120	9 Malay	160
10 German	100	10 Bengali	150
11 French	70	11 Japanese	120
12 Panjabi	70	12 German	100
13 Javanese	65	13 Urdu	85
14 Bihari	65	14 Italian	60
15 Italian	60	15 Korean	60
16 Korean	60	16 Vietnamese	60
17 Telugu	55	17 Persian	55
18 Tamil	55	18 Tagalog	50
19 Marathi	50	19 Thai	50
20 Vietnamese	50	20 Turkish	50

SPEAKERS OF ENGLISH

The first column gives figures for countries where English is used as a mother-tongue or first language; for countries where no figure is given, English is not the first language of a significant number of people. (A question-mark indicates that no agreed estimates are available.) The second column gives total population figures (mainly 1990 figures) for countries where English has official or semi-official status as a medium of communication. These totals are likely to bear little correlation with the real use of English in the area.

Country	First language speakers of English	Country population
Anguilla	8 000 –	8 000
Antigua and Barbuda	80 600 –	80 600
Australia	14 000 000	17 073 000
Bahamas	253 000	253 000
Bangladesh	?	113 005 000 +
Barbados	257 000 +	257 000 +
Belize	100 000 +	189 000 +
Bermuda	59 300 +	59 300 +
Bhutan	?	1 442 000 +
Botswana		1 295 000 –
Brunei		259 000 +
Cameroon		11 900 000 +
Canada	17 000 000 +	26 620 000 +
Dominica	50 000 +	82 200 –
Fiji		740 000 +
Ghana		15 020 000
Gibraltar		30 689 +
Grenada	101 000 +	101 000 +
Guyana	700 000 +	756 000
Hong Kong	?	5 841 000 –
India	?	853 373 000 +
Irish Republic	3 515 000	3 515 000
Jamaica	2 300 000 +	2 391 000
Kenya		24 872 000
Kiribati		71 100 +
Lesotho		1 760 000
Liberia		2 595 000
Malawi		8 831 000
Malaysia (East)		14 300 000
Malta		353 000
Mauritius		1 080 000
Montserrat	12 000	12 000
Namibia		1 302 000
Nauru		9 000 +
Nepal	?	18 910 000 +
New Zealand	3 000 000	3 389 000
Nigeria	?	119 812 000 +
Pakistan	?	122 666 000 +
Papua New Guinea		3 671 000
Philippines		61 480 000
St Christopher and Nevis	44 100	44 100
St Lucia	?	151 000 +
St Vincent and the Grenadines	100 000 +	115 000 +
Senegambia		600 000
Seychelles		68 700
Sierra Leone		4 151 000
Singapore	?	2 718 000
Solomon Islands		319 000 +
South Africa	2 000 000 +	30 797 000
Sri Lanka	?	17 103 000 +
Suriname		411 000
Swaziland		770 000
Tanzania		24 403 000
Tonga		96 000 +
Trinidad and Tobago	1 233 000	1 233 000
Tuvalu		9 100 +
Uganda		16 928 000
UK	57 000 000 +	57 384 000
USA	215 000 000	249 246 000 +
US territories in Pacific		300 000 –
Vanuatu		150 000
Western Samoa		165 000 +
Zambia		8 456 000
Zimbabwe	200 000 +	9 369 000
Other British territories	30 000 +	30 000 +
TOTALS	317 043 000 +	1 895 079 100 +

FOREIGN WORDS AND PHRASES

ab initio (Lat) 'from the beginning'.
à bon marché (Fr) 'good market'; at a good bargain, cheap.
ab ovo (Lat) 'from the egg'; from the beginning.
absit omen (Lat) a superstitious formula; may there be no ill omen (as in a reference just made).
a cappella (Ital) 'in the style of the chapel'; sung without instrumental accompaniment.
achtung (Ger) 'Look out!, Take care!'.
acushla (Ir) term of endearment; darling.
addendum *plural* **addenda** (Lat) 'that which is to be added'; supplementary material for a book.
à deux (Fr) 'for two'; often denotes a dinner or conversation of a romantic nature.
ad hoc (Lat) 'towards this'; for this special purpose.
ad hominem (Lat) 'to the man'; appealing not to logic or reason but to personal preferences or feelings.
ad infinitum (Lat) 'to infinity'; denotes endless repetition.
ad litem (Lat) 'for the lawsuit'; used of a guardian appointed to act in court (eg because of insanity or insufficient years of the litigant).
ad nauseam (Lat) 'to the point of sickness'; disgustingly endless or repetitive.
ad referendum (Lat) 'for reference'; to be further considered.
ad valorem (Lat) 'to value'; 'according to what it is worth' often used of taxes etc.
advocatus diaboli (Lat) 'devil's advocate'; person opposing an argument in order to expose any flaws in it.
affaire (Fr) liaison, intrigue; an incident arousing speculation and scandal.
afflatus (Lat) 'blowing or breathing'; inspiration (often divine).
aficionado (Span) 'amateur'; an ardent follower; a 'fan'.
a fortiori (Lat) 'from the stronger' (argument); denotes the validity and stronger reason of a proposition.
agent provocateur (Fr) 'provocative agent'; someone who incites others, by pretended sympathy to commit crimes.
aggiornamento (Ital) 'modernization'; reform (often political).
aide-de-camp (Fr) 'assistant on the field'; an officer who acts as a confidential personal assistant for an officer of higher rank.
aide-mémoire (Fr) 'help-memory'; a reminder; memorandum-book; a written summary of a diplomatic agreement.
à la carte (Fr) 'from the menu'; each dish individually priced.
à la mode (Fr) 'in fashion, fashionable'; also in cooking, of meat braised and stewed with vegetables; with ice-cream (American English).
al dente (Ital) 'to the tooth'; culinary term denoting (usually) pasta fully cooked but still firm.
al fresco (Ital) 'fresh'; painting on fresh or moist plaster; in the fresh, cool or open air.
alma mater (Lat) 'bountiful mother'; one's former school, college, or university; official college or university song (American English).
aloha (Hawaiian) 'love'; a salutation, 'hello' or 'goodbye'.
alumnus *plural* **alumni** (Lat) 'pupil' or 'foster son'; a former pupil or student.
ambiance (Fr) surroundings, atmosphere.
amende honorable (Fr) a public apology satisfying the honour of the injured party.
amour-propre (Fr) 'own love, self-love'; legitimate self-esteem, sometimes exaggerated; vanity, conceit.
ancien régime (Fr) 'old regime'; a superseded and outdated political system or ruling elite.
angst (Ger) 'anxiety'; an unsettling feeling produced by awareness of the uncertainties and paradoxes inherent in the state of being human.
anno Domini (Lat) 'in the year of the Lord'; used in giving dates of the Christian era, counting forward from the year of Christ's birth.
annus mirabilis (Lat) 'year of wonders'; a remarkably successful or auspicious year.
anschluss (Ger) 'joining together'; union, especially the political union of Germany and Austria in 1938.
ante-bellum (Lat) 'before the war'; denotes a period before a specific war, especially the American Civil War.
ante meridiem (Lat) 'before midday'; between midnight and noon, abbreviated to am.
à point (Fr) 'into the right condition'; to a nicety, a culinary term.

FOREIGN WORDS AND PHRASES (cont.)

a posteriori (Lat) 'from the later'; applied to reasoning from experience, from effect to cause.
apparatchik (Ger) a Communist spy or agent; (humorous) any bureaucratic hack.
appellation contrôlée (Fr) 'certified name'; used in the labelling of French wines, a guarantee of specified conditions of origin, strength, etc.
après-ski (Fr) 'after-ski'; pertaining to the evening's amusements after skiing.
a priori (Lat) 'from the previous'; denotes argument from the cause to the effect; deductive reasoning.
atelier (Fr) a workshop, an artist's studio.
au contraire (Fr) 'on the contrary'.
au fait (Fr) 'to the point'; highly skilled; knowledgeable or familiar with something.
au fond (Fr) 'at the bottom'; fundamentally.
au naturel (Fr) 'in the natural state'; naked; also as a culinary term: cooked plainly, raw, or without dressing.
au pair (Fr) 'on an equal basis'; originally an arrangement of mutual service without payment; now used of a girl (usually foreign) who performs domestic duties for board, lodging and pocket money.
auto-da-fé (Port) 'act of the faith'; the public declaration or carrying out of a sentence imposed on heretics in Spain and Portugal by the Inquisition, eg burning at the stake.
avant-garde (Fr) 'front guard'; applied to those in the forefront of an artistic movement.
ave atque vale (Lat) hail and farewell.

babushka (Russ) 'grandmother'; granny; a triangular headscarf worn under the chin.
bain-marie (Fr) 'bath of Mary'; a water-bath; a vessel of boiling water in which another is placed for slow and gentle cooking, or for keeping foods warm.
baksheesh (Persian) a gift or present of money, particularly in the East (India, Turkey, Egypt, etc).
bal costumé (Fr) a fancy-dress ball.
banzai (Jap) a Japanese battle cry, salute to the emperor, or exclamation of joy.
barrio (Span) 'district, suburb'; a (usually poor) community of Spanish-speaking immigrants (esp American English).
batik (Javanese) 'painted'; method of producing patterns on fabric by drawing with wax before dyeing.
beau geste (Fr) 'beautiful gesture'; a magnanimous action.
belle époque (Fr) 'fine period'; the time of gracious living for the well-to-do immediately preceding World War I.
bête noire (Fr) 'black beast'; a bugbear; something one especially dislikes.
Bildungsroman (Ger) 'educational novel'; a novel concerning its hero's early spiritual and emotional development and education.
blasé (Fr) 'cloyed'; dulled to enjoyment.
blitzkrieg (Ger) 'lightning war'; a sudden overwhelming attack by ground and air forces; a burst of intense activity.
bodega (Span) a wine shop that usually sells food as well; a building for wine storage.
bona fides (Lat) 'good faith'; genuineness.
bonne-bouche (Fr) 'good mouth'; a delicious morsel eaten at the end of a meal.
bonsai (Jap) art of growing miniature trees in pots; a dwarf tree grown by this method.
bonvivant (Fr) 'good living (person)'; one who lives well, particularly enjoying good food and wine; a jovial companion.
bon voyage (Fr) have a safe and pleasant journey.
bourgeois (Fr) 'citizen'; a member of the middle class; a merchant; conventional, conservative.

camera obscura (Lat) 'dark room'; a light-free chamber in which an image of outside objects is thrown upon a screen.
canard (Fr) 'duck'; a false rumour; a second wing fitted as a horizontal stabilizer near the nose of an aircraft.
carpe diem (Lat) 'seize the day'; enjoy the pleasures of the present moment while they last.
carte blanche (Fr) 'blank sheet of paper'; freedom of action.

FOREIGN WORDS AND PHRASES (cont.)

casus belli (Lat) 'occasion of war'; whatever sparks off or justifies a war or quarrel.
cause célèbre (Fr) a very notable or famous trial; a notorious controversy.
caveat emptor (Lat) 'let the buyer beware'; warns the buyer to examine carefully the article he is about to purchase.
c'est la vie (Fr) 'that's life'; denotes fatalistic resignation.
chacun à son goût (Fr) 'each to his own taste'; implies surprise at another's choice.
chambré (Fr) 'put into a room'; (of red wine) at room temperature.
chargé-d'affaires (Fr) a diplomatic agent of lesser rank; an ambassador's deputy.
chef d'oeuvre (Fr) a masterpiece, the best piece of work by a particular artist, writer, etc.
chicano (Span) *mejicano* 'Mexican'; or an American of Mexican descent.
chutzpah (Yiddish) effrontery, nerve to do or say outrageous things.
cinéma-vérité (Fr) 'cinema truth'; realism in films usually sought by photographic scenes of real life.
cinquecento (Ital) 'five hundred'; of the Italian art and literature of the 16th century Renaissance period.
circa (Lat) 'surrounding'; of dates and numbers, approximately.
cliché (Fr) 'stereotype printing block'; the impression made by a die in any soft metal; a hackneyed phrase or concept.
cognoscente *plural* **cognoscenti** (Lat) 'one who knows'; one who professes critical knowledge of art, music, etc; a connoisseur.
coitus interruptus (Lat) 'interrupted intercourse'; coitus intentionally interrupted by withdrawal before semen is ejaculated; anticlimax when something ends prematurely.
comme il faut (Fr) 'as it is necessary'; correct; genteel.
compos mentis (Lat) 'having control of one's mind'; sane.
contra mundum (Lat) 'against the world'; denotes defiant perseverance despite universal criticism.
cordon bleu (Fr) 'blue ribbon'; denotes food cooked to a very high standard; a dish made with ham and cheese and a white sauce.
coup de foudre (Fr) 'flash of lightning'; a sudden and astonishing happening; love at first sight.
coup de grâce (Fr) 'blow of mercy'; a finishing blow to end pain; a decisive action which ends a troubled enterprise.
coup d'état (Fr) 'blow of state'; a violent overthrow of a government or subversive stroke of state policy.
coupé (Fr) 'cut'; (usually) two-door motor-car with sloping roof.
crème de la crème (Fr) 'cream of the cream'; the very best.
cuisine minceur (Fr) 'slenderness cooking'; a style of cooking characterized by imaginative use of light, simple, low-fat ingredients.
cul-de-sac (Fr) 'bottom of the bag'; a road closed at one end.
cum grano salis (Lat) with a grain (pinch) of salt.
curriculum vitae (Lat) 'course of life'; denotes a summary of someone's educational qualifications and work experience for presenting to a prospective employer.

décolleté (Fr) 'with bared neck and shoulders'; with neck uncovered; (of dress) low cut.
de facto (Lat) 'from the fact'; in fact, actually, irrespective of what is legally recognized.
de gustibus non est disputandum (Lat) (often in English shortened for convenience to *de gustibus*) 'there is no disputing about tastes'; there is no sense in challenging people's preferences.
déjà vu (Fr) 'already seen'; in any of the arts, original material; an illusion of having experienced something before; something seen so often it has become tedious.
de jure (Lat) 'according to law'; denotes the legal or theoretical position, which may not correspond with reality.
delirium tremens (Lat) 'trembling delirium'; psychotic condition caused by alcoholism, involving anxiety, shaking, hallucinations, etc.
deo volente (Lat) 'God willing'; a sort of good-luck talisman.
de rigueur (Fr) 'of strictness'; compulsory; required by strict etiquette.
derrière (Fr) 'behind'; the buttocks.
déshabillé (Fr) 'undressed', state of being only partially dressed, or of being casually dressed.

FOREIGN WORDS AND PHRASES (cont.)

de trop (Fr) 'of too much'; superfluous; in the way.
deus ex machina (Lat) 'a god from a machine'; a contrived solution to a difficulty in a plot.
distingué (Fr) 'distinguished'; having an aristocratic or refined demeanour; striking.
dolce far niente (Ital) 'sweet doing nothing'; denotes the pleasure of idleness.
doppelgänger (Ger) 'double goer'; a ghostly duplicate of a living person, a wraith; someone who looks exactly like someone else.
double entendre (Fr) 'double meaning'; ambiguity (normally with indecent connotations).
doyen (Fr) 'dean'; most distinguished member or representative by virtue of seniority, experience, and often also excellence.
droit de seigneur (Fr) 'the lord's right'; originally the alleged right of a feudal superior to take the virginity of a vassal's bride; any excessive claim imposed on a subordinate.
dummkopf (Ger) 'dumb-head'; blockhead; idiot.

echt (Ger) 'real, genuine'; denotes authenticity, typicality.
eheu fugaces (Lat); opening of a quotation (Horace *Odes* II, XIV, 1–2) 'alas! the fleeting years slip away'; bemoans the brevity of human existence.
élan (Fr) 'dash, rush, bound'; flair, flamboyance.
el dorado (Span) 'the gilded man'; the golden land (or city) imagined by the Spanish conquerors of America; any place which offers the opportunity of acquiring fabulous wealth.
embarras de richesse (Fr) 'embarrassment of wealth'; a perplexing amount of wealth or an abundance of any kind.
embonpoint (Fr) *en bon point* 'in fine form'; well-fed, stout, plump.
emeritus (Lat) 'having served one's time'; eg of a retired professor, honourably discharged from a public duty; holding a position on an honorary basis only.
éminence grise (Fr) someone exerting power through their influence over a superior.
enfant terrible (Fr) 'terrible child'; a precocious child whose sayings embarrass its parents; a person whose behaviour is indiscreet, embarrassing to his associates.
ennui (Fr) world-weary listlessness, boredom.
en passant (Fr) 'in passing'; by the way, incidentally; applied in chess to the taking of a pawn that has just moved two squares as if it had moved only one.
en route (Fr) on the way, on the road; let us go.
entente (Fr) 'understanding'; a friendly agreement between nations.
épater les bourgeois (Fr) 'shock the middle class'; to disconcert the prim and proper; commonly used of artistic productions which defy convention.
erratum *plural* **errata** (Lat) an error in writing or printing.
ersatz (Ger) 'replacement, substitute'; connotes a second-rate substitute; a supplementary reserve from which waste can be made good.
et al (Lat) *et alii* 'and other things'; used to avoid giving a complete and possibly over-lengthy list of all items eg of authors.
et tu, Brute (Lat) 'you too, Brutus' (Caesar's alleged exclamation when he saw Brutus among his assassins); denotes surprise and dismay that a supposed friend has joined in a conspiracy against one.
eureka (Gr) *heureka* 'I have found!'; cry of triumph at a discovery.
ex cathedra (Lat) 'from the seat'; from the chair of office; authoritatively, judicially.
ex gratia (Lat) 'from favour'; of a payment; one that is made as a favour, without any legal obligation and without admitting legal liability.
ex officio (Lat) 'from office, by virtue of office'; used as a reason for membership of a body.
ex parte (Lat) 'from (one) part'; 'from (one) side'; on behalf of one side only in legal proceedings; partial, prejudiced.

fait accompli (Fr) 'accomplished fact'; already done or settled, and therefore irreversible.
fata Morgana (Ital) a striking kind of mirage, attributed to witchcraft.

FOREIGN WORDS AND PHRASES (cont.)

fatwa (Arabic) 'the statement of a formal legal opinion'; a formal legal opinion delivered by an Islamic religious leader.
faute de mieux (Fr) 'for lack of anything better'.
faux ami (Fr) 'false friend'; a word in a foreign language that does not mean what it appears to.
faux-naïf (Fr) 'falsely naive'; seeming or pretending to be unsophisticated, innocent, etc.
faux pas (Fr) 'false step'; a social blunder.
femme fatale (Fr) 'fatal woman'; an irresistibly attractive woman who brings difficulties or disasters on men; a siren.
fidus Achates (Lat) 'the faithful Achates' (Aeneas' friend); a loyal follower.
film noir (Fr) 'black film'; a bleak and pessimistic film.
fin de siècle (Fr) 'end of the century'; of the end of the 19th-c in Western culture or of an era; decadent.
floruit (Lat) 'he or she flourished'; denotes a period during which a person lived.
fons et origo (Lat) 'the source and origin'.
force de frappe (Fr) 'strike force'; equivalent of the 'independent nuclear deterrent'.
force majeure (Fr) 'superior force'; an unforseeable or uncontrollable course of events, excusing one from fulfilling a contract, a legal term.
führer (Ger) 'leader, guide'; an insulting term for anyone bossily asserting authority.

gastarbeiter (Ger) 'guest-worker'; an immigrant worker, especially one who does menial work.
gauleiter (Ger) 'district leader'; a chief official of a district under the Nazi régime; an overbearing wielder of petty authority.
gemütlich (Ger) amiable, comfortable, cosy.
gestalt (Ger) 'form, shape'; original whole or unit, more than the sum of its parts.
gesundheit (Ger) 'health'; 'your health', said to someone who has just sneezed.
glasnost (Russ) 'publicity'; the policy of openness and forthrightness followed by the Soviet government, initiated by Mikhail Gorbachev.
gnothi seauton (Gr) 'know thyself'.
götterdämmerung (Ger) 'twilight of the gods'; the downfall of any once powerful system.
goy plural **goys** or **goyim** (Hebrew) non-Jewish, a gentile.
grand mal (Fr) 'large illness'; a violently convulsive form of epilepsy.
grand prix (Fr) 'great prize'; any of several international motor races; any competition of similar importance in other sports.
gran turismo (Ital) 'great touring, touring on a grand scale'; a motor car designed for high speed touring in luxury (abbreviation GT).
gratis (Lat) *gratiis* 'kindness, favour'; free of charge.
gravitas (Lat) 'weight'; seriousness, weight of demeanour, avoidance of unseemly frivolity.
gringo (Mexican-Spanish) 'foreigner'.
guru (Hindi) a spiritual teacher; a revered instructor or mentor.

habeas corpus (Lat) 'you should have the body'; a writ to a jailer to produce a prisoner in person, and to state the reasons for detention; maintains the right of the subject to protection from unlawful imprisonment.
haiku (Jap) 'amusement poem'; a Japanese poem consisting of only three lines, containing respectively five, seven, and five syllables.
hajj (Arabic) 'pilgrimage'; the Muslim pilgrimage to Mecca.
haka (Maori) a Maori ceremonial war dance; a similar dance performed by New Zealanders eg before a rugby game.
halal (Arabic) 'lawful'; meat from an animal killed in strict accordance with Muslim law.
haute couture (Fr) 'higher tailoring'; fashionable, expensive dress designing and tailoring.
haut monde (Fr) 'high world'; high society, fashionable society, composed of the aristocracy and the wealthy.
hic jacet (Lat) 'here lies'; the first words of an epitaph; memorial inscription.
hoi polloi (Gr) 'the many'; the rabble, the vulgar.

FOREIGN WORDS AND PHRASES (cont.)

hombre (Span) 'man'.
honoris causa (Lat) 'for the sake of honour'; a token of respect; used to designate honorary university degrees.
hors concours (Fr) 'out of the competition'; not entered for a contest; unequalled.

ibidem (Lat) 'in the same place'; used in footnotes to indicate that the same book (or chapter) has been cited previously.
id (Lat) 'it'; the sum total of the primitive instinctive forces in an individual.
idée fixe (Fr) 'a fixed idea'; an obsession.
idem (Lat) 'the same'.
ikebana (Jap) 'living flowers'; the Japanese art of flower arrangement.
in absentia (Lat) 'in absence'; used for occasions, such as the receiving of a degree award, when the recipient would normally be present.
in camera (Lat) 'in the room'; in a private room, in secret.
incommunicado (Span) 'unable to communicate'; deprived of the right to communicate with others.
in extremis (Lat) 'in the last'; at the point of death; in desperate circumstances.
in flagrante delecto (Lat) 'with the crime blazing'; in the very act of committing the crime.
infra dig (Lat) 'below dignity'; below one's dignity.
in loco parentis (Lat) 'in place of a parent'.
in shallah (Arabic) 'if God wills'; *see* **deo volente**.
inter alia (Lat) 'among other things'; used to show that a few examples have been chosen from many possibilities.
in vitro (Lat) 'in glass'; in the test tube.
ipso facto (Lat) 'by the fact itself'; thereby.

je ne sais quoi (Fr) 'I do not know what'; an indefinable something.
jihad 'struggle'; a holy war undertaken by Muslims against unbelievers.
Jugendstil (Ger) 'youth style'; the German term for art nouveau.

kamikaze (Jap) 'divine wind'; Japanese pilots making a suicide attack; any reckless, potentially self-destructive, act.
kanaka (Hawaiian) 'man'; used by Europeans (and Australians) to mean South Sea islander.
karaoke (Jap) 'empty orchestra'; in bars, clubs, etc members of the public sing a solo to a recorded backing.
karma (Sanskrit) 'act'; the concept that the actions in a life determine the future condition of an individual.
kibbutz (Hebrew) A Jewish communal agricultural settlement in Israel.
kitsch (Ger) 'rubbish'; work in any of the arts that is pretentious and inferior or in bad taste.
kvetch (Yiddish) 'complain, whine (incessantly)'.

la dolce vita (Ital) 'the sweet life'; the name of a film made by Frederico Fellini in 1960 showing a life of wealth, pleasure and self-indulgence.
laissez-faire (Fr) 'let do'; a general principle of non-interference.
lebensraum (Ger) 'life space'; room to live; used by Hitler to justify his acquisition of land for Germany.
leitmotiv (Ger) 'leading motive'; a recurrent theme.
lèse majesté (Fr) 'injured majesty'; offence against the sovereign power; treason.
lingua franca (Ital) 'Frankish language'; originally a mixed Italian trading language used in the Levant, subsequently any language chosen as a means of communication among speakers of different languages.
locum tenens (Lat) 'place holder'; a deputy or substitute, especially for a doctor or a clergyman.

macho (Mexican/Span) 'male'; originally a positive term denoting masculinity or virility, it has come in English to describe an ostentatious virility.
magnum opus (Lat) 'great work'; a person's greatest achievement, especially a literary work.
maharishi (Sanskrit) a Hindu sage or spiritual leader, a guru.

FOREIGN WORDS AND PHRASES (cont.)

mañana (Span) 'tomorrow'; an unspecified time in the future.
mea culpa (Lat) 'through my fault'; originally part of the Latin mass; an admission of fault and an expression of repentance.
memento mori (Lat) 'remember that you must die'; an object, such as a skull, or anything to remind one of mortality.
ménage à trois (Fr) 'household of three'; a household comprised of a husband and wife and the lover of one of them.
mens sana in corpore sano (Lat) 'a sound mind in a sound body' (Juvenal X, 356); the guiding rule of the 19th-c English educational system.
mirabile dictu (Lat) 'wonderful to tell'; an expression of (sometimes ironic) amazement.
modus operandi (Lat) 'mode of working'; the characteristic methods employed by a particular criminal.
modus vivendi (Lat)'mode of living'; an arrangement or compromise by means of which those who differ may get on together for a time.
mot juste (Fr) 'exact word'; the word which fits the context exactly.
multum in parvo (Lat) 'much in little'; a large amount in a small space.
mutatis mutandis (Lat) 'with the necessary changes made'.

négociant (Fr) 'merchant, trader'; often used for *négociant en vins* 'wine merchant'.
ne plus ultra (Lat) 'not more beyond'; extreme perfection.
netsuke (Jap) a small Japanese carved ornament used to fasten small objects, eg a purse, tobacco pouch, or medicine box, to the sash of a kimono. They are now collectors' pieces.
noblesse oblige (Fr) 'nobility obliges'; rank imposes obligations.
non sequitur (Lat) 'it does not follow'; a conclusion that does not follow logically from the premise; a remark that has no relation to what has gone before.
nostalgie de la boue (Fr) 'hankering for mud'; a craving for a debased physical life without civilized refinements.
nota bene (Lat) 'observe well, note well'; often abbreviated NB.
nouveau riche (Fr) 'new rich'; one who has only lately acquired wealth (without acquiring good taste).
nouvelle cuisine (Fr) 'new cooking'; a style of simple French cookery which aims to produce dishes that are light and healthy, utilizing fresh fruit and vegetables, and avoiding butter and cream.
nouvelle vague (Fr) 'new wave'; a movement in the French cinema aiming at imaginative quality films.

obiter dictum (Lat) 'something said in passing'; originally a legal term for something said by a trial judge which was incidental to the case in question.
origami (Jap) 'paper-folding'; Japanese art of folding paper to make shapes suggesting birds, boats, etc.
O tempora! O mores! (Lat) 'O the times! O the manners' (Cicero *In Catalinam*) a condemnation of present times, as contrasted with a past which is seen as golden.
outré (Fr) 'gone to excess'; beyond what is customary or proper; eccentric.

pace (Lat) 'peace'; by your leave (indicating polite disagreement).
panem et circenses (Lat) 'bread and circuses', or 'food and the big match' (Juvenal *Satires* X, 80); amusements which divert the populace from unpleasant realities.
passim (Lat) 'everywhere, throughout'; dispersed through a book.
per capita (Lat) 'by heads'; per head of the population in statistical contexts.
perestroika (Russ) 'reconstruction'; restructuring of an organization.
persona non grata (Lat) one who is not welcome or favoured (originally a term in diplomacy).
pied à terre (Fr) 'foot to the ground'; a flat, small house, etc kept for temporary or occasional accommodation.
plus ça change (Fr) abbreviated form of **plus ça change, plus ça la mĕme chose** 'The more things change, the more they stay the same'; a comment on the unchanging nature of the world.
post meridiem (Lat) 'after midday, after noon.'

FOREIGN WORDS AND PHRASES (cont.)

post mortem (Lat) 'after death'; an examination of a body in order to determine the cause of death; an after-the-event discussion.
poule de luxe (Fr) 'luxurious hen'; a sexually attractive promiscuous young woman; a prostitute.
pour encourager les autres (Fr) 'to encourage the others' (Voltaire *Candide*, on the execution of Admiral Byng); exemplary punishment.
premier cru (Fr) 'first growth'; wine of the highest quality in a system of classification.
prêt-à-porter (Fr) 'ready to wear'; refers to 'designer' clothes that are made in standard sizes as opposed to made-to-measure clothes.
prima donna (Ital) 'first lady'; leading female singer in an opera; a person who is temperamental and hard to please.
prima facie (Lat) 'at first sight'; a legal term for evidence that is assumed to be true unless disproved by other evidence.
primus inter pares (Lat) 'first among equals.'
prix fixe (Fr) 'fixed price'; used of a meal in a restaurant offered at a set price for a restricted choice.
pro bono publico (Lat) 'for the public good'; something done for no fee.

quid pro quo (Lat) 'something for something'; something given or taken as equivalent to another, often as retaliation.
quod erat demonstrandum (Lat) 'which was to be shown'; often used in its abbreviated form **qed**.

raison d'être (Fr) 'reason for existence'.
rara avis (Lat) 'rare bird' (Juvenal, VI, 165); something or someone remarkable and unusual.
realpolitik (Ger) 'politics of realism'; practical politics based on the realities and necessities of life, rather than moral or ethical ideas.
recherché (Fr) 'sought out'; carefully chosen; particularly choice; rare or exotic.
reculer pour mieux sauter (Fr) 'move backwards in order to jump better'; a strategic withdrawal to wait for a better opportunity.
reductio ad absurdum (Lat) 'reduction to absurdity'; originally used in logic to mean the proof of a proposition by proving the falsity of its contradictory; the application of a principle so strictly that it is carried to absurd lengths.
répondez, s'il vous plaît (Fr) 'reply, please'; in English mainly in its abbreviated form, **RSVP**, on invitations.
revenons à nos moutons (Fr) 'let us return to our sheep'; let us get back to our subject.
rijsttafel (Dutch) 'rice table'; an Indonesian rice dish served with a variety of foods.
risqué (Fr) 'risky, hazardous'; audaciously bordering on the unseemly.
rus in urbe (Lat) 'the country in the town' (Martial XII, 57, 21); the idea of country charm in the centre of a city.

salus populi suprema est lex (Lat) 'let the warfare of the people be the chief law' (Cicero *De Legibus* III, 3).
samizdat (Russ) 'self-publisher'; the secret printing and distribution of banned literature in the USSR and other Eastern European countries under Communist rule.
sanctum sanctorum (Lat) 'holy of holies'; the innermost chamber of the temple, where the Ark of the Covenant was kept; any private room reserved for personal use.
sang froid (Fr) 'cold blood'; self possession; coolness under stress.
savoir faire (Fr) 'knowing what to do'; knowing what to do and how to do it in any situation.
schadenfreude (Ger) 'hurt joy'; pleasure in others' misfortunes.
shlimazel (Yiddish) 'bad luck'; a persistently unlucky person.
shlock (Yiddish) 'broken or damaged goods'; inferior, shoddy.
shmaltz (Yiddish) 'melted fat, grease'; showy sentimentality, particularly in writing, music, art, etc.'
shmuck (Yiddish) 'penis'; a (male) stupid person.
shogun (Jap) 'leader of the army'; ruler of feudal Japan.

FOREIGN WORDS AND PHRASES (cont.)

sic (Lat) 'so, thus'; used in brackets within printed matter to show that the original is faithfully reproduced even if incorrect.
sic transit gloria mundi (Lat) 'so passes away earthly glory'.
sine die (Lat) 'without a day'; the adjournment of a meeting (often in court), indicating that no day has been fixed for its resumption; an indefinite adjournment.
sine qua non (Lat) 'without which not'; an indispensable condition.
sotto voce (Ital) 'below the voice'; in an undertone; aside.
status quo (Lat) 'the state in which'; the existing condition.
sub judice (Lat) 'under a judge'; under consideration by a judge or a court of law.
subpoena (Lat) 'under penalty'; a writ commanding attendance in court.
sub rosa (Lat) 'under the rose'; in secret, privately.
succès de scandale (Fr) 'success of scandal'; the success of a book, film, etc due not to merit but to its connection with, or reference to, a scandal.
summa cum laude (Lat) 'with the highest praise'; with great distinction; the highest class of degree award that can be gained by a US college student.
summum bonum (Lat) 'the chief good'.

table d'hôte (Fr) 'host's table'; a set meal at a fixed price. Compare **prix fixe**.
tabula rasa (Lat) 'scraped table'; a cleaned tablet; a mind not yet influenced by outside impressions and experience.
tai chi (Chin) 'great art of boxing'; a system of exercise, and self-defence in which good use of balance and co-ordination allows effort to be minimized.
tempus fugit (Lat) 'time flies'; delay cannot be tolerated.
terra incognita (Lat) 'unknown land'; an unknown land (so marked on early maps); an area of study about which very little is known.
touché (Fr) 'touched'; claiming or acknowledging a hit made in fencing; claiming or acknowledging a point scored in an argument.
tour de force (Fr) 'turning movement'; feat of strength or skill.
trompe l'oeil (Fr) 'deceives the eye'; an appearance of reality achieved by the use of perspective and detail in painting, architecture, etc.
tsunami (Jap) 'wave in harbour'; a wave generated by movement of the earth's surface underwater; commonly (and erroneously) called a 'tidal wave'.

übermensch (Ger) 'over-person'; superman.
ultra vires (Lat) 'beyond strength, beyond powers'; beyond one's power or authority.
urbi et orbi (Lat) 'to the city and the world'; used of the Pope's pronouncements; to everyone.

vade-mecum (Lat) 'go with me'; a handbook, pocket companion.
vin du pays (Fr) 'wine of the country'; a locally produced wine for everyday consumption.
vis-à-vis (Fr) 'face to face'; one who faces or is opposite another; in relation to.
viva voce (Lat) 'with the living voice'; in speech, orally; an oral examination, particularly at a university (commonly 'viva' alone).
volte-face (Fr) 'turn-face'; a sudden and complete change in opinion or in views expressed.
vox populi (Lat); 'voice of the people'; public or popular opinion.

weltschmerz (Ger) 'world pain'; sympathy with universal misery; thoroughgoing pessimism.
wunderkind (Ger) 'wonder-child'; a 'child prodigy'; one who shows great talent and/or achieves great success at an early (or comparatively early) age.

zeitgeist (Ger) 'time-spirit'; the spirit of the age.

COMMON ABBREVIATIONS

See also **Computer Languages** p 331

AA	Alcoholics Anonymous
AA	Automobile Association
AAA	Amateur Athletics Association
AAA	American Automobile Association
ABA	Amateur Boxing Association
ABA	American Booksellers Association
ABC	American Broadcasting Association
ABC	Australian Broadcasting Corporation
ABM	antiballistic missile
ABTA	Association of British Travel Agents
AC/ac	alternating current
ACAS	Advisory, Conciliation, and Arbitration Service
ACLU	American Civil Liberties Union
ACT	Australian Capital Territory
ACTH	adrenocorticotrophic hormone
ACTU	Australian Council of Trade Unions
AD	anno Domini (in the year of Our Lord)
A-D	analog-to-digital (in computing)
ADH	antidiuretic hormone
ADP	adenosine diphosphate
AEA	Atomic Energy Authority (UK)
AEC	Atomic Energy Commission (USA)
AFC	American Football Conference
AFL/CIO	American Federation of Labor/ Congress of Industrial Organizations
AFV	armoured fighting vehicle
AGM	annual general meeting
AGR	advanced gas-cooled reactor
AH	anno Hegirae (in the year of Hegira)
AHF	anti-haemophilic factor
AI	artificial intelligence
AID	artificial insemination by donor
AIDS	Acquired Immune Deficiency Syndrome
AIF	Australian Imperial Force
AIH	artificial insemination by husband
ALCM	air-launched cruise missile
ALP	Australian Labor Party
ALU	arithmetic and logic unit
AM	amplitude modulation
am	ante meridiem (before noon)
AMA	American Medical Association
amu	atomic mass unit
ANC	African National Congress
ANS	autonomic nervous system
ANSI	American National Standards Institute
ANZAC	Australian and New Zealand Army Corps
ANZUS	Australia, New Zealand and the United States
AOB	any other business
AONB	Area of Outstanding Natural Beauty
APEX	Association of Professional, Executive, Clerical, and Computer Staff
APR	annual percentage rate
APRA	Alianza Popular Revolutionaria Americana (American Popular Revolutionary Alliance)
AR	aspect ratio
ARCIC	Anglican Roman Catholic International Commission
A/S	Advanced/Supplementary
ASA	American Standards Association
ASCII	American Standards Code for Information Interchange
ASDIC	Admiralty Submarine Detection Investigation Committee
ASEAN	Association of South-East Asian Nations
ASL	American Sign Language
ASLEF	Associated Society of Locomotive Engineers and Firemen
ASLIB	Association of Special Libraries and Information Bureaux
ASM	air-to-surface missile
ASPCA	American Society for the Prevention of Cruelty to Animals
ASSR	Autonomous Soviet Socialist Republic
ASTMS	Association of Scientific, Technical, and Managerial Staffs
ATP	adenosine triphosphate
ATS	Auxiliary Territorial Service
ATV	Associated Television
AU	astronomical unit
AV	audio-visual
AVC	Additional Voluntary Contribution
AWACS	Airborne Warning and Control System
AWU	Australian Workers' Union
BAFTA	British Academy of Film and Television Arts
BALPA	British Airline Pilots' Association
B&W	black and white
BASIC	(English) British American Scientific International Commercial
BBC	British Broadcasting Association
BC	before Christ
BCD	binary coded decimal
BCE	Before the Common Era
BCG	bacille (bacillus) Calmette Guérin
BCS	Bardeen, Cooper & Schrieffer (theory)
BEF	British Expeditionary Force
BEV	Black English Vernacular

COMMON ABBREVIATIONS (cont.)

BIA	Bureau of Indian Affairs
BIS	Bank for International Settlements
BLAISE	British Library Automated Information Service
BMA	British Medical Association
BOSS	Bureau of State Security (South Africa)
BP	blood pressure
BSE	bovine spongiform encephalopathy
BSI	British Standards Institution
BST	British Summer Time
btu	British thermal unit
BUF	British Union of Fascists
BUPA	British United Provident Association
CAB	Citizen's Advice Bureau
CACM	Central American Common Market
CAD	computer aided design
CAI	computer aided instruction
CAL	computer aided learning
CAM	computer aided manufacture
CAP	Common Agricultural Policy
CARICOM	Caribbean Community
CARIFTA	Caribbean Free Trade Area
CATV	cable television
CB	citizen's band (radio)
CBE	Commander of the (Order of the) British Empire
CBI	Confederation of British Industry
CCD	charge-coupled device
CCK	cholecystokinin-pancreozymin
CCR	camera cassette recorder
CCTV	closed circuit television
CD	Civil Defence
CDROM	compact disc read-only memory
CDU	Christian Democratic Union
CE	Common Era
CENTO	Central Treaty Organization
CERN	Organisation Européene pour la Recherche Nucléaire (formerly, Conseil Européen pour la Recherche Nucléaire)
CFC	chlorofluorocarbon
CGS	centimetre-gram-second
CGT	capital gains tax
CGT	Confédération Générale du Travail
CH	Companion of Honour
CHAPS	Clearing House Automated Clearance System
CHIPS	Clearing House Interbank Payments System
CIA	Central Intelligence Agency
CID	Criminal Investigation Department
CIO	Congress of Industrial Organizations
CIS	Commonwealth of Independent States
CM	Congregation of the Mission
CMG	Companion of (the Order of) St Michael & St George
CNAA	Council for National Academic Awards
CND	Campaign for Nuclear Disarmament
CNES	Centre National d'Espace
CNS	central nervous system
COMECON	Council for Mutual Economic Assistance
CORE	Congress of Racial Equality
CP	Congregation of the Passion
CPI	Consumer Price Index
CP/M	control program monitor
CPR	cardio-pulmonary resuscitation
CPU	central processing unit
CRO	cathode-ray oscilloscope
CRT	cathode-ray tube
CSE	Certificate of Secondary Education
CSF	cerebrospinal fluid
CSIRO	Commonwealth Scientific and Industrial Research Organization
CSO	colour separation overlay
CTT	capital transfer tax
CV	cultivar
CVO	Commander of the Royal Victorian Order
CVS	chorionic villus sampling
CWA	County Women's Association
CWS	Co-operation Wholesale Society
D-A	digital-to-analog (in computing)
DALR	dry adiabatic lapse rate
D&C	dilation and curettage
DBE	Dame Commander of the (Order of the) British Empire
DBMS	database management system
DBS	direct broadcasting from satellite
DC/dc	direct current
DCF	discounted cash flow
DCMG	Dame Commander of (the Order of) St Michael and St George
DCVO	Dame Commander of the Royal Victorian Order
DDT	dichloro-diphenyl-trichloroethane
DES	Department of Education and Science
DES	diethylstilboestrol
DFC	Distinguished Flying Cross
DHA	District Health Authority
DIA	Defense Intelligence Agency

COMMON ABBREVIATIONS (cont.)

DLP Democratic Labor Party (Australia)
DMSO dimethyl sulphoxide
DNA deoxyribonucleic acid
DOS Disk Operating System
DSN Deep Space Network
DSO Distinguished Service Order
DST daylight saving time
DTP desk top publishing

EAC European Atomic Commission
EAROM electrically alterable read-only memory
EBCDIC Extended Binary-Coded Decimal Interchange Code
EBU European Boxing Union
EBU European Broadcasting Union
EC European Community
ECA European Commission on Agriculture
ECF extracellular fluid
ECG electrocardiograph
ECM European Common Market
ECO European Coal Organization
ECOSOC Economic and Social Council (of the United Nations)
ECOWAS Economic Community of West African States
ECSC European Coal and Steel Community
ECT electroconvulsive therapy
ECTG European Channel Tunnel Group
ECU European Currency Unit
EDC European Defence Community
EDF European Development Fund
EDVAC Electronic Discrete Variable Automatic Computer
EEC European Economic Community
EEG electroencephalography
EEOC Equal Employment Opportunity Commission
EEROM electrically erasable read-only memory
EFA European Fighter Aircraft
EFC European Forestry Commission
EFTA European Free Trade Association
EGF epidermal growth factor
EI Exposure Index
ELDO European Launcher Development Organization
ELF Eritrea Liberation Front
emf electromotive force
EMS European Monetary System
emu electromagnetic units
ENIAC Electronic Numeral Indicator and Calculator
EOKA Ethniki Organosis Kipriakou Agonos (National Organization of Cypriot Struggle)
EP European Parliament
EPA Environmental Protection Agency
EPR Einstein-Podolsky-Rosen (paradox)
EPR electron paramagnetic resonance
EPROM electronically programmable read-only memory
ERNIE Electronic Random Number Indicator Equipment
ERW enhanced radiation weapon
ESA Environmentally Sensitive Area
ESA European Space Agency
ESC electronic stills camera
ESCU European Space Operations Centre
ESO European Southern Observatory
ESP extra-sensory perception
ESRO European Space Research Organization
ESTEC European Space Research and Technology Centre
ETU Electricians Trade Union
EUFA European Union Football Associations
EURATOM European Atomic Energy Community

FA Football Association
FAA Federal Aviation Administration
FAO Food and Agriculture Organization
FBI Federal Bureau of Investigation
FCA Farm Credit Administration
FCC Federal Communications Commission
FDIC Federal Deposit Insurance Corporation
FIFA Fédération Internationale de Football Association (International Association Football Federation)
FIMBRA Financial Intermediaries, Managers and Brokers Regulatory Association
FLN Front de Liberation Nationale
FM/fm frequency modulation
FORTRAN Formula Translation
FPS foot-pound-second
FRELIMO Frente de Libertação de Moçambique
FSH follicle-stimulating hormone
FTC Federal Trade Commission

GAR Grand Army of the Republic
GATT General Agreement on Tariffs and Trade
GBE Knight/Dame Grand Cross of (the Order of the) British Empire

COMMON ABBREVIATIONS (cont.)

GC	George Cross
GCC	Gulf Co-operation Council
GCE	General Certificate of Education
GCHQ	Government Communications Headquarters
GCMG	Knight/Dame Grand Cross of (the Order of) St Michael and St George
GCSE	General Certificate of Secondary Education
GCVO	Knight/Dame Grand Cross of the Royal Victorian Order
GDI	gross domestic income
GDP	gross domestic product
GEO	geosynchronous Earth orbit
GESP	generalized extra-sensory perception
GH	growth hormone
GLC	gas-liquid chromatography
GLCM	ground-launched cruise missile
GM	George Medal
GMC	General Medical Council
GMT	Greenwich Mean Time
GNP	gross national product
GnRH	gonadotrophin-releasing hormone
GP	General Practitioner
GPSS	General Purpose System Simulator
GUTS	grand unified theories
HCG	human chorionic gonadotrophin
HE	His/Her Excellency
HEP	hydro-electric power
HF	high frequency
HGV	heavy goods vehicle
HIH	His/Her Imperial Highness
HIM	His/Her Imperial Majesty
HLA	human leucocyte antigen
HM	His/Her Majesty
HMG	His/Her Majesty's Government
HMI	His/Her Majesty's Inspectorate
HMO	Health Maintenance Organization
HMS	His/Her Majesty's Ship/Service
HMSO	His/Her Majesty's Stationery Office
HNC	Higher National Certificate
HND	Higher National Diploma
hp	horsepower
HR	House of Representatives
HRH	His/Her Royal Highness
IAEA	International Atomic Energy Agency
IBRD	International Bank for Reconstruction and Development
IC	integrated circuit
ICAO	International Civil Aviation Organization
ICFTU	International Confederation of Free Trade Unions
ICI	Imperial Chemical Industries
IDA	International Development Agency
IFAD	International Fund for Agricultural Development
IFC	International Finance Corporation
ILO	International Labour Organization
IMCO	Intergovernmental Maritime Consultative Organization
IMF	International Monetary Fund
INLA	Irish National Liberation Army
INRI	Iesus Nazarenus Rex Iudeorum (Jesus of Nazareth, King of the Jews)
IPA	International Phonetic Alphabet
IQ	intelligence quotient
IR	infrared
IRA	Irish Republican Army
IRB	Irish Republican Brotherhood
IRBM	intermediate-range ballistic missile
ISBN	International Standard Book Number
ISO	International Organization for Standardization
ISSN	International Standard Serial Number
ita	International Teaching Alphabet
ITCZ	intertropical convergence zone
ITN	Independent Television News
ITT	International Telephone and Telegraph Corporation
ITU	International Telecommunication Union
ITV	Independent Television
IUCN	International Union for the Conservation of Nature and Natural Resources
IUD	intra-uterine device
IUPAC	International Union of Pure and Applied Chemistry
IUPAP	International Union of Pure and Applied Physics
IVF	in vitro fertilization
IVR	International Vehicle Registration
IWW	Industrial Workers of the World
JP	Justice of the Peace
JET	Joint European Torus

COMMON ABBREVIATIONS (cont.)

KADU Kenya African Democratic Union
KANU Kenya African National Union
KB Knight Bachelor; Knight of the Bath
KBE Knight Commander of the (Order of the) British Empire
KC King's Counsel
KCB Knight Commander of the Bath
KCMG Knight Commander of (the Order of) St Michael and St George
KCVO Knight Commander of the Royal Victorian Order
KG Knight of the Order of the Garter
KGB Komitet Gosudarstvennoye Bezhopaznosti (Committee of State Security)
KKK Ku Klux Klan
KMT Kuomintang
kpc kiloparsec
KT Knight of the Thistle

LAFTA Latin-American Free Trade Association
LAN local area network
LAUTRO Life Assurance and Unit Trust Companies
LCD liquid crystal display
LDC less developed country
LEA Local Education Authority
LED light-emitting diode
LEO low Earth orbit
LFA Less Favoured Area
LH luteinizing hormone
LHRH luteinizing-hormone-releasing hormone
LIFFE London International Financial Futures Exchange
LISP List Processing
LMS London Missionary Society
LPG liquefied petroleum gas
LSD lysergic acid diethylamide
LSI large-scale integration
LVO Lieutenant of the Royal Victorian Order

MAC Multiplexed Analog Component
MAO monoamine oxidase
MATV Master Antenna Television
MBE Member of the Order of the British Empire
MCA Monetary Compensation Amount
MCC Marylebone Cricket Club
MDMA methylenedioxymethamphetamine
ME myalgic encephalomyelitis
MH Medal of Honor
MHD magnetohydrodynamics
MICR magnetic ink character recognition
Mired micro reciprocal degrees
MIRV multiple independently targetted re-entry vehicle
MKSA metre-kilogram-second-ampere
MLR minimum lending rate
mmf magnetomotive force
MMI man-machine interaction
MOH Medal of Honor
mpc megaparsec
MPS marginal propensity to save
MPTP methylphenyltetrahydropyridine
MRA Moral Rearmament
MS multiple sclerosis
MSC Manpower Services Commission
MSG monosodium glutamate
MSH melanocyte-stimulating hormone
MVD Ministerstvo Vnutrennikh Del (Ministry for Internal Affairs)
MVO Member of the Royal Victorian Order

NAACP National Association for the Advancement of Colored People
NANC non-adrenergic, non-cholinergic
NASA National Aeronautics and Space Administration
NASDA National Space Development Agency
NATO North Atlantic Treaty Organization
NDE near-death experience
NEDC National Economic Development Office
NEP New Economic Policy
NF National Front
NFC National Football Conference
NGC New General Catalogue
NGF nerve growth factor
NHL National Hockey League
NHS National Health Service
NIH National Institutes of Health
NKVD Narodnyi Komitet Vnutrennikh Del (People's Commissariat of Internal Affairs)
NLRB National Labor Relations Board
NMR nuclear magnetic resonance
NOW National Organization for Women
NPT Non-Proliferation Treaty
NRA National Recovery Administration
NRAO National Radio Astronomy Observatory
NSF National Science Foundation
NSPCC National Society for the Prevention of Cruelty to Children

COMMON ABBREVIATIONS (cont.)

NTSC National Television System Commission
NUM National Union of Mineworkers
NUT National Union of Teachers
NVC non-verbal communication

OAPEC Organization of Arab Petroleum Exporting Countries
OAS Organisation de l'Armée Secrète (Secret Army Organization)
OAS Organization of American States
OAU Organization of African Unity
OB Order of the Bath
OB outside broadcast
OBE Officer of the (Order of the) British Empire
OCarm Order of the Brothers of the Blessed Virgin Mary of Mount Carmel
OCart Order of Carthusians
OCR optical character recognition/reader
OCSO Order of the Reformed Cistercians of the Strict Observance
OD ordnance datum
ODC Order of Discalced Carmelites
ODECA Organización de Estados Centro-americanos (Organization of Central American States)
OECD Organization for Economic Co-operation and Development
OEEC Organization for European Economic Co-operation
OEM Original Equipment Manufacturer
OFM Order of Friars Minor
OFMCap Order of Friars Minor Capuchin
OFMConv Order of Friars Minor Conventual
OGPU Otdelenie Gosudarstvenni Politcheskoi Upravi (Special Government Political Administration)
OM Order of Merit
OMCap Order of Friars Minor of St Francis Capuccinorum
OOBE out-of-the-body experience
OP Order of Preachers
OPEC Organization of Petroleum Exporting Countries
OSA Order of the Hermit Friars of St Augustine
OSB Order of St Benedict
OSFC Order of Friars Minor of St Francis Capuccinorum
OTC over-the-counter (stocks and shares, drugs)
OTEC ocean thermal energy conversion
OU Open University
OXFAM Oxford Committee for Famine Relief

PAC Pan-African Congress
PAC political action committee
PAL phase alternation line
PAYE pay as you earn
pc parsec
PC personal computer
PC Poor Clares
PCP phenylcyclohexylpiperidine
PDGF platelet-derived growth factor
PDR precision depth recorder
PEN International Association of Poets, Playwrights, Editors, Essayists, and Novelists
PEP Political and Economic Planning
PF Patriotic Front
PGA Professional Golfers' Association
PH Purple Heart
PIN personal identification number
PK psychokinesis
PKU phenylketonuria
PLA People's Liberation Army
plc public limited company
PLO Palestine Liberation Organization
pm post meridiem (after noon)
PM of F Presidential Medal of Freedom
PNLM Palestine National Liberation Movement
POW prisoner of war
PPI plan position indicator
PR proportional representation
PRO Public Record Office
PRO public relations officer
PSBR public sector borrowing requirement
PTA parent-teacher association
PTFE polytetrafluorethylene
PVA polyvinyl acetate
PVC polyvinyl chloride
PWA Public Works Administration
PWR pressurized-water reactor
PYO pick-your-own

QC Queen's Counsel
QCD quantum chromodynamics
QED quantum electrodynamics

COMMON ABBREVIATIONS (cont.)

RA Royal Academy
R&A Royal & Ancient Golf Club of St Andrews
RAAF Royal Australian Air Force
RADA Royal Academy of Dramatic Art
RAF Royal Air Force
RAM random access memory
RAM Royal Academy of Music
RAN Royal Australian Navy
RDA recommended daily allowance
REM rapid eye movement
RHA Regional Health Authority
RISC reduced interaction set computer
RKKA Rabochekrest'yanshi Krasny (Red Army of Workers and Peasants)
RM Royal Marines
rms root-mean-square
RN Royal Navy
RNA ribonucleic acid
RNLI Royal National Lifeboat Institution
ROM read-only memory
RP received pronunciation
RPI retail price index
RPM resale price maintenance
rpm revolutions per minute
RS Royal Society
RSPB Royal Society for the Protection of Birds
RSPCA Royal Society for the Prevention of Cruelty to Animals
RSVP répondez s'il vous plaît (please reply)
RTG radio-isotope thermo-electric generator
RVO Royal Victorian Order

SA Sturm Abteilung (Storm Troopers)
sae stamped addressed envelope
SALR saturated adiabatic lapse rate
SALT Strategic Arms Limitation Talks
SAS Special Air Service
SAT scholastic aptitude test
SBR styrene butadiene rubber
SCID severe combined immuno-deficienty
SCLC Southern Christian Leadership Conference
SDI selective dissemination of information
SDI strategic defense initiative
SDP Social Democratic Party
SDR special drawing rights
SDS Students for a Democratic Society
SDU Social Democratic Union
SEAQ Stock Exchange Automated Quotations
SEATO South East Asia Treaty Organization
SEC Securities and Exchange Commission
SECAM Séquence Electronique Couleur avec Mémoire (Electronic Colour Sequence with Memory)
SERPS State Earnings Related Pension Scheme
SHAEF Supreme Headquarters Allied Expeditionary Force
SHAPE Supreme Headquarters Allied Powers, Europe
SHF super high frequency
SI Système International (International System)
SIB Securities and Investments Board
SIOP Single Integrated Operation Plan
SJ Society of Jesus
SLBN submarine-launched ballistic missile
SLCM sea-launched cruise missile
SLDP Social and Liberal Democratic Party
SLE systemic lupus erythematosus
SLR single lens reflex
SNCC Student Non-Violent Co-ordinating Committee
SNP Scottish National Party
SOCist Cistercians of Common Observance
SOE Special Operations Executive
SONAR sound navigation and ranging
SP starting price
SQUID superconducting quantum interference device
SR Socialist Revolutionaries
SRO self-regulatory organization
SS Schutzstaffel (Protective Squad)
SSR Soviet Socialist Republic
SSSI Site of Special Scientific Interest
START Strategic Arms Reduction Talks
STOL short take-off and landing
SWAPO South West Africa People's Organization
SWS slow wave sleep

TAB Totalisator Agency Board
TARDIS Time and Relative Dimensions in Space
TASS Telegrafnoe Agentsvo Sovetskovo Soyuza (Telegraph Agency of the Soviet Union)
TCDD tetrachlorodibenzo-p-dioxin
TEFL Teaching English as a Foreign Language
TESL Teaching English as a Second Language
TGWU Transport and General Workers Union

COMMON ABBREVIATIONS (cont.)

TNT trinitrotoluene
TSB Trustee Savings Bank
TT Tourist Trophy
TTL through the lens
TUC Trades Union Congress
TV television
TVA Tennessee Valley Authority

UAE United Arab Emirates
UAP United Australia Party
UCAR Union of Central African Republics
UCCA University Central Council on Admissions
UDA Ulster Defence Association
UDI Unilateral Declaration of Independence
UEFA Union of European Football Association
UFO unidentified flying object
UHF ultra high frequency
UHT ultra high temperature
UK United Kingdom
UN United Nations
UNCTAD United Nations Conference on Trade and Development
UNDC United Nations Disarmament Commission
UNDP United Nations Development Programme
UNEP United Nations Environment Programme
UNESCO United Nations Economic, Scientific, and Cultural Organization
UNFAO United Nations Food and Agriculture Organization
UNGA United Nations General Assembly
UNHCR United Nations High Commission for Refugees
UNHRC United Nations Human Rights Commission
UNICEF United Nations International Children's Emergency Fund
UNIDO United Nations Industrial Development Organization
UNO United Nations Organization
UNRWA United Nations Relief and Works Agency for Palestine Refugees in the Near East
UNSC United Nations Security Council
UNSG United Nations Secretary General
UNTT United Nations Trust Territory
UPU Universal Postal Union
USA United States of America
USAF United States Air Force
USCG United States Coast Guard
USIS United States Information Service
USSR Union of Soviet Socialist Republics

VA Veterans Administration
VAT value-added tax
VC Victoria Cross
VCR video cassette recorder
VD venereal disease
VDU visual display unit
VHF very high frequency
VHS Video Home Service
VIP vasoactive intestinal polypeptide
VIP very important person
VLF very low frequency
VLSI very large scale interpretation
VOA Voice of America
VSEPR valence shell electron pair repulsion
VSO Voluntary Service Overseas
VTOL vertical take-off and landing
VTR video tape recorder

WAAC Women's Auxiliary Army Corps
WAAF Women's Auxiliary Air Force
WAC Women's Army Corps
WASP White Anglo-Saxon Protestant
WBA World Boxing Association
WBC World Boxing Council
WCC World Council of Churches
WEA Workers' Educational Association
WFTU World Federation of Trade Unions
WHO World Health Organization
WI (National Federation of) Women's Institutes
WIPO World Intellectual Property Organization
WMO World Meteorological Organization
WPA Work Projects Administration
WRAC Women's Royal Army Corps
WRAF Women's Royal Air Force
WRNS Women's Royal Naval Service
WRVS Women's Royal Voluntary Service
WVS Women's Voluntary Service
WWF World Wide Fund for Nature

YHA Youth Hostels Association
YMCA Young Men's Christian Association
YMHA Young Men's Hebrew Association
YWCA Young Women's Christian Association
YWHA Young Women's Hebrew Association

ALPHABETS

There is no agreement over the use of a single transliteration system in the case of Hebrew. The equivalents given below are widely used; but several other possibilities can be found.

HEBREW

Letter	Name	Trans-literation
א	'aleph	
ב	beth	b
ג	gimel	g
ד	daleth	d
ה	he	h
ו	waw	w
ז	zayin	z
ח	heth	h
ט	teth	t
י	yodh	y, j
כ ך	kaph	k
ל	lamedh	l
מ ם	mem	m
נ ן	nun	n
ס	samekh	s
ע	ayin	
פ ף	pe	p, f
צ ץ	saddhe	s
ק	qoph	q
ר	resh	r
ש	shin	sh, ṡ
ש	sin	ṡ
ת	taw	t

GREEK

Letter	Name	Trans-literation
Α α	alpha	a
Β β	beta	b
Γ γ	gamma	g
Δ δ	delta	d
Ε ε	epsilon	e
Ζ ζ	zeta	z
Η η	eta	e, ė
Θ θ	theta	th
Ι ι	iota	i
Κ κ	kappa	k
Λ λ	lambda	l
Μ μ	mu	m
Ν ν	nu	n
Ξ ξ	xi	x
Ο ο	omicron	o
Π π	pi	p
Ρ ρ	rho	r
Σ σ,ς	sigma	s
Τ τ	tau	t
Υ υ	upsilon	y
Φ φ	phi	ph
Χ χ	chi	ch, kh
Ψ ψ	psi	ps
Ω ω	omega	o, ȯ

NATO ALPHABET

Letter	Code name	Pronunciation
A	Alpha	AL-FAH
B	Bravo	BRAH-VOH
C	Charlie	CHAR-LEE
D	Delta	DELL-TAH
E	Echo	ECK-OH
F	Foxtrot	FOKS-TROT
G	Golf	GOLF
H	Hotel	HOH-TELL
I	India	IN-DEE-AH
J	Juliet	JEW-LEE-ETT
K	Kilo	KEY-LOH
L	Lima	LEE-MAH
M	Mike	MIKE
N	November	NO-VEM-BER
O	Oscar	OSS-CAH
P	Papa	PAH-PAH
Q	Quebec	KEY-BECK
R	Romeo	ROW-ME-OH
S	Sierra	SEE-AIR-RAH
T	Tango	TAN-GO
U	Uniform	YOU-NEE-FORM
V	Victor	VIK-TAH
W	Whiskey	WISS-KEY
X	Xray	ECKS-RAY
Y	Yankee	YANG-KEY
Z	Zulu	ZOO-LOO

MORSE & BRAILLE

Letters	Morse	Braille
A	·–	⠁
B	–···	⠃
C	–·–·	⠉
D	–··	⠙
E	·	⠑
F	··–·	⠋
G	––·	⠛
H	····	⠓
I	··	⠊
J	·–––	⠚
K	–·–	⠅
L	·–··	⠇
M	––	⠍
N	–·	⠝
O	–––	⠕
P	·––·	⠏
Q	––·–	⠟
R	·–·	⠗
S	···	⠎
T	–	⠞
U	··–	⠥
V	···–	⠧
W	·––	⠺
X	–··–	⠭
Y	–·––	⠽
Z	––··	⠵

TYPEFACES

The typefaces shown are modern versions of the main groups under which most typefaces may be classified. The dates indicating the introduction of each group are approximate.

Gothic

ABCDEFGHIJKLMNOPQRSTUVWXYZ
abcdefghijklmnopqrstuvwxyz
15 & 7pt Old English Text (c.1450)

Venetian

ABCDEFGHIJKLMNOPQRSTUVWXYZ
abcdefghijklmnopqrstuvwxyz
15 & 7pt Centaur (c.1470)

Old Face

ABCDEFGHIJKLMNOPQRSTUVWXYZ
abcdefghijklmnopqrstuvwxyz
15 & 7pt Caslon Old Face (c.1495)

Transitional

ABCDEFGHIJKLMNOPQRSTUVWXYZ
abcdefghijklmnopqrstuvwxyz
15 & 7pt Baskerville (c.1761)

Modern

ABCDEFGHIJKLMNOPQRSTUVWXYZ
abcdefghijklmnopqrstuvwxyz
15 & 7pt Bodoni (c.1765)

Sans Serif

ABCDEFGHIJKLMNOPQRSTUVWXYZ
abcdefghijklmnopqrstuvwxyz
15 & 7pt Univers (c.1816)

Egyptian

ABCDEFGHIJKLMNOPQRSTUVWXYZ
abcdefghijklmnopqrstuvwxyz
12 & 7pt Rockwell (c.1830)

Old Style

ABCDEFGHIJKLMNOPQRSTUVWXYZ
abcdefghijklmnopqrstuvwxyz
15 & 7pt Goudy Old Style (c.1850)

Newspaper

ABCDEFGHIJKLMNOPQRSTUVWXYZ
abcdefghijklmnopqrstuvwxyz
12pt Century Bold & Century Roman (c.1890)

Contemporary

ABCDEFGHIJKLMNOPQRSTUVWXYZ
abcdefghijklmnopqrstuvwxyz
12 & 7pt Times New Roman (c.1932)

FIRST NAME MEANINGS IN THE UK AND USA

The meanings of the most popular first names in the UK and USA are given below, along with a few other well-known names.

Name Original meaning

Aaron high mountain (*Hebrew*)
Adam redness (*Hebrew*)
Alan harmony (*Celtic*)
Albert nobly bright (*Germanic*)
Alexander defender of men (*Greek*)
Alison *French diminutive of* Alice; of noble kind
Amanda fit to be loved (*Latin*)
Amy loved (*French*)
Andrea *female form of* Andrew
Andrew manly (*Greek*)
Angela messenger, angel (*Greek*)
Ann(e) *English form of* Hannah
Anthony *Roman family name*
April name of the month
Arthur ?bear, stone (*Celtic*)
Barbara strange, foreign (*Greek*)
Barry spear, javelin (*Celtic*)

Name Original meaning

Beatrice bringer of joy (*Latin*)
Benjamin son of my right hand (*Hebrew*)
Bernard bear + brave (*Germanic*)
Beth *pet form of* Elizabeth
Betty *pet form of* Elizabeth
Bill/Billy *pet form of* William
Bob *pet form of* Robert
Brandi *variant of* Brandy, *from the common noun*
Brandon *place name*; broom-covered hill (*Germanic*)
Brian ?hill (?*Celtic*)
Candice *meaning unknown*
Carl man, husbandman (*Germanic*)
Carol(e) *forms of* Caroline, *Italian female form of* Charles
Catherine pure (*Greek*)

FIRST NAME MEANINGS (cont.)

Name Original meaning

Charles man, husbandman (*Germanic*)
Christine *French form of* Christina *ultimately from* Christian; anointed
Christopher carrier of Christ (*Greek*)
Claire bright, shining (*Latin*)
Colin *form of* Nicholas
Craig rock (*Celtic*)
Crystal *female use of the common noun*
Daniel God is my judge (*Hebrew*)
Danielle *female form of* Daniel
Darren *Irish surname*
Darryl *surname; uncertain origin*
David beloved, friend (*Hebrew*)
Dawn *female use of the common noun*
Dean *surname*; valley *or* leader
Deborah bee (*Hebrew*)
Dennis of Dionysus (*Greek*), *the god of wine*
Derek *form of* Theodoric; ruler of the people (*Germanic*)
Diane *French form of* Diana; divine (*Latin*)
Donald world mighty (*Gaelic*)
Donna lady (*Latin*)
Doreen *from* Dora, *a short form of* Dorothy; gift of God
Doris woman from Doris (*Greek*)
Dorothy gift of God (*Greek*)
Ebony *female use of the common noun*
Edward property guardian (*Germanic*)
Eileen *Irish form of* ?Helen
Elizabeth oath/perfection of God (*Hebrew*)
Emily *Roman family name*
Emma all-embracing (*Germanic*)
Eric ruler of all (*Norse*)
Erica *female form of* Eric
Eugenie *French form of* Eugene; well-born (*Greek*)
Frank *pet form of* Francis; Frenchman
Frederick peaceful ruler (*Germanic*)
Gail *pet form of* Abigail; father rejoices (*Hebrew*)
Gareth gentle (*Welsh*)
Gary *US place name*
Gavin *Scottish form of* Gawain; hawk + white (*Welsh*)
Gemma gem (*Italian*)
Geoffrey ?peace (*Germanic*)
George husbandman, farmer (*Greek*)
Graham *Germanic place name*
Hannah grace, favour (*Hebrew*)
Harold army power/ruler (*Germanic*)
Harry *pet form of* Henry; home ruler (*Germanic*)

Name Original meaning

Hayley *English place name*; hay-meadow
Heather *plant name*
Helen bright/shining one (*Greek*)
Ian *modern Scottish form of* John
Irene peace (*Greek*)
Jacqueline *French female form of* Jacques (James)
James *Latin form of* Jacob; one who takes by the heel (*Hebrew*)
Jane *from Latin* Johanna, *female form of* John
Janet *diminutive form of* Jane
Jason *form of* Joshua; Jehovah is salvation (*Hebrew*)
Jeffrey *US spelling of* Geoffrey
Jean *French form of* Johanna, *from* John
Jennifer fair/white + yielding/smooth (*Celtic*)
Jeremy *English form of* Jeremiah; Jehova exalts (*Hebrew*)
Jessica he beholds (*Hebrew*)
Joan *contracted form of* Johanna, *from* John
Joanne *French form of* Johanna, *from* John
John Jehovah has been gracious (*Hebrew*)
Jonathan Jehovah's gift (*Hebrew*)
Joseph Jehovah adds (*Hebrew*)
Joyce ?joyful (*?Latin*)
Julie *French female form of Latin* Julius; descended from Jove
Karen *Danish form of* Katarina (Catherine)
Katherine *US spelling of* Catherine
Kathleen *English form of Irish* Caitlin (*from* Catharine)
Kelly *Irish surname*; warlike one
Kenneth *English form of Gaelic*; fair one *or* fire-sprung
Kerry *Irish place name*
Kevin handsome at birth (*Irish*)
Kimberly *South African place name*
Lakisha La + ?Aisha; woman (*Arabic*)
Latoya La + *form of* Tonya (Antonia)
Laura bay, laurel (*Latin*)
Lauren *diminutive of* Laura
Lee *Germanic place name*; wood, clearing
Leslie *Scottish place name*
Lilian lily (*Italian*)
Linda serpent (symbol of wisdom) (*Germanic*)
Lindsay *Scottish place name*
Lisa *pet form of* Elizabeth
Margaret pearl (*Greek*)
Marjorie *from* Marguerite, *French form of* Margaret
Mark *English form of* Marcus, *from* Mars, *god of war*

FIRST NAME MEANINGS (cont.)

Name Original meaning

Martin *from* Mars, *god of war* (*Latin*)
Mary *Greek form of* Miriam (*Hebrew*); *unknown meaning*
Matthew gift of the Lord (*Hebrew*)
Melissa bee (*Greek*)
Michael like the Lord (*Hebrew*)
Michelle *English spelling of French* Michèle, *from* Michael
Nancy *pet form of* Ann
Natalie birthday of the Lord (*Latin*)
Neil champion (*Irish*)
Nicholas victory people (*Greek*)
Nicola *Italian female form of* Nicholas
Nicole *French female form of* Nicholas
Pamela ?all honey (*Greek*)
Patricia noble (*Latin*)
Paul small (*Latin*)
Pauline *French female form of* Paul
Peter stone, rock (*Greek*)
Philip fond of horses (*Greek*)
Rachel ewe (*Hebrew*)
Rebecca ?noose (*Hebrew*)
Richard strong ruler (*Germanic*)
Robert fame bright (*Germanic*)
Ronald counsel + power (*Germanic*)
Ruth ?vision of beauty (*Hebrew*)
Ryan *Irish surname*
Sally *pet form of* Sarah

Name Original meaning

Samantha *female form of* Samuel; heard/name of God (*Hebrew*)
Sandra *pet form from* Alexandra
Sarah princess (*Hebrew*)
Scott *surname*; from Scotland
Sharon the plain (*Hebrew*)
Shaun *English spelling of Irish* Sean, *from* John
Shirley bright clearing (*Germanic*)
Simon *form of* Simeon; listening attentively (*Hebrew*)
Stephanie *French female form of* Stephen
Stephen crown (*Greek*)
Stuart steward (*Germanic*)
Susan *short form of* Susannah; lily (*Hebrew*)
Teresa woman of Theresia (*Greek*)
Thomas twin (*Hebrew*)
Tiffany manifestation of God (*Greek*)
Timothy honouring God (*Greek*)
Trac(e)y *?pet form of* Teresa
Vera faith (*Slavic*)
Victoria victory (*Latin*)
Vincent conquer (*Latin*)
Virginia maiden (*Latin*)
Walter ruling people (*Germanic*)
Wayne *surname*; wagon-maker
William will + helmet (*Germanic*)
Zoë life (*Greek*)

FORMS OF ADDRESS

In the formulae given below, *F* stands for forename and *S* for surname.

- ☐ Very formal ceremonial styles for closing letters are now seldom used: 'Yours faithfully' is assumed below, unless otherwise indicated.
- ☐ Forms of spoken address are given only where a special style is followed.
- ☐ Holders of courtesy titles are addressed according to their rank, but without 'The', 'The Right Hon.' or 'The Most Hon.'.
- ☐ Ranks in the armed forces, and ecclesiastical and ambassadorial ranks, precede titles in the peerage, eg 'Colonel the Earl of ——' or 'The Rev the Marquess of ——'.
- ☐ Although the correct forms of address are given below for members of the Royal Family, it is more normal practice for letters to be addressed to their private secretary, equerry, or lady-in-waiting.
- ☐ More detailed information about forms of address is to be found in Debrett's *Correct Form* and Black's *Titles and Forms of Address.*

Ambassadors (foreign)

Address on envelope: 'His/Her Excellency the Ambassador of ——' or 'His/Her Excellency the —— Ambassador'. (The wife of an ambassador is not entitled to the style 'Her Excellency'.) *Begin:* 'Your Excellency'. (Within the letter, refer to 'Your Excellency' once, thereafter as 'you'.) *Close:* 'I have the honour to be, Sir/Madam (or according to rank), Your Excellency's obedient servant'. *Spoken address:* 'Your Excellency' at least once, and then 'Sir' or 'Madam' by name.

FORMS OF ADDRESS (cont.)

Archbishop (Anglican communion)
Address on envelope: 'The Most Reverend the Lord Archbishop of ——'. (The Archbishops of Canterbury and York are Privy Counsellors, and should be addressed as 'The Most Reverend and Right Hon. the Lord Archbishop of ——'.) *Begin:* 'Dear Archbishop' or 'My Lord Archbishop'. *Spoken address:* 'Your Grace'. *Begin an official speech:* 'My Lord Archbishop'.

Archbishop (Roman Catholic)
Address on envelope: 'His Grace the Archbishop of ——'. *Begin:* 'My Lord Archbishop'. *Close:* 'I remain, Your Grace, Yours faithfully' or 'Yours faithfully'. *Spoken address:* 'Your Grace'.

Archdeacon
Address on envelope: 'The Venerable the Archdeacon of ——'. *Begin:* 'Dear Archdeacon' or 'Venerable Sir'. *Spoken address:* 'Archdeacon'. *Begin an official speech:* 'Venerable Sir'.

Baron
Address on envelope: 'The Right Hon. the Lord ——'. *Begin:* 'My Lord'. *Spoken address:* 'My Lord'.

Baron's wife (Baroness)
Address on envelope: 'The Right Hon. the Lady [S——]'. *Begin:* 'Dear Madam'. *Spoken address:* 'Madam'.

Baroness (in her own right)
Address on envelope: either as for Baron's wife, or 'The Right Hon. the Baroness [S——]'. Otherwise, as for Baron's wife.

Baronet
Address on envelope: 'Sir [F—— S——], Bt'. *Begin:* 'Dear Sir'. *Spoken address:* 'Sir [F——]'.

Baronet's wife
Address on envelope: 'Lady [S——]'. If she has the title 'Lady' by courtesy, 'Lady [F—— S——]'. If she has the courtesy style 'The Hon.', this precedes 'Lady'. *Begin:* 'Dear Madam'. *Spoken address:* 'Madam'.

Bishop (Anglican communion)
Address on envelope: 'The Right Reverend the Lord Bishop of ——'. (The Bishop of London is a Privy Counsellor, so is addressed as 'The Right Rev and Right Hon. the Lord Bishop of London'. The Bishop of Meath is styled 'The Most Reverend'.) *Begin:* 'Dear Bishop' or 'My Lord'. *Spoken address:* 'Bishop'. *Begin an official speech:* 'My Lord'.

Bishop (Episcopal Church in Scotland)
Address on envelope: 'The Right Reverend [F—— S——], Bishop of ——'. Otherwise as for a bishop of the Anglican communion. The bishop who holds the position of Primus is addressed as 'The Most Reverend the Primus'. *Begin:* 'Dear Primus'. *Spoken address:* 'Primus'.

Bishop (Roman Catholic)
Address on envelope: 'His Lordship the Bishop of ——' or 'The Right Reverend [F—— S——], Bishop of ——'. In Ireland, 'The Most Reverend' is used instead of 'The Right Reverend'. If an auxiliary bishop, address as 'The Right Reverend [F—— S——], Auxiliary Bishop of ——'. *Begin:* 'My Lord' or (more rarely) 'My Lord Bishop'. *Close:* 'I remain, my Lord' or (more rarely), 'my Lord Bishop'. Yours faithfully', or simply 'Yours faithfully'. *Spoken address:* 'My Lord' or (more rarely) 'My Lord Bishop'.

Cabinet Minister *see* **Secretary of State**

Canon (Anglican communion)
Address on envelope: 'The Reverend Canon [F—— S——]'. *Begin:* 'Dear Canon' or 'Dear Canon [*S*——]'. *Spoken address:* 'Canon' or 'Canon [S——]'.

Canon (Roman Catholic)
Address on envelope: 'The Very Reverend Canon [F—— S——]'. *Begin:* 'Very Reverend Sir'. *Spoken address:* 'Canon [*S*——]'.

FORMS OF ADDRESS (cont.)

Cardinal
Address on envelope: 'His eminence Cardinal [S——]'. If an archbishop, 'His Eminence the Cardinal Archbishop of ——'. *Begin:* 'Your Eminence' or (more rarely) 'My Lord Cardinal'. *Close:* 'I remain, Your Eminence (or 'My Lord Cardinal'), Yours faithfully'. *Spoken:* 'Your Eminence'.

Clergy (Anglican communion)
Address on envelope: 'The Reverend [F—— S——]'. *Begin:* 'Dear Sir' or 'Dear Mr [S——]'.

Clergy (Roman Catholic)
Address on envelope: 'The Reverend [F—— S——]'. If a member of a religious order, the initials of the order should be added after the name. *Begin:* 'Dear Reverend Father'.

Clergy (Other churches)
Address on envelope: 'The Reverend [F—— S——]'. *Begin:* 'Dear Sir/Madam' or 'Dear Mr/Mrs etc. [S——]'.

Countess
Address on envelope: 'The Right Hon. the Countess of ——'. *Begin:* 'Dear Madam'. *Spoken address:* 'Madam'.

Dean (Anglican)
Address on envelope: 'The Very Reverend the Dean of ——'. *Begin:* 'Dear Dean' or 'Very Reverend Sir'. *Spoken address:* 'Dean'. *Begin an official speech:* 'Very Reverend Sir'.

Doctor
Physicians, anaesthetists, pathologists and radiologists are addressed as 'Doctor'. Surgeons, whether they hold the degree of Doctor of Medicine or not, are known as 'Mr/Mrs'. In England and Wales, obstetricians and gynaecologists are addressed as 'Mr/Mrs', but in Scotland, Ireland and elsewhere as 'Doctor'. In addressing a letter to the holder of a doctorate, the initials DD, MD, etc. are placed after the ordinary form of address, eg 'The Rev John Smith, DD', the 'Rev Dr Smith' and 'Dr John Brown' are also used.

Dowager
Address on envelope: On the marriage of a peer or baronet, the widow of the previous holder of the title becomes 'Dowager' and is addressed 'The Right Hon. the Dowager Countess of ——', 'The Right Hon. the Dowager Lady ——', etc. If there is already a Dowager still living, she retains this title, the later widow being addressed 'The Most Hon. [F——], Marchioness of ——', 'The Right Hon. [F——], Lady ——', etc. However, many Dowagers prefer the style which includes their Christian names to that including the title Dowager. *Begin*, etc. as for a peer's wife.

Duchess
Address on envelope: 'Her Grace the Duchess of ——'. *Begin:* 'Dear Madam'. *Spoken address:* 'Your Grace'. (For Royal Duchess, *see* Princess.)

Duke
Address on envelope: 'His Grace the Duke of ——'. *Begin:* 'My Lord Duke'. *Spoken address:* 'Your Grace'. (For Royal Duke, *see* Prince.)

Earl
Address on envelope: 'The Right Hon. the Earl of ——'. *Begin:* 'My Lord'. *Spoken address:* 'My Lord'. (For Earl's wife, *see* Countess.)

Governor of a colony or **Governor-General**
Address on envelope: 'His Excellency [ordinary designation], Governor(-General) of ——'. (The Governor-General of Canada has the rank of 'Right Honourable', which he retains for life.) The wife of a Governor-General is styled 'Her Excellency' within the country her husband administers. *Begin:* according to rank. Close: 'I have the honour to be, Sir (or 'My Lord', if a peer), Your Excellency's obedient servant'. *Spoken address:* 'Your Excellency'.

FORMS OF ADDRESS (cont.)

Judge, High Court
Address on envelope: if a man, 'The Hon. Mr Justice [S——]'; if a woman, 'The Hon. Mrs Justice [S——]'. *Begin:* 'Dear Sir/Madam'; if on judicial matters, 'My Lord/Lady'. *Spoken address:* 'Sir/Madam'; only on the bench or when dealing with judicial matters should a High Court Judge be addressed as 'My Lord/Lady' or referred to as 'Your Lordship/Ladyship'.

Judge, Circuit
Address on envelope: 'His/Her Honour Judge [S——]'. If a Knight, 'His Honour Judge Sir [F—— S——]'. *Begin:* 'Dear Sir/Madam'. *Spoken address:* 'Sir/Madam'; address as 'Your Honour' only when on the bench or dealing with judicial matters.

Justice of the Peace (England and Wales)
When on the bench, refer to and address as 'Your Worship'; otherwise according to rank. The letters 'JP' may be added after the person's name in addressing a letter, if desired.

Knight Bachelor
As Baronet, except that 'Bt' is omitted. Knight of the Bath, of St Michael and St George, etc. *Address on envelope:* 'Sir [F—— S——], with the initials 'GCB', KCB', etc. added. *Begin:* 'Dear Sir'.

Knight's wife
As Baronet's wife, or according to rank.

Lady Mayoress
Address on envelope: 'The Lady Mayoress of ——'. *Begin:* 'My Lady Mayoress'. *Spoken address:* '(My) Lady Mayoress'.

Lord Mayor
Address on envelope: The Lord Mayors of London, York, Belfast, Cardiff, Dublin and also Melbourne, Sydney, Adelaide, Perth, Brisbane and Hobart are styled 'The Right Hon. the Lord Mayor of ——'. Other Lord Mayors are styled 'The Right Worshipful the Lord Mayor of ——'. *Begin:* 'My Lord Mayor', even if the holder of the office is a woman. *Spoken address:* '(My) Lord Mayor'.

Marchioness
Address on envelope: 'The Most Hon. the Marchioness of ——'. *Begin:* 'Dear Madam'. *Spoken address:* 'Madam'.

Marquess
Address on envelope: 'The Most Hon. the Marquess of ——'. *Begin:* 'My Lord'. *Spoken address:* 'My Lord'.

Mayor
Address on envelope: 'The Worshipful the Mayor of ——'; in the case of cities and certain towns, 'The Right Worshipful'. *Begin:* 'Mr Mayor'. *Spoken address:* 'Mr Mayor'.

Mayoress
Address on envelope: 'The Mayoress of ——'. *Begin:* 'Madam Mayoress' is traditional, but some now prefer 'Madam Mayor'. *Spoken address:* 'Mayoress' (or 'Madam Mayor').

Member of Parliament
Address on envelope: Add 'MP' to the usual form of address. *Begin:* according to rank.

Monsignor
Address on envelope: 'The Reverend Monsignor [F—— S——]'. If a canon, 'The Very Reverend Monsignor (Canon) [F—— S——]'. *Begin:* 'Reverend Sir'. *Spoken address:* 'Monsignor [S——]'.

Officers in the Armed Forces
Address on envelope: The professional rank is prefixed to any other rank, eg 'Admiral the Right Hon. the Earl of ——', 'Lieut.-Col. Sir [F—— S——], KCB'. Officers below the rank of Rear-Admiral, and Marshal of the Royal Air Force, are entitled to 'RN' (or 'Royal Navy') and 'RAF' respectively after their name. Army officers of the rank of Colonel or below may follow their name with the name of their regiment or corps (which may be abbreviated). Officers in the women's services add 'WRNS', 'WRAF', 'WRAC'. *Begin:* according to social rank.

FORMS OF ADDRESS (cont.)

Officers (retired and former)

Address on envelope: Officers above the rank of Lieutenant (in the Royal Navy), Captain (in the Army) and Flight Lieutenant may continue to use and be addressed by their armed forces rank after being placed on the retired list. The word 'retired' (or in an abbreviated form) should not normally be placed after the person's name. Former officers in the women's services do not normally continue to use their ranks.

Pope

Address on envelope: 'His Holiness, the Pope'. *Begin:* 'Your Holiness' or 'Most Holy Father'. *Close:* if a Roman Catholic, 'I have the honour to be your Holiness's most devoted and obedient child' (or 'most humble child'); if not Roman Catholic, 'I have the honour to be (or 'remain') Your Holiness's obedient servant'. *Spoken address:* 'Your Holiness'.

Prime Minister

Address on envelope: according to rank. The Prime Minister is a Privy Counsellor (see separate entry) and the letter should be addressed accordingly. *Begin,* etc. according to rank.

Prince

Address on envelope: If a Duke, 'His Royal Highness the Duke of ——'; if not a Duke, 'His Royal Highness the Prince [F——]', if a child of the sovereign; otherwise 'His Royal Highness Prince [F——] of [Kent or Gloucester]'. *Begin:* 'Sir'. Refer to as 'Your Royal Highness'. *Close:* 'I have the honour to remain (or be), Sir, Your Royal Highness's most humble and obedient servant'. *Spoken address:* 'Your Royal Highness' once, thereafter 'Sir'.

Princess

Address on envelope: If a Duchess, 'Her Royal Highness the Duchess of ——'; if not a Duchess, the daughter of a sovereign is addressed as 'Her Royal Highness the Princess [F——]', followed by any title she holds by marriage. 'The' is omitted in addressing a princess who is not the daughter of a sovereign. A Princess by marriage is addressed 'HRH Princess [husband's F——] of ——'. *Begin:* 'Madam'. Refer to as 'Your Royal Highness'. *Close:* as for Prince, substituting 'Madam' for 'Sir'. *Spoken address:* 'Your Royal Highness' once, thereafter 'Ma'am'.

Privy Counsellor

Address on envelope: If a peer, 'The Right Hon. the Earl of ——, PC'; if not a peer, 'The Right Hon. [F—— S——]', without the 'PC'. *Begin,* etc. according to rank.

Professor

Address on envelope: 'Professor [F—— S——]'; the styles 'Professor Lord [S——]' and 'Professor Sir [F—— S——]' are often used, but are deprecated by some people. If the professor is in holy orders, 'The Reverend Professor'. *Begin:* 'Dear Sir/Madam', or according to rank. *Spoken address:* according to rank.

Queen

Address on envelope: 'Her Majesty the Queen'. *Begin:* 'Madam, with my humble duty'. Refer to as 'Your Majesty'. *Close:* 'I have the honour to remain (or 'be'), Madam, Your Majesty's most humble and obedient servant'. *Spoken address:* 'Your Majesty' once, thereafter 'Ma'am'. *Begin an official speech:* 'May it please Your Majesty'.

Rabbi

Address on envelope: 'Rabbi [initial and S——]' or, if a doctor, 'Rabbi Doctor [initial and S——]'. *Begin:* 'Dear Sir'. *Spoken address:* 'Rabbi [S——]' or '[Doctor S——]'.

Secretary of State

Address on envelope: 'The Right Hon. [F—— S——], MP, Secretary of State for ——', or 'The Secretary of State for ——'. Otherwise according to rank.

Viscount

Address on envelope: 'The Right Hon. the Viscount ——'. *Begin:* 'My Lord'. *Spoken address:* 'My Lord'.

Viscountess

Address on envelope: 'The Right Hon. the Viscountess ——'. *Begin:* 'Dear Madam'. *Spoken address:* 'Madam'.

COMPUTER LANGUAGES (HIGH-LEVEL)

Name	Full name	Main use
Ada	—	Complex on-line real-time monitoring and control (eg military applications)
AED	Algol extended for design	Computer-aided design
ALGOL	Algorithmic Orientated Language	Concise expression of mathematical and logical processes and the control of these processes
APL	A Programming Language	Educational; mathematical problems particularly those concerned with multidimensional arrays
APT	Automatically Programmed Tools	Operate machine tools using numeric codes
BASIC	Beginners All-purpose Symbolic Instruction Code	Education, games
BCPL	B Combined Programming Language	Mathematical, scientific, systems programming
C	—	Operating systems (eg UNIX), business, scientific, games
CHILL	—	Real-time language used for programming computer-based telecommunication systems and computer-controlled telephone exchanges
COBOL	Common Business Oriented Language	Business data processing
COGO	Co-ordinate Geometry	Solving coordinate geometry problems in civil engineering
COMAL	Common algorithmic language	Education
CORAL	Computer On-line Real-time Application Language	Military applications
FORTH	—	Astronomy, robotics, control applications
FORTRAN	Formula Translation	Mathematical, engineering, scientific
GPSS	General Purpose Systems Simulation	Simulation programs
LISP	List Processing	Linguistics, Artificial Intelligence, manipulation of mathematical and arithmetic logic
LOGO	—	Education, turtle graphics
ML	Meta Language	Dynamic programming
MODULA-2	—	Parallel computations (derivative of Pascal)
OCCAM	—	Artificial Intelligence applications
Pascal	—	Education
PL/1	Programming Language 1	Educational; commercial and scientific work
PL/M	Programming Language for Microcomputers	Educational; commercial and scientific work
PROLOG	Programming in logic	Artificial intelligence, expert systems
SIMULA	Simulation language	Simulation programs
SNOBOL	String Oriented Symbolic Language	Manipulation of textual data
SQL	Structured Query Language	Database querying

NEWS AGENCIES

Press name	Full name	Date founded	Location
AAP	Australian Associated Press	1935	Sydney
AASA	Agence Arabe Syrienne d'Information	1966	Damascus
ADN	Allgemeiner Deutscher Nachrichtendienst	1946	Berlin
AE	Agence Europe	1952	Brussels
AFP	Agence France-Presse	1944	Paris
AIO	Agencia Informativa Orbe de Chile	1952	Santiago
AIP	Agence Ivoirienne de Presse	1961	Abidjan
ALD	Agencia Los Diarios	1910	Buenos Aires
ALI	Agencia Lusa de Informacao	1987	Lisbon
AM	Agencia Meridional	1931	Rio de Janeiro
ANA	Athenagence	1896	Athens
ANP	Algemeen Nederlands Persbureau	1934	The Hague
ANSA	Agenzia Nazionale Stampa Associate	1945	Rome
ANTARA	Indonesian National News Agency	1937	Jakarta
AN	Agencia Nacional	1946	Brasilia
APA	Austria Presse-Agentur	1946	Vienna
APP	Agence Parisienne de Presse	1949	Paris
APP	Associated Press of Pakistan	1948	Islamabad
APS	Agence de Presse Senegalaise	1959	Dakar
APS	Algeria Presse Service	1962	Algiers
AP	Associated Press	1848	New York
ATA	Albanian Telegraphic Agency	1945	Tirana
AUP	Australian United Press	1928	Melbourne
BELGA	Agence Belga	1920	Brussels
BER-NAMA	Malaysia National News Agency	1967	Kuala Lumpur
BOPA	Botswana Press Agency	1981	Gaborone
BTA	Bulgarska Telegrafitscheka Agentzia	1898	Sofia
CANA	Caribbean News Agency	–	Bridgetown
CIP	Centre d'Information de Presse	1946	Brussels
CNA	Central News Agency	1924	Taipei
CNA	Cyprus News Agency	1976	Nicosia
CNS	China News Service	1952	Beijing
COL-PRENSA	Colprensa	1980	Bogota
CP	Canadian Press	1917	Toronto
CTK	Ceskoslovenska Tiskova Kancelar	1918	Prague
DPA	Deutsche Presse-Agentur	1949	Hamburg
EFE	Agencia EFE	1939	Madrid
ENA	Eastern News Agency	1970	Dhaka
EXTEL	Exchange and Telegraph Company	1872	London
FIDES	Agenzia Internazionale Fides	1926	Vatican City
GNA	Agence Guinéenne de Presse	1981	Conakry
GNA	Ghana News Agency	1957	Accra
GNA	Guyana News Agency	1981	George-town
HHA	Hurriyet Haber Ajasi	1963	Istanbul
IC	Inforpress Centroamericana	1972	Guatemala
INA	Iraqi News Agency	1959	Baghdad
IPS	Inter Press Service	1964	Rome
IRNA	Islamic Republic News Agency	1936	Tehran
JAM-PRESS	Jampress	1984	Kingston
JANA	Jamahiriya News Agency	–	Tripoli
JIJI	Jiji Tsushin-Sha	1945	Tokyo

NEWS AGENCIES (cont.)

Press name	Full name	Date founded	Location
JTA	Jewish Telegraphic Agency	1919	Jerusalem
KCNA	Korean Central News Agency	1946	Pyongyang
KNA	Kenya News Agency	1963	Nairobi
KPL	Khao San Pathet Lao	1968	Vientiane
KUNA	Kuwait News Agency	1976	Kuwait City
KYODO	Kyodo Tsushin	1945	Tokyo
LAI	Logos Agencia de Informacion	1929	Madrid
MENA	Middle East News Agency	1955	Cairo
MTI	Magyar Tavariti Iroda	1880	Budapest
NAB	News Agency of Burma	1963	Rangoon
NAEWOE	Naewoe Press	1974	Seoul
NAN	News Agency of Nigeria	1978	Lagos
NA	Noticias Argentinas	1973	Buenos Aires
NOTIMEX	Noticias Mexicanas	1968	Mexico City
NOVOSTI	Agentstvo Pechati Novosti	1961	Moscow
NPS	Norsk Presse Service	1960	Oslo
NTB	Norsk Telegrambyra	1867	Oslo
NZPA	New Zealand Press Agency	1879	Wellington
OPA	Orbis Press Agency	1977	Prague
OTT-FNB	Oy Suomen Tietoimisto Notisbyran Ab	1887	Helsinki
PANA	Pan-African News Agency	1979	Dakar
PAP	Polska Agencija Prasowa	1944	Warsaw
PA	Press Association	1868	London
PETRA	Jordan News Agency	1965	Amman
PNA	Philippines News Agency	1973	Manila
PPI	Pakistan Press International	1959	Karachi
PRELA	Prensa Latina	1959	Havana
PS	Presse Services	1929	Paris
PTI	Press Trust of India	1949	Bombay
RB	Ritzaus Bureau	1866	Copenhagen
REUTERS	Reuters	1851	London
ROM-PRESS	Romanian News Agency	1949	Bucharest
SAPA	South Africa Press Association	1938	Johannesburg
SDA	Schweizerische Depeschenagentur	1894	Berne
SIP	Svensk-Internationella Pressbyran	1927	Stockholm
SLENA	Sierre Leone News Agency	1980	Freetown
SOFIA-PRES	Sofia Press Agency	1967	Sofia
SOPAC-NEWS	South Pacific News Service	1948	Wellington
SPA	Saudi Press Agency	1970	Riyadh
TANJUG	Novinska Agencija Tanjug	1943	Belgrade
TAP	Tunis Afrique Presse	1961	Tunis
TASS	Telegraph Agency of the Sovereign States	1925	Moscow
TT	Tidningarnes Telegrambyra	1921	Stockholm
UNI	United News of India	1961	New Dehli
UPI	United Press International	1958	New York
UPP	United Press of Pakistan	1949	Karachi
XINHUA	Xinhua	1937	Beijing
YONHAP	Yonhap (United) Press Agency	1980	Seoul
ZIANA	Zimbabwe Inter-Africa News Agency	1981	Harare

NATIONAL NEWSPAPERS—Europe

Name	Location	Circulation[1]	Date founded
ABC	Madrid	247 200	1905
Algemeen Dagblad	Rotterdam	410 400	1946
Apogevmatini	Athens	130 000	1956
Avriani	Athens	115 000	1980
B.T.	Copenhagen	202 600	1916
Berliner Zeitung	Berlin	296 300	1877
Berlingske Tidende	Copenhagen	128 800	1749
Bild am Sonntag (s)	Hamburg	2 400 000	1956
Bild Zeitung	Hamburg	5 124 000	1952
Correio do Manha	Lisbon	70 000	1979
Corriere della Sera	Milan	468 100	1876
De Standaard/ Het Nieuwsblad/ De Gentenaar	Brussels	378 700	N/A
De Telegraaf	Amsterdam	723 800	1893
De Volkskrant	Amsterdam	323 000	1919
Diario de Noticias	Lisbon	58 900	1864
Diario Popular	Lisbon	62 200	1942
Die Welt	Bonn	225 000	1946
Die Zeit (weekly)	Hamburg	468 000	1946
Ekstra Bladet	Copenhagen	229 500	1904
El Pais	Madrid	380 000	1976
El Periodico	Barcelona	150 000	1978
Ethnos	Athens	150 500	1981
Evening Herald	Dublin	132 300	1891
Evening Press	Dublin	129 700	1954
France-Dimanche (s)	Paris	721 000	N/A
France-Soir	Paris	410 700	1944
Frankfurter Allgemeine Zeitung	Frankfurt	360 000	1949
Het Laatste Nieuws	Brussels	301 306	1888
Il Giornale	Milan	176 900	1974
Il Giorno	Milan	211 600	1965
Il Messaggero	Rome	330 000	1878
International Herald Tribune	Paris	174 200	1887
Irish Independent	Dublin	174 800	1905
Irish Times	Dublin	88 700	1859
La Libre Belgique	Brussels	80 800	1884
La Dernière Heure	Brussels	92 600	1906
La Lanterne	Brussels	132 800	1944
La Republica	Rome	486 000	1976
La Stampa	Turin	433 400	1867
La Vanguardia	Barcelona	225 000	1881
Le Figaro	Paris	433 500	1828
Le Monde	Paris	362 400	1944
Le Parisien Libère	Paris	339 300	1944
Le Soir	Brussels	208 900	1887
L'Humanité	Paris	117 000	1904
L'Humanité Dimanche (s)	Paris	360 000	1946
Luxemburger Wort/ La Voix du Luxembourg	Luxembourg	83 200	1848
Politiken	Copenhagen	152 200	1884
Suddeutsche Zeitung	Munich	378 400	1945
Sunday Independent (s)	Dublin	222 400	1905
Sunday Press (s)	Dublin	266 000	1949
Sunday World (s)	Dublin	366 800	1973
Ta Nea	Athens	155 000	1944
Welt am Sonntag (s)	Hamburg	336 000	–
Ya	Madrid	380 000	1935

(s) published on Sundays only
[1]1991 figures (rounded to nearest 100)

NATIONAL NEWSPAPERS—UK

Name	Location	Circulation[1]	Date founded
Daily Express	London	1 570 400	1900
Daily Mail	London	1 739 800	1896
Daily Mirror	London	3 171 700	1903
Daily Telegraph	London	1 105 400	1855
Financial Times	London	285 900	1880
The Guardian	London	431 700	1821
The Herald	Glasgow	122 100	1783
The Independent on Sunday (s)	London	375 000	1990
The Independent	London	422 700	1986
The Mail on Sunday (s)	London	1 944 000	1982
News of the World (s)	London	5 249 300	1843
Observer (s)	London	749 600	1791
The People (s)	London	2 932 500	1881
Scotland on Sunday (s)	Edinburgh	72 900	1988
The Scotsman	Edinburgh	85 900	1817
The Sun	London	4 195 000	1964
The Sunday Mirror (s)	London	2 814 600	1963
The Sunday Post (s)	Dundee	1 432 600	1920
The Sunday Telegraph (s)	London	648 300	1961
The Sunday Times (s)	London	1 272 600	1822
The Times	London	450 600	1785
Today	London	601 900	1986

(s) published on Sundays only
[1] 1991 figures (rounded to nearest 100)

MAJOR NEWSPAPERS—USA

Includes national newspapers and local newspapers having an all-day, morning, or evening circulation of 250 000 or more.

Name	Location	Circulation[1]	Date founded
Atlanta Constitution	Atlanta, Ga	315 000	1868
Baltimore Sun	Baltimore, Md	406 000	1837
Boston Globe	Boston, Mass	519 000	1872
Boston Herald	Boston, Mass	364 000	1892
Buffalo News	Buffalo, NY	312 000	1880
Chicago Sun-Times	Chicago, Ill	534 000	1948
Chicago Tribune	Chicago, Ill	730 000	1847
Christian Science Monitor[2]	Boston, Mass	106 000	1908
Cleveland Plain Dealer	Cleveland, Ohio	438 000	1842
Columbus Dispatch	Columbus, Ohio	252 000	1871
Dallas Morning News	Dallas, Texas	375 000	1885
Denver Rocky Mountain News	Denver, Colo	353 000	1859
Detroit Free Press	Detroit, Mich	638 000	1831
Detroit News	Detroit, Mich	526 000	1873
Fort Worth Star-Telegram	Fort Worth, Texas	254 000	1906
Houston Chronicle	Houston, Texas	433 000	1901
Houston Post	Houston, Texas	324 000	1885
Kansas City Star	Kansas City, Mo	300 000	1880
Los Angeles Times	Los Angeles, Cal	1 159 000	1881
Miami Herald	Miami, Fla	428 000	1910
Milwaukee Sentinel	Milwaukee, Wisc	276 000	1837
Minneapolis Star Tribune	Minneapolis, Minn	408 000	1867
New Orleans Times-Picayune	New Orleans, La	278 000	1837
New York Daily News	New York, NY	1 212 000	1919
New York Post	New York, NY	521 000	1801
New York Times[2]	New York, NY	1 092 000	1851
Newark Star-Ledger	Newark, NJ	477 000	1832
Newsday	Melville, NY	699 000	1940
Orange County Register	Santa Ana, Cal	346 000	1905
Orlando Sentinel	Orlando, Fla	272 000	1876
Philadelphia Inquirer	Philadelphia, Pa	513 000	1829
Phoenix Republic	Phoenix, Ariz	350 000	1890
Portland Oregonian	Portland, Ore	321 000	1850
Sacramento Bee	Sacramento, Cal	261 000	1857
San Diego Union	San Diego, Cal	270 000	1868
San Francisco Chronicle	San Francisco, Cal	566 000	1865
San Jose Mercury News	San Jose, Cal	280 000	1851
St Louis Post-Dispatch	St Louis, Mo	380 000	1878
St Petersburg Times	St Petersburg, Fla	345 000	1884
Tampa Tribune	Tampa, Fla	285 000	1893
USA Today[2]	Arlington, Va	1 356 000	1982
Wall Street Journal[2]	New York, NY	1 887 000	1889
Washington Post	Washington, DC	802 000	1877

[1] 1991 figures (rounded to nearest 1 000)
[2] National newspapers

SYMBOLS IN GENERAL USE

&,	ampersand (*and*)
&c.	et cetera
@	at; per (in costs)
×	by (measuring dimensions, eg 3 × 4)
£	pound
$	dollar (also peso, escudo, etc in certain countries)
¢	cent (also centavo, etc in certain countries)
©	copyright
®	registered
¶	new paragraph
§	new section
"	ditto
*	born (in genealogy)
†	died
*	hypothetical or unacceptable form (in linguistics)
☠	poison; danger
♂, □	male
♀, ○	female
✠	bishop's name follows
☏	telephone number follows
☞	this way
✂ ✂…	cut here

In astronomy

●	new moon
☽	moon, first quarter
○	full moon
☾	moon, last quarter

In meteorology

 cold front (in meteorology)

 warm front

 stationary front

 occluded front

In cards

♥	hearts
♦	diamonds
♠	spades
♣	clubs

CLOTHES CARE SYMBOLS

 Do not iron

 Can be ironed with *cool* iron (up to 110°C)

 Can be ironed with *warm* iron (up to 150dC)

 Can be ironed with *hot* iron (up to 200°C)

 Hand wash only

Can be washed in a washing machine
The number shows the most effective washing temperature (in °C)

Reduced (medium) washing conditions

Much reduced (minimum) washing conditions (for wool products)

 Do not wash

 Can be tumble dried (one dot within the circle means a low temperature setting; two dots for higher temperatures)

 Do not tumble dry

 Do not dry clean

Dry cleanable (letter indicates which solvents can be used)
A: all solvents

Dry cleanable
F: white spirit and solvent 11 can be used

Dry cleanable
P: perchloroethylene (tetrachloroethylene), white spirit, solvent 113 and solvent 11 can be used

Dry cleanable, if special care taken

Chlorine bleach may be used with care

 Do not use chlorine bleach

CAR INDEX MARKS—UK

AA	Bournemouth
AB	Worcester
AC	Coventry
AD	Gloucester
AE	Bristol
AF	Truro
AG	Hull
AH	Norwich
AJ	Middlesbrough
AK	Sheffield
AL	Nottingham
AM	Swindon
AN	Reading
AO	Carlisle
AP	Brighton
AR	Chelmsford
AS	Inverness
AT	Hull
AU	Nottingham
AV	Peterborough
AW	Shrewsbury
AX	Cardiff
AY	Leicester
BA	Manchester
BB	Newcastle upon Tyne
BC	Leicester
BD	Northampton
BE	Lincoln
BF	Stoke-on-Trent
BG	Liverpool
BH	Luton
BJ	Ipswich
BK	Portsmouth
BL	Reading
BM	Luton
BN	Manchester
BO	Cardiff
BP	Portsmouth
BR	Newcastle upon Tyne
BS	Inverness
BT	Leeds
BU	Manchester
BV	Preston
BW	Oxford
BX	Haverfordwest
BY	London NW
CA	Chester
CB	Manchester
CC	Bangor
CD	Brighton
CE	Peterborough
CF	Reading
CG	Bournemouth
CH	Nottingham
CJ	Gloucester
CK	Preston
CL	Norwich
CM	Liverpool
CN	Newcastle upon Tyne
CO	Exeter
CP	Huddersfield
CR	Portsmouth
CS	Glasgow
CT	Lincoln
CU	Newcastle upon Tyne
CV	Truro
CW	Preston
CX	Huddersfield
CY	Swansea
DA	Birmingham
DB	Manchester
DC	Middlesbrough
DD	Gloucester
DE	Haverfordwest
DF	Gloucester
DG	Gloucester
DH	Dudley
DJ	Liverpool
DK	Manchester
DL	Portsmouth
DM	Chester
DN	Leeds
DO	Lincoln
DP	Reading
DR	Exeter
DS	Glasgow
DT	Sheffield
DU	Coventry
DV	Exeter
DW	Cardiff
DX	Ipswich
DY	Brighton
EA	Dudley
EB	Peterborough
EC	Preston
ED	Liverpool
EE	Lincoln
EF	Middlesbrough
EG	Peterborough
EH	Stoke-on-Trent
EJ	Haverfordwest
EK	Liverpool
EL	Bournemouth
EM	Liverpool
EN	Manchester
EO	Preston
EP	Swansea
ER	Peterborough
ES	Dundee
ET	Sheffield
EU	Bristol
EV	Chelmsford
EW	Peterborough
EX	Norwich
EY	Bangor
FA	Stoke-on-Trent
FB	Bristol
FC	Oxford
FD	Dudley
FE	Lincoln
FF	Bangor
FG	Brighton
FH	Gloucester
FJ	Exeter
FK	Dudley
FL	Peterborough
FM	Chester
FN	Maidstone
FO	Gloucester
FP	Leicester
FR	Preston
FS	Edinburgh
FT	Newcastle upon Tyne
FU	Lincoln
FV	Preston
FW	Lincoln
FX	Bournemouth
FY	Liverpool
GA	Glasgow
GB	Glasgow
GC	London SW
GD	Glasgow
GE	Glasgow
GF	London SW
GG	Glasgow
GH	London SW
GJ	London SW
GK	London SW
GL	Truro
GM	Reading
GN	London SW
GO	London SW
GP	London SW

CAR INDEX MARKS—UK (cont.)

GR Newcastle upon Tyne
GS Luton
GT London SW
GU London SE
GV Ipswich
GW London SE
GX London SE
GY London SE

HA Dudley
HB Cardiff
HC Brighton
HD Huddersfield
HE Sheffield
HF Liverpool
HG Preston
HH Carlisle
HJ Chelmsford
HK Chelmsford
HL Sheffield
HM London (Central)
HN Middlesbrough
HO Bournemouth
HP Coventry
HR Swindon
HS Glasgow
HT Bristol
HU Bristol
HV London (Central)
HW Bristol
HX London (Central)
HY Bristol

JA Manchester
JB Reading
JC Bangor
JD London (Central)
JE Peterborough
JF Leicester
JG Maidstone
JH Reading
JJ Maidstone
JK Brighton
JL Lincoln
JM Reading
JN Chelmsford
JO Oxford
JP Liverpool
JR Newcastle upon Tyne
JS Inverness
JT Bournemouth
JU Leicester
JV Lincoln
JW Birmingham
JX Huddersfield
JY Exeter

KA Liverpool
KB Liverpool
KC Liverpool
KD Liverpool
KE Maidstone
KF Liverpool
KG Cardiff
KH Hull
KJ Maidstone
KK Maidstone
KL Maidstone
KM Maidstone
KN Maidstone
KO Maidstone
KP Maidstone
KR Maidstone
KS Edinburgh
KT Maidstone
KU Sheffield
KV Coventry
KW Sheffield
KX Luton
KY Sheffield

LA London NW
LB London NW
LC London NW
LD London NW
LE London NW
LF London NW
LG Chester
LH London NW
LJ Bournemouth
LK London NW
LL London NW
LM London NW
LN London NW
LO London NW
LP London NW
LR London NW
LS Edinburgh
LT London NW
LU London NW
LV Liverpool
LW London NW
LX London NW
LY London NW

MA Chester
MB Chester
MC London NE
MD London NE
ME London NE
MF London NE
MG London NE
MH London NE
MJ Luton
MK London NE
ML London NE
MM London NE
MN *(not used)*
MO Reading
MP London NE
MR Swindon
MS Edinburgh
MT London NE
MU London NE
MV London SE
MW Swindon
MX London SE
MY London SE

NA Manchester
NB Manchester
NC Manchester
ND Manchester
NE Manchester
NF Manchester
NG Norwich
NH Northampton
NJ Brighton
NK Luton
NL Newcastle upon Tyne
NM Luton
NN Nottingham
NO Chelmsford
NP Worcester
NR Leicester
NS Glasgow
NT Shrewsbury
NU Nottingham
NV Northampton
NW Leeds
NX Dudley
NY Cardiff

OA Birmingham
OB Birmingham
OC Birmingham
OD Exeter
OE Birmingham
OF Birmingham

CAR INDEX MARKS—UK (cont.)

OG	Birmingham
OH	Birmingham
OJ	Birmingham
OK	Birmingham
OL	Birmingham
OM	Birmingham
ON	Birmingham
OO	Chelmsford
OP	Birmingham
OR	Portsmouth
OS	Glasgow
OT	Portsmouth
OU	Bristol
OV	Birmingham
OW	Portsmouth
OX	Birmingham
OY	London NW
PA	Guildford
PB	Guildford
PC	Guildford
PD	Guildford
PE	Guildford
PF	Guildford
PG	Guildford
PH	Guildford
PJ	Guildford
PK	Guildford
PL	Guildford
PM	Guildford
PN	Brighton
PO	Portsmouth
PP	Luton
PR	Bournemouth
PS	Aberdeen
PT	Newcastle upon Tyne
PU	Chelmsford
PV	Ipswich
PW	Norwich
PX	Portsmouth
PY	Middlesbrough
RA	Nottingham
RB	Nottingham
RC	Nottingham
RD	Reading
RE	Stoke-on-Trent
RF	Stoke-on-Trent
RG	Newcastle upon Tyne
RH	Hull
RJ	Manchester
RK	London NW
RL	Truro
RM	Carlisle
RN	Preston
RO	Luton
RP	Northampton
RR	Nottingham
RS	Aberdeen
RT	Ipswich
RU	Bournemouth
RV	Portsmouth
RW	Coventry
RX	Reading
RY	Leicester
SA	Aberdeen
SB	Glasgow
SC	Edinburgh
SCY	Truro (Isles of Scilly)
SD	Glasgow
SE	Aberdeen
SF	Edinburgh
SG	Edinburgh
SH	Edinburgh
SJ	Glasgow
SK	Inverness
SL	Dundee
SM	Glasgow
SN	Dundee
SO	Aberdeen
SP	Dundee
SR	Dundee
SS	Aberdeen
ST	Inverness
SU	Glasgow
SV	*Spare*
SW	Glasgow
SX	Edinburgh
SY	*Spare*
TA	Exeter
TB	Liverpool
TC	Bristol
TD	Manchester
TE	Manchester
TF	Reading
TG	Cardiff
TH	Swansea
TJ	Liverpool
TK	Exeter
TL	Lincoln
TM	Luton
TN	Newcastle upon Tyne
TO	Nottingham
TP	Portsmouth
TR	Portsmouth
TS	Dundee
TT	Exeter
TU	Chester
TV	Nottingham
TW	Chelmsford
TX	Cardiff
TY	Newcastle upon Tyne
UA	Leeds
UB	Leeds
UC	London (Central)
UD	Oxford
UE	Dudley
UF	Brighton
UG	Leeds
UH	Cardiff
UJ	Shrewsbury
UK	Birmingham
UL	London (Central)
UM	Leeds
UN	Exeter
UO	Exeter
UP	Newcastle upon Tyne
UR	Luton
US	Glasgow
UT	Leicester
UU	London (Central)
UV	London (Central)
UW	London (Central)
UX	Shrewsbury
UY	Worcester
VA	Peterborough
VB	Maidstone
VC	Coventry
VD	*Series withdrawn*
VE	Peterborough
VF	Norwich
VG	Norwich
VH	Huddersfield
VJ	Gloucester
VK	Newcastle upon Tyne
VL	Lincoln
VM	Manchester
VN	Middlesbrough
VO	Nottingham
VP	Birmingham
VR	Manchester
VS	Luton
VT	Stoke-on-Trent
VU	Manchester
VV	Northampton

CAR INDEX MARKS—UK (cont.)

VW	Chelmsford
VX	Chelmsford
VY	Leeds
WA	Sheffield
WB	Sheffield
WC	Chelmsford
WD	Dudley
WE	Sheffield
WF	Sheffield
WG	Sheffield
WH	Manchester
WJ	Sheffield
WK	Coventry
WL	Oxford
WM	Liverpool
WN	Swansea
WO	Cardiff
WP	Worcester
WR	Leeds
WS	Bristol
WT	Leeds
WU	Leeds
WV	Brighton
WW	Leeds
WX	Leeds
WY	Leeds
YA	Taunton
YB	Taunton
YC	Taunton
YD	Taunton
YE	London (Central)
YF	London (Central)
YG	Leeds
YH	London (Central)
YJ	Brighton
YK	London (Central)
YL	London (Central)
YM	London (Central)
YN	London (Central)
YO	London (Central)
YP	London (Central)
YR	London (Central)
YS	Glasgow
YT	London (Central)
YU	London (Central)
YV	London (Central)
YW	London (Central)
YX	London (Central)
YY	London (Central)

CAR INDEX MARKS—International

A	Austria
ADN	Yemen PDR
AFG	Afghanistan
AL	Albania
AND	Andorra
AUS	Australia*
B	Belgium
BD	Bangladesh*
BDS	Barbados*
BG	Bulgaria
BH	Belize
BR	Brazil
BRN	Bahrain
BRU	Brunei*
BS	Bahamas*
BUR	Burma
C	Cuba
CDN	Canada
CH	Switzerland
CI	Côte d'Ivoire
CL	Sri Lanka*
CO	Colombia
CR	Costa Rica
CS	Czechoslovakia
CY	Cyprus*
D	W Germany
DK	Denmark
DOM	Dominican Republic
DY	Benin
DZ	Algeria
E	Spain
EAK	Kenya*
EAT	Tanzania*
EAU	Uganda*
EAZ	Tanzania*
EC	Ecuador
ES	El Salvador
ET	Egypt
ETH	Ethiopia
F	France
FJI	Fiji*
FL	Liechtenstein
FR	Faroe Is
GB	UK*
GBA	Alderney*
GBG	Guernsey*
GBJ	Jersey*
GBM	Isle of Man*
GBZ	Gibraltar
GCA	Guatemala
GH	Ghana
GR	Greece
GUY	Guyana*
H	Hungary
HK	Hong Kong*
HKJ	Jordan
I	Italy
IL	Israel
IND	India*
IR	Iran
IRL	Ireland*
IRQ	Iraq
IS	Iceland
J	Japan*
JA	Jamaica*
K	Kampuchea
KWT	Kuwait
L	Luxembourg
LAO	Laos
LAR	Libya
LB	Liberia
LS	Lesotho*
M	Malta*
MA	Morocco
MAL	Malaysia*
MC	Monaco
MEX	Mexico
MS	Mauritius*
MW	Malawi*
N	Norway
NA	Netherlands Antilles
NIC	Nicaragua
NL	Netherlands
NZ	New Zealand*
P	Portugal
PA	Panama
PAK	Pakistan*
PE	Peru
PL	Poland
PNG	Papua New Guinea*

CAR INDEX MARKS—International (cont.)

PY	Paraguay	**RSM**	San Marino	**USA**	USA
RA	Argentina	**RU**	Burundi	**V**	Vatican City
RB	Botswana*	**RWA**	Rwanda	**VN**	Vietnam
RC	Taiwan	**S**	Sweden	**WAG**	Gambia
RCA	Central African Republic	**SD**	Swaziland*	**WAL**	Sierra Leone
RCB	Congo	**SF**	Finland	**WAN**	Nigeria
RCH	Chile	**SGP**	Singapore*	**WD**	Dominica*
RH	Haiti	**SME**	Suriname*	**WG**	Grenada*
RI	Indonesia*	**SN**	Senegal	**WL**	St Lucia*
RIM	Mauritania	**SU**	CIS	**WS**	W Samoa
RL	Lebanon	**SWA**	Namibia*	**WV**	St Vincent and the Grenadines*
RM	Madagascar	**SY**	Seychelles*		
RMM	Mali	**SYR**	Syria	**YU**	Yugoslavia
RN	Niger	**T**	Thailand*	**YV**	Venezuela
RO	Romania	**TG**	Togo	**Z**	Zambia*
ROK	Korea, Republic of	**TN**	Tunisia	**ZA**	South Africa*
ROU	Uruguay	**TR**	Turkey	**ZRE**	Zaire
RP	Philippines	**TT**	Trinidad and Tobago*	**ZW**	Zimbabwe*

*In countries so marked, the rule of the road is drive on the left; in other countries, drive on the right.

UK AIRPORTS

Alderney Channel Islands
Baltasound Unst, Shetlands
Belfast City
Belfast International
Benbecula Hebrides
Biggin Hill Kent
Blackpool Lancashire
Bournemouth Dorset
Bristol Avon
Cambridge
Cardiff
Coventry West Midlands
Dundee
Dyce Aberdeen
East Midlands Derbyshire
Exeter Devon
Fair Isle Shetlands
Gatwick London
Glenegedale Islay
Glasgow
Grimsetter Orkney
Guernsey Channel Islands
Heathrow London
Humberside
Inverness
Jersey Channel Islands
Kirkwall Orkney
Leeds-Bradford
Liverpool
London City
Luton Bedfordshire
Lydd Kent
Manchester
Newcastle
North Bay Barra, Hebrides
Norwich Norfolk
Penzance Cornwall
Plymouth (Roborough) Devon
Prestwick Ayrshire
Ronaldsway Isle of Man
Saint Mary's Scilly Isles
Sandown Isle of Wight
Scatsa Shetlands
Southampton Hampshire
Southend Essex
Stansted London
Stornoway Hebrides
Sumburgh Shetlands
Swansea
Teeside Cleveland
Tingwall Lerwick, Shetlands
Tiree Hebrides
Tresco Scilly Isles
Turnhouse Edinburgh
West Midlands Birmingham
Westray Orkney
Wick Caithness

INTERNATIONAL AIRPORTS

Alborg Roedslet Norresundbyr, Denmark
Abadan International Iran
Abu Dhabi United Arab Emirates
Adana Turkey
Adelaide Australia
Agno Lugano, Switzerland
Ain el Bay Constantine, Algeria
Albany County New York, USA
Albuquerque New Mexico, USA
Alexandria Egypt
Alfonso Bonilla Aragon Cali, Columbia
Alicante Spain
Almeria Spain
Amarillo Texas, USA
Amborovy Majunga, Madagascar
Amilcar Cabral International Sal I, Cape Verde
Aminu International Kano, Nigeria
Anchorage Alaska, USA
Archangel Russia
Arlanda Stockholm, Sweden
Arnos Vale St Vincent
Arrecife Lanzarote, Canary Is
Arturo Marino Benitez Santiago, Chile
Asturias Spain
Ataturk Istanbul, Turkey
Auckland New Zealand
Augusto C Sandino Managua, Nicaragua
Baghdad International Iraq
Bahrain International Bahrain
Bali International/Ngurah Rai Denpasar, Indonesia
Balice Kracow, Poland
Bandar Seri Begawan Brunei
Baneasa Bucharest, Romania
Bangkok International Thailand
Barajas Madrid, Spain
Barcelona Spain
Basle-Mulhouse Basle, Spain
Beijing (Peking) China
Beira Mozambique
Beirut International Khaldeh, Lebanon
Belfast International UK
Belgrade Yugoslavia
Belize City International Belize
Ben Gurion Tel Aviv, Israel
Benina Benghazi, Libya
Benito Juarez Mexico City, Mexico
Berlin-Schonefeld Berlin, Germany
Berline-Tegel Berlin, Germany
Berne Switzerland
Billund Denmark
Birmingham Alabama, USA
Blackburne/Plymouth Montserrat (Leeward I)
Blagnac Toulouse, France
Bole Addis Ababa, Ethiopia
Bombay India
Borispol Kiev, Ukraine
Boukhalef Tangier, Morocco
Boulogne France
Bourgas Bulgaria
Bradley International Hartford, Connecticut, USA
Brasilia International Brazil
Bremen Germany
Brisbane Australia
Brnik Ljubljana, Yugoslavia
Bromma Stockholm, Sweden
Brussels National Belgium
Buffalo New York, USA
Bujumbura Burindi
Bulawayo Zimbabwe
Butmir Sarajevo, Yugoslavia
Cairns Queensland, Australia
Cairo International Egypt
Calabar Nigeria
Calcutta India
Calgary International Canada
Cancun Mexico
Cannon International Reno, Nevada, USA
Canton Akron, Ohio, USA
Capodichino Naples, Italy
Carrasco Montevideo, Uruguay
Carthage Tunis, Tunisia
Cebu Philippines
Chang Kai Shek Taipei, Taiwan
Changi Singapore
Charleroi (Gossilies) Belgium
Charles de Gaulle Paris, France
Charleston South Carolina, USA
Charleston West Virginia, USA
Charlotte North Carolina, USA
Château Bougon Nantes, France
Christchurch New Zealand
Ciampino Rome, Italy
Cologne-Bonn Cologne, Germany
Columbus Ohio, USA
Congonhas São Paulo, Brazil
Copenhagen International Kastrup, Denmark
Cork Republic of Ireland
Costa Smeralda Olbia, Sardinia
Côte d'Azure Nice, France
Cotonou Benin
Cristoforo Colombo Genoa, Italy

INTERNATIONAL AIRPORTS (cont.)

Crown Point Scarborough, Tobago
Cuscatlan Comalapa, El Salvador
D F Malan Cape Town, South Africa
Dalaman Turkey
Dallas/Fort Worth Dallas, Texas, USA
Damascus Syria
Dar-es-Salaam Tanzania
Darwin Australia
Des Moines Iowa, USA
Detroit-Wayne County Detroit, Michigan, USA
Deurne Antwerp, Belgium
Dhahran International Al Khobar, Saudi Arabia
Djibouti Djibouti
Doha Qatar
Dois de Julho International Salvador, Brazil
Domodedovo Moscow, Russia
Don Miguel Hidalgo y Castilla Guadalajara, Mexico
Dorval International Montreal, Canada
Douala Cameroon
Dresden Germany
Dubai United Arab Emirates
Dublin Republic of Ireland
Dubrovnik Yugoslavia
Dulles International Washington DC, USA
Dusseldorf Germany
Ecterdingen Stuttgart, Germany
Edmonton International Canada
Eduardo Gomes Manaus, Brazil
Eindhoven Netherlands
El Alto La Paz, Bolivia
El Dorado Bogata, Colombia
El Paso Texas, USA
Elat Israel
Elmas Cagliari, Italy
Entebbe Uganda
Entzheim Strasbourg, France
Eppley Airfield Omaha, Nebraska, USA
Erie Pennsylvania, USA
Ernesto Cortissoz Barranquilla, Colombia
Esbjerg Denmark
Esenboga Ankara, Turkey
Faleolo Apia, Samoa
Faro Portugal
Ferihegy Budapest, Hungary
Findel Luxembourg
Fiumicino (Leonardo da Vinci) Rome, Italy
Flesland Bergen, Norway
Fontanarossa Catonia, Sicily
Fornebu Oslo, Norway
Fort de France Lamentin, Martinique
Fort Lauderdale Florida, USA
Fort Myers Florida, USA
Frankfurt am Main Germany
Freeport International Bahamas
Frejorgues Montpellier, France
Fuenterrabia San Sebastian, Spain
Fuerteventura Canary Is
Fuhlsbuttel Hamburg, Germany
G Marconi Bologna, Italy
Galileo Galilei Pisa, Italy
Gatwick London, UK
G'Bessia Conakry, Guinea Republic
General Abelard L Rodriguez Tijuana, Mexico
General Juan N Alvarez Acapulco, Mexico
General Manuel Marquez de Leon La Paz, Mexico
General Mariano Escobedo Monterrey, Mexico
General Mitchell Milwaukee, Wisconsin, USA
General Rafael Buelna Mazatlan, Mexico
Geneva Switzerland
Gerona/Costa Brava Gerona, Spain
Gillot St Denis de la Reunion, Indian Ocean
Golden Rock St Kitts
Goleniow Szczecin, Poland
Glasgow UK
Granada Spain
Grantley Adams International Bridgetown, Barbados
Greater Cincinnati Ohio, USA
Greater Pittsburgh Pennsylvania, USA
Guam Guam
Guararapes International Recife, Brazil
Guarulhos International São Paulo, Brazil
Halifax Canada
Halim Perdanakusama Jakarta, Indonesia
Hamilton Kindley Field Hamilton, Bermuda
Hancock Field Syracuse, New York State, USA
Hanover-Langenhagen Hanover, Germany
Hanoi Vietnam
Harare Zimbabwe
Harrisburg Pennsylvania, USA
Hartsfield Atlanta, Georgia, USA
Hassan Laayoune, Morocco
Hato Curaao, Netherlands Antilles
Hahaya International Moroni, Comoros
Hanedi Tokyo, Japan
Heathrow London, UK
Hellenikon Athens, Greece
Henderson Field Honiari, Solomon Is
Heraklion Crete, Greece
Hewanorra International St Lucia
Ho Chi Minh City Vietnam
Hong Kong International Hong Kong
Hongqiao Shanghai, China

INTERNATIONAL AIRPORTS (cont.)

Honolulu Hawaii, USA
Hopkins Cleveland, Ohio, USA
Houari Boumedienne International Dar-el-Beida, Algeria
Houston Texas, USA
Ibiza Balearics, Spain
Indianapolis Indiana, USA
Indira Ghandi International Delhi, India
Inezgane Agadir, Morocco
Islamabad Pakistan
Isle Verde San Juan, Puerto Rico
Izmir Turkey
Itazuke Fukuoka, Japan
Ivanka Bratislava, Czechoslovakia
Ivato Antananarivo, Madagascar
J F Kennedy New York, USA
Jackson Field Port Moresby, Papua New Guinea
Jacksonville Florida, USA
James M Cox Dayton, Ohio, USA
Jan Smuts Johannesburg, South Africa
Jomo Kenyatta Nairobi, Kenya
Jorge Chavez International Lima, Peru
Jose Marti International Havana, Cuba
Juan Santa Maria International Alajuela, Costa Rica
Kagoshima Japan
Kalmar Sweden
Kamazu Lilongwe, Malawi
Kansas City Missouri, USA
Kaohsiung Taiwan
Karachi Pakistan
Karpathos Karpathos, Greece
Katunayake Colombo, Sri Lanka
Keflavik Reykjavik, Iceland
Kent County Grand Rapids, Michigan, USA
Kerkyra Corfu, Greece
Key West Florida, USA
Khartoum Sudan
Khoramaksar Aden, Yemen Arab Republic
Khwaja Rawash Kabul, Afghanistan
Kigali Rwanda
Kimpo International Seoul, South Korea
King Abdul Aziz Jeddah, Saudi Arabia
King Khaled Riyadh, Saudi Arabia
Kingsford Smith Sydney, Australia
Kjevik Kristiansand, Norway
Klagenfurt Austria
Komaki Nagoya, Japan
Kos Greece
Kota Kinabulu Sabah, Malaysia
Kotoka Accra, Ghana
Kranebitten Innsbruck, Austria
Kuching Sarawak, Malaysia
Kungsangen Norrkoping, Sweden
Kuwait International Kuwait
La Aurora Guatemala City, Guatemala
La Coruna Spain
La Guardia New York, USA
La Mesa San Pedro Sula, Honduras
La Parra Jerez de la Frontera, Spain
Lahore Pakistan
Landvetter Gothenburg, Sweden
Larnaca International Cyprus
Las Americas International Santo Domingo, Dominican Republic
Las Palmas Gran Canaria, Canary Is
Le Raizet Point-à-Pitre, Guadeloupe
Leipzig Germany
Les Angades Oujda, Morocco
Lesquin Lille, France
Lester B Pearson International Toronto, Canada
Libreville Gabon
Lic Gustavo Diaz Ordaz Puerto Vallarta, Mexico
Lic Manuel Crecencio Rejon Merida, Mexico
Liège (Bierset) Belgium
Linate Milan, Italy
Lincoln Nebraska, USA
Lindbergh International San Diego, USA
Linz Austria
Lisbon Portugal
Little Rock Arkansas, USA
Llabanère Perpignan, France
Logan International Boston, Massachusetts, USA
Lomé Togo
London City UK
Long Beach California, USA
Los Angeles California, USA
Loshitsa Minsk, Byelorussia
Louis Botha Durban, South Africa
Louisville Kentucky, USA
Lourdes/Tarbes Juillan, France
Luanda Angola
Luano Lubumashi, Zaire
Lubbock Texas, USA
Luis Munoz Marin International San Juan, Puerto Rico
Lungi Freetown, Sierra Leone
Luqa Malta
Lusaka Zambia

INTERNATIONAL AIRPORTS (cont.)

Luxor Egypt
Maastricht Netherlands
McCarran International Las Vegas, Nevada, USA
McCoy International Orlando, Florida, USA
Mactan International Cebu, Philippines
Mahon Menorca
Mais Gate Port au Prince, Haiti
Malaga Spain
Male' Maldives
Malpensa Milan, Italy
Managua Nicaragua
Manchester New Hampshire, USA
Manchester UK
Maputo Mozambique
Marco Polo Venice, Italy
Mariscal Sucre Quito, Ecuador
Maseru Lesotho
Matsapha Manzini, Swaziland
Maupertus Cherbourg, France
Maxglan Salzburg, Austria
Maya Maya Brazaville, Congo
Medina Saudi Arabia
Meenambakkam International Madras, India
Mehrabad International Teheran, Iran
Melita Djerba, Tunisia
Memphis Tennessee, USA
Menara Marrakech, Morocco
Merignac Bordeaux, France
Miami Florida, USA
Midway Chicago, Illinois, USA
Mingaladon,Yangon Myanmar, Malaysia
Ministro Pistarini Buenos Aires, Argentina
Minneapolis/St Paul Minneapolis, USA
Mirabel Montreal, Canada
Mogadishu Somalia
Mohamed V Casablanca, Morocco
Moi International Mombasa, Kenya
Monroe County Rochester, New York State, USA
Morelos Mexico City, Mexico
Münster/Osnabrück Germany
Murmansk Russia
Murtala Muhammed Lagos, Nigeria
Nadi International Fiji
Nagasaki Japan
Narita Tokyo, Japan
Narssarsuaq Greenland
Nashville Tennessee, USA
Nassau International Bahamas
Nauru Nauru
N'djamena Chad
N'Djili Kinshasa, Zaire
Nejrab Aleppo, Syria
Newcastle UK
New Orleans Louisiana, USA
Newark New York, USA
Niamey Niger
Ninoy Aquino International Manila, Philippinnes
Nis Yugoslavia
Norfolk International Virginia, USA
Norman Manley International Kingston, Jamaica
North Front Gibraltar
Nouadhibou Mauritania
Nouakchott Mauritania
Novo-Alexeyevka Tblisi, Georgia
Nuremberg Germany
Oakland International California, USA
Octeville Le Havrets, France
Odense Denmark
O'Hare Chicago, Illinois, USA
Okecie Warsaw, Poland
Okinawa Naha, Japan
Oran Algeria
Orebro Sweden
Orlando Florida, USA
Orly Paris, France
Osaka Japan
Osvaldo Veira Bissau, Guinea Bissau
Otopeni Bucharest, Romania
Ouagadougou Burkino Faso
Owen Roberts Grand Cayman, West Indies
Pago Pago Samoa
Palese Bari, Italy
Palma Majorca
Pamplona Spain
Panama City Panama
Paphos Cyprus
Papola Casale Brindisi, Italy
Paradisi Rhodes, Greece
Patenga Chittagong, Bangladesh
Penang Malaysia
Peninsula Monterey, California, USA
Peretola Florence, Italy
Perth Australia
Peshawar Pakistan
Peterson Field Colorado Springs, Colorado, USA
Philadelphia Pennsylvania, USA
Piarco Port of Spain, Trinidad
Pleso Zagreb, Yugoslavia
Pochentong Phnom Penh, Cambodia
Point Salines Grenada

INTERNATIONAL AIRPORTS (cont.)

Pointe Noire Congo
Polonia Medan, Indonesia
Ponta Delgado São Miguel, Azores
Port Bouet Abidjan, Ivory Coast
Port Harcourt Nigeria
Portland Maine, USA
Portland Oregon, USA
Port Sudan Sudan
Porto Pedra Rubras Oporto, Portugal
Praia Cape Verde
Prestwick UK
Princess Beatriz Aruba, Netherlands Antilles
Provence Marseille, France
Pula Yugoslavia
Pulkovo St Petersburg, Russia
Punta Arenas International Chile
Punta Raisi Palermo, Sicily
Queen Alia Amman Jordan
Releigh/Durham North Carolina, USA
Ras al Khaimah United Arab Emirates
Rebiechowo Gdańsk, Poland
Regina Canada
Reina Sofia Tenerife
Rejon Merida, Mexico
Richmond Virginia, USA
Riem Munich, Germany
Rio de Janeiro International Brazil
Riyadh International Saudi Arabia
Roberts International Monrovia, Liberia
Rochambau Cayenne, French Guiana
Robert Mueller Municipal Airport Austin, Texas, USA
Ronchi dei Legionari Trieste, Italy
Rotterdam Netherlands
Ruzyne Prague, Czechoslovakia
Saab Linkoping, Sweden
Saint Eufemia Lamezia Terma, Italy
Saint Louis Missouri, USA
Saint Thomas Virgin Is
Sainte Foy Quebec, Canada
Sale Rabat, Morocco
Salgado Filho International Porto Alegre, Brazil
Salt Lake City Utah, USA
San Antonio Texas, USA
San Diego California, USA
San Francisco California, USA
San Giusto Pisa, Italy
San Javier Murcia, Spain
San José California, USA
San Pablo Seville, Spain
San Salvador El Salvador
Sanaa International Yemen
Sangster International Montego Bay, Jamaica
Santa Caterina Funchal, Madeira
Santa Cruz La Palma, Canary Is
Santa Isabel Malabo, Guinea
Santander Spain
Santiago Spain
Santos Dumont Rio de Janeiro, Brazil
São Tomé São Tomé
Satolas Lyon, France
Schipol Amsterdam, Netherlands
Schwechat Vienna, Austria
Seeb Muscat, Oman
Senou Bamako, Mali
Seychelles International Mahe, Seychelles
Sfax Tunisia
Shannon Republic of Ireland
Sharjah United Arab Emirates
Sheremetyevo Moscow, Russia
Silvio Pettirossi Asuncion, Paraguay
Simon Bolivar Caracas, Venezuela
Simon Bolivar Guayaquil, Ecuador
Sir Seewoosagur Ramgoolam Plaisance, Mauritius
Sir Seretse Khama Gaborone, Botswana
Skanes Monastir, Morocco
Skopje Yugoslavia
Sky Harbour Phoenix, Arizona, USA
Snilow Lwow, Ukraine
Sofia International Bulgaria
Sola Stavanger, Norway
Sondica Bilbao, Spain
Søndre Strømfjord Greenland
Spilve Riga, Latvia
Split Yugoslavia
Spokane Washington, USA
Stansted UK
Stapleton International Denver, Colorado, USA
Sturup Malmö, Sweden
Subang International Kuala Lumpur, Malaysia
Sunan Pyongyang, North Korea
Tacoma Seattle, USA
Tallahassee Florida, USA
Tamatve Madagascar
Tampa Florida, USA
Tegucigalpa Toncontin, Honduras
Thalerhof Graz, Austria
Theodore Francis Providence, Rhode I, USA
Thessalonika Greece
Timehri International Georgetown, Guyana
Timişoara Romania
Tirana Albania

INTERNATIONAL AIRPORTS (cont.)

Tito Menniti Reggio Calabria, Italy
Tontouta Noumea, New Caledonia
Townsville Australia
Tribhuyan Kathmandu, Nepal
Tripoli Libya
Trivandrum India
Truax Field Madison, Wisconsin, USA
Tucson Arizona, USA
Tullamarine Melbourne, Australia
Turin Italy
Turku Finland
Turnhouse Edinburgh, UK
Ulemiste Tallinn, Estonia
Unokovo Moscow, Russia
Uplands Ottawa, Canada
V C Bird International Antigua
Vaasa Finland
Vagar Faeroe Is
Valencia Spain
Vancouver International Canada
Vantaa Helsinki, Finland
Varna International Bulgaria
Verona Italy
Victoria British Columbia, Canada
Vigie St Lucia
Vigo Spain
Vilnius Lithuania
Vilo de Porto Santa Maria, Azores
Viracopos Sao Paulo, Brazil
Vitoria Spain
Washington International Baltimore, Maryland, USA
Wattay Vientiane, Laos
Wellington New Zealand
Wichita Kansas, USA
Will Rogers Oklahoma City, Oklahoma, USA
Winnipeg International Manitoba, Canada
Yoff Dakar, Senegal
Yundam Banjul, Gambia
Zakynthos Greece
Zia International Dhaka, Bangladesh
Zürich Switzerland

AIRLINE DESIGNATORS

Code	Airline	Country
AA	American Airlines	USA
AC	Air Canada	Canada
AF	Air France	France
AH	Air Algerie	Algeria
AI	Air India	India
AM	Aeromexico	Mexico
AN	Ansett Australia	Australia
AQ	Aloha Airlines	Hawaii
AR	Aerolineas Argentinas	Argentina
AS	Alaska Airlines	USA
AT	Royal Air Maroc	Morocco
AV	Avianca	Colombia
AY	Finnair	Finland
AZ	Alitalia	Italy
BA	British Airways	UK
BB	Sansa	Costa Rica
BC	Brymon Airways	UK
BD	British Midland	UK
BG	Biman Bangladesh Airlines	Bangladesh
BH	Augusta Airways	Australia
BI	Royal Brunei Airlines	Brunei
BO	Bouraq Indonesia Airlines	Indonesia
BP	Air Botswana	Botswana
BU	Braathens SAFE	Norway
BW	BWIA International Trinidad and Tobego Airways	Trinidad
BY	Britannia Airways	UK
CA	Air China	China
CI	China Airlines	Taiwan
CM	COPA (Compania Panamena de Aviación)	Panama
CO	Continental Airlines	USA
CO	Air Micronesia	Mariana Is
CP	Canadian Airlines International	Canada
CU	Cubana	Cuba
CW	Air Marshall Islands	Marshall Is
CX	Cathay Pacific Airways	Hong Kong
CY	Cyprus Airways	Cyprus
DA	Dan-Air Services	UK
DI	Delta Air Regionalflug	Germany
DL	Delta Air Lines	USA
DO	Dominicana De Aviación	Dominican Republic
DS	Air Senegal	Senegal
DT	TAAG-Angola Airlines	Angola
DX	Danair	Denmark
DY	Alyemda-Democratic Yemen Airlines	Republic of Yemen

AIRLINE DESIGNATORS (cont.)

Code	Airline	Country
EI	Aer Lingus	Ireland
EK	Emirates	United Arab Emirates
ET	Ethiopian Airlines	Ethiopia
EU	Ecuatoriana	Ecuador
EW	Eastwest Airlines	Australia
EX	A/S Norving	Norway
FF	Tower Air	USA
FG	Afriana Afgan Airlines	Afghanistan
FI	Icelandair	Iceland
FJ	Air Pacific	Fiji
FO	Western New South Wales Airlines	Australia
FR	Ryanair	Ireland
FU	Air Littoral	France
GA	Garuda Indonesia	Indonesia
GC	Lina Congo	Congo
GF	Gulf Air	Bahrain
GH	Ghana Airways	Ghana
GI	Air Guinée	Guinea
GL	Gronlandsfly	Greenland
GN	Air Gabon	Gabon
GR	Aurigny Air Services	Channel Is
GT	GB Airways	Gibraltar
GY	Guyana Airways	Guyana
HA	Hawaiian Airlines	USA
HM	Air Seychelles	Seychelles
HP	America West Airlines	USA
HV	Transavia Airlines	Netherlands
IB	Iberia	Spain
IC	Indian Airlines	India
IE	Solomon Airlines	Solomon Is
IP	Airlines of Tasmania	Australia
IR	Iran Air	Iran
IY	Yemenia Yemen Airways	Yemen Arab Republic
JE	Manx Airlines	Isle of Man
JG	Swedair	Sweden
JL	Japan Airlines	Japan
JM	Air Jamaica	Jamaica
JP	Adria Airways	Yugoslavia
JQ	Trans Jamaica Airlines	Jamaica
JS	Chosonminhang Korean Airways	DPR of Korea
JU	JAT (Jugoslovenski Aerotransport)	Yugoslavia
JY	Jersey European Airways	Channel Is
KA	Dragonair	Hong Kong
KE	Korean Air	Rep. of Korea
KH	Kyrnair	Corsica
KL	KLM	Netherlands
KM	Air Malta	Malta
KP	Flitestar	South Africa
KQ	Kenya Airways	Kenya
KU	Kuwait Airways	Kuwait
KV	Transkei Airways	South Africa
LA	LAN-Chile	Chile
LC	Loganair	UK
LE	Link Airways	South Africa
LF	Linjeflyg	Sweden
LG	Luxair	Luxembourg
LH	Lufthansa	Germany
LJ	Sierra National Airlines	Sierra Leone
LL	Bell-Air	New Zealand
LM	ALM (Antillean Airlines)	Netherlands Antilles
LN	Jamahiriya Libyan Arab Airlines	Libya
LO	LOT-Polish Airlines	Poland
LR	LACSA	Costa Rica
LT	LTU (Lufttransport-Unternehmen GMBH)	Germany
LU	Theron Airways	South Africa
LX	Crossair	Switzerland
LY	El Al Israel Airlines	Israel
MA	Malev	Hungary
MD	Air Madagascar	Madagascar
ME	Middle East Airlines	Lebanon
MH	Malaysian Airlines	Malaysia
MK	Air Mauritius	Mauritius
MN	Commercial Airways	South Africa
MR	Air Mauritanie	Mauritania
MS	Egyptair	Egypt
MV	Ansett WA	Australia
MX	Mexicana	Mexico
NG	Lauda Air	Austria
NH	All Nippon Airways	Japan
NJ	Namakwaland Ludgiens	South Africa
NM	Mount Cook Airlines	New Zealand
NN	Air Martinique	Martinique
NO	Aus-Air	Australia
NR	Norontair	Canada
NS	NFD	Germany
NU	Southwest Airlines	Japan
NV	Northwest Territorial Airways	Canada
NW	Northwest Airlines	USA
NX	Nationair Canada	Canada
NZ	Air New Zealand	New Zealand
OA	Olympic Airways	Greece
OG	Air Guadeloupe	French W Indies
OK	Czechoslovak Airlines	Czechoslovakia
OM	Air Mongol-MIAT	Mongolian P R
ON	Air Nauru	Australia
OO	Skywest Airlines	Australia
OR	Air Comores	Comoros

AIRLINE DESIGNATORS (cont.)

Code	Airline	Country
OS	Austrian Airlines	Austria
PB	Air Burundi	Burundi
PC	Fiji Air	Fiji
PK	Pakistan International Airlines	Pakistan
PL	Aeroperu	Peru
PR	Philippine Airlines	Philippines
PU	Pluna (Primerias Lineas Uruguayas de Navegación Aerea)	Uruguay
PX	Air Niugini	Papua New Guinea
PY	Surinam Airways	Suriname
PZ	LAP (Lineas Aereas Paraguayas)	Paraguay
QC	Air Zaire	Zaire
QF	Qantas Airways	Australia
QL	Lesotho Airways	Lesotho
QM	Air Malawi	Malawi
QU	Uganda Airlines	Uganda
QV	Lao Aviation	Laos
QX	Horizon Air	USA
QZ	Zambia Airways	Zambia
RA	Royal Nepal Airlines	Nepal
RB	Syrian Arab Airlines	Syria
RG	Varig	Brazil
RJ	Royal Jordanian	Jordan
RK	Air Afrique	Côte d'Ivoire
RL	Aeronica	Nicaragua
RO	Tarom	Romania
RR	Royal Air Force	UK
RY	Air Rwanda	Rwanda
SA	South African Airways	South Africa
SB	Air Caledonie International	New Caledonia
SC	Cruzeiro	Brazil
SD	Sudan Airways	Sudan
SH	Sahsa (Servicio Aero de Honduras)	Honduras
SJ	Southern Air	New Zealand
SK	SAS (Scandinavian Airlines)	Sweden
SM	Aberdeen Airways	UK
SN	Sabena Belgian World Airlines	Belgium
SQ	Singapore Airlines	Singapore
SR	Swissair	Switzerland
SU	Aeroflot	Russia
SV	Saudia	Saudi Arabia
SW	Air Namibia	Namibia
TC	Air Tanzania	Tanzania
TG	Thai Airways International	Thailand
TK	Turkish Airlines	Turkey
TM	LAM (Linhas Aereas de Moçambique)	Mozambique
TN	Australian Airlines	Australia
TP	TAP Air Portugal	Portugal
TR	Transbrasil S/A Linhas Aereas	Brazil
TU	Tunis Air	Tunisia
TW	TWA (Trans World Airlines)	USA
UA	United Airlines	USA
UC	Ladeco	Chile
UK	Air UK	UK
UL	Air Lanka	Sri Lanka
UM	Air Zimbabwe	Zimbabwe
UN	Eastern Australia Airlines	Australia
UP	Bahamasair	Bahamas
US	USAir	USA
UT	UTA (Union de Transports Aériens)	France
UY	Cameroon Airlines	Cameroon
VA	VIASA (Venezolana Internacional de Aviación)	Venezuela
VB	Birmingham European Airways	UK
VE	Avensa	Venezuela
VH	Air Burkina	Burkina Faso
VK	Air Tungaru	Republic of Kiribati
VN	Vietnam Airlines	Vietnam
VO	Tyrolean Airways	Austria
VP	VASP (Viacão Aèrea São Paulo)	Brazil
VR	Transportes Aereos de Cabo Verde	Cape Verde Is
VS	Virgin Atlantic Airways	UK
VT	Air Tahiti	Tahiti
VU	Air Ivoire	Côte d'Ivoire
VX	Aces (Aerolineas Centrales de Colombia)	Colombia
WI	Rottnest Airbus	Australia
WJ	Labrador Airways	Canada
WN	Southwest Airlines	USA
WR	Royal Tongan Airlines	Tonga
WT	Nigeria Airways	Nigeria
WX	Ansett Express	Australia
WY	Oman Aviation Services	Oman
YK	Cyprus Turkish Airlines	Cyprus
YN	Air Creebec	Canada
YP	Aero Lloyd	Germany
YU	Dominair	Dominican Republic
YZ	Transportes Aereos Da Guiné-Bissau	Guinea Bissau
ZA	Zas Airline of Egypt	Egypt
ZB	Monarch Airlines	UK
ZC	Royal Swazi National Airways	Swaziland
ZP	Virgin Air	Virgin Is
ZQ	Ansett New Zealand	New Zealand
ZX	Air BC	Canada

AIR DISTANCES

Air distances between some major cities, given in statute miles. To convert to kilometres, multiply number given by 1.6093.

*Shortest route.

	Amsterdam	Anchorage	Beijing	Buenos Aires	Cairo	Chicago	Delhi	Hong Kong	Honolulu	Istanbul	Johannesburg	Lagos	London	Los Angeles	Mexico City	Montreal	Moscow	Nairobi	Paris	Perth	Rome	Santiago	Sydney	Tokyo
Anchorage	4475																							
Beijing	6566	4756																						
Buenos Aires	7153	8329	12000																					
Cairo	2042	6059	6685	7468																				
Chicago	4109	28	7599	5587	6135																			
Delhi	3985	8925	2368	8340	2753	8119																		
Hong Kong	5926	5063	1235	3124	5098	7827	2345																	
Honolulu	8368	2780	6778	8693	9439	4246	7888	5543																
Istanbul	1373	6024	4763	7783	764	5502	2833	5998	9547															
Johannesburg	5606	1042	10108	5725	4012	8705	6765	6728	12892	4776														
Lagos	3161	7587	8030	4832	2443	7065	5196	7541	10367	3207	2854													
London	217	4472	5054	6985	2187	3956	4169	5979	7252	1552	5640	3115												
Los Angeles	5559	2333	6349	6140	7589	1746	8717	7231	2553	6994	10443	7716	5442											
Mexico City	5724	3751	7912	4592	7730	1687	9806	8794	4116	7255	10070	7343	5703	1563										
Montreal	3422	3100	7557	5640	5431	737	7421	8564	4923	4795	8322	5595	3252	2482	2307									
Moscow	1338	4291	3604	8382	1790	5500	2698	4839	8802	1089	6280	4462	1550	6992	6700	4393								
Nairobi	4148	8714	8888	7427	2203	8177	4956	7301	11498	2967	1809	2377	4246	9688	9949	7498	3951							
Paris	261	4683	5108	6892	1995	4140	4089	5987	7463	1394	5422	2922	220	5633	5714	3434	1540	4031						
Perth	9118	8368	4987	9734	7766	11281	5013	3752	7115	7846	5564	10209	9246	9535	11098	12402	8355	7373	12587					
Rome	809	5258	5306	6931	1329	4828	3679	5773	8150	852	4802	2497	898	6340	6601	5431	1478	3349	688	8309				
Santiago	7714	7919	13622	710	8029	5328	12715	3733	8147	10109	5738	6042	8568	5594	4168	5551	10118	7547	461	15129	7548			
Sydney	1039	8522	5689	7760	9196	9324	6495	4586	5078	9883	7601	11700	10565	7498	9061	9980	9425	9410	10150	2037	10149	13092		
Tokyo	6006*	3443	1313	13100	6362	6286	3656	1807	3831	5757	8535	9130*	6218	5451	7014	6913	4668	8565	6208*	4925	6146	11049	4640	
Washington	3854	3430	7930	6097	5859	590	7841	8385	4822	5347	8199	5472	3672	2294	1871	493	4884	7918	3843	11829	4495	5061	9792	6763

FLYING TIMES

Approximate flying times between some major cities. Timings quoted (in hours and minutes) are for 'flying time' only. In many cases in order to travel between two points chosen, it is necessary to change aircraft one or more times. Time between flights has not been included.

	Amsterdam	Anchorage	Beijing	Buenos Aires	Cairo	Chicago	Delhi	Hong Kong	Honolulu	Istanbul	Johannesburg	Lagos	London	Los Angeles	Mexico City	Montreal	Moscow	Nairobi	Paris	Perth	Rome	Santiago	Sydney	Tokyo
Anchorage	9.00																							
Beijing	16.50	11.45																						
Buenos Aires	17.45	10.48	28.31																					
Cairo	4.20	13.20	13.15	20.40																				
Chicago	8.35	5.44	15.15	15.40	18.40																			
Delhi	8.15	16.50	6 40	26.20	7.00	20.05																		
Hong Kong	15.15	11.40	3.00	29.35	10.55	17.05	6.05																	
Honolulu	16.42	5.45	10.55	19.00	22.50	9.25	16.50	13.05																
Istanbul	3.15	12.15	15.40	18.45	2.00	12.20	7.35	17.35	21.05															
Johannesburg	13.15	19.50	20.10	12.30	8.55	21.40	23.45	14.55	30.25	16.30														
Lagos	6.40	14.55	22.35	9.55	8.20	14.55	14.55	22.30	23.40	8.05	6.55													
London	1.05	8.30	18.05	16.35	5.35	8.30	10.35	16.05	17.15	3.50	13.10	6.25												
Los Angeles	11.15	6.13	15.25	13.45	21.00	5.00	19.30	15.50	5.15	14.50	24.10	17.25	11.00											
Mexico City	12.27	10.49	18.45	10.25	16.47	5.15	20.42	19.10	8.35	15.42	25.42	19.07	14.35	3.20										
Montreal	7.40	7.91	27.30	16.00	12.35	2.20	17.35	23.05	12.50	10.15	20.10	13.25	7.00	6.40	4.45									
Moscow	3.15	12.15	8.40	22.05	5.25	12.15	7.35	18.00	21.00	4.40	13.30	10.10	3.45	14.45	18.10	10.45								
Nairobi	8.15	17.00	16.00	24.55	4.55	17.00	10.45	12.45	25.45	7.15	3.45	6.20	8.30	19.30	20.42	15.30	12.50							
Paris	1.10	9.00	16.35	15.35	5.05	9.00	10.45	16.40	18.05	3.10	15.50	7.45	1.05	12.50	13.25	6.25	4.00	9.20						
Perth	20.35	17.25	11.15	25.20	17.10	23.00	9.30	8.15	17.25	15.25	14.20	25.55	19.30	19.30	22.50	26.30	19.40	23.00	21.40					
Rome	2.20	12.00	16.10	14.40	3.25	11.35	8.50	15.10	19.13	2.35	12.25	6.55	2.25	14.35	5.35	8.10	4.10	7.20	1.55	20.00				
Santiago	20.50	19.13	22.34	2.10	25.10	17.15	29.05	19.15	8.35	21.00	19.55	24.25	21.55	16.00	12.00	14.50	24.05	29.05	19.45	26.00	18.50			
Sydney	23.05	16.35	16.15	20.45	17.20	21 10	13.50	10.35	11.50	18.40	31.50	28.35	21.55	18.10	18.05	24.50	19.40	31.35	25.05	4.35	23.50	24.30		
Tokyo	11.40	7.20	3.50	28.30	19.40	12.55	9.45	4.20	7.05	14.05	25.00	18.40	11.50	11.55	16.25	18.55	9.25	19.55	16.45	10.05	17.40	27.55	9.15	
Washington	8.55	7.25	25.50	11.00	14.20	1.45	20.10	24.15	10.55	11.25	21.20	14.45	8.10	5.25	7.50	2.50	12.30	17.10	9.25	22.45	12.40	17.40	23.35	12.40

DEEPWATER PORTS OF THE WORLD

Aalborg Denmark
Aarhus Denmark
Abadan Iran
Aberdeen UK
Abidjan Ivory Coast
Abu Dhabi United Arab Emirates
Acajutla El Salvador
Acapulco Mexico
Adelaide Australia
Aden South Yemen
Agadir Morocco
Ajaccio Corsica
Alcudia Majorca
Alexandria Egypt
Algeciras Spain
Algiers Algeria
Alicante Spain
Almeria Spain
Amsterdam Netherlands
Anchorage USA
Ancona Italy
Annaba Algeria
Antofagasta Chile
Antwerp Belgium
Apia Samoa
Aqaba Jordan
Archangel Russia
Arica Chile
Ashdod Israel
Asuncion Paraguay
Auckland New Zealand
Aveiro Portugal
Aviles Spain

Bahia Blanca Argentina
Balboa Panama
Baltimore USA
Bandar Abbas Iran
Bangkok Thailand
Banjul Gambia
Barcelona Spain
Bari Italy
Barranquilla Colombia
Basrah Iraq
Beira Mozambique
Beirut Lebanon
Belem Brazil
Belfast UK
Belize City Belize
Benghazi Libya
Bergen Norway
Bilbao Spain
Bissau Guinea-Bissau
Bizerta Tunisia
Bombay India
Bordeaux France
Boston USA
Boulogne France
Bourgas Bulgaria
Brazzaville Congo
Bremen Germany
Brest France
Bridgetown Barbados
Brindisi Italy
Brisbane Australia
Bristol UK
Buena Ventura Colombia
Buenos Aires Argentina
Buffalo USA
Busan South Korea

Cabinda Angola
Cadiz Spain
Caen France
Cagliari Sardinia
Calabar Nigeria
Calais France
Calcutta India
Caldera Costa Rica
Calicut India
Callao Peru
Cape Town South Africa
Cardiff UK
Cartagena Colombia
Cartagena Spain
Casablanca Morocco
Catania Sicily
Cayenne French Guiana
Cebu Philippines
Charleston USA
Cherbourg France
Chiba Japan
Chicago USA
Chittagong Bangladesh
Cienfuegos Cuba
Cleveland USA
Coatzacoalcos Mexico
Cochin India
Cologne Germany
Colombo Sri Lanka
Conakry Guinea
Constanta Romania
Copenhagen Denmark
Corinto Nicaragua
Cork Republic of Ireland
Corunna Spain
Cotonou Benin

Dakar Senegal
Dalian China
Dammam Saudi Arabia
Dampier Australia
Dar es Salaam Tanzania
Darwin Australia
Davao Philippines
Detroit USA
Dieppe France
Djibouti Djibouti
Doha Qatar
Dordrecht Netherlands
Douala Cameroon
Douglas Isle of Man
Dover UK
Dubai United Arab Emirates
Dublin Republic of Ireland
Dubrovnik Yugoslavia
Duisburg Germany
Duluth USA
Dundee UK
Dunedin New Zealand
Dunkirk France
Durban South Africa
Durres Albania

East London South Africa
Eilat Israel
Emden Germany
Esbjerg Denmark

Famagusta Cyprus
Faro Portugal
Felixstowe UK
Flensburg Germany
Flushing Netherlands
Folkestone UK
Fortaleza Brazil
Fort-de-France Martinique
Frankfurt Germany
Fredericia Denmark
Frederikshavn Denmark
Fredrikstad Norway
Freeport Bahamas
Freeport USA
Freetown Sierra Leone
Fremantle Australia
Funchal Madeira

Galveston USA
Galway Republic of Ireland
Gateshead UK

DEEPWATER PORTS OF THE WORLD (cont.)

Gavle Sweden
Gdansk Poland
Gdynia Poland
Geelong Australia
Genoa Italy
Georgetown Cayman Is
Georgetown Guyana
Ghent Belgium
Gibraltar Gibraltar
Gijon Spain
Glasgow UK
Godthaab Greenland
Goole UK
Gothenburg Sweden
Grangemouth UK
Gravesend UK
Great Yarmouth UK
Greenock UK
Grimsby UK
Guayaquil Ecuador

Haifa Israel
Hakodate Japan
Halifax Canada
Halmstad Sweden
Hamburg Germany
Hamilton Bermuda
Hamilton Canada
Harstad Norway
Hartlepool UK
Harwich UK
Havana Cuba
Hay Point Australia
Helsingborg Sweden
Helsinki Finland
Hiroshima Japan
Hobart Australia
Ho Chi Minh City Vietnam
Hodeida Yemen Arab Republic
Holyhead UK
Hong Kong Hong Kong
Honiari Solomon Is
Honolulu Hawaian Is
Houston USA
Hull UK

Ibiza Ibiza
Inchon South Korea
Iskenderun Turkey
Istanbul Turkey
Izmir Turkey

Jacksonville USA
Jakarta Indonesia
Jarrow UK
Jeddah Saudi Arabia

Kagoshima Japan
Kalmar Sweden
Kandla India
Kaohsiung Taiwan
Karachi Pakistan
Kawasaki Japan
Khulna Bangladesh
Kiel Germany
Kingston Jamaica
Kirkcaldy UK
Kitakyushu Japan
Klaipeda Lithuania
Kobe Japan
Kompong Som Cambodia
Koper Yugoslavia
Kota Kinabalu Malaysia
Kristiansand Norway
Kuching Malaysia
Kushiro Japan
Kuwait Kuwait

Lagos Nigeria
La Guaira Venezuela
Langesund Norway
La Plata Argentina
Larnaca Cyprus
Larne UK
Las Palmas Grand Canary
La Spezia Italy
Lattakia Syria
La Union El Salvador
Le Havre France
Leith UK
Libreville Gabon
Liege Belgium
Limassol Cyprus
Limerick Republic of Ireland
Lisbon Portugal
Liverpool UK
Livingstone Guatemala
Livorno Italy
Lobito Angola
London UK
Long Beach USA
Los Angeles USA
Lowestoft UK
Luanda Angola
Lubeck Germany
Luda China

Madras India
Malaga Spain
Malmo Sweden
Manchester UK
Manila Philippines
Mannheim Germany
Manzanillo Mexico
Maputo Mozambique
Mar del Plata Argentina
Maracaibo Venezuela
Mariehamn Finland
Marsala Sicily
Marseilles France
Masan South Korea
Matanzas Cuba
Melbourne Australia
Mersin Turkey
Messina Sicily
Miami USA
Middlesbrough UK
Milwaukee USA
Mina Qaboos Oman
Mina Sulman Bahrain
Mindelo Cape Verde
Mizushima Japan
Mobile USA
Mogadishu Somalia
Mombasa Kenya
Monrovia Liberia
Montego Bay Jamaica
Montevideo Uruguay
Montreal Canada
Mormugao India
Moulmein Burma
Murmansk Russia

Nacala Mozambique
Nagasaki Japan
Nagoya Japan
Nampo North Korea
Nantes France
Napier New Zealand
Naples Italy
Narvik Norway
Nassau Bahamas
Natal Brazil
Nelson New Zealand
New Amsterdam Guyana
Newcastle Australia
Newcastle UK
New Haven USA
New Mangalore India
New Orleans USA

DEEPWATER PORTS OF THE WORLD (cont.)

New Plymouth New Zealand
Newport UK
New York USA
Nice France
Nouakchott Mauritania
Noumea New Caledonia
Novorossiysk Russia
Nukualofa Tonga
Nyborg Denmark

Oakland USA
Odense Denmark
Odessa Ukraine
Oporto Portugal
Oran Algeria
Osaka Japan
Oslo Norway
Ostend Belgium
Oulu Finland

Pago Pago Samoa
Palermo Sicily
Palma Majorca
Palm Beach USA
Panama Canal Panama
Papeete Tahiti
Paradip India
Paramaribo Suriname
Paranagua Brazil
Paris France
Pasajes Spain
Pasir Gudang Malaysia
Penang Malaysia
Philadelphia USA
Phnom-Penh Cambodia
Piraeus Greece
Plymouth UK
Point-a-Pitre Guadeloupe
Pointe-Noire Congo
Pondicherry India
Ponta Delgada Azores
Poole UK
Port-au-Prince Haiti
Port Cartier Canada
Port Elizabeth South Africa
Port Georgetown Guyana
Port Gentil Gabon
Port Harcourt Nigeria
Port Hedland Australia
Port Kelang Malaysia
Port Kembla Australia
Portland USA
Port Limon Costa Rica
Port Louis Mauritius
Port Moresby Papua New Guinea
Port of Spain Trinidad
Port Said Egypt
Port Sudan Sudan
Port Talbot UK
Port Victoria Seychelles
Porto Alegre Brazil
Portsmouth UK
Prince Rupert Canada
Providence USA
Puerto Cortes Honduras
Pula Yugoslavia
Punta Arenas Chile

Quebec Canada

Ramsgate UK
Rangoon Burma
Ravenna Italy
Recife Brazil
Reykjavik Iceland
Richards Bay South Africa
Richmond USA
Riga USSR
Rijeka Yugoslavia
Rio de Janeiro Brazil
Rio Grande Brazil
Rosaria Argentina
Rostock Germany
Rotterdam Netherlands
Rouen France

Sacramento USA
Safi Morocco
Saint George's Grenada
Saint Helier Jersey
Saint John Canada (New Brunswick)
Saint John's Antigua
Saint John's Canada (Newfoundland)
Saint Malo France
Saint Nazaire France
Saint Petersburg Russia
Sakai Japan
Salerno Italy
Salina Cruz Mexico
Salonica Greece
Salvador Brazil
Samsun Turkey
San Diego USA
San Francisco USA
San Jose Guatemala
San Juan Puerto Rico
San Juan del Sur Nicaragua
San Lorenzo Argentina
San Pedro Ivory Coast
San Remo Italy
Santa Cruz de Tenerife Tenerife
Santa Fe Argentina
Santa Marta Colombia
Santander Spain
Santiago de Cuba Cuba
Santo Domingo Dominican Republic
Santos Brazil
São Tomé São Tomé
Sasebo Japan
Sassandra Ivory Coast
Savannah USA
Savona Italy
Seattle USA
Seville Spain
Sfax Tunisia
Shanghai China
Shimizu Japan
Singapore Singapore
Sitra Bahrain
Sittwe Burma
Sousse Tunisia
Southampton UK
Split Yugoslavia
Stavanger Norway
Stockholm Sweden
Stockton USA
Stralsund Germany
Suez Egypt
Sunderland UK
Sundsvall Sweden
Surabaya Indonesia
Suva Fiji
Swansea UK
Sydney Australia
Sydney Canada
Syracuse Sicily
Szczecin Poland

Tacoma USA
Takamatsu Japan
Tampa USA
Tampico Mexico
Tanga Tanzania
Tangier Morocco
Taranto Italy
Tarragona Spain
Tauranga New Zealand

DEEPWATER PORTS OF THE WORLD (cont.)

Three Rivers (Trois Rivières) Canada
Thunder Bay Canada
Timaru New Zealand
Tianjin China
Toamasina Madagascar
Tokyo Japan
Toledo USA
Toronto Canada
Torshavn Faroes
Toulon France
Townsville Australia
Toyama Japan
Trebizond Turkey
Trieste Italy
Tripoli Lebanon
Tripoli Libya
Trondheim Norway
Tunis Tunisia
Turku Finland
Tuticorin India

Ulsan South Korea

Vaasa Finland
Valencia Spain
Valetta Malta
Valparaiso Chile
Vancouver Canada
Varna Bulgaria
Venice Italy
Velsen Netherlands
Veracruz Mexico
Vigo Spain
Visakhapatnam India
Vitoria Brazil
Vlaardingen Netherlands

Wellington New Zealand
Willemstad Netherlands Antilles
Wilmington USA

Xingang China

Yokohama Japan

Zamboanga Philippines
Zanzibar Tanzania
Zeebrugge Belgium
Zhdanov Ukraine

INTERNATIONAL E-ROAD NETWORK ('Euroroutes')

Reference and intermediate roads (class A roads) have two-digit numbers; branch, link, and connecting roads (class B roads, not listed here), have three-digit numbers.

North-South orientated reference roads have two-digit odd numbers ending in the figure 5, and increasing from west to east. East-West orientated roads have two-digit even numbers ending in the figure 0, and increasing from north to south.

Intermediate roads have two-digit odd numbers (for N-S roads) or two-digit even numbers (for E-W roads) falling within the numbers of the reference roads between which they are located.

Only a selection of the towns and cities linked by E-roads are given here.

[···] indicates a sea crossing.

West-East orientation
Reference roads

E10 Narvik — Kiruna — Luleå
E20 Shannon — Dublin ··· Liverpool — Hull ··· Esbjerg — Nyborg ··· Korsør-Køge — Copenhagen ··· Malmö — Stockholm ··· Tallin — Leningrad
E30 Cork — Rosslare ··· Fishguard — London — Felixstowe ··· Hook of Holland — Utrecht — Hanover — Berlin — Warsaw — Smolensk — Moscow
E40 Calais — Brussels — Aachen — Cologne — Dresden — Krakow — Kiev — Rostov na Donu
E50 Brest — Paris — Metz — Nurenberg — Prague — Mukačevo
E60 Brest — Tours — Besançon — Basle — Innsbruck — Vienna — Budapest — Bucharest — Constanţa
E70 La Coruña — Bilbao — Bordeaux — Lyon — Torino — Verona — Trieste — Zagreb — Belgrade — Bucharest — Varna
E80 Lisbon — Coimbra — Salamanca — Pau — Toulouse — Nice — Genoa — Rome — Pescara ··· Dubrovnik — Sofia — Istanbul — Erzincan — Iran
E90 Lisbon — Madrid — Barcelona ··· Mazara del Vallo — Messina ··· Reggio di Calabria — Brindisi ··· Igoumenitsa — Thessaloniki — Gelibolu ··· Lapseki — Ankara — Iraq

Intermediate roads

E06 Olderfjord—Kirkenes
E12 Mo i Rana — Umeå ··· Vaasa — Helsinki
E14 Trondheim—Sundsvall
E16 Londonderry — Belfast ··· Glasgow — Edinburgh
E18 Craigavon — Larne ··· Stranraer —

INTERNATIONAL E-ROAD NETWORK ('Euroroutes')

Intermediate roads (cont.)

Newcastle ··· Stavanger — Oslo — Stockholm — Kappelskär ··· Mariehamn ··· Turku — Helsinki — Leningrad
E22 Holyhead — Manchester — Immingham ··· Amsterdam — Hamburg — Sassnitz ··· Trelleborg — Norrköping
E24 Birmingham—Ipswich
E26 Hamburg—Berlin
E28 Berlin—Gdańsk
E32 Colchester—Harwich
E34 Antwerp—Bad Oeynhausen
E36 Berlin—Legnica
E42 Dunkirk—Aschaffenburg
E44 Le Havre — Luxembourg — Giessen
E46 Cherbourg—Liège
E48 Schweinfurt—Prague
E52 Strasbourg—Salzburg
E54 Paris—Basle—Munich
E56 Nuremberg—Sattledt
E58 Vienna—Bratislava
E62 Nantes—Geneva—Tortona
E64 Turin—Brescia
E66 Fortezza—Székesfehérvár
E68 Szeged—Braşov
E72 Bordeaux—Toulouse
E74 Nice—Alessandria
E76 Migliarino—Florence
E78 Grosseto—Fano
E82 Porto—Tordesillas
E84 Keşan—Silivri
E86 Krystalopigi—Yefira
E88 Ankara—Refahiye
E92 Igoumenitsa—Volos
E94 Corinth—Athens
E96 Izmir—Sivrihisar
E98 Topbogazi—Syria

North-South orientation

Reference roads

E05 Greenock — Birmingham — Southampton ··· Le Havre — Paris — Bordeaux — Madrid — Algeciras
E15 Inverness — Edinburgh — London — Dover ··· Calais — Paris — Lyon — Barcelona — Algeciras
E25 Hook of Holland — Luxembourg — Strasbourg — Basle — Geneva — Turin — Genoa
E35 Amsterdam — Cologne — Basle — Milan — Rome
E45 Gothenburg ··· Frederikshavn — Hamburg — Munich — Innsbruck — Bologna — Rome — Naples — Villa S Giovanni ··· Messina — Gela
E55 Kemi-Tornio — Stockholm — Helsingborg ··· Helsingør — Copenhagen — Gedser ··· Rostock — Berlin — Prague — Salzburg — Rimini — Brindisi ··· Igoumenitsa — Kalamata
E65 Malmö — Ystad ··· Świnoujście — Prague — Zagreb — Dubrovnik — Bitolj — Antirrion ··· Rion — Kalamata ··· Kissamos — Chania
E75 Karasjok — Helsinki ··· Gdańsk — Budapest — Belgrade — Athens ··· Chania — Sitia
E85 Černovcy — Bucharest — Alexandropouli
E95 Leningrad—Moscow—Yalta

Intermediate roads

E01 Larne — Dublin — Rosslare ··· La Coruña — Lisbon — Seville
E03 Cherbourg—La Rochelle
E07 Pau—Zaragoza
E09 Orléans—Barcelona
E11 Vierzon—Montpellier
E13 Doncaster—London
E17 Antwerp—Beaune
E19 Amsterdam—Brussels—Paris
E21 Metz—Geneva
E23 Metz—Lausanne
E27 Belfort—Aosta
E29 Cologne—Sarreguemines
E31 Rotterdam—Ludwigshafen
E33 Parma—La Spezie
E37 Bremen—Cologne
E39 Kristiansand—Aalborg
E41 Dortmund—Altdorf
E43 Würzburg—Bellinzona
E47 Nordkap — Oslo — Copenhagen — Rødby ··· Puttgarden — Lübeck
E49 Magdeburg—Vienna
E51 Berlin—Nuremberg
E53 Plzeň—Munich
E57 Sattledt—Ljubljana
E59 Prague—Zagreb
E61 Klagenfurt—Rijeka

INTERNATIONAL E-ROAD NETWORK ('Euroroutes')

Intermediate roads (cont.)

E63 Sodankylä — Naantali ··· Stockholm — Gothenburg
E67 Warsaw—Prague
E69 Tromsø—Tornio
E71 Košice—Budapest—Split
E73 Budapest—Metković
E77 Gdańsk—Budapest
E79 Oradea — Calafat ··· Vidín — Thessaloniki
E81 Halmeu—Piteśti
E83 Bjala—Sofia
E87 Tulcea — Eceabat ··· Çanakkale — Antalya
E89 Gerede—Ankara
E91 Toprakkale—Syria
E93 Orel—Odessa
E97 Trabzon—Aşkale
E99 Doğubeyazit—Ş Urfa

MAP OF EUROPE

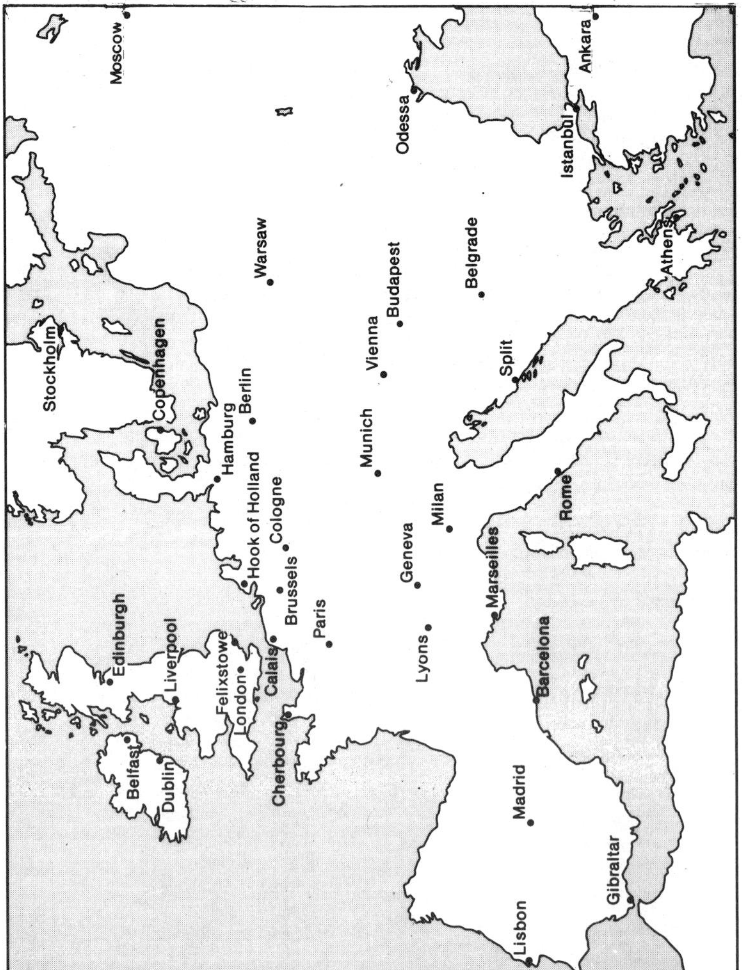

EUROPEAN ROAD DISTANCES

Road distances between some cities, given in kilometres.
To convert to statute miles, multiply number given by 0.6214

	Athens	Barcelona	Brussels	Calais	Cherbourg	Cologne	Copenhagen	Geneva	Gibraltar	Hamburg	Hook of Holland	Lisbon	Lyons	Madrid	Marseilles	Milan	Munich	Paris	Rome	Stockholm
Barcelona	3313																			
Brussels	2963	1318																		
Calais	3175	1326	204																	
Cherbourg	3339	1294	583	460																
Cologne	2762	1498	206	409	785															
Copenhagen	3276	2218	966	1136	1545	760														
Geneva	2610	803	677	747	853	1662	1418													
Gibraltar	4485	1172	2256	2224	2047	2436	3196	1975												
Hamburg	2977	2018	597	714	1115	460	460	1118	2897											
Hook of Holland	3030	1490	172	330	731	269	269	895	2428	550										
Lisbon	4532	1304	2084	2052	1827	2290	2971	1936	676	2671	2280									
Lyons	2753	645	690	739	789	714	1458	158	1817	1159	863	1778								
Madrid	3949	636	1558	1550	1347	1764	2498	1439	698	2198	1730	668	1281							
Marseilles	2865	521	1011	1059	1101	1035	1778	425	1693	1479	1183	1762	320	1157						
Milan	2282	1014	925	1077	1209	911	1537	328	2185	1238	1098	2250	328	1724	618					
Munich	2179	1365	747	977	1160	583	1104	591	2565	805	851	2507	724	2010	1109	331				
Paris	3000	1033	285	280	340	465	1176	513	1971	877	457	1799	471	1273	792	856	821			
Rome	817	1460	1511	1662	1794	1497	2050	995	2631	1751	1683	2700	1048	2097	1011	586	946	1476		
Stockholm	3927	2868	1616	1786	2196	1403	650	2068	3886	949	1500	3231	2108	3188	2428	2187	1754	1827	2707	
Vienna	1991	1802	1175	1381	1588	937	1455	1019	2974	1155	1205	2935	1157	2409	1363	898	428	1249	1209	2105

UK ROAD DISTANCES

Road distances between British centres are given in statute miles, using routes recommended by the Automobile Association based on the quickest travelling time. To convert to kilometres, multiply number given by 1.6093.

	Aberdeen	Birmingham	Bristol	Cambridge	Cardiff	Dover	Edinburgh	Exeter	Glasgow	Holyhead	Hull	Leeds	Liverpool	Manchester	Newcastle	Norwich	Nottingham	Oxford	Penzance	Plymouth	Shrewsbury	Southampton	Stranraer	York
Birmingham	430																							
Bristol	511	85																						
Cambridge	468	101	156																					
Cardiff	532	107	45	191																				
Dover	591	202	198	121	234																			
Edinburgh	130	293	373	337	395	457																		
Exeter	584	157	81	233	119	248	446																	
Glasgow	149	291	372	349	393	490	45	444																
Holyhead	457	151	232	246	209	347	325	305	319															
Hull	361	136	227	157	246	278	229	297	245	215														
Leeds	336	115	216	143	236	265	205	288	215	163	59													
Liverpool	361	98	178	195	200	295	222	250	220	104	126	72												
Manchester	354	88	167	153	188	283	218	239	214	123	97	43	34											
Newcastle	239	198	291	224	311	348	107	361	150	260	121	91	170	141										
Norwich	501	161	217	62	252	167	365	295	379	309	153	173	232	183	258									
Nottingham	402	59	151	82	170	202	268	222	281	174	92	73	107	71	156	123								
Oxford	497	63	74	82	109	148	361	152	354	218	188	171	164	153	253	144	104							
Penzance	696	272	195	346	232	362	561	112	559	419	411	401	366	355	477	407	336	265						
Plymouth	624	199	125	275	164	290	488	45	486	347	341	328	294	281	410	336	265	193	78					
Shrewsbury	412	48	128	142	110	243	276	201	272	104	164	116	64	69	216	205	85	113	315	242				
Southampton	571	128	75	133	123	155	437	114	436	296	253	235	241	227	319	192	171	67	227	155	190			
Stranraer	241	307	386	361	406	503	130	457	88	332	259	232	234	226	164	393	295	371	572	502	287	447		
York	325	128	221	153	241	274	191	291	208	190	38	24	100	71	83	185	86	185	406	340	144	252	228	
London	543	118	119	60	155	77	405	170	402	263	215	196	210	199	280	115	128	56	283	215	162	76	419	209

SCIENCE, ENGINEERING AND MEASUREMENT

SCIENTISTS

Airy, Sir George Biddell (1802–92) English astronomer and geophysicist, born Alnwick. Astronomer Royal (1835–81) who reorganized the Greenwich Observatory. Initiated measurement of Greenwich Mean Time, determined the mass of the Earth from gravity experiments in mines, and carried out extensive work in optics.

Alzheimer, Alois (1864–1915) German psychiatrist and neuropathologist, born Markbreit. Gave full clinical and pathological description of pre-senile dementia (Alzheimer's disease) (1907). Also made important contributions to the preparation of microscopical sections of brain tissue.

Ampère, André Marie (1775–1836) French mathematician and physicist, born Lyons. Laid the foundations of the science of electrodynamics. His name is given to the basic SI unit of electric current (ampere, amp).

Appleton, Sir Edward Victor (1892–1965) English physicist, born Bradford. Researched propagation of wireless waves, and discovered the existence of a layer of electrically charged particles in the upper atmosphere (the Appleton layer) which plays an essential role in radio communication. Received Nobel prize for physics (1947) for studies of Earth's atmosphere.

Archimedes (c.287–212 BC) Greek mathematician, born Syracuse. Discovered formulae for the areas and volumes of plane and solid geometrical figures using methods which anticipated theories of integration to be developed 1800 years later. Also founded the science of hydrostatics; in popular tradition remembered for the cry of 'Eureka' when he discovered the principle of upthrust on a floating body.

Aristotle (384–322 BC) Greek philosopher and scientist, born Stagira. One of the most influential figures in the history of Western thought and scientific tradition. Wrote enormous amounts on biology, zoology, physics and psychology.

Avogadro, Amedeo (1776–1856) Italian physicist, born Turin. Formulated the hypothesis (Avogadro's Law) that equal volumes of gas contain equal numbers of molecules, when at the same temperature and pressure.

Axelrod, Julius (1912–) American pharmacologist, born New York City. Discovered the substance which inhibits neural impulses, laying the basis for significant advances in the treatment of disorders such as schizophrenia. Joint winner of the 1970 Nobel prize for physiology or medicine.

Babbage, Charles (1791–1871) English mathematician, born Teignmouth. Attempted to build two calculating machines – the 'difference engine', to calculate logarithms and similar functions by repeated addition performed by trains of gear wheels, and the 'analytical engine', to perform much more varied calculations. The idea of the versatile mechanical computer was too ambitious to be realized by the mechanical devices available at the time, but Babbage is regarded as the pioneer of modern computers.

Bacon, Francis, Baron Verulam of Verulam, Viscount St Albans (1561–1626) English statesman and natural philosopher, born London. Creator of scientific induction; stressed the importance of experiment in interpreting nature, giving significant impetus to future scientific investigation.

Baird, John Logie (1888–1946) Scottish engineer, born Helensburgh. Gave first demonstration of a television image in 1926. Also researched radar and infrared television, and succeeded in producing 3-D and colour images (1944), as well as projection onto a screen and stereophonic sound.

Barnard, Christian Neethling (1922–) South African surgeon, born Beaufort West. Performed first successful heart transplant in December 1967 at Groote Schuur Hospital. Although the recipient died 18 days later from pneumonia, a second patient operated on in January 1968 survived for 594 days.

Beaufort, Sir Francis (1774–1857) Irish naval officer and hydrographer, born Navan, County Meath. Devised the Beaufort scale of wind force and a tabulated system of weather registration.

Becquerel, Antoine Henri (1852–1908) French physicist, born Paris. While researching fluorescence (the ability of substances to give off

SCIENTISTS (cont.)

visible light), discovered radioactivity in the form of rays emitted by uranium salts, leading to the beginnings of modern nuclear physics. For this he shared the 1903 Nobel prize for physics with Marie and Pierre Curie.

Bell, Alexander Graham (1847–1922) Scottish–American inventor, born Edinburgh. After researching and teaching methods in speech therapy and experimenting with various acoustical devices, produced the first intelligible telephonic transmission on 5 June 1875, and patented the telephone in 1876. Founded the Bell Telephone Company in 1877; other inventions include the photophone, the graphophone and the tetrahedral kite.

Bohr, Niels Henrik David (1885–1962) Danish physicist, born Copenhagen. Greatly extended the theory of atomic structure by explaining the spectrum of hydrogen by means of an atomic model and the quantum theory (1913). Awarded the Nobel prize for physics in 1922. Assisted in atom bomb research in America during World War II.

Boltzmann, Ludwig Eduard (1844–1906) Austrian physicist, born Vienna. Carried out important work on the kinetic theory of gases and established Boltzmann's law, or the principle of equipartition of energy.

Boyle, The Hon Robert (1627–91) Irish physicist and chemist, born Munster. One of the first members of the Royal Society. Carried out experiments on air, vacuum, combustion and respiration and in 1662 arrived at Boyle's law, which states that the pressure and volume of a gas are inversely proportional at constant temperature. Also researched alchemy and chemistry and was the first to prepare phosphorus.

Brahe, Tycho or **Tyge** (1546–1601) Danish astronomer, born Knudstrup, Sweden (then under Danish crown). After seeing the partial solar eclipse of 1569 became obsessed about astronomy. Accurately measured and compiled catalogues of the positions of stars, providing vital information for later astronomers and recorded unique observations of a new star in Cassiopeia in 1572 (a nova now known as Tycho's star).

Brunel, Isambard Kingdom (1806–59) English engineer and inventor, born Portsmouth. Helped to plan the Thames Tunnel and later planned the Clifton suspension bridge. Designed the first steamship to cross the Atlantic, the first ocean screw-steamer. In 1833 appointed engineer to the Great Western Railway and constructed all tunnels, bridges and viaducts on that line; also constructed and improved many docks.

Celsius, Anders (1701–44) Swedish astronomer, born Uppsala. Devised the centigrade, or 'Celsius', scale of temperature. Also advocated the introduction of the Gregorian calendar, and made observations of the aurora borealis, or northern lights.

Chadwick, Sir James (1891–1974) English physicist, born near Macclesfield. Studied radioactivity and as a result of the Curies' work, was able to confirm the existence of the neutron which Rutherford had postulated in 1920. Built Britain's first cyclotron in 1935 and assisted in atomic bomb research in America during World War II.

Copernicus, Nicolaus (1473–1543) Polish astronomer, born Toruń. Studied mathematics, optics, perspective and canon law before a varied career involving law, medicine and astronomy. Published theory in 1543 that the Sun is at the centre of the Universe; this was not initially accepted due to opposition from the Church which held that the Universe is Earth-centred.

Coulomb, Charles Augustin de (1736–1806) French physicist, born Angoulême. Experimented on friction, and invented the torsion balance for measuring the force of magnetic and electrical attraction. The unit of electric charge (coulomb) is named after him.

Crick, Francis Harry Compton (1916–) English biologist, born Northampton. Constructed a molecular model of the complex genetic material deoxyribonucleic acid (DNA). Later research on nucleic acids led to far-reaching discoveries concerning the genetic code. Joint winner of the Nobel prize for medicine and physiology in 1962.

Curie, Marie (originally **Manya**) née **Sklodowska** (1867–1934) Polish–French physicist, born Warsaw. After graduating from the Sorbonne worked on magnetism and radioactivity, isolating radium and polonium. Shared the Nobel prize for physics in 1903 with her husband Pierre Curie and Antoine Henri Becquerel. Became professor of physics at the Sorbonne in 1906; awarded the Nobel prize for chemistry in 1911.

Curie, Pierre (1859–1906) French chemist and physicist, born Paris. Carried out research on magnetism and radioactivity with his wife, Marie Curie, for which they were jointly awarded the Nobel prize for physics in 1903, with Antoine Henri Becquerel.

SCIENTISTS (cont.)

Cuvier, Georges (Léopold Chrétien Frédéric Dagobert) (1769–1832) French anatomist, born Montbéliard. Known as the father of comparative anatomy and palaeontology. Opponent of the Theory of Descent, and originated the natural system of animal classification. Linked comparative anatomy and palaeontology through studies of animal and fish fossils.

Dalton, John (1766–1844) English chemist, born Eaglesfield, near Cockermouth. Researched mixed gases, the force of steam, the elasticity of vapours and deduced the law of partial pressures, or Daltons's law. Also made important contributions in atomic theory.

Darwin, Charles Robert (1809–82) English naturalist, born Shrewsbury. Recommended as naturalist for a scientific survey of South American waters (1831–36) on HMS *Beagle* during which he made many geological and zoological discoveries which led him to speculate on the origin of species. In 1859 published theory of evolution in *The Origin of Species by Means of Natural Selection.*

Davy, Sir Humphry (1778–1829) English chemist, born Penzance. Experimented with newly-discovered gases, and discovered the anaesthetic effect of laughing gas. Discovered the new metals potassium, sodium, barium, strontium, calcium and magnesium. Also investigated volcanic action, devised safety lamps for use in mining and was important in promoting science within industry.

Delbrück, Max (1906–81) German–American biophysicist, born Berlin. Made significant contributions in the creation of bacterial and bacteriophage genetics, and in 1946 showed that viruses can recombine genetic material. Joint winner of the 1969 Nobel prize for physiology or medicine for his work in viral genetics.

Descartes, René (1596–1650) French philosopher and mathematician, born near Tours. Creator of analytical or coordinate geometry, also named after him as Cartesian geometry. Also theorized extensively in physics and physiology, and is regarded as the father of modern philosophy.

Dirac, Paul Adrien Maurice (1902–84) English mathematical physicist, born Bristol. Published complete mathematical formulation of the relativity theory of Albert Einstein after work on quantum mechanics. Joint winner of the Nobel prize for physics in 1933.

Doppler, Christian Johann (1803–53) Austrian physicist, born Salzburg. The Doppler effect, described in a paper in 1842, explains the increase and decrease of wave frequency observed when a wave source and the observer respectively approach or recede from one another.

Duchenne, Guillaume Benjamin Amand (1806–75) French physician, born Boulogne. Pioneer in electrophysiology and founder of electrotherapeutics. First to describe locomotor ataxia, in 1858.

Dulbecco, Renato (1914–) Italian–American biologist, born Catanzaro. Showed how certain viruses can transform some cells into a cancerous state, giving a valuable simple model system for which he shared the 1975 Nobel prize for physiology or medicine.

Edison, Thomas Alva (1847–1931) American inventor and physicist, born Milan, Ohio. Took out more than 1000 patents, including the gramophone (1877), the incandescent light bulb (1879) and an improved microphone for Bell's telephone. Also discovered thermionic emission, formerly called the Edison effect.

Ehrlich, Paul (1854–1915) German bacteriologist, born Strehlen (now Strzelin), Silesia. Pioneer in haematology and chemotherapy, synthesized salvarsan as a treatment for syphilis and propounded the side-chain theory in immunology. Joint winner of the 1908 Nobel prize for physiology or medicine.

Einstein, Albert (1879–1955) German–Swiss–American mathematical physicist, born Ulm, Bavaria. Achieved world fame through his special and general theories of relativity; also studied gases and discovered the photoelectric effect, for which he was awarded the Nobel prize in 1921.

Euler, Leonhard (1707–83) Swiss mathematician, born Basel. Published over 800 different books and papers on mathematics, physics and astronomy, introducing many new functions and carrying out important work in calculus. Introduced the notations *e* and *gp*, still used today. Also studied motion and celestial mechanics.

Eysenck, Hans Jurgen (1916–) German–British psychologist, born Berlin. Researched the variations in human personality and intelligence, and frequently championed the view that genetic factors are to a large extent responsible for psychological differences between people.

Fahrenheit, Gabriel Daniel (1686–1736) German physicist, born Danzig. Devised alcohol thermo-

SCIENTISTS (cont.)

meter (1709) and later invented the mercury thermometer (1714). Also devised the temperature scale named after him, and was the first to show that the boiling point of liquids varies at different atmospheric pressures.

Faraday, Michael (1791–1867) English chemist and physicist, born Grenoble. Discovered electromagnetic induction (1831), the laws of electrolysis (1833) and the rotation of polarized light by magnetism (1845). First to isolate benzene and to synthesize chlorocarbons.

Fermi, Enrico (1901–54) Italian–American nuclear physicist, born Rome. Published method of calculating atomic particles, and in 1943 succeeded in splitting the nuclei of uranium atoms, producing artificial radioactive substances. Awarded the 1938 Nobel prize for physics, and constructed the first American nuclear reactor at Chicago (1942). The element fermium was named after him.

Feynman, Richard Phillips (1918–88) American physicist, born New York. Made considerable theoretical advances in quantum electrodynamics, for which he was joint winner of the Nobel prize for physics in 1965. Involved in building the first atomic bomb during World War II.

Fleming, Sir Alexander (1881–1955) Scottish bacteriologist, born Loudoun, Ayrshire. First to use anti-typhoid vaccines on humans and pioneered the use of salvarsan to treat syphilis. In 1928 discovered penicillin by chance, for which he was joint winner of the 1945 Nobel prize for physiology or medicine.

Foucault, Jean Bernard Léon (1819–68) French physicist, born Paris. Determined the velocity of light by the revolving mirror method and proved that light travels more slowly in water than in air (1850). In 1851 by means of a freely suspended pendulum, he proved that the Earth rotates. In 1852 constructed the gyroscope and in 1857 the Foucault prism.

Frisch, Karl von (1886–1982) Austrian ethologist and zoologist, born Vienna. Developed ethology using field observation of animals combined with ingenious experiments. Showed that forager bees communicate information (on the location of food sources) in part by use of coded dances. Joint winner of the Nobel prize for physiology or medicine in 1973.

Gajdusek, Daniel Carleton (1923–) American virologist, born Yonkers, New York. Studied the origin and dissemination of infectious diseases amongst the Fore people of Papua New Guinea. Joint winner of the 1976 Nobel prize for physiology or medicine.

Galilei, Galileo, known as **Galileo** (1564–1642) Italian astronomer, mathematician and natural philosopher, born Pisa. Inferred the value of a pendulum for exact measurement of time, proved that all falling bodies, great or small, descend due to gravity at the same rate. Perfected the refracting telescope and pursued astronomical observations which revealed mountains and valleys on the Moon, four satellites of Jupiter and sunspots, and convinced him of the correctness of the Copernican theory. His advocation of the Copernican theory led to his imprisonment by the Inquisition; he remained under house arrest until his death.

Gauss, Carl Friedrich (1777–1855) German mathematician, astronomer and physicist, born Brunswick. Made significant new advances in number theory, studied errors of observation and devised the method of least squares. Also carried out much work on pure mathematics, studied the Earth's magnetism and was involved in the development of the magnetometer, as well as giving a mathematical theory of optical systems of lenses.

Geiger, Hans Wilhelm (1882–1945) German physicist, born Neustadt-an-der-Haart. Investigated beta-ray radioactivity and, with Walther Müller, devised a counter to measure it.

Halley, Edmond (1656–1742) English astronomer and mathematician, born London. Studied the Solar System and correctly predicted the return (in 1758, 1835 and 1910) of a comet that had been observed in 1583, and is now named after him. Also first to make a complete observation of the transit of Mercury, established the law connecting barometric pressure with heights above sea-level (on the basis of Boyle's law) and studied weather and magnetic variations of the Earth. Appointed Astronomer Royal in 1720.

Harvey, William (1578–1657) English physician, born Folkestone. Discovered the circulation of the blood.

Hawking, Stephen William (1942–) English theoretical physicist, born Oxford. Research on relativity led him to study gravitational singularities such as the 'big bang' where the Universe originated and 'black holes', which result from the death of stars. His book *A Brief History of Time* is a popular account of modern cosmology. Since the 1960s he has suffered from a highly disabling progressive neuromotor disease.

SCIENTISTS (cont.)

Heisenberg, Werner Karl (1901–76) German theoretical physicist, born Würzburg. Developed quantum mechanics and formulated the principle of indeterminacy (uncertainty principle). Awarded the 1932 Nobel prize for physics. In 1958, with Wolfgang Pauli, announced the formulation of a unified field theory.

Helmholtz, Hermann (Ludwig Ferdinand von) (1821–94) German physiologist and physicist, born Potsdam. Researched physiology of vision, the ear and the nervous system and well as making important contributions in fluid dynamics, studies of vibrations and the spectrum, and studies of the development of electric current within a galvanic battery.

Henle, Friedrich Gustav Jakob (1809–85) German anatomist, born Fürth. Discovered the tubules in the kidney which are named after him and wrote treatises on systematic anatomy.

Herschel, Sir John Frederick William (1792–1871) English astronomer, born Slough. Son of Sir William Herschel; continued his father's research and discovered 525 nebulae and clusters. Pioneered celestial photography and researched photoactive chemicals and the wave theory of light.

Herschel, Sir (Frederick) William (1738–1822) German–British astronomer, born Hanover. Made (1773–74) a reflecting telescope with which he discovered the planet Uranus in 1781. Also discovered satellites of Uranus and Saturn, the rotation of Saturn's rings and Saturn's rotation period. Researched binary stars, nebulae and the Milky Way.

Hertz, Heinrich Rudolph (1857–94) German physicist, born Hamburg. Confirmed James Clerk Maxwell's predictions in 1887 by his discovery of invisible electromagnetic waves, of the same fundamental form as light waves.

Hooke, Robert (1635–1703) English chemist, physicist and architect, born Freshwater, Isle of Wight. Anticipated the invention of the steam engine, formulated Hooke's Law of the extension an compression of elastic bodies, and anticipated Isaac Newton's inverse square law of gravitation. Constructed first Gregorian telescope and inferred rotation of Jupiter. Materially invented the microscope, the quadrant and a marine barometer.

Hubble, Edwin Powell (1889–1953) American astronomer, born Marshfield, Missouri. Demonstrated that some nebulae are independent galaxies, and in 1929 discovered galaxy 'redshift', that distant galaxies are receding from us and that the apparent speed of recession of a galaxy is proportional to its distance from us.

Hutton, James (1726–97) Scottish geologist, born Edinburgh. Formed the basis of modern geology with the Huttonian theory, emphasizing the igneous origin of many rocks and deprecating the assumption of causes other than those still seen at work.

Huxley, Thomas Henry (1825–95) English biologist, born Ealing. Assistant surgeon on surveying expedition to the South Seas (1846–50), during which he collected marine animal specimens; became foremost scientific supporter of Charles Darwin's theory of evolution. Also studied fossils and later turned to philosophy.

Huygens, Christiaan (1629–93) Dutch physicist, born The Hague. Made pendulum clock (1657) on Galileo's suggestion, and developed the doctrine of accelerated motion under gravity. Discovered the rings and fourth satellite of Saturn and the laws of collision of elastic bodies. In optics, first propounded the undulatory theory of light, and discovered polarization.

Jansky, Karl Guthe (1905–50) American radio engineer, born Norman, Oklahoma. Discovered astronomical radio sources by chance while investigating interference on short-wave radio telephone transmissions, initiating the science of radio astronomy. The SI unit of radio emission strength, the jansky, is named after him.

Jeans, Sir James Hopwood (1877–1946) English physicist and astronomer, born Ormskirk, near Southport. Made important contributions to the dynamical theory of gases, radiation, quantum theory and stellar evolution; best known for his role in popularizing physics and astronomy.

Joule, James Prescott (1818–89) English physicist, born Salford. Showed experimentally that heat is a form of energy and established the mechanical equivalent of heat; this became the basis for the theory of conservation of energy. With Lord Kelvin studied temperatures of gases and formulated the absolute scale of temperature.

Kant, Immanuel (1724–1804) German philosopher, born Königsberg, Prussia (now Kaliningrad, Russia). Researched astronomy and geophysics, and predicted the existence of the planet Uranus before its discovery. Philosophical works had enormous influence.

Katz, Sir Bernard (1911–) German–British biophysicist, born Leipzig. Discovered how the neural transmitter acetylcholine is released by

SCIENTISTS (cont.)

neural impulses. Joint winner of the 1970 Nobel prize for physiology or medicine.

Kelvin, William Thomson, 1st Baron (1824–1907) Irish–Scottish physicist and mathematician, born Belfast. Solved important problems in electrostatics, proposed the absolute, or Kelvin, temperature scale and established the second law of thermodynamics simultaneously with Rudolf Clausius. Also investigated geomagnetism and hydrodynamics, and invented innumerable instruments.

Kepler, Johann (1571–1630) German astronomer, born Weil der Stadt, Württemberg. Formulated laws of planetary motion describing elliptical orbits and forming the starting point of modern astronomy. Also made discoveries in optics, general physics and geometry.

Kirchhoff, Gustav Robert (1824–87) German physicist, born Königsberg. Carried out important research in electricity, heat, optics and spectrum analysis, his work leading to the discovery of caesium and rubidium (1859).

Krebs, Sir Hans Adolf (1900–81) German–British biochemist, born Hildesheim. Discovered the series of chemical reactions known as the urea cycle (1932). Joint winner of the 1953 Nobel prize for physiology or medicine for research into metabolic processes, particularly the 'Kreb's cycle'.

Lamarck, Jean (Baptiste Pierre Antoine de Monet) Chevalier de (1744–1829) French naturalist, born Bazentin. Made the basic distinction between vertebrates and invertebrates. On evolution he postulated that acquired characters can be inherited by later generations, preparing the way for the Darwinian theory of evolution.

Leibniz, Gottfried Wilhelm (1646–1716) German mathematician and philosopher, born Leipzig. Discovered calculus around the same time as Isaac Newton; also made original contribution in the fields of optics, mechanics, statistics, logic and probability, and laid the foundations of 18th-century philosophy.

Leishman, Sir William Boog (1865–1926) Scottish bacteriologist, born Glasgow. Discovered an effective vaccine for inoculation against typhoid and was first to discover the parasite of the disease kala-azar.

Linnaeus, Carolus (Carl von Linné) (1707–78) Swedish naturalist and physician, born Raceshult. Founder of modern scientific nomenclature for plants and animals.

Lorentz, Hendrik Antoon (1853–1928) Dutch physicist, born Arnhem. Carried out important work in electromagnetism; joint winner of the Nobel prize for physics in 1902 for explaining the effect whereby atomic spectral lines are split in the presence of magnetic fields. Also showed that current scientific controversy regarding the 'ether' could be resolved if moving bodies contract very slightly in the direction of motion; this result was later to emerge from Einstein's special theory of relativity.

Lorenz, Konrad Zacharias (1903–89) Austrian zoologist and ethologist, born Vienna. Regarded as the father of ethology, favouring the study of the instinctive behaviour of animals in the wild. In 1935 published observations on imprinting in young birds by which hatchlings 'learn' to recognize substitute parents, and argued that while aggressive behaviour in man is inborn, it may be channelled into other forms of activity, whereas in other animals it is purely survival-motivated.

Lyell, Sir Charles (1797–1875) Scottish geologist, born Kinnordy, Fife. Established the principle of uniformitarianism in geology, that geological changes have been gradual and produced by forces still at work, instead of including catastrophic changes as previously believed. His work significantly influenced Charles Darwin, although Lyell never accepted the theory of evolution by natural selection.

Mach, Ernst (1838–1916) Austrian physicist and philosopher, born Turas, Moravia. Carried out experimental work on projectiles and the flow of gases. His name has been given to the ratio of the speed of flow of a gas to the speed of sound (Mach number) and to the angle of a shock wave to the direction of motion (Mach angle).

Malpighi, Marcello (1628–94) Italian anatomist, born near Bologna. Discovered capillary blood vessels and made many pioneering discoveries in microscopic anatomy.

Marconi, (Marquis) Guglielmo (1874–1937) Italian physicist and inventor, born Bologna. Experimented in converting electromagnetic waves into electricity and achieved wireless telegraphy in 1895. In 1898 transmitted signals across the English Channel and in 1901 succeeded in sending Morse code signals across the Atlantic. Joint winner of the 1909 Nobel prize for physics. Later developed short-wave radio equipment and established a worldwide radio telegraph network for the British government.

Maxwell, James Clerk (1831–79) Scottish physicist, born Edinburgh. Produced mathematical

SCIENTISTS (cont.)

theory of electromagnetism and identified light as electromagnetic radiation. Also suggested that invisible electromagnetic waves could be generated in a laboratory, as later carried out by Hertz. Other research included the kinetic theory of gases, the nature of Saturn's rings, colour perception and colour photography.

Medawar, Sir Peter Brian (1915–87) British zoologist and immunologist, born Rio de Janeiro. Pioneered experiments in skin grafting and the prevention of rejection in transplant operations. Joint winner of Nobel prize for physiology or medicine in 1960.

Mendel, Gregor Johann (1822–84) Austrian biologist and botanist, born near Udrau, Silesia. Became abbot in 1868. Researched inheritance characters in plants leading to the formulation of Mendel's law of segregation and the law of independent assortment; his principles became the basis of modern genetics.

Mendeleyev, Dmitri Ivanovich (1834–1907) Russian chemist, born Tobolsk. Formulated the periodic law from which he predicted the existence of several elements which were subsequently discovered. Element 101 is named mendelevium after him.

Michaelis, Leonor (1875–1949) German–American biochemist, born Berlin. Made early deductions on enzyme action and is best known for the Michaelis–Menten equation on enzyme-catalyzed reactions.

Michelson, Albert Abraham (1852–1931) German–American physicist, born Strelno (now Strzelno, Poland). Carried out famous Michelson–Morley experiment which confirmed the non-existence of the 'ether', a result which set Einstein on the road to the theory of relativity. First American scientist to win a Nobel prize in 1907. Also invented an interferometer and an echelon grating as well as carrying out important work on the spectrum.

Millikan, Robert Andrews (1868–1953) American physicist, born Illinois. Awarded the Nobel prize for physics in 1923 for determining the charge on the electron, and carried out important work on cosmic rays.

Newton, Sir Isaac (1642–1727) English scientist and mathematician, born Woolsthorpe, Lincolnshire. Formulated complete theory of gravitation by 1684; also carried out important work in optics, concluding that the different colours of light making up white light have different refrangibility, developed the reflecting telescope, and invented calculus around the same time as Leibniz.

Parkinson, James (1755–1824) English physician, born London. Gave first description of paralysis agitans, or Parkinson's disease. Described appendicitis and perforation, and was first to recognize perforation as a cause of death.

Pascal, Blaise (1623–62) French mathematician and physicist, born Clermont-Ferrand. Carried out important work in geometry, invented a calculating machine, demonstrated that air pressure decreases with altitude as previously predicted and developed probability theory. The SI unit of pressure (pascal) and the modern computer programming language, Pascal, are named after him.

Pasteur, Louis (1822–95) French chemist, born Dôle. Father of modern bacteriology. Discovered possibility of attenuating the virulence of injurious micro-organisms by exposure to air, by variety of culture, or by transmission through various animals, and demonstrated that the attenuated organisms could be used for immunization. From this he developed vaccinations against anthrax and rabies. Also introduced pasteurization (moderate heating) to kill disease-producing organisms in wine, milk and other foods, and disymmetry in molecules.

Pauli, Wolfgang (1900–58) Austrian–American theoretical physicist, born Vienna. Formulated the exclusion principle (1924), that no two electrons can be in the same energy state, producing important advances in the application of quantum theory to the periodic table of elements; for this he was awarded the Nobel prize for physics in 1945. Made other important contributions in particle physics, and postulated the existence of an electrically neutral particle later discovered as the neutrino.

Pavlov, Ivan Petrovich (1849–1936) Russian physiologist, born near Ryazan. Studied physiology of circulation, digestion and 'conditioned' or acquired reflexes, believing the brain's only function to be to couple neurones to produce reflexes. Awarded the Nobel prize for physiology or medicine in 1904.

Perutz, Max Ferdinand (1914–) Austrian–British biochemist, born Vienna. Studied the structure of haemoglobin. Joint winner of the 1962 Nobel prize for chemistry.

Planck, Max Karl Ernst (1858–1947) German theoretical physicist, born Kiel. Researched

SCIENTISTS (cont.)

thermodynamics and black-body radiation, leading him to formulate quantum theory (1900), which assumes energy changes take place in abrupt instalments or quanta. Awarded Nobel prize for physics in 1918.

Ptolemy, or **Claudius Ptolemaeus** (c.90–168) Egyptian astronomer and geographer, believed born Ptolemaeus Hermion. Corrected and improved the astronomical work of his predecessors to form the Ptolemaic System, described by Plato and Aristotle, with the Earth at the centre of the Universe and heavenly bodies revolving round it; beyond this lay the sphere of the fixed stars. Also compiled geographical catalogues and maps.

Purkinje, Jan Evangelista (1787–1869) Czech physiologist, born Libochowitz. Carried out research on the eye, brain, muscles, embryology, digestion and sweat glands, studying 'Purkinje's figure', an effect by which one can see in one's own eye the shadows of the retinal blood vessels, and 'Purkinje's cells', cells in the middle layer of the cerebellar cortex.

Pythagoras (6th century BC) Greek mathematician and philosopher, born Samos. Associated with mathematical discoveries involving the chief musical intervals, the relations of numbers and the relations between the lengths of sides of right-angled triangles (Pythagoras's theorem). Profoundly influenced Plato and later astronomers and mathematicians.

Ramón y Cajal, Santiago (1852–1934) Spanish physician and histologist, born Petilla de Aragon. Carried out important work on the brain and nerves, isolated the neuron and discovered how nerve impulses are transmitted to brain cells. Joint winner of the 1906 Nobel prize for physiology or medicine.

Rathke, Martin Heinrich (1793–1860) German biologist, born Danzig. Discovered gill-slits and gill-arches in embryo birds and mammals. 'Rathke's pocket' is the name given to the small pit on the dorsal side of the oral cavity of developing vertebrates.

Rayleigh, John William Strutt, 3rd Baron (1842–1919) English physicist, born near Maldon, Essex. Carried out valuable research on vibratory motion, the theory of sound and the wave theory of light. With Sir William Ramsay discovered argon (1894). Awarded Nobel prize for physics in 1904.

Richter, Charles Francis (1900–85) American seismologist, born near Hamilton, Ohio. Devised the scale of earthquake strength which bears his name (1927–35).

Röntgen, Wilhelm Konrad von (1845–1923) German physicist, born Lennep, Prussia. Discovered the electromagnetic rays which he called X-rays (also known as Röntgen rays) in 1895. For his work on X-rays he was joint winner of the Rumford medal in 1896 and winner of the 1901 Nobel prize for physics. Also carried out important work on the heat conductivity of crystals, the specific heat of gases, and the electromagnetic rotation of polarized light.

Rutherford, Ernest Rutherford, 1st Baron Rutherford of Nelson (1871–1937) New Zealand–British physicist, born Spring Grove, near Nelson. Made first successful wireless transmissions over two miles, discovered the three types of uranium radiations, formulated a theory of atomic disintegration and determined the nature of alpha particles; this led to a new atomic model in which the mass is concentrated in the nucleus. Also discovered that alpha-ray bombardment could produce atomic transformation and predicted the existence of the neutron. Awarded Nobel prize for chemistry in 1908.

Schrödinger, Erwin (1887–1961) Austrian physicist, born Vienna. Originated the study of wave mechanics as part of the quantum theory with the celebrated Schrödinger wave equation, for which he was joint winner of the 1933 Nobel prize for physics. Also made contributions to field theory.

Schwann, Theodor (1810–82) German physiologist, born Neuss. Discovered the enzyme pepsin, investigated muscle contraction, demonstrated the role of micro-organisms in putrefaction and extended the cell theory, previously applied to plants, to animal tissues.

Sörensen, Sören Peter Lauritz (1868–1939) Danish biochemist, born Havrabjerg, Slagelsi. Carried out pioneering research on hydrogen concentration and invented the pH scale for measuring acidity in 1909.

Szent-Györgyi, Albert von Nagyrapolt (1893–1986) Hungarian–American biochemist, born Budapest. Discovered actin, isolated vitamin C and was awarded the Nobel prize for physiology or medicine in 1937. Also made important studies of

SCIENTISTS (cont.)

biological combustion, muscular contraction and cellular oxidation.

Thomson, Sir Joseph John (1856–1940) English physicist, born Cheetham Hill, near Manchester. Studied gaseous conductors of electricity and the nature of cathode rays; this led to his discovery of the electron. Also pioneered mass spectrometry and discovered the existence of isotopes of elements. Awarded the Nobel prize for physics in 1906.

Thompson, Sir William *see* **Kelvin, Lord**

Tinbergen, Nikolaas (1907–88) Dutch ethologist, born The Hague. Co-founder with Konrad Lorenz of the science of ethology (study of animal behaviour in natural surroundings). Analyzed social behaviour of certain animals and insects as an evolutionary process with considerable relevance to human behaviour, especially courtship and aggression. Joint winner of the 1973 Nobel prize for physiology or medicine.

Van de Graaff, Robert Jemison (1901–67) American physicist, born Tuscaloosa, Alabama. Conceived of an improved type of electrostatic generator, in which electric charge could be built up on a hollow metal sphere; constructed first model, later to be known as the Van de Graaff generator, giving possibility of generating potentials of over a million volts. Developed the generator for use as a particle accelerator for atomic and nuclear physicists. Generator was also adapted to produce high-energy X-rays for cancer treatment and examination of the interior structure of heavy ordnance.

Van der Waals, Johannes Dederik (1837–1923) Dutch physicist, born Leiden. Discovered van der Waals's equation, defining the physical state of a gas or liquid and investigated the weak attractive forces (van der Waals's forces) between molecules. Awarded the Nobel prize for physics in 1910.

Volta, Alessandro Giuseppe Anastasio, Count (1745–1827) Italian physicist, born Como. Developed the theory of current electricity, discovered the electric composition of water, invented an electric battery, the electrophorus, an electroscope and made investigations into heat and gases. His name is given to the SI unit of electric potential difference, the volt.

Warburg, Otto Heinrich (1883–1970) German biochemist, born Freiburg Baden. Carried out important cancer research. Awarded the 1931 Nobel prize for physiology or medicine, but as a Jew was prevented from accepting it by Hitler.

Watt, James (1736–1819) Scottish engineer and inventor, born Greenock. Developed and improved early models of the steam engine, and manufactured it from 1774. The watt, a unit of power, is named after him, and the term horsepower was first used by him.

Wien, Wilhelm (1864–1928) German physicist, born Gaffken, E Prussia. Awarded Nobel prize for physics for work on the radiation of energy from black bodies. Research also included investigation of X-rays and hydrodynamics.

Young, Thomas (1773–1829) English physicist and physician, born Milverton, Somerset. Expounded the phenomenom of interference, which established the undulatory theory of light. Also made valuable contributions in insurance, haemodynamics and deciphering the inscriptions on the Rosetta Stone.

FIELDS OF SCIENTIFIC STUDY

acoustics The science of mechanical waves including production and propagation properties.

actinobiology The study of the effects of radiation upon living organisms.

aerodynamics That part of the mechanics of fluids that deals with the dynamics of gases. Particularly, the study of forces acting upon bodies in motion in air.

aerology The study of the free atmosphere.

aeronautics All activities concerned with aerial locomotion.

aerothermodynamics Particular branch of thermodynamics relating to the heating effects associated with the dynamics of a gas; in particular the physical effects produced in the air flowing over a vehicle during launch and re-entry.

FIELDS OF SCIENTIFIC STUDY (cont.)

aetiology, etiology The medical study of the causation of disease.

algology The study of algae.

angiology The study or scientific account of the anatomy of blood and lymph vascular systems.

astronautics The science of space flight.

astronomy The study of all classes of celestial object and the universe as a whole.

astrophysics That branch of astronomy which applies the laws of physics to the study of interstellar matter and the stars, their constitution, evolution, luminosity etc.

autecology The study of the ecology of any individual species. *See* **synecology**.

autonomics Study of self-regulating systems for process control, optimizing performance.

autoradiography Originally used to show the distribution of radioactive molecules in cells and tissues after injecting the organism with, or growing the cells in a medium containing a radioactive precursor. It is now widely used to show the distribution of radiolabelled molecules separated on the basis of size, charge etc. Photographic film or emulsion is exposed after applying it to the section, fixed cell or separating medium and the distribution of developed grains viewed directly or under the microscope. Similar procedures exist for fluorescent and other labels.

bacteriology The scientific study of bacteria.

ballistics The study of the dynamics of the path taken by an object moving under the influence of a gravitational field.

balneology The scientific study of baths and bathing, and of their application to disease.

bioclimatology The study of the effects of climate on living organisms.

biology The study of living organisms and systems; the life sciences collectively, including botany, anatomy, physiology, zoology etc.

biometeorology The study of the effects of atmospheric conditions on living things.

biophysics The physics of vital processes; study of biological phenomena in terms of physical principles.

biosystematics The study of relationships with reference to the laws of classification of organisms; taxonomy.

biotechnology The use of organisms or their components in industrial or commercial processes, which can be aided by the techniques of genetic manipulation in developing eg novel plants for agriculture or industry.

botany The study of living organisms and systems.

bronchography The radiological examination of the trachea, bronchi, or the bronchial tree after the introduction of a contrast medium.

cardiology That part of medical science concerned with the function and diseases of the heart.

chemistry The study of the composition of substances and the changes that they undergo.

chromatics The science of colours as affected by phenomena determined by their differing wavelengths.

cladistics Method of classifying organisms into groups (taxa) based on 'recency of common descent' as judged by the possession of shared derived (ie not primitive) characteristics.

climatology The study of climate and its causes.

cosmology The study of the universe on the largest scales of length and time, particularly the propounding theories concerning its origin, nature, structure and evolution. A cosmology is any model said to represent the observed universe. Western cosmology is entirely scientific in its approach, and has produced two famous models, the Big Bang and steady-state cosmology.

cryogenics The study of materials at very low temperatures.

crystallography Study of internal arrangements (ionic and molecular) and external form of crystal species, and their classification into types.

cybernetics The study of control and communications in complex electronic systems and in animals, especially humans.

cytogenetics Study of the chromosomal complement of cells, and of chromosomal abnormalities and their inheritance.

cytology The study of the structure and functions of cells.

dendrochronology Science of reconstructing past climates from the information stored in tree trunks as annual radial increments of growth.

dermatology That branch of medical science which deals with the skin and its diseases.

dynamics That branch of applied mathematics which studies the way in which force produces motion.

ecology The scientific study of the interrelations between living organisms and their environment, emphasizing both relations between species and within species; the scientific study of the distribution and abundance of living organisms (ie exactly where they occur and precisely how many there are).

FIELDS OF SCIENTIFIC STUDY (cont.)

econometrics The application of statistical methods to economic phenomena.

ecophysiology Branch of physiology concerned with how organisms are adapted to their natural environment.

electrocardiography The study of electric currents produced in cardiac muscular activity.

electrokinetics Science of electric charges in motion, without reference to the accompanying magnetic field.

electromagnetics or **electromagnetism** Science of the properties of, and relationships between, magnetism and electric currents.

electromyography The study of electric currents set up in muscle fibres by bodily movement.

electronics The study and application of the movement of electrons.

electrophysiology The study of electrical phenomena associated with living organisms, particularly nervous conduction.

electrostatics Section of science of electricity which deals with the phenomena of electric charges substantially at rest.

embryology The study of the formation and development of embryos.

endocrinology The study of the internal secretory glands.

energetics The abstract study of the energy relations of physical and chemical changes. *See* **thermodynamics**.

entomology The branch of zoology which deals with the study of insects.

epidemiology The study of disease in the population, defining its incidence and prevalence, examining the role of external influences such as infection, diet or toxic substances, and examining appropriate preventive or curative measures.

epistemics The scientific study of the perceptual, intellectual and linguistic processes by which knowledge and understanding are acquired and communicated.

ergonomics The application of various human studies to the area of work and leisure; includes anatomy, physiology and psychology.

ethology Describes an approach to the study of animal behaviour in which attempts to explain behaviour combine questions about its immediate causation, development, function and evolution.

etiology *see* **aetiology**

eugenics Study of the means whereby the characteristics of human populations might be improved by the application of genetics.

exobiology The study of (possible) living systems which probably must exist elsewhere in the universe.

fluidics The science of liquid flow in tubes etc which strongly simulates electron flow in conductors and conducting plasma. The interaction of streams of fluid can be used for the control of instruments or industrial processes without the use of moving parts.

fractography The microscopic study of fractures in metal surfaces.

genecology The branch of ecology which seeks genetic explanations of the patterns of distribution of plants and animals in time and space.

genetics The study of heredity; of how differences between individuals are passed on from one generation to the next; and of how the information in the genes is used in the development and functioning of the adult organism.

geochronology Study of time with respect to the history of the Earth, primarily through the use of absolute and relative age-dating methods.

geology The study of the planet Earth. It embraces mineralogy, petrology, geophysics, geochemistry, physical geology, palaeontology and stratigraphy. It increasingly involves the use of the chemical, physical, mathematical and biological sciences.

geophysics Study of physical properties of the Earth; it makes use of the data available in Earth measurement, seismology, meteorology and oceanography, as well as that relating to atmospheric electricity, terrestrial magnetism and tidal phenomena.

gerontology The scientific study of the processes of aging.

gynaecology, gynecology That branch of medical science which deals with the functions and diseases peculiar to women.

histology The study of the minute structure of tissues in organisms.

horology The science of time measurement, or of the construction of timepieces.

hydraulics The science relating to the flow of fluids.

hydrodynamics That branch of dynamics which studies the motion produced in fluids by applied forces.

hydrogeology The study of the geological aspects of the Earth's water.

hydrography The study, determination, and publication of the conditions of seas, rivers and lakes, which involves surveying and charting of coasts,

FIELDS OF SCIENTIFIC STUDY (cont.)

rivers, estuaries and harbours, and supplying particulars of depth, bottom, tides, currents etc.

hydrology The study of water, including rain, snow and water on the Earth's surface, covering its properties, distribution, utilization etc.

hydroponics Technique of growing plants without soil. The roots can be in either a nutrient solution or in an inert medium percolated by such a solution.

hydrostatics Branch of statics which studies the forces arising from the presence of fluids.

immunology The study of the biological responses of a living organism to its invasion by living bacteria, viruses, or parasites, and its defence against these; also the study of the body's reaction to foreign substances.

kinematics That branch of applied mathematics which studies the way in which velocities and accelerations of various parts of a moving system are related.

kinetics The study of the rates at which chemical reactions and biological processes proceed.

laryngology That branch of medical science which treats diseases of the larynx and adjacent parts of the upper respiratory tract.

limnology The study of lakes.

lithography The systematic description of rocks, more especially sedimentary rocks. *See* **petrology**.

magnetohydrodynamics The study of the motions of an electrically conducting fluid in the presence of a magnetic field. The motion of the fluid gives rise to induced electric currents which interact with the magnetic field which in turn modifies the motion. The phenomenon has applications both to magnetic fields in space and to the possibility of generating electricity.

magnetostatics Study of steady-state magnetic fields.

malacology The study of molluscs.

mathematics May be defined as the study of the logical consequences of sets of axioms. Pure mathematics, roughly speaking, comprises those branches studied for their own sake or their relation to other branches. The most important of these are algebra, analysis and topology. The term applied mathematics is usually restricted to applications in physics. Applications in other fields, eg economics, mainly statistical, are sometimes referred to as applicable mathematics.

mechanics The study of forces on bodies and of the motions they produce. *See* **dynamics**, **kinematics**, **statics**.

metallography The study of metals and their alloys with the aid of various procedures eg microscopy, X-ray diffraction etc.

meteorology The study of the Earth's atmosphere in its relation to weather and climate.

metrology The science of measuring.

micropalaeontology The study of microfossils.

mineralogy The study of the chemical composition, physical properties and occurrence of minerals.

morphology The study of the structure and forms of organisms, as opposed to the study of their functions.

mycology The study of fungi.

myology The study of muscles.

neuroendocrinology The study of interactions between the nervous system and endocrine organs, particularly pituitary gland and hypothalamic region of brain.

neurology The study of the nervous system.

neuropathology The study of pathology of diseases of the nervous system.

nosology Systematic classification of diseases; the branch of medical science which deals with this.

nucleonics The science and technology of nuclear studies.

obstetrics That branch of medical science which deals with the problems and management of pregnancy and labour.

oceanography The study of the oceans, including geological, chemical, physical and biological processes.

odontology Study of the physiology, anatomy, pathology etc of the teeth.

oncology That part of medical science dealing with new growths (tumours) of body tissue.

oölogy The study of ova.

ophthalmology The study of the eye and its diseases.

optics The study of light. Physical optics deals with the nature of light and its wave properties; geometrical optics ignores the wave nature of light and treats problems of reflection and refraction from the ray aspect.

organography A descriptive study of the external form of plants, with relation to function.

ornithology The study of birds.

orthopaedics, orthopedics That branch of sur-

FIELDS OF SCIENTIFIC STUDY (cont.)

gery which deals with deformities arising from injury or disease of bones or of joints.

osteology The study of bones.

otology That part of surgical science dealing with the organ of hearing and its diseases.

otorhinolaryngology That part of surgical science which deals with diseases of the ear, nose and throat.

palaeoclimatology The study of climatic conditions in the geological record, using evidence from fossils, sediments and their structures, geophysics and geochemistry.

palaeoecology The study of fossil organisms in terms of their mode of life, their interrelationships, their environment, their manner of death and their eventual burial.

palaeogeography The study of the relative positions of land and water at particular periods in the geological past.

palaeontology The study of fossil animals and plants.

palaeopathology Study of disease of previous eras from examination of bodily remains or evidence from ancient writings.

palaeozoology The study of fossil animals. *See* **palaeontology**.

palynology The study of fossil spores and pollen. They are very resistant to destruction and in many sedimentary rocks are the only fossils that can be used to determine the relationships of strata.

parapsychology The study of certain alleged phenomena, the paranormal, that is beyond the scope of ordinary psychology, eg ESP, psychokineses etc.

parasitology The study of parasites and their habits (usually confined to animal parasites).

pathology That part of medical science which deals with the causes and nature of disease, and with the bodily changes brought about by disease.

pedology The study of soil.

petrology That study of rocks which includes consideration of their mode of origin, present conditions, chemical and mineral composition, their alteration and decay.

pharmacodynamics The science of the action of drugs; pharmacology.

pharmacology The scientific study of the action of chemical substances on living systems.

phenology The study of plant development in relation to the seasons.

phenomenology In philosophy, the study of the psychic awareness that accompanies experience and that is the source of all meaning for the individual. In psychiatry, it refers to the description and classification of an individual's mental activity, including subjective experience and perceptions, mental performance (eg memory) and the somatic accompaniments of mental events (eg heart rate).

phonetics Study of speech and vocal acoustics. Used to describe the system of symbols which uniquely represent the spoken word of any language in writing, enabling the reader to pronounce words accurately in spite of spelling irregularities.

photobiology The study of light as it affects living organisms.

phycology The study of the algae.

physics Study of electrical, luminescent, mechanical, magnetic, radioactive and thermal phenomena with respect to changes in energy states without change of chemical composition.

physiography The science of the surface of the Earth and the inter-relations of air, water and land.

phytology *see* **botany**

phytopathology Plant pathology. The study of plant diseases, especially of plants in relation to their parasites.

phytosociology The study of the association of plant species.

planetology The study of the composition, origin and distribution of matter in the planets of the solar system.

planigraphy *see* **tomography**

prosthetics That branch of surgical science concerned with prosthesis.

proxemics The study of the spatial features of human social interaction, eg personal space.

psychodynamics A theory of the working of an individual's mind.

psychometrics The application of mathematical and statistical concepts to psychological data, particularly in the areas of mental testing and experimental data.

psychopathology The study of psychological disorders.

psychopharmacology Refers to the study and use of drugs that influence behaviour, emotions, perception and thought, by acting on the central nervous system.

psychophysics The branch of psychology that studies the relationship between characteristics of the physical stimulus and the psychological experience they produce.

FIELDS OF SCIENTIFIC STUDY (cont.)

radiobiology Branch of science involving study of effect of radiation and radioactive materials on living matter.
radiology The science and application of X-rays, gamma-rays and other penetrating ionizing or non-ionizing radiations.
rheology The science of the flow of matter. The critical study of elasticity, viscosity and plasticity.
robotics The study of the design and use of robots, particularly for their use in manufacture and related processes.
röntgenology *see* **radiology**
seismology The study of earthquakes, particularly their shock waves. Studies of the speed and refraction of seismic waves enable the deeper structure of the Earth to be investigated.
semeiology The branch of medical science which is concerned with the symptoms of disease.
semiotics The study of communication.
serology The study of serums.
sonics General term for study of mechanical vibrations in matter.
spelaeology, speleology The study of the fauna and flora of caves.
statics That branch of applied mathematics which studies the way in which forces combine with each other usually so as to produce equilibrium. Until the early part of the 20th century the term also embraced the study of gravitational attractions, but this is now normally regarded as a separate subject.
statistics The branch of mathematics which deals with the collection and analysis of numerical data.
stratigraphy The definition and description of the stratified rocks of the Earth's crust, their relationships and structure, their arrangement into chronological groups, their mineral mass and the conditions of their formation, and their fossil contents.
superaerodynamics Aerodynamics at very low air densities occurring above 100 000ft/30 480 m, ie for spacecraft on ascending and re-entry trajectories.
symptomatology The study of symptoms; a discourse or treatise on symptoms; the branch of medical science concerning symptoms of disease.
synecology The study of relationships between communities and their environment. *See* **autecology**.
systematics The branch of biology which deals with classification and nomenclature.
tectonics The study of the major structural features of the Earth's crust.
teleology The interpretation of animal or plant structures in terms of purpose and utility.
teratology The study of monstrosities, as an aid to the understanding of normal development.
thermionics The study of the processes involved in the emission of electrons from hot bodies.
thermodynamics The study of heat and heat-related phenomena.
topology The study of those properties of shapes and space that are independent of distance.
toxicology The branch of medical science dealing with the nature and effects of poisons.
urodynamics The study of urine flow.
urology That part of medical science which deals with diseases and abnormalities of the urinary tract and their treatment.
virology The study of viruses.
zoogeography The study of animal distribution.
zoology The study of all aspects of animals.
zootaxy The science of the classification of animals.

SCIENTIFIC TERMS

Bold type indicates that a definition of a word or phrase in an entry is given elsewhere in the glossary.

In this glossary 10^{12} is used to mean 1 followed by 12 zeros and 10^{-27} is used to mean 1 occurring 27 places after a decimal point.

aberration In an image-forming system, such as a curved mirror or lens, the failure to produce a true image when different colours of light or light incident on different parts of the mirror or lens are focused to different positions.
absolute alcohol Water-free **ethanol**.
absolute zero The least possible temperature for all substances, when the **molecules** of any substance possess no heat energy. A figure of −273.15°C is generally accepted as the value of absolute zero.
ac *see* **alternating current**
acid rain Rain that is unnaturally **acid** as a result of pollution of the atmosphere with oxides of

SCIENTIFIC TERMS (cont.)

nitrogen and sulphur from the burning of coal and oil.

acid Normally, a substance which (a) dissolves in water with the formation of hydrogen **ions**, (b) dissolves metals with the liberation of hydrogen gas, or (c) more generally, a substance which tends to lose a **proton** or to accept an **electron** pair.

acoustic imaging Determination of distance and direction of objects, such as submarines, by the reception of the reflection of a sound pulse. Also known as sonar.

acquired character In zoology, a modification of an organ during the lifetime of an individual due to use or disuse, and not inherited from a previous generation. *See* **natural selection**.

adaptation In zoology, any structural, physiological or behavioural characteristic which fits an organism to the conditions under which it lives; the genetic or developmental processes by which such characteristics arise. *See* **natural selection**.

adiabatic process In physics, a process which occurs without interchange of heat with surroundings.

adsorption In chemistry, the taking up of one substance at the surface of another.

aerosol (1) A system in the form of a **colloid**, such as a mist or a fog, in which the dispersion medium is a gas. (2) Pressurized container with built-in spray mechanism used for packaging insecticides, deodorants, paints etc.

aerospace The Earth's atmosphere together with the space beyond; the branch of technology or of industry concerned with the flight of spacecraft through this.

algae A group of simple plants containing **chlorophyll** but without roots, stems or leaves, which live in aquatic conditions.

alkali A substance which, when dissolved in water, forms a solution containing hydroxyl **ions**, negatively charged ions containing oxygen and hydrogen, and with a **pH value** of more than 7.

allotropy The existence of two or more forms of an **element** in one phase of matter (ie solid, liquid or gas), called allotropes.

alloy A mixture of metals, or of a metal with a non-metal in which the metal is the major component.

alpha particle The **nucleus** of a helium **atom**, emitted from natural or radioactive **isotopes**. Often written α-particle. *See* **radioactivity**.

alternating current Generally abbreviated to ac. Electric **current** whose flow alternates in direction.

AM (amplitude modulation) *see* **modulation**

amino acid A fatty acid in which an amino group (NH_2) and a carboxyl group (COOH) are attached to an **organic molecule**. Play an important part in the bodies of animals and plants, often combining in different forms to produce **protein**.

amorphous Noncrystalline.

amu *see* **atomic mass unit**

anaerobic Living in the absence of oxygen. Anaerobic respiration is the liberation of energy which does not require the presence of oxygen.

anion Negative **ion**, ie **atom** or **molecule** which has gained one or more **electrons**.

anisotropic Said of crystalline material for which physical properties, such as its ability to conduct electrical **current**, depend on the direction relative to the crystal axes.

annihilation Spontaneous conversion of a particle and its **antiparticle** into **radiation**.

annual A plant that flowers and dies within a period of one year from germination.

annulus A plane surface bounded by two concentric circles, like a washer.

anode Positively charged **conductor** used in conjunction with a **cathode** to lead an electric current into or out of a solid, liquid or gas.

antibody Defensive substance produced in an organism in response to the action of a foreign body, such as the toxin of a **parasite**.

anticyclone A distribution of atmospheric pressure in which the pressure increases towards the centre. Winds in such a system circulate in a clockwise direction in the northern hemisphere and in a counterclockwise direction in the southern hemisphere.

antigen A substance which stimulates the production of an **antibody**.

antiparticle The antiparticle of a given particle has the same mass but opposite values for all its other properties such as charge. A particle and its antiparticle, eg the **electron** and **positron**, destroy each other on contact in the process of **annihilation**.

aperture (1) The opening, usually circular, through which light enters an optical system, such as a camera lens; its area may be varied by an iris diaphragm to control the amount of light passing. *See* **f-number**. (2) The rectangular opening at which motion picture film is exposed in a camera or projector.

SCIENTIFIC TERMS (cont.)

Archimedes' principle The principle that when a body is wholly or partly immersed in a fluid it experiences an upwards force equal to the weight of fluid it displaces.

aromatic compounds Organic compounds containing **benzene** or with similar chemical properties.

asteroid One of thousands of rocky objects found in the **solar system**, normally between the orbits of Mars and Jupiter, ranging in size from 1 to 1 000 km.

astigmatism (1) In medicine, unequal curvature of the focusing surfaces of the eye, which prevents incident light rays from reaching a common focus point on the retina, resulting in blurred eyesight. (2) In physics, a defect in an optical system on account of which, instead of a point image being formed of a point object, two short line images (focal lines) are produced at slightly different positions and at right angles to each other.

astronomical unit Mean distance of the Earth from the Sun, about 149 600 000 km or 93 000 000 ml.

atom The smallest particle of an element which can take part in a chemical reaction. A central nucleus containing **protons** and **neutrons** is surrounded by shells of **electrons**.

atomic mass unit Exactly one twelfth the mass of a neutral **atom** of the most abundant **isotope** of carbon (1.660×10^{-27} kg).

aurora Luminous curtains or streamers of light seen in the night sky at high latitudes, caused when electrically charged particles from the Sun are guided by the Earth's magnetic field to the polar regions, there colliding with atoms in the upper atmosphere. In the northern hemisphere known as aurora borealis and in the southern as aurora australis.

background radiation **Radiation** which causes **ionization** coming from natural sources such as the Earth's rocks, soil and atmosphere.

bacteriophage A **virus** which infects bacteria.

benthos Collectively, the immobile animal and plant life living on the sea bottom.

benzene A **molecule** consisting of a ring or closed chain of six carbon **atoms** each with a hydrogen atom attached.

beta decay Radioactive disintegration with the emission of an **electron** or **positron**. *See* **radioactivity**.

biennial A plant that flowers and dies between its first and second years from germination and which does not flower in its first year.

Big Bang Hypothetical model of the universe which postulates that all matter and energy were once concentrated into an unimaginably dense state, from which it has been expanding from a creation event some 13 000 000 000 and 20 000 000 000 years ago.

bioassay Quantitative determination of a substance by measuring its biological effect on eg growth, ie the use of an organism to test the environment.

biogenesis The formation of living organisms from their ancestors and of minute **cell** structures from their predecessors.

bioluminescence The production of light by living organisms, as such as glow-worms, some deep-sea fish, some bacteria and some fungi.

biosphere The part of the Earth (upwards at least to a height of 10 000 m, and downwards to the depths of the ocean, and a few hundred m below the land surface) and the atmosphere surrounding it, which is able to support life. The term may be expanded theoretically to other planets.

bit In computer science, a digit in binary notation, ie 0 or 1. It is the smallest unit of storage (from Binary digIT).

black hole A region in space from which matter and energy cannot escape. A black hole could be a **star** or the central part of a **galaxy** which has collapsed in on itself to the point where the speed required for matter to escape exceeds the speed of light.

buckyballs **Molecules** consisting of 60 carbon **atoms** arranged symmetrically. Familiar name for buckminsterfullerene.

byte In computer science, a fixed number of **bits**, often corresponding to a single character and operated on as a unit.

calculus Branch of mathematics dealing with continuously varying quantities or functions.

carat Also karat. (1) A standard weight for precious stones equal to 200 milligrams. (2) The standard of fineness for gold, such that 24 carats represents pure gold, and 23 carat gold has $\frac{1}{24}$ part impurity.

carbohydrates Compounds of carbon, hydrogen and oxygen, the last two being in the same proportion as in water. Form the main source of energy in food as sugars and starches.

carbon dating Or radiocarbon dating. Estimating the date of death of an **organic** material from

SCIENTIFIC TERMS (cont.)

the amount of a radioactive **isotope** of carbon in it. The quantity of the radioactive carbon naturally decreases with time. *See* **radioactivity**.

carcinogen Substance which encourages the growth of cancer.

carnivore A flesh-eating mammal.

catalysis The acceleration or retardation of a chemical reaction by a substance, a catalyst, which itself undergoes no permanent chemical change, or which can be recovered when the chemical reaction is completed.

cathode Negatively charged **conductor** used in conjunction with an **anode** to lead an electric current into or out of a solid, liquid or gas.

caustic Said of a material which is destructive or corrosive to living tissue; an agent which burns or destroys living tissue.

cell In biology, the unit from which plants and animals are composed.

cellulose A **carbohydrate** forming the chief component of **cell** walls in plants and in wood.

Celsius scale **SI** name for centigrade scale. Temperature scale in which the freezing point of water is 0°C and the boiling point is 100°C.

centigrade scale *see* **Celsius scale**

centrifuge Machine which uses the force produced by rotation to separate molecules from solution, particles and solids from liquids, and liquids which do not mix from each other.

CGS unit Abbreviation for Centimetre-Gram-Sec unit, based on the centimetre, the gram and the sec as the fundamental units of length, mass and time. For most purposes superseded by **SI** units.

chaos theory Theory which describes how the behaviour of a system which obeys well-known physical laws can become unpredictable if a very large number of accurately known quantities or a very extensive description of its initial state is required to predict its development. This leads to unpredictability in eg weather forecasting.

chip Popular name for an **integrated circuit**.

chlorophylls Green pigments involved in the process of **photosynthesis**. *Chlorophyll a* is the primary photosynthetic pigment in all organisms that release oxygen, ie all plants and **algae**.

cholesterol An white crystalline solid found in nerve tissues, gall stones, and in other tissues of the body.

chromosome Rod-like structures found in the **nucleus** of a **cell**, which perform an important role in cell division and transmission of hereditary features.

clone Organisms, **cells** or micro-organisms all derived from a single progenitor. They have therefore an almost identical **genotype**.

colloid A solid dispersed through a liquid such that, though apparently dissolved, it cannot pass through a membrane.

comet A small member of the solar system, made of ice, dust and gas, becoming visible as it approaches the Sun. A bright nucleus is often seen, and sometimes a tail which points away from the Sun.

conductor A material used for the transference of heat or electrical energy.

congenital Said of diseases or deformities dating from birth, but not passed on from a previous generation.

continental drift A hypothesis to explain the distribution of the continents and oceans and the structural, geological and physical similarities which exist between them. The continents were believed to have been formed from one large land mass and to have drifted apart. *See* **plate tectonics**.

convection The transfer of heat in a fluid by the circulation flow due to temperature differences. The regions of higher temperature, being less dense, rise, while the regions of lower temperature move down to take their place.

Coriolis effect The effect whereby an object falling freely towards the Earth is slightly deviated from a straight line and will fall to a point east of the point directly below its initial position, due to the rotation of the Earth underneath as it falls.

cosmic rays Highly penetrating rays from interstellar space, consisting of particles such as **protons**, **electrons** and **positrons**.

cracking Breaking down heavier crude-oil **molecules** to form lighter molecules by heat, pressure and the use of **catalysis**.

current Flow of electric charge in a substance, solid, liquid or gas.

cyclone (1) A region of low pressure, or depression. (2) A tropical revolving storm in the Arabian Sea, Bay of Bengal and South Indian Ocean.

Darwinian theory *see* **natural selection**

desertification Formation of deserts from zones previously supporting plant life by the action of drought and/or increased populations of humans and grass-eating animals.

diffraction The spreading of light or other waves passing through a narrow opening or by the edge of an opaque body.

SCIENTIFIC TERMS (cont.)

diffusion General transport of matter whereby **molecules** or **ions** mix through normal movement of particles due to their heat energy.

dimorphism (1) In chemistry, the crystallization into two distinct forms of an **element** or compound, eg carbon as diamond and graphite. (2) In biology, the condition of having two different forms, as animals which show marked differences between male and female (sexual dimorphism), animals which have two different kinds of offspring, and colonial animals in which the members of the colony are of two different kinds.

direct current Generally abbreviated to dc. Electric current which flows in one direction only.

dispersion The separation of visible light into its various colours when passing between media of different density, such as air and glass. Occurs because light passing between the media is deviated from a straight path by an amount which depends on the wavelength, ie the colour.

diurnal During a day. The term is used in astronomy and meteorology to indicate the variations of an astronomical quantity or weather phenomenon during an average day.

DNA, deoxyribose nucleic acid In its double-stranded form the genetic material of organisms. Usually, two strands of DNA form a double-helix, the strands running in opposite directions.

dominant Describes a **gene** which shows its effect in those individuals who received it from only one parent. Also describes an inherited feature due to a dominant gene.

Doppler effect The apparent change of frequency of light or sound because of the relative motion of the source of radiation and the observer. For example, the change in frequency of sound heard when a train or aircraft is moving towards or away from an observer.

dry ice Solid (frozen) carbon dioxide, used in refrigeration (storage) and engineering.

dwarf star The name given to a small low-luminosity star. *See* **white dwarf**.

ecosystem Conceptual view of a plant and animal community, emphasizing the interactions between living and non-living parts, and the flow of materials and energy between these parts.

El Niño An occasional warm tropical ocean current that moves from the East Indies to the South American coast, sometimes causing devastating changes in weather patterns leading to torrential rain and flooding in some areas, and drought in others.

electric field Region in which forces are exerted on any electric charge present.

electrode **Conductor** whereby an electric current is lead into or out of a solid, liquid or gas.

electrolysis Chemical change, generally decomposition of a compound, effected by a flow of current through a solution of the chemical, or its molten state, based on **ionization**.

electromagnetic wave A wave comprising two interdependent mutually perpendicular transverse waves of **electric** and **magnetic fields**. The spectrum of electromagnetic waves comprises **gamma-radiation**, **X-rays**, **ultraviolet radiation**, visible light, **infrared radiation**, **microwaves** and **radio waves**. The speed in free space for all such waves is around 300 000 km (186 000 ml) per sec.

electron A subatomic particle with negative electric charge, which with the **proton** and **neutron**, is a basic constituent of the **atom**.

element A simple substance, composed of **atoms**, which cannot be resolved into simpler substances by normal chemical means.

emulsion (1) In chemistry, a suspension in the form of a **colloid** of one liquid in another. (2) In photography, a suspension of finely divided crystals in a medium such as gelatine which provides the light-sensitive coating on film, glass plates and paper.

endothermic Said of a chemical reaction which is accompanied by the absorption of heat.

entropy In thermal processes, a quantity which measures the extent to which the energy of a system is available for conversion to work.

enzyme A protein which provides **catalysis**, which is restricted to a limited set of reactions.

epicentre That point on the surface of the Earth lying immediately above the focus of an earthquake or nuclear explosion.

equinox Either of the two instants of time at which the Sun crosses the projected plane of the Earth's equator, around 21 March and 23 September.

ethanol Or ethyl alcohol. An alcohol with chemical formula C_2H_5OH, the active substance in alcoholic drinks.

evolution In biology, changes in the genetic composition of a population during successive generations. The gradual development of more complex organisms from simpler ones.

exothermic Said of a chemical reaction which is accompanied by the evolution of heat.

f-number A measure of the **aperture** of a lens,

SCIENTIFIC TERMS (cont.)

representing its light transmission; it expresses the diameter of the lens diaphragm as a fraction of its focal length, eg f/8, also written f:8 or f8.

Fahrenheit scale Temperature scale in which the freezing point of water is 32°F and the boiling point is 212°F.

fault A fracture in rocks along which some displacement has taken place. The displacement may vary from a few millimetres to thousands of metres. Movement along faults is the most common cause of earthquakes.

feedback Occurs when part of an output signal is fed back into the input of the system, which often occurs in electro-acoustic systems in which the microphone and loudspeaker are in the same room.

fermentation A slow decomposition process of **organic** substances induced by micro-organisms or **enzymes**. An important fermentation process is the alcoholic fermentation of sugar.

fibre optics *see* **optical fibre**

field theory As yet unverified attempt to link the properties of all force fields in physics into a unified system.

fission (1) In biology, reproduction of some single-cell organisms from a single parent in which the **cell** divides into two more or less equal parts. (2) In physics, the spontaneous or induced disintegration of a heavy atomic **nucleus** into two or more lighter fragments. The energy released in the process is referred to as **nuclear energy**.

fossil The relic or trace of some plant or animal which has been preserved by natural processes in rocks of the past.

fractal A geometrical entity characterized by a basic pattern that is repeated at ever decreasing sizes.

fraternal twins *see* **twins**

fusion (1) The process of forming a new atomic **nucleus** by combining lighter ones. The energy released in the process is referred to as nuclear energy or fusion energy. (2) The conversion of a solid into a liquid state. *See* **atom**.

Galaxy (1) The name given to the belt of faint stars which encircles the heavens and which is known as the Milky Way. (2) The name is also used for the entire system of dust, gases and stars within which the Sun moves. (3) More generally, galaxy is used to mean any extra-galactic nebula, each being a vast collection of stars, dust and gas.

galvanized iron Iron which has been subjected to galvanizing, eg zinc coating, to prevent corrosion due to moisture.

gamma-radiation **Electromagnetic waves** of high energy emitted after **nuclear reactions** or by radioactive atoms during the process of radioactive decay. *See* **radioactivity.**

gene One of the units of **DNA**, arranged in linear fashion on the **chromosomes**, responsible for passing on specific features from parents to offspring.

genetic code The system by which **genes** pass on instructions that ensure transmission of features inherited from previous generations.

genetic engineering Biological science whose aims include the control of hereditary defects by the modification or elimination of certain **genes**, and the mass production of useful biological substances (eg insulin) by the transplanting of genes.

genome The full set of **chromosomes** of an individual; the total number of **genes** in such a set.

genotype The genetic constitution of an individual; a group of individuals all of which possess the same genetic constitution.

genus In biology, a taxonomic rank of closely related forms, which is lower than family and is further subdivided into species.

geomorphology The structure and development of land forms, including those under the sea; the study of this.

geostationary Said of an orbit lying above the equator, in which an artificial satellite moves at the same speed as the Earth rotates, thus maintaining position above a fixed point on the Earth's surface. Such a satellite would have an altitude of 35 800 km above the Earth's surface.

geothermal power Power generated by using the heat energy of rocks in the Earth's crust.

gestation In mammals, the act of retaining and nourishing the young in the uterus; pregnancy.

giant star A large and luminous star with low average density.

gravitational waves Waves which move through a gravitational field. Accelerating masses are expected to radiate gravitational waves, but so far this has not been observed directly.

greenhouse effect Phenomenon by which thermal radiation from the Sun is trapped by water vapour and carbon dioxide on a planet's surface. This leads to the temperature at the planet's surface being considerably higher than would otherwise be the case.

gyroscope Or gyro. An apparatus in which a heavy

SCIENTIFIC TERMS (cont.)

flywheel or top rotates at high speed, the turning movement resisting change of direction of axis.

herbaceous A soft and green plant organ or a plant without persistent woody tissues above ground.

herbivore Grass-eating animals.

hermaphrodite A person whose reproductive organs are anatomically ambiguous, so that they are not exclusively male or female.

histamine A substance present in all tissues of the body, being liberated into the blood, eg when the skin is cut or burnt or during allergic reactions, eg hay fever; large releases cause the contraction of nearly all smooth muscle, a fall of arterial blood pressure and shock.

hologram A photograph made without use of a lens by means of interference between two parts of a split **laser** beam, which when suitably illuminated shows as a three-dimensional image.

hormone A substance released by glands into the bloodstream which carries it to remote sites in the body where it has a specific physiological action activating or repressing function.

hybrid In biology, the offspring of a cross between two different strains, varieties, races or species.

identical twins *see* **twins**

igneous rocks Rock masses generally accepted as being formed by the solidification of the Earth's internal molten **magma**.

immunity A state of having a high resistance to a disease due to the formation of **antibodies** in response to the presence of **antigens**.

imprinting In biology, an aspect of learning in some species, through which attachment to the important parental figure develops and their social preferences become restricted to their own species.

in vitro fertilization Reproduction of the natural process of fertilization outside the living body, in laboratory apparatus.

indigenous Native; not imported.

inertia The property of a body, proportional to its mass, which opposes a change in the motion of the body.

infinity A number which is larger than any quantified concept. For many purposes it may be considered as one divided by zero.

infrared radiation **Electromagnetic waves** in the wavelength range from 0.000075 to 0.1 cm, approximately, lying between the visible and **microwave** regions of the spectrum.

infrasound Sound of frequencies below the usual audible limit, ie of less than around 20 cycles per sec or hertz.

inorganic Said of chemical **elements** and their compounds, other than the compounds of carbon.

integrated circuit A very small circuit consisting of interconnected **semiconductor** devices in a single structure which cannot be subdivided without destroying its intended function.

ion Strictly, any **atom** or **molecule** which has resultant electric charge due to loss or gain of **electrons**. Free electrons are sometimes loosely classified as negative ions.

ionization Formation of **ions** by separating **molecules**, or adding or subtracting **electrons** from **atoms** by various methods.

isobar A line drawn on a map through places having the same atmospheric pressure at a given time.

isomerism The existence of more than one substance having a given molecular composition and molecular mass but differing in constitution or structure.

isotope One of a set of chemically identical species of **atom** which have the same number of **protons**, but different numbers of **neutrons**.

jet stream A fairly well-defined core of strong wind, around 200–300 ml (320–480 km) wide with wind speeds up to around 200 ml per hour (320 km per hour) occurring more than 20 000 ft (7 000 m) above the Earth.

Kelvin scale Temperature scale in which **absolute zero** is assigned the value zero and the temperature interval is the same as that of the Celsius scale. The unit is abbreviated as K; the freezing point of water (0°C) on this scale is 273.15 K.

La Niña An occasional cold ocean current that moves westerly along the equator, sometimes causing devastating changes in weather patterns leading to torrential rain and flooding in some areas, and drought in others.

laser Light Amplification by Stimulated Emission of Radiation. A source of intense light of a very narrow wavelength range in the ultraviolet, visible or infrared region of **electromagnetic waves**.

LED *see* **light-emitting diode**

light-emitting diode **Semiconductor** device which emits light when an electric current is passed through it, as used eg for displays in digital clocks and electronic calculators. Abbreviated as LED.

light-year An astronomical measure of distance, being the distance travelled by light in space dur-

SCIENTIFIC TERMS (cont.)

ing a year, which is approximately 9.46×10^{12} km or 5.88×10^{12} ml.

lipids, lipoids General terms for oils, fats, waxes and related products found in living tissues.

litmus A material of **organic** origin used as an indicator; its colour changes to red in the presence of **acids**, and to blue in the presence of **alkalis**.

luminescence Emission of light otherwise than due to heating, and so at a relatively cool temperature.

Mach number The ratio of the speed of a body, or of the flow of a fluid, to the speed of sound in the same medium. At Mach 1, the speed of the body is that of sound; below Mach 1, it is **subsonic**; above Mach 1, it is **supersonic**.

magma Molten rock, including dissolved water and other gases. It is formed by melting at depth in the Earth and rises either to the surface, as lava, or to whatever level it can reach before crystallizing again.

magnetic field A field of force which exists around a magnetized body. Also associated with electric **currents** and the motions of **electrons** in **atoms**.

magnetic tape Flexible plastic tape, typically 6 to 50 mm wide, coated on one side with magnetic material, in which signals are registered for subsequent reproduction. Used for storing television images, sound or computer data.

magnetism Science covering **magnetic fields** and their effects on materials.

magnitude A measure of the apparent or absolute brightness of an astronomical object. The brightest naked-eye stars are of around first magnitude and the dimmest around the sixth.

matrix A system of numbers arranged in a square or rectangular formation.

metamorphic rocks Rocks formed by alteration of existing rocks by heat, pressure or other processes in the Earth's crust.

meteor A 'shooting star'. A small body which enters the Earth's atmosphere from the space between the planets and burns up due to friction, flashing across the sky and generally ceasing to be visible before it falls to Earth.

microwave background A weak **radio wave** signal which is detectable in every direction in the sky with almost identical intensity. It is believed to be the relic of the early hot phase in the **Big Bang** universe.

microwaves Those electromagnetic waves with wavelengths between 1 mm and 30 cm, lying between **radio waves** and **infrared radiation** in the spectrum.

Milky Way *see* **Galaxy**

minor planet Term used generally in professional astronomy for **asteroid**. Also known as planetoid.

MKSA Metre-Kilogram(me)-Sec-Ampere system of units, adopted by the International Electrotechnical Commission, in place of all other systems of units. *See* **SI**.

modulation The process of impressing information (code, speech, video, data etc.) onto a higher frequency carrier wave. In frequency modulation (FM) the information is recorded as a variation in frequency, with constant amplitude, and in amplitude modulation (AM) as a variation in amplitude at constant frequency. Used in radio broadcasting.

mole The amount of substance that contains as many entities (**atom**, **molecules**, **ions**, **electrons**, **photons** etc) as there are atoms in 12 of a certain **isotope** of carbon.

molecule An **atom** or a finite group of atoms which is capable of independent existence and has properties characteristic of the substance of which it is the basic unit. Molecular substances are those which have discrete molecules, such as water. Diamond and sodium chloride are examples of non-molecular substances.

mutation In biology, a genetic change that can be transmitted to offspring as an inheritable divergence from previous generations.

natural selection An evolutionary theory which postulates the survival of the best-adapted forms of a species, with the inheritance of those characteristics wherein their fitness lies, and which arise as random variations due to **mutation**; it was first propounded by Charles Darwin, and is often referred to as Darwinism or the Darwinian Theory.

neap tides High tides occurring when the Sun's tidal influence is working against that of the Moon.

nebula A term applied to any astronomical object which appears as a hazy smudge of light in an optical telescope, its usage predating photographic astronomy. It is now more properly restricted to true clouds of interstellar medium. **Galaxies** are sometimes referred to as extragalactic nebulae.

neuron, neurone A nerve cell and its processes.

neutrino A fundamental particle with zero charge

SCIENTIFIC TERMS (cont.)

and zero mass which only interacts weakly with matter and is therefore difficult to detect.

neutron star A small body of very high density resulting from a **supernova** explosion in which a massive **star** collapses under its own gravitational forces, the **electrons** and **protons** combining to form **neutrons**.

neutron An uncharged subatomic particle, with mass approximately equal to that of the **proton**, which is found in the **nucleus** of the **atom**.

noble gases Elements helium, neon, argon, krypton, xenon and radon, which due to their stable structures do not take part in all the usual chemical reactions. Also known as inert gases, rare gases.

node The location of a minimum in the sound, pressure or particle motion when waves superimpose and result in standing waves.

nova Classically, any new star which suddenly becomes visible to the unaided eye. In modern astronomy, a star late in its evolutionary track which suddenly brightens by a factor of 10 000 or more.

nuclear energy In principle, the energy stored in an atomic **nucleus** which binds together the constituent particles. More usually, the energy released during nuclear reactions involving regrouping of such particles (eg **fission** or **fusion** processes).

nuclear fission The spontaneous or induced disintegration of the **nucleus** of a heavy **atom** into two lighter atoms. The process involves a loss of mass which is converted into **nuclear energy**.

nuclear fusion The process of forming **atoms** of new elements by the fusion of atoms of lighter ones. Usually the formation of helium by the fusion of hydrogen and its **isotopes**. The process involves a loss of mass which is converted into **nuclear energy**.

nuclear reaction A process in which an atomic **nucleus** interacts with another nucleus or particle, producing changes in energy and nuclear structure.

nucleon General name for a **neutron** or **proton**.

nucleus (1) In biology, the compartment within a **cell** bounded by a double membrane and containing the genomic **DNA**. (2) In physics, the structure within an **atom** composed of **protons** and **neutrons** which constitutes almost all the mass of the atom.

omnivore An animal which eats both plants and animals.

oncogene A type of **gene** involved in the onset and development of cancer.

optical fibre Fibres of ultra-pure glass, having properties such that light can be transmitted through them by continuously reflecting round bends. Used eg in some communications systems.

order of magnitude The approximate size or number of something, usually measured in a scale from one value to ten times that value.

organic Said of the compounds of carbon. Owing to the ability of carbon atoms to combine together in long chains, these compounds are far more numerous than those of other elements and are the basis of living matter.

orogenesis The tectonic process whereby mountain chains are formed through movement of the Earth's crust.

orthogenesis The evolution of organisms systematically in definite directions and not accidentally in many directions; determinate variation.

osmosis Diffusion of a solvent through a semi-permeable membrane into a more concentrated solution, tending to equalize the concentrations on both sides of the membrane.

oxidation The addition of oxygen to a compound. More generally, any reaction involving the loss of **electrons** from an **atom**. It is always accompanied by reduction.

ozone layer The region of the Earth's atmosphere, between about 20 and 40 km above the surface, where ozone makes up a greater proportion of the air than at any other height. This layer exerts a vital influence by absorbing much of the **ultraviolet radiation** in sunlight and preventing it from reaching the Earth's surface where it has considerable biological effect.

parasite An organism which lives in or on another organism and derives subsistence from it without rendering it any service in return.

parsec The unit of length used for distances beyond the solar system, approximately equal to 3.26 **light-years**.

parthenogenesis The development of a new individual from a single, unfertilized reproductive cell, often an egg.

pasteurization Reduction of the number of microorganisms in milk by maintaining it in a holder at a temperature of from 62.8° to 65.5°C for 30 minutes.

pathogen An organism, eg **parasite**, bacterium or **virus**, which causes disease.

SCIENTIFIC TERMS (cont.)

perennial A plant that lives for more than two years.

periodic table Table displaying classification of chemical **elements** into periods (corresponding to the filling of successive shells of electrons in the atom) and groups (corresponding to the number of outer electrons present).

pH value A number used to express degrees of acidity or alkalinity in solutions, where a pH above 7 indicates alkalinity and below 7 indicates acidity. *See* **acid** and **alkali**.

phage *see* **bacteriophage**

phosphorescence (1) In biology, production of light, usually (in animals) with little production of heat, as in glow-worms. (2) *See* **luminescence**.

photochemical reaction Chemical reaction brought about by light or **ultraviolet radiation**.

photoelectric effect Any phenomenon resulting from the absorption of **photon** energy by **electrons**, leading to their release from a surface, when the photon energy exceeds that binding the electron to the surface, or otherwise allowing conduction when the photon energy exceeds the amount of energy binding an electron to the **atom**.

photon A unit of radiation in the **quantum theory** of light in which light is required to have particle character. May also be regarded as a unit of energy. Photons travel at the speed of light.

photosensitive Property of being sensitive to action of visible or invisible radiation.

photosynthesis The use of energy from light to drive chemical reactions, most notably the building-up of complex compounds by the **chlorophyll** apparatus of plants.

plankton Animals and plants floating in the waters of seas, rivers, ponds and lakes, as distinct from animals which are attached to, or crawl upon, the bottom; especially minute organisms and forms, possessing weak powers of motion.

plasma (1) In physics, a gaseous discharge containing **ions** in which there is no resultant charge, the number of positive and negative ions being equal, in addition to unionized **molecules** or **atoms**. (2) In biology, the bounding membrane of **cells** which controls the entry of molecules and the interaction of cells with their environment.

plate tectonics The interpretation of the Earth's structures and processes (including midocean ridges, mountain building, earthquake zones and volcanic belts) in terms of the movements of large plates of the Earth's crust acting as rigid slabs floating on the layer beneath.

polarization (1) In chemistry, the separation of the positive and negative charges of a molecule by an external agent. (2) In physics, nonrandom orientation of electric and magnetic fields of an **electromagnetic wave**, ie the restriction of the vibrations of light in certain planes.

Polaroid Trademark for a range of photographic and optical products, including a transparent light-polarizing plastic sheet and methods of instant photography in black-and-white and colour. *See* **polarization**.

polymer A plastic material built up from a series of smaller units. The molecular size of the polymer helps to determine the mechanical properties of the plastic material and ranges from a few hundred of the basic units to perhaps hundreds of thousands.

polymorphism (1) The presence in a population of two or more forms of a particular gene. (2) The occurrence of different structural forms at different stages of the life-cycle of the individual.

positron Particle of the same mass as and opposite charge to the (negative) **electron**. The **antiparticle** to the electron.

precession of the equinoxes The variation in the direction of the Earth's axis of rotation caused mainly by the attraction of the Sun and Moon on the equatorial bulge of the Earth, the change describing a full cone with a period of around 25 800 years.

primary colours Those from which all other colours can be derived; red, yellow and blue.

protein Any member of a group of complex substances containing nitrogen that play an important part in the bodies of plants and animals.

proton The **nucleus** of the hydrogen **atom**, of positive charge. With **neutrons**, protons form the nuclei of all atoms.

quantum mechanics A branch of mechanics based on the **quantum theory**, used in predicting the behaviour of elementary particles.

quantum theory Theory of emission and absorption of energy not in continuous measures but in finite steps, applied to elementary particles.

quark A fundamental subatomic particle, currently seen as any of six types: bottom, top, up, down, charmed and strange. Although not yet observed directly, these are suggested to be the units out of which all other subatomic particles are formed.

quasar A distant, compact object far beyond our **Galaxy** which looks star-like on a photograph but appears to be much more distant than a star that

SCIENTIFIC TERMS (cont.)

we would be able to observe. The word is a contraction of quasi-stellar object. Thought to be the most luminous objects in the universe, their mechanisms are possibly related to **black holes**.

radar In general, a system using pulsed **radio waves** to measure the distance and direction of a target (from *RA*dio *D*etection *A*nd *R*anging).

radiation The dissemination of energy from a source. The term is applied to **electromagnetic waves** and to emitted particles (**protons, neutrons** etc).

radio galaxy A **galaxy** emitting a particularly high amount of **radio waves**.

radio waves **Electromagnetic waves** of frequency suitable for radio transmission, of wavelength greater than around 10 cm, ie of longer wavelength than **microwaves**.

radioactivity Spontaneous disintegration of certain natural heavy **elements** (eg radium, actinium, uranium, thorium). The ultimate end-product of radioactive disintegration is an **isotope** of lead.

rational number A number which can be expressed as the ratio of two integers, eg $\frac{3}{4}$.

recessive Describes a **gene** which shows its effect only in individuals that received it from both parent. Also describes an inheritable feature due to a recessive gene.

recombination Reassortment of genes or inheritable features in combinations different from what they were in the parents.

red giant A large, cool, luminous star with its hydrogen exhausted by **nuclear reaction** to helium.

redshift Generally, the decrease in frequency of light observed when a light source moves away from an observer due to the **Doppler effect**. Often referred to in the sense of redshifts observed in light from distant galaxies, indicating the expansion of the universe.

reduction Any process in which an electron is added to an **atom** or an **ion**. Always occurs accompanied by **oxidation**.

refraction Deflection of waves (light, sound etc) which occurs when passing from one medium to another of different density.

relative atomic mass Mass of atoms of an element given on the scale where 1 unit is equal to 1.660×10^{-27} kg. Devised by assigning the value 12 to a specific **isotope** of carbon.

relativity Einstein's Special Theory of Relativity (1905) postulates that all motion is relative and that the velocity of light is the same for all observers, and predicts the effects of these assumptions including variations in the size and mass of objects and in the rate of passage of time, depending on the speed of the observer. His General Theory of Relativity (1916) predicts the variations involved due to acceleration and gravitation.

remote sensing A method in which remote detectors are used to collect data for transmission to a central computer; observation and collection of scientific data without direct contact, especially observation of the Earth's surface from the air or from space using **electromagnetic waves**.

resonance If a vibrating system is set into forced vibrations by a periodic driving force and the applied frequency is at or near the natural vibration frequency of the system, then resonance occurs, producing vibrations of maximum velocity amplitude.

respiration Breathing; the taking in of oxygen and giving out of carbon dioxide, with associated physiological processes.

Richter scale A scale of measurement from 1 to 10, used to indicate the magnitude of an earthquake.

RNA, ribonucleic acid Nucleic acid containing ribose, present in the living cells, where it plays an important part in the development of **proteins**. Can hold genetic information as in **viruses**, but is also the primary agent for transferring information from the **genome** to the protein synthetic machinery of the cell.

saprophyte A plant that feeds on dead organic matter.

saturated compounds Compounds to which no hydrogen atoms or their equivalent can be added, ie which contain neither a double nor a triple bond.

sedimentary rocks All those rocks which result from the wastage of pre-existing rocks. They include the fragments of rocks deposited as sheets of sediment on the floors of seas, lakes and rivers and on land and also deposits formed of the hard parts of organisms. **Igneous** and **metamorphic** rocks are excluded.

semiconductor Said of a material (an **element** or a compound) having higher resistance to the flow of electricity than a **conductor**, but lower resistance than an insulator.

sex determination In many organisms (including vertebrates) sex is determined by the possession of a particular combination of **chromosomes**. In

SCIENTIFIC TERMS (cont.)

mammals, the female's chromosomes are designated XX and the male's are known as XY.

SI System of coherent metric units (Système International d'Unités) proposed for international acceptance in 1960.

sidereal time Time measured by considering the rotation of the Earth relative to the distant stars (rather than the Sun, which is the basis of civil time).

silicon chip *see* **chip**

sine wave A mathematical function which describes a waveform of a single frequency, indefinitely repeated in time. Its displacement can be expressed as the sine (or cosine) of a linear function of time or distance, or both.

software package Fully documented computer program, or set of programs, designed to perform a particular task.

solar system The term designating the Sun and the attendant bodies moving about it under gravitational attraction; comprises nine major planets, and a vast number of **asteroids**, **comets** and **meteors**.

solstice One of the two instants in the year when the Sun reaches its greatest excursion north or south of the equator, or the point reached then. The summer solstice occurs around 21 June, when the Sun reaches the tropic of Cancer, and the winter solstice occurs around 21 December, when the Sun reaches the tropic of Capricorn.

sonar *see* **acoustic imaging**

sonic boom Noise phenomenon due to the shock waves projected from an aircraft travelling at **supersonic** speed. The waves create pressures which may be of sufficient intensity to cause damage to buildings etc.

species A group of individuals that actually or potentially interbreed with each other but not with other such groups and show continuous **variation** within the group but which is distinct from other such groups.

spore A single-cell asexual reproductive body, sometimes extended to other reproductive bodies.

spring tides Those high tides occurring when the Sun and Moon are acting together to produce a maximum tide.

stalactite A deposit of calcium carbonate which hangs icicle-like from the roofs of limestone caverns.

stalagmite An upward-growing conical formation of calcium carbonate, precipitated from dripping solutions on the floors and walls of limestone caverns.

star Sphere of matter held together entirely by its own gravitational field and generating energy by means of **nuclear fusion** reactions in its deep interior.

stellar evolution The sequence of events and changes covering the entire life cycle of a star.

subsonic Said of an object or flow which moves with a speed less than that of sound. *See* **Mach number**, **supersonic**.

superconductivity Property of some pure metals and metallic alloys at very low temperature of having negligible resistance to the flow of an electric current. Each material has its own critical temperature above which it is a normal conductor. When a current is established, it persists almost indefinitely.

supergiant star Star of very high luminosity, enormous size and low density.

supernova A very bright **nova** resulting from an explosion which blows a star's material into space, leaving an expanding cloud of gas and sometimes a central compact object.

supersonic Faster than the speed of sound in that medium. Erroneously used for ultrasonic. *See* **Mach number**, **subsonic**, **ultrasonic**.

symbiosis Mutually beneficial partnership between organisms of different kinds, especially such an association where one lives within the other.

Système International d'Unités *see* **SI**

thermonuclear energy Energy released by a nuclear **fusion** reaction that occurs because of the high thermal energy of the interacting particles.

tornado An intensely destructive, advancing whirlwind formed from strongly ascending air current; also, in West Africa, the squall following thunderstorms between the wet and dry seasons.

transition metal One of the group which have an incomplete inner electron shell. Also known as transition element. *See* **atom**.

transuranic elements Elements of atomic number greater than that of uranium, ie with 93 or more protons in the atomic nuclei. These do not occur naturally but more than 12 have been artificially produced, including neptunium, plutonium, curium and lawrencium.

tsunami A series of waves produced in the ocean by violent movement of the sea floor, most commonly submarine faulting accompanied by an

SCIENTIFIC TERMS (cont.)

earthquake. Its amplitude in mid-ocean is very small; as it approaches land, the amplitude builds up and all the energy of the original disturbance is concentrated with devastating results. Erroneously called a tidal wave.

turbulence Particle motion which at any point varies rapidly in magnitude and direction.

twins (1) Identical twins arise from the same fertilized egg which has subsequently divided into two, each half developing into a separate individual. (2) In mammals, non-identical twins are produced from separate eggs fertilized at the same time.

typhoon A tropical revolving storm, in the China Sea and western North Pacific.

ultrasonic Said of sound frequencies above the upper limit of the normal range of hearing, at or about 20 000 cycles per sec, or 20 kilohertz. Ultrasonics is the general term for the study and application of ultrasonic sound and vibrations.

ultrasound **Ultrasonic** sound used by some animals (eg bats, dolphins) for localization and communication, and in a variety of industrial applications.

ultraviolet radiation **Electromagnetic waves** in a wavelength range from 0.00004 to 0.000001 cm approximately, ie between the visible and X-ray regions of the spectrum.

uncertainty principle The principle that there is a fundamental limit to the precision with which a position co-ordinate of a particle and its momentum in that direction can be simultaneously known. Also, there is a fundamental limit to the knowledge of the energy of a particle when it is measured for a finite time.

unified field theory *see* **field theory**.

valency A measure of the combining power of an **atom**, **molecule** or **ion**; the valency of an ion is equal to its charge.

Van Allen radiation belts Two belts encircling the Earth within which electrically charged particles from the Sun are trapped.

variation In biology, the differences between the offspring of a single mating; the differences between the individuals of a race, subspecies, or species; the differences between analogous groups of higher rank.

vector In mathematics, a vector or vector quantity is one which has magnitude and direction, eg force or velocity.

very high frequencies Those between 30 000 000 and 300 000 000 cycles per sec or between 30 and 300 megahertz. Abbreviated as VHF.

virtual reality Computer simulation which takes into account the motion of an observer to produce the illusion of reality in a computer-created situation, using complex graphics and sound reproduction.

virus A **pathenogen**, usually protein-coated particles of **DNA** or **RNA**, capable of increasing rapidly inside a living cell.

vitamins **Organic** substances required in relatively small amounts in the diet for the proper functioning of the organism, comprising vitamins A, C, D, E, K and the vitamins of the B complex.

white dwarf Small dim star in the final stages of its evolution. The masses of known white dwarfs do not exceed 1.4 times that of the Sun, with a typical diameter about the same as that of the Earth.

X-chromosome *see* **sex determination**

X-rays **Electromagnetic waves** in a wavelength range from 0.0000000001 to 0.000001 cm approximately, ie between the ultraviolet and gamma-ray regions of the spectrum.

Y-chromosome *see* **sex determination**

zenith In astronomy, the point on the celestial sphere vertically above the observer's head.

zodiac A name, of Greek origin, given to the belt of stars, about 18° wide, through which the Sun appears to pass through the year. The zodiac lies approximately in the plane of the motions of the Sun, Moon and planets.

TABLE OF ELEMENTS

Atomic weights are taken from the 1983 list of the International Union of Pure and Applied Chemistry. For radioactive elements, the mass number of the most stable isotope is given in square brackets.

Symbol	Element	Derived from	Atomic No.	Weight	Discovered by	Date
Ac	actinium	Greek, *aktis* = ray	89	[227]	Debierne	1899
Ag	silver	Anglo-Saxon, *seolfor*	47	107.8682	Prehistoric	—
Al	aluminium	Latin, *alumen* = alum	13	26.98154	Wöhler	1828
Am	americium	America	95	[243]	Seaborg, James and others	1944
Ar	argon	Greek, *argos* = inactive	18	39.948	Rayleigh and Ramsay	1894
As	arsenic	Latin, *arsenicum*	33	74.9216	Schröder	1649
At	astatine	Greek, *astatos* = unstable	85	[210]	Corson, Mackenzie and Segrè	1940
Au	gold	Anglo-Saxon, *gold*	79	196.9665	Prehistoric	—
B	boron	Persian, *būrah*	5	10.811	Davy	1808
Ba	barium	Greek, *barys* = heavy	56	137.33	Davy	1808
Be	beryllium	Greek, *beryllion* = beryl	4	9.01218	Wöhler	1828
Bi	bismuth	German (origin unknown)	83	208.9804	Valentine	1450
Bk	berkelium	Berkeley, California	97	[247]	—	1950
Br	bromine	Greek, *bromos* = stench	35	79.904	Balard	1826
C	carbon	Latin, *carbo* = charcoal	6	12.011	Prehistoric	—
Ca	calcium	Latin, *calx* = lime	20	40.078	Davy	1808
Cd	cadmium	Greek, *kadmeia* = calamine	48	112.41	Stromeyer	1817
Ce	cerium	Planet Ceres	58	140.12	Berzelius	1803
Cf	californium	California	98	[251]	—	1950
Cl	chlorine	Greek, *chloros* = green	17	35.453	Scheele	1774
Cm	curium	Pierre and Marie Curie	96	[249]	Seaborg, James and others	1944
Co	cobalt	German, *Kobold* = goblin	27	58.9332	Brandt	1739
Cr	chromium	Greek, *chroma* = colour	24	51.9961	Vauquelin	1797
Cs	cesium/ caesium	Latin, *caesium* = bluish-grey	55	132.9054	Bunsen	1860
Cu	copper	Cyprus	29	63.546	Prehistoric	—
Dy	dysprosium	Greek, *dysprositos*	66	162.50	Boisbaudran	1886
Er	erbium	Ytterby, a Swedish town	68	167.26	Mosander	1843
Es	einsteinium	Einstein	99	[252]	—	1952
Eu	europium	Europe	63	151.96	Demarcay	1896
F	fluorine	Latin, *fluo* = flow	9	18.998403	Scheele	1771
Fe	iron	Anglo-Saxon, *iren*	26	55.847	Prehistoric	—
Fm	fermium	Fermi	100	[257]	—	1952
Fr	francium	France	87	[223]	Mlle Perey	1939
Ga	gallium	Latin, *Gallia* = France	31	69.723	Boisbaudran	1875
Gd	gadolinium	Gadolin, a Finnish chemist	64	157.25	Marignac	1880
Ge	germanium	Latin, *Germania*	32	72.59	Winkler	1886
H	hydrogen	Greek, *hydor* = water + *gen*	1	1.00794	Cavendish	1766
He	helium	Greek, *helios* = sun	2	4.002602	Ramsay	1895
Hf	hafnium	Hafnia = Copenhagen	72	178.49	Coster and Hevesey	1923
Hg	mercury	Mercury (myth)	80	200.59	Prehistoric	—
Ho	holmium	*Holmia* = Stockholm	67	164.9304	Cleve	1879
I	iodine	Greek, *iodes* = violet	53	126.9045	Courtois	1811
In	indium	Its indigo spectrum	49	114.82	Reich and Richter	1863
Ir	iridium	Latin, *iris* = a rainbow	77	192.22	Tennant	1803
K	potassium	English, *potash*	19	39.0983	Davy	1807

TABLE OF ELEMENTS (cont.)

Kr	krypton	Greek, *kryptos* = hidden	36	83.80	Ramsay and Travers	1898
La	lanthanum	Greek, *lanthanō* = conceal	57	138.9055	Mosander	1839
Li	lithium	Greek, *lithos* = stone	3	6.941	Arfvedson	1817
Lu	lutetium	Lutetia, ancient name of Paris	71	174.967	Urbain and Welsbach	1907
Lw	lawrencium	Lawrence, US physicist	103	[260]	—	1961
Md	mendelevium	Mendeléev, Russian chemist	101	[258]	—	1955
Mg	magnesium	Magnesia, district in Thessaly	12	24.305	Bussy	1829
Mn	manganese	Latin, *magnes* = magnet	25	54.9380	Gahn	1774
Mo	molybdenum	Greek, *molybdos* = lead	42	95.94	Hjelm	1782
N	nitrogen	Greek, *nitron* = salpetre	7	14.0067	D Rutherford	1772
Na	sodium	English, *soda*	11	22.98977	Davy	1807
Nb	niobium	Niobe (Greek myth)	41	92.9064	Hatchett	1801
Nd	neodymium	Gereek *neos* = new and *didymos* = twin	60	144.24	Welsbach	1885
Ne	neon	Greek, *neos* = new	10	20.179	Ramsay and Travers	1898
Ni	nickel	Swedish, abbreviation of *kopparnickel*	28	58.69	Cronstedt	1751
No	nobelium	Nobel	102	[259]	—	1957
Np	neptunium	Planet Neptune	93	[237]	McMillan and Abelson	1940
O	oxygen	Greek, *oxys* = acid + *gen*	8	15.9994	Priestley	1774
Os	osmium	Greek, *osme* = odour	76	190.2	Tennant	1803
P	phosphorus	Latin, from Greek 'light-bearing'	15	30.97376	Brandt	1669
Pa	protactinium	Greek, *protos* = first + *actinium*	91	[231]	Hahn and Meitner	1917
Pb	lead	Anglo-Saxon, *lead*	82	207.2	Prehistoric	—
Pd	palladium	Planet Pallas	46	106.42	Wollaston	1804
Pm	promethium	Prometheus, stealer of fire from heaven (Greek myth)	61	[145]	Clinton Laboratories, Oak Ridge, Tenn.	1940
Po	polonium	Poland	84	[209]	Mme Curie	1898
Pr	praseodymium	Greek, *prasios* = green and *didymos* = twin	59	140.9077	Welsbach	1885
Pt	platinum	Spanish, *platina* = silver	78	195.08	Wood	1741
Pu	plutonium	Planet Pluto	94	[244]	Seaborg, McMillan, Wahl and Kennedy	1940
Ra	radium	Latin, *radius* = ray	88	[226]	Mme and M. Curie and Bémont	1898
Rb	rubidium	Latin, *rubidus* = red	37	85.4678	Bunsen	1860
Re	rhenium	German, *Rhein*	75	186.207	Noddack and Tacke	1925
Rh	rhodium	Greek, *rhodon* = rose	45	102.9055	Wollaston	1804
Rn	radon	Radium emanation	86	[222]	Dorn	1901
Ru	ruthenium	Ruthenia	44	101.07	Claus	1845
S	sulphur/sulfur	Latin, *sulfur*	16	32.066	Prehistoric	—
Sb	antimony	L. Latin, *antimonium*	51	121.75	Valentine	1450
Sc	scandium	Scandinavia	21	44.95591	Nilson	1879
Se	selenium	Greek, *selene* = moon	34	78.96	Berzelius	1817
Si	silicon	Latin, *silex* = flint	14	28.0855	Berzelius	1823
Sm	samarium	Samarski, a Russian savant	62	150.36	Boisbaudran	1879
Sn	tin	Anglo-Saxon, *tin*	50	118.710	Prehistoric	—
Sr	strontium	Strontian, a Scottish village	38	87.62	Davy	1808
Ta	tantalum	Tantalus (Greek myth)	73	180.9479	Ekeberg	1802
Tb	terbium	Ytterby, a Swedish town	65	158.9254	Mosander	1843

TABLE OF ELEMENTS (cont.)

Tc	technetium	Greek, *technetos* = artificial	43	[99]	Perrier and Segrè	1937
Te	tellurium	Latin, *tellus* = earth	52	127.60	Reichenstein	1782
Th	thorium	God Thor	90	232.0381	Berzelius	1828
Ti	titanium	Latin, *Titanes* = sons of the earth	22	47.88	Gregor	1789
Tl	thallium	Greek, *thallos* = budding twig	81	204.383	Crookes	1862
Tm	thulium	Greek and Roman Thule = Northland	69	168.9342	Cleve	1879
U	uranium	Planet Uranus	92	238.0289	Klaproth	1789
Une	unnilennium		109	[266]		
Unh	unnilhexium		106	[263]		
Unp	unnilpentium		105	[262]		
Unq	unnilquadium		104	[261]		
Uns	unnilseptium		107	[262]		
V	vanadium	Goddess Vanadis (Freya)	23	50.9415	Sefström	1830
W	tungsten	Swedish, heavy stone	74	183.85	d'Elhujar	1781
Xe	xenon	Greek, *xenos* = stranger	54	131.29	Ramsay and Travers	1898
Y	yttrium	Ytterby, a Swedish town	39	88.9059	Gadolin	1794
Yb	ytterbium	Ytterby, a Swedish town	70	173.04	Marignac	1878
Zn	zinc	German, *zink*	30	65.39	—	before 1500
Zr	zirconium	Persian, *zargun* = gold-coloured	40	91.224	Berzelius	1824

PHYSICAL CONSTANTS

1986 recommended values of the main fundamental physical constants of physics and chemistry.

Quantity	Symbol	Value	Units
Universal constants			
speed of light in vacuum	c	299792458	$\mathrm{m\,s^{-1}}$
permeability of vacuum	μ_0	$4\pi \times 10^{-7}$	$\mathrm{N\,A^{-2}}$
		$= 12.566370614\ldots$	$10^{-7}\,\mathrm{N\,A^{-2}}$
permittivity of vacuum, $1/\mu_0\gamma^2$	ε_0	$8.854187817\ldots$	$10^{-12}\,\mathrm{F\,m^{-1}}$
Newtonian constant of gravitation	G	6.67259	$10^{-11}\,\mathrm{m^3\,kg^{-1}\,s^{-2}}$
Planck constant	h	6.6260755	$10^{-34}\,\mathrm{J\,s}$
$h/2\pi$	$\hbar$	1.05457266	$10^{-34}\,\mathrm{J\,s}$
Electromagnetic constants			
elementary charge	e	1.60217733	$10^{-19}\,\mathrm{C}$
	e/h	2.41798836	$10^{14}\,\mathrm{A\,J^{-1}}$
magnetic flux quantum, $h/2e$	Φ_0	2.06783461	$10^{-15}\,\mathrm{Wb}$
Josephson frequency-voltage quotient	$2e/h$	4.8359767	$10^{14}\,\mathrm{Hz\,V^{-1}}$
Bohr magneton, $e\hbar/2m_e$	μ_B	9.2740154	$10^{-24}\,\mathrm{J\,T^{-1}}$
nuclear magneton, $e\hbar/2m_p$	μ_N	5.0507866	$10^{-27}\,\mathrm{J\,T^{-1}}$
Atomic constants			
fine-structure constant, $\mu_0 ce^2/2h$	α	7.29735308	10^{-3}
	α^{-1}	137.0359895	
Rydberg constant, $m_e c\alpha^2/2h$	R_∞	10973731.534	$\mathrm{m^{-1}}$
Bohr radius, $\alpha/4\pi R_\infty$	a_0	0.529177249	$10^{-10}\,\mathrm{m}$
quantum of circulation	$h/2m_e$	3.63694807	$10^{-4}\,\mathrm{m^2\,s^{-1}}$
	h/m_e	7.27389614	$10^{-4}\,\mathrm{m^2\,s^{-1}}$

PHYSICAL CONSTANTS (cont.)

Electron			
electron mass	m_e	9.1093897	10^{-31} kg
		5.48579903	10^{-4} u
electron-muon mass ratio	m_e/m_μ	4.83633218	10^{-3}
electron-proton mass ratio	m_e/m_p	5.44617013	10^{-4}
electron specific charge	$-e/m_e$	−1.75881962	10^{11} C kg^{-1}
Compton wavelength, $h/m_e c$	λ_C	2.42631058	10^{-12} m
$\lambda_C/2\pi = \alpha a_0 = \alpha^2/4\pi R_\infty$	$\bar{\lambda}_C$	3.86159323	10^{-13} m
classical electron radius, $\alpha^2 a_0$	r_e	2.81794092	10^{-15} m
electron magnetic moment	μ_e	928.47701	10^{-26} J T^{-1}
electron g factor, $2(1 + a_e)$	g_e	2.002319304386	
electron-proton magnetic moment ratio	μ_e/μ_p	658.2106881	
Muon			
muon mass	m_μ	1.8835327	10^{-28} kg
		0.113428913	u
muon magnetic moment	μ_μ	4.4904514	10^{-26} J T^{-1}
muon g factor, $2(1 + a_\mu)$	g_μ	2.002331846	
muon-proton magnetic moment ratio	μ_μ/μ_p	3.18334547	
Proton			
proton mass	m_p	1.6726231	10^{-27} kg
		1.007276470	u
proton Compton wavelength, $h/m_p c$	$\lambda_{C,p}$	1.32141002	10^{-15} m
$\lambda_{C,p}/2\pi$	$\bar{\lambda}_{C,p}$	2.10308937	10^{-16} m
proton magnetic moment	μ_p	1.41060761	10^{-26} J T^{-1}
in Bohr magnetons	μ_p/μ_B	1.521032202	10^{-3}
in nuclear magnetons	μ_p/μ_N	2.792847386	
proton gyromagnetic ratio	γ_p	26752.2128	10^4 s^{-1} T^{-1}
	$\gamma_p/2\pi$	42.577469	MHz T^{-1}
uncorrected (H_2O, sph., 25°C)	γ'_p	26751.5255	10^4 s^{-1} T^{-1}
	$\gamma'_p/2\pi$	42.576375	MHz T^{-1}
Neutron			
neutron mass	m_n	1.6749286	10^{-27} kg
		1.008664904	u
neutron Compton wavelength, $h/m_n c$	$\lambda_{C,n}$	1.31959110	10^{-15} m
$\lambda_{C,n}/2\pi$	$\lambda_{C,n}$	2.10019445	10^{-16} m
Physico-chemical constants			
Avogadro constant	N_A, L	6.0221367	10^{23} mol^{-1}
atomic mass constant $m_u = \frac{1}{12}m(^{12}C)$	m_u	1.6605402	10^{-27} kg
Faraday constant, $N_A e$	F	96485.309	C mol^{-1}
molar gas constant	R	8.314510	J mol^{-1} K^{-1}
Boltzmann constant, R/N_A	k	1.380658	10^{-23} J K^{-1}
molar volume (ideal gas), RT/p			
$T = 273.15$ K, $p = 101\,325$ Pa	V_m	0.02241410	m^3 mol^{-1}
Stefan-Boltzmann constant, $(\pi^2/60)\,k^4/\hbar^3c^2$	σ	5.67051	10^{-8} W m^{-2} K^{-4}
first radiation constant, $2\pi hc^2$	c_1	3.74177749	10^{-16} W m^2
second radiation constant, hc/k	c_2	0.01438769	m K

RADIATION

Radiation	Approximate wavelengths	Discovered by	Date	Uses
Radio waves	>10 cm	Heinrich Hertz (German)	1888	communications; radio and TV broadcasting
Microwaves	1 mm–10 cm	Heinrich Hertz (German)	1886	communications; radar; microwave ovens
Infrared	10^{-3}–7.8×10^{-7} m	William Herschel (German–British)	1800	night and smoke vision systems; intruder alarms; weather forecasting; missile guidance systems
Visible	7.8×10^{-7}–3×10^{-7} m	—	—	human eyesight
Ultraviolet	3×10^{-7}–10^{-8} m	Johann Ritter (German)	1801	forensic science; medical treatment
X-rays	10^{-8}–3×10^{-11} m	Wilhelm Röntgen (German)	1895	medical X-ray photographs; material structure analysis
Gamma rays	$<3\times10^{-11}$ m	Ernest Rutherford (British)	1902	medical diagnosis

PROPERTIES OF METALS

Name	Symbol	Valence no.	Atomic no.	Melting point (°C)
Aluminium	Al	3	13	660.37
Antimony (stibium)	Sb	3 or 5	51	630.74
Barium	Ba	2	56	725
Beryllium	Be	2	4	1278 ± 5
Bismuth	Bi	3 or 5	83	271.3
Cadmium	Cd	1 or 2	48	320.9
Caesium	Cs	1	55	28.40 ± 0.01
Calcium	Ca	2	20	839 ± 2
Cerium	Ce	3 or 4	58	798
Chromium	Cr	2, 3, or 6	24	1857 ± 20
Cobalt	Co	2 or 3	27	1495
Copper (cuprum)	Cu	1 or 2	29	$1083.4\pm.2$
Gallium	Ga	3	31	29.78
Gold (aurum)	Au	1 or 3	79	1064.43
Iridium	Ir	2 or 4	77	2410
Iron (ferrum)	Fe	2 or 3	26	1535
Lanthanum	La	3	57	918
Lead (plumbum)	Pb	2 or 4	82	327.5
Lithium	Li	1	3	180.5
Magnesium	Mg	2	12	648.8 ± 0.5
Manganese	Mn	2, 3, 4, 6, or 7	25	1244 ± 3
Mercury (hydrargyrum)	Hg	1 or 2	80	-38.87
Molybdenum	Mo	2 or 6	42	2617
Nickel	Ni	2 or 3	28	1453
Osmium	Os	2 or 8	76	3045 ± 30
Palladium	Pd	2 or 4	46	1554
Platinum	Pt	3 or 4	78	1772
Plutonium	Pu	—	94	641
Potassium (kalium)	K	1	19	63.25
Rubidium	Rb	1	37	38.89
Silver (argentum)	Ag	1	47	961.93
Sodium (natrium)	Na	1	11	97.81 ± 0.03
Tin (stannum)	Sn	2 or 4	50	231.97
Titanium	Ti	3 or 4	22	1660 ± 10
Tungsten (wolfram)	W	4 or 6	74	3410 ± 20
Uranium	U	2 or 6	92	1132 ± 0.8
Vanadium	V	5	23	1890 ± 10
Zinc	Zn	2	30	419.58

PROPERTIES OF POLYMERS

Polymer	Density ($kg\ m^{-3}$)	Tensile strength ($MN\ m^{-2}$)	Heat capacity ($J\ g^{-1}K^{-1}$)	Resistivity (Ω cm)
Acetals	1420	65	1.46	10^{15}
Cellulose	1480–1530	80–240	1.3–1.5	10^{7}–10^{14}
Cellulose acetate				
Moulded	1220–1340	12–58	1.26–1.8	10^{10}–10^{14}
Sheet	1280–1320	30–52	1.26–2.1	10^{11}–10^{15}
Cellulose nitrate (celluloid)	1350–1400	50	1.3–1.7	10^{10}
Epoxy cast resins	1110–1400	26–85	1.0	10^{12}–10^{17}
Nylon-6 (Poly-E-caprolactam)	1120–1170	45–90	1.6	10^{12}–10^{15}
Nylon-66 (Polyhexa-methylene-adipamide)	1130–1150	60–80	1.7	10^{14}–10^{15}
Polyacrylonitrile	1160–1180	200	—	10^{14}
Polycarbonates	1200	52–62	1.17–1.25	10^{16}
Polyethylene				
Low density	910–925	4–15	—	10^{15}–10^{18}
Medium density	926–940	8–22	—	10^{15}–10^{18}
High density	940–965	20–36	—	10^{15}–10^{18}
Polyisoprene				
Natural rubber	906–13	—	1.88	10^{6}
Hard rubber	1130–1180	39	1.38	10^{16}
Polypropylene	902–906	28–36	1.92	$>10^{16}$
Polystyrene	1040–1090	30–100	1.3–1.5	$>10^{16}$
Polyurethane				
Cast liquid	1100–1500	1–65	1.8	10^{11}–10^{15}
Elastomer	1110–1250	29–55	1.8	10^{11}–10^{13}
Polyvinylchloride	1300–1400	50	0.84–1.17	10^{16}
Silicone cast resin	1300	—	—	10^{14}–10^{15}

SI UNITS (international system of units)

Concept	Symbol	Name of Unit	Abbreviation of Unit Name
Length	l	metre	m
Mass	m	kilogramme	kg
Time	t	second	s
Electric current	I	ampere	A
Thermodynamic temperature	T	kelvin	K
Luminous intensity	I	candela	cd
Amount of substance		mole	mol
Plane angle	α, β, θ, etc	radian	rad
Solid angle	Ω, ω	steradian	sr
Area	A, a	square metre	m^2
Volume	V, v	cubic metre	m^3
Velocity	v, u	metre/second	$m\ s^{-1}$
Acceleration	a	metre/second^2	$m\ s^{-2}$
Density	ρ	kilogramme/metre^3	$kg\ m^{-3}$
Mass rate of flow	$\dot{m}, \dot{M}$	kilogramme/sec	$kg\ s^{-1}$
Volume rate of flow	$\dot{V}$	cubic metre/sec	$m^3\ s^{-1}$

SI UNITS (international system of units) (cont.)

Concept	Symbol	Name of Unit	Abbreviation of Unit Name
Moment of inertia	I	kilogramme metre^2	kg m^2
Momentum	p	kilogramme metre/sec	kg m s^{-1}
Angular momentum	$I\omega$	kilogramme metre^2/sec	kg m^2 s^{-1}
Force	F	newton	N
Torque (moment of force)	T (M)	newton metre	N m
Work (energy, heat)	W (E)	joule	J
Potential energy	V	joule	J
Kinetic energy	T (W)	joule	J
Heat (enthalpy)	Q (H)	joule	J
Power	P	watt	W
Pressure (stress)	p (σ, f)	newton/metre^2	N m^{-2}
Surface tension	γ (σ)	newton/metre	N m^{-1}
Viscosity, dynamic	η, μ		N s m^{-1}
Viscosity, kinematic	v		m^2 s^{-1}
Temperature	θ, T	degree Celsius, kelvin	°C, K
Velocity of light	c	metre/second	m s^{-1}
Permeabiity of vacuum	μ_0	henry/metre	H m^{-1}
Permittivity of vacuum	ε_0	farad/metre	F m^{-1}
Electric charge	Q	coulomb	C
Electric potential (potential difference)	V	volt	V
Electric field strength (electric force)	E	volt/metre	V m^{-1}
Electric resistance	R	ohm	Ω
Conductance	G	siemens	S
Electric flux	Ψ	coulomb	$\Psi = Q$
Electric flux density (displacement)	D	coulomb/metre^2	C m^{-2}
Frequency	f	hertz	Hz
Permittivity	ε	farad/metre	F m^{-1}
Relative permittivity	ε_r		
Magnetic field strength	H	amp. turn/metre	At m^{-1}
Magnetic flux	Φ	weber	Wb
Magnetic flux density	B	telsa	T
Permeability	μ	henry/metre	H m^{-1}
Relative permeability	μ_r		
Mutual inductance	M	henry	H
Self inductance	L	henry	H
Capacitance	C	farad	F
Reactance	X	ohm	Ω
Impedance	Z	ohm	Ω
Susceptance	B	siemens	S
Admittance	Y	siemens	S
Total voltamperes	S	volt amp	VA
Reactive voltamperes	Q	volt amp reactive	VAr
Power factor	p.f.	—	—
Luminous flux	Φ	lumen	lm
Illumination	E	lux	lx

SI CONVERSION FACTORS

This table gives the conversion factors for many British and other units which are still in common use, showing their equivalents in terms of the international system of units (SI). The column labelled 'SI equivalent' gives the SI value of one unit of the type named in the first column, eg 1 calorie is 4.186 J.

Unit name	Symbol	Quantity	SI equivalent	Unit
acre		area	0.405	hm^2
ångström+	Å	length	0.1	nm
astronomical unit	AU	length	0.150	Tm
atomic mass unit	amu	mass	1.661×10^{-27}	kg
bar+	bar	pressure	0.1	MPa
barn+	b	area	100	fm^2
barrel (US) = 42 US gal	bbl	volume	0.159	m^3
British thermal unit	Btu	energy	1.055	kJ
calorie	cal	energy	4.186	J
cubic foot	ft^3	volume	0.028	m^3
cubic inch	in^3	volume	16.387	cm^3
cubic yard	yd^3	volume	0.765	m^3
curie+	Ci	activity of radionuclide	37	GBq
degree = 1/90 rt angle	°	plane angle	$\pi/180$	rad
degree Celsius	°C	temperature	1	K
degree Centigrade	°C	temperature	1	K
degree Fahrenheit	°F	temperature	5/9	K
degree Rankine	°R	temperature	5/9	K
dyne	dyn	force	10	μN
electronvolt	eV	energy	0.160	aJ
erg	erg	energy	0.1	μJ
fathom (6 ft)		length	1.829	m
fermi		length	1	fm
foot	ft	length	30.48	cm
foot per second	$ft\,s^{-1}$	velocity	0.305 1.097	$m\,s^{-1}$ $km\,h^{-1}$
gallon (UK)+	gal	volume	4.546	dm^3
gallon (US)+ = 231 in^3	gal	volume	3.785	dm^3
gallon (UK) per mile		consumption	2.825	$dm^3\,km^{-1}$
gauss	Gs, G	magnetic flux density	100	μT
grade = 0.01 rt angle		plane angle	$\pi/200$	rad
grain	gr	mass	0.065	g
hectare+	ha	area	1	hm^2
horsepower	hp	energy	0.746	kW
inch	in	length	2.54	cm
kilogram-force	kgf	force	9.807	N
knot+		velocity	1.852	$km\,h^{-1}$
light year	l.y.	length	9.461×10^{15}	m
litre	l	volume	1	dm^3
maxwell	Mx	magnetic flux	10	nWb
metric carat		mass	0.2	g
micron	μ	length	1	μm
mile (nautical)+		length	1.852	km
mile (statute)		length	1.609	km
mile per hour (mph)	$mile\,h^{-1}$	velocity	1.609	$km\,h^{-1}$
minute = (1/60)°	′	plane angle	$\pi/10800$	rad
oersted	Oe	magnetic field strength	$1/(4\pi)$	$kA\,m^{-1}$

SI CONVERSION FACTORS (cont.)

Unit name	Symbol	Quantity	SI equivalent	Unit
ounce (avoirdupois)	oz	mass	28.349	g
ounce (troy) = 480 gr		mass	31.103	g
parsec	pc	length	30857	Tm
phot	ph	illuminance	10	klx
pint (UK)	pt	volume	0.568	dm^3
poise	p	viscosity	0.1	Pa s
pound	lb	mass	0.454	kg
pound-force	lbf	force	4.448	N
pound-force/in^{-2}		pressure	6.895	kPa
poundal	pdl	force	0.138	N
pounds per square inch	psi	pressure	6.895×10^3	K Pa
rad⁺	rad	absorbed dose	0.01	Gy
rem⁺	rem	dose equivalent	0.01	Sv
right angle = $\pi/2$ rad		plane angle	1.571	rad
röntgen⁺	R	exposure	0.258	mC kg^{-1}
second = (1/60)′	″	plane angle	$\pi/648$	mrad
slug		mass	14.594	kg
solar mass	M	mass	1.989×10^{30}	kg
square foot	ft^2	area	9.290	dm^2
square inch	in^2	area	6.452	cm^2
square mile (statute)		area	2.590	km^2
square yard	yd^2	area	0.836	m^2
standard atmosphere	atm	pressure	0.101	MPa
stere	st	volume	1	m^3
stilb	sb	luminance	10	kcd m^{-2}
stokes	St	viscosity	1	$cm^2\ s^{-1}$
therm = 10^5 Btu		energy	0.105	GJ
ton = 2240 lb		mass	1.016	Mg
ton-force	tonf	force	9.964	kN
ton-force/in^{-2}		pressure	15.444	MPa
tonne	t	mass	1	Mg
torr / mmHg	torr	pressure	0.133	kPa
X unit		length	0.100	pm
yard	yd	length	0.915	m

⁺In temporary use with SI.

SI PREFIXES

Factor	Prefix	Symbol	Factor	Prefix	Symbol	Factor	Prefix	Symbol	Factor	Prefix	Symbol
10^{18}	exa	E	10^6	mega	M	10^{-1}	deci	d	10^{-9}	nano	n
10^{15}	peta	P	10^3	kilo	k	10^{-2}	centi	c	10^{-12}	pico	p
10^{12}	tera	T	10^2	hecto	h	10^{-3}	milli	m	10^{-15}	femto	f
10^9	giga	G	10^1	deca	da	10^{-6}	micro	μ	10^{-18}	atto	a

TEMPERATURE CONVERSION

To convert	To	Equation	To convert	To	Equation
°Fahrenheit	°Celsius	$-32, \times 5, \div 9$	°Celsius	°Réaumur	$\times 4, \div 5$
°Fahrenheit	°Rankine	$+459.67$	Kelvin	°Celsius	-273.15
°Fahrenheit	°Réaumur	$-32, \times 4, \div 9$	°Rankine	°Fahrenheit	-459.67
°Celsius	°Fahrenheit	$\times 9, \div 5, +32$	°Réaumur	°Fahrenheit	$\times 9, \div 4, +32$
°Celsius	Kelvin	$+273.15$	°Réaumur	°Celsius	$\times 5, \div 4$

Carry out operations in sequence.

TEMPERATURE CONVERSION

Degrees Fahrenheit (F) → Degrees Celsius (Centigrade) (C)

°F	°C	°F	°C	°F	°C	°F	°C
1	−17.2	54	12.2	107	41.7	160	71.1
2	−16.7	55	12.8	108	42.2	161	71.7
3	−16.1	56	13.3	109	42.8	162	72.2
4	−15.5	57	13.9	110	43.3	163	72.8
5	−15.0	58	14.4	111	43.9	164	73.3
6	−14.4	59	15.0	112	44.4	165	73.9
7	−13.9	60	15.5	113	45.0	166	74.4
8	−13.3	61	16.1	114	45.5	167	75.0
9	−12.8	62	16.7	115	46.1	168	75.5
10	−12.2	63	17.2	116	46.7	169	76.1
11	−11.6	64	17.8	117	47.2	170	76.7
12	−11.1	65	18.3	118	47.8	171	77.2
13	−10.5	66	18.9	119	48.3	172	77.8
14	−10.0	67	19.4	120	48.9	173	78.3
15	−9.4	68	20.0	121	49.4	174	78.9
16	−8.9	69	20.5	122	50.0	175	79.4
17	−8.3	70	21.1	123	50.5	176	80.0
18	−7.8	71	21.7	124	51.1	177	80.5
19	−7.2	72	22.2	125	51.7	178	81.1
20	−6.7	73	22.8	126	52.2	179	81.7
21	−6.1	74	23.3	127	52.8	180	82.2
22	−5.5	75	23.9	128	53.3	181	82.8
23	−5.0	76	24.4	129	53.9	182	83.3
24	−4.4	77	25.0	130	54.4	183	83.9
25	−3.9	78	25.5	131	55.0	184	84.4
26	−3.3	79	26.1	132	55.5	185	85.0
27	−2.8	80	26.7	133	56.1	186	85.5
28	−2.2	81	27.2	134	56.7	187	86.1
29	−1.7	82	27.8	135	57.2	188	86.7
30	−1.1	83	28.3	136	57.8	189	87.2
31	−0.5	84	28.9	137	58.3	190	87.8
32	0	85	29.4	138	58.9	191	88.3
33	0.5	86	30.0	139	59.4	192	88.8
34	1.1	87	30.5	140	60.0	193	89.4
35	1.7	88	31.1	141	60.5	194	90.0
36	2.2	89	31.7	142	61.1	195	90.5
37	2.8	90	32.2	143	61.7	196	91.1
38	3.3	91	32.8	144	62.2	197	91.7
39	3.9	92	33.3	145	62.8	198	92.2
40	4.4	93	33.9	146	63.3	199	92.8
41	5.0	94	34.4	147	63.9	200	93.3
42	5.5	95	35.0	148	64.4	201	93.9
43	6.1	96	35.5	149	65.0	202	94.4
44	6.7	97	36.1	150	65.5	203	95.0
45	7.2	98	36.7	151	66.1	204	95.5
46	7.8	99	37.2	152	66.7	205	96.1
47	8.3	100	37.8	153	67.2	206	96.7
48	8.9	101	38.3	154	67.8	207	97.2
49	9.4	102	38.9	155	68.3	208	97.8
50	10.0	103	39.4	156	68.9	209	98.3
51	10.5	104	40.0	157	69.4	210	98.9
52	11.1	105	40.5	158	70.0	211	99.4
53	11.7	106	41.1	159	70.5	212	100.0

Degrees Celsius (Centigrade) (C) → Degrees Fahrenheit (F)

°C	°F	°C	°F
1	33.8	51	123.8
2	35.6	52	125.6
3	37.4	53	127.4
4	39.2	54	129.2
5	41.0	55	131.0
6	42.8	56	132.8
7	44.6	57	134.6
8	46.4	58	136.4
9	48.2	59	138.2
10	50.0	60	140.0
11	51.8	61	141.8
12	53.6	62	143.6
13	55.4	63	145.4
14	57.2	64	147.2
15	59.0	65	149.0
16	60.8	66	150.8
17	62.6	67	152.6
18	64.4	68	154.4
19	66.2	69	156.2
20	68.0	70	158.0
21	69.8	71	159.8
22	71.6	72	161.6
23	73.4	73	163.4
24	75.2	74	165.2
25	77.0	75	167.0
26	78.8	76	168.8
27	80.6	77	170.6
28	82.4	78	172.4
29	84.2	79	174.2
30	86.0	80	176.0
31	87.8	81	177.8
32	89.6	82	179.6
33	91.4	83	181.4
34	93.2	84	183.2
35	95.0	85	185.0
36	96.8	86	186.8
37	98.6	87	188.6
38	100.4	88	190.4
39	102.2	89	192.2
40	104.0	90	194.0
41	105.8	91	195.8
42	107.6	92	197.6
43	109.4	93	199.4
44	111.2	94	201.2
45	113.0	95	203.0
46	114.8	96	204.8
47	116.6	97	206.6
48	118.4	98	208.4
49	120.2	99	210.2
50	122.0	100	212.0

NUMERICAL EQUIVALENTS

Arabic	Roman	Greek	Binary numbers
1	I	α'	1
2	II	β'	10
3	III	γ'	11
4	IV	δ'	100
5	V	ε'	101
6	VI	ς'	110
7	VII	ζ'	111
8	VIII	η'	1000
9	IX	θ'	1001
10	X	ι'	1010
11	XI	ια'	1011
12	XII	ιβ'	1100
13	XIII	ιγ'	1101
14	XIV	ιδ'	1110
15	XV	ιε'	1111
16	XVI	ις'	10000
17	XVII	ιζ'	10001
18	XVIII	ιη'	10010
19	XIX	ιθ'	10011
20	XX	κ'	10100
30	XXX	λ'	11110
40	XL	μ'	101000
50	L	ν'	110010
60	LX	ξ'	111100
70	LXX	ο'	1000110
80	LXXX	π'	1010000
90	XC	͵ο'	1011010
100	C	ρ'	1100100
200	CC	σ'	11001000
300	CCC	τ'	100101100
400	CD	υ'	110010000
500	D	φ'	111110100
1 000	M	͵α	1111101000
5 000	V̄	͵ε	1001110001000
10 000	X̄	͵ι	10011100010000
100 000	C̄	͵ρ	11000011010100000

Fraction	Decimal
1/2	0.5000
1/3	0.3333
2/3	0.6667
1/4	0.2500
3/4	0.7500
1/5	0.2000
2/5	0.4000
3/5	0.6000
4/5	0.8000
1/6	0.1667
5/6	0.8333
1/7	0.1429
2/7	0.2857
3/7	0.4286
4/7	0.5714
5/7	0.7143
6/7	0.8571
1/8	0.1250
3/8	0.3750
5/8	0.6250
7/8	0.8750
1/9	0.1111
2/9	0.2222
4/9	0.4444
5/9	0.5556
7/9	0.7778
8/9	0.8889
1/10	0.1000
3/10	0.3000
7/10	0.7000
9/10	0.9000
1/11	0.0909
2/11	0.1818
3/11	0.2727
4/11	0.3636
5/11	0.4545
6/11	0.5454
7/11	0.6363
8/11	0.7272
9/11	0.8181
10/11	0.9090
1/12	0.0833
5/12	0.4167
7/12	0.5833
11/12	0.9167
1/16	0.0625
3/16	0.1875
5/16	0.3125
7/16	0.4375
9/16	0.5625
11/16	0.6875
13/16	0.8125
15/16	0.9375
1/20	0.0500
3/20	0.1500
7/20	0.3500
9/20	0.4500
11/20	0.5500
13/20	0.6500
17/20	0.8500
19/20	0.9500
1/32	0.0312
3/32	0.0937
5/32	0.1562
7/32	0.2187
9/32	0.2812
11/32	0.3437
13/32	0.4062
15/32	0.4687
17/32	0.5312
19/32	0.5937
21/32	0.6562
23/32	0.7187
25/32	0.7812
27/32	0.8437
29/32	0.9062
31/32	0.9687

NUMERICAL EQUIVALENTS (cont.)

%	Decimal	Fraction	%	Decimal	Fraction	%	Decimal	Fraction	%	Decimal	Fraction
1	0.01	1/100	15	0.15	3/20	30	0.30	3/10	45	0.45	9/20
2	0.02	1/50	16	0.16	4/25	31	0.31	31/100	46	0.46	23/50
3	0.03	3/100	$16\frac{2}{3}$	0.167	1/6	32	0.32	8/25	47	0.47	47/100
4	0.04	1/25	17	0.17	17/100	33	0.33	33/100	48	0.48	12/25
5	0.05	1/20	18	0.18	9/50	$33\frac{1}{3}$	0.333	1/3	49	0.49	49/100
6	0.06	3/50	19	0.19	19/100	34	0.34	17/50	50	0.50	1/2
7	0.07	7/100	20	0.20	1/5	35	0.35	7/20	55	0.55	11/20
8	0.08	2/25	21	0.21	21/100	36	0.36	9/25	60	0.60	3/5
$8\frac{1}{3}$	0.083	1/12	22	0.22	11/50	37	0.37	37/100	65	0.65	13/20
9	0.09	9/100	23	0.23	23/100	38	0.38	19/50	70	0.70	7/10
10	0.10	1/10	24	0.24	6/25	39	0.39	39/100	75	0.75	3/4
11	0.11	11/100	25	0.25	1/4	40	0.40	2/5	80	0.80	4/5
12	0.12	3/25	26	0.26	13/50	41	0.41	41/100	85	0.85	17/20
$12\frac{1}{2}$	0.125	1/8	27	0.27	27/100	42	0.42	21/50	90	0.90	9/10
13	0.13	13/100	28	0.28	7/25	43	0.43	43/100	95	0.95	19/20
14	0.14	7/50	29	0.29	29/100	44	0.44	11/25	100	1.00	1

MULTIPLICATION TABLE

	2	**3**	**4**	**5**	**6**	**7**	**8**	**9**	**10**	**11**	**12**	**13**	**14**	**15**	**16**	**17**	**18**	**19**	**20**	**21**	**22**	**23**	**24**	**25**
2	4	6	8	10	12	14	16	18	20	22	24	26	28	30	32	34	36	38	40	42	44	46	48	50
3	6	9	12	15	18	21	24	27	30	33	36	39	42	45	48	51	54	57	60	63	66	69	72	75
4	8	12	16	20	24	28	32	36	40	44	48	52	56	60	64	68	72	76	80	84	88	92	96	100
5	10	15	20	25	30	35	40	45	50	55	60	65	70	75	80	85	90	95	100	105	110	115	120	125
6	12	18	24	30	36	42	48	54	60	66	72	78	84	90	96	102	108	114	120	126	132	138	144	150
7	14	21	28	35	42	49	56	63	70	77	84	91	98	105	112	119	126	133	140	147	154	161	168	175
8	16	24	32	40	48	56	64	72	80	88	96	104	112	120	128	136	144	152	160	168	176	184	192	200
9	18	27	36	45	54	63	72	81	90	99	108	117	126	135	144	153	162	171	180	189	198	207	216	225
10	20	30	40	50	60	70	80	90	100	110	120	130	140	150	160	170	180	190	200	210	220	230	240	250
11	22	33	44	55	66	77	88	99	110	121	132	143	154	165	176	187	198	209	220	231	242	253	264	275
12	24	36	48	60	72	84	96	108	120	132	144	156	168	180	192	204	216	228	240	252	264	276	288	300
13	26	39	52	65	78	91	104	117	130	143	156	169	182	195	208	221	234	247	260	273	286	299	312	325
14	28	42	56	70	84	98	112	126	140	154	168	182	196	210	224	238	252	266	280	294	308	322	336	350
15	30	45	60	75	90	105	120	135	150	165	180	195	210	225	240	255	270	285	300	315	330	345	360	375
16	32	48	64	80	96	112	128	144	160	176	192	208	224	240	256	272	288	304	320	336	352	368	384	400
17	34	51	68	85	102	119	136	153	170	187	204	221	238	255	272	289	306	323	340	357	374	391	408	425
18	36	54	72	90	108	126	144	162	180	198	216	234	252	270	288	306	324	342	360	378	396	414	432	450
19	38	57	76	95	114	133	152	171	190	209	228	247	266	285	304	323	342	361	380	399	418	437	456	475
20	40	60	80	100	120	140	160	180	200	220	240	260	280	300	320	340	360	380	400	420	440	460	480	500
21	42	63	84	105	126	147	168	189	210	231	252	273	294	315	336	357	378	399	420	441	462	483	504	525
22	44	66	88	110	132	154	176	198	220	242	264	286	308	330	352	374	396	418	440	462	484	506	528	550
23	46	69	92	115	138	161	184	207	230	253	276	299	322	345	368	391	414	437	460	483	506	529	552	575
24	48	72	96	120	144	168	192	216	240	264	288	312	336	360	384	408	432	456	480	501	528	552	576	600
25	50	75	100	125	150	175	200	225	250	275	300	325	350	375	400	425	450	475	500	525	550	575	600	625

MATHEMATICAL SIGNS AND SYMBOLS

$+$	plus; positive; underestimate
$-$	minus; negative; overestimate
$\pm$	plus or minus; positive or negative; degree of accuracy
$\mp$	minus or plus; negative or positive
$\times$	multiplies (colloq. 'times') (6×4)
$\cdot$	multiplies (colloq. 'times') (6.4); scalar product of two vectors ($A \cdot B$)
$\div$	divided by ($6 \div 4$)
/	divided by; ratio of (6/4)
—	divided by; ratio of ($\frac{6}{4}$)
$=$	equals
$\neq$, $\neq$	not equal to
$\equiv$	identical with
$\not\equiv$, $\not\equiv$	not identical with
:	ratio of (6:4); scalar product of two tensors (Y:Z)
::	proportionately equals (1:2::2:4)
$\approx$	approximately equal to; equivalent to; similar to
$>$	greater than
$\gg$	much greater than
$\ngtr$	not greater than
$<$	less than
$\ll$	much less than
$\nless$	not less than
$\geqslant, \geqq, \gtreqqless$	equal to or greater than
$\leqslant, \leqq, \lesseqqgtr$	equal to or less than
$\propto$	directly proportional to
( )	parentheses
[ ]	brackets
{ }	braces
—	vinculum: division ($\overline{a-b}$); chord of circle or length of line ($\overline{AB}$); arithmetic mean ($\overline{X}$)

∞	infinity
$\rightarrow$	approaches the limit
$\sqrt{}$	square root
$\sqrt[3]{}, \sqrt[4]{}$	cube root, fourth root, etc.
!	factorial ($4! = 4 \times 3 \times 2 \times 1$)
%	percent
$'$	prime; minute(s) of arc; foot/feet
$''$	double prime; second(s) of arc; inch(es)
$\frown$	arc of circle
$^\circ$	degree of arc
$\angle, \angle^s$	angle(s)
$\veebar$	equiangular
$\perp$	perpendicular
$\parallel$	parallel
○, ⓢ	circle(s)
$\triangle, \triangle_s$	triangle(s)
□	square
▭	rectangle
▱	parallelogram
$\cong$	congruent to
$\therefore$	therefore
$\because$	because
$\overset{m}{=}$	measured by
$\triangle$	increment
$\sum$	summation
$\prod$	product
$\int$	integral sign
∇	del: differential operator
$\cup$	union
$\cap$	interaction

SQUARES AND ROOTS

No.	Square	Cube	Square root	Cube root
1	1	1	1.000	1.000
2	4	8	1.414	1.260
3	9	27	1.732	1.442
4	16	64	2.000	1.587
5	25	125	2.236	1.710
6	36	216	2.449	1.817
7	49	343	2.646	1.913
8	64	512	2.828	2.000
9	81	729	3.000	2.080
10	100	1 000	3.162	2.154
11	121	1 331	3.317	2.224
12	144	1 728	3.464	2.289
13	169	2 197	3.606	2.351
14	196	2 744	3.742	2.410
15	225	3 375	3.873	2.466
16	256	4 096	4.000	2.520
17	289	4 913	4.123	2.571
18	324	5 832	4.243	2.621
19	361	6 859	4.359	2.668
20	400	8 000	4.472	2.714
25	625	15 625	5.000	2.924
30	900	27 000	5.477	3.107
40	1 600	64 000	6.325	3.420
50	2 500	125 000	7.071	3.684

COMMON MEASURES

Metric units

Length		Imperial equiv.
	1 millimetre	0.03937 in
10 mm	1 centimetre	0.39 in
10 cm	1 decimetre	3.94 in
100 cm	1 metre	39.37 in
1 000 m	1 kilometre	0.62 mile

Area		Imperial equiv.
	1 square millimetre	0.0016 sq in
	1 square centimetre	0.155 sq in
100 sq cm	1 square decimetre	15.5 sq in
10000 sq cm	1 square metre	10.76 sq ft
10000 sq m	1 hectare	2.47 acres

Volume		Imperial equiv.
	1 cubic centimetre	0.016 cu in
1 000 cu cm	1 cubic decimetre	61.024 cu in
1 000 cu dm	1 cubic metre	35.31 cu ft
		1.308 cu yds
Liquid volume		
	1 litre	1.76 pints
100 litres	1 hectolitre	22 gallons

Weight		Imperial equiv.
	1 gram	0.035 oz
1 000 g	1 kilogram	2.2046 lb
1 000 kg	1 tonne	0.0842 ton

Imperial units

Length		Metric equiv.
	1 inch	2.54 cm
12 in	1 foot	30.48 cm
3 ft	1 yard	0.9144 m
1 760 yd	1 mile	1.6093 km

Area		Metric equiv.
	1 square inch	6.45 sq cm
144 sq in	1 square foot	0.0929 m^5
9 sq ft	1 square yard	0.836 m^2
4840 sq yd	1 acre	0.405 ha
640 acres	1 square mile	259 ha

Volume		Metric equiv.
	1 cubic inch	16.3871 cm^3
1 728 cu in	1 cubic foot	0.028 m^3
27 cu ft	1 cubic yard	0.765 m^3
Liquid volume		
	1 pint	0.57 litre
2 pints	1 quart	1.14 litres
4 quarts	1 gallon	4.55 litres

Weight		Metric equiv.
	1 ounce	28.3495 g
16 oz	1 pound	0.4536 kg
14 lb	1 stone	6.35 kg
8 stones	1 hundredweight	50.8 kg
20 cwt	1 ton	1.016 tonnes

CONVERSION FACTORS

Imperial to metric

Length			Multiply by
inches	→	millimetres	25.4
inches	→	centimetres	2.54
feet	→	metres	0.3048
yards	→	metres	0.9144
statute miles	→	kilometres	1.6093
nautical miles	→	kilometres	1.852

Area			Multiply by
square inches	→	square centimetres	6.4516
square feet	→	square metres	0.0929
square yards	→	square metres	0.8361
acres	→	hectares	0.4047
square miles	→	square kilometres	2.5899

Volume			Multiply by
cubic inches	→	cubic centimetres	16.3871
cubic feet	→	cubic metres	0.0283
cubic yards	→	cubic metres	0.7646

Capacity			Multiply by
UK fluid ounces	→	litres	0.0284
US fluid ounces	→	litres	0.0296
UK pints	→	litres	0.5682
US pints	→	litres	0.4732
UK gallons	→	litres	4.546
US gallons	→	litres	3.7854

Weight			Multiply by
ounces (avoirdupois)	→	grams	28.3495
ounces (troy)	→	grams	31.1035
pounds	→	kilograms	0.4536
tons (long)	→	tonnes	1.016

Metric to imperial

Length			Multiply by
millimetres	→	inches	0.0394
centimetres	→	inches	0.3937
metres	→	feet	3.2808
metres	→	yards	1.0936
kilometres	→	statute miles	0.6214
kilometres	→	nautical miles	0.54

Area			Multiply by
square centimetres	→	square inches	0.155
square metres	→	square feet	10.764
square metres	→	square yards	1.196
hectares	→	acres	2.471
square kilometres	→	square miles	0.386

CONVERSION FACTORS (cont.)

Metric to imperial

Volume			Multiply by
cubic centimetres	→	cubic inches	0.061
cubic metres	→	cubic feet	35.315
cubic metres	→	cubic yards	1.308

Capacity			Multiply by
litres	→	UK fluid ounces	35.1961
litres	→	US fluid ounces	33.8150
litres	→	UK pints	1.7598
litres	→	US pints	2.1134
litres	→	UK gallons	0.2199
litres	→	US gallons	0.2642

Weight			Multiply by
grams	→	ounces (avoirdupois)	0.0353
grams	→	ounces (troy)	0.0322
kilograms	→	pounds	2.2046
tonnes	→	tons (long)	0.9842

CONVERSION TABLES: LENGTH

in	cm	in	cm	cm	in	cm	in	in	mm	mm	in
⅛	0.3	16	40.6	1	0.39	24	9.45	⅛	3.2	1	0.04
¼	0.6	17	43.2	2	0.79	25	9.84	¼	6.4	2	0.08
⅜	1	18	45.7	3	1.18	26	10.24	⅜	9.5	3	0.12
½	1.3	19	48.3	4	1.57	27	10.63	½	12.7	4	0.16
⅝	1.6	20	50.8	5	1.97	28	11.02	⅝	15.9	5	0.2
¾	1.9	21	53.3	6	2.36	29	11.42	¾	19	6	0.24
⅞	2.2	22	55.9	7	2.76	30	11.81	⅞	22.2	7	0.28
1	2.5	23	58.4	8	3.15	31	12.2	1	25.4	8	0.31
2	5.1	24	61	9	3.54	32	12.6	2	50.8	9	0.35
3	7.6	25	63.5	10	3.94	33	12.99	3	76.2	10	0.39
4	10.2	26	66	11	4.33	34	13.39	4	101.6	11	0.43
5	12.7	27	68.6	12	4.72	35	13.78	5	127	12	0.47
6	15.2	28	71.1	13	5.12	36	14.17	6	152.4	13	0.51
7	17.8	29	73.7	14	5.51	37	14.57	7	177.8	14	0.55
8	20.3	30	76.2	15	5.91	38	14.96	8	203.2	15	0.59
9	22.9	40	101.6	16	6.3	39	15.35	9	228.6	16	0.63
10	25.4	50	127	17	6.69	40	15.75	10	254	17	0.67

Exact conversions
1 in = 2.540 cm
1 cm = 0.3937 in
1 in = 25.40 mm
1 mm = 0.0394 in

CONVERSION TABLES: LENGTH (cont.)

ft	m	m	ft	yd	m	m	yd	ml*	km	km	ml*
1	0.3	1	3.3	1	0.9	1	1.1	1	1.6	1	0.6
2	0.6	2	6.6	2	1.8	2	2.2	2	3.2	2	1.2
3	0.9	3	9.8	3	2.7	3	3.3	3	4.8	3	1.9
4	1.2	4	13.1	4	3.7	4	4.4	4	6.4	4	2.5
5	1.5	5	16.4	5	4.6	5	5.5	5	8.0	5	3.1
6	1.8	6	19.7	6	5.5	6	6.6	6	9.7	6	3.7
7	2.1	7	23.0	7	6.4	7	7.7	7	11.3	7	4.3
8	2.4	8	26.2	8	7.3	8	8.7	8	12.9	8	5.0
9	2.7	9	29.5	9	8.2	9	9.8	9	14.5	9	5.6
10	3.0	10	32.8	10	9.1	10	10.9	10	16.1	10	6.2
15	4.6	15	49.2	15	13.7	15	16.4	15	24.1	15	9.3
20	6.1	20	65.5	20	18.3	20	21.9	20	32.2	20	12.4
25	7.6	25	82.0	25	22.9	25	27.3	25	40.2	25	15.5
30	9.1	30	98.4	30	27.4	30	32.8	30	48.3	30	18.6
35	10.7	35	114.8	35	32.0	35	38.3	35	56.3	35	21.7
40	12.2	40	131.2	40	36.6	40	43.7	40	64.4	40	24.9
45	13.7	45	147.6	45	41.1	45	49.2	45	72.4	45	28.0
50	15.2	50	164.0	50	45.7	50	54.7	50	80.5	50	31.1
75	22.9	75	246.1	75	68.6	75	82.0	55	88.5	55	34.2
100	30.5	100	328.1	100	91.4	100	109.4	60	96.6	60	37.3
200	61.0	200	656.2	200	182.9	200	218.7	65	104.6	65	40.4
300	91.4	300	984.3	220	201.2	220	240.6	70	112.7	70	43.5
400	121.9	400	1312.3	300	274.3	300	328.1	75	120.7	75	46.6
500	152.4	500	1640.4	400	365.8	400	437.4	80	128.7	80	49.7
600	182.9	600	1968.5	440	402.3	440	481.2	85	136.8	85	52.8
700	213.4	700	2296.6	500	457.2	500	546.8	90	144.8	90	55.9
800	243.8	800	2624.7	600	548.6	600	656.2	95	152.9	95	59.0
900	274.3	900	2952.8	700	640.1	700	765.5	100	160.9	100	62.1
1000	304.8	1000	3280.8	800	731.5	800	874.9	200	321.9	200	124.3
1500	457.2	1500	4921.3	880	804.7	880	962.4	300	482.8	300	186.4
2000	609.6	2000	6561.7	900	823.0	900	984.2	400	643.7	400	248.5
2500	762.0	2500	8202.1	1000	914.4	1000	1093.6	500	804.7	500	310.7
3000	914.4	3000	9842.5	1500	1371.6	1500	1640.4	750	1207.0	750	466.0
3500	1066.8	3500	11482.9	2000	1828.8	2000	2187.2	1000	1609.3	1000	621.4
4000	1219.2	4000	13123.4	2500	2286.0	2500	2734.0	2500	4023.4	2500	1553.4
5000	1524.0	5000	16404.2	5000	4572.0	5000	5468.1	5000	8046.7	5000	3106.9

*Statute miles

Exact conversions
1 ft = 0.3048 m
1 m = 3.2808 ft
1 yd = 0.9144 m
1 m = 1.0936 yd
1 ml = 1.6093 km
1 km = 0.6214 ml

CONVERSION TABLES: AREA

sq in	sq cm	sq cm	sq in	sq ft	sq m	sq m	sq ft	acres	hectares	hectares	acres
1	6.45	1	0.16	1	0.09	1	10.8	1	0.40	1	2.5
2	12.90	2	0.31	2	0.19	2	21.5	2	0.81	2	4.9
3	19.35	3	0.47	3	0.28	3	32.3	3	1.21	3	7.4
4	25.81	4	0.62	4	0.37	4	43.1	4	1.62	4	9.9
5	32.26	5	0.78	5	0.46	5	53.8	5	2.02	5	12.4
6	38.71	6	0.93	6	0.56	6	64.6	6	2.43	6	14.8
7	45.16	7	1.09	7	0.65	7	75.3	7	2.83	7	17.3
8	51.61	8	1.24	8	0.74	8	86.1	8	3.24	8	19.8
9	58.06	9	1.40	9	0.84	9	96.9	9	3.64	9	22.2
10	64.52	10	1.55	10	0.93	10	107.6	10	4.05	10	24.7
11	70.97	11	1.71	11	1.02	11	118.4	11	4.45	11	27.2
12	77.42	12	1.86	12	1.11	12	129.2	12	4.86	12	29.7
13	83.87	13	2.02	13	1.21	13	139.9	13	5.26	13	32.1
14	90.32	14	2.17	14	1.30	14	150.7	14	5.67	14	34.6
15	96.77	15	2.33	15	1.39	15	161.5	15	6.07	15	37.1
16	103.23	16	2.48	16	1.49	16	172.2	16	6.47	16	39.5
17	109.68	17	2.64	17	1.58	17	183	17	6.88	17	42
18	116.13	18	2.79	18	1.67	18	193.8	18	7.28	18	44.5
19	122.58	19	2.95	19	1.77	19	204.5	19	7.69	19	46.9
20	129.03	20	3.10	20	1.86	20	215.3	20	8.09	20	49.4
25	161.29	25	3.88	25	2.32	25	269.1	25	10.12	25	61.8
50	322.58	50	7.75	50	4.65	50	538.2	50	20.23	50	123.6
75	483.87	75	11.63	75	6.97	75	807.3	75	30.35	75	185.3
100	645.16	100	15.50	100	9.29	100	1076.4	100	40.47	100	247.1
125	806.45	125	19.38	250	23.23	250	2691	250	101.17	250	617.8
150	967.74	150	23.25	500	46.45	500	5382	500	202.34	500	1235.5
				750	69.68	750	8072.9	750	303.51	750	1853.3
				1000	92.90	1000	10763.9	1000	404.69	1000	2471.1
								1500	607.03	1500	3706.6

Exact conversions

1 in^2 = 6.4516 cm^2
1 cm^2 = 0.155 in^2

1 ft^2 = 0.929 m^2
1 m^2 = 10.7639 ft^2

1 acre = 0.4047 hectare
1 hectare = 2.471 acres

CONVERSION TABLES: AREA

sq ml*	sq km	sq km	sq ml*	sq ml*	sq km	sq km	sq ml*	sq ml*	sq km	sq km	sq ml*
1	2.6	1	0.39	18	46.6	18	6.95	300	777.0	300	115.83
2	5.2	2	0.77	19	49.2	19	7.34	400	1036.0	400	154.44
3	7.8	3	1.16	20	51.8	20	7.72	500	1295.0	500	193.05
4	10.4	4	1.54	21	54.4	21	8.11	600	1554.0	600	231.66
5	12.9	5	1.93	22	57.0	22	8.49	700	1813.0	700	270.27
6	15.5	6	2.32	23	59.6	23	8.88	800	2072.0	800	308.88
7	18.1	7	2.70	24	62.2	24	9.27	900	2331.0	900	347.49
8	20.7	8	3.09	25	64.7	25	9.65	1000	2590.0	1000	386.1
9	23.3	9	3.47	30	77.7	30	11.58	1500	3885.0	1500	579.2
10	25.9	10	3.86	40	103.6	40	15.44	2000	5180.0	2000	772.2

Exact conversions
1 sq ml = 2.589999 sq km
1 sq km = 0.3861 sq ml

*Statute miles

CONVERSION TABLES: VOLUME

cu in	cu cm	cu cm	cu in	cu ft	cu m	cu m	cu ft	cu yd	cu m	cu m	cu yd
1	16.39	1	0.61	1	0.03	1	35.3	1	0.76	1	1.31
2	32.77	2	1.22	2	0.06	2	70.6	2	1.53	2	2.62
3	49.16	3	1.83	3	0.08	3	105.9	3	2.29	3	3.92
4	65.55	4	2.44	4	0.11	4	141.3	4	3.06	4	5.23
5	81.93	5	3.05	5	0.14	5	176.6	5	3.82	5	6.54
6	93.32	6	3.66	6	0.17	6	211.9	6	4.59	6	7.85
7	114.71	7	4.27	7	0.20	7	247.2	7	5.35	7	9.16
8	131.10	8	4.88	8	0.23	8	282.5	8	6.12	8	10.46
9	147.48	9	5.49	9	0.25	9	317.8	9	6.88	9	11.77
10	163.87	10	6.10	10	0.28	10	353.1	10	7.65	10	13.08
15	245.81	15	9.15	15	0.42	15	529.7	15	11.47	15	19.62
20	327.74	20	12.20	20	0.57	20	706.3	20	15.29	20	26.16
50	819.35	50	30.50	50	1.41	50	1765.7	50	38.23	50	65.40
100	1638.71	100	61.00	100	2.83	100	3531.5	100	76.46	100	130.80

Exact conversions
$1\ in^3 = 16.3871\ cm^3$
$1\ cm^3 = 0.0610\ in^3$

$1\ ft^3 = 0.0283\ m^3$
$1\ m^3 = 35.3147\ ft^3$

$1\ yd^3 = 0.7646\ m^3$
$1\ m^3 = 1.3080\ yd^3$

CONVERSION TABLES: CAPACITY

Liquid measure

UK fluid ounces	litres	US fluid ounces	litres	litres	UK fluid ounces	US fluid ounces
1	0.0284	1	0.0296	1	35.2	33.8
2	0.0568	2	0.0592	2	70.4	67.6
3	0.0852	3	0.0888	3	105.6	101.4
4	0.114	4	0.118	4	140.8	135.3
5	0.142	5	0.148	5	176.0	169.1
6	0.170	6	0.178	6	211.2	202.9
7	0.199	7	0.207	7	246.4	236.7
8	0.227	8	0.237	8	281.6	270.5
9	0.256	9	0.266	9	316.8	304.3
10	0.284	10	0.296	10	352.0	338.1
11	0.312	11	0.326	11	387.2	372.0
12	0.341	12	0.355	12	422.4	405.8
13	0.369	13	0.385	13	457.5	439.6
14	0.397	14	0.414	14	492.7	473.4
15	0.426	15	0.444	15	527.9	507.2
20	0.568	20	0.592	20	703.9	676.3
50	1.42	50	1.48	50	1759.8	1690.7
100	2.84	100	2.96	100	3519.6	3381.5

Exact conversions
1 fl oz = 0.0284 l
1 fl oz = 0.0296 l

1 l = 35.1961 UK fl oz
1 l = 33.8140 US fl oz

CONVERSION TABLES: CAPACITY

UK pints	litres
1	0.57
2	1.14
3	1.70
4	2.27
5	2.84
6	3.41
7	3.98
8	4.55
9	5.11
10	5.68
11	6.25
12	6.82
13	7.38
14	7.95
15	8.52
20	11.36
50	28.41
100	56.82

US pints	litres
1	0.47
2	0.95
3	1.42
4	1.89
5	2.37
6	2.84
7	3.31
8	3.78
9	4.26
10	4.73
11	5.20
12	5.68
13	6.15
14	6.62
15	7.10
20	9.46
50	23.66
100	47.32

litres	UK pints	US pints
1	1.76	2.11
2	3.52	4.23
3	5.28	6.34
4	7.04	8.45
5	8.80	10.57
6	10.56	12.68
7	12.32	14.79
8	14.08	16.91
9	15.84	19.02
10	17.60	21.13
11	19.36	23.25
12	21.12	25.36
13	22.88	27.47
14	24.64	29.59
15	26.40	31.70
20	35.20	105.67
50	87.99	211.34
100	175.98	422.68

Exact conversions

1 UK pt = 0.5682 l
1 UK pt = 1.20 US pt

1 US pt = 0.4732 l
1 US pt = 0.83 UK pt

1 l = 1.7598 UK pt, 2.1134 US pt
1 US cup = 8 fl oz

UK gallons	litres
1	4.55
2	9.09
3	13.64
4	18.18
5	22.73
6	27.28
7	31.82
8	36.37
9	40.91
10	45.46
11	50.01
12	54.55
13	59.10
14	63.64
15	68.19
16	72.74
17	77.28
18	81.83
19	86.37
20	90.92
25	113.65
50	227.30
75	340.96
100	454.61

US gallons	litres
1	3.78
2	7.57
3	11.36
4	15.14
5	18.93
6	22.71
7	26.50
8	30.28
9	34.07
10	37.85
11	41.64
12	45.42
13	49.21
14	52.99
15	56.78
16	60.57
17	64.35
18	68.14
19	71.92
20	75.71
25	94.63
50	189.27
75	283.90
100	378.54

UK litres	US gallons	gallons
1	0.22	0.26
2	0.44	0.53
3	0.66	0.79
4	0.88	1.06
5	1.10	1.32
6	1.32	1.58
7	1.54	1.85
8	1.76	2.11
9	1.98	2.38
10	2.20	2.64
11	2.42	2.91
12	2.64	3.17
13	2.86	3.43
14	3.08	3.70
15	3.30	3.96
16	3.52	4.23
17	3.74	4.49
18	3.96	4.76
19	4.18	5.02
20	4.40	5.28
25	5.50	6.60
50	11.00	13.20
75	16.50	19.81
100	22.00	26.42

Exact conversions

1 UK gall = 4.546 l

1 US gall = 3.7854 l

1 l = 0.220 UK gall, 0.2642 US gall

CONVERSION TABLES: CAPACITY

UK gall	US gall	UK gall	US gall	UK gall	US gall
1	1.2	7	8.4	13	15.6
2	2.4	8	9.6	14	16.8
3	3.6	9	10.8	15	18
4	4.8	10	12	20	24
5	6	11	13.2	25	30
6	7.2	12	14.4	50	60

US gall	UK gall	US gall	UK gall	US gall	UK gall
1	0.8	7	5.8	13	10.8
2	1.7	8	6.7	14	11.7
3	2.5	9	7.5	15	12.5
4	3.3	10	8.3	20	16.6
5	4.2	11	9.2	25	20.8
6	5	12	10	50	41.6

Exact conversions
1 UK gall = 1.200929 US gall

1 US gall = 0.832688 UK gall

Dry capacity measures

UK bushels	cu m	litres
1	0.037	36.4
2	0.074	72.7
3	0.111	109.1
4	0.148	145.5
5	0.184	181.8
10	0.369	363.7

US bushels	cu m	litres
1	0.035	35.2
2	0.071	70.5
3	0.106	105.7
4	0.141	140.9
5	0.175	176.2
10	0.353	352.4

Exact conversions
1 UK bushel = 0.0369 m^3
1 UK bushel = 36.3677 l

1 US bushel = 0.9353 m^3
1 US bushel = 35.2381 l

cu m	UK bushels	US bushels
1	27.5	28.4
2	55.0	56.7
3	82.5	85.1
4	110	113
5	137	142
10	275	284

litres	UK bushels	US bushels
1	0.027	0.028
2	0.055	0.057
3	0.082	0.085
4	0.110	0.114
5	0.137	0.142
10	0.275	0.284

Exact conversions
1 m^3 = 27.4962 UK bu
1 m^3 = 28.3776 US bu

1 l = 0.0275 UK bu
1 l = 0.0284 US bu

UK pecks	litres	US pecks	litres
1	9.1	1	8.8
2	18.2	2	17.6
3	27.3	3	26.4
4	36.4	4	35.2
5	45.5	5	44
10	90.9	10	88.1

litres	UK pecks	US pecks
1	0.110	0.113
2	0.220	0.226
3	0.330	0.339
4	0.440	0.454
5	0.550	0.567
10	1.100	1.135

Exact conversions
1 UK pk = 9.0919 l 1 US pk = 8.8095 l 1 l = 0.1100 UK pk, 0.1135 US pk

CONVERSION TABLES: CAPACITY

Dry capacity measures (cont.)

US quarts	cu m	litres
1	1101	1.1
2	2202	2.2
3	3304	3.3
4	4405	4.4
5	5506	5.5
10	11012	11

US pints	cu m	litres
1	551	0.55
2	1101	1.10
3	1652	1.65
4	2202	2.20
5	2753	2.75
10	5506	5.51

Exact conversions
1 US qt = 1101.2209 cm^3
1 US qt = 1.1012 l

1 US pt = 550.6105 cm^3
1 US pt = 0.5506 l

CONVERSION TABLES: TYRE PRESSURES

lb per sq in	kg per sq cm	lb per sq in	kg per sq cm
10	0.7	26	1.8
15	1.1	28	2
20	1.4	30	2.1
24	1.7	40	2.8

CONVERSION TABLES: WEIGHT

ounces*	grams	grams	ounces*
1	28.3	1	0.04
2	56.7	2	0.07
3	85	3	0.11
4	113.4	4	0.14
5	141.7	5	0.18
6	170.1	6	0.21
7	198.4	7	0.25
8	226.8	8	0.28
9	255.1	9	0.32
10	283.5	10	0.35
11	311.7	20	0.71
12	340.2	30	1.06
13	368.5	40	1.41
14	396.9	50	1.76
15	425.2	60	2.12
16	453.6	70	2.47
		80	2.82
		90	3.18
		100	3.53

pounds	kilo-grams	pounds	kilo-grams
1	0.45	19	8.62
2	0.91	20	9.07
3	1.36	25	11.34
4	1.81	30	13.61
5	2.27	35	15.88
6	2.72	40	18.14
7	3.18	45	20.41
8	3.63	50	22.68
9	4.08	60	27.24
10	4.54	70	31.78
11	4.99	80	36.32
12	5.44	90	40.86
13	5.90	100	45.36
14	6.35	200	90.72
15	6.80	250	113.40
16	7.26	500	226.80
17	7.71	750	340.19
18	8.16	1000	453.59

kilo-grams	pounds	kilo-grams	pounds
1	2.2	19	41.9
2	4.4	20	44.1
3	6.6	25	55.1
4	8.8	30	66.1
5	11	35	77.2
6	13.2	40	88.2
7	15.4	45	99.2
8	17.6	50	110.2
9	19.8	60	132.3
10	22	70	154.4
11	24.3	80	176.4
12	26.5	90	198.5
13	28.7	100	220.5
14	30.9	200	440.9
15	33.1	250	551.2
16	35.3	500	1102.3
17	37.5	750	1653.5
18	39.7	1000	2204.6

*avoirdupois

Exact conversions
1 oz (avdp) = 28.3495 g
1 g = 0.0353 oz (avdp)

1 lb = 0.454 kg
1 kg = 2.205 lb

CONVERSION TABLES: WEIGHT

Tons: long, UK 2240 lb; short, US 2000 lb

UK tons	tonnes
1	1.02
2	2.03
3	3.05
4	4.06
5	5.08
10	10.16
15	15.24
20	20.32
50	50.80
75	76.20
100	101.60

US tons	tonnes
1	0.91
2	1.81
3	2.72
4	3.63
5	4.54
10	9.07
15	13.61
20	18.14
50	45.36
75	68.04
100	90.72

UK tons	US tons
1	1.12
2	2.24
3	3.36
4	4.48
5	5.6
10	11.2
15	16.8
20	22.4
50	56
75	84
100	102

tonnes	UK tons	US tons
1	0.98	1.10
2	1.97	2.20
3	2.95	3.30
4	3.94	4.40
5	4.92	5.50
10	9.84	11.02
15	14.76	16.53
20	19.68	22.05
50	49.21	55.11
75	73.82	82.67
100	98.42	110.23

US tons	UK tons
1	0.89
2	1.79
3	2.68
4	3.57
5	4.46
10	8.93
15	13.39
20	17.86
50	44.64
75	66.96
100	89.29

Exact conversions
1 UK ton = 1.0160 tonnes   1 US ton = 0.9072 tonne   1 UK ton = 1.1199 US tons
1 tonne = 0.9842 UK ton = 1.1023 US tons   1 US ton = 0.8929 UK ton

Hundredweights: long, UK 112 lb; short, US 100 lb

UK cwt	kilograms
1	50.8
2	102
3	152
4	203
5	254
10	508
15	762
20	1016
50	2540
75	3810
100	5080

US cwt	kilograms
1	45.4
2	90.7
3	136
4	181
5	227
10	454
15	680
20	907
50	2268
75	3402
100	4536

UK cwt	US cwt
1	1.12
2	2.24
3	3.36
4	4.48
5	5.6
10	11.2
15	16.8
20	22.4
50	56
75	84
100	102

kilograms	UK cwt	US cwt
1	0.0197	0.022
2	0.039	0.044
3	0.059	0.066
4	0.079	0.088
5	0.098	0.11
10	0.197	0.22
15	0.295	0.33
20	0.394	1.44
50	0.985	1.10
75	1.477	1.65
100	1.970	2.20

US cwt	UK cwt
1	0.89
2	1.79
3	2.68
4	3.57
5	4.46
10	8.93
15	13.39
20	17.86
50	44.64
75	66.96
100	89.29

Exact conversions
1 UK cwt = 50.8023 kg   1 US cwt = 45.3592 kg   1 UK cwt = 1.1199 US cwt
1 kg = 0.0197 UK cwt = 0.0220 US cwt   1 US cwt = 0.8929 UK cwt

stones	pounds	stones	pounds	stones	pounds
1	14	8	112	15	210
2	28	9	126	16	224
3	42	10	140	17	238
4	56	11	154	18	252
5	70	12	168	19	266
6	84	13	182	20	280
7	98	14	196		

stones	kilograms	stones	kilograms
1	6.35	6	38.10
2	12.70	7	44.45
3	19.05	8	50.80
4	25.40	9	57.15
5	31.75	10	63.50

Exact conversions
1 st = 14 lb
1 lb = 0.07 st

1 st = 6.350 kg
1 kg = 0.1575 st

INTERNATIONAL CLOTHING SIZES

Size equivalents are approximate, and may display some variation between manufacturers.

Women's suits/dresses

UK	USA	UK/ Continent
8	6	36
10	8	38
12	10	40
14	12	42
16	14	44
18	16	46
20	18	48
22	20	50
24	22	52

Women's hosiery

UK/USA	UK/ Continent
8	0
8½	1
9	2
9½	3
10	4
10½	5

Men's suits and overcoats

UK/USA	Continental
36	46
38	48
40	50
42	52
44	54
46	56

Men's socks

UK/USA	UK/ Continent
9½	38–39
10	39–40
10½	40–41
11	41–42
11½	42–43

Men's shirts

UK/USA	UK/ Continent
12	30–31
12½	32
13	33
13½	34–35
14	36
14½	37
15	38
15½	39–40
16	41
16½	42
17	43
17½	44–45

Adults' shoes

UK	USA (ladies)	UK/ Continent
4	5½	37
4½	6	38
5	6½	38
5½	7	39
6	7½	39
6½	8	40
7	8½	41
7½	8½	42
8	9½	42
8½	9½	43
9	10½	43
9½	10½	44
10	11½	44
10½	11½	45
11	12	46

Children's shoes

UK/USA	UK/ Continent
0	15
1	17
2	18
3	19
4	20
5	22
6	23
7	24
8	25
8½	26
9	27
10	28
11	29
12	30
13	32

INTERNATIONAL PATTERN SIZES

Young junior/teenage

Size	Bust		Waist		Hip		Back waist length	
	cm	in	cm	in	cm	in	cm	in
5/6	71	28	56	22	79	31	34.5	13½
7/8	74	29	58	23	81	32	35.5	14
9/10	78	30½	61	24	85	33½	37	14½
11/12	81	32	64	25	89	35	38	15
13/14	85	33½	66	26	93	36½	39	15⅜
15/16	89	35	69	27	97	38	40	15¾

INTERNATIONAL PATTERN SIZES (cont.)

Misses

Size	Bust cm	Bust in	Waist cm	Waist in	Hip cm	Hip in	Back waist length cm	Back waist length in
6	78	30½	58	23	83	32½	39.5	15½
8	80	31½	61	24	85	33½	40	15¾
10	83	32½	64	25	88	34½	40.5	16
12	87	34	67	26½	92	36	41.5	16¼
14	92	36	71	28	97	38	42	16½
16	97	38	76	30	102	40	42.5	16¾
18	102	40	81	32	107	42	43	17
20	107	42	87	34	112	44	44	17¼
Half-size								
10½	84	33	69	27	89	35	38	15
12½	89	35	74	29	94	37	39	15¼
14½	94	37	79	31	99	39	39.5	15½
16½	99	39	84	33	104	41	40	15¾
18½	104	41	89	35	109	43	40.5	15⅞
20½	109	43	96	37½	116	45½	40.5	16
22½	114	45	102	40	122	48	41	16⅛
24½	119	47	108	42½	128	50½	41.5	16¼
Women's								
38	107	42	89	35	112	44	44	17¼
40	112	44	94	37	117	46	44	17⅜
42	117	46	99	39	122	48	44.5	17½
44	122	48	105	41½	127	50	45	17⅝
46	127	50	112	44	132	52	45	17¾
48	132	52	118	46½	137	54	45.5	17⅞
50	137	54	124	49	142	56	46	18

INTERNATIONAL PAPER SIZES

A series	mm	in	B series	mm	in	C series	mm	in
A0	841 × 1189	33.11 × 46.81	B0	1000 × 1414	39.37 × 55.67	C0	917 × 1297	36.00 × 51.20
A1	594 × 841	23.39 × 33.1	B1	707 × 1000	27.83 × 39.37	C1	648 × 917	25.60 × 36.00
A2	420 × 594	16.54 × 23.39	B2	500 × 707	19.68 × 27.83	C2	458 × 648	18.00 × 25.60
A3	297 × 420	11.69 × 16.54	B3	353 × 500	13.90 × 19.68	C3	324 × 458	12.80 × 18.00
A4	210 × 297	8.27 × 11.69	B4	250 × 353	9.84 × 13.90	C4	229 × 324	9.00 × 12.80
A5	148 × 210	5.83 × 8.27	B5	176 × 250	6.93 × 9.84	C5	162 × 229	6.40 × 9.00
A6	105 × 148	4.13 × 5.83	B6	125 × 176	4.92 × 6.93	C6	114 × 162	4.50 × 6.40
A7	74 × 105	2.91 × 4.13	B7	88 × 125	3.46 × 4.92	C7	81 × 114	3.20 × 4.50
A8	52 × 74	2.05 × 2.91	B8	62 × 88	2.44 × 3.46	DL	110 × 220	4.33 × 8.66
A9	37 × 52	1.46 × 2.05	B9	44 × 62	1.73 × 2.44	C7/6	81 × 162	3.19 × 6.38
A10	26 × 37	1.02 × 1.46	B10	31 × 44	1.22 × 1.73			

All sizes in these series have sides in the proportion of $1:\sqrt{2}$.
A series is used for writing paper, books and magazines. B series for posters. C series for envelopes.

ENGINEERING: BRIDGES

When a single date is given it is the date for completion of construction

Name	Location	Length (m[1])	Type	Date
Akashi-Kaikyo Bridge	Honshu–Shikoku, Japan	4000 (main span 1990)	suspension	begun 1978, due for completion 1998
Ambassador	Detroit, Michigan, USA	564	suspension	1929
Annacis (renamed Alex Fraser)	Fraser River, Vancouver, Canada	465	(longest) cable stay	1986
Arthur Kill	Staten Island–New Jersey, USA	170	movable	1959
Astoria	Astoria, Oregon	376	truss	1966
Bayonne (Kill van Kull)	New Jersey–Staten Island, USA	504	arch	1932
Bendorf	R Rhine, Coblenz, Germany	1030	cement girder	1965
Benjamin Franklin	Philadelphia–Camden, USA	534	suspension	1926
Bosporus	Golden Horn, Istanbul, Turkey	1074	suspension	1973
Bosporus II	Istanbul, Turkey	1090	suspension	1986–8
Bridge of Sighs	Doge's Palace–Pozzi prison, Venice, Italy	c.5	enclosed arch	16th-c
Britannia tubular rail	Menai Strait, Wales	420	plate girder	1845–50
Brooklyn	Brooklyn–Manhattan Island, New York City, USA	486	suspension	1869–83
Chao Phraya	Bangkok, Thailand	450	(longest single-plane) cable stay	1989
Cincinnati	Cincinnati, Ohio, USA	332	suspension	1867
Commodore Barry	Chester, Pennsylvania, USA	501	cantilever	1974
Cooper River	Charleston, S Carolina, USA	488	truss	1989
Delaware River	Chester, Pennsylvania, USA	501	cantilever	1971
Duisburg-Neuenkamp	Duisburg, Germany	350	cable braced	1970
Erskine	Glasgow, Scotland	305	cable braced	1970
Evergreen	Seattle, Washington, USA	longest span 2293	floating pontoon	1963
Firth of Forth (rail)	South Queensferry, Scotland	1658 (spans 521)	cantilever	1882–90
Firth of Forth (road)	South Queensferry, Scotland	1006	suspension	1958–64
George Washington	Hudson River, New York City, USA	1067	suspension	1927–31
Gladesville	Sydney, Australia	305	(longest) concrete arch	1964
Golden Gate	San Francisco, California, USA	1280	suspension	1937
Grand Trunk rail-road	Niagara Falls, New York, USA	suspension	1855 (survived until 1897)	
Greater New Orleans	Mississippi River, Louisiana, USA	480	cantilever	1958
Howrah (railroad)	Hooghly River, Calcutta, India	457	cantilever	1936–43
Humber Estuary	Hull–Grimsby, England	1410	(longest) suspension	1973–81

ENGINEERING: BRIDGES (cont.)

Name	Location	Length (m^1)	Type	Date
Kincardine	R Forth, Scotland	822 (swing span 111)	movable	1936
Kniebrücke	Düsseldorf, Germany	320	cable braced	1969
Lake Pontchartrain Causeway	Maudeville–Jefferson, Louisiana, USA	38 km	twin concrete trestle	1963
Lower Yarra	Melbourne, Australia	336	cable braced	1970
Lions Gate	Vancouver, Canada	473	suspension	1938
London	Southwark–City of London	centre span 46	concrete arch	1973
Mackinac	Michigan, USA	1158	suspension	1957
McCall's Ferry	USA	110	wooden covered	1815
Menai Strait	Menai Strait, N Wales	177	suspension	1820–6 (reconstructed 1940)
Minami Bisan–Seto	Honshu–Shikoku, Japan	1723	suspension	1988
New River Gorge	Fayetteville, West Virginia, USA	518	(longest) arch	1977
Nord Sundet	Norway	223	lattice	1989
Plauen	Plauen, Germany	a span of 90	(longest) masonry arch	1903
Pont d'Avignon	R Rhône, France	c.60	arch	1177–87
Pontypridd	S Wales	43	single span arch	1750
Port Mann	Fraser River, British Columbia, Canada	366	arch	1964
Quebec (railroad)	St Lawrence, Canada	549	(largest-span) cantilever	1918
Rainbow	Canada–USA, Niagara Falls	300	steel arch	1941
Rialto	Grand Canal, Venice, Italy	25	single span arch	1588–92
Rio-Niteroi	Guanabara Bay, Brazil	centre span 300, length 14 km	box and plate girder	1972
Salazar	Tagus River, Lisbon, Portugal	1014	suspension	1966
Severn	Beachley, England	988	suspension	1961–6
Severn	Ironbridge, Shropshire, England	31	(first) cast-iron arch	1779
Sky Train Bridge (rail)	Vancouver, Canada	340	cable stay	1989
Sydney Harbour	Sydney, Australia	503	(widest) arch	1923–32
Tacoma Narrows II	Puget Sound, Washington, USA	854	suspension	1950
Tay (road)	Dundee, Scotland	2246	box girder	1966
Thatcher Ferry	Panama Canal, C America	344	arch	1962
Tower	R Thames, London	76	movable	1886–94
Transbay	San Francisco, USA	705	suspension	1933
Trois-Rivières	St Lawrence River, Quebec, Canada	336	steel arch	1962

ENGINEERING: BRIDGES (cont.)

Name	Location	Length (m[1])	Type	Date
Verrazano Narrows	Brooklyn–Staten Island, New York Harbour, USA	1298	suspension	1959–64
Victoria Jubilee	St Lawrence River, Montreal, Canada	open steel	1854–9	
Wheeling	Wheeling, Virginia, USA	308	suspension	1849
Yokohama Bay (road)	Japan	855	suspension	1989
Zoo	Cologne, Germany	259	steel box girder	1966

[1]To convert m to ft, multiply by 3.2808

ENGINEERING: TUNNELS

When a single date is given it is the date for completion of construction

Name	Use	Location	Length	Date
Aki	rail	Japan	13 km	1975
Baltimore Harbour	road	Baltimore, Maryland, USA	2 km	1957
Box	rail	Wiltshire, England	3 km	1841
Cascade	rail	Washington, USA	13 km	1929
Channel	rail	Cheriton, England–Sargette, France	50 km	begun 1987, due to be opened 1993
Chesapeake Bay Bridge-Tunnel	road	USA	28 km	1964
Chesbrough	water supply	Chicago, USA	3 km	1867
Dai-shimizu	rail	Honshu, Japan	22 km	1979
Delaware Aqueduct		Catskill Mt, New York City, USA	169 km	1937–44
Detroit River	rail	Detroit, Michigan, USA–Windsor, Ontario, Canada	2 km	1910
Eupalinus	water supply	Samos	1037 m	c.525 BC
Flathead	rail	Washington, USA	13 km	1970
Fréjus	rail	Modane, France–Bardonecchia, Italy	13 km	1857–71
Fucino	drainage	Lake Fucino, Italy	6 km	41
Great Apennine	rail	Vernio, Italy	19 km	1934
Hokuriku	rail	Japan	15 km	1962
Holland	road	Hudson River, New York City–Jersey City, New Jersey, USA	3 km	1927
Hoosac	rail	Massachusetts	8 km	1876
Hyperion	sewer	Los Angeles, California, USA	8 km	1959
Kanmon	rail	Kanmon Strait, Japan	19 km	1975
Keijo	rail	Japan	11 km	1970
Kemano	hydro-power	British Columbia, Canada	430 m	1954
Kilsby Ridge	rail	London–Birmingham line	2 km	1838
Languedoc	Canal du Midi	Malpas, France	157 m	c.1681
Lierasen	rail	Norway	11 km	1973

ENGINEERING: TUNNELS (cont.)

Name	Use	Location	Length	Date
London and Southwark Subway	rail	London, England	11 km	1890
Lötschberg	rail	Switzerland	15 km	1913
Mersey	road	Mersey River, Birkenhead–Liverpool, England	4 km	1934
Moffat	rail	Colorado, USA	10 km	1928
Mont Blanc	road	France–Italy	12 km	1965
Mt MacDonald	rail	Canada	15 km	1989
Orange-Fish River	irrigation	South Africa	(longest irrigation tunnel) 82 km	1975
Owingsburg Landing	canal	Pennsylvania, USA	137 m	1828
Posilipo	road	Naples–Pozzuoli, Italy	6 km	c.36 BC
Rogers Pass	rail	Calgary–Vancouver	15 km	1982–8
Rogers Pass	road	British Columbia, Canada	35 km	1989
Rokko	rail	Ōsaka–Kōbe, Japan	16 km	1972
Scheldt River	road-rail	Antwerp, Belgium	686 m	1969
Seikan	rail	Tsugaru Strait, Honshu–Hokkaido, Japan	(longest undersea rail) 54 km	1964–88
Shin-shimizu	rail	Japan	13 km	1961
Simplon I and II	rail	Brigue, Switzerland–Iselle, Italy	20 km	1906 and 1922
St Gotthard	rail	Switzerland	15 km	1882
St Gotthard	road	Göschenen, Switzerland–Airolo, Italy	16 km	1980
(First) Thames	pedestrian, rail after 1865	Wapping–Rotherhithe, London, England	366 m	1825–43
Tower Subway	rail	London, England	411 m	1869–70
Tronquoy	canal	France	1099 m	1810

To convert m to ft, multiply by 3.2808
To convert km to ml, multiply by 1.6092

ENGINEERING: MAJOR DAMS

When a single date is given, it is the date for completion of construction

Name	River, country	Height (m[1])	Date
Afsluitdijk Sea	Zuider Zee, Netherlands	20 (largest sea dam, length 32 km)	1927–32
Aswan High	Nile, Egypt	111	1970
Ataturk	Euphrates, Turkey	184	1990
Bakun	Rajang, Malaysia	204	under construction
Boguchany	Angara, Russia	79	1989
Bratsk	Angara, Russia	125	1961
Chapeton	Paraná, Argentina	35	under construction

ENGINEERING: MAJOR DAMS (cont.)

Name	River, country	Height (m[1])	Date
Chicoasen	Grijalva, Mexico	263	1980
Grand Coulee	Columbia (Franklin D Roosevelt Lake), USA	168	1933–42
Grand Dixence	Dixence, Switzerland	285	1961
Guavio	Guaviare, Colombia	245	1989
Hoover	Colorado (Lake Mead), USA	221	1931–6
Haipu	Parana, Paraguay/Brazil border	189	1982
Inguri	Inguri, Georgia	272	1980
Kariba	Zambezi (L Kariba), Zambia/ Zimbabwe border	128	1959
Kiev	Dneiper, Ukraine	256 (longest dam, length 412 km)	1964
LaGrande 2A	LaGrande, Canada	168	under con-struction
Mauvoisin	Drance de Bagnes, Switzerland	237	1957
Mica	Columbia, Canada	244	1973
Nurek	Vakhsh, Tadzhikistan	310	1980
Poti	Paraná, Argentina	109 (length 150 km, most massive: volume 238 180 000 m^3)	under con-struction
Rogun	Vakhsh, Tadzhikistan	335 (tallest)	1973–90
Sayansk	Yenisey, Russia	236	1980
Sera da Mesa	Tocantins, Brazil	144	under con-struction
Thames Barrier	Thames, UK	spans 520 (largest tidal barrier)	1984
Vaiont	Vaiont, Italy	262	1961 (damaged by landslide 1963)

[1] To convert m to ft, multiply by 3.2808

ENGINEERING: TALLEST BUILDINGS

Name	Location	Height (m[1])	Date of con-struction
Sears Tower	Chicago, USA	443	1973–4
World Trade Centre	New York City, USA	417	1972
Empire State Building	New York City, USA	381	1931
Bank of China	Hong Kong	368	1988–9
Standard Oil Building	Chicago, USA	346	1971
John Hancock Center	Boston, USA	344	1967
Chrysler Building	New York City, USA	319	1930
Library Tower	Los Angeles, USA	310	1989
Texas Commercial Plaza	Houston, USA	305	1981
Allied Bank Plaza	Houston, USA	302	1983

[1] To convert m to ft, multiply by 3.2808

INVENTIONS

Name	Date	Inventor (nationality*)
adding machine	1642	Blaise Pascal (Fr)
adhesive (rubber-based glue)	1850	anon
adhesive (epoxy resin)	1958	Certas Co.
aeroplane (steam powered)	1886	Clement Ader (Fr)
aeroplane	1903	Orville and Wilbur Wright (US)
aeroplane (swing-wing)	1954	Grumman Co. (US)
aerosol	1926	Erik Rotheim (Nor)
airship (non-rigid)	1851	Henri Giffard (Fr)
airship (rigid)	1900	Graf Ferdinand von Zeppelin (Ger)
ambulance	1792	Jean Dominique Larrey (Fr)
aspirin (synthesization)	1859	Heinrich Kolbe (Ger)
aspirin (introduction into medicine)	1899	Heinrich Dreser (Ger)
atomic bomb	1939–45	Otto Frisch (Aus), Niels Bohr (D) and Rudolf Peierls (Ger)
balloon	1783	Jacques and Joseph Montgolfier (Fr)
barbed wire (first patent)	1867	Lucien B Smith (US)
barbed wire (manufacture)	1874	Joseph Glidden (US)
barbiturates (preparation of barbituric acid)	1863	Adolf von Baeyer (Ger)
	1903	Emil Herman von Fischer and Emil von Behring (Ger)
barometer	1643	Evanglelista Torricelli (Ital)
battery (electric)	1800	Alessandro Volta (Ital)
bicycle	1839–40	Kirkpatrick MacMillan (UK)
bifocal lens	1780	Benjamin Franklin (US)
blood (artificial)	1966	Clark and Gollan (US)
bronze (copper with tin)	c.3700 BC	Pre-dynastic Egypt
bunsen burner	1855	Robert Wilhelm Bunsen (Pruss)
burglar alarm	1858	Edwin T Holmes (US)
cable-car	1866	W Ritter (Ger) or anon (US)
calendar (modern)	525	Dionysius Exiguus (Scythian)
canning	1810	Nicolas Appert (Fr)
cannon	2nd-c BC	Archimedes (Gr)
car (three-wheeled steam tractor)	1769	Nicolas Cugnot (Fr)
car (internal combustion)	1884	Gottlieb Daimler (Ger)
car (petrol)	1886	Karl Benz (Ger)
car (air-conditioning)	1902	J Wilkinson (US)
car (disc brakes)	1902	Frederick W Lanchester (UK)
car (speedometer)	1902	Thorpe & Salter (UK)
carbon fibres	1964	Courtaulds Ltd. (UK)
carburettor	1876	Gottlieb Daimler (Ger)
carpet sweeper	1876	Melville Bissell (US)
cash register	1892	William Burroughs (US)
celluloid	1870	John W Hyatt (US)
cement (Portland)	1824	Joseph Aspdin (UK)
chocolate (solid)	1819	François-Louis Cailler (Swiss)
chocolate (solid, milk)	1875	Daniel Peter (Swiss)
chronometer	1735	John Harrison (UK)
cinema	1895	Auguste and Louis Lumière (Fr)
cinema (wide screen)	1900	Raoul Grimoin-Sanson (Fr)
clock (mechanical)	725	I-Hsing (Chinese)
clock (pendulum)	1656	Christiaan Huygens (NL)
clock (quartz)	1929	Warren Alvin Marrison (US)

INVENTIONS (cont.)

Name	Date	Inventor (nationality*)
coffee (instant)	1937	Nestlé (Swiss)
compact disc	1979	Philips (NL) and Sony (Japanese)
compass (discovery of magnetite)	1st-c	China
compass (first record of mariner's compass)	1187	Alexander Neckam (UK)
computer	1835	Charles Babbage (UK)
computer (electronic, digital)	1946	J Presper Eckert and John W Mauchly (US)
concrete	1st-c	Rome
concrete (reinforced)	1892	François Hennebique (Fr)
contact lenses	1887	Adolph E Fick (Ger)
contraceptive pill	1950	Gregor Pincus (US)
corrugated iron	1853	Pierre Carpentier (Fr)
credit card	1950	Ralph Scheider (US)
crossword	1913	Arthur Wynne in *New York World*
crystal	c.1450	anon, Venice
decompression chamber	1929	Robert H Davis (UK)
dental plate	1817	Anthony A Plantson (US)
dental plate (rubber)	1854	Charles Goodyear (US)
detergents	1916	anon, Germany
diesel engine	1892	Rudolf Diesel (Ger)
dishwasher (automatic)	1889	Mrs W A Cockran (US)
drill (pneumatic)	1861	Germain Sommelier (Fr)
drill (electric, hand)	1895	Wilhelm Fein (Ger)
electric chair	1888	Harold P Brown and E A Kenneally (US)
electric flat iron	1882	Henry W Seeley (US)
electric generator	1831	Michael Faraday (UK)
electric guitar	1931	Adolph Rickenbacker, Barth and Beauchamp (US)
electric heater	1887	W Leigh Burton (US)
electric light bulb	1879	Thomas Alva Edison (US)
electric motor (DC)	1870	Zenobe Gramme (Belg)
electric motor (AC)	1888	Nikola Tesla (US)
electric oven	1889	Bernina Hotel, Switzerland
electocardiography	1903	Willem Einthoven (NL)
electromagnet	1824	William Sturgeon (UK)
encyclopedia	c.47 BC	Marcus Terentius Varro
endoscope	1827	Pierre Segalas (Fr)
escalator	1892	Jesse W Reno (US)
explosives (nitroglycerine)	1847	Ascanio Sobrero (Ital)
explosives (dynamite)	1866	Alfred Nobel (Swed)
extinguisher	1866	François Carlier (Fr)
facsimile machine (fax)	1907	Arthur Korn (Ger)
ferrofluids	1968	Ronald Rosensweig (US)
film (moving outlines)	1874	Jules Janssen (Fr)
	1888	Louis Le Prince (Fr)
	1891	Thomas Alva Edison (US)
film (with soundtrack)	1896	Lee De Forest (US)
food processor	1947	Kenneth Wood
forceps (obstetric)	c.1630	Peter Chamberlen
freeze-drying	1906	Arsene D'Arsonval and Georges Bordas (Fr)
galvanometer	1834	André Marie Ampère (Fr)

INVENTIONS (cont.)

Name	Date	Inventor (nationality*)
gas lighting	1792	William Murdock (UK)
gearbox (automatic)	1910	Hermann Fottinger (Ger)
glass (heat-resistant)	1884	Carl Zeiss (Ger)
glass (stained)	pre 850	Europe
glass (toughened)	1893	Leon Appert (Fr)
glass fibre	1713	Renée de Reaumur (Fr)
glass fibre (industrial)	1931	Owens Illinois Glass Co. (US)
glassware	c.2600 BC	
glider	1853	George Cayley (UK)
gramophone	1877	Thomas Alva Edison (US)
gun	245 BC	Ctesibius (Gr)
gyro-compass	1911	Elmer A Sperry (US)
heart (artificial)	1937	Vladimir P Demikhov (USSR)
heat pump	1851	William Thompson, Lord Kelvin (UK)
helicopter	1907	Louis and Jacques Breguet (Fr)
holography	1948	Denis Gabor (Hung/UK)
hovercraft	1955	Christopher Cockerell (UK)
integrated circuit (concept)	1952	Geoffrey Dummer (UK)
interferometry	1802	Thomas Young (UK)
interferometer	1856	J-C Jamin (Fr)
iron (working of)	c.1323 BC	Hittites (Anatolia)
jeans	1872	Levi-Strauss (US)
kidney (artificial)	1945	Willem Kolff (NL)
laser	1960	Theodore Maiman (US)
launderette	1934	J F Cantrell (US)
lawnmower	1902	James Edward Ransome (UK)
lift (mechanical)	1851	Elisha G Otis (US)
lightning conductor	1752	Benjamin Franklin (US)
linoleum	1860	Frederick Walton (UK)
lithography	1796	Aloys Senefelder (Bav)
locomotive (railed)	1804	Richard Trevithick (UK)
lock	c.4000 BC	Mesopotamia
loom (power)	1785	Edmund Cartwright (UK)
loudspeaker	1900	Horace Short (UK)
machine gun	1718	James Puckle (UK)
maps	c.2250 BC	Mesopotamia
margarine	1868	Hippolyte Mergé-Mouriès (Fr)
match	1680	Robert Boyle (UK)
match (safety)	1845	Anton von Schrotter (Ger)
microchip	1958	Jack Saint Clair Kilby (US)
microphone	1876	Alexander Graham Bell (US) and Thomas Alva Edison (US)
microprocessor	1971	Marcian E Hoff (US)
microscope	1590	Zacharias Janssen (NL)
microscope (electron)	1933	Max Knoll and Ernst Ruska (Ger)
microscope (scanning tunnelling)	1982	Gerd Binnig and Heinrich Rohrer (Swiss)
microscope (atomic force)	1985	Gerd Binnig and Heinrich Rohrer (Swiss)
microwave oven	1945	Percy Le Baron Spencer (US)
missile (air-to-air)	1943	Herbert Wagner (Ger)
motorcycle	1885	Gottlieb Daimler (Ger)
neon lamp	1910	Georges Claude (Fr)
newspaper	59 BC	Julius Caesar (Roman)
non-stick pan	1954	Marc Grégoir (Fr)

INVENTIONS (cont.)

Name	Date	Inventor (nationality*)
novel (serialized)	1836	Charles Dickens, Chapman and Hall publishers (UK)
nylon	1938	Wallace H Carothers (US)
optical fibres	c.1955	Navinder S Kapany (Ind)
optical sound recording	1920	Lee De Forest (US)
pacemaker (implantable)	1956	Wilson Greatbach (US)
paint (fluorescent)	1933	Joe and Bob Switzer (US)
paint (acrylic)	1964	Reeves Ltd. (UK)
paper	AD 105	Ts'ai Lun (Chinese)
paper clip	1900	Johann Vaaler (Nor)
parachute	c.2nd-c BC	China
parachute (jump)	1797	André-Jacques Garnerin (Fr)
parachute (patent)	1802	André-Jacques Garnerin (Fr)
parchment	2nd-c BC	Eumenes II of Pergamum (reigned 197–159 BC)
parking meter	1932	Carlton C Magee (US)
pasteurization	1863	Louis Pasteur (Fr)
pen (fountain)	1884	Lewis Waterman (US)
pen (ball-point)	1938	Laszlo Biro (Hung)
pencil	1795	Nicholas Jacques Conté (Fr)
photoelectric cell	1896	Julius Elster and Hans F Geitel (Ger)
phototypesetting	1894	Eugene Porzott (Hung)
photographic lens (for camera obscura)	1812	William H Wollaston (UK)
photographic film	1889	Georges Eastman (US)
photography (on metal)	1816	Joseph Nicéphore Niepce (Fr)
photography (on paper)	1838	William Henry Fox Talbot (UK)
photography (colour)	1861	James Clerk Maxwell (UK)
pianoforte	1720	Bartolomeo Cristofori (Ital)
plastics	1868	John W Hyatt (US)
pocket calculator	1972	Jack Saint Clair Kilby, James Van Tassell and Jerry D Merryman (US)
porcelain	c.960	China
pressure cooker	1954	Frederic Jean and Henri Lescure (Fr)
printing press (wooden)	c.1450	Johannes Gutenberg (Ger)
printing press (rotary)	1845	Richard Hoe (US)
propeller (boat, hand-operated)	1775	David Bushnell (US)
propeller (ship)	1844	Isambard Kingdom Brunel (UK)
radar (theory)	1900	Nikola Tesla (Croat)
radar (theory)	1922	Guglielmo Marconi (Ital)
radar (application)	c.1930	A Hoyt Taylor and Leo C Young (US)
radio telegraphy (discovery and production of sound waves)	1888	Heinrich Hertz (Ger)
radio (transatlantic)	1901	Guglielmo Marconi (Ital)
rails (iron)	1738	Abraham Barby (UK)
railway (underground)	1843	Charles Pearson (UK)
railway (electric)	1878	Ernst Werner von Siemens (Ger)
rayon	1883	Joseph Swan (UK)
razor (safety)	1895	King Camp Gillette (US)
razor (electric)	1928	Jacob Schick (US)
record (flat disc)	1888	Emil Berliner (Ger)
record (long-playing microgroove)	1948	Peter Goldmark (US)
refrigerator (compressed ether)	1855	James Harrison (UK)
refrigerator (absorption)	1857	Ferdinand Carré (Fr)

INVENTIONS (cont.)

Name	Date	Inventor (nationality*)
revolver	1835	Samuel Colt (US)
Richter seismographic scale	1935	Charles Francis Richter (US)
rocket (missile)	1232	Mongols (China)
rubber (latex foam)	1929	E A Murphy, W H Chapman and John Dunlop (US)
rubber (butyl)	1937	Robert Thomas and William Sparks, Exxon (US)
rubber (vulcanized)	1939	Charles Goodyear (US)
Rubik cube	1975	Erno Rubik (Hung)
safety-pin	1849	Walter Hunt (US)
satellite (artificial)	1957	USSR
saw	c.4000 BC	Egypt
scanner	1973	Godfrey N Hounsfield (UK)
scotch tape	1930	Richard Drew (US)
screw	3rd-c BC	Archimedes (Gr)
serotherapy	1890	Emil von Behring (Ger)
sewing machine	1830	Barthelemy Thimonnier (Fr)
ship (steam)	1775	Jacques C Perier (Fr)
ship (turbine)	1894	Charles Parsons (UK)
ship (metal hull and propeller)	1844	Isambard Kingdom Brunel (UK)
silk (reeling)	c.2640 BC	Hsi Ling Shi (Chinese)
skin (artificial)	c.1980	John Tanner (US), Bell (US), Neveu (Fr), Ioannis Yannas (Gr), Howard Green (US) and Jacques Thivolet (Fr)
skyscraper	1882	William Le Baron Jenney (US)
slide rule	1621	William Oughtred (UK)
soap	2500 BC	Sumer, Babylonia
soda (extraction of)	c.16th-c BC	Egypt
spectacles	c.1280	Alessandro della Spina, Salvino degli Armati (Ital)
spinning frame	1768	Richard Arkwright (UK)
spinning jenny	c.1764	James Hargreaves (UK)
spinning-mule	1779	Samuel Crompton (UK)
stapler	1868	Charles Henry Gould (UK)
starter motor	1912	Charles F Kettering (US)
steam engine	1698	Thomas Savery (UK)
steam engine (condenser)	1769	James Watt (UK)
steam engine (piston)	1705	Thomas Newcomen (UK)
steel (production)	1854	Henry Bessemer (UK), William Kelly (US)
steel (stainless)	1913	Henry Brearley (UK)
stethoscope	1816	René Théophile Hyacinthe Laënnec (Fr)
stereotype	1725	William Ged (UK)
submarine	c.1620	Cornelis Brebbel or Van Drebbel (NL)
sun-tan cream	1936	Eugene Schueller (Fr)
suspension bridge	25 BC	China
syringe (scientific)	1646	Blaise Pascal (Fr)
syringe (hypodermic)	c.1835	Charles Gabriel Pravaz (Fr)
table tennis	1890	James Gibb (UK)
tampon	1930	Earl Hass (US)
tank	1916	Ernest Swinton (UK)
telegraph (electric)	1774	Georges Louis Lesage (Swiss)
telegraph (transatlantic cable)	1866	William Thompson, Lord Kelvin (UK)
telegraph code	1837	Samuel F B Morse (US)

INVENTIONS (cont.)

Name	Date	Inventor (nationality*)
telephone (first practical)	1876	Alexander Graham Bell (US)
telephone (automatic exchange)	1889	Alman B Strowger (US)
telescope (refractor)	1608	Hans Lippershey (NL)
television (mechanical)	1926	John Logie Baird (UK)
television (colour)	1940	Peter Goldmark (US)
tennis	1873	Walter G Wingfield (UK)
thermometer	3rd-c BC	Ctesibius (Gr)
thermometer (mercury)	1714	Gabriel Fahrenheit (Ger)
timeclock	1894	Daniel M Cooper (US)
toaster	1927	Charles Strite (US)
traffic lights	1868	J P Knight (UK)
traffic lights (automatic)	1914	Alfred Benesch (US)
transformer	1831	Michael Faraday (UK)
tranquillizers	1952	Henri Laborit (Fr)
transistor	1948	John Bardeen (US), Walter Brattain (US), William Shockley (US)
travel agency	1841	Thomas Cook (UK)
traveller's cheques	1891	American Express Travel Agency
turbojet	1928	Frank Whittle (UK)
typewriter	1829	William Burt (US)
typewriter (electric)	1872	Thomas Edison (US)
tyre (pneumatic, coach)	1845	Robert William Thomson (UK)
tyre (pneumatic, bicycle)	1888	John Boyd Dunlop (UK)
ultrasonography (obstetric)	1979	Ian Donald (UK)
universal joint	c.140 BC	Fang Feng (Chinese)
vacuum cleaner (steam powered)	1871	Ives W McGaffrey (US)
vacuum cleaner (electric)	1901	Hubert Cecil Booth (UK)
vending machine	1883	Percival Everitt (UK)
ventilator	1858	Theophile Guibal (Fr)
videophone	1927	American Telegraph & Telephone Co.
video recorder	1956	Ampex Co. (US)
washing machine (electric)	1907	Hurley Machine Co. (US)
watch	1462	Bartholomew Manfredi (Ital)
watch (waterproof)	1927	Rolex (Swiss)
wheel	c.3500 BC	Mesopotamia
windmill	c.600	Syria
writing (pictography)	c.3000 BC	Egypt
xerography	1938	Chester Carbon (US)
zip-fastener	1893	Whitcomb L Judson (US)

*Aus: Austrian
Belg: Belgian
Croat: Croatian
D: Danish
Fr: French
Ger: German
Gr: Greek
Hung: Hungarian
Ind: Indian
Ital: Italian
NL: Dutch
Nor: Norwegian
Pruss: Prussian
Swed: Swedish

INDUSTRIALISTS AND ENTREPRENEURS

Agnelli, Giovanni (1866–1945) Italian. Founder of Fiat (Fabbrica Italiana Automobili Torino) in 1899. Appointed as a senator in 1923 and mobilized Italian industry in World War II.

Astor, John Jacob, 1st Baron Astor of Hever (1886–1971) English–American, born New York. Elected MP for Dover (1922) and chairman of the Times Publishing Company.

Astor, William Waldorf, 1st Viscount Astor (1848–1919) English–American, born New York. After period as US minister to Italy, emigrated to Britain to become newspaper proprietor, acquiring the *Pall Mall Gazette*, *Pall Mall Magazine* and in 1911, *The Observer*.

Austin, Herbert, 1st Baron Austin of Longbridge (1866–1941) English, born Buckinghamshire. After working in engineering shops in Australia, returned to England and produced his first three-wheel car with the Wolseley Company in 1895, forming his own company in 1905. Conservative MP from 1918 to 1924.

Barclay, Robert (1843–1913) English. Founder of Barclay and Company Limited with the merger of 20 banks in 1896. In 1917 the name was changed to Barclay's Bank Limited.

Beaverbrook, Max (William Maxwell Aitken), 1st Baron (1879–1964) English–Canadian, born Maple, Ontario. Originally stockbroker, before entering British parliament (1911–16); became minister of information (1918). Later acquired a number of major British newspapers, including the *Daily Express*.

Benz, Karl Friedrich (1844–1929) German, born Karlsruhe. Engineer and car manufacturer who developed two-stroke engine. Founded Benz & Co. and produced one of the earliest petrol-driven vehicles; company later merged to become Daimler-Benz & Co.

Birdseye, Clarence (1886–1956) American, born Brooklyn, New York. Co-founder of the General Seafoods Company in 1924, after developing a process for freezing foods in small packages. Later president of Birdseye Frosted Foods (1930–34) and Birdseye Electric Company (1935–38). He is credited with around 300 patents.

Boeing, William Edward (1881–1956) American, born Detroit, Michigan. Formed Pacific Aero Products Co. in 1916 to build seaplanes. Renamed as the Boeing Airplane Co. in 1917, it became the largest aircraft manufacturer in the world. Also formed civilian airline Boeing Air Transport Co. in 1927.

Bond, Alan (1938–) English–Australian, born London. At the age of 19 established his own company; the Bond Corporation developed extensive interests in Australian newspapers, television, brewing, oil and gas, and gold mining.

Burrell, Sir William (1861–1958) Scottish, born Glasgow. Ship-owner and art collector. Accumulated 8 000 works of art from all over the world, which he donated to the city of Glasgow in 1944.

Butlin, Sir William Edmund (1899–1980) English, born South Africa. Holiday camp promoter; opened first camp at Skegness in 1936 and expanded business in the UK and abroad after World War II.

Cadbury, George (1839–1922) English, born Birmingham. Quaker businessman, son of John Cadbury. Took over father's business in 1861 and established for the workers the model village of Bournville, near Birmingham. Became proprietor of the *Daily News* in 1902.

Cadbury, John (1801–89) English, born Birmingham. Quaker businessman, founder of Cadburys cocoa and chocolate business.

Carnegie, Andrew (1835–1918) Scottish, born Dunfermline. Invested in oil lands and a business which grew into the largest iron and steel works in America. Retired in 1901, a multimillionaire.

Chandos, Oliver Lyttelton, 1st Viscount (1893–1972) English, born London. Managing director of the British Metal Corporation from 1928. In 1940 entered the House of Commons and was made president of the board of trade. Resigned from politics to return to business in 1954.

Christie, James (1730–1803) English, born London. Founder of Christie's auctioneers in 1766.

Citroën, André Gustave (1878–1935) French, born Paris. Responsible for mass production of armaments during World War I. Later manufacturer of small low-priced cars but in 1934 lost control of the Citroën company.

Conran, Sir Terence Orby (1931–) English, born Esher, Surrey. Businessman and designer who founded and ran the Habitat Company (1971). Has since been involved in management of Richard Shops, Conran Stores and Habitat Mothercare.

Cunard, Sir Samuel (1787–1865) Canadian, born Halifax. Merchant and shipowner who emigrated to Britain in 1838 to found the British and North American Royal Mail Steam Packet Company, later known as the Cunard Line, for the new steam mail service between Britain and America.

INDUSTRIALISTS AND ENTREPRENEURS (cont.)

Du Pont Nemours, Eleuthère Irénée (1771–1834) French–American, born Paris. Worked in father's printing plant until 1797. Emigrated to USA and in 1802 established a gunpowder factory which developed into one of the world's largest chemical concerns.

Du Pont, Pierre Samuel (1870–1954) American, born Wilmington, Delaware. Joined family gunpowder company. As its president (1915–20) introduced and developed many new industrial management techniques. Became president of General Motors in 1920.

Dunlop, John Boyd (1840–1921) Scottish, born Dreghorn, Ayrshire. Credited with inventing the pneumatic tyre. In 1889 formed business which became the Dunlop Rubber Company Ltd; produced pneumatic tyres for bicycles, and later cars.

Firestone, Harvey Samuel (1868–1938) American, born Columbiana, Ohio. Sold solid rubber carriage tyres in Chicago and in 1900 founded Firestone Tire and Rubber Company, which grew to be one of the biggest industrial corporations in the USA. Pioneered pneumatic tyres for Ford model T, and non-skid treads. Started rubber plantations in Liberia in 1924.

Ford, Henry II (1917–87) American, born Dearborn, Michigan. Seized control of the Ford Motor Company from his grandfather Henry Ford in 1945. Stepped down as chief executive officer in 1979 and as chairman in 1980, but remained as member of the board of directors.

Ford, Henry (1863–1947) American, born Greenfield, Michigan. Apprentice to a machinist at age of 15, produced his first petrol-driven car in 1893. In 1903 founded Ford Motor Company and pioneered mass-production techniques.

Frick, Henry Clay (1849–1919) American, born West Overton, Pennsylvania. Millionaire at 30 after forming company to supply the Pittsburgh steelworks with coke. Became chairman of the Carnegie steel company in 1889. A ruthless employer, he was shot and stabbed after forcefully breaking a strike in 1892, but subsequently recovered. Became a director of United States Steel in 1901.

Getty, Jean Paul (1892–1976) American, born Minneapolis, Minnesota. Entered oil business in his early twenties and went on to acquire and control more than 100 companies. Also acquired an enormous and valuable art collection.

Guinness, Sir Benjamin Lee (1798–1868) Irish, born Dublin. Inherited Guinness's Brewery (1759) and made it the largest business of its kind in the world. First lord mayor of Dublin (1851) and MP (1865–8).

Gulbenkian, Calouste Sarkis (1869–1955) British–Ottoman–Turkish, born Scutari. Entered father's oil business in Baku in 1888. Later organized international oil company mergers and negotiated oil concessions between America and Saudi Arabia.

Hammer, Armand (1899–1990) American, born New York. Exported grain to the USSR in exchange for furs, dealing with Lenin and subsequent Soviet leaders. Founded the A Hammer Pencil Company in 1925 and maintained strong connections with the USSR, occasionally acting as intermediary between USSR and US governments. Bought and expanded the small Occidental Petroieum Corporation in 1957, and founded Hammer Galleries Inc in New York in 1930.

Harmsworth, Harold Sydney, 1st Viscount Rothermere (1868–1940) Irish, born London. Newspaper magnate, founder of the *Glasgow Daily Record* and the *Sunday Pictorial*. Also controlled the *Daily Mail*, *Sunday Dispatch* and the *Daily Mirror*, for which he developed a circulation of three million in 1922.

Heinz, Henry John (1844–1919) American, born Pittsburgh, Pennsylvania. Co-founder of food manufacturing and packing company F & J Heinz, and president of the reorganized business H J Heinz Co. from 1905 to 1919. Promoted pure food movement in the USA, and pioneered staff welfare work.

Hilton, Conrad Nicholson (1887–1979) American, born San Antonio, New Mexico. Took over family inn in 1918, then built up a chain of hotels in major cities in the USA. Formed Hilton Hotels Corporation in 1946 and Hilton International in 1948, and continued to expand until 1966 when his son became president.

Honda, Soichiro (1906–91) Japanese, born Iwata Gun. Became garage apprentice in 1922, and opened his own garage in 1928. By 1934 had opened a piston-ring production factory and later produced motor cycles. President of Honda Corporation (1948–1973), remaining as a director, and appointed 'supreme advisor' in 1983.

Hoover, William Henry (1849–1932) American, born Ohio. After running a tannery business, bought patent of an electric cleaning machine from a janitor and formed Electric Suction Sweeper Co in 1908 (later renamed Hoover) to manufacture and market it throughout the world.

INDUSTRIALISTS AND ENTREPRENEURS (cont.)

Hughes, Howard Robard (1905–76) American, born Houston, Texas. Inherited father's oil-drilling equipment company and used profits to make Hollywood films. After working as a pilot, became involved in designing, building and flying aircraft, then abruptly returned to filmmaking. From 1966 lived in complete seclusion but continued to control his vast business interests.

Iacocca, Lee (Lido Anthony) (1924–) American, born Allentown, Pennsylvania. Worked for Ford Motor Company, rising to become president in 1970. In 1978 joined Chrysler Corporation as president and chief executive officer, restoring profitability during serious financial difficulties.

Krupp, Alfred (1812–87) German, born Essen. Inherited father's iron forge and began manufacturing arms in 1837. Established a steel plant and became an international arms supplier. Also acquired large mines, collieries and docks.

Lyons, Sir Joseph (1848–1917) English, born London. Starting with a teashop in Piccadilly, made J Lyons and Co Ltd. one of the largest catering businesses in Britain.

Marks, Simon, 1st Baron Marks of Broughton (1888–1964) English, born Leeds. Son of a Jewish immigrant from Poland from whom he inherited 60 Marks and Spencer 'penny bazaars'. With Israel (later Lord) Seif, established Marks and Spencer as a major high-quality retail chain.

Maxwell, (Ian) Robert (1923–91) English, born Czechoslovakia. Founder of Pergamon Press and Labour MP (1964–70). As well as controlling Mirror Group Newspapers and the Maxwell Communication Corporation, Maxwell had extensive private business interests. After his death in 1991 massive debts were revealed.

Murdoch, (Keith) Rupert (1931–) Australian–American, born Melbourne. After becoming Australia's second largest publisher, expanded abroad acquiring newspapers in London and New York, including the *Sun, The Times* and the New York *Post.* Expanded communications empire in 1989 with the purchase of Collins the publishers and inaugurated Sky Television.

Nobel, Alfred (1833–96) Swedish, born Stockholm. Explosives expert who invented dynamite and gelignite. Created an industrial empire to manufacture his many inventions and left his fortune to endow annual Nobel prizes.

Nuffield, William Richard Morris, 1st Viscount (1877–1963) English, born Worcester. Started in bicycle repair business and by 1910 was manufacturing prototypes of Morris Oxford cars at Cowley in Oxford. First British manufacturer to develop mass production of cheap cars.

Olivetti, Adriano (1901–60) Italian, born Ivrea. Vastly increased and developed father's typewriter firm. Widely noted for his social concerns.

Onassis, Aristotle Socrates (1906–75) Greek, born Smyrna, Turkey. Made fortune in tobacco trade and built up one of the world's largest independent fleets of ships. Also pioneer in construction of supertankers. Married Jaqueline Kennedy, widow of US president John F Kennedy.

Packer, Kerry Francis Bullmore (1937–) Australian, born Sydney. Inherited from his father the Australian Consolidated Press, newspaper publisher with television and radio interests. Involved in disputes and legal battles with national cricket bodies due to his creation and broadcasting of 'World Series Cricket'.

Pilkington, Sir Lionel Alexander Bethune (Sir Alastair) (1920–) English, born Calcutta. Member of family firm of glass-makers, who researched and developed methods of producing defect-free plate glass.

Pulitzer, Joseph (1847–1911) Hungarian–American, born Makó, Hungary. In 1846 emigrated to join US army. Later in St Louis he became a reporter, then began to acquire and revitalize old newspapers, including the New York *World* (1883). Established in his will annual Pulitzer prizes for literature, drama, music and journalism.

Rockefeller, John Davison (1839–1937) American, born Richford, New York. Founded the Standard Oil Co. in 1870 and through it secured control of the oil trade of America. Gave over 500 million dollars in aid of medical research, universities and Baptist churches; in 1913 established Rockefeller Foundation 'to promote the well-being of mankind'.

Roddick, Anita Lucia (1943–) English, born Brighton. Founder of the Body Shop International plc to sell natural cosmetics. Company has around 300 stores.

Rolls, Charles Stewart (1877–1910) English, born London. Motor car manufacturer, founded C S Rolls & Co in 1902, and later Rolls-Royce Ltd with Sir Henry Royce. In 1910 made first non-stop double crossing of the English Channel by aeroplane.

INDUSTRIALISTS AND ENTREPRENEURS (cont.)

Rowntree, Joseph (1836–1925) English, born York. With his brother became a partner in a cocoa factory in York in 1869, and built up welfare organizations for employees.

Royce, Sir (Frederick) Henry (1863–1933) English, born near Peterborough. Founder of electrical and mechanical engineering firm Royce Ltd (1884) and co-founder of Rolls-Royce Ltd, manufacturer of car and aeroplane engines. Designed engines used in Spitfires and Hurricanes in World War II.

Sainsbury, Alan John, Baron Sainsbury of Drury Lane (1902–) English, born Hornsey, Middlesex. Joined family grocery business in 1921 and since 1967 has been joint president of major supermarket chain J Sainsbury PLC.

Selfridge, Harry Gordon (1858–1947) English–American, born Ripon, Wisconsin. Chicago trader who in 1906 on a visit to London initiated the Selfridge business; the Oxford Street store opened in 1909.

Sieff, Israel Moses, Baron Sieff of Brimpton (1889–1972) English, born Manchester. With Simon Marks, developed Marks and Spencer. Joint managing director from 1926 to 1967 and succeeded Lord Marks as chairman (1964–1967).

Sinclair, Sir Clive (Marles) (1940–) English, born Surrey. Launched electronics company which has developed and successfully marketed calculators, miniature televisions, personal computers. Also manufactured Sinclair C5 'personal transport' vehicle powered by a washing-machine motor and rechargeable batteries.

Tate, Sir Henry (1819–99) English, born Chorley, Lancashire. Patented method for cutting sugar cubes (1872) and formed major sugar refinery. Gave nation Tate Gallery (1897) containing his own valuable private collection.

Tiffany, Charles Lewis (1812–1902) American, born Killingby, Connecticut. Goldsmith and jeweller who began dealing in 1837, and by 1883 was one of the largest silverware manufacturers in America. Held appointments to 23 royal patrons, including the tsar of Russia and Queen Victoria.

Wang, An (1920–89) American–Chinese, born Shanghai. Graduated in science from Shanghai, then studied applied physics at Harvard. Invented the magnetic core memory and founded Wang Laboratories in Boston in 1951, now one of the world's largest automation system firms. Also introduced desktop computers and calculators.

Woolworth, Frank Winfield (1852–1919) American, born Rodman, Jefferson County, New York. From inexpensive fixed-price goods stores built up a chain of over a thousand stores controlled from a New York headquarters. Most development outside America was after the death of the founder.

ENVIRONMENTAL DISASTERS ON LAND

Location	Event	Date	Consequence
Basle, Switzerland	Fire in Sandez factory warehouse resulted in major chemical spill.	November 1980	River Rhine rendered lifeless for 200 km/124 ml.
Beirut	Toxic waste dumped by Italian company.	July–September 1988	Italy forced to take back its poison drums.
Bhopal, India	Toxic gas leaked from a Union Carbide pesticide plant and enveloped a nearby slum area housing 200 000 people.	December 1984	Possibly 10 000 people died (officially 2352). Survivors suffer ravaged lungs and/or blindness. 100 km^2/39 ml^2 affected by the gas.
Camelford, Cornwall	20 tonnes of aluminium sulphate were flushed down local rivers after an accident at a water treatment works.	July 1988	60 000 fish killed. Local people suffered from vomiting, diarrhoea, blisters, mouth ulcers, rashes and memory loss.
Chernobyl, Ukraine	Nuclear reactor exploded, releasing a radioactive cloud over Europe.	April 1986	Fewer than 50 people were killed, but the radioactive cloud spread as far as Britain, contaminating farmland. 100 000 Soviet citizens may die of radiation-induced cancer, a further 30 000 fatalities are possible worldwide. 250 000 people evacuated from the area in five years.
Cubatao, Brazil	Uncontrolled pollution from nuclear industry.	1980s	Local population suffer serious ailments and genetic deformities. 30% of deaths are caused by pollution-related diseases and damage to respiratory systems.
Cumbria, England	Fire in Windscale plutonium production reactor burned for 24 hours and ignited 3 tonnes of uranium.	October 1957	Radioactive material spread throughout the countryside. In 1983 the British government said 39 people probably died of cancer as a result. Unofficial sources say 1000.
Decatur, Alabama, USA	Fire at Browns Ferry reactor caused by a technician checking for air leaks with a lighted candle.	March 1975	$100 million damage. Electrical controls burned out, lowering cooling water to dangerous levels.
Detroit, Michigan, USA	Malfunction in sodium cooling system at the Enrico Fermi demonstration breeder reactor.	October 1966	Partial core meltdown. Radiation was contained.
Erwin, Tennessee, USA	Highly enriched uranium released from top-secret nuclear fuel plant.	August 1979	1000 people contaminated (with up to 5 times as much radiation as would normally be received in a year).
Flixborough, England	Container of cyclohexane exploded.	1974	28 people died.

ENVIRONMENTAL DISASTERS ON LAND (cont.)

Location	Event	Date	Consequence
Goiânia, Brazil	Major radioactive contamination incident involving an abandoned radiotherapy unit containing radioactive caesium chloride salts.	September–October 1987	People evacuated; homes demolished; 249 people affected by sickness or death.
Gore, Oklahoma, USA	A cylinder of nuclear material burst after being improperly heated at Kerr-McGee plant.	January 1986	1 worker died, 100 hospitalized.
Idaho Falls, Idaho, USA	Accident at experiment reactor.	January 1961	3 workers killed. Damage contained, despite high radiation levels at the plant.
Kasli, Russia	Chemical explosion in tanks containing nuclear waste.	1957	Radioactive material spread. Major evacuation of area.
Kuwait	Iraqi forces set alight 600 oil wells.	February 1991	Air pollution consisted of clouds of soot and oil particles which obscured the sun and fell as 'black rain'. Threat that it would turn into sulphur dioxide and fall as acid rain. Incidence of fatal bronchitis expected to increase. Possible serious contamination of agricultural land and water supplies particularly in Iraq's Tigris and Euphrates valleys.
Love Canal, near Niagara Falls, New York, USA	Dumping of drums containing hazardous waste at Love Canal, which by the 1970s were leaking toxic chemicals.	1940s to 1952	More than 240 families evacuated, countryside contaminated.
Lucens Vad, Switzerland	Coolant malfunction in an experimental underground reactor.	January 1969	Large amount of radiation released into cavern, which was then sealed.
Minimata Bay, Japan	Dumping of chemicals, including methyl mercury.	1953	Minimata disease, characterized by cerebral palsy, had killed more than 300 people by 1983. Thousands more suffered genetic abnormalities, brain disease and nervous disorders.
Monongahela River, Pennsylvania, USA	Storage tank ruptured and spilled 3 800 000 gallons of diesel oil into the Monongahela river.	January 1988	Water supply to 23 000 residents of Pittsburgh cut off. Oil slick spread into W Virginia, growing to 77 km/48 ml, and reached Steubenville, Ohio.
Monticello, Minnesota, USA	Water-storage space at Northern States Power Company's reactor overflowed.	November 1971	50 000 gallons of radioactive waste water dumped in Mississippi River. St Paul water system contaminated.

ENVIRONMENTAL DISASTERS ON LAND (cont.)

Location	Event	Date	Consequence
Rochester, New York, USA	Steam-generator pipe broke at the Rochester Gas & Electric Company's plant.	January 1982	Small amounts of radioactive steam escaped.
Seveso, N Italy	Leak of toxic TCDD gas containing the poison dioxin.	July 1976	Local population still suffering; in worst contaminated area, topsoil had to be removed and buried in a giant plastic-coated pit.
Tennessee, USA	100 000 gallons of radioactive coolant leaked into the containment building of the TVA's Sequoyah 1 plant.	February 1981	8 workers contaminated.
Three Mile Island, Harrisburg, Pennsylvania, USA	Water pump broke down releasing radioactive steam.	March 1979	Pollution by radioactive gases. Some authorities claimed regional cancer, child deformity. Massive clean-up operation resulted in 150 tonnes of radioactive rubble and 250 000 gallons of radioactive water.
Tsuruga, Japan	Accident during repairs of a nuclear plant.	April 1981	100 workers exposed to radioactive material.

OIL SPILLS AT SEA

Name	Location	Date	Consequence
AmocoCadiz, Cyprus-registered tanker, grounded and spilled 65 562 000 gallons	near Portshall, France	March 1978	marine pollution, 160 km/99 ml of French coast polluted
Aragon spilled 7 350 000 gallons	—	1989	marine pollution
Atlantic Empress and *Aegean Captain*; collision between tankers caused spillage of 88 200 000 gallons	off Trinidad and Tobago	July 1979	marine pollution
Burmah Agate collided and spilled 10 700 000 gallons	Galveston Bay, Texas	November 1979	marine pollution

OIL SPILLS AT SEA (cont.)

Name	Location	Date	Consequence
Castillo de Beliver tanker; fire caused spillage of 73 500 000 gallons	off Cape Town, South Africa	August 1983	marine pollution
Ekofisk oil field; blow-out caused spillage of 8 200 000 gallons	North Sea	April 1977	marine pollution
Exxon Valdez, US tanker, grounded on Bligh Reef and spilled 10 080 000 gallons	Prince William Sound, Alaska	March 1989	1770 km/1162 ml of Alaskan coastline polluted. More than 3600 sq km/1390 sq ml of water fouled. Thousands of animals killed.
Gulf; Iraq pumped oil at a rate of 4 200 000 gallons a day into the sea	10 ml off coast near Kuwait City	January–February 1991	Threat to desalination plants and therefore to water supply. Devastating effect on all areas of marine environment.
Ixtoc oil well; blow-out caused spillage of 176 400 000 gallons	Gulf of Mexico	June 1979	marine pollution
Hawaiian Patrol; fire caused spillage of 29 106 000 gallons	N Pacific	February 1977	marine pollution
Keo; hull failure caused spillage of 88 200 000 gallons	off Massachusetts, USA	November 1969	marine pollution
Khark 5, Iranian supertanker, spilled 19 000 000 gallons of light crude oil after an explosion in its hull	700 km/435 ml N of the Canary Is, Atlantic Ocean	December 1989	370 km/230 ml oil slick almost reached Morocco. About 40% evaporated and much sank to ocean floor, endangering fish and oysters.
Kirki, Greek tanker, broke up and spilled 5 880 000 gallons of light crude oil	off Cervantes, W Australia	July 1991	pollution of conservation zones and lobster fishery

OIL SPILLS AT SEA (cont.)

Name	Location	Date	Consequence
Nowruz oil field; blow-out caused spillage of about 176 400 000 gallons	Persian Gulf	February 1983	marine pollution
Othello collided and spilled 17 640 000–29 400 000 gallons	Tralhavet Bay, Sweden	—	marine pollution
Sea Star collided and spilled 33 810 000 gallons	Gulf of Oman	December 1972	marine pollution
Sewaren storage tank rupture caused spillage of 8 400 000 gallons	New Jersey	November 1969	marine pollution
Torrey Canyon grounded and spilled 34 986 000 gallons	off Lands's End, England	March 1967	marine pollution
Urquiola grounded and spilled 29 400 000 gallons	La Coruna, Spain	May 1976	marine pollution
World Glory; hull failure caused spillage of 13 524 000 gallons	off South Africa	June 1968	marine pollution

ACID RAIN

A term generally used for polluted rainfall associated with the burning of fossil fuels.

It is implicated in damage to forests and the stonework of buildings, and increases the acid content of soils and lakes, harming crops and fish.

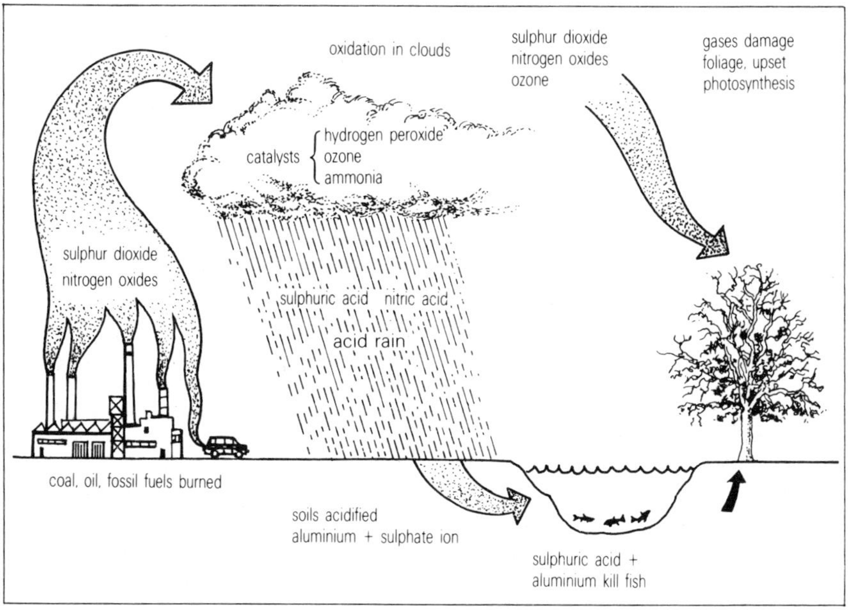

ARTS AND CULTURE

NOVELISTS

Selected works are listed.

Abrahams, Peter (Henry) (1919–) South African novelist, born Vrededorp, near Johannesburg; *The View from Coyoba* (1985).

Achebe, Chinua (Albert Chinualumogu) (1930–) Nigerian novelist, born Ogidi; *Things Fall Apart* (1959), *Anthills of the Savannah* (1988).

Ackroyd, Peter (1949–) British novelist, poet, critic, born London; *The Last Testament of Oscar Wilde* (1983), *Chatterton* (1988), *First Light* (1989).

Adams, Douglas (Noel) (1952–) English novelist, short-story writer; *The Hitch Hiker's Guide to the Galaxy* (1979), *Dirk Gently's Holistic Detective Agency* (1987).

Adams, Richard (George) (1920–) English novelist, short-story writer, born Newbury, Berkshire; *Watership Down* (1972), *Shardik* (1974), *The Girl in a Swing* (1980).

Aldiss, Brian (1925–) British novelist, poet, short-story writer, playwright, born East Dereham, Norfolk; *The Helliconia Trilogy* (1985), *Forgotten Life* (1988), *Dracula Unbound* (1991).

Aldridge, (Harold Edward) James (1918–) Australian novelist, short-story writer, playwright, born While Hills, Victoria; *The Diplomat* (1949), *The Hunter* (1950), *The Last Exile* (1961).

Alvarez, A(lfred) (1929–) English novelist, poet, critic, born London; *The Savage God: A Study of Suicide* (non-fiction) (1971), *Hers* (1974), *Day of Atonement* (1991).

Ambler, Eric (1909–) British novelist, playwright, born London; *The Mask of Dimitrios* (1939), *A Kind of Anger* (1964), *The Care of Time* (1981).

Amis, Kingsley (William) (1922–) English novelist, poet, born London; *Lucky Jim* (1954), *That Uncertain Feeling* (1955), *Jake's Thing* (1978).

Amis, Martin (Louis) (1949–) English novelist, short-story writer, born Oxford; *The Rachel Papers* (1973), *Money* (1984), *London Fields* (1990), *Time's Arrow* (1991).

Anand, Mulk Raj (1905–) Indian novelist, short-story writer, born Peshawar; *Untouchable* (1935), *The Big Heart* (1945).

Angelou, Maya (Marguerita Johnson) (1928–) American novelist, poet, playwright, born St Louis, Missouri; *I Know Why The Caged Bird Sings* (1969), *All God's Children Need Travelling Shoes* (1986).

Apuleius, Lucius (c.123 – after 161) Roman writer, born Madaura, Numidia, Africa; *Golden Ass* (the only Roman novel to survive complete), *Apologia*.

Archer, Jeffrey (Howard) (1940–) English novelist, short-story writer, born Somerset; *Not a Penny More, Not a Penny Less* (1975), *Kane and Abel* (1979), *First Among Equals* (1984), *A Twist in the Tale* (1989).

Asimov, Isaac (1920–92) American novelist, short-story writer, born Petrovichi, USSR; *I Robot* (1950), *Foundation* (1951), *The Disappearing Man and other stories* (1985), *Nightfall* (1990).

Atwood, Margaret (Eleanor) (1939–) Canadian novelist, poet, short-story writer, born Ottowa; *Bluebeards' Egg* (1983), *The Handmaid's Tale* (1986), *Cat's Eye* (1989).

Auchinclos, Louis (Stanton) (1917–) American novelist, short-story writer, born Lawrence, New York; *The Great World and Timothy Colt* (1957), *A World of Profit* (1968), *Diary of a Yuppie* (1986).

Austen, Jane (1775–1817) English novelist, born Steventon, Hampshire; *Sense and Sensibility* (1811), *Pride and Prejudice* (1813), *Mansfield Park* (1814), *Emma* (1816), *Persuasion* (1818).

Bainbridge, Beryl (1934–) English novelist, born Liverpool; *The Dressmaker* (1973), *Injury Time* (1977).

Ballantyne, R(obert) M(ichael) (1825–94) Scottish novelist, born Edinburgh; *The Coral Island* (1857), *The Gorilla Hunters* (1862).

Ballard, J(ames) G(raham) (1930–) English novelist, born Shanghai, China; *The Drowned World* (1962), *The Terminal Beach* (1964), *Empire of the Sun* (1984).

Balzac, Honoré de (1799–1850) French novelist, born Tours; *Comédie humaine* (1827–47), *Illusions perdues* (1837–43).

Banks, Iain (1954–) Scottish novelist; *The Wasp Factory* (1984), *The Bridge* (1986).

Banks, Lynne Reid (1929–) English novelist,

NOVELISTS (cont.)

playwright, born London; *The L-Shaped Room* (1961), *Defy the Wilderness* (1981), *The Warning Bell* (1987).

Barnes, Julian (1946–) English novelist, born Leicester; *Flaubert's Parrot* (1984), *Staring at the Sun* (1986), *A History of the World in 10½ Chapters* (1989).

Barstow, Stan(ley) (1928–) English novelist, short-story writer, playwright, born Horbury, Yorkshire; *A Kind of Loving* (1961), *A Raging Calm* (1968), *Just You Wait and See* (1986).

Barth, John (Simmons) (1930–) American novelist, short-story writer, born Cambridge, Maryland; *The Floating Opera* (1956), *Chimera* (1974), *The Tidewater Tales* (1987).

Bates, H(erbert) E(rnest) (1905–74) English novelist and short-story writer, born Rushden, Northamptonshire; *Fair Stood the Wind for France* (1944), *The Jacaranda Tree* (1949), *Love for Lydia* (1952), *The Darling Buds of May* (1958).

Bawden, Nina (née **Mabey**) (1925–) English, born London; *The Birds on the Trees* (1970), *The Peppermint Pig* (children's) (1975), *Walking Naked* (1981), *The Ice House* (1983).

Bedford, Sybille (née **Schoenebeck**) (1911–) British novelist, born Charlottenburg, Germany; *A Legacy* (1956), *Jigsaw: An Unsentimental Education* (1989).

Beerbohm, Sir (Henry) Max(imilian) (1872–1956) English novelist, born London; *Zuleika Dobson* (1912).

Behn, Aphra (1640–89) English novelist, playwright, born Wye, Kent; *The Rover* (play) (1678), *Oroonoko* (1688).

Bellow, Saul (1915–) Canadian novelist, born Lachine, Quebec; *Henderson the Rain King* (1959), *Herzog* (1964), *Humboldt's Gift* (1974); Nobel Prize for Literature 1976.

Bely, Andrei (**Boris Nikolayvich Bugayev**) (1880–1934) Russian Novelist, poet, born Moscow; *The Silver Dove* (1910), *Petersburg* (1913).

Benedictus, David (Henry) (1938–) English novelist, playwright, born London; *The Fourth of June* (1962), *A World of Windows* (1971), *Local Hero* (novelization of screenplay) (1983).

Bennett, (Enoch) Arnold (1867–1931) English novelist, born Hanley, Staffordshire; *Anna of the Five Towns* (1902), *The Old Wives' Tale* (1908), *Clayhanger* series (1910–18).

Berger, John (Peter) (1926–) English novelist, playwright, born Stoke Newington, London; *A Painter of Our Time* (1958), *A Fortunate Man* (non-fiction) (1967), *G.* (1972).

Berger, Thomas (Louis) (1924–) American novelist, born Cincinnati, Ohio; *Reinhart in Love* (1962), *Arthur Rex* (1978), *The Houseguest* (1988).

Binchy, Maeve (1940–) Irish novelist, short-story writer, born Dublin; *Light a Penny Candle* (1982), *Echoes* (1985), *Firefly Summer* (1987), *Circle of Friends* (1990).

Blackmore, R(ichard) D(odderidge) (1825–1900) English novelist, born Longworth, Berkshire; *Lorna Doone* (1869).

Bleasdale, Alan (1946–) English novelist, playwright, born Liverpool; *Scully* (1975), *Boys from the Blackstuff* (1983).

Böll, Heinrich (1917–) German novelist, born Cologne; *And Never Said a Solitary Word* (1953), *The Unguarded House* (1954), *The Bread of Our Early Years* (1955); Nobel Prize for Literature 1972.

Borges, Jorge Luis (1899–1986) Argentinian poet, short-story writer, born Buenos Aires; *Labyrinths* (1953), *Ficciones* (1945), *El Aleph* (1949).

Bowen, Elizabeth (Dorothea Cole) (1899–1973) Anglo-Irish novelist, short-story writer, born Dublin; *The Death of the Heart* (1938), *The Heat of the Day* (1949).

Bowles, Paul (Frederick) (1910–) American novelist, short-story writer, born New York City; *The Sheltering Sky* (1949), *Pages from Cold Point and other stories* (1968).

Boyd, William (1952–) British, born Accra, Ghana; *A Good Man in Africa* (1982), *An Ice-Cream War* (1983), *Brazzaville Beach* (1990).

Bradbury, Malcolm (Stanley) (1932–) English novelist, born Sheffield; *Eating People is Wrong* (1959), *The History Man* (1975).

Bradbury, Ray(mond) (Douglas) (1920–) American novelist, short-story writer, born Waukegan, Illinois; *The Martian Chronicles* (1950), *Fahrenheit 451* (1954), *Something Wicked this Way Comes* (1962).

Bradford, Barbara Taylor (1933–) English novelist; *A Woman of Substance* (1979), *Hold the Dream* (1985).

Bragg, Melvin (1939–) English novelist, playwright, short-story writer, born Carlisle; *The Hired Man* (1969), *A Time to Dance* (1991).

Braine, John (Gerard) (1922–86) English novelist, born Bradford; *Room at the Top* (1957).

Brink, André (Philippus) (1935–) South African novelist, short-story writer, playwright, *born Vrede, Orange Free State; Looking on Dark-*

NOVELISTS (cont.)

ness (1974), *Rumours of Rain* (1978), *A Dry White Season* (1979), *States of Emergency* (1988).

Brittain, Vera (Mary) (1893–) English novelist, poet, born Newcastle under Lyme, Staffordshire; *Testament of Youth* (1933), *Testament of Friendship* (1940), *Testament of Experience* (1957) (all autobiographies).

Bromfield, Louis (1896–1956) American novelist, short-story writer, born Mansfield, Ohio; *Early Autumn* (1926), *Until the Day Break* (1942).

Brontë, Anne (1820–49) English novelist, poet, born Thornton, Yorkshire; *Agnes Grey* (1847), *The Tenant of Wildfell Hall* (1848).

Brontë, Charlotte (1816–55) English novelist, poet, born Thornton, Yorkshire; *Jane Eyre* (1847), *Shirley* (1849), *Villette* (1853).

Brontë, Emily (1818–48) English novelist, poet, born Thornton, Yorkshire; *Wuthering Heights* (1847).

Brooke-Rose, Christine (1926–) British novelist, born Geneva, Switzerland; *The Languages of Love* (1957), *Thru* (1975), *Amalgamemnon* (1984).

Brookner, Anita (1938–) English novelist, born London; *Hotel du Lac* (1984), *Family and Friends* (1985) *Brief Lives* (1991).

Brophy, Brigid (Antonia) (1929–) British novelist, short-story writer, playwright, born London; *The Crown Princess and Other Stories* (1953), *The King of a Rainy Country* (1956), *In Transit* (1969)

Brown, George Douglas (1869–1902) Scottish novelist, born Ochiltree, Ayrshire; *House with the Green Shutters* (1901).

Brown, George MacKay (1921–) Scottish novelist, poet, short-story writer, playwright, born Orkney; *Greenvoe* (1972).

Buchan, John (1875–1940) Scottish novelist, poet, born Perth; *The Thirty-Nine Steps* (1915), *Greenmantle* (1916), *Sir Walter Scott* (biography) (1932).

Buck, Pearl (née **Sydenstricker**) (1892–1973) American novelist, born Hillsboro, W Virginia; *The Good Earth* (1913), *Pavilion of Women* (1946); Nobel Prize for Literature 1938.

Bulgakov, Mikhail (Afanasievich) (1891–1940) Russian novelist, short-story writer, born Kiev; *Diavoliada* (1925), *The Master and Margarita* (1967).

Bunyan, John (1628–88) English novelist, born Elstow, near Bedford; *Pilgrim's Progress* (1678).

Burgess, Anthony (John Anthony Burgess Wilson) (1917–) English novelist, born Manchester; *A Clockwork Orange* (1962), *The Malayan Trilogy* (1972), *Earthly Powers* (1980), *Kingdom of the Wicked* (1985), *Any Old Iron* (1989).

Burney, Fanny (Frances, Mme d'Arblay) (1752–1840) English novelist, born King's Lynn; *Evelina* (1778), *Cecilia* (1782).

Burroughs, Edgar Rice (1875–1950) American novelist, born Chicago; *Tarzan of the Apes* (1914), *The Land that Time Forgot* (1924).

Burroughs, William S(eward) (1914–) American novelist, born St Louis, Missouri; *The Naked Lunch* (1959), *The Soft Machine* (1961), *The Wild Boys* (1971), *Exterminator!* (1974).

Byatt, A(ntonia) S(usan) (1936–) English novelist, born Sheffield; *The Shadow of a Sun* (1964), *The Virgin in the Garden* (1978), *Possession* (1989), Booker Prize.

Calvino, Italo (1923–87) Italian novelist, short-story writer, born Santiago de Las Vegas, Cuba; *Invisible Cities* (1972), *The Castle of Crossed Destinies* (1969), *If on a Winter's Night a Traveller* (1979).

Camus, Albert (1913–60) French novelist, playwright, born Mondovi, Algeria; *The Outsider* (1942), *The Plague* (1948), *The Fall* (1957); Nobel Prize for Literature 1957.

Canetti, Elias (1905–) Bulgarian novelist, born Russe, Bulgaria; *Auto da Fé* (1935, trans 1946), *Crowds and Power* (1960, trans 1962); Nobel Prize for Literature 1981.

Capote, Truman (1924–84) American playwright, novelist, short-story writer, born New Orleans; *Other Voices, Other Rooms* (1948), *Breakfast at Tiffany's* (1958).

Carey, Peter (1943–) Australian novelist, short-story writer, born Bacchus Marsh, Victoria; *Bliss* (1981), *Illywhacker* (1985), *Oscar and Lucinda* (1989), Booker Prize.

Carter, Angela (1940–92) English novelist, poet, playwright, born London; *The Magic Toyshop* (1967), *The Infernal Desire Machines of Dr Hoffman* (1972), *Nights at the Circus* (1984), *Wise Children* (1991).

Cartland, (Mary) Barbara (Hamilton) (1901–) English novelist, born Birmingham; prolific writer, over 400 titles, eg *The* Husband Hunters (1976), *Wings on My Heart* (1954), *The Castle Made for Love* (1985).

Cather, Willa (Silbert) (1876–1947) American novelist, poet, born near Winchester, Virginia; *O Pioneers!* (1913), *My Antonia* (1918), *One*

NOVELISTS (cont.)

of Ours (1922), *The Professor's House* (1925), *My Mortal Enemy* (1926), *Death Comes for the Archbishop* (1927), *Sapphira and the Slave Girl* (1940).

Cervantes Saavedra, Miguel de (1547–1616) Spanish novelist and poet, born Alcala de Henares; *La Galatea* (1585), *Don Quixote* (1605–15).

Chandler, Raymond (1888–1959) American novelist, born Chicago; *The Big Sleep* (1939), *Farewell, My Lovely* (1940), *The High Window* (1942), *The Lady in the Lake* (1943), *The Long Goodbye* (1953).

Chesterton, G(ilbert) K(eith) (1874–1936) English novelist, poet, born London; *The Napoleon of Notting Hill* (1904), *The Innocence of Father Brown* (1911).

Christie, Dame Agatha (Mary Clarissa) (1890–1976) English novelist, born Torquay, Devon; *Murder on the Orient Express* (1934), *Death on the Nile* (1937), *Ten Little Niggers* (1939), *Curtain* (1975).

Clarke, Arthur C(harles) (1917–) English novelist, short-story writer, born Minehead, Somerset; *Childhood's End* (1953), *The Fountains of Paradise* (1979), *The Garden of Rama* (1991).

Clavell, James (du Maresq) (1922–) American novelist, playwright, born England; *King Rat* (1962), *Tai-Pan* (1966), *Shotgun* (1975).

Cleary, Jon (Stephen) (1917–) Australian novelist, born Sydney; *You Can't See Around Corners* (1947), *The Safe House* (1975), *Pride's Harvest* (1991).

Coetze, J(ohn) M(ichael) South African novelist, born Cape Town; *Life and Times of Michael K* (1983).

Colette, Sidonie Gabrielle (1873–1954) French novelist, born Saint-Sauveur-en-Puisaye, Burgundy; *Claudine à l'école* (1900), *Chéri* (1920), *La Fin de Chéri* (1926), *Gigi* (1943).

Collins, (William) Wilkie (1824–89) English novelist, born London; *The Woman in White* (1860), *No Name* (1862), *Armadale* (1866), *The Moonstone* (1868).

Compton–Burnett, Dame Ivy (1884–1969) English novelist, born Pinner, Middlesex; *A House and its Head* (1935), *A Family and a Fortune* (1939), *Manservant and Maidservant* (1947).

Condon, Richard (Thomas) (1915–) American novelist, born New York City; *The Manchurian Candidate* (1959), *Winter Kills* (1974), *Prizzi's Honour* (1982).

Connell, Evan S(helby) (1924–) American novelist, born Kansas City, Missouri; *Mrs Bridge* (1958), *Mr Bridge* (1969), *The Diary of a Rapist* (1966).

Conrad, Joseph (originally **Jozef Teodor Konrad Nalecz Korzeniowski**) (1857–1924), Polish/British novelist, short-story writer, born Berdichev, Ukraine; *Lord Jim* (1900), *Heart of Darkness* (1902), *Nostromo* (1904), *The Secret Agent* (1907), *Chance* (1914).

Cookson, Catherine Ann (1906–) English novelist, born Tyne Dock, County Durham; prolific author, over 40 titles eg *Tilly Trotter* (1956), *The Glass Virgin* (1969).

Cooper, Jilly (1937–) English novelist; *Men and Supermen* (1972), *Class* (1979), *Riders* (1985), *Rivals* (1988), *Polo* (1990).

Cooper, William (Harry Summerfield Hoff) (1910–) English novelist, born Crewe, Cheshire; *Scenes from Provincial Life* (1950), *Disquiet and Peace* (1956), *Immortality At Any Price* (1991).

Crane, Stephen (1871–1900) American novelist, born New Jersey; *The Red Badge of Courage* (1895).

Davidson, Lionel (1922–) English novelist, born Hull, Yorkshire; *The Rose of Tibet* (1962), *Smith's Gazelle* (1971), *The Chelsea Murders* (1978).

Davies, (William) Robertson (1913–) Canadian novelist, short-story writer, playwright, born Thamesville, Ontario; *The Rebel Angels* (1981), *'The Deptford Trilogy'* (1970–75), *What's Bred in the Bone* (1985).

de Beauvoir, Simone (1908–86) French novelist, born Paris; *The Second Sex* (1949, trans 1953), *Les Mandarins* (1954), *Memoirs of a Dutiful Daughter* (1959).

Defoe, Daniel (1660–1731) English novelist, born Stoke Newington, London; *Robinson Crusoe* (1719), *Moll Flanders* (1722), *A Journal of the Plague Year* (1722).

Deighton, Len (Leonard Cyril) (1929–) English novelist, born London; *The Ipcress File* (1962), *Spy Hook* (1988), *Spy Line* (1989), *Spy Sinker* (1990).

Delafield, E M (Edmée Elizabeth Monica Dashwood) (1890–1943) English novelist, born Llandogo, Monmouth; *The Diary of a Provincial Lady* (1931).

DeLillo, Don (1936–) American novelist, born New York City; *End Zone* (1972), *Ratner's Star* (1976), *The Names* (1982), *White Noise* (1985).

NOVELISTS (cont.)

de Quincey, Thomas (1785–1859) English novelist, born Manchester; *Confessions of an English Opium Eater* (1822).

Desai, Anita (née **Mazumbar**) (1937–) Indian novelist, short-story writer, born Mussoorie; *Cry, The Peacock* (1963), *Fire on the Mountain* (1977), *In Custody* (1985).

De Vries, Peter (1910–) American novelist, born Chicago, Illinois; *The Tunnel of Love* (1954), *The Meckerel Plaza* (1958), *Slouching Towards Kalamazoo* (1983).

Dickens, Charles (1812–70) English novelist, born Landport, Portsmouth; *Oliver Twist* (1837–9), *David Copperfield* (1849–50), *Bleak House* (1852–3), *Great Expectations* (1860–1).

Dickens, Monica (1915–) English novelist, born London; *One Pair of Hands* (1939), *Spring Comes to the World's End* (1973).

Didion, Joan (1934–) American novelist, born Sacramento, California; *Run River* (1963), *A Book of Common Prayer* (1977), *Democracy* (1984).

Dinesen, Isak (**Karen Blixen**) (1885–1962) Danish novelist, born Rungsted; *Seven Gothic Tales* (1934), *Out of Africa* (1937).

Disraeli, Benjamin (1804–81) English novelist, born London; *Coningsby* (1844), *Sybil* (1846), *Tancred* (1847).

Donleavy, J(ames P(atrick) (1926–) Irish-American novelist, playwright, born Brooklyn, New York; *The Ginger Man* (1955), *Shultz* (1980), *Are You Listening, Rabbi Löw?* (1987).

Dos Passos, John Roderigo (1896–1970) American novelist, born Chicago; *Manhatten Transfer* (1925), *USA* (1930–6).

Dostoevsky, Fyodor Mikhailovich (1821–81) Russian novelist, born Moscow; *Notes from Underground* (1864), *Crime and Punishment* (1866), *The Brothers Karamazov* (1880).

Doyle, Sir Arthur Conan (1859–1930) Scottish novelist, short-story writer, born Edinburgh; *The Memoirs of Sherlock Holmes* (1894), *The Hound of the Baskervilles* (1902), *The Lost World* (1912).

Drabble, Margaret (1939–) English novelist, short-story writer, born Sheffield; *The Millstone* (1965), *Jerusalem the Golden* (1967), *The Ice Age* (1977).

Duffy, Maureen (Patricia) (1933–) English novelist, playwright, born Worthing, Sussex; *That's How It Was* (1962), *The Paradox Players* (1967), *The Microcosm* (1966).

Dumas, Alexandre (père) (Alexandre Dumas Davy de la Pailleterie) (1802–70) French novelist and playwright, born Villers-Cotterets, Aisne; *The Three Musketeers* (1844–5).

Dumas, Alexandre (fils) (1824–95) French novelist, playwright, born Paris; *La Dame aux camélias* (1848).

du Maurier, Dame Daphne (1907–89) English novelist, born London; *Rebecca* (1938), *My Cousin Rachel* (1951).

Dunn, Nell (1936–) English novelist, playwright, born London; *Poor Cow* (1967), *Tears His Head Off His Shoulders* (1974), *The Only Child* (1978).

Durrell, Gerald Malcolm (1925–90) English writer, born Jamshedpur, India; *The Overloaded Ark* (1953), *My Family and Other Animals* (1956).

Durrell, Lawrence George (1912–90) English novelist, poet, born Julundur, India; *'Alexandria Quartet'* (1957–60).

Eco, Umberto (1932–) Italian novelist, born Alessandria, Piedmont; *The Name of the Rose* (1980), *Foucault's Pendulum* (1989).

Edgeworth, Maria (1767–1849) Irish novelist, born Blackbourton, Oxfordshire; *Castle Rackrent* (1800), *The Absentee* (1809).

Eliot, George (originally **Mary Ann**, later **Marian Evans**) (1819–80) English novelist, born Arbury, Warwickshire; *Adam Bede* (1858), *The Mill on the Floss* (1860), *Middlemarch* (1871–2), *Daniel Deronda* (1874–6).

Elkin, Stanley (Lawrence) (1930–) American novelist, short-story writer, born Brooklyn, New York; *Criers and Kibitzers, Kibitzers and Criers* (1966), *The Living End* (1979), *George Mills* (1982), *The Magic Kingdom* (1985).

Ellis, Alice Thomas (**Anna Margaret Haycraft**, née **Lindholm**) (1932–) English, born Liverpool; *The Sin Eater* (1977), *The 27th Kingdom* (1982), *The Inn at the Edge of the World* (1990).

Fairbairns, Zoë (Ann) (1948–) English novelist, born Tunbridge Wells, Kent; *Stand We At Last* (1983), *Here Today* (1984), *Daddy's Girl* (1991).

Farmer, Philip José (1918–) American novelist, short-story writer; *To Your Scattered Bodies Go* (1977), *The Magic Labyrinth* (1980).

Fast, Howard (Melvin) (1914–) American novelist, playwright, born New York City; *The Last Frontier* (1941), *Spartacus* (1951), *The Immigrants* (1977).

Faulkner, William Harrison (1897–1962) American novelist, born near Oxford, Mississippi; *Sar-*

NOVELISTS (cont.)

toris (1929), *The Sound and the Fury* (1929), *Absalom, Absalom!* (1936); Nobel Prize for Literature 1949.

Feinstein, Elaine (1930–) English novelist, poet, born Bootle, Lancashire; *The Circle* (1970), *The Border* (1989), *All You Need* (1991).

Fielding, Henry (1707–54) English novelist, born Sharpham Park, near Glastonbury, Somerset; *Joseph Andrews* (1742), *Tom Jones* (1749).

Figes, Eva (née **Unger**) (1932–) British novelist, born Germany; *Winter Journey* (1967), *Light* (1983), *The Tree of Knowledge* (1990).

Fitzgerald, F(rancis) Scott (Key) (1896–1940) American novelist, short-story writer, born St Paul, Minnesota; *The Great Gatsby* (1925), *Tender is the Night* (1934).

Fitzgerald, Penelope (Mary) (née **Knox**) (1916–) *The Bookshop* (1978), *Offshore* (1979) Booker Prize, *The Gate of Angels* (1990).

Flaubert, Gustave (1821–80) French novelist, born Rouen; *Madame Bovary* (1857), *Salammbô* (1862).

Fleming, Ian (Lancaster) (1908–64) English novelist; author of the 'James Bond' novels eg *Casino Royale* (1953), *From Russia with Love* (1957), *Dr No* (1958), *Goldfinger* (1959), *The Man with the Golden Gun* (1965).

Ford, Ford Madox (**Ford Hermann Hueffer**) (1873–1939) English novelist, poet, born Merton, Surrey; *The Fifth Queen* (1906), *The Good Soldier* (1915), *Parade's End* (1924–8).

Forrester, C(ecil) S(cott) (1899–1966) British novelist, born Cairo, Egypt; *Payment Deferred* (1926), *The African Queen* (1935), *The Happy Return* (1937).

Forster, E(dward) M(organ) (1879–1970) English novelist, short-story writer, born London; *A Room with a View* (1908), *Howards End* (1910), *A Passage to India* (1922–4).

Forsyth, Frederick (1938–) English novelist, short-story writer, born Ashford, Kent; *The Day of the Jackal* (1971), *The Odessa File* (1972), *The Fourth Protocol* (1984).

Fowles, John (Robert) (1926–) English novelist, born Leigh-on-Sea; *The Magus* (1965, revised 1977), *The French Lieutenant's Woman* (1969).

Frame, Janet Paterson (1924–) New Zealand novelist, short-story writer, born Dunedin; *The Lagoon: Stories* (1952), *Scented Gardens for the Blind* (1963), *Living in the Maniototo* (1979).

Francis, Dick (Richard Stanley) (1920–) English novelist, born Tenby, Pembrokeshire; *Dead Cert* (1962), *Slay-Ride* (1973), *The Edge* (1988), *Comeback* (1991).

Fraser, Antonia (Lady Antonia Pinter) (1932–) English novelist, born London; *Mary, Queen of Scots* (1969), *Quiet as a Nun* (1977), *A Splash of Red* (1981).

Frayn, Michael (1933–) English novelist, playwright, born Mill Hill, London; *The Tin Men* (1965), *A Very Private Life* (1968), *Sweet Dreams* (1973).

Freeling, Nicholas (1927–) English novelist, born London; *Love in Amsterdam* (1962), *Tsing-Boum* (1969), *Sand Castles* (1990).

French, Marilyn (1929–) American novelist, born New York City; *The Women's Room* (1977), *The Bleeding Heart* (1980), *Her Mother's Daughter* (1987).

Fuller, Roy (Broadbent) (1912–91) English novelist, poet, born Failsworth, Lancashire; *The Second Curtain* (1953), *The Ruined Boys* (1959), *My Child, My Sister* (1965).

Gaddis, William (1922–) American novelist, born New York City; *The Recognitions* (1955), *JR* (1976), *Carpenter's Gothic* (1985).

Galsworthy, John (1867–1933) English novelist, playwright, born Coombe, Surrey; *The Man of Property* (1906), *The Forsyte Saga* (1906–31); Nobel Prize for Literature 1932.

Garcia Márquez, Gabriel (1928–) Colombian novelist, born Aracataca; *One Hundred Years of Solitude* (1970), *Chronicle of a Death Foretold* (1982); Nobel Prize for Literature 1982.

Garner, Helen (1942–) Australian novelist, born Geelong; *Monkey Gripp* (1977).

Gaskell, Mrs Elizabeth (Cleghorn) (1810–65) English novelist, born Cheyne Row, Chelsea, London; *Mary Barton* (1848), *Cranford* (1853), *North and South* (1855), *Sylvia's Lovers* (1863).

Gerhardie, William Alexander (1895–1977) English novelist, born St Petersburg, Russia; *The Polyglots* (1925), *Resurrection* (1934).

Gibbon, Lewis Grassic (**James Leslie Mitchell**) (1901–35) Scottish novelist, born near Auchterless, Aberdeenshire; *Sunset Song* (1932), *Cloud Howe* (1933), *Grey Granite* (1934).

Gibbons, Stella (Dorothea) (1902–89) English novelist, born London; *Cold Comfort Farm* (1933).

Gide, André (Paul Guillaume) (1860–1951) French novelist, born Paris; *The Immoralist* (1902), *The Vatican Cellars* (1914).

Gilliat, Penelope (Ann Douglas, née **Conner)** (1924–) English novelist, short-

NOVELISTS (cont.)

story writer, born London; *One by One* (1965), *The Cutting Edge* (1978), *Mortal Matters* (1983).

Gissing, George Robert (1857–1903) English novelist, short-story writer, born Wakefield, Yorkshire; *New Grub Street* (1891), *The Private Papers of Henry Ryecroft* (1902).

Glasgow, Ellen (1873–1945) American novelist, born Richmond, Virginia; *Barren Ground* (1925), *The Sheltered Life* (1932), *In This Our Life* (1941).

Godden, (Margaret) Rumer (1907–) English, born Sussex; *Black Narcissus* (1939), *Breakfast with the Nikolides* (1942), *The Greengage Summer* (1958), *Coromandel Sea Change* (1991).

Godwin, William (1756–1836) English novelist, born Wisbech; *Caleb Williams* (1794), *Mandeville* (1817).

Goethe, Johann Wolfgang von (1749–1832) German novelist, poet, born Frankfurt-am-Main; *The Sorrows of Young Werther* (1774).

Gogol, Nikolai Vasilievich (1809–52) Russian novelist, short-story writer, playwright, born Sorochinstsi, Poltava; *The Overcoat* (1835), *Diary of a Madman* (1835), *Dead Souls* (1842), *The Odd Women* (1893).

Gold, Herbert (1924–) American novelist, born Cleveland, Ohio; *Birth of a Hero* (1951), *The Man Who Was Not With It* (1956), *My Last Two Thousand Years* (autobiography) (1972).

Golding, (Sir) William (Gerald) (1911–) English novelist, born St Columb Minor, Cornwall; *The Lord of the Flies* (1954), *The Inheritors* (1955), *Pincher Martin* (1956), *The Spire* (1964), *Darkness Visible* (1979), *Rites of Passage* (1980), *The Paper Men* (1984), *Close Quarter* (1987), *Fire Down Below* (1989); Nobel Prize for Literature 1983.

Goldman, William (1931–) American novelist, playwright, born Chicago, Illinois; *Boys and Girls Together* (1964), *The Princess Bride* (1973), *The Silent Gondoliers* (1984).

Goldsmith, Oliver (1728–74) Anglo-Irish playwright, novelist, poet, born Pallasmore, County Longford; *The Vicar of Wakefield* (1766).

Gordimer, Nadine (1923–) South African novelist, short-story writer, born Springs, Transvaal; *Occasion for Loving* (1963), *A Guest of Honour* (1970), *The Conservationist* (1974), *A Sport of Nature* (1987); Nobel Prize for Literature 1991.

Gorky, Maxim (Aleksei Maksimovich Peshkov) (1868–1936) Russian novelist, short-story writer, born Nizhni Novgorod (New Gorky); *The Mother* (1906–7), *Childhood* (1913), *The Life of Klim Samgin (1925–36).*

Gosse, Sir Edmund William (1849–1928) English novelist, poet, born London; *Father and Son* (1907).

Graham, Winston (Mawdsley) (1911–) English, born Victoria Park, Manchester; *Ross Poldark* (1945), *The Little Walls* (1955), *Marnie* (1961).

Grass, Günter (Wilhelm) (1927–) German novelist, born Danzig; *The Tin Drum* (1959), *The Meeting at Telgte* (1979).

Graves, Robert von Ranke (1895–1985) English novelist, poet, born London; *I Claudius* (1934), *Claudius the God* (1934).

Gray, Alasdair (1934–) Scottish novelist, short-story writer, poet, born Glasgow; *Lanark* (1981), *Unlikely Stories, Mostly* (1983), *1982 Janine* (1984).

Greene, (Henry) Graham (1904–91) English novelist, playwright, born Berkhamstead, Hertfordshire; *Brighton Rock* (1938), *The Power and the Glory* (1940), *The Third Man* (1950), *The Honorary Consul* (1973).

Grossmith, George (1847–1912) and **Weedon** (1852–1919) English writers, entertainers; *The Diary of A Nobody* (1892).

Haggard, Sir (Henry) Rider (1856–1925) British novelist, born Bradenham Hall, Norfolk; *King Solomon's Mines* (1885), *She* (1887), *Allan Quatermain* (1887).

Hailey, Arthur (1920–) Anglo-Canadian novelist, playwright, born Luton, Bedfordshire; *Flight into Danger* (1958), *Airport* (1968), *The Evening News* (1990).

Hardy, Thomas (1840–1928) English novelist, poet, born Higher Bockhampton, Dorset; *Far from the Madding Crowd* (1874), *The Mayor of Casterbridge* (1886), *Tess of the D'Urbervilles* (1891), *Jude the Obscure* (1895).

Hartley, L(eslie) P(oles) (1895–1972) English novelist, short-story writer, born near Peterborough; *The Shrimp and the Anemone* (1944), *The Go-Between* (1953), *The Hireling* (1957).

Hawthorne, Nathaniel (1804–64) American novelist, short-story writer, born Salem, Massachusetts; *The Scarlet Letter* (1850), *The House of the Seven Gables* (1851).

Hazzard, Shirley (1931–) American novelist, short-story writer, born Sydney, Australia; *People in Glass Houses* (1967), *The Transit of Venus* (1980).

NOVELISTS (cont.)

Heinlein, Robert A(nson) (1907–88) American novelist; *Stranger in a Strange Land* (1962), *The Moon is a Harsh Mistress* (1967).

Heller, Joseph (1923–) American novelist, born Brooklyn, New York; *Catch-22* (1961), *Something Happened* (1974), *Picture This* (1988).

Hemingway, Ernest (Millar) (1899–1961) American novelist, short-story writer, born Oak Park (Chicago), Illinois; *A Farewell to Arms* (1929), *For Whom the Bell Tolls* (1940), *The Old Man and the Sea* (1952); Nobel Prize for Literature 1954.

Hesse, Herman (1877–1962) German novelist, born Calw in Württemberg; *Siddshartha* (1922), *Steppenwolf* (1927), *The Glass Bead Game* (1943); Nobel Prize for Literature 1946.

Heyer, Georgette (1902–74) English novelist, born London; 56 novels eg *The Black Moth* (1929), *Footsteps in the Dark* (1932), *Regency Buck* (1935), *The Corinthian* (1940), *Friday's Child* (1944), *The Grand Sophy* (1950), *Bath Tangle* (1955), *Venetia* (1958), *The Nonesuch* (1962), *Frederica* (1965).

Highsmith, Patricia (Mary Patricia Plangman) (1921–) American novelist, short-story writer, born Fort Worth, Texas; *This Sweet Sickness* (1960), *The Cry of the Owl* (1962), *The Boy Who Followed Ripley* (1980).

Hill, Susan (Elizabeth) (1942–) English novelist, short-story writer, born Scarborough, Yorkshire; *I'm the King of the Castle* (1970), *Strange Meeting* (1972), *The Woman in Black* (1983).

Hilton, James (1900–54) English novelist, born Leigh, Lancashire; *Lost Horizon* (1933), *Goodbye Mr Chips* (1934).

Hines, (Melvin) Barry (1939–) English novelist, playwright, born Barnsley, S Yorkshire; *A Kestrel for a Knave* (1968), *The Gamekeeper* (1975).

Hoban, Russell (Conwell) (1925–) American novelist, playwright, born Lansdale, Pennsylvania; *Turtle Diary* (1975), *Riddley Walker* (1980), *Pilgermann* (1983).

Hogg, James (the **'Ettrick Shepherd'**) (1770–1835) Scottish novelist, poet, born Ettrick, Selkirkshire; *Confessions of a Justified Sinner* (1824).

Holt, Victoria (Eleanor Alice Burford Hibbert) (1906–) English novelist, prolific output, also writes as Philippa Carr, Jean Plaidy; *Catherine de 'Medici* (1969 – as JP), *Will You Love Me in September* (1981 – as PC), *The Captive* (1989 – as VH).

Holtby, Winifred (1898–1935) English novelist, born Yorkshire; *The Crowded Street* (1924), *The Land of Green Ginger* (1927), *South Riding* (1936).

Horgan, Paul (1903–) American novelist, poet, short-story writer, born Buffalo, New York; *The Fault of Angels* (1933), *Rome Eternal* (1957), *Mexico Bay* (1982).

Howard, Elizabeth Jane (1923–) English novelist, born London; *The Sea Change* (1959), *After Julius* (1965), *The Light Years* (1990). *Making Time* (1991).

Hughes, Thomas (1822–96) English novelist, born Uffington, Berkshire; *Tom Brown's Schooldays* (1857).

Hugo, Victor (Marie) (1802–85), French novelist, dramatist, poet, born Besançon; *Notre Dame de Paris* (1831), *Les Misérables* (1862).

Hulme, Keri (1947–) New Zealand novelist, born Christchurch; *The Bone People* (1983), *Lost Possessions* (1985).

Hunter, Evan (Salvatore A Lombino) (1926–) American novelist, playwright, short-story writer, born New York City; *The Blackboard Jungle* (1954), *Strangers When We Meet* (1958), *The Paper Dragon* (1966), *Last Summer* (1968).

Hurston, Zora Neale (1903–60) American novelist, born Eatonville, Florida; *Their Eyes Were Watching God* (1937), *Moses Man of the Mountain* (1939).

Huxley, Aldous (Leonard) (1894–1963) English novelist, born Godalming, Surrey; *Brave New World* (1932), *Eyeless in Gaza* (1936), *Island* (1962).

Innes, (Ralph) Hammond (1913–) English novelist, playwright, born Horsham, Sussex; *The Trojan Horse* (1940), *Atlantic Fury* (1962), *Isvik* (1991).

Irving, John (1942–) American novelist, short-story writer; *The World According to Garp* (1978), *The Hotel New Hampshire* (1981), *A Prayer for Owen Meany* (1989).

Isherwood, Christopher (William Bradshaw) (1904–) English/American novelist, born Disley, Cheshire; *Mr Norris Changes Trains* (1935), *Goodbye to Berlin* (1939), *Down there on a Visit* (1962)

Ishiguru, Kazuo (1954–) British novelist, short-story writer, born Japan; *The Remains of the Day* (1989).

James, Henry (1843–1916) American novelist, born New York; *Portrait of a Lady* (1881), *The Bostonians* (1886), *The Turn of the Screw* (1898), *The Awkward Age* (1899), *The Ambassadors* (1903), *The Golden Bowl* (1904).

NOVELISTS (cont.)

James, P(hyliss) D(orothy) (1920–) English novelist, born Oxford; *Cover Her Face* (1966), *Taste for Death* (1986).

Jhabvala, Ruth Prawer (1927–) British/Polish novelist, born Cologne, Germany; *Heat and Dust* (1975), *In Search of Love and Beauty* (1983).

Jong, Erica (née **Mann**) (1942–) American novelist, poet, born New York City; *Fear of Flying* (1973), *Fanny, Being the True History of the Adventures of Fanny Hackabout-Jones* (1980), *Serenissima* (1987).

Joyce, James (Augustine Aloysius) (1882–1941) Irish novelist, poet, born Dublin; *Dubliners* (1914), *A Portrait of the Artist as a Young Man* (1914–15), *Ulysses* (1922), *Finnegan's Wake* (1939).

Kafka, Franz (1883–1924) Austrian novelist, short-story writer, born Prague; *The Metamorphosis* (1916), *The Trial* (1925), *The Castle* (1926), *America* (1927).

Kaplan, Johanna (1942–) American novelist, short-story writer, born New York City; *Other People's Lives* (1975), *O My America!* (1980).

Kazantzakis, Nikos (1883–1957) Greek novelist, poet, playwright, born Heraklion, Crete; *Zorba the Greek* (1946).

Keane, Molly (1904–) Anglo-Irish novelist, born County Kildare, Ireland; *Devoted Ladies* (1934), *Good Behaviour* (1981), *Time After Time* (1983).

Kelman, James (Alexander) (1946–) Scottish novelist, short-story writer, playwright, born Glasgow; *The Busconductor Hines* (1984), *A Chancer* (1985), *Greyhound for Breakfast* (1987), *A Disaffection* (1989).

Keneally, Thomas (Michael) (1935–) Australian novelist, short-story writer, playwright, born Sydney; *Bring Larks and Heroes* (1967), *Three Cheers for a Paraclete* (1968), *The Survivor* (1969), *Schindler's Ark* (1982).

Kennedy, Margaret (Moore) (1896–1967) English novelist, playwright, born London; *The Ladies of Lyndon* (1923), *The Constant Nymph* (1924), *The Fool of the Family* (1930).

Kerouac, Jack (Jean-Louis) (1922–69) American novelist, born Lowell, Massachusetts; *On the Road* (1957), *The Dharma Brums* (1958).

Kesey, Ken (Elton) (1935–) American novelist, short-story writer, born La Junta, Colorado; *One Flew Over the Cuckoo's Nest* (1962).

King, Francis (Henry) (1923–) English novelist, short-story writer, born Adelboden, Switzerland; *To the Dark Tower* (1946), *The Widow* (1957), *The Custom House* (1961), *Visiting Cards* (1990).

King, Stephen (Edwin) (1947–) American novelist, short-story writer; *Carrie* (1974), *The Shining* (1977), *Christine* (1983).

Kingsley, Charles (1819–75) English novelist, born Holne vicarage, Dartmoor; *Westward Ho!* (1855), *The Water-Babies* (1863), *Hereward the Wake* (1866).

Kipling, Rudyard (1865–1936) English novelist, poet, short-story writer, born Bombay, India; *Barrack–room Ballads* (1892), *The Jungle Book* (1894), *Kim* (1901), *Just So Stories* (1902); Nobel Prize for Literature 1907.

Kundera, Milan (1929–) French/Czech novelist, born Brno; *Life is Elsewhere* (1973), *The Farewell Party* (1976), *The Unbearable Lightness of Being* (1984), *Immortality* (1991).

Laclos, Pierre (Ambroise François) Choderlos de (1741–1803) French novelist, born Amiens; *Les Liasons Dangereuses* (Dangerous Liaisons) (1782).

La Fayette, Marie Madeleine Pioche de Lavergne, Comtesse de (1634–93) French novelist, born Paris; *Zaide* (1670), *La Princesse de Clèves* (1678).

Lamming, George (Eric) (1927–) Barbadian novelist, born Carrington Village; *In the Castle of My Skin* (1953), *Season of Adventure* (1960).

Lampedusa Giuseppe Tomasi di (1896–1957) Italian novelist, born Palermo, Sicily; *Il Gattopardo* (The Leopard) (1958).

Lawrence, D(avid) H(erbert) (1885–1930) English novelist, poet, short-story writer, born Eastwood, Nottinghamshire; *Sons and Lovers* (1913), *The Rainbow* (1915), *Women in Love* (1920), *Lady Chatterley's Lover* (1928).

Le Carré, John (David John Moore Cornwell) (1931–) English novelist, born Poole, Dorset; *Tinker, Tailor, Soldier, Spy* (1974), *Smiley's People* (1980), *The Little Drummer Girl* (1983).

Lee, (Nelle) Harper (1926–) American novelist, born Monroeville, Alabama; *To Kill a Mockingbird* (1960).

Lee, Laurie (1914–) English novelist, poet, born Slad, Gloucestershire; *Cider with Rosie* (1959), *As I Walked Out One Midsummer Morning* (1969).

Le Fanu, (Joseph) Sheridan (1814–73) Irish novelist, short-story writer, born Dublin; *Uncle Silas* (1864), *In a Glass Darkly* (1872).

NOVELISTS (cont.)

Le Guin, Ursula K(roeber) (1929–) American novelist, poet, short-story writer, born Berkeley, California; *Rocannon's World* (1966), *The Left Hand of Darkness* (1969), *Searoad* (1991).

Lehmann, Rosamond (Nina) (1903–90) English novelist, born London; *Dusty Answer* (1927), *Invitation to the Waltz* (1932), *The Ballad and the Source* (1944).

Lessing, Doris (1919–) British novelist, short-story writer, born Kermanshah, Iran; *The Grass is Singing* (1950), *The Golden Notebook* (1962), *Canopus in Argus Archives* (1979–83).

Levi, Primo (1919–87) Italian novelist, born Turin; *If this is a Man* (1947), *The Periodic Table* (1984).

Lewis, (Harry) Sinclair (1885–1951) American novelist, born Sauk Center, Minnesota; *Main Street* (1920), *Babbitt* (1922), *Martin Arrowsmith* (1925), *Elmer Gantry* (1927); Nobel Prize for Literature 1930.

Lively, Penelope (Margaret) (né **Low**) (1933–) British, born Cairo, Egypt; *The Road to Lichfield* (1977), *Moon Tiger* (1987), Booker Prize, *City of the Mind* (1991).

Lodge, David (1935–) English novelist, born London; *The British Museum is Falling Down* (1965), *Changing Places* (1975), *Small World* (1984).

London, Jack (John) Griffith (1876–1916); American novelist, born San Francisco; *Call of the Wild* (1903), *White Fang* (1907), *Martin Eden* (1909).

Lowry (Clarence) Malcolm (1909–57) English novelist, born Cheshire; *Under The Volcano* (1947).

Lurie, Alison (1926–) American novelist, born Chicago, Illinois; *Love and Friendship* (1962), *The War Between the Tates* (1974), *The Truth about Lorin Jones* (1988).

Macaulay, Dame (Emilie) Rose (1881–1958) English novelist, born Rugby, Warwickshire; *Dangerous Ages* (1921), *The World, My Wilderness* (1950), *The Tower of Trebizond* (1956).

MacDonald, George (1824–1905) Scottish novelist, born Huntly, Aberdeenshire; *Robert Falconer* (1868), *The Princess and the Goblin* (1872), *Lilith* (1895).

McEwan, Ian (Russell) (1948–) English novelist, short-story writer, playwright, born Aldershot, Hampshire; *First Love, Last Rites* (1975), *The Cement Garden* (1978), *The Child in Time* (1987), *The Innocent* (1990).

McIlvanney, William (1936–) Scottish novelist, poet, born Kilmarnock, Ayrshire; *Remedy is None* (1966), *Docherty* (1975), *The Big Man* (1985).

MacInnes, Colin (1914–76) English novelist, born London; *City of Spades* (1957), *Absolute Beginners* (1957).

MacKenzie, Sir (Edward Morgan) Compton (1883–1972) English novelist, born West Hartlepool; *Whisky Galore* (1942).

MacKenzie, Henry (1745–1831) Scottish novelist, born Edinburgh; *The Man of Feeling* (1771)

MacLean, Alistair (1922–87) Scottish novelist, born Glasgow; *The Guns of Navarone* (1957), *Where Eagles Dare* (1967).

Mailer, Norman (Kingsley) (1923–) American novelist, born Long Beach, New Jersey; *The Naked and the Dead* (1949), *Barbary Shore* (1951), *An American Dream* (1965), *The Executioner's Song* (1979).

Malamud, Bernard (1914–86) American novelist, born Brooklyn; *The Fixer* (1966), *The Tenants* (1971).

Mankowitz, (Cyril) Wolf (1924–) English novelist, short-story writer, playwright, born London; *Make Me an Offer* (1952), *A Kid for Two Farthings* (1953), *My Old Man's a Dustman* (1956).

Mann, Thomas (1875–1955) German novelist, born Lubeck; *Death in Venice* (1912), *The Magic Mountain* (1924).

Manning, Olivia (1908–80) English novelist, short-story writer, born Portsmouth; *The Balkan Trilogy* (1960–5), *The Levant Trilogy* (1977–80).

Mansfield, Katherine (Katherine Mansfield Beauchamp) (1888–1923) New Zealand short-story writer, born Wellington; *Prelude* (1918), *Bliss, and other stories* (1920), *The Garden Party, and other stories* (1922).

Markandaya, Kamala (Kamala Purnaiya Taylor) (1924–) Indian novelist; *Nectar in a Sieve* (1954), *A Silence of Desire* (1960), *The Coffer Dams* (1969).

Mars-Jones, Adam (1954–) English short-story writer, critic, born London; *Lantern Lecture and Other Stories* (1981), *The Darker Proof: Stories From a Crisis* (with Edmund White) (1987).

Marsh, Ngaio (1899–1982) New Zealand novelist, born Christchurch; *Death in a White Tie* (1958), *A Grave Mistake* (1978).

Massie, Allan (1938–) British novelist, born Singapore; *Change and Decay in All Around I See* (1978), *The Last Peacock* (1980), *A Question of Loyalties* (1989).

NOVELISTS (cont.)

Maugham, (William) Somerset (1874–1965) English novelist, born Paris; *Of Human Bondage* (1915), *The Moon and Sixpence* (1919), *The Razor's Edge* (1945).

Maupassant, Guy de (1850–93) French short-story writer, novelist, born Miromesnil; *Claire de Lune* (1884), *Bel Ami* (1885).

Mauriac, François (1885–1970) French novelist, born Bordeaux; *Le Baiser au Lépreux* (1922); Nobel Prize for Literature 1952.

Melville, Herman (1819–91) American novelist, poet, born New York; *Moby Dick* (1851).

Meredith, George (1828–1909) English novelist, poet, born Portsmouth; *The Egoist* (1879), *Diana of the Crossways* (1885).

Michener, James A(lbert) (1907–) American novelist, short-story writer; *Tales of the South Pacific* (1947), *Hawaii* (1959), *Chesapeake* (1978).

Miller, Henry Valentine (1891–1980) American novelist, born New York; *Tropic of Cancer* (1934), *Tropic of Capricorn* (1938), *The Rosy Crucifixion Trilogy* (1949–60).

Mishima, Yukio (Kimitake Hiraoka) (1925–70) Japanese novelist, born Tokyo; *Confessions of a Mask* (1960), *The Temple of the Golden Pavilion* (1959), *The Sea of Fertility* (1969–71).

Mitchell, (Charles) Julian (Humphrey) (1935–) English novelist, playwright, born Epping, Essex; *The White Father* (1964), *The Undiscovered Country* (1968).

Mitchell, Margaret (1900–49) American novelist, born Atlanta, Georgia; *Gone with the Wind* (1936).

Mitchison, Naomi (1897–) Scottish novelist, poet, playwright, born Edinburgh; *The Corn King and the Spring Queen (1931), The Big House* (1950).

Mitford, Nancy (1904–73) English novelist, born London; *Love in a Cold Climate* (1949), *Don't Tell Alfred* (1960).

Mo, Timothy (1950–) born Hong Kong; *The Monkey King* (1978), *Sour Sweet* (1982), *An Insular Possession* (1986).

Monsarrat, Nicholas (John Turney) (1910–79) English novelist, born Liverpool; *The Cruel Sea* (1951), *The Story of Esther Costello* (1953).

Moorcock, Michael (1939–) English novelist, short-story writer, born London; *Gloriana* (1978), *Byzantium Endures* (1983), *The City in the Autumn Stars* (1986).

Moore, Brian (1921–) Irish–Canadian novelist, born Belfast, Northern Ireland; *The Luck of Ginger Coffey* (1960), *The Temptation of Eileen Hughes, Lies of Silence* (1990).

Morrison, Toni (1931–) American novelist, born Ohio; *The Bluest Eye* (1970), *Song of Solomon* (1977), *Tar Baby* (1981).

Mortimer, John (Clifford) (1923–) English novelist, short-story writer, playwright, born London; *A Cat Among the Pigeons* (1964), *Rumpole of the Bailey* (1978), *Paradise Postponed* (1985).

Mortimer, Penelope (Ruth) (née **Fletcher**) (1918–) *A Villa in Summer* (1954), *The Pumpkin Eater* (1962), *My Friend Says It's Bullet-Proof* (1968), *The Home* (1971).

Mosley, Nicholas (1923–) English novelist, born London; *Spaces of the Dark* (1951), *Accident* (1965), *Hopeful Monsters* (1991).

Murdoch, Iris (1919–) Irish novelist, born Dublin; *The Bell* (1958), *The Sea, The Sea* (1978), *The Philosopher's Pupil* (1983).

Nabokov, Vladimir Vladimirovich (1899–1977) Russian/US novelist, poet, born St Petersburg; *Lolita* (1955), *Look at the Harlequins!* (1974)

Naipaul, V(idiadhar) S(urajprasad) (1932–) Trinidadian novelist, born Trinidad; *A House for Mr Biswas* (1961), *In a Free State* (1971), *A Bend in the River* (1979).

Newby, P(ercy H(oward) (1918–) English novelist, born Crowborough, Sussex; *The Picnic at Sakkara, Revolution and Roses* (1957), *The Barbary Light* (1962).

Ngugi wa Thiong'o (formerly wrote as **James T Ngugi**) (1938–) Kenyan novelist, short-story writer, playwright, born Kamiriithu, near Limura; *Weep Not, Child* (1964), *A Grain of Wheat* (1967), *Petals of Blood* (1977).

Nye, Robert (1939–) English novelist, poet, short-story writer, playwright, born London; *Falstaff* (1976), *Merlin* (1978), *The Life and Death of My Lord Gilles de Rais* (1990).

Oates, Joyce Carol (1938–) American novelist, short-story writer, born Millersport, New York; *A Garden of Earthly Delights* (1967), *Them* (1969), *Wonderland* (1971).

O'Brien, Edna (1932–) Irish novelist, short-story writer, born Tuamgraney, County Clare; *The Country Girls* (1960), *August is a Wicked Month* (1964), *A Pagan Place* (1971).

O'Flaherty, Liam (1897–1984) Irish novelist, short-story writer, born Inishmore, Aran Islands; *The Informer* (1926), *Two Lovely Beasts* (1948).

NOVELISTS (cont.)

O'Hara, John (Henry) (1905–70) American novelist, short-story writer, born Pottsville, Pennsylvania; *Spring Sowing* (1924), *Appointment in Samarra* (1934), *The Doctor's Son* (1935), *Butterfield 8* (1935), *Paul Joey* (1940).

Okri, Ben (1959–) Nigerian novelist, born Minna; *The Famished Road* (1991), Booker Prize.

Oliphant, Margaret (1828–97) Scottish novelist, born Wallyford, Midlothian; *The Athelings* (1857), *Salem Chapel* (1863).

Orwell, George (Eric Arthur Blair) (1903–50) English novelist, born Bengal; *Down and Out in Paris and London* (1933), *The Road to Wigan Pier* (1937), *Animal Farm* (1945), *Nineteen Eighty-Four* (1949).

Ouida (Marie-Louise de la Ramée) (1839–1908) English novelist, born Bury St Edmunds; *Held in Bondage* (1865), *Under Two Flags* (1867), *Folle-Farine* (1871).

Ozick, Cynthia (1928–) American novelist, short-story writer, born New York City; *Trust* (1966), *The Pagan Rabbit and Other Stories* (1971), *The Cannibal Galaxy* (1983).

Pasternak, Boris (Leonidovich) (1890–1960) Russian novelist, born Moscow; *Doctor Zhivago* (1957); Nobel Prize for Literature 1958.

Paton, Allan (Stewart) (1903–88) South African novelist, short-story writer, born Pietermaritzburg, Natal; *Cry, the Beloved Country* (1948).

Peacock, Thomas Love (1785–1866) English novelist, poet, born Weymouth; *Melincourt* (1817), *Nightmare Abbey* (1818).

Peake, Mervyn (Laurence) (1911–68) English novelist, poet, born Kuling, China; *Titus Groan* (1946), *Gormenghast* (1950), *Titus Alone* (1959).

Plaidy, Jean *see* **Holt, Victoria**

Poe, Edgar Allan (1809–49) American short-story writer, poet, born Boston; *Tales of the Grotesque and Arabesque* (eg 'The Fall of the House of Usher') (1840), *The Pit and the Pendulum* (1843).

Porter, Harold (Hal) (1911–84) Australian novelist, playwright, poet, short-story writer, born Melbourne; *A Handful of Pennies* (1958), *The Right Thing* (1971).

Porter, Katherine Anne (Maria Veronica Callista Russell) (1890–1980) American novelist, short-story writer, born Indian Creek, Texas; *Pale Horse, Pale Rider* (1939), *Ship of Fools* (1962).

Powell, Anthony (Dymoke) (1905–) English novelist, born London; *A Dance to the Music of Time* (1951–75), *The Fisher King* (1986).

Powys, John Cowper (1872–1963) English novelist, born Shirley, Derbyshire; *Wolf Solent* (1929), *Owen Glendower* (1940).

Priestley, J(ohn) B(oynton) (1894–1984) English novelist, playwright, born Bradford; *The Good Companions* (1929), *Angel Pavement* (1930).

Pritchett, Sir V(ictor S(awdon) (1900–) English novelist, short-story writer, playwright, born Ipswich, Suffolk; *Nothing like Leather* (1935), *Dead Man Leading* (1937), *Mr Beluncle* (1951).

Proust, Marcel (1871–1922) French novelist, born Paris; *Remembrance of Things Past* (1913–27).

Puzo, Mario (1920–) American novelist, born New York City; *The Godfather* (1969).

Pynchon, Thomas (1937–) American novelist, born Long Island; *V* (1963), *Gravity's Rainbow* (1973).

Queen, Ellery (Patrick Dannay (1905–82) and his cousin **Manfred B Lee** (1905–71)) American novelists and short-story writers, both born Brooklyn, New York; *The French Powder Mystery* (1930), *The Tragedy of X* (1940), *The Glass Village* (1954).

Radcliffe, Ann (1764–1823) English novelist, born London; *The Mysteries of Udolpho* (1794), *The Italian* (1797).

Rao, Raja (1909–) Indian novelist, short-story writer, born Hassan, Mysore; *Kanthapura* (1938), *The Serpent and the Rope* (1960), *The Cat and Shakespeare* (1965).

Raphael, Frederic (Michael) (1931–) American novelist, short-story writer, playwright, born Chicago, Illinois; *The Earlsdon Way* (1958), *The Limits of Love* (1960), *Lindmann* (1963), *Heaven and Earth* (1985).

Read, Piers Paul (1941–) English novelist, born Beaconsfield, Buckinghamshire; *The Junkers* (1968), *Monk Dawson* (1969), *The Villa Golitsyn* (1981).

Reid Banks, Lynne (1929–) English novelist, born London; *The L-Shaped Room* (1960), *Defy the Wilderness* (1981).

Remarque, Erich Maria (1898–1970) German novelist, born Osnabrück; *All Quiet on the Western Front* (1929), *The Road Back* (1931), *The Black Obelisk* (1957).

Renault, Mary (Eileen Mary Challans) (1905–83) English novelist, born London; *The King Must Die* (1958), *Fire from Heaven* (1969), *The Persian Boy* (1972).

NOVELISTS (cont.)

Rendell, Ruth (1930–) English novelist, born London; *A Judgement in Stone* (1977), *The Killing Doll* (1980), *Heartstones* (1987); as **Barbara Vine** *The House of Stairs* (1989).

Rhys, Jean (Ella Gwendolyn Rees Williams) (1894–1979) British novelist, short-story writer, born Dominica, West Indies; *After Leaving Mackenzie* (1930), *Wide Sargasso Sea* (1966), *Tigers are Better Looking* (1968).

Richardson, Dorothy M(iller) (1873–1957) English novelist, born Abingdon, Berkshire; *Pilgrimage* (12 volumes, 1915–38).

Richardson, Harry Handel (Ethel Florence Lindesay Richardson) (1870–1946) Australian novelist, born Melbourne; *The Getting of Wisdom* (1910), *Ultima Thule* (1929).

Richardson, Samuel (1689–1761) English novelist, born near Derby; *Pamela* (1740), *Clarissa* (1747–8), *Sir Charles Grandison* (1753–4).

Richler, Mordecai (1931–) Canadian novelist, born Montreal, Quebec; *The Apprenticeship of Duddy Kravitz* (1959), *St Urbain's Horseman* (1971), *Solomon Gursky Was Here* (1989).

Rolfe, Frederick William (Baron Corvo) (1860–1913) English novelist, born London; *Hadrian the Seventh* (1904), *The Desire and Pursuit of the Whole* (1934).

Roth, Henry (1906–) American novelist, short-story writer, born Tysmenica, Austria-Hungary; *Call It Sleep* (1934).

Roth, Philip Milton (1933–) American novelist, short-story writer, born Newark, New Jersey; *Portnoy's Complaint* (1969), *The Great American Novel* (1973), *My Life as a Man* (1974).

Rushdie, Salman (1947–) British novelist, short-story writer, born Bombay; *Midnight's Children* (1981), *Shame* (1983), *The Satanic Verses* (1988).

Sackville-West, Vita (Victoria May) (1892–1962) English poet, novelist, short-story writer, born Knole, Kent; *The Edwardians* (1930), *All Passion Spent* (1931).

Sade, Donatien Alphonse François, Comte de, (known as **Marquis**) (1740–1814) French novelist, born Paris; *Les 120 Journées de Sodome* (1784), *Justine* (1791), *Le Philosophie dans le boudoir* (1793), *Juliette* (1798), *Les Crimes de l'amour* (1800).

Saki (Hector Hugh Munro) (1870–1916) British novelist, short-story writer, born Akyab, Burma; *The Chronicles of Clovis* (1912), *The Unbearable Bassington* (1912).

Salinger, J(erome) D(avid) (1919–) American novelist, born New York; *The Catcher in the Rye* (1951), *Franny and Zooey* (1961).

Sand, George (Amandine Aurore Lucille Dupin) (1804–76) French novelist, born Paris; *Lélia* (1833), *La Petite Fadette* (1849).

Saroyan, William (1908–81) American novelist, playwright, short-story writer, born Fresno, California; *The Daring Young Man on the Flying Trapeze* (1934), *My Name is Aram* (1940), *The Human Comedy* (1942).

Sartre, Jean-Paul (1905–80) French novelist, playwright, born Paris; *Nausea* (1949), *The Roads to Freedom* (1945–7); Nobel Prize for Literature 1964.

Sayers, Dorothy L (1893–1957) English novelist, short-story writer, born Oxford; *Lord Peter Views the Body* (1928), *Gaudy Night* (1935).

Schreiner, Olive (1855–1920) South African novelist, born Wittebergen Mission Station, Cape of Good Hope; *The Story of an African Farm* (1883), *Trooper Peter Halkett of Mashonaland* (1897).

Scott, Sir Walter (1771–1832) Scottish novelist, poet, born Edinburgh; *Waverley* (1814), *The Heart of Midlothian* (1818), *The Bride of Lammermoor* (1819), *Ivanhoe* (1820).

Selby, Hubert, Jr (1928–) American novelist, born Brooklyn, New York; *Last Exit to Brooklyn* (1964), *The Room* (1971), *Requiem for a Dream* (1978).

Sharpe, Tom (Thomas Ridley) (1928–) British novelist, born London; *Riotous Assembly* (1971), *Porterhouse Blue* (1974), *Blott on the Lanscape* (1975), *Wilt* (1976).

Shelley, Mary (Wollstonecraft) (1797–1851) English novelist, born London; *Frankenstein* (1818), *The Last Man* (1826), *Perkin Warbeck* (1830).

Sholokhov, Mikhail Alexandrovich (1905–84) Russian novelist, born near Veshenskayal; *And Quiet Flows the Don* (1928–40), *The Upturned Soil* (1940); Nobel Prize for Literature 1965.

Shute, Nevil (Nevil Shute Norway) (1899–1960) English/Australian novelist, born Ealing; *The Pied Piper* (1942), *A Town Like Alice* (1950), *On the Beach* (1957).

Sillitoe, Alan (1928–) English novelist, poet, short-story writer, born Nottingham; *Saturday Night and Sunday Morning* (1958), *The Loneliness of the Long Distance Runner* (1959).

Simenon, Georges (1903–89) Belgian-born

NOVELISTS (cont.)

French writer, born Liège; almost 100 novels feathering Jules Maigret, 400 other novels.

Singer, Isaac Bashevis (1904–91) American novelist, playwright, born Radzymin, Poland; *The Family Moskat* (1950), *The Satan in Goray* (1955); Nobel Prize for Literature 1978.

Smith, Iain Crichton (Iain Mac A'Ghobhainn) (1928–) Scottish novelist, poet, short-story writer, playwright, born Glasgow; *Consider the Lilies* (1968), *Murdo and Other Stories* (1981), *The Dream* (1990).

Smollett, Tobias George (1721–71) Scottish novelist, born Dalquharn, Dunbartonshire; *Roderick Random* (1748), *The Adventures of Peregrine Pickle* (1751), *The Expedition of Humphrey Clinker* (1771).

Snow, C(harles) P(ercy) (1905–80) English novelist, born Leicester; *Strangers and Brothers* (1940–70).

Solzhenitsyn, Aleksandr Isayevich (1918–) Russian novelist, born Kislovodsk, Caucasus; *One Day in the Life of Ivan Denisovich* (1962), *Cancer Ward* (1968),*The First Circle* (1969); Nobel Prize for Literature 1970.

Spark, Muriel (1918–) Scottish novelist, short-story writer, poet, born Edinburgh; *The Ballad of Peckham Rye* (1960), *The Prime of Miss Jean Brodie* (1962), *The Girls of Slender Means* (1963).

Spring, Howard (1889–1965) Welsh novelist, born Cardiff; *Oh Absalom* (1938).

Stead, C(hristian) K(arlson) (1932–) New Zealand novelist, poet, born Auckland; *Smith's Dream* (1971), *All Visitor's Ashore* (1984), *Sister Hollywood* (1990).

Stein, Gertrude (1874–1946) American novelist, short-story writer, born Allegheny, Pennsylvania; *Three Lives* (1909), *Tender Buttons* (1914).

Steinbeck, John Ernest (1902–68) American novelist born Salinas, California; *Of Mice and Men* (1937), *The Grapes of Wrath* (1939), *Cannery Row* (1945), *East of Eden* (1952); Nobel Prize for Literature 1962.

Stendhal (Henri Marie Beyle) (1788–1842) French novelist, born Grenoble; *Le Rouge et le noir* (1830), *La Chartreuse de Parme* (1839).

Sterne, Lawrence (1713–68) Irish novelist, born Clonmel, Tipperary; *Tristram Shandy* (1759–67), *A Sentimental Journey* (1768).

Stevenson, Robert Louis (Balfour) (1850–94) Scottish novelist, short-story writer, poet, born Edinburgh; *Travels with a Donkey* (1879), *Treasure Island* (1883), *Kidnapped* (1886), *The Strange Case of Dr Jekyll and Mr Hyde* (1886), *Weir of Hermiston* (1896).

Stewart, J(ohn) I(nnes) M(ackintosh (Michael Innes) (1906–) British novelist, born Edinburgh; *A Use of Riches* (1957), *The Last Tresilians* (1963); as Michael Innes: *Hamlet, Revenge!* (1937), *Appleby and the Ospreys* (1986).

Stewart, Mary (1916–) English novelist, born Sunderland; *This Rough Magic* (1964), *The Last Enchantment* (1979).

Stoker, Bram (Abraham) (1847–1912) Irish novelist, short-story writer, born Dublin; *Dracula* (1897).

Storey, David (Malcolm) (1933–) British novelist, playwright, born Wakefield, Yorkshire; *This Sporting Life* (1960), *Radcliffe* (1963), *A Prodigal Child* (1982).

Stowe, Harriet (Elizabeth) Beecher (1811–96) American novelist, born Litchfield, Connecticut; *Uncle Tom's Cabin* (1852).

Styron, William (Clark) (1925–) American novelist, born Newport News, Virginia; *Lie Down in Darkness* (1951), *The Confessions of Nat Turner* (1967), *Sophie's Choice* (1979).

Suskind, Patrick (1949–) German novelist; *Perfume, the story of a murderer* (1985).

Swift, Graham (Colin) (1949–) English novelist, born London; *The Sweet Shop Owner* (1980), *Waterland* (1984), *Out of This World* (1988).

Swift, Jonathan (1667–1754) Irish novelist, poet, born Dublin; *A Tale of a Tub* (1704), *Gulliver's Travels* (1726).

Symons, Julian (Gustave) (1912–) English novelist, poet, short-story writer, playwright, born London; *The Thirty-First of February* (1950), *The Colour of Murder* (1957), *Sweet Adelaide* (1980).

Tennant, Emma (1937–) English novelist, born London; *Hotel de Dream* (1978), *Alice Fell* (1980).

Thackeray, William Makepeace (1811–63) English novelist, born Calcutta; *Vanity Fair* (1847–8), *Pendennis* (1848–50).

Theroux, Paul (Edward) (1941–) American novelist, short-story writer, born Medford, Massachusetts; *The Mosquito Coast* (1981), *Doctor Slaughter* (1984), *My Secret History* (1989).

Thiong'o, Ngugi Wa (1938–) Kenyan novelist, born Limura; *The River Between* (1963), *A Grain of Wheat* (1967).

Thomas, D(onald) M(ichael) (1935–) British novelist, poet, born Redruth, Cornwall; *The White Hotel* (1981), *Ararat* (1983), *Lying Together* (1990).

NOVELISTS (cont.)

Tolkien, J(ohn) R(onald) R(euel) (1892–1973) English novelist, born Bloemfontein, South Africa; *The Hobbit* (1937), *The Lord of the Rings* (1954–5).

Tolstoy, Count Leo Nikolayevich (1828–1910) Russian novelist, born Yasnaya Polyana, Central Russia; *War and Peace* (1863–9), *Anna Karenina* (1873–7), *Resurrection* (1899).

Tranter, Nigel Godwin (1909–) Scottish novelist, born Glasgow; *The Steps to the Empty Throne* (1969), *The Path of the Hero King* (1970), *The Price of the King's Peace* (1971).

Tremain, Rose (née **Thomson**) (1943–) British novelist, short-story writer, playwright, born London; *The Cupboard* (1981), *The Colonel's Daughter and Other Stories* (1984), *Restoration* (1989).

Trevor, William (**William Trevor Cox**) (1928–) Irish novelist, short-story writer, born Mitchelstown, Co Cork; *Fools of Fortune* (1983), *The Silence in the Garden* (1988), *Two Lives* (1991).

Trollope, Anthony (1815–82) English novelist, born London; *Barchester Towers* (1857), *Can You Forgive Her?* (1864), *The Way We Live Now* (1875).

Tuohy, (John) Frank (1925–) British novelist, short-story writer, born Uckfield, Sussex; *The Animal Game* (1957), *The Warm Nights of January* (1960), *The Ice Saints* (1964).

Turgenev, Ivan Sergeevich (1818–83) Russian novelist, born province of Orel; *Sportsman's Sketches* (1952), *Fathers and Children* (1862).

Tutuola, Amos (1920–) Nigerian novelist, short-story writer, born Abeokuta; *The Palm-Wine Drinkard and His Dead Palm-Wine Tapster in the Deads' Town* (1952), *The Wild Hunter in the Bush of the Ghosts* (1982), *The Village Witchdoctor and Other Stories* (1990).

Twain, Mark (**Samuel Langhorne Clemens**) (1835–1910) American novelist, born Florida, Missouri; *The Celebrated Jumping Frog of Calaveras County* (1865), *The Adventures of Tom Sawyer* (1876), *The Prince and the Pauper* (1882), *The Adventures of Huckleberry Finn* (1884), *A Connecticut Yankee in King Arthur's Court* (1889).

Updike, John (Hoyer) (1932–) American novelist, short-story writer, born Shillington, Pennsylvania; *Rabbit, Run* (1960), *Pigeon Feathers and other stories* (1962).

Upward, Edward (Falaise) (1903–) English novelist, born Romford, Essex; *Journey to the Border* (1938), *In the Thirties (1962), The Rotten Elements* (1969).

Uris, Leon (Marcus) (1924–) American novelist, born Baltimore, Maryland; *Battle Cry* (1953), *Exodus* (1958), *The Haj* (1984).

Van der Post, Sir Laurens (Jan) (1906–) South African novelist, playwright, born Philippolis; *Flamingo Feather* (1955), *Journey into Russia* (1964), *A Far-Off Place* (1974).

Vansittart, Peter (1920–) English novelist, born Bedford; *Quintet* (1976), *The Death of Robin Hood* (1981), *Parsifal* (1988).

Vargas Llosa, Mario (1936–) Peruvian novelist; *The Time of the Hero* (1963), *Aunt Julia and the Scriptwriter* (1977), *The War at the End of the World* (1982), *The Green House* (1986).

Verne, Jules (1828–1905) French novelist, born Nantes; *Voyage to the Centre of the Earth* (1864), *Twenty Thousand Leagues under the Sea* (1870).

Vidal, Gore (Eugene Luther Vidal, Jr) (1925–) American novelist, short-story writer, playwright, born West Point, New York; *The Season of Comfort* (1949), *Myra Breckenridge* (1968), *Kalki* (1978).

Voltaire, François-Marie Arouet de (1694–1778) French novelist, poet, born Paris; *Zadig* (1747), *Candide* (1759).

Vonnegut, Kurt (1922–) American novelist, short-story writer, born Indianapolis, Indiana; *Cat's Cradle* (1963), *Slaughterhouse-Five* (1969).

Wain, John (Barrington) (1925–) English novelist, poet, short-story writer, playwright, born Stoke-on-Trent, Staffordshire; *Hurry on Down* (1953), *The Young Visitors* (1965), *Where the Rivers Meet* (1988).

Walker, Alice (1944–) American novelist, short-story writer, born Eatonville, Georgia; *The Third Life of Grange Copeland* (1970), *In Love and Trouble* (1973), *The Color Purple* (1983).

Walpole, Horace (1717–97) English novelist, poet, born London; *Letter from Xotto to his friend Lien Chi at Pekin* (1757), *Anecdotes of Painting in England* (1761–71), *The Castle of Otranto* (1764), *The Mysterious Mother* (1768), *Historic Doubts on the Life and Reign of King Richard the Third* (1768).

Warner, Marina (1946–) English novelist, born London; *In a Dark Wood* (1977), *The Skating Party* (1982), *The Lost Father* (1988).

Warren, Robert Penn (1905–89) American novelist, poet, born Guthrie, Kentucky; *Night Rider* (1939), *All the King's Men* (1943).

Waterhouse, Keith (Spencer) (1929–) English

NOVELISTS (cont.)

novelist, playwright, born Leeds, Yorkshire; *Billy Liar* (1959), *Office Life* (1978), *Bimbo* (1990).

Waugh, Evelyn (Arthur St John) (1903–66) English novelist, born Hampstead; *Decline and Fall* (1928), *A Handful of Dust* (1934), *Brideshead Revisited* (1945).

Weldon, Fay (1933–) English novelist, born Alvechurch, Worcestershire; *Down Among the Women* (1971), *Female Friends* (1975), *Life and Loves of a She-Devil* (1983).

Wells, H(erbert) G(eorge) (1866–1946) English novelist, born Bromley, Kent; *The Time Machine* (1895), *The War of the Worlds* (1898), *The History of Mr Polly* (1910).

Welty, Eudora (1909–) American novelist, short-story writer, born Jackson, Mississippi; *A Curtain of Green* (1941), *The Golden Apples* (1949), *The Ponder Heart* (1954), *The Optimist's Daughter* (1972).

Wesley, Mary (née **Farmar)** (1912–) British novelist, born Englefield Green, Berkshire; *The Camomile Lawn* (1984), *A Sensible Life* (1990).

West, Morris (Langlo) (1916–) Australian novelist, playwright, born Melbourne, Victoria; *Children of the Sun* (non-fiction) (1957), *Summer of the Red Wolf* (1971), *The World is Made of Glass* (1983).

West, Dame Rebecca (Cecily Isabel Fairfield) (1892–1983) Irish novelist, born County Kerry, Ireland; *The Harsh Voice* (1935), *The Mountain Overflows* (1957).

Wharton, Edith (Newbold) (1862–1937) American novelist, short-story writer, born New York; *The House of Mirth* (1905), *Ethan Frome* (1911), *The Age of Innocence* (1920).

White, Antonia (Eirene Adeline Botting) (1899–1980) English novelist, born London; *Frost in May* (1983), *Beyond the Glass* (1954).

White, Patrick Victor Martindale (1912–) Australian novelist, playwright, short-story writer, born London; *Voss* (1957), *The Vivisector* (1970), *A Fringe of Leaves* (1976); Nobel Prize for Literature 1973.

White, T(erence) H(anbury) (1906–64) English novelist, poet, born Bombay; *Darkness at Pemberley* (1932), *The Once and Future King* (1958).

Wilde, Oscar (1854–1900) Irish novelist, short-story writer, playwright, poet, born Dublin; *The Happy Prince and Other Tales* (1888), *The Picture of Dorian Gray* (1890), *The Importance of Being Earnest* (play) (1895).

Wilder, Thornton Niven (1897–1976) American novelist, playwright, born Madison, Wisconsin; *The Bridge of San Luis Rey* (1927) *The Woman of Andros* (1930), *Heaven's My Destination* (1935).

Wilding, Michael (1942–) Australian novelist, short-story writer, born Worcester, England; *Living Together* (1974), *The West Midland Underground* (1975), *Pacific Highway* (1982).

Wilson, A(ndrew) N(orman) (1950–) English novelist, born London; *Kindly Light* (1979), *Wise Virgin* (1982), *Daughters of Albion* (1991).

Winterson, Jeanette (1959–) English novelist, born Lancashire; *Oranges Are Not the Only Fruit* (1987), *The Passion* (1987), *Sexing the Cherry* (1989).

Wodehouse, Sir P(elham) G(renville) (1881–1975) English novelist, short-story writer, born Guildford; *The Inimitable Jeeves* (1923), *Carry on, Jeeves* (1925).

Wolfe, Thomas Clayton (1900–38) American novelist, born Asheville, North Carolina; *Look Homeward, Angel* (1929), *Of Time and the River* (1935), *From Death to Morning* (1935).

Wolfe, Tom (Thomas Kennerley) (1931–) American novelist, born Richmond, Virginia; *The Electric Kool-Aid Acid Test* (1968), *The Right Stuff* (1979), *The Bonfire of the Vanities* (1988).

Woolf, (Adeline) Virginia (1882–1941) English novelist, born London; *Mrs Dalloway* (1925), *To The Lighthouse* (1927), *Orlando* (1928), *A Room of One's Own* (1929), *The Waves* (1931).

Wouk, Herman (1915–) American novelist, playwright, born New York City; *The Caine Mutiny* (1951), *The Winds of War* (1971), *War and Remembrance* (1978).

Wright, Richard Nathaniel (1908–60) American novelist, short-story writer, born Mississippi; *Native Son* (1940), *Eight Men* (1961).

Yerby, Frank (Garvin) (1916–91) American novelist, born Augusta, Georgia; *The Golden Hawk* (1948), *The Dahomean* (1971), *A Darkness at Ingraham's Crest* (1979).

Yourcenar, Marguerite (Marguerite de Crayencour) (1903–87) French novelist, poet, born Brussels; *Memoirs of Hadrian* (1941).

Zamyatin, Evgeny Ivanovich (1884–1937) Russian novelist, short-story writer, born Lebedyan; *We* (1921), *The Dragon: Fifteen Stories* (1966).

Zola, Émile (1840–1902) French novelist, born Paris; *Thérèse Raquin* (1867), *Les Rougon-Macquart* (1871–93), *Germinal* (1885).

POETS

Selected volumes of poetry are listed.

Abse, Dannie (Daniel) (1923–) Welsh, born Cardiff; *After Every Green Thing* (1948), *Tenants of the House* (1957).

Adcock, (Kareen) Fleur (1934–) New Zealander, born Papakura; *The Eye of the Hurricane* (1964), *The Incident Book* (1986).

Aiken, Conrad (Potter) (1889–1973) American, born Georgia; *Earth Triumphant (1914), Preludes for Memnon* (1931).

Akhamatova, Anna (pseudonym of **Anna Andreevna Gorenko**) (1889–1966) Russian, born Odessa; *Evening* (1912), *Poem without a Hero* (1940–62), *Requiem* (1963).

Angelou, Maya (pseudonym of **Marguerite Annie Johnson**) (1928–) American, born St Louis, Missouri; *And Still I Rise* (1978), *I Shall Not Be Moved* (1990).

Apollinaire, Guillame (1880–1918) French, born Rome; *Alcools* (1913), *Calligrammes* (1918).

Aristo, Ludovico (1474–1535) Italian, born Reggio; *Furioso* (1532).

Auden, W(ystan) H(ugh) (1907–73) British, naturalized American citizen, born York; *Another Time* (1940), *The Sea and the Mirror* (1944), *The Age of Anxiety* (1947).

Baudelaire, Charles (Pierre) (1821–67) French, born Paris; *Les Fleurs du mal* (1857).

Beer, Patricia (1924–) English, born Exmouth, Devon; *The Loss of the Magyar (1959), The Lie of the Land* (1983).

Belloc, (Joseph) Hillaire (Pierre) (1870–1953) British, born St Cloud, France; *Cautionary Tales* (1907), *Sonnets and Verse* (1923).

Berryman, John (1914–72) American, born McAlester, Oklahoma; *Homage to Mistress Bradsheet* (1966), *Dream Songs* (1969).

Betjeman, John (1906–84) English, born Highgate; *Mount Zion* (1931), *New Bats in Old Belfries* (1945), *A Nip in the Air* (1972).

Bishop, Elizabeth (1911–79) American, born Worcester, Massachusetts; *North and South* (1946), *Geography III* (1978).

Blake, William (1757–1827) English, born London; *The Marriage of Heaven and Hell* (1793), *The Vision of the Daughter of Albion* (1793), *Songs of Innocence and Experience* (1794), *Vala, or The Four Zoas* (1800), *Milton* (1810).

Blunden, Edmund (Charles) (1896–1974) English, born Yalding, Kent; *The Waggoner and Other Poems* (1920), *Undertones of War* (1928).

Brooke, Rupert (Chawner) (1887–1915) English, born Rugby; *Poems* (1911), *1914 and Other Poems* (1915), *New Numbers* (1915).

Brooks, Gwendolyn (1917–) American, born Topeka, Kansas; *A Street in Bronzeville* (1945), *Annie Allen* (1949), *In The Mecca* (1968).

Browning, Elizabeth Barrett (1806–61) English, born Coxhoe Hall, near Durham; *Sonnets from the Portuguese* (1850), *Aurora Leigh* (1855).

Browning, Robert (1812–89) English, born Camberwell; *Bells and Pomegranates, Dramatic Lyrics, Men and Women* (1855), *The Ring and the Book* (1868–9).

Burns, Robert (1759–96) Scottish, born Alloway, Ayr; *Poems Chiefly in the Scottish Dialect* (1786), *Tam O'Shanter* (1790).

Byron, George Gordon (1788–1824) English, born London; *Hours of Idleness* (1807), *Childe Harolde* (1817), *Don Juan* (1819–24).

Catullus, Gaius Valerius (c.84–c.54 BC) Roman, born Verona; lyric poet, over one hundred poems survive.

Causley, Charles (1917–) English, born Lanceton, Cornwall; *Union St* (1957), *Johnny Alleluia* (1961), *Underneath the Water* (1968).

Chaucer, Geoffrey (c.1343–1400) English, born London; *Book of the Duchess* (1370), *Troilus and Cressida* (c.1385), *The Canterbury Tales* (1387–1400).

Clampitt, Amy (1920–) American, born Iowa; *The Kingfisher* (1983), *Archaic Figure* (1987).

Clare, John (1793–1864) English, born Helpstone, Northamptonshire.

Coleridge, Samuel Taylor (1722–1834) English, born Otterly St Mary, Devonshire; *Poems on Various Subjects* (1796), *'Kubla Khan'* (1797), *'The Rime of the Ancient Mariner'* (1798), *Christabel and Other Poems* (1816), *Sybylline Leaves* (1817).

Cowper, William (1731–1800) English, born Great Berkhampstead, Hertfordshire; *The Task* (1785).

Crabbe, George (1754–1823) English, born Aldeburgh, Suffolk; *The Village* (1783).

cummings, e(dward) e(stlin) (1894–1962) American, born Cambridge, Massachusetts; *Tulips and Chimneys* (1923), *XLI Poems* (1925), *is 5* (1926).

Dante, Alighieri (1265–1321) Italian, born Florence; *Vita nuova* (1294), *Divine Comedy* (1321).

Day Lewis, Cecil (1904–72) Irish, born Ballintogher, Sligo; *Overtures to Death* (1938), *The Aeneid of Virgil* (1952).

de la Mare, Walter (1873–1956) English, born

POETS (cont.)

Charleston, Kent; *The Listeners* (1912), *The Burning Glass and Other Poems* (1945).

Dickinson, Emily (Elizabeth) (1830–86) American, born Amherst, Massachusetts; only 7 poems published in her lifetime; posthumous publications, eg *Poems* (1890).

Donne, John (?1572–1631) English, born London; *Satires & Elegies* (1590s), *Holy Sonnets* (1610–11), *Songs and Sonnets* (most verse published posthumously).

Doolittle, Hilda (known as **H D**) (1886–1961) American, born Bethlehem, Pennsylvania; *Sea Garden* (1916), *The Walls Do Not Fall* (1944), *Helen in Egypt* (1961).

Dryden, John (1631–1700) English, born Aldwinckle All Saints, Northamptonshire; *'Astrea Redux'* (1660), *'Absalom and Achitophel'* (1681), *'MacFlecknoe'* (1684).

Dunbar, William (c.1460–c.1520) Scottish, birthplace probably E Lothian; *'The Thrissill and the Rois'* (1503), *'Lament for the Makaris'* (c.1507)

Dunn, Douglas (Eaglesham) (1942–) Scottish, born Inchinnann; *Elegies* (1985), *Love or Nothing* (1974).

Dutton, Geoffrey (Piers Henry) (1922–) Australian, born Anlaby; *Antipedes in Shoes* (1955), *Poems Soft and Loud* (1968).

Eliot, T(homas), S(tearns) (1888–1965) American (British citizen 1927), born St Louis, Missouri; *Prufrock and Other Observations* (1917), *The Waste Land* (1922), *Ash Wednesday* (1930), *Four Quartets* (1944).

Éluard, Paul (pseudonym of **Eugène Grindal**) (1895–1952) French, born Saint-Denis; *La Vie immédiate* (1934), *Poésie et vérité* (1942).

Emerson, Ralph Waldo (1803–84) American, born Boston; poems published posthumously in *Complete Works* (1903–4).

Empson, Sir William (1906–84) English, born Yokefleet, E Yorkshire; *Poems* (1935), *The Gathering Storm* (1940).

Fitzgerald, Edward (1809–83) English, born near Woodbridge, Suffolk; translater of *The Rubaiyat of Omar Khayyam* (1859).

Fitzgerald, Robert (David) (1902–) Australian, born Hunters Hill, New South Wales; *To Meet the Sun* (1929), *The Wind at Your Door* (1959), *Product* (1974).

Frost, Robert (Lee) (1874–1963) American, born San Francisco; *North of Boston* (1914), *Mountain Interval* (1916), *New Hampshire* (1923), *In the Clearing* (1962).

Ginsberg, Allen (1926–) American, born Newark, New Jersey; *Howl and Other Poems* (1956), *Empty Mirror* (1961), *The Fall of America* (1973).

Graves, Robert (van Ranke) (1895–1985) English, born London; *Fairies and Fusiliers* (1917).

Gunn, Thom(son William) (1929–) English, born Gravesend, Kent; *The Sense of Movement* (1957), *Touch* (1967), *Jack Straw's Castle* (1976).

Heaney, Seamus (Justin) (1939–) Irish, born Castledawson, County Derry; *Death of a Naturalist* (1966), *Door into the Dark* (1969), *Field Work* (1979).

Henri, Adrian (Maurice) (1932–) English, born Birkenhead; *Tonight at Noon* (1968), *City* (1969), *From the Loveless Motel* (1980).

Henryson, Robert (c.1430–1506) Scottish, birthplace unknown; *Testament of Cresseid, Morall Fabels of Esope the Phrygian.*

Herbert, George (1593–1633) English, born Montgomery; *The Temple* (1633).

Herrick, Robert (1591–1674) English, born London; *Hesperides* (1648).

Hill, Geoffrey (1932–) English, born Bromsgrove, Worcestershire; *King Log* (1968), *Mercian Hymns* (1971).

Hodgson, Ralph (Edwin) (1871–1962) English, born Yorkshire; *Poems* (1917), *The Skylark and Other Poems* (1958).

Homer (10th–8th-c BC) Greek, birthplace and existence disputed; he is credited with the writing or writing down of *The Iliad* and *The Odyssey.*

Hopkins, Gerard Manley (1844–89) English, born Stratford, London; *'The Wreck of the Deutschland'* (1876), posthumously published *Poems* (1918).

Horace, Quintus Horatius Flaccus (65–8 BC) Roman, born Venusia, Apulia; *Epodes* (30 BC), *Odes* (23–13 BC).

Housman, A(lfred) E(dward) (1859–1936) English, born Flockbury, Worcestershire; *A Shropshire Lad* (1896), *Last Poems* (1922).

Hughes, Ted (1930–) English, born Mytholmroyd, Yorkshire; *The Hawk in the Rain* (1957), *Lupereal* (1960), *Wodwo* (1967), *Crow* (1970), *Care Birds* (1975), *Season Songs* (1976), *Gaudete* (1977), *Moortown* (1979).

Jennings, Elizabeth (Joan) (1926–) English, born Boston, Lincolnshire; *Poems* (1953), *The Animals' Arrival* (1969), *The Mind Has Mountains* (1966).

Johnson, Samuel (1709–84) English, born Lichfield, Staffordshire; *The Vanity of Human Wishes* (1749).

POETS (cont.)

Kavanagh, Patrick (1905–67) Irish, born Inniskeen; *Ploughman and Other Poems* (1936), *The Great Hunger* (1942).

Keats, John (1795–1821) English, born London; *Endymion* (1818), *Lamia and Other Poems* (1820).

Keyes, Sidney (Arthur Kilworth) (1922–43) English, born Dartford, Kent; *The Iron Laurel* (1942), *The Cruel Solstice* (1943).

La Fontaine, Jean de (1621–95) French, born Château-Thierry, Champagne; *Contes et nouvelles en vers* (1665), *Fables choisies mises en vers* (1668).

Langland, William (c.1332–c.1400) English, birthplace uncertain, possibly Ledbury, Herefordshire; *Piers Plowman* (1362–99).

Larkin, Philip (Arthur) (1922–85) English, born Coventry; *The North Ship* (1945), *The Whitsun Weddings* (1964), *High Windows* (1974).

Longfellow, Henry (Wadsworth) (1807–82) American, born Portland, Maine; *Voices of the Night* (1839), *Ballads and Other Poems* (1842), *Hiawatha* (1855), *'Divina Comedia'* (1872).

Lowell, Amy (Laurence) (1874–1925) American, born Brookline, Massachusetts; *A Dome of Many-Colored Glass* (1912), *Legends* (1921).

Lowell, Robert (Traill Spence, Jr) (1917–77) American, born Boston, Massachusetts; *Lord Weary's Castle* (1946), *Life Studies* (1959), *Prometheus Bound* (1967).

Macaulay, Thomas (Babington) (1800–59) English, born Rothey Temple, Leicestershire; *The Lays of Ancient Rome* (1842).

MacCaig, Norman (Alexander) (1910–) Scottish, born Edinburgh; *Far Cry* (1943), *Riding Lights* (1955), *A Round of Applause* (1962), *A Man in My Position* (1969), *Voice-Over* (1988).

MacDiarmid, Hugh (pseudonym of **Christopher Murray Grieve**) (1892–1978) Scottish, born Langholm, Dumfriesshire; *A Drunk Man Looks at the Thistle* (1926).

McGough, Roger (1937–) English, educated Liverpool; *Waving at Trains* (1982), *The Mersey Sound: Penguin Modern Poets 10* (with Adrian Henri and Brian Patten) (1967), *An Imaginary Menagerie* (1988).

MacLean, Sorley (Somhairle Macgill-Eain) (1911–) Scottish, born Isle of Raasay; *Reothairt is Contraigh* (Spring Tide and Neap Tide) (1977).

MacNeice, (Frederick) Louis (1907–63) Irish, born Belfast; *Blind Fireworks* (1929), *Solstices* (1961).

Mallarmé, Stéphane (1842–98) French, born Paris; *L'Après-midi d'un faune* (1876), *Poésies* (1899).

Marvell, Andrew (1621–78) English, born Winestead, near Hull; *Miscellaneous Poems by Andrew Marvell, Esq.* (1681).

Masefield, John (Edward) (1878–1967) English, born Ledbury, Herefordshire; *Salt-Water Ballads* (1902).

Millay, Edna St Vincent (1892–1950) American, born Rockland, Maine; *A Few Figs from Thistles* (1920), *The Ballad of Harp-Weaver* (1922).

Milton, John (1608–74) English, born London; *Lycidas* (1637), *Paradise Lost* (1667, 74), *Samson Agonistes* (1667).

Moore, Marianne (Craig) (1887–1972) American, born Kirkwood, Missouri; *The Pangolin and Other Verse* (1936).

Muir, Edwin (1887–1959) Scottish, born Deerness, Orkney; *First Poems* (1925), *Chorus of the Newly Dead* (1926), *Variations on a Time Theme* (1934), *The Labyrinth* (1949), *New Poems* (1949–51).

Nash, (Frederick) Ogden (1902–71) American, born New York; *Free Wheeling* (1931).

O'Hara, Frank (Francis Russell) (1926–66) American, born Baltimore, Maryland; *A City Winter and Other Poems* (1952), *Lunch Poems* (1964).

Ovid (Publius Ovidius Naso) (43 BC – c.17 AD) Roman, born Sulmo; *Amores* (c.16 BC), *Metamorphoses, Ars Amatoria.*

Owen, Wilfred (Edward Salter) (1893–1918) English, born Oswestry, Shropshire; most poems published posthumously, 1920 by Siegfried Sassoon.

Paz, Octavio (1914–) Mexican, born Mexico City; *Liberty on Parole, Salamander, Collected Poems* (1988); Nobel Prize for Literature 1990.

Petrarch, (Francesco Petrarca) (1304–74) Italian, born Arezzo; *Canzoniere.*

Plath, Sylvia (1932–63) American, born Boston, Massachusetts; *The Colossus and Other Poems* (1960), *Ariel* (1965), *Crossing the Water* (1971), *Winter Trees* (1972).

Porter, Peter (Neville Frederick) (1929–) Australian, born Brisbane; *Poems, Ancient and Modern* (1964), *English Subtitles* (1981).

Pound, Ezra (Weston Loomir) (1885–1972) **American, born Haile, Idaho;** *The Cantos* (1917, 48, 59).

Pushkin, Aleksandr (Sergeevich) (1799–1837) Russian, born Moscow; *Eugene Onegin* (1828), *Ruslam and Lyudmilla* (1820).

POETS (cont.)

Raine, Kathleen (Jessie) (1908–) English, born London; *Stone and Flower* (1943).

Rich, Adrienne (Cecile) (1929–) American, born Baltimore, Maryland; *The Diamond Cutters and Other Poems* (1955), *Snapshots of a Daughter-in-Law* (1963).

Riding, Laura (Laura Reichenthal) (1901–91) American, born New York; *The Close Chaplet* (1926).

Rilke, Rainer Maria (1875–1926) Austrian, born Prague; *Die Sonnettean Orpheus* (1923).

Rimbaud, (Jean Nicholas) Arthur (1854–91) French, born Charleville, Ardennes; *Les Illuminations* (1886).

Rochester, John Wilmot, Earl of (1647–80) English, born Ditchley, Oxfordshire; *A Satyre against Mankind* (1675).

Roethke, Theodore Huebner (1908–63) American, born Saginaw, Michigan; *Open House* (1941), *The Lost Son and Other Poems* (1948).

Rosenberg, Isaac (1890–1918) English, born Bristol; *Night and Day* (1912), *Youth* (1915), *Poems* (1922).

Saint-Jean Perse (pseudonym of **Marie René Auguste Alexis Saint-Léger Léger**) (1887–1975) French, born St Léger des Feuilles; *Anabase* (1924), *Exil* (1942), *Chroniques* (1960); Nobel Prize for Literature 1960.

Sassoon, Siegfried (Lorraine) (1886–1967) English, born Kent; *Counter-Attack and Other Poems* (1917), *The Road to Ruin* (1933).

Schwarz, Delmore (1913–66) American, born New York; *In Dreams Begin Responsibilities* (1938), *Vaudeville for a Princess and Other Poems* (1950).

Shelley, Percy Bysshe (1792–1822) English, born Field Place, Horesham, Sussex; *'Love's Philosophy', 'Alastor'* (1816), *'The Revolt of Islam'* (1818), *'Julian and Maddalo'* (1818), *'The Triumph of Life'* (1822).

Sidney, Sir Philip (1554–86) English, born Penshurst, Kent; *Arcadia* (1580), *Astrophel and Stella* (1591).

Sitwell, Dame Edith (Louisa) (1887–1964) English, born Scarborough; *Façade* (1922), *Colonel Fantock* (1926).

Smart, Christopher (1722–71) English, born Shipborne, Kent; *Jubilate Agno* (first published 1939).

Smith, Stevie (pseudonym of **Florence Margaret Smith**) (1902–71) English, born Hull; *Not Waving but Drowning : Poems* (1957).

Spender, Stephen (Harold) (1909–) English, born London; *Poems* (1933).

Spenser, Edmund (1552–99) English, born London; *The Shepheardes Calender* (1579), *The Faerie Queene* (1590, 96).

Stevens, Wallace (1879–1955) American, born Reading, Pennsylvania; *Harmonium* (1923), *Transport to Summer* (1947).

Tennyson, Alfred, Lord (1809–92) English, born Somersby Rectory, Lincolnshire; *Poems* (1832) (eg 'The Lotos-Eaters' and 'The Lady of Shalott'), *The Princess* (1847), *In Memoriam* (1850), *Idylls of the King* (1859), *Maud* (1885).

Thomas, Dylan (Marlais) (1914–53) Welsh, born Swansea; *Twenty-five Poems* (1936), *Deaths and Entrances* (1946), *In Country Sleep and Other Poems* (1952).

Thomas, (Philip) Edward (1878–1917) English, born London; *Six poems* (1916), *Last Poems* (1918).

Thomas, R(onald) S(tuart) (1913–) Welsh, born Cardiff; *The Stones of the Field* (1946), *Song at the Year's Turning* (1955).

Thomson, James (1700–48) Scottish, born Ednam, Roxburghshire; *The Seasons* (1730), *The Castle of Indolence* (1748).

Verlaine, Paul (1844–96) French, born Metz; *Fêtes galantes* (1869), *Sagesse* (1881).

Virgil, Publius Vergilius Maro (70–19 BC) Roman, born near Mantua; *Eclogues* (37 BC), *Georgics* (29 BC), *The Aeneid* (19 BC).

Webb, Francis Charles (1925–73) Australian, born Adelaide; *A Drum for Ben Boyd* (1948), *The Ghost of the Cock* (1964).

Whitman, Walt (1819–92) American, born West Hills, Long Island, New York; *Leaves of Grass* (1855–89).

Wordsworth, William (1770–1850) English, born Cockermouth; *Lyrical Ballads* (with S T Coleridge, 1798), *The Prelude* (1799, 1805, 1850), *The Excursion* (1814).

Wright, Judith (1915–) Australian, born Armidale, New South Wales; *The Moving Image* (1946), *The Two Fires* (1955), *Birds* (1962).

Wyatt, Thomas (1503–42) English, born Allington Castle, Kent; poems first published in *Tottel's Miscellany* (1557).

Yeats, W(illiam) B(utler) (1865–1939) Irish, born Sandymount, County Dublin; *The Wanderings of Oisin and Other Poems* (1889), *The Wind Among the Reeds* (1894), *The Wild Swans at Coole* (1917), *Michael Robartes and the Dancer* (1921), *The Winding Stair and Other Poems* (1933); Nobel Prize for Literature 1923.

POETS LAUREATE

1617 Ben Jonson[1]
1638 Sir William Davenant[1]
1668 John Dryden
1689 Thomas Shadwell
1692 Nahum Tate
1715 Nicholas Rowe
1718 Laurence Eusden
1730 Colley Cibber
1757 William Whitehead
1785 Thomas Warton
1790 Henry Pye
1813 Robert Southey
1843 William Wordsworth
1850 Alfred, Lord Tennyson
1896 Alfred Austin
1913 Robert Bridges
1930 John Masefield
1968 Cecil Day Lewis
1972 Sir John Betjeman
1984 Ted Hughes

[1]The post was not officially established until 1668.

PLAYWRIGHTS

Selected plays are listed.

Aeschylus (c.525–c.456 BC), Athenian; *The Oresteia trilogy (Agamemnon, Choephoroe, Eumenides)* (458 BC), *Prometheus Bound, Seven Against Thebes.*

Albee, Edward Franklin (1928–) American, born Washington DC; *The American Dream* (1961), *Who's Afraid of Virginia Woolf?* (1962).

Amos, Robert (1920–) Australian, born Austria; *When the Gravediggers Come* (1961).

Anouilh, Jean (1910–87) French, born Bordeaux; *Antigone* (1944), *Médée* (1946), *L'Alouette* (1953), *Beckett; or, the Honour of God* (1960).

Aristophanes (c.448–380 BC), Athenian; *The Acharnians* (425), *The Knights, The Clouds, The Wasps, The Birds* (414), *Lysistrata* (411), *The Frogs* (405).

Ayckbourn, Alan (1939–) English, born London; *Absurd Person Singular* (1973), *Absent Friends* (1975), *Joking Apart* (1979).

Beaumont, Sir Francis (1584–1616) English, born Grace-Dieu, Leicestershire, and **John Fletcher**; *Philaster* (1609), *The Maid's Tragedy* (1610).

Beckett, Samuel (Barclay) (1906–89) Irish, born Foxrock, near Dublin; *Waiting for Godot* (1955), *Endgame* (1958), *Krapp's Last Tape* (1958), *Happy Days* (1961), *Not I* (1973); Nobel Prize for Literature 1969.

Beynon, Richard (1925–) Australian, born Carlton, Melbourne; *The Shifting Heart* (1956), *Time and Mr Strachan* (1958).

Bond, (Thomas) Edward (1934–) English, born North London; *Early Morning* (1969), *Lear* (1971), *Summer* (1982).

Brecht, (Eugen) Bertolt (Friedrich) (1898–1956) German, born Augsburg; *Galileo* (1938–9), *Mutter Courage und ihre Kinder* (Mother Courage and her Children) (1941), *Der Gute Mensch von Setzuan* (The Good Woman of Setzuan) (1943), *Der Kaukasische Kreidekreis* (The Caucasian Chalk Circle) (1949).

Brieux, Eugène (1858–1932) French, born Paris; *Les Trois Filles de M Dupont* (1897), *The Red Robe* (1900).

Chapman, George (c.1559–1634) English, born near Hitchin, Hertfordshire; *Bussy D'Ambois* (1607).

Chekhov, Anton Pavlovich (1860–1904) Russian, born Taganrog; *The Seagull* (1895), *Uncle Vanya* (1900), *Three Sisters* (1901), *The Cherry Orchard* (1904).

Congreve, William (1670–1729) English, born Bardsey, near Leeds; *Love for Love* (1695), *The Way of the World* (1700).

Corneille, Pierre (1606–84) French, born Rouen; *Le Cid* (1636), *Horace* (1639), *Polyeucte* (1640).

Coward, Noël (1899–1973) English, born Teddington, Middlesex; *Hay Fever* (1925), *Private Lives* (1933), *Blithe Spirit* (1941).

Dekker, Thomas (c.1570–1632) English, born London; *The Whore of Babylon* (1606).

Dryden, John (1631–1700) English, born Aldwinkle; *The Indian Queen* (1664), *Marriage à la Mode* (1672), *All for Love* (1678), *Amphitryon* (1690).

Eliot, T(homas) S(tearns) (1888–1965) American naturalized British, born St Louis, Missouri; *Murder in the Cathedral* (1935), *The Family Reunion* (1939), *The Cocktail Party* (1950).

Esson, Thomas Louis Buvelot Australian, born Edinburgh; *The Drovers* (1920), *Andeganora* (1937).

Euripides (c.480–406 BC) Athenian; *Medea* (431), *Electra* (413), *The Bacchae* (407).

Fletcher, John (1579–1625) English, born Rye, Sussex; *The Faithful Shepherdess* (1610), *A Wife for a Month* (1624).

PLAYWRIGHTS (cont.)

Fo, Dario (1926–) Italian, born Lombardy; *Accidental Death of an Anarchist* (1970), *Can't Pay! Won't Pay!* (1978).

Ford, John (1586–c.1640) English, born Devonshire; *'Tis Pity She's a Whore* (1633), *Perkin Warbeck* (1634).

Galsworthy, John (1867–1933) English, born Coombe, Surrey; *Strife* (1909), *Justice* (1910); Nobel Prize for Literature 1932.

Genet, Jean (1910–86) French, born Paris; *The Maids* (1948), *The Balcony* (1956).

Giraudoux, Jean (1882–1944) French, born Bellac; *Judith* (1931), *Ondine* (1939).

Goethe, Johann Wolfgang von (1749–1832) German, born Frankfurt am Main; *Faust* (1808, 1832).

Gogol, Nikolai (Vasilievich) (1809–52) Russian, born Ukraine; *The Inspector General* (1836).

Goldsmith, Oliver (1728–74) Irish, born Pallas, County Longford; *She Stoops to Conquer* (1773).

Gray, Oriel (1921–) Australian, born Sydney; *The Torrents* (1955), *Burst of Summer* (1960).

Greene, Robert (1558–92) English, born Norwich; *Orlando Furioso* (1594), *James the Fourth* (1598).

Hauptmann, Gerhart (1862–1946) German, born Obersalzbrunn, Silesia; *Before Sunrise* (1889), *The Weavers* (1892); Nobel Prize for Literature 1912.

Hayes, Alfred (1911–85) American, born England; *The Girl on the Via Flaminia* (1954).

Hebbel (Christian) Friedrich (1813–63) German, born Wesselburen, Dithmarschen; *Judith* (1841), *Maria Magdalena* (1844).

Hewett, Dorothy (1923–) Australian, born Wickepin, West Australia; *The Chapel Perilous* (1972), *This Old Man Comes Rolling Home* (1976).

Heywood, Thomas (c.1574–1641) English, born Lincolnshire; *A Woman Killed with Kindness* (1603), *The Fair Maid of the West* (1631), *The English Traveller* (1633).

Hibberd, Jack (1940–) Australian, born Warracknabeal, Victoria; *Dimboola* (1969), *White with Wire Wheels* (1970), *A Stretch of the Imagination* (1973).

Howard, Sidney (Coe) (1891–1939) American, born Oakland, California; *They Knew What They Wanted* (1924), *The Silver Cord* (1926).

Ibsen, Henrik (1828–1906) Norwegian, born Skien; *Peer Gynt* (1867), *A Doll's House* (1879), *The Pillars of Society* (1880), *The Wild Duck* (1884), *Hedda Gabler* (1890), *The Master Builder* (1892).

Inge, William (1913–73) American, born Kansas; *Picnic* (1953), *Where's Daddy?* (1966).

Ionesco, Eugène (1912–) French, born Romania; *The Bald Prima Donna* (1948), *The Picture* (1958), *Le Rhinocéros* (1960).

Jonson, Ben(jamin) (c.1572–1637) English, born Westminster; *Every man in his Humour* (1598), *Sejanus* (1603), *Volpone* (1606), *The Alchemist* (1610), *Bartholomew Fair* (1614).

Kaiser, Georg (1878–1945) German, born Magdeburg; *The Burghers of Calais* (1914), *Gas* (1920).

Kyd, Thomas (1558–94) English, born London; *The Spanish Tragedy* (1587).

Lawler, Ray(mond Evenor) (1922–) Australian, born Footscrag; *The Summer of the Seventeenth Doll* (1955), *The Man Who Shot the Albatross* (1970).

Lorca, Federico Garcia (1899–1936) Spanish, born Fuente Vaqueros; *Blood Wedding* (1933), *The House of Bernarda Alba* (1945).

Maeterlink, Maurice (1862–1949) Belgian, born Gand; *La Princesse Maleine* (1889), *Pelleas et Melisande* (1892), *The Blue Bird* (1909).

Mamet, David Alan (1947–) American, born Chicago; *Sexual Perversity in Chicago* (1974), *Duck Variations* (1974), *American Buffalo* (1975), *Edmond* (1982).

Marlowe, Christopher (1564–1593) English, born Canterbury; *Tamburlaine the Great* (in two parts, 1587), *Dr Faustus* (1588), *The Jew of Malta* (c.1589), *Edward II* (1592).

Marston, John (1576–1634) English, born Wardington, Oxfordshire; *Antonio's Revenge* (1602), *The Malcontent* (1604).

Miller, Arthur (1915–) American, born New York; *All My Sons* (1947), *Death of a Salesman* (1949), *The Crucible* (1952), *A View from the Bridge* (1955), *The Misfits* (1961), *After the Fall* (1964).

Molière (pseudonym of **Jean-Baptiste Poquelin**) (1622–73) French, born Paris; *Le Bourgeois Gentilhomme* (The Bourgeois Gentleman) (1660), *Tartuffe* (1664), *Le Misanthrope* (The Misanthropist) (1666), *Le Malade Imaginaire* (The Hypocondriac) (1673).

Oakley, Barry (1931–) Australian, born Melbourne; *The Feet of Daniel Mannix* (1975), *Bedfellows* (1975).

O'Casey, Sean (originally **John Casey**) (1880–1964) Irish, born Dublin; *Juno and*

PLAYWRIGHTS (cont.)

the Paycock (1924), *The Plough and the Stars* (1926).

O'Neill, Eugene (1888–1953) American, born New York; *Beyond the Horizon* (1920), *Desire under the Elms* (1924), *Mourning Becomes Electra* (1931), *Long Day's Journey into Night* (1941), *The Iceman Cometh* (1946); Nobel Prize for Literature 1936.

Orton, Joe (John Kingsley) (1933–67) English, born Leicester; *Entertaining Mr Sloane* (1964), *Loot* (1965), *What the Butler Saw* (1969).

Osborne, John (James) (1929–) Welsh, born Fulham, London; *Look Back in Anger* (1956), *The Entertainer* (1957), *Inadmissible Evidence* (1964).

Otway, Thomas (1652–1685) English, born Milland, Sussex; *Don Carlos* (1676), *The Orphan* (1680), *Venice Preserv'd* (1682).

Patrick, John (1905–) American, born Louisville, Kentucky; *The Teahouse of the August Moon* (1953).

Pinter, Harold (1930–) English, born East London; *The Birthday Party* (1958), *The Caretaker* (1960), *The Homecoming* (1965).

Pirandello, Luigi (1867–1936) Italian, born near Agrigento, Sicily; *Six Characters in Search of an Author* (1921), *Henry IV* (1922); Nobel Prize for Literature 1934.

Plautus, Titus Maccius (c.254–184 BC) Roman; *Menachmi, Miles Gloriosus.*

Porter, Hal (1911–84) Australian, born Melbourne; *The Tower* (1963), *The Professor* (1966), *Eden House* (1969).

Racine, Jean (1639–99) French, born near Soissons; *Andromaque* (1667), *Phèdre* (1677), *Bajazet* (1672), *Esther* (1689).

Romeril, John (1945–) Australian, born Melbourne; *Chicago, Chicago* (1970), *I Don't Know Who to Feel Sorry For* (1973).

Sackville, Thomas (1553–1608) English, born Buckhurst, Sussex; *Gorboduc* (1592).

Sartre, Jean-Paul (1905–80) French, born Paris; *The Flies* (1943), *Huis Clos* (1945), *The Condemned of Altona* (1961).

Schiller, Johann Christoph Friedrich von (1759–1805) German, born Marbach; *The Robbers* (1781), *Wallenstein* (1799), *Maria Stuart* (1800).

Seneca, Lucius Annaeus (c.4 BC–AD 65) Roman, born Corduba; *Hercules, Medea, Thyestes.*

Seymour, Alan (1927–) Australian, born Perth; *The One Day of the Year* (1962), *Swamp Creatures* (1958), *Danny Johnson* (1960).

Shakespeare, William *see* PLAYS OF SHAKESPEARE p 456.

Shaffer, Peter (Levin) (1926–) English, born Liverpool; *The Royal Hunt of the Sun* (1964), *Equus* (1973), *Amadeus* (1979).

Shaw, George Bernard (1856–1950) Irish, born Dublin; *Arms and the Man* (1894), *Man and Superman* (1903), *Pygmalion* (1913), *Saint Joan* (1924); Nobel Prize for Literature 1925.

Shepard, Sam (Samuel Shepard Rogers) (1943–) American, born Illinois; *La Turista* (1967), *The Tooth of Crime* (1972), *Buried Child* (1978), *True West* (1979), *Fool for Love* (1983).

Sheridan, Richard Brinsley (1751–1816) Irish, born Dublin; *The Rivals* (1775), *The School for Scandal* (1777), *The Critic* (1779).

Sherwood, Robert (Emmet) (1896–1955) American, born New York; *Idiot's Delight* (1936), *Abe Lincoln in Illinois* (1938), *There Shall Be No Night* (1940).

Sophocles (496–406 BC) Athenian, born Colonus; *Antigone, Oedipus Rex, Oedipus at Colonus.*

Soyinka, Wole (Akinwande Olnwole Soyinka) (1934–) Nigerian, born Abeokata, West Nigeria; *The Swamp Dwellers* (1958), *The Bacchae of Euripides* (1973).

Stoppard, Tom (Thomas Straussler) (1937–) English, born Czechoslovakia; *Rosencrantz and Guildenstern are Dead* (1966), *The Real Inspector Hound* (1968), *Travesties* (1974).

Strindberg, (Johan) August (1849–1912) Swedish, born Stockholm; *Miss Julie* (1888), *Master Olof* (1877), *The Dance of Death* (1901).

Synge, (Edmund) J(ohn) M(illington) (1871–1909) Irish, born near Dublin; *The Well of Saints* (1905), *The Playboy of the Western World* (1907).

Webster, John (c.1578–c.1632) English, born London; *The White Devil* (1612), *The Duchess of Malfi* (1614).

Wilde, Oscar (Fingal O'Flahertie Wills) (1854–1906) Irish, born Dublin; *Lady Windermere's Fan* (1892), *The Importance of Being Earnest* (1895), *Salomé* (1896).

Wilder, Thornton (Niven) (1897–1975) American, born Wisconsin; *Our Town* (1938), *The Merchant of Yonkers* (1938), *The Skin of Our Teeth* (1942), *The Matchmaker* (1954, later a musical *Hello, Dolly!*, 1964).

PLAYWRIGHTS (cont.)

Williams, Tennessee (originally **Thomas Lanier Williams**) (1911–83) American, born Mississippi; *The Glass Menagerie* (1944), *A Streetcar Named Desire* (1947), *Cat on a Hot Tin Roof* (1955), *Sweet Bird of Youth* (1959).

Williamson, David Keith (1942–) Australian, born Melbourne; *The Removalists* (1971), *Don's Party* (1971).

Wycherely, William (1641–1715) English, born Clive, near Shrewsbury; *The Gentleman Dancing-Master* (1672), *The Country Wife* (1675), *The Plain-Dealer* (1676).

PLAYS OF SHAKESPEARE

William Shakespeare (1564–1616), English playwright and poet, born Stratford-upon-Avon.

Title	Date	Category
The Two Gentleman of Verona	1590–1	comedy
Henry VI Part One	1592	history
Henry VI Part Two	1592	history
Henry VI Part Three	1592	history
Titus Andronicus	1592	tragedy
Richard III	1592–3	history
The Taming of the Shrew	1593	comedy
The Comedy of Errors	1594	comedy
Love's Labour's Lost	1594–5	comedy
Richard II	1595	history
Romeo and Juliet	1595	tragedy
A Midsummer Night's Dream	1595	comedy
King John	1596	history
The Merchant of Venice	1596–7	comedy
Henry IV Part One	1596–7	history
The Merry Wives of Windsor	1597–8	comedy
Henry IV Part Two	1597–8	history
Much Ado About Nothing	1598	dark comedy
Henry V	1598–9	history
Julius Caesar	1599	Roman
As You Like It	1599–1600	comedy
Hamlet, Prince of Denmark	1600–1	tragedy
Twelfth Night, or What You Will	1601	comedy
Troilus and Cressida	1602	tragedy
Measure for Measure	1603	dark comedy
Othello	1603–4	tragedy
All's Well That Ends Well	1604–5	dark comedy
Timon of Athens	1605	romantic drama
The Tragedy of King Lear	1605–6	tragedy
Macbeth	1606	tragedy
Antony and Cleopatra	1606	tragedy
Pericles	1607	romance
Coriolanus	1608	Roman
The Winter's Tale	1609	romance
Cymbeline	1610	comedy
The Tempest	1611	comedy
Henry VIII	1613	history

FILM AND TV ACTORS

Selected films and television productions are listed.
Original and full names of actors are given in parentheses.

Adams, Brooke (1949–) American born New York City; *Invasion of the Body Snatchers* (1978), *A Man, a Woman, and a Bank* (1980), *Dead Zone* (1983), *Lace* (TV 1984), *Lace 2* (TV 1985), *Moonlighting* (TV 1987).

Adjani, Isabelle (1955–) French born Paris; *The Story of Adele H* (1975), *Nosferatu* (1978), *Possession* (1980), *Quartet* (1981), *One Deadly Summer* (1983), *Subway* (1985), *Ishtar* (1987), *Camille Claudel* (1988), *La Reine Margot* (1992).

Agutter, Jenny (1952–) British born Taunton; *The Railway Children* (1970), *Walkabout* (1970), *Logan's Run* (1976), *The Eagle has Landed* (1977), *Equus* (1977), *The Man in the Iron Mask* (1977), *An American Werewolf in London* (1981), *Silas Marner* (TV 1985), *Child's Play 2* (1990).

Aiello, Danny (1935–) American born New York City; *Fort Apache The Bronx* (1981), *Once Upon a Time in America* (1984), *The Purple Rose of Cairo* (1984), *Moonstruck* (1987), *Do the Right Thing* (1988), *Harlem Nights* (1989).

Aimée, Anouk (Françoise Sorya) (1934–) French born Paris; *Les Amants de Verone* (1949), *La Dolce Vita* (1960), *Lola* (1961), *Un Homme et un Femme* (1966), *Justine* (1969).

Albert, Eddie (Eddie Albert Heimberger) (1908–) American born Rock Island, Illinois; *Brother Rat* (1938), *Four Wives* (1939), *Smash Up* (1947), *Carrie* (1952), *Leave it to Larry* (TV 1952), *Roman Holiday* (1953), *Oklahoma!* (1955), *I'll Cry Tomorrow* (1955), *Attack!* (1956), *The Teahouse of the August Moon* (1956), *The Roots of Heaven* (1958), *Orders to Kill* (1958), *The Miracle of the White Stallions* (1962), *Green Acres* (TV 1965-70), *The Longest Yard* (1974), *Escape to Witch Mountain* (1975), *Switch* (TV 1975-6), *Yes, Giorgio* (1982), *Dreamscape* (1984).

Alda, Alan (1936–) American born New York City; *Paper Lion* (1968), *Catch 22* (1970), *M*A*S*H* (TV 1972-83), *California Suite* (1978), *Same Time Next Year* (1978), *The Four Seasons* (1981), *Sweet Liberty* (1986), *A New Life* (1988), *Crimes and Misdemeanors* (1990), *Betsy's Wedding* (1990).

Allen, Karen (1951–) American born Carrollton, Illinois; *Animal House* (1978), *The Wanderers* (1979), *East of Eden* (TV 1980), *Raiders of the Lost Ark* (1981), *Shoot the Moon* (1981), *Starman* (1984), *The Glass Menagerie* (1987), *Scrooged* (1988), *Secret Weapon* (TV 1990).

Allen, Nancy (1950–) American born New York City; *Carrie* (1976), *I Wanna Hold Your Hand, 1941* (1979), *Dressed to Kill* (1980), *Blow Out* (1981), *The Philadelphia Experiment* (1984), *The Gladiator* (TV 1986), *Robocop* (1987), *Poltergeist III* (1988), *Robocop 2* (1990).

Allen, Woody (Allen Stewart Konigsberg) (1935–) American born Brooklyn, New York; *What's New Pussycat* (1965), *Casino Royale* (1967), *Bananas* (1971), *Play it Again Sam* (1972), *Sleeper* (1973), *Annie Hall* (1977), *Manhattan* (1979), *Stardust Memories* (1980), *Hannah and Her Sisters* (1986), *New York Stories* (1989), *Crimes and Misdemeanors* (1989), *Scenes from the Mall* (1990), *Shadows and Fog* (1992).

Alley, Kirstie (1955–) American born Wichita, Kansas; *Star Trek II: The Wrath of Khan* (1982), *Blind Date* (1983), *Champions* (1983), *Runaway* (1984), *North and South* (TV 1986), *Summer School* (1987), *Cheers* (TV 1987–), *Shoot to Kill* (1988), *Look Who's Talking* (1989), *Madhouse* (1990), *Loverboy* (1990), *Sibling Rivalry* (1990), *Look Who's Talking Too* (1991).

Allyson, June (Ella Geisman) (1917–) American born Westchester, New York; *Two Girls and a Sailor* (1944), *Music for Millions* (1944), *Little Women* (1949), *The Glen Miller Story* (1954), *The Shrike* (1955), *The June Allyson Show* (TV 1959-61).

Ameche, Don (Dominic Felix Amici) (1908–) American born Kenosha, Wisconsin; *Ramona* (1936), *In Old Chicago* (1938), *The Three Musketeers* (1939), *Midnight* (1939), *The Story of Alexander Graham Bell* (1939), *Swanee River* (1939), *Four Sons* (1940), *Down Argentine Way* (1940), *That Night in Rio* (1941), *Heaven Can Wait* (1943), *Happy Land* (1943), *Trading Places* (1983), *Cocoon* (1985), *Bigfoot and the Hendersons* (1987), *Coming to America* (1988), *Things Change* (1988), *Cocoon: The Return* (1988).

Anderson, Dame Judith (Frances Margaret Anderson) (1898–1992) Australian born Adelaide, also stage, *Rebecca* (1940), *The Ten Commandments* (1956), *Cat on a Hot Tin Roof* (1958), *A Man Called Horse* (1970), *Star Trek III: The Search for Spock* (1984), *Santa Barbara* (TV 1984–).

FILM AND TV ACTORS (cont.)

Andress, Ursula (1936–) Swiss born Berne; *Dr No* (1963), *She* (1965), *What's New Pussycat?* (1965), *Casino Royale* (1967), *The Clash of the Titans* (1981).

Andrews, Anthony (1948–) British born London; *Danger UXB* (TV 1978), *Brideshead Revisited* (TV 1981), *The Scarlet Pimpernel* (TV 1982), *Under the Volcano* (1984), *The Lighthorsemen* (1987).

Andrews, Julie (Julia Elizabeth Wells) (1935–) British born Walton-on-Thames, Surrey; *Mary Poppins* (1964), *The Americanization of Emily* (1964), *The Sound of Music* (1965), *Torn Curtain* (1966), *Thoroughly Modern Millie* (1967), *Star!* (1968), *S.O.B.* (1981), *Victor/Victoria* (1982).

Ann-Margret (Ann-Margret Olsson) (1941–) Swedish/American born Valsobyn, Jamtland, Sweden; *State Fair* (1962), *Bye Bye Birdie* (1962), *The Cincinnati Kid* (1965), *Carnal Knowledge* (1971), *52 Pick-Up* (1986), *A New Life* (1988).

Anthony, Lysette (1963–) British born London; *Krull* (1983), *Three Up, Two Down* (TV 1987–8), *Jack the Ripper* (TV 1988), *Without a Clue* (1988), *The Lady and the Highway Man* (1989), *Campion* (TV 1989–90).

Archer, Anne (1947–) American born Los Angeles; *Bob and Carol and Ted and Alice* (TV 1973), *Paradise Alley* (1978), *Green Ice* (1980), *Fatal Attraction* (1987), *Love at Large* (1990), *Narrow Margin* (1990).

Arquette, Rosanna (1959–) American born New York City; *Shirley* (1979 TV), *S.O.B.* (1981), *Johnny Belinda* (TV 1982), *The Executioner's Song* (TV 1982), *Desperately Seeking Susan* (1983), *Silverado* (1985), *After Hours* (1985), *Nobody's Fool* (1985), *Eight Million Ways to Die* (1987), *The Big Blue* (1988), *New York Stories* (1989), *The Black Rainbow* (1990).

Ashcroft, Dame Peggy (1907–91) British born Croydon; also stage; *The Thirty-nine Steps* (1935), *Quiet Wedding* (1940), *Edward and Mrs Simpson* (TV 1978), *A Passage to India* (1984), *The Jewel in the Crown* (TV 1984), *Madame Sousatzka* (1988), *She's Been Away* (TV 1990).

Asher, Jane (1946–) British born London; *The Masque of the Red Death* (1964), *Deep End* (1971), *Dreamchild* (1985).

Astaire, Fred (Frederick Austerlitz) (1899–1987) American born Omaha, Nebraska; *Flying Down to Rio* (1933), *The Gay Divorcee* (1934), *Top Hat* (1935), *Funny Face* (1957), *It Takes a Thief* (TV 1965–9), *Finian's Rainbow* (1968).

Astor, Mary (Lucille Langhanke) (1906–87) American born Quincy, Illinois; *Beau Brummell* (1924), *Don Juan* (1926), *Dodsworth* (1936), *The Prisoner of Zenda* (1937), *The Great Lie* (1941), *The Maltese Falcon* (1941), *The Palm Beach Story* (1942), *Meet Me in St Louis* (1944), *Act of Violence* (1948), *Little Women* (1949), *Return to Peyton Place* (1961).

Atkinson, Rowan (1955–) British; *The Black Adder* (TV 1984), *Blackadder II* (TV 1985), *Blackadder III* (TV 1986), *Blackadder Goes Forth* (TV 1989), *The Tall Guy* (1989), *The Witches* (1990).

Attenborough, Sir Richard (1923–) British born Cambridge; *In Which We Serve* (1942), *The Man Within* (1942), *Brighton Rock* (1947), *The Guinea Pig* (1949), *The Great Escape* (1963).

Avalon, Frankie (Francis Thomas Avallone) (1940–) American born Philadelphia, Pennsylvania; *The Alamo* (1960), *Voyage to the Bottom of the Sea* (1962), *Beach Blanket Bingo* (1965), *Fireball 500* (1966), *Grease* (1978).

Aykroyd, Dan (1952–) Canadian born Ottowa, Ontario; *1949* (1979), *The Blues Brothers* (1980), *Neighbours* (1981), *Twilight Zone* (1983), *Ghostbusters* (1984), *Spies Like Us* (1986), *Dragnet* (1987), *The Couch Trip* (1988), *The Great Outdoors* (1988), *Caddyshack II* (1988), *Ghostbusters II* (1989), *My Stepmother is an Alien* (1989), *Driving Miss Daisy* (1989), *Loose Cannons* (1990).

Bacall, Lauren (Betty Joan Perske) (1924–) American born New York City; *To Have and Have Not* (1944), *The Big Sleep* (1946), *How to Marry a Millionaire* (1953), *The Fan* (1981), *Mr. North* (1988).

Bacon, Kevin (1958–) American born Philadelphia, Pennsylvania; *Animal House* (1978), *Friday the 13th* (1980), *Diner* (1982), *Footloose* (1984), *She's Having a Baby* (1988), *Tremors* (1989), *Flatliners* (1990), *The Big Picture* (1990).

Baker, Carroll (1931–) American born Johnstown, Pennsylvania; *Giant* (1956), *The Carpetbaggers* (1964).

Baker, Joe Don (1936–) American born Groesbeck, Texas; *Cool Hand Luke* (1967), *Mongo's Back in Town*

FILM AND TV ACTORS (cont.)

(TV 1971), *Charley Varrick* (1972), *Walking Tall* (1972), *Mitchell* (1974), *The Natural* (1984), *Fletch* (1984), *Getting Even* (1985), *The Living Daylights* (1987).

Baker, Tom (1935–) British; *Nicholas and Alexandra* (1971), *Doctor Who* (TV 1975-81), *The Life and Loves of a She-Devil* (TV 1987), *The Chronicles of Narnia* (TV 1990).

Baldwin, Alec (1958–) American born Massapequa, New York; *Sweet Revenge* (TV 1984), *She's Having a Baby* (1988), *Beetlejuice* (1988), *Working Girl* (1988), *Married to the Mob* (1988), *The Hunt for Red October* (1989), *Miami Blues* (1990), *The Marrying Man* (1990), *Alice* (1991).

Ball, Lucille (1910–89) American born Celaron, New York; *Top Hat* (1935), *Stage Door* (1937), *The Affairs of Annabel* (1938), *Five Came Back* (1939), *The Big Street* (1942), *Du Barry was a Lady* (1943), *Without Love* (1945), *Ziegfeld Follies* (1946), *Easy to Wed* (1946), *Her Husband's Affairs* (1947), *Fancy Pants* (1950), *I Love Lucy* (TV 1951–5), *The Long Long Trailer* (1954), *The Facts of Life* (1956), *The Lucy Show* (TV 1962-8), *Yours Mine and Ours* (1968), *Here's Lucy* (TV 1968-73), *Life with Lucy* (TV 1976).

Bancroft, Anne (Anna Maria Italiano) (1931–) American born Bronx, New York; *The Miracle Worker* (1962), *The Graduate* (1968), *Silent Movie* (1976), *The Elephant Man* (1980), *84 Charing Cross Road* (1986), *Torch Song Trilogy* (1988), *Bert Rigby, You're a Fool* (1989).

Bankhead, Tallulah (1902–68) American born Huntsville, Texas; *Tarnished Lady* (1931), *A Royal Scandal* (1945).

Bardot, Brigitte (Camille Javal) (1934–) French born Paris; *And God Created Woman* (1956), *En Cas de Malheur* (1958), *Viva Maria!* (1965).

Barkin, Ellen (1959–) American born Bronx, New York; *Diner* (1982), *The Adventures of Buckeroo Banzai* (1984), *The Big Easy* (1986), *Siesta* (1987), *Sea of Love* (1990), *Johnny Handsome* (1990), *Switch* (1991).

Barrymore, Drew (1975–) American born Los Angeles; *E.T.* (1982), *Firestarter* (1984), *Irreconcilable Differences* (1984), *Cat's Eye* (1984).

Barrymore, Ethel (Edith Blythe) (1879–1959) American born Philadelphia, Pennsylvania; *Rasputin and the Empress* (1932), *None but the Lonely Heart* (1944), *The Farmer's Daughter* (1947), *Young at Heart* (1954).

Barrymore, John (John Blythe) (1882–1942) American born Philadelphia, Pennsylvania; *Dr Jekyll and Mr Hyde* (1920), *Show of Shows* (1929), *Rasputin and the Empress* (1932), *Dinner at 8* (1933), *Midnight* (1939), *The Great Profile* (1940).

Barrymore, Lionel (Lionel Blythe) (1878–1954) American born Philadelphia, Pennsylvania; *Peter Ibbetson* (1917), *The Copperhead* (1918), *The Bells* (1926), *Sadie Thompson* (1928), *A Free Soul* (1931), *The Man I Killed* (1932), *Arsène Lupin* (1932), *Rasputin and the Empress* (1932), *Dinner at 8* (1933), *Grand Hotel* (1932), *David Copperfield* (1934), *Captains Courageous* (1937), *A Family Affair* (1937), *Young Dr Kildare* (1938), *Calling Dr Gillespie* (1942), *On Borrowed Time* (1939), *Three Wise Fools* (1946), *It's a Wonderful Life* (1946), *Duel in the Sun* (1946), *Key Largo* (1948).

Basinger, Kim (1953–) American born Athens, Georgia; *From Here to Eternity* (TV 1980), *Hard Country* (1981), *Never Say Never Again* (1983), *The Natural* (1984), *9½ Weeks* (1985), *No Mercy* (1986), *Blind Date* (1987), *Nadine* (1987), *Batman* (1989), *My Stepmother is an Alien* (1989), *The Marrying Man* (1990).

Bates, Alan (1934–) British born Allestree, Derbyshire; *A Kind of Loving* (1962), *Whistle Down the Wind* (1962), *Zorba the Greek* (1965), *Far from the Madding Crowd* (1967), *Women in Love* (1969), *The Rose* (1979), *A Prayer for the Dying* (1987), *We Think the World of You* (1988), *Hamlet* (1990).

Beart, Emmanuelle (1965–) French born Gassin; *Manon des Sources* (1986).

Beatty, Ned (1937–) American born Louisville, Kentucky; *Deliverance* (1972), *Nashville* (1975), *Network* (1976), *All the Presidents' Men* (1976), *Exorcist II: The Heretic* (1977), *Superman* (1978), *Friendly Fire* (TV 1979), *Incredible Shrinking Woman* (1981), *Superman II* (1981), *The Toy* (1983), *Hopscotch* (1983), *Stoker Ace* (1983), *Restless Natives* (1986), *The Big Easy* (1987), *The Fourth Protocol* (1987), *Switching Channels* (1988), *The Unholy* (1988), *Midnight Crossing* (1988), *After the Rain* (1988), *Purple People Eater* (1988).

Beatty, Warren (Henry Warren Beaty) (1937–) American born Richmond, Virginia; *Splendour in the Grass* (1961), *The Roman Spring of Mrs Stone* (1961), *All Fall Down* (1962), *Bonnie and Clyde* (1967), *The Parallax View* (1974), *Shampoo* (1975), *Heaven Can Wait* (1978), *Reds* (1981), *Ishtar* (1987), *Dick Tracy* (1990), *Bugsy* (1991).

FILM AND TV ACTORS (cont.)

Bedelia, Bonnie (1952–) American born New York City; *They Shoot Horses Don't They* (1970), *Love and Other Strangers* (1970), *Heart Like a Wheel* (1983), *The Prince of Pennsylvania* (1988), *Die Hard* (1988), *Die Hard II: Die Harder* (1990), *Presumed Innocent* (1990).

Belmondo, Jean-Paul (1933–) French born Neuilly-sur-Seine, Paris; *A Bout de Souffle* (1959), *Moderato Cantabile* (1960), *Un Singe en Hiver* (1962), *That Man from Rio* (1964).

Belushi, James (1954–) American born Chicago; *Trading Places* (1983), *Salvador* (1986), *About Last Night* (1987), *Red Heat* (1988), *Only the Lonely* (1991), *Curly Sue* (1991).

Belushi, John (1949–82) American born Chicago; *Animal House* (1978), *1941* (1979), *The Blues Brothers* (1981), *Neighbors* (1981).

Bennett, Jill (1931–90) British born Penang, Malaysia; also stage; *Inadmissable Evidence* (1968), *For Your Eyes Only* (1981).

Berenger, Tom (1950–) American born Chicago; *The Big Chill* (1983), *Platoon* (1987), *Shoot to Kill* (1988), *Betrayed* (1988), *Last Rites* (1988).

Bergen, Candice (1946–) American born Beverly Hills, California; *The Group* (1966), *The Magus* (1969), *Carnal Knowledge* (1971), *Rich and Famous* (1981), *Gandhi* (1982).

Bergman, Ingrid (1915–82) Swedish born Stockholm; *Intermezzo* (1939), *Dr Jekyll and Mr Hyde* (1941), *Casablanca* (1943), *For Whom the Bell Tolls* (1943), *Gaslight* (1943), *Spellbound* (1945), *Anastasia* (1946), *Notorious* (1946): *Stromboli* (1950), *Indiscreet* (1958), *Cactus Flower* (1969), *Murder on the Orient Express* (1974), *Autumn Sonata* (1978).

Berkoff, Stephen (1937–) British born London; *Octopussy* (1983), *Beverly Hills Cop* (1984), *Rambo* (1985), *War and Remembrance* (TV 1989).

Bernhardt, Sarah (1844–1923) (Henriette Rosine Bernhardt) French born Paris; stage, plus a few films; *Queen Elizabeth* (1912).

Bisset, Jacqueline (1944–) British born Weybridge, Surrey; *Cul-de-Sac* (1966), *Casino Royale* (1967), *Bullitt* (1968), *The Grasshopper* (1970), *Murder on the Orient Express* (1974), *The Deep* (1977), *Rich and Famous* (1981), *Class* (1983), *Under the Volcano* (1984), *High Season* (1987), *Scenes from the Class Struggle in Beverly Hills* (1989), *Wild Orchid* (1990).

Bloom, Claire (1931–) British born London; *Look Back in Anger* (1959), *The Haunting* (1963), *The Spy who Came in from the Cold* (1966).

Bogarde, Dirk (Derek Niven Van Den Bogaerde) (1921–) Dutch/British born Hampstead; *A Tale of Two Cities* (1958), *Victim* (1961), *The Servant* (1963), *Darling* (1965), *Death in Venice* (1973), *Providence* (1977), *These Foolish Things* (1990).

Bogart, Humphrey (De Forest) (1899-1957) American born New York City; *Broadway's Like That* (1930), *The Petrified Forest* (1936), *High Sierra* (1941), *The Maltese Falcon* (1941), *Casablanca* (1942), *To Have and Have Not* (1944), *The Big Sleep* (1946), *The Treasure of the Sierra Madre* (1947), *The African Queen* (1952), *The Barefoot Contessa* (1954), *The Caine Mutiny* (1954).

Bonham-Carter, Helena (1966–) British born London; *Oxford Blues* (1984), *Lady Jane* (1985), *A Room with a View* (1985), *Hamlet* (1990), *Where Angels Fear to Tread* (1991).

Borgnine, Ernest (Ermes Borgnino) (1918–) American born Hamden, Connecticut; *From Here to Eternity* (1953), *Bad Day at Black Rock* (1954), *Marty* (1955), *The Catered Affair* (1956), *The Best Things in Life Are Free* (1956), *The Vikings* (1958), *Pay or Die* (1960), *McHale's Navy* (TV 1962–5), *The Dirty Dozen* (1967), *Ice Station Zebra* (1968), *The Wild Bunch* (1969), *The Poseidon Adventure* (1972), *Convoy* (1978), *The Black Hole* (1979), *Escape from New York* (1981), *Deadly Blessing* (1981), *Codename Wildgeese* (1984), *Airwolf* (TV 1984–6), *The Dirty Dozen – The Next Mission* (TV 1985).

Bosley, Tom (1927–) American born Chicago; *Love with the Proper Stranger* (1964), *Debbie* (TV 1969), *Happy Days* (TV 1975), *Private Sessions* (TV 1985), *Fatal Confession* (TV 1987).

Bow, Clara (1905–65) American born Brooklyn, New York; *Mantrap* (1926), *It* (1927), *Wings* (1927).

Bowie, David (David Robert Jones) (1947–) British born Brixton, South London; *The Man Who Fell to*

FILM AND TV ACTORS (cont.)

Earth (1976), *Cat People* (1982), *The Hunger* (1983), *Merry Christmas Mr Lawrence* (1983), *Into the Night* (1985), *Labyrinth* (1986), *The Last Temptation of Christ* (1988).

Braga, Sonia (1951–) Brazilian born Maringa; *Kiss of the Spider Woman* (1985), *Moon over Parador* (1988), *The Milagro Beanfield War* (1988), *The Rookie* (1990).

Branagh, Kenneth (1960–) British; also stage; *High Season* (1987), *A Month in the Country* (1988), *Henry V* (1989), *Dead Again* (1991).

Brandauer, Klaus Maria (1944–) Austrian born Alt Aussee; *Mephisto* (1980), *Never Say Never Again* (1983), *Colonel Red* (1984), *Out of Africa* (1985), *Streets of Gold* (1986), *Hanussen* (1988), *The Russia House* (1990), *White Fang* (1991), *Becoming Colette* (1991).

Brando, Marlon (1924–) American born Omaha, Nebraska; *A Streetcar Named Desire* (1951), *Viva Zapata* (1952), *Julius Caesar* (1953), *The Wild One* (1953), *On the Waterfront* (1954), *Guys and Dolls* (1955), *The Teahouse of the August Moon* (1956), *The Young Lions* (1958), *One-Eyed Jacks* (1961), *Mutiny on the Bounty* (1962), *The Chase* (1966), *The Godfather* (1972), *Last Tango in Paris* (1972), *Superman* (1978), *Apocalypse Now* (1979), *A Dry White Season* (1988), *The Freshman* (1990), *Hearts of Darkness* (doc) (1991), *Christopher Columbus: The Discovery* (1992).

Bridges, Jeff (1949–) American born Los Angeles; *The Last Picture Show* (1971), *Hearts of the West* (1975), *Stay Hungry* (1976), *King Kong* (1976), *Somebody Killed Her Husband* (1978), *Winter Kills* (1979), *Tron* (1982), *Against All Odds* (1983), *Starman* (1984), *The Jagged Edge* (1985), *8 Million Ways to Die* (1985), *The Morning After* (1986), *Nadine* (1987), *Tucker: The Man and His Dream* (1987), *The Fabulous Baker Boys* (1989), *Texasville* (1990), *The Fisher King* (1991), *The Vanishing* (1992).

Bridges, Lloyd (1913–) American born San Leandro, California; *Home of the Brave* (1949), *Try and Get Me* (1951), *The Rainmaker* (1956), *Sea Hunt* (TV 1957-60), *The Goddess* (1958), *The Love War* (TV 1970), *Roots* (TV 1977).

Broderick, Matthew (1963–) American born New York City; *War Games* (1983), *Ladyhawke* (1984), *Ferris Bueller's Day Off* (1986), *Biloxi Blues* (1988), *Torch Song Trilogy* (1988), *Family Business* (1989), *Glory* (1989), *The Freshman* (1990).

Bronson, Charles (Charles Buchinski) (1920–) American born Ehrenfield, Pennsylvania; *Drumbeat* (1954), *Vera Cruz* (1954), *The Magnificent Seven* (1960), *This Property is Condemned* (1966), *The Dirty Dozen* (1967), *Chato's Land* (1972), *The Mechanic* (1972), *The Valachi Papers* (1972), *Death Wish* (1974), *Hard Times* (1975), *Telefon* (1977), *Death Wish II* (1982), *Death Wish III* (1985), *Death Wish IV* (1987), *Murphy's Law* (1987). *Messenger of Death* (1988), *Kinjite: Forbidden subjects* (1989), *The Indian Runner* (1991).

Brooks, Louise (Leslie Gettman) (1906–85) American born Cherryvale, Kansas; *Pandora's Box* (1929), *Diary of a Lost Girl* (1930).

Brooks, Mel (Melvin Kaminski) (1926–) American born New York City; *The Twelve Chairs* (1969), *Blazing Saddles* (1974), *Silent Movie* (1976), *High Anxiety* (1978), *History of the World Part One* (1981), *Spaceballs* (1987).

Brown, Bryan (1947–) Australian born Panania; *A Town Like Alice* (TV 1981), *The Thorn Birds* (TV 1983), *Eureka Stockade* (TV 1985), *F/X: Murder by Illusion* (1985), *Rebel* (1985), *Taipan* (1985), *The Shiralee* (TV 1987), *Cocktail* (1988), *Gorillas in the Mist* (1988).

Brynner, Yul (1915–85) Swiss/Russian, naturalized American born Sakhalin, Siberia; *The King and I* (1956), *The Brothers Karamazov* (1958), *The Magnificent Seven* (1960), *Return of the Seven* (1966).

Burton, Richard (Richard Jenkins) (1925–84) British born Pontrhydfen, S Wales; *My Cousin Rachel* (1952), *Alexander the Great* (1956), *Look Back in Anger* (1959), *Cleopatra* (1962), *The Night of the Iguana* (1964), *The Spy Who Came in from the Cold* (1965), *Who's Afraid of Virginia Woolf?* (1966), *The Taming of the Shrew* (1967), *Where Eagles Dare* (1969), *Equus* (1977), *Exorcist II: The Heretic* (1977), *Absolution* (1979), *1984* (1984).

Caan, James (1939–) American born Bronx, New York; *Brian's Song* (TV 1971), *The Godfather* (1972), (*part II*–1974), *Rollerball* (1975), *A Bridge Too Far* (1977), *Alien Nation* (1989), *Dick Tracy* (1990).

Cage, Nicolas (Nicholas Coppola) (1964–) American born Long Beach, California; *Fast Times at Ridgemont*

FILM AND TV ACTORS (cont.)

High (1982), *Rumblefish* (1983), *Racing with the Moon* (1984), *The Cotton Club* (1984), *Birdy* (1985), *Peggy Sue Got Married* (1986), *Raising Arizona* (1987), *Moonstruck* (1987), *Vampire's Kiss* (1988), *Wild At Heart* (1990), *Wings of the Apache* (1990).

Cagney, James (Francis Jr) (1899-1986) American born New York City; *Public Enemy* (1931), *Lady Killer* (1933), *A Midsummer Night's Dream* (1935), *The Roaring Twenties* (1939), *Yankee Doodle Dandy* (1942), *White Heat* (1949), *Love Me or Leave Me* (1955), *Mister Roberts* (1955), *One, Two, or Three* (1961), *Ragtime* (1981).

Caine, Michael (Maurice Micklewhite) (1933–) British born London; *Zulu* (1963), *The Ipcress File* (1965), *Alfie* (1966), *The Italian Job* (1969), *Sleuth* (1972), *The Man Who Would Be King* (1975), *The Eagle Has Landed* (1976), *California Suite* (1978), *Beyond the Poseidon Adventure* (1979), *Dressed to Kill* (1980), *Death Trap* (1983), *Educating Rita* (1983), *Hannah and Her Sisters* (1986), *The Whistle Blower* (1987), *Without a Clue* (1988), *Bullseye* (1990), *Shock to the System* (1990), *Mr Destiny* (1990), *Noises Off* (1992), *Blue Ice* (1992).

Callow, Simon (1949–) British born London; also stage; *Amadeus* (1984), *A Room With a View* (1985), *Maurice* (1987).

Candy, John (1950–) Canadian born Toronto, Ontario; *Stripes* (1981), *Brewster's Millions* (1984), *Splash!* (1984), *Summer Rental* (1984), *Little Shop of Horrors* (1987), *Spaceball* (1987), *Planes, Trains, and Automobiles* (1988), *The Greeat Outdoors* (1988), *Who's Harry Crumb?* (1989), *Uncle Buck* (1989), *Only the Lonely* (1991).

Cardinale, Claudia (1939–) Italian born Tunis, Tunisia; *The Pink Panther* (1963), *Once Upon a Time in the West* (1969), *Escape to Athena* (1979), *Fitzcarraldo* (1982).

Caron, Leslie (Claire Margaret) (1931–) French born Boulogne-Billancourt, near Paris; *An American in Paris* (1951), *Lili* (1953), *The Glass Slipper* (1954), *Daddy Long Legs* (1955), *Gigi* (1958), *Fanny* (1961), *The L-Shaped Room* (1962), *Father Goose* (1964), *QB VII* (TV 1974).

Carradine, David (John Arthur Carradine) (1936–) American born Hollywood, California; *Shane* (TV 1966), *Kung Fu* (1972-4), *Death Race 2000* (1975), *Bound for Glory* (1976), *North and South* (TV 1986), *Crime Zone* (1988), *The Misfit Brigade* (1988), *Bird on a Wire* (1990).

Carradine, John (Richmond Reed Carradine) (1906–88) American born New York City; *Five Came Back* (1939), *Stagecoach* (1939), *The Grapes of Wrath* (1940), *Bluebeard* (1944), *House of Frankenstein* (1945), *The Man Who Shot Liberty Valance* (1962), *Peggy Sue Got Married* (1986).

Carradine, Keith (Ian) (1950–) American born San Mateo, California; *Thieves Like Us* (1973), *Nashville* (1975), *The Longriders* (1980), *Southern Comfort* (1981), *Blackout* (1985), *Murder Ordained* (TV 1987), *The Moderns* (1988).

Carrera, Barbara (1945–) Nicaraguan/American born Managua, Nicaragua; *The Master Gunfighter* (1975), *Embryo* (1976), *The Island of Dr. Moreau* (1977), *Condorman* (1981), *Never Say Never Again* (1983), *Codename: Wildgeese II* (1984), *Dallas* (TV 1984–5), *Loverboy* (1990).

Cassavetes, John (1929–89) American born New York City; *Johnny Staccato* (TV 1959), *The Dirty Dozen* (1967), *Rosemary's Baby* (1969), *Minnie and Moskovitz* (1979), *The Fury* (1978), *Whose Life is it Anyway?* (1981), *Tempest* (1983).

Cates, Phoebe (1963–) American born New York City; *Fast Times at Ridgemont High* (1982), *Paradise* (1982), *Private School* (1983), *Gremlins* (1984), *Lace* (TV 1984), *Lace 2* (TV 1985), *Bright Lights, Big City* (1988), *Shag* (1988), *Gremlins 2: The New Batch* (1990), *Heart of Dixie* (1990).

Chamberlain, Richard (1935–) American born Beverly Hills, California; *Dr Kildare* (TV 1961-6), *The Music Lovers* (1970), *Lady Caroline Lamb* (1972), *The Slipper and the Rose* (1976), *The Man in the Iron Mask* (1977), *The Last Wave* (1978), *Shogun* (TV 1980), *The Thorn Birds* (TV 1983), *Island Son* (TV 1989–).

Chaplin, Sir Charles (Spencer) (1889–1977) British born London; *The Champion* (1915), *The Tramp* (1915), *Easy Street* (1917), *A Dog's Life* (1918), *Shoulder Arms* (1918), *The Kid* (1920), *The Idle Class* (1921), *The Gold Rush* (1924), *City Lights* (1931), *Modern Times* (1936), *The Great Dictator* (1940), *Limelight* (1952), *A King in New York* (1957).

FILM AND TV ACTORS (cont.)

Chaplin, Geraldine (1944–) American born Santa Monica, California; *Doctor Zhivago* (1965), *The Three Musketeers* (1974), *Nashville* (1975), *Hidden Talent* (1984), *White Mischief* (1987), *The Moderns* (1988), *Mama Turns 100* (1988).

Charisse, Cyd (Tula Ellice Funklea) (1922–) American born Amarillo, Texas; *Ziegfeld Follies* (1945), *The Unfinished Dance* (1947), *Singin' in the Rain* (1952), *The Band Wagon* (1953), *Brigadoon* (1954), *It's Always Fair Weather* (1955), *Invitation to the Dance* (1957), *Two Weeks in Another Town* (1962).

Chase, Chevy (Cornelius Crane Chase) (1943–) American born New York City; *Foul Play* (1978), *Caddyshack* (1980), *Seems Like Old Times* (1980), *Vacation* (1983), *European Vacation* (1984), *Fletch* (1985), *Spies Like Us* (1985), *The Three Amigos* (1986), *The Couch Trip* (1988), *Caddy Shack II* (1988), *Funny Farm* (1988), *Fletch Lives* (1988), *Christmas Vacation* (1989).

Cher (Cher Bono, formerly Cherilyn Sarkisian) (1946–) American born El Centro, California; *Silkwood* (1983), *Mask* (1985), *Moonstruck* (1987), *Suspect* (1987), *The Witches of Eastwick* (1987), *Mermaids* (1990).

Chevalier, Maurice (1888–1972) French born Paris; *The Innocents of Paris* (1929), *One Hour with You* (1932), *Love Me Tonight* (1932), *The Love Parade* (1932), *Gigi* (1958).

Christie, Julie (1941–) British born Chukua, Assam, India; *The Fast Lady* (1963), *Billy Liar* (1963), *Doctor Zhivago* (1965), *Darling* (1965), *Farenheit 451* (1966), *Far from the Madding Crowd* (1967), *The Go-Between* (1971), *Don't Look Now* (1974), *Shampoo* (1975), *Heaven Can Wait* (1978), *Heat and Dust* (1982), *Power* (1985), *The Gold Diggers* (1988).

Clark, Petula (1932–) British born Epsom, Surrey; *Finian's Rainbow* (1968), *Goodbye Mr Chips* (1969).

Cleese, John (Marwood) (1939–) British born Weston-super-Mare; *The Frost Report* (TV 1966), *At Last the 1948 Show* (TV 1967), *Monty Python's Flying Circus* (TV 1969-74), *Monty Python and the Holy Grail* (1974), *Fawlty Towers* (TV 1975 & 1979), *The Life of Brian* (1979), *Time Bandits* (1982), *The Meaning of Life* (1983), *Clockwise* (1985), *A Fish Called Wanda* (1988), *Erik the Viking* (1989).

Clift, (Edward) Montgomery (1920–66) American born Omaha, Nebraska; *Red River* (1946), *The Search* (1948), *A Place in the Sun* (1951), *From Here to Eternity* (1953), *Freud* (1962), *Suddenly Last Summer* (1968).

Close, Glenn (1947–) American born Greenwich, Connecticut; *The World According to Garp* (1982), *The Big Chill* (1983), *The Natural* (1984), *Something About Amelia* (TV 1984), *Jagged Edge* (1985), *Maxie* (1985), *Fatal Attraction* (1987), *Dangerous Liaisons* (1988), *Immediate Family* (1989), *Reversal of Fortune* (1990), *Hamlet* (1990), *Meeting Venus* (1991), *Hook* (1991).

Cobb, Lee J (Lee Jacoby) (1911–76) American born New York City; *Golden Boy* (1939), *The Moon is Down* (1943), *Anna and the King of Siam* (1946), *The Dark Past* (1948), *On the Waterfront* (1954), *The Man in the Grey Flannel Suit* (1956), *Twelve Angry Men* (1957), *The Brothers Karamazov* (1958), *The Virginian* (TV 1962–6), *Come Blow Your Horn* (1963), *Death of a Salesman* (TV 1966), *Coogan's Bluff* (1968), *They Came to Rob Las Vegas* (1968), *The Young Lawyers* (TV 1970–1), *The Exorcist* (1973).

Coburn, James (1928–) American born Laurel, Nebraska; *The Magnificent Seven* (1960), *The Great Escape* (1963), *Charade* (1963), *Our Man Flint* (1966), *In Like Flint* (1966), *A Fistful of Dynamite* (1971), *California Suite* (1978), *Loving Couples* (1980), *Young Guns II* (1990).

Coleman, Dabney (1932–) American born Austin, Texas; *This Property is Condemned* (1966), *That Girl* (TV 1966-70), *Nine to Five* (1980), *On Golden Pond* (1981), *Tootsie* (1982), *War Games* (1983), *Buffalo Bill* (TV 1983), *The Man With One Red Shoe* (1985), *Dragnet* (1987), *Where the Heart Is* (1990).

Collins, Joan (Henrietta) (1933–) British born London; *Lady Godiva Rides Again* (1951), *The Virgin Queen* (1955), *The Bitch* (1979), *Dynasty* (TV 1981–9).

Connery, Sean (Thomas Connery) (1930–) British born Edinburgh; *Dr. No* (1963), *Marnie* (1964), *From Russia With Love* (1964), *Goldfinger* (1965), *The Hill* (1965), *Thunderball* (1965), *A Fine Madness* (1966), *You Only Live Twice* (1967), *The Molly Maguires* (1969), *The Anderson Tapes* (1970), *Diamonds are Forever* (1971), *The Offence* (1972), *Zardoz* (1973), *Murder on the Orient Express* (1974), *The Man Who Would Be*

FILM AND TV ACTORS (cont.)

King (1975), *Robin and Marian* (1976), *Meteor* (1979), *Outland* (1981), *Time Bandits* (1981), *Never Say Never Again* (1983), *Highlander* (1985), *The Name of the Rose* (1986), *The Untouchables* (1987), *The Presidio* (1988), *Indiana Jones and the Last Crusade* (1989), *Family Business* (1989), *The Hunt for Red October* (1990), *The Russia House* (1990), *Highlander II, The Quickening* (1991), *Medicine Man* (1992), *The Rising Sun* (1992), *Dreadnought* (1992), *Broken Dreams* (1992).

Conti, Tom (1941–) British born Paisley; *Merry Christmas Mr Lawrence* (1983), *Reuben Reuben* (1983), *Saving Grace* (1984), *Miracles* (1985), *Heavenly Pursuits* (1985), *Shirley Valentine* (1989).

Cooper, Gary (Frank J Cooper) (1901–61) American born Helena, Montana; *The Winning of Barbara Worth* (1926), *Lilac Time* (1928), *The Virginian* (1929), *A Farewell to Arms* (1932), *City Streets* (1932), *The Lives of a Bengal Lancer* (1935), *Sergeant York* (1941), *For Whom the Bell Tolls* (1943), *The Fountainhead* (1949), *High Noon* (1952), *Friendly Persuasion* (1956).

Costner, Kevin (1955–) American born Los Angeles; *Night Shift* (1982), *American Flyers* (1984), *Silverado* (1985), *The Untouchables* (1987), *No Way Out* (1987), *Bull Durham* (1988), *Field of Dreams* (1989), *Revenge* (1990), *Dances With Wolves* (1990), *Robin Hood, Prince of Thieves* (1991), *JFK* (1991), *The Bodyguard* (1992).

Cotten, Joseph (1905–) American born Petersburg, Virginia; *Citizen Kane* (1941), *The Magnificent Ambersons* (1942), *Journey into Fear* (1942), *Shadow of a Doubt* (1943), *I'll Be Seeing You* (1945), *Portrait of Jennie* (1948), *The Third Man* (1949), *Niagara* (1952), *Tora! Tora! Tora!* (1971).

Courtenay, Tom (1937–) British born Hull; also stage; *The Loneliness of the Long Distance Runner* (1962), *Billy Liar* (1963), *Doctor Zhivago* (1965), *The Dresser* (1983), *Let Him Have It* (1991).

Cox, Ronny (1938–) American born Cloudcroft, New Mexico; *Deliverance* (1972), *The Onion Field* (1978), *Taps* (1981), *Vision Quest* (1985), *Beverly Hills Cop* (1985), *Beverly Hills Cop II* (1987), *Robocop* (1987), *St Elsewhere* (TV 1989), *Total Recall* (1990).

Crawford, Joan (Lucille Le Sueur) (1906–77) American born San Antonio, Texas; *Our Dancing Daughters* (1928), *Our Blushing Brides* (1933), *Dancing Lady* (1933), *The Women* (1939), *Mildred Pierce* (1945), *Possessed* (1947), *Whatever Happened to Baby Jane?* (1962), *Trog* (1970).

Crenna, Richard (1926–) American born Los Angeles; *Pride of St. Louis* (1952), *Star!* (1968), *Body Heat* (1981), *Death Ship* (1981), *First Blood* (1982), *Breakheart Pass* (1983), *Table for Five* (1983), *The Flamingo Kid* (1984), *The Rape of Richard Beck* (TV 1985), *Summer Rental* (1985), *Rambo* (1986), *Rambo III* (1988), *Leviathan* (1989).

Crosby, Bing (Harry Lillis Crosby) (1904–77) American born Tacoma, Washington; *King of Jazz* (1930), *Mississippi* (1935), *Anything Goes* (1936), *Road to Singapore* (1940), *Road to Zanzibar* (1941), *Holiday Inn* (1942), *Road to Morrocco* (1942), *Going My Way* (1944), *The Bells of St Mary's* (1945), *Blue Skies* (1946), *A Connecticut Yankee in King Arthur's Court* (1949), *White Christmas* (1954), *The Country Girl* (1954), *High Society* (1956), *Road to Hong Kong* (1962).

Cruise, Tom (Tom Cruise Mapother IV) (1962–) American born Syracuse, New York; *Taps* (1981), *Endless Love* (1981), *The Outsiders* (1983), *Legend* (1984), *Risky Business* (1984), *Top Gun* (1985), *The Color of Money* (1986), *Cocktail* (1988), *Rain Man* (1988), *Born on the Fourth of July* (1989), *Days of Thunder* (1990), *Far And Away* (1992), *A Few Good Men* (1992).

Crystal, Billy (1947–) American born Long Beach, New York; *This Is Spinal Tap* (1983), *Throw Momma from the Train* (1987), *The Princess Bride* (1988), *When Harry Met Sally ...* (1989), *City Slickers* (1991), *Mr Saturday Night* (1992).

Culp, Robert (1930–) American born Oakland, California; *I Spy* (TV 1965–7), *Bob and Carol and Ted and Alice* (1969), *The Greatest American Hero* (TV 1981-2), *The Gladiator* (TV 1986).

Curtis, Jamie Lee (1958–) American born Los Angeles; *Operation Petticoat* (TV 1978), *Halloween* (1979), *The Fog* (1980), *Halloween II* (1981), *Love Letters* (1983), *Trading Places* (1983), *Perfect* (1985), *A Fish Called Wanda* (1988), *Dominick and Eugene* (1988), *Blue Steel* (1990).

Curtis, Tony (Bernard Schwarz) (1925–) American born New York City; *Houdini* (1953), *Trapeze* (1956), *The Vikings* (1958), *Some Like it Hot* (1959), *Spartacus* (1960), *The Boston Strangler* (1968).

FILM AND TV ACTORS (cont.)

Cusack, Cyril James (1910–) Irish born Durban, S Africa; *Odd Man Out* (1947), *The Blue Lagoon* (1949), *Jacqueline* (1965), *The Spy Who Came in From the Cold* (1965), *Fahrenheit 451* (1966), *Day of the Jackal* (1973), *1984* (1984), *Little Dorrit* (1987), *My Left Foot* (1989), *The Fool* (1990).

Cusack, Sinead (1948–) Irish; *David Copperfield* (1969), *Tam Ling* (1971), *Rocket Gibraltar* (1988).

Cushing, Peter (1913–) British born Kenley, Surrey; *The Man in the Iron Mask* (1939), *Hamlet* (1947), *1984* (TV 1955), *The Curse of Frankenstein* (1957), *Dracula* (1958), *The Mummy* (1959), *The Hound of the Baskervilles* (1959), *Cash on Demand* (1963), *Dr Who and the Daleks* (1965), *Dalek's Invasion of Earth* (1966), *Sherlock Homes* (TV 1968), *Tales from the Crypt* (1972), *Horror Express* (1972), *Star Wars* (1977), *Biggles* (1988).

Dafoe, Willem (1955–) American born Appleton, Wisconsin; *Heaven's Gate* (1980), *Platoon* (1986), *The Last Temptation of Christ* (1988), *Mississippi Burning* (1988), *Triumph of the Spirit* (1989), *Born on the Fourth of July* (1989), *Wild At Heart* (1990), *Cry Baby* (1990), *Flight of The Intruder* (1990), *Light Sleeper* (1992), *Body of Evidence* (1992).

Dalton, Timothy (1946–) British born Wales; *The Lion in Winter* (1968), *Wuthering Heights* (1970), *Mary Queen of Scots* (1971), *Agatha* (1979), *Flash Gordon* (1980), *Centenniel* (TV 1981–2), *The Living Daylights* (1987), *License to Kill* (1989).

Dance, Charles (1946–) British born Rednal, Worcestershire; *For Your Eyes Only* (1981), *The Jewel in the Crown* (TV 1984), *The Golden Child* (1985), *Plenty* (1985), *Good Morning Babylon* (1987), *White Mischief* (1987), *Pascali's Island* (1988), *Phantom of the Opera* (TV 1990).

D'Angelo, Beverly (1953–) American born Columbus, Ohio; *First Love* (1977), *Every Which Way But Loose* (1978), *Hair* (1979), *Coal Miner's Daughter* (1980), *Paternity* (1981), *Honky Tonk Freeway* (1981), *Vacation* (1984), *European Vacation* (1985), *Aria* (1987), *High Spirits* (1988), *Christmas Vacation* (1989).

Daniels, William (1927–) American born Brooklyn, New York; *Captain Nice* (TV 1966), *The Graduate* (1967), *1776* (1972), *The Parallax View* (1974), *The Blue Lagoon* (1981), *Reds* (1981), *St Elsewhere* (TV 1982-9), *Blind Date* (1987).

Danson, Ted (1947–) American born Flagstaff, Arizona; *The Onion Field* (1979), *Body Heat* (1981), *Cheers* (1981–), *Creepshow* (1982), *Something About Amelia* (TV 1984), *Three Men and a Baby* (1988), *Cousins* (1989), *Dad* (1990), *Three Men and a Little Lady* (1990).

Darren, James (James Ercolani) (1936–) American born Philadelphia, Pennsylvania; *Gidget* (1959), *The Guns of Navarone* (1961), *For Those Who Think Young* (1964), *Time Tunnel* (TV 1966), *T. J. Hooker* (TV 1983–6).

Davenport, Nigel (1928–) British born Fambridge; *A Man for All Seasons* (1966), *The Virgin Soldiers* (1969), *Living Free* (1972), *The Island of Dr Moreau* (1977).

Davis, Bette (Ruth Elizabeth Davis) (1908–89) American born Lowell, Massachusetts; *Bad Sister* (1931), *Dangerous* (1935), *Jezebel* (1938), *All About Eve* (1950), *Whatever Happened to Baby Jane?* (1962), *The Great Lie* (1941), *Strangers* (TV 1979), *The Whales of August* (1987).

Davis, Geena (1957–) American born Wareham, Massachusetts; *Tootsie* (1982), *Fletch* (1985), *The Fly* (1986), *Beetlejuice* (1988), *The Accidental Tourist* (1989), *Earth Girls Are Easy* (1989).

Davis, Judy (1956–) Australian born Perth; *My Brilliant Career* (1979), *Who Dares Wins* (1982), *A Passage to India* (1987), *High Tide* (1987).

Day, Doris (Doris von Kappelhoff) (1924–) American born Cincinnati, Ohio; *Romance on the High Seas* (1948), *Storm Warning* (1950), *Calamity Jane* (1953), *Young at Heart* (1954), *Love Me or Leave Me* (1955), *The Pajama Game* (1957), *Pillow Talk* (1959), *That Touch of Mink* (1962), *With Six You Get Egg Roll* (1968), *The Doris Day Show* (TV 1968-73).

Day-Lewis, Daniel (1958–) Irish born London; *Gandhi* (1983), *My Beautiful Laundrette* (1985), *Room with a View* (1985), *The Unbearable Lightness of Being* (1988), *Stars and Bars* (1988), *Nanou* (1988), *My Left Foot* (1989), *The Last of the Mohicans* (1992), *Age of Innocence* (1992).

FILM AND TV ACTORS (cont.)

Dean, James (Byron) (1931–55) American born Fairmount, Indiana; *East of Eden* (1955), *Rebel without a Cause* (1955), *Giant* (1956).

De Havilland, Olivia (1916–) British born Tokyo, Japan; *Midsummer Night's Dream* (1935), *The Adventures of Robin Hood* (1938), *Gone with the Wind* (1939), *The Dark Mirror* (1946), *To Each his Own* (1946), *The Heiress* (1949).

Delon, Alain (1935–) French born Paris; *Rocco and his Brothers* (1960), *The Leopard* (1962), *Swann in Love* (1984).

De Luise, Dom (1933–) American born Brooklyn, New York; *The Twelve Chairs* (1969), *The Cannonball Run* (1980), *Going Bananas* (1988).

De Mornay, Rebecca (1962–) American born Los Angeles, California; *Risky Business* (1984), *Runaway Train* (1985), *And God Created Woman* (1988), *Dealers* (1988), *Feds* (1988).

Dench, Dame Judi (Judith Olivia Dench) (1934–) British born York; also stage; *The Third Secret* (1964), *Four in the Morning* (1966), *A Fine Romance* (TV 1981–4), *A Room With a View* (1985), *84 Charing Cross Road* (1987), *A Handful of Dust* (1988), *Henry V* (1989) *Behaving Badly* (TV 1989).

Deneuve, Catherine (Catherine Dorleac) (1943–) French born Paris; *Les Parapluies de Cherbourg* (1964), *Repulsion* (1965), *Belle de Jour* (1967), *Tristana* (1970), *The Hunger* (1983).

De Niro, Robert (1943–) American born New York City; *Bang the Drum Slowly* (1973), *Mean Streets* (1973), *The Godfather, Part II* (1974), *1900* (1976), *Taxi Driver* (1976), *The Deer Hunter* (1978), *Raging Bull* (1980), *King of Comedy* (1982), *Brazil* (1985), *Angel Heart* (1987), *The Untouchables* (1987), *Midnight Run* (1988), *Jacknife* (1989), *Stanley & Iris* (1989), *We're No Angels* (1990), *GoodFellas* (1990), *Awakenings* (1990), *Backdraft* (1991), *Cape Fear* (1991), *The Mistress* (1992), *Mad Dog and Glory* (1992), *Night and The City* (1992), *This Boy's Life* (1992).

Dennehy, Brian (1940–) American born Bridgeport, Connecticut; *Foul Play* (1978), *Butch and Sundance* (1979), *Big Shamus Little Shamus* (TV 1979), *First Blood* (1982), *Gorky Park* (1983), *Cocoon* (1985), *Silverado* (1985), *Legal Eagles* (1986), *Belly of an Architect* (1987), *Best Seller* (1987), *Miles from Home* (1988), *Cocoon: The Return* (1988), *Return to Snowy River Part II* (1988), *Presumed Innocent* (1990).

Depardieu, Gérard (1948–) French born Châteauroux; *1900* (1976), *Get Out Your Handkerchiefs* (1977), *Loulou* (1980), *The Last Metro* (1980), *The Return of Martin Guerre* (1981), *Danton* (1982), *The Moon in the Gutter* (1983), *Police* (1985), *Jean de Florette* (1986), *Streets of Departure* (1986), *Under the Sun of Satan* (1987), *The Woman Next Door* (1987), *Cyrano de Bergerac* (1990), *Green Card* (1990), *Uranus* (1991), *Merci la Vie* (1991), *Mon Père, Ce Héros* (1991), *Tous les Matins du Monde* (1991), *Christopher Columbus* (1992), *Germinal* (1992).

Derek, Bo (Mary Cathleen Collins) (1956–) American born Long Beach, California; *Orca* (1977), *'10'* (1979), *Tarzan, the Ape Man* (1981), *Bolero* (1984), *Ghosts Can't Do It* (1990).

Dern, Bruce (MacLeish) (1936–) American born Chicago; *Marnie* (1964), *They Shoot Horses Don't They?* (1969), *Silent Running* (1972), *The Great Gatsby* (1974), *Family Plot* (1975), *Smile* (1975), *Coming Home* (1978), *The Driver* (1978), *Tattoo* (1981), *Middle Age Crazy* (1981), *That Championship Season* (1982), *Big Town* (1987), *1969* (1988), *World Gone Wild* (1988), *The 'Burbs* (1989), *After Dark My Sweet* (1990).

Dern, Laura (Elizabeth) (1966–) American born California; *Mask* (1985), *Smooth Talk* (1986), *Blue Velvet* (1986), *Wild at Heart* (1990).

Devane, William (1937–) American born Albany, New York; *Missiles of October* (TV 1973), *Fear on Trial* (TV 1975), *Family Plot* (1975), *From Here to Eternity* (TV 1979), *Yanks* (1979), *Honky Tonk Freeway* (1981), *Knots Landing* (TV 1984–).

De Vito, Danny (1944–) American born Neptune, New Jersey; *One Flew Over the Cuckoo's Nest* (1975), *Taxi* (TV 1978-82), *Romancing the Stone* (1983), *Terms of Endearment* (1984), *The Jewel of the Nile* (1985), *Ruthless People* (1986), *Tin Men* (1987), *Throw Momma from the Train* (1987), *War of the Roses* (1989), *Batman Returns* (1992).

Dey, Susan (1953–) American born Pekin, Illinois; *First Love* (1977), *Looker* (1981); *The Partridge Family* (TV 1970–4), *L.A. Law* (1986–).

FILM AND TV ACTORS (cont.)

Dickinson, Angie (Angeline Brown) (1932–) American born Kulm, North Detroit; *Rio Bravo* (1951), *Big Bad Mama* (1974), *Police Woman* (TV 1975-8), *Dressed to Kill* (1980).

Dietrich, Marlene (Maria Magdalena von Losch) (1901–92) German/American born Berlin; *The Blue Angel* (1930), *Morocco* (1930), *Blond Venus* (1932), *Shanghai Express* (1932), *The Scarlet Empress* (1934), *The Devil is a Woman* (1935), *Desire* (1936), *Destry Rides Again* (1939), *A Foreign Affair* (1948), *Rancho Notorious* (1952), *Judgement at Nuremberg* (1961).

Dillon, Matt (1964–) American born Larchmont, New York; *Tex* (1982), *The Outsiders* (1983), *Rumble Fish* (1983), *The Flamingo Kid* (1984), *Target* (1985), *Big Town* (1987), *Kansas* (1988), *Drugstore Cowboy* (1989).

Donat, Robert (1905–58) British born Withington; *The Count of Monte Cristo* (1934), *The Thirty-Nine Steps* (1935), *The Ghost Goes West* (1936), *The Citadel* (1938), *Goodbye Mr Chips* (1939), *The Winslow Boy* (1948), *Inn of the Sixth Happiness* (1958).

Donohoe, Amanda British; *Castaway* (1987), *The Lair of the White Worm* (1988), *L.A. Law* (TV 1989–), *The Rainbow* (1989), *Paper Mask* (1990).

Dors, Diana (Diana Fluck) (1931–84) British born Swindon, Wiltshire; *Oliver Twist* (1948), *Yield to the Night* (1956), *Deep End* (1970), *There's a Girl in My Soup* (1970), *The Amazing Mr Blunden* (1972), *Theatre of Blood* (1973), *Steaming* (1984).

Douglas, Kirk (Issur Danielovitch Demsky) (1916–) American born Amsterdam, New York; *The Strange Love of Martha Ivers* (1946), *Lust for Life* (1956), *Gunfight at the OK Corral* (1957), *Paths of Glory* (1957), *The Vikings* (1958), *Spartacus* (1960), *The Man from Snowy River* (1982).

Douglas, Michael (1944–) American born New Brunswick, New Jersey; *The Streets of San Francisco* (TV 1972-5), *Coma* (1978), *The China Syndrome* (1980), *The Star Chamber* (1983), *Romancing the Stone* (1984), *The Jewel of the Nile* (1985), *Fatal Attraction* (1987), *Wall Street* (1987), *Black Rain* (1989), *War of the Roses* (1989), *Shining Through* (1991), *Basic Instinct* (1992), *Falling Down* (1992).

Dukakis, Olympia (1931–) American born Massachusetts; *Moonstruck* (1987), *Working Girl* (1988), *Dad* (1990).

Dreyfuss, Richard (1947–) American born Brooklyn, New York; *American Graffiti* (1973), *The Apprenticeship of Duddy Kravitz* (1974), *Jaws* (1975), *Close Encounters of the Third Kind* (1977), *The Goodbye Girl* (1977), *Whose Life is it Anyway?* (1981), *Down and Out in Beverly Hills* (1986), *Stakeout* (1987), *Tin Men* (1987), *Moon over Parador* (1988), *Always* (1989), *The Proud and the Free* (1991), *What About Bob?* (1991), *Prisoners of Honour* (1991).

Dunaway, (Dorothy) Faye (1941–) American born Bascom, Florida; *Bonnie and Clyde* (1967), *Little Big Man* (1970), *The Getaway* (1972), *Chinatown* (1974), *The Towering Inferno* (1974), *Network* (1976), *The Eyes of Laura Mars* (1978), *The Champ* (1979), *Mommie Dearest* (1981), *Barfly* (1987), *Midnight Crossing* (1988), *Burning Secret* (1988), *The Handmaid's Tale* (1990), *Scorchers* (1991), *Silhouette* (TV 1991), *Three Weeks in Jerusalem* (1991), *American Dreamers* (1992).

Dunne, Griffin (1955–) American born New York City; *The Fan* (1981), *An American Warewolf in London* (1981), *Almost You* (1984), *After Hours* (1985), *Who's That Girl?* (1987), *Secret Weapon* (TV 1990).

Durbin, Deanna (Edna Mae Durbin) (1921–) Canadian born Winnipeg, Manitoba; *Three Smart Girls* (1936), *One Hundred Men and a Girl* (1937), *Mad About Music* (1938), *That Certain Age* (1938), *Three Smart Girls Grow Up* (1939), *It Started With Eve* (1941), *Christmas Holiday* (1944), *Lady on a Train* (1945).

Duvall, Robert (1930–) American born San Diego, California; *To Kill a Mockingbird* (1963), *The Godfather* (1972), (*part II* – 1974), *Ike* (TV 1979), *Apocalypse Now* (1979), *The Great Santini* (1980), *Tender Mercies* (1983), *The Natural* (1984), *Colors* (1988).

Duvall, Shelley (1949–) American born Houston, Texas; *Thieves Like Us* (1974), *Annie Hall* (1977), *The Shining* (1980), *Popeye* (1980), *Time Bandits* (1981), *Roxanne* (1987).

Eastwood, Clint (1930–) American born San Francisco, California; *Rawhide* (TV 1958-65), *A Fistful of Dollars* (1964), *For a Few Dollars More* (1965), *The Good, The Bad, and the Ugly* (1966), *Paint Your Wagon* (1969), *Coogan's Bluff* (1968), *Where Eagles Dare* (1969), *Play Misty for Me* (1971), *Dirty Harry* (1972),

FILM AND TV ACTORS (cont.)

High Plains Drifter (1973), *Magnum Force* (1973), *The Enforcer* (1976), *The Outlaw Josey Wales* (1976), *Every Which Way But Loose* (1978), *Escape from Alcatraz* (1979), *Any Which Way You Can* (1980), *Firefox* (1982), *Honky Tonk Man* (1982), *Sudden Impact* (1983), *Tightrope* (1984), *Heartbreak Ridge* (1986), *Pink Cadillac* (1989), *The Dead Pool* (1989), *White Hunter Black Heart* (1990), *The Rookie* (1990), *The Unforgiven* (1992).

Eden, Barbara (Barbara Huffman) (1934–) American born Tucson, Arizona; *Voyage to the Bottom of the Sea* (1961), *I Dream of Jeannie* (TV 1965-70), *Harper Valley PTA* (1978), *Harper Valley PTA* (TV 1981).

Ekberg, Anita (1931–) Swedish born Malmo, Sweden; *La Dolce Vita* (1959), *The Summer is Short* (1962).

Ekland, Britt (Britt-Marie Ekland) (1942–) Swedish born Stockholm; *The Man with the Golden Gun* (1974), *Casanova* (1977), *Scandal* (1989).

Elliott, Denholm (1922–) British born London; *Nothing but the Best* (1964), *Here We Go Round the Mulberry Bush* (1967), *A Bridge too Far* (1977), *Raiders of the Lost Ark* (1981), *Brimstone and Treacle* (1982), *Trading Places* (1983), *The Razor's Edge* (1984), *A Private Function* (1984), *A Room with a View* (1985), *Defence of the Realm* (1985), *Maurice* (1987), *Indiana Jones and the Last Crusade* (1989).

Estevez, Emilio (1962–) American born New York City; *The Outsiders* (1983), *Repo Man* (1984), *Breakfast Club* (1984), *St Elmo's Fire* (1985), *Stakeout* (1987), *Young Guns* (1988), *Young Guns 2* (1990).

Evans, Dame Edith (1888–1976) British born London; also stage; *The Queen of Spades* (1948), *The Importance of Being Earnest* (1951).

Everett, Rupert (1960–) British born Norfolk; *Another Country* (1984), *Dance with a Stranger* (1985), *The Comfort of Strangers* (1990).

Fairbanks, Douglas Sr (Douglas Elton Ullman) (1883–1939) American born Denver, Colorado; *The Mark of Zorro* (1920), *The Three Musketeers* (1921), *Robin Hood* (1922), *The Thief of Baghdad* (1924), *The Black Pirate* (1926).

Fairbanks, Douglas Jnr (1907–) American born New York City; *Catherine the Great* (1934), *The Prisoner of Zenda* (1937), *Sinbad the Sailor* (1947).

Falk, Peter (1927–) American born New York City; *It's a Mad Mad Mad Mad World* (1963), *The Great Race* (1965), *Columbo* (TV 1971–8), *The Princess Bride* (1987), *Cookie* (1988), *Vibes* (1988), *Wings of Desire* (1988), *Aunt Julia and the Scriptwriter* (1991).

Farentino, James (1938–) American born Brooklyn, New York; *Cool Million* (TV 1971), *Jesus of Nazareth* (TV 1977), *Dynasty* (1981), *Hill Street Blues* (TV 1982–8).

Farrow, Mia (Maria Farrow) (1945–) American born Los Angeles; *Peyton Place* (TV 1964-7), *Rosemary's Baby* (1968), *Blind Terror* (1971), *The Great Gatsby* (1973), *Death on the Nile* (1978), *A Wedding* (1978), *A Midsummer Night's Sex Comedy* (1982), *The Purple Rose of Cairo* (1985), *Hannah and Her Sisters* (1986), *Another Woman* (1988), *New York Stories* (1989), *Alice* (1991).

Fawcett, Farah (1947–) American born Corpus Christi, Texas; *Somebody Killed Her Husband* (1978), *Logan's Run* (1978), *Charlie's Angles* (TV 1976), *The Cannonball Run* (1980), *Extremities* (1986).

Fell, Norman (1924–) American born Philadelphia, Pennsylvania; *The Graduate* (1967), *Bullitt* (1968), *The Man from UNCLE* (TV 1968), *Three's Company* (TV 1977–8), *The Ropers* (TV 1979–80), *Paternity* (1981).

Field, Sally (1946–) American born Pasadena, California; *Gidget* (TV 1965), *The Flying Nun* (TV 1967–9), *Sybil* (TV 1976), *Stay Hungry* (1976), *Heroes* (1977), *Smokey and the Bandit* (1977), *Hooper* (1978), *Norma Rae* (1979), *Beyond the Poseidon Adventure* (1979), *Smokey and the Bandit II* (1980), *Absence of Malice* (1981), *Places in the Heart* (1984), *Punchline* (1988), *Steel Magnolias* (1990), *Not Without my Daughter* (1991), *Soapdish* (1991).

Fields, W C (William Claude Dunkenfield) (1879–1946) American born Philadelphia, Pennsylvania; *Pool Sharks* (1915), *International House* (1933), *It's a Gift* (1934), *The Old Fashioned Way* (1934), *David Copperfield* (1935), *My Little Chickadee* (1940), *The Bank Dick* (1940), *Never Give a Sucker an Even Break* (1941).

FILM AND TV ACTORS (cont.)

Finch, Peter (William Mitchell) (1916–77) British born London; *The Shiralee* (1957), *The Nun's Story* (1959), *No Love for Johnnie* (1961), *Far from the Madding Crowd* (1967), *Sunday Bloody Sunday* (1971), *Network* (1976).

Finney, Albert (1936–) British born Salford, Lancashire; *The Entertainer* (1960), *Saturday Night and Sunday Morning* (1960), *Tom Jones* (1963), *Charlie Bubbles* (1968), *Murder on the Orient Express* (1974), *Shoot the Moon* (1981), *Annie* (1982), *The Dresser* (1983), *Under the Volcano* (1984), *The Green Man* (TV 1990), *Miller's Crossing* (1990).

Firth, Peter (1953–) British born Bradford, Yorkshire; *Equus* (1973), *Tess* (1980), *Life Force* (1985), *Letter to Brezhnev* (1985).

Fisher, Carrie (1956–) American born Beverly Hills, California; *Shampoo* (1975), *Star Wars* (1977), *The Blues Brothers* (1980), *The Empire Strikes Back* (1980), *Under the Rainbow* (1981), *Return of the Jedi* (1983), *The Man With One Red Shoe* (1985), *Hannah and Her Sisters* (1986), *The 'Burbs* (1989), *When Harry Met Sally ...* (1989), *Loverboy* (1990), *Sibling Rivalry* (1990).

Fletcher, Louise (1934–) American born Birmingham, Alabama; *One Flew Over the Cuckoo's Nest* (1975), *Exorcist II: The Heretic* (1977), *The Cheap Detective* (1978), *Brainstorm* (1983), *Firestarter* (1984), *The Boy Who Could Fly* (1985), *Two Moon Junction* (1988).

Flynn, Errol (1909–59) Australian/American born Hobart, Tasmania; *In the Wake of the Bounty* (1933), *Captain Blood* (1935), *The Charge of the Light Brigade* (1936), *The Adventures of Robin Hood* (1938), *The Sea Hawk* (1940), *The Sun Also Rises* (1957).

Fonda, Henry (James) (1905-82) American born Grand Island, Nebraska; *The Moon's Our Home* (1936), *A Farmer Takes a Wife* (1938), *Young Mr Lincoln* (1939), *The Grapes of Wrath* (1940), *The Lady Eve* (1941), *The Oxbow Incident* (1943), *My Darling Clementine* (1946), *Twelve Angry Men* (1957), *Stage Struck* (1957), *Fail Safe* (1964), *The Boston Strangler* (1968), *On Golden Pond* (1981).

Fonda, Jane (Seymour) (1937–) American born New York City; *Walk on the Wild Side* (1961), *Barbarella* (1968), *They Shoot Horses Don't They?* (1969), *Klute* (1971), *Julia* (1977), *Coming Home* (1978), *The Electric Horseman* (1979), *The China Syndrome* (1980), *Nine to Five* (1981), *On Golden Pond* (1981), *The Dollmaker* (TV 1983), *The Morning After* (1986), *Old Gringo* (1989), *Stanley And Iris* (1989).

Fonda, Peter (1939–) American born New York City; *Easy Rider* (1969), *Futureworld* (1976), *Cannonball Run* (1981), *Mercenary Fighters* (1988).

Fontaine, Joan (Joan de Havilland) (1917–) British born Tokyo, Japan; *Rebecca* (1940), *Suspicion* (1941), *Jane Eyre* (1943), *Frenchman's Creek* (1944), *From This Day Forward* (1946), *Letter from an Unknown Woman* (1948), *Born to Be Bad* (1950).

Ford, Harrison (1942–) American born Chicago; *Dead Heat on a Merry-Go-Round* (1966), *American Graffiti* (1974), *Star Wars* (1977), *Heroes* (1977), *Force 10 from Navarone* (1978), *The Frisco Kid* (1979), *Hanover Street* (1979), *Apocalypse Now* (1979), *The Empire Strikes Back* (1980), *Raiders of the Lost Ark* (1981), *Blade Runner* (1982), *Return of the Jedi* (1983), *Indiana Jones and the Temple of Doom* (1984), *Witness* (1985), *Mosquito Coast* (1986), *Frantic* (1988), *Working Girl* (1988), *Indiana Jones and the Last Crusade* (1989), *Presumed Innocent* (1990), *Regarding Henry* (1991), *Patriot Games* (1992).

Forrest, Steve (William Forrest Andrews) (1924–) American born Huntsville, Texas; *The Baron* (TV 1965), *S.W.A.T.* (TV 1975–6), *Hollywood Wives* (1984), *Spies Like Us* (1986), *Dallas* (TV 1986).

Foster, Jodie (Ariane Munker) (1962–) American born Bronx, New York; *Bob and Carol and Ted and Alice* (TV 1973), *Paper Moon* (TV 1974), *Alice Doesn't Live Here Anymore* (1974), *Bugsy Malone* (1976), *Taxi Driver* (1976), *The Little Girl Who Lives Down the Lane* (1976), *Candleshoe* (1977), *Freaky Friday* (1977), *Siesta* (1987), *The Accused* (1988), *5 Corners* (1988), *Stealing Home* (1988), *Catchfire* (1990), *Silence of the Lambs* (1991), *Little Man Tate* (1991), *Shadows And Fog* (1992), *Newsby* (1992).

Fox, James (1939–) British born London; *The Magnet* (1950), *The Loneliness of the Long Distance Runner* (1963), *Those Magnificent Men in Their Flying Machines* (1965), *Thoroughly Modern Millie* (1967), *Performance* (1970), *A Passage to India* (1984), *Greystoke* (1984), *The Whistle Blower* (1987), *High Season* (1987), *She's Been Away* (TV 1990).

FILM AND TV ACTORS (cont.)

Fox, Michael J (1961–) Canadian born Edmonton, Alberta; *Letters from Frank* (TV 1979), *Family Ties* (TV 1983–), *Poison Ivy* (TV 1985), *Back to the Future* (1985), *Teenwolf* (1985), *The Secret of My Success* (1987), *Bright Lights, Big City* (1988), *Casualties of War* (1989), *Back to the Future II* (1989), *Back to the Future III* (1990), *The Hard Way* (1991), *'Doc' Hollywood* (1991).

Francis, Anne (1932–) American born Ossining, New York; *Summer Holiday* (1948), *Susan Slept Here* (1954), *Forbidden Planet* (1956), *Funny Girl* (1968), *My Three Sons* (TV 1971).

Funicello, Annette (1942–) American born Utica, New York; *Johnny Tremain* (1957), *The Shaggy Dog* (1961), *Babes in Toyland* (1961), *Beach Blanket Bingo* (1964), *Fireball 500* (1966), *Back to the Beach* (1987).

Gabin, Jean (Jean-Alexis Moncorgé) (1904–76) French born Paris; *Chacun Sa Chance* (1930), *Pepé le Moko* (1936), *La Grande Illusion* (1937), *Quai des Brumes* (1938), *Le Jour Se Lève* (1939), *Touchez Pas Au Grisbi* (1953), *Archimède Le Clochard* (1958), *Un Singe en Hiver* (1962), *Le Chat* (1971), *L'Année Sainte* (1976).

Gable, (William) Clark (1901–60) American born Cadiz, Ohio; *Red Dust* (1932), *It Happened One Night* (1934), *Mutiny on the Bounty* (1935), *San Francisco* (1936), *Gone with the Wind* (1939), *The Hucksters* (1947), *Mogambo* (1953), *Never Let Me Go* (1953), *Teacher's Pet* (1958), *The Misfits* (1961).

Gabor, Zsa Zsa (Sari Gabor) (1918–) Hungarian born Budapest; *Lovely to Look at* (1952), *Moulin Rouge* (1952), *Lili* (1953), *Public Enemy Number One* (1954), *Queen of Outer Space* (1959), *Up the Front* (1972).

Gambon, Michael (1940–) Irish born Dublin; *Turtle Diary* (1985), *The Singing Detective* (TV 1986), *Paris by Night* (1989), *The Cook, the Thief, His Wife and her Lover* (1989).

Garbo, Greta (Greta Lovisa Gustafsson) (1905–90) Swedish/American born Stockholm; *Flesh and the Devil* (1927), *Anna Christie* (1930), *Grand Hotel* (1932), *Queen Christina* (1933), *Anna Karenina* (1935), *Camille* (1936), *Ninotchka* (1939).

Gardner, Ava (Lucy Johnson) (1922–90) American born Smithfield, North Carolina; *The Killers* (1946), *The Hucksters* (1947), *Show Boat* (1951), *Pandora and the Flying Dutchman* (1951), *The Snows of Kilimanjaro* (1952), *Magambo* (1953), *The Barefoot Contessa* (1954), *The Sun Also Rises* (1957), *The Night of the Iguana* (1964).

Garland, Judy (Frances Gumm) (1922–69) American born Grand Rapids, Minnesota; *The Wizard of Oz* (1939), *Babes in Arms* (1939), *For Me and My Gal* (1942), *Meet Me in St Louis* (1944), *Ziegfeld Follies* (1945), *The Clock* (1945), *Easter Parade* (1948), *Summer Stock* (1950), *A Star is Born* (1954).

Garner, James (James Scott Baumgarner) (1928–) American born Norman, Oklahoma; *Maverick* (TV 1957–62), *The Great Escape* (1963), *The Americanization of Emily* (1964), *The Skin Game* (1971), *Rockford Files* (TV 1974-80), *The Fan* (1980), *Victor/Victoria* (1982).

Garr, Teri (1949–) American born Lakewood, Ohio; *Young Frankenstein* (1974), *Oh God* (1977), *Close Encounters of the Third Kind* (1977), *The Black Stallion* (1978), *Honky Tonk Freeway* (1981), *One from the Heart* (1982), *Tootsie* (1982), *The Sting II* (1982), *The Black Stallion Returns* (1983), *Mr Mom* (1983), *First Born* (1984), *After Hours* (1985), *Full Moon in Blue Water* (1988).

Gassman, Vittorio (1922–) Italian born Genoa; *Il Cavaliere Misterioso* (1948), *Riso Amaro* (1948), *La Vie est un Roman* (1983).

Gazzara, Ben (Biago Gazzara) (1930–) American born New York City; *Anatomy of Murder* (1959), *Arrest and Trial* (TV 1963), *Run for Your Life* (TV 1965-7), *QB VII* (TV 1974), *Voyage of the Damned* (1976).

Gere, Richard (1949–) American born Philadelphia, Pennsylvania; *Yanks* (1979), *American Gigolo* (1980), *An Officer and a Gentleman* (1982), *Breathless* (1983), *The Cotton Club* (1984), *No Mercy* (1986), *Miles from Home* (1988), *Internal Affairs* (1990), *Pretty Woman* (1990), *Rhapsody In August* (1991), *Final Analysis* (1992), *Mr North* (1992), *Newsby* (1992).

Gibson, Henry (1935–) American born Germantown, Pennsylvania; *Kiss Me Stupid* (1964), *The Blues Brothers* (1981), *The Incredible Shrinking Woman* (1981), *Innerspace* (1987), *Switching Channels* (1988).

Gibson, Mel (1956–) American/Australian born Peekskill, New York; *Tim* (1979), *Mad Max* (1979), *Gallipoli* (1981), *Mad Max 2: The Road Warrior* (1982), *The Year of Living Dangerously* (1982), *Mad Max*

FILM AND TV ACTORS (cont.)

Beyond Thunderdome (1985), *Lethal Weapon* (1987), *Tequila Sunrise* (1988), *Lethal Weapon 2* (1989), *Bird on a Wire* (1990), *Air America* (1990), *Hamlet* (1990), *Lethal Weapon 3* (1992), *The Rest of Daniel* (1992).

Gielgud, Sir John (Arthur) (1904–) British born London; also stage; *Julius Caesar* (1953), *The Charge of the Light Brigade* (1968), *Oh What a Lovely War* (1969), *Murder on the Orient Express* (1974), *Providence* (1977), *Brideshead Revisited* (TV 1981), *Arthur* (1981), *Gandhi* (1982), *The Whistle Blower* (1987), *Arthur 2: On the Rocks* (1988), *Loser Takes All* (1989), *Prospero's Books* (1991).

Gish, Lillian (Diana) (Lillian de Guiche) (1896–) American born Springfield, Ohio; *An Unseen Enemy* (1912), *Birth of a Nation* (1914), *Intolerance* (1916), *Broken Blossoms* (1919), *Way Down East* (1920), *Duel in the Sun* (1946), *Night of the Hunter* (1955), *The Whales of August* (1987).

Glover, Danny (1947–) American born San Francisco, California; *Silverado* (1985), *Witness* (1985), *Lethal Weapon* (1987), *Bat 21* (1988), *Lethal Weapon 2* (1989), *Predator 2* (1990), *Lethal Weapon 3* (1992).

Godunov, Alexander (Aleksandr Godunov) (1949–) Soviet born Sakhalin Island, USSR; *Witness* (1985), *Die Hard* (1989).

Goldberg, Whoopi (Caryn Johnson) (1949–) American born Manhattan, New York; *The Color Purple* (1985), *Burglar* (1985), *Jumping Jack Flash* (1986), *Clara's Heart* (1988), *The Telephone* (1988), *Ghost* (1990), *Soapdish* (1991), *Sister Act* (1992), *Change of Heart* (1992), *Serafina!* (1992), *The Player* (1992).

Goldblum, Jeff (1952–) American born Pittsburgh, Pennsylvania; *California Split* (1974), *Death Wish* (1974), *Nashville* (1975), *Invasion of the Body Snatchers* (1978), *Escape from Athena* (1979), *The Right Stuff* (1983), *The Big Chill* (1983), *Into the Night* (1985), *Silverado* (1985), *The Fly* (1985), *Life Story* (TV 1987), *Vibes* (1988), *The Tall Guy* (1989), *Earth Girls Are Easy* (1989), *Mister Frost* (1990).

Goodman, John (1953–) American born St Louis, Missouri; *True Stories* (1986), *The Big Easy* (1987), *Rosanne* (TV 1988–), *Punchline* (1988), *Sea of Love* (1990), *Always* (1990), *Stella* (1990), *Arachnophobia* (1990).

Gossett, Louis Jr (1936–) American born Brooklyn, New York; *Travels with My Aunt* (1972), *Roots* (TV 1977), *The Lazarus Syndrome* (TV 1979), *An Officer and a Gentleman* (1982), *The Powers of Matthew Starr* (TV 1982), *Jaws 3D* (1983), *Iron Eagle* (1985), *Iron Eagle II* (1988), *Cover Up* (1991).

Granger, Stewart (James Lablanche Stewart) (1913–) British born London; *The Man in Grey* (1943), *Waterloo Road* (1944), *Love Story* (1944), *Caesar and Cleopatra* (1945), *Captain Boycott* (1947), *King Solomon's Mines* (1950), *Scaramouch* (1952), *The Prisoner of Zenda* (1952), *Beau Brummell* (1954), *The Wild Geese* (1977).

Grant, Cary (Archibald Alexander Leach) (1904–86) British born Bristol; *This is the Night* (1932), *She Done Him Wrong* (1933), *The Awful Truth* (1937), *Bringing Up Baby* (1938), *His Girl Friday* (1940), *Arsenic and Old Lace* (1944), *Notorious* (1946), *To Catch a Thief* (1953), *North by Northwest* (1959).

Grant, Lee (Lyova Rosenthal) (1930–) American born New York City; *Detective Story* (1951), *The Landlord* (1970), *Shampoo* (1975), *The Voyage of the Damned* (1976), *Damien: Omen II* (1978), *Big Town* (1987).

Greene, Lorne (1915–87) Canadian born Ottowa; *Peyton Place* (1957), *Bonanza* (TV 1959–71), *Earthquake* (1974), *Tidal Wave* (1975), *Battle Star Galactica* (TV 1978), *Griff* (1974), *Battle Star Galactica 1980* (TV 1980), *Code Red* (TV 1981).

Grenfell, Joyce (Joyce Phipps) (1910–75) British born London; also stage; *The Happiest Days of Your Life* (1949), *Laughter in Paradise* (1951), *The Bells of St Trinians* (1954).

Greenwood, Joan (1921–87) British born Chelsea; *Whisky Galore* (1949), *Kind Hearts and Coronets* (1949), *The Man in the White Suit* (1951), *The Importance of Being Earnest* (1952), *Tom Jones* (1963), *Little Dorrit* (1987).

Griffith, Melanie (1957–) American born New York City; *Something Wild* (1987), *Cherry 2000* (1988), *Working Girl* (1988), *Stormy Monday* (1988), *Pacific Heights* (1990), *Bonfire of the Vanities* (1990), *Paradise* (1991), *Shining Through* (1992), *Close to Eden* (1992).

Guinness, Sir Alec (1914–) British born London; also stage; *Oliver Twist* (1948), *Kind Hearts and Coronets* (1949), *The Mudlark* (1950), *The Lavander Hill Mob* (1951), *The Man in the White Suit* (1951), *The Card* (1952), *Father Brown* (1954), *The Ladykillers* (1955), *The Bridge on the River Kwai* (1957), *The*

FILM AND TV ACTORS (cont.)

Horse's Mouth (1958), *Our Man in Havana* (1960), *Tunes of Glory* (1962), *Lawrence of Arabia* (1962), *Doctor Zhivago* (1966), *Star Wars* (1977), *Tinker Tailor Soldier Spy* (TV 1979), *Smiley's People* (TV 1981), *Return of the Jedi* (1983), *A Passage to India* (1984), *Little Dorrit* (1987), *A Handful of Dust* (1988), *Kafka* (1991).

Guttenberg, Steve (1958–) American born Massapequa, New York; *Diner* (1981), *Police Academy* (1984), *Police Academy II* (1985), *Cocoon* (1985), *Short Circuit* (1986), *The Bedroom Window* (1986), *Three Men and a Baby* (1988), *High Spirits* (1988), *Cocoon: The Return* (1988), *Three Men and a Little Lady* (1990).

Gwynne, Fred (1926–) American born New York City; *Car 54 Where are You?* (TV 1961–2), *The Munsters* (TV 1964–5); *On the Waterfront* (1954), *Munster Go Home* (1966), *The Cotton Club* (1984), *Fatal Attraction* (1987), *Kane and Abel* (TV 1988), *Pet Sematary* (1989).

Hackman, Gene (1931–) American born San Bernardino, California; *Bonnie and Clyde* (1967), *I Never Sang for my Father* (1969), *French Connection* (1971), *The Poseidon Adventure* (1972), *Young Frankenstein* (1974), *French Connection II* (1975), *A Bridge Too Far* (1977), *Superman* (1978), *Superman II* (1981), *Target* (1985), *Superman IV* (1987), *Another Woman* (1988), *Bat 21* (1988), *Full Moon in Blue Water* (1988), *Split Decisions* (1988), *Missisippi Burning* (1989), *The Package* (1989), *Loose Cannons* (1990), *Postcards from the Edge* (1990), *Narrow Margin* (1990), *Class Action* (1990), *Company Business* (1991), *The Unforgiven* (1992).

Hagman, Larry (Larry Hageman) (1931–) American born Weatherford, Texas; *Ensign Pulver* (1964), *I Dream of Jeannie* (TV 1965–70), *The Eagles Has Landed* (1976), *Superman* (1978), *Dallas* (TV 1978–90).

Hamill, Mark (1952–) American born Oakland, California; *Star Wars* (1977), *The Big Red One* (1979), *The Empire Strikes Back* (1980), *The Night the Lights Went out in Georgia* (1981), *Return of the Jedi* (1983), *Slipstream* (1988).

Hamilton, George (1939–) American born Memphis, Tennessee; *Home from the Hill* (1960), *All the Fine Young Cannibals* (1960), *Act One* (1963), *Roots* (TV 1977), *Love at First Bite* (1979), *Zorro the Gay Blade* (1981), *Dynasty* (TV 1985), *Spies* (TV 1986).

Hamlin, Harry (1951–) American born Pasadena, California; *Clash of the Titans* (1981), *Dragonslayer* (1981), *Space* (TV 1985), *LA Law* (TV 1986–).

Hanks, Tom (1957–) American born Oakland, California; *Bachelor Party* (1983), *Splash!* (1984), *The Man With One Red Shoe* (1985), *Dragnet* (1987), *Big* (1988), *Punchline* (1988), *The 'Burbs* (1989), *Turner and Hooch* (1990), *Joe Versus the Volcano* (1990), *Bonfire of the Vanities* (1991), *A League of Their Own* (1992), *Benny And Joon* (1992).

Hannah, Daryl (1960–) American born Chicago; *Blade Runner* (1982), *Splash!* (1984), *Clan of the Cave Bear* (1986), *Legal Eagles* (1986), *Roxanne* (1987), *Wall Street* (1987), *High Spirits* (1988), *Steel Magnolias* (1989), *Crazy People* (1990), *At Play in the Fields of the Lord* (1991).

Hardy, Oliver (Norvell Hardy Junior) (1892–1957) American born near Atlanta, Georgia; many Laurel and Hardy films including *Putting Pants on Philip* (1927), *The Battle of the Century* (1927), *Two Tars* (1928), *The Perfect Day* (1929), *Laughing Gravy* (1931), *The Music Box* (1932), *Babes in Toyland* (1934), *Bonnie Scotland* (1935), *Way Out West* (1937), *The Flying Deuces* (1939), *Atoll K* (1950).

Harlow, Jean (Harlean Carpentier) (1911–37) American born Kansas City, Missouri; *Red Dust* (1932), *Hell's Angels* (1930), *Platinum Blonde* (1931), *Red-Headed Woman* (1932), *Bombshell* (1933), *Dinner at 8* (1933), *Libelled Lady* (1936).

Harmon, Mark (1951–) American born Burbank, California; *The Dream Merchants* (1980), *Flamingo Road* (TV 1981–2), *Beyond the Poseidon Adventure* (1983), *Moonlighting* (TV 1987), *St Elsewhere* (TV 1987–9), *The Presidio* (1988).

Harris, Julie (Julia Harris) (1925–) American born Grosspoint, Michigan; *The Member of the Wedding* (1953), *East of Eden* (1955), *The Haunting* (1963).

Harris, Richard (1930–) Irish born County Limerick; *The Guns of Navarone* (1961), *Mutiny on the Bounty* (1962), *This Sporting Life* (1963), *Camelot* (1967), *A Man Called Horse* (1969), *Cromwell* (1970), *The*

FILM AND TV ACTORS (cont.)

Cassandra Crossing (1977), *Orca–Killer Whale* (1977), *The Wild Geese* (1978), *Tarzan the Ape Man* (1981), *The Field* (1990).

Harrison, Sir Rex (Reginald Carey Harrison) (1908-90) British born Huyton, Lancashire; *Major Barbara* (1940), *Blithe Spirit* (1945), *Anna and the King of Siam* (1946), *The Ghost and Mrs Muir* (1947), *The Reluctant Debutante* (1958), *The Constant Husband* (1955), *Cleopatra* (1962), *My Fair Lady* (1964), *Dr Doolittle* (1967).

Hauer, Rutger (1944–) Dutch born Amsterdam; *Nighthawks* (1981), *Blade Runner* (1982), *Eureka* (1983), *The Osterman Weekend* (1983), *The Hitcher* (1985), *Flesh and Blood* (1985), *Wanted Dead or Alive* (1986), *The Legend of the Holy Drinker* (1989), *Blind Fury* (1990).

Hawn, Goldie (Jeanne) (1945–) American born Washington D.C.; *Laugh In* (TV 1968–73); *Cactus Flower* (1969), *There's a Girl in My Soup* (1970), *Butterflies are Free* (1971), *Sugarland Express* (1974), *Shampoo* (1975), *Foul Play* (1978), *Seems Like Old Times* (1980), *Private Benjamin* (1980), *Best Friends* (1982), *Swing Shift* (1984), *Bird on a Wire* (1990), *CrissCross* (1991), *Deceived* (1991), *Housesitter* (1992), *Death Becomes Her* (1992).

Hay, Will (1889–1949) British born Stockton-on-Tees; *Good Morning Boys* (1937), *Old Bones of the River* (1938), *Oh Mr Porter* (1938), *Ask a Policeman* (1939), *The Ghost of St Michaels* (1941), *My Learned Friend* (1944).

Hayward, Susan (Edythe Marrenner) (1917–75) American born Brooklyn, New York; *Smash-Up: The Story of a Woman* (1947), *With A Song In My Heart* (1952), *I'll Cry Tomorrow* (1955), *I Want to Live!* (1958), *Where Love Has Gone* (1964), *Valley of the Dolls* (1967), *The Revengers* (1972).

Hayworth, Rita (Margarita Carmen Cansino) (1918–87) American born New York City; *Only Angels Have Wings* (1939), *The Lady in Question* (1940), *The Strawberry Blonde* (1940), *Blood and Sand* (1941), *You'll Never Get Rich* (1941), *Cover Girl* (1944), *Gilda* (1946), *The Lady from Shanghai* (1948), *Separate Tables* (1958).

Hemmingway, Mariel (1961–) American born Ketchum, Indiana; *Manhattan* (1979), *Superman IV* (1987), *The Suicide Club* (1987), *Sunset* (1988).

Hepburn, Audrey (Audrey Hepburn-Ruston) (1929–) British/Dutch born Brussels, Belgium; *Roman Holiday* (1953), *War and Peace* (1956), *Funny Face* (1957), *The Nun's Story* (1959), *Breakfast at Tiffany's* (1961), *My Fair Lady* (1964), *How to Steal a Million* (1966), *Wait Until Dark* (1967), *Robin and Marian* (1976), *Always* (1989).

Hepburn, Katharine (1907–) American born Hartford, Connecticut; *A Bill of Divorcement* (1932), *Morning Glory* (1933), *Stage Door* (1937), *Bringing Up Baby* (1938), *Holiday* (1938), *The Philadelphia Story* (1940), *Woman of the Year* (1942), *Adam's Rib* (1949), *The African Queen* (1951), *Long Day's Journey into Night* (1962), *Guess Who's Coming to Dinner?* (1967), *Suddenly Last Summer* (1968), *The Lion in Winter* (1968), *The Glass Menagerie* (TV 1973), *Rooster Cockburn* (1975), *On Golden Pond* (1981).

Hershey, Barbara (formerly Barbara Seagull, originally Herzstein) (1948–) American born Hollywood, California; *Last Summer* (1968), *Diamonds* (1975), *The Flood* (TV 1976), *The Stunt Man* (1978), *Angel on My Shoulder* (TV 1980), *The Entity* (1983), *The Right Stuff* (1983), *The Natural* (1984), *Passion Flower* (TV 1985), *Hannah and Her Sisters* (1986), *Tin Men* (1987), *A World Apart* (1988), *The Last Temptation of Christ* (1988), *Beaches* (1988), *Barton Fink* (1990), *Naked Lunch* (1991).

Heston, Charlton (John Charlton Carter) (1922–) American born Evanston, Illinois; *Arrowhead* (1953), *The Ten Commandments* (1956), *Touch of Evil* (1958), *Ben Hur* (1959), *El Cid* (1961), *The Greatest Story Ever Told* (1965), *The War Lord* (1965), *Khartoum* (1966), *Planet of the Apes* (1968), *Will Penny* (1968), *Earthquake* (1973).

Hillerman, John (1932–) American born Denison, Texas; *Paper Moon* (1973), *The Betty White Show* (TV 1977), *Magnum* (TV 1980–9), *History of the World Part One* (1981).

Hiller, Wendy (1912–) British born Bramhall, Cheshire; also stage; *Major Barbara* (1940), *I Know Where I'm Going* (1945), *Separate Tables* (1958), *Sons and Lovers* (1960), *A Man for All Seasons* (1966), *Murder*

FILM AND TV ACTORS (cont.)

on the Orient Express (1974), *Voyage of the Damned* (1976), *The Elephant Man* (1980), *The Lonely Passion of Judith Hearne* (1987).

Hoffman, Dustin (1937–) American born Los Angeles; *The Graduate* (1967), *Midnight Cowboy* (1969), *Little Big Man* (1970), *Papillon* (1973), *Lenny* (1974), *All the President's Men* (1976), *Kramer Vs Kramer* (1979), *Tootsie* (1982), *Death of a Salesman* (TV 1984), *Rain Man* (1989), *Dick Tracy* (1990), *Billy Bathgate* (1991), *Hook* (1991), *Hero* (1992).

Hogan, Paul (1939–) Australian born New South Wales; *Crocodile Dundee* (1986), *Crocodile Dundee II* (1988), *Almost an Angel* (1990).

Holbrook, Hal (Harold Holbrook) (1925–) American born Cleveland, Ohio; *The Group* (1966), *The Bold Ones* (1970–1), *That Certain Summer* (TV 1972), *Magnum Force* (1973), *All the President's Men* (1976), *Julia* (1977), *Capricorn One* (1976), *The Fog* (1980), *Creepshow* (1982), *The Star Chamber* (1982).

Holden, William (William Franklin Beedle Jr) (1918-82) American born O'Fallon, Illinois; *Golden Boy* (1939), *Rachel and the Stranger* (1948), *Sunset Boulevard* (1950), *Born Yesterday* (1950), *Stalag 17* (1953), *Love is a Many-Splendored Thing* (1955), *Picnic* (1955), *The Bridge on the River Kwai* (1957), *Casino Royale* (1967), *The Wild Bunch* (1969), *The Towering Inferno* (1974), *Network* (1976), *Damien: Omen II* (1978), *Escape to Athena* (1979), *The Earthling* (1980), *S.O.B.* (1981), *When Time Ran Out* (1981).

Hope, Bob (Leslie Townes Hope) (1903–) British/American born Eltham; *Thanks for the Memory* (1938), *The Cat and the Canary* (1939), *Road to Singapore* (1940), *The Ghost Breakers* (1940), *Road to Zanzibar* (1941), *My Favorite Blonde* (1942), *Road to Morocco* (1942), *The Paleface* (1948), *Fancy Pants* (1950), *The Facts of Life* (1960), *Road to Hong Kong* (1961), *How to Commit Marriage* (1969).

Hopkins, Anthony (1941–) British born Port Talbot, Wales; *The Lion in Winter* (1968), *When Eight Bells Toll* (1971), *War and Peace* (TV 1972), *The Lindbergh Kidnapping Case* (TV 1976), *Magic* (1978), *The Elephant Man* (1980), *The Bunker* (TV 1981), *The Bounty* (1983), *84 Charing Cross Road* (1986), *Desperate Hours* (1991), *Silence of the Lambs* (1991), *Spotswood* (1991), *Freejack* (1992), *Howard's End* (1992), *Charlie* (1992), *The Innocent* (1992).

Hopper, Dennis (1936–) American born Dodge City, Kansas; *Rebel Without a Cause* (1955), *Giant* (1956), *Cool Hand Luke* (1967), *Easy Rider* (1969), *Apocalypse Now* (1979), *Blue Velvet* (1986), *River's Edge* (1986), *Blood Red* (1990), *Catchfire* (1990), *Paris Trout* (1991), *The Indian Runner* (1991), *Money Men* (1992).

Hordern, Sir Michael (1911–) British born Berkhampsted; also stage; *The Constant Husband* (1955), *The Spanish Gardener* (1956), *Dr Syn – Alias the Scarecrow* (1963), *A Funny Thing Happened on the Way to the Forum* (1966), *The Bed-Sitting Room* (1969), *The Slipper and the Rose* (1976), *The Missionary* (1982), *Paradise Postponed* (TV 1986), *The Fool* (1990).

Hoskins, Bob (Robert William) (1942–) British born Bury St Edmunds, Suffolk; *Pennies from Heaven* (TV 1978), *The Long Good Friday* (1980), *Pink Floyd: The Wall* (1982), *The Honorary Consul* (1983), *The Cotton Club* (1984), *Brazil* (1985), *Sweet Liberty* (1985), *Mona Lisa* (1986), *A Prayer for the Dying* (1987), *Who Framed Roger Rabbit* (1988), *Heart Condition* (1990), *Mermaids* (1990), *Shattered* (1991), *Hook* (1991), *The Favour, The Watch And The Very Big Fish* (1991), *The Inner Circle* (1992).

Howard, Leslie (Leslie Howard Stainer) (1890-1943) British born London; *Of Human Bondage* (1934), *The Scarlet Pimpernel* (1935), *Pygmalion* (1938), *Gone with the Wind* (1939).

Howard, Trevor (Wallace) (1916–88) British born Cliftonville, Kent; *The Way Ahead* (1944), *Brief Encounter* (1946), *Green for Danger* (1946), *The Third Man* (1949), *The Heart of the Matter* (1953), *The Key* (1958), *Sons and Lovers* (1960), *Mutiny on the Bounty* (1962), *The Charge of the Light Brigade* (1968), *Ryan's Daughter* (1970), *The Night Visitor* (1971), *Catholics* (TV 1973), *Conduct Unbecoming* (1975), *Meteor* (1979), *Staying On* (TV 1980), *Gandhi* (1982), *White Mischief* (1987), *The Unholy* (1988).

Hudson, Rock (Roy Scherer Jr) (1925–85) American born Winnetka, Illinois; *Magnificent Obsession* (1954), *Giant* (1956), *Written on the Wind* (1956), *The Tarnished Angel* (1957), *Pillow Talk* (1959), *Send Me No Flowers* (1964), *Seconds* (1966), *Darling Lili* (1969), *McMillan and Wife* (TV 1971–5), *McMillan* (TV 1976), *Embryo* (1976), *The Martian Chronicles* (TV 1980), *Dynasty* (TV 1985).

FILM AND TV ACTORS (cont.)

Hulce, Tom (1953–) American born Plymouth, Michigan; *September 30, 1955* (1977), *Animal House* (1978), *Amadeus* (1984), *Dominick and Eugene* (1988), *Parenthood* (1989).

Hunt, Linda (1945–) American born Morristown, New Jersey; *The Year of Living Dangerously* (1983), *The Bostonians* (1984), *Silverado* (1985), *Dune* (1985), *Waiting for the Moon* (1987), *She Devil* (1989).

Huppert, Isabelle (1955–) French born Paris; *César et Rosalie* (1972), *La Dentellière* (1977), *Violette Nozière* (1978), *Heaven's Gate* (1980), *The Possessed* (1987), *Une Affaire des Femmes* (1988), *Madame Bovary* (1991).

Hunter, Kim (Janet Cole) (1922–) American born Detroit, Michigan; *A Matter of Life and Death* (1945), *A Streetcar Named Desire* (1951), *Deadline U.S.A.* (1952), *Planet of the Apes* (1967), *The Swimmer* (1968), *Beneath the Planet of the Apes* (1970), *Escape from the Planet of the Apes* (1971).

Hurt, John (1940–) British born Chesterfield, Derbyshire; also stage; *A Man for All Seasons* (1966), *10 Rillington Place* (1971), *The Naked Civil Servant* (TV 1975), *Midnight Express* (1978), *Alien* (1979), *The Elephant Man* (1980), *History of the World Part One* (1981), *Champions* (1983), *1984* (1984), *Spaceballs* (1987), *Aria* (1987), *White Mischief* (1987), *Scandal* (1989), *Frankenstein Unbound* (1990).

Hurt, William (1950–) American born Washington DC; *Altered States* (1981), *The Janitor* (1981), *Body Heat* (1981), *The Big Chill* (1983), *Gorky Park* (1983), *Kiss of the Spider Woman* (1985), *Children of a Lesser God* (1986), *Broadcast News* (1987), *A Time of Destiny* (1988), *The Accidental Tourist* (1989), *Love You to Death* (1990), *Alice* (1990), *Until The End of The World* (1991), *The Doctor* (1991), *The Plague* (1992).

Hussey, Olivia (1951–) British born Buenos Aires, Argentina; *Romeo and Juliet* (1968), *Lost Horizon* (1973), *Jesus of Nazareth* (TV 1977), *Death on the Nile* (1978), *The Man With Bogart's Face* (1980).

Huston, Anjelica (1952–) Irish/American born Ireland; *The Last Tycoon* (1976), *Frances* (1982), *This is Spinal Tap* (1983), *Prizzi's Honor* (1985), *The Dead* (1987), *Gardens of Stone* (1987), *A Handful of Dust* (1988), *Mr. North* (1988), *The Witches* (1990), *The Grifters* (1990), *The Addams Family* (1991), *Bitter Moon* (1992).

Hutton, Timothy (1960–) American born Malibu, California; *Ordinary People* (1980), *Taps* (1981), *Daniel* (1983), *The Falcon and the Snowman* (1985), *Made in Heaven* (1987).

Hutton, Lauren (Mary Hutton) (1943–) American born Charleston, South Carolina; *A Wedding* (1978), *American Gigolo* (1980), *Zorro the Gay Blade* (1981).

Hyde-White, Wilfrid (1903–91) British born Gloucester; *The Third Man* (1949), *My Fair Lady* (1964), *The Associates* (TV 1979), *Buck Rogers* (TV 1980-2), *Oh God Book Two* (1980), *The Fog* (1982).

Ireland, Jill (1936–90) British born London; *Shane* (TV 1966), *Rider on the Rain* (1970), *The Mechanic* (1972), *Wild Horses* (1973), *Death Wish II* (1982).

Irons, Jeremy (1948–) British born Cowes; *The French Lieutenant's Woman* (1981), *Brideshead Revisited* (TV 1981), *Swann in Love* (1984), *The Mission* (1985), *Dead Ringers* (1988), *Reversal of Fortune* (1990), *Kafka* (1991), *Waterland* (1992), *Damage* (1992), *M. Butterfly* (1992).

Jackson, Glenda (1936–) British born Liverpool; also stage; *Women in Love* (1969), *Sunday Bloody Sunday* (1971), *Mary Queen of Scots* (1971), *Elizabeth R* (TV 1971), *A Touch of Class* (1972), *Hedda* (1975), *Stevie* (1978), *The Patricia Neal Story* (TV 1981), *Turtle Diary* (1985), *Business as Usual* (1987), *Salome's Last Dance* (1988), *The Rainbow* (1989), *Doombeach* (1990), *A Murder of Quality* (TV 1991).

Jackson, Gordon (1923–89) British born Glasgow; *Whisky Galore* (1948), *Tunes of Glory* (1960), *The Great Escape* (1982), *The Ipcress File* (1965), *The Prime of Miss Jean Brodie* (1969), *Upstairs Downstairs* (TV 1970–5), *Kidnapped* (1972), *The Medusa Touch* (1977), *The Professionals* (TV 1977–81), *A Town Like Alice* (TV 1980), *The Shooting Party* (1984), *The Whistle Blower* (1987), *Beyond Therapy* (1987).

Jacobi, Derek (1938–) British born Leytonstone, London; also stage; *The Odessa File* (1964), *I Claudius* (TV 1976), *Burgess and MacLean* (TV 1977), *Mr Pye* (TV 1986), *Little Dorrit* (1987), *The Fool* (1990).

Johnson, Don (1950–) American born Flatt Creek, Missouri; *From Here to Eternity* (1979), *Miami Vice* (TV 1984–90), *The Long Hot Summer* (TV 1985), *Dead Bang* (1988), *The Hot Spot* (1990), *Harley Davidson and the Marlboro Man* (1991).

FILM AND TV ACTORS (cont.)

Jones, James Earl (1931–) American born Tate County, Missouri; *The Great White Hope* (1970), *Jesus of Nazareth* (TV 1977), *Exorcist II: The Heretic* (1977), *Roots II* (TV 1979), *Conan the Barbarian* (1982), *Beastmaster* (1982), *Coming to America* (1988), *Field of Dreams* (1988), *Three Fugitives* (1988), *The Hunt for Red October* (1989), *Best of the Best* (1990).

Jones, Jennifer (Phyllis Isley) (1919–) American born Tulsa, Oklahoma; *The Song of Bernadette* (1943), *Duel in the Sun* (1976), *Portrait of Jennie* (1948), *Carrie* (1951), *Love is a Many-Splendored Thing* (1955), *A Farewell to Arms* (1958), *Tender is the Night* (1961), *Towering Inferno* (1974).

Julia, Raul (1940–) Puerto Rican born San Juan, Puerto Rico; *The Eyes of Laura Mars* (1978), *One From the Heart* (1982), *Tempest* (1982), *Kiss of the Spider Woman* (1985), *The Morning After* (1986), *Moon over Parador* (1988), *The Penitent* (1988), *Tequila Sunrise* (1989), *Romero* (1990), *Presumed Innocent* (1990), *The Rookie* (1990), *Frankenstein Unbound* (1990).

Karloff, Boris (William Henry Pratt) (1887-1969) British/American born London; *Frankenstein* (1931), *The Mask of Fu Manchu* (1931), *The Lost Patrol* (1934), *The Raven* (1935), *The Bride of Frankenstein* (1935), *The Body Snatcher* (1945).

Kaye, Danny (David Daniel Kominski) (1913–87) American born New York City; *Up in Arms* (1944), *The Secret Life of Walter Mitty* (1947), *Hans Christian Anderson* (1952), *White Christmas* (1954), *The Court Jester* (1956), *The Five Pennies* (1959), *Skokie* (TV 1981).

Keach, Stacy (1941–) American born Savannah, Georgia; *Jesus of Nazareth* (TV 1977), *Up in Smoke* (1978), *Princess Daisy* (TV 1983), *Mike Hammer* (TV 1983–4), *Mistral's Daughter* (TV 1984).

Keaton, Buster (Joseph Francis Keaton) (1895–1966) American born Pickway; *Our Hospitality* (1923), *The Navigator* (1924), *The General* (1927), *San Diego I Love You* (1944), *Sunset Boulevard* (1950), *Limelight* (1952), *It's a Mad, Mad, Mad, Mad World* (1963).

Keaton, Diane (Diane Hall) (1946–) American born Los Angeles, California; *The Godfather* (1972), (*part II*–1974), *Sleeper* (1973), *Annie Hall* (1977), *Manhattan* (1979), *Reds* (1981), *Shoot the Moon* (1982), *Mrs Soffel* (1984), *Baby Boom* (1987), *The Good Mother* (1988), *The Godfather Part III* (1990), *Success* (1991).

Keaton, Michael (Michael Douglas) (1951–) American born Carapolis, Pennsylvania; *Night Shift* (1982), *Mr Mom* (1983), *Beetlejuice* (1988), *Batman* (1989), *The Dream Team* (1989), *Clean and Sober* (1989), *Pacific Heights* (1990), *Batman Returns* (1992).

Keitel, Harvey (1947–) American born Brooklyn, New York; *Mean Streets* (1973), *Taxi Driver* (1976), *Bad Timing* (1980), *The Men's Club* (1986), *The Last Temptation of Christ* (1988), *The January Man* (1989).

Kelly, Gene (Eugene Curran Kelly) (1912–) American born Pittsburgh, Pennsylvania; *For Me and My Girl* (1942), *Cover Girl* (1944), *Anchors Aweigh* (1945), *Ziegfeld Follies* (1946), *The Pirate* (1948), *The Three Musketeers* (1948), *Take Me Out to the Ball Game* (1949), *On the Town* (1949), *Summer Stock* (1950), *An American in Paris* (1951), *Singin' in the Rain* (1952), *Brigadoon* (1954), *Invitation to Dance* (1956), *Les Girls* (1957), *Marjorie Morningstar* (1958), *Inherit the Word* (1960), *Sins* (TV 1987).

Kelly, Grace (Patricia) (1928-82) American born Philadelphia, Pennsylvania; *High Noon* (1952), *Mogambo* (1953), *Dial M for Murder* (1954), *Rear Window* (1954), *The Country Girl* (1954), *To Catch a Thief* (1955), *High Society* (1956).

Kennedy, George (1925–) American born New York City; *Charade* (1963), *The Flight of the Phoenix* (1967), *The Dirty Dozen* (1967), *Cool Hand Luke* (1967), *Sarge* (TV 1971), *Thunderbolt and Lightfoot* (1974), *Earthquake* (1974), *The Blue Knight* (TV 1975-6), *The Eiger Sanction* (1977), *Death on the Nile* (1979), *Bolero* (1984), *Delta Force* (1985), *Creepshow 2* (1987), *Dallas* (TV 1988–91).

Kensit, Patsy (1968–) British; *The Great Gatsby* (1973), *Hanover Street* (1979), *Absolute Beginners* (1986), *Lethal Weapon 2* (1989), *Chicago Joe and the Showgirl* (1990), *Twenty-one* (1991).

Kerr, Deborah (Deborah Jane Kerr-Trimmer) (1921–) British born Helensburgh, Scotland; *Major Barbara* (1940), *Love on the Dole* (1941), *The Life and Death of Colonel Blimp* (1943), *Perfect Strangers* (1945), *I See a Dark Stranger* (1945), *Black Narcissus* (1947), *From Here to Eternity* (1953), *The King and I* (1956), *Tea and Sympathy* (1956), *An Affair to Remember* (1957), *Separate Tables* (1958), *The Sundowners* (1960), *The Innocents* (1961), *The Night of the Iguana* (1964), *Casino Royale* (1967), *Prudence and the Pill* (1968), *The Assam Garden* (1985).

FILM AND TV ACTORS (cont.)

Kingsley, Ben (Krishna Banji) (1943–) Anglo-Indian born Snaiton, Yorkshire; *Gandhi* (1982), *Betrayal* (1982), *Turtle Diary* (1985), *Testimony* (1987), *Pascali's Island* (1988), *Without a Clue* (1988).

Kinnear, Roy (1934–88) British; *The Three Musketeers* (1974), *The Four Musketeers* (1975), *A Man for All Seasons* (1988), *Return of the Musketeers* (1989).

Kinski, Klaus (Claus Gunther Nakszynski) (1926–) Polish born Sopot (Zoppot), Danzig (now Poland); *For a Few Dollars More* (1965), *Dr Zhivago* (1965), *Aguirre Wrath of God* (1972), *Nosferatu* (1978), *Fitzcarraldo* (1982), *Codename Wildgeese* (1984).

Kinski, Nastassja (Nastassja Nakszynski) (1960–) German born Berlin; *Tess* (1979), *Cat People* (1982), *One from the Heart* (1982), *Paris, Texas* (1984).

Kline, Kevin (1947–) American born St Louis, Missouri; *Sophie's Choice* (1983), *The Big Chill* (1983), *Silverado* (1985), *Cry Freedom* (1987), *A Fish Called Wanda* (1988), *January Man* (1989), *Love You to Death* (1990), *Soap Dish* (1991).

Ladd, Alan (1913–64) American born Hot Springs, Arkansas; *This Gun for Hire* (1942), *The Glass Key* (1942), *The Blue Dahlia* (1946), *The Great Gatsby* (1949), *Shane* (1953), *The Carpetbaggers* (1964).

Ladd, Diane (Diane Ladnier) (1939–) American born Meridian, Missouri; *Chinatown* (1974), *Alice Doesn't Live Here Any More* (1975), *All Night Long* (1981), *Grace Kelly* (TV 1983), *Something Wicked This Way Comes* (1983), *Plain Clothes* (1988), *Wild at Heart* (1990).

Lamarr, Hedy (Hedwig Kiesler) (1913–) Austrian born Vienna; *Algiers* (1938), *White Cargo* (1942), *Samson and Delilah* (1949).

Lambert, Christopher (1957–) French born New York City; *Greystoke* (1984), *Subway* (1985), *Highlander* (1985), *The Sicilian* (1987), *Why Me?* (1990).

Lamour, Dorothy (Dorothy Kaumeyer) (1914–) American born New Orleans, Louisiana; *The Jungle Princess* (1936), *The Hurricane* (1937), *Road to Singapore* (1940), *Road to Zanzibar* (1941) etc, *Manhandled* (1948), *Creepshow 2* (1987).

Lancaster, Burt (Stephen Burton) (1913–) American born New York City; *The Killers* (1946), *Brute Force* (1947), *The Flame and the Arrow* (1950), *Come Back Little Sheba* (1953), *From Here to Eternity* (1953), *Vera Cruz* (1954), *Gunfight at the OK Corral* (1957), *Elmer Gantry* (1960), *Birdman of Alcatraz* (1962), *The Professionals* (1966), *The Swimmer* (1967), *1900* (1976), *Atlantic City* (1980), *Local Hero* (1983), *Rocket Gibraltar* (1988), *Field of Dreams* (1988).

Lane, Diane (1963–) American born New York City; *The Fury* (1978), *Outsiders* (1983), *Rumble Fish* (1983), *Streets of Fire* (1984), *The Cotton Club* (1984), *Big Town* (1987).

Lange, Hope (1933–) American born Redding Ridge, Connecticut; *Bus Stop* (1956), *Peyton Place* (1957), *Death Wish* (1974), *Nightmare on Elm Street II* (1985), *Blue Velvet* (1986).

Lange, Jessica (1949–) American born Cloquet, Minnesota; *King Kong* (1976), *All That Jazz* (1979), *The Postman Always Rings Twice* (1981), *Tootsie* (1982), *Frances* (1982), *Country* (1984), *Sweet Dreams* (1985), *Crimes of the Heart* (1986), *Far North* (1988), *Music Box* (1989), *Men Don't Leave* (1990), *Blue Sky* (1991), *Cape Fear* (1991), *Night and The City* (1992).

Lansbury, Angela (Brigid) (1925–) American born London; *National Velvet* (1944), *Gaslight* (1944), *The Picture of Dorian Gray* (1945), *The Private Affairs of Bel Ami* (1947), *The Three Musketeers* (1948), *The Reluctant Debutante* (1958), *The Long Hot Summer* (1958), *The Dark at the Top of the Stairs* (1960), *The Manchurian Candidate* (1962), *The Greatest Story Ever Told* (1965), *Bedknobs and Broomsticks* (1971), *Death on the Nile* (1978), *The Lady Vanishes* (1979), *Lace* (TV 1984), *Company of Wolves* (1984), *Murder She Wrote* (TV 1984–).

Laughton, Charles (1899–1962) British born Scarborough; *The Sign of the Cross* (1932), *The Private Life of Henry VIII* (1932), *The Barretts of Wimpole Street* (1934), *Ruggles of Red Gap* (1935), *Mutiny on the Bounty* (1935), *Les Miserables* (1935), *Rembrandt* (1936), *The Hunchback of Notre Dame* (1939), *Hobsons Choice* (1954), *Witness for the Prosecution* (1957), *Advise and Consent* (1962).

Laurel, Stan (Arthur Stanley Jefferson) (1890–1965) British/American born Ulverston, Lancashire; *Nuts in May* (1917), *Monsieur Don't Care* (1925); for films with Hardy *see* **Hardy, Oliver**.

FILM AND TV ACTORS (cont.)

Laurie, Piper (Rosetta Jacobs) (1932–) American born Detroit, Michigan; *The Hustler* (1961), *Carrie* (1976), *Tim* (1979), *Mae West* (TV 1982), *The Thorn Birds* (TV 1983), *Tender is the Night* (TV 1985), *Return to Oz* (1985), *Children of a Lesser God* (1986), *Tiger Warsaw* (1988), *Twin Peaks* (TV 1991).

Lee, Christopher (1922–) British born London; *The Curse of Frankenstein* (1956), *Dracula* (1958), *The Man Who Could Cheat Death* (1959), *The Mummy* (1959), *The Face of Fu Manchu* (1965), *Rasputin the Mad Monk* (1965), *Horror Express* (1972), *The Three Musketeers* (1973), *The Man With the Golden Gun* (1974), *Return from Witch Mountain* (1976), *Howling II* (1985), *The Land of Faraway* (1988).

Lee, Spike (Shelton Jackson Lee) (1957–) American born Atlanta, Georgia; *She's Gotta Have It* (1986), *School Daze* (1988), *Do the Right Thing* (1989), *Mo' Better Blues* (1990).

Leigh, Janet (Jeanette Helen Morrison) (1927–) American born Merced, California; *Little Women* (1949), *The Forsyte Woman* (1949), *Houdini* (1953), *My Sister Eileen* (1955), *The Vikings* (1958), *Psycho* (1960), *The Manchurian Candidate* (1962), *The Fog* (1980).

Leigh, Vivien (Vivien Hartley) (1913–67) British born Darjeeling, India; *Dark Journey* (1937), *A Yank at Oxford* (1938), *Gone with the Wind* (1939), *Lady Hamilton* (1941), *Caesar and Cleopatra* (1945), *Anna Karenina* (1948), *A Streetcar Named Desire* (1951), *The Roman Spring of Mrs Stone* (1961), *Ship of Fools* (1965).

Lemmon, Jack (John Uhler Lemmon III) (1925–) American born Boston, Massachusetts; *It Should Happen to You* (1953), *Mister Roberts* (1955), *Some Like It Hot* (1959), *The Apartment* (1960), *Irma La Douce* (1963), *The Great Race* (1965), *The Odd Couple* (1968), *The Prisoner of Second Avenue* (1975), *The China Syndrome* (1979), *Missing* (1982), *Dad* (1990), *JFK* (1991), *The Player* (1992), *Glengarry Glen Ross* (1992).

Lewis, Jerry (Joseph Levitch) (1926–) American born Newark, New Jersey; *My Friend Irma* (1949), *The Bellboy* (1960), *Cinderfella* (1960), *The Nutty Professor* (1963), *It's a Mad, Mad, Mad, Mad World* (1963), *The Family Jewels* (1965), *King of Comedy* (1983), *Smorgasbord* (1983), *Cookie* (1988).

Lithgow, John (1945–) American born Rochester, New York; *Blow Out* (1973), *High Anxiety* (1978), *The World According to Garp* (1982), *The Twighlight Zone* (1983), *Terms of Endearment* (1983), *The Day After* (TV 1983), *2010* (1984), *Footloose* (1984), *Distant Thunder* (1988), *Memphis Belle* (1990).

Lloyd, Christopher (1938–) American born Stanford, Connecticut; *Star Trek III: The Search for Spock* (1984), *Back to the Future* (1985), *Who Framed Roger Rabbit* (1988), *Track 29* (1988), *Eight Men Out* (1988), *Back to the Future II* (1989), *Back to the Future III* (1990), *Why Me?* (1990).

Lloyd, Emily (1970–) British born London; *Wish You Were Here* (1987), *Cookie* (1988), *In Country* (1989), *Chicago Joe and the Showgirl* (1989).

Lloyd, Harold (Clayton) (1893–1971) American born Burchard, Nebraska; *High and Dizzy* (1920), *Grandma's Boy* (1922), *Safety Last* (1923), *Why Worry?* (1923), *The Freshman* (1925), *The Kid Brother* (1927), *Feet First* (1930), *Movie Crazy* (1932).

Loggia, Robert (1930–) American born Staten Island, New York; *T.H.E. Cat* (TV 1966), *First Love* (1977), *S.O.B.* (1981), *An Officer and a Gentleman* (1982), *Psycho 2* (1982), *Scarface* (1983), *Jagged Edge* (1985), *Over the Top* (1987), *Big* (1988), *Prizzi's Honour* (1988), *Mancuso FBI* (TV 1989–).

Lockwood, Margaret (Margaret Day) (1916–90) British born Karachi, India; *Lorna Doone* (1934), *The Beloved Vagabond* (1936), *The Lady Vanishes* (1938), *Night Train to Munich* (1940), *The Man in Grey* (1943), *The Wicked Lady* (1945), *Cast a Dark Shadow* (1947), *The Slipper and the Rose* (1976).

Lollobrigida, Gina (1927–) Italian born Subiaco; *Belles de Nuit* (1952), *Bread, Love and Dreams* (1953), *Trapeze* (1956), *Woman of Straw* (1964), *Falcon Crest* (TV 1984).

Lom, Herbert (Herbert Charles Angelo Kuchacevich ze Schluderpacheru) (1917–) Czechoslovakian born Prague; *The Seventh Veil* (1946), *Duel Alibi* (1947), *State Secret* (1950), *The Ladykillers* (1950), *El Cid* (1961), *Phantom of the Opera* (1962), *A Shot in the Dark* (1964), *Murders in the Rue Morgue* (1972), *The Return of the Pink Panther* (1974), *The Pink Panther Strikes Again* (1977), *Revenge of the Pink Panther* (1978), *The Lady Vanishes* (1979), *Hopscotch* (1980), *The Dead Zone* (1983), *Whoops Apocalypse* (1986), *Going Bananas* (1988).

FILM AND TV ACTORS (cont.)

Loren, Sophia (Sofia Scicolone) (1934–) Italian born Rome; *Woman of the River* (1955), *Boy on a Dolphin* (1957), *The Key* (1958), *El Cid* (1961), *Two Women* (1961), *The Millionairess* (1961), *Marriage Italian Style* (1964), *Cinderella Italian Style* (1967), *A Special Day* (1977).

Lorre, Peter (Laszlo Lowenstein) (1904-64) Hungarian born Rosenberg; *M* (1931), *Mad Love* (1935), *Crime and Punishment* (1935), *The Maltese Falcon* (1941), *Casablanca* (1942), *The Mask of Dimitrios* (1944), *Arsenic and Old Lace* (1944), *The Beast With Five Fingers* (1946), *My Favourite Brunette* (1947), *20,000 Leagues Under the Sea* (1954), *The Raven* (1963).

Lowe, Rob (1964–) American born Charlottesville, Virginia; *Class* (1983), *Oxford Blues* (1984), *St Elmo's Fire* (1985), *Youngblood* (1985), *About Last Night* (1987), *Illegally Yours* (1987), *Masquerade* (1988), *Bad Influence* (1990).

Lugosi, Bela (Bela Ferenc Denzso Blasko) (1882–1956) Hungarian/American born Lugos (now Romania); *Dracula* (1930), *The Murders in the Rue Morgue* (1931), *White Zombie* (1932), *International House* (1933), *The Black Cat* (1934), *Son of Frankenstein* (1939), *Abbott and Costello Meet Frankenstein* (1948), *Plan 9 from Outer Space* (1956).

Lumley, Joanna (1946–) British born Kashmir; *On Her Majesty's Secret Service* (1969), *General Hospital* (TV 1974-5), *The New Avengers* (TV 1976-7), *Sapphire and Steel* (TV 1979), *Trail of the Pink Panther* (1982), *Curse of the Pink Panther* (1983), *Shirley Valentine* (1989).

McCallum, David (1933–) British born Glasgow; *Violent Playground* (1958), *The Great Escape* (1963), *The Man From UNCLE* (TV 1964–7), *The Greatest Story Ever Told* (1965), Colditz (TV 1972), The Invisible Man (TV 1975), Sapphire and Steel (TV 1979), *The Watcher in the Woods* (1980), *Return of the Man from UNCLE* (TV 1983), *Mother Love* (1989).

McCarthy, Andrew (1963–) American born New York City; *Class* (1983), *Pretty in Pink* (1986), *Mannequin* (1987), *Less Than Zero* (1987), *Fresh Horses* (1988), *Kansas* (1988).

McCarthy, Kevin (1914–) American born Seattle, Washington; *Death of a Salesman* (1952), *Invasion of the Body Snatchers* (1956), *The Misfits* (1961), *The Prize* (1963), *Invasion of the Body Snatchers* (1978), *Piranha* (1978), *The Howling* (1981), *S.O.B.* (1981), *Private Benjamin* (1982), *My Tutor* (1983), *Twilight Zone* (1983), *Innerspace* (1987); *Flamingo Road* (1980–1).

McDowall, Roddy (1928–) British born London; *How Green Was My Valley* (1941), *Planet of the Apes* (1967), *Escape from the Planet of the Apes* (1971) etc, *The Poseidon Adventure* (1972), *Embryo* (1977), *Fright Night* (1985), *Don' Time on Planet Earth* (1988).

McGillis, Kelly (1957–) American born Newport Beach, California; *Reuben* (1982), *Sweet Revenge* (TV 1984), *Witness* (1985), *Top Gun* (1985), *Accused* (1988), *The House on Carroll Street* (1988), *Cat Chaser* (1989).

McKern, Leo (Reginald) (1920–) Australian born Sydney; *Time without Pity* (1957), *The Mouse That Roared* (1959), *A Jolly Bad Fellow* (1964), *A Man for All Seasons* (1966), *Ryan's Daughter* (1971), *The Omen* (1976), *Candleshoe* (1977), *Rumpole of the Bailey* (TV 1978-80), *The Blue Lagoon* (1980), *The French Lieutenant's Woman* (1981), *Ladyhawke* (1984), *Monsignor Quixote* (TV 1986), *Travelling North* (1986).

MacLaine, Shirley (Shirley Beaty) (1934–) American born Richmond, Virginia; *The Trouble with Harry* (1955), *Ask any Girl* (1959), *The Apartment* (1959), *Irma La Douce* (1963), *Sweet Charity* (1968), *Terms of Endearment* (1983), *Madame Sousatzka* (1988), *Postcards from the Edge* (1990), *Defending Your Life* (1991), *Used People* (1992).

McQueen, Steve (Terence Steven McQueen) (1930-80) American born Slater, Missouri; *Wanted Dead or Alive* (TV 1958), *The Blob* (1958), *The Magnificent Seven* (1960), *The Great Escape* (1962), *Love with the Proper Stanger* (1963), *The Cincinnatti Kid* (1965), *Bullitt* (1968), *Le Mans* (1971), *Getaway* (1972), *Papillon* (1973), *Towering Inferno* (1974), *An Enemy of the People* (1977).

Madonna (Madonna Louise Veronica Ciccone) (1958–) American born Bay City, Michigan; *Desperately Seeking Susan* (1985), *Shanghai Suprise* (1986), *Who's That Girl?* (1987), *Dick Tracy* (1990).

Malkovich, John (1953–) American born Christopher, Illinois; *The Killing Fields* (1984), *Places in the*

FILM AND TV ACTORS (cont.)

Heart (1984), *Empire of the Sun* (1987), *Miles from Home* (1988), *Dangerous Liaisons* (1988), *Crazy People* (1990), *The Sheltering Sky* (1990).

Mansfield, Jayne (Vera Jayne Palmer) (1933–67) American born Bryn Mawr, Pennsylvania; *The Girl Can't Help It* (1957), *The Sheriff of Fractured Jaw* (1959), *Too Hot to Handle* (1960), *The Challenge* (1960), *Promises! Promises!* (1965).

Martin, Steve (1945–) American born Waco, Texas; *Sgt. Peppers Lonely Hearts Club Band* (1978), *The Jerk* (1978), *Muppet Movie* (1979), *Pennies from Heaven* (1981), *Dead Men Don't Wear Plaid* (1982), *The Man With Two Brains* (1983), *The Lonely Guy* (1984), *All of Me* (1984), *The Three Amigos* (1986), *The Little Shop of Horrors* (1986), *Planes, Trains, and Automobiles* (1987), *Roxanne* (1987), *Dirty, Rotten Scoundrels* (1989), *Parenthood* (1989), *My Blue Heaven* (1990), *L.A. Story* (1991), *Father of the Bride* (1991), *Grand Canyon* (1991), *Housesitter* (1992).

Marvin, Lee (1924–87) American born New York City; *The Wild One* (1954), *Attack* (1957), *The Killers* (1964), *Cat Ballou* (1965), *The Dirty Dozen* (1967), *Paint Your Wagon* (1969), *Gorky Park* (1983), *Dirty Dozen 2: The Next Mission* (TV 1985).

Marx Brothers, The: Chico (Leonard Marx) (1886–1961); **Harpo** (Adolph Marx) (1988–1964); **Groucho** (Julius Henry Marx) (1890–1977); **Zeppo** (Herbert Marx) (1901–); all American born New York City; (joint) *The Cocoanuts* (1929), *Monkey Business* (1931), *Horse Feathers* (1932), *Duck Soup* (1933), *A Night at the Opera* (1935), *A Day at the Races* (1937), *A Night in Casablanca* (1946).

Mason, James (1909–84) British born Huddersfield; *I Met a Murderer* (1939), *The Night Has Eyes* (1942), *The Man in Grey* (1943), *Fanny by Gaslight* (1944), *The Seventh Veil* (1945), *The Wicked Lady* (1946), *Odd Man Out* (1946), *Pandora and the Flying Dutchman* (1951), *The Desert Fox* (1951), *Five Fingers* (1952), *The Prisoner of Zenda* (1952), *Julius Caesar* (1953), *20,000 Leagues Under the Sea* (1954), *A Star is Born* (1954), *Journey to the Center of the Earth* (1959), *Lolita* (1962), *The Pumpkin Eater* (1964), *Georgy Girl* (1966), *The Blue Max* (1966), *The Deadly Affair* (1967), *Voyage of the Damned* (1976), *Heaven Can Wait* (1978), *The Boys from Brazil* (1978), *Murder by Decree* (1979), *Evil Under the Sun* (1982), *The Verdict* (1982), *Yellowbeard* (1983), *The Shooting Party* (1984).

Massey, Anna (Raymond) (1937–) British born London; also stage; *Burning Lake is Missing* (1965), *A Doll's House* (1973), *Rebecca* (TV 1979), *The Chain* (1985).

Massey, Raymond (1896–1983) American born Toronto; *The Old Dark House* (1932), *The Scarlet Pimpernel* (1934), *Things to Come* (1936), *The Prisoner of Zenda* (1937), *Abe Lincoln in Illinois* (1940), *Arsenic and Old Lace* (1944), *The Fountainhead* (1949), *East of Eden* (1955), *I Spy* (TV 1955), *Dr Kildare* (TV 1961–6).

Mastroianni, Marcello (1924–) Italian born Fontana Liri, near Frosinone; *I Miserabili* (1947), *White Nights* (1957), *La Dolce Vita* (1959), *Yesterday, Today and Tomorrow* (1963), *Divorce Italian Style* (1962), *8½* (1963), *Casanova* (1970), *Diamonds for Breakfast* (1968), *Ginger and Fred* (1985), *Black Eyes* (1987), *The Two Lives of Mattia Pascal* (1988), *Traffic Jam* (1988), *Used People* (1992).

Matthau, Walter (1920–) American born New York City; *A Face in the Crowd* (1957), *King Creole* (1958), *Charade* (1963), *Mirage* (1965), *The Fortune Cookie* (1966), *A Guide to the Married Man* (1967), *The Odd Couple* (1968), *Hello Dolly* (1969), *Cactus Flower* (1969), *Kotch* (1971), *Earthquake* (1974), *The Taking of Pelham One Two Three* (1974), *Hopscotch* (1980), *Pirates* (1986), *The Couch Trip* (1988).

Mature, Victor (1915–) American born Louisville, Kentucky; *One Million BC* (1940), *My Darling Clementine* (1946), *Kiss of Death* (1947), *Samson and Delilah* (1949), *The Robe* (1953), *The Egyptian* (1954), *Safari* (1956), *The Long Haul* (1957), *After the Fox* (1966).

Maura, Carmen (1945–) Spanish born Madrid; *Dark Habits* (1983), *What Have I Done to Deserve This?* (1984), *Law of Desire* (1987), *Women on the Verge of a Nervous Breakdown* (1988), *Baton Rouge* (1988).

Mercouri, Melina (1915–) Greek born Athens; *Stella* (1954), *Never on Sunday* (1960), *Topkapi* (1964).

Midler, Bette (1945–) American born Honolulu, Hawaii; *The Rose* (1979), *Down and Out in Beverly Hills* (1986), *Ruthless People* (1986), *Outrageous Fortune* (1987), *Beaches* (1988), *Big Business* (1988), *Stella* (1989), *Scenes from The Mall* (1991), *For the Boys* (1991).

Mills, Hayley (1946–) British born London; *Tiger Bay* (1959), *Pollyanna* (1960), *The Parent Trap* (1961),

FILM AND TV ACTORS (cont.)

Whistle Down the Wind (1961), *The Moonspinners* (1965), *Forbush and the Penguins* (1971), *Parent Trap II* (TV 1986).

Mills, Sir John (Lewis Ernest Watts) (1908–) British born Felixstowe, Suffolk; *Those Were the Days* (1934), *Cottage to Let* (1941), *In Which We Serve* (1942), *Waterloo Road* (1944), *The Way to the Stars* (1945), *Great Expectations* (1946), *The October Man* (1947), *Scott of the Antarctic* (1948), *The History of Mr Polly* (1949), *The Rocking Horse Winner* (1950), *The Colditz Story* (1954), *Hobson's Choice* (1954), *Town on Trial* (1957), *Tiger Bay* (1959), *Swiss Family Robinson* (1959), *Tunes of Glory* (1960), *Ryan's Daughter* (1970), *Lady Caroline Lamb* (1972), *The Big Sleep* (1978), *The 39 Steps* (1978), *Quatermass* (TV 1979), *Young at Heart* (TV 1980–1), *Gandhi* (1982), *Sahara* (1983), *Who's That Girl?* (1987).

Minnelli, Liza (1946–) American born Los Angeles; *Cabaret* (1972), *New York New York* (1977), *Arthur* (1981), *Arthur 2: On the Rocks* (1988), *Rent-a-Cop* (1988), *Stepping Out* (1991).

Mirren, Helen (1945–) British born London; also stage; *Miss Julie* (1973), *Excalibur* (1981), *Cal* (1984), *2010* (1985), *Heavenly Pursuits* (1985), *White Nights* (1986), *Mosquito Coast* (1986), *Pascali's Island* (1988), *The Cook, The Thief, His Wife and Her Lover* (1989), *The Comfort of Strangers* (1990), *Where Angels Fear To Tread* (1991).

Mitchum, Robert (1917–) American born Bridgeport, Connecticut; *The Story of G.I. Joe* (1945), *Pursued* (1947), *Crossfire* (1947), *Out of the Past* (1947), *The Big Steal* (1949), *Night of the Hunter* (1955), *Home from the Hill* (1960), *The Sundowners* (1960), *Cape Fear* (1962), *The List of Adrian Messanger* (1963), *Ryan's Daughter* (1971), *Farewell My Lovely* (1975), *The Big Sleep* (1978), *The Winds of War* (TV 1983), *War and Remembrance* (TV 1987), *Mr. North* (1988), *Scrooged* (1988), *Cape Fear* (1991).

Modine, Matthew (1959–) American born Utah; *Private School* (1983), *Birdy* (1984), *Mrs Soffel* (1984), *Vision Quest* (1985), *Full Metal Jacket* (1988), *Streamers* (1983), *Married to the Mob* (1989), *Memphis Belle* (1990), *Pacific Heights* (1990).

Monroe, Marilyn (Norma Jean Mortenson or Baker) (1926–62) American born Los Angeles; *How to Marry a Millionaire* (1953), *Gentlemen Prefer Blondes* (1953), *The Seven Year Itch* (1955), *Bus Stop* (1956), *Some Like It Hot* (1959), *The Misfits* (1960).

Montand, Yves (Ivo Levi) (1921–91) French born Monsumagno, Italy; *The Wages of Fear* (1953), *Let's Make Love* (1962), *Jean de Florette* (1986), *Manon des Sources* (1986).

Moore, Demi (Demi Guines) (1962–) American born Roswell, New Mexico; *St Elmo's Fire* (1986), *About Last Night* (1987), *The Seventh Sign* (1988), *We're No Angels* (1990), *Ghost* (1990), *The Butcher's Wife* (1991).

Moore, Dudley (1935–) British born Dagenham, Essex; *Bedazzled* (1967), *Foul Play* (1978), *'10'* (1979), *Arthur* (1981), *Lovesick* (1983), *Unfaithfully Yours* (1983), *Micki and Maude* (1984), *Best Defense* (1985), *Santa Claus* (1985), *Arthur 2: On the Rocks* (1988), *Like Father, Like Son* (1989), *Crazy People* (1990).

Moore, Roger (George) (1927–) British born London; *Ivanhoe* (TV 1957), *The Saint* (TV 1963-8), *The Persuaders* (TV 1971-2), *Live and Let Die* (1973), *The Man With the Golden Gun* (1974), *Shout at the Devil* (1976), *The Spy Who Loved Me* (1977), *The Wild Geese* (1978), *Escape to Athena* (1979), *Moonraker* (1979), *For Your Eyes Only* (1981), *The Cannonball Run* (1981), *Octopussy* (1983), *A View to a Kill* (1985).

Moorehead, Agnes (1906–74) American born Chinton, Massachusetts; *Citizen Kane* (1941), *The Magnificent Ambersons* (1942), *Jane Eyre* (1943), *The Lost Moment* (1947), *The Woman in White* (1948), *Johnny Belinda* (1948), *Summer Holiday* (1948), *The Bat* (1959), *How the West was Won* (1963), *Bewitched* (TV 1964–71).

Moranis, Rick (1954–) Canadian born Toronto, Ontario; *Strange Brew* (1982), *Ghostbusters* (1984), *Brewster's Millions, Little Shop of Horrors* (1986), *Space Balls* (1987), *Ghostbusters II* (1989), *Parenthood* (1989), *Honey, I Shrunk the Kids* (1990), *My Blue Heaven* (1990).

Moreau, Jeanne (1928–) French born Paris; *Les Amants* (1958), *Ascenseur Pour L'Echafaud* (1957), *Jules et Jim* (1961), *Eva* (1962), *The Trial* (1963), *Journal D'une Femme de Chambre* (1964), *Viva Maria* (1965), *Nikita* (1990).

FILM AND TV ACTORS (cont.)

Morgan, Frank (Francis Phillip Wupperman) (1890-1949) American born New York City; *Hallelujah I'm a Bum* (1933), *Bombshell* (1933), *The Affairs of Cellini* (1934), *The Great Ziegfeld* (1936), *Trouble for Two* (1936), *Piccadilly Jim* (1936), *Dimples* (1936), *The Last of Mr Cheyney* (1937), *The Wizard of Oz* (1939), *Boom Town* (1940), *The Vanishing Virginian* (1942), *Tortilla Flat* (1942), *The Human Comedy* (1943), *The Three Musketeers* (1948).

Morgan, Harry (Harry Bratsburg) (1915–) American born Detroit, Michigan; *High Noon* (1952), *December Bride* (TV 1954–8), *The Teahouse of the August Moon* (1956), *Dragnet* (TV 1969), *M*A*S*H* (TV 1976-83), *Aftermash* (TV 1983), *Dragnet* (TV 1987).

Murphy, Eddie (1961–) American born Brooklyn, New York; *48 Hours* (1982), *Trading Places* (1983), *Beverly Hills Cop* (1985), *The Golden Child* (1986), *Beverly Hills Cop II* (1987), *Coming to America* (1988), *Harlem Nights* (1989), *Another 48 Hours* (1990), *Boomerang* (1992), *Distinguished Gentleman* (1992).

Murray, Bill (1950–) American born Evanston, Illinois; *Meatballs* (1977), *Caddyshack* (1980), *Stripes* (1981), *Tootsie* (1982), *Ghostbusters* (1984), *Razor's Edge* (1984), *Little Shop of Horrors* (1986), *Scrooged* (1988), *Ghostbusters II* (1989), *What About Bob?* (1991).

Neal, Patricia (1926–) American born Packard, Kentucky; *The Fountainhead* (1949), *The Hasty Heart* (1950), *Diplomatic Courier* (1952), *Breakfast at Tiffany's* (1961), *Hud* (1963), *A Face in the Crowd* (1957), *All Quiet on the Western Front* (TV 1980).

Neeson, Liam (1952–) British born Ballymena, Northern Ireland; *Excalibur* (1981), *Suspect* (1987), *Satisfaction* (1988), *High Spirits* (1988), *The Good Mother* (1988), *The Dead Pool* (1988), *The Big Man* (1990), *Dark Man* (1990).

Neill, Sam (1948–) New Zealander; *The Final Conflict* (1982), *Reilly Ace of Spies* (TV 1983), *Robbery Under Arms* (TV 1985), *Plenty* (1985), *Kane and Abel* (TV 1988), *A Cry in the Dark* (1988), Evil Angels (1988), *The Hunt for Red October* (1990).

Newman, Paul (1925–) American born Cleveland, Ohio; *Somebody Up There Likes Me* (1956), *The Long Hot Summer* (1958), *The Hustler* (1961), *Hud* (1963), *The Prize* (1963), *Torn Curtain* (1966), *Cool Hand Luke* (1967), *Butch Cassidy and the Sundance Kid* (1969), *Judge Roy Bean* (1972), *The Sting* (1973), *Absence of Malice* (1981), *The Verdict* (1982), *The Color of Money* (1986), *Blaze* (1990), *Mr & Mrs Bridge* (1990).

Nicholson, Jack (1937–) American born Neptune, New Jersey; *The Little Shop of Horrors* (1960), *Easy Rider* (1969), *Five Easy Pieces* (1970), *Carnal Knowledge* (1971), *The Last Detail* (1974), *Chinatown* (1974), *One Flew Over the Cuckoo's Nest* (1975), *Tommy* (1975), *The Shining* (1980), *The Postman Always Rings Twice* (1981), *Reds* (1981), *Terms of Endearment* (1983), *Prizzi's Honour* (1985), *Broadcast News* (1987), *Ironweed* (1987), *The Witches of Eastwick* (1987), *Batman* (1989), *Two Jakes* (1990), *The Death of Napoleon* (1991), *Man Trouble* (1992), *A Few Good Men* (1992), *Hoffa* (1992).

Nielsen, Leslie (1926–) Canadian born Regina, Saskatchewan; *Forbidden Planet* (1956), *Incident in San Francisco* (TV 1970), *The Poseidon Adventure* (1972), *Airplane* (1980), *Prom Night* (1980), *Police Squad* (TV 1982), *Soul Man* (TV 1986), *The Patriot* (TV 1987), *Fatal Confession* (TV 1987), *The Naked Gun* (1988), *Repossessed* (1990), *Naked Gun $2\frac{1}{2}$: the Smell of Fear* (1991).

Nimoy, Leonard (1931–) American born Boston, Massachusetts; *Star Trek* (TV 1966-8), *Mission Impossible* (TV 1970-2), *Invasion of the Body Snatchers* (1978), *Star Trek: The Motion Picture* (1979), *Star Trek 2: The Wrath of Khan* (1982), *Star Trek 3: The Search for Spock* (1984), *Star Trek 4: The Voyage Home* (1986), *Star Trek V: The Final Frontier* (1989).

Niven, David (James David Graham Niven) (1910-83) British born London; *Thank You Jeeves* (1936), *The Prisoner of Zenda* (1937), *Wuthering Heights* (1939), *Bachelor Mother* (1939), *Raffles* (1940), *The Way Ahead* (1944), *A Matter of Life and Death* (1946), *Carrington V.C.* (1955), *Around the World in Eighty Days* (1956), *Separate Tables* (1958), *The Guns of Navarone* (1961), *The Pink Panter* (1964), *Casino Royale* (1967), *Candleshoe* (1977), *Death on the Nile* (1978), *Escape to Athena* (1979), *Trail of the Pink Panther* (1982), *Curse of the Pink Panther* (1982).

Nolte, Nick (1940–) American born Omaha, Nebraska; *Rich Man Poor Man* (TV 1976), *Cannery Row*

FILM AND TV ACTORS (cont.)

(1982), *48 Hours* (1982), *Down and Out in Beverly Hills* (1986), *Weeds* (1987), *New York Stories* (1989), *Three Fugitives* (1989), *Another 48 Hours* (1990), *Cape Fear* (1991), *Prince of Tides* (1991), *The Player* (1992), *Lorenzo's Oil* (1992).

Novak, Kim (Marilyn Pauline Novak) (1933–) American born Chicago; *Vertigo* (1958), *Of Human Bondage* (1964), *Kiss Me Stupid* (1964), *The Amorous Adventures of Molly Flanders* (1965).

Oldman, Gary (1959–) British born New Gross, S London; *Sid and Nancy* (1986), *Prick Up Your Ears* (1987), *We Think the World of You* (1988), *Track 29* (1988).

Oberon, Merle (Estelle Merle O'Brien Thompson) (1911–79) British/Indian born Bombay, India; *The Dark Angel* (1935), *The Scarlet Pimpernel* (1935), *The Divorce of Lady X* (1938), *Wuthering Heights* (1939), *That Uncertain Feeling* (1941), *Forever and a Day* (1943), *A Song to Remember* (1943), *The Oscar* (1966), *Hotel* (1967), *Interval* (1973).

Olivier, Sir Laurence (Kerr) (1907–89) British born Dorking; also stage; *The Divorce of Lady X* (1938), *Wuthering Heights* (1939), *Rebecca* (1940), *Pride and Prejudice* (1940), *Henry V* (1944), *Hamlet* (1948), *Richard III* (1956), *The Prince and the Showgirl* (1958), *The Devil's Disciple* (1959), *The Entertainer* (1960), *Sleuth* (1972), *Marathon Man* (1976), *A Bridge Too Far* (1977), *Brideshead Revisited* (TV 1981), *A Voyage Round My Father* (TV 1982).

O'Neal, Ryan (Patrick Ryan O'Neal) (1941–) American born Los Angeles; *Peyton Place* (TV 1964–8), *Love Story* (1970), *What's Up, Doc?* (1972), *Paper Moon* (1973), *Nickelodeon* (1976), *A Bridge Too Far* (1977), *Green Ice* (1980).

O'Neal, Tatum (1963–) American born Los Angeles; *Paper Moon* (1973), *Nickelodeon* (1976), *International Velvet* (1978), *Little Darlings* (1980).

O'Sullivan, Maureen (1911–) Irish born Boyle; *Tarzan the Ape Man* (1932), *Tarzan and His Mate* (1934) etc, *The Barretts of Wimpole Street* (1934), *Pride and Prejudice* (1940), *Never Too Late* (1965), *Hannah and Her Sisters* (1986), *Peggy Sue Got Married* (1986).

O'Toole, Peter (Seamus) (1932–) Irish born Kerry, Connemara; *Lawrence of Arabia* (1962), *How to Steal a Million* (1966), *The Lion in Winter* (1968), *Goodbye Mr Chips* (1969), *The Ruling Class* (1972), *The Stunt Man* (1980), *My Favourite Year* (1982), *The Last Emperor* (1987), *High Spirits* (1988), *Wings of Fame* (1989), *Isabelle Eberhardt* (1990), *King Ralph* (1991).

Pacino, Al (Alfredo Pacino) (1940–) American born New York City; *The Godfather* (1972), (*part II* – 1974, *part III* – 1990), *Dog Day Afternoon* (1975), *Scarface* (1983), *Revolution* (1984), *Sea of Love* (1990), *Dick Tracy* (1990), *Frankie and Johnny in the Claire De Lune* (1991), *Glengarry Glen Ross* (1992), *Scent Of A Woman* (1992), *Damon* (1992).

Page, Geraldine (1924–) American born Kirksville, Missouri; *Summer and Smoke* (1961), *Sweet Bird of Youth* (1962), *Dear Heart* (1965), *The Happiest Millionaire* (1966), *Interiors* (1978), *Harry's War* (1980), *Honky Tonk Freeway* (1981), *The Pope of Greenwich Village* (1984), *The Trip to Bountiful* (1985).

Palance, Jack (Walter Palanuik) (1920–) American born Lattimer, Pennsylvania; *Panic in the Streets* (1950), *Shane* (1953), *The Big Knife* (1953), *Arrowhead* (1953), *They Came to Rob Las Vegas* (1968), *Oklahoma Crude* (1973), *Hawk the Slayer* (1980), *Believe It or Not* (TV 1982–), *Gor* (1988), *Bagdad Cafe* (1988), *Batman* (1988).

Palin, Michael (1943–) British born Sheffield; *Monty Python's Flying Circus* (TV 1969–74), *And Now for Something Completely Different* (1970), *Monty Python and the Holy Grail* (1974), *Three Men in a Boat* (TV 1975), *Jabberwocky* (1976), *Ripping Yarns* (TV 1976–80), *The Life of Brian* (1978), *Time Bandits* (1980), *The Meaning of Life* (1982), *The Missionary* (1982), *A Private Function* (1984), *Brazil* (1985), *A Fish Called Wanda* (1988), *Around the World in 80 Days* (TV 1990), *American Friends* (1990).

Peck, Gregory (Eldred) (1916–) American born La Jolla, California; *The Keys to the Kingdom* (1944), *Spellbound* (1945), *Duel in the Sun* (1946), *Gentleman's Agreement* (1947), *The Macomber Affair* (1947), *The Paradine Case* (1947), *Twelve O'Clock High* (1949), *The Gunfighter* (1950), *Captain Horatio Hornblower* (1951), *The Million Pound Note* (1954), *The Purple Plain* (1955), *The Man in the Grey Flannel Suit* (1956), *The Big Country* (1958), *The Guns of Navarone* (1961), *Cape fear* (1962), *To Kill a Mockingbird* (1963), *The Omen* (1976), *Old Gringo* (1989), *Other People's Money* (1991), *Cape Fear* (1991).

FILM AND TV ACTORS (cont.)

Penn, Sean (1960–) American born Burbank, California; *Taps* (1981), *Fast Times At Ridgemont High* (1982), *Racing with the Moon* (1984), *The Falcon and the Snowman* (1985), *At Close Range* (1986), *Shanghai Surprise* (1986), *Colors* (1988), *Judgement in Berlin* (1988), *Casualties of War* (1989), *We're No Angels* (1989), *State of Grace* (1990).

Perkins, Anthony (1932–) American born New York City; *The Actress* (1953), *Desire Under the Elms* (1957), *Fear Strikes Out* (1957), *This Angry Age* (1958), *Psycho* (1960), *Five Miles to Midnight* (1962), *Murder on the Orient Express* (1974), *For the Term of His Natural Life* (TV 1982), *Psycho II* (1983), *Crimes of Passion* (1985), *Psycho III* (1986), *Destroyer* (1988).

Pesci, Joe (1943–) American born Newark, New Jersey; *Raging Bull* (1980), *Lethal Weapon 2* (1989), *Goodfellas* (1990), *Home Alone* (1990), *My Cousin Vinny* (1992), *Lethal Weapon 3* (1992).

Pfeiffer, Michelle (1957–) American born Santa Ana, California; *Grease 2* (1982), *Scarface* (1983), *Sweet Liberty* (1982), *Into the Night* (1985), *Witches of Eastwick* (1987), *Dangerous Liaisons* (1988), *Tequila Sunrise* (1988), *Married to the Mob* (1989), *The Fabulous Baker Boys* (1989), *The Russia House* (1990), *Frankie and Johnny in the Claire De Lune* (1991), *Batman Returns* (1992), *Age of Innocence* (1992).

Philipe, Gérard (1922–59) French born Cannes; *The Idiot* (1946), *Le Diable au Corps* (1947), *Une Si Jolie Petite Plage* (1949), *Fanfan la Tulipe* (1951), *Les Belles de Nuit* (1952), *Knave of Hearts* (1954), *Montparnasse* (1957), *Les Liaisons Dangereuses* (1959).

Phoenix, River (1970–) American born Madras, Oregon; *Explorers* (1985), *Mosquito Coast* (1986), *Running on Empty* (1988), *Jimmy Reardon* (1988), *Little Nikita* (1988), *Indiana Jones and the Last Crusade* (1989), *I Love You to Death* (1990), *Dogfight* (1991), *My Own Private Idaho* (1991), *Speakers* (1992).

Pickford, Mary (Gladys Mary Smith) (1893-1979) Canadian born Toronto, Ontario; *The Violin Maker of Cremona* (1909), *Rebecca of Sunnybrook Farm* (1917), *Poor Little Rich Girl* (1917), *Pollyanna* (1919), *Little Lord Fauntleroy* (1921), *Tess of the Storm Country* (1922), *The Taming of the Shrew* (1929), *Coquette* (1929), *Secrets* (1933).

Pickup, Ronald (Alfred) (1940–) British born Chester; *Day of the Jackal* (1973), *The 39 Steps* (1978), *Nijinski* (1980), *Never Say Never Again* (1983), *Fortunes of War* (TV 1987), *Testimony* (1987).

Pleasence, Donald (1919–) British born Worksop; *Robin Hood* (TV 1955–7), *Battle of the Sexes* (1959), *Dr Crippen* (1962), *The Great Escape* (1963), *The Caretaker* (1964), *Cul-de-Sac* (1966), *Fantastic Voyage* (1966), *You Only Live Twice* (1967), *Escape to Witch Mountain* (1975), *The Eagle Has Landed* (1977), *Oh! God* (1977), *Telefon* (1977), *Halloween* (1978), *Sgt. Peppers Lonely Hearts Club Band* (1979), *Escape from New York* (1981), *Halloween 4* (1988), *Hanna's War* (1988), *Ground Zero* (1988).

Plowright, Joan (1929–) British born Scunthorpe, Brigg, Lincolnshire; also stage; *The Entertainer* (1960), *Drowning by Numbers* (1988), *Love You to Death* (1990).

Plummer, Christopher (1927–) Canadian born Toronto, Ontario; *The Fall of the Roman Empire* (1964), *The Sound of Music* (1965), *Waterloo* (1970), *The Man Who Would Be King* (1975), *The Return of the Pink Panther* (1975), *International Velvet* (1978), *Hanover Street* (1979), *Somewhere in Time* (1980), *The Janitor* (1981), *Dreamscape* (1984), *Where the Heart Is* (1990).

Poitier, Sidney (1924–) American born Miami, Florida; *No Way Out* (1950), *Cry, the Beloved Country* (1952), *The Blackboard Jungle* (1955), *The Defiant Ones* (1958), *Porgy and Bess* (1959), *Lilies of the Field* (1963), *To Sir with Love* (1967), *In the Heat of the Night* (1967), *Guess Who's Coming to Dinner* (1967), *Little Nikita* (1988), *Shoot to Kill* (1988), *Separate But Equal* (TV 1991), *Sneakers* (1992).

Powell, Robert (1944–) British born Salford, Lancashire; *The Italian Job* (1969), *Jesus of Nazareth* (TV 1977), *The 39 Steps* (1978), *Pygmalion* (TV 1981), *Frankenstein* (TV 1984), *Hannay* (TV 1988).

Powers, Stefanie (Stefania Federkiewicz) (1942–) American born Hollywood, California; *Experiment in Terror* (1962), *Fanatic* (1964), *Stagecoach* (1966), *The Girl from UNCLE* (1966), *Herbie Rides Again (1973), Escape to Athena* (1979), *Hart to Hart* (1979-83), *Family Secrets* (TV 1984) .

Presley, Elvis (Aaron) (1935–77) American born Tupelo, Mississippi; *Love Me Tender* (1956), *Jailhouse Rock* (1957), *Loving You* (1957), *King Creole* (1958), *G.I. Blues* (1960), *Girl Happy* (1965), *That's the Way It Is* (1971).

FILM AND TV ACTORS (cont.)

Price, Vincent (1911–) American born St Louis, Missouri; *Tower of London* (1940), *Dragonwyck* (1946), *His Kind of Woman* (1941), *House of Wax* (1953), *The Story of Mankind* (1957), *The Fly* (1958), *The Fall of the House of Usher* (1961), *The Raven* (1963), *The Tomb of Ligeia* (1964), *City Under the Sea* (1965), *House of a Thousand Dolls* (1967), *The House of Long Shadows* (1983), *The Whales of August* (1987), *Dead Heat* (1988), *Edward Scissorhands* (1991).

Quaid, Dennis (1954–) American born Houston, Texas; *Breaking Away* (1978), *Caveman* (1980), *The Night the Lights Went Out in Georgia* (1980), *Bill* (TV 1981), *All Night Long* (1981), *Johnny Belinda* (TV 1982), *The Right Stuff* (1983), *Jaws 3D* (1983), *Dreamscape* (1984), *The Big Easy* (1986), *Innerspace* (1987), *Suspect* (1987), *D.O.A.* (1988), *Great Balls of Fire* (1989), *Come See the Paradise* (1990), *Postcards from the Edge* (1990), *Wilder Napalm* (1992).

Quaid, Randy (1950–) American born Houston, Texas; *The Last Picture Show* (1971), *What's Up Doc?* (1972), *Paper Moon* (1973), *Midnight Express* (1978), *Vacation* (1983), *Parents* (1988), *Caddyshack II* (1988), *Christmas Vacation* (1989), *Days of Thunder* (1990), *Texasville* (1990).

Quayle, Sir Anthony (1913–89) British born Ainsdale, Lancashire; *Ice Cold in Alex* (1958), *The Guns of Navarone* (1961), *Lawrence of Arabia* (1962).

Quick, Diana (1946–) British born Kent; *Nicholas and Alexandra* (1971), *The Big Sleep* (1981), *Brideshead Revisited* (TV 1981), *Ordeal by Innocence* (1985), *Wilt* (1989).

Quinn, Anthony Rudolph Oaxaca (1915–) Irish/American born Chihuahua, Mexico; *Viva Zapata* (1952), *La Strada* (1954), *Lust for Life* (1956), *The Guns of Navarone* (1961), *Zorba the Greek* (1964), *The Shoes of the Fisherman* (1968), *Revenge* (1989), *Ghosts Can't Do It* (1990).

Rampling, Charlotte (1946–) British born Sturmer; *Georgy Girl* (1966), *The Damned* (1969), *Zardoz* (1973), *Orca* (1977), *Stardust Memories* (1980), *The Verdict* (1982), *Max mon Amour* (1986), *Angel Heart* (1987), *Paris by Night* (1988), *D.O.A.* (1988).

Randall, Tony (Leonard Rosenberg) (1920–) American born Tulsa, Oklahoma; *Mr Peepers* (TV 1952–5), *Seven Faces of Dr Lau* (1956), *Pillow Talk* (1959), *Send Me No Flowers* (1964), *The Odd Couple* (TV 1970–4), *Everything You Always Wanted to Know About Sex* (1972).

Rathbone, Basil (Philip St John) (1892–1967) British born Johannesburg, South Africa; *David Copperfield* (1935), *Anna Karenina* (1935), *Captain Blood* (1935), *Romeo and Juliet* (1936), *The Adventures of Robin Hood* (1938), *The Hound of the Baskervilles* (1939), *The Adventures of Sherlock Holmes* (1939) etc, *Spider Woman* (1944), *Heartbeat* (1946), *The Court Jester* (1956).

Reagan, Ronald (Wilson) (1911–) American born Tampico, Illinois; *King's Row* (1941), *Desperate Journey* (1942), *The Hasty Heart* (1949), *Bedtime for Bonzo* (1951), *The Killer* (1964).

Redford, (Charles) Robert (1937–) American born Santa Monica, California; *Barefoot in the Park* (1967), *Butch Cassidy and the Sundance Kid* (1969), *The Candidate* (1972), *The Great Gatsby* (1973), *The Sting* (1973), *The Way We Were* (1973), *All the President's Men* (1976), *The Electric Horseman* (1979), *The Natural* (1984), *Out of Africa* (1985), *Legal Eagles* (1986), *Havana* (1990), *Sneakers* (1992).

Redgrave, Lynn (1943–) British born London; *Tom Jones* (1963), *Georgy Girl* (1966), *Girl With Green Eyes* (1964), *Everything You Always Wanted to Know About Sex* (1972), *The Happy Hooker* (1976), *House Calls* (TV 1980–1).

Redgrave, Sir Michael (Scudamore) (1908–85) British born Bristol; also stage; *The Lady Vanishes* (1938), *The Way to the Stars* (1945), *The Browning Version* (1951), *The Importance of Being Earnest* (1952), *The Dam Busters* (1955), *The Quiet American* (1958), *The Innocents* (1961), *Nicholas and Alexandra* (1971).

Redgrave, Vanessa (1937–) British born London; also stage; *Morgan!* (1965), *Blow-Up* (1966), *Camelot* (1967), *Mary, Queen of Scots* (1971), *Julia* (1977), *Playing for Time* (TV 1980), *The Bostonians* (1984), *Wetherby* (1985), *Three Sovereigns for Sarah* (TV 1985). *Prick Up Your Ears* (1987), *Consuming Passions* (1988), *The Ballad of The Sad Café* (1991), *What Ever Happened To Baby Jane!* (1991), *Howard's End* (1992).

Reed, Oliver (Robert Oliver Reed) (1938–) British born Wimbledon, London; *The Damned* (1962), *The System* (1964), *The Jokers* (1966), *Women in Love* (1969), *The Brood* (1980), *Condorman* (1981), *Castaway* (1987), *Gor* (1988), *Return of the Musketeers* (1989).

FILM AND TV ACTORS (cont.)

Reeve, Christopher (1952–) American born New York City; *Superman* (1978), (*part II* – 1980, *III* – 1983, *IV* – 1987), *Somewhere in Time* (1980), *Monsignor* (1982), *Death Trap* (1982), *The Bostonians* (1984), *Switching Channels* (1988).

Reeves, Keanu (1965–) American; *River's Edge* (1986), *Prince of Pennsylvania* (1988), *The Night Before* (1988), *Dangerous Liaisons* (1988), *Permanent Record* (1988), *Bill and Ted's Excellent Adventures* (1989), *Parenthood* (1989), *Love You to Death* (1990), *Bill and Ted's Bogus Journey* (1991), *My Own Private Idaho* (1991), *Dracula* (1992).

Reinhold, Judge (Edward Ernest Reinhold Jr) (1956–) American born Wilmington, Delaware; *Stripes* (1981), *Fast Times at Ridgemont High* (1982), *Beverly Hills Cop* (1984), *Gremlins* (1984), *Ruthless People* (1986), *Beverly Hills Cop II* (1987), *Vice-Versa* (1988), *Rosalie Goes Shopping* (1989).

Remick, Lee (1935–91) American born Quincy, Massachusetts; *Anatomy of a Murder* (1959), *Experiment in Terror* (1962), *Days of Wine and Roses* (1963), *No Way to Treat a Lady* (1968), *Jennie* (TV 1975), *The Omen* (1976), *The Medusa Touch* (1977), *Mistral's Daughter* (TV 1984).

Reynolds, Burt (1935–) American born Waycross, Georgia; *Gunsmoke* (TV 1965–7), *Hunters Are for Killing* (TV 1970), *Deliverance* (1972), *Nickelodeon* (1976), *Smokey and the Bandit* (1977), *Hooper* (1978), *Starting Over* (1979), *Smokey and the Bandit II* (1980), *The Cannonball Run* (1981), *Sharkey's Machine* (1981), *The Best Little Whorehouse in Texas* (1982), *Stroker Ace* (1983), *The Man Who Loved Women* (1983), *City Heat* (1984), *Rent-a-Cop* (1988), *Switching Channels* (1988), *Breaking In* (1989), *Evening Shade* (TV 1991–).

Richardson, Miranda (1958–) British born Liverpool; *Dance with a Stranger* (1984), *The Innocent* (1985), *Blackadder II* (TV 1986), *Empire of the Sun* (1987), *A Month in the Country* (1988), *Die Kinder* (TV 1990).

Richardson, Sir Ralph (1902–83) British born Cheltenham; also stage; *Bulldog Jack* (1935), *Q Planes* (1939), *The Four Feathers* (1939), *Anna Karenina* (1948), *The Fallen Idol* (1948), *The Heiress* (1949), *Richard III* (1956), *Oscar Wilde* (1960), *Long Day's Journey into Night* (1962), *Dr Zhivago* (1966), *The Wrong Box* (1967), *A Doll's House* (1973), *The Man in the Iron Mask* (1977), *Time Bandits* (1980), *Dragonslayer* (1981), *Greystoke* (1984).

Rigg, Diana (1938–) British born Doncaster, Yorkshire; *The Avengers* (TV 1965-7), *On Her Majesty's Secret Service* (1969), *Theatre of Blood* (1973), *Evil Under the Sun* (1981), *Mother Love* (TV 1989).

Ringwald, Molly (1968–) American born Rosewood, California; *The Facts of Live* (TV), *The Tempest* (1982), *Space Hunter 3D: Adventures in the Forbidden Zone* (1983), *Packin' It In* (TV 1983), *Sixteen Candles* (1984), *The Breakfast Club* (1985), *Pretty in Pink* (1986), *Maybe Baby* (1987), *The Pick-up Artist* (1987), *Fresh Horses* (1988), *For Keeps?* (1988), *Loser Takes All* (1989), *Betsy's Wedding* (1990).

Robards, Jason (Jnr) (1922–) American born Chicago, Illinois; *Tender is the Night* (1961), *Long Day's Journey into Night* (1962), *The Hour of the Gun* (1967), *Once Upon a Time in the West* (1969), *Tora! Tora! Tora!* (1970), *All the President's Men* (1976), *Julia* (1977), *Melvin and Howard* (1980), *The Legend of the Lone Ranger* (1981), *The Day After* (TV 1983), *Sakharov* (TV 1984), *The Long Hot Summer* (TV 1985), *Bright Lights, Big City* (1988), *The Good Mother* (1988), *Parenthood* (1989), *Reunion* (1989).

Robbins, Tim (1958–) American born New York City; *Bull Durham* (1988), *Cadillac Man* (1990), *Jacob's Ladder* (1990), *Mo'Betta Blues* (1990), *The Player* (1992), *Bob Roberts* (1992).

Roberts, Eric (1956–) American born Biloxi, Missouri; *King of the Gypsies* (1978), *The Pope of Greenwich Village* (1984), *The Coca Cola Kid* (1985), *Runaway Train* (1985), *Nobody's Fool* (1986), *Best of the Best* (1989), *Blood Red* (1990).

Roberts, Julia (1967–) American born Smyrna, Georgia; *Satisfaction* (1988), *Mystic Pizza* (1988), *Steel Magnolias* (1989), *Pretty Woman* (1990), *Flatliners* (1990), *Sleeping with the Enemy* (1991), *Dying Young* (1991), *Hook* (1991), *The Player* (1992).

Robertson, Cliff (Clifford Parker Robertson III) (1925–) American born La Jolla, California; *Picnic* (1955), *The Girl Most Likely* (1957), *PT 109* (1963), *The Best Man* (1964), *The Honey Pot* (1967), *Charly* (1968), *Washington Behind Closed Doors* (TV 1977), *Class* (1983), *Brainstorm* (1983).

FILM AND TV ACTORS (cont.)

Robinson, Edward G (Emanuel Goldenberg) (1893–1973) American born Bucharest, Romania; *Little Caesar* (1930), *Five Star Final* (1931), *The Whole Town's Talking* (1935), *The Last Gangster* (1937), *A Slight Case of Murder* (1938), *The Amazing Dr Clitterhouse* (1938), *Dr Ehrlich's Magic Bullet* (1940), *Brother Orchid* (1940), *The Sea Wolf* (1941), *Double Indemnity* (1944), *The Woman in the Window* (1944), *Scarlet Street* (1945), *All My Sons* (1948), *Key Largo* (1948), *House of Strangers* (1949), *Two Weeks in Another Town* (1962), *The Cincinnati Kid* (1965), *Soylent Green* (1973).

Rogers, Ginger (Virginia Katherine McMath) (1911–) American born Independence, Missouri; *Young Man of Manhattan* (1930), *42nd Street* (1933), *Flying Down to Rio* (1933), *The Gay Divorcee* (1934), *Top Hat* (1935), *Follow the Fleet* (1936), *Stage Door* (1937), *Bachelor Mother* (1939), *Kitty Foyle* (1940), *Roxie Hart* (1942), *Lady in the Dark* (1944).

Rogers, Will (William Penn Adair) (1879–1935) American born Colagah, Indian Territory (now Oklahoma); *Jubilo* (1919), *State Fair* (1933), *Judge Priest* (1934), *David Harum* (1934), *Handy Andy* (1934), *Life Begins at Forty* (1935), *Steamboat round the Bend* (1935).

Rooney, Mickey (Joe Yule Jr) (1920–) American born Brooklyn, New York; *A Midsummer Night's Dream* (1935), *Ah Wilderness* (1935), *A Family Affair* (1937), *Judge Hardy's Children* (1938), *Boys' Town* (1938), *Babes in Arms* (1939), *The Human Comedy* (1943), *National Velvet* (1944), *Summer Holiday* (1948), *The Bold and the Brave* (1956), *Breakfast at Tiffany's* (1961), *It's a Mad, Mad, Mad, Mad World* (1963), *Leave 'Em Laughing* (TV 1980), *Bill* (TV 1981), *Erik the Viking* (1989), *Home for Christmas* (TV 1990).

Rossellini, Isabella (1952–) Italian born Rome; *White Nights* (1985), *Blue Velvet* (1986), *Siesta* (1987), *Zelly and Me* (1988), *Cousins* (1989), *Wild at Heart* (1990).

Rourke, Mickey (1956–) American born Schenectady, New York; *Body Heat* (1981), *Rumble Fish* (1983), *9½ Weeks* (1985), *The Year of the Dragon* (1985), *Angel Heart* (1987), *A Prayer for the Dying* (1987), *Johnny Handsome* (1990), *Wild Orchid* (1990), *Harley Davidson and the Marlboro Man* (1991), *Desperate Hours* (1991).

Rowlands, Gena (Virginia) (1934–) American born Cambria, Wisconsin, *The High Cost of Loving* (1958), *Lonely Are The Brave* (1962), *A Woman Under The Influence* (1972), *Thursday's Child* (TV 1983), *A Night on Earth* (1991).

Russell, Jane (1921–) American born Bemidji, Minnesota; *The Outlaw* (1943), *The Paleface* (1948), *Gentleman Prefer Blondes* (1953).

Russell, Kurt (1951–) American born Springfield, Massachusetts; *The Quest* (TV 1976), *Elvis* (TV 1979), *Escape from New York* (1981), *The Thing* (1982), *Silkwood* (1983), *Swing Shift* (1984), *Big Trouble in Little China* (1986), *Tequila Sunrise* (1988), *Tango and Cash* (1990), *Backdraft* (1991).

Rutherford, Dame Margaret (1892–1972) British born London; also stage; *Blithe Spirit* (1945), *The Happiest Days of Your Life* (1950), *The Importance of Being Earnest* (1952), *The Smallest Show on Earth* (1957), *Murder She Said* (1961), *The V.I.P.s* (1963), *Murder Most Foul* (1964), *Murder Ahoy* (1964).

Ryan, Meg (1962–) American born Fairfield, Connecticut; *Rich and Famous* (1981), *Top Gun* (1985), *Innerspace* (1987), *D.O.A.* (1988), *Promised Land* (1988), *The Presidio* (1988), *When Harry Met Sally ...* (1989), *Joe Versus the Volcano* (1990), *The Doors* (1991).

Ryan, Robert (1909–73) American born Chicago; *Gangway for Tomorrow* (1943), *Crossfire* (1947), *The Set-Up* (1949), *Clash by Night* (1952), *God's Little Acre* (1958), *Odds Against Tomorrow* (1959), *Billy Budd* (1962), *The Dirty Dozen* (1967), *The Wild Bunch* (1969).

Ryder, Winona (1971–) American born Winona, Michigan; *Beetlejuice* (1988), *1969* (1988), *Heathers* (1989), *Great Balls of Fire* (1989), *Mermaids* (1990).

Sabu (Sabu Dastagir) (1924–63) Indian born Karapur, Mysore, India; *Elephant Boy* (1937), *The Thief of Baghdad* (1940), *The Jungle Book* (1942), *The End of the River* (1947), *Black Narcissus* (1947).

Saint, Eva Marie (1924–) American born Newark, New Jersey; *On the Waterfront* (1954), *A Hatful of Rain* (1957), *North by Northwest* (1959), *Loving* (1970), *The Best Little Girl in the World* (TV 1982), *Fatal Vision* (TV 1984), *The Last Days of Patton* (TV 1986), *Moonlighting* (TV 1987).

FILM AND TV ACTORS (cont.)

Sanders, George (1906–73) British born St Petersburg, Russia; *Lancer Spy* (1937), *Rebecca* (1940), *The Saint* (1940–2), *The Moon and Sixpence* (1942), *The Picture of Dorian Gray* (1944), *Scandal in Paris* (1946), *The Ghost and Mrs Muir* (1947), *Forever Amber* (1947), *The Private Affairs of Bel Ami* (1947), *Lady Windermere's Fan* (1949), *All About Eve* (1950), *Village of the Damned* (1960), *A Shot in the Dark* (1964).

Sands, Julian (1958–) British born Yorkshire; *Oxford Blues* (1982), *The Killing Fields* (1984), *A Room with a View* (1985), *Gothic* (1987), *Siesta* (1987), *Vibes* (1988), *Warlock* (1989), *Arachnaphobia* (1990).

Sara, Mia (1968–) American born Brooklyn, New York; *Legend* (1985), *Ferris Bueller's Day Off* (1986), *Queenie* (TV 1988), *Apprentice to Murder* (1988).

Sarandon, Chris (1942–) American born Beckley, West Virginia; *Dog Day Afternoon* (1975), *Fright Night* (1985), *The Princess Bride* (1988), *Child's Play* (1988).

Sarandon, Susan (Susan Abigail Tomalin) (1946–) American born New York City; *The Front Page* (1974), *Dragonfly* (1977), *Atlantic City* (1981), *Tempest* (1982), *The Hunger* (1983), *The Witches of Eastwick* (1987), *Bull Durham* (1988), *A Dry White Season* (1989), *White Palace* (1991), *Thelma and Louise* (1991), *Light Sleeper* (1991), *Lorenzo's Oil* (1992).

Savalas, Telly (Aristotle Savalas) (1925–) Greek/American born Garden City, New York; *Birdman of Alcatraz* (1982), *The Battle of the Bulge* (1985), *The Dirty Dozen* (1967), *On Her Majesty's Secret Service* (1969), *Horror Express* (1972), *Visions of Death* (1972), *Kojak* (TV 1973–7), *Escape to Athena* (1979), *Kojak* (TV 1989–).

Scheider, Roy (1932–) American born Orange, New Jersey; *Paper Lion* (1968), *French Connection* (1971), *Jaws* (1975), *Jaws 2* (1978), *All That Jazz* (1979), *Blue Thunder* (1982), *Still of the Night* (1982), *2010* (1984), *52 Pick Up* (1986), *Night Game* (1989).

Schwarzenegger, Arnold (1947–) American born Braz, Austria; *Stay Hungry* (1976), *Pumping Iron* (1977), *Conan the Barbarian* (1982), *Conan the Destroyer* (1984), *The Terminator* (1984), *Red Sonja* (1985), *Commando* (1985), *Raw Deal* (1986), *Predator* (1987), *The Running Man* (1987), *Red Heat* (1989), *Total Recall* (1990), *Kindergarten Cop* (1990), *T2 – Terminator 2: Judgment Day* (1991).

Scofield, (David) Paul (1922–) British born Hurstpierpoint, Sussex; also stage; *That Lady* (1955), *A Man for All Seasons* (1966), *Hamlet* (1990).

Scott, George C (1927–) American born Wise, Virginia; *Anatomy of a Murder* (1959), *The Hustler* (1962), *The List of Adrian Messenger* (1963), *Dr Strangelove* (1963), *Patton* (1970), *The Hospital* (1972), *Fear on Trial* (TV 1976), *The Changeling* (1980), *Taps* (1981), *Oliver Twist* (1982), *Firestarter* (1984), *A Christmas Carol* (TV 1984), *The Last Days of Patton* (TV 1986), *The Exorcist III* (1990).

Segal, George (1934–) American born New York City; *King Rat* (1965), *Who's Afraid of Virginia Woolf?* (1966), *The Owl and the Pussycat* (1970), *The Last Married Couple in America* (1980), *Look Who's Talking* (1989).

Selleck, Tom (1945–) American born Detroit, Michigan; *Coma* (1977), *Magnum* (TV 1981–9), *High Road to China* (1983), *Lassiter* (1984), *Runaway* (1984), *Three Men and a Baby* (1988), *Three Men and a Little Lady* (1990), *Tokyo Diamond* (1991).

Sellers, Peter (1925-80) British born Southsea; *The Smallest Show on Earth* (1957), *The Ladykillers* (1959), *I'm Alright Jack* (1959), *Only Two Can Play* (1962), *Lolita* (1962), *Dr Strangelove* (1963), *The Pink Panther* (1963), *A Shot in the Dark* (1964), *Return of the Pink Panther* (1975), *The Pink Panther Strikes Again* (1976), *Revenge of the Pink Panther* (1978), *Being There* (1979).

Seymour, Jane (Joyce Frankenberg) (1951–) British born Hillingdon, Middlesex; *Live and Let Die* (1972), *Battle Star Galactica* (TV 1978), *East of Eden* (TV 1981), *Somewhere in Time* (1980), *The Scarlet Pimpernel* (TV 1982), *War and Remembrance* (TV 1987–9), *Matters of the Heart* (1991), *Angel of Death* (1991).

Sharif, Omar (Michael Shalhouz) (1932–) Egyptian born Alexandria; *Lawrence of Arabia* (1962), *Doctor Zhivago* (1965), *Green Ice* (1980).

Shatner, William (1931–) Canadian born Montreal, Quebec; *Star Trek* (TV 1966–8), *Horror at 37,000 Feet* (TV 1974), *Big Bad Mama* (1974), *Star Trek: The Motion Picture* (1979), *The Kidnapping of the President* (1980), *Star Trek 2: The Wrath of Khan* (1982), *T. J. Hooker* (TV 1982–6), *Star Trek 3: The Search for Spock* (1984), *Star Trek 4: The Voyage Home* (1987), *Star Trek V: The Final Frontier* (1989).

FILM AND TV ACTORS (cont.)

Shearer, Moira (Moira King) (1926–) British born Dunfermline, Fife; *The Red Shoes* (1948), *Tales of Hoffman* (1950), *The Man Who Loved Redheads* (1954), *Peeping Tom* (1959), *Black Tights* (1961).

Sheedy, Ally (1962–) American born New York City; *Wargames* (1983), *The Breakfast Club* (1985), *St. Elmo's Fire* (1986), *Short Circuit* (1986), *Heart of Dixie* (1990), *Betsy's Wedding* (1990).

Sheen, Charlie (Carlos Irwin Estevez) (1965–) American born Santa Monica, California; *Ferris Bueller's Day Off* (1986), *Wall Street* (1987), *Platoon* (1987), *Eight Men Out* (1988), *Major League* (1989), *The Rookie* (1990), *Catchfire* (1990), *Navy Seals* (1991).

Sheen, Martin (Ramon Estevez) (1940–) American born Dayton, Ohio; *Catch 22* (1970), *Badlands* (1973), *The Execution of Private Slovik* (TV 1974), *The Little Girl Who Lives Down the Lane* (1976), *Apocalypse Now* (1979), *Gandhi* (1982), *That Championship Season* (1982), *The Dead Zone* (1983), *Firestarter* (1984), *Wall Street* (1987), *Siesta* (1987), *Da* (1988), *Judgement in Berlin* (1988), *Stockade* (1990).

Shepard, Sam (Samuel Shepard Rogers) (1943–) American born Fort Sheridan, Illinois; *Frances* (1982), *The Right Stuff* (1983), *Country* (1984), *Crimes of the Heart* (1986), *Baby Boom* (1987).

Shepherd, Cybill (1950–) American born Memphis, Tennesee; *The Last Picture Show* (1971), *Taxi Driver* (1976), *The Lady Vanishes* (1979), *The Long Hot Summer* (TV 1985), *Moonlighting* (TV 1985–9), *Texasville* (1990), *Alice* (1991).

Shields, Brooke (1965–) American born New York City; *The Blue Lagoon* (1980), *Endless Love* (1981), *Sahara* (1982).

Signoret, Simone (Simon-Henriette Charlotte Kaminker) (1921–85) French born Wiesbaden, Germany; *La Ronde* (1950), *Casque d'Or* (1952), *Les Diaboliques* (1952), *Room at the Top* (1959), *Ship of Fools* (1965), *Le Chat* (1971), *Madame Rosa* (1973).

Sim, Alastair (1900–76) British born Edinburgh; *Inspector Hornleigh* (1939), *Green for Danger* (1946), *The Happiest Days of Your Life* (1950), *Scrooge* (1951), *Laughter in Paradise* (1951), *The Bells of St Trinians* (1954).

Simmons, Jean (1929–) British born London; *Great Expectations* (1946), *Black Narcissus* (1946), *Hamlet* (1948), *The Blue Lagoon* (1948), *The Big Country* (1958), *Elmer Gantry* (1960), *Spartacus* (1960), *The Grass is Greener* (1961), *The Thorn Birds* (TV 1982), *Going Undercover* (1988), *Great Expectations* (TV 1991).

Sinatra, Frank (Francis Albert Sinatra) (1915–) American born Hoboken, New Jersey; *Anchors Aweigh* (1945), *On the Town* (1949), *From Here to Eternity* (1953), *The Man With the Golden Gun* (1955), *Pal Joey* (1957), *The Manchurian Candidate* (1962), *The Detective* (1963).

Sinden, Donald (1923–) British born Plymouth, England; *Doctor in the House* (1954), *The National Health* (1973), *The Day of the Jackal* (1973), *The Island at the Top of the World* (1973), *Two's Company* (TV 1977–80), *Never the Twain* (TV 1983–).

Singer, Marc (1948–) Canadian born Vancouver; *Beast Master* (1982), *If You Could See What I Hear* (1982), *V* (TV 1983), *V– The Final Battle* (TV 1984–5), *Dallas* (TV 1986), *Born to Race* (1988).

Skerritt, Tom (1933–) American born Detroit Michigan; *M*A*S*H* (1970), *Big Bad Mama* (1974), *Run, Run, Joe* (TV 1974), *The Devil's Rain* (1975), *Up in Smoke* (1978), *Alien* (1979), *Ice Castles* (1979), *The Dead Zone* (1983), *Top Gun* (1986), *Wisdom* (1986), *Cheers* (TV 1987–8), *Space Camp* (1988), *Poltergeist III* (1988).

Slater, Christian (1969–) American born New York City; *The Name of the Rose* (1986), *Tucker: The Man and His Dream* (1988), *Heathers* (1989), *Young Guns II* (1990), *Pump Up the Volume* (1990), *Robin Hood, Prince of Thieves* (1991).

Smith, Sir C. Aubrey (Charles Aubrey Smith) (1863-1948) British born London; *Love Me Tonight* (1932), *Morning Glory* (1933), *Lives of a Bengal Lancer* (1935), *The Prisoner of Zenda* (1937), *The Four Feathers* (1939), *Rebecca* (1940), *And Then There Were None* (1945), *An Ideal Husband* (1947), *Little Women* (1949).

Smith, Maggie (1934–) British born Ilford, Essex; also stage; *The V.I.P.s* (1963), *The Pumpkin Eater* (1964), *The Prime of Miss Jean Brodie* (1969), *Travels with My Aunt* (1972), *California Suite* (1978), *A Private Function* (1984), *A Room With a View* (1985), *The Lonely Passion of Judith Hearne* (1987).

FILM AND TV ACTORS (cont.)

Soul, David (David Solberg) (1943–) American born Chicago; *Magnum Force* (1973), *Starsky and Hutch* (TV 1975–80), *China Hand* (1987).

Spacek, Sissy (Mary Elizabeth Spacek) (1949–) American born Quitman, Texas; *Badlands* (1973), *Carrie* (1976), *Coal Miner's Daughter* (1980), *Missing* (1982), *The River* (1984), *Crimes of the Heart* (1986).

Spader, James American; *Pretty in Pink* (1986), *Mannequin* (1987), *Less Than Zero* (1987), *Baby Boom* (1987), *Jack's Back* (1988), *Sex, Lies and Videotape* (1989), *The Rachel Papers* (1989), *Bad Influence* (1990), *White Palace* (1991).

Stallone, Sylvester (1946–) American born New York City; *The Lords of Flatbush* (1973), *Rocky* (1976), (*part II*–1979, *III* – 1982, *IV* – 1985, *V* – 1990), *Paradise Alley* (1978), *Victory* (1981), *Nighthawks* (1981), *First Blood* (1981), *Rambo* (1985), *Over the Top* (1987), *Rambo III* (1988), *Lock Up* (1989), *Tango and Cash* (1990), *Oscar* (1991), *Stop, Or My Mom Will Shoot* (1992), *Bartholomew Vs Neff* (1992), *Cliffhanger* (1992).

Stamp, Terence (1939–) British born Stepney; *The Collector* (1965), *Far from the Madding Crowd* (1967), *Superman* (1978), *Superman II* (1981), *Company of Wolves* (1985), *Legal Eagles* (1986), *Wall Street* (1987), *The Sicilian* (1988), *Alien Nation* (1988).

Stanton, Harry Dean (1926–) American born Kentucky; *How the West Was Won* (1962), *Cool Hand Luke* (1967), *The Godfather* (*Part II*–1974), *Alien* (1979), *The Rose* (1979), *Private Benjamin* (1980), *Young Doctors in Love* (1982), *Christine* (1983), *Repo Man* (1984), *Paris, Texas* (1984), *Pretty in Pink* (1986), *Mr. North* (1988), *Stars and Bars* (1988).

Stanwyck, Barbara (Ruby Shaw) (1907–90) American born Brooklyn, New York; *Broadway Nights* (1927), *Miracle Woman* (1931), *Night Nurse* (1931), *The Bitter Tea of General Yen* (1933), *Baby Face* (1933), *Annie Oakley* (1935), *Stella Dallas* (1937), *Union Pacific* (1939), *The Lady Eve* (1941), *Meet John Doe* (1941), *Ball of Fire* (1941), *Double Indemnity* (1944), *The Strange Love of Martha Ivers* (1946), *Sorry Wrong Number* (1948), *The Furies* (1950), *Executive Suite* (1954), *Walk on the Wild Side* (1962), *The Big Valley* (TV 1965–9), *The Thorn Birds* (TV 1983).

Steele, Tommy (Thomas Hicks) (1936–) British born London; *The Tommy Steele Story* (1957), *The Happiest Millionaire* (1967), *Half a Sixpence* (1967), *Finian's Rainbow* (1968).

Steiger, Rod (Rodney Stephen Steiger) (1925–) American born Westhampton, New York; *On the Waterfront* (1954), *Oklahoma!* (1955), *The Court Martial of Billy Mitchell* (1955), *The Harder They Fall* (1956), *Al Capone* (1958), *The Pawnbroker* (1964), *Doctor Zhivago* (1965), *In the Heat of the Night* (1967), *A Fistful of Dynamite* (1971), *The Amityville Horror* (1979), *Hollywood Wives* (TV 1984), *American Gothic* (1988), *The January Man* (1988).

Stewart, James (Maitland) (1908–) American born Indiana, Pennsylvania; *Seventh Heaven* (1937), *You Can't Take It With You* (1938), *Mr Smith Goes to Washington* (1939), *Destry Rides Again* (1939), *The Shop around the Corner* (1940), *The Philadelphia Story* (1940), *It's a Wonderful Life* (1946), Harvey (1950), *Broken Arrow* (1950), *The Glen Miller Story* (1953), *Rear Window* (1954), *The Man from Laramie* (1955), *Vertigo* (1958), *Anatomy of a Murder* (1959), *Mr Hobbs Takes a Vacation* (1962), *Shenandoah* (1965), *North and South II* (TV 1986).

Stockwell, Dean (1935–) American born Hollywood, California; *The Green Years* (1946), *The Boy with Green Hair* (1948), *Kim* (1950), *Compulsion* (1959), *Sons and Lovers* (1959), *McCloud: Twas the Fight Before Christmas* (TV 1977), *Paris, Texas* (1984), *Dune* (1984), *The Legend of Billie Jean* (1985), *Blue Velvet* (1986), *Gardens of Stone* (1987), *Tucker: The Man and His Dream* (1988), *The Blue Iguana* (1988), *Married to the Mob* (1988), *Quantum Leap* (TV 1989–).

Stoltz, Eric (1961–) American born California; *Fast Times at Ridgemont High* (1982), *Mask* (1985), *Highway to Hell, Some Kind of Wonderful* (1987), *Sister Sister* (1988), *Haunted Summer* (1988), *Fly II* (1989), *Memphis Belle* (1990).

Stone, Sharon (1964–) American born Meadsville, Pennsylvania; *Deadly Blessing* (1981), *King Solomon's Mines, Police Academy IV, Action Jaction* (1987), *Above the Law* (UK: *Nico*) (1988), *Total Recall* (1990).

Strauss, Peter (1947–) American born New York City; *Rich Man Poor Man* (TV 1976), *Masada* (TV 1980), *Spacehunter 3D: Adventures in the Forbidden Zone* (1983), *Tender is the Night* (TV 1985), *Penalty Phase* (TV 1986), *Kane and Abel* (TV 1988).

FILM AND TV ACTORS (cont.)

Streep, Meryl (Mary Louise Streep) (1949–) American born Summit, New Jersey; *Julia* (1977), *The Deer Hunter* (1978), *Kramer Vs Kramer* (1979), *Manhattan* (1979), *The French Lieutenant's Woman* (1981), *Sophie's Choice* (1982), *Still of the Night* (1982), *Silkwood* (1983), *Plenty* (1985), *Out of Africa* (1986), *Ironweed* (1987), *A Cry in the Dark* (1988), *Evil Angels* (1988), *She-Devil* (1989), *Postcards from the Edge* (1990), *Defending Your Life* (1991), *Death Becomes Her* (1992).

Streisand, Barbra (Joan) (1942–) American born Brooklyn, New York; *Funny Girl* (1968), *Hello Dolly* (1969), *On a Clear Day You Can See Forever* (1970), *Whats Up, Doc?* (1972), *The Way We Were* (1973), *A Star is Born* (1976), *Yentl* (1983), *Nuts* (1987), *Prince of Tides* (1991).

Sutherland, Donald (1934–) Canadian born St John, New Brunswick; *The Dirty Dozen* (1967), *M*A*S*H* (1970), *Klute* (1971), *Casanova* (1976), *1900* (1976), *The Eagle Has Landed* (1977), *Animal House* (1978), *Invasion of the Body Snatchers* (1978), *Ordinary People* (1980), *Apprentice to Murder* (1988), *Lock Up* (1989), *A Dry White Season* (1989), *Backdraft* (1991).

Sutherland, Kiefer (1967–) American born Los Angeles; *Bright Lights, Big City* (1985), *Stand By Me* (1987), *The Lost Boys* (1987), *The Killing Time* (1987), *1969* (1988), *Promised Land* (1988), *Young Guns* (1988), *Renegades* (1989), *Chicago Joe and the Showgirl* (1989), *Flatliners* (1990), *Young Guns II* (1990), *Article 99* (1991).

Suzman, Janet (1939–) S African born Johannesburg; also stage; *Nicholas and Alexandra* (1972), *Voyage of the Damned* (1976), *The Draughtsman's Contract* (1982), *Mountbatten* (TV 1985), *A Dry White Season* (1989), *Nuns on the Run* (1990).

Swanson, Gloria (Gloria May Josephine Svensson) (1897–1983) American born Chicago; *Male and Female* (1919), *The Affairs of Anatol* (1921), *Manhandled* (1924), *Sadie Thompson* (1928), *Queen Kelly* (1928), *The Trespasser* (1929), *Sunset Boulevard* (1950).

Swayze, Patrick (1954–) American born Houston, Texas; *The Outsiders* (1983), *Red Dawn* (1984), *Young Blood* (1985), *North and South* (TV 1986), *North and South II* (TV 1986), *Dirty Dancing* (1987), *Tiger Warsaw* (1988), *Road House* (1989), *Next of Kin* (1989), *Ghost* (1990), *Point Break* (1991), *City Of Joy* (1992).

Tandy, Jessica (1909–) British born London; *Dragonwyck* (1946), *The Birds* (1963), *Honky Tonk Freeway* (1981), *The World According to Garp* (1982), *Still of the Night* (1982), *The Bostonians* (1984), *Cocoon* (1985), *The House on Carroll Street* (1988), *Cocoon: The Return* (1988), *Driving Miss Daisy* (1989).

Taylor, Elizabeth (Rosemond) (1932–) British born London; *National Velvet* (1944), *Little Women* (1949), *The Father of the Bride* (1950), *A Place in the Sun* (1951), *Giant* (1956), *Raintree Country* (1957), *Cat on a Hot Tin Roof* (1958), *Butterfield 8* (1960), *Cleopatra* (1962), *Who's Afraid of Virginia Woolf?* (1966), *Reflections in a Golden Eye* (1967), *The Taming of the Shrew* (1967), *Suddenly Last Summer* (1968), *A Little Night Music* (1977), *The Mirror Crack'd* (1981), *Malice in Wonderland* (TV 1985), *Poker Alice* (TV 1986), *Young Toscanini* (1988), *Sweet Bird of Youth* (TV 1989), *Faithful* (1992).

Taylor, Robert (Spangler Arlington Brugh) (1911–69) American born Filley, Nebraska; *Magnificent Obsession* (1935), *Camille* (1936), *Three Comrades* (1938), *Yank at Oxford* (1938), *Waterloo Bridge* (1940), *Bataan* (1943), *Song of Russia* (1943), *Quo Vadis* (1951), *Ivanhoe* (1952), *Knights of the Round Table* (1953), *Party Girl* (1958), *The Detectives* (TV 1959–61), *The Miracle of the White Stallions* (1962).

Taylor, Rod (Robert Taylor) (1929–) Australian born Sydney; *The Time Machine* (1960), *The Birds* (1963), *The V.I.P.s* (1963), *Thirty-Six Hours* (1964), *The Glass Bottom Boat* (1966).

Tearle, Sir Godfrey (1884–1953) British born New York City; also stage; *Romeo and Juliet* (1908), *The Thirty-nine Steps* (1935), *One of Our Aircraft is Missing* (1942), *The Titfield Thunderbolt* (1953).

Temple, Shirley (1927–) American born Santa Monica, California; *Little Miss Marker* (1934), *Curly Top* (1935), *Dimples* (1936), *Heidi* (1937), *The Little Princess* (1939).

Terry-Thomas (Thomas Terry Hoar Stevens) (1911–90) British born Finchley, London; *Private's Progress* (1956), *Carleton Browne of the FO* (1958), *The Naked Truth* (1958), *I'm All Right, Jack* (1959), *It's a Mad, Mad, Mad, Mad World* (1963), *How to Murder Your Wife* (1965), *Those Magnificent Men in Their Flying Machines* (1965), *Don't Look Now* (1968).

FILM AND TV ACTORS (cont.)

Thompson, Lea (1962–) American born Minneapolis, Minnesota; *Jaws 3D* (1983), *Red Dawn* (1984), *Back to the Future* (1985), (*part II*–1989), *Howard: A New Breed of Hero* (1985), *SpaceCamp* (1986), *The Wizard of Loneliness* (1988), *Casual Sex?* (1988), *Going Undercover* (1988), *Article 99* (1991).

Thornton, Sigrid (1959–) Australian born Queensland; *Prisoner: Cell Block H* (TV 1970–1), *The Man from Snowy River* (1982), *The Far Country* (TV 1986), *Slate, Wyn, and Me* (1987), *The Light Horsemen* (1987), *Return to Snowy River Part II* (1988), *Paradise* (1988).

Tierney, Gene (Eliza) (1920–91) American born Brooklyn, New York; *The Return of Frank James* (1940), *Tobacco Road* (1941), *Belle Star* (1941), *Heaven Can Wait* (1943), *Laura* (1944), *Leave Her to Heaven* (1945), *The Ghost and Mrs. Muir* (1947), *Whirlpool* (1949), *Toys in the Attic* (1963), *The Pleasure Seekers* (1964).

Tilly, Meg (1960–) Canadian born Texada; *Fame* (1980), *The Big Chill* (1983), *Psycho II* (1983), *Agnes of God* (1985), *Masquerade* (1988), *Valmont* (1989), *The Tow Jakes* (1991).

Tomlin, Lily (1939–) American born Detroit, Michigan; *Nine to Five* (1980), *The Incredible Shrinking Woman* (1981), *All of Me* (1984), *Big Business* (1988).

Tracy, Spencer (1900–67) American born Milwaukee, Wisconsin; *Twenty Thousand Years in Sing Sing* (1932), *The Power and the Glory* (1933), *A Man's Castle* (1933), *Fury* (1936), *San Francisco* (1936), *Libeled Lady* (1936), *Captains Courageous* (1937), *Boy's Town* (1938), *Stanley and Livingstone* (1939), *Northwest Passage* (1939), *Edison the Man* (1940), *Dr Jekyll and Mr Hyde* (1941), *Woman of the Year* (1942), *The Seventh Cross* (1944), *State of the Union* (1948), *Adam's Rib* (1949), *Father of the Bride* (1950), *Bad Day at Black Rock* (1955), *The Last Hurrah* (1958), *Inherit the Wind* (1960), *Judgment at Nuremberg* (1961), *It's a Mad, Mad, Mad, Mad World* (1963), *Guess Who's Coming to Dinner* (1967).

Travolta, John (1954–) American born Englewood, New Jersey; *Welcome Back Kotter* (TV 1975–8), *Carrie* (1976), *Saturday Night Fever* (1977), *Grease* (1978), *Blow Out* (1981), *Staying Alive* (1983), *Two of a Kind* (1984), *Perfect* (1985), *Look Who's Talking* (1989), *Look Who's Talking Too* (1991), *Chains of Gold* (1991).

Turner, Kathleen (1954–) American born Springfield, Missouri; *The Doctors* (TV 1977–8), *Body Heat* (1981), *The Man With Two Brains* (1983), *Romancing the Stone* (1984), *Crimes of Passion* (1984), *The Jewel of the Nile* (1985), *Prizzi's Honour* (1985), *Peggy Sue Got Married* (1986), *Switching Channels* (1988), *Julia and Julia* (1988), *The Accidental Tourist* (1989), *War of the Roses* (1989), *V.I. Warshawski* (1991), *House of Cards* (1992).

Turner, Lana (Julia Jean Mildred Frances Turner) (1921–) American born Wallace, Indiana; *Dr Jekyll and Mr Hyde* (1940), *Somewhere I'll Find You* (1942), *The Three Musketeers* (1948), *Peyton Place* (1957).

Turturro, John (1957–) American born Brooklyn, New York; *Raging Bull* (1980), *Hannah and Her Sisters* (1986), *Do the Right Thing* (1989), *Miller's Crossing* (1990), *Barton Fink* (1991), *Mac* (1992).

Tushingham, Rita (1940–) British born Liverpool; *A Taste of Honey* (1961), *Girl with Green Eyes* (1964), *The Knack* (1965), *Dr Zhivago* (1965), *Judgment in Stone* (1986).

Ullman, Liv (1939–) Norwegian born Tokyo, Japan; *Persona* (1966), *The Emigrants* (1972), *Face to Face* (1975), *Autumn Sonata* (1978), *Dangerous Moves* (1983), *Gaby—The True Story* (1987), *La Amiga* (1988), *The Rose Garden* (1989), *Mindwalk* (1990), *The Ox* (1991).

Ustinov, Peter Alexander (1921–) British born London; *Private Angelo* (1949), *Hotel Sahara* (1951), *Quo Vadis* (1951), *Beau Brummell* (1954), *The Sundowners* (1960), *Spartacus* (1960), *Romanoff and Juliet* (1961), *Topkapi* (1964), *Logan's Run* (1976), *Death on the Nile* (1978), *Evil Under the Sun* (1982), *Appointment With Death* (1988).

Valentino, Rudolph (Rodolpho Alphonso Guglielmi di Valentina d'Antonguolla) (1895–1926) Italian/US born Castellaneta; *The Four Horsemen of the Apocalypse* (1921), *The Sheikh* (1921), *Blood and Sand* (1922), *The Young Rajah* (1922), *Monsieur Beaucaire* (1924), *The Eagle* (1925), *The Son of the Sheikh* (1926).

Van Cleef, Lee (1925-89) American born Somerville, New Jersey; *High Noon* (1952), *For a Few Dollars More* (1967), *The Good, the Bad, and the Ugly* (1967), *Return of Sabata* (1971), *The Magnificent Seven Ride* (1972), *Escape from New York* (1981), *Code name: Wildgeese II* (1986).

Van Dyke, Dick (1925–) American born West Plains, Missouri; *The Dick Van Dyke Show* (TV 1961–6), *Mary Poppins* (1964), *Chitty Chitty Bang Bang* (1968), *The Cosmic* (1969), *Dropout Father* (TV 1982).

FILM AND TV ACTORS (cont.)

Vaughan, Peter (Peter Ohm) (1923–) British born Shropshire; *Village of the Damned* (1960), *Bofors Gun* (1968), *Zulu Dawn* (1979), *Time Bandits* (1981), *The French Lieutenant's Woman* (1981), *The Missionary* (1982), *The Razor's Edge* (1984), *Brazil* (1985), *Haunted Honeymoon* (1986), *War and Remembrance* (TV 1987), *The Bourne Identity* (1988).

Vaughn, Robert (Francis Vaughn) (1932–) American born New York City; *The Magnificant Seven* (1960), *The Towering Inferno* (1974), *Washington Behind Closed Doors* (TV 1976), *Superman III* (1983), *The Man from UNCLE* (TV 1964–7).

Vincent, Jan-Michael (1944–) American born Denver, Colorado; *The Mechanic* (1972), *The World's Greatest Athlete* (1973), *Bite the Bullet* (1974), *Hooper* (1978), *Hard Country* (1981), *Airwolf* (TV 1982–6), *The Winds of War* (TV 1983).

Von Stroheim, Erich (Hans Erich Maria Stroheim Von Nordenwall) (1885–1957) Austrian born Vienna; *Foolish Wives* (1921), *La Grande Illusion* (1937), *Five Graves to Cairo* (1943), *Sunset Boulevard* (1950).

Von Sydow, Max (Carl Adolf) (1929–) Swedish born Lund; *The Seventh Seal* (1956), *The Face* (1959), *The Greatest Story Ever Told* (1965), *Hawaii* (1966), *Through a Glass Darkly* (1966), *Hour of the Wolf* (1967), *The Shame* (1968), *The Emigrants* (1972), *The Exorcist* (1973), *Exorcist II: The Heretic* (1977), *Flash Gordon* (1980), *Never Say Never Again* (1983), *Hannah and Her Sisters* (1986), *Pelle, the Conquerer* (1988), *Awakenings* (1990), *Dr. Grassler* (1990), *The Father* (1990), *The Ox* (1991), *The Touch* (1992).

Wagner, Lindsay (1949–) American born Los Angeles; *Bionic Woman* (TV 1964–7), *The Paper Chase* (1973).

Wagner, Robert (John Jr) (1930–) American born Detroit, Michigan; *The Silver Whip* (1953), *Prince Valiant* (1954), *A Kiss Before Dying* (1956), *The True Story of Jesse James* (1957), *All the Fine Young Cannibals* (1959), *The Condemned of Altona* (1963), *The Pink Panther* (1963), *It Takes a Thief* (TV 1965–9), *Colditz* (TV 1972–3), *The Towering Inferno* (1974), *Switch* (TV 1975–7), *Hart to Hart* (TV 1979–84).

Wahl, Ken (957–) American born Chicago; *Every Which Way But Loose* (1979), *The Champ* (1979), *The Wanderers* (1979), *Fort Apache—The Bronx* (1981), *Code Name The Soldier* (1982), *The Gladiator* (TV 1986).

Walken, Christopher (1943–) American born Astoria, New York; *The Anderson Tapes* (1970), *Annie Hall* (1977), *The Deer Hunter* (1978), *The Dogs of War* (1981), *Pennies from Heaven* (1981), *The Dead Zone* (1983), *Brainstorm* (1983), *A View to a Kill* (1984), *At Close Range* (1986), *The Milagro Beanfield War* (1987), *Biloxi Blues* (1988), *Puss in Boots* (1988), *The Comfort of Strangers* (1990), *Batman Returns* (1992).

Walters, Julie (1950–) British born Birmingham; *Educating Rita* (1983), *She'll Be Wearing Pink Pajamas* (1984), *Car Trouble* (1986), *Prick Up Your Ears* (1987), *Personal Services* (1987), *Buster* (1987), *Killing Dad* (1989).

Wanamaker, Sam (1919–) American born Chicago; *Those Magnificent Men in Their Flying Machines* (1965), *The Spy Who Came in from the Cold* (1965), *Voyage of the Damned* (1976), *Death on the Nile* (1978), *Private Benjamin* (1980), *Raw Deal* (1986), *Superman IV* (1986), *Baby Boom* (1987).

Ward, Rachel (1957–) British born London; *Sharky's Machine* (1981), *Dead Men Don't Wear Plaid* (1982), *The Thorn Birds* (TV 1983), *The Good Wife* (1986), *Hotel Colonial* (1987), *How to Get Ahead in Advertising* (1989), *After Dark My Sweet* (1990).

Warner, David (1941–) British born Manchester; *Morgan* (1966), *The Bofors Gun* (1968), *The Engagement* (1970), *The French Lieutenant's Woman* (1971), *The Omen* (1976), *Holocaust* (TV 1978), *The 39 Steps* (1978), *Time Bandits* (1981), *Tron* (1982), *The Man with Two Brains* (1983), *Company of Wolves* (1984), *Mr North* (1988), *Hanna's War* (1988), *The Secret Life of Ian Fleming* (1990).

Washington, Denzel (1954–) American born Mt. Vernon, New York; *St Elsewhere* (1982–9), *Cry Freedom* (1987), *Queen and Country* (1988), *Glory* (1989), *Mo' Better Blues* (1990), *Mississippi Masala* (1991), *Ricochet* (1991), *Malcolm X* (1992).

Waterman, Dennis (1948–) British born London; *Up the Junction* (1967), *The Sweeney* (TV 1974–8), *The Sweeney* (1977), *Minder* (TV 1979-86), *The Life and Loves of a She-Devil* (TV 1986).

Wayne, John (Marion Michael Morrison) (1907-79) American born Winterset, Iowa; *The Big Trail* (1930),

FILM AND TV ACTORS (cont.)

Stagecoach (1939), *The Long Voyage Home* (1940), *Red River* (1948), *She Wore a Yellow Ribbon* (1949), *Sands of Iwo Jima* (1949), *The Quiet Man* (1952), *The High and the Mighty* (1954), *The Searchers* (1956), *Rio Bravo* (1959), *The Alamo* (1960), *True Grit* (1969), *The Shootist* (1976).

Weaver, Sigourney (Susan Weaver) (1949–) American born New York City; *Alien* (1979), *The Janitor* (1981), *The Year of Living Dangerously* (1982), *Ghostbusters* (1984), *Aliens* (1986), *Gorillas in the Mist* (1988), *Working Girl* (1988), *Ghostbusters II* (1989).

Welch, Raquel (Raquel Tejada) (1940–) American born Chicago; *Fantastic Voyage* (1966), *One Million Years B.C.* (1967), *Myra Breckenridge* (1970), *The Three Musketeers* (1974), *The Four Musketeers* (1975).

Weld, Tuesday (Susan Kerr Weld) (1943–) American born New York City; *Return to Peyton Place* (1961), *The Cincinnati Kid* (1963), *Pretty Poison* (1968), *Author! Author!* (1982), *Once Upon a Time in America* (1984).

Welles, Orson (1915–85) American born Kenosha, Wisconsin; *Citizen Kane* (1941), *Journey into Fear* (1942), *The Stranger* (1945), *The Lady from Shanghai* (1947), *The Third Man* (1949), *The Trial* (1962), *Touch of Evil* (1965), *A Man For All Seasons* (1966), *Casino Royale* (1967), *Voyage of the Damned* (1976), *History of the World Part One* (1981).

West, Mae (1892–1980) American born Brooklyn, New York; *She Done Him Wrong* (1933), *I'm No Angel* (1933), *My Little Chickadee* (1939), *Myra Breckinridge* (1970).

Widmark, Richard (1914–) American born Sunrise, Minnesota; *Kiss of Death* (1947), *Night and the City* (1950), *How the West Was Won* (1963), *The Bedford Incident* (1965), *Madigan* (1968), *Madigan* (TV 1972), *Murder on the Orient Express* (1974), *Who Dares Wins* (1982), *Hanky Panky* (1982), *Against all Odds* (1983).

Wilder, Gene (Jerome Silberman) (1935–) American born Milwaukee, Wisconsin; *Bonnie and Clyde* (1967), *The Producers* (1967), *Willy Wonka and the Chocolate Factory* (1971), *Blazing Saddles* (1974), *Young Frankenstein* (1974), *The Frisco Kid* (1979), *Stir Crazy* (1982), *Hanky Panky* (1982), *The Woman in Red* (1984), *Haunted Honeymoon* (1986), *See No Evil Hear No Evil* (1989), *Funny About Love* (1991).

Williams, Kenneth (1926–88) British born London; *Carry on Sergeant* (1958), *Carry on Dick* (1974) etc, *Follow that Camel* (1968).

Williams, Robin (1952–) American born Chicago; *Mork and Mindy* (TV 1978–82), *Popeye* (1980), *The World According to Garp* (1982), *Good Morning Vietnam* (1987), *Dead Poets' Society* (1989), *Cadillac Man* (1990), *Awakenings* (1990), *Dead Again* (1991), *The Fisher King* (1991), *Hook* (1991), *Toys* (1992), *Ferngully* (1992), *Being Human* (1992).

Williams, Treat (Richard Williams) (1951–) American born Rowayton, Connecticut; *The Eagle Has Landed* (1977), *Hair* (1977), *1941* (1979), *Once Upon a Time in America* (1984), *Dempsey* (TV 1985), *Smooth Talk* (1985), *A Street Car Named Desire* (1986), *The Men's Club* (1986), *Dead Heat* (1988), *Heart of Dixie* (1990).

Williamson, Nicol (1938–) British born Hamilton, Scotland; *Inadmissable Evidence* (1967), *The Bofors Gun* (1968), *The Reckoning* (1969), *Excalibur* (1981), *Sakharov* (TV 1985), *Return to Oz* (1985), *Black Widow* (1986), *The Exorcist III* (1990).

Willis, Bruce (1955–) American born Penns Grove, New Jersey; *Moonlighting* (TV 1985–9), *Blind Date* (1987), *Die Hard* (1988), *Sunset* (1988), *In Country* (1989), *Die Hard 2: Die Harder* (1990), *Bonfire of the Vanities* (1991), *Hudson Hawk* (1991), *Billy Bathgate* (1991), *The Last Boy Scout* (1991), *Death Becomes Her* (1992).

Winger, Debra (1955–) American born Columbus, Ohio; *Urban Cowboy* (1980), *Cannery Row* (1981), *An Officer and a Gentleman* (1982), *Terms of Endearment* (1983), *Legal Eagles* (1985), *Black Widow* (1987), *Made in Heaven* (1987), *Betrayed* (1988), *The Sheltering Sky* (1990), *Wilder Napalm* (1992).

Winters, Shelley (Shirley Schrift) (1922–) American born St. Louis, Missouri; *A Double Life* (1948), *The Big Knife* (1955), *The Night of the Hunter* (1955), *The Diary of Anne Frank* (1959), *Lolita* (1962), *A Patch of Blue* (1965), *Alfie* (1966), *The Poseidon Adventure* (1972), *S.O.B.* (1981), *Purple People Eater* (1988).

FILM AND TV ACTORS (cont.)

Wisdom, Norman (1918–) British born London; *Trouble in Store* (1955), *Man of the Moment* (1955), *Just My Luck* (1958), *There was a Crooked Man* (1960), *On the Beat* (1962), *A Stitch in Time* (1963), *Sandwich Man* (1966), *The Night They Raided Minsky's* (1968), *What's Good for the Goose* (1969).

Wood, Natalie (Natasha Gurdin) (1938–81) American born San Francisco, California; *Miracle on 34th Street* (1947), *The Ghost and Mrs. Muir* (1947), *Rebel Without a Cause* (1955), *The Searchers* (1956), *Marjorie Morningstar* (1958), *All The Fine Young Cannibals* (1959), *Splendour in the Grass* (1961), *Westside Story* (1961), *Love with the Proper Stranger* (1964), *The Great Race* (1965), *This Property is Condemned* (1966), *Bob and Carol and Ted and Alice* (1969), *From Here to Eternity* (TV 1979), *Meteor* (1979), *Brainstorm* (1983).

Woods, James (1947–) American born Vernal, Utah; *The Choirboys* (1977), *Videodrome* (1984), *Salvador* (1986), *Best Seller* (1987), *Cop* (1988), *The Boost* (1988).

Woodward, Joanne (1930–) American born Thomasville, Georgia; *Three Faces of Eve* (1957), *No Down Payment* (1957), *The Long Hot Summer* (1958), *The Stripper* (1963), *A Big Hand for the Little Lady* (1966), *Rachel, Rachel* (1968), *Summer Wishes, Winter Dreams* (1973), *The Glass Menagerie* (1987), *Mr and Mrs Bridge* (1990).

York, Michael (1942–) British born Fulmer; *Accident* (1967), *Romeo and Juliet* (1968), *Cabaret* (1972), *Lost Horizon* (1973), *The Three Musketeers* (1973), *The Four Musketeers* (1974), *Jesus of Nazareth* (TV 1977), *The Island of Dr Moreau* (1977), *The White Lions* (1980), *Space* (TV 1985), *The Far Country* (TV 1986), *Sword of Gideon* (TV 1986), *Return of the Musketeers* (1989).

Young, Sean (1960–) American born Louisville, Kentucky; *Blade Runner* (1982), *Dune* (1984), *Baby, Secret of the Lost Legend* (1985), *Wall Street* (1987), *The Boost* (1988), *Cousins* (1989), *Wings of the Apache* (1990).

MOTION PICTURE ACADEMY AWARDS

	Best film	Best actor	Best actress
1970	*Patton* (Franklin J Schaffner)	George C Scott *Patton*	Glenda Jackson *Women in Love*
1971	*The French Connection* (William Friedkin)	Gene Hackman *The French Connection*	Jane Fonda *Klute*
1972	*The Godfather* (Francis Ford Coppola)	Marlon Brando *The Godfather*	Liza Minnelli *Cabaret*
1973	*The Sting* (George Roy Hill)	Jack Lemmon *Save the Tiger*	Glenda Jackson *A Touch of Class*
1974	*The Godfather Part II* (Francis Ford Coppola)	Art Carney *Harry and Tonto*	Ellen Burstyn *Alice Doesn't Live Here Anymore*
1975	*One Flew Over the Cuckoo's Nest (Milos Forman)*	Jack Nicholson *One Flew Over the Cuckoo's Nest*	Louise Fletcher *One Flew Over the Cuckoo's Nest*
1976	*Rocky* (John G Avildsen)	Peter Finch *Network*	Faye Dunaway *Network*
1977	*Annie Hall* (Woody Allen)	Richard Dreyfuss *The Goodbye Girl*	Diane Keaton *Annie Hall*
1978	*The Deer Hunter* (Michael Cimino)	Jon Voight *Coming Home*	Jane Fonda *Coming Home*
1979	*Kramer vs Kramer* (Robert Beaton)	Dustin Hoffman *Kramer vs Kramer*	Sally Field *Norma Rae*
1980	*Ordinary People* (Robert Redford)	Robert de Niro *Raging Bull*	Sissy Spacek *Coal Miner's Daughter*

MOTION PICTURE ACADEMY AWARDS (cont.)

	Best film	Best actor	Best actress
1981	*Chariots of Fire* (Hugh Hudson)	Henry Fonda *On Golden Pond*	Katharine Hepburn *On Golden Pond*
1982	*Gandhi* (Richard Attenborough)	Ben Kingsley *Ghandi*	Meryl Streep *Sophie's Choice*
1983	*Terms of Endearment* (James L Brooks)	Robert Duval *Tender Mercies*	Shirley MacLaine *Terms of Endearment*
1984	*Amadeus* (Milos Forman)	F Murray Abraham *Amadeus*	Sally Field *Places in the Heart*
1985	*Out of Africa* (Sydney Pollack)	William Hurt *Kiss of the Spider Woman*	Geraldine Page *The Trip to Bountiful*
1986	*Platoon* (Oliver Stone)	Paul Newman *The Color of Money*	Marlee Matlin *Children of a Lesser God*
1987	*The Last Emperor* (Bernardo Bertolucci)	Michael Douglas *Wall Street*	Cher *Moonstruck*
1988	*Rain Man* (Barry Levinson)	Dustin Hoffman *Rain Man*	Jody Foster *The Accused*
1989	*Driving Miss Daisy* (Bruce Beresford)	Daniel Day-Lewis *My Left Foot*	Jessica Tandy *Driving Miss Daisy*
1990	*Dances with Wolves* (Kevin Costner)	Jeremy Irons *Reversal of Fortune*	Kathy Bates *Misery*
1991	*The Silence of the Lambs* (Jonathan Demme)	Anthony Hopkins *The Silence of the Lambs*	Jody Foster *The Silence of the Lambs*

DIRECTORS

Aldrich, Robert (1918–83) American, born Cranston, Rhode Island; *Apache* (1954), *Vera Cruz* (1954), *Kiss Me Deadly* (1955), *Attack!* (1957), *What Ever Happened to Baby Jane?* (1962), *The Dirty Dozen* (1967).

Allen, Woody (Allen Stewart Konigsberg) (1935–) American, born Brooklyn, New York; *What's Up Tiger Lily?* (1966), *Bananas* (1971), *Everything You Wanted to Know About Sex, But Were Afraid to Ask* (1972), *Play it Again, Sam* (1972), *Sleeper* (1973), *Love and Death* (1975), *Annie Hall* (1977), *Interiors* (1978), *Manhattan* (1979), *Stardust Memories* (1980), *A Midsummer Night's Sex Comedy* (1982), *Broadway Danny Rose* (1984), *The Purple Rose of Cairo* (1985), *Hannah and Her Sisters* (1986), *Radio Days* (1987), *Crimes and Misdemeanors* (1990), *Alice* (1991), *Shadows and Fog* (1992).

Almódovar, Pedro (1951–) Spanish, born Calzada de Calatrava; *Dark Habits* (1983), *Law of Desire* (1987), *Women on the Verge of a Nervous Breakdown* (1988), *Tie Me Up! Tie Me Down!* (1990), *High Heels* (1991).

Altman, Robert (1925–) American, born Kansas City, Missouri; *The James Dean Story* (1957), *M*A*S*H* (1970), *McCabe and Mrs Miller* (1971), *The Long Goodbye* (1973), *Nashville* (1975), *A Wedding* (1978), *Popeye* (1980), *Come Back to the 5 & Dime Jimmy Dean Jimmy Dean* (1982), *Streamers* (1983), *Fool for Love* (1985), *Aria* (1987), *Vincent and Theo* (1990), *The Player* (1992).

Asquith, Anthony (1902–68) British, born London; *Shooting Stars* (1928), *Underground* (1930), *Pygmalion* (1937), *French without Tears* (1939), *Quiet Wedding* (1940), *The Demi–Paradise* (1943), *Fanny by Gaslight* (1944), *The Way to the Stars* (1945), *The Browning Version* (1950), *The Importance of Being Earnest* (1952), *Orders to Kill* (1958), *The VIPs* (1963).

Attenborough, Sir Richard Samuel (1923–) British, born Cambridge; *Oh! What a Lovely War* (1968), *A Bridge Too Far* (1977), *Gandhi* (1982), *A Chorus Line* (1985), *Cry Freedom* (1987), *Charlie* (1992).

Badham, John (1939–) American, born Luton,

DIRECTORS (cont.)

England; *The Law* (TV 1974), *Saturday Night Fever* (1977), *Whose Life is it Anyway?* (1981), *Blue Thunder* (1982), *War Games* (1983), *American, Flyers* (1984), *Short Circuit* (1986), *Stakeout* (1987), *Bird on a Wire* (1989).

Beatty, Warren (Henry Warren Beaty) (1937–) American, born Richmond, Virginia; *Heaven Can Wait* (1978), *Reds* (1981), *Dick Tracy* (1990).

Bergman, (Ernst) Ingmar (1918–) Swedish, born Uppsala; *Crisis* (1945), *Prison* (1948), *Sawdust and Tinsel* (1953), *The Face* (1955), Smiles of a Summer Night (1955), *The Seventh Seal* (1957), *Wild Strawberries* (1957), *The Virgin Spring* (1959), *Through a Glass Darkly* (1961), *The Silence* (1963), *Shame* (1968), *Cries and Whispers* (1972), *The Magic Flute* (1974), *Autumn Sonata* (1978), *Fanny and Alexander* (1983).

Bertolucci, Bernardo (1940–) Italian, born Parma; *Love and Anger* (1969), *The Conformist* (1970), *Last Tango in Paris* (1972), *1900* (1976), *The Last Emperor* (1987), *The Sheltering Sky* (1990).

Besson, Luc (1959–) French, born Paris; *The Last Battle* (1983), *Subway* (1985), *The Big Blue* (1988), *Nikita* (1990).

Bogdanovich, Peter (1939–) American, born Kingston, New York; *Targets* (1967), *The Last Picture Show* (1971), *Paper Moon* (1973), *What's Up, Doc?* (1972), *Nickelodeon* (1976), *Mask* (1985), *Illegally Yours* (1987), *Texasville* (1990), *Noises Off* (1992).

Boorman, John (1933–) English, born Epsom, Surrey; *Point Blank* (1967), *Hell in the Pacific* (1969), *Deliverance* (1972), *Zardoz* (1974), *Exorcist II: The Heretic* (1977), *Excalibur* (1981), *The Emerald Forest* (1984), *Hope and Glory* (1987), *Where the Heart Is* (1990).

Brook, Sir Peter (Stephen Paul) (1925–) British, born London; theatre, opera, and film director; *Lord of the Flies* (1963), *King Lear* (1971), *Carmen* (1983).

Brooks, Mel (Melvin Kaminski) (1926–) American, born Brooklynm, New York; *The Producers* (1966), *Blazing Saddles* (1974), *Young Frankenstein* (1974), *High Anxiety* (1978), *History of the World, Part 1* (1981), *Space Balls* (1987), *Life Stinks* (1991).

Buñuel, Luis (1900–83) Spanish, born Calanda; *Un Chien Andalou* (with Salvador Dali) (1928), *L'Age d'Or* (1930), *Los Olvidados* (1950), *Robinson Crusoe* (1952), *El* (1953), *Nazarin* (1958), *Viridiana* (1961), *The Exterminating Angel* (1962), *Belle de Jour* (1967), *The Discreet Charm of the Bourgeoisie* (1972), *The Phantom of the Liberty* (1974), *That Obscure Object of Desire* (1977).

Burton, Tim (1958–) American born Burbank, California; *Peewee's Big Adventure* (1985), *Beetlejuice* (1988), *Batman* (1989), *Edward Scissorhands* (1990), *Batman Returns* (1992).

Capra, Frank (1897–91) Italian/American, born Bisacquino, Sicily; *Platinum Blonde* (1932), *American Madness* (1932), *Lady for a Day* (1933), *It Happened One Night* (1934), *Mr Deeds Goes to Town* (1936), *Lost Horizon* (1937), *You Can't Take It With You* (1938), *Mr Smith Goes to Washington* (1939), *Meet John Doe* (1941), *Arsenic and Old Lace* (1944), *It's a Wonderful Life* (1946).

Carpenter, John (1948–) American, born Carthage, New York; *Dark Star* (1974), *Assault on Precinct 13* (1976), *Halloween* (1978), *Elvis – the Movie* (TV 1979), *The Fog* (1979), *Escape from New York* (1981), *The Thing* (1982), *Christine* (1983), *Starman* (1984), *Big Trouble in Little China* (1986), *Prince of Darkness* (1987), *Memoirs of an Invisible Man* (1992).

Clair, René (originally **René Lucien Chomette**) (1898–1981) French, born Paris; *An Italian Straw Hat* (1927), *Sous Les Toits de Paris* (1929), *Le Million* (1931), *A Nous la liberté* (1931), *I Married a Witch* (1942), *It Happened Tomorrow* (1944), *And Then There Were None* (1945), *Les Belles de Nuit* (1952), *Porte des Lila* (1956), *Tout l'or du Monde* (1961).

Cocteau, Jean (1889–1963) French, born Maisons-Lafitte; *Le Sang d'un poète* (1930), *La Belle et La Bête* (1946), *Orphée* (1950), *Le Testament d'Orphée* (1959).

Coppola, Francis Ford (1939–) American, born Detroit, Michigan; *The Godfather* (1972), (*Part II* – 1974, *Part III* – 1991), *Apocalypse Now* (1979), *One from the Heart* (1982), *The Outsiders* (1983), *Rumble Fish* (1983), *The Cotton Club* (1984), *Peggy Sue Got Married* (1987), *Gardens of Stone* (1987), *Tucker: The Man and His Dream* (1988), *Dracula* (1992).

Corman, Roger (1926–) American, born Detroit, Michigan; *Not of this Earth* (1957), *Bucket of Blood* (1960), *Fall of the House of Usher* (1960), *Little Shop of Horrors* (1960), *The Intruder* (1961), *The Raven* (1963), *X–The Man with X-ray Eyes* (1963), *The Masque of the Red Death* (1964), *The Tomb of Ligeia* (1965), *Frankenstein Unbound* (1990).

DIRECTORS (cont.)

Cohen, Ethan and **Joel** *Blood Simple* (1984), *Raising Arizona* (1987), *Miller's Crossing* (1990), *Barton Fink* (1991).

Costner, Kevin (1955–) American, born Los Angeles; *Dances with Wolves* (1990).

Cronenberg, David (1943–) Canadian, born Toronto; *Shivers* (1976), *Rabid* (1977), *The Brood* (1978), *Scanners* (1980), *Videodrome* (1982), *The Dead Zone* (1983), *The Fly* (1985), *Dead Ringers* (1988), *Naked Lunch* (1991).

Curtiz, Michael (Mihály Kertész) (1888–1962) American/Hungarian, born Budapest, Hungary; *Noah's Ark* (1929), *Mammy* (1930), *Doctor X* (1932), *The Mystery of the Wax Museum* (1933), *British Agent* (1934), *Black Fury* (1935), *Captain Blood* (1935), *Charge of the Light Brigade* (1936), *The Adventures of Robin Hood* (1938), *Angels with Dirty Faces* (1938), *The Sea Hawk* (1940), *The Sea Wolf* (1941), *Yankee Doodle Dandy* (1942), *Casablanca* (1943), *Mildred Pierce* (1945), *White Christmas* (1954), *We're No Angels* (1955), *King Creole* (1958).

Dante, Joe (1946–) American, born Morristown, New Jersey; *Piranha* (1978), *The Howling*, *Gremlins* (1984), *Explorers* (1985), *Innerspace* (1987), *The 'Burbs* (1989), *Amazon Women on the Moon* (1987), *Gremlins 2: The New Batch* (1990).

de Mille, Cecil B(lount) (1881–1959) American, born Ashfield, Massachusetts; *Male and Female* (1919), *King of Kings* (1927), *The Ten Commandments* (1923 & 1956), *The Greatest Show on Earth* (1952).

Demme, Jonathan (1944–) American, born Long Island, New York; *Citizen Band* (1977), *Swing Shift* (1984), *Something Wild* (1987), *Swimming to Cambodia* (1987), *Married to the Mob* (1988), *The Silence of the Lambs* (1991).

de Palma, Brian (1940–) American, born Newark, New Jersey; *Greetings* (1968), *Carrie* (1976), *The Fury* (1978), *Dressed to Kill* (1980), *Blow Out* (1981), *Scarface* (1983), *Body Double* (1984), *The Untouchables* (1987), *Casualties of War* (1989).

Donner, Richard (c.1939–) American; *The Omen* (1976), *Superman* (1978), *Inside Moves* (1980), *The Final Conflict* (1981), *The Toy* (1982), *Ladyhawke* (1984), *The Goonies* (1985), *Lethal Weapon* (1987), *Scrooged* (1988), *Lethal Weapon 2* (1989), *Lethal Weapon 3* (1992).

Eisenstein, Sergei Mikhailovich (1898–1948) Soviet, born Riga; *Stride* (1924), *Battleship Potemkin* (1925), *Alexander Nevsky* (1938), *Ten Days That Shook The World* (1928), *The Magic Seed* (1941), *Ivan the Terrible* (1942–6).

Fassbinder, Rainer Werner (1946–82) German, born Bad Wörishofen; *Warnung von einer heiligen Nutte* (1971), *Satan's Brew* (1976).

Fellini, Federico (1920–) Italian, born Rimini; *I Vitelloni* (1953), *La Strada* (1954), *La Dolce Vita* (1960), *8½* (1963), *Satyricon* (1969), *Fellini's Rome* (1972), *Casanova* (1976), *Orchestra Rehearsal* (1979), *City of Women* (1981), *The Ship Sails On* (1983), *Ginger and Fred* (1986).

Fleming, Victor (1883–1949) American, born Pasadena, California; *Mantrap* (1926), *The Virginian* (1929), *The Wet Parade* (1932), *Red Dust* (1932), *Treasure Island* (1934), *Test Pilot* (1938), *Gone with the Wind* (1939), *The Wizard of Oz* (1939), *Dr Jekyll and Mr Hyde* (1941), *A Guy Named Joe* (1943).

Friedkin, William (1939–) American, born Chicago; *The French Connection* (1971), *The Exorcist* (1973), *The Guardian* (1990).

Gilliam, Terry (1940–) American, born Minneapolis, Minnesota; *Jabberwocky* (1977), *The Time Bandits* (1980), *Brazil* (1985), *The Adventures of Baron Munchausen* (1988), *The Fisher King* (1991).

Godard, Jean-Luc (1930–) French, born Paris; *A Bout de Souffle* (1960), *Alphaville* (1965), *Le Plus Vieux Métier du Monde* (1967).

Griffith, D(avid) W(ark) (1875–1948) American, born La Grange, Kentucky; *Judith of Bethulia* (1913), *The Birth of a Nation* (1915), *Intolerance* (1916), *Hearts of the World* (1918), *Broken Blossoms* (1919), *Orphans of the Storm* (1922).

Hall, Sir Peter (Reginald Frederick) (1930–) British, born Bury St Edmunds, Suffolk; theatre and film director; *Work is a Four Letter Word* (1968), *Perfect Friday* (1971), *Akenfield* (1974).

Hawks, Howard Winchester (1896–1977) American, born Goshen, Indiana; *The Dawn Patrol* (1930), *Scarface* (1932), *Twentieth Century* (1934), *Barbary Coast* (1935), *Bringing Up Baby* (1938), *His Girl Friday* (1940), *To Have and Have Not* (1944), *The Big Sleep* (1946), *Red River* (1948), *Gentleman Prefer Blondes* (1953), *Rio Bravo* (1959).

Hill, George Roy (1922–) American, born Minneapolis, Minnesota; *The World of Henry Orient* (1964), *Thorougly Modern Millie* (1967), *Butch Cassidy and the Sundance Kid* (1969), *Slaughter-*

DIRECTORS (cont.)

house 5 (1972), *The Sting* (1973), *The World According to Garp* (1982).

Hitchcock, Sir Alfred Joseph (1899–1980) British, born Leytonstone, London; *The Lodger* (1926), Blackmail (1929), *Murder* (1930), *The Thirty-Nine Steps* (1935), *The Lady Vanishes* (1938), *Rebecca* (1940), *Lifeboat* (1944), *Spellbound* (1945), *Notorious* (1946), *The Paradine Case* (1947), *Strangers on a Train* (1951), *Dial M for Murder* (1954), *Rear Window* (1954), *To Catch a Thief* (1955), *Vertigo* (1958), *North by Northwest* (1959), *Psycho* (1960), *The Birds* (1963), *Marnie* (1964), *Frenzy* (1972); *Alfred Hitchcock Presents* (TV 1955–61).

Huston, John Marcellus (1906–87) Irish/American, born Nevada, Missouri; *Murders in the Rue Morgue* (1932), *Juarez* (1939), *High Sierra* (1941), *The Maltese Falcon* (1941), *Key Largo* (1948), *The Treasure of the Sierra Madre* (1948), *The Asphalt Jungle* (1950), *The African Queen* (1951), *Moulin Rouge* (1952), *The Misfits* (1960), *Freud* (1962), *Night of the Iguana* (1964), *Casino Royale* (1967), *Fat City* (1972), *The Man Who Would Be King* (1975), *Annie* (1982), *Prizzi's Honour* (1985), *The Dead* (1987).

Ivory, James Francis (1928–) American, born Berkeley, California; *Shakespeare Wallah* (1965), *Heat and Dust* (1982), *The Bostonians* (1984), *A Room with a View* (1985), *Maurice* (1987), *Mr and Mrs Bridge* (1990), *Howard's End* (1992).

Jarman, (Michael) Derek (1942–) British, born Northwood, Middlesex; *Sebastiane* (1976), *Jubilee* (1977), *The Tempest* (1979), *Caravaggio* (1985), *The Last of England* (1987), *The Garden* (1990), *Edward II* (1991).

Kasdan, Lawrence (1949–) American, born Miami Beach, Florida; *Body Heat* (1981), *The Big Chill* (1983), *Silverado* (1985), *The Accidental Tourist* (1989), *Love You to Death* (1990), *Grand Canyon* (1991).

Kaufman, Philip (1936–) American, born Chicago, Illinois; *Invasion of the Body Snatchers* (1978), *The Wanderers* (1979), *The Right Stuff* (1983), *The Unbearable Lightness of Being* (1988), *Henry and June* (1990).

Kazan, Elia (originally **Elia Kazanjoglou**) (1909–) American, born Istanbul, Turkey; *Boomerang* (1947), *Gentleman's Agreement* (1947), *Pink* (1949), *A Streetcar Named Desire* (1951), *Viva Zapata* (1952), *On the Waterfront* (1954), *East of Eden* (1955), *Baby Doll* (1956), *A Face in the Crowd* (1957), *Splendour in the Grass* (1962), *America, America* (1963), *The Arrangement* (1969), *The Visitors* (1972), *The Last Tycoon* (1976).

Kubrick, Stanley (1928–) American, born The Bronx, New York; *The Killing* (1956), *Paths of Glory* (1957), *Spartacus* (1960/91), *Lolita* (1962), *Dr Strangelove* (1964), *2001: A Space Odyssey* (1968), *A Clockwork Orange* (1971), *Barry Lyndon* (1975), *The Shining* (1980), *Full Metal Jacket* (1987).

Kurosawa, Akira (1910–) Japanese, born Tokyo; *Rashomon* (1950), *The Idiot* (1951), *Living* (1952), *Seven Samurai* (1954), *Throne of Blood* (1957), *The Lower Depths* (1957), *The Hidden Fortress* (1958), *Dersu Uzala* (1975), *The Shadow Warrior* (1981), *Ran* (1985), *Dreams* (1990), *Rhapsody in August* (1991).

Landis, John (1950–) American, born Chicago, Illinois; *Schlock* (1971), *Kentucky Fried Movie* (1977), *Animal House* (1978), *The Blues Brothers* (1980), *An American Werewolf in London* (1981), *Twilight Zone* (1983), *Trading Places* (1983), *Into the Night* (1985), *Spies Like Us* (1985), *The Three Amigos* (1986), *Coming to America* (1988), *Oscar* (1991), *Innocent Blood* (1992).

Lang, Fritz (1890–1976) German, born Vienna; *Destiny* (1921), *Dr Mabuse the Gambler* (1922), *Siegfried* (1923), *Metropolis* (1926), *Spies* (1927), *M* (1931), *The Testament of Dr Mabuse* (1932), *You Only Live Once* (1937), *The Return of Frank James* (1940), *The Woman in the Window* (1944), *The Big Heat* (1953), *Beyond a Reasonable Doubt* (1956), *While the City Sleeps* (1955).

Lean, Sir David (1908–91) English, born Croydon; *Pygmalion* (1938), *In Which We Serve* (1942), *Blithe Spirit* (1945), *Brief Encounter* (1946), *Great Expectations* (1946), *The Sound Barrier* (1952), *Hobson's Choice* (1954), *Summer Madness* (1955), *Bridge on the River Kwai* (1957), *Lawrence of Arabia* (1962), *Doctor Zhivago* (1965), *Ryan's Daughter* (1970), *A Passage to India* (1984).

Levinson, Barry (1942–) American, born Baltimore, Maryland; *Diner* (1982), *The Natural* (1984), *The Young Sherlock Holmes* (1985), *Tin Men* (1987), *Good Morning Vietnam* (1987), *Rain Man* (1988), *Avalon* (1990), *Bugsy* (1991), *Toys* (1992).

Lucas, George (1944–) American, born Modesto, California; *THX–1138* (1971), *American Graffiti* (1973), *Star Wars* (1977).

Lynch, David K (1946–) American, born Missoula, Montana; *Eraserhead* (1976), *The Elephant*

DIRECTORS (cont.)

Man (1980), *Dune* (1984), *Blue Velvet* (1986), *Wild at Heart* (1990), *Twin Peaks: Fire Walk with me* (1992); *Twin Peaks* (TV 1990–1).

McBride, Jim (1941–) American; *Breathless* (1983), *The Big Easy* (1986), *Great Balls of Fire* (1989).

Mankiewicz, Joseph Leo (1909–) American, born Wilkes-Barre, Pennsylvania; *All About Eve* (1950), *The Barefoot Contessa* (1954), *Guys and Dolls* (1954), *Suddenly Last Summer* (1959), *Sleuth* (1972).

Miller, George (1945–) Australian, born Brisbane; *Mad Max* (1979), *Mad Max 2: The Road Warrior* (1982), *Mad Max Beyond Thunderdome* (1985), *Witches of Eastwick* (1987).

Miller, Jonathan Wolfe (1934–) British, born London; theatre and opera director; *The Magic Flute* (1986), *The Tempest* (1988).

Minnelli, Vincente (1913–86) American, born Chicago; *Ziegfeld Follies* (1946), *An American in Paris* (1951), *Lust for Life* (1956), *Gigi* (1958).

Nunn, Trevor Robert (1940–) British, born Ipswich; theatre, opera, and film director; *Lady Jane* (1985); stage: *Cats* (1981), *Starlight Express* (1984), *Aspects of Love* (1989).

Olivier, Sir Laurence Kerr (1907–89) English, born Dorking, Surrey; *Henry V* (1944), *Hamlet* (1948), *Richard III* (1956), *The Prince and The Showgirl* (1958), *The Entertainer* (1960).

Parker, Alan (1944–) British, born London; *Bugsy Malone* (1976), *Midnight Express* (1978), *Fame* (1980), *Shoot the Moon* (1981), *Pink Floyd: The Wall* (1982), *Birdy* (1985), *Angel Heart* (1987), *Mississippi Burning* (1988), *Come See the Paradise* (1990), *The Commitments* (1991).

Pasolini, Pier Paolo (1922–75) Italian, born Bologna; *Accatone!* (1961), *The Gospel According to St Matthew* (1964), *Oedipus Rex* (1967), *Medea* (1970).

Polanski, Roman (1933–) Polish, born Paris; *Knife in the Water* (1962), *Repulsion* (1965), *Cul-de-Sac* (1966), *Rosemary's Baby* (1968), *Macbeth* (1971), *Chinatown* (1974), *Tess* (1979), *Pirates* (1985), *Frantic* (1988), *Bitter Moon* (1992).

Pollack, Sydney (1934–) American, born South Bend, Indiana; *They Shoot Horses Don't They?* (1969), *The Electric Horseman* (1979), *Absence of Malice* (1981), *Tootsie* (1982), *Out of Africa* (1985), *Havana* (1990).

Powell, Michael Latham (1905–90) British, born Bekesbourne, near Canterbury; with **Emeric Pressburger** (1902–88) Hungarian/British, born Miskolc, Hungary: *The Spy in Black* (1939), *The Thief of Baghdad* (1940), *The Life and Death of Colonel Blimp* (1943), *Black Narcissus* (1946), *The Red Shoes* (1948), *A Matter of Life and Death* (1946); *Peeping Tom* (1959).

Redford, (Charles) Robert (1937–) American, born Santa Monica, California; *Ordinary People* (1980), *The Milagro Beanfield War* (1987), *A River Runs Through It (1992).*

Reed, Sir Carol (1906–76) British, born London; *The Young Mr Pitt* (1942), *The Way Ahead* (1944), *The Fallen Idol* (1948), *The Third Man* (1949), *An Outcast of the Islands* (1952), *The Man Between* (1953), *Our Man in Havana* (1959), *Oliver!* (1968).

Reiner, Carl (1922–) American, born The Bronx, New York; *Oh God* (1977), *The Jerk* (1979), *Dead Men Don't Wear Plaid* (1982), *The Man with Two Brains* (1983), *Summer School* (1987).

Reiner, Rob (1945–) American, born The Bronx, New York; *This is Spinal Tap* (1984), *Stand by Me* (1987), *The Princess Bride* (1988), *When Harry Met Sally ...* (1989), *Misery* (1990), *A Few Good Men* (1992).

Renoir, Jean (1894–1979) French, born Paris; *Une Partie de Campagne* (1936), *La Règle du Jeu* (1939), *The Southerner* (1945).

Roeg, Nicolas Jack (1928–) British, born London; *Performance* (1970), *Walkabout* (1971), *Don't Look Now* (1973), *The Man Who Fell to Earth* (1976), *Bad Timing* (1979), *Eureka* (1983), *Insignificance* (1985), *Castaway* (1986), *Black Widow* (1988), *Track 29* (1988), *The Witches* (1990).

Rossellini, Roberto (1906–77) Italian, born Rome; *The White Ship* (1940), *Rome, Open City* (1945), *Paisan* (1946), *Germany, Year Zero* (1947), *Stromboli* (1950), *Voyage to Italy* (1953), *General Della Rovera* (1959).

Russell, Ken (Henry Kenneth Alfred Russell) (1927–) British, born Southampton; *Women in Love* (1969), *The Music Lovers* (1970), *The Devils* (1971), *Crimes of Passion* (1984), *Gothic* (1987), *Lair of the White Worm* (1989), *The Rainbow* (1989), *Whore* (1991).

Schlesinger, John Richard (1926–) British, born London; *A Kind of Loving* (1962), *Billy Liar!* (1963), *Midnight Cowboy* (1969), *Sunday, Bloody Sunday* (1971), *Marathon Man* (1976), *Honky Tonk Freeway* (1981), *An Englishman Abroad* (TV 1982), *Madame Sousatzka* (1988), *Pacific Heights* (1990).

Scorsese, Martin (1942–) American, born Queens, New York; *Boxcar Bertha* (1972), *Mean*

DIRECTORS (cont.)

Streets (1973), *Alice Doesn't Live Here Any More* (1974), *Taxi Driver* (1976), *Raging Bull* (1980), *King of Comedy* (1982), *After Hours* (1985), *The Mission* (1986), *The Color of Money* (1986), *The Last Temptation of Christ* (1988), *GoodFellas* (1990), *Cape Fear* (1991), *Age of Innocence* (1992).

Scott, Ridley (1937–) British, born South Shields; *Alien* (1979), *Blade Runner* (1982), *No Way Out* (1989), *Thelma & Louise* (1991), *1492* (1992).

Siegel, Don (1912–91) American, born Chicago; *Riot in Cell Block 11* (1954), *Invasion of the Body Snatchers* (1956), *Baby Face Nelson* (1957), *Coogan's Bluff* (1968), *Two Mules for Sister Sara* (1969), *Dirty Harry* (1971), *Charley Varrick* (1973), *The Shootist* (1976), *Telefon* (1977), *Escape from Alcatraz* (1979).

Spielberg, Steven (1947–) American, born Cincinnati, Ohio; *Duel* (TV 1972), *Sugarland Express* (1973), *Jaws* (1975), *1941* (1979), *Close Encounters of the Third Kind* (1977), *Raiders of the Lost Ark* (1981), *ET* (1982), *Twilight Zone* (1983), *The Color Purple* (1985), *Indiana Jones and the Temple of Doom* (1984), *Empire of the Sun* (1987), *Indiana Jones and the Last Crusade* (1989), *Hook* (1992).

Stevenson, Robert (1905–86) British, born Buxton, Derbyshire; *King Solomon's Mines* (1937), *Mary Poppins* (1964), *The Love Bug* (1968), *Bedknobs and Broomsticks* (1971).

Stone, Oliver (1946–) American, born New York City; *Platoon* (1987), *Wall Street* (1987), *Born on the Fourth of July* (1989), *The Doors* (1991), *JFK* (1991).

Tati, Jacques (Jacques Tatischeff) (1908–82) French, born Le Pecq; *Jour de fête* (1947), *Monsieur Hulot's Holiday* (1952), *Mon Oncle* (1958), *Playtime* (1968), *Traffic* (1981).

Truffaut, François (1932–84) French, born Paris; *Jules et Jim* (1961), *The Bride Wore Black* (1967), *Baisers volés* (1968), *L'Enfant Sauvage* (1969), *Day for Night* (1973), *The Last Metro* (1980).

Visconti, Count Luchino (Luchino Visconti di Modrone) (1906–76) Italian, born Milan; *The Leopard* (1963), *Ossessione* (1942), *The Damned* (1969), *Death in Venice* (1971).

Weir, Peter (1944–) Australian born Sydney; *The Cars that Ate Paris* (1974), *Picnic at Hanging Rock* (1975), *The Last Wave* (1977), *Gallipoli* (1981), *The Year of Living Dangerously* (1982), *Witness* (1985), *Mosquito Coast* (1986), *Dead Poet's Society* (1989), *Green Card* (1990).

Welles, (George) Orson (1915–85) American, born Kenosha, Wisconsin; *Citizen Kane* (1941), *The Magnificent Ambersons* (1942), *Jane Eyre* (1943), *Macbeth* (1948), *Othello* (1951), *Touch of Evil* (1958), *The Trial* (1962), *Chimes at Midnight* (1966).

Wise, Robert (1914–) American, born Winchester Indiana; *The Body Snatcher* (1945), *The Day the Earth Stood Still* (1951), *West Side Story* (1961), *The Sound of Music* (1965), *Star Trek The Motion Picture* (1979).

Zeffirelli, Franco (1922–) Italian, born Florence; *The Taming of the Shrew* (1966), *Romeo and Juliet* (1968), *Brother Sun, Sister Moon* (1973), *Jesus of Nazareth* (TV 1977), *The Champ* (1979), *Endless Love* (1981), *La Traviata* (1982), *Otello* (1986), *Hamlet* (1990).

Zemeckis, Robert (1951–) American, born Chicago; *I Wanna Hold Your Hand* (1978), *Romancing The Stone* (1984), *Back to the Future* (1985), *Who Framed Roger Rabbit?* (1988), *Back to the Future II* (1989), *Back to the Future III* (1990), *Death Becomes Her* (1992).

Zinnemann, Fred (1907–) American/Austrian, born Vienna, Austria; *High Noon* (1952), *From Here to Eternity* (1953), *A Man for All Seasons* (1966), *Five Days One Summer* (1982).

COMPOSERS

Albéniz, Issac (1860–1909) Spanish, born Camprodón, Catalonia; works include operas and works for piano based on Spanish folk music (eg *Iberia*).

Bach, Johann Sebastian (1685–1750) German, born Eisenach; prolific composer, works include over 190 cantatas and oratorios, concertos, chamber music, keyboard music, and orchestral works (eg *Toccata and Fugue in D minor, The Well-tempered Clavier, Six Brandenburg Concertos, St Matthew Passion, Mass in B minor, Goldberg Variations, The Musical Offering, The Art Of Fugue*).

Bartók, Béla (1881–1945) Hungarian, born Nagyszentmiklós; six string quartets, *Sonata for 2 pianos and percussion*, concertos (for piano, violin, viola, and notably the *Concerto for Orchestra*), opera, (*Duke Bluebeard's Castle*), two ballets (*The Wooden Prince, The Miraculous Mandarin*), songs, choruses, folksong arrangements.

Beethoven, Ludwig van (1770–1827) German, born Bonn; works include 33 piano sonatas (eg the 'Pathetique', 'Moonlight', *Waldstein, Appassionata*), nine symphonies (eg *Eroica*, 'Pastoral', *Choral* Symphony (no. 9)), string quartets, concertos, *Lebewohl* and the opera *Fidelio*.

Berg, Alban (1885–1935) Austrian, born Vienna; works include songs (*Four Songs*), operas (*Wozzeck, Lulu*, unfinished), a violin concerto and a string quartet (*Lyric Suite*).

Berio, Luciano (1925–) Italian, born Oneglia; works include compositions using tapes and electronic music (eg *Mutazioni, Omaggio a James Joyce*), works for solo instruments (*Sequenzas*), stage works (eg *Laborintus II, Opera*) and symphonies (*Synfonia*).

Berlioz, (Louis) Hector (1803–69) French, born Côte St André, near Grenoble; works include the overture *Le carnival romain*, the cantata (*La Damnation de Faust*), symphonies (eg *Symphonie Fantastique, Romeo et Juliette*) and operas (eg *Béatrice et Bénédict, Les Toyens*).

Bernstein, Leonard (1918–90) American, born Laurence, Massachusetts; works include ballets (*Jeremiah, The Age of Anxiety, Kaddish*), symphonies (eg *Fancy Free, The Dybbuk*), and musicals, (eg *Candide, West Side Story, On The Town, Songfest, Halil*).

Bizet, Georges (1838–75) French, born Paris; works include opera (eg *Carmen, Les Pêcheurs de Perles, La Jolie Fille de Perth*) incidental music to Daudet's play *L'Arlésienne* and a symphony.

Boulez, Pierre (1925–) French, born Montbrison; works include three piano sonatas and works for piano and flute (eg *Sonatine*).

Brahms, Johannes (1833–97) German, born Hamburg; works include songs, four symphonies, two piano concertos, choral work (eg *German Requiem*), orchestral work (eg *Variations on a Theme of Haydn*), programme work (eg *Tragic overture*), also the *Academic Festival Overture* and *Hungarian Dances*.

Bruckner, Anton (1824–96) Austrian, born Ansfelden; works include nine symphonies, a string quartet, choral-orchestral Masses and other church music (eg *Te Deum*).

Cage, John (1912–) American, born Los Angeles; works include unorthodox modern compositions, eg *Sonatas and Interludes for the prepared piano*.

Carter, Elliott Cook Jr (1908–) American, born New York City; works include quartets, symphonies, concertos, songs and chamber music.

Chabrier, Emmanuel (1841–94) French, born Ambert; works include operas (*Gwendoline, Le Roi malgré lui, Briséis*) and an orchestral rhapsody (*España*).

Chausson, Ernest (1855–99) French, born Paris; works include songs and orchestral works (eg *Poème*).

Chopin, Frédéric François (1810–49) Polish, born Zelazowa Wola, near Warsaw; wrote almost exclusively for piano – nocturnes, polonaises, mazurkas, preludes, concertos, and a funeral march.

Copland, Aaron (1900–90) American, born Brooklyn, New York; ballets (eg *Billy The Kid, Appalachian Spring*), film scores (eg *Our Town, The Hucis*), symphonies (eg *Symphonie Ode, Connotations, Clarinet Concerto*).

Corelli, Arcangelo (1653–1713) Italian, born Fusignano, near Bologna; works include 12 concertos (eg *Concerto for Christmas Night*), and solo and trio sonatas for violin.

COMPOSERS (cont.)

Couperin, François (1668–1733) French, born Paris; works include chamber music, four books containing 240 harpsichord pieces, motets and other church music.

Debussy, Claude Achille (1862–1918) French, born St Germaine-en-Laye, near Paris; songs (eg the cantata *L'Enfant prodigue*), opera (*Pelléas et Mélisande*), orchestral works (eg *Prèlude à l'après-midi d'un faune, La Mer*), chamber and piano music (eg *Feux d'artifice, La Cathédrale engloutie*).

Delius, Frederick (1862–1934) English (of German Scandinavian descent), born Bradford; works include songs (eg *A Song of Summer, Idyll, Songs of Farewell*), concertos, operas (eg *Koanga, A Village Romeo and Juliette*), chamber music and orchestral variations (eg *Appalachia, Sea Drift, A Mass of Life*).

Dukas, Paul (1865–1935) French, born Paris; works include a symphonic poem (*L'Apprenti sorcier*) and opera (*Ariane et Barbe-Bleue*).

Dutilleux, Henri (1916–) French, born Angers; works include a piano sonata, two symphonies, a violin concerto, a string quartet (*Ainsi la nuit*), compositions for two pianos and other orchestral works.

Dvořák, Antonin (1841–1904) Czech, born near Prague; works include songs, concertos, choral (eg *Hymnus*) and chamber music, symphonies (notably 'From the New World'), operas (eg *Rusalka* (The Water Nymph), *Armida, Slavonic Dances*).

Elgar, Sir Edward (William) (1857–1934) English, born Broadheath, near Worcester; works include chamber music, two symphonies, oratorios (eg *The Dream of Gerontius, The Apostles, The Kingdom*), and the orchestral work *Enigma Variations*.

Falla, Manuel de (1876–1946) Spanish, born Cadiz; works include opera (eg *La Vida Breve, Master Peter's Puppet Show*), ballet (eg *The Three-Cornered Hat, Love the Magician*) and orchestral suites (eg *Nights in the Gardens of Spain*).

Fauré, Gabriel Urbain (1845–1924) French, born Pamiers; works include songs (eg *Après un rêve*), chamber music, choral music (eg the *Requiem*), operas and orchestral music (eg *Marques et bergamasques*).

Franck, César Auguste (1822–90) naturalized French, born Liège, Belgium; works include tone-poems, (eg *Les Béatitudes*), sonatas for violin and piano, symphony in D minor and *Variations symphoniques* for piano and orchestra.

Gershwin, George (1898–1937) American, born Brooklyn, New York; Broadway musicals (eg *Lady Be Good, Of Thee I Sing*), symphonies, songs (notably 'I Got Rhythm', 'The Man I Love'), operas (eg *Porgy and Bess*), and concert works (eg *Rhapsody in Blue, Concerto in F, An American in Paris*).

Grainger, Percy Aldridge (1882–1961) Australian, born Melbourne; works include songs, piano and chamber music (eg *Molly on the Shore, Mock Morris, Shepherds Hey*).

Grieg, Edvard Hagerup (1843–1907) Norwegian, born Bergen; works include songs, a piano concerto, orchestral suites, violin sonatas, choral music and incidental music for *Peer Gynt* and *Sigurd Jorsalfar*.

Handel, George Frideric (1685–1759) naturalized English, born Halle, Saxony; prolific output including over 27 operas (eg *Almira, Rinaldo, Beggar's Opera*), 20 oratorios (eg *The Messiah, Saul, Israel in Egypt, Samson, Jephthah*), orchestral suites (eg the *Water Music* and *Music for the Royal Fireworks*), organ concertos and chamber music.

Haydn, (Franz) Joseph (1732–1809) Austrian, born Rohrau, Lower Austria; prolific output including 104 symphonies (eg the 'Salomon' or 'London' Symphonies), string quartets and oratorios (notably *The Creation, The Seasons*).

Holst, Gustav Theodore (originally von Holst) (1874–1934) English of Swedish origin, born Cheltenham; works include choral and ballet music, operas (eg *The Perfect Fool, At the Boar's Head*), orchestral suites (eg *The Planets, St Paul's Suite for Strings*), choral music (eg *The Hymn of Jesus, Ode to Death*), and *Concerto for Two Violins*.

Honegger, Arthur (1892–1955) French, born Le Harve; works include five symphonies and dramatic oratorios (*King David, Joan of Arc at the Stake*).

Ireland, John Nicholson (1879–1962) English, born Bowden, Cheshire; works include sonatas (eg Violin

COMPOSERS (cont.)

Sonata in A), piano music, songs (eg 'Sea Fever'), the rhapsody *Mai-dun* and orchestral works (eg *The Forgotten Rite, These Things Shall Be*).

Ives, Charles (1874–1954) American, born Danbury, Connecticut; works include five symphonies, chamber music (eg *Concord Sonata*) and many songs.

Janáček, Leoš (1854–1928) Czech, born Hukvaldy, Moravia; works include chamber, orchestral and choral music (eg the song cycle *The Diary of One Who Has Vanished*), operas (eg *Janufa, The Cunning Little Vixen, The Excursions of Mr Brouček, From the House of the Dead*), two string quartets and a mass.

Lalo, (Victor Antoine) Édouard (1823–92) French, born Lille. Works include compositions for violin (eg *Symphonie espagnole*), opera (eg *Le Roi d'Ys*) and ballet (*Namouna*).

Ligeti, Györgi Sándor (1923–) Hungarian, born Dicsöszentmárton; works include orchestral compositions (eg *Apparitions, Lontano, Double Concerto*), choral works (eg *Requiem*) and music for harpsichord, organ and wind and string ensembles.

Liszt, France (1811–1886) Hungarian, born Raiding; 400 original compositions including symphonic poems, piano music and masses (eg *The Legend of St Elizabeth, Christus*).

Mahler, Gustav (1860–1911) Austrian, born Kalist, Bohemia; works include ten symphonies, songs, the cantata *Das klagende Lied*, and the song-symphony *Das lied von der Erde* (The Song of the Earth).

Mendelssohn, (Jacob Ludwig) Felix (1809–47) German, born Hamburg; prolific output, including concerto overtures (eg *Fingal's Cave, Midsummer Night's Dream, Hebrides, Scotch Symphony*), symphonies (Symphony in C minor), quartets (B minor Quartet), operas (eg *Camacho's Wedding*), and oratorios (eg *Elijah*).

Messiaen, Olivier Eugène Prosper Charles (1908–) French, born Avignon; works include compositions for piano (*Vingt regards sur l'enfant Jésus, Catalogue d'oiseaux*), the symphony *Turangalila*, an oratorio (*La Transfiguration de Notre Seigneur Jésus-Christ*) and an opera (*St François d'Assisi*).

Milhaud, Darius (1892–1974) French, born Aix-en-Provence; works include several operas, incidental music for plays, ballets (eg the jazz ballet *La Création du monde*), symphonies and orchestral, choral and chamber works.

Monteverdi, Claudio (Giovanni Antonio) (1567–1643) Italian, born Cremona; works include masses (eg *Mass* and *Vespers* of the Virgin), cantatas and operas (eg *Orfeo, Il Ritorno d'Ulisse, L'Incoronazione di Poppea* (The Coronation of Poppea)).

Mozart, (Johann Chrysostom) Wolfgang Amadeus (1756–91) Austrian, born Salzburg; 600 compositions including symphonies (eg 'Jupiter', *Linz, Prague*), concertos, string quartets, sonatas, operas (eg *Marriage of Figaro, Don Giovanni, Cosi fan tutte*) and the Singspiels *The Abduction from the Seraglio, Die Zauberflöte*.

Mussorgsky, Modeste (1839–81) Russian, born Karevo, government of Pskov; works include operas (eg *Boris Godunov*), song cycles and instrumental works (eg *Pictures from an Exhibition, Night on the Bare Mountain*).

Nielsen, Carl August (1865–1931) Danish, born Furen; works include operas (eg *Saul and David, Masquerade*), symphonies (eg 'The Four Temperaments'), string quartets, choral and piano music.

Palestrina, Giovanni Pierluigi da (c.1525–1594) Italian, born Palestrina, near Rome; works include chamber music and the organ work *Commotion*, masses, choral music (eg *Song of Songs*), madrigals.

Prokofiev, Sergei (1891–1953) Russian, born Sontsovka in the Ukraine; works include 11 operas (eg *The Gambler, The Love for the Three Oranges, The Fiery Angels, Semyon Kotko, Betrothal in a Monastery, War and Peace, The Story of a Real Man*), ballets (eg *Romeo and Juliet, Cinderella*), concertos, sonatas, cantatas (eg *We are Seven, Hail to Stalin*), film scores (eg *Alexander Nevsky*), and the 'children's piece' *Peter and the Wolf*.

Puccini, Giacomo (Antonio Domenico Michele Secondo Maria) (1858–1924) Italian, born Lucca; 12 operas (eg *Manon Lescaut, La Bohème, Tosca, Madama Butterfly, Turandot*).

Purcell, Henry (1659–95) English, born London; works include songs (eg 'Nymphs and Shepherds', 'Arise, ye Subterranean Winds'), sonatas, string fantasies, church music and opera (eg *Dido and Aeneas*).

COMPOSERS (cont.)

Rachmaninov, Sergei Vasilyevich (1873–1943) Russian, born Nizhi-Novgorod; works include operas, three symphonies, four piano concertos (eg *Prelude in C Sharp Minor*), the tone-poem *The Isle of the Dead*, and *Rhapsody on a Theme of Paganini* for piano and orchestra.

Rameau, Jean Philippe (1683–1764) French, born Dijon; works include over 30 ballets and operas (eg *Hippolyte et Aricie, Castor et Pollux*) and harpsichord pieces.

Ravel, Maurice (1875–1937) French, born Ciboure, in the Basque country; works include piano compositions (eg *Sonatina, Miroirs, Ma Mère L'Oye, Gaspard de la nuit*), string quartets, operas (eg *L'Heure espagnol, L'Enfant et les sortilèges*), ballets (eg *Daphnis and Chloë*), the 'choreographic poem' *La Valse* and the miniature ballet *Boléro*.

Rimsky-Korsakov, Nikolai Andreievich (1844–1908) Russian, born Tikhvin, Novgorod; works include orchestral music (eg the symphonic suite *Sheherazade, Capriccio Espagnol, Easter Festival*) and 15 operas (eg *Sadko, The Snow Maiden, The Tsar Sultan, The Invisible City of Kitesh, The Goldern Cockerel*).

Rossini, Gioacchino Antonio (1792–1868) Italian, born Pesaro; works include many operas (eg *Il Barbiere de Seviglia, Otella, Guillaume Tell*) and a number of vocal and piano pieces.

Roussel, Albert (1869–1937) French, born Tourcoing; works include four symphonies, numerous choral works (eg *Évocations*), ballets (eg *Bacchus and Ariane, Le Festin de l'araignée*) and an opera (*Padmâvati*).

Saint-Saëns, (Charles) Camille (1835–1921) French, born Paris; works include four symphonic poems (eg *Danse macabre*), piano (*Le Rouet d'Omphale, Phaëton, La Jeunesse d'Hercule*), violin and cello concertos, symphonies, the opera *Samson et Dalila*, church music (eg *Messe solennelle*), and *Carnival des animaux* for two pianos and orchestra.

Satie, Erik Alfred Leslie (1866–1925) French, born Honfleur; works include ballets (eg *Parade*), lyric dramas and whimsical pieces.

Scarlatti, (Guiseppe) Domenico (1685–1757) Italian, born Naples; works include over 600 harpsichord sonatas.

Schönberg, Arnold (1874–1951) naturalized American, born Vienna; works include chamber music (eg *Chamber Symphony*), concertos (eg *Piano Concerto*), and symphonic poems (eg *Pelleas und Melisande*), the choral-orchestral *Gurrelieder*, string quartets, the oratorio *Die Jacobsiter*, and opera (*Von Heute auf Morgen, Moses und Aaron*).

Schubert, Franz Peter (1797–1828) Austrian, born Vienna; prolific output, works include symphonies, piano sonatas, string quartets and songs (eg *Gretchen am Spinnrade, Erlkönig, Die schöne Müllerin, Winterreise, Who is Sylvia?, Hark, Hark the Lark, Schwanengesang* ('Swan-song')).

Schumann, Robert Alexander (1810–56) German, born Zwickau, Saxony; works include piano music (eg *Fantasiestücke*), songs (eg The Fool's Song in *Twelfth Night*, the Chamisso songs *Frauenliebe und Leben* or 'Woman's Love and Life'), chamber music, and four symphonies (eg the *Rhenish*).

Scriabin, Alexander (1872–1915) Russian, born Moscow; works include a piano concerto, three symphonies, two tone poems (eg *Poem of Ecstasy*), 10 sonatas, studies and preludes.

Shostakovich, Dmitri (1906–75) Russian, born St Petersburg; works include 15 symphonies, operas (eg *The Nose, A Lady Macbeth of Mtensk*), concertos, string quartets and film music.

Sibelius, Jean (1865–1957) Finnish, born Tavastehus; works include symphonic poems (eg *Swan of Tuonela, En Saga*), songs, a violin concerto, and seven symphonies.

Stockhausen, Karlheinz (1928–) German, born Mödrath, near Cologne; works include orchestral (eg *Gruppen*), choral and instrumental compositions.

Strauss, Johann (the Younger) (1825–99) Austrian, born Vienna; works include over 400 waltzes (eg *The Blue Danube, Wine, Women, and Song, Perpetuum Mobile, Artist's Life, Tales from the Vienna Woods, Voices from Spring, The Emperor*), and operettas (eg *Die Flederamaus, A Night in Venice*).

Strauss, Richard (1864–1949) German, born Munich; works include symphonic poems (eg *Don Juan, Till Eulenspiegel, Also Sprach Zarathustra, Tod und Verklärung ('Death and Transfiguration'), Don Quixote, Ein Heldenleben*) and operas (eg *Der Rosenkavalier, Ariadne auf Naxos, Capriccio*).

COMPOSERS (cont.)

Stravinsky, Igor (1882–1971) Russian, born Oranienbaum, near St Petersburg (naturalized French, then American); works include operas (eg *The Rake's Progress*), oratorios (eg *Oedipus Rex, Symphony of Psalms*), concertos, ballets (eg *The Firebird, The Rite of Spring, Petrushka, Pulcinella, Apollo Musogetes, The Card Game, Orpheus, Agon*), and a musical play *Elegy for J.F.K* for voice and clarinets.

Tchaikovsky, Piotr Ilyich (1840–93) Russian, born Kamsko-Votinsk; works include ten operas (eg *Eugene Onegin, The Queen of Spades*), a violin concerto, six symphonies, two piano concertos, three ballets (*The Nutcracker, Swan Lake, The Sleeping Beauty*) and tone-poems (eg *Romeo and Juliet, Italian Capriccio*).

Telemann, George Philipp (1681–1767) German, born Magdeburg; prolific composer, works include 600 overtures, 40 operas, 200 concertos, sonatas, suites, and overtures (eg *Der Tag de Gerichts, Die Tageszeiten*).

Tippett, Sir Michael Kemp (1905–) English, born London; works include operas (eg *The Midsummer Marriage, King Priam, The Knot Garden, The Ice Break*), concertos, symphonies, cantatas and oratorios (eg *A Child of our Time, The Vision of St Augustine*).

Varèse, Edgar (1883–1965) American, born Paris; works are alost entirely orchestral (eg *Metal, Ionization, Hyperprism*).

Vaughan Williams, Ralph (1872–1958) English, born Down Ampney, Gloucestershire; works include songs, symphonies (eg *London Symphony, Pastoral Symphony*), choral-orchestral works (eg *Sea Symphony, Magnificat*), operas (eg *Hugh the Drover, The Pilgrim's Progress*), a ballet *Job*, and film music (eg for *Scott of the Antarctic*).

Verdi, Giuseppe (1813–1901) Italian, born le Roncole, near Busseto; church music (eg *Requiem*), operas (eg *Oberto, Nabucco, Rigoletto, Il Trovatore, La Traviata, Un Ballo in Maschera, La Forza del Destino, Aïda, Otello, Falstaff*).

Vivaldi, Antonio (1678–1741) Italian, born Venice; prolific output, works include over 400 concertos (eg *L'Estro Armonico, The Four Seasons*), 40 operas and an oratorio, *Juditha triumphans.*

Wagner, (Wilhelm) Richard (1813–83) German, born Leipzig; operas include *Lohengin, Rienzi*, the *Ring* cycle (*Das Rheingold, Die Walküre, Siegfried, Götterdämmerung*), *Die Meistersinger, Tristan und Isolde, Parsifal.*

Walton, Sir William Turner (1902–83) English, born Oldham; works include concertos, operas (*Troilus and Cressida, The Bear*), a cantata (*Belshazzar's Feast*), ballet music for *The Wise Virgins*, a song-cycle (*Anon in Love*) and film music.

Weber, Carl Maria von (1786–1826) German, born Eutin, near Lübeck; works include operas (eg *Oberon, Euryanthe, Silvana*), concertos, symphonies, sonatas, scenas, cantatas (eg *Kampf and Sieg*) and songs.

Webern, Anton von (1883–1945) Austrian, born Vienna; works include a symphony, three cantatas, *Four Pieces for Violin and Pianoforte, Fives Pieces for Orchestra*, a concerto for nine instruments and songs.

Xenakis, Iannis (1922–) Greek, born Romania; works include compositions for piano and orchestra (eg *Erikhthon*), *Shaar* for strings, *Tetras* for string quartet and solo pieces (eg *Nomos Alpha* for cello, *Herma* for piano), *Pithoprakta* for 50 instruments.

SONGWRITERS

A selection of songs is listed.

Arlen, Harold (Hyman Arluck) (1905–86) American, born Buffalo, New York; over 500 songs, including 'Between the Devil and the Deep Blue Sea', 'Stormy Weather', 'Get Happy' (lyrics by Ted Koehler), *A Star is Born* (1953) ('The Man that Got Away') (lyrics by Ira Gershwin); *The Wizard of Oz* (1939) ('Over the Rainbow') (lyrics by E Y Harburg, 1896–1981).

Berlin, Irving (originally **Israel Baline**) (1888–1989) American, born Temus, Siberia; composer; *Annie Get Your Gun* (1946), *Call Me Madam* (1950); over 900 songs, including 'There's No Business Like Show Business', 'White Christmas', 'God Bless America', 'Oh, How I Hate to Get Up in the Morning'.

SONGWRITERS (cont.)

Bernstein, Leonard (1918–90) American composer of opera, symphonies, songs, born Laurence, Massachusetts; *West Side Story* (1958) (lyrics by Stephen Sondheim); songs include 'You Got Me', 'New York, New York'.

Britten, Baron (Edward) Benjamin, of Aldeburgh (1913–76) English, born Lowestoft; composer of choral symphonic works, opera, song cycles eg *Our Hunting Fathers, On This Island* (text by WH Auden).

Brown, Nacio Herb (1896–1954) American, born Deming, New Mexico; composer; *Broadway Melody* (lyrics by Arthur Field, 1894–1973); *Singin' in the Rain* (1952); songs include 'You were Meant for Me'.

Cahn, Sammy (Samuel) (1913–) American lyricist, born New York; 'I've Heard That Song Before', 'I'll Walk Alone', 'It's Magic' (with Jule Styne); 'All the Way', 'High Hopes' (with Jimmy van Heusen).

Cohan, George M(ichael) (1878–1942) American composer, lyricist, born Providence, Rhode Island; *Little Johnny Jones* (1904) ('Give My Regards to Broadway'); 'The Talk of the Town' (1907).

Coward, Sir Noël Pierce (1899–1973) English composer, lyricist, playwright, born Teddington; *Words and Music* (revue) (1932) ('Mad Dogs and Englishmen', 'Someday I'll Find You').

Dylan, Bob (Robert Allen Zimmermann) (1941–) American songwriter, musician, born Duluth, Minnesota; 'Blowin' in the Wind', 'With God on Our Side', 'The Times They are A–Changing', 'It's Alright Ma, I'm Only Bleeding', 'Mr Tambourine Man', 'Subterranean Homesick Blues', 'Like a Rolling Stone', 'Leopard-Skin Pill-Box Hat', 'Knockin' on Heaven's Door'.

Ellington, (Edward Kennedy) 'Duke' (1899–1974) American pianist, composer, bandleader, born Washington DC; 2000 works, including songs, instrumentals, film music: 'It Don't Mean a Thing if it Ain't Got That Swing' (lyrics Irving Mills), 'Best Wishes' (lyrics Ted Koehler), 'Creole Love Call' (vocal, no lyrics).

Fields, Dorothy (1905–74) American lyricist, born Allenhurst, New Jersey; 'I Can't Give You Anything But Love' (with Jimmy McHugh, from *Blackbirds* (1928)), 'On the Sunny Side of the Street (with Jimmy McHugh), 'Exactly Like You', 'Lovely to Look At' and 'The Way You Look Tonight' (with Jerome Kern); *Stars in Your Eyes* (1939) (with Arthur Schwartz); *Sweet Charity* (1966) ('Big Spender') (with Cy Coleman).

Gershwin, George (originally **Jacob Gershvin**) (1898–1937) American composer, born Brooklyn, New York, and **Ira Gershwin** (originally **Israel Gershvin**) (1896–1983) American lyricist, born New York; *Lady, Be Good!* ('The Man I Love', 'How Long Has This Been Going On?'), *Girl Crazy, Porgy and Bess* ('Summertime') (lyrics by Ira Gershwin and Du Bose Heyward); songs include 'You Can't Take That Away from Me', 'Nice Work if You Can Get It', 'Love Walked in', 'They All Laughed'.

Gilbert, Sir William Schwenck (1836–1911) English librettist, born London, and **Sir Arthur Sullivan Seymour** (1842–1900) English composer, born London; operettas and songs include *H.M.S. Pinafore* (1878), *The Mikado* (1885), *The Gondoliers* (1889).

Herman, Jerry (1932–) American composer, lyricist, born New York; *Hello Dolly!* (1964), *Mame* (1966).

Kern, Jerome (David) (1885–1945) American composer, born New York; 'The Way You Look Tonight' (lyrics Dorothy Fields), 'Ol' Man River', 'They Didn't Believe Me' (lyrics Herbert Reynold); *Show Boat* (1927) (lyrics Oscar Hammerstein II (1895–1960) American lyricist, born New York).

Lennon, John (Winston) (1940–80) English songwriter, musician, born Liverpool, and **(James) Paul McCartney** (1942–) English songwriter, musician, born Liverpool; 'Please Please Me', 'Yesterday', 'All You Need is Love', 'Strawberry Fields', 'I Want to Hold Your Hand', 'Michelle', 'Eleanor Rigby', 'Ticket to Ride', 'Dear Prudence', 'Help!'.

Livingston, Jay (1915–) American composer, lyricist, born McDonald, Pennsylvania; and **Ray Evans** (1915–) American lyricist, born Salamanca, New York; 'The Cat and the Canary', 'Mona Lisa', 'Whatever Will Be, Will Be (Que Sera Sera)', 'Dear Heart'.

Lloyd Webber, Sir Andrew (1948–) English composer, born London, with **Tim Rice** (1944–) English lyricist, born Amersham, Buckinghamshire: *Joseph and the Amazing Technicolor Dreamcoat* (1968) ('Any Dream Will Do'); *Jesus Christ Superstar* (1970) ('Jesus Christ Superstar', 'I Don't Know How to Love Him'), *Evita* (1978) ('Don't Cry for Me, Argentina'); *Cats* (1981) (libretto TS Eliot), *Phantom of the Opera* (1986), *Aspects of Love* (1989).

SONGWRITERS (cont.)

Loesser, Frank (Henry) (1910–69) American composer, lyricist, born New York; *Guys and Dolls* (1950) ('I've never Been in Love Before', 'Luck Be a Lady'); *The Perils of Pauline* (1947) (words and music); lyrics for 'The Boys in the Back Room' (music by Frederick Hollander); lyrics for 'The Lady's in Love with You' and 'Some Like it Hot', from the film *Some Like it Hot* (1959).

McHugh, Jimmy (James Frances McHugh) (1896–1969) American composer, born Boston, Massachusetts; with Dorothy Fields, as above; 'I'm Shooting High' (with Ted Koehler), 'Exactly Like You' (with Al Dubin).

Mancini, Henry (1924–) American composer of songs and film music, born Cleveland, Ohio; over 80 films eg *Breakfast at Tiffany's* (1961); songs include 'Moon River' (lyrics Johnny Mercer), 'Days of Wine and Roses', 'Charade'.

Mercer, Johnny H (1909–76) American lyricist, born Savannah, Georgia; 1500 songs for over 70 films and 7 Broadway musicals; songs with Mancini, as above; 'Blues in the Night' (music by Harold Arlen), 'That Old Black Magic' (music by Harold Arlen), 'Jeepers Creepers' (music by Henry Warren); lyrics for *Seven Brides for Seven Brothers.*

Porter, Cole (1891–1964) American composer, lyricist, born Peru, Indiana; *Gay Divorcee* (1932), *Anything Goes* (1934), *Du Barry Was a Lady* ('Well, Did You Evah!') (1939), *Kiss Me Kate* (1948) ('So in Love'); songs include 'I'm in Love Again', 'Let's Do It, Let's Fall in Love', 'Just one of Those Things'.

Rodgers, Richard (1902–79) American composer, born Long Island, New York; with **Lorenz Hart** (1895–1943) American lyricist, born New York: *The Girl Friend* (1926), *Babes in Arms* (1937), 'Manhattan'; with **Oscar Hammerstein II** (1895–1960) American lyricist, born New York: *Oklahoma!* (1943) ('Oh, What a Beautiful Morning'), *South Pacific* (1949), *The King and I* (1959) ('Shall We Dance?'), *The Sound of Music* (1959) ('Do–Re–Mi', 'Edelweiss').

Romberg, Sigmund (1887–1951) American composer, born Nagykanizsa, Hungary; *The Desert Song* (1926), *The New Moon* (1928) ('Lover Come Back to Me'), *The Student Prince* (1924), *Girl of the Golden West* (film, 1938).

Schubert, Franz (Peter) (1797–1828) Austrian composer, born Vienna; works include 145 songs, texts by Schiller and Goethe, among others.

Schumann, Robert (Alexander) (1810–56) German composer, born Zwickau; songs to texts by Heine, among others, 1840.

Simon, Paul (1942–) American songwriter, musician, born Newark, New Jersey; 'I am a Rock', 'Bridge over Troubled Water', 'Mrs Robinson', 'Cecilia', 'Keep the Customer Satisfied', 'Homeward Bound', 'The Boxer', 'The Sound of Silence'.

Sondheim, Stephen (Joshua) (1930–) American composer, lyricist, born New York; lyrics for Bernstein's *West Side Story* (1958), *A Funny Thing Happened on the Way to the Forum* (1962), *A Little Night Music* (1973) ('Send in the Clowns') (lyrics and music).

Stynge, Jule (1905–) American composer, born London; 'There Goes that Song Again', 'I'll Walk Alone', 'It's Magic' (with Sammy Cahn)'; *Gentlemen Prefer Blondes* (1949) ('Diamonds are a Girl's Best Friend') with Leo Robin.

Warren, Harry (1893–1981) American composer of songs, film scores, born Brooklyn, New York; 'You're My Everything', 'We're in the Money', 'Chattanooga Choo–Choo', 'Jeepers Creepers' (with Mercer); with **Al Dubin** (1891–1945) American lyricist, born Zurich, Switzerland: *42nd Street* (1932), 'The Boulevard of Broken Dreams', 'I Only Have Eyes for You'.

Weill, Kurt (1900–50) German composer, born Dessau; songs, opera, with **Bertolt Eugene Friedrich Brecht** (1898–1956) German lyricist, playwright, born Augsburg: *Threepenny Opera* (1928) ('Mack the Knife'); *Lady in the Dark* (1941) (lyrics Ira Gershwin), *Street Scene* (1947) (lyrics Langston Hughes), *Lost in the Stars* (1949) (lyrics Maxwell Anderson).

OPERAS AND OPERETTAS

Name	Composer	Date
Aida	Verdi	1871
Akhnaten	Philip Glass	1984
Albert Herring	Britten	1947
Alceste	Gluck	1767
Andrea Chénier	Umberto Giordano	1896
Ariadne auf Naxos	Richard Strauss	1916
Armide et Renaud	Lully	1686
Un Ballo in Maschera	Verdi	1859
The Barber of Seville	Rossini	1816
The Bartered Bride	Smetana	1866
Béatrice et Bénédict	Berlioz	1862
The Beggar's Opera	Gay	1728
Bluebeard's Castle	Bartók	1918
Billy Budd	Britten	1951
La Bohème	Puccini	1896
Boris Godunov	Mussorgsky	1874
Capriccio	Richard Strauss	1942
Carmen	Bizet	1875
Cavalleria Rusticana	Mascagni	1890
La Cenerentola (Cinderella)	Rossini	1817
La Clemenza di Tito	Mozart	1791
The Consul	Gian-Carlo Menotti	1950
Cosi Fan Tutte	Mozart	1790
The Cunning Little Vixen	Janáček	1924
The Damnation of Faust	Berlioz	1846
Death in Venice	Britten	1973
Dido and Aeneas	Purcell	1689
Don Carlos	Verdi	1867
Don Giovanni	Mozart	1787
Don Pasquale	Donizetti	1843
Duke Bluebeard's Castle	Bartók	1918
The Egyptian Helen	Richard Strauss	1928
Einstein on the Beach	Philip Glass	1976
Elegy for Young Lovers	Hans Werner Henze	1961
Elektra	Richard Strauss	1909
Eugene Onegin	Tchaikovsky	1879
The Fair Maid of Perth	Bizet	1867
Falstaff	Verdi	1893
Faust	Gounod	1859
La Fille du Régiment	Donizetti	1840
Fidelio	Beethoven	1814
Die Fledermaus	Johann Strauss	1874
The Flying Dutchman	Wagner	1843
La Gioconda	Amilcare Ponchielli	1876
The Golden Cockerel	Rimsky-Korsakov	1909
The Gondoliers	Gilbert and Sullivan	1889
Le Grand Macabre	Ligeti	1978
Hansel and Gretel	Humperdinck	1893
H.M.S. Pinafore	Gilbert and Sullivan	1878
Hugh the Drover	Vaughan Williams	1924
The Ice Break	Tippett	1977
Idomeneo	Mozart	1781
L'Incoronazione di Poppea	Monteverdi	1642
Iphigénie en Tauride	Gluck	1779
Jenufa	Janáček	1904
Katya Kabanova	Janáček	1921
King Priam	Tippet	1962
Lady Macbeth of Mtsensk	Shostakovich	1934
Lohengrin	Wagner	1850
The Love for the Three Oranges	Prokofiev	1920
Lucia di Lammermoor	Donizetti	1835
Lucrezia Borgia	Donizetti	1833
Lulu	Berg	1937
Macbeth	Verdi	1847
Madama Butterfly	Puccini	1904
The Magic Flute	Mozart	1791
Les Mamelles de Tirésias	Poulenc	1947
Manon	Massenet	1884
Manon Lescaut	Puccini	1893
The Marriage of Figaro	Mozart	1786
Maskarade	Nielsen	1906
Mask of Orpheus	Harrison Birtwhistle	1986
Der Meistersinger von Nürnberg	Wagner	1868
The Merry Wives of Windsor	Otto Nicolai	1849
The Midsummer Marriage	Tippett	1955
The Mikado	Gilbert and Sullivan	1885
Moses und Aron	Schönberg	1954
Nabucco	Verdi	1842
Nixon in China	Peter Adams	1990
Norma	Bellini	1831
Noye's Fludde	Britten	1958

OPERAS AND OPERETTAS (cont.)

Name	Composer	Date
Oedipus Rex	Stravinsky	1927
Orfeo ed Euridice	Gluck	1762
Orpheus in the Underworld	Offenbach	1858
Otello	Verdi	1887
Pagliacci	Leoncavallo	1892
Parsifal	Wagner	1882
The Pearl Fishers	Bizet	1863
Pelléas et Mélisande	Debussy	1902
Peter Grimes	Britten	1945
Porgy and Bess	Gershwin	1935
Punch and Judy	Harrison Birtwhistle	1968
I Puritani	Bellini	1835
The Rake's Progress	Stravinsky	1951
The Rape of Lucretia	Britten	1946
Rigoletto	Verdi	1851
The Ring	Wagner	1876
Der Rosenkavalier	Richard Strauss	1911
Le Rossignol	Stravinsky	1914
Salome	Richard Strauss	1911
Samson et Dalila	Saint-Saëns	1877
Semele	Handel	1744
Simon Boccanegra	Verdi	1857
La Sonnambula	Bellini	1831
The Tales of Hoffman	Offenbach	1881
Tannhäuser	Wagner	1845
The Threepenny Opera	Weill	1928
Tosca	Puccini	1900
La Traviata	Verdi	1853
Tristan und Isolde	Wagner	1865
The Trojans	Berlioz	1863
Il Trovatore	Verdi	1853
Turandot	Puccini	1926
The Turn of the Screw	Britten	1954
I Vespri Siciliani	Verdi	1855
Werther	Massenet	1892
Where the Wild Things Are	Oliver Knussen	1980
William Tell	Rossini	1829
Wozzeck	Berg	1925

OPERA SINGERS

Allen, Thomas (1944–) English baritone, born Seaham.

Anderson, Marian (1902–) American contralto, born South Philadelphia.

Angeles, Victoria de Los (originally **Victora Gómez Cima**) (1923–) Spanish soprano, born Barcelona.

Austral, Florence (originally **Florence Wilson**) (1892–1968) Australian soprano, born Richmond, West Melbourne.

Bailey, Norman (Stanley) (1933–) English baritone, born Birmingham.

Baker, Dame Janet (Abbott) (1933–) English mezzo-soprano, born Hatfield, Yorkshire.

Barstow, Josephine (Clare) (1940–) English soprano, born Sheffield.

Battistini, Mattia (1856–1928) Italian baritone, born Rome.

Berganza, Teresa (1935–) Spanish mezzo-soprano, born Madrid.

Bonci, Alessandro (1870–1940) Italian tenor, born Cesena.

Butt, Dame Clara (1872–1936) English contralto, born Southwick, Sussex.

Callas, Maria (originally **Maria Anna Sofia Cecilia Kalogeropoulos**) (1923–77) American soprano of Greek parents, born New York.

Carreras, José (1946–) Spanish tenor, born Barcelona.

Caruso, Enrico (1873–1921) Italian tenor, born Naples.

Collier, Maria (1926–71) Australian soprano, born Ballarat.

Crossley, Ada (Jessica) (1874–1929) Australian mezzo-soprano, born Tarraville, Gippsland.

Davies, Arthur (1950–) Welsh tenor, born Wrexham, Wales.

Davies, Ryland (1943–) Welsh tenor, born Cwym, Ebbw Vale, Wales.

de Luca, Giuseppe (1876–1950) Italian baritone, born Rome.

De Lucia, Fernando (1860–1925) Italian tenor, born Naples.

de Reszke, Jean (originally **Jan Mieczislaw**) (1850–1925) Polish tenor, born Warsaw.

Del Monaco, Mario (1915–82) Italian tenor, born Florence.

OPERA SINGERS (cont.)

Domingo, Placido (1941–) Spanish tenor, born Madrid.
Evans, Sir Geraint (Llewellyn) (1922–) Welsh baritone, born Pontypridd, South Wales.
Farrar, Geraldine (1882–1967) American soprano, born Meltrose, Massachusetts.
Farrell, Eileen (1920–) American soprano, born Willimantic, Connecticut.
Ferrier, Kathleen (1912–53) English contralto, born Higher Walton, Lancashire.
Field, Helen (1951–) Welsh soprano, born Awyd, North Wales.
Fischer-Dieskau, Dietrich (1925–) German baritone, born Zehlendorf, Berlin.
Flagstad, Kirsten (1895–1962) Norwegian soprano, born Hamar.
Forrester, Maureen (1930–) Canadian contralto, born Montreal.
Fremstad, Olive (1871–1951) American soprano, born Stockholm.
Galli-Curci, Amelita (1882–1963) Italian soprano, born Milan.
Galli-Marie, Celestine (1840–1905) French mezzo-soprano, born Paris.
Gigli, Beniamino (1890–1957) Italian tenor, born Recanati.
Harper, Heather (1930–) Irish soprano, born Belfast.
Jurinac, Sena (1921–) Yugoslav soprano, born Travnik.
Lehmann, Lilli (1848–1929) German soprano, born Würzburg.
Lehmann, Lotte (1888–1976) German soprano, born Perleberg.
Lind, Jenny ('the Swedish Nightingale') (1820–87) Swedish soprano, born Stockholm.
Ludwig, Christa (Deiber) (1928–) German mezzo-soprano, born Berlin.
Meier, Johanna (1938–) American soprano, born Chicago.
Melba, Madam Nellie (originally **Helen Mitchell**) (1861–1931) Australian soprano, born Burnle, near Richmond.
Melchior, Lauritz (1890–1973) Danish tenor, born Copenhagen.
Nilsson, Birgit (1918–) Swedish soprano, born near Karup.
Norman, Jessye (1945–) American soprano, born Augusta, Georgia.
Patti, Adelina (Adela Juana Maria) (1843–1919) Italian soprano, born Madrid.
Pavarotti, Luciano (1935–) Italian tenor, born Modena.
Pears, Sir Peter (1910–86) English tenor, born Farnham, Surrey.
Pinza, Enzio (1892–1957) Italian bass, born Rome.
Popp, Lucia (1939–) Czech soprano, born Llhorsaká.
Schumann, Elsabeth (1888–1952) German soprano, born Merseburg.
Schwarzkopf, Elizabeth (1915–) German soprano, born Jarotschin, near Poznan, Poland.
Smirnov, Dimitri (1882–1944) Russian tenor, born Moscow.
Söderström, Elisabeth (1927–) Swedish soprano, born Stockholm.
Sutherland, Joan (1926–) Australian soprano, born Sydney.
Tear, Robert (1939–) Welsh tenor, born Barry, South Wales.
Te Kanawa, Dame Kiri (1944–) New Zealand soprano, born Gisborne.
Tetrazzini, Luisa (1871–1940) Italian soprano, born Florence.
Wiener, Otto (1913–) Austrian baritone, born Vienna.

ORCHESTRAS

Name	Date founded	Location
Academy of Ancient Music	1973	UK (London)
Academy of St Martin-in-the-Fields	1959	UK (London)
Berliner Philharmonic	1882	Germany
Boston Symphony Orchestra	1881	USA
BBC Northern Symphony Orchestra	1934	UK
BBC Scottish Symphony Orchestra	1935	UK (Glasgow)
BBC Symphony Orchestra	1930	UK (London)
BBC Welsh Symphony Orchestra	1935	UK (Cardiff)
Chicago Symphony Orchestra	1891	USA
Cleveland Symphony Orchestra	1918	USA
Concertgebouw Orchestra	1888	Netherlands (Amsterdam)
Detroit Symphony Orchestra	1914	USA
English Chamber Orchestra	1948	UK (London)
Hallé Orchestra	1858	UK (Manchester)
Israel Philharmonic Orchestra	1936	Israel(Tel Aviv)
Leningrad Philharmonic Orchestra	1921	USSR
London Philharmonic Orchestra	1904	UK
London Symphony Orchestra	1904	UK
Los Angeles Philharmonic Orchestra	1904	USA
Melbourne Symphony Orchestra	1906	Australia
Milan La Scala Orchestra	1778	Italy
NBC Symphony Orchestra	1937-54	USA (New York)
National Symphony Orchestra	1931	USA (Washington DC)
New Orleans Philharmonic Symphony Orchestra	1936	USA
New York Philharmonic Orchestra	1842	USA
New York Symphony Orchestra	1878	USA
Orchestre Symphonique de Monréal	1842	Canada
Oslo Philharmonic	1919	Norway
Philadelphia Orchestra	1900	USA
The Philharmonic Orchestra	1945	UK (London)
Pittsburgh Symphony Orchestra	1926	USA
Royal Philharmonic Orchestra	1946	UK (London)
San Francisco Symphony Orchestra	1911	USA
Santa Cecelia Academy Orchestra	1895	Italy (Rome)
Scottish Chamber Orchestra	1974	UK (Edinburgh)
Scottish National Orchestra	1890	UK (Glasgow)
Seattle Symphony Orchestra	1903	USA
Staatskapelle Orchestra	1923	Germany (Dresden)
Sydney Symphony Orchestra	1934	Australia
Ulster Orchestra	1966	UK (Belfast)
Vienna Philharmonic	1842	Austria
Vienna Symphony Orchestra	1900	Austria

POP AND ROCK MUSICIANS AND SINGERS

Selected singles and albums are listed.

Abba Swedish group, 1970s to early 1980s; members include Bjorn Ulvaeus (1945–) singer, guitarist, born Gothenburg; Agnetha Faltskog (1950–) singer, born Jankoping; Anni-Frid Lyngstad (1945–) singer, born Narvik, Norway; Benny Andersson (1946–) singer, keyboardist, born Stockholm; *Waterloo* (1974), *Arrival* (1976), *Voulez-Vous* (1979), *Super Trouper* (1980).

ABC British group, 1980s to present; members include Martin Fry (1958–) vocalist, born Manchester; Mark White (1961–) guitarist, born Sheffield; Stephen Singleton (1959–) saxophonist, born Sheffield; 'Poison Arrow', 'When Smokey Sings', *The Lexicon of Love* (1982), *Alphabet City* (1987).

Abdul, Paula (1963–) American singer; dancer, born Los Angeles; 'Straight Up', 'Cold Hearted', *Forever Your Girl* (1988), *Shut Up And Dance* (1989).

AC/DC Australian heavy metal group, mid-1970s to present; members include Bon Scott (originally Ronald Belford Scott) (1946–80) vocalist, born Kirriemuir, Scotland; Brian Johnson (1947–) vocalist, born North Shields; Angus Young (1959–) guitarist, born Glasgow, Scotland; Malcolm Young (1953–) guitarist, born Glasgow, Scotland; Phil Rudd (1954–) drummer, born Melbourne, Australia; *High Voltage* (1976), *If you want blood, you've got it* (1978), *Highway to Hell* (1979), *Dirty Deeds Done Dirt Cheap* (1981), *For Those About to Rock* (1981), *Blow Up Your Video* (1988).

Adams, Bryan (1959–) Canadian singer, guitarist, songwriter, born Vancouver; 'Everything I do', *Cuts Like a Knife* (1983), *You Want It, You Got It* (1984), *Reckless* (1985).

Aerosmith American group, 1970s to present; members include Steven Tyler (1948–) vocalist, born New York City; Joe Perry (1950–) guitarist, born Boston; Tom Hamilton (1951–) bassist, born Colorado Springs; Joey Kramer (1950–) drummer, born New York City; 'Come Together', 'Dream On', 'Angel', 'Dude Looks Like a Lady', 'Rag Doll', 'Love in an Elevator', 'Jamie's got a Gun', *Aerosmith* (1973), *Toys in the Attic* (1975), *Permanent Vacation* (1987), *Pump* (1989).

The Animals British group, 1960s; members include Eric Burdon (1941–) vocalist, born Newcastle-upon-Tyne; Alan Price (1942–) keyboardist, born Fairfield, County Durham; 'House of the Rising Sun', 'We've Gotta Get Out Of This Place', *Animals* (1964), *Ark* (1983).

Ant, Adam (originally **Stuart Leslie Goddard**) (1954–) British singer/songwriter, guitarist, born London; (with the Ants) 'Prince Charming', 'Stand and Deliver', 'Goody Two-Shoes', 'Apollo Nine', *King of the Wild Frontier* (1980), *Prince Charming* (1980); *Friend or Foe* (1982), *Vive Le Rock* (1985).

Armatrading, Joan (1950–) British singer, guitarist, born St Kitts Island, Caribbean; *Joan Armatrading* (1976), *To the Limit* (1978), *Walk Under Ladders* (1981), *The Key* (1983), *Sleight of Hand* (1986).

Asia British group, 1980s; Steve Howe (1947–) guitarist, born London; Carl Palmer (1951–) drummer, born Birmingham; John Wetton (1949–) bassist, vocalist, born Derby; Geoff Downes, keyboardist; 'Heat of the Moment', 'Only Time Will Tell', *Asia* (1982), *Alpha* (1983).

Baez, Joan (1941–) American singer, guitarist, born Staten Island, New York; 'The Night They Drove Ol' Dixie Down' (1972), *Any Day Now* (1968), *Farewell, Anjelica* (1975), *Diamonds and Rust* (1975), *Recently* (1987).

The Bangles American group, 1980s; Susannah Hoffs guitarist; Vicky Peterson guitarist; Debbie Peterson drummer; Michael Steele bassist; all singers; 'Manic Monday', 'If He knew what She Wants', 'Walk like an Egyptian', 'Eternal Flame', 'Be with You', *All over the Place* (1984), *Different Light* (1986), *Everything* (1988).

Bassey, Shirley (1937–) British singer, born Tiger Bay, Cardiff, Wales; 'Goldfinger', 'Big Spender', 'Diamonds are Forever'.

The Bay City Rollers Scottish 1970s band; members include Derek Longmuir (1955–) drummer; Alan Longmuir (1953–) bassist; Les McKeown (1955–) guitarist, vocalist; all born Edinburgh; 'Bye Bye Baby', 'Give Me a Little Love', 'Saturday Night'.

The Beach Boys American group, 1960s to present; members include Brian (1942–) bassist, Dennis (1944–83) drummer, and Carl (1946–) Wilson drummer, keyboardist; all born Hawthorne, California;

POP AND ROCK MUSICIANS AND SINGERS (cont.)

Mike Love (1941–) vocalist; 'Surfin' USA', 'Help Me Rhonda', 'Barbara Ann', 'Good Vibrations', 'Fun, Fun, Fun', 'I Get Around', 'California Girls', 'Little Deuce Coupe', 'God Only Knows', 'Wouldn't It Be Nice'.

The Beatles British group, 1960s; John (Winston) Lennon (1940–80) singer/songwriter, guitarist; (James) Paul McCartney (1942–) singer/songwriter, guitarist; George Harrison (1943–) singer/songwriter, guitarist; Ringo Starr (originally Richard Starkey) (1940–) singer/songwriter, drummer; all born Liverpool; 'Love Me Do', 'She Loves You', 'From Me to You', 'I Want to Hold your Hand', 'Yesterday', 'Day Tripper', 'Paperback Writer', 'You've Got to Hide Your Love Away', 'Penny Lane', 'Strawberry Fields Forever', 'Hey Jude', *Please Please Me* (1963), *With the Beatles* (1963), *A Hard Day's Night* (1964), *Beatles for Sale* (1964), *Help!* (1965), *Rubber Soul* (1965), *Revolver* (1966), *Sergeant Pepper's Lonely Hearts Club Band* (1967), *Magical Mystery Tour* (1967), *Yellow Submarine* (1968), *The White Album* (1968), *Abbey Road* (1969), *Let it Be* (1970).

The Bee Gees British/Australian group; members include Barry (1946–), Robin (1949–), and Maurice (1949–) Gibb; all born Isle of Man; 'Massachusetts', 'Jive Talkin'', 'How Deep is Your Love?', 'Staying Alive', 'Night Fever', *Children of the World* (1976).

Benatar, Pat (originally **Pat Andrzejewski**) (1953–) American singer/songwriter, born Brooklyn, New York; *Crimes of Passion, In the Heat of the Night, Live From Earth, Precious Time, Get Nervous* (1982), *Tropico* (1984), *Seven the Hard Way* (1986), *Wide Awake In Dreamland* (1988).

Berry, Chuck (originally **Charles Edward Anderson Berry**) (1926–) American singer/songwriter, guitarist; born St Louis, Missouri; 'Maybelline', 'Sweet Little Sixteen', 'Too Much Monkey Business', 'Rock and Roll Music', 'School Days', 'No Particular Place to Go', 'Johnny B Goode', 'Nadine', 'My Ding a Ling'.

B-52s American group, 1970s to present; members include Cindy Wilson (1957–) vocalist; Ricky Wilson (1953–85) guitarist; Keith Strickland (1953–) drummer; all born Athens, Georgia; Fred Schneider (1954–) vocalist, born Newark, Georgia; Kate Pierson (1948–) vocalist, keyboardist, born Weehawken, New Jersey; 'Rock Lobster', 'Love Shack', 'Roam', 'Deadbeat Club', *Wild Planet* (1980), *Mesopotamia* (1982), *Whammy* (1983), *Bouncing off the Satellites* (1986), *Cosmic Thing.*

Black Sabbath British heavy metal group, 1970s to present; members include Ozzy Osbourne (1948–) vocalist, born Birmingham; *Paranoid* (1971).

Blondie American group, 1970s to 1980s; members include Deborah Harry (1945–) vocalist, born Miami, Florida (solo 'Island of Lost Souls', 'French Kissin' in the USA', 'Free to Fall', 'I want that Man', *Rockbird, Def, Dumb, and Blonde*); Chris Stein (1950–) guitarist, born Brooklyn; 'Denis', 'Heart of Glass', 'Union City Blue', 'Call Me', 'The Tide is High', *Blondie, Plastic Letters, Eat to the Beat, Parallel Lines, AutoAmerican.*

Blue Oyster Cult American group, 1970s to present; Eric Bloom vocalist; Buck Dharma (born Donald Roeser) guitarist; Alan Lanier guitarist, keyboardist; Joe Bouchard bassist, vocalist; Albert Bouchard drummer, vocalist; Rick Downey drummer; 'Don't Fear the Reaper', *Blue Oyster Cult* (1972), *Agents of Fortune* (1976), *Cultosaurus Erectus* (1980), *Fire of Unknown Origin* (1981), *Revolution by Night* (1983).

Bolan, Marc (and T Rex) (originally **Mark Feld**) (1947–77) British singer/songwriter, guitarist, born London; 'Get It On', 'Metal Guru', 'Children Of The Revolution', 'Jeepster', *Unicorn* (1970).

Booker T and the MG's American group, 1960s; Booker T Jones (1944–) vocalist, organist, born Memphis, Tennessee; Donald 'Duck' Dunn (1941–) bassist, born Memphis; Steve Cropper (1941–) guitarist, born Willow Springs, Missouri; 'To be a Lover', *Green Onions* (1962).

Boomtown Rats Irish group, mid 1970s to early 1980s; members include Bob Geldof (1954–) singer/songwriter, born Dublin (solo *Deep in the Heart of Nowhere* (1986)); 'Rat Trap', 'I Don't Like Mondays', 'Banana Republic', *Tonic for the Troops* (1978).

Bowie, David (originally **David Robert Jones**) (1947–) British singer/songwriter, guitarist, born Brixton, London; 'The Laughing Gnome', 'Space Oddity', 'Life on Mars', 'Jean Genie', 'Andy Warhol', 'Rebel, Rebel', 'Ashes to Ashes', 'Blue Jean', 'China Girl', 'Let's Dance', 'Modern Love', *The Man who Sold the World* (1970), *Hunky Dory* (1971), *The Rise and Fall of Ziggy Stardust and the Spiders from Mars* (1972), *Diamond Dogs* (1974), *Heroes* (1977), *Scary Monsters* (1980), *Let's Dance* (1983).

POP AND ROCK MUSICIANS AND SINGERS (cont.)

Brown, James (1928–) American singer/songwriter, drummer, pianist, born Barnwell, South Carolina; 'Papa's Got a Brand New Bag', 'It's a Man's Man's Man's World', 'Ain't It Funky Now', 'Sex Machine', 'Get Up offa That Thing'.

Bush, Kate (1958–) British singer/songwriter, keyboardist, born Plumstead; 'Wuthering Heights', 'The Man with the Child in His Eyes', 'Wow', 'Running Up That Hill', *Never Forever* (1980), *The Dreaming* (1982), *Hounds of Love* (1986).

The Byrds American group, 1960s to present; Roger McGuinn (1942–) guitarist, born Chicago; Chris Hillman (1942–) bassist, mandolin player, vocalist, born Los Angeles; David Crosby vocalist, guitarist; Michael Clarke (1943–) drummer, born New York City; 'Mr Tambourine Man', 'Eight Miles High', *Mr Tambourine Man* (1965), *Turn, Turn, Turn* (1966), *Fifth Dimension* (1966).

Carnes, Kim (1945–) American singer/songwriter, born Los Angeles; 'Don't Fall In Love With A Dreamer', 'Bette Davis Eyes', 'Voyeur', *Gideon* (1980), *Mistaken Identity* (1991).

The Carpenters American group, 1970s to 1980s; members include Karen Carpenter (1950–83) vocalist, drummer; Richard Carpenter (1946–) vocalist, keyboardist; both born New Haven, Connecticut; *Close to You* (1970), *Yesterday Once More* (1974), *Voice of the Heart* (1983).

Cars American group, 1970s to present; Ric Ocasek singer/songwriter, guitarist, born Baltimore; Ben Orr (originally Benjamin Orzechowski) born Cleveland; Greg Hawkes keyboardist; 'My Best Friend's Girl', 'Just What I Needed', 'Since You're Gone', 'Shake it Up', 'Drive', 'You Might Think', *The Cars* (1978), *Candy-O* (1979), *Heartbeat City* (1984).

Cash, Johnny (1932–) American singer/songwriter, guitarist, born Kingsland, Arkansas; 'Don't Take Your Guns to Town', 'Rings of Fire', 'A Boy Named Sue', 'The Man in Black', 'A Thing Called Love'.

Charles, Ray (originally **Ray Charles Robinson**) (1930–) American singer/songwriter, pianist, born Albany, Georgia; 'I Got a Woman', 'Lonely Avenue', 'You Are My Sunshine', 'Crying Time', 'Hit the Road, Jack', *The Genius of Ray Charles* (1959).

Cheap Trick American group, 1970s to present; Rick Nielsen (1946–) guitarist; Tom Peterson (1950–) bassist; both born Rockford, Illinois; Bun E Carlos (originally Brad Carlson) drummer; Robin Zander (1952–) vocalist, born Loves Park, Illinois; 'I Want You to Want Me', 'Surrender', 'The Flame', *Heaven Tonight* (1978), *Dream Police* (1979), *One on One* (1982).

Cher (originally **Cherilyn Sarkasian La Pierre**) (1946–) American singer/songwriter, born El Centro, California; (with Sonny Bono) 'I Got You Babe', 'Just You', 'All I Ever Need Is You'; 'All I Really Want To Do', 'Gypsys, Tramps and Thieves', 'Half Breed', 'Dark Lady', 'The Shoop Shoop Song'.

Clapton, Eric (1945–) British singer/songwriter, guitarist, born Ripley, Surrey (was in 1960s groups Cream and The Yardbirds); 'Layla', 'Lay Down Sally', 'Wonderful Tonight', 'I Shot the Sheriff', 'Tulsa Time', 'Cocaine', 'I've Got a Rock 'n Roll Heart', *Derek and the Dominos* (with Duane Allman) (1970); *461 Ocean Boulevard* (1974), *Slowhand* (1977), *Just One Night* (1980), *Money and Cigarettes* (1983), *August* (1986), *Journey Man* (1989), *24 Nights*.

The Clash British group, late 1970s to 1980s; members include Joe Strummer (originally John Mellors) (1952–) guitarist, vocalist, born Ankara, Turkey; Mick Jones (1955–) guitarist, vocalist, born London ; Paul Simonon (1956–) bassist, born London; 'Topper' Headon (1956–) drummer, born Dover; 'I Fought the Law', 'Rock the Casbah', 'Should I Stay or Should I Go', *The Clash* (1977), *Cost of Living* (1979), *London Calling* (1979), *Combat Rock, Cut the Crap* (1985).

Cochran, Eddie (1938–60) American singer, guitarist, born Oklahoma City; 'Three Steps to Heaven', 'Summertime Blues', 'C'mon Everybody', 'Something Else'.

Cocker, Joe (1944–) British singer/songwriter, born Sheffield, England; 'With a Little Help from My Friends', 'You Are So Beautiful', 'Up Where We Belong' (with Jennifer Warnes), *Mad Dogs and the Englishmen* (1970), *I Can Stand a Little Rain* (1974), *Unchain My Heart* (1987).

Cohen, Leonard (1934–) Canadian singer/songwriter, guitarist, born Montreal; 'Suzanne', 'Famous Blue Raincoat', *Songs of Leonard Cohen* (1968), *Songs of Love and Hate* (1970), *Various Positions* (1984), *I'm Your Man* (1988).

POP AND ROCK MUSICIANS AND SINGERS (cont.)

Cooke, Sam (originally **Sam Cook**) (1935–64) American singer/songwriter, born Chicago, Illinois; 'You Send Me', 'A Change Is Gonna Come', 'Wonderful World' (1960), *Sam Cooke at the Copa* (1964), *Sam Cooke – The Man And His Music* (1986).

Cooper, Alice (originally **Vincent Furnier**) (1948–) American singer/songwriter, born Detroit; 'School's Out', 'Poison', 'Hey Stoopid', *Love it to Death* (1971), *School's Out* (1972).

Cope, Julien (1957–) British singer/songwriter, born Bargoed, Wales; 'Trampoline', 'Beautiful World', 'World Shut Your Mouth', *World Shut Your Mouth* (1984), *St Julien* (1987).

Costello, Elvis (originally **Declan Patrick McManus**) (1955–) British singer/songwriter, guitarist, born Paddington, London; 'Watching the Detectives', '(I Don't Want To Go To) Chelsea', 'Accidents Will Happen', 'Alison', 'Shipbuilding', 'Every Day I Write the Book', 'Don't Let Me Be Misunderstood', *My Aim is True* (1977), *This Years Model* (with The Attractions) (1978), *Armed Forces* (1979), *Almost Blue* (1981), *Imperial Bedroom* (1982), *Punch the Clock* (1983), *Goodbye Cruel World* (1984), *King of America* (1986).

Cray, Robert (1953–) American singer, blues guitarist, born Columbus, Georgia; 'Phone Booth', *False Accusations* (1985), *Showdown!* (1985).

Cream British group, late 1960s; members include Eric Clapton (1945–) singer, guitarist; Jack Bruce singer, bass; Ginger Baker drummer; 'I Feel Free', 'Sunshine of Your Love', 'Strange Brew', 'Badge', 'Crossroads', *Fresh Cream* (1966), *Disraeli Gears* (1967), *Wheels on Fire* (1968), *Goodbye* (1969).

Creedance Clearwater Revival American group, late 1960s to early 1970s; members include John Cameron Fogerty (1945–90) (solo 'Rockin' All Over the World', *Centerfield* (1985)), Tom Fogerty (1941–), both guitarists and vocalists, born Berkeley, California; Doug Clifford (1945–) drummer, born Palo Alto; Stu Cook (1945–) bassist, born Oakland; 'Susie Q', 'Proud Mary', 'Bad Moon Risin', 'Green River', 'Born on the Bayou', 'Down on the Corner', 'I Heard it through the Grapevine', 'Fortunate Son', 'Travellin' Band', 'Up, around the Bend', *Creedance Clearwater Revival* (1968), *Pendulum* (1970), *Mardi Gras* (1972).

Crosby, Bing (originally **Harry Lillis**) (1903–77) American singer, born Spokane, Washington; 'Swingin' on a Star', 'White Christmas', 'True Love' (with Grace Kelly).

Crosby, Stills, Nash and Young American group, late 1960s to present; David Crosby (originally David van Cortland) (1941–) guitarist, vocalist, born Los Angeles; Graham Nash (1942–) vocalist, born Blackpool, England; Stephen Stills guitarist, vocalist, pianist; Neil Young guitarist, vocalist, pianist; 'Ohio', *Déjà vu* (1970), *Four Way Street* (1971), *Allies* (1983).

The Cult British group, 1980s to present; members include Ian Astbury (1962–) vocalist, born London; Billy Duffy (1961–) guitarist; 'Fat Man' (as Southern Death Cult), 'She Sells Sanctuary', 'Rain', 'Love Removal Machine', *Dreamtime* (1984), *Love* (1985), *Electric* (1987).

Culture Club British group, 1980s; members include Boy George (originally George O'Dowd) vocalist, born Eltham; Jon Moss (1957–) drummer, born London; 'Karma Chameleon', *Colour By Numbers.*

The Cure British group, mid-1970s to present; members include Robert Smith (1957–) guitarist, singer/songwriter, born Crawley, Sussex; Laurence Tolhurst drummer, keyboardist; 'Killing an Arab', 'Boys Don't Cry', 'Love Cats', 'The Caterpillar', 'Close to Me', 'Standing on the Beach', 'In Between Days', *Boy's Don't Cry* (1980), *Faith* (1981), *Pornography* (1982), *The Head on the Door* (1985), *Disintegration* (1989).

Davis, Sammy, Jr (1925–90) American singer, born New York City; 'Something's Gotta Give', 'That Old Black Magic', 'Candy Man', *Starring Sammy Davis Jr* (1955), *Just for Lovers* (1955), *The Wham of Sam* (1960).

Dead Kennedys American group, late 1970s to 1980s; members include Jello Biafra vocalist; East Bay Ray (aka Ray Valium) guitarist; Klaüs Flouride bassist; Ted drummer; 'California Uber Alles', 'Kill the Poor' (1980), 'Too Drunk to Fuck' (1981), 'Holiday in Cambodia', *Fresh Fruit for Rotten Vegetables* (1980), *Plastic Surgery Diaster* (1982), *Frankenchrist* (1985).

Deep Purple British heavy metal group, late 1960s to 1980s; members include Ian Gillan (1945–) vocalist, born Hounslow; David Coverdale (1951–) vocalist, born Saltburn; Ritchie Blackmore (1945–) guitarist born Weston-super-Mare; Jon Lord (1941–) keyboardist, born Leicester; Roger Glover

POP AND ROCK MUSICIANS AND SINGERS (cont.)

(1945–) bassist; Ian Paice (1948–) drummer; 'Black Night', 'Smoke on the Water', *Shades of Deep Purple* (1968), *Deep Purple* (1969), *Deep Purple In Rock* (1970), *Machine Head* (1972), *Made in Japan* (1972), *Perfect Strangers* (1984).

Def Leppard British heavy metal group, 1980s to present; members include Joe Elliott (1960–) vocalist; Rick Savage bassist; Pete Willis guitar, replaced by Phil Collen; Steve Clark (d.1991) guitarist; Rick Allen (c.1963–) drummer; 'Photograph', 'Foolin'', 'Rock of Ages', 'Animal', 'Women', 'Pour Some Sugar on Me', *On Through the Night* (1980), *High and Dry* (1981), *Pyromania* (1983), *Hysteria* (1987).

Denver, John (originally **John Henry Deutschendorf**) (1943–) American singer/songwriter, born New Mexico; 'Take Me Home Country Roads', 'Annie's Song', 'I'm Sorry', *Back Home Again* (1974), *An Evening With John Denver* (1975).

Depêche Mode British group, 1980s to present; Andy Fletcher (1961–); Martin Gore (1961–); Vince Clarke; Alan Wilder (1963–) keyboardist; *Speak and Spell* (1981), *Black Celebration* (1986), *Music for the Masses* (1987).

Devo American group, 1970s to 1980s; Jerry Casale bassist, singer/songwriter; Bob Casale and Mark Mothersbaugh keyboardists, guitarists, vocalists; Bob Mothersbaugh guitarist, vocalist; Alan Myers drummer; 'Satisfaction', 'Whip It', *Q:Are We Not Men? A:We Are Devo!* (1978), *Shout* (1984).

Diamond, Neil (Leslie) (1941–) American singer/songwriter, guitarist, born Coney Island, New York; 'Song Sung Blue', 'You Don't Bring Me Flowers' (with Barbra Streisand), 'Love on the Rocks', *Beautiful Noise* (1976), *The Jazz Singer* (1980), *Heartlight* (1982), *Headed for the Future* (1986).

Diddley, Bo (originally **Ellas McDaniel**) (1928–) American singer, guitarist, born McComb, Mississippi; 'Bo Diddley'/'I'm a Man', 'Road Runner', 'Do Wah Diddy Diddy', *Got My Own Bag of Tricks* (1971).

Dio, Ronnie James (originally **Ronald Padavona**) (1949–) American heavy metal singer, born Cortland, New York; 'Hungry for Heaven', 'Rock 'n Roll Children', *Holy Diver* (1983), *The Last in Line* (1984), *Sacred Heart* (1985), *Dream Evil* (1987).

Dire Straits British group, late 1970s to present; members include Mark Knopfler (1949–) singer/songwriter, guitarist, born Glasgow (solo soundtrack *Local Hero*); David Knopfler guitarist replaced by Hal Lindes; John Illsley (1949–) bassist, born London; Pick Withers drummer; Alan Clark keyboardist; 'Romeo and Juliet', 'Tunnel of Love', 'So Far Away', 'Money for Nothing', 'Walk of Life', *Dire Straits* (1978), *Communiqué* (1979), *Making Movies, Love over Gold* (1983), *Alchemy* (1984), *Brothers in Arms* (1985), *Money for Nothing* (1988).

Domino, Fats (originally **Antoine Domino**) (1928–) American singer, pianist, born New Orleans, Louisiana; 'Every Night About This Time', 'It's Midnight', 'Ain't That a Shame', 'Blue Monday', 'Blueberry Hill'.

Donovan (originally **Donovan Philips Leitch**) (1946–) British singer/songwriter, guitarist, born Glasgow; 'Mellow Yellow', 'Sunshine Superman', *The Universal Soldier* (1966).

Doobie Brothers American group, 1970s; John Hartman (1950–) drummer, born Falls Church, Virginia; Tom Johnston vocalist, guitarist, born Visalia, California; Tiran Porter bassist, born San Francisco; Patrick Simmons (1950–) vocalist, guitarist, born Aberdeen, Washington; Michael Hossack (1950–) drummer, born Paterson, New York replaced by Keith Knudson (1952–) born Ames, Iowa; Jeff 'Skunk' Baxter (1948–) guitarist, born Washington DC; Michael McDonald keyboardist, vocalist, born St Louis (solo *Sweet Freedom* (1986)); 'Listen to the Music', 'Black Water', 'Fool', *What Were Once Vices Are Now Habits* (1974).

The Doors American group, late 1960s to early 1970s; members include Jim Morrison (1943–71), singer/songwriter, born Melbourne, Florida; Ray Manzarek (1939–) keyboardist, born Chicago; Robby Krieger (1946–) guitarist, born Los Angeles; John Densmore (1945–) drummer, born Los Angeles; 'Light My Fire', 'The End', 'When the Music's Over', 'L.A. Woman', 'Hello, I Love You', 'Five To One', 'Touch Me', 'Riders on the Storm', *The Doors* (1967), *Strange Days* (1967), *Waiting for the Sun* (1968), *L.A. Woman* (1970), *An American Prayer* (1978).

POP AND ROCK MUSICIANS AND SINGERS (cont.)

Duran Duran British group, 1980s to present; members include Simon Le Bon (1958–) vocalist, born Watford, Herfordshire; Nick Rhodes (originally Nicholas Bates) (1962–) keyboardist, born Birmingham; John Taylor (1960–) bassist, born Birmingham; Roger Taylor drummer; Andy Taylor guitarist; 'Planet Earth', 'Hungry Like the Wolf', 'Save a Prayer', 'Rio', 'Union of the Snake', 'Wild Boys', *Duran Duran* (1981), *Rio* (1982), *Seven and the Ragged Tiger* (1983), *Arena* (1984), *Notorious* (1986).

Dury, Ian (1942–) British singer/songwriter, born Upminster, Essex; (with Blockheads) 'Sex & Drugs & Rock 'n' Roll', 'Hit Me with your Rhythm Stick', *New Boots And Panties* (1977), *Do It Yourself, Laughter* (1980); 'Profoundly in Love with Pandora'.

Dylan, Bob (originally **Robert Allan Zimmerman**) (1941–) American singer/songwriter, guitarist, born Duluth, Minnesota; 'Blowin in the Wind', 'Mr Tambourine Man', 'Desolation Row', 'Like a Rolling Stone', 'Maggie's Farm', 'All Along the Watchtower', 'Lay Lady Lay', *The Freewheelin' Bob Dylan* (1963), *The Times They Are A-changin'* (1963), *Another Side of Bob Dylan* (1964), *Bringing It All Back Home* (1965), *Blonde on Blonde* (1966), *John Wesley Harding* (1968), *Nashville Skyline* (1969), *Blood on the Tracks* (1974), *The Basement Tapes* (1975), *Slow Train Coming* (1979), *Infidels* (1983).

The Eagles American group, 1970s; members include Glenn Frey (1948–) singer, guitarist, born Detroit, Michigan; Donn Henley (1947–) singer, drummer, born Texas (solo 'Dirty Laundry', 'Boys of Summer', *Building the Perfect Beast* (1984)); Bernie Leadon (1947–) guitarist replaced by Joe Walsh (1947–) guitarist, singer/songwriter, born Wichita, Kansas (solo 'Life's Been Good', *But Seriously Folks* (1976), *Got Any Gum?* (1987)); Randy Meisner (1946–) bassist, born Nebraska; 'Best of My Love', 'Lyin' Eyes', 'New Kid in Town', 'Heartache Tonight', *Eagles* (1972), *Desperado* (1973), *One of these Nights* (1975), *Hotel California* (1976), *The Long Run* (1979).

Earth, Wind and Fire American group, 1970s to present; Maurice White (1941–) vocalist, drummer, born Memphis, Tennessee; Verdine White (1951–) bassist; Philip Bailey (1951–) vocalist, born Denver, Colorado; Larry Dunn (1953–) keyboardist, born Colorado; Johnny Graham (1951–) guitarist, born Kentucky; Al McKay (1948–) guitarist, born Louisiana; Andre Woolfolk (1950–) reeds, born Texas; Ralph Johnson (1951–) drummer, born California; 'Shining Star', 'Got to Get you into My Life', 'Boogie Wonderland', *Open Our Eyes* (1974), *That's The Way of the World* (1975).

Easton, Sheena (originally **Sheena Orr**) (1959–) British singer, born Bellshill, Scotland; 'Morning Train', 'For Your Eyes Only', 'Sugar Walls'.

Electric Light Orchestra British group, 1970s to 1980s; members include Jeff Lynne (1947–) guitarist, vocalist; Roy Wood (1946–); Bev Bevan (1946–) drummer; all born Birmingham; 'Roll Over Beethoven', 'Evil Woman', 'Hold On Tight', 'Mr Blue Sky', 'Last Train to London', 'Calling America', *Xanadu* (1980)

Emerson, Lake and Palmer British group, 1970s; members include Keith Emerson (1944–) keyboardist, vocalist, born Todmorton; Greg Lake (1948–) guitarist, vocalist, born Bournemouth; Carl Palmer (1941–) drummer, born Birmingham; 'I Believe in Father Christmas', 'Honky Tonk Train Blues'.

Eno, Brian (1948–) British singer/songwriter, keyboardist, born Woodbridge, Suffolk; *My Life In the Bush Of Ghosts* (with David Byrne) (1981).

Eurythmics British group, 1980s; members include David Allan Stewart (1952–) songwriter, keyboardist, guitarist, born Sunderland, England; Annie Lennox (1954–) singer/songwriter, born Aberdeen, Scotland; 'Love is a Stranger', 'Who's that Girl?', 'Here Comes the Rain Again', 'Sexcrime', 'Thorn in My Side', 'It's Alright (Baby's Coming Back)', 'Sisters are Doin' it for themselves' (with Aretha Franklin), 'When Tomorrow Comes', *Sweet Dreams are Made of This* (1982), *Touch* (1983), *1984* (1984), *Be Yourself Tonight* (1985), *Revenge* (1986), *Savage* (1987), *We Too are One* (1989).

Everly Brothers American group; Don (1937–), Phil (1939–), born Brownie, Kentucky; 'Bye Bye Love', 'Little Susie', 'Dream', *EB 84* (1984).

Fairport Convention British group, mid 1960s to 1970s; members include Ashley Hutchings (1945–), Simon Nicol (1950–), Richard Thompson singer/songwriter, guitarist; Martin Lamble (1949–69) drummer; Judy Dyble (1948–) singer/songwriter replaced by Sandy Denny (1941–); Dave Swarbrick (1941–)

POP AND ROCK MUSICIANS AND SINGERS (cont.)

fiddler; all born London; Ian Matthews (1946–) born Scunthorpe; 'Meet on a Ledge', 'A Sailor's Life', *Rosie* (1973), *Fairport 9*.

Ferry, Bryan (1945–) British singer, born Washington, County Durham; 'Tokyo Joe', 'The Price of Love', 'Slave to Love', 'Don't Stop the Dance'; *Let's Stick Together* (1976), *Bête Noire* (1987).

Flack, Roberta (1939–) American singer/songwriter, pianist; 'Killing Me Softly With His Song', 'Back Together Again', Tonight I Celebrate My Love', *And Donny Hathaway* (1972), *Killing Me Softly* (1973).

Fleetwood Mac British/American group, late 1960s to present; members include Peter Green (originally Peter Greenbaum) (1946–) singer/songwriter, guitarist, born London; Mick Fleetwood (1942–) drummer; John McVie (1945–) bassist; Christine McVie singer, keyboardist; Lindsey Buckingham (1947–) singer, guitarist, born Palo Alto, California; Stevie (Stephanie) Nicks (1948–) singer/songwriter, born Phoenix, Arizona (solo *Bella Donna* (1982), *The Wild Heart* (1983), *Rock A Little* (1985), *The Other Side of the Mirror*); 'Sara', 'Big Love', 'Little Lies', *Fleetwood Mac* (1975), *Rumours* (1977), *Mirage* (1982), *Tango in the Night* (1987).

Fogelberg, Dan (1951–) American singer/songwriter; 'Longer', 'Hard To Say', Leader Of The Band', *Phoenix* (1979), *Innocent Age* (1981), *Wild Places* (1990).

Foreigner British/American group, late 1970s to late 1980s; members include Mick Jones (1947–) guitarist, born England; Dennis Elliott (1950–) drummer, born London; Lou Gramm (1950–) vocalist, born Rochester, New York; 'Hot Blooded', 'Urgent', 'Waiting for a Girl Like You', 'I Want to Know what Love is', 'That Was Yesterday' *Double Vision* (1978), *Records* (1982), *Agent Provocateur* (1984).

Frankie Goes to Hollywood British group, early 1980s; Holly Johnson (1960–) and Paul Rutherford (1959–) vocalists; Mark O'Toole (1964–) bassist; Peter Gill (1960–) drummer; Brian Nash (1963–) guitarist; 'Relax!', 'Two Tribes', 'The Power of Love', 'Ferry Across the Mersey', *Welcome to the Pleasure Dome* (1984).

Franklin, Aretha (1942–) American singer, born Memphis, Tennessee; 'Think', 'Respect', *I Never Loved A Man The Way I Love You* (1967), *Lady Soul* (1968), *Amazing Grace* (1972), *Everything I Feel in Me* (1974), *Almighty Fire* (1978), *Love All The Hurt Away* (1981), *Get It Right* (1983), *Aretha* (1986).

Free British group, late 1960s to early 1970s; members include Paul Rodgers (1949–) vocalist, born Middlesborough; Paul Kosoff (1950–76), guitarist, born London; Andy Fraser (1952–) bassist, born London; Simon Kirke (1948–) drummer, born Shropshire; 'Alright Now', 'My Brother Jake'.

Gaye, Marvin (Pentz) (1939–84) American singer/songwriter, pianist, drummer, born Washington DC; 'Hitch Hike', 'Can I Get a Witness', 'I Heard it through the Grapevine', 'What's Goin' On', 'Sexual Healing', *What's Goin' On* (1971), *Let's Get it On* (1973), *Here My Dear* (1979), *In Our Lifetime* (1981), *Midnight Love* (1982).

Genesis British group, late 1960s to present; members include (at various times) Peter Gabriel (1950–) singer/songwriter, born Cobham, Surrey; Phil Collins (1951–) singer/songwriter, drummer, born London; Tony Banks (1950–) keyboardist; Michael Rutherford (1951–) guitarist, bassist, vocalist; all have worked as solo artists; *Selling England by the Pound* (1973), *Nursery Cryme* (1971), *The Lamb Lies Down on Broadway* (1974).

Glitter, Gary (originally **Paul Gadd**) (1944–) British singer/songwriter, born Banbury, Oxfordshire; 'I'm the Leader of the Gang (I Am)', 'I Love You Love Me Love'.

The Go-Go's American group, 1980s; Jane Wiedlin (1958–) guitarist, born Oconomowoc, Wisconsin (solo 'Cool Places' (with Sparks), 'Blue Kiss', 'Rush Hour', *Fur* (1988)); Belinda Carlisle (1958–) singer, born Hollywood (solo *Heaven on Earth, Runaway Horses*); Charlotte Caffey (1953–) guitarist, born Santa Monica; Gina Schock (1957–) drummer, born Baltimore; Kathy Valentine (1959–) bassist, born Austin, Texas; 'Our Lips Are Sealed', 'We Got The Beat', *Beauty and the Beast* (1981), *Vacation* (1982), *Talk Show* (1984).

Grateful Dead American group, late 1960s to present; members include Jerry Garcia (originally Jerome Garcia) (1942–) guitarist, born San Francisco, California; 'Dark Star', *Live Dead* (1970), *Europe* (1972), *Blues for Allah* (1975), *In the Dark* (1987), *Dylan and the Dead* (with Bob Dylan) (1988).

Guns 'n' Roses American group, late 1980s to present; W Axl Rose singer; Slash guitarist; Matt Sorum

POP AND ROCK MUSICIANS AND SINGERS (cont.)

drummer; 'Sweet Child O' Mine', 'Welcome to the Jungle', 'Night Train', 'Patience', 'You Could Be Mine' *Appetite for Destruction, G 'n' R Lies.*

Haley, Bill (1925–81) American singer/songwriter, guitarist, born Highland Park, Michigan; (with The Comets) 'Crazy Man Crazy', 'Shake Rattle and Roll', 'Rock Around the Clock', 'See You Later, Alligator', 'Rudy's Rock'.

Hall & Oates American duo, 1970s to present; Daryl Hall (originally Daryl Hohl) (1948–) singer, born Pottsdown, Pennsylvania; John Oates (1949–) singer, guitarist, born New York City; 'She's Gone', 'Sara Smile, 'Rich Girl', 'Kiss On My List', 'I Can't Go For That (No Can Do), 'Maneater', 'Out of Touch', *Abandoned Luncheonette* (1973), *Private Eyes* (1981), *Rock 'n' Soul Part I, Bigbamboom* (1985), *Live At the Apollo* (1985).

Hancock, Herbie (Herbert Jeffrey Hancock) (1940–) American singer/songwriter, keyboardist, born Chicago; 'Gimme the Night', 'Rockit', *Maiden Voyage* (1965), *Blow-Up* (1966), *Sextant* (1972), *Head Hunters* (1973), *Thrust* (1974), *Future Shock* (1983), *Sound System* (1983).

Harrison, George (1943–) British singer/songwriter, guitarist, born Liverpool; 'My Sweet Lord', 'All Those Years Ago', 'Got My Mind Set On You', 'When We Was Fab'; *All Things Must Pass* (1970), *Cloud Nine* (1987).

Hendrix, Jimi (originally **James Marshall Hendrix**) (1942–70) American singer/songwriter, guitarist, born Seattle, Washington; (with the Experience) 'Voodoo Chile', 'Hey Joe', 'Purple Haze', 'The Wind Cries Mary', 'Crosstown Traffic', 'All Along the Watchtower', *Are You Experienced?* (1967), *Electric Ladyland* (1968), *Axis: Bold As Love* (1968).

Herman's Hermits British group, 1960s; members include Peter 'Herman' Noone (1947–) singer, pianist, guitarist, born Manchester; Karl Green (1947–) guitarist, harmonica player, born Salford; Keith Hopwood (1946–) guitarist, born Manchester; Derek 'Lek' Leckenby (1945–) guitarist, born Leeds; Barry Whithman (1946–) drummer, born Manchester; 'I'm Into Something Good', 'Mrs Brown, You've Got a Lovely Daughter', 'I'm Henry VIII, I Am'.

The Hollies British group, 1960s to present; members include Allan Clarke (1942–) vocalist, born Salford; Graham Nash (1942–) guitarist, vocalist, born Blackpool replaced by Terry Sylvester (1945–) born Liverpool; Tony Hicks (1943–) guitarist, born Nelson; Eric Haydock (1943–) bassist, born Stockport replaced by Bernie Calvert (1943–) born Burnley; Bobby Elliott (1943–) drummer, born Burnley; 'Searchin'', 'Just One Look', 'He Ain't Heavy, He's My Brother', 'The Air That I Breathe', 'Stop In the Name of Love'.

Holly, Buddy (originally **Charles Hardin Holley**) (1936–59) American singer/songwriter, guitarist, violinist, born Lubbock, Texas; (with the Crickets) 'That'll Be the Day', 'Oh Boy!', 'Not Fade Away', 'Peggy Sue', 'Every Day', 'Rave On', 'Peggy Sue Got Married'.

Houston, Whitney (1963–) American singer, born Newark, New Jersey; 'Saving All My Love For You', 'How Will I Know', 'Greatest Love', 'I Wanna Dance With Somebody (Who Loves Me)', 'Where Do Broken Hearts Go', 'My Name is Not Sue', *Whitney Houston, Whitney* (1987).

Human League British group, late 1970s to present; members include Philip Oakey (1955–) singer; Susanne Sully (1963–) singer; Joanne Catherall (1962–) singer; Ian Burden (1957–) bassist; Jo Callis (1951–) guitarist; 'Don't You Want Me' (1981), '(Keep Feeling) Fascination', 'Mirror Man', 'Louise', *Dare* (1981), *Crash* (1986).

Idol, Billy (originally **William Michael Albert Broad**) (1955–) British singer/songwriter, guitarist, born Stanmore, Essex; 'Dancing With Myself', 'Mony Mony', 'Hot in the City', 'White Wedding', 'Rebel Yell', 'Eyes Without a Face', 'To Be A Lover', *Billy Idol* (1982), *Rebel Yell* (1984), *Whiplash Smile* (1986), *Charmed Life* (1990).

Inxs Australian group, 1980s to present; Michael Hutchence (1960–) singer, born Sydney; Andrew Farriss keyboardist; Jon Farriss drummer; Tim Farriss guitarist; Kirk Pengilly guitarist, saxophonist; Garry Beer Beers drummer; 'Original Sin', 'This Time', 'Never Tear Us Apart', 'Need You Tonight', *Shabooh Shoobah* (1982), *The Swing* (1984), *Listen Like Thieves* (1985), *Kick* (1987), *X* (1990).

POP AND ROCK MUSICIANS AND SINGERS (cont.)

Iron Maiden British heavy metal group, mid 1970s to present; members include Steve Harris (1957–) bassist, born Leytonstone, London; Dave Murray (1958–) guitarist, born Clapham, London; Adrian Smith (1957–) guitarist, born London; Paul Di'anno (1959–) singer, born Chingford, Essex replaced by Bruce Dickenson (1958–) born Sheffield; Nicko McBain (1954–) drummer, born London; 'Running Free', 'Run to the Hills', *Iron Maiden* (1980), *Number of the Beast, Power Slave* (1984), *Live After Death* (1985), *Somewhere In Time* (1986).

Isley Brothers American group; Kelly (originally O'Kelly) (1937–86), Rudolph (1939–), Ronald (1941–) Isley; all born Cincinnati, Ohio; 'Shout', 'Twist and Shout', 'This Old Heart of Mine (Is Weak For You)', *Harvest for the World* (1976).

J Geils Band American group, late 1960s to present; members include Jerome Geils (1946–) guitarist, born New York City; Magic Dick (originally Richard Salwitz) (1945–) harmonica player, born New London, Connecticut; Danny Klein (1946–) bassist, born Worcester, Massachusetts; Peter Wolf (originally Peter Blankfield) (1946–) vocalist, born New York City; Stephen Jo Bladd (1942–) drummer, born Boston; Seth Justman (1951–) keyboardist, born Washington DC; 'Centerfold', *Bloodshot* (1973), *Love Stinks* (1980), *Freeze-Frame* (1981), *Showtime!* (1982).

Jackson, Janet (1966–) American singer/songwriter, born Gary, Indiana; 'When I Think Of You', *Control* (1986).

Jackson, Michael (Joe) (1958–) American singer/songwriter, born Gary, Indiana; 'Billy Jean', 'Beat It'; 'The Girl is Mine', 'Say Say Say' (with Paul McCartney); 'I Can't Stop Loving You' (with Siedah Garrett), *Ben* (1972), *Off the Wall* (1979), *Thriller* (1982), *Bad* (1987) (was in the Jacksons, American group, 1960s to 1970s).

The Jam British group, mid 1970s to early 1980s; members include Paul Weller (1958–) singer/songwriter, guitarist, born Woking, Surrey; Bruce Foxton (1955–) bassist, born Woking; Rick Butler (1955–) drummer; 'Going Underground', 'Eton Rifles', 'Town Called Malice', 'Beat Surrender', 'Dream of Children'.

Jarre, Jean-Michel (1949–) French keyboardist, composer, born Lyons; *Oxygène* (1977), *Equinoxe* (1978).

The Jefferson Airplane/Jefferson Starship/Starship American group, mid 1960s to present; many different members, often changing, include Grace Slick (originally Grace Wing) (1939–) singer/songwriter, born Chicago, Illinois; 'White Rabbit', 'We Built this City', 'Sara', 'Nothing's Gonna Stop Us Now', *Surrealistic Pillow* (1967), *Crown of Creation* (1968), *Red Octopus* (1975), *Spitfire* (1976), *Knee Deep in Hoopla* (1986), *No Protection* (1987).

Jethro Tull British group, late 1960s to present; members include Ian Anderson (1947–) flautist, guitarist, vocalist, saxophonist, born Edinburgh; Martin Barre (1946–) guitarist, born London; Glenn Cornick (1947–) bassist, born Barrow-in-Furness; Clive Bunker (1946–) drummer; 'Sweet Dream', 'Witch's Promise', *Aqaulung* (1971), *Living In The Past* (1972), *Songs From The Wood* (1977), *Crest of a Knave* (1987).

Joel, Billy (William Martin Joel) (1949–) American singer/songwriter, pianist, born Hicksville, Long Island, New York; 'Say Goodbye to Hollywood', 'Just The Way You Are', 'My Life', 'It's Still Rock 'n Roll to Me', 'Tell Her About it', 'Uptown Girl', 'We Didn't Start the Fire', *The Stranger* (1977), *52nd Street* (1978), *Glass House* (1980), *The Nylon Curtain* (1982), *An Innocent Man* (1983), *The Bridge* (1986), *Storm Front* (1989).

John, Elton (originally **Reginald Kenneth Dwight**) (1947–) British singer/songwriter, pianist, born Pinner, Middlesex; 'Your Song', 'Crocodile Rock', 'Don't Go Breakin' My Heart' (with Kiki Dee), 'Little Jeannie', 'Wrap Her Up', 'Nikita', 'No Sacrifice', *Tumbleweed Connection* (1970), *Don't Shoot Me, I'm Only The Piano Player* (1973), *Good Bye Yellow Brick Road* (1973), *A Single Man* (1979), *Too Low for Zero, Ice on Fire* (1985).

Jones, Grace (1952–) Jamaican singer/songwriter, born Jamaica, West Indies; 'Private Life', 'Love is the Drug', 'Pull up to the Bumper', 'Slave to the Rhythm'.

Jones, Tom (originally **Thomas Jones Woodward**) (1940–) British singer, drummer, born Pontypridd,

POP AND ROCK MUSICIANS AND SINGERS (cont.)

S Wales; 'It's Not Unusual', 'What's New Pussycat?', 'Green Green Grass of Home', 'I'll Never Fall In Love Again', 'Delilah'.

Joplin, Janis (1943–1970) American singer/songwriter, born Port Arthur, Texas; 'Piece of My Heart', *Cheap Thrills* (1968), *I Got dem ole Kozmic Blues Again Mama* (1969), Pearl (1971).

Journey American group, 1970s to 1980s; members include Steve Perry (1949–) vocalist, born Hanford, California; Ross Valory (1950–) bassist, born San Francisco; Neal Schon (1955–) guitarist, born San Mateo, California; Steve Smith drummer; Gregg Rolie (1948–) keyboardist replaced by Jonathan Cain, born Chicago; 'Who's Crying Now', 'Open Arms', 'Faithfully', *Infinity* (1978), *Evolution* (1979), *Departure* (1980), *Captured* (1981), *Escape* (1981), *Frontiers* (1983), *Raised on Radio* (1986).

Joy Division/New Order British group, late 1970s to mid-1980s; members include Ian Curtis (1957–80) vocalist, born Macclesfield; changed to New Order in 1981; members include Bernard Albrecht (originally Barney Sumner) (1956–) vocalist, guitarist, born Salford, Lancashire; Peter Hook (1956–) bassist; Stephen Morris (1957–) drummer; (as Joy Division) 'Transmission', 'Love Will Tear Us Apart', *Unknown Pleasures* (1979); (as New Order) 'Blue Monday', 'Shellshock', *Movement* (1981), *Low Life* (1985).

Khan, Chaka (originally **Yvette Marie Stevens**) (1953–) American singer/songwriter, born Great Lakes, Illinois; (with Rufus) *Rags to Rufus* (1974); *Chaka* (1978), *I Feel For You* (1984).

King, B B (originally **Riley B King**) (1925–) American guitarist, singer/songwriter, born Itta Bena, near Indianola, Mississippi; *Live at the Regal* (1965), *Confessin' the Blues* (1966), *Blues Is King* (1967), *Indianola Mississippi Seeds* (1970), *Live in Stock County Jail* (1971), *There Must Be A Better World Somewhere* (1981), *Six Silver Strings* (1985).

King, Ben E (originally **Benjamin Earl Nelson**) (1938–) singer, born Henderson, N Carolina; 'Stand By Me'.

King, Carole (originally **Carole Klein**) (1942–) American singer/songwriter; 'It Might As Well Rain Until September' 'Its Too Late' 'You've Got A Friend' 'Will You Love Me Tomorow', *Tapestry* (1971), *Wrap Around Joy* (1974), *Pearls* (1980).

The Kinks British group, 1960s to 1980s; Ray Davies (1944–) singer/songwriter, guitarist (solo 'A Quiet Life'); Dave Davies (1947–) singer, guitarist; both born Muswell Hill, London; Mike Avory (1944–) drummer, born Hampton, Middlesex; Peter Quaife (1943–) bassist, born Tavistock, Devon; 'You Really Got Me', 'All Day and All of the Night', 'Dedicated Follower of Fashion', 'Sunny Afternoon', 'Waterloo Sunset', 'Autumn Almanac', 'Lola', 'Come Dancing', 'Don't Forget to Dance', *Village Green Preservation Society* (1968), *Lola vs. Powerman & The Moneyground Pt 1* (1970), *State of Confusion* (1983).

Kiss American group, 1970s to present; members include Paul Stanley (originally Paul Stanley Eisen) (1952–) guitarist, born New York City; Gene Simmons (originally Gene Klein) (1949–) bassist, born Haffa, Israel; Peter Criss (originally Peter Crisscoula) (1947–) drummer, born New York City; Ace (Paul) Frehley (1951–) guitarist, born New York City; 'Rock And Roll All Nite', 'Beth', 'I was Made for Lovin' You', 'Tears are Fallin', *Dressed to Kill* (1975), *Double Platinum* (1978), *Lick It Up* (1983), *Crazy Nights* (1987).

Knight, Gladys (1944–) American singer, band leader (The Pips – American group, late 1950s), born Atlanta, Georgia; (with The Pips) 'I Heard It Through The Grapevine', 'Help Me Make It Through The Night', 'Midnight Train To Georgia', 'On And On', *Imagination* (1973), *Visions* (1983), *Life* (1985).

Kraftwerk German group, 1970s to present; Ralph Hutter and Florian Schneider; 'Radio Activity', 'The Model', 'Trans Europe Express', 'Computer Love', 'Tour de France', *Autobahn* (1975), *Man Machine* (1978), *Computer World* (1981).

Lauper, Cyndi (1954–) American singer, born New York City; 'Time After Time', 'Girls Just Want To Have Fun', 'All Through The Night', 'She Bop', *She's So Unusual* (1983), *True Colours* (1986).

Led Zeppelin British group, late 1960s to 1970s; members include Jimmy Page (1944–) guitarist, born Heston, London; Robert Plant (1948–) vocalist, born Bromwich, Staffordshire; John Paul Jones (originally John Baldwin) (1946–) bassist, born Sidcup; John Bonham (1948–80) drummer, born Redditch; *Led Zeppelin I* (1969), *Led Zeppelin II* (1970), *Led Zeppelin III* (1970), *Led Zeppelin IV* (1971), *Houses of the Holy* (1973), *Physical Graffiti* (1975), *In Through The Out Door* (1979).

POP AND ROCK MUSICIANS AND SINGERS (cont.)

Lee, Peggy (originally **Norma Delores Egstrom**) (1920–) American singer, born Jamestown, North Dakota; 'Manana', 'Fever'.

Lennon, John Winston (1940–80) British singer/songwriter, guitarist, keyboardist, born Liverpool; 'Give Peace A Chance', 'Working Class Hero', 'Jealous Guy', 'Merry Xmas (War Is Over)', 'Whatever Gets You Through The Night', *Imagine* (1971), *Rock 'n' Roll* (1975), *Double Fantasy* (1980).

Lewis, Huey (originally **Hugh Cregg**) (1950–) American singer, born New York; (with The News – American group, 1980s to present); 'Do You Believe in Love', 'Heart and Soul', 'I Want A New Drug', 'The Heart Of Rock & Roll', 'Walking On A Thin Line', 'Power Of Love', 'Stuck With You', *Picture This* (1982), *Sports* (1983), *Fore* (1986).

Lewis, Jerry Lee (1935–) American pianist, singer, born Ferriday, Louisiana; 'Great Balls of Fire', 'Whole Lotta Shakin' Goin' On', 'High School Confidential', 'Breathless'.

Little Richard (originally **Richard Wayne Penniman**) (1935–) American singer/songwriter, pianist, born Macon, Georgia; 'Tutti Frutti', 'Long Tall Sally', 'Rip It Up', 'The Girl Can't Help It', 'Lucille', 'Jenny, Jenny', 'Good Golly, Miss Molly', 'Lawdy Miss Clawdy', *Life Time Friend* (1986).

Lovin' Spoonful American group, 1960s to 1970s; John Sebastian (1944–) vocalist, guitarist; Zal Yanovsky (1944–) guitarist; Steve Boone (1943–) bassist; Joe Butler (1944–) drummer; 'Daydream', 'Summer In The City', *Daydream* (1966), *Best Of* (1967).

Lowe, Nick (1949–) British singer/songwriter, bassist, guitarist, born Woodbridge, Suffolk; 'I Love The Sound Of Breaking Glass', 'Cruel To Be Kind'.

Lulu (originally **Marie McDonald McLaughlin Lawrie**) (1948–) British singer, born Glasgow; (with The Luvvers) 'Shout', 'Leave A Little Love'; 'To Sir With Love', 'Boom Bang-A-Bang', 'The Man Who Sold The World' (with David Bowie).

Lynyrd Skynyrd American group, 1970s; members include Ronnie Van Zandt (1949–77) vocalist, born McCombe, Minnesota; 'Sweet Home Alabama', 'Freebird', 'Whiskey rock'n'roller', *Pronounced Leh-nerd Skin-nerd* (1973), *Second Helping* (1974), *Street Survivors* (1977), *Gold and Platinum* (1979).

McCartney, Paul (1942–) British singer/songwriter, guitarist, born Liverpool; 'Wonderful Christmastime', 'Coming Up', 'Ebony & Ivory' (with Stevie Wonder), 'No More Lonely Nights', *Tug of War* (1982), *Pipes of Peace* (1983).

McLean, Don (1945–) singer/songwriter, born New Rochelle, New York; 'And I Love You So', 'Vincent', 'Castles in the Air', *American Pie* (1971), *Chain Lightning* (1981), *Dominion* (1983).

Madness British group, late 1970s to 1980s; members include Graham 'Suggs' McPherson (1961–) vocalist, born Hastings, Sussex; Mike Barson (1958–) keyboardist, Lee Thompson (1957–) saxophonist; *Chris Foreman* (1958–) guitarist; Mark Bedford (1961–) bassist; Daniel 'Woody' Woodgate (1960–) drummer; Chas Smash (originally Carl Smith) (1959–) vocalist, trumpeter; 'House Of Fun', 'Our House', 'Baggy Trousers', 'Ghost Train', *One Step Beyond* (1979), *Complete Madness* (1982), *Mad Not Mad* (1985).

Madonna (originally **Madonna Louise Veronica Ciccone**) (1958–) American singer/songwriter, born Rochester, Michigan; 'Holiday', 'Crazy For You', 'Gambler', 'Into The Groove', 'Live To Tell', 'Vogue', *Madonna* (1983), *Like a Virgin* (1984), *True Blue* (1986), *Who's that Girl?* (1987), *Like a Prayer* (1989), *The Immaculate Collection* (1990).

The Mamas and the Papas American group, late 1960s; members include John Philips (1935–) singer/songwriter, guitarist, born Parris Island, South Carolina; Dennis Doherty (1941–) born Halifax, Nova Scotia; Michelle Phillips (originally Holly Michelle Gilliam) (1944–) born Long Beach, California; Cass Elliott (originally Ellen Naomi Cohen) (1943–74) vocalist, born Baltimore, Maryland; 'California Dreamin'', 'Monday, Monday', 'Dedicated to the one I love', 'San Francisco'.

Manfred Mann British group, 1960s to 1980s; members include Manfred Mann (originally Michael Lubowitz) (1940–) keyboardist, born Johannesburg, South Africa; Paul Jones (originally Paul Pond) (1942–) vocalist, harmonica player, born Portsmouth; '5-4-3-2-1', 'Do Wah Diddy Diddy', 'If You Gotta Go, Go Now', 'The Mighty Quinn', 'Pretty Flamingo', 'Blinded By The Light'.

POP AND ROCK MUSICIANS AND SINGERS (cont.)

Manilow, Barry (originally **Barry Alan Pinkins**) (1946–) American singer/songwriter, pianist, born Brooklyn, New York; 'Mandy', 'I Write the Songs', 'Looks Like We Made It', 'Copacabana (At the Copa)', *Barry Manilow I, Barry Manilow II, Tryin' to Get the Feeling, This One's for You, Barry Manilow Live, Even Now, One Voice.*

Marillion British group, 1980s to present; members include Fish (Derek William Dick) (1958–) singer/songwriter, born Dalkeith, near Edinburgh; Steve Rothery (1959–) guitarist, born Bromton, Yorkshire; Mark Kelly (1961–) keyboardist, born Dublin; Pete Trewavas (1959–) bassist, born Middlesbrough; Ian Mosley (1953–) drummer, born Paddington, London; 'Market Square Heroes', 'Kayleigh', 'Lavender', 'Heart of Lothian', *Script For A Jester's Tear* (1983), *Fugazi* (1984), *Real to Reel* (1984), *Misplaced Childhood* (1985), *Clutching At Straws.*

Marley, Bob (originally **Robert Nesta Marley**) (1945–81) Jamaican singer/songwriter, guitarist, born Rhoden Hall, St Ann's Parish, Jamaica; (with The Wailers) 'No Woman, No Cry', 'I Shot the Sheriff', 'Exodus', 'Buffalo Soldier', *Catch a Fire* (1972), *Rastaman Vibration* (1976), *Uprising* (1980).

Mayall, John (1933–) British singer/songwriter, guitarist, harmonica player, born Macclesfield; *Bluesbreakers – John Mayall with Eric Clapton* (1965), *Crusader* (1967), *A Hard Road* (1967), *The Turning Point* (1970).

Mellencamp, John Cougar (1951–) American singer/songwriter, guitarist, born Seymour, Indiana; 'I Need A Lover', 'Hurt So Good', 'Jack and Diane', 'Crumblin' Down', 'Pink Houses', *American Fool* (1982), *Uh-Huh* (1983), *Scarecrow* (1985).

Michael, George (originally **Yorgos Kyriatou Panayiotou**) (1963–) British singer/songwriter (was in Wham! – British 1980s group), born Finchley, London; 'Careless Whisper', 'Different Corner', 'I Want Your Sex', *Faith* (1987).

Midler, Bette (1945–) American singer, born Honolulu, Hawaii; 'From A Distance', *The Divine Miss M* (1972), *The Rose* (1979), *No Frills* (1983).

Miller, Steve (1943–) American singer/songwriter, guitarist, born Milwaukee, Wisconsin; 'Rock'n Me', *The Joker* (1973), *Fly Like An Eagle* (1976), *Abracadabra* (1982), *Living In The 20th Century* (1986).

Minogue, Kylie (1968–) Australian singer, born Melbourne; 'I Should Be So Lucky', *Kylie* (1987).

Mitchell, Joni (originally **Roberta Joan Anderson**) (1943–) Canadian singer/songwriter, guitarist, born McLeod, Alberta; 'Help Me', *Joni Mitchell* (1968), *Clouds* (1969), *Ladies of the Canyon* (1970), *Blue* (1971), *Dog Eat Dog* (1986), *Chalk Mark in a Rain Storm* (1988).

The Monkees American group, late 1960s; members include Mickey Dolenz (1945–) vocalist, drummer, born Los Angeles; Davy Jones (1946–) vocalist, guitarist, born Manchester, England; Peter Tork (originally Peter Torkelson) (1944–) bassist, born Washington DC; Mike Nesmith guitarist; 'I'm a Believer', 'Daydream Believer', *Pool It* (1987).

The Moody Blues British group, mid 1960s to 1970s; members include Justin Hayward guitarist; John Lodge bassist; Mike Pindar keyboardist; Graem Edge drummer; Ray Thomas flautist, saxophonist, and vocalist; 'Nights in White Satin', *Days of Future Passed* (1967).

Morrison, Van (originally **George Ivan Morrison**) (1945–) Irish singer/songwriter, guitarist, born Belfast; 'Brown Eyed Girl', *Blowin' Your Mind* (1967); (with Them – Irish group, 1960s) 'Baby Please Don't Go'.

Motley Crue American heavy metal group, late 1970s to present; Nikki Sixx bassist; Mick Mars guitarist; Vince Neil (originally Vincent Neil Wharton) vocalist; 'Smokin' In The Boys' Room', 'Without You', *Too Fast For Love* (1982), *Shout At The Devil* (1983), *Theatre Of Pain* (1983), *Girls, Girls, Girls* (1986), *Dr Feelgood* (1989).

Motörhead British heavy metal group, late 1970s to present; members include Lemmy (originally Ian Kilminster) (1945–) vocalist, born Stoke-on-Trent; *Overkill* (1979), *Bomber* (1979), *Ace of Spades* (1980), *No Sleep Till Hammersmith* (1981), *Orgasmatron* (1986).

Mott The Hoople British band, late 1960s to mid 1970s; members include Ian Hunter (1946–) vocalist,

POP AND ROCK MUSICIANS AND SINGERS (cont.)

guitarist, born Shrewsbury; Mick Ralphs (1944–) guitarist, born Hereford; Overend (Peter) Watts (1947–) bassist, born Birmingham; Verden Allen (1944–) keyboardist, born Hereford; Dale 'Buffin' Griffin (1948–) drummer, born Ross-on-Wye; 'All The Way To Memphis', *All The Young Dudes* (1972), *Mott* (1973).

Moyet, Alison 'Alf' (1961–) British singer, born Basildon; 'All Cried Out', 'That Ole Devil Called Love', 'Weak In The Presence Of Beauty', *Alf* (1984), *Chasing Rain* (1987).

Nelson, Ricky (originally **Eric Hilliard Nelson**) (1940–85) American singer, guitarist, born Teaneck, New Jersey; 'Travelin' Man', 'Hello Mary Lou', *Garden Party* (1972).

The Neville Brothers American group; Arthur Lanon Neville (1937–) keyboardist, vocalist, percussionist; Charles Neville (1938–) saxophonist, flautist, percussionist; Aaron Neville (1941–) keyboardist, vocalist; Cyril Neville (1948–) vocalist, percussionist; all born New Orleans, Louisiana.

New Kids On The Block American group, 1980s to present; members include Jonathan Knight, Jordan Knight, Joe McIntyre, Donnie Wahlberg, Danny Wood; 'You Got It (The Right Stuff)', 'I'll Be Loving You Forever', 'Merry Merry Christmas', '*Hanging Tough*' (1988), *Step By Step* (1990).

Newman, Randy (originally **Randolph Newman**) (1944–) American singer/songwriter, pianist, born Los Angeles; 'I Love L.A.', 'Gone Dead Train', *Sail Away* (1972), *Trouble In Paradie* (1983).

Newton-John, Olivia (1948–) Australian/British singer, born Cambridge, England; 'Make A Move On Me', 'Twist Of Fate', *Grease* (1978), *Xanadu* (1980), *Physical* (1981), *Soul Kiss* (1985).

New York Dolls American group, 1970s; Johnny Thunders (originally Johnny Genzale); Sylvain Sylvain guitarist; Arthur Kane bassist; Billy Murcia (1951–72) drummer, born London replaced by Jerry Nolan; David Johansen (1950–) singer, born Staten Island, New York; *New York Dolls* (1973).

Ocean, Billy (1950–) British vocalist, born Trinidad; 'Love Really Hurts Without You', 'Red Light Spells Danger', 'Caribbean Queen', 'Loverboy', 'When The Going Gets Tough, The Tough Get Going', 'There'll Be Sad Songs', *Suddenly* (1984), *Love Zone* (1986).

Oldfield, Mike (1953–) British multi-instrumentalist, composer, born Reading, Berkshire; 'Blue Peter', 'Moonlight Shadow', *Tubular Bells* (1973), *Hergest Ridge* (1974), *Ommadawn* (1975), *Killing Fields* (1984).

Orbison, Roy (1936–88) American singer/songwriter, guitarist, born Vernon, Texas; 'Only the Lonely', 'Crying', 'Dream Baby', '(Oh) Pretty Woman', 'In Dreams', 'Blue Bayou'.

Osbourne, Ozzy (originally **John Osbourne**) (1948–) American hard rock singer (with Blizzard of Ozz, 1980s to present); 'Shot In The Dark', *The Ultimate Sin* (1986), *Tribute* (1987), *No Rest For The Wicked* (1989).

The Osmonds American group, 1970s; members include Alan (1949–), Wayne (1951–), Merrill (1953–), Jay (1955–), Donny (originally Donald Clark Osmond) (1957–), and Marie Osmond (1959–); all born Ogden, Utah; Jimmy (1963–) born Canoga Park, California.

Palmer, Robert (1949–) British singer, born W Yorkshire, England; 'Every Kinda People', 'Bad Case Of Loving You (Doctor Doctor)', 'Some Guys Have All The Luck', 'Addicted To Love', 'She Makes My Day', *Riptide* (1985).

Peter, Paul and Mary American trio, 1960s to present; Peter Yarrow (1938–) guitarist and vocalist, born New York City; Paul Stookey (1937–) guitarist and vocalist, born Baltimore, Maryland; Mary Travers (1937–) vocalist, born Louisville, Kentucky; 'If I Had A Hammer', 'Blowin' In The Wind', 'Puff The Magic Dragon', 'Leavin' On A Jet Plane', *Peter, Paul & Mary* (1962), *In The Wind* (1963), *Peter, Paul & Mommy* (1969), *No Easy Walk To Freedom* (1986).

Petty, Tom (1953–) American singer/songwriter, guitarist, born Gainsville; (with The Heartbreakers — mid 1970s to present) 'Don't Come Around Here No More', *Damn the Torpedoes* (1979), *Hard Promises* (1981), *Southern Accents* (1985), *Into The Great Wide Open* (1991); *Songs From The Garage* (1988), *Full Moon Fever* (1989).

Pickett, Wilson (1941–) American singer, born Prattville, Alabama; 'In The Midnight Hour', '634-5789', 'Hey Jude'.

POP AND ROCK MUSICIANS AND SINGERS (cont.)

Pink Floyd British group, late 1960s to present; members include 'Syd' (Roger Keith) Barrett (1946–) singer/songwriter, guitarist; Roger Waters (1944–) singer/songwriter; David Gilmour (1944–) singer/songwriter, guitarist; all born Cambridge; *The Piper at the Gates of Dawn* (1967), *A Saucerful of Secrets* (1968), Ummagumma (1969), *Meddle* (1971), *Dark Side of the Moon* (1973), *Wish you were Here* (1975), *The Wall* (1979), *The Final Cut* (1983), *A Momentary Lapse of Reason* (1987), *A Delicate Sound of Thunder* (1988).

Pitney, Gene (1941–) American singer, born Hartford, Connecticutt; 'The Man Who Shot Liberty Valance', '24 Hours From Tulsa'.

The Pogues British/Irish group, 1980s to present; members include Philip Chevron (originally Philip Ryan) (1957–) guitarist, born Dublin; James Fearnley (1954–) accordionist, born Manchester; Andrew Ranken (1953–) drummer, born London; Jem Finer (originally Jeremy Max Finer (1955–) banjo player, born Dublin; Spider Stacy (originally Peter Richard Stacy) (1958–) tin whistle player, born Eastbourne; 'Dirty Old Town', 'Sally Maclennane', 'A Pair of Brown Eyes', 'Irish Rover' (with the Dubliners), *Red Roses For Me* (1984), *Rum, Sodomy & The Lash* (1985).

Pointer Sisters American group, 1970s to 1980s; Ruth (1946–), Anita (1948–), Bonnie (1950–), June (1954–) Pointer; all born Oakland, California; 'Fairy Tale', 'Fire', 'Slow Hand', 'Jump (For My Love)', 'Automatic', 'Neutron Dance', *So Excited!* (1982), *Break Out* (1983), *Serious Slammin'* (1988).

Police British group, late 1970s to present; members include Sting (originally Gordon Sumner) (1951–), singer/songwriter, bassist, born Wallsend, Northumberland (solo 'Set Them Free', 'Russians', *The Dream of the Blue Turtles* (1985), *Nothing Like The Sun* (1987)); Stewart Copeland (1952–) drummer, born Alexandria, Virginia; Andy Summers (1942–) guitarist, born Lancaster; 'Can't Stand Losing You' (1978), 'Roxanne', 'Message In A Bottle', 'Walking On The Moon', 'Don't Stand So Close To Me', 'Every Little Thing She Does Is Magic', 'Every Breath You Take', *Outlandos d'Amour* (1978), *Regatta de Blanc* (1979), *Zenyatta Mondatta* (1980), *Ghost in the Machine* (1981), *Synchronicity* (1983).

Pop, Iggy (originally **James Newell Osterburg**) (1947–) American singer/songwriter, drummer, born Ypsilanti, Michigan; 'I Wanna Be Your Dog', *The Stooges* (1969), *Raw Power* (1973) (with the Stooges); 'Nightclubbing', 'The Passenger', 'Real Wild Child', 'Well Did You Evah' (with Deborah Harry), *The Idiot* (1976), *Lust for Life* (1977), *Blah Blah Blah* (1986), *Instinct* (1988).

Presley, Elvis (Aaron) (1935–77) American singer, guitarist, born Tupelo, Mississippi; 'Heartbreak Hotel' (1956), 'Hound Dog' (1956), 'Love Me Tender' (1956), 'All Shook Up' (1957), 'Jailhouse Rock' (1957), 'One Night' (1959), 'A Fool Such as I' (1959), 'It's Now or Never' (1960), *G I Blues* (1961), *Blue Hawaii* (1961), 'Suspicious Minds' (1969), 'In the Ghetto' (1969).

The Pretenders British group, late 1970s to present; members include Chrissie Hynde (1951–) singer/songwriter, guitarist, born Akron, Ohio; 'Back on the Chain Gang', 'Brass in Pocket', *Pretenders* (1979), *Single Records* (1988).

Prince (originally **Prince Rogers Nelson**) (1958–) American singer/songwriter, guitarist, keyboardist, drummer born Minneapolis, Minnesota; 'Little Red Corvette', 'Delirious', 'When Doves Cry', 'Let's Go Crazy', 'Raspberry Beret', 'Kiss', *Prince* (1979), *Dirty Mind* (1980), *Controversy* (1981), *1999* (1982), *Purple Rain* (with the Revolution) (1984), *Around The World In A Day* (1985), *Parade* (1986), *Sign o' the Times* (1987), *Love Sexy* (1988).

The Psychedelic Furs British group, late 1970s; members include Richard 'Butler Rep' Butler vocalist; Tim Butler bassist; John Ashton guitarist; 'Heaven', 'Pretty In Pink', *Mirror Moves* (1984), *Midnight To Midnight* (1986).

Public Image Limited (P.I.L.) British group, late 1970s to present; members include John Lyndon; 'This Is Not A Love Song', 'Rise', *Flowers Of Romance* (1981), *Album* (1986), *The Greatest Hits So Far* (1990).

Quatro, Suzi (1950–) American singer/songwriter, born Detroit, Michigan; 'Can The Can', 'Devil Gate Drive', 'Stumblin' In'.

Queen British group, 1970s to present; members include Freddie Mercury (originally Frederick Bulsara) (1946–91) singer/songwriter, born Zanzibar; Brian May (1947–) guitarist, born Hampton, Middlesex; John Deacon (1951–) bassist, born Leicester; Roger Taylor (originally Roger Meadows-Taylor)

POP AND ROCK MUSICIANS AND SINGERS (cont.)

(1949–) drummer, born Norfolk; 'Seven Seas of Rhye', 'Killer Queen', 'Bohemian Rhapsody', 'We are the Champions', 'Somebody to Love', 'Another one Bites the Dust', 'Crazy Little Thing Called Love', 'Under Pressure' (with David Bowie), 'Radio Ga-Ga', *Queen II* (1974), *Shear Heart Attack* (1974), *A Night at the Opera* (1975), *A Day at the Races* (1976), *The Game* (1980), *Hot Space* (1982), *The Works* (1984).

Quiet Riot American heavy metal group, late 1970s to present; members include Kevin DuBrow vocalist; Rhandy Rhoads guitarist replaced by Carlos Cavazo; Rudy Sarzo bassist; Frankie Banali drummer; 'Cum On Feel The Noize', 'Bang Your Head (Metal Health)', *Metal Health* (1983), *Condition Critical* (1984), *QRIII* (1986), *Wild, Young And Crazee* (1987).

The Ramones American group, late 1970s to present; members include Joey Ramone (originally Jeffrey Hyman) (1952–) vocalist, born New York; Johnny Ramone (originally John Cummings) (1952–) guitarist; Dee Dee Ramone (originally Douglas Colvin) (1952–) bassist; Tommy Ramone (originally Tom Erdelyi) (1952–) drummer, born Budapest replaced by Marky Ramone (originally Mark Bell); 'Beat The Brat', 'Now I Wanna Sniff Some Glue', 'Do You Remember Rock'n'Roll Radio?', 'Baby I Love You', *Ramones* (1976), *The Century* (1980), *Pleasant Dreams* (1981), *Too Tough To Die* (1985), *Halfway To Sanity* (1988).

Ray, Johnnie (1927–90) American singer, born Rosebud, Oregon; 'Cry'/'The Little White Cloud That Cried', 'Walkin' My Baby Back Home', 'Just Walking In The Rain', 'You Don't Owe Me A Thing', 'I'll Never Fall In Love Again', *The Big Beat* (1957).

Redding, Otis (1941–67) American singer/songwriter, born Dawson, Georgia; 'I've Been Loving You Too Long', 'Try a Little Tenderness', 'Mr Pitiful', 'Satisfaction', '(Sittin' On The) Dock of the Bay', 'Respect', *King and Queen, The Otis Redding Story* (1968), *The Dock of the Bay* (1987).

Reed, Lou (originally **Louis Firbank**) (1944–) American singer/songwriter, born Long Island, New York; 'Walk On The Wild Side', 'I Love You Suzanne', *Lou Reed* (1972), *Transformer* (1972), *Rock 'n' Roll Animal* (1974), *Coney Island Baby* (1976), *Street Hassle* (1978), *New Sensations* (1984), *New York* (1989).

Martha Reeves and The Vandellas American group, 1960s; members include Martha Reeves (1941–) singer; Rosalind Ashford (1943–) singer; Betty Kelly (1944–) singer; all born Detroit; 'Nowhere To Run', 'I'm Ready For Love', 'Jimmy Mack', 'Dancing In The Street'.

R.E.M. American group, 1980s to present; members include Michael Stipe (1960–) vocalist; Peter Buck (1956–) guitarist; Michael Mills (1958–) bassist; Bill Berry (1958–) drummer; 'World Leader Pretend', 'The One I Love', 'Stand', 'The End of the World', 'Superman', 'Orange Crush', 'Losing my Religion', 'Shiny Happy People', *Murmur* (1983), *Reckoning* (1984), *Life's Rich Pageant* (1986), *Number 5: Document* (1987), *Green* (1989), *Out of Time* (1991).

REO Speedwagon American group, late 1960s to present; members include Alan Gratzer (1948–) drummer, born Syracuse, New York; Neal Doughty (1946–) keyboardist, born Evanston, Illinois; Gary Richrath (1949–) guitarist, born Peoria, Illinois; Kevin Cronin singer; 'Keep On Lovin' You', 'Take It On The Run', 'Can't Fight This Feeling', *Hi Fidelity* (1980), *Good Trouble* (1982), *Wheels Are Turnin'* (1984), *Life As We Know It* (1987).

Richard, Cliff (originally **Harry Roger Webb**) (1940–) British singer/songwriter, guitarist, born Lucknow, India; over 100 hits including 'Livin' Doll', 'The Young Ones', 'Summer Holiday', 'Congratulations', *21 Today* (1961), *Rock & Roll Juvenile* (1971), *We Don't Talk Anymore* (1979), *Love Songs* (1981).

Richie, Lionel (originally **Lionel Brockman Richie Jnr.**) (1949–) American singer/songwriter, pianist, born Tuskegee, Alabama; 'All Night Long', 'Say You', *Can't Slow Down.*

The Righteous Brothers American duo, 1960s to 1970s; Bobby Hatfield (1940–) singer, born Beaver Dam, Wisconsin; Bill Medley (1940–) singer, born Los Angeles; 'You've Lost That Lovin' Feelin'', 'Just Once In My Life', 'Unchained Melody', 'Ebb Tide', 'Rock And Roll Heaven'.

Robinson, Smokey (originally **William Robinson Jr**) (1940–) American singer/songwriter, born Detroit, Michigan; (with The Miracles – American group, 1960s) 'Shop Around', 'The Tracks Of My Tears', 'I Second That Emotion'; 'Being With You', *Where There's Smoke* (1979), *Smoke Signals* (1986).

The Rolling Stones British group, 1960s to present; members include 'Mick' (Michael Philip) Jagger (1943–) vocalist, harmonica-player, born Dartford, Kent (solo 'Just Another Night', 'Dancing In The

POP AND ROCK MUSICIANS AND SINGERS (cont.)

Street' (with David Bowie), *She's The Boss* (1985)); Keith Richard (originally Richards) (1943–) guitarist, born Dartford, Kent; Bill Wyman (originally William Perks) (1936–) bassist, born Penge, London; Charlie Watts (1941–) drummer, born Neasden, London; Brian Jones (originally Lewis Brian Hopkin-Jones) (1942–69) guitarist, born Cheltenham replaced by Mick Taylor (1948–) born Hertfordshire replaced by Ron Wood (1947–) born Hillingdon, Middlesex; Ian Stewart (1938–85) keyboardist; 'It's All Over Now', 'Little Red Rooster', 'The Last Time', '(I Can't Get No) Satisfaction', 'Get Off of My Cloud', '19th Nervous Breakdown', 'Paint It Black', 'Mother's Little Helper', 'Let's Spend The Night Together', 'Jumpin' Jack Flash', 'Sympathy For The Devil', (1968), 'Honky Tonk Women', 'You Can't Always Get What You Want', 'Brown Sugar', 'Miss you', *The Rolling Stones* (1964), *Aftermath* (1966), *Beggar's Banquet* (1968), *Let it Bleed* (1969), *Get Yer Ya–Ya's Out* (1970), *Sticky Fingers* (1971), *Exile on Main Street* (1972), *Goat's Head Soup* (1973), *Some Girls* (1978), *Emotional Rescue* (1980), *Tattoo You* (1981), *Undercover* (1983), *Dirty Work* (1986), *Steel Wheels* (1989), *Flashpoint* (1990).

Ronstadt, Linda Marie (1946–) American singer, born Tuscon, Arizona; 'Blue Bayou', 'Somewhere Out There' (with James Ingram), *Heart Like A Wheel* (1974), *Simple Dreams* (1977), *Living In The USA* (1978), *Canciones de Mi Padre* (1988).

Ross, Diana (1944–) American singer, born Detroit, Michigan; with the Supremes – 1960s group: 'Ain't No Mountain High Enough', 'Baby Love', 'Stop! In the Name of Love', 'You Can't Hurry Love', 'You Keep Me Hangin' On', 'Where Did Our Love Go', 'I'm Gonna Make You Love Me'; with Lionel Richie: 'Endless Love'; 'Upside Down', 'I'm Coming Out', 'My Old Piano', 'Chain Reaction', *Diana* (1980), *Eaten Alive* (1985).

Roxy Music British group, 1970s to early 1980s; members include Bryan Ferry (1945–) singer, born Washington, County Durham; Brian Eno (1948–) songwriter, keyboardist, born Woodbridge, Suffolk; Paul Manzanera (originally Philip Targett-Adams) (1941–) guitarist, born London; Andy Mackay (1946–) saxophonist; 'Virginia Plain', 'Do The Strand', 'Street Life', 'Love is a Drug', 'Dance Away', 'Angel Eyes', 'Jealous Guy', 'My Only Love', *Roxy Music* (1972), *Stranded* (1973), *Siren* (1975), *Manifesto* (1980), *Avalon* (1982).

Runrig Scottish group, 1970s to present; members include Iain Bayne (1960–) drummer, born St Andrews; Malcolm Jones (1959–) guitarist, born Inverness; Calum MacDonald (1953–) percussionist, songwriter, born Lochmaddy, N Uist; Rory MacDonald (1949–) bassist, songwriter, born Domoch, Sutherland; Donnie Munro (1953–) lead singer, born Uig, Skye; Peter Wishart (1962–) keyboarder, born Dunfermline, Fife.

Rush Canadian heavy metal group, 1970s to present; members include Geddy Lee (1953–) vocalist, bassist, born Willowdale; Alex Lifeson (1953–) guitarist, born Fernie, British Columbia; Neil Peart (1952–) drummer, born Hamilton; *2112* (1976), *All The World's A Stage* (1976), *Moving Pictures* (1981), *Power Windows* (1985), *Hold Your Fire* (1987).

Sade (originally **Helen Folasade Adu**) (1959–) British/Nigerian singer/songwriter, born Ibadan, Nigeria; 'Smooth Operator', 'Paradise', *Diamond Life* (1984), *Promise* (1985), *Stronger than Pride* (1988).

Santana, Carlos (1947–) Mexican guitarist, vocalist, born Autlan de Novarra, Jalisco, Mexico; (with band Santana – late 1960s to present) 'Black Magic Woman', *Santana* (1969), *Abraxas* (1970), *Amigos* (1976), *Moonflower* (1977), *Zebop!* (1981), *Freedom* (1987).

Sayer, Leo (originally **Gerard Hugh Sayer**) (1948–) British singer, born Shoreham-on-Sea, Sussex; 'The Show Must Go On', 'Long Tall Glasses (I Can Dance)', 'You Make Me Feel Like Dancing', 'When I Need You', 'More Than I Can Say', *Leo* (1984).

Sedaka, Neil (1939–) American singer/songwriter; 'Breaking Up Is Hard To Do', 'Laughter In The Rain', 'Bad Blood', *Laughter And Tears: Best of Neil Sedaka Today* (1976).

Bob Seger (1945–) American singer/songwriter, born Ann Arbor, Michigan; (with the Silver Bullet Band – mid 1970s to present) 'Still The Same', 'Hollywood Nights', 'Shame On The Moon', *Night Moves* (1976), *Stranger in Town* (1978), *Against The Wind* (1980), *The Distance* (1982), *Like A Rock* (1986).

Sex Pistols British punk group, 1970s; members include Johnny Rotten (originally John Lydon) (1956–) vocalist; Steve Jones (1955–) guitarist; Paul Cook (1956–) drummer; Sid Vicious (originally John

POP AND ROCK MUSICIANS AND SINGERS (cont.)

Simon Ritchie) (1958–79) singer, bassist; 'Anarchy in the U.K.', 'God Save The Queen', 'Pretty Vacant', 'Holidays In The Sun', 'My Way', 'Something Else', 'C'mon Everybody', 'Silly Thing', *Never Mind the Bollocks – Here's The Sex Pistols* (1977), *Some Product* (1978), *Flogging a Dead Horse* (1979), *The Great Rock 'n' Roll Swindle* (1980).

The Shadows British group, late 1950s to present; members include Hank Marvin (originally Brian Rankin) (1941–) guitarist, born Newcastle; Bruce Welch (1941–) guitarist, born Newcastle; Jet Harris (originally Terry Harris) (1939–) bassist, born London; Tony Meehan (1943–) drummer, born London; 'Apache', 'Kon Tiki', 'Wonderful Land', 'Dance On', 'Foot Tapper', 'Don't Cry For Me Argentina', *Moonlight Shadows* (1986).

Sha Na Na American group, late 1960s to present; members include John 'Bowzer' Baumann pianist; Scott Powell, Johnny Contardo, Frederic Dennis Greene, Don York singers; Chico Ryan bassist; Elliot Randall guitarist; Scott Simon pianist; Jocko Marcellion drummer; Lennie Baker saxophonist; *The Golden Age of Rock'n'Roll* (1973).

The Shangri-las American group, mid 1960s; Betty Weiss singer; Mary Weiss; Marge and Mary Ann Ganser; 'Leader Of The Pack', 'Past, Present, And Future'.

Shannon, Del (1939–90) American singer, born Coopersville, Michigan; 'Runaway', *Little Town Flirt* (1963), *Drop Down And Get Me* (1983).

Sharkey, Feargal (1958–) Irish singer, born Londonderry, Northern Ireland; (with The Undertones – Irish band, late 1970s to early 1980s) 'Teenage Kicks', 'My Perfect Cousin', *All Wrapped Up* (1983); 'Listen To Your Father', 'A Good Heart', *Feargal Sharkey* (1985), *Wish* (1987).

Shaw, Sandie (originally **Sandra Goodrich**) (1947–) British singer, born Dagenham, Essex; 'There's Always Something There To Remind Me', 'Long Live Love', 'Puppet on a String, 'Hand In Glove', 'Are You Ready To Be Heartbroken?'.

Shocked, Michelle (c.1962–) singer/songwriter, born Texas; *Texas Campfire Tapes* (1987), *Short Sharp Shocked* (1988).

Simon, Carly (1945–) singer/songwriter, born New York City; 'You're So Vain', 'Nobody Does It Better', 'Coming Round Again', 'Let The River Run', *No Secrets* (1972).

Simon, Paul (1941–) American singer/songwriter, guitarist, born Newark, New Jersey; 'You Can Call Me Al', *Paul Simon* (1972), *Graceland* (1986), *Rhythm of the Nations* (1990) (was in Simon and Garfunkel, 1960s, formerly Tom and Gerry, with Art Garfunkel (1942–) singer, born Forest Hills, New York; 'The Sound of Silence', 'Mrs Robinson', 'Bridge over Troubled Water', 'The Boxer', 'Scarborough Fair', 'Homeward Bound', *Bridge over Troubled Water* (1970).

Simone, Nina (originally **Eunice Waymon**) (1933–) American singer, born Tryon, N Carolina; *My Baby Just Cares For Me.*

Simple Minds British group, late 1970s to present; members include Jim Kerr singer, born Glasgow; Charlie Burchill guitarist; Mel Gaynor drummer; Derek Forbes bassist replaced by John Giblin; Mick McNeil keyboardist; Duncan Barnwell guitarist; 'Don't You (Forget about Me)', 'Belfast Child', *New Gold Dream* (1982), *Sparkle In The Rain* (1984), *Once upon a Time* (1985), *Live in the City of Light* (1987).

Simply Red British group, 1980s; members include Mick Hucknall singer/songwriter; Tony Bowers bassist; Chris Joyce drummer; Fritz McIntyre keyboardist; Sylvan Richardson guitarist; 'Money's Too Tight To Mention', 'Holding Back The Years', *Picture Book* (1985), *Men And Women* (1987).

Sinatra, Frank (Francis Albert) (1915–) American singer, born Hoboken, New Jersey; 'I've Got You Under My Skin', 'Strangers In The Night', 'The Lady Is A Tramp', 'Theme From New York, New York', 'My Way'.

Siouxsie and the Banshees British group, late 1970s to present; members include Siouxsie Sioux (originally **Susan Janet Dallion**) (1957–) singer/songwriter, born London; Steve Severin (originally Steve Bailey) (1955–) bassist, born London; Budgie (originally Peter Clarke) (1957–) drummer, born St Helens, Lancashire; 'Wheel's On Fire', *The Scream* (1979), *Tinderbox, Kaleidoscope* (1980), *Tinderbox* (1986), *Through The Looking Glass* (1987), *Peepshow* (1988).

POP AND ROCK MUSICIANS AND SINGERS (cont.)

Slade British group, late 1960s to present; Noddy Holder (originally Neville Holder) (1950–) guitarist, vocalist, born Walsall, Staffordshire; Jim Lea (1952–) bassist, vocalist, pianist, born Wolverhampton; Dave Hill (1952–) drummer, born Devon; Don Powell (1950–) drummer, born Bilston, Staffordshire; 'Coz I Love You', 'Mama Weer All Crazee Now', 'Cum On Feel The Noize', 'Skweeze Me, Pleeze Me', 'Merry Xmas Everybody', 'My Oh My', *Play It Loud* (1970), *We'll Bring The House Down* (1981), *Amazing Kamikazi Syndrome* (1983), *Rogues Gallery* (1985), *You Boyz Make Big Noize* (1987).

Sly and the **Family Stone** American group, 1960s to present; members include Sly Stone (originally Sylvester Stewart) (1944–) vocalist, guitarist, keyboardist; Freddie Stone (1946–) guitarist; Cynthia Robinson (1946–) trumpeter; Larry Graham (1946–) guitarist; Rosemary Stone (1945–) vocalist, pianist; 'Dance To The Music', 'Everyday People', *Greatest Hits* (1970), *There's A Riot Goin' On* (1971).

Smith, Patti (1946–) American singer/songwriter, born Chicago; 'Because the Night', *Horses* (1976), *Easter* (1978), *Dream Of Life* (1988).

The Smiths British group, 1980s; members include (Steven Patrick) Morrissey (1959–) singer/songwriter (solo 'Everyday Is Like Sunday', *Viva Hate* (1988)); Johnny Marr (1963–) guitarist, songwriter; both born Manchester; 'Hand In Glove', 'Bigmouth Strikes Again', 'Boy With The Thorn In His Side', 'Panic', *The Smiths* (1984), *Meat Is Murder* (1985), *Hatful of Hollow* (1985), *The Queen Is Dead* (1986), *Strangeways, Here We Come* (1987).

Spandau Ballet British group, 1980s to present; members include Tony Hadley (originally Anthony Patrick Hadley) (1959–) vocalist, born Islington; Gary Kemp (1960–) guitarist, songwriter; Martin Kemp (1961–) bassist; both born London; John Keeble (1959–) drummer; Steve Norman (1960–) guitarist; 'Gold', *True* (1983), *Parade* (1984), *Through The Barricades* (1986).

Springfield, Dusty (originally **Mary O'Brien**) (1939–) British singer, born Hampstead, London; 'I Only Want To Be With You', 'You Don't Have To Say You Love Me', *Dusty In Memphis* (1969).

Springfield, Rick (1949–) Australian singer/songwriter, guitarist, born Sydney; 'Jessie's Girl', *Working Class Dog* (1981), *Success Hasn't Spoiled Me Yet* (1982), *Living In Oz* (1983), *Tao* (1985), *Rock Of Life* (1988).

Springsteen, Bruce (Frederick Joseph) (1949–) American singer/songwriter, guitarist, born Freehold, New Jersey; 'Hungry Heart', 'Dancing In The Dark', 'Brilliant Disguise', *Greetings from Ashbury Park, NJ* (1973), *Born to Run* (1975), *Darkness on the Edge of Town* (1978), *The River* (1980), *Nebraska* (1982), *Born in the USA* (1985), *Tunnel of Love* (1987).

Squeeze British group, mid 1970s to present; members include Glen Tilbrook (1957–); Chris Difford (1954–); both guitarists, vocalists, songwriters; Jools Holland (1954–) keyboardist replaced by Paul Carrack (1951–) born Sheffield; John Bentley (1951–) bassist; Gilson Lavis (1951–) drummer; 'Goodbye Girl', 'Up The Junction', *Cool For Cats* (1979), *East Side Story* (1981), *Cosi Fan Tutti Frutti* (1985), *Babylon And On* (1987).

Status Quo British group, 1970s to present; members include Francis Rossi (1949–) guitarist, vocalist; Richard Parfitt (1948–) guitarist, vocalist; Alan Lancaster (1949–) bassist; John Coghland (1946–) drummer; all born London; 'Down, Down', 'Caroline', 'You're in the Army Now', *Piledriver* (1973), *Hello* (1973), *On The Level* (1975), *Blue For You* (1976), *Rockin' all over the World* (1978), *1982*.

Steeleye Span British group, 1970s to present; members include Tim Hart guitarist, vocalist; Maddy Prior; Martin Carthy guitarist, vocalist; Peter Knight fiddler; Rick Kemp bassist; Bob Johnson guitarist; Nigel Pegrum drummer, flautist; *All Around My Hat* (1975), *Back In Line* (1986).

Steely Dan American group, 1970s; Walter Becker (c.1950–) bassist, guitarist; Donald Fagen (c.1950–) keyboardist; 'Reelin' Back The Years', *Aja* (1977).

Steppenwolf Canadian group, late 1960s to early 1970s; members include John Kay (originally Joachim Krauledat) (1944–) guitarist, vocalist, born East Germany; Jerry Edmonton (1946–) drummer; Goldy McJohn (1945–) keyboardist; 'Born to Be Wild', 'Magic Carpet Ride', *Steppenwolf* (1968), *The Second* (1968), *Steppenwolf Live* (1970), *Hour Of The Wolf* (1975).

POP AND ROCK MUSICIANS AND SINGERS (cont.)

Stevens, Cat (originally **Steven Demitri Georgiou**) (1947–) singer/songwriter, born London; 'Lady D'Arbanville', 'Wild World', 'Peace Train', 'Morning Has Broken', *Tea For The Tillerman* (1971), *Teaser & The Firecat* (1971), *Catch Bull At Four* (1972), *Foreign* (1973), *Buddha And The Chocolate Box* (1974).

Stevens, Shakin' (originally **Michael Barratt**) (1948–) British singer, born Ely, Wales; 'This Ole House', 'Green Door', 'Oh Julie', *Lipstick Powder And Paint* (1985).

Stewart, Rod(erick David) (1945–) British singer/songwriter, guitarist, born London; *First Step* (1977) and *Long Player* (1971) (with the Faces); 'Maggie May', 'You Wear It Well', 'Sailing', 'Do Ya Think I'm Sexy?', 'I Don't Want To Talk About It', 'Passion', 'Baby Jane', 'Stay with Me', 'Young Turks', 'The Motown Song', *Every Picture Tells A Story* (1971), *Atlantic Crossing* (1975), *Blondes Have More Fun* (1978), *Tonight I'm Yours* (1981), *Body Wishes* (1983), *Every Beat Of My Heart* (1986), *Out Of Order* (1988).

The Stranglers British group, mid 1970s to present; members include Hugh Cornwell (1949–) vocalist, guitarist; Jean-Jacques Burnel, vocalist, bassist; 'Peaches', 'Walk On By', 'Golden Brown', 'Always The Sun', '96 Tears', *Rattus Norvegicus* (1977), *No More Heroes* (1977), *Feline* (1983), *Aural Structure* (1984), *Dreamtime* (1986), *Ten* (1990).

Stray Cats American group, early 1980s; Brian Setzer (1960–) singer/songwriter, guitarist, born New York City; Lee Rocker (originally Lee Drucher) bassist; Slim Jim Phantom (originally James McDonell) drummer; 'Runaway Boys', 'Stray Cat Strut', 'Rock This Town', 'Sexy and 17', *Stray Cats* (1981), *Gonna Ball* (1982), *Built For Speed* (1982), *Rant'n'Rave* (1983).

Streisand, Barbra (Joan) (1942–) American singer/songwriter, born Brooklyn, New York; (with Neil Diamond) 'You Don't Bring Me Flowers'; 'Guilty', *Stoney End* (1971), *The Way We Were* (1974), *Streisand Superman* (1977), *Emotion* (1984), *One Voice* (1987); 30 gold albums.

Style Council British group, 1980s; members include Paul Weller singer, guitarist; Mick Talbot (1959–) keyboardist; 'You're The Best Thing', 'Shout To The Top', 'Walls Come Tumbling Down', *Café Blue* (1984), *My Favourite Shop* (1985), *The Cost Of Living* (1987).

Summer, Donna (originally **LaDonna Adrian Gaines**) (1948–) American singer, born Boston, Massachusetts; 'Love To Love You Baby', 'I Feel Love', 'Last Dance', 'Hot Stuff', 'Highway Runner', 'He's A Rebel', 'Forgive Me', 'Dinner With Gershwin', *Live And More* (1978), *Bad Girls* (1979), *The Wanderer* (1980), *She Works Hard For The Money* (1983), *All Systems Go* (1987).

Survivor American group, late 1970s to present; members include Jim Petrik keyboardist, guitarist; Frankie Sullivan guitarist; David Bickler vocalist replaced by Jimi Jamison; 'Eye Of The Tiger', 'American Heartbeat', 'I Can't Hold Back', 'Burning Heart', *Vital Signs* (1984).

Talking Heads American group, mid 1970s to present; members include David Byrne (1952–) singer/songwriter, guitarist, born Dumbarton, Scotland; Chris Frantz (1951–) drummer, born Fort Campbell, Kentucky; Martina 'Tina' Weymouth (1950–) bassist, born Coronado, California; Jerry Harrison (1949–) keyboardist, born Milwaukee, Wisconsin; 'Psycho Killer', 'Burning Down the House', 'Road to Nowhere', 'And She Was', *Talking Heads* (1977), *Fear of Music* (1979), *Remain in the Light* (1980), *Speaking In Tongues* (1983), *Little Creatures* (1985), *True Stories* (1986), *Naked* (1988).

Taylor, James (1948–) American singer/songwriter, guitarist; born Boston, Massachusetts; 'You've Got A Friend', *Mud Slide Slim And The Blue Horizon* (1971), *One Man Dog* (1972), *Gorilla* (1975), *That's Why I'm Here* (1986), *Never Die Young* (1988).

Teardrop Explodes British group, late 1970s to early 1980s; members include Julian Cope (1957–) singer, bassist, born Bargoed, Wales; Mick Finkler guitarist replaced by Troy Tate; Gary Dwyer drummer; Jeff Hammer keyboardist; 'Reward', 'Treason', *Kilimanjaro* (1980), *Wilder* (1981), *Everybody Wants To Shag The Teardrop Explodes* (1991).

Tears For Fears British group, 1980s; members include Curt Smith (1961–) singer, bassist; Roland Orzabol (1961–) singer, guitarist; 'Pale Shelter', 'Shout', 'Mothers Talk', 'Everybody Wants To Rule The World', 'Head Over Heels', *The Hurting* (1983), *Songs From The Big Chair* (1985).

POP AND ROCK MUSICIANS AND SINGERS (cont.)

The Temptations Black American group, 1960s to present; members have included David Ruffin (1941–) singer; Eddie Kendricks (1939–) singer; Dennis Edwards (1943–) singer; Melvin Franklin (1942–), Otis Williams (1941–), Damon Harris, (1950–); over 80 hit singles since 1962; 'Just My Imagination (Running Away With Me)', 'Treat Her Like a Lady', 'Papa Was A Rolling Stone', *Diana Ross & The Supremes Join The Temptations* (1968), *All Directions* (1972).

10cc British group, 1970s to early 1980s; members include Graham Gouldman (1946–) vocalist, bassist, keyboardist; Lol Creme (1947–) vocalist, guitarist; Kevin Godley (1945–) vocalist, drummer; all born Manchester; 'Donna', 'Rubber Bullets', 'I'm Not In Love', 'Dreadlock Holiday', *Bloody Tourists* (1983).

Thin Lizzy Irish heavy metal group, 1970s to mid 1980s; members include Phil Lynott (1951–86) vocalist, bassist (solo 'Yellow Pearl', 'Nineteen'); Brian Downey (1951–) drummer; Eric Bell (1947–) guitarist, born Belfast; Gary Moore vocalist, guitarist; both born Dublin; Brian Robertson (1956–) guitarist, born Glasgow; Scott Gorham (1951–) guitarist, born Santa Monica, California; 'Whiskey In The Jar', 'Boys Are Back In Town', *Jailbreak* (1976), *Live And Dangerous* (1978), *Black Rose* (1979).

Thompson Twins British group, 1980s; members include Tom Bailey (1956–) singer, bassist, born Halifax; Joe Leeway (1957–) percussionist, born London; Alannah Currie (1957–) saxophonist, born Auckland, New Zealand; 'Hold Me Now', 'Doctor, Doctor', 'Don't Mess With Doctor Dream', 'King For One Day', *Into The Gap* (1984), *Here's To Future Days* (1985), *Close To The Bone* (1987).

Toto American group, 1980s; members include Jeff Porcaro (1954–) drummer; Steve Porcaro keyboardist; David Paich keyboardist; David Hungate bassist; Steve Lukather guitarist; Bobby Kimball (originally Robert Toteaux) vocalist; 'Rosanna', 'Africa', *Toto* (1978), *Toto IV* (1982), *The Seventh One* (1988).

Turner, Tina (originally **Annie Mae Bullock**) (1938–) American singer/songwriter, born Nutbush, Tennessee; (with Ike Turner (1931–) singer, pianist, born Clarksdale, Mississipi) 'River Deep, Mountain High', 'Nutbush City Limits', *The Best of Ike and Tina Turner* (1976); solo: 'Let's Stay Together', 'What's Love Got to Do with It', 'Better Be Good To Me', 'We Don't Need Another Hero', *Private Dancer* (1984), *Break Every Rule* (1986).

Twisted Sister American heavy metal group, 1980s to present; members include Dee Snider (1955–) vocalist; Jay Jay French guitarist; Mark 'The Animal' Mendoza bassist; J J Pero drummer; *Under The Blade* (1982), *You Can't Stop Rock'n'Roll* (1983), *Stay Hungry* (1984), *Come Out And Play* (1985), *Love Is For Suckers* (1987).

Tyler, Bonnie (1953–) British singer, born Skewen, S Wales; 'It's A Heartache', 'Total Eclipse Of The Heart', 'Holding Out For A Hero', *Faster Than The Speed Of Night* (1983), *Sweet Dreams And Forbidden Fire* (1986).

UB40 British group, 1980s to present; members include Ali Campbell (1959–) singer, guitarist; Robin Campbell (1954–) guitarist, Jim Brown (1957–) drummer; Brian Travers (1959–) saxophonist; Earl Falconer (1959–) bassist; Norman Hassan (1958–) percussionist; Mickey Virtue (1957–) keyboardist; 'Red Red Wine', 'I Got You Babe', 'Don't Break My Heart', 'Sing Our Own Song', *Signing Off* (1982), *Labour Of Love* (1983), *Baggariddim* (1985), *Rat In The Kitchen* (1986).

Ultravox British group, mid 1970s to 1980s; members include John Foxx (originally Dennus Leigh) singer born Chorley, Lancashire; Chris Cross (originally Chris Allen) (1952–) bassist; Warren Cann (1952–) drummer, born Canada; Billy Currie (1952–) keyboardist/violinist; Midge Ure (originally James Ure) (1953–) singer, guitarist, born Glasgow (solo 'If I Was', *The Gift* (1985)); *Vienna* (1980), *U-Vox* (1986).

U2 Irish group, 1980s to present; members include Bono (originally Paul Hewson) (1960–) vocalist, born Dublin; The Edge (originally David Evans) (1961–) guitarist, Larry Mullen (1961–) drummer; Adam Clayton (1960–) bassist; 'New Year's Day', 'Pride (In The Name of Love)', 'Sunday, Bloody Sunday', 'With Or Without You', 'Desire', *War* (1983), *Live Under a Blood Red Sky* (1983), *The Unforgettable Fire* (1984), *The Joshua Tree* (1987), *Rattle and Hum* (1988).

Valens, Ritchie (originally **Richard Valenzuela**) (1941–59) American singer/songwriter, guitarist, born Pacoima, California; 'Come On, Let's Go', 'Donna', 'La Bamba'.

POP AND ROCK MUSICIANS AND SINGERS (cont.)

Vandross, Luther (1951–) American soul singer; 'Never Too Much', 'Here And Now', *Give Me The Reason* (1986), *Any Love* (1988).

Van Halen American group, late 1970s to present; members include David Lee Roth (1955–) vocalist, born Bloomingdale, Indiana (solo 'California Girls', 'Yankee Rose', *Eat 'Em and Smile* (1986), *Skyscraper* (1987)); Sammy Hagar (1951–) singer/songwriter, guitarist, born Monterey, California (solo 'I've Done Everything For You', 'You're Love is Driving Me Crazy', 'Two Sides of Love', 'I Can't Drive 55', *Three Lock Box* (1983), *Voice of America* (1984)); Eddie Van Halen guitarist; Alex Van Halen drummer; both born Holland; Michael Anthony bassist; 'You Really Got Me', 'Jump', 'Panama', 'Hot For Teacher', 'Why Can't This Be Love', *Van Halen* (1978), *Van Halen II* (1979), *Women And Children First* (1980), *Fair Warning* (1981), *Diver Down* (1982), *1984* (1984), *5150* (1986), *OU812* (1988), *For Unlawful Carnal Knowledge* (1991).

Vega, Suzanne American singer/songwriter, guitarist; 'Marlene On The Wall', 'Small Blue Thing', 'Left Of Center', 'Luka', 'Tom's Diner', *Suzanne Vega* (1985), *Solitude Standing* (1987).

The Velvet Underground American group, late 1960s; members include John Cale (1940–) guitarist, viola player, born Garnant, Wales; Nico (originally Christa Paffgen) (d.1988) vocalist, born Cologne, Germany; Lou Reed (originally Louis Firbank) (1944–) singer/songwriter, guitarist, born Long Island, New York; *The Velvet Underground & Nico* (1967), *White Light, White Heat* (1968), *The Velvet Underground* (1969).

Vincent, Gene (Vincent Eugene Craddock) (1935–71) American singer, born Norfolk, Virginia; (with the Blue Caps) 'Be-Bop-a-Lula', 'Pistol Packin' Mama', 'Bird Doggin''.

Vinton, Bobby (1935–) American singer, multi-instrumentalist, born Canonsburg, Pennsylvania; 'Roses Are Red', 'Blue Velvet', 'There, I Said It Again', *Mr Lonely* (1965), *Melodies Of Love* (1974).

Waits, Tom (1949–) American singer/songwriter, pianist, born Pamona, California; *Small Change* (1976), *Swordfishtrombone* (1983), *The Asylum Years* (1984), *Rain Dogs* (1985).

Warwick, Dionne (also **Marie Dionne Warwicke**) (1940–) American singer/songwriter, pianist, born East Orange, New Jersey; 'There Came You' (with The Spinners); (Dionne & Friends) 'That's What Friends Are For'; *Dionne, Heartbreaker* (1982).

Was (Not Was) Don Was; David Was; 'Spy In The House Of Love', *Born To Laugh At Tornadoes* (1983), *What's Up Dog?* (1988).

Wham! British group, 1980s; George Michael (originally Yorgos Kyriatou Panayiotou) (1963–) singer/songwriter, born Finchley, London; Andrew Ridgely (1963–) singer, guitarist, born Bushey, Hertfordshire; 'Young Guns (Go For It)', 'Club Tropicana', 'Wake Me Up Before You Go-Go', 'Freedom', 'Last Christmas', 'I'm Your Man', 'Edge Of Heaven', *Fantastic* (1983), *Make It Big* (1984), *The Final* (1986).

White, Barry (1944–) American, born Galveston, Texas; 'Can't Get Enough Of Your Love, Babe', *Can't Get Enough* (1974), *Right Now Barry White* (1987).

Whitesnake British heavy metal group, late 1970s to present; members include David Coverdale singer; 'Fool For Your Loving', 'In The Heat Of The Night', 'Here I Go Again', *Love Hunter* (1979), *Ready An' Willing' (1980), Saints And Sinners* (1982), *Slide It In* (1984), *White Snake* (1987).

The Who British group, late 1960s to 1980s; members include Pete Townsend (1945–) singer/songwriter, guitarist (solo *Who Came First* (1972)); Roger Daltrey (1944–) vocalist, born London (solo *After The Fire* (1985)); John Entwistle (1944–) bassist, French horn player; Keith Moon (1947–78) drummer; all born London; 'Substitute', 'Won't Get Fooled Again', 'You Better You Bet', *My Generation* (1966), *The Who Sell Out* (1967), *Tommy* (1969), *Who's Next* (1971), *Quadrophenia* (1973), *Face Dances* (1981), *It's Hard* (1982).

Wings British group, 1970s; members include Paul McCartney (1942–) singer/songwriter, guitarist; 'Give Ireland Back to the Irish', 'Venus and Mars', 'Live and Let Die', 'Crossroads', 'Mull Of Kintyre', *Band On The Run* (1973), *Wild Life* (1973), *Wings over America.*

Wonder, Stevie (originally **Steveland Judkins** or **Stevland Morris**) (1950–) American singer/songwriter, harmonica-player, keyboardist, born Saginaw, Michigan; 'Fingertips', 'Superstition', 'You Are The Sunshine Of My Life', 'Isn't She Lovely', 'Master Blaster', 'Happy Birthday', 'I Just Called to Say I Love

POP AND ROCK MUSICIANS AND SINGERS (cont.)

You', 'Part-Time Lover', 'Ebony and Ivory' (with Paul McCartney), *Stevie Wonder/The 12 Year Old Genius* (1961), *Music Of My Mind* (1972), *Talking Book* (1972), *Innervisions* (1973), *Songs in the Key of Life* (1976), *Hotter than July* (1980), *In Square Circle* (1985), *Characters* (1987).

Yankovic, Weird Al American accordionist, parodist; 'Eat It', 'King Of Suede', 'I Lost On Jeopardy', *In 3-D* (1984), *Dare To Be Stupid* (1985), *Even Worse* (1988).

Yardbirds British group, 1960s; members include Keith Relf (1943–76) singer, harmonica player, born Richmond, Surrey; Paul Samwell-Smith (1943–) bassist, born Twickenham, Middlesex; Chris Dreja (1946–) guitarist, born Surbiton, Surrey; Eric Clapton guitarist; Jeff Beck guitarist; Jimmy Page bassist, guitarist; 'Good Morning Little Schoogirl', 'For Your Love', 'I'm A Man', 'Happening Ten Years Time Ago'.

Yes British group, 1970s to present; members include Jon Anderson (1944–) vocalist, born Lancashire; Rick Wakeman (1949–) keyboardist, born London; Steve Howe guitarist; Chris Squire (1948–) bassist, born London; 'Owner Of A Lonely Heart', *Fragile* (1972), *Close To The Edge* (1972), *90125* (1983), *Big Generator* (1987).

Young, Neil (1945–) Canadian singer/songwriter, guitarist, born Toronto; 'Heart Of Gold', *After the Gold Rush* (1970), *Harvest* (1972), *Tonight's the Night* (1975), *Zuma* (1975), *Rust Never Sleeps* (1979), *Reactor* (1981), *Landing On Water* (1986), *Freedom* (1989).

Young, Paul (1956–) British singer, born Luton, Bedfordshire; 'Where I Leave My Hat', 'Come Back And Stay', 'Love Of The Common People', 'Everytime You Go Away', *No Parlez* (1983), *The Secret Of Association* (1985).

Zappa, Frank Vincent (originally **Francis Vincent Zappa Jr**) (1940–) American singer/songwriter, guitarist, band leader (The Mothers of Invention – American 1970s group), born Baltimore, Maryland; 'Valley Girl', *Apostrophe* (1974), *Joe's Garage* (1979), *Ship Arriving Too Late To Save A Drowning Witch* (1982), *The Perfect Stranger And Other Works* (1985).

ZZ Top American group, 1970s to present; Billy Gibbons vocalist, guitarist; Dusty Hill vocalist, bassist; Frank Beard drummer; 'Gimme All Your Lovin'', 'Sharp Dressed Man', 'Legs', 'Sleeping Bag', *Tres Hombres* (1973), *Tejas* (1976), *Deguello* (1979), *Eliminator* (1983), *Afterburner* (1985).

JAZZ MUSICIANS AND SINGERS

Selected songs, compositions and albums are mentioned.

Adderley, 'Cannonball' (Julian Edwin) (1928–75) American alto saxophonist, bandleader and composer, born Tampa, Florida. Played blues and funk, one of the first to electrify the saxophone; made hits out of Afro-American themes; 'Sermonette', 'This here', 'Work Song'.

Armstrong, Louis (Daniel) ('Satchmo') (1900–71) American trumpeter and singer, born New Orleans. First major jazz virtuoso and exponent of 'scat' singing (vocal imitation of an instrument); appeared in more than 50 films, also very successful commercially; 'Mack the Knife', 'Blueberry Hill', 'Hello, Dolly!'.

Ayler, Albert (1936–70) American tenor saxophonist, born Cleveland, Ohio. Influenced from youth by gospel and religious bands; debut at 16 with Little Walter as sax player; developed Free Jazz style; 'Bells', 'Ghosts'.

Baker, Chet (Chesney H) (1929–88) One of the most lyrical trumpeters in jazz history, at centre of West Coast 'cool jazz' scene; had success with Gerry Mulligan's pianoless quartet with 'My Funny Valentine'.

Barbieri, Gato (Leandro J) (1934–) Argentinian clarinettist, tenor saxophonist and composer, born Rosario, Argentina. Made debut playing the requinto (clarinet) in the 'milonga' bands, then developed own styles, from Free Jazz to Latin; tenor player of tropical alcoves and clubs; won Grammy for film soundtrack *Last Tango in Paris* (1972).

Basie, 'Count' (William Allen) (1904–84) American pianist and bandleader, born Red Bank, New Jersey. Major big (16-piece) band leader of the swing era; Kansas City style music; compositions include 'One o'clock Jump' and 'Jumpin' at the Woodside'.

Bechet, Sydney (1897–1959) American clarinettist and soprano saxophonist, born New Orleans. Began in New Orleans style; contributed to the popularization of jazz, mingling tradition with

JAZZ MUSICIANS AND SINGERS (cont.)

accessible tunes; 'Les Oignons', 'Petite Fleur', 'Dans les Rues d'Antibes'; music for ballet *La Nuit est une Sorcière*.

Beiderbecke, Bix (Leon) (1903–31) American cornetist and pianist, born Davenport, Iowa. First great white jazz musician, characterized by his richly harmonic tone and soft, warm sonority; 'I'm comin' Virginia', 'In the Dark', 'In a Mist' (piano solo).

Blakey, Art ('Bu') (Buhaina, Abdullah ibn) (1919–90) American drummer and bandleader, born Pittsburgh, Pennsylvania. Leading exponent of 'hard bop' style; played in double time; studied African rhythms; leader of The Jazz Messengers; composed score for 1985 film *Des Femmes Disparaissent*, *Oh, By the Way, New York Scene*.

Bley, Carla (née **Borg**) (1938–) American pianist, bandleader and composer, born Oakland, California. Elegant rhythm 'n' blues, blended bebop and folk; leader of own band and record company; compositions include 'Ida Lupina', 'Sing Me Softly of the Blues' and Gary Burton's masterpiece 'A Genuine Tong Funeral'.

Broonzy, Big Bill (Conley, William Lee) (1893–1958) American singer, musician and composer, born Scott, Mississippi. Guitar accompanist and composer to the great blues players of his generation; played in ragtime style, also encompassing folksong, rural and urban blues; 'See See Rider', 'Trouble in Mind', his own 'Texas Tornado' and 'Bossie Woman' and recordings of John Hampton's 1938–9 *Spirituals to Sing* concerts.

Brown, James ('Soul Brother No 1') (1928–) American singer, drummer, pianist and composer, born Barnwell, South Carolina. Archetypal funk, then electro-funk of the new hip-hop generation. First hit 'Please, Please, Please' with the Famous Flames; over 100 others including 'Do the Mashed Potatoes', 'Papa's Got a Brand New Bag', 'It's a Man's Man's Man's World', 'Living in America' for the film *Rocky IV* (1985).

Brown, Sandy (Alexander) (1929–) Anglo-Indian clarinettist, bandleader and composer, born Izatnagar, India. Outstanding blues player. Originally influenced by Louis Armstrong's Hot Five and the New Orleans style, then by West Indian calypso and African folk. Leader of the Fairweather All-Stars.

Brubeck, Dave (David Warren) (1920–) American pianist, bandleader and composer, born Concord, California. Pupil of Schoenberg and Milhaud; uses odd rhythms, the rondo form, fugue-like passages; made popular by Paul Desmond's 'Take Five'; compositions include 'The Duke', 'In Your own Sweet Way', 'Unsquare Dance'.

Burton, Gary (1943–) American vibraphonist and bandleader, born Anderson, India. Has habit of 'discovering' new talent, eg Tommy Smith. Also involved in music education and publishing. Many successful album recordings, including Carly Bley's *Genuine Tong Funeral* and *Alone at Last*.

Byrd, Charlie (1925–) American guitarist, born Chuckatuck, Virginia. Specialist on nylon string guitar; very versatile; plays jazz, classical and South American in the same concerts; prolific recordings include *Jazz/Samba* with Stan Getz.

Charles, Ray ('The Genius') (Robinson, Ray Charles) (1930–) American singer, pianist and composer, born Albany, Georgia. Successful soul artist (despite blindness) with sensitive, vibrant voice and sincere, expressive preacher's tone; often accompanied by big bands; 'Sewanee River Rock', 'What'd I Say', 'Georgia on My Mind', 'Hit the Road Jack', 'I Can't Stop Loving You', film theme 'Ruby'.

Cherry, Don(ald Eugene) (1936–) American trumpeter, cornetist, bandleader and composer, born Oklahoma City. Exponent of improvised music; considered himself not playing the trumpet but singing with it; came to prominence in Ornette Coleman's Free Jazz quartet and on the John Coltrane quartet album *The Avant-Garde*.

Christian, Charlie (1916–42) American guitarist, born Dallas, Texas. Electric guitar pioneer, establishing it as a solo instrument; one who helped lay basis of bebop revolution in Minton's Playhouse; played with Benny Goodman. Early death due to TB. Shared composer credit with Goodman for 'Solo Flight' and 'Seven Come Eleven'; also 'Blues in C', 'Waitin' for Benny'.

Clarke, Kenny ('Klook') (Kenneth Spearman) (1914–85) American drummer, bandleader and composer, born Pittsburgh, Pennsylvania. Inventor of bebop drums; father of modern percussionists; co-led Clarke–Boland big band. Compositions include 'Epistrophy' with Thelonious Monk, 'Salt Peanuts' with Dizzy Gillespie.

JAZZ MUSICIANS AND SINGERS (cont.)

Cole, Nat 'King' (Coles, Nathaniel Adams) (1930–) American singer, pianist and composer, born Montgomery, Alabama. Inventor of modern concept of trio, using piano, guitar and double bass. Won popularity as a singer; 'Straighten up and Fly Right', 'Too Young', 'Unforgettable', 'Answer Me, My Love', 'Ballerina', 'Stardust'.

Coleman, Ornette (1930–) American alto and tenor saxophonist, trumpeter and composer, born Fort Worth, Texas. Experimented in free-form jazz and atonality to mixed acclaim; now regarded as major innovator; invented word 'harmelodic' (improvised coloration). Albums include *Something Else!* and *The Shape of Jazz to Come.*

Coltrane, John (William) (1926–67) American tenor and soprano saxophonist, bandleader and composer, born Hamlet, North Carolina. One of the most influential performers of the post-bebop era. Developed and experimented with improvisation, influenced by Indian ragas, African pentatonic scales and the polyphonic music of the Pygmys; 'Giant Steps', 'A Love Supreme'.

Corea, Chick (Corea, Armando Anthony) (1941–) Italo-American pianist and composer, born Chelsea, Massachusetts. His taste for diversity makes him hard to classify; plays from acoustics to electronics and from Latin rhythms to bebop, Free Jazz to classical; replaced Herbie Hancock in Miles Davis's group for *In a Silent Way* and *Bitches Brew*; 'Return to Forever', 'Crystal Silence', 'Armando's Rhumba', *Now He Sings, Now He Sobs.*

Dankworth, John (Philip William) (1927–) British alto saxophonist, bandleader and composer, born London. A student of the Royal Academy of Music, he later converted stables at his home to be a workshop for young musicians. Hits include novelty 'Experiments with Mice', 'African Waltz'; ballet *Lysistrata*; film score *Saturday Night and Sunday Morning*; piece for orchestra *What the Dickens.*

Davis, Miles (Dewey III) ('Prince of Darkness') (1926–91) American trumpeter and bandleader, born Alton, Illinois. One of the most popular and adapatable jazz musicians of all time. Recording debut with 'Now's the Time', 'Billie Bounce', 'Koko'. Working with Gil Evans, he led a nonet that inspired the 'cool jazz' school. Albums include *The Birth of the Cool* (a turning point in jazz history), *Kind of Blue*; recorded music for Louis Malle's film *Ascenseur pour l'Echafaud* (1957).

Dolphy, Eric (Allan) (1928–64) American alto saxophonist, clarinettist, flautist and composer, born Los Angeles, California. Music rooted in Afro-American tradition but with birdsong-like improvisation comprising screeches, airiness and wild escapades eg in 'Gazelloni' on *Out to Lunch* and 'Jim Crow' on *Other Aspects.*

Dorsey, Tommy (Thomas Francis) ('The Sentimental Gentleman of Swing') (1905–56) American trombonist and big-band leader, born Shenandoah, Pennsylvania. Characteristic sweet-toned instrumental style with seamless legato; formed Dorsey Brothers Orchestra in 1928 with brother Jimmy, one of the most popular swing dance bands. Nearly 200 hits 1935–53 including 'Treasure Island', 'Marie', 'Satan Takes a Holiday', 'Indian Summer', 'In the Blue of Evening' (with Sinatra), 'Boogie Woogie'.

Eldridge, Roy (David Roy) ('Little Jazz') (1911–89) American trumpeter, pianist, drummer, bass player and bandleader, born Pittsburgh, Pennsylvania. Virtuoso who influenced Louis Armstrong and Dizzy Gillespie. Famous trumpet soloist, often playing in the high register; played with top bands eg McKinney's Cotton Pickers and the Fletcher Henderson Orchestra; vocal duet hit with Anita O'Day 'Let Me Off Uptown', also countless records, including *Dale's Wail* with Oscar Peterson, *the Trumpet Battle* with Charlie Shavers and Lester Young.

Ellington, 'Duke' (Edward Kennedy) (1899–1974) American pianist, bandleader and composer, born Washington DC. One of the most important jazz composers and players. Produced about 2 000 works including 'Mood Indigo', 'Sophisticated Lady', 'Take the A Train', film music for *Anatomy of a Murder (1959)* and *Paris Blues* (1961).

Ellis, Don(ald Johnson) (1934–78) American trumpeter, bandleader and composer, born Los Angeles. Worked in both jazz and contemporary music, experimenting with oriental instruments and compositions, and incorporating string quartets; music full of virtuosity collages and improvisation, but poorly represented on disc.

Evans, Bill (William John) (1929–80) American pianist and composer, born Plainfield, New Jersey. Most influential pianist of his generation. Won several Grammies, eg for *Conversations with Myself*; 'Waltz for Debby', 'N Y C 's No Lark' (for Sonny Clark).

JAZZ MUSICIANS AND SINGERS (cont.)

Evans, Gil (Green, Ian Ernst Gilmore) (1912–88) Canadian composer, pianist and bandleader, born Toronto. Collaboration with Miles Davis led to emergence of 'cool jazz' style; one of the first modern jazz arrangers to combine electronics and rock influences with bebop and swing. Compositions include 'Boplicity' and 'Moon Dreams' for Davis's *Birth of the Cool*, 'Concierto de Aranjuez' for *Sketches of Spain*, electric album *Svengali*.

Fitzgerald, Ella (1918–) American singer, born Newport News, Virginia. Unequalled jazz singer; famous for scat singing (vocal imitation of an instrument) and improvisation; starred in drummer Chick Webb's orchestra; sang with Duke Ellington's and Count Basie's bands; performed *Porgy and Bess* with Louis Armstrong; 'Stone Cold Dead in the Market', 'Mack the Knife', 'Party Blues'.

Franklin, Aretha ('Lady Soul', 'Queen of Soul') (1942–) American singer, born Memphis, Tennessee. Daughter of Detroit preacher and gospel singer; many million-selling singles; recorded 'Respect' with Ray Charles and 'Lady Soul' with Otis Redding; masterpiece album *Amazing Grace*; *Love All the Hurt Away*, *One Lord, One Faith, One Baptism*.

Garbarek, Jan (1947–) Norwegian saxophonist, born Mysen, Norway. Despite being inspired by Coltrane, his influence is very much European, drawing on the moods and haunting melodies from his Scandinavian roots; has played and recorded with George Russsell's sextet and orchestra in Sweden; style described as 'distilled thought'.

Garner, Erroll (1921–77) American pianist, born Pittsburgh, Pennsylvania. Self-taught artist with a gift for melody; combined old and new styles; his own lingering style became known as the 'Garner amble'; known for 'Play Piano Play', 'Laura', 'Misty'; awarded gold disc for *Concert by the Sea* (1958).

Getz, Stan(ley) ('The Sound') (1927–91) American tenor saxophonist and bandleader, born Philadelphia. Most important white jazz saxophonist for 40 years of his life. Characteristic smooth, light tone and articulate phrasing. Popularized bossa nova jazz style in the 1960s; 'Focus', 'Desafinado', 'The Girl from Ipanema'.

Gillespie, 'Dizzy' (John Birks) (1917–) American trumpeter, bandleader and composer, born Cheraw, South Carolina. Great pioneering virtuoso and innovator; created bebop style (with Charlie Parker); introduced African rhythms into jazz; compositions include classics 'Night in Tunisia', 'Groovin' High', 'Dizzy Atmosphere', 'Anthropology'.

Goodman, Benny (Benjamin David) ('The King of Swing') (1909–86) American clarinettist, bandleader and composer, born Chicago. The first to integrate coloured musicians into his own band; in 1962 played in first US jazz band to perform in the Soviet Union; clean, joyful style; sextet recordings include 'Six Appeal', 'Seven Come Eleven', 'Wholly Cats', 'Breakfast Feud'; 'Jersey Bounce', 'Why Don't You Do Right' (sung by Peggy Lee).

Gordon, Dexter (Keith) (1923–90) American tenor saxophonist, born Los Angeles. One of the first to play bop tenor; developed modern ballad style and keen harmonic tone (which Coltrane and Rollins studied); 'The Chase', 'The Duel', 'Daddy Plays the Horn', *Gotham City*; also acted in play *The Connection* and film *Round Midnight*.

Grappelli, Stephane (1908–) French violinist, born Paris. Founder member (with Django Reinhardt) of Quintette du Hot Club in France, which had a European influence on jazz in the 1930s. Adapted violin to jazz; master of swing-based style; recorded swing versions of the 'Marseillaise' called 'Echoes of France', and of J S Bach's *Concerto in D Minor*. Duets with Yehudi Menuhin include *Tea for Two* and *Strictly for the Birds*.

Guy, Buddy (1936–) American singer and guitarist, born Lettsworth, Louisiana. Began at 13 with home-made guitar and progressed to centre of Chicago blues scene in the 1950s and 1960s; 'Stone Crazy', debut album *A Man And His Blues, compilation with other Chicago bands In The Beginning*.

Hampton, Lionel ('Hamp') (1909–) American vibraphonist, born Louisville, Kentucky. Made vibraphone a solo instrument, first recording with Louis Armstrong; played in Benny Goodman's band before forming own big band in 1940; 'Flyin' Home' (famous solo by Illinois Jacquet).

Hancock, Herbie (Herbert Jeffrey) (1940–) American pianist and composer, born Chicago. Child classical musician, but dedicated to jazz; played in Miles Davis's quintet for five years, seeing developments towards jazz rock; with own band turned to electric and electronic means. Music blends rhythm 'n' blues and soul blues, or blues and swing; 'Watermelon Man', 'Rock It'; soundtrack of Bertrand's Tavernier's film *'Round Midnight* (1986) won an Oscar.

JAZZ MUSICIANS AND SINGERS (cont.)

Hawkins, Coleman (Randolph) ('Bean', 'Hawk') (1904–69) American tenor saxophonist, born St Joseph, Missouri. Elevated tenor sax to status of solo instrument, hence title 'father' of the saxophone. Abandoned staccato style to develop melodic fluid tone. Compositions include 'Queer Notions'. Hits include masterpiece 'Body and Soul', 'The Man I Love', 'Picasso'.

Henderson, (James) Fletcher ('Smack') (1897–1952) American bandleader, pianist and arranger, born Cuthbert, Georgia. Pioneer of the big band formation. Perfected technique of writing for separate sections and set standard for the swing era. Joined Benny Goodman's band as pianist and arranger and contributed to its success with 'King Porter Stomp' and 'Blue Skies'.

Herman, Woody (Woodrow Charles) (1913–87) American clarinettist, saxophonist, singer, bandleader and composer, born Milwaukee, Wisconsin. A forerunner of 'cool jazz', his first band, The Band That Plays The Blues, had 1939 hit 'Woodchopper's Ball'. His first Herd band was famous: Igor Stravinsky composed *Ebony Concerto* for him; the second had 'Four Brothers' reed section and recorded 'Early Autumn', which includes Stan Getz's influential solo.

Hines, Earl (Kenneth) ('Fatha') (1903–83) American pianist and bandleader, born Duquesne. Often associated with trumpeter Louis Armstrong (they had an influential duet recording 'Weather Bird'), Hines's trumpet-style of piano playing was a significant development among jazz pianists. His big band had a 12-year residency at the *Grand Terrace Ballroom*. One of the first jazz pianists to play and record solo; 'Boogie Woogie on St Louis Blues', 'Jelly Jelly', 'Second Balcony Jump', 'The Earl', 'Rosetta' (composition).

Hodges, Johnny ('Jeep', 'Rabbit') (Hodge, Cornelius) (1906–70) American alto and soprano saxophonist, born Cambridge, Massachusetts. Dominant in alto scene before Charlie Parker; constant member of Duke Ellington's band (except 1951–5); technically orthodox but aesthetically inimitable, known for 'I Got It Bad', 'On the Sunny Side of the Street', 'Warm Valley' and 'In a Sentimental Mood' (later recorded by Coltrane in his honour).

Holiday, Billie ('Lady Day') (Fagan, Eleanora) (1915–59) American singer, born Baltimore. Talented singer with a tragic destiny; noticed as a cabaret singer, she became famous alongside Benny Goodman and Lester Young, toured with Artie Shaw and made a film *New Orleans* with Louis Armstrong before drug addiction killed her; 'Strange Fruit', 'Lover Man', 'God Bless the Child'.

Hooker, John Lee (1917–) American singer and guitarist, born Clarksdale, Mississippi. Popular blues musician with relaxed vocal style; often sang alone and accompanied himself on guitar; began in gospel choirs and became one of the most influential of trad bluesmen; 'Boogie Chillen', 'Boogie With the Hook', 'It Serves Me Right to Suffer'; made *Hooker and Heat* with band Canned Heat; own albums include *Do the Boogie* and *Sittin' Here Thinkin'*.

Jackson, 'Milt' (Milton) ('Bags') (1923–) American vibraphonist, born Detroit. Most important vibraphonist of the bebop era. Co-founder with John Lewis of Modern Jazz Quartet, with which his career is linked; 'La Ronde' and 'Vendome' are the MJQ's mascots.

Jarrett, Keith (1945–) American pianist and composer, born Allentown, Pennsylvania. With his idiosyncratic style of playing, going wild on the keys and embellishing his solos with big 'free' lyrical passages, he became very popular; played with Miles Davis, among others; *Facing You, Sun Bear Concerts*.

Johnson, J J (James Louis) (1924–) American trombonist, pianist, baritone saxophonist and composer, born Indianapolis, Indiana. Father of the modern jazz trombone who invented bebop trombone playing, being the first slide trombonist to match the requirements of speed and articulation, as shown when he played with Charlie Parker; compositions include 'Rodeo for Quartet and Orchestra'; *All-Star Jam, The Eminent J J Johnson, The Bosses*.

Johnson, James P(rice) (1894–1955) American pianist and composer, born New Brunswick, New Jersey. Pioneer of stride with 'Carolina Shout'; often accompanied the great female blues singers; swinging style influential on eg Duke Ellington and Thelonious Monk; composer of symphonic works and hits 'Old Fashioned Love', 'Charleston' (with Cecil Mack).

Johnston, Lonny (Alonzo) (1889–1970) American guitarist, born New Orleans. Major blues figure in New Orleans, introduced guitar in its modern form as a solo instrument; invented style of playing note by note; 'Stardust', 'Confused', 'Swinging with Lonnie'.

JAZZ MUSICIANS AND SINGERS (cont.)

Jones, Elvin (Ray) (1927–) American drummer, born Pontiac, Michigan. Versatile, inventive, self-taught drummer who eschewed the restrictions of continuous tempo and created complicated polyrhythms, producing the river, a new tornado of sound in jazz. Played in Coltrane's quartet for six years; *Live at the Village Vanguard, Heart to Heart* (with Davis); appeared in film dedicated to him *Different Drummer.*

Jones, Quincy (Delight) (1933–) American trumpeter, bandleader, composer and arranger, born Illinois. Famous as arranger and producer, but successful also solo musician. Michael Jackson's mentor and producer of the *Thriller* album; 'Killer Joe '70', 'Just Once', 'Summer in the City' (Grammy winner).

Joplin, Scott (1866–1917) American ragtime pianist and composer, born Texarkana, Texas. Originator and exponent of 'Ragtime' music. First score *Multiple Leaf Rag* sold more than a million copies, but he died unfulfilled; Gunther Schiller made *Treemonisha* into a Broadway hit in the 1970s; 'The Entertainer' was used in the soundtrack of the film *The Sting* (1973).

Kenton, Stan (ley Newcomb) (1912–79) American pianist, composer and bandleader, born Wichita, Kansas. Exponent of 1950s big band 'progressive' jazz style; later bands had unusual five-trombone sections. Music considered loud and pretentious by some, but innovatory by others; won Grammy 1961 for *West Side Story.*

King, B B (Riley B) (1925–) American blues singer and guitarist, born Itta Bena, Mississippi. Famous as singer and influential for economical guitar style. Prolific recording success includes 'Three O'clock Blues', 'Sweet Black Angel' and 1981 Grammy-winner *There Must be a Better World Somewhere.*

Kirk, (Rhasaan) Roland (1936–77) American multi-instrumentalist, born Columbus, Ohio. Music rooted in gospel and blues; polyinstrumentalist despite blindness; could play three saxophones at once, sang into his flute and played whistle, siren, bagpipes etc.

Krupa, Gene (1909–73) American drummer and bandleader, born New York City. Exuberant soloist who made the drummer a solo instrumentalist; played with Benny Goodman; formed own band; had hit 'Sing Sing Sing' with Goodman small group, and 'Rockin' Chair' with trumpeter Roy Eldridge; also 'Chickery Chick', 'Bonaparte's Retreat' and compilation *World's Greatest Drummer*; appeared in several films eg *Some Like It Hot* (1939) and *The Benny Goodman Story* (1956).

Lacy, Steve (Lackritz, Steven) (1934–) American soprano saxophonist and compser, born New York City. Concentrated on soprano sax and developed own rough-edged tone; in the 1950s was sideman to the best soloists of the revival and Swing, then was partner to Cecil Taylor (*In Transition*), then to Thelonious Monk; first record in his own name, *Soprano today*, included some of Monk's music, as did much of his work.

Lewis, John (Aaron) (1920–) American pianist and composer, born LaGrange, Illinois. Succeeded Monk as pianist in Dizzy Gillespie's big band; influential in the first bebop era; recorded with Charlie Parker and Miles Davis; formed the Modern Jazz Quartet in 1951; uncluttered, confident yet bluesy style; celebrated Monk with version of 'Round Midnight'; also composed 'Toccata for Trumpet' which shows Bach's influence, 'Move' and 'Rouge' in Davis's *Birth of the Cool.*

Lunceford, Jimmie (James Melvin) (1902–47). His band, the chickasaw Syncopaters, was a great addition to the history of big bands, playing music by Sy Oliver and having outstanding success with ''Tain't What You Do (It's The Way That You Do It)', 'Rhythm is Our Business' and 'Blues in the Night'; 'Honeydripper', 'Got a Right to Cry', 'Rag Mop', 'Pink Champagne'.

Lyttelton, Humphrey ('Humph') (1921–) British trumpeter and bandleader, born Eton, England. Mainstream jazz musician; celebrated 40 continuous years as bandleader in 1988; pioneer in the British revivalist movement; introduced three-saxophone section and original tunes from English and W Indian folk roots; albums include *Bad Penny Blues.*

McLaughlin, John (1942–) British electric guitarist and bandleader, born Yorkshire. Impressive speed and rhythm technique; music developed into synthesis of Afro-American and Indian music. Took part in birth of jazz-rock with Miles Davis; formed Mahavishnu orchestra; first album *Extrapolation*; plays one track in 1986 film soundtrack *Round Midnight.*

Marsalis, Wynton (1961–) American trumpeter and bandleader, born New Orleans. Classical soloist and jazz performer; played Haydn's *Concerto for Trumpet* at age 14; joined Art Blakey's Jazz Messengers at 18; first recording was with the 'giants' Herbie Hancock, Ron Carter and Tony Williams; style combines extension of bebop with sense of swing; won Grammy 1984 as both best classical and jazz soloist. Albums include 1987 *Standard Time.*

JAZZ MUSICIANS AND SINGERS (cont.)

Metheny, Pat (1954–) American guitarist and composer, born Lee's Summit, Missouri. Musically open-minded, appeals to bebop, rock and Free Jazz fans; blends acoustics and electronics; composed music for John Schlesinger's *The Falcon and the Snowman* (sung by David Bowie); *Song X* (with Ornette Coleman), *Bright Side of Life, American Gargage, Offramp.*

Mezzrow, Mezz (Mesirow, Milton) (1899–1972) American reeds player (especially clarinet), born Chicago, Illinois. Began playing sax in jail; played as a professional musician with eg Eddie Condon, Sidney Bechet; *Paris* and two volumes of *The King Jazz Story* with Bechet.

Miller, (Alton) Glenn (1904–44) American bandleader and trombonist, born Clarinda, Iowa. Very popular as dance band leader, especially during war years. Characteristic style was produced by doubling the lead tenor with a clarinet; 'In the Mood', 'Moonlight Serenade'.

Mingus, Charles (Jr) (1922–79) American double bassist, pianist, composer and bandleader, born Nogales, Arizona. One of the most important composers in 20th-century black music; 'Pussy Cat Dues', 'Boogie Stop Shuffle', 'Jelly Roll', 'Goodbye Pork Pie Hat', *Tijuana Moods.*

Monk, Thelonious (Sphere) (1917–82) American pianist and composer, born Rocky Mount, North Carolina. Famous 'Prophet' or 'High Priest' of bebop, with which he experimented at Minton's Playhouse in Harlem. Leading composer in jazz history; 'Round Midnight' and 'Straight No Chaser' are classics.

Montgomery, Wes (John Lesley) (1923–68) American guitarist, born Indianapolis, Indiana. Influential, innovative and versatile self-taught guitarist; worked with Lionel Hampton; mellow sound due to plucking strings with thumb instead of plectrum; *The Incredible Jazz Guitar of Wes Montgomery.*

Morton, Jelly Roll (LaMenthe, Ferdinand-Joseph) (1890–1941) American bandleader, composer and pianist, born New Orleans. First great composer in jazz, and a link between ragtime and jazz; formed successful band the Red Hot Peppers, who may have been the first to combine arranged ensemble pieces with improvisation; 'Georgia Stomp', 'Grandpa's Spells', 'Wolverine Blues', 'King Porter Stomp'.

Mulligan, Gerry (Gerald Joseph) ('Jeru') (1927–) American baritone saxophonist, born New York. Talented arranger and popular musician who made the baritone saxophone a solo instrument; wrote 'Jeru', 'Boplicity', 'Venus de Milo' and 'Godchild' for Davis's *Birth of the Cool.*

Oliver, King (Joseph) (1885–1938) American cornetist and bandleader, born New Orleans. By the collective improvisation of Oliver's 'Dippermouth Blues', jazz was freed from the polyphonic concept of the New Orleans style; the Chicago style developed which retained swing but had many elements (marches, melodies, polkas etc). Oliver thus one of the 'fathers' of jazz; innovative cornet player, using newly-invented mute; 'landmark' hits include 'West End Blues', 'Canal Street Blues' and 'Doctor Jazz'.

Ory, Kid (Edward) (1886–1973) American trombonist, singer, bandleader and composer, born La Prince, Louisiana. A master of New Orleans 'tailgate' trumpet style, playing rhythmic bass as well as solo; led and played in various successful bands eg Kid Ory's Sunshine Orchestra, the first black jazz band to record, and Louis Armstrong's Hot Five. From 1942 he was active in the New Orleans Revival, though he'd been there from the start. Compositions include 'Muskrat Ramble'; appeared as bandleader in *The Benny Goodman Story* (1956); albums include *Kid Ory's Creole Jazz Band 1944–45.*

Parker, Charlie (Charles Christopher) ('Bird', 'Yardbird') (1920–55) American alto saxophonist, bandleader and composer, born Kansas City. Influential modern jazz performer in post-1940s, whose ideas formed the basis of the bebop style; innovative association with trumpeter Dizzy Gillespie in bebop quintets; compositions include 'Now's the Time' and 'Ornithology'.

Pass, Joe (Passalaqua, Giuseppe) (1929–) American guitarist. Most influential swing guitarist since Wes Montgomery, comparable to pianist Oscar Peterson in speed and vigour; world-famous as sideman with eg Peterson, Count Basie, Ella Fitzgerald, Duke Ellington; own albums include *Virtuoso* and *University of Akron concert.*

Peterson, Oscar (Emmanuel) (1925–) Canadian pianist and composer, born Montreal. Reliable accompanist and flamboyant soloist; permanent member of Jazz at the Philharmonic; also performed with double-bass player Niels-Henning Orsted Pederson and guitarist Joe Pass; solo albums include *My Favourite Instrument, At Salle Playel*; others eg *Affinity* and *Jazz Portrait of Frank Sinatra.*

Pine, Courtney (1964–) English tenor and soprano saxophonist and bass clarinettist, bandleader and composer, born London. Originally Coltrane-inspired, this talented saxophonist of Jamaican origin has

JAZZ MUSICIANS AND SINGERS (cont.)

formed two bands, The Jazz Warriors and The World's First Saxophone Posse; 1986 album *Journey to the Urge Within* includes tune 'Miss Interpret'; also contributed to soundtrack of film *Angel Heart* (1987).

Portal, Michel (1935–) American soprano, alto and tenor saxophonist and clarinettist, born Bayonne, New Jersey. Jazz and classical, uses different instruments for each style; a pioneer of Free Jazz in France; founded 'Unit', an open, informed group where American and European guests were welcomed; film music includes *La Cecilia* and *L'Ombre Rouge*.

Powell, Bud (Earl) (1924–66) American pianist and composer, born New York City. A great virtuoso, very important in bebop movement, and in jazz history generally; encouraged by Thelonious Monk in the 1940s, he made many recordings with other virtuosos and solo, including 'Cheryl', 'Dana Lee', 'Chasin' the Bird', 'Un Poco Loco', 'Passion Thoroughfare', 'Bouncing With Bud'; the character Gordon in 1986 film *Round Midnight* is based on Powell.

Reinhardt, Django (Jean-Baptiste) (1910–53) Belgian guitarist, born Liverchies, Belgium. Self-taught musician of gipsy background and the first European to have an influence on swing-style American guitarists, despite losing two fingers in a caravan fire; joined with Stephane Grappelli to form the Quintette du Hot Club de France, which inaugurated a French-style jazz; toured with the Duke Ellington orchestra, changing from acoustic to electric guitar; produced swing version of Bach's *First Movement of the Concerto in D Minor*; compositions include 'Love's Melody' and 'Improvisation', also (with Grappelli) 'H.Q.C. Strut', 'Daphne', 'Djangology'.

Roach, Max(well) (1925–) American drummer, bandleader and composer, born New York City. Key member of bebop movement and a 'giant' of modern jazz; being the first to 'swing' on the drums and use them for 'melody', he created the very influential legato rhythmic feeling; *The Freedom Suite* (waltzes), *We Insist – Freedom Now Suite, Money Jungle* (with Duke Ellington), *Drums Unlimited*.

Rollins, Sonny (Theodore Walter) ('Newk') (1930–) American tenor saxophonist and composer, born New York City. Powerful improviser and important voice in the 'hard bop' movement, joining Clifford Brown and Max Roach; used Caribbean calypso eg in 'Saint Thomas' and 'Don't Stop the Carnival'; 'Tenor Madness', 'Oleo', 'Airegin', *Saxophone Colossus*.

Shaw, Artie (Arshawsky, Arthur Jacob) (1910–) American clarinettist, bandleader and composer, born Norwalk, Connecticut. Like Benny Goodman in tone and innovation, he was also one of the first to present a mixed black and white band, which had a 'cooler' atmosphere due to its reliance on strings; 'Begin the Beguine', 'Summit Ridge Drive', 'Frenesi', 'Dancing in the Dark'.

Shepp, Archie (1937–) American saxophonist, pianist, singer and bandleader, born Fort Lauderdale, Florida. Created formula of three horns, bass and drums which became the Free Jazz standard; developed frantic solo style in orchestral context; jazz for him was 'Great Black Music'; faithful to blues and gospel traditions and embraced W African trends eg in *Mama Too Tight* and *Magic of Ju-Ju*; also *Four for Trane* and *Ascension* with Coltrane.

Shorter, Wayne (1933–) American tenor and soprano saxophonist, bandleader and composer, born Newark, New Jersey. Played in Art Blakey's Jazz Messengers and Miles Davis's quintet (whose development towards jazz rock he helped; formed own group Weather Report, then continued in electric jazz style; the ethereal 'Mysterious Traveller' and dance-like 'Heavy Weather' contributed to *Round Midnight* film soundtrack.

Silver, Horace (Ward Martin Tavares) (1928–) American pianist, bandleader and composer, born Norwalk, Connecticut. Leading figure, with Art Blakey, of the hard bop style, and main exponent of funky jazz; first pianist and musical director of The Jazz Messengers; compositions have flavour of blues and gospel: 'Doodlin'', 'The Preacher', 'Señor Blues' and 'Opus de Funk'.

Simone, Nina (Wayman, Eunice) (1933–) American singer, pianist and composer, born North Carolina. Performance varied from gospel through blues and soul to modern jazz, excelling in all registers; repertoire included Gerschwin; best known composition 'To Be Young, Gifted and Black'; 'I Loves You Porgy', 'Mississippi Goddam', 'Central Park Blues', 'My Baby Just Cares For Me'.

Smith, Bessie (1894–1937) American singer, born Chattanooga, Tennessee. Advertised as 'The Empress of the Blues'; hers was a blues-based repertoire including recordings accompanied by leading musicians (eg Louis Armstrong). Realistic songs depict poverty and love pains often flavoured by angry feminism, eg 'Downhearted Blues'; made short film *St Louis Blues* (1929).

Smith, Tommy (1967–) British saxophonist and composer, born Luton, England. Cosmopolitan musician

JAZZ MUSICIANS AND SINGERS (cont.)

with broad ideas and lavish tonality; disciple of John Coltrane, with a 'European' feeling for textures and moods in his playing; in his first album *Step By Step* he plays his own compositions, with John Scofield and Jack De Johnette; also *Peeping Tom.*

Solal, Martial (1927–) Algerian pianist, composer and bandleader, born Algiers. Born improviser with boundless imagination who defies classification, and who can render standard pieces unrecognizable by his artistry; compositions include *Suite in D Flat* for jazz quartet, and for the film *A Bout De Souffle.*

Sun Ra (Blount, Herman or **Lee, Sonny)** (1914–) American pianist, composer and bandleader, born Birmingham, Alabama. Pioneer of electronic music, little is known of him before the 1950s; his influential Arkestra functioned as a cooperative, and combined the traditions of the swing era with the freedom of improvisation and the rhythmic agility of bop; dedicated his music 'to the Creator of the Universe'.

Surman, John (1944–) British multi-instrumentalist, composer and bandleader, born Tavistock, England. Emerging from a classical background with folk, ethnic and church music roots, Surman was sideman of French-born bluesman Alexis Korner before becoming world famous as soloist; *The Trio, The Amazing Adventures of Simon Simon.*

Taylor, Cecil (Percival) (1933–) American pianist, bandleader and composer, born New York City. An exponent of the avant-garde due to his powerful free style of improvisation; very energetic and fast player who treats his piano like a percussion instrument; worked with saxophonist Jimmy Lyons for many years; *Conquistador, Unit Structures, For Olim.*

Teagarden, Jack ('Mr T') (1905–64) American trombonist and bandleader, born Texas. Great classical jazz figure with warm, natural tone; inventor of jazz trombone; also sang with Louis Armstrong; 'That's an Awful Serious Thing', 'I'm Gonna Stomp Mr Henry Lee' (with Eddie Condon), 'You Rascal You', 'Chances Are', 'Someone Stole Gabriel's Horn', 'A Hundred Years From Today'.

Tatum, Art(hur, Jr) (1909–56) American pianist, born Toledo, Ohio. The most influential of the swing-style pianists, and considered unequalled; despite near-blindness from birth his technique was astonishing and he became famous as the greatest in the history of jazz; 'Body and Soul', 'Tea For Two', 'Tiger Rag'.

Thielemans, 'Toots' (Jean-Baptiste) (1922–) Belgian guitarist and harmonica player, born Brussels. Converted from the accordian to the guitar and harmonica by Django Reinhardt, he also played with Benny Goodman, Lester Young, Count Basie and Stan Getz in America and Europe; Quincy Jones's favourite soloist; played film soundtrack *Midnight Cowboy*; successes include album *Affinity*, and 'Bluesette', a composition which followed an evening improvising with Stephane Grappelli.

Tracey, Stan (1926–) British pianist, bandleader and composer, born London. Important contributor to European jazz scene; being self-taught meant an unconventional and individual technique; percussive piano style; compositions include jazz suites *Under Milk Wood, The Bracknell Connection, Genesis*, also for album *We Love You Madly.*

Tristano, Lennie (Leonard Joseph) (1919–78) American pianist and composer, born Chicago. Blind by age 11; 'Pianist of the Year' 1948; great jazz teacher and 'father confessor to all the avant-garde musicians in the city (Chicago)'; anticipated the 1960s Free Jazz movement in eg 'Intuition', 'Digression', 'Yesteryear'.

Tyner, McCoy (Alfred) (1938–) American pianist and composer, born Philadelphia, Pennsylvania. Part of epochal Coltrane quartet, where the calmness of his playing was a background to the furious solos; later joined Ike and Tina Turner for *Sahara*; 1973 best record prize for *Enlightenment*; *Double Trios* includes revived standard and classic bebop numbers eg 'Lover Man'.

Vaughan, Sarah (Lois) ('Sassy', 'The Divine One') (1924–90) American singer, born Newark, New Jersey. Encouraged by Ella Fitzgerald, she began her career in Earl Hines's and Billy Eckstein's bands; wide vocal range, keen sense of improvisation; attracted by new bebop, she recorded with its inventors eg Dizzy Gillespie and Charlie Parker; 'Things Must Change, 'Make Yourself Comfortable', 'Whatever Lola Wants', 'Broken-Hearted Melody'.

Walker, T-Bone (Aaron Thibeaux) (1910–75) American guitarist, singer and songwriter, born Linden, Texas. One who achieved perfect cohesion between voice and electric sound; teenage friends with Charlie Christian (both were influential in guitar-playing field); made name as blues player with 'T-Bone Blues' in 1939; 'Call It Stormy Monday'; won Grammy 1968 for *Good Feelin'*.

Waller, Fats (Thomas Wright) (1904–43) American pianist, singer, bandleader and composer, born New York City. Professional musican at 15 and master of the New York 'Stride' piano style; talented musician

JAZZ MUSICIANS AND SINGERS (cont.)

but popular for singing and humour; prolific composer; 'Honeysuckle rose', 'Ain't Misbehavin', 'Black and Blue', 'I'm Crazy Bout My Baby', 'Two Sleepy People'; appeared in films eg 1943 *Stormy Weather.*

Washington, Dinah (Jones, Ruth Lee) (1924–63) American singer, born Tuscaloosa, Alabama. Originally 'discovered' by Lionel Hampton, she became the 'Queen of the blues' whose vibrato voice expressed the aspirations and disappointments of the Black community; 'Baby, Get Lost', 'This Bitter Earth', 'What a Difference a Day Makes', 'Baby (You've Got What It Takes)', 'It Could Happen To You'.

Waters, Ethel (1900–1977) American singer, born Chester, Pennsylvania. Began in blues style and became a highly-regarded 1930s pop singer; also worked in cabaret and film; 'Stormy Weather', 'A Hundred Years From Today' (with Benny Goodman and Jack Teagarden), 'Come Up and See Me Sometime' (from Mae West film).

Waters, Muddy (Morganfield, McKinley) (1915–83) American singer, guitarist, bandleader and composer, born Rolling Fork, Mississippi. Popular blues player from 1943; sang with passionate gravelly voice; achieved fame worldwide and his pupils too are many of the 'greats' in jazz; 'Rolling Stone', 'I've Got My Mojo Working', 'Hoochie Coochie Man', 'She's 19 Years Old'.

Weber, Eberhard (1940–) German bass player, bandleader and composer, born Stuttgart. Exponent of European (rather than American) music. Plays with five-string 'electro-bass', having made it a front-line instrument for rhythm to melody and improvisation; eshews American blues roots and, like Jan Garbarek, blends romanticism with evocative or moody sounds; successful first album *The Colours of Chloe.*

Williams, Tony (1945–) American drummer and composer, born Chicago. Contributed to evolution of jazz-rock; percussionist in Miles Davis's quartet; made fame as 1970s symbol of modern drumming; drummer for Eric Dolphy's *Out to Lunch* and Davis's *Filles de Kilimanjaro*; now plays modern jazz and jazz fusion; *Spring, Lifetime, Emergency, Turn It Over, The Joy of Flying.*

Winding, Kai (1922–83) Danish-American trombonist, born Aarhus. Played with many of the jazz 'greats' eg co-leading quintet with J J Johnson, restoring trombone to important position; toured with Gillespie, Monk and Hampton; played on Davis's *Birth of the Cool*; had hit with 'More' (1963 *Mondo Cane* film theme), also *More Brass, Betwixt And Between Jazz Showcase.*

Young, Lester (Willis) ('Prez') (1909–59) American tenor saxophonist, born Woodville, Mississippi. A forerunner of 'cool jazz', which was the opposite of the 1930s saxophone style (eg Coleman Hawkins); pioneer of linear improvisation (J J Johnson); eschewed accepted concepts of melody, rhythm and swing; made reputation with Count Basie's Band: recordings with them include 'Tickle Toe', 'Every Tub', 'One O'Clock Jump'; also 'Lady Be Good', 'Taxi War Dance', 'Rock-A-Bye Basie'.

BALLET DANCERS

Ashley, Merrill (Linda Michelle Merrill) (1950–) American, born St Paul, Minnesota.

Barishnikov, Mikhail (Nikolaievich) (1948–) Russian, born Riga.

Buchones, Fernando (1955–) American, born Florida.

Danilova, Alexandra (Dionysievna) (1904–) Russian/American, born Peterhof.

Dolin, Sir Anton (Sydney Francis Patrick Chippendall Healey-Kay) (1904–83) British, born Slinfold.

Dowell, Anthony (1943–) British, born London.

Duncan, Isadora (1878–1927) American, born San Francisco.

Dunham, Katherine (1912–) American, born Chicago.

Eglevsky, André (1917–77) Russian/American, born Moscow.

Elssler, Fanny (Franziska Elsller) (1810–1884) Austrian, born Gumpendorf.

Farrell, Suzanne (1945–) American, born Cincinnati, Ohio.

Fonteyn, Dame Margot (Peggy Hookham) (1919–91) British, born Reigate.

Fracci, Carla (1936–) Italian, born Milan.

Genée, Dame Adelin (Anina Jensen) (1878–1970) Danish, born Hinnerup.

Gilpin, John (1830–83) British, born Southsea.

Gopal, Ram (1920–) Indian, born Bangalore.

BALLET DANCERS (cont.)

Gore, Walter (1910–79) British, born Waterside, Scotland.
Gorsky, Alexander Alexeivich (1871–1924) Russian, born St Petersburg.
Graham, Martha (1894–1991) American, born Pittsburgh.
Gregory, Cynthia (1946–) American, born Los Angeles.
Grisi, Carlotta (1819–99) Italian, born Visinada.
Hamilton, Gordon (1918–59) Australian, born Sydney.
Haydée, Marcia (Marcia Haydee Salaverry Pereira de Silva) (1939–) Brazilian, born Niteroi.
Helpmann, Sir Robert (1909–86) Australian, born Mount Gambier.
Jasinski, Roman (Roman Czeslaw) (1912–) Polish/American, born Warsaw.
Kain, Karen (1951–) Canadian, born Hamilton, Ontario.
Karsavina, Tamara Platonovna (1885–1978) Russian/British, born St Petersburg.
Kent, Allegra (1938–) American, born Los Angeles.
Kirkland, Gelsey (1953–) American, born Bethlehem, Pennsylvania.
Leclerq, Tanquil (1929–) American, born Paris.
Lichine, David (David Lichenstein) (1910–72) Russian/American, born Rostov-on-Don.
Markova, Dame Alicia (Lilian Alicia Marks) (1910–) British, born London.
Martins, Peter (1946–) Danish, born Copenhagen.
Mauri, Rosita (1849–1923) Spanish, born Tarragona.
Neary, Patricia (1942–) American, born Miami, Florida.
Nemchinova, Vera (Nicolayevna) (1899–1984) Russian, born Moscow.
Nijinsky, Vaslav Fomich (1889–1950) Russian, born Kiev.
Nureyev, Rudolf Hametovich (1938–) Russian/British, born on a train between Lake Baikal and Irkutsk, Siberia.
Page, Ruth (1905–) American, born Indianapolis.
Panov, Valeri (Matvevich) (1938–) Russian, born Vitebsk.
Panova, Galina (1949–) Russian, born Archangel.
Pavlova, Anna (Pavlovna) (1881–1931) Russian, born St Petersburg.
Petipa, Lucien (1815–98) French, born Marseilles.
Petipa, Marie (Mariusovna II) (1857–1930) Russian, born St Petersburg.
Rambert, Dame Marie (Cyvia Rambam, then **Miriam Ramberg)** (1888–1982) Polish/British, born Warsaw.
Riabochinska, Tatiana (1917–) Russian/American, born Moscow.
Rubinstein, Ida Lvovna (1885–1960) Russian, born St Petersburg.
Seymour, Lynn (Lynn Springbett) (1939–) Canadian, born Wainwright.
Shearer, Moira (Moira King) (1926–) British, born Dunfermline.
Shearer, Sybil (1918–) American, born Toronto.
Sibley, Antoinette (1939–) British, born Bromley.
Somes, Michael (1917–) British, born Horsley.
Spessivtseva, Olga Alexandrovna (1895–91) Russian/American, born Rostov.
Taglioni, Marie (1804–84) Swedish/Italian, born Stockholm.
Tallchief, Maria (1925–) American, born Fairfax, Oklahoma.
Taras, John (1919–) American, born New York.
Trefilova, Vera Alexandrovna (1875–1943) Russian, born St Petersburg.
Ulanova, Galina (Sergeyevna) (1910–) Russian, born St Petersburg.
Villella, Edward (1936–) American, born Bayside, New York.

BALLET COMPANIES

Name	Date founded	Location
American Ballet Theatre	1940	New York, USA
The Australian Ballet	1962	Melbourne, Australia
Australian Dance Theatre	1965	Adelaide, Australia
Ballets des Champs Elysées	1944	Paris, France
Ballet Joos	1933	Cambridge, UK
Ballets de Paris	1948	France
Ballet Rambert	1926	UK
Ballet Russe de Monte Carlo	1938	Monte Carlo
Ballets Russes of Sergei Diaghilev now Kirov Ballet	1909-29	Paris and St Petersburg
Ballet-Théâtre Contemporain	1968	Amiens, France
Ballet du Xième Siècle	1960	Brussels, Belgium
Bolshoi Ballet	1776	Moscow, Russia
Borovansky Ballet	1942	Melbourne, Australia
Kirov Ballet	1935	St Petersburg, Russia
London Festival Ballet (originally Festival Ballet)	1949	UK
National Ballet of Canada	1951	Toronto
New York City Ballet	1948	USA
Northern Ballet (formed from part of Western Theatre Ballet)	1969	Manchester, UK
Royal Ballet (formerly Sadler's Wells Ballet)	1936	Covent Garden, UK
Royal Danish Ballet	ballets from 2nd half 16th-c	Copenhagen
Royal Swedish Ballet	1st court ballet 1638	Stockholm
Royal Winnipeg Ballet	1938	Canada
The San Francisco Ballet (formerly the San Francisco Opera Ballet)	1933	USA
School of American Ballet (now the American Ballet)	1933	New York, USA
Scottish Ballet (formed from part of Western Theatre Ballet)	1969	Glasgow, UK
Stanislavsky Ballet (Stanislavsky and Nemirovich-Danchenko Music Theatre Ballet)	1929	Moscow, USSR
Stuttgart Ballet	court ballets from 1609	Germany
Western Theatre Ballet (divided 1969 to form Northern Ballet, Scottish Ballet)	1957	Bristol, UK

BALLETS

Ballet	Composer	Choreographer	First performance
Anastasia	Tchaikovksy, Martinu	MacMillan	1971
Apollo	Stravinsky	Balanchine	1928
L'Après-midi d'un faune	Debussy	Nijinsky	1912
La Bayadère	Minkus	Petipa	1877
Les Biches	Poulenc	Nijinska	1924
Billy the Kid	Copland	Loring	1938
Bolero	Ravel	Bejart	1961
La Boutique Fantasque	Rossini, arr. Respighi	Massine	1919
Carmen	Bizet	Petit	1949
Checkmate	Bliss	de Valois	1937
Cinderella	Prokofiev	Ashton	1948
Coppélia	Delibes	St Léon	1870
Don Quixote	Minkus	Petipa	1869
Duo Concertant	Stravinsky	Balanchine	1972
Façade	Walton	Ashton	1931
Fall River Legend	Gould	de Mille	1948
Fancy Free	Bernstein	Robbins	1944
The Firebird	Stravinsky	Fokine	1910
The Four Temperaments	Hindemith	Balanchine	1946
Giselle	Adam	Coralli and Perro (later revised by Petipa)	1841
Las Hermanas	Martin	MacMillan	1963
Jewels	Fauré, Stravinsky and Tchaikovsky	Balanchine	1967
Les Noces	Stravinsky	Nijinska	1923
The Nutcracker	Tchaikovsky	Ivanov	1892
Ondine	Henze	Ashton	1958
Onegin	Tchaikovsky, arr. Stolze	Cranko	1965
Orpheus	Stravinsky	Balanchine	1948
Parade	Satie	Massine	1917
Petroushka	Stravinsky	Fokine	1911
Pineapple Poll	Sullivan, orch. Mackerras	Cranko	1951
Prince Igor	Borodin	Fokine	1909
The Prodigal Son	Prokofiev	Balanchine	1929
The Rake's Progress	Gordon	de Valois	1935
Raymonda	Glazounov	Petipa	1898
Les Rendezvous	Auber, arr. Lambert	Ashton	1933
Requiem	Fauré	MacMillan	1976
Rhapsody	Rachmaninov	Ashton	1980
The Rite of Spring	Stravinsky	MacMillan	1962
Rodeo	Copland	de Mille	1942
Romeo and Juliet	Prokofiev	Lavrovsky	1940
Le Sacré du printemps (The Rite of Spring)	Stravinsky	Nijinsky	1913
Schéhérazade	Rimsky-Korsakov	Fokine	1910
The Sleeping Beauty	Tchaikovsky	Petipa	1890
Song of the Earth	Mahler	MacMillan	1965
Spartacus	Khachaturian	Grigorovich	1968
La Spectre de la Rose	Weber	Fokine	1911
Swan Lake	Tchaikovsky	Petipa and Ivanov	1895
La Sylphide	Løvenskjold	Bournonville	1836
Les Sylphides (Chopiniana)	Chopin, variously orchestrated	Fokine	1909
Tales of Hoffman	Offenbach, arr. Lanchberg	Darrell	1973
The Three-Cornered Hat	de Falla	Massine	1919
La Ventana	Lumbye and Holm	Bournonville	1854
A Wedding Bouquet	Berners	Ashton	1937

BALLET CHOREOGRAPHERS

Ashton, Sir Frederick William Mallandaine (1904–88) English, born Guayaquil, Ecuador; *Façade* (1931), *Les Rendezvous* (1933), *Cinderella* (1948), *Daphnis and Chloe* (1951), *Ondine* (1958), *The Two Pigeons* (1961), *The Dream* (1964), *Rhapsody* (1980).

Balanchine, George (Georgi Balanchivadze) (1904–83) Russian/American, born St Petersburg; *Apollo* (1928), *The Prodigal Son* (1929), *Bourrée Fantasque* (1949), *Jeu de cartes* (1937), *Agon* (1957), *The Seven Deadly Sins* (1958), *Davidsbundlertauze* (1980).

Bournonville, August (1805–79) Danish, born Copenhagen; *La Sylphide* (1836), *Napoli* (1842), *La Ventana* (1854).

Cranko, John (1927–73) South African, born Rustenburg; *Beauty and the Beast* (1949), *Pineapple Doll* (1951), *The Prince of the Pagodas* (1957), *Jeu de Cartes* (1965), *Onegin* (1965), *Taming of the Shrew* (1969), *Traces* (1973).

Darrell, Peter (1929–) British, born Richmond, Surrey; *A Wedding Present* (1962), *Beauty and the Beast* (1969), *Tales of Hoffman* (1972), *Swan Lake* (1977).

de Mille, Agnes (1909–) American, born New York City; *Three Virgins and a Devil* (1941), *Rodeo* (1942), *Fall River Legend* (1948), and for Broadway – *Oklahoma!* (1943), *Gentleman Prefer Blondes* (1949).

de Valois, Dame Ninette (Edris Stannus) (1898–) Irish, born Baltiboys, County Wicklow; *Job* (1931), *La Création du monde* (1931), *The Rake's Progress* (1935), *Checkmate* (1937), *Don Quixote* (1950).

Diaghilev, Sergei Pavlovich (1872–1929) Russian, born Selistchev barracks, province of Novgorod; producer, impressario, and founder of Ballet Russes; not a choreographer himself, he fostered the talents of Balanchine, Fokine, Nijinsky.

Fokine, Michel (Mikhail Mikhaylovich Fokine) (1880–1942) Russian/American dancer and choreographer, born St Petersburg; *Les Sylphides* (1907), *Petroushka* (1911).

Ivanov, Lev (Ivanovich) (1834–1901) Russian, born Moscow; *The Enchanted Forest* (1887), *The Nutcracker* (1892), *Swan Lake* (with Petipa, 1895).

Jooss, Kurt (1901–79) German, born Waaseralfingen; *Petrushka* (1930), *The Green Table* (1932), *Pulcinella* (1932), *The Mirror* (1935).

Lorring, Eugene (1914–) American, born Milwaukee; *Yankee Clipper* (1937), *Billy the Kid* (1938).

MacMillan, Sir Kenneth (1929–) British, born Dunfermline, Scotland; *The Rite of Spring* (1962), *Las Hermanas* (1963), *Romeo and Juliet* (1965), *Anastasia* (1971), *The Four Seasons* (1975), *Mayerling* (1978), *Isadora* (1981).

Massine, Léonide (Fedorovich) (1895–1979) Russian/American, born Moscow; *Parade* (1917), *La Boutique Fantasque* (1919), *The Three-Cornered Hat* (1919), *Bachanale* (1939).

Nijinska, Bronislova (Fominitshna) (1891–1972) Russian/Polish/American, born Minsk; *Le Renard* (1922), *Les Noces* (1923, 66), *Les Biches* (1924, 64), *La Valse* (1929), *The Snow Maiden* (1942).

Perrot, Jules (Joseph) (1810–94) French, born Lyons; *Ondine* (1843), *Les Elements* (1847), *Faust* (1848), *Markobomba* (1854).

Petipa, Marius (1818–1910) French, born Marseilles; *Pharoah's Daughter* (1862), *La Bayadère* (1877), *The Sleeping Beauty* (1890), *Cinderella* (1893), *Swan Lake* (1895), *Raymonda* (1898).

Robbins, Jerome (Jerome Rabinowitz) (1918–) American, born New York; *Fancy Free* (1944), *Interplay* (1945), *The Pied Piper* (1951), *Afternoon of a Fawn* (1953), *West Side Story* (musical, 1957), and for Broadway, eg *The King and I* (1951).

St-Léon, Arthur (1821–70) French, born Paris; *Le Violon du diable* (1849), *La Fille mal gardée* (1866), *La Source* (1866), *Coppélia* (1870).

Tudor, Antony (William Cook) (1908–87) English, born London; *Undertow* (1945), *Lady of the Camellias* (1951), *Shadowplay* (1967), *The Tiller in the Field* (1978).

ARTISTS

Selected paintings are listed.

Altdorfer, Albrecht (c.1480–1538) German, born Regensburg; *Danube Landscape* (1520), *Alexander's Victory* (1529).

Andrea del Sarto (Andrea d'Agnolo di Francesco) (1486–1530) Italian, born Florence; *Miracles of S Filippo Benizzi* (1509–10), *Madonna del Saeco* (1525).

Angelico, Fra (Guido di Pietro) (c.1400–55) Italian, born Vicchio, Tuscany; *Coronation of the Virgin* (1430–5), *San Marco altarpiece* (c.1440).

Auerbach, Frank (1931–) German/British, born Berlin; *Mornington Crescent* (1967).

Bacon, Francis (1909–92) British, born Dublin; *Three Figures at the Base of a Crucifixion* (1945), *Two figures with a Monkey* (1973), *Triptych Inspired by the Oresteia of Aeschylus* (1981).

Beardsley, Aubrey (Vincent) (1872–98) British, born Brighton; illustrations to Malory's *Morte d'Arthur* (1893), Wilde's *Salome* (1894).

Bell, Vanessa (1879–1961) British, born Kensington, London; *Still Life on Corner of a Mantlepiece* (1914).

Bellini, Gentile (c.1429–1507) Italian, born Venice; *Procession of the Relic of the True Cross* (1496), *Miracle at Ponte di Lorenzo* (1500).

Blackadder, Elizabeth (1931–) Scottish, born Falkirk; *Interior with Self-Portrait* (1972), *White Anemones* (1983), *Texas Flame* (1986).

Blake, William (1757–1827) British, born London; illustrations for his own *Songs of Innocence and Experience* (1794), *Newton* (1795), illustrations for the *Book of Job* (1826)

Böcklin, Arnold (1827–1901) Swiss, born Basel; *Pan in the Reeds* (1857), *The Island of the Dead* (1880).

Bomberg, David (1890–1957) British, born Birmingham; *In the Hold* (1913–14), *The Mud Bath* (1913–14).

Bonnard, Pierre (1867–1947) French, born Paris; *Young Woman in Lamplight* (1900), *Dining Room in the Country* (1913), *Seascape of the Mediterranean* (1941).

Bosch, Hieronymus (Jerome von Aken) (c.1460–1516) Dutch, born 's-Hertogenbosch, Brabant; *The Temptation of St Anthony, The Garden of Earthly Delights* (work undated).

Botticelli, Sandro (Alessandro di Mariano Filipepi) (1444–1510) Italian, born Florence; *Primavera* (c.1478), *The Birth of Venus* (c.1485), *Mystic Nativity* (1500).

Braque, Georges (1882–1963) French, born Argenteuil-sur-Seine; *Still Life with Violin* (1910), *The Portuguese* (1911), *Blue Wash-Basin* (1942).

Brueghel, Pieter (the Elder) (c.1525–69) Dutch, born Bruegel, near Breda; *Road to Calvary* (1564), *Massacre of the Innocents* (c.1566), *The Blind Leading the Blind* (1568), *The Peasant Wedding* (1568), *The Peasant Dance* (1568).

Burne-Jones, Sir Edward (Coley) (1833–98) British, born Birmingham; *The Beguiling of Merlin* (1874), *The Arming of Perseus* (1877), *King Cophetea and the Beggar Maid* (1880–4).

Burra, Edward (1905–76) British, born London; *Dancing Skeletons* (1934), *Soldiers* (1942), *Scene in Harlem (Simply Heavenly)* (1952).

Canaletto (Giovanni Antonio Canal) (1697–1768) Italian, born Venice; *Stone Mason's Yard* (c.1730).

Caravaggio, Michelangelo (Merisi da) (1573–1610) Italian, born Caravaggio, near Burgamo; *The Supper at Emmaus* (c.1598–1600), *Martyrdom of St Matthew* (1599–1600), *The Death of the Virgin* (1605–6).

Cézanne, Paul (1839–1906) French, born Aix-en-Provence; *The Black Marble Clock* (c.1869–70), *Maison du Pendu* (c.1873), *Bathing Women* (1900–5), *Le Jardinier* (1906).

Chagall, Marc (1887–1985) Russian/French, born Vitebsk; *The Musician* (1912–13), *Bouquet of Flying Lovers* (1947).

Chirico, Giorgio de (1888–1978) Italian, born Volos, Greece; *Portrait of Guillame Apollinaire* (1914), *The Jewish Angel* (1916), *The Return of Ulysses* (1968).

Cimabué (Cenni de Pepo) (c.1240–c.1302) Italian, born Florence; *Crucifix* (date unknown), *Saint John the Evangelist* (1302).

ARTISTS (cont.)

Claude Lorraine (le Lorrain) (Claude Gèllée) (1600–82) French, born near Nancy; *The Mill* (1631), *The Embarkation of St Ursula* (1641), *Ascanius Shooting the Stag of Silvia* (1682).

Constable, John (1776–1837) English, born East Bergholt, Suffolk; *A Country Lane* (c.1810), *The White Horse* (1819), *The Hay Wain* (1821), *Stonehenge* (1835).

Corot, Jean Baptiste Camille (1796–1875) French, born Paris; *Bridge at Narni* (1827), *Souvenir de Marcoussis* (1869), *Woman Reading in a Landscape* (1869).

Correggio (Antonio Allegri de) (c.1494–1534) Italian, born Corregio; *The Agony in the Garden* (c.1528).

Courbet, (Jean Désiré) Gustave (1819–77) French, born Ornans; *The After-Dinner at Ornans* (1848–9), *The Bathers* (1853), *The Painter's Studio* (1855), *The Stormy Sea* (1869).

Cranach, Lucas (the Elder) (1472–1553) German, born Kronach, near Bamberg; *The Crucifixion* (1503), *The Fountain of Youth* (1550).

Dalí, Salvador (Felipe Jacinto) (1904–89) Spanish, born Figueras, Gerona; *The Persistence of Memory* (1931), *The Transformation of Narcissus* (1934), *Christ of St John of the Cross* (1951).

David, Jacques Louis (1748–1825) French, born Paris; *Death of Socrates* (1788), *The Death of Marat* (1793), *The Rape of the Sabines* (1799), *Madame Récamier* (1800).

Degas, Edgar (Hilaire Germain Edgar de Gas) (1834–1917) French, born Paris; *Cotton-brokers Office* (1873), *L'Absinthe* (1875–6), *Little Fourteen-year-old Dancer* (sculpture) (1881), *Dancer at the Bar* (c.1900).

Delacroix, (Ferdinand Victor) Eugène (1798–1863) French, born St-Maurice-Charenton; *Dante and Vergil in Hell* (1822), *Liberty Guiding the People* (1831), *Jacob and the Angel* (1853–61).

Delvaux, Paul (1897–) Belgian, born Antheit, near Huys; *Vénus endormie* (1932), *Phases of the Moon* (1939), *In Praise of Melancholy* (1951).

Doré, (Louis Auguste) Gustave (1832–1883) French, born Strasbourg; Illustrations to Dante's *Inferno* (1861), Milton's *Paradise Lost* (1866).

Duccio di Buoninsegna (c.1260–c.1320) Italian; *Maestà (Siena Cathedral altarpiece) (1308–11).*

Duchamp, (Henri Robert) Marcel (1887–1968) French/American, born Blainville, Normandy; *Nude descending a Staircase* (1912), *The Bride Stripped Bare by her Bachelors Even* (1915–23).

Dufy, Raoul (1877–1953) French, born Le Havre; *Posters at Trouville* (1906), illustrations to Guillame Appollinaire's *Bestiary* (1911), *Riders in the Wood* (1931).

Eardley, Joan (1921–63) British, born Warnham, Sussex; *Winter Sea IV* (1958), *Two Children* (1962).

Ernst, Max(imillian) (1891–1976) German/American/French, born Brühl, near Cologne, Germany; *Europe after the Rain* (1940–2), *The Elephant Célébes* (1921), *Moonmad* (1944) (sculpture), *The King Playing with the Queen* (1959) (sculpture).

Eyck, Jan van (c.1389–1441) Dutch, born Maaseyck, near Maastricht; *The Adoration of the Holy Lamb* (Ghent altarpiece) (1432), *Man in a Red Turban* (1433), *Arnolfni Marriage Portrait* (1434), *Madonna by the Fountain* (1439).

Fini, Léonor (1908–) Italian/Argentine, born Buenos Aires; *The End of the World* (1944).

Freud, Lucian (1922–) German/British, born Berlin; *Woman with a Daffodil* (1945), *Interior in Paddington* (1951), *Hotel Room* (1953–4).

Friedrich, Caspar David (1774–1840) German, born Pomerania; *The Cross in the Mountains* (1807-8).

Fuseli, Henri (Johann Heinrich Füssli) (1741–1825) Swiss/English, born Zurich; *The Nightmare* (1781), *Appearance of the Ghost* (1796).

Gainsborough, Thomas (1727–88) English, born Sudbury, Suffolk; *Peasant Girl Gathering Sticks* (1782), *The Watering Place* (1777).

Gauguin, (Eugène Henri) Paul (1848–1903) French, born Paris; *The Vision after the Sermon* (1888), *Still Life with Three Puppies* (1888), *The White Horse* (1898), *Women of Tahiti* (1891), *Tahitian Landscape* (1891), *Where Do We Come From? What Are We? Where Are We Going?* (1897–8), *Golden Bodies* (1901).

ARTISTS (cont.)

Géricault, Theodore (1791–1824) French, born Rouen; *Officer of Light Horse* (c.1812), *Raft of the Medusa* (1819).

Ghirlandaio, Domenico (Domenico di Tommaso Bigordi) (1449–1494) Italian, born Florence; *Virgin of Mercy* (1472), *St Jerome* (1480), *Nativity* (1485).

Giorgione (da Castelfranco), or Giorgio Barbarelli (c.1478–1511) Italian, born Castelfranco; *The Tempest* (c.1508), *Three Philosophers* (c.1508), *Portrait of a Man* (1510).

Giotto (di Bondone) (c.1266–1337) Italian, born near Florence; frescoes in *Arena Chapel*, Padua (1304–12), *Ognissanti Madonna* (1311–12).

Goes, Hugo van der (c.1440–82) Dutch, born probably Ghent; *Portinari Alterpiece* (1475), *Ghent Altarpiece* (1495).

Goya (y Lucientes), Francisco (José) de (1746–1828) Spanish, born Fuendetotos; *Family of Charles IV* (1799), *Los Desastres de la Guerra* (1810–14), *Black Paintings* (1820s).

Greco, El (Domenico Theotocopoulos) (1541–1614) Greek, born Candia, Crete; *Lady in Fur Wrap* (c.1577–8), *El Espolio* (The Disrobing of Christ) (1577–9), *The Saviour of the World* (1600), *Portrait of Brother Hortensio Felix Paravicino* (1609), *Toledo Landscape* (c.1610).

Grünewald, Matthias (Mathis Nithardt or **Gothardt)** (c.1480–1528) German, born probably Würzburg; *Isenheim Altarpiece* (1515).

Hilliard, Nicholas (c.1547–1619) English, born Exeter; miniature of *Queen Elizabeth I* (1572), *Henry Wriothesley* (1594).

Hockney, David (1937–) British, born Bradford, Yorkshire; *We Two Boys Together Clinging* (1961), *The Rake's Progress* (1963), *A Bigger Splash* (1967), *Invented Man Revealing a Still Life* (1975), *Dancer* (1980).

Hogarth, William (1697–1764) English, born Smithfield, London; *Before and After* (1731), *A Rake's Progress* (1733–5).

Hokusai, Katsushika (1760–1849) Japanese, born Tokyo; *Tametomo and the Demon* (1811), *Mangwa* (1814–19), *Hundred Views of Mount Fuji* (1835).

Holbein, Hans, 'the younger' (1497–1543) German, born Augsburg; *Bonifacius Amerbach* (1519), *Solothurn Madonna* (1522), *Anne of Cleves* (1539).

Hundertwasser, Fritz (Friedrich Stowasser) (1928–) Austrian, born Vienna; *Many Transparent Heads* (1949–50), *The End of Greece* (1963), *The Court of Sulaiman* (1967).

Hunt, (William) Holman (1827–1910) English, born London; *The Hireling Shepherd* (1852), *Claudio and Isabella* (1853), *The Light of the World* (1854), *Isabella and the Pot of Basil* (1867).

Ingres, Jean Auguste Dominique (1780–1867) French, born Montauban; *Gilbert* (1805), *La Sources* (1807–59), *Bather* (1808), *Turkish Bath* (1863).

John, Augustus (Edwin) (1878–1961) British, born Tenby; *The Smiling Woman* (1908), *Portrait of a Lady in Black* (1917).

John, Gwen (1876–1939) British, born Haverfordwest, Pembrokeshire; *Girl with bare shoulders* (1909–10).

Kandinsky, Vasily (1866–1944) Russian/French, born Moscow; *Kossacks* (1910–11), *Swinging* (1925), *Two Green Points* (1935), *Sky Blue* (1940).

Kirchner, Ernst Ludwig (1880–1938) German, born Aschaffenburg; *Recumbent Blue Nude with Straw Hat* (1908–9), *The Drinker* (1915), *Die Amselfluh* (1923).

Kitaj, R(onald) B(rooks) (1932–) American, born Cleveland, Ohio; *The Orientalists*, *The Ohio Gang* (1964), *If not, not* (1975–6).

Klee, Paul (1879–1940) Swiss, born Münchenbuchsee, near Berne; *Der Vollmond* (1919), *Rosegarden* (1920), *A tiny tale of a tiny dwarf* (1925), *Fire in the Evening* (1929), *Twittering Machine.*

Klimt, Gustav (1862–1918) Austrian, born Baumgarten, near Vienna; *Music* (1895), *The Kiss* (1907–8), *Judith II* (Salome) (1909).

ARTISTS (cont.)

Kokoschka, Oskar (1886–1980) Austrian/British, born Pöchlarn; *The Dreaming Boys* (1908).

Landseer, Sir Edwin (Henry) (1803–73) English, born London; *The Old Shepherd's Chief Mourner* (1837), *The Monarch of the Glen* (1850).

La Tour, Georges (Dumesnil) de (1593–1652) French, born Vic-sur-Seille, Lorraine; *St Jerome Reading* (1620s), *The Denial of St Peter* (1650).

Léger, Fernand (1881–1955) French, born Argentan; *Contrast of Forms* (1913), *Black Profile* (1928), *The Great Parade* (1954).

Lely, Sir Peter (Pieter van der Faes) (1618–80) Dutch/British, born Soest, Westphalia; *The Windsor Beauties* (1668), *Admirals* series (1666–7).

Leonardo da Vinci (Leonardo di Ser Piero da Vince) (1452–1519) Italian, born Vinci; *The Last Supper* (1495–7), *Madonna and Child with St Anne* (begun 1503), *Mona Lisa* (1500–6), *The Virgin of the Rocks* (c.1508).

Lichtenstein, Roy (1923–) American, born New York City; *Whaam!* (1963), *As I Opened Fire* (1964).

Lippi, Fra Filippo, called **Lippo** (c.1406–69) Italian, born Florence; *Tarquinia Madonna* (1437), *Barbadori Altarpiece* (begun 1437).

Lochner, Stefan (c.1400–1451) German, born Meersburg am Bodenese; *The Adoration of the Magi* (c.1448), triptych in Cologne Cathedral.

Macke, August (1887–1914) German, born Meschede; *Greeting* (1912), *The Zoo* (1912), *Girls Under Trees* (1914).

Magritte, René (François Ghislain) (1898–1967) Belgian, born Lessines, Hainault; *The Menaced Assassin* (1926), *Loving Perspective* (1935), *Presence of Mind* (1960).

Manet, Édouard (1832–83) French, born Paris; *Déjeuner sur l'herbe* (1863), *A Bar at the Foliès-Bergère* (1882), *Ball at the Opera* (1893–4).

Mantegna, Andrea (1431–1506) Italian, born Vicenza; *Madonna of Victory* (altarpiece), *San Zeno Altarpiece* (1457–9), *Triumphs of Caesar* (c.1486–94).

Martin, John (1789–1854) English, born Haydon Bridge; *Joshua Commanding the Sun to Stand Still* (1816), *The Last Judgement* (1851–4).

Martini, or **Memmi, Simone (Simone di Martino)** (c.1284–1344) Italian, born Siena; *S Caterina Polyptych* (1319), *Annunciation* (1333).

Masaccio (Tomasso di Giovanni di Simone Guidi) (1401–28) Italian, born Castel San Giovanni di Val d'Arno; *polyptych* for the *Carmelite Church* in Pisa (1426), frescoes in *Sta Maria del Carmine,* Florence, (1424–7).

Masson, André (Aimé René) (1896–1987) French, born Balgny, Oise; *Massacres* (1933), *The Labyrinth* (1939).

Matisse, Henri (Emile Benoît) (1869–1954) French, born Le Cateau-Cambrésis; *La Desserte* (1908), *Notre Dame* (1914), *The Large Red Studio* (1948), *L'Escargot* (1953).

Michelangelo (Michelagniolo di Lodovico Buonarroti) (1475–1564) Italian, born Caprese, Tuscany; *The Pietà* (1497) (sculpture), *David* (1501–4) (sculpture), *Madonna* (c.1502), ceiling of the *Sistine Chapel,* Rome (1508–12), *The Last Judgement* (begun 1537).

Millais, Sir John Everett (1829–96) English, born Southampton; *Ophelia* (1851–2), *The Bridesmaid* (1851), *Tennyson* (1881), *Bubbles* (1886).

Millet, Jean-François (1814–75) French, born Grouchy; *Sower* (1850), *The Gleaners* (1857).

Mondrian, Piet (Pieter Cornelius Mondriaan) (1872–1944) Dutch, born Amersfoort; *Still Life with Gingerpot II* (1911), *Composition with red, black, blue, yellow, and grey* (1920), *Broadway Boogie-Woogie* (1942–3).

Monet, Claude (1840–1926) French, born Paris; *Impression: Sunrise* (1872), *Haystacks* (1890–1), *Rouen Cathedral* (1892–5), *Water-lilies* (1899 onwards).

ARTISTS (cont.)

Moreau, Gustave (1826–89) French, born Paris; *Oedipus and the Sphinx* (1864), *Apparition* (1876), *Jupiter and Semele* (1889–95).

Morisot, Berthe (Marie Pauline) (1841–95) French, born Bourges; *The Harbour at Cherbourg* (1874), *In the Dining Room* (1886).

Morris, William (1834–96) British, born Walthamstow; *Queen Guinevere* (1858).

Motherwell, Robert (Burns) (1915–91) American, born Aberdeen, Washington; *Gauloises* (1967), *Opens* (1968–72).

Munch, Edvard (1863–1944) Norwegian, born Löten; *The Scream* (1895), *Mother and Daughter* (c.1897), *Self-Portrait between the clock and the bed* (1940–2).

Nash, Paul (1899–1946) British, born London; *We Are Making a New World* (1918), *Menin Road* (1919).

Newman, Barnett (1905–70) American, born New York; *The Moment* (1946), *Onement I* (1948), *Vir Heroicus Sublimis* (1950–1).

Nicholson, Ben (1894–1982) British, born Denham, London; *White Relief* (1935), *November 11, 1947* (1947).

Nicholson, Winifred (1893–1981) British, born Oxford; *Honeysuckle and Sweet Peas* (1950), *The Copper and Capari* (1967), *The Gate to The Isles* (1980).

Nolde, Emil (Emil Hansen) (1867–1956) German, born Nolde; *The Missionary* (1912), *Candle Dancers* (1912).

Oliver, Isaac (c.1560–1617) French/English, born Rouen; *Self-Portrait* (c.1590), *Henry, Prince of Wales* (c.1612).

Palmer, Samuel (1805–81) English, born London; *Repose of the Holy Family* (1824), *The Magic Apple Tree* (1830), *Opening the Fold* (1880).

Parmigiano, or **Parmigianino (Girolamo Francesco Maria Mazzola)** (1503–40) Italian, born Parma; frescoes in *S Giovanni Evangelista*, Parma (c.1522), *Self-Portrait in a convex mirror* (1524), *Vision of St Jerome* (1526–7), *Madonna Altarpiece*, Bologna (c.1528–30), *The Madonna of the Long Neck* (c.1535).

Pasmore, (Edwin John) Victor (1908–) British, born Chelsham, Surrey; *The Evening Star* (1945–7), *Black Symphony – the Pistol Shot* (1977).

Peploe, S(amuel) J(ohn) (1871–1935) Scottish, born Edinburgh; one of the 'Scottish colourists'; *Boats of Royan* (1910).

Perugino (Pietro di Cristoforo Vannucci) (c.1450–1523) Italian, born Città della Pieve, Umbria; *Christ giving the Keys to Peter* (fresco in the Sistine Chapel) (c.1483).

Picabia, Francis (Marie) (1879–1953) French, born Paris; *I See Again in Memory my Dear Undine* (1913), *The Kiss* (1924).

Picasso, Pablo (Ruiz) (1881–1973) Spanish, born Málaga; *Mother and Child* (1921), *Three Dances* (1925), *Guernica* (1937), *The Charnel House* (1945), *The Artist and his Model* (1968).

Piero della Francesca (c.1420–92) Italian, born Borgo san Sepolcro; *Madonna of the Misericordia* (1445–8), *Resurrection* (c.1450).

Piper, John (1903–92) English, born Epsom; *Windsor Castle* watercolours (1941–2), *Council Chamber, House of Commons* (1941); also stage designs and illustrated publications.

Pissarro, Camille (Jacob) (1830–1903) French, born St Thomas, Danish W Indies; *Landscape at Chaponval* (1880), *The Boieldieu Bridge at Rouen* (1896), *Boulevard Montmartre* (1897).

Pollock, (Paul) Jackson (1912–56) American, born Cody, Wyoming; *No 14* (1948), *Guardians of the Secret* (1943).

Poussin, Nicolas (1594–1665) French, born Les Andelys, Normandy; *The Adoration of the Golden Calf* (1624), *Inspiration of the Poet* (c.1628), *Seven Sacraments* (1644–8), *Self-Portrait* (1650).

Raeburn, Sir Henry (1756–1823) Scottish, born Edinburgh; *Rev Robert Walker Skating* (1784), *Isabella McLeod, Mrs James Gregory* (c.1798).

ARTISTS (cont.)

Ramsay, Allan (1713–84) Scottish, born Edinburgh; *The Artist's Wife* (1754–5).

Raphael (Raffaello Santi, or **Sanzio)** (1483–1520) Italian, born Urbino; *Assumption of the Virgin* (1504), *Madonna of the Meadow* (1505–6), *Transfiguration* (1518–20).

Redon, Odilon (Betran-Jean Redon) (1840–1916) French, born Bordeaux; *Woman with outstretched arms* (c.1910–14).

Redpath, Anne (1895–1965) Scottish, born Galashiels; *Pinks* (1947).

Rembrandt (Rembrandt Harmensz van Rijn) (1606–69) Dutch, born Leiden; *Anatomy Lesson of Dr Tulp* (1632), *Blinding of Samson* (1636), *The Night Watch* (1642), *The Conspiracy of Claudius* (1661–2).

Renoir, (Jean) Pierre Auguste (1841–1919) French, born Limoges; *Woman in Blue* (1874), *Woman Reading* (1876), *The Bathers* (1887).

Reynolds, Sir Joshua (1723–92) English, born Plympton Earls, near Plymouth; *Portrait of Miss Bowles with her dog* (1775), *Master Henry Hoare* (1788).

Riley, Bridget (Louise) (1931–) British, born London; *Pink Landscapes* (1959–60), *Zig-Zag* (1961), *Fall* (1963), *Apprehend* (1970).

Rosa, Salvator (1615–73) Italian, born Arenella, near Naples; *Self-Portrait with a Skull* (1656), *Humana Fragilitas* (c.1657).

Rosetti, Dante Gabriel (1828–82) British, born London; *Beata Beatrix* (1849–50), *Ecce Ancilla Domini!* (1850), *Astarte Syriaca* (1877).

Rothko, Mark (Marcus Rothkovitch) (1903–70) Latvian/American, born Dvinsk; *The Omen of the Eagle* (1942), *Red on Maroon* (1959).

Rousseau, Henri (Julien Félix), known as **Le Douanier** (1844–1910) French, born Laval; *Monsieur et Madame Stevene* (1884), *Sleeping Gipsy* (1897), *Portrait of Joseph Brunner* (1909).

Rubens, Sir Peter Paul (1577–1640) Flemish, born Siegen, Westphalia; *Marchesa Brigida Spinola-Doria* (1606), *Hélène Fourment with two of her Children* (c.1637).

Sargent, John Singer (1856–1925) American, born Florence; *Madame X* (1884), *Lady Agnew* (1893), *Gassel* (1918).

Schiele, Egon (1890–1918) Austrian, born Tulln; *Autumn Tree* (1909), *Pregnant Woman and Death* (1911), *Edith Seated* (1917–18).

Seurat, Georges (Pierre) (1859–91) French, born Paris; *Bathers at Asnières* (1884), *Sunday on the Island of La Grande Jatte* (1885--6), *Le Cirque* (1891).

Sickert, Walter (Richard) (1860–1942) British, born Munich; *La Hollandaise* (1905–6), *Ennui* (c.1914).

Sisley, Alfred (1839–99) French, born Paris; *Avenue of Chestnut Trees near La Celle Saint-Cloud* (1868), *Mosley Weir, Hampton Court* (1874).

Spencer, Sir Stanley (1891–1959) British, born Cookham-on-Thames, Berkshire; *The Resurrection* (1927), *The Leg of Mutton Nude* (1937).

Steen, Jan (Havicksz) (1627–79) Dutch, born Leiden; *A Woman at her Toilet* (1663), *The World upside Down* (1663).

Stubbs, George (1724–1806) English, born Liverpool; *James Stanley* (1755), *Anatomy of the Horse* (1766), *Hambletonian, Rubbing Town* (1799).

Sutherland, Graham (Vivian) (1903–80) British, born London; *Entrance to a Lane* (1939), *Crucifixion* (1946), *A Bestiary and some Correspondences* (1968).

Tanguy, Yves (1900–55) French/American, born Paris; *He did what he wanted* (1927), *The Invisibles* (1951).

Tintoretto (Jacopo Robusti) (1518–94) Italian, born probably Venice; *The Miracle of the Slave* (1548), *St George and the Dragon* (c.1558), *The Golden Calf* (c.1560).

ARTISTS (cont.)

Titian (Tiziano Veccellio) (c.1488–1576) Italian, born Pieve di Cadore; *The Assumption of the Virgin* (1516–18), *Bacchus and Ariadne* (1522–3), *Pesaro Madonna* (1519–26), *Crowning with Thorns* (c.1570).

Toulouse-Lautrec, Henri (Marie Raymond de) (1864–1901) French, born Albi; *The Jockey* (1899), *At the Moulin Rouge* (1895), *The Modiste* (1900).

Turner, Joseph Mallord William (1775–1851) English, born London; *Frosty Morning* (1813), *The Shipwreck* (1805), *Crossing the Brook* (1815), *The Fighting Téméraire* (1839), *Rain, Steam and Speed* (1844).

Uccelo, Paolo (Paolo di Dono) (c.1396–1475) Italian, born Pratovecchio; *The Flood* (c.1445), *The Rout of San Romano* (1454–7).

Utamaro, Kitagawa (1753–1806) Japanese, born Edo (modern Tokyo); *Ohisa* (c.1788), *The Twelve Hours of the Green Houses* (c.1795).

Van Dyck, Sir Anthony (1599–1641) Flemish, born Antwerp; *Marchesa Elena Grimaldi* (c.1625), *The Deposition* (1634–5), *Le Roi à la chasse* (c.1638).

Van Gogh, Vincent (Willem) (1853–90) Dutch, born Groot-Zundert, near Breda; *The Potato Eaters* (1885), *Self-Portrait with Bandaged Ear* (1888), *The Harvest* (1888), *The Sunflowers* (1888), *Starry Night* (1889), *Cornfields with Flight of Birds* (1890).

Velázquez, Diego (Rodriguez de Silva y) (1599–1660) Spanish, born Seville; *The Immaculate Conception* (c.1618), *The Waterseller of Seville* (c.1620), *The Surrender of Breda* (1634–5), *Pope Innocent X* (1650), *Las Meninas* (c.1656).

Vermeer, Jan (Johannes) (1632–75) Dutch, born Delft; *The Astronomer* (1668), *Christ in the House of Mary and Martha* (date unknown), *A Lady with a Gentleman at the Virginals* (c.1665), *The Lacemaker* (date unknown).

Veronese, Paolo (Paolo Caliari) (1528–88) Italian, born Verona; *The Feast in the House of Levi* (1573), *Marriage at Cana* (1573), *Triumph of Venice* (c.1585).

Verrocchio, Andrea del (Andrea de 'Cioni) (c.1435–c.1488) Italian, born Florence; *Baptism of Christ* (c.1470), *David* (c.1475) (sculpture).

Warhol, Andy (Andrew Warhola) (1928–87) American, born McKeesport, Pennsylvania; *Marilyn* (1962), *Electric Chair* (1963).

Watteau, (Jean) Antoine (1684–1721) French, born Valenciennes; *The Pilgrimage to the Island of Cythera* (1717), *L'Enseigne de Gersaint* (1721).

Whistler, James (Abbott) McNeill (1834–1903) American, born Lowell, Massachusetts; *The Artist's Mother* (1871), *Nocturne in blue and silver: Old Battersea Bridge* (1872–5), *Falling Rocket* (1875).

Wilkie, Sir David (1785–1841) Scottish, born Cults, Fife; *The Village Politicians* (1806), *Chelsea Pensioners Reading the Waterloo Despatch* (1822).

Wood, Grant (1891–1942) American, born Iowa; *American Gothic* (1930), *Spring Turning* (1936).

Wright, Joseph ('of Derby') (1734–97) English, born Derby; *Experiment with an Air Pump* (1766), *The Alchemist in Search of the Philosopher's Stone Discovers Phosphorous* (1795).

Wyeth, Andrew (Newell) (1917–) American, born Chadds Ford, Pennsylvania; *Christina's World* (1948).

ARCHITECTS

Aalto, (Hugo) Alvar (Henrik) (1898–1976) Finnish, born Kuortane; *Convalescent Home*, Paimio, near Turku (1929–30), *Town Hall*, Saynatsab (1950–2), *Finlandia Concert Hall*, Helsinki (1971).

Adam, Robert (1728–92) Scottish, born Kirkcaldy; *Adelphi*, London (1769–71, demolished 1936), *General Register House* (begun 1774), *Charlotte Square* (1791), *Edinburgh University* (1789–94) — all Edinburgh; *Culzean Castle*, Ayrshire (1772–92).

Adam, William (1689–1748) Scottish, born Maryburgh; *Hopetoun House*, near Edinburgh (1721).

ARCHITECTS (cont.)

Alberti, Leone Battista (1404–72) Italian, born Genoa; facade of the *Palazzo Recellai*, Florence (1460), *San Andrea*, Mantua (1470).

Anthemias of Tralles (dates unknown) Greek, born Tralles, Lydia; *Hagia Sophia*, Constantinople (now Istanbul) (532–7).

Apollodorus of Damascus (dates unknown) Greek, born Syria; *Trajan's Forum*, Rome, *The Baths of Trajan*, Rome.

Arnolfo di Cambio (1232–1302) Italian, born Colledi Valdelsa, Tuscany; *Florence Cathedral* (1299–1310).

Asplund, Erik Gunnar (1885–1940) Swedish, born Stockholm; *Stockholm City Library* (1924–7), *Law Courts*, Gothenburg (1934–7).

Baker, Sir Herbert (1862–1946) English, born Kent; *Groote Schuur*, near Cape Town (1892–1902), *Union Government Buildings*, Pretoria (1907).

Barry, Sir Charles (1795–1860) English, born London; *Royal Institution of the Arts*, Manchester (1824), *Houses of Parliament*, London (opened 1852).

Behrens, Peter (1868–1940) German, born Hamburg; *Turbine Assembly Works*, Berlin (1909), *German Embassy*, St Petersburg (1912).

Berlage, Hendrick Petrus (1856–1934) Dutch, born Amsterdam; *Amsterdam Bourse* (1903), *Holland House*, London (1914), *Gemeente Museum*, the Hague (1934).

Bernini, Gian Lorenzo (1598–1680) Italian, born Naples; *St Peter's Baldacchino*, Rome (1625).

Borromini, Francesco (1599–1667) Italian, born Bissone, on Lake Lugano; *S Carlo alle Quattro Fontane* (1637–41), *S Ivo* (1642–61), both Rome.

Boullée, Étienne-Louis (1728–99) French, born Paris; *Hôtel de Brunoy*, Paris (1772), *Monument to Isaac Newton* (never built) (1794).

Bramante, Donato (Donato di Pascuccion d'Antonio) (1444–1514) Italian, born near Urbino; *San Maria presso S Satiro*, Milan (begun 1482), *Tempietto of S Pietro*, Rome (1502).

Breuer, Marcel Lajos (1902–81) Hungarian–American, born Pécs; *UNESCO Building*, Paris (1953–8).

Brosse, Salomon de (1565–1626) French, born Verneuil-sur-Oise; *Luxembourg Palace*, Paris (1615–20), *Louis XIII's Hunting Lodge*, Versailles (1624–6).

Brunelleschi, Filippo (1377–1446) Italian, born Florence; *San Lorenzo*, Florence (begun 1418), *dome* of *Florence Cathedral* (begun 1420), *Ospedale degli Innocenti*, Florence (1419).

Bryce, David (1803–76) Scottish, born Edinburgh; *Fettes College* (1863–9), *Royal Infirmary* (begun 1870) — both Edinburgh.

Burnham, David Hudson (1846–1912) American, born Henderson, New York; *Reliance Building*, Chicago (1890–5), *Monadnock Building*, Chicago (1890–1), *Selfridge Building*, London (1908).

Burton, Decimus (1800–81) English, born London; *Regents Park Colosseum* (1823), *Arch at Hyde Park Corner* (1825) — both London.

Butterfield, William (1814–1900) English, born London; *Keble College*, Oxford (1866–86), *St Augustine's College*, Canterbury (1844–73), *All Saints'*, Margaret Street, London (1849–59).

Campen, Jacob van (1595–1657) Dutch, born Haarlem; *Maurithuis*, The Hague (1633), *Amsterdam Theatre* (1637), *Amsterdam Town Hall* (1647–55).

Candela, Felix (1910–) Spanish–Mexican, born Madrid; *Sports Palace* for Olympic Games, Mexico City (1968).

Chambers, Sir William (1726–96) Scottish, born Stockholm; *Somerset House* (1776), pogoda in *Kew Gardens* (1757) — both London.

Chermayeff, Serge (1900–) American, born the Caucasus; *De La Warr Pavilion*, Bexhill-on-Sea (1933–5).

Churriguera, Don José (1650–1725) Spanish, born Salamanca; *Salamanca Cathedral* (1692–4).

ARCHITECTS (cont.)

Coates, Wells Wintemute (1895–1958) English, born Tokyo; *BBC Studios* (1932), *EKCO Laboratories,* (1936), *Cinema,* Festival of Great Britain Exhibition (1951).

Cockerell, Charles Robert (1788–1863) English, born London; *Taylorian Institute,* Oxford (1841–5), *Fitzwilliam Museum,* Cambridge (1837–40).

Cortona, Pietro Berrettini da (1596–1669) Italian, born Cortona; *Villa Sacchetti,* Castel Fusano (1626–7), *San Firenze,* Florence (1645).

Dance, George the elder (1700–68) English, born London; *Mansion House,* London (1739).

Dance, George the younger (1741–1825) English, born London; rebuilt *Newgate Prison* (1770–83).

Delorme, Philibert (c.1510–70) French, born Lyons; *Tuileries* (1565–70), *Châteaux of Anet,* Meudon (1547–55).

Doesburg, Theo van (originally **Cristian Emil Marie Kupper**) (1883–1931) Dutch, born Utrecht; *L'Art Nouveau Shop,* Paris (1896), *Keller und Reiner Art Gallery,* Berlin (1898).

Doshi, Balkrishna Vithaldas (1927–) Indian, born Poona; *City Hall,* Toronto (1958), *Indian Institute of Management,* Ahmedabad (1951–7).

Dudok, Willem Marinus (1884–1974) Dutch, born Amsterdam; *Hilversum Town Hall* (1928–30), *Bijenkorf Department Store,* Rotterdam (1929).

Engel, Johann Carl Ludwig (1778–1840) Finnish, born Berlin; layout of Helsinki (1818–26).

Erickson, Arthur Charles (1924–) Canadian, born Vancouver; *Simon Fraser University Buildings,* British Columbia (1963), *Lethbridge University,* Alberta (1971).

Fischer von Erlach, Johann Bernard (1656–1723) Austrian, born Graz; *Kariskirche,* Vienna (1716), *Hofbibliotek,* Vienna (1723), *Kollegienkirche,* Salzburg (1707).

Foster, Norman (1935–) English, born Manchester; *Willis Faber Dumas Building,* Ipswich (1975), *Sainsbury Centre,* University of East Anglia (1978), *Hong Kong and Shanghai Bank,* Hong Kong (1979–85).

Francesco di Giorgio (1439–1501/2) Italian, born Siena; *Church of San Bernardino all'Osservanza,* Siena (1474–84), *Palazzo Ducale,* Gubbio (1476–82).

Gabriel, Ange-Jacques (1698–1782) French, born Paris; *Pavillon de Pompadour,* Fontainebleu (begun 1749), Paris; layout of *Place de la Concorde,* Paris (1753), *Petit Trianon,* Versailles (1761–8).

Garnier, Tony (Antoine) (1869–1948) French, born Lyons; *Grange Blanche Hospital,* Lyons (1911–27), *Stadium,* Lyons (1913–18), *Hôtel de Ville,* Boulogne-Bilancourt (1931–3).

Gaudi, Antonio y Cornet (1852–1926) Spanish, born Reus, Tarragona; *Casa Vicens* (1878–80), *Sagrada Familia* (1884 onwards), *Casa Batlló* (1904–17), *Casa Milá* (1905–9) – all Barcelona.

Geddes, Sir Patrick (1854–1932) Scottish, born Perth; *Ramsay Gardens,* Edinburgh (1892), *Edinburgh Zoo* (1913), *Scots College,* Montpelier, France (1924).

Gibbs, James (1682–1754) Scottish, born Aberdeen; *St-Martin-in-the-Fields,* London (1722–6), *King's College Fellows' Building,* Cambridge (1724–49).

Gilbert, Cass (1859–1934) American, born Zanesville, Ohio; *Woolworth Building,* New York City, 1913.

Gilly, Friedrich (1772–1800) German, born Berlin; *Funerary Precinct and Temple* to Frederick II, the Great of Prussia (1796), *Prussian National Theatre,* Berlin (1798).

Giotto de Bondone (c.1266–1337) Italian, born Vespignano, near Florence; *Campanile,* Florence Cathedral (from 1334).

Giulio Romano (properly **Giulio Pippi de' Giannuzzi**) (c.1492–1546) Italian, born Rome; *Oakazzi dek Te',* Mantua (1524), church of *S Petronio* façade, Bologna (1546).

Greenway, Francis Howard (1777–1837) British/Australian, born Bristol; *Macquarie Lighthouse,* Sydney Harbour (1818), *St James' Church,* Sydney (1824).

Gropius, Walter (1883–1969) German/American, born Berlin; *Fagus Shoe Factory,* Alfeld (1911), *The Bauhaus,* Dessau (1925) – both Germany; *Harvard University Graduate Centre* (1950), USA.

ARCHITECTS (cont.)

Guarini, Guarino, (originally **Camillo**) (1624–83) Italian, born Modena; *San Lorenzo* church, Turin (1668–80), *Capella della SS Sindone* church, Turin (1668), *Palazzo Carignano*, Racconigi (1679).

Hamilton, Thomas (1784–1858) Scottish, born Glasgow; *Royal High School* (1825–9), *Royal College of Physicians Hall* (1844–5), *George IV Bridge* (1827–34) — all Edinburgh.

Haussmann, Georges Eugène (1809–91) French, born Paris; layout of *Bois de Boulogne, Bois de Vincennes*, Paris (1853–1870).

Hawksmoor, Nicholas (1661–1736) English, born Nottinghamshire; *St Mary Woolnoth* church (1716–24), *St George's*, Bloomsbury (1716–30) — both London.

Hildebrandt, Johann Lukas von (1668–1745) Austrian, born Genoa; *Lower and Upper Belvedere*, Vienna, (1714–15, 1720–3).

Hoffmann, Josef (1870–1956) Austrian architect, born Pirnitz; *Purkersdorf Sanatorium* (1903–5), *Stociet House*, Brussels (1905–11).

Holland, Henry (1746–1806) English, born London; *Carlton House*; London (1783–96), *Brighton Pavilion* (1787).

Howard, Sir Ebenezer (1850–1928) English, born London; *Letchworth Garden City* (1903).

Itkinos and **Callicrates** (dates and place of birth unknown) Greek; *The Parthenon*, Athens (447/6–438 BC).

Jacobsen, Arne (1902–71) Danish, born Copenhagen; *Town Hall of Aarhus* (with Erik Moller, 1938–42), *Town Hall of Rodovre* (1955–6), *SAS Tower*, Copenhagen (1960) – all Denmark; new *St Catherine's College*, Oxford (1959).

Jefferson, Thomas (1743–1826) American, born Shadwell, Virginia; *'Monticello'*, Albermale County (1769), *Virginia State Capitol* (1796).

Johnson, Philip Cortelyou (1906–) American, born Cleveland, Ohio; *Glass House*, New Canaan, Connecticut (1949–50), *Seagram Building*, New York City (1945), *Amon Carter Museum of Western Art*, Texas (1961), *New York State Theater*, Lincoln Center (1964).

Jones, Inigo (1573–1652) English, born London; *The Queen's House*, Greenwich (1616–18, 1629–35), *Banqueting House*, Whitehall, London (1619–22).

Kahn, Louis Isadore (1901–74) American architect, born Osel (now Saaremaa, Estonia); *Richards Medical Research Building*, Pennsylvania (1957–61), *City Tower Municipal Building*, Philadelphia (1952–7).

Kent, William (1685–1748) English, born Bridlington; *Holkham Hall* (begun 1734).

Labrouste, (Pierre François) Henri (1801–75) French, born Paris; *Bibliothèque Sainte Geneviève* (1838–50), *Bibliothèque Nationale* reading room (1860–7) — both Paris.

Lasdun, Sir Denys Louis (1914–) English, born London; *Royal College of Musicians* (1958–64), *National Theatre* (1965–76) — both London.

Le Corbusier (Charles-Edouard Jeanneret) (1887–1966) French, born La Chaux-de-Fonds, Switzerland; *Salvation Army Hostel*, Paris (begun 1929), *Chapel of Ronchamp*, near Belfort (1950–4), *Museum of Modern Art*, Tokyo (1957).

Ledoux, Claude Nicolas (1736–1806) French, born Dormans, Champagne; *Château*, Louveciennes (1771–3), *Theatre*, Besançon (1771–3).

Leonardo da Vinci (1452–1519) Italian, born Vinci; *Mariolo de Guiscardi House*, Milan (1497), *La Veruca Fortress*, near Pisa (1504), *Villa Melzi*, Vaprio, Milan (1513).

Lescot, Pierre (c.1510–78) French, born Paris; rebuilt one wing of the *Louvre*, Paris (1546), screen of *St Germain l'Auxerrois* (1541–4).

Lethaby, William Richard (1857–1931) English, born Barnstaple; *Avon Tyrell*, Christchurch, Hampshire (1891–2), *Eagle Insurance Buildings*, Birmingham (1899–1900).

Le Vau, or **Levau, Louis** (1612–70) French, born Paris; *Hôtel Lambert*, Paris (1640–4), part of *Palace of Versailles* (from 1661), *Collège des Quatre Nations*, Paris (1661).

ARCHITECTS (cont.)

Loos, Adolf (1870–1933) Austrian, born Bruno, Moravia; *Steiner House*, Vienna (1910).

Lorimer, Sir Robert Stodart (1864–1929) Scottish, born Edinburgh; *Thistle Chapel, St Giles*, Edinburgh (1909–11), *Scottish National War Memorial*, Edinburgh Castle (1923–8).

Lutyens, Sir Edwin Landseer (1869–1944) English, born London; *Cenotaph*, Whitehall, London (1919–20), *Liverpool Roman Catholic Cathedral* (1929–c.1941), *Viceroy's House*, New Delhi (1921–5).

Mackintosh, Charles Rennie (1868–1928) Scottish, born Glasgow; *Glasgow School of Art* (1897–9), *Hill House*, Helensburgh (1902–3).

Mackmurdo, Arthur Heygate (1851–1942) English, born London; *Gordon Institute for Boys*, St Helens (1890).

Maderna, or **Maderno, Carlo** (1556–1629) Italian, born Capalago; façade of *St Peter's* (1606–12), *S Susanna* (1597–1603), *Palazzo Barberini* (1628–38) — all Rome.

Mansard, or **Mansart, François** (1598–1666) French, born Paris; north wing of *Château de Blois* (1635), *Sainte-Marie de la Visitation*, Paris (1632).

Mansard, or **Mansart, Jules Hardouin** (1645–1708) French, born Paris; *Grand Trianon, Palace of Versailles* (1678–89).

Mendelsohn, Eric (1887–1953) German, born Allenstein; *De La Warr Pavilion*, Bexhill, UK (1934–5), *Anglo-Palestine Bank*, Jerusalem (1938), Israel.

Michelozzo di Bartolommeo (1396–1472) Italian, born Florence; *Villa Medici*, Fiesole (1458–61), *San Marco*, Florence (begun 1437).

Mies van der Rohe, Ludwig (1886–1969) German–American, born Aachen; *Seagram Building*, New York City (1956–8), *Public Library*, Washington (1967).

Nash, John (1752–1835) English, born London; layout of *Regent's Park* and *Regent Street*, London (1811 onwards), *Brighton Pavilion* (1815).

Nervi, Pier Luigi (1891–1979) Italian, born Sondrio; *Berta Stadium*, Florence (1930–2), *Olympic Stadia*, Rome (1960), *San Francisco Cathedral* (1970).

Neumann, (Johann) Balthasar (1687–1753) German, born Eger; *Würzburg Palace* (1730–43), *Schloss Bruchsal* (1738–53).

Niemeyer, Oscar (1907–) Brazilian, born Rio de Janeiro; *Church of St Francis of Assisi*, Pampúlha, Belo Horizonte, Brazil (1942–4), *Niemeyer House*, Rio de Janeiro (1953).

Oud, Jacobus Johann Pieter (1890–1963) Dutch, born Purmerend; *Alida Hartog-Ond House*, Purmerend (1906), *Café de Unie*, Rotterdam (1924), *Convention Centre*, The Hague (1957–63).

Palladio, Andrea (1508–80) Italian, born Padua; *Godi-Porto* (villa at Lonedo) (1540), *La Malcontenta* (villa near Padua) (1560), *San Giorgio Maggiore*, Venice (begun 1566).

Paxton, Sir Joseph (1801–65) English, born Milton-Bryant, near Woburn; building for *Great Exhibition* of 1851, later re-erected as the *Crystal Palace*, Sydenham (1852–4).

Pei, Ieoh Meng (1917–) Chinese–American, born Canton; *Mile High Center*, Denver (1954–9), *John Hancock Tower*, Boston (1973), *Glass Pyramids*, the Louvre, Paris (1983–9).

Perret, Auguste (1874–1954) French, born Brussels; *Théâtre des Champs Élysées*, Paris (1911–13), *Musée des travaux publics*, Paris (1936).

Piranesi, Giambattista (1720–78) Italian, born Venice; *Santa Maria Arentina*, Rome (1764–6).

Pisano, Nicola (c.1225–c.1284) Italian, born Tuscany; *Pisa Baptistry* (1260), façade renovation of *Pisa Cathedral* (1260–70).

Playfair, William Henry (1789–1857) Scottish, born London; *National Gallery of Scotland* (1850–7), *Royal Scottish Academy* (1832–5), *Surgeon's Hall* (1829–32) — all Edinburgh.

Poelzig, Hans (1869–1936) German, born Berlin; *Exhibition Hall*, Posen (1910–11), *Salzburg Festival Theatre* (1920–2).

ARCHITECTS (cont.)

Pugin, August Welby Northmore (1812–52) English, born London; decorations and sculpture for the *Houses of Parliament*, London (1836–7), *Birmingham Cathedral* (1839–41).

Rietveld, Gerrit Thomas (1888–1964) Dutch, born Utrecht; *Schröder House*, Utrecht (1924), *Van Gogh Museum*, Amsterdam (1963–4).

Rogers, Richard (1933–) English, born Florence; *Pompidou Centre*, Paris (1971–9), *Lloyds*, London (1979–85).

Saarinen, (Gottlieb) Eliel (1873–1950) Finnish–American, born Rantasalmi; *Cranbrook Academy of Art*, Michigan (1934–40).

Saarinen, Eero (1910–61) Finnish–American, born Kirkknonummi; *Jefferson Memorial Arch*, St Louis (1948–64), *American Embassy*, London (1955–60).

Sanmichele, Michele (c.1484–1559) Italian, born Verona; *Capella Pelegrini*, Verona (1527–57), *Palazzo Grimani*, Venice (1551–9).

Sansovino, Jacopo (1486–1570) Italian, born Florence; *Library* and *Mint*, Venice.

Schinkel, Karl Friederich (1781–1841) German, born Neurippen, Brandenburg; *Old Museum*, Berlin (1823–30), *War Memorial on the Kreuzberg* (1818).

Scott, Sir George Gilbert (1811–78) English, born Gawcott, Buckinghamshire; *Albert Memorial*, London (1862–3), *St Pancras station and hotel*, London (1865), *Glasgow University* (1865).

Serlio, Sebastiano (1475–1554) Italian, born Bologna; *Grand Ferrare*, Fontainebleau (1541–8), *Château*, Ancy-le-Franc, Tonnerre (from 1546).

Shaw, (Richard) Norman (1831–1912) English, born Edinburgh; *Old Swan House*, Chelsea (1876), *New Scotland Yard*, London (1888).

Smirke, Sir Robert (1781–1867) English, born London; *Covent Garden Theatre*, London (1809), *British Museum*, London (1823–47).

Smythson, Robert (c.1535–1614) English, place of birth unknown; *Wollaton Hall*, Nottingham (1580–8), *Hardwick Hall*, Derbyshire (1591–7).

Soane, Sir John (1753–1837) English, born near Reading; altered interior of *Bank of England* (1788–1833), *Dulwich College Art Gallery* (1811–14).

Sottsass, Ettore Jnr (1917–) Italian, born Innsbruck; *Apartment Building*, Turin (1934), *Galleria del Cavalliro*, Venice (1956).

Soufflot, Jacques Germain (1713–80) French, born Irancy; *Hôtel Dieu*, Lyons (1741), *St Geneviève* (Panthéon), Paris (begun 1757).

Spence, Sir Basil Urwin (1907–76) Scottish, born India; pavilions for *Festival of Britain*, Heavy Industries Exhibition, London (1951), *New Coventry Cathedral* (1951).

Stirling, Sir James (1926–92) Scottish; *Department of Engineering*, Leicester University (1959–63) (with James Gowan), *History Faculty*, Cambridge (1965–8), *Florey Building*, Queen's College, Oxford (1966), *Neue Staatsgalerie*, Stuttgart (1980–4).

Street, George Edmund (1824–81) English, born Woodford, Essex; *London Law Courts* (1870–81).

Stuart, James (1713–88) English architect, born London; rebuilt interior, *Chapel of Greenwich Hospital* (1779).

Sullivan, Louis Henry (1856–1924) American, born Boston; *Wainwright Building*, St Louis (1890), *Carson, Pirie and Scott Store*, Chicago (1899–1904).

Tange, Kenzo (1913–) Japanese, born Tokyo; *Hiroshima Peace Centre* (1949–55), *Shizoka Press and Broadcasting Centre*, Tokyo (1966–7).

Utzon, Jørn (1918–) Danish, born Copenhagen; *Sydney Opera House* (1956–68), *Kuwait House of Parliament* (begun 1972).

Vanbrugh, Sir John (1664–1726) English, born London; *Castle Howard* (1699–1726), *Blenheim Palace* (1705–20).

ARCHITECTS (cont.)

Velde, Henri Clemens van de (1863–1957) Belgian, born Antwerp; *Werkbund Theatre*, Cologne (1914), *Museum Kröller-Muller*, Otterloo (1937–54).

Vignola, Giacomo Barozzi da (1507–73) Italian, born Vignola; *Villa di Papa Giulio* (1550–5), church of the *Il Gesu*, Rome (1586–73).

Viollet-le-Duc, Eugène Emmanuel (1814–79) French, born Paris; restored cathedral of *Notre Dame*, Paris (1845–64), *Château de Pierrefonds* (1858–70).

Voysey, Charles Francis Annesley (1857–1941) English, born London; *Grove Town Houses*, Kensington (1891–2), *Sanderson's Wallpaper Factory*, Chiswick (1902).

Wagner, Otto (1841–1918) Austrian, born Penzing, near Vienna; stations for *Vienna Stadtbahn* (1894–7), *Post Office Savings Bank*, Vienna (1904–6).

Waterhouse, Alfred (1830–1905) English, born Liverpool; *Manchester Town Hall* (1867–77), *Natural History Museum*, South Kensington, London (1873–81).

Webb, Philip (1831–1915) English, born Oxford; *Red House*, Bexley (1859), *Clouds*, Wiltshire (1881–6), *Standen*, East Grinstead (1891).

Webb, Sir Aston (1849–1930) English, born London; eastern façade of *Buckingham Palace* (1912), *Admiralty Arch* (1903–10), *Imperial College of Science* (1906) — all London.

Wood, John, the elder (1704–1754) *Royal Crescent*, Bath (1767–75), *Queen Square*, Bath (c.1773).

Wren, Sir Christopher (1632–1723) English, born East Knoyle, Wiltshire; *Pembroke College Chapel*, Cambridge (1663–5), *The Sheldonian Theatre*, Oxford (1664), *Royal Greenwich Observatory* (1675–6), *St Paul's*, London (1675–1710), *Greenwich Hospital* (1696).

Wright, Frank Lloyd (1869–1959) American, born Richland Center, Wisconsin; *Larkin Building*, Buffalo (1904), *Robie House*, Chicago (1908), *Johnson Wax Factory*, Racine, Wisconsin (1936–9), *Guggenheim Museum*, New York (begun 1942).

Wyatt, James (1746–1813) English, born Staffordshire; *London Pantheon* (1772), *Gothic Revival Country House*, Fonthill Abbey, Wiltshire (1796–1813).

SCULPTORS

Selected works are listed.

Arp, Hans (Jean) (1887–1966) French, born Strasbourg; *Eggboard* (1922), *Kore* (1958).

Barlach, Ernst (1870–1938) German, born Wedel; *Moeller-Jarke Tomb* (1901), *Have Pity!* (1919).

Bernini, Gianlorenzo (1598–1680) Italian, born Naples; *Neptune and Triton* (1620), *David* (1623), *Ecstasy of St Theresa* (1640s), *Fountain of the Four Rivers* (1648–51).

Bologna, Giovanni da (Jean de Boulogne) (1529–1608) French, born Douai; *Mercury* (1564–5), *Rape of the Sabines* (1579–83).

Brancusi, Constantin (1876–1957) Romanian/French, born Hobitza, Gorj; *The Kiss* (1909), *Torso of a Young Man* (1922).

Calder, Alexander (1898–1976) American, born Philadelphia, Pennsylvania; *Stabiles and Mobiles* (1932), *A Universe* (1934).

Caro, Sir Anthony (1924–) English, born London; *Sailing Tonight* (1971–74), *Veduggio Sound* (1973), *Ledge Piece* (1978).

Cellini, Benvenuto (1500–71) Italian, born Florence; salt cellar of *Neptune and Ceres* (1543), *Cosimo de 'Medici* (1545–7), *Perseus with the Head of Medusa* (1564).

Donatello (Donato di Niccolo di Betti di Bardi) (c.1386–1466) Italian, born Florence; *St Mark* (1411–12), *St George Killing the Dragon* (c.1417), *Feast of Herod* (1423–37), *David*, *Judith and Holofernes*, Piazza della Signoria, Florence.

SCULPTORS (cont.)

Epstein, Sir Jacob (1880–1959) American/British, born New York; *Rima* (1925), *Genesis* (1930), *Ecce Homo* (1934–5), *Christ in Majesty* (Llandaff Cathedral), *St Michael and the Devil* (on the façade of Coventry Cathedral) (1958–9), *Adam* (1939).

Frink, Dame Elizabeth (1930–) British, born Thurlow, Suffolk; *Horse Lying Down* (1975), *Running Man* (1985), *Seated Man* (1986).

Gaudier-Brzeska, Henri (1891–1915) French, born St Jean de Braye, near Orléans; *Red stone dancer* (1913).

Ghiberti, Lorenzo (di Cione di Ser Buonaccorso) (c.1378–1455) Italian, born in or near Florence; *St John the Baptist* (1412–15), *St Matthew* (1419–22), *The Gates of Paradise* (1425–52).

Giacometti, Alberto (1901–66) Swiss, born Bogonova, near Stampa; *Head* (c.1928), *Woman with her Throat Cut* (1932).

Goldsworthy, Andy (1956–) British, born Cheshire; *Hazel Stick Throws* (1980), *Slate Cone* (1988), *The Wall* (1988–9).

González, Julio (1876–1942) Spanish, born Barcelona; *Angel* (1933), *Woman Combing her Hair* (1936), *Cactus People* (1930–40).

Hepworth, Dame (Jocelyn) Barbara (1903–75) British, born Wakefield, Yorkshire; *Figure of a Woman* (1929–30), *Large and Small Forms* (1945), *Single Form* (1963).

Leonardo Da Vinci (1452–1519) Italian, born Vinci, between Pisa and Florence; *St John the Baptist.*

Michelangelo (Michelangelo di Lodovico Buonarotti) (1475–1564) Italian, born Caprese, Tuscany; *Cupid* (1495), *Bacchus* (1496), *Pieta* (1497), *David* (c.1500).

Moore, Henry (Spencer) (1898–1986) British, born Castleford, Yorkshire; *Recumbent figure* (1938), *Fallen Warrior* (1956–7).

Paolozzi, Eduardo Luigi (1924–) Scottish, born Leith, Edinburgh; *Krokodeel* (c.1956–7), *Japanese War God* (1958), *Medea* (1964), *Piscator* (1981), *Manuscript of Monte Cassino*, Edinburgh (1991).

Pheidias (c.490–c.417 BC) Greek, born Athens; *Athena Promachos* (460–450 BC), marble sculptures of the *Parthenon* (447–432 BC).

Pisano, Andrea (c.1270–1349) Italian, born Pontedera; bronze doors of the *Baptistry* of Florence (1330–6).

Pisano, Giovanni (c.1248–c.1320) Italian, born Pisa; *Fontana Magiore*, Perugia (1278), *Duomo pulpit*, Pisa (1302–10).

Pisano, Nicola (c.1225–c.1248) Italian, birthplace unknown; *Baptistry* at Pisa (1260).

Praxiteles (5th-c BC) Greek, born probably Athens; *Hermes Carrying the Boy Dionysus* (date unknown).

Robbia, Luca della (Luca di Simone di Marco) (c.1400–1482) Italian, born Florence; *Cantoria* (1432–7).

Rodin, (François) Auguste (René) (1840–1917) French, born Paris; *The Age of Bronze* (1875–6), *The Gates of Hell* (1880–1917), *The Burghers of Calais* (1884), *The Thinker* (1904).

Schwitters, Kurt (1887–1948) German, born Hanover; *Merzbau* (1920–43).

Tinguely, Jean (1925–91) Swiss, born Fribourg; *Baluba No 3* (1959), *Métamécanique No 9* (1959), *Homage to New York* (1960), *EOSX* (1967).

PHOTOGRAPHERS

Adams, Ansel (Easton) (1902–84) American, born San Francisco. Notable for broad landscapes of the western USA, especially the Yosemite in the 1930s. One of the founders of the f/64 Group (1932). Publications included *Taos Pueblo* and *Born Free and Equal.*

Adams, Marcus Algenon (1875–1959) English, born Southampton. Portrait photographer who established studio in 1919 specializing in formal children's portraits with soft-focus style. His portraits of three generations of the British royal family taken from 1926 until his retirement in 1957 were published worldwide.

Adamson, Robert (1821–48) Scottish, born Berunside. Pioneer in photography. With David Octavius Hill applied the calotype process of making photographic prints on silver chloride paper for a commission to portray the founders of the Scottish Free Church in 1843.

Akiyama, Shotaru (1920–) Japanese, born Tokyo. Worked for a Japanese motion picture company before becoming a freelance photographer for a number of publishers in 1951. Chairman of the Japan Advertising Photographers Association since 1979.

Anschütz, Ottomar (1846–1907) German, born Yugoslavia. Pioneer of instantaneous photography and one of the first to make a series of pictures of moving animals and people, making a substantial contribution to the invention of the cinematograph.

Arbus, Diane, née **Nemerov** (1923–71) American, born New York City. After work in conventional fashion photography, sought to portray people 'without their masks'. Achieved fame in the 1960s with ironic studies of social poses and the deprived classes, but became increasingly depressed, eventually taking her own life.

Atget, (Jean) Eugène (Auguste) (1856–1927) French, born Libourne, near Bordeaux. Studied at the Conservatoire d'Art Dramatique, Paris (1879–81), before working as a stage actor, comedian and painter. His photographic work (1898–1925) was discovered in 1926 in Paris by Berenice Abbott.

Avedon, Richard (1923–) American, born New York City. Studied photography at the New School for Social Research, New York and served in the photography section of the US merchant navy (1942–44). Established his own studio in New York and worked free-lance for *Harper's Bazaar, Vogue* and *Life.* Received Photographer of the Year award from the American Society of Magazine Photographers in 1985.

Bailey, David (Royston) (1938–) British, born London. Originally specialized in free-lance fashion photography from 1959, later extending to portraits expressing the spirit of the 1960s and to studies of the nude. Also writes extensively on photography and has been director of television commercials and documentaries since the 1970s.

Beaton, Sir Cecil (Walter Hardy) (1904–80) British, born London. Outstanding photographer of fashion and celebrities, including royalty. Also designed scenery and costumes for ballet, operatic, theatrical and film productions. Publications include *My Royal Past* (1939), *The Glass of Fashion* (1959), *The Magic Image* (1975), as well as several volumes of autobiography (1961–78).

Bischof, Werner (1916–54) Swiss, born Zurich. Freelance graphic artist and photographer in Zurich (1932–6) and later magazine photographer for *Life, Picture Post* and *Paris Match.*

Blumenfeld, Erwin (1897–1969) American, born Berlin, Germany. Self-taught photographer, associated with Dadaist artists in Amsterdam (1918–23). Worked as a fashion photographer for *Verve* and *Vogue* in Paris before opening a studio in New York in 1943.

Bourke-White, Margaret (White, Margaret) (1904–71) American, born New York City. Photojournalist for *Fortune* magazine (1929) and later *Life* magazine from 1936, for which she covered World War II. First woman photographer to be attached to US armed forces. Also produced reports of the siege of Moscow (1941) and opening of the concentration camps in 1944, later covering troubles around the world. Books include *Eyes on Russia* (1931), *Halfway to Freedom* (1946) and an autobiography, *Portrait of Myself* (1963).

Brady, Matthew B (1823–96) American, born near Lake George, New York. Operated portrait studio in New York using daguerrotype from 1844, and later recorded the American Civil War with the Union armies, an effort which ruined him financially so that he died in poverty in a New York almshouse.

Brandt, Bill (1904–83) British, born London. Studied with Man Ray in Paris in 1929. In 1930s produced striking social records and during World War II worked for ministry of information recording conditions in London in the Blitz. Subsequently turned to landscape and studies of the nude. Collections include *The English at Home*

PHOTOGRAPHERS (cont.)

(1936), *A Night in London* (1938), *Perspective of Nudes* (1961), *Shadows of Light* (1966).

Brassaï (Halász, Gyula) (1899–1984) French, born Brasso, Transylvania, Hungary (now Romania). From 1930 recorded underworld and nightlife of Paris. Refused to photograph during the German occupation, but worked in Picasso's studios, returning to photography after the war.

Bullock, Wynn (Percy Wingfield Bullock) (1902–75) American, born Chicago, Illinois. Studied photography at the Art Center School, Los Angeles (1938–40). Worked in commercial postcard photography and later taught at the Institute of Design at the University of California.

Cameron, Julia Margaret, née **Pattle** (1815–79) British, born Calcutta, India. Became outstanding amateur photographer in the 1860s, and received permanent acclaim for close-up portraits of Victorian celebrities.

Capa, Robert (Friedmann, André) (1913–54) American, born Budapest, Hungary. Recorded the Spanish Civil War (1935–37), China under Japanese attack (1938), World War II in Europe and subsequently the early days of the state of Israel. Killed by a land mine in the Indo-China fighting.

Cartier-Bresson, Henri (1908–) French, born Paris. Presented his first photographic exhibition in 1933; later visited Mexico and USA and worked as assistant to film director Jean Renoir. After World War II developed his human interest style of black-and-white photography in worldwide travels. Publications include *Images á la sauvette* (The Decisive Moment, 1952), *The Europeans* (1955).

Chim, David Seymour (David Szymin) (1911–56) American, born Warsaw, Poland. Freelance photographer who worked for *Vu* and *Ce Soir* in Paris, and throughout Europe and north Africa. Established his own studio in New York (1940–42) and was a co-founder of Magnum Photos, Paris and New York.

Clergue, Lucien (Georges) (1934–) French, born Arles. Self-taught freelance teacher at Arles from 1960. Founder of Rencontres Internationales de la Photographie, Arles (1970) and recipient of Photographer of the Year award, Photo Festival of Japan (1986).

Coburn, Alvin Langdon (1882–1966) British, born Boston, Massachusetts. Established a studio in New York (1901–2) and worked as an independent photographer in Boston, London, California and Wales. Associated with the Vorticist Group in London (1917–18).

Cosindas, Marie (1925–) American, born Boston, Massachusetts. Attended photography workshops under Ansel Adams in Boston in 1961 and has worked as a freelance photographer since 1960. Received Guggenheim Fellowship in 1967.

Crawford, Osbert Guy Stanhope (1886–1957) English, born Bombay. Identified potential of aerial photography in archaeology, resulting in the collection *Wessex from the Air* (1928).

Cunningham, Imogen (1883–1976) American, born Portland, Oregon. Opened portrait studio in Seattle (1910) specializing in soft-focus sentimental-style portraits and still-life flower studies. Later converted to sharply defined images, and was still teaching at the Art Institute in San Francisco in her nineties.

Curtis, Edward Sheriff (1868–1952) American, born Madison, Wisconsin. From 1896 recorded the North American Indian tribes and their way of life, publishing first 20 volumes in 1907. Took around 40 000 negatives, stressing the Indians' peaceful arts and culture.

Daguerre, Louis Jacques Mandé (1787–1851) French, born Cormeilles. Inventor of the 'daguerrotype', a process in which a photographic image is obtained on a copper plate coated with a layer of metallic silver sensitized to light by iodine vapour.

Davidson, Bruce (1933–) American, born Chicago, Illinois. Studied photography at Rochester Institute of Technology and since 1958 has worked freelance for *Life*, *Queen*, *Vogue* and other magazines in New York, Paris and Los Angeles. Received Guggenheim Fellowship in 1962.

Dodgson, Charles Lutwidge (Carroll, Lewis) (1832–98) English, born Daresbury, near Warrington. Pioneer photographer, mainly interested in portrait photography.

Doisneau, Robert (1912–) French, born Gentilly, Seine. Studied lithography in Paris (1926–29) and has worked as a photographer since 1930, including in industrial photography and as a photojournalist. Awarded the Kodak Prize (1947) and the Niépce Prix (1956).

Draper, Henry (1837–82) American, born Prince Edward County, Virginia. Pioneer of astronomical photography who produced photographs of the Orion nebula and over 100 stellar spectra.

Duclos du Hauron, Louis (1837–1920) French, born Langon. Outlined principles of additive and subtractive colour separation in *Les Couleurs en*

PHOTOGRAPHERS (cont.)

Photographie (1869). Described practical photographic methods which he patented in *Photographie en Couleur* (1878), and proposed the anaglyph method of viewing stereoscopic images.

Eakins, Thomas (1844–1916) American, born Philadelphia, Pennsylvania. Extended advances made by Muybridge in his studies of figures in motion. His composite plates inspired Duchamp's *Nude Descending the Staircase*.

Eastman, George (1854–1932) American, born Waterville, New York. Produced a successful roll-film (1884), the 'Kodak' box camera (1888) and pioneer of experiments which made possible the moving-picture industry. Formed the Eastman Kodak Co in 1892 and produced the Brownie camera in 1900.

Edgerton, Harold Eugene (1903–90) Engineer who specialized in high-speed photography. Produced a krypton–xenon gas arc which was employed in photographing the capillaries in the white of the eye without harming the patient.

Eisenstaedt, Alfred (1898–) American, born Dirschau, West Prussia (now Tczew, Poland). One of the original photojournalists on *Life* magazine (1936–72). Voted Photographer of the Year in 1951. Publications include *Witness to Our Time* (1966), *The Eye of Eisenstaedt* (1969) and *Photojournalism* (1971).

Evans, Walker (1903–75) American, born St Louis, Missouri. Architectural and social photographer who recorded rural life in the Southern states and people in New York City subways. Publications include *American Photographs* (1938), *Many Are Called* (1966).

Feininger, Andreas (Bernhard Lyonel) (1906–) American, born Paris. Self-taught photographer, involved in industrial and architectural photography in Stockholm (1933–39). Worked as a freelance photographer in New York and as a war photographer for the US Office of War Information (1941–2).

Fenton, Roger (1819–69) English, born Lancashire. Photographed in Russia in 1852 and was a founder of the Photographic Society (later the Royal) in 1853; Queen Victoria became its patron and Fenton photographed the royal family at Balmoral and Windsor. In 1855 went to the Crimea as the world's first accredited war photographer. Later travelled in Britain producing architectural and landscape studies.

Firth, Francis (1822–98) English, born Chesterfield. Topographical photographer who produced the first photographic traveller's records to be seen in Britain during travel in Egypt and the near east between 1856 and 1859. Established nationwide service of photographs of local scenes as prints in Britain, a business which survived commercially until 1971.

Frank, Robert (1924–) Swiss, born Zurich. After working as a photographer in Zurich (1943–4) moved to the USA in 1947 and worked freelance for *Harper's Bazaar* and *Life* in New York. Later worked in film-making and received the Guggenheim Fellowship (1955).

Genthe, Arnold (1869–1942) American, born Berlin. Commercial portrait photographer who emigrated to the USA in 1896 and established a studio in San Francisco (1897–1906). Concentrated on dance and theatrical portraits.

Gill, Sir David (1843–1914) Scottish, born Aberdeen. Astronomer who pioneered use of photography for charting the heavens.

Godwin, Fay Simmonds (1931–) English, born Berlin. Best known for landscape photography, including Welsh and Scottish scenes. Publications include *The Oldest Road* (1975, co-authored with J R C Anderson).

Haas, Ernst (1921–86) Austrian, born Vienna. Studied photography in Vienna and worked freelance for *Vogue* and *Life* in Paris (1948–50) before moving to the USA in 1950.

Halsman, Philippe (1906–79) American, born Riga, Latvia. Self-taught photographer who established a studio in Paris and worked for *Vogue* and *Voila* (1931–40). Emigrated to the USA in 1940 and became President of the American Society of Magazine Photographers, New York (1944, 1954) and received a Life Achievement Award (1975).

Hardy, Bert (1913–) English, born London. Photojournalist on staff of *Picture Post* until 1957, except for service as Army photographer from 1942 to 1946, during which he recorded concentration camps. Later assignments took him to the Korean and Vietnam Wars. Became involved in advertising until his retirement in 1967.

Hill, David Octavius (1802–70) Scottish, born Perth. Pioneer in photography. With Robert Adamson applied the calotype process of making photographic prints on silver chloride paper for a commission to portray the founders of the Scottish Free Church in 1843.

Hine, Lewis W(ickes) (1874–1940) American, born Oshkosh, Wisconsin. Expressed social concern through photographic studies of Ellis Island

PHOTOGRAPHERS (cont.)

immigrants and child labour. During World War I documented the plight of refugees for the American Red Cross and in 1930–1 recorded the construction of the Empire State Building in *Men at Work* (1932). Later registered the effects of the Depression for a US government project.

Hiro (Yasuhiro Wakabayahi) (1930–) Japanese, born Shanghai, China. Moved to New York in 1954 and established a studio there in 1958. Worked free-lance for *Harper's Bazaar* from 1958, and received the Photographer of the Year award from the American Society of Magazine Photographers (1969).

Karsh, Yousef (1908–) Canadian, born Mardin, Turkey. Apprenticed to a Boston portraitist (1928–31) and in 1932 opened studio in Ottawa. Appointed official portrait photographer to the Canadian government in 1935. Produced wartime studies of national leaders and has continued to portray statesmen, artists and writers throughout the world.

Kertész, André (1894–1985) Hungarian–American, born Budapest. Photographer with Hungarian army during World War I and later an acclaimed reporter of the 'human condition' in Paris. Worked for Condé-Nast publications and other magazines in New York in the 1930s and 1940s. After a major retrospective exhibition at the New York Museum of Modern Art in 1964 received belated official recognition.

Lange, Dorothea, originally **Nutzhorn** (1895–1965) American, born Hoboken, New Jersey. Established studio in San Francisco in 1919, and later recorded rural life in the south and west of the USA during the depression years from 1935. With her husband collaborated on the book *An American Exodus: A Record of Human Erosion* (1939). After World War II worked as a freelance reporter in Asia, South America and the Middle East.

Lartigue, Jacques-Henri (Charles Auguste) (1894–1986) French, born Courbvoie, Seine. Adopted informal approach to photography, elevating the snapshot into a creative art form. *Diary of a Century* is a collection recording the elegance of the inter-war years in France.

Lichfield, Patrick, 5th Earl of (1939–) English. After working as an assistant opened his own studio and since 1981 has achieved success in travel and publicity photography and royal portraits.

Lichtsteiner, Rudolf (1938–) Swiss, born Winterthur. Freelance photographer in Zurich from 1972 and in Switzerland from 1987. Recipient of the Niepce Prix (1966).

Marey, Étienne Jules (1830–1903) French, born Beaune. Physiologist who pioneered scientific cinematography in studies of animal movement (1887–1900). Improved camera design and reduced exposure time to around 1/25 000 of a second to photograph insect flight.

Martin, Paul (1864–1942) English–French, born Herbenville, France. Made use of a disguised camera to record working people in the streets of London and on holiday at the seaside (1888–98), recording the realities of late-Victorian everyday life in *London by Gaslight* (1896). Turned professional in 1899.

McBean, Angus Rowland (1904–90) Welsh, born Newbridge, Monmouth. Theatrical photographer from 1934, noted for an individual approach to portraiture, use of photographic montage, collage and double-exposure to achieve surrealistic effects. Later photographed in the world of pop music and withdrew from professional photography after 1969.

McCullin, Don(ald) (1935–) British, born London. Studied painting (1948–50) and later became a photographic assistant in aerial reconnaissance with the RAF (1953–55). Worked abroad as freelance photographer and as staff photographer for *The Sunday Times* (1964–84).

Moholy-Nagy, László (Nagy, László) (1895–1946) American, born Bucsborsod, near Mohol, south Hungary. Produced first 'photograms' (non-representational photographic images made directly without a camera) in 1923 and later became recognized as a leading avant-garde artist in Germany in the European New Photographers movement (1925–35), his work including film-making and typography integrated with photographic illustration. Moved to USA in 1937.

Mountford, Charles Pearcy (1890–1976) Australian, born Hallett, South Australia. Ethnologist who wrote a series of books about Aboriginals and their culture containing his award-winning photography. Later directed feature films on Aboriginal life from 1950.

Muybridge, Eadweard (Muggeridge, Edward James) (1830–1904) English–American, born Kingston-on-Thames. Became professional photographer in 1866 and later chief photographer to the US government. In 1880 devised the zoopraxiscope to show picture sequences, achieving a

PHOTOGRAPHERS (cont.)

rudimentary kind of cinematography. *Animal Locomotion* (1887) gives the results of his extensive survey of animal and human movement carried out for the University of Pennsylvania.

Nadar (Tournachon, Gaspard-Felix) (1820–1910) French, born Paris. Photographer, artist and journalist who produced lively portraits of distinguished literary and artistic contemporaries and the first 'photo-interview', series of photographs captioned with the sitter's replies to his questions. Proposed the use of aerial photographs for map-making and in 1858 took the first photographs from a balloon, of Paris.

Newman, Arnold (Abner) (1918–) American, born New York City. Assistant portrait photographer (1938–39) and later Director of the Newman Portrait Studio, Miami Beach (1942–45). President since 1946 of Arnold Newman Studios Inc., New York, and recipient of the gold medal, Biennale Internazionale della Fotografica, Venice (1963).

Newton, Helmut (1920–) Australian, born Berlin, Germany. Apprentice to a theatre and fashion photographer in Berlin (1936–40) and freelance photographer for *Elle*, *Queen*, *Marie-Claire* and *Vogue* since 1958. Received the Best Photography Award, Art Directors Club, Tokyo (1976).

Niepce, Joseph Nicéphore (1765–1833) French, born Chalon-sur-Saône. Chemist who succeeded in producing a photograph on metal (1826), said to be the world's first. Later cooperated with others in further research.

Nilsson, Lennart (1922–) Swedish, born Rome. Freelance press photographer, acclaimed for several portraits such as *Sweden in Profiles* (1954) who later pioneered microfilm showing the anatomy of plants and animals. Perfected special lenses to film inside the human body, enabling him to produce pictures of the human foetus in the womb from conception to birth. *Ett barn blir till* (1965, The Everyday Miracle: A Child is Born) won the American National Press Association Picture of the Year Award.

Parer, Damien (1912–44) Australian, born Malvern, Victoria. Official cameraman with the 2nd Australian Imperial Forces. Filmed action at the siege of Tobruk in the Middle East, later working in Greece, Syria and New Guinea. His documentary film *Kokoda Front* was the first Australian film to win an Oscar. Killed while filming American troops landing at Peleliu, Caroline Islands.

Parkinson, Norman, originally **Parkinson Smith, Ronald William** (1913–90) English, born London. Opened studio in 1934 and became a well-known portrait and fashion photographer, his work being used widely in quality magazines. Later advertising work in the 1950s involved worldwide travel. Settled in Tobago in 1963.

Parks, Gordon (Alexander Buchanan) (1912–) American, born Fort Scott, Kansas. Self-taught photographer; worked for the US Office of War Information (1943–45) and as a freelance fashion photographer in Minneapolis (1937–42). After working as a documentary film-maker in the USA and Saudi Arabia, became an independent photographer, film writer and director for Warner Brothers, MGM and Paramount Pictures (1962–71).

Penn, Irving (1917–) American, born Plainfield, New Jersey. Served as an ambulance driver and documentary photographer in the American Field Service in Italy and India (1944–5). Later worked for *Vogue* in New York (1943–4) and as a freelance advertising photographer from 1952.

Porter, Eliot (Furness) (1901–) American, born Winnetka, Illinois. Self-taught photographer who concentrated on his photographic career from 1939, in particular in landscape and wildlife photography. Received the Conservation Award from the US Department of the Interior (1967).

Ray, Man (Rabinovich, Emanuel) (1890–1976) American, born Philadelphia, Pennsylvania. After making a number of Surrealist films in Paris, published and exhibited many photographs and 'rayographs' (photographic images made without a camera) in the 1930s, returning to the USA in 1940. Awarded the gold medal at the Biennale of Photography in Venice (1961). Published his autobiography, *Self Portrait*, in 1963.

Robinson, Henry Peach (1830–1901) English, born Ludlow. Opened studio in Leamington Spa in 1857, but moved from formal portraiture to 'high art photography', often creating scenes using composites of several separate images of costumed models and painted settings in the mid-Victorian style. A founder member of The Linked Ring (1892), an association of photographers seeking artistic creation, which developed into the international Photo-Secession. Wrote *Pictorial Effect in Photography*.

Rodchenko, Alexander Mikhailovich (1891–1956) Russian, born St Petersburg. Photographer, painter and designer whose most original photo-

PHOTOGRAPHERS (cont.)

graphic works were documentary photographs of the new communist society.

Rosenblum, Walter (1919–) American, born New York City. After studying photography in New York, worked as a photographer for the US army in Europe (1943–5), becoming the most decorated photographer in the army. Editor of *Photo Notes* (1939–41) and chairman of the Exhibition Committee (1941–2) in New York. Awarded the Guggenheim Fellowship in 1979.

Rothstein, Arthur (1915–) American, born New York City. Photo officer for the US army in India, Burma and China (1943–6) and picture editor for the Office of War Information, New York (1941–3). Founder of the American Society of Magazine Photographers (1941) and recipient of the Lifetime Arts Achievement award from the New York Council of the Arts (1985).

Saint Joseph, John Kenneth Sinclair (1912–) English, born Worcestershire. Professor of aerial photographic studies at Cambridge (1948–80), developing large photographic archive with emphasis on systematic reconnaissance, and low-level oblique photography of natural landscapes and of archaeological monuments in their landscape setting. *Monastic Sites from the Air* (1952), *Medieval England: An Aerial Survey* (1958, 1979), *Roman Britain from the Air* (1983) are collections of some of the results.

Salomon, Erich (1886–1944) German, born Berlin. Prisoner-of-war in France (1915–18). Began freelance photographic career in 1927, working for *L'Illustration* of Paris and *Fortune* of New York. Died at Auschwitz with his wife and son.

Sander, August (1876–1964) German, born Herdorf am Sieg. Planned a massive photographic documentary study, *Men in the 20th Century*, but only the first part *Faces of Our Times* (1929) was published as his social realism was discouraged by the Nazi Ministry of Culture after 1934. Surviving material has provided penetrating portraits of all levels of German life in the early part of the century.

Sheeler, Charles (1883–1965) American, born Philadelphia. Worked as industrial photographer from 1912, producing creative industrial records, especially the skyscrapers of Manhattan in *Mannahatta* (1920). Commissioned to record the building of the Ford Motor installation at River Rouge, Michigan (1927), and staff photographer at the New York Museum of Modern Art (1942–5).

Sielmann, Heinz (1917–) German, born Königsberg. Interested in animal photography, started making films in 1938, for which he won three German Oscars (1953–5). Developed techniques enabling photography in inaccessible animal lairs which have revolutionized the study of animal behaviour.

Siskind, Aaron (1903–91) American, born New York City. Self-taught freelance photographer from 1932. Member of Film and Photo League of New York and later photography teacher. Co-editor of the Chicago poetry and photographic magazine *Choice* (1961–70). Received Guggenheim Fellowship (1966).

Smith, W(illiam) Eugene (1918–78) American, born Wichita, Kansas. Staff photographer for *Newsweek* in New York (1937–8) and later freelance for magazines including *Harper's Bazaar*, and *Life*. Pacific war correspondent (1942–5) and photographer for Hitachi in New York and Japan (1959–77). Received Honor Award from the American Society of Magazine Photographers (1959).

Smythe, Francis Sydney (1900–49) English, born Maidstone. Mountaineer whose many books, including *Kamet Conquered* (1932), *Camp Six* (1937), *Adventures of a Mountaineer* (1940), *Over Welsh Hills* (1941) contained acclaimed mountain photography.

Snowdon, Antony Charles Robert Armstrong-Jones, 1st Earl of (1930–) English, born London. Freelance photographer from 1951 and artistic adviser to many publications. Famous for informal portraits of the famous, he has also recorded the plight of the handicapped and disabled and has produced documentaries for television on similar themes.

Steichen, Edward Jean (1879–1973) American, born Luxembourg. Practised painting and photography in Europe until 1914. Member of The Linked Ring in England and noted for his studies of the nude. A founder of the American Photo-Secession Group, he later served in the photographic division of the US army during World War I, and in the 1920s achieved success in fashion photography. Head of US Naval Film Services during World War II and director of photography at the New York Museum of Modern Art (1945–62), organizing the world-famous exhibition *The Family of Man* (1945).

Stieglitz, Alfred (1864–1946) American, born Hoboken, New Jersey. Studied engineering and photography in Berlin and later was a founder of

PHOTOGRAPHERS (cont.)

the Photo-Secession Group in 1902, devoted to artistic expression in photography. Exerted great influence through his magazine *Camera Work* (1903–17) and his gallery of modern art. Other work included studies of New York architecture, clouds and portraits.

Strand, Paul (1890–1976) American, born New York. Became commercial photographer in 1912, committed to 'straight' photography of precision and clarity. Produced documentary films during the 1920s and 1930s, but from the 1940s concentrated on still photography for records of his life in many different parts of the world.

Sutcliffe, Frank Meadow (1853–1941) English, born near Whitby, Yorkshire. Received numerous international awards for studies of the vanishing world of English farmhands and fisher-folk in the local country and seacoast between 1881 and 1905. From late 1890s made use of new lightweight cameras to obtain natural snapshots rather than formal poses. A fully illustrated account of his work was published in 1974.

Talbot, William Henry Fox (1800–77) British, born Melbury, Dorset. Announced his invention of photography, a system of making photographic prints on silver chloride paper, in 1839. In 1841 patented the calotype, the first process for photographic negatives from which prints could be made and was awarded the Rumford Medal of the Royal Society in 1842. Also discovered a method of instantaneous flash photography and his *Pencil of Nature* (1844) was the first photographically illustrated book to be published.

Van der Elskin, Ed(uard) (1925–) Dutch, born Amsterdam. Self-taught freelance photographer in Amsterdam (1947–50), Paris (1950–5) and Edam, the Netherlands since 1955. Also freelance filmmaker.

Weston, Edward (Henry) (1886–1958) American, born Highland Park, Illinois. Became recognized as modernist, emphasizing sharp images and precise definition in landscapes, portraits and still-life. Member of Group f/64 in California from 1932. First photographer to receive a Guggenheim Fellowship with which he travelled widely throughout the American West. Illustrated an edition of Walt Whitman's *Leaves of Grass*.

White, Minor (Martin) (1908–76) American, born Minneapolis, Minnesota. Developed the realism of the photographic sequence and the abstraction of the 'equivalent', the visual metaphor in which he continued Stieglitz's symbolism of natural formations. In 1946 moved to San Francisco and worked with Ansel Adams. Founded the periodicals *Aperture* (1952) and *Image* (1953–57) and was appointed professor of creative photography at the Massachussets Institute of Technology (1965–76).

Winogrand, Garry (1928–84) American, born New York. Studied photography in New York from 1951. Received Guggenheim Fellowship (1964, 69 and 78).

FASHION DESIGNERS

Amies, Sir (Edwin) Hardy (1909–) English, born London. Couturier and dressmaker by appointment to Queen Elizabeth. Renowned especially for tailored suits for women. Founded his own fashion house in 1946 and started designing for men also in 1959.

Armani, Giorgio (1935–) Italian, born Piacenza. Became designer for Nino Cerruti in 1961 and also freelanced before setting up the Giorgio Armani company in 1975. Designed first for men, then women, including loose-fitting jackets and blazers.

Ashley, Laura née **Mountney** (1925–85) Welsh, born Merthyr Tydfil. Started business with husband Bernard Ashley in 1953, manufacturing furnishing materials and wallpapers with patterns based mainly on 19th-century document sources. Later experimented with designing and making clothes, transforming the business from one shop to an international chain of boutiques.

Balenciaga, Cristóbal (1895–1972) Spanish, born Guetaria. Opened dressmaking and tailoring shops in Madrid and Barcelona in 1915. Moved to Paris in 1937 because of the Spanish Civil War. His clothes were noted for dramatic simplicity and elegant design.

Balmain, Pierre Alexandre (1914–82) French, born St Jean-de-Maurienne. Worked for Edward Molyneux and Lucien Lelong before opening his own house in 1945. Famous for elegant simplicity, his designs included evening dresses, tailored suits, sportswear and stoles. Also designed for the theatre and cinema.

Cardin, Pierre (1922–) French, born Venice.

FASHION DESIGNERS (cont.)

Worked in fashion houses and on costume design in Paris after World War II and opened his own house in 1953. Since then has been prominent in fashion for both women and men.

Chanel, Gabrielle, known as **Coco** (1883–1971) French, born Saumur. Orphaned at an early age, she worked with her sister as a milliner until 1912, when she opened a shop of her own. Later opened couture houses in Deauville and Paris, producing designs combining simple elegance and comfort. Also introduced the vogue for costume jewellery and the evening scarf. Retired in 1938, but made a successful comeback in 1954.

Conran, Jasper (1959–) English, born London. Son of Sir Terence Conran, he trained in art and design in New York before joining Fiorucci briefly as a designer in 1977. Produced his first collection of easy-to-wear, quality clothes in London in 1978.

Courrèges, André (1923–) French, born Pau. Trained by Balenciaga from 1952 to 1960, he opened his own house in 1961. Famous for stark, futuristic, 'Space Age' designs, he introduced the miniskirt (1964) and has featured white boots and trouser suits for women.

De la Renta, Oscar (1932–) American, born Santo Domingo, Dominican Republic. Worked at Balenciaga's couture house in Madrid, joined the house of Lanvin-Castillo in Paris (1961) then Elizabeth Arden in New York (1963), before starting his own company in 1965. Has reputation for opulent, ornately trimmed clothes, particularly evening dresses, but also designs daywear and accessories.

Dior, Christian (1905–57) French, born Granville, Normandy. Began designing clothes in 1935, and founded his own Paris house in 1947. Achieved worldwide fame with his long-skirted 'New Look' and subsequently the 'A-line' and 'the Sack'.

Garavani, Valentino (1933–) Italian, born Rome. Studied fashion in Milan and Paris, then worked for Dessès and Guy Laroche in Paris. Opened his own house in Rome in 1959, but achieved worldwide recognition with his 1962 show in Florence.

Gaultier, Jean-Paul (1952–) French. Worked with Cardin for two years (1969–71), then at Paton. In 1976, began working as a freelance designer, drawing inspiration from the London street-scene, which he glamorized for the Paris market. He is now one of the most influential Paris designers.

Givenchy, Hubert James Marcel Taffin de (1927–) French, born Beauvais. After training and working with a number of well-known designers, opened his own house in 1952. His Bettina blouse in white cotton became internationally famous, and his clothes are noted for their elegance and quality.

Hamnett, Katherine (1952–) English, born Gravesend, Kent. After studying fashion at St Martin's School of Art in London, worked as a freelance designer, setting up a short-lived company (1969–74) and then her own business in 1979. Draws inspiration for designs from workwear and from movements such as the peace movement.

Hartnell, Sir Norman (Bishop) (1901–78) English, born Honiton, Devon. Started his own couturier business in 1923, receiving the Royal Warrant in 1940. Produced costumes for leading actresses, wartime 'utility' dresses, the WRAC uniform and Princess Elizabeth's wedding and coronation gowns.

Kenzo, Takada (1940–) Japanese, born Kyoto. After studying art, worked in Japan before producing freelance collections in Paris from 1964. Started a shop called Jungle Jap in 1970. Creates clothes with both oriental and western influences, and is a trendsetter in the field of knitwear.

Klein, Anne Hannah, née **Hannah Golofski** (1921–74) American, born New York. Started as sketcher on Seventh Avenue in 1938, and established Anne Klein & Co in 1968. Designed practical sportswear for women.

Klein, Calvin Richard (1942–) American, born New York. Graduated from New York's Fashion Institute of Technology in 1962, and set up his own firm in 1968. Quickly achieved recognition and is known for understatement and the simple but sophisticated style of his clothes, including 'designer jeans'.

Lacroix, Christian (1951–) French couturier, born Arles, Provence. After studying fashion history, worked for a leather firm with Guy Paulin, a ready-to-wear designer. In 1981 joined Jean Patou; in 1987 opened the House of Lacroix in Paris. Made his name with ornate and frivolous clothes.

Lagerfeld, Karl (1939–) German, born Hamburg. Won an International Wool Secretariat competition in 1954 and worked with Balmain in Paris. After three years he left to begin freelance work with a number of design houses, including Chloe, Ballantyne, Fendi and Valentino. His tal-

FASHION DESIGNERS (cont.)

ents lie particularly in meticulous cut, extravagant beading, furs and knitwear. He is renowned for his flamboyant fashion shows.

Laroche, Guy (1923–89) French, born La Rochelle, near Bordeaux. Worked in millinery, first in Paris then on Seventh Avenue, New York, before returning to Paris where he worked for Dessès for eight years; started his own business in 1957, achieving a reputation for skilful cutting. From 1966 his designs included menswear.

Lauren, Ralph, originally **Ralph Lipschitz** (1939–) American, born the Bronx, New York City. In 1967 joined Beau Brummel Neckwear and created the Polo range for men, later including womenswear. Famous for his American styles, such as the 'prairie look' and 'frontier fashions'.

Mainbocher, originally **Main Rousseau Bocher** (1891–1976) American, born Chicago. After service in World War I stayed on in Paris, eventually becoming a fashion artist with *Harper's Bazaar* and later editor of French *Vogue* until 1929. Started his couture house in Paris in 1930; created the Duchess of Windsor's wedding dress (1937).

Missoni, Tai Otavio (1921–) Italian, born Yugoslavia. Founded the Missoni company in Milan with his wife, Rosita, in 1953. At first manufactured knitwear to be sold under other labels, but later created, under their own label, innovative knitwear notable for its sophistication and distinctive colours and patterns.

Miyake, Issey (1938–) Japanese, born Hiroshima. Spent six years in Paris and New York fashion houses before showing his first collection in Tokyo in 1963. Distinctive style combines eastern and western influences in garments which have an almost theatrical quality, frequently in subdued colours.

Molyneux, Edward Henry (1891–1974) English, born London. After studying art, worked for Lucile. Opened his own couture house in Paris in 1919 with branches in London, Monte Carlo, Cannes and Biarritz, and became famous for the elegant simplicity of tailored suits with pleated skirts and evening wear.

Mortensen, Erik (1926–) Danish. Since 1948, attached to the Balmain fashion house in Paris, becoming artistic director in 1960 and taking over the management after the death of Pierre Balmain in 1982. Awarded the Golden Thimble of the French Haute Couture in 1983 and 1987.

Muir, Jean Elizabeth (1933–) English, born London. Started as sales assistant with Liberty's in London, then moved to Jaeger in 1956. In 1961 started on her own as Jane & Jane and in 1966 established her company Jean Muir. Her clothes are noted for their classic shapes, softness and fluidity.

Oldfield, Bruce (1950–) English, born London. As a freelance designer sold sketches to Yves Saint Laurent and designed for Bendel's store in New York. Showed his first collection in 1975 in London. His designs include evening dresses for royalty and screen stars and ready-to-wear clothes.

Patou, Jean (1880–1936) French, born Normandy. In 1912 opened Maison Parry in Paris and in 1913 sold his collection outright to an American buyer. After war service he successfully opened again as couturier in 1919. Noted for his designs for sports stars and actresses and for his perfume 'Joy'.

Poiret, Paul (1879–1944) French, born Paris. Worked for Jacques Doucet and Worth before opening his own fashion house in 1904. Influenced by the exotic oriental costumes of the Ballets Russes, his designs featured turbans and harem pants and he became a leader of fashion rather than a designer for individual clients. After World War I did not re-establish his prominence and died in poverty.

Pucci, Emilio, Marchese di Barsento (1914–) Italian, born Naples. Member of Italy's Olympic ski team (1933–34) and later member of the Italian parliament (1963–72), he started designing ski clothes in 1947 and in 1950 opened his own couture house, creating print dresses for women. Became renowned for use of bold patterns and brilliant colour.

Quant, Mary (1934–) English, born London. Began fashion design when she opened a small boutique in Chelsea in 1955. Her clothes became extremely fashionable in the 1960s when the geometric simplicity of her designs and the originality of her colours became an essential feature of the 'swinging Britain' era.

Rhodes, Zandra (1940–) English, born Chatham, Kent. After studying art, designed and printed textiles and, with others, opened The Fulham Road Clothes Shop, afterwards setting up on her own. Showed her first dress collection in 1969, and is noted for distinctive, exotic designs in chiffons and silks.

Saint Laurent, Yves, originally **Henri Donat**

FASHION DESIGNERS (cont.)

Mathieu (1936–) French, born Oran, Algeria. Employed by Christian Dior in 1955 after winning an International Wool Secretariat design competition. Took over the house on Dior's death in 1957. In 1962 opened his own house and launched the first of his 160 Rive Gauche boutiques in 1966, selling ready-to-wear clothes, a trend which many other designers were to follow.

Schiaparelli, Elsa (1890–1973) Italian–French, born Rome. After living in the USA, moved to Paris and started in business in 1929. Her designs were inventive and sensational, and she was noted for her use of bright colour and traditional fabrics, featuring zippers and buttons, and outrageous hats. Opened a salon in New York in 1949, and retired in 1954.

Ungaro, Emanuel Maffeolti (1933–) French, born Aix-en-Provence. Worked for small Paris tailoring firm and later with Balenciaga, before opening his own house in 1965 with Sonia Knapp designing his fabrics. Initially featured rigid lines, but later produced softer styles. Produced his first ready-to-wear lines in 1968.

Westwood, Vivienne (1941–) English, born Tintwhistle. After one term at Harrow Art School, left to train as a teacher. After meeting Malcolm McLaren, was drawn into the design world again, their anarchic style being inspired by rebellious urban youth: rockers, teddy boys and punks. In 1971, opened a shop (originally 'Let it Rock') in London's King's Road: this was joined by a second shop 'Nostalgia of Mud' in the West End in 1982.

Worth, Charles Frederick (1825–95) English–French, born Bourn, Lincolnshire. Achieved success as a fashion designer in Paris, gaining the patronage of the Empress Eugénie. His establishment in the Rue de la Paix became the centre of the fashion world.

Yamamoto, Yohji (1943–) Japanese, born Tokyo. Started his own company in 1972 producing his first collection in 1976 in Tokyo. After some time in Paris, opened a new headquarters in London in 1987. Designs loose, functional clothes for men and women, which conceal rather than emphasize the body.

PHILOSOPHERS

Anaxagoras (500–428BC) Greek, born Clazomenae. Believed that matter is infinitely divisible into particles containing a mixture of all qualities and that mind is a pervasive formative agency in the creation of material objects. Prosecuted for impiety and banished from Athens.

Anaximander (611–547BC) Greek, born Miletus. Proposed that basic matter is the *apeiron*, the infinite or indefinite. Speculated that the Earth is unsupported at the centre of the Universe and that human beings developed from another species.

Aquinas, St Thomas (c.1225–74) Italian, born Roccasecca, near Aquino. Believed in the teachings of Aristotle. Wrote on principles of natural religion in *Summa contra Gentiles* (1259–64) and on proving the existence of God in *Summa Theologiae* (1266–73). Had considerable influence on theological thought of following ages.

Aristotle (384–322BC) Greek, born Stagira, Macedonia. One of the most important philosophers and scientists in the history of Western thought, writing extensively on logic, metaphysics, ethics, politics, rhetoric, poetry, biology, zoology, physics and psychology. Best-known works include the *Metaphysics*, *Nicomachean Ethics*, *Politics*, *Poetics*, the *De Anima*, the *Organon*.

Augustine of Hippo, St (354–430) Italian, born North Africa. Involved in Manicheanism, the attempt to offer a solution to the problem of evil and influenced by scepticism and neoplatonism. Converted to Christianity in 386. Famous works are the *Confessions* (400), *The City of God* (412–27).

Austin, John L(angshaw) (1911–60) English, born Lancaster. Professor at Oxford University and leading figure in 'Oxford Philosophy' movement. Examined ordinary linguistic usage to resolve philosophical perplexities. Best-known works: *Philosophical Papers* (1961), *Sense and Sensibilia* (1962), *How to do Things with Words* (1962).

Averrhoes, Ibn Ruoshd (1126–98) Muslim, born Cordova, Spain. Famous medieval Islamic philosopher who also wrote on jurisprudence and medicine. Most important works were the *Commentaries on Aristotle* which offered a partial synthesis of Greek and Arabic philosophical traditions.

Ayer, Sir Alfred (Jules) (1910–89) British, born London. Professor at London and Oxford Universit-

PHILOSOPHERS (cont.)

ies. *Language, Truth and Logic* (1936) gives an account of the antimetaphysical doctrines which he became involved with in the 1930s, and aroused great hostility when published. Later publications include *The Problem of Knowledge* (1956), *The Central Questions of Philosophy* (1972). Knighted in 1970.

Bacon, Francis, Viscount St Albas (1561–1626) English, born London. Important philosopher and statesman, knighted in 1603. Abandoned deductive logic of Aristotle and stressed the importance of experiment in interpretation of nature. Philosophical works include *The Advancement of Learning* (1605), *De Augmentis Scientiarum* (1623), *Novum Organum* (1620). Bacon also wrote many religious and professional works.

Bacon, Roger (c.1214–92) English, born probably Ilchester, Somerset. Philosopher and scientist with reputation for unconvential learning in magic and alchemy, and imprisoned for heresy. Also published many works on mathematics, philosophy, and logic whose importance was recognized in later centuries.

Bentham, Jeremy (1748–1832) English, born London. Philosopher, jurist and social reformer: advocated utilitarianism in *A Fragment on Government* (1776), *Introduction to the Principles of Morals and Legislation* (1789). Published many works on penal and social reform, economics and politics.

Berkeley, Bishop George (1685–1753) Irish, born near Kilkenny. Developed the belief that the contents of the material world are 'ideas' that only exist when perceived by a mind in *Essay towards a New Theory of Vision* (1709), *A Treatise concerning the Principles of Human Knowledge* (1710), *Three Dialogues between Hylas and Philonous* (1713). Expressed concern about social corruption and national decadence and wrote on social reforms and religion.

Berlin, Sir Isaiah (1909–) British, born Riga, USSR. Oxford professor whose philosophical works include *Karl Marx* (1939), *Historical Inevitability* (1954), *Two Concepts of Liberty* (1953), *Vico and Herder* (1976) and four volumes of essays.

Boethius, Anicius Manlius Severinus (c.475–524) Roman, born probably Rome. Produced translations of and commentaries on Aristotle. Wrote *De Consolatione Philosophiae*, which explains the mutability of all earthly fortune and demonstrates that happiness can only be attained by virtue, during a year of imprisonment after accusations of treason before being executed.

Buber, Martin (1878–1965) Jewish, born Vienna. Published many works on social and ethical problems and is best known for the religious philosophy expounded in *Ich und Du* (1923), contrasting personal relationships of mutuality and reciprocity with utilitarian or objective relationships.

Burke, Edmund (1729–87) Irish, born Dublin. Statesman and philosopher whose political thought has become the philosophy of modern Conservatism. Works include *Observations on the Present State of the Nation* (1769), *On the Causes of the Present Discontents* (1770).

Carnap, Rudolf (1891–1970) German–American, born Wuppertal. Leading member of the 'Vienna Circle' of logical positivists who dismissed most traditional metaphysics as a source of meaningless answers to pseudo-problems. Works include *Der logische Aufbau der Welt* (1928), *Logische Syntax der Sprache* (1934), *Meaning and Necessity* (1947), *The Logical Foundations of Probability* (1950).

Comte, Auguste (1798–1857) French, born Montpelier. Usually regarded as the founder of sociology. His 'Positivism' sought to expound the laws of social evolution, to describe the organization of all branches of human knowledge, and to establish a science of society as a basis for social planning. Works include *Cours de Philosophie positive* (1830–42), *Système de Politique positive* (1851–54).

Confucius (Ku'ng Fu-tse, 'the Master K'ung') (551–479BC) Chinese, born state of Lu (modern Shantung). Moral teacher who tried to replace old religious observances with moral values as the basis of social and political order, emphasizing the importance of respect and benevolence. 'Confucianism' became, and remained until recently, the state religion of China. His teachings are recorded in the *Analects*, written by his pupils after his death.

Copleston, Frederick (Charles) (1907–) English, born near Taunton. Catholic philosopher; published many critical studies of philosophers and wrote *A History of Philosophy* (1946–66).

Cousin, Victor (1792–1867) French, born Paris. An eclectic in philosophy; published many historical studies and commentaries on other philosophers. Most original work was *Du Vrai, du Beau, et du Bien* (1854).

Croce, Benedetto (1866–1952) Italian, born Pes-

PHILOSOPHERS (cont.)

casserolli. Developed phenomenology of the mind in which four principle activities, art and philosophy (theoretical), political economy and ethics (practical), complement each other. His theory of aesthetics is described in *Lo Spirito* and his opposition to totalitarianism is expressed in *History as the Story of Liberty* (trans 1941).

Cudworth, Ralph (1617–88) English, born Aller, Somerset. Leading member of the Cambridge Platonists. *The True Intellectual System of the Universe* (1678) aimed to refute determinism and materialism and to establish the reality of a supreme divine intelligence; *Treatise concerning Eternal and Immutable Morality* is a posthumous publication discussing ethics.

de Beauvoir, Simone (1908–80) French, born Paris. Sorbonne professor, novelist and feminist who contributed substantially to the existentialist movement. Works include *Le Deuxième Sexe* (1949), translated as *The Second Sex* (1953).

Democritus (c.460–370BC) Greek, born Abdera, Thrace. Prolific ancient philosopher publishing works on ethics, physics, mathematics, cosmology and music, although only fragments of his writings remain. Best known for physical speculations, in particular the belief that the world consists of an infinite number of minute particles whose different combinations account for different properties.

Descartes, René (1596–1650) French, born La Haye, near Tours. Usually regarded as the founder of modern philosophy. *Discourse de la Méthode* (1637), the *Meditationes de Prima Philosophia* (1641) and *Principia Philosophiae* (1644) set out his ideas on philosophical methods, propositions and religious beliefs. He also made important contributions in astronomy and mathematics.

Dewey, John (1859–1952) American, born Burlington, Vermont. Exponent of pragmatism whose philosophy stressed the instrumental function of ideas and judgments in problem solving. Also published widely on psychology and education. Works include *The School and Society* (1899), *Reconstruction in Philosophy* (1920), *Experience and Nature* (1925), *The Quest for Certainty* (1929), *Experience and Education* (1938).

Diogenes (412–323BC) Greek, born Sinope, Pontus. Continued the pre-Socratic tradition of speculation about the primary constituent of the world, which he identified as air, operating as an active and intelligent life-force.

Duns Scotus, John (c.1266–1308) Scottish, born probably Duns, Berwickshire. Philosopher whose beliefs represented a strong reaction against Aristotle and Aquinas; he propounded the primacy of the individual and the freedom of the individual will. His writings were mainly commentaries on the bible and other philosophers.

Empedocles (490–430BC) Greek, born Acragas, Sicily. Philosopher, poet, doctor, statesman and soothsayer who described a cosmic cycle in which earth, air, fire and water periodically combine and separate under the forces of Love and Hate as well as beliefs on the transmigration and redemption of souls.

Epicurus (341–270BC) Greek, born Samos. Advocated a philosophy designed to promote detachment, serenity and freedom from fear, and the belief that pleasure is the only good and the only goal of morality.

Erasmus, Desiderius (1466–1536) Dutch, born Rotterdam. Influential Renaissance humanist and scholar who published many popular works including *Adagia* (Adages, 1500, 1508), *Enchiridion Militis Christiani* (*Handbook of a Christian Soldier*, 1503) and Encomium Moriae (*In Praise of Folly*, 1509).

Feuerbach, Ludwig (Andreas) (1804–72) German, born Landshut, Bavaria. Attacked conventional Christianity in *Das Wesen des Christentums* (1847), translated as *The Essence of Christianity*, and agreed that religion is 'the dream of the human mind', projecting on to an illusory God our own human ideals and nature.

Fichte, Johann Gottlieb (1762–1814) German, born Rammenau, Saxony. Posited the Ego as the basic reality, affirming itself in the act of consciousness and constructing the external world as its field of action. He elaborates this system in *Grundlage des Naturrechts* (1796) and *System der Sittenlehre* (1798).

Foucault, Michel (1926–84) French, born Poitiers. Believed that prevailing social attitudes are manipulated by those in power to define such categories as insanity, illness, sexuality and criminality and to use these to identify and oppress 'deviants'. Translations of his work included *Madness and Civilization* (1971), *The Order of Things* (1970), *The Archaeology of Knowledge* (1972), *The History of Sexuality* (1984).

Frege, (Friedrich Ludwig) Gottlob (1848–1925) German, born Wismar. Regarded as the founder of moder mathematical logic and the philosophy of language. Main works are *Begriffschrift* (1879),

PHILOSOPHERS (cont.)

Die Grundlagen der Arithmetik (1884) and *Die Grundgesetze der Arithmetik* (1893, 1903).

Gödel, Kurt (1906–78) American, born Brünn, Austria-Hungary (now Brno, Czechoslovakia). Logician and mathematician whose theorem, published in 1931, demonstrated the existence of formally undecidable elements in any formal system of arithmetic.

Gorgias (c.485–380BC) Greek, born Leontini, Sicily. Advocated a philosophy which was an extreme form of scepticism or nihilism: that nothing exists, that if it did it would be unknowable, that if it were knowable it would be incommunicable to others. He is portrayed in Plato's dialogue, the *Gorgias*.

Hamilton, Sir William (1788–1856) Scottish, born Glasgow. Philosopher whose main work *Lectures on Metaphysics and Logic*, published posthumously (1856–60), presented views on perception and knowledge. Important figure in the revival of philosophy in Britain at this time.

Hegel, Georg Wilhelm Friedrich (1770–1831) German, born Stuttgart. Idealist philosopher whose major works include *Phänomenologie des Geistes* (1807), *Wissenschaft der Logik* (1812, 1816), *Encyclopädie der philosophischen Wissenschaften in Grundrisse* (1817). Although his philosophy is difficult and obscure it has remained influential until the present.

Hejdegger, Martin (1889–1976) German, born Messkirch, Baden. Philosopher whose writings examine the nature and predicament of human existence, classify modes of 'Being' and discuss the human mode of existence characterized by participation and involvement in the world of objects. His major work was *Sein und Zeit* (*Being and Time*, 1927).

Heraclitus (c.540–460BC) Greek, born Ephesus. Believed that everything is in a state of flux and that fire is the ultimate constituent of the world. Only fragments remain of his book *On Nature*.

Herbert of Cherbury, Edward (1st Baron) (1583–1648) English, born Eyton, Shropshire. Soldier, statesman and philosopher who proved in *De Religione Gentilum* (1645) that all religions recognize five main articles, from the acknowledgement of a supreme God to the concept that there are rewards and punishments in a future state.

Hobbes, Thomas (1588–1679) English, born Malmesbury. Political philosopher whose major work *Leviathan* (1651) presented and connected his thoughts on metaphysics, psychology and political philosophy. His materialistic philosophy described how the world is a mechanical system consisting of bodies in motion in which human beings are wholly selfish and enlightened self-interest explains the existence of the sovereign state and prevents 'a war of every man against every man'. He was banned from publishing in England in 1666 after being accused of being an atheist.

Hume, David (1711–76) Scottish, born Edinburgh. Philosopher and historian whose beliefs concerning perception, causation, personal identity, and ethics are still influential. Most important works included *A Treatise of Human Nature* (1739–40), *Essays Moral and Political* (1741, 1742), *Enquiry concerning Human Understanding* (1748), *Dialogues concerning Natural Religion* (1759), *Political Discourses* (1752).

Husserl, Edmund (Gustav Albrecht) (1859–1938) German, born Prossnitz, Austrian Empire. Defender of philosophy as an *a priori* discipline who presented a programme for the systematic investigation of consciousness and its objects by suspending belief in the empirical world.

James, William (1842–1910) American, born New York City. Philosopher and psychologist who developed the pragmatist ideas of Charles Peirce; beliefs are true because they work, not vice versa. These ideas, and discussions of ethics and religion are given in *The Will to Believe* (1907), *Pragmatism* (1907), *Varieties of Religious Experience* (1902), *The Meaning of Truth* (1909).

Jaspers, Karl (Theodor) (1883–1969) German, born Oldenburg. One of the founders of existentialism; his beliefs are developed in *Philosophie* (1932).

Kant, Immanuel (1724–1804) German, born Königsberg, Prussia. Influential scientist and philosopher who argued that the immediate objects of perception depend not only on our sensations but also on our perceptual equipment and that some properties we observe in objects are due to the nature of the observer. Ethics, aesthetics and politics are also discussed in *Critique of Pure Reason* (1781), *Critique of Practical Reason* (1788), *Critique of Judgment* (1790), *Perpetual Peace* (1795).

Kierkegaard, Søren Aabye (1813–55) Danish, born Copenhagen. A founder of existentialism who tried to reinstate the central importance of the individual and the significant choices each of us makes in forming our future selves and wrote in

PHILOSOPHERS (cont.)

many works about the necessity for individual choice rather than prescribed dogma.

Langer, Suzanne K(nauth) (1895–1985) American, born New York City. Published important works in linguistic analysis and aesthetics: *Philosophy in a New Key* (1942), *Feeling and Form* (1953), *Problems of Art* (1957), *Mind: an Essay on Human Feeling* (1967–82).

Leibniz, Gottfried Wilhelm (1647–1716) German, born Leipzig. Mathematician and philosopher who believed that the world is composed of an infinity of simple immaterial 'monads' which form a hierarchy, the highest of which is God; had greatest influence as a mathematician.

Locke, John (1632–1704) English, born Wrington, Somerset. Philosopher who defended natural rights, constitutional law and the liberty of the individual. *Essay concerning Human Understanding* (1690) explores the nature and scope of human reason and seeks to establish that 'all knowledge is founded on and ultimately derives from sense ... or sensation'.

Lukacs, George (1885–1971) Hungarian, born Budapest. Marxist philosopher who wrote prolifically on literature and aesthetics. His major work on Marxism was *History and Class Consciousness* (1923).

Mach, Ernst (1838–1916) Austrian, born Turas, Moravia. Physicist and philosopher whose writings laid the foundations of logical positivism.

Maimonides, Moses (Moses ben Maimon) (1135–1204) Jewish, born Cordoba. Physician and philosopher who tried to harmonize the thought of Aristotle and Judaism in *Guide to the Perplexed* (1190).

Marcuse, Herbert (1898–1979) American, born Berlin. Radical political theorist who analysed the repressions imposed by the unconscious mind in *Eros and Civilization* (1955) and condemned the 'repressive tolerance' of modern industrial society which both stimulated and satisfied superficial material desires of the masses at the cost of more fundamental needs and freedoms in *One Dimensional Man* (1964).

Mencius (Meng-tzu) (372–298BC) Chinese, born Shantung. Philosopher who popularized and developed Confucian ideas and made many proposal for social and political reform; his beliefs are recorded in a book compiled after his death, *Book of Meng-tzu*.

Merleau-Ponty, Maurice (1908–61) French, born Rochefort-sur-mer. Philosopher who rejected extremes of both behaviouristic psychology and subjectivist accounts; the world is neither wholly 'given', nor wholly 'constructed' for the perceiving subject, but is essentially ambiguous and enigmatic. Major works are *La Structure du Comportement* (1942) and *Phénoménologie de la Perception* (1945).

Mill, J(ohn) S(tuart) (1806–73) English, born London. Philosopher and social reformer, leading exponent of the British empiricism and utilitarian traditions who also restored the importance of cultural values. Active in politics, he campaigned for women's suffrage and supported the Advanced Liberals. Major works included *A System of Logic* (1843), *On Liberty* (1859), *The Subjection of Women* (1869).

Moore, George (Edward) (1873–1958) English, born London. Cambridge professor of mental philosophy and logic who emphasized the intellectual virtues of clarity, precision and honesty, identifying as a principal task of philosophy the analysis of ordinary concepts and arguments. Works included *Principia Ethica* (1903), *Ethics* (1916).

More, Henry (The 'Cambridge Platonist') (1614–87) English, born Grantham, Lincolnshire. Followed the philosophies of Plato, Plotinus and Descartes and attempted to demonstrate the compatibility of reason and faith. Later became interested in occultism and mysticism. Main works: *Philosophical Poems* (1647), *An Antidote against Atheism* (1653), *The Immortality of the Soul* (1659), *Enchiridion Ethicum* (1666), *Divine Dialogues* (1668).

Nietzsche, Friedrich (Wilhelm) (1844–1900) German, born Röcken, Saxony. Philosopher who produced many unconventional works expressing repudiation of Christian and liberal ethics, detestaton of democratic ideals, the celebration of the *Übermensch* (superman) who can create and impose his own law, the death of God. Best-known writings include *Unzeitgemässe Betrachtungen* (Untimely Meditations, 1873–76), *Die Fröliche Wissenschaft* (The Joyous Science, 1882), *Also Sprach Zarathustra* (Thus Spake Zarathustra, 1883–92), *Jenseits von Gut und Böse* (Beyond Good and Evil, 1886).

Ockham, William of (1285–1349) English, born Ockham, Surrey. Philosopher, theologian and political writer whose controversial religious views led to disputes with the Catholic church. Defended nominalism against realism and introduced 'Ockham's razor'; the belief that a theory should not

PHILOSOPHERS (cont.)

propose the existence of anything more than is needed for its explanations. Works include *Summa Logicae, Quodlibta Septem.*

Ortega y Gasset, José (1883–1955) Spanish, born Madrid. Argued that great philosophies demarcate the cultural horizons of their epochs. Works include *Meditaciones del Quijote* (1914), *Tema de nuestro tiempa* (1923), *La Rebelión de Las Masas* (1930).

Parmenides (c.515–445BC) Greek, born Elea, S Italy. Argued in *On Nature* for the impossibility of motion, plurality and change, and set an agenda of problems for subsequent pre-Socratic philosophers.

Peirce, Charles (Sanders) (1839–1914) American, born Cambridge, Massachusetts. Philosopher, logician and mathematician, best known as the founder of pragmatism.

Philo Judeaus (c.20BC–AD40) Hellenistic Jew, born Alexandria. Prolific author who attempted to synthesize Greek philosophy and Jewish scripture.

Plato (c.427–347BC) Greek, born probably Athens. One of the most important philosophers of all time. Pupil of Socrates and teacher of Aristotle, his writings consist of philosophical dialogues and letters discussing the definition of moral virtues, the theory of knowledge as recollection, the immortality of the soul, and contrasts of transient and timeless aspects of the world. The *Republic* presents Plato's political utopia.

Plotinus (205–70) Greek, born possibly Lycopolis, Egypt. Neoplatonist philosopher who advocated ascetism and the contemplative life, and greatly influenced early Christian theology.

Popper, Sir Karl (Raimund) (1902–) Austrian, born Vienna. Rejected philosophical systems with totalitarian political implications from Plato to Marx and stressed the importance of 'falsifiability'; true scientific theories must specify in advance the conditions under which they could be tested and refuted. Main works include *Die Logik der Forschung* (1934, trans *The Logic of Scientific Discovery*, 1959), *The Open Society and its Enemies* (1945), *The Poverty of Historicism* (1957).

Protagorus (c.490–421BC) Greek, born Abdera. Believed to have taken a sceptical or relativistic view of human knowledge; his many works are lost and most information about him comes from Plato's dialogues.

Pythagoras (6th-cBC) Greek, born Samos. Philosopher and mathematician whose life is surrounded in myth and legend. Emphasized moral ascetism and purification; also associated with mathematical discoveries involving musical intervals and relations of numbers. He had a profound influence on later philosophers and scientists.

Quine, Willard Van Orman (1908–) American, born Akron, Ohio. Influential professor of philosophy who challenged the standard sharp distinctions between analysis and synthetic truths and between science and metaphysics; also presented a systematic linguistic philosophy. Best-known works: *Two Dogmas of Empiricism* (1951), *From a Logical Point of View* (1953), *Word and Object* (1960), *The Roots of Reference* (1973).

Reichenbach, Hans (1891–1953) German, born Hamburg. Made important technical contributions to technical probability theory and wrote widely on logic and the philosophical bases of science in *Philosophie der Raum-Zeit-Lehre* (1927–28), *Elements of Symbolic Logic* (1947), *The Rise of Scientific Philosophy* (1951).

Russell, Bertrand (Arthur William, 3rd Earl) (1872–1970) British, born Trelleck, Monmouthshire. Philosopher, mathematician, prolific author and controverisal figure, who was imprisoned in 1918 during World War I as an active pacifist and in 1961 for taking part in a sit-down demonstration in Whitehall. Wrote wide-ranging literature on mathematics, philosophy, politics, education and morals, such as *The Principles of Mathematics* (1903), *The Problems of Philosophy* (1912), *Theory and Practice of Bolshevism* (1919), *On Education* (1926), *Marriage and Morals* (1932).

Ryle, Gilbert (1900–76) English, born Brighton, Sussex. Influential exponent of linguistic philosophy. *The Concept of Mind* (1949) was directed against the traditional theory that mind and matter were distinct and problematically related. Other works; *Dilemmas* (1954), *Plato's Progress* (1966).

Santayana, George (Jorge Augustin Nicola Ruiz de Santayana) (1863–1952) Spanish–American, born Madrid. Naturalistic and materialistic critic of the transcendental claims of religion and German idealism, who believed that our knowledge of the external world depends on an act of 'animal faith'. Main philosophical works: *The Sense of Beauty* (1896), *The Life of Reason* (1905–06), *Scepticism and Animal Faith* (1923), *Realms of Being* (1927–40), *Platonism and the Spiritual Life* (1927).

Sartre, Jean-Paul (1905–80) French, born Paris. Philosopher, dramatist and novelist who devel-

PHILOSOPHERS (cont.)

oped characteristic atheistic existentialist doctrines from an early anarchistic tendency; these are expressed in the autobiographical novel *La Nausée* (1938) and in *Le Mur* (1938). Awarded, but declined to accept, the Nobel prize for literature in 1964.

Schelling, Friedrich (Wilhelm Joseph) von (1775–1854) German, born Leonburg. Idealist philosopher who examined the relation of the self to the objective world and argued that consciousness itself is the only immediate object of knowledge and that only in art can the mind become fully aware of itself. Works include *Ideen zur einer Philosophie der Natur* (1797), *System des transzendentalen Idealismus* (1800).

Schlick, Moritz (1882–1936) German, born Berlin. Leader of the 'Vienna Circle' of logical positivists who wrote on ethics, which he argued was a fractal science of the causes of human actions. Main publications *Allgemeine Erkenntnislehre* (General Theory of Knowledge, 1918), *Fragen der Ethik* (Problem of Ethics, 1930).

Schopenhaur, Artur (1788–1960) German, born Danzig. Philosopher who emphasized the active role of Will as the creative but covert and irrational force in human nature and argued that art represented the sole kind of knowledge that was not subservient to the Will; his work is often characterized as a systematic philosophical pessimism. Major work: *Die Welt als Wille und Vorstellung* (The World as Will and Idea, 1819).

Shaftesbury, Anthony Ashley Cooper, 3rd Earl of (1671–1713) English, born London. Moral philosopher and politician who argued that we possess natural 'mora: sense' and affections directed to the good of the species and in harmony with the larger cosmic order in *Characteristics of Men, Manners, Opinions, Times* (1711).

Socrates (469–399BC) Greek, born Athens. One of the most important philosophers in history, responsible for a decisive shift of philosophical interest from speculation about the natural world and cosmology to ethics and conceptual analysis. His reputation for eliciting contradictions in the philosophies of others may have contributed to demands for his conviction for 'impiety' and 'corrupting the youth'; he was sentenced to die by drinking hemlock.

Spencer, Herbert (1820–1903) British, born Derby. Philosopher with interest in evolutionary theory which he expounded in *Principles of Psychology* (1855). Also applied his evolutionary theories to ethics and sociology and became an advocate of 'social Darwinism', that societies naturally evolve in competition for resources and that the 'survival of the fittest' is therefore morally justified. Works included *System of Synthetic Philosophy* (1862–93), *Social Statistics* (1851), *Education* (1861), *The Man Versus the State* (1884).

Spinoza, Baruch (Benedict de) (1632–77) Dutch, born Amsterdam. Rationalist philosopher who advocated a strictly historical approach to the interpretation of biblical sources and argued that complete freedom of philosophical and scientific speculation was appropriate. His major work, the *Ethics* (1677, posthumous) described a complete, deductive metaphysical system intended to be a proof derived with mathematical certainty of what is good for human beings.

Tarski, Alfred (1902–83) Polish, born Warsaw. Logician and mathematician who gave a definition of 'truth' in formal logical languages in *Der Wahrheitsbetriff in den Formalisierten Sprachen* (The Concept of Truth in Formalized Languages, 1933).

Thales (c.620–c.555BC) Greek, born Miletus. Traditionally the founder of European philosophy. Proposed the first natural cosmology, identifying water as the original substance and the basis of the universe. Also had wide-ranging practical and scientific interests.

Tillich, Paul (Johannes) (1886–1965) German, born Starzeddel, Prussia. Protestant theologian and philosopher, an early critic of the Nazis whose main work *Systematic Theology* (1951–63) combines elements of existentialism and the ontological tradition in Christian thought. He explained faith as a reality transcending finite existence rather than a belief in a personal God, leading to oversimplified accusations of atheism. Popular works were *The Courage to Be* (1952), *Dynamics of Faith* (1957).

Weil, Simone (1909–43) French, born Paris. Combined sophisticated scholarly and philosophical interests with dedicated involvement with interests of the oppressed and exploited. Translated philosophical and spiritual works include *Gravity and Grace* (1952), *The Need for Roots* (1952), *Waiting for God* (1951), *Oppression and Liberty* (1958).

Whitehead, A(lfred) N(orth) (1861–1947) English, born Ramsgate. Mathematician and idealist philosopher. *Process and Reality* (1929) attempted a metaphysics comprising psychologi-

PHILOSOPHERS (cont.)

cal as well as physical experience, with events as the ultimate component of reality. Other works include *Adventures of Ideas* (1933) and *Modes of Thought* (1938).

Wittgenstein, Ludwig (Josef Johann) (1889–1951) Austrian, born Vienna. Philosopher who studied the nature and limits of language. *Logisch-philosophische Abhandlung* (1921) describes how meaningful language must consist in propositions that are 'pictures' of the facts of which the world is composed and many claims of speculative philosophy must be rejected. *Philosophical Investigations* (1953, posthumous) comes to different conclusions, pointing to the variety and subtlety in language and exploring its functions.

Zeno of Elea (c.490–c.420BC) Greek, born Elea, Italy. A disciple of Parmenides who devised famous paradoxes which purported to show the impossibility of motion and spatial division.

LITERARY PRIZES

Booker Prize (UK)

1970 Bernice Rubens *The Elected Member*
1971 V S Naipaul *In a Free State*
1972 John Berger *G*
1973 J G Farrell *The Siege of Krishnapur*
1974 Nadine Gordimer *The Conservationist*; Stanley Middleton *Holiday*
1975 Ruth Prawer Jhabvala *Heat and Dust*
1976 David Storey *Saville*
1977 Paul Scott *Staying On*
1978 Iris Murdoch *The Sea, The Sea*
1979 Penelope Fitzgerald *Offshore*
1980 William Golding *Rites of Passage*
1981 Salman Rushdie *Midnight's Children*
1982 Thomas Keneally *Schindler's Ark*
1983 J M Coetzee *Life and Times of Michael K*
1984 Anita Brookner *Hotel du Lac*
1985 Keri Hulme *The Bone People*
1986 Kingsley Amis *The Old Devils*
1987 Penelope Lively *Moon Tiger*
1988 Peter Carey *Oscar and Lucinda*
1989 Kazuo Ishiguro *The Remains of the Day*
1990 A S Byatt *Possession*
1991 Ben Okri *The Famished Road*

Prix Goncourt (France)

1970 Michel Tournier *Le Roi des aulnes*
1971 Jacques Laurent *Les Bêtises*
1972 Jean Carrière *L'Epervier de Maheux*
1973 Jacques Chessex *L'Ogre*
1974 Pascal Lainé *La Dentellière*
1975 Emile Ajar *La Vie devant soi*
1976 Patrick Grainville *Les Flamboyants*
1977 Didier Decoin *John L'Enfer*
1978 Patrick Modiano *Rue des boutiques obscures*
1979 Antonine Maillet *Pelagie-la-Charrette*
1980 Yves Navarre *Le Jardin d'acclimation*
1981 Lucien Bodard *Anne Marie*
1982 Dominique Fernandez *Dans la Main de l'ange*
1983 Frederick Tristan *Les Égares*
1984 Marguerite Duras *L'Amant*
1985 Yann Queffelec *Les Noces barbares*
1986 Michel Host *Valet de Nuit*
1987 Tahar ben Jalloun *La Nuit sacrée*
1988 Erik Orsenna *L'Exposition coloniale*
1989 Jean Vautrin *Un Grand Pas Vers le Bon Dieu*
1990 Jean Rouaud *Les Champs d'Honneur*
1991 Pierre Combescot *Les Filles du Calvaire*

Pulitzer Prize in Letters (USA)

1970 Jean Stafford *Collected Stories*
1972 Wallace Stegner *Angle of Repose*
1973 Eudora Welty *The Optimist's Daughter*
1975 Michael Shaara *The Killer Angels*
1976 Saul Bellow *Humboldt's Gift*
1978 James Alan McPherson *Elbow Room*
1979 John Cheever *The Stories of John Cheever*
1980 Norman Mailer *The Executioner's Song*
1981 John Kennedy Toole *A Confederacy of Dunces*
1982 John Updike *Rabbit is Rich*
1983 Alice Walker *The Color Purple*
1984 William Kennedy *Ironweed*
1985 Alison Lurie *Foreign Affairs*
1986 Larry McMurtry *Lonesome Dove*
1987 Peter Taylor *A Summons to Memphis*
1988 Toni Morrison *Beloved*
1989 Anne Tyler *Breathing Lessons*
1990 Oscar Hijuelos *The Mambo Kings Play Songs of Love*
1991 John Updike *Rabbit at Rest*

NOBEL PRIZES 1970–91

Year	Peace	Literature	Economic Science	Chemistry	Physics	Physiology/Medicine	Year
1970	Norman E Borlaug	Alexandr Solzhenitsyn	Paul A Samuelson	Luis Federico Leloir	Louis Eugène Néel Hannes Olof Alvén	Julius Axelrod Bernard Katz Ulf von Euler	1970
1971	Willy Brandt	Pablo Neruda	Simon Kuznets	Gerhard Herzberg	Dennis Gabor	Earl W Sutherland	1971
1972	*none*	Heinrich Böll	John R Hicks Kenneth J Arrow	Stanford Moore William H Stein Christian B Anfinsen	John Bardeen Leon N Cooper John R Schrieffer	Gerald M Edelman Rodney R Porter	1972
1973	Henry A Kissinger Le Duc Tho (*declined*)	Patrick White	Wassily Leontief	Ernst Otto Fischer Geoffrey Wilkinson	Leo Esaki Ivar Giaever Brian D Josephson	Konrad Lorenz Nikolaas Tinbergen Karl von Frisch	1973
1974	Sean MacBride Sato Eisaku	Eyvind Johnson Harry Martinson	Gunnar Myrdal Friedrich A von Hayek	Paul J Flory	Martin Ryle Antony Hewish	Albert Claude George Emil Palade Christian de Duve	1974
1975	Andrei D Sakharov	Eugenio Montale	Leonid V Kantorovich Tjalling C Koopmans	John W Cornforth Vladimir Prelog	Aage N Bohr Ben R Mottelson L James Rainwater	David Baltimore Renato Dulbecco Howard M Temin	1975
1976	Mairead Corrigan Betty Williams	Saul Bellow	Milton Friedman	William N Lipscomb	Burton Richter Samuel Chao Chung Ting	Baruch S Blumberg Daniel C Gajdusek	1976
1977	Amnesty International	Vicente Aleixandre	James E Meade Bertil Ohlin	Ilya Prigogine	Philip W Anderson Nevill F Mott John H van Vleck	Rosalyn S Yalow Roger C L Guillemin Andrew V Schally	1977
1978	Menachem Begin Anwar al-Sadat	Isaac B Singer	Herbert A Simon	Peter Mitchell	Pjotr L Kapitza Arno A Penzias Robert W Wilson	Werner Arber Daniel Nathans Hamilton O Smith	1978
1979	Mother Teresa	Odysseus Elytis	Arthur Lewis Theodore W Schultz	Herbert C Brown George Wittig	Steven Weinberg Sheldon L Glashow Abdus Salam	Allan M Cormack Godfrey N Hounsfield	1979
1980	Adolfo Pérez Esquivel	Czesław Miłosz	Lawrence R Klein	Paul Berg Walter Gilbert Frederick Sanger	James W Cronin Val L Fitch	Baruj Benacerraf George D Snell Jean Dausset	1980

1981	Office of the UN High Commissioner for Refugees	Elias Canetti	James Tobin	Kenichi Fukui Roald Hoffman	Nicolaas Bloembergen Arthur L Schawlow Kai M Siegbahn	Roger W Sperry David H Hubel Torsten N Wiesel	1981
1982	Alfonso García Robles Alva Myrdal	Gabriel García Márquez	George J Stigler	Aaron Klug	Kenneth G Wilson	Sune K Bergström Bengt I Samuelsson John R Vane	1982
1983	Lech Walesa	William Golding	Gerard Debreu	Henry Taube	Subrahmanyan Chandrasekhar William A Fowler	Barbara McClintock	1983
1984	Desmond Tutu	Jaroslav Seifert	Richard Stone	Robert B Merrifield	Carlo Rubbia Simon van der Meer	Niels K Jerne Georges J F Köhler César Milstein	1984
1985	International Physicians for the Prevention of Nuclear War	Claude Simon	Franco Modigliani	Herbert Hauptman Jerome Karle	Klaus von Klitzing	Joseph L Goldstein Michael S Brown	1985
1986	Elie Wiesel	Wole Soyinka	James M Buchanan	Dudley R Herschbach Yuan Tseh Lee John C Polanyi	Gerd Binnig Heinrich Rohrer Ernst Ruska	Stanley Cohen Rita Levi-Montalcini	1986
1987	Oscar Arias Sánchez	Joseph Brodsky	Robert M Solow	Charles Pedersen Donald Cram Jean-Marie Lehn	George Bednorz Alex Müller	Susumu Tonegawa	1987
1988	UN Peacekeeping Forces	Naguib Mahfouz	Maurice Allais	Johann Deisenhofer Robert Huber Hartmut Michel	Leon Lederman Melvin Schwartz Jack Steinberger	James Black Gertrude Elion George Hitchings	1988
1989	Tenzin Ciyatso (Dalai Lama)	Camilo José Cela	Trygve Haavelmo	Sydney Altman Thomas Cech	Hans Dehmelt Wolfgang Paul Norman Ramsay	J Michael Bishop Harold E Varmus	1989
1990	Mikhail Gorbachev	Octavio Paz	Harry M Markovitz Merton Miller William Sharpe	Elias James Corey	Jerome Friedman Henry Kendall Richard Taylor	Joseph E Murray E Donnall Thomas	1990
1991	Aung San Suu Kyi	Nadine Gordimer	Ronald Coase	Richard R Ernst	Pierre-Gilles de Gennes	Erwin Neher Bert Sakmann	1991

MUSEUMS AND ART GALLERIES — Europe

A selection of the most important museums and galleries is given.

Amsterdam, Netherlands
Anne Frank's House
Dortmond Museum of Handwriting
Museum of Amsterdam
Rijksmuseum
Stedelijk Museum

Ankara, Turkey
Archaeological Museum

Antwerp, Belgium
Butcher's Hall
Folklore Museum
Maritime Museum
Royal Museum of Fine Art
Rubens's House

Athens, Greece
Acropolis Museum
Byzantine Museum
Goulandris Natural History Museum
National Archaeological Museum

Barcelona, Spain
Catalan Museum of Art
Ethnological Museum
Joán Miró Foundation
Museum of Costume
Picasso Museum

Basle, Switzerland
Basle Historical Museum

Berlin, Germany
The Bauhaus Archives and Museum of Design
Berlin Museum
Memorial Museum of the German Resistance
Museum of German Ethnology
Museum of Transport and Technology

Bruges, Belgium
Folklore Museum
Memling Museum
Museum of Our Lady of the Pottery

Brunswick, Germany
Museum of Brunswick
Museum of Lower Saxony

Brussels, Belgium
Museum of Brussels
Museum of Costume and Lace
Railway Museum
Royal Museum of the Army

Budapest, Hungary
Hungarian National Museum

Cologne, Germany
Diocesan Museum
Museum of the City of Cologne
Schnütgen Museum
Wallraf Richartz Museum

Copenhagen, Denmark
Copenhagen City Museum
National Museum
State Museum of Art
Theatre Museum

Delphi, Greece
Delphi Museum

Dresden, Germany
Semper Gallery
State Gallery of Art

Dublin, Ireland
Dublin Civic Museum
Guinness Museum
National Gallery of Ireland
National Museum of Ireland
National Transport Museum

Essen, Germany
Folkwang Museum

Florence, Italy
Accademia Gallery
Bardini Museum
Bargello Museum
Museum of the History of Science
Uffizi Gallery

Frankfurt, Germany
German Postal Museum
Goethe Museum
Historical Museum

Freiberg im Breisgau, Germany
Augustiner Museum
Museum of Modern Art
Museum of Natural History

Geneva, Switzerland
Museum of Art and History
Voltaire Museum

Genoa, Italy
Gallery of Modern Art
Palazzo Bianco
Palazzo Rosso

Haarlem, Netherlands
Frans Hals Museum

Hamburg, Germany
Altona Museum
Hamburg Art Gallery
Museum Village

Helsinki, Finland
Helsinki City Museum
Museum of Applied Arts
Museum of Finnish Architecture
Sports Museum of Finland

Istanbul, Turkey
Archaeological Museum
Hagia Sophia Museum
Museum of the Ancient Orient
Topkapi Palace Museum

Leipzig, Germany
Museum of Art

MUSEUMS AND ART GALLERIES — Europe (cont.)

Liège, Belgium
Liège Print Collection
Museum of Firearms
Museum of Walloon Life

Lisbon, Portugal
Calouste Gulbenkian Museum
Museum of Archaeology and Ethnology
Museum of Art
Museum of Contemporary Art
Vasco da Gama Aquarium

Madrid, Spain
Museum of Madrid
Museum of the Navy
National Museum of Ethnology
Palace of El Pardo
The Prado Museum

Milan, Italy
Brera Art Gallery
Castle of the Sforzas
Gallery of Modern Art
La Scala Museum of Theatre History
Leonardo da Vinci Museum of Science and Technology

Moscow, Russia
Armory Museum
Central Lenin Museum
Pushkin Museum of Fine Arts
Tretyakov Art Gallery

Munich, Germany
Bavarian National Museum
City Museum
Deutsches Museum
Residence Museum
State Collection of Minerals

Naples, Italy
Aquarium
Archaeological Museum
Palazzo Capodimonte

Olympia, Greece
Museum of Ancient Olympia

Oslo, Norway
Edvard Munch Museum
National Gallery
Norwegian Folk Museum
Ski Museum

Paris, France
Auguste Rodin Museum
Carnavalet Museum
The Louvre
Musée d'Orsay
Museum of Modern Art at the Pompidou Centre
Museum of Technology

Prague, Czechoslovakia
National Museum
State Jewish Museum

Rome, Italy
Borghese Gallery
National Gallery of Ancient Art
National Museum of Popular Art
Vatican Museums

Rotterdam, Netherlands
Rotterdam Museum: The Double Palmtree
Rotterdam Museum: Schielandshuis

St Petersburg, Russia
Museum of the History of Religion and Atheism
Russian Museum
State Hermitage Museum

Salzburg, Austria
Mozart's Birthplace
Residence Gallery

Siena, Italy
Siena Art Gallery
Siena Museum

Stockholm, Sweden
National Museum of Antiquities
Nordic Museum
Stockholm City Museum

The Hague, Netherlands
Netherlands Costume Museum
Sikkens Museum of Signs

Thessaloniki, Greece
Archaeological Museum
Macedonian Folk Art Museum

Toledo, Spain
El Greco Museum
Museum of the Alcazar of Toledo

Utrecht, Netherlands
Catharine Convent State Museum
Netherlands Railway Museum

Venice, Italy
Accademia Gallery
Correr Museum
Treasury of St Mark's

Versailles, France
Château de Versailles
Lambinet Museum

Vienna, Austria
Belvedere Gallery
Museum of the History of Art
Museum of Lower Austria
Treasury of the Holy Roman Empire

Warsaw, Poland
National Museum

Zürich, Switzerland
House for Art
Swiss National Museum

MUSEUMS AND ART GALLERIES — UK

Aberdeen, Scotland
Aberdeen Art Gallery

Bangor, Wales
Museum of Welsh Antiquities
Bangor Art Gallery

Bath, England
Victoria Art Gallery
Burrows Toy Museum

Belfast, Northern Ireland
Ulster Museum

Birmingham, England
The Barber Institute of Fine Arts
City Museum and Art Gallery
National Motocycle Museum
Cambridge and County Folk Museum

Cambridge, England
The Fitzwilliam Museum
Kettle's Yard
Museum of Classical Archaeology

Cardiff, Wales
National Museum of Wales
Welsh Folk Museum (at St Fagans)

Edinburgh, Scotland
City Art Centre
The Georgian House
Gladstone's Land
Museum of Childhood
National Gallery of Scotland
Royal Museum of Scotland (previously the Royal Scottish Museum and the National Museum of Antiquities of Scotland)
Scottish National Gallery of Modern Art
Scottish National Portrait Gallery

Glasgow, Scotland
Art Gallery and Museum
The Burrell Collection
Hunterian Art Gallery and Museum
Museum of Transport
People's Palace Museum
The Tenement House

Leeds, England
City Art Gallery
Leeds Industrial Museum

Leicester, England
East Midlands Gas Museum

Liverpool, England
Lark Lane Motor Museum
Liverpool Museum

London, England
The British Museum
Courtauld Institute Galleries
Dulwich College Picture Gallery
Imperial War Museum
Institute of Contemporary Arts
London Toy and Model Museum
London Transport Museum
Museum of London
Museum of Mankind
The National Gallery
National Maritime Museum
The National Portrait Gallery
Natural History Museum
Pollock's Toy Museum
Royal College of Music, Museum of Instruments
Science Museum
The Serpentine Gallery
The Tate Gallery
Victoria and Albert Museum
The Wallace Collection
The Wellcome Museum of the History of Medicine

Manchester, England
Greater Manchester Museum of Science and Industry
Manchester City Art Gallery
Manchester Jewish Museum
The Manchester Museum
Whitworth Art Gallery

Newcastle upon Tyne, England
Blackfriars Museum of Antiquities
Museum of Science and Engineering

Oxford, England
Ashmolean Museum of Art and Archaeology
The Bate Collection of Historical Instruments
Museum of Modern Art
Museum of the History of Science
Pitt-Rivers Museum

Reading, England
Museum of English Rural Life

Sheffield, England
Abbeydale Industrial Hamlet
Kelham Island Industrial Museum
Sheffield City Museum

Southampton, England
Southampton Art Gallery
Southampton Maritime Museum

Swansea, Wales
Glynn Vivian Art Gallery and Museum
Swansea Maritime and Industrial Museum

York, England
National Railway Museum
York Castle Museum
York City Art Gallery
Yorkshire Museum

MUSEUMS AND ART GALLERIES — USA

Atlanta, Georgia
High Museum of Art

Baltimore, Maryland
Baltimore Museum of Art
Walters Art Gallery

Boston, Massachusetts
Isabella Stewart Gardner Museum
Museum of Fine Arts
Museum of Science and Hayden Planetarium

Buffalo, New York
Albright-Knox Art Gallery
Buffalo Fine Arts Academy

Cambridge, Massachusetts
Botanical Museum
Fogg Art Museum
Peabody Museum of Archaeology and Ethnology

Charleston, South Carolina
Charleston Museum
Museum of Coastal History

Chicago, Illinois
Art Institute of Chicago
Field Museum of Natural History

Cincinnati, Ohio
Cincinnati Art Museum

Cleveland, Ohio
Cleveland Museum of Art

Dallas, Texas
Dallas Museum of Fine Arts

Denver, Colorado
Denver Art Museum
Museum of Natural History

Des Moines, Iowa
Des Moines Art Center
Living History Farms (at Urbandale)

Detroit, Michigan
Detroit Institute of Arts
Henry Ford Museum

Dodge City, Kansas
Boot Hill Museum

Duluth, Minnesota
Canal Park Marine Museum

Fort Myers, Florida
Edison Winter Home

Gainsville, Florida
Florida State Museum

Hartford, Connecticut
Wadsworth Atheneum

Honolulu, Hawaii
Bishop Museum
Honolulu Academy of Arts

Houston, Texas
Baker Planetarium, and the Museum of Medical Science
Houston Museum of Natural Science, Burke
Museum of Fine Arts

Indianapolis, Indiana
Children's Museum
Herron Museum of Art
Indianapolis Museum of Art

Kansas City, Missouri
Nelson Atkins Museum of Art
St Louis Art Museum

Los Angeles, California
California Museum of Science and Industry
George C Page Museum of La Brea Discoveries
Jean Paul Getty Museum (at Malibu)
Los Angeles County Museum of Art
Museum of Contemporary Art
Southwest Museum

Minneapolis, Minnesota
Minneapolis Institute of Arts
Walker Art Center

Mystic, Connecticut
Mystic Seaport Museum

Nashville, Tennessee
Carl Van Vechter Gallery

New Orleans, Louisiana
Delgado Museum of Art
Louisiana State Museum

New York City, New York
American Museum of Natural History
Asia House Gallery
Brooklyn Museum
Frick Collection
Gallery of Modern Art
Guggenheim Museum
Metropolitan Museum of Art and the Cloisters Morgan Library
Museum of Holography
Museum of Modern Art
Museum of the American Indian
Museum of the City of New York
Solomon R Guggenheim Museum
Whitney Museum of American Art

Oklahoma City, Oklahoma
National Cowboy Hall of Fame

Orlando, Florida
Beal-Maltbie Shell Museum
Morse Gallery of Art

Philadelphia, Pennsylvania
Academy of Natural Sciences
Barnes Foundation Collection (in Merion, Pennsylvania)
Franklin Institute Science Museum
Pennsylvania Academy of the Fine Arts
Philadelphia Museum of Art
Rodin Museum
University Museum of Archaeology and Anthropology

Pittsburgh, Pennsylvania
Carnegie Institute Museum of Art

MUSEUMS AND ART GALLERIES — USA (cont.)

Plymouth, Massachusetts
Plymoth Plantation

Portland, Oregon
Oregon Art Institute

Reno, Nevada
Harrah's Auto Collection

Rochester, New York
Rochester Memorial Art Gallery

Salt Lake City, Utah
The Museum of Church History and Art

San Francisco, California
Asian Art Museum
California Academy of Sciences
California Palace of the Legion of Honor
M H De Young Memorial Museum
San Francisco Museum of Art

Santa Fé, California
El Rancho de las Golondririas (at Cienega)
Museum of Indian Art and Culture
Museum of International Folk Art

San Marino, California
Huntington Library and Art Gallery

Sarasota, Florida
Ringling Museum of Art

Seattle, Washington
Seattle Art Museum

Toledo, Ohio
Toledo Museum of Art

Tulsa, Oklahoma
Philbrook Art Centre

Washington, District of Columbia
Corcoran Gallery of Art
Dumbarton Oaks Collection
Freer Gallery of Art
Museum of Modern Art of Latin America
National Air and Space Museum
National Archives
National Gallery of Art
National Museum of American Art
National Museum of American History
Smithsonian Institute
Washington Gallery of Modern Art

Williamsburg, Virginia
Abby Aldrich
Rockefeller Folk Art Collection
Colonial Willamsburg

Williamstown, Massachusetts
Sterling and Francine Clark Art Institute

UNIVERSITIES — Europe (EC)

This includes all universities with enrolments of 5 000 or more in 1991–2.

Belgium

Name	Location	Year founded	Enrolment
Free University of Brussels (Flemish)	Brussels	1834, present status 1970	7 500
Free University of Brussels (French)	Brussels	1834, present status 1970	14 878
State University of Ghent	Ghent	1817	14 164
University of Liège	Liège	1817	10 068
Catholic University Of Louvain (Flemish)	Louvain	1425, present status 1970	23 953
Catholic University Of Louvain (French)	Louvain-le-Neuve	1425, present status 1970	17 998

Denmark

Name	Location	Year founded	Enrolment
Aalborg Universitets Center	Aalborg	1974	8 500
University of Aarhus	Aarhus	1928	13 000
University of Copenhagen	Copenhagen	1479	26 355
University of Odense	Odense	1964	7 240
Technical Univesity of Denmark	Copenhagen	1829	5 655

France

Name	Location	Year founded	Enrolment
Université d'Aix-Marseille I (Université de Provence)	Marseilles	1970	18 687
Université d'Aix-Marseille II	Marseilles	1973	19 160
Université d'Aix-Marseille III (Université de Droit, d'Economie et des Sciences)	Aix-en-Provence	1973	18 118
Université de Bordeaux I	Talence	—	18 647
Université de Bordeaux II	Bordeaux	—	14 565
Université de Bordeaux III	Talence	—	14 686
Université de Bourgogne	Dijon	—	20 572
Université de Bretagne Occidentale	Brest	—	15 420
Université de Caen	Caen	1432, reorganized 1985	22 500
Université de Clermont-Ferrand I	Clermont-Ferrand	1976, present status 1985	9 638
Université de Clermont-Ferrand II (Université Blaise Pascal)	Clermont-Ferrand	1810, present status 1984	13 645
Université de Franche-Comté	Besançon	1422 at Dôle, 1691 at Besançon	16 000
Université de Grenoble I (Université Joseph Fourier)	Grenoble	—	13 585
Université de Grenoble II (Université Pierre Mendès-France)	Grenoble	1970	18 500
Université de Grenoble III (Université Stendhal)	Grenoble	1810	5 772
Université Jean Monnet (Université de Saint Étienne)	Saint Étienne	1969, present name 1991	11 679

UNIVERSITIES — Europe (EC) (cont.)

France (cont.)

Name	Location	Year founded	Enrolment
Université de Lille I (Université des Sciences et Techniques de Lille Flandres Artois)	Villeneuve d'Ascq	1855 as Faculty of Sciences, present status 1971	19 124
Université de Lille II (Droit et Santé)	Lille	1969	17 481
Université de Lille III (Sciences Humaines, Lettres et Arts)	Villeneuve d'Ascq	1560, present status 1985	21 826
Université de Limoges	Limoges	1808; closed 1840; reopened 1965	11 615
Université Lyon I (Université Claude-Bernard)	Villeurbanne	1970	23 000
Université Lyon II	Lyons	—	19 914
Université Lyon III (Université Jean Moulin)	Lyons	1973	15 136
Université de Maine	Le Mans	1969	7 821
Université de Metz	Metz	1971	10 635
Université de Montpellier I	Montpellier	1970	17 880
Université de Montpellier II (Université des Sciences et Techniques de Languedoc)	Montpellier	—	11 000
Université de Montpellier III (Université Paul Valéry)	Montpellier	1970	15 500
Université de Nancy I	Nancy	1970	15 083
Université de Nancy II	Nancy	1970	17 028
Université de Nantes	Nantes	—	—
Université de Nice	Nice	1971	21 749
Université d'Orléans	Orléans	1971	12 200
Université de Paris I (Panthéon-Sorbonne)	Paris	1971	36 795
Université de Paris II (Université Panthéon-Assas)	Paris	1970	18 654
Université de Paris III (Sorbonne-Nouvelle)	Paris	1970	—
Université de Paris IV (Paris-Sorbonne)	Paris	1970	23 630
Université de Paris V (René Descartes)	Paris	1970	32 386
Université de Paris VI (Pierre et Marie Curie)	Paris	—	—
Université de Paris VII	Paris	1970	30 000
Université de Paris VIII (Vincennes à St-Denis)	St Denis	1969	22 350
Université de Paris IX (Paris-Dauphine)	Paris	1968	5 600
Université de Paris X (Paris-Nanterre)	Nanterre	—	32 000
Université de Paris XI (Paris-Sud)	Orsay	1970	25 000
Université de Paris XII (Paris-Val-de-Marne)	Créteil	1970	18 000
Université de Paris XIII (Pais-Nord)	Villetaneuse	1970	13 459
Université de Pau et des Pays de l'Adour	Pau	1970	11 000
Université de Picardie	Amiens	1965	10 000
Université de Poitiers	Poitiers	1432	22 000
Université de Reims Champagne-Ardenne	Reims	1548	20 500
Université de Rennes I	Rennes	—	23 500
Université de Rennes II (Université de Haute Bretagne)	Rennes	—	13 000
Université de Rouen	Mont-Saint-Aignan	1966	19 908
Université de Savoie (Chambéry)	Chambéry	1970	6 705
Université de Strasbourg I (Université Louis Pasteur)	Strasbourg	1971	14 321

UNIVERSITIES — Europe (EC) (cont.)

Name	Location	Year founded	Enrolment
Université de Strasbourg II (Sciences Humaines)	Strasbourg	1538	11 000
Université de Strasbourg III (Université Robert Schumann)	Strasbourg	—	8 300
Université de Toulouse I (Sciences Sociales)	Toulouse	1229	14 700
Université de Toulouse II (Le Mirail)	Toulouse	—	20 111
Université de Toulouse III (Université Paul Sabatier)	Toulouse	—	—
Université de Tours (Université François Rabelais)	Tours	1970	22 000
Université de Valenciennes et du Hainaut-Cambresis	Valenciennes	1964	8 000

Germany

Name	Location	Year founded	Enrolment
Rheinisch-Westfälische Technische Hochschule Aachen	Aachen	1870, university status 1880	37 043
Universität Augsburg	Augsburg	1970	12 766
Otto Friedrich Universität Bamberg	Bamberg	1647	7 500
Universität Bayreuth	Bayreuth	1972	8 500
Humboldt-Universität zu Berlin	Berlin	1809	21 000
Hochschule für Ökonomie 'Bruno Leuschner'	Berlin	1950	—
Freie Universität Berlin	Berlin	1948	60 000
Technische Universität Berlin	Berlin	Bauakademie (f.1799) and Gewer beakademie (f.1821), amalgamated 1879 as Technische Hochschule; opened under present title 1946	35 000
Universität Bielefeld	Bielefeld	1969	13 500
Ruhr-Universität Bochum	Bochum	1961	36 000
Rheinische Friedrich-Wilhelms-Universität Bonn	Bonn	founded 1786; refounded 1818	38 000
Technische Universität Carolo Wilhelmina zu Braunschweig	Braunschweig	1745, present title 1968	17 000
Universität Bremen	Bremen	1971	13 100
Technische Universität (Karl-Marx-Stadt) Chemnitz	Chemnitz	1836	8 000[1]
Technische Hochschule Darmstadt	Darmstadt	1836, university status 1895	17 900
Universität Dortmund	Dortmund-Eichlinghafen	1966	21 777
Technische Universität Dresden	Dresden	1828, university status 1961	15 500, incl 1 200 external students[1]
Universität Duisburg Gesamthochschule	Duisburg	1972	14 500
Heinrich-Heine-Universität Düsseldorf	Düsseldorf	1965 (formerly Medizinische Akademie f.1907)	16 000

UNIVERSITIES — Europe (EC) (cont.)

Germany (cont.)

Name	Location	Year founded	Enrolment
Friedrich-Alexander-Universität Erlangen-Nürnberg	Erlangen	1743	27 500
University Essen-Gesamtshochschule	Essen	1972	c.17 500
Johann Wolfgang Goethe-Universität Frankfurt	Frankfurt am Main	1914	34 373
Justus-Liebig-Universität Giessen	Giessen	1607	20 500
Georg-August-Universität Göttingen	Göttingen	1737	30 000
Albert-Ludwigs-Universität Freiburg	Freiburg	1457	23 600
Martin Luther-Universität Halle-Wittenberg	Halle	1502 Wittenberg; 1694 Halle; 1817 Halle-Wittenberg	8 642[1]
Universität Hamburg	Hamburg	—	43 114
Universität Hannover	Hanover	1831	28 200
Ruprecht-Karls-Universität Heidelberg	Heidelberg	1386	27 500
Universität Hohenheim	Stuttgart (Hohenheim)	1818	6 200
Friedrich-Schiller Universität	Jena	1548, university status 1558	5 105
Universität Kaiserslautern	Kaiserslautern	1970	9 394
Universität Fridericiana Karlsruhe	Karlsruhe	1825	21 153
Gesamthochschule Kassel	Kassel	1970	14 938
Christian-Albrechts Universität zu Kiel	Kiel	1665	18 600
Universität Konstanz	Konstanz	1966	8 977
Deutsche Sporthochschule Köln	Cologne	1947	c.6 000
Universitat zu Köln	Cologne	1388	54 000
Universität Leipzig	Leipzig	1409	c.14 800[1]
Johannes Gutenberg-Universität Mainz	Mainz	1477; closed 1816; reopened 1946	26 000
Universität Mannheim	Mannheim	1907, university status 1967	c.9 800
Philipps-Universität Marburg	Marburg	1527	16 909
Ludwig-Maximilians-Universität München	Munich	1472	60 000
Technische Universität München	Munich	1868	24 123
Westfälische Wilhelms-Universität Münster	Münster	1780	45 942
Universität Oldenburg	Oldenburg	1974	10 949
Universität Osnabrück	Osnabruck	1973	c.8 750
Open University	Hagen	1974	30 008 full- and part-time, 10 735 associate
Universität-Gesamthochschule Paderborn	Paderborn	1972	16 300
Universität Passau	Passau	1972	7 876

UNIVERSITIES — Europe (EC) (cont.)

Name	Location	Year founded	Enrolment
Universität Regensburg	Regensburg	1962	c.13 000
Universität Rostock	Rostock	1419	6 000
Universität Des Saarlandes	Saarbrücken	1948	20 000
Universität-Gesamthochschule Siegen	Siegen	1972	11 500
Universität Stuttgart	Stuttgart	1829, university status 1967	21 300
Universität Trier	Trier	1970	9 770
Eberhard-Karls-Universität Tübingen	Tübingen	1477	24 866
Univesität Ulm	Ulm	1967	5 500
Bergische Universität-Gesamthochschule Wuppertal	Wuppertal	1972	16 500
Bayerische-Julius-Maximilians-Universität Würzburg	Würzburg	1582	18 281

Greece

Name	Location	Year founded	Enrolment
Aristotelian University of Thessaloniki	Thessaloniki	1925	56 000
'Demokritos' University of Thrace	Komotini	1973	6 856
National and Capodistrian University of Athens	Athens	1837	45 000
National Technical University of Athens	Athens	1836	8 019
University of Ioannina	Ioannina	1964 as part of Aristotelian University; independent status 1970	9 100
University of Macedonia	Thessaloniki	1957	6 509
University of Patras	Patras	1964	8 900

Republic of Ireland

Name	Location	Year founded	Enrolment
University of Dublin Trinity College	Dublin	1592	9 250
National University of Ireland	Dublin	1908	
Three constituent colleges:			
University College Dublin	Dublin	1909	12 544
University College Cork	Cork	1845 as Queen's College; 1908	7 117
University College Galway	Galway	1845 as Queen's College; 1908	5 613
University of Limerick	Limerick	1970, university status 1989	5 925

Italy

Name	Location	Year founded	Enrolment
Università degli Studi di Ancona	Ancona	1969	6 731
Università degli Studi di Bari	Bari	1924	42 439
Università degli Studi	Bologna	11th-c	59 111
Università degli Studi di Brescia	Brescia	1982	6 134

UNIVERSITIES — Europe (EC) (cont.)

Italy (cont.)

Name	Location	Year founded	Enrolment
Università di Cagliari	Cagliari, Sardinia	1606	c.18 000
Università di Calabria	Commenda di Rende	1972	6 000
Università di Camerino	Camerino	1336, university status 1727	5 000
Università degli Studi di Cassino	Cassino	1982	—
Università di Catania	Catania	1434	35 421
Università degli Studi	Ferrara	1391	6 019
Università degli Studi	Florence	1321	46 355
Università degli Studi di Genova	Genoa	1471	30 411
Università degli Studi dell' Aquila	L'Aquila	1952	8 260
Università degli Studi di Lecce	Lecce	1956	12 000
Università degli Studi di Macerata	Macerata	1290	7 144
Università degli Studi	Messina	1548	28 602, incl 6 754 part-time
Università degli Studi di Milano	Milan	1924	77 463
Università degli Studi	Modena	1175	8 156
Università degli Studi del Molise	Campobasso	1982	—
Università degli Studi	Naples	1224	c.100 000
Università degli Studi di Padua	Padua	1222	c.49 861
Università degli Studi	Palermo	1777	c.20 000
Università degli Studi	Parma	1064	c.17 000
Università degli Studi di Pavia	Pavia	1361	25 003
Università degli Studi di Perugia	Perugia	1200	19 266
Università degli Studi	Pisa	1343	28 000
Università di Reggio Calabria	Reggio Calabria	1982	—
Università degli Studi di Roma 'La Sapienza'	Rome	1303	180 000
Università degli Studi di Roma 'Tor Vergata'	Rome	1985	—
Università degli Studi di Salerno	Fisciano (Salerno)	1970	—
Università degli Studi	Sassari	1562	9 500
Università degli Studi	Siena	1240	11 000
Università degli Studi di Torino	Turin	1404	50 058
Università degli Studi di Trento	Trento	1962	9 051
Università degli Studi di Trieste	Trieste	1938	18 565
Università degli Studi della Tuscia	Viterbo	1981	—
Università degli Studi di Udine	Udine	1977	8 000
Università degli Studi di Urbino	Urbino	1506	15 700
Università degli Studi di Venezia	Venice	1868	18 059
Università degli Studi di Verona	Verona	1982	9 308
Politecnico di Milàno	Milan	1863	43 771
Politecnico di Torino	Turin	1859	17 742
Catholic University of the Sacred Heart	Milan	1920, present status 1924	28 200
Università Commerciale Luigi Bocconi	Milan	1902	10 500
Università Italiana per Stranieri	Perugia	1921	c.7 000

UNIVERSITIES — Europe (EC) (cont.)

The Netherlands

Name	Location	Year founded	Enrolment
University of Amsterdam	Amsterdam	1632	27 000
Free University, Amsterdam	Amsterdam	1880	12 000
Delft University of Technology	Delft	1842	14 500
Eindhoven University of Technology	Eindhoven	1956	7 041
Twente University of Technology	Enschede	1961	6 500
University of Groningen	Groningen	1614	18 000
Open University	Heerlen	1984	50 000
Leiden University	Leiden	1575	17 933
University of Limburg	Maastricht	1976	6 000
Catholic University Nijmegen	Nijmegen	1923	c.13 000
Erasmus University Rotterdam	Rotterdam	1973	18 000
Tilburg University	Tilburg	1927	9 000
Utrecht University	Utrecht	1636	23 000
Agricultural University	Wageningen	1918	6 000

Portugal

Name	Location	Year founded	Enrolment
Universidade Autónoma de Lisboa 'Luis de Camões'	Lisbon	1977	5 000
Universidade Católica Portuguesa	Lisbon	1968	8 400
Universidade de Coímbra	Coímbra	1290 (in Lisbon)	13 090
Universidade de Lisboa	Lisbon	1288, restored 1911	17 195
Universidade de Minho	Braga	1973	6 200
Universidade do Porto	Porto	1911	18 000
New University of Lisbon	Lisbon	1973	6 853
Universidade Técnica de Lisboa	Lisbon	1930	14 058

Spain

Name	Location	Year founded	Enrolment
Open University	Madrid	1972	104 135
Universidad de Alcalá de Henares	Alcalá de Henares (Madrid)	1977	14 777
Universidad de Alicante	Alicante	1979	11 000
Universitat de Barcelona	Barcelona	1450	80 566
Universitat Autónoma de Barcelona	Barcelona Bellaterra (Barcelona)	1968	36 118
Universidad de Cádiz	Cádiz	1979	14 822
Universidad de Cantabria	Santander	1972 as Universidad de Santander	12 019
Universidad de Castilla-la-Mancha	Ciudad Real	1982	12 000
Universidad Pontificia 'Comillas'	Madrid	1890 in Santander; moved to Madrid 1960	15 819

UNIVERSITIES — Europe (EC) (cont.)

Spain (cont.)

Name	Location	Year founded	Enrolment
Universidad de Córdoba	Córdoba	1972	14 000
Universidad de Deusto	Bilbao	1886	14 386
Universidad de Extremadura	Cáceres	1973	12 320
Universidad de Granada	Granada	1526	56 231
Universidad de La Laguna	La Laguna, Canary Is	1701	16 000
Universidad de Las Palmas de Gran Canaria	Las Palmas, Canary Is	1980	10 000
Universidad de León	León	1979	10 299
Universidad Complutense de Madrid	Madrid	1508	126 617
Universidad Autónoma de Madrid	Madrid	1968	28 000
Universidad de Málaga	Málaga	1972	23 058
Universidad de Murcia	Murcia	1915	26 437
Universidad de Navarra	Pamplona	1952	15 341
Universidad de Oviedo	Oviedo	1608	28 670
University of the Basque Country	Bilbao	1968, reorganized 1980	46 748
Universitat de Les Illes Balears	Palma de Mallorca	1978	8 570
Universidad Pontificia de Salamanca	Salamanca	1134 as Ecclesiastical School, university status 1219; defunct by end 18th-c, restored 1940	8 500
Universidad de Salamanca	Salamanca	1218, reorganized 1254	c.24 000
Universidad de Sevilla	Seville	1502	46 677
Universitat de València	Valencia	1510	55 317
Universidad de Valladolid	Valladolid	13th-c	36 000
Universidad de Zaragoza	Zaragoza	1583	40 000

[1]1989–90 figures

UNIVERSITIES — UK

Name	Location	Year founded	Enrolment (1990–1)
University of Aberdeen	Aberdeen	1495	7 200
Anglia Polytechnic University	main campuses Chelmsford and Cambridge	1905[1] as Chelmsford School of Science and Art	10 700, incl part-time
Aston University	Birmingham	1966	4 791
University of Bath	Bath	1966	4 336
The University of Birmingham	Birmingham	1900	9 742

UNIVERSITIES — UK (cont.)

Name	Location	Year founded	Enrolment (1990–1)
Bournemouth University	Poole	1976[1] as Dorset Institute of Higher Education	6 419, incl sandwich; 1 778 part-time; 522 post graduate
University of Bradford	Bradford	1966	5 305
University of Brighton	Brighton	1970	6 232
The University of Bristol	Bristol	1909	8 429
Brunel University	Uxbridge	1966	c.3 123
University of Buckingham	Buckingham	1983	8 627[2]
The University of Cambridge	Cambridge		10 382[2] (in residence)
Christ's		1505	
Churchill		1960	
Clare		1326	
Clare Hall		1966	
Corpus Christi		1352	
Darwin		1964	
Downing		1800	
Emmanuel		1584	
Fitzwilliam		1966	
Girton		1869	
Gonville & Caius		1348	
Homerton		1824	
Hughes Hall		1885	
Jesus		1496	
King's		1441	
Lucy Cavendish		1965	
Magdalene		1542	
New Hall		1954	
Newham		1871	
Pembroke		1347	
Peterhouse		1284	
Queen's		1448	
Robinson		1977	
St Catherine's		1473	
St Edmund's		1896	
St John's		1511	
Selwyn		1882	
Sidney Sussex		1596	
Trinity		1546	
Trinity Hall		1350	
Wolfson		1965	
City University	London	1966	4 468
University of Central England in Birmingham	Birmingham	1971[1]	6 000 full-time; 7 000 part-time
University of Central Lancashire	Preston	1956[1]	5 500 full-time; 4 000 part-time

UNIVERSITIES — UK (cont.)

Name	Location	Year founded	Enrolment (1990–1)
City of London University	London	1970[1]	15 000, incl part-time
Coventry University	Coventry	1970[1]	8 314
Cranfield Institute of Technology	Bedford	1969	2 091
De Montfort University	Leicester	1969[1]	6 325 full-time; 2 300 part-time
University of Dundee	Dundee	1967	4 308
The University of Durham	Durham	1832	5 592
The University of East Anglia	Norwich	1963	4 786
University of East London	London	1970[1]	6 100 full-time; 2 600 part-time
University of Edinburgh	Edinburgh	1583	12 158
The University of Essex	Colchester	1964	3 293
The University of Exeter	Exeter	1955	6 819
University of Glamorgan	Pontypridd	1913[1] as mining college	4 944 full-time; 1 629 part-time
University of Glasgow	Glasgow	1451	13 142
Glasgow Polytechnic (awaiting university title)	Glasgow	Queen's College 1875; Glasgow Polytechnic 1971[1]; merged 1992	Queen's College 1 773; Glasgow Polytechnic 5 605 full-time; 2 522 part-time
University of Greenwich	Woolwich	1890[1]	10 000
University of Hertfordshire	Hatfield	1952[1]	8 000
University of Huddersfield	Huddersfield	1841[1]	5 900 full-time; 2 500 part-time
Heriot-Watt University	Edinburgh	1966	6 000
The University of Hull	Hull	1954	6 819
University of Humberside	Hull	1978[1]	8 000
The University of Keele	Newcastle under Lyme	1962	3 715
University of Kent at Canterbury	Canterbury	1965	4 886
Kingston University	Kingston-upon-Thames	1970[1]	6 860
The University of Lancaster	Lancaster	1964	5 318
The University of Leeds	Leeds	1904	12 393
Leeds Metropolitan University	Leeds	1970[1]	8 105 full-time; 6 189 part-time
The University of Leicester	Leicester	1957	6 203
The University of Liverpool	Liverpool	1903	9 504
Liverpool John Moores University	Liverpool	1970[1]	9 008 full-time; 4 585 part-time

UNIVERSITIES — UK (cont.)

Name	Location	Year founded	Enrolment (1990–1)
The University of London	London	1836	54 521 internal; 24 856 external
Birkbeck College		1823	332 full-time; 3 619 part-time
Goldsmiths' College		1904	3 600
Imperial College of Science, Technology, and Medicine		1907	6 569
Institute of Education		1902; controlled by London University since 1932; School of London University since 1987	1 209 full-time; 1 429 part-time
King's College London		1829	6 873
London School of Economics and Political Science		1895	4 123 full-time; 729 part-time
Queen Mary and Westfield College		Queen Mary 1887; Westfield 1882; merged 1989	5 454
Royal Holloway and Bedford New College	Egham	Royal Holloway 1886; Bedford 1849; merged 1985	3 327
Royal Veterinary College		1791	424
School of Oriental and African Studies		1916	1 285
School of Pharmacy		1842	523
University College		1826	9 138
Wye College	Ashford	1447	700
Loughborough University of Technology	Loughborough	1966	5 887
The University of Manchester	Manchester	1851	13 000
University of Manchester Institute of Science and Technology	Manchester	1824	5 100
Manchester Polytechnic	Manchester	1970[1]	9 621 full-time; 2 689 sandwich; 6 400 part-time
Middlesex University	London	1973[1]	4 869 full-time; 3 268 sandwich; 1 777 part-time
Napier University	Edinburgh	1964[1]	c.4 800 full-time; 3 500 part-time
The University of Newcastle upon Tyne	Newcastle upon Tyne	1852	9 090
University of North London	London	1971[1]	7 500, incl part-time

UNIVERSITIES — UK (cont.)

Name	Location	Year founded	Enrolment (1990–1)
University of Northumbria at Newcastle	Newcastle	1969[1]	8 870 full-time; 4 092 part-time
City University Nottingham	Nottingham	1970[1]	9 618 full-time; 4 453 part-time
The University of Nottingham	Nottingham	1948	8 500
The Open University	Milton Keynes	1969	185 000
The University of Oxford	Oxford		139 487[2] (in residence)
All Souls		1438	
Balliol		1263	
Brasenose		1509	
Christ Church		1546	
Corpus Christi		1517	
Exeter		1314	
Green		1979	
Hertford		1874	
Jesus		1571	
Keble		1868	
Lady Margaret Hall		1878	
Linacre		1962	
Lincoln		1427	
Magdalen		1458	
Merton		1263	
New College		1379	
Nuffield		1937	
Oriel		1326	
Pembroke		1624	
Queen's		1340	
Rewley House		1990	
St Anne's		1952	
St Antony's		1950	
St Catherine's		1962	
St Cross		1965	
St Edmund Hall		c.1278	
St Hilda's		1938	
St Hugh's		1886	
St John's		1555	
St Peter's		1929	
Somerville		1879	
Trinity		1554	
University		1249	
Wadham		1612	
Wolfson		1966	
Worcester		1714	
Oxford Polytechnic (awaiting university title)		1970	6 450 full-time; 2 900 part-time

UNIVERSITIES — UK (cont.)

Name	Location	Year founded	Enrolment (1990–1)
University of Paisley		1897	4 092 full-time; 995 part-time
University of Plymouth	Plymouth	1970[1]	7 700 full-time; 1 100 part-time
University of Portsmouth	Portsmouth	1870[1]	7 100 full-time; 1 000 part-time
The Queen's University of Belfast	Belfast	1908	7 867
The University of Reading	Reading	1926	7 600
Robert Gordon University	Aberdeen	1885[1]	4 479
University of St Andrews	St Andrews	1411	4 298
University of Salford	Salford	1967	328
The University of Sheffield	Sheffield	1905	8 884[3]
Sheffield Hallam University	Sheffield	1969[1]	8 931 full-time; 4 789 part-time
South Bank University	London	1970[1]	11 000
The University of Southampton	Southampton	1952	7 822
Staffordshire University	Stoke-on-Trent	1970[1]	3 706 full-time; 1 952 sandwich; 2 400 part-time
University of Stirling	Stirling	1967	3 600
University of Strathclyde	Glasgow	1964	8 500
University of Sunderland	Sunderland	1969[1]	4 376 full-time; 1 401 part-time
University of Surrey	Guildford	1966	4 546
The University of Sussex	Brighton	1961	6 014
University of Teesside	Middlesbrough	1929[1]	7 000
Thames Valley University	W London	1991[4]	5 900 full-time; 9 000 part-time
University of Ulster	Coleraine	1984	11 140
The University of Wales	Cardiff	1893	24 449
University College of Wales	Aberystwyth	1872	4 332
University College of North Wales	Bangor	1884	2 999
University of Wales College of Cardiff	Cardiff	1988	9 000
St David's College, Lampeter	Lampeter	1827, present status 1971	1 100
University College, Swansea	Swansea	1920	5 800
University of Wales College of Medicine	Cardiff	1931, present status 1984	1 218
The University of Warwick	Coventry	1965	7 222
University of the West of England	Bristol	1969[1]	7 000 full-time; 5 000 part-time

UNIVERSITIES — UK (cont.)

Name	Location	Year founded	Enrolment (1990–1)
University of Westminster	London	1970[1]	5 000 full-time; 6 500 part-time; 18 000 short course
University of Wolverhampton	Wolverhampton	1969[1]	7 362 full-time; 4 885 part-time
The University of York	York	1963	4 516
Royal College of Art	London	1837	635

[1]Founded as a polytechnic or other college; university status applied for in 1992; 1991–2 enrolment figures
[2]1991–2 enrolment figures
[3]1989–90 enrolment figures
[4]Formerly Ealing College of Higher Education

AMERICAN COLLEGES AND UNIVERSITIES

This listing includes the following categories of accredited undergraduate four-year colleges (institutions awarding a bachelor's as their highest undergraduate degree) in the United States: independent (nonprofit), independent-religious, state, district, city, state and local, and state-related colleges with total enrolments of 10 000 or more; colleges founded before 1800, regardless of total enrolment; and well-known colleges, regardless of total enrolment.

Name	Location	Year founded	Enrolment (1990–1)
Abilene Christian University	Abilene, Texas	1906	4 053
Adelphi University	Garden City, New York	1896	8 754
American University	Washington, DC	1893	10 153
Amherst College	Amherst, Massachusetts	1821	1 580
Appalachian State University	Boone, North Carolina	1899	11 483
Arizona State University	Tempe	1885	42 952
Auburn University	Auburn University, Alabama	1856	21 537
Ball State University	Muncie, Indiana	1918	19 344
Barnard College	New York, New York	1889	19 250
Baruch College of the City University of New York		1968	15 853
Baylor University	Waco, Texas	1845	12 109
Bellarmine College	Louisville, Kentucky	1950	2 479
Boise State University	Boise, Idaho	1932	12 848
Boston College	Chestnut Hill, Massachusetts	1863	14 515
Boston University		1839	24 071
Bowdoin College	Brunswick, Maine	1794	1 350
Bowling Green State University	Bowling Green, Ohio	1910	18 040
Brandeis University	Waltham, Massachusetts	1948	3 793
Brigham Young University	Provo, Utah	1875	27 380
Brooklyn College of the City University of New York		1930	16 042
Brown University	Providence, Rhode Island	1764	7 577
Bryn Mawr College	Bryn Mawr, Pennsylvania	1885	1 885
Bucknell University	Lewisburg, Pennsylvania	1846	3 634

AMERICAN COLLEGES AND UNIVERSITIES (cont.)

Name	Location	Year founded	Enrolment (1990–1)
California Institute of Technology	Pasadena	1891	1 861
California Polytechnic State University	San Luis Obispo	1901	17 758
California Polytechnic State University	Pomona	1938	19 472
California State University	Bakersfield	1970	5 452
California State University	Chico	1887	16 641
California State University, Dominguez Hills	Carson	1960	9 450
California State University	Fresno	1911	19 586
California State University	Fullerton	1957	25 602
California State University	Hayward	1957	13 000
California State University	Long Beach	1949	33 991
California State University	Los Angeles	1847	21 596
California State University	Northridge	1958	31 166
California State University	Sacramento	1947	26 339
California State University	San Bernardino	1965	11 927
Carnegie Mellon University	Pittsburgh, Pennsylvania	1900	7 056
Case Western Reserve University	Cleveland, Ohio	1826	8 557
Catholic University of America	Washington, DC	1887	6 600
Central Connecticut State University	New Britain	1849	10 568
Central Michigan University	Mount Pleasant	1892	16 866
Central Missouri State University	Warrensburg	1871	11 429
Central State University	Edmond, Oklahoma	1890	14 214
The Citadel, The Military College of South Carolina	Charleston	1842	3 670
City College of the City University of New York		1847	14 090
Clarkson University	Potsdam, New York	1896	3 329
Clemson University	Clemson, South Carolina	1889	16 303
Cleveland State University	Cleveland, Ohio	1964	19 220
Colgate University	Hamilton, New York	1819	2 710
College of the Holy Cross	Worcester, Massachusetts	1843	2 738
College of Staten Island of the City University of New York		1955	12 185
College of William and Mary	Williamsburg, Virginia	1693	7 672
Colorado School of Mines	Golden	1874	2 446
Colorado State University	Fort Collins	1862	20 795
Columbia College	New York, New York	1754	3 243
Columbia University School of Engineering and Applied Science	New York, New York	1864	2 036
Columbia University School of General Studies	New York, New York	1754	1 196
Converse College	Spartanburg, South Carolina	1889	1 224
Cooper Union for the Advancement of Science and Art	New York, New York	1859	1 036
Cornell University	Ithaca, New York	1865	18 389
Creighton University	Omaha, Nebraska	1878	6 168
Dartmouth College	Hanover, New Hampshire	1769	5 500
DePaul University	Chicago, Illinois	1898	15 718
Dickinson College	Carlisle, Pennsylvania	1773	2 003
Drake University	Des Moines, Iowa	1881	8 028
Drew University	Madison, New Jersey	1866	2 276

AMERICAN COLLEGES AND UNIVERSITIES (cont.)

Name	Location	Year founded	Enrolment (1990–1)
Drexel University	Philadelphia, Pennsylvania	1891	11 927
Duke University	Durham, North Carolina	1838	11 178
Duquesne University	Pittsburg, Pennsylvania	1878	6 975
East Carolina University	Greenville, North Carolina	1907	16 500
Eastern Illinois University	Charleston	1895	10 301
Eastern Michigan University	Ypsilanti	1849	26 031
East Tennessee State University	Johnson City	1911	11 750
Emory University	Atlanta, Georgia	1836	9 390
Fairfield University	Fairfield, Connecticut	1942	4 821
Fairleigh-Dickinson University, Teaneck-Hackensack Campus	Teaneck, New Jersey	1954	5 468
Fashion Institute of Technology	New York, New York	1944	12 771
Ferris State University	Big Rapids, Michigan	1884	12 076
Florida Atlantic University	Boca Raton	1961	12 758
Florida International University	Miami	1965	21 999
Florida State University	Tallahassee	1857	28 327
Fordham University	New York, New York	1841	13 158
Gallaudet University	Washington, DC	1856	2 373
George Mason University	Fairfax, Virginia	1957	20 308
Georgetown University	Washington, DC	1789	11 525
George Washington University	Washington, DC	1821	14 752
Georgia Institute of Technology	Atlanta	1885	12 241
Georgia Southern University	Statesboro	1906	11 238
Georgia State University	Atlanta	1913	23 386
Gonzaga University	Spokane, Washington	1887	4 178
Grand Valley State University	Allendale, Michigan	1960	11 726
Grinnell College	Grinnell, Iowa	1846	1 251
Hamilton College	Clinton, New York	1812	1 668
Hampden-Sydney College	Hampden-Sydney, Virginia	1776	956
Hartwick College	Oneonta, New York	1797	1 498
Harvard University	Cambridge, Massachusetts	1636	15 601
Haverford College	Haverford, Pennsylvania	1833	1 147
Hofstra University	Hempstead, New York	1935	12 225
Howard University	Washington, DC	1867	11 236
Hunter College of the City University of New York		1870	19 645
Illinois State University	Normal	1857	22 694
Indiana State University	Terre Haute	1865	11 783
Indiana State University at Kokomo		1945	3 438
Indiana University at South Bend		1922	7 215
Indiana University at Bloomington		1820	35 453
Indiana University Northwest	Gary	1959	5 078
Indiana University of Pennsylvania	Indiana, Pennsylvania	1875	14 398
Indiana University – Purdue University at Fort Wayne		1917	11 879

AMERICAN COLLEGES AND UNIVERSITIES (cont.)

Name	Location	Year founded	Enrolment (1990–1)
Indiana University – Purdue University at Indianapolis		1969	27 518
Indiana University Southeast	New Albany	1941	5 642
Iowa State University of Science and Technology	Ames	1858	25 339
Ithaca College	Ithaca, New York	1892	6 433
James Madison University	Harrisonburg, Virginia	1908	11 011
John Carroll University	University Heights, Ohio	1886	4 551
Johns Hopkins University	Baltimore, Maryland	1876	4 335
Juilliard School	New York, New York	1905	843
Kansas State University	Manhattan	1863	21 137
Kean College of New Jersey	Union	1855	13 329
Kent State University	Kent, Ohio	1910	24 434
Lamar University	Beaumont, Texas	1923	11 848
La Salle University	Philadelphia, Pennsylvania	1863	6 478
Lehigh University	Bethlehem, Pennsylvania	1865	6 663
Liberty University	Lynchburg, Virginia	1971	5 198
Long Island University, Brooklyn Campus	Brooklyn, New York	1926	4 600
Long Island University, CW Post Campus	Brookville, New York	1954	8 964
Louisiana State University and A&M College	Baton Rouge	1860	25 307
Louisiana Technical University	Ruston	1894	10 011
Loyola Marymount University	Los Angeles, California	1911	4 809
Loyola University Chicago		1870	14 780
Loyola University New Orleans		1912	5 400
Mankato State University	Mankato, Minnesota	1867	16 185
Marquette University	Milwaukee, Wisconsin	1881	11 775
Marshall University	Huntington, West Virginia	1837	12 406
Massachusetts Institute of Technology	Cambridge	1861	9 628
Memphis State University	Memphis, Tennessee	1912	20 681
Metropolitan State College	Denver, Colorado	1965	17 341
Miami University	Oxford, Ohio	1809	15 841
Michigan State University	East Lansing	1855	44 317
Middle Tennessee State University	Murfreesboro, Tennessee	1911	14 865
Mississippi State University	Mississippi State, Mississippi	1878	14 391
Montana State University	Bozeman	1893	10 392
Montclair State College	Upper Montclair, New Jersey	1908	13 083
Moravian College	Bethlehem, Pennsylvania	1742	1 802
National University	San Diego, California	1971	9 059
New Mexico State University	Las Cruces	1888	14 809
New York Institute of Technology	Old Westbury, New York	1955	12 744
New York University	New York, New York	1831	32 756
North Carolina State University	Raleigh	1887	26 683
Northeastern Illinois University	Chicago	1961	10 453
Northeastern University	Boston, Massachusetts	1898	30 515
Northeast Louisiana University	Monroe	1931	10 686
Northern Arizona University	Flagstaff	1899	16 994

AMERICAN COLLEGES AND UNIVERSITIES (cont.)

Name	Location	Year founded	Enrolment (1990–1)
Northern Illinois University	De Kalb	1895	24 509
Northwestern University	Evanston, Illinois	1851	14 684
Nova University	Fort Lauderdale, Florida	1964	9 562
Oakland University	Rochester, Michigan	1957	12 400
Oberlin College	Oberlin, Ohio	1833	2 815
Ohio State University	Columbus	1870	54 094
Ohio University	Athens	1804	17 000
Oklahoma State University	Stillwater	1890	19 591
Old Dominion University	Norfolk, Virginia	1930	16 729
Oral Roberts University	Tulsa, Oklahoma	1963	3 550
Oregon State University	Corvallis	1868	16 024
Pace University	New York, New York	1906	8 355
Parsons School of Design, New School for Social Research	New York, New York	1896	7 033
Pennsylvania State University, University Park Campus	University Park, Pennsylvania	1855	38 864
Pomona College	Claremont, California	1887	1 375
Portland State University	Portland, Oregon	1946	14 758
Pratt Institute	Brooklyn, New York	1887	3 384
Princeton University	Princeton, New Jersey	1746	6 321
Purdue University	West Lafayette, Indiana	1869	35 647
Purdue University Calumet	Hammond, Indiana	1951	7 698
Purdue University North Central	Westville, Indiana	1967	3 446
Queens College of the City University of New York	Flushing, New York	1937	18 071
Rensselaer Polytechnic Institute	Troy, New York	1824	6 508
Rhode Island School of Design	Providence	1877	1 912
Rice University	Houston, Texas	1912	4 016
Rochester Institute of Technology	Rochester, New York	1829	11 147
Rutgers, State University of New Jersey, Douglass College	New Brunswick	1918	3 227
Rutgers, State University of New Jersey, Livingston College	New Brunswick	1969	3 776
Rutgers, State University of New Jersey, Newark College of Arts and Science	Newark	1946	3 396
Rutgers, State University of New Jersey, Rutgers College	New Brunswick	1766	8 377
Rutgers, State University of New Jersey, University College – New Brunswick		1934	3 087
St Cloud State University	St Cloud, Minnesota	1869	17 076
St John's University	Jamaica, New York	1870	19 105
Saint Louis University	St Louis, Missouri	1818	11 884
Sam Houston State University	Huntsville, Texas	1879	12 753
San Diego State University	San Diego, California	1897	35 021
San Francisco State University	San Francisco, California	1899	28 120
San Jose State University	San Jose, California	1857	29 847

AMERICAN COLLEGES AND UNIVERSITIES (cont.)

Name	Location	Year founded	Enrolment (1990–1)
Santa Clara University	Santa Clara, California	1851	7 710
Sarah Lawrence College	Bronxville, New York	1926	1 200
Seton Hall University	South Orange, New Jersey	1856	8 166
Skidmore College	Saratoga Springs, New York	1903	2 139
Smith College	Northampton, Massachusetts	1871	2 765
Southern Connecticut State University	New Haven	1893	13 618
Southern Illinois University at Carbondale		1869	24 083
Southern Illinois University at Edwardsville		1957	11 686
Southern Methodist University	Dallas, Texas	1911	8 798
Southern University and A&M College	Baton Rouge, Louisiana	1880	9 122
Southwest Missouri State University	Springfield	1905	19 480
Southwest Texas State University	San Marcos	1899	20 944
Stanford University	Stanford, California	1891	13 441
State University of New York at Albany		1844	15 218
State University of New York at Binghamton		1946	12 202
State University of New York at Buffalo		1946	24 678
State University of New York at Stony Brook		1957	15 465
State University of New York, College at Brockport		1867	8 138
State University of New York, College at Buffalo		1867	12 142
State University of New York, College at Cortland		1868	6 170
State University of New York, College at Fredonia		1826	5 041
State University of New York, College at Geneseo		1867	5 599
State University of New York, College at New Paltz		1828	8 637
State University of New York, College at Old Westbury		1965	4 262
State University of New York, College at Oneonta		1889	6 000
State University of New York, College at Oswego		1861	8 200
State University of New York, College at Plattsburgh		1889	6 555
State University of New York, College at Potsdam		1816	4 826
State University of New York, Empire State College	Saratoga Springs	1971	6 522
Stephen F Austin State University	Nacogdoches, Texas	1923	12 815
Stephens College	Columbia, Missouri	1833	1 191
Swarthmore College	Swarthmore, Pennsylvania	1864	1 317
Syracuse University	Syracuse, New York	1870	16 700
Temple University	Philadelphia, Pennsylvania	1884	26 421
Temple University, Ambler Campus	Ambler, Pennsylvania	1910	4 842
Texas A&M University	College Station	1876	41 171

AMERICAN COLLEGES AND UNIVERSITIES (cont.)

Name	Location	Year founded	Enrolment (1990–1)
Texas Technical University	Lubbock	1923	25 363
Towson State University	Towson, Maryland	1866	15 034
Trinity University	San Antonio, Texas	1869	2 538
Tufts University	Medford, Massachusetts	1852	7 634
Tulane University	New Orleans, Louisiana	1834	11 485
Tuskegee University	Tuskegee, Alabama	1881	3 627
Union College	Schenectady, New York	1795	2 240
University of Akron	Akron, Ohio	1870	28 801
University of Alabama	Tuscaloosa	1831	19 828
University of Alabama at Birmingham		1969	16 286
University of Alabama in Huntsville		1950	8 139
University of Alaska Anchorage		1954	7 990
University of Alaska Fairbanks		1917	4 480
University of Arizona	Tucson	1885	35 735
University of Arkansas	Fayetteville	1871	14 600
University of Arkansas at Little Rock		1927	11 362
University of Arkansas at Pine Bluff		1873	3 672
University of California at Berkeley		1868	30 638
University of California, Davis		1906	23 910
University of California, Irvine		1965	16 761
University of California, Los Angeles		1919	36 427
University of California, Riverside		1954	8 716
University of California, San Diego	La Jolla	1959	17 805
University of California, Santa Barbara		1891	18 391
University of California, Santa Cruz		1965	10 052
University of Central Florida	Orlando	1963	21 225
University of Chicago		1891	11 063
University of Cincinnati		1819	18 676
University of Colorado at Boulder		1876	25 176
University of Connecticut	Storrs	1881	17 867
University of Dayton	Dayton, Ohio	1850	10 092
University of Delaware	Newark	1743	17 781
University of Florida	Gainesville	1853	34 198
University of Georgia	Athens	1785	23 395
University of Hawaii at Hilo		1970	4 449
University of Hawaii at Manoa	Honolulu	1907	18 874
University of Houston		1927	32 289
University of Houston – Clear Lake	Houston	1971	7 560
University of Houston – Downtown	Houston	1974	8 702
University of Idaho	Moscow	1889	9 533
University of Illinois at Chicago		1965	25 182
University of Illinois at Urbana – Champaign	Urbana	1867	35 766
University of Iowa	Iowa City	1947	28 045
University of Kansas	Lawrence	1866	28 909
University of Kentucky	Lexington	1865	23 100
University of Louisville		1798	23 600
University of Lowell	Lowell, Massachusetts	1894	11 179
University of Maine	Orono	1865	13 278
University of Maryland Baltimore County	Baltimore	1966	10 150

AMERICAN COLLEGES AND UNIVERSITIES (cont.)

Name	Location	Year founded	Enrolment (1990–1)
University of Maryland College Park	College Park	1856	34 837
University of Maryland University College	College Park	1947	40 385
University of Massachusetts at Amherst		1863	23 000
University of Massachusetts at Boston		1964	11 018
University of Miami	Coral Gables	1925	13 686
University of Michigan	Ann Arbor	1817	36 306
University of Michigan – Dearborn		1959	7 684
University of Michigan – Flint		1956	6 600
University of Minnesota, Twin Cities Campus	Minneapolis	1851	40 972
University of Mississippi	University, Mississippi	1844	10 894
University of Missouri – Columbia		1839	24 972
University of Missouri – Kansas City		1933	11 357
University of Missouri – Rolla		1870	5 439
University of Missouri – St Louis		1963	13 161
University of Montana	Missoula	1893	10 055
University of Nebraska at Kearney		1903	10 114
University of Nebraska at Omaha		1908	16 661
University of Nebraska – Lincoln		1869	24 453
University of Nevada, Las Vegas		1957	18 216
University of Nevada, Reno		1874	10 753
University of New Hampshire	Durham	1866	11 468
University of New Mexico	Albuquerque	1889	24 600
University of New Orleans		1958	15 322
University of North Carolina at Asheville		1927	3 310
University of North Carolina at Chapel Hill		1795	23 852
University of North Carolina at Charlotte		1946	14 323
University of North Carolina at Greensboro		1891	11 892
University of North Carolina at Wilmington		1947	6 978
University of Northern Colorado	Greeley	1890	10 239
University of North Dakota	Grand Forks	1883	11 885
University of Northern Colorado	Greeley	1890	10 239
University of Northern Iowa	Cedar Falls	1876	12 638
University of North Texas	Denton	1890	27 160
University of Notre Dame	Notre Dame, Indiana	1842	9 900
University of Oklahoma	Norman	1890	19 246
University of Oregon	Eugene	1872	18 043
University of Pennsylvania	Philadelphia	1740	21 903
University of Pittsburgh		1787	28 120
University of Pittsburgh at Johnstown		1927	3 210
University of Rhode Island	Kingston	1892	12 111
University of South Alabama	Mobile	1963	11 584
University of South Carolina	Columbia	1801	25 613
University of South Carolina at Spartanburg		1967	3 501
University of South Carolina – Coastal Carolina College	Conway	1954	4 080
University of Southern California	Los Angeles	1880	28 895
University of Southern Maine	Portland	1878	10 487
University of Southern Mississippi	Hattiesburg	1910	11 912
University of South Florida	Tampa	1956	32 360

AMERICAN COLLEGES AND UNIVERSITIES (cont.)

Name	Location	Year founded	Enrolment (1990–1)
University of Southwestern Louisiana	Lafayette	1898	15 826
University of Tennessee at Chattanooga		1886	7 725
University of Tennessee at Martin		1927	5 369
University of Tennessee, Knoxville		1794	25 414
University of Texas at Arlington		1895	24 783
University of Texas at Austin		1883	49 617
University of Texas at Dallas	Richardson	1969	8 685
University of Texas at El Paso		1913	16 524
University of Texas at San Antonio		1969	15 489
University of Texas at Tyler		1972	3 720
University of Texas – Pan American	Edinburg	1927	12 220
University of the District of Columbia	Washington, DC	1976	11 990
University of the State of New York, Regents College	Albany	1971	13 500
University of Toledo	Toledo, Ohio	1872	24 781
University of Utah	Salt Lake City	1850	24 311
University of Vermont	Burlington	1791	9 466
University of Virginia	Charlottesville	1819	17 662
University of Washington	Seattle	1861	33 536
University of Wisconsin – Eau Claire		1916	10 644
Indiania University at South Bend		1922	7 215
University of Wisconsin – Green Bay		1968	4 801
University of Wisconsin – La Crosse		1909	8 759
University of Wisconsin – Madison		1848	40 905
University of Wisconsin – Milwaukee		1956	25 380
University of Wisconsin – Oshkosh		1871	11 093
University of Wisconsin – Parkside	Kenosha	1968	5 112
University of Wisconsin – Platteville		1866	5 430
University of Wisconsin – River Falls		1874	5 243
University of Wisconsin – Stevens Point		1894	8 805
University of Wisconsin – Stout	Menomonie	1891	7 445
University of Wisconsin – Whitewater		1868	10 185
University of Wyoming	Laramie	1886	12 524
Utah State University	Logan	1888	12 650
Valparaiso University	Valparaiso, Indiana	1859	3 862
Vanderbilt University	Nashville, Tennessee	1873	9 236
Vassar College	Poughkeepsie, New York	1861	2 459
Villanova University	Villanova, Pennsylvania	1842	11 265
Virginia Commonwealth University	Richmond	1838	21 764
Virginia Polytechnic Institute and State University	Blacksburg	1872	23 365
Wake Forest University	Winston-Salem, North Carolina	1834	5 505
Washington and Jefferson College	Washington, Pennsylvania	1781	1 205
Washington and Lee University	Lexington, Virginia	1749	2 032
Washington College	Chestertown, Maryland	1782	1 003
Washington State University	Pullman, Washington	1892	17 494
Washington University	St Louis, Missouri	1853	9 701
Wayne State University	Detroit, Michigan	1868	33 872
Weber State College	Ogden, Utah	1889	13 449

AMERICAN COLLEGES AND UNIVERSITIES (cont.)

Name	Location	Year founded	Enrolment (1990–1)
Wellesley College	Wellesley, Massachusetts	1870	2 279
Wesleyan University	Middletown, Connecticut	1831	3 417
West Chester University of Pennsylvania	West Chester	1871	12 076
Western Illinois University	Macomb	1899	13 750
Western Kentucky University	Bowling Green	1906	15 240
Western Michigan University	Kalamazoo	1903	26 995
West Virginia University	Morgantown	1867	20 854
Wheaton College	Norton, Massachusetts	1834	1 264
Wichita State University	Wichita, Kansas	1895	16 668
William Paterson College of New Jersey	Wayne	1855	10 041
Williams College	Williamstown, Massachusetts	1793	2 120
Wright State University	Dayton, Ohio	1964	17 380
Xavier University	Cincinnati, Ohio	1831	6 680
Yale University	New Haven, Connecticut	1701	10 842
Yeshiva University	New York, New York	1886	4 670
Youngstown State University	Youngstown, Ohio	1908	15 454

SPORTS AND GAMES

OLYMPIC GAMES

First Modern Olympic Games took place in 1896, founded by Frenchman Baron de Coubertin; held every four years; women first competed in 1900; first separate Winter Games celebration in 1924.

Venues

Summer Games

1896 Athens, Greece
1900 Paris, France
1904 St Louis, USA
1908 London, UK
1912 Stockholm, Sweden
1920 Antwerp, Belgium
1924 Paris, France
1928 Amsterdam, Holland
1932 Los Angeles, USA
1936 Berlin, Germany
1948 London, UK
1952 Helsinki, Finland
1956 Melbourne, Australia
1960 Rome, Italy
1964 Tokyo, Japan
1968 Mexico City, Mexico
1972 Munich, West Germany
1976 Montreal, Canada
1980 Moscow, USSR
1984 Los Angeles, USA
1988 Seoul, South Korea
1992 Barcelona, Spain
1996 Atlanta, USA

Winter Games

1924 Chamonix, France
1928 St Moritz, Switzerland
1932 Lake Placid, New York, USA
1936 Garmisch-Partenkirchen, Germany
1948 St Moritz, Switzerland
1952 Oslo, Norway
1956 Cortina, Italy
1960 Squaw Valley, California, USA
1964 Innsbruck, Austria
1968 Grenoble, France
1972 Sapporo, Japan
1976 Innsbruck, Austria
1980 Lake Placid, New York, USA
1984 Sarajevo, Yugoslavia
1988 Calgary, Canada
1992 Albertville, France
1994 Lillehammer, Norway
1998 Nugano, Japan

Olympic games were also held in 1906 to commemorate the 10th anniversary of the birth of the Modern Games.

The 1956 equestrian events were held at Stockholm, Sweden, due to quarantine laws in Australia.

Leading Medal Winners

Summer Games	Gold	Silver	Bronze	Total
1 USA	783	594	512	1889
2 Unified Team[1]	440	361	328	1129
3 West Germany[2]	190	228	235	653
4 Great Britain	178	225	218	621
5 France	161	173	192	526
6 Sweden	132	146	173	451
7 Italy	153	126	132	411
8 East Germany	153	129	127	409
9 Hungary	135	124	143	402
10 Finland	98	77	112	287

Winter Games	Gold	Silver	Bronze	Total
1 CIS[1]	88	63	67	218
2 Norway	63	66	59	188
3 USA	47	51	36	134
4 Austria	34	45	40	119
5 Finland	36	44	37	117
6 East Germany	39	36	35	110
7 West Germany[2]	36	36	29	101
8 Sweden	37	25	34	96
9 Switzerland	24	25	27	76
10 Canada	16	16	19	51

[1]Includes medals won as USSR
[2]Includes medals won as Germany 1896–1964 and 1992

COMMONWEALTH GAMES

First held as the British Empire Games in 1930; take place every four years and between Olympic celebrations; became the British Empire and Commonwealth Games in 1954; current title adopted in 1970.

Venues

1930	Hamilton, Canada
1934	London, England
1938	Sydney, Australia
1950	Auckland, New Zealand
1954	Vancouver, Canada
1958	Cardiff, Wales
1962	Perth, Australia
1966	Kingston, Jamaica
1970	Edinburgh, Scotland
1974	Christchurch, New Zealand
1978	Edmonton, Canada
1982	Brisbane, Australia
1986	Edinburgh, Scotland
1990	Auckland, New Zealand
1994	Victoria, Canada

Leading Medal Winners

Nation	Gold	Silver	Bronze	Total
1 England	420	368	368	1 156
2 Australia	397	374	382	1 153
3 Canada	287	301	299	887
4 New Zealand	94	121	161	376
5 Scotland	56	74	109	239
6 South Africa	60	44	47	151
7 Wales	32	39	60	131
8 India	37	36	31	104
9 Kenya	35	24	33	92
10 Northern Ireland	15	20	34	69

SPORTS

aikido Ancient Japanese art of self-defence; combination of karate and judo deriving from ancient jujitsu; two main systems: *tomiki* and *uyeshiba*.

American football *see* **football**

angling Fishing with rod, line and hook in the form of freshwater, fly, game and deep-sea fishing. Rules govern time of year when different types of fishing take place, and type and amount of bait used. Oldest fishing club is in Ellem, Scotland.

archery Shooting with a bow and arrow at a circular target divided into 10 scoring zones, the smallest of which is coloured gold and worth 10 points; popular as sport from 17th century. In competition, arrows are fired from 30, 50, 70 and 90 metres (men), and 30, 50, 60 and 70 metres(women).

athletics Tests of running, jumping, throwing and walking skills. The running or **track** events range from the 100m (328ft) sprint to the 42.2km/26.2ml marathon; jumping and throwing or **field** events consist of high jump, long jump, triple jump and pole vault (men only), and the discus throw, shot put, javelin throw and hammer throw (men only). Multi-event competitions are the **decathlon** (10) for men and the **heptathlon** (7) for women. Athletics dates to c.3800BC Egypt; International Amateur Athletic Federation founded 1912.

badminton Indoor game, two or four players, played on court 13.4m/44ft long and 5.2m/17ft wide (6.1m/20ft wide for doubles), using rackets, a shuttlecock (cork or plastic half sphere with 'feathers') and a raised central net; object is to volley the shuttlecock over the net so that the opponent is unable to return it; name derives from Badminton House, the seat of the Duke of Beaufort, where game played 19th century, but it dates from China over 2 000 years ago.

bagatelle Restricted form of billiards, played on a table with nine numbered cups instead of pockets; takes many different forms which vary according to local conditions.

baseball Team game played by two sides of 25 possible players on a diamond-shaped field which has bases at the corners each 27.43m/90ft apart. Essential pieces of equipment are long cylindrical bats, the solid ball 'pitched' from the 'mound', and the glove worn by each fielder; team 'at bat' tries to score most runs by having its players circle the three bases and touch home plate before being put out by the team 'in the field'; players out if their hit is caught, if they are tagged with the ball when 'off-base', if the base is touched by the ball before they arrive at it, or if they 'strike out', ie fail to hit the ball after three pitches have been judged strikes by the umpire; 'home run' scored when player hits ball, circles all three bases and crosses home plate; game consists of nine innings; believed to have been

SPORTS (cont.)

invented in 1839 by a West Point cadet, Abner Doubleday, at Cooperstown, NY.

basketball Five-a-side team ball game played on a hard surface court approx 26m/84ft by 14m/45ft 9in, with a bottomless basket 3.05m/10ft above the ground at each end; object is to move the ball by a series of passing and bouncing moves and throw it through the opponents' basket; invented by James Naismith in 1891 at Springfield, Massachusetts, but similar game believed to have been played in 10th-century Mexico.

biathlon Combined test of cross-country skiing and rifle shooting. It is used as a form of military training, based on the old military patrol race. Men's individual competitions are over 10 and 20km (6.2 and 12.4ml), and women's over 5 and 10km (3.1 and 6.2ml). At designated points on the course, competitors have to fire either standing or prone at a fixed target.

billiards Indoor table game played in many different forms. The standard green baize-covered table measures 3.66m/12ft by 1.83m/6ft and has six pockets, into which the players use a tapered pole or *cue* to 'pot' the one red or two white balls to score, the balls going in off another ball. Scoring also achieved by making 'cannons' (hitting the white ball so that it successively hits the two others). Originally an outdoor game, its origins are uncertain; an early reference is 1429 when Louis XI of France owned a billiard table.

bobsledding Propelling oneself along snow or ice on a sledge, popular as a sport since 19th century; special luge run was created at Davros, Switzerland, in 1879. Most popular competitive forms: **luge tobogganing** on a small sledge and **bobsleighing** in a steel-bodied two- or four-person toboggan down special tracks at speeds of up to 130kph/80mph; earliest known sledge dates to c.6500BC Finland.

bowling Delivering a rubber or plastic ball along a 18.3m/60ft wooden lane to knock down pins: in **tenpin bowling** these are often mechanically replaced; popularized by third- and fourth-century German churchgoers, who would roll a ball at a *kegel*, a club used for protection: a hit would absolve them from sin. The game of nine pins was taken to the USA by Dutch and German immigrants; when outlawed, 10th pin introduced as a way around the legislation.

bowls Indoor or outdoor game played as singles, pairs, triples or fours. **Lawn bowls** ('flat green') is played on a flat level rink; **crown green bowls** is played on an uneven green raised at the centre (usually singles and pairs only); object is to deliver your bowl nearest to the *jack*, a small target ball; similar game believed to have been played by the Egyptians in c.5200BC. Glasgow solicitor William Mitchell drew up rules for modern bowls in 1848.

boxing Fist-fighting between two people, usually men, in a roped ring 4.3–6.1m/14–20ft square. Professional championship bouts constitute 12 three-minute rounds; amateur bouts three rounds, unless one fighter is knocked out or retires, the referee halts the fight, or a fighter is disqualified. The 17 weight divisions range from straw-weight for fighters under 48kg/105lb to heavyweight, normally over 88kg/195lb. Boxing dates from Greek and Roman times; first known match in Britain 1681 when Duke of Albemarle organized one between his butler and butcher in New Hall, Essex. First rules drawn up 1743, when each round lasted until one fighter was knocked down; gloves and three-minute rounds introduced 1867.

bull-fighting National sport in Spain, where it is called *corrida de toros* and the leading *matadors* are national heroes. *Picadors* are sent into the bull ring to weaken the bull before the matador enters the arena to make the final killing.

caber tossing Throwing a 3–4m/12–18ft tree trunk or *caber*, often practised in Highland Games gatherings in Scotland. The competitor has the caber placed vertically in his hands; he runs with it and tosses it so that it revolves longitudinally and lands with the base as near to the 12 o'clock position from him as possible.

canoeing Water sport practised by one to four people in canoes, developed 1865 by the British barrister John Macgregor. Two types of competition canoe: the *kayak*, which has a keel (the canoeist sits in the boat), and the *Canadian canoe*, which has no keel (the canoeist kneels).

clay-pigeon shooting or **trap shooting** Pastime and sport in which shotguns are fired at clay targets (*clays*) in the air; these simulate birds' flight and are released by an automatic machine.

cricket Bat and ball 11-a-side team game. A wicket consisting of three stumps (wooden sticks) surmounted by a pair of bails (smaller sticks) is placed at each end of a grassy pitch 22m/22yd in length. Each team takes it in turn to bat (with long flat-sided wooden bats) and bowl (with a solid ball), the object being to defend the two wickets while trying to score as many

SPORTS (cont.)

runs as possible. A bowler delivers an 'over' of (usually) six balls to a batsman standing in front of one of the wickets before a different bowler attacks the other wicket. If the batsman hits a ball (and in certain other circumstances), he may exchange places with the other batsman, thus scoring at least one run. A ball reaching the boundary of the field scores four runs automatically, and six if it has not bounced on the way. A batsman can be got out by being 'bowled' (the ball from the bowler knocks the wicket down), 'stumped' (the wicket-keeper knocks the wicket down with the ball while the defending batsman is standing outside his 'safe ground' or 'crease', 'run out' (the wicket towards which one of the batsmen is running is knocked down before the safe ground is reached) and 'leg before wicket' or 'lbw' (when the lower part of the batsman's leg prevents the ball from the bowler from reaching the wicket). Once 10 batsmen have been dismissed, the innings comes to a close, but a team can stop its innings or 'declare' if it thinks it has made enough runs. Each team has two innings, and the one with the greater number of runs at the end of the match wins. A similar game was played in the mid-16th century; first known county match 1719; test matches usually last five days; county championship three or four, and limited-over competitions normally concluded in one day, lasting for a specific number of overs per side. Earliest known laws: 1744; Marylebone Cricket Club (MCC) founded 1787; first test match: Melbourne 1877.

croquet A ball-and-mallet game for two to four players, played on a lawn about 32m/35yd long and 25m/28yd wide, on which six hoops have been arranged, with a small stake in the centre of the lawn. The object is to strike your own ball (blue, red, yellow or black) through the hoops in a prescribed order, a process which can be delayed by an opponent's ball hitting your ball out of the way. The central peg marks the finish and the first to hit it with his/her ball is the winner.

curling Similar to bowls but played on ice using special disc-shaped stones fitted with handles. The object is to deliver the stones, which are curled in one direction or another depending on the twist as they are released, near to a target, or *tee*. A match lasts for a certain number of *heads* or shots, or by time. Sweeping the ice in front of a stone can make it travel further.

cycling Bicycle riding as a sport can take several forms: *time trials* are raced against the clock; *cyclocross* is a mixture of cycling and cross-country running, carrying the bike; *track racing* takes place on purpose-built concrete or wooden velodromes; *criteriums* are races around town or city centres; *road races* are normally in excess of 150km/100ml in length, between two points or several circuits of a predetermined course; *stage races* involve many days' racing over more than 100 miles. First cycle race Paris 1868, won by James Moore of England.

cyclocross *see* **cycling**

darts Indoor game of throwing three 13cm/5in darts or 'arrows' from a distance of 2.4m/8ft at a circular board which has its 'bull' or centre 1.7m/5ft 8in from the floor. The standard board is divided into 20 segments numbered 1–20, (not in numerical order); each have progressively smaller segments inside which either double or treble that number's score if hit. The centre ring (the bull) is worth 50 points, and the area around it (the outer) is worth 25 points. Most popular game '501': players start at that figure and deduct all scores from it; final shot must consist of a double.

decathlon Ten-event track-and-field discipline held over two days, comprising, in order, 100 metres, long jump, shot, high jump, 400m, 110m hurdles, discus, pole vault, javelin, and 1500m. Points are awarded in each event.

discus throw Athletics field event using a circular disc of wood with metal plates, weighing 2kg/4.4lb for men and 1kg/2.2lb for women. It is thrown with one hand from within the confines of a circle 2.5m/8ft 2in in diameter.

diving Jumping from an elevated rigid or sprung board into a swimming pool, often performing a variety of twists and somersaults. Style gains marks, as does successfully completing the dive, based on the level of difficulty of each attempt (which is used as a multiplying factor). Springboard events take place from a board 3m/9ft 10in above the water; platform diving form a rigid board 10m/30ft 5in above the water.

falconry Sport in which birds of prey are trained to hunt animals and other birds, also known as **hawking**. Two kinds of falcon: *long-winged* birds (eg the peregrine), used in open country, which swoop on their prey from a great height, and *short-winged* birds, or accipiters, which perch on the falconer's gloved fist or tree branch until they see their prey, and then rely on speed.

SPORTS (cont.)

The birds are hooded until such time as they are ready to 'work'.

fencing Sword fighting, using a light foil, heavier *épée, or sabre* (curved handle, narrow blade). Different target areas exist for each weapon, and protective clothing registers hits electronically. It can be traced back to the Egyptians of c.1300BC and was popular in the Middle Ages.

fishing *see* **angling**

fives A handball game played on a three or four-walled court (which in Rugby fives is 5.49m/18ft wide, 8.54m/28ft long, with front wall 4.57m/15ft high, back wall 1.83m/6ft high and side walls sloping) by two or four players with a hard white ball, hit with gloved hands. It is derived from the French game *jeu de paume.* First recorded game 1825 at Eton school; another variation is Winchester fives.

football A field team game using an inflated ball, which has developed several different forms:

1 Association football or **soccer** An 11-a-side team game played on a grass or synthetic pitch measuring 90–120m/100-130yd in length, and 45–90m/50–100yd wide; goal nets measure 7.3m/8yd wide by 2.4m/8ft high; object is to move the ball around using the foot or head until it can be put into the net, thus scoring a goal. Only the goalkeeper within a specific area is allowed to touch the ball with the hand while it is in play. Ancient Greeks, Chinese, Egyptians and Romans all played a form of football; it became an organized game in 19th-century Britain, in schools and universities; standard rules drawn up 1848; Football Association formed 1863; first FA Cup final played 1872; first World Cup Uruguay 1930.

2 American football Played Oct–Jan in the USA, it resembles rugby in some respects, but the players wear heavy padding and helmets, and forward passing of the ball is permitted; played on a rectangular field 91m/100yd by 49m/53yd, divided gridiron-like into 4.6m/5yd segments; object is to score touchdowns, similar to tries in rugby, but progress has to be made upfield by a series of 'plays': a team must make 9.1m/10yds of ground with four plays, otherwise they lose possession of the ball. Six points are awarded for a touchdown and one for a 'point after', for kicking the ball between the posts and over the crossbar – the equivalent of a conversion in rugby. A goal kicked from anywhere on the field (a 'field goal') is worth three points. Teams consist of more than 40 members, but only 11 are allowed on the field at any one time; special units of players have different roles so they change eg when the team changes from attacking to being on the defence.

3 Australian Rules football A handling and kicking game with few rules, a cross between Association football and rugby, with 18 players on an oval pitch measuring c.165m/180yd long by c.137m/150yd wide. The object is to score by kicking the ball between the opponent's goal posts (six points). Smaller posts are positioned either side of the main goal: a ball kicked through that area scores one point; first recorded game played 1858.

4 Gaelic football Mixture of rugby, soccer and Australian Rules football, played by teams of 15 on a rectangular pitch 77–91m/84–100yd wide and 128–146m/140–160yd long with goals resembling rugby posts with soccer-style nets attached; points scored by either putting the ball into the goal net (three), or over the crossbar and between the uprights (one); first game resembling Gaelic football took place 1712 at Slane, Ireland.

5 rugby football *see* **rugby**

foxhunting Mounted blood sport involving chasing and killing a wild fox using foxhounds (similar in shape and colour to the beagle, but slightly larger); hunt is controlled by a Master of Hounds, the hounds by the Huntsman; season lasts November to April. It developed in the UK in the late 17th century. Since 1949 there has been a movement to try to get the sport banned in the UK.

golf Outdoor sport played on a course 4 000–6 000m/5 000–7 000yd long, usually with 18 but sometimes 9, 12 or 15 holes; object is to hit a small rubber-cored ball using a long-handled iron or wooden-faced club from a flat starting point or *tee* along a *fairway* to a hole positioned on an area of smooth grass or *green*, up to 450m/500yd away; additional hazards: trees, bushes, streams, sand-filled bunkers and the *rough*, or uncut grass beside the fairway; winner completes the course using the lowest number of strokes. The *par* is the expected number of strokes a good player needs to hole a ball; one stroke below par is a *birdie*; two strokes below an *eagle*; three strokes below an *albatross*; an occasional possibility is a *hole in one*; similar game played by the Dutch c.1300, known as *kolf* or *colf*. *Gouf* was definitely played in Scotland in the 15th century; world's first club, the Gentlemen Golfers of Edinburgh, formed 1744.

greyhound racing Spectator sport which takes

SPORTS (cont.)

place on an enclosed circular or oval track where greyhound dogs (on whose success bets are usually placed) are lured to run by a mechanical hare; invented California 1919.

gymnastics Physical exercises. Men compete on the parallel bars, pommel horse, horizontal bar, rings, horse vault and floor exercise, and women on the asymmetrical bars, beam, horse vault and floor exercise. Judges award marks out of 10, looking for control, suppleness, balance and ingenuity. The ancient Greeks and Romans performed such exercises for health purposes; modern techniques date from late 18th-century Germany.

hammer throw Athletics field event; hammer weighing 7.6kg/16lb is thrown using one hand from within the confines of a 2.13m/7ft circle (protected by a wire cage). Six throws are allowed, the object being to attain the greatest distance.

handball Indoor and outdoor game first played in Germany c.1890; resembles Association football, but played with the hands. Indoor game played seven-a-side on a court 40m/43.8yd long and 20m/21.9yd wide, with goals 2m/6ft 6in high and 3m/9ft 10in wide; outdoor game (**field handball**) played on a field with 11 on each side.

hang gliding Flying in a glider with a delta-shaped wing, usually having launched from a high place. The pilot is suspended by a harness from the light frame holding the wing, and controls the direction of the craft by body movement. Providing the angle of attack is maintained, lift is generated. A hang glider with a motor and wing span increased to 10m/33ft is called a *microlight*, which typically has a speed of 90kph/55mph. Hang gliding was pioneered in the 1890s in Germany.

harness racing Horse race with rider seated in a small two-wheeled cart or *sulky*; horses trot or pace; races run on an oval dirt track measuring 400–1 500 m/0.5–1ml in circumference; first introduced 1554 Holland, popularized mid-19th century USA.

hawking *see* **falconry**

heptathlon Seven-event track-and-field competition (usually women's): 100m hurdles, shot put, high jump, 200m, long jump, javelin and 800m; held over two days; replaced pentathlon in 1981.

high jump Athletics field event; competitors attempt to clear a bar without any aids; height increased gradually: three failed attempts means disqualification. The winner clears the greatest height, or has the least failures.

hockey or **field hockey** Stick-and-ball game played by two teams of 11 on a pitch 91m/100yd long and 54m/60yd wide, the object being to move the ball around with the sticks until a player can score from within the semicircle of radius 14.64m/16yd in front of the opposing side's goal; game is split into two halves of 35 minutes; ancient Greeks played a similar game c.2500BC; modern hockey dates from 1875.

horse racing Racing of horses against one another, each ridden by a jockey. Two categories: **flat racing** for thoroughbred horses on a flat grass or dirt surface over a predetermined distance from 1 to 4km/5 furlongs to 2.5ml, and **national hunt racing** in which the horses negotiate either movable hurdles or fixed fences over a distance up to 6.5km/4.5ml. The ancient Egyptians took part in horse races in c.1200BC; popularized in 12th-century England. Most monarchs have supported the sport, hence name the 'sport of kings'. See also **harness racing, hurdling** and **steeplechasing**.

hurdling 1 Athletics event; foot racing while clearing obstacles (hurdles) en route; race distances: 110m and 400m for men, 100m and 400m for women; hurdle height varies: 106.7cm/3ft 6in for the 110m; 91.4cm/3ft for the 400m and 84cm/2ft 9in for the 100m.

2 Horse race in which the horses have to clear hurdles.

hurling or **hurley** Irish 15-a-side field game played with curved sticks and a ball; object to hit ball into opposing team's goal: under the crossbar scores three points; above the crossbar but between the posts scores one; played since 1800 BC; standardized in 1884 following the formation of the Gaelic Athletic Association.

ice hockey Fast game played by two teams of six on an ice rink 56–61m/184–200ft long and 26–30m/85–98ft wide with sticks and a small rubber puck; players wear ice skates and protective clothing; possibly played 1850s Canada.

ice skating 1 figure skating Artistic dancing on ice for individuals and pairs; first known skating club formed mid-18th century London; first artificial rink opened 1876 Baker Street.

2 speed skating Competitors race against one another on an oval ice track over distances between 500 and 10 000m/550 and 11 000yd.

javelin throw Athletics field event; throwing a

SPORTS (cont.)

spear-like javelin which consists of three parts: pointed metal head, shaft and grip; men's javelin is 2.6–2.7m/8ft 6in–8ft 10in in length and weighs 800g/1.8lb; women's is 2.2–2.3m/7ft 2in–7ft 6in and weighs at least 600g/1.3lb; the competitor runs to a specified mark with the javelin in one hand, and throws it; for throw to count, metal head must touch ground before any other part; first mark made by the head is the point used for measuring the distance achieved.

judo Unarmed combat sport of late 19th-century Japanese origin. Contestants wear a *judogi* or loose-fitting suit and compete on a mat which breaks their falls. When one cannot break a hold, surrender is signalled by slapping the mat; ability is graded from fifth to first Kyu, and then first to 12th Dan – only Dr Jigoro Kano, who devised the sport, has been awarded 12th Dan. Different coloured belts indicate grades: eg white for novice, brown (three degrees) and black (nine degrees).

jujitsu Japanese art of unarmed offence and self-defence used by the Samurai; forms basis of judo, aikido and karate; thought to have been introduced early 17th century by Chinese monk, Chen Yuan-ping.

karate Martial art of unarmed combat, dating from 17th century; developed Japan 20th century; name adopted 1930s; aim is to be in total control of the body's muscular power, so it can be used with great force and accuracy at any instant. Experts may show their mental and physical training by eg breaking various thicknesses of wood, but in fighting an opponent, blows do not actually make contact; levels of prowess symbolized by coloured belts.

kendo Japanese martial art of sword fighting, now practised with *shiani*, or bamboo swords; object is to land two scoring blows on opponent's target area. *Kendokas* (participants) wear traditional dress of the Samurai period, including face masks and aprons; grades according to ability are from sixth to first Kyu, then from first to 10th Dan; earliest reference is AD789.

kung fu Chinese unarmed combat dating from the sixth century, when it was practised at the Shaolin Temple; best known form is *wing chun*.

lacrosse Stick-and-ball field game; teams of 10 (men's) or 12 (women's) play on a pitch measuring about 100–110m/110–120yd by 55–75m/60–85yd; stick measures at least 90cm/3ft and has thongs forming a triangular net at one end in which ball is caught and carried, and thrown into opponents' goal (just under 2m/6ft square); derived from N American Indian's game of *baggataway*; stick supposedly resembled a bishop's crozier, so French settlers called it *la crosse*; played since 15th century; spread to Europe early 19th century, and to Britain 1867.

long jump Athletics field event; contestant has a running stride to the take-off mark and jumps into a sandpit; length of the jump measured from front of take-off line to nearest break in the sand made by any part of the competitor's body; sometimes called **broad jump**.

lugeing Travelling across ice on a toboggan sled, usually made of wood with metal runners; rider sits upright or lies back (but lies on the stomach in tobogganing). Competitors in single or two-seater luges race against time on a predetermined run of at least 1 000m/1 094yd; luge is approximately 1.5m/5ft in length, steered by the feet and a hand rope. See also **bobsledding**.

marathon Long-distance running race, normally on open roads, over 42km 195m/26ml 385yd (distance first used at 1908 London Olympics so competitors could finish exactly in front of the royal box); race introduced at the 1896 Olympic Games to commemorate the run of the Greek courier (according to legend, Pheidippides) who ran the c.24ml/39km from Marathon to Athens in 490BC with the news of a Greek victory over the Persian army. In the 1980s the **half marathon** over 21km/13ml 194yd also became popular.

martial arts *see* **aikido**, **judo**, **jujitsu**, **karate**, **kendo**, **kung fu**, **taekwondo**.

moto-cross or **scrambling** Motorcycle racing over a circuit of rough terrain, taking advantage of natural hazards eg streams and hills; uses sturdier motorcycles than those for road use; competitions usually categorized by engine size; first moto-cross held 1924 at Camberley, Surrey.

motorcycle racing Speed competitions for motorcycles which for the annual season-long grand prix are categorized for the engine sizes 80cc, 125cc, 250cc, 500cc and sidecar. Other forms include speedway moto-cross and motorcycle trials riding.

motor racing Racing finely-tuned motor cars, either purpose-built or modified production vehicles; season-long (Mar–Nov) Formula One world championship involves usually 16 races at different venues worldwide; other popular forms include stock-car racing, hill-climbing, sports-car

SPORTS (cont.)

racing and rallying; first race 1894, between Paris and Rouen.

mountaineering Climbing a mountain aided by ropes and other accessories, which for tall peaks can take weeks; most popular form in UK is **rock climbing**; in higher places elsewhere the form is **snow and ice climbing**.

netball Women's seven-a-side court game invented in the USA and developed from basketball; court is 30.5m/100ft long and 15.25m/50ft wide; object is to score goals by passing the inflated ball between players and throwing it through opponent's hoop suspended on a post 3.05m/10ft high. Players must not touch each other or run with the ball.

octopush A form of hockey played underwater, first introduced 1960s in South Africa; teams of six; players use miniature hockey sticks and a puck, which must hit the opposing end of the swimming pool to score a goal.

orienteering Cross-country running and route-finding aided by map and compass; competitors set off at intervals and have to find their way to check-points where their cards are marked; devised as a sport in Sweden in 1918, based on military training techniques; became an international sport 1960s.

paddle tennis Bat-and-ball game for two or four people, invented USA c.1920; rules similar to lawn tennis, but court is half the size, bat wooden and ball made of sponge.

parachuting Jumping out of an aircraft and landing with the aid of a parachute; competitions involve landing within a specific area; participant can choose to freefall for a few thousand feet before opening the chute, normally c.750m/2 500ft.

pelota Generic name for various hand, glove, racket or bat-and-ball games, all developed from French *jeu de paume*; most popular form **Pelote Basque**: it uses a walled court (*trinquete*), players wear a shaped wicker basket attached to their forearm in which they catch and propel the ball. Pelota is one of the world's fastest games.

pentathlon 1 Five track-and-field events, usually for women: 100m hurdles, shot put, high jump, long jump, and 800m; replaced by **heptathlon** 1981.
2 modern pentathlon Five-sport competition based on military training, comprising cross-country riding on horseback, épée fencing, pistol shooting, swimming and cross-country running.

platform tennis Variation of paddle tennis, a cross between lawn tennis and squash rackets; side walls can be used to bring the ball into court; popular USA winter sport.

point-to-point Horse races for amateur riders over a cross-country course, normally farmland; organized by hunts; horses used are regular hunting horses; original courses went from one point to another (hence name), but are now often over circular or oval courses with mixture of artificial and natural fences.

pole vault Athletics field event; jumping contest for height using fibreglass pole for leverage to clear a bar, which is raised progressively; three attempts may be made to clear the height before attempting a new one.

polo Largest stick-and-ball game; played by teams of four on horseback on a pitch measuring 274m/300yd by 146m/160yd; object is to hit the ball into the opposing team's 7.3m/8yd-wide and 3m/10ft-high goal using a long-handled mallet; match lasts about an hour, divided into seven-minute *chukkas*, the number of which varies according to competition; a pony is not expected to play more than two chukkas; name derives its name from Tibetan *pulu*; first played in C Asia c.500BC.

pool American table game played in many forms, using 15 balls, a *cue* similar to that used in billiards and snooker, and a table half the size of a standard billiard table, with six round pockets; UK most popular form is eight-ball pool, where the object is to pot all balls of your colour and finally the black (or No.8) ball.

potholing or **spelunking** (US) Exploration and study of caves and other underground features, originally to survey extent, physical history and structure, and natural history. When practised as a hobby people descend through access points (potholes) to follow courses of underground rivers and streams; scientific term: **speleology**.

powerboat racing Inshore and offshore racing of boats fitted with high-powered and finely-tuned engines; first race of note Calais to Dover 1903.

pyramids Ball game played on standard billiard table in which 15 coloured balls, usually red, are placed in a triangle, the apex ball on the pyramid (pink-ball) spot; object is to pot more balls than opponent; 19th century forerunner of snooker.

quoits Outdoor game demanding great accuracy; metal ring is thrown at a peg; became popular mid-14th-century England; horseshoe pitching developed from quoits.

SPORTS (cont.)

rackets or **raquets** (US) Racket-and-ball game; played by two or four players on walled court; probably forerunner to many racket-and-ball games; thought to have originated Middle Ages, and to have developed 18th century at the Fleet debtor's prison, London.

rally Motor racing on open roads and in forests, sometimes lasting several days; driver and navigator require skill and endurance; uses modified production cars.

real tennis Indoor racket-and-ball game similar to rackets; played on walled court with specifically designed hazards; derivation of the 11th-century *jeu de paume*; racket developed 16th century and the game became very popular in the 17th; also known as 'royal' or 'court' tennis, and a minority sport today.

rodeo US sport: mainly competitive riding and a range of skills deriving from cowboy ranching practices; events include bronco riding with and without saddle (where the cowboy must stay on a wild bucking horse for a set time holding with only one hand, points being awarded for style to the horse and rider), bull riding, steer wrestling, calf roping and team roping.

roller skating First seen 1760 in Liège, Belgium; developed as a sport late 19th century, following invention of the modern four-wheeled skate in 1863. Competitions exist as for ice skating: individual, pairs, dancing and speed skating on a track.

rounders Outdoor bat-and-ball game; baseball may derive from it; teams of nine players; object, after hitting the ball, which is bowled from the centre of the pitch, is to score a rounder by running around outside of the four posts without being put out (by the ball being caught, the batter being tagged between posts, or the post ahead of the batter being 'stopped' by a fielder touching it with the hand holding the ball); first reference to rounders 1744.

rowing Propulsion of a boat by oars; involves two or more people, each with an oar, and often with a coxswain (one rower with two oars: **sculling**); as an organized sport, dates from 1715 (first rowing of the Doggetts Coat and Badge race on the R Thames, London).

rugby football Team ball game played with oval ball on a pitch 69m/75yd long and 100m/110yd wide; developed 1823 from football (when William Webb Ellis of Rubgy school picked up the ball and ran with it); H-shaped goalposts at each end of field are 5.6m/18ft 6in wide, with a crossbar 3m/10ft above the ground; object is to score a *try* by grounding ball in opposing scoring area behind goal line. **Rugby union** is the amateur game (15-a-side); **rugby league** now considered the professional game; it has teams of 13 and was formed by the breakaway Northern Union after a dispute with the Rugby Football Union about pay in 1895. Some rule differences eg the scoring (League in brackets): try 5 (4), conversion 2 (2), penalty 3 (2), dropped goal 3 (1).

sailing Travelling over water in a suitable craft, usually a small single or double-sided dinghy, often with outboard motor or auxiliary engine for use in no wind; **yachting** involves racing small, light sailing vessels with crews of one, two or three; large ocean-going yachts may be 25m/80ft or more in length; several classes of racing yacht in Olympic and international competitions – eg the Admiral's Cup and Americas Cup.

scrambling *see* **motocross**

sculling *see* **rowing**

sepek takrow Three-a-side court game played on badminton court with ball made from rattan palm; ball is propelled over centre net (lower than in badminton) by players using any part of the body other than arms or hands; popular in SE Asia, particularly Philippines, Malaysia (as 'kick') and Thailand (as 'rattan ball').

shinty Twelve-a-side stick-and-ball game originating in Ireland more than 1 500 years ago, now popular in the Scottish Highlands; played on pitch up to 155m/150yd long and 73m/80yd wide; aim is to score goals by propelling the leather-covered cork and worsted ball, using curved sticks or *camans*, into the opposing team's goal or *hail*.

shooting Competitive shooting takes many forms and uses different types of weapon; most popular weapons: the standard pistol, small bore rifle, full bore rifle, air rifle and air pistol. All events involve shooting at still or moving targets (*see* **clay pigeon shooting**). Using firearms for sport developed in the 15th century. Hunting for game, eg grouse or pheasant shooting, has specifically defined seasons.

shot put Athletics field event; the shot is a brass or iron sphere weighing 7.3kg/16lb for men and 3.6kg/8lb 13 oz for women. It is propelled, using only one hand, from a starting position under the chin. The thrower must not leave the 2.1m/7ft diameter throwing circle. In competition six throws are allowed.

SPORTS (cont.)

skiing Propelling oneself along snow while standing on skis, aided by poles; named from Norwegian *ski*, 'snowshoe'; two forms of competition skiing: **alpine skiing**, consisting of the downhill, slalom (zigzag courses through markers) and ski jumping, and **Nordic skiing** (on narrower skis to which only the toe is attached), incorporating cross-country skiing and the **biathlon**. Other forms: **ski-flying** (hang gliding on skis) and **skijoring** (being towed behind a vehicle or horse).

skydiving or **freefalling** Jumping from an aircraft and freefalling, often performing a wide range of stunts or forming patterns by holding hands with other skydivers, to a height of 600m/2 000ft, when the parachute must be opened.

snooker Indoor game played on a standard billiards table by two (or occasionally four) players; aim is to 'pot' the 21 coloured balls (arranged on the table at the start) by hitting them with the white ball, itself hit using a tapered pole or *cue*. Fifteen of the balls are red; these must be potted alternately with the coloured ones. This sequence is called a *break* and continues until a mistake is made; reds remain in pockets but coloureds are returned to the table until no reds are left, when they are potted in ascending order; game ends when the black is finally potted. Points 1–7 relate to colours, in order: red, yellow, green, brown, blue, pink, black.

soccer *see* **football**

softball Smaller version of **baseball**, played on diamond-shaped pitch of sides measuring 18.3m/60ft; ball is larger as well as softer; teams of nine; game lasts for nine innings per team, each innings lasting until a team has three players out; object is to complete a circuit of the diamond without being put out, eg by being tagged between bases by a player with the ball. Pitching is underarm in softball, overarm in baseball; two forms: *fast pitch* and *slow pitch*; in the latter the bowler must deliver ball in arc at least 2.4m/8ft high.

speedway Motorcycle racing on machines with no brakes and only one gear, usually on an oval track and involving four riders at once. Other forms include *long track* racing and *ice speedway*.

squash or **squash rackets** Strenuous indoor racket-and-ball game played (in English singles) on an enclosed court measuring 9.75m/32ft long by 6.4m/21ft wide; small rubber ball is hit alternately by players against the front wall, so that it cannot be returned; developed 1817 from **rackets** at Harrow school; called *rackets* in the USA.

steeplechase National hunt horse racing; horses negotiate fixed fences normally 0.9–1.2m/3–4ft high; first one in Ireland in 1752; most famous is Grand National. See **horse racing**.

stock-car racing Motor racing; in USA: highly supercharged production cars race around concreted tracks; in UK: 'bangers' (old cars) race on round or oval track intending to be last car still moving at the end of the race; some 'rough' tactics are allowed to try to eliminate other drivers.

stoolball Eleven-a-side bat-and-ball game resembling cricket and rounders; batter defends wicket, a 30cm/1ft square wooden board 1.4m/4ft 8in from the ground, which underarm bowler attempts to hit; runs scored in similar way to cricket; uses wooden bat, similar in shape to tennis racket.

street hockey Hockey played on roller skates, popular in USA and Europe and becoming so in UK; five members to each team play on an enclosed rink.

sumo wrestling A Japanese national sport; competition takes place in a 3.66m/12ft diameter circle; object is to force opponent out of ring or to ground; sumo wrestlers are very heavy and eat vast amounts of food to increase weight and body size.

surfing Riding waves, either with the body alone, or with the aid of a board; object is to ride along the face of a wave before it breaks; board is usually about 1.8m/6ft long, but a longer one is used for competition; originated in Oceania, developed in Hawaii and has flourished in modern times there and in California and Australia.

swimming Propelling oneself through water without mechanical aids. Four strokes: *breast stroke*, the slowest stroke, developed in the 16th century; *front crawl* or *freestyle*, the fastest stroke; *backstroke*; and *butterfly*, developed in the USA in the 20th century. In competitions there are also relays, involving four swimmers, and medley races, combining all four strokes; Olympic-size pool is 50m/55yd long, with eight lanes; race lengths from 50m/55yd to 1 500m/1 640yd; earliest reference to swimming as a sport is 36BC Japan.

table tennis or **ping pong** Indoor bat-and-ball game played by two or four players; uses small wooden bats covered in rubber or sponge and a hollow plastic ball; table measures 2.75m/9ft by 1.52m/5ft and has a 15.25cm/6in-high net across

SPORTS (cont.)

it; ball must be hit over the net and into opposing half of table, to be returned without volleying; object is to play unreturnable shots; in doubles, players must hit ball alternately and in order; winner is first to reach 21 points with at least a two-point lead; thought to have been played 1880s.

taekwondo Martial art developed in Korea by General Choi Hong Hi; officially part of Korean tradition and culture since 1955, now popular as a sport.

tenpin bowling *see* **bowling**

tennis, lawn Racket-and-ball game for two or four players; court measures 23.77m/78ft long by 8.23m/27ft wide (singles), or 10.97m/36ft wide (doubles); net 0.9m/3ft high is stretched across centre; rackets have oval heads strung with nylon or gut; playing surface can be grass, clay, shale, concrete, wood, or other man-made materials; object is to play unreturnable strokes, thus scoring points; progression of scoring is 15, 30, 40, deuce if both reach 40, and game; set won by winning six games with a two-game lead (or one in a 'short' set). In doubles, players may hit ball in any order, but must serve in rotation. 'Field tennis' was played 18th century but game similar to modern game was invented 1873 as *sphairstike* in Wales by Walter Wingfield.

tobogganing *see* **bobsledding** and **lugeing**

trampolining Performing acrobatics on a sprung canvas sheet stretched across a frame, first used at turn of 20th century as a circus attraction; developed as a sport following design of modern trampoline in 1936. In competition, marks gained for performing difficult manoevres; popular forms are synchronized trampolining and tumbling.

trap shooting *see* **clay pigeon shooting**

triple jump Athletics field event; takes place in same place as long jump, governed by same rules. After the run-up, competitors must take off and hop on the same foot; second phase is a step onto the other foot, followed by a jump; previously called the *hop, step and jump.*

tug of war Athletics event of strength; two teams (normally eight men) pull against each other from opposite ends of a long thick rope; aim is to pull the opponents over a predetermined mark. Ancient Chinese and Egyptians participated in similar events; first rules drawn up 1879.

volleyball Indoor court game; two teams of six play on a court measuring 18m/59ft by 9m/29ft which has a raised net stretched across the centre; aim is to score points by grounding the inflated ball on opponents' side after hitting it over net with the arms or hands; ball may not be hit more than three times on one team's side of the net.

walking Either a leisurely pursuit (eg **fell walking**) or a competitive sport on roads or tracks which has strict rules: eg raised foot must touch ground before the other leaves it.

water polo Sport played by two seven-a-side teams in a swimming pool; aim is to score by propelling inflated ball into opposing team's goal at end of the pool, without touching the bottom; developed in Britian in 1869; originally called 'football in water'.

water skiing Being towed by a motor boat on one or two skis, using a 23m/75ft-long rope. Competitions held for jumping, slalom and acrobatics.

weightlifting Test of strength by lifting weights attached to both ends of a metal pole or *barbell.* Competitors have to make two successful lifts: the *snatch,* taking the bar to an outstretched position above the head in one movement (held for two seconds), and the *clean and jerk* or *jerk* which is achieved in two movements, first onto the chest, then above the head with outstretched arms; aggregate weight of the two lifts gives a competitor's total, and the weights are gradually increased. Another form is *powerlifting,* which calls for sheer strength rather than technique, and takes three forms: the *squat, dead lift* and *bench press.* Weightlifting was part of Ancient Olympic Games; introduced as sport c.1850.

wrestling Fighting person to person without using fists; aim is to throw opponent to the ground; most popular forms are *freestyle,* where the legs can be used to hold and trip, and *Graeco-Roman* where holds below the waist are not allowed. Ten weight divisions: light-flyweight (under 48kg) to super-heavyweight (over 100kg). Other forms: *sumo,* the national sport in Japan; *Sambo* from the USSR; *Kushti* in Iran; *Glima* in Iceland; *Schwingen* in Switzerland; and *Yagli,* the national sport in Turkey; also UK variations *Devon and Cornwall* and *Cumberland and Westmoreland.*

yachting *see* **sailing**

CHAMPIONS 1980–1992

For 1992 Summer Olympic events the designation (UT) is given for members of the Unified Team (Armenia, Azerbaijan, Byelorussia, Georgia, Kazakhstan, Kirghizia, Moldavia, Tadzhikistan, Turkmenistan, Ukraine and Uzbekistan).

AEROBATICS

World Championships
First held in 1960 and every two years since then except 1974.

Recent winners (Men)

1968 Erwin Bloske (East Germany)
1970 Igor Egorov (USSR)
1972 Charlie Hillard (USA)
1976 Vikto Letsko (USSR)
1978 Ivan Tucek (Czechoslovakia)
1980 Leo Loudenslager (USA)
1982 Viktor Smolin (USSR)
1984 Petr Jirmus (Czechoslovakia)
1986 Petr Jirmus (Czechoslovakia)
1988 Henry Haigh (USA)
1990 Claude Bessière (France)

Recent winners (Women)

1968 Madelyne Delcroix (France)
1970 Svetlana Savitskaya (USSR)
1972 Mary Gaffaney (USA)
1976 Lidia Leonova (USSR)
1978 Valentina Yaikova (USSR)
1980 Betty Stewart (USA)
1982 Betty Stewart (USA)
1984 Khalide Makagonova (USSR)
1986 Liubov Nemkova (USSR)
1988 Catherine Maunoury (France)
1990 Natalya Sergeyeva (USSR)

AMERICAN FOOTBALL

Superbowl
First held in 1967; takes place each January; an end-of-season meeting between the champions of the two major US leagues, the National Football Conference (NFC) and the American Football Conference (AFC).

Recent winners

1980 Pittsburgh Steelers (AFC)
1981 Oakland Raiders (NFC)
1982 San Francisco 49ers (NFC)
1983 Washington Redskins (NFC)
1984 Los Angeles Raiders (AFC)
1985 San Francisco 49ers (NFC)
1986 Chicago Bears (NFC)
1987 New York Giants (NFC)
1988 Washington Redskins (NFC)
1989 San Francisco 49ers (NFC)
1990 San Francisco 49ers (NFC)
1991 New York Giants (NFC)
1992 Washington Redskins (NFC)

Most wins: (4), Pittsburgh Steelers 1975–6, 1979–80; (4) San Francisco 49ers 1982, 1985, 1989–90

ANGLING

World Fresh Water Championship
First held in 1957; takes place annually.

Recent winners (Individual)

1979 Gerard Heulard (France)
1980 Wolf-Rüdiger Kremkus (West Germany)
1981 David Thomas (England)
1982 Kevin Ashurst (England)
1983 Wolf-Rüdiger Kremkus (West Germany)
1984 Bobby Smithers (Ireland)
1985 David Roper (England)
1986 Lud Wever (Holland)
1987 Clive Branson (Wales)
1988 Jean-Pierre Fouquet (France)
1989 Tom Pickering (England)
1990 Bobb Nudd (England)
1991 Bob Nudd (England)

Recent winners (Team)

1979 France
1980 West Germany
1981 France
1982 Holland
1983 Belgium
1984 Luxembourg
1985 England
1986 Italy
1987 England
1988 England
1989 Wales
1990 France
1991 England

Most wins: Individual (3), Robert Tesse (France) 1959–60, 1965. Team (12), France, 1959, 1963–4, 1966, 1968, 1972, 1974–5, 1978–9, 1981, 1990.

Angling (cont.)

World Fly Fishing Championship
First held in 1981; takes place annually.

Winners (Individual)

1981 C. Wittkamp (Holland)
1982 Viktor Diez y Diez (Spain)
1983 Segismondo Fernandez (Spain)
1984 Tony Pawson (England)
1985 Leslaw Frasik (Poland)
1986 Slivoj Svoboda (Czechoslovakia)
1987 Brian Leadbetter (England)
1988 John Pawson (England)
1989 Wladyslaw Trzebuinia (Poland)
1990 Franciszek Szajnik (Poland)
1991 Brian Leadbetter (England)

Winners (Team)

1981 Holland
1982 Italy
1983 Italy
1984 Italy
1985 Poland
1986 Italy
1987 England
1988 England
1989 Poland
1990 Czechoslovakia
1991 New Zealand

Most wins: Individual (no-one has won more than one title). Team (4), Italy, as above.

ARCHERY

World Championships
First held in 1931; took place annually until 1959; since then, every two years.

Recent winners
Individual (Men)

1969 Hardy Ward (USA)
1971 John Williams (USA)
1973 Vikto Sidoruk (USSR)
1975 Darrell Pace (USA)
1977 Richard McKinney (USA)
1979 Darrell Pace (USA)
1981 Kysti Laasonen (Finland)
1983 Richard McKinney (USA)
1985 Richard McKinney (USA)
1987 Vladimir Yesheyev (USSR)
1989 Stanislav Zabrodsky (USSR)
1991 Simon Fairweather (Australia)

Recent winners
Team (Men)

1969 USA
1971 USA
1973 USA
1975 USA
1977 USA
1979 USA
1981 USA
1983 USA
1985 South Korea
1987 South Korea
1989 USSR
1991 South Korea

Most wins: Individual (4), Hans Deutgen (Sweden) 1947–50. Team (14), USA 1957–83.

Recent winners
Individual (Women)

1969 Dorothy Lidstone (Canada)
1971 Emma Gapchenko (USSR)
1973 Linda Myers (USA)
1975 Zebiniso Rustamova (USSR)
1977 Luann Ryon (USA)
1979 Jin-Ho Kim (South Korea)
1981 Natalia Butuzova (USSR)
1983 Jin-Ho Kim (South Korea)
1985 Irina Soldatova (USSR)
1987 Ma Xiagjun (China)
1989 Soo Nyung-Kim (South Korea)
1991 Soo Nyung-Kim (South Korea)

Recent winners
Team (Women)

1969 USSR
1971 Poland
1973 USSR
1975 USSR
1977 USA
1979 South Korea
1981 USSR
1983 South Korea
1985 USSR
1987 USSR
1989 South Korea
1991 South Korea

Most wins: Individual (7), Janina Kurkowska (Poland) 1931–4, 1936, 1939, 1947. Team (8), USA 1952, 1957–9, 1961, 1963, 1965, 1977.

ASSOCIATION FOOTBALL

FIFA World Cup

Association Football's premier event; first contested for the Jules Rimet Trophy in 1930; Brazil won it outright after winning for the third time in 1970; since then teams have competed for the FIFA (*Féderation Internationale de Football Association*) World Cup; held every four years.

Post-war winners

1950 Uruguay
1954 West Germany
1958 Brazil
1962 Brazil
1966 England
1970 Brazil
1974 West Germany
1978 Argentina
1982 Italy
1986 Argentina
1990 West Germany

Most wins: (3), Brazil, as above; (3) Italy, 1934, 1938, 1982. (3) West Germany, as above

European Championship

Held every four years since 1960; qualifying group matches held over the two years preceding the final.

Winners

1960 USSR
1964 Spain
1968 Italy
1972 West Germany
1976 Czechoslovakia
1980 West Germany
1984 France
1988 Holland

Most wins: (2), West Germany, as above.

South American Championship

First held in 1916, for South American national sides; discontinued in 1967, but revived eight years later; now played every two years.

Recent winners

1956 Uruguay
1957 Argentina
1959[1] Argentina
1959[1] Uruguay
1963 Bolivia
1967 Uruguay
1975 Peru
1979 Paraguay
1983 Uruguay
1987 Uruguay
1989 Brazil
1991 Argentina

[1] There were two tournaments in 1959.

Most wins: (13), Uruguay, 1916–17, 1920, 1923–4, 1926, 1935, 1942, 1956, 1959, 1967, 1983, 1987

European Champions Cup

The leading club competition in Europe; open to the League champions of countries affiliated to UEFA (Union of European Football Associations); commonly known as the 'European Cup'; inaugurated in the 1955–6 season; played annually.

Recent winners

1979 Nottingham Forest (England)
1980 Nottingham Forest (England)
1981 Liverpool (England)
1982 Aston Villa (England)
1983 SV Hamburg (West Germany)
1984 Liverpool (England)
1985 Juventus (Italy)
1986 Steaua Bucharest (Romania)
1987 FC Porto (Portugal)
1988 PSV Eindhoven (Holland)
1989 AC Milan (Italy)
1990 AC Milan (Italy)
1991 Red Star Belgrade (Yugoslavia)

Most wins: (6), Real Madrid (Spain), 1956–60, 1966.

Football Association Challenge Cup

The world's oldest club knockout competition (the 'FA cup'), held annually; first contested in the 1871–2 season; first final at the Kennington Oval on 16 March 1872; first winners were The Wanderers.

Recent winners

1979 Arsenal
1980 West Ham United
1981 Tottenham Hotspur
1982 Tottenham Hotspur
1983 Manchester United
1984 Everton
1985 Manchester United
1986 Liverpool
1987 Coventry City
1988 Wimbledon
1989 Liverpool
1990 Manchester United
1991 Tottenham Hotspur

Most wins: (8), Tottenham Hotspur, 1901, 1921, 1961–2, 1967, 1981–2, 1991.

Association Football (cont.)

Football League
The oldest league in the world, and regarded as the toughest; founded in 1888; consists of four divisions; the current complement of 92 teams achieved in 1950.

Recent winners	
1979–80	Liverpool
1980–1	Aston Villa
1981–2	Liverpool
1982–3	Liverpool
1983–4	Liverpool
1984–5	Everton
1985–6	Liverpool
1986–7	Everton
1987–8	Liverpool
1988–9	Arsenal
1989–90	Liverpool
1990–1	Arsenal

Most wins: (18), Liverpool, 1901, 1906, 1922–3, 1947, 1964, 1966, 1973, 1976–7, 1979–80, 1982–4, 1986, 1988, 1990.

ATHLETICS

World Championships
First held in Helsinki, Finland in 1983, then in Rome, Italy in 1987; take place every four years.

Event	Winners (Men)
1983	
100 m	Carl Lewis (USA)
200 m	Calvin Smith (USA)
400 m	Bert Cameron (Jamaica)
800 m	Willi Wüllbeck (East Germany)
1 500 m	Steve Cram (UK)
5 000 m	Eamonn Coghlan (Ireland)
10 000 m	Alberto Cova (Italy)
Marathon	Rob de Castella (Austria)
3000 m steeplechase	Patriz Ilg (West Germany)
110 m hurdles	Greg Foster (USA)
400 m hurdles	Ed Moses (USA)
20 km walk	Ernesto Canto (Mexico)
50 km walk	Ronald Weigel (East Germany)
4 × 100 m relay	USA
4 × 400 m relay	USSR
High jump	Gennadiy Avdeyenko (USSR)
Long jump	Carl Lewis (USA)
Triple jump	Zdzislaw Hoffman (Poland)
Pole vault	Sergey Bubka (USSR)
Shot	Edward Sarul (Poland)
Discus	Imrich Bugar (Czechoslovakia)
Hammer	Sergey Litvinov (USSR)
Javelin	Detlef Michel (East Germany)
Decathlon	Daley Thompson (UK)
1987	
100 m	Ben Johnson (Canada)
200 m	Calvin Smith (USA)
400 m	Thomas Schoenlebe (East Germany)
800 m	Billy Konchellah (Kenya)
1 500 m	Abdi Bile (Somalia)
5 000 m	Said Aouita (Morocco)
10 000 m	Paul Kipkoech (Kenya)
Marathon	Douglas Waikihuru (Kenya)
3 000 m steeplechase	Francesco Panetta (Italy)
110 m hurdles	Greg Foster (USA)
400 m hurdles	Ed Moses (USA)
20 km walk	Maurizio Damilano (Italy)
50 km walk	Hartwig Gauder (East Germany)
4 × 100 m relay	USA
4 × 400 m relay	USA
High jump	Patrik Sjoeberg (Sweden)
Long jump	Carl Lewis (USA)
Triple jump	Khristo Markov (Bulgaria)
Pole vault	Sergey Bubka (USSR)
Shot	Werner Gunthoer (Switzerland)
Discus	Jurgen Schult (East Germany)
Hammer	Sergey Litvinov (USSR)
Javelin	Seppo Raty (Finland)
Decathlon	Torsten Voss (East Germany)

Athletics (cont.)

1991	
100 m	Carl Lewis (USA)
200 m	Michael Johnson (USA)
400 m	Antonio Pettigrew (USA)
800 m	Billy Konchellah (Kenya)
1 500 m	Noureddine Morceli (Algeria)
5 000 m	Yobes Ondieki (Kenya)
10 000 m	Moses Tanui (Kenya)
Marathon	Hiromi Taniguchi (Japan)
3000 m steeplechase	Moses Kiptanui (Kenya)
100 m hurdles	Greg Foster (Zambia)
400 m hurdles	Samuel Matete (Zambia)
20 km walk	Maurizio Damilano (Italy)
50 km walk	Alexandr Potashov (USSR)
4 × 100 m relay	USA
4 × 400 m relay	UK
High jump	Charles Austin (USA)
Long jump	Mike Powell (USA)
Triple jump	Kenny Harrison (USA)
Pole vault	Sergey Bubka (USSR)
Shot	Werner Gunthor (Switzerland)
Discus	Lars Riedel (Germany)
Hammer	Yuriy Sedykh (USSR)
Javelin	Kimmo Kinnunen (Finland)
Decathlon	Dan O'Brien (USA)

Event	Winners (Women)
1983	
100 m	Marlies Göhr (East Germany)
200 m	Marita Koch (East Germany)
400 m	Jarmila Kratochvilova (Czechoslovakia)
800 m	Jarmila Kratochvilova (Czechoslovakia)
1 500 m	Mary Decker (USA)
3000 m	Mary Decker (USA)
Marathon	Greta Waitz (Norway)
100 m hurdles	Bettina Jahn (East Germany)
400 m hurdles	Ekaterina Fesenko (USSR)
4 × 100 m relay	East Germany
4 × 400 m relay	East Germany
High jump	Tamara Bykova (USSR)
Long jump	Heike Daute (East Germany)
Shot	Helene Fibingerova (Czechoslovakia)
Discus	Martina Opitz (East Germany)
Javelin	Tiina Lillak (Finland)
Heptathlon	Tamona Neubert (East Germany)
1987	
100 m	Silke Gladisch (East Germany)
200 m	Silke Gladisch (East Germany)
400 metres	Olga Bryzgina (USSR)
800 m	Sigrun Wodars (East Germany)
1 500 m	Tatyana Samolenko (USSR)
3000 m	Tatyana Samolenko (USSR)
Marathon	Rosa Mota (Portugal)
100 m hurdles	Ginka Zagorcheva (Bulgaria)
400 m hurdles	Sabine Busche (East Germany)
10 km walk	Irinia Strakhova (USSR)
4 × 100 m relay	USA
4 × 400 m relay	East Germany
High jump	Stefka Kostadinova (Bulgaria)
Long jump	Jackie Joyner-Kersee (USA)
Shot	Natalya Lisovskaya (USSR)
Discus	Martina Hellman (*née* Opitz) (East Germany)
Javelin	Fatima Whitbread (UK)
Heptathlon	Jackie Joyner-Kersee (USA)
1991	
100 m	Katrin Krabbe (Germany)
200 m	Katrin Krabbe (Germany)
400 m	Marie-Jose Perec (France)
800 m	Lilia Nurutdinova (USSR)
1 500 m	Hassiba Boulmerka (Algeria)
3000 m	Tatyana Dorovskikh (USSR)

Athletics (cont.)

10 000 m	Liz McColgan (UK)
Marathon	Wanda Panfil (Poland)
100 m hurdles	Lyudmila Narozhilenko (USSR)
400 m hurdles	Tatyana Ledovskaya (USSR)
10 km walk	Alina Ivanova (USSR)
4 × 100 m relay	Jamaica
4 × 400 m relay	USSR
High jump	Heike Henkel (Germany)
Long jump	Jackie Joyner-Kersee (USA)
Shot	Huang Zhihong (China)
Discus	Tsvetanka Khristova (Bulgaria)
Javelin	Xu Demei (China)
Heptathlon	Sabine Braun (Germany)

AUSTRALIAN RULES FOOTBALL

Victoria Football League

The top prize is the Australian Football League Trophy (Victoria Football League 1897–1989); inaugural winners in 1897 were Essendon.

Recent winners

1979 Carlton
1980 Richmond
1981 Carlton
1982 Carlton
1983 Hawthorn
1984 Essendon
1985 Essendon
1986 Hawthorn
1987 Carlton
1988 Hawthorn
1989 Hawthorn
1990 Collingwood
1991 Hawthorn

Most wins: (15), Carlton, 1906–8, 1914–15, 1938, 1945, 1947, 1968, 1970, 1972, 1979, 1981–2, 1987.

BADMINTON

World Championships

First held in 1977; initially took place every three years; since 1983 every two years.

Singles winners (Men)

1977 Flemming Delfs (Denmark)
1980 Rudy Hartono (Indonesia)
1983 Icuk Sugiarto (Indonesia)
1985 Han Jian (China)
1987 Yang Yang (China)
1989 Yang Yang (China)
1991 Zhao Jianhua (China)

Singles winners (Women)

1977 Lene Koppen (Denmark)
1980 Wiharjo Verawatay (Indonesia)
1983 Li Lingwei (China)
1985 Han Aiping (China)
1987 Han Aiping (China)
1989 Li Lingwei (China)
1991 Tang Jiuhong (China)

Most titles: (3), Han Aiping (2 singles as above, women's doubles 1985).

Thomas Cup

An international team event for men's teams; inaugurated 1949, now held every two years.

Recent winners

1964 Indonesia
1967 Malaysia
1970 Indonesia
1973 Indonesia
1976 Indonesia
1979 Indonesia
1982 China
1984 Indonesia
1986 China
1988 China
1990 China

Most wins: (8), Indonesia, 1958–61, 1964, 1970–9, 1984.

Uber Cup

An international event for women's teams; first held in 1957; now held every two years.

Recent winners

1963 USA
1966 Japan
1969 Japan
1972 Japan
1975 Indonesia
1978 Japan
1981 Japan
1984 China
1986 China
1988 China
1990 China

Most wins: (5), Japan, as above.

Badminton (cont.)

All-England Championship
Badminton's premier event prior to the inauguration of the World Championships; first held in 1899.

Recent winners
Singles (Men)

1980 Prakash Padukone (Indonesia)
1981 Liem Swie King (Indonesia)
1982 Morten Frost (Denmark)
1983 Luan Jin (China)
1984 Morten Frost (Denmark)
1985 Zhao Jianhua (China)
1986 Morten Frost (Denmark)
1987 Morten Frost (Denmark)
1988 Ib Frederikson (Denmark)
1989 Yang Yang (China)
1990 Zhao Jianhua (China)
1991 Ardi Wiranata (Indonesia)
1992 Liu Jun (China)

Recent winners
Singles (Women)

1980 Lene Koppen (Denmark)
1981 Sun Ai Hwang (Korea)
1982 Zang Ailing (China)
1983 Zang Ailing (China)
1984 Li Lingwei (China)
1985 Han Aiping (China)
1986 Yun-Ja Kim (Korea)
1987 Kirsten Larsen (Denmark)
1988 Gu Jiaming (China)
1989 Li Lingwei (China)
1990 Susi Susanti (Indonesia)
1991 Susi Susanti (Indonesia)
1992 Tang Jiuhong (China)

Most titles: (21: 4 singles, 9 men's doubles, 8 mixed doubles), George Thomas (England) 1903–28.

BASEBALL

World Series
First held in 1903; takes place each October, the best of seven matches; professional Baseball's leading event, the end-of-season meeting between the winners of the two Major Baseball leagues in the USA, the National League (NL) and American League (AL).

Recent winners

1979 Pittsburgh Pirates (NL)
1980 Philadelphia Phillies (NL)
1981 Los Angeles Dodgers (NL)
1982 St Louis Cardinals (NL)
1983 Baltimore Orioles (AL)
1984 Detroit Tigers (AL)
1985 Kansas City Royals (AL)
1986 New York Mets (NL)
1987 Minnesota Twins (AL)
1988 Los Angeles Dodgers (NL)
1989 Oakland Athletics (AL)
1990 Cincinatti Reds (NL)
1991 Minnesota Twins (AL)

Most wins: (22), New York Yankees, 1923, 1927–8, 1932, 1936–9, 1941, 1943, 1947, 1949–53, 1956, 1958, 1961–2, 1977–8.

World Amateur Championship
Instituted in 1938; since 1974 held every two years.

Recent winners

1972 Cuba
1973 Cuba & USA (*shared*)
1974 USA
1976 Cuba
1978 Cuba
1980 Cuba
1982 South Korea
1984 Cuba
1986 Cuba
1988 Cuba
1990 Cuba

Most wins: (20), Cuba, 1939–40, 1942–43, 1950, 1952–3, 1961, 1969–73, 1976–80, 1984–86, 1988, 1990.

BASKETBALL

World Championship
First held 1950 for men, 1953 for women; takes place every four years.

Winners (Men)

1950 Argentina
1954 USA
1959 Brazil
1963 Brazil
1967 USSR
1970 Yugoslavia
1974 USSR
1978 Yugoslavia
1982 USSR
1986 USA
1990 Yugoslavia

Most wins: (3), USSR, as above, Yugoslavia, as above.

Basketball (cont.)

Winners (Women)

1953 USA
1957 USA
1959 USSR
1964 USSR
1967 USSR
1971 USSR
1975 USSR
1979 USA
1983 USSR
1987 USA
1991 USA

Most wins: (6), USSR, as above.

National Basketball Association Championship
First held in 1947; the major competition in professional basketball in the USA, end-of-season NBA Play-off involving the champion teams from the Eastern (EC) Conference and Western Conference (WC).

Recent winners

1979 Seattle Supersonics (WC)
1980 Los Angeles Lakers (WC)
1981 Boston Celtics (EC)
1982 Los Angeles Lakers (WC)
1983 Philadelphia 76ers (EC)
1984 Boston Celtics (EC)
1985 Los Angeles Lakers (WC)
1986 Boston Celtics (EC)
1987 Los Angeles Lakers (WC)
1988 Los Angeles Lakers (WC)
1989 Detroit Pistons (EC)
1990 Detroit Pistons (EC)
1991 Chicago Bulls (EC)

Most wins: (16), Boston Celtics, 1957, 1959–66, 1968–9, 1974, 1976, 1981, 1984, 1986.

BIATHLON

World Championships
First held in 1958; take place annually; the Olympic champion is the automatic world champion in Olympic years; women's championship first held in 1984.

Recent winners
Individual (Men)

10 km (15 km since 1988)
1979 Frank Ullrich (East Germany)
1980 Frank Ullrich (East Germany)
1981 Frank Ullrich (East Germany)
1982 Eirik Kvalfoss (Norway)
1983 Eirik Kvalfoss (Norway)
1984 Eirik Kvalfoss (Norway)
1985 Frank-Peter Rötsch (East Germany)
1986 Valeriy Medvetsev (USSR)
1987 Frank-Peter Rötsch (East Germany)
1988 Frank-Peter Rötsch (East Germany)
1989 Frank Luck (East Germany)
1990 Mark Kirchner (East Germany)
1991 Mark Kirchner (Germany)
1992 Mark Kirchner (Germany)

20 km
1979 Klaus Siebert (East Germany)
1980 Anatoliy Alyabyev (USSR)
1981 Heikki Ikola (Finland)
1982 Frank Ullrich (East Germany)
1983 Frank Ullrich (East Germany)
1984 Peter Angerer (West Germany)
1985 Yuriy Kashkarov (USSR)
1986 Valeriy Medvetsev (USSR)
1987 Frank-Peter Rötsch (East Germany)
1988 Frank-Peter Rötsch (East Germany)
1989 Eric Kralfoss (Norway)
1990 Valeriy Medvetsev (USSR)
1991 Mark Kirchner (Germany)
1992 Evgeny Redkine (CIS)

Most individual titles: (6), Frank Ullrich (East Germany), as above plus 1978 10 km.

Recent winners
Individual (Women)

5 km (7.5 km since 1988)
1984 Venera Chernyshova (USSR)
1985 Sanna Gronlid (Norway)
1986 Kaya Parva (USSR)
1987 Yelena Golovina (USSR)
1988 Petra Schaaf (West Germany)
1989 Anna Elvebakk (Norway)
1990 Anna Elvebakk (Norway)
1991 Ingeborg Nykelmo (Norway)
1992 Anfissa Restzova (CIS)

10 km (15 km since 1988)
1984 Venera Chernyshova (USSR)
1985 Kaya Parva (USSR)
1986 Eva Korpela (Sweden)
1987 Sanna Gronlid (Norway)
1988 Anna Elvebakk (Norway)
1989 Petra Schaaf (West Germany)
1990 Svetlana Davydova (USSR)
1991 Petra Schaaf (Germany)
1992 Antje Misersky (Germany)

BILLIARDS

World Professional Championship
First held in 1870, organized on a challenge basis; became a knockout event in 1909; discontinued in 1934; revived in 1951 as a challenge system; reverted to a knockout event in 1980.

Recent winners

1980 Fred Davis (England)
1981 *not held*
1982 Rex Williams (England)
1983 Rex Williams (England)
1984 Mark Wildman (England)
1985 Ray Edmonds (England)
1986 Robbie Foldvari (Australia)
1987 Norman Dagley (England)
1988 Norman Dagley (England)
1989 Mike Russell (England)
1990 *not held*
1991 Mike Russell (England)

Most wins: (knockout) (6), Tom Newman (England), 1921–2, 1924–7. (challenge) (8), John Roberts, Jnr (England), 1870–85.

BOBSLEIGHING AND TOBOGGANING

World Championships
First held in 1930 (four-man) and in 1931 (two-man); Olympic champions automatically become world champions.

Recent winners (Two-man)

1980 Erich Schärer/Josef Benz (Switzerland)
1981 Bernhard Germeshausen/Hans-Jürgen Gerhardt (East Germany)
1982 Erich Schärer/Josef Benz (Switzerland)
1983 Ralf Pichler/Urs Leuthold (Switzerland)
1984 Wolfgang Hoppe/Dietmar Schauerhammer (East Germany)
1985 Wolfgang Hoppe/Dietmar Schauerhammer (East Germany)
1986 Wolfgang Hoppe/Dietmar Schauerhammer (East Germany)
1987 Ralf Pichler/Celest Poltera (Switzerland)
1988 Janis Kipurs/Vladimir Kozlov (USSR)
1989 Wolfgang Hoppe/Bogdan Musiol (East Germany)
1990 Gustav Weder/Bruno Gerber (Switzerland)
1991 Rudi Lochner/Marcus Zimmermann (Germany)
1992 Gustav Weder/Donat Acklin (Switzerland)

Recent winners (Four-man)

1980 East Germany
1981 East Germany
1982 Switzerland
1983 Switzerland
1984 East Germany
1985 East Germany
1986 Switzerland
1987 Switzerland
1988 Switzerland
1989 Switzerland
1990 Switzerland
1991 Germany
1992 Austria

Most wins: (Two-man) (8), Eugenio Monti (Italy) 1957–61, 1963, 1966, 1968. (Four-man) (14), Switzerland, 1939, 1947, 1954–5, 1957, 1971, 1973, 1975, 1982–3, 1986–9.

Luge World Championships
First held in 1955; annually until 1981, then every two years; up to 1980 the Olympic champions were also world champions if the event was included in the Olympic programme.

Recent winners
Men's single-seater

1976 Detlef Günther (East Germany)
1977 Hans Rinn (East Germany)
1978 Paul Hildgartner (Italy)
1979 Detlef Günther (East Germany)
1980 Bernhard Glass (East Germany)
1981 Sergey Danilin (USSR)
1983 Miroslav Zajonc (Canada)
1985 Michael Walter (East Germany)
1987 Markus Prock (Austria)
1989 George Hack (West Germany)
1991 A Huber (Italy)

Most wins: (3), Thomas Köhler (East Germany), 1962, 1964, 1967.

Recent winners
Women's single-seater

1976 Margrit Schumann (East Germany)
1977 Margrit Schumann (East Germany)
1978 Vera Sosulya (USSR)
1979 Melitta Sollmann (East Germany)
1980 Vera Sosúlya (USSR)
1981 Melitta Sollman (East Germany)
1983 Steffi Martin (East Germany)
1985 Steffi Martin (East Germany)
1987 Cerstin Schmidt (East Germany)
1989 Susi Erdmann (East Germany)
1991 Susi Erdmann (Germany)

Most wins: (5), Margrit Schumann (East Germany), 1973–7.

BOWLS

World Championships

Instituted for men in 1966 and for women in 1969; held every four years.

Men's Singles

1966 David Bryant (England)
1972 Malwyn Evans (Wales)
1976 Doug Watson (South Africa)
1980 David Bryant (England)
1984 Peter Bellis (New Zealand)
1988 David Bryant (England)

Men's Pairs

1966 Australia
1972 Hong Kong
1976 South Africa
1980 Australia
1984 USA
1988 New Zealand

Men's Triples

1966 Australia
1972 USA
1976 South Africa
1980 England
1984 Ireland
1988 New Zealand

Men's Fours

1966 New Zealand
1972 England
1976 South Africa
1980 Hong Kong
1984 England
1988 Ireland

Leonard Trophy

Team award, given to the nation with the best overall performances in the men's world championship.

Winners

1966 Australia
1972 Scotland
1976 South Africa
1980 England
1984 Scotland
1988 England

Most wins: (6), David Bryant (singles as above, plus Triples and Team 1980, 1988).

Women's Singles

1969 Gladys Doyle (Papua New Guinea)
1973 Elsie Wilke (New Zealand)
1977 Elsie Wilke (New Zealand)
1981 Norma Shaw (England)
1985 Merle Richardson (Australia)
1988[1] Janet Ackland (Wales)

Women's Pairs

1969 South Africa
1973 Australia
1977 Hong Kong
1981 Ireland
1985 Australia
1988[1] Ireland

Women's Triples

1969 South Africa
1973 New Zealand
1977 Wales
1981 Hong Kong
1985 Australia
1988[1] Australia

Women's Fours

1969 South Africa
1973 New Zealand
1977 Australia
1981 England
1985 Scotland
1988[1] Australia

Women's Team

1969 South Africa
1973 New Zealand
1977 Australia
1981 England
1985 Australia
1988[1] England

Most wins: (3), Merle Richardson (Fours 1977; Singles and Pairs 1985).

[1] The women's event was advanced to Dec 1988 (Australia)

World Indoor Championships

First held in 1979; take place annually.

Winners

1979 David Bryant (England)
1980 David Bryant (England)
1981 David Bryant (England)
1982 John Watson (Scotland)
1983 Bob Sutherland (Scotland)
1984 Jim Baker (Ireland)
1985 Terry Sullivan (Wales)
1986 Tony Allcock (England)
1987 Tony Allcock (England
1988 Hugh Duff (Scotland)

Bowls (cont.)

1989	Richard Corsie (Scotland)
1990	John Price (Wales)
1991	Richard Corsie (Scotland)
1992	Ian Schuback (Australia)

Most wins: (3), David Bryant (England), as above.

Waterloo Handicap
First held in 1907 and annually at Blackpool's Waterloo Hotel; the premier event of Crown Green Bowling.

Recent winners	
1979	Brian Duncan
1980	Vernon Lee
1981	Roy Nicholson
1982	Dennis Mercer
1983	Stan Frith
1984	Steve Ellis
1985	Tommy Johnstone
1986	Brian Duncan
1987	Brian Duncan
1988	Ingham Gregory
1989	Brian Duncan
1990	John Bancroft
1991	John Eccles

Most wins: (4), Brian Duncan, as above.

BOXING

World Heavyweight Champions
The first world heavyweight champion under Queensbury Rules with gloves was James J Corbett in 1892.

Champions since 1978		Recognizing Body
1978	Leon Spinks (USA)	UND
1978	Ken Norton (USA)	WBC
1978	Muhammad Ali (USA)	WBA
1978	Larry Holmes (USA)	WBC
1979	John Tate (USA)	WBA
1980	Mike Weaver (USA)	WBA
1982	Mike Dokes (USA)	WBA
1983	Gerry Coetzee (South Africa)	WBA
1984	Larry Holmes (USA)	IBF
1984	Tim Witherspoon (USA)	WBC
1984	Pinklon Thomas (USA)	WBC
1984	Greg Page (USA)	WBA
1985	Michael Spinks (USA)	IBF
1985	Tony Tubbs (USA)	WBA
1986	Tim Witherspoon (USA)	WBA
1986	Trevor Berbick (Canada)	WBC
1986	Mike Tyson (USA)	WBC
1986	James Smith (USA)	WBA
1987	Tony Tucker (USA)	IBF
1987	Mike Tyson (USA)	WBA/WBC
1987	Mike Tyson (USA)	UND
1989	Francesco Damiani (Italy)	WBO
1989	Mike Tyson (USA)	WBA/WBC/IBF
1990	James (Buster) Douglas (USA)	WBA/WBC/IBF
1990	Evandes Holyfield (USA)	WBA/WBC/IBF
1991	Ray Mercer (USA)	WBO

UND = Undisputed Champion
WBC = World Boxing Council
WBA = World Boxing Association
IBF = International Boxing Federation
WBO = World Boxing Organization

CANOEING

Olympic Games
The most prestigious competition in the canoeing calendar, included at every Olympic celebration since 1936; the Blue Riband event in the men's competition is the Kayak Singles over 1000 metres, and in the women's the Kayak Singles over 500 metres.

Single kayak (Men)	
1936	Gregor Hradetzky (Austria)
1948	Gert Fredriksson (Sweden)
1952	Gert Fredriksson (Sweden)
1956	Gert Fredriksson (Sweden)
1960	Erik Hansen (Denmark)
1964	Rolf Peterson (Sweden)
1968	Mihaly Hesz (Hungary)
1972	Aleksandr Shaparenko (USSR)
1976	Rüdiger Helm (East Germany)
1980	Rüdiger Helm (East Germany)
1984	Alan Thompson (New Zealand)
1988	Greg Barton (USA)
1992	Clint Robinson (Australia)

Single kayak (Women)	
1948	Keren Hoff (Denmark)
1952	Sylvi Saimo (Finland)
1956	Elisaveta Dementyeva (USSR)
1960	Antonina Seredina (USSR)
1964	Lyudmila Khvedosyuk (USSR)
1968	Lyudmila Pinayeva (USSR)
1972	Yulia Ryabchinskaya (USSR)
1976	Carola Zirzow (East Germany)
1980	Birgit Fischer (East Germany)
1984	Agneta Andersson (Sweden)
1988	Vania Guecheva (USSR)
1992	Birgit Schmidt (Germany)

Most wins: Men (3), Gert Fredriksson as above. No woman has won more than one title.

CHESS

World Champions

World Champions have been recognized since 1886. The first international tournament was held in London in 1851, and won by Adolf Anderssen (Germany), first women's champion recognized in 1927.

Post-war champions (Men)

1948–57 Mikhail Botvinnik (USSR)
1957–8 Vassiliy Smyslov (USSR)
1958–60 Mikhail Botvinnik (USSR)
1960–1 Mikhail Tal (USSR)
1961–3 Mikhail Botvinnik (USSR)
1963–9 Tigran Petrosian (USSR)
1969–72 Boris Spassky (USSR)
1972–5 Bobby Fischer (USA)
1975–85 Anatoliy Karpov (USSR)
1985– Gary Kasparov (USSR)

Longest reigning champion: 27 years, Emanuel Lasker (Germany) 1894–1921.

Champions (Women)

1927–44 Vera Menchik-Stevenson (UK)
1950–3 Lyudmila Rudenko (USSR)
1953–6 Elizaveta Bykova (USSR)
1956–8 Olga Rubtsova (USSR)
1958–62 Elizaveta Bykova (USSR)
1962–78 Nona Gaprindashvili (USSR)
1978–91 Maya Chiburdanidze (USSR)
1991– Xie Jun (China)

Longest reigning champion: 17 years, Vera Menchik-Stevenson (UK), as above.

CONTRACT BRIDGE

World Team Championship

The game's biggest championship; men's contest (The Bermuda Bowl) first held in 1951, and now takes place every two years; women's contest (The Venice Cup) first held in 1974, and since 1985 is concurrent with the men's event.

Recent winners (Men)

1973 Italy
1974 Italy
1975 Italy
1976 USA
1977 USA
1979 USA
1981 USA
1983 USA
1985 USA
1987 USA
1989 Brazil

Most wins: (13), Italy, 1957–9, 1961–3, 1965–7, 1969, 1973–5.

Recent winners (Women)

1974 USA
1976 USA
1978 USA
1981 UK
1983 not held
1985 UK
1987 Italy
1989 USA

Most wins: (4), USA, as above.

World Team Olympiad

First held in 1960; since then, every four years.

Winners (Men)

1960 France
1964 Italy
1968 Italy
1972 Italy
1976 Brazil
1980 France
1984 Poland
1988 USA

Winners (Women)

1960 United Arab Emirates
1964 UK
1968 Sweden
1972 Italy
1976 USA
1980 USA
1984 USA
1988 Denmark

Most wins: Men (3), Italy, as above; women (3), USA, as above.

CRICKET

World Cup

First played in England in 1975; held every four years; the 1987 competition was the first to be played outside England, in India and Pakistan.

Winners

1975 West Indies
1979 West Indies

Cricket (cont.)

1983 India
1987 Australia
1992 Pakistan

County Championship
The oldest cricket competition in the world; first won by Sussex in 1827; not officially recognized until 1890, when a proper points system was introduced.

Recent winners

1979 Essex
1980 Middlesex
1981 Nottinghamshire
1982 Middlesex
1983 Essex
1984 Essex
1985 Middlesex
1986 Essex
1987 Nottinghamshire
1988 Worcestershire
1989 Worcestershire
1990 Middlesex
1991 Essex

Most outright wins: (29), Yorkshire, 1893, 1896, 1898, 1900–2, 1905, 1908, 1912, 1919, 1922–5, 1931–3, 1935, 1937–9, 1946, 1959–60, 1962–3, 1966–8.

Refuge Assurance League
First held in 1969; known as the John Player League until 1987.

Recent winners

1979 Somerset
1980 Warwickshire
1981 Essex
1982 Sussex
1983 Yorkshire
1984 Essex
1985 Essex
1986 Hampshire
1987 Worcestershire
1988 Worcestershire
1989 Lancashire
1990 Derbyshire
1991 Nottinghamshire

Most wins: (3), Kent, 1972–3, 1976; Essex, as above; Lancashire 1969–70, 1989.

NatWest Bank Trophy
First held in 1963; known as the Gillette Cup until 1981.

Recent winners

1979 Somerset
1980 Middlesex
1981 Derbyshire
1982 Surrey
1983 Somerset
1984 Middlesex
1985 Essex
1986 Sussex
1987 Nottinghamshire
1988 Middlesex
1989 Warwickshire
1990 Lancashire
1991 Hampshire

Most wins: (5), Lancashire, 1970–2, 1975, 1990.

Benson and Hedges Cup
First held in 1972.

Recent winners

1979 Essex
1980 Northamptonshire
1981 Somerset
1982 Somerset
1983 Middlesex
1984 Lancashire
1985 Leicestershire
1986 Middlesex
1987 Yorkshire
1988 Hampshire
1989 Nottinghamshire
1990 Lancashire
1991 Worcestershire
1992 Hampshire

Most wins: (3), Kent, 1973, 1976, 1978; Leicestershire, 1972, 1975, 1985.

Sheffield Shield
Australia's leading domestic competition; contested inter-state since 1891–2.

Recent winners

1980 Victoria
1981 Western Australia
1982 South Australia
1983 New South Wales
1984 Western Australia
1985 New South Wales
1986 New South Wales
1987 Western Australia
1988 Western Australia
1989 Western Australia
1990 New South Wales
1991 Victoria
1992 Western Australia

Cricket (cont.)

Most wins: 40, New South Wales, 1896–7, 1900, 1902–7, 1909, 1911–12, 1914, 1920–1, 1923, 1926, 1929, 1932–3, 1938, 1940, 1949–50, 1952, 1954–62, 1965–6, 1983, 1985–6, 1990.

CROQUET

McRobertson Shield

Croquet's leading tournament; held spasmodically since 1925; contested by teams from Great Britain, New Zealand and Australia.

Winners

1925 Great Britain
1928 Australia
1930 Australia
1935 Australia
1937 Great Britain
1950 New Zealand
1956 Great Britain
1963 Great Britain
1969 Great Britain
1974 Great Britain
1979 New Zealand
1982 Great Britain
1986 New Zealand
1990 Great Britain

Most wins: (8), Great Britain, as above.

CROSS COUNTRY RUNNING

World Championships

First international championship held in 1903, but only included runners from England, Ireland, Scotland and Wales; recognized as an official world championship from 1973; first women's race in 1967.

Recent winners
Individual (Men)

1980 Craig Virgin (USA)
1981 Craig Virgin (USA)
1982 Mohamed Kedir (Ethiopia)
1983 Bekele Debele (Ethiopia)
1984 Carlos Lopes (Portugal)
1985 Carlos Lopes (Portugal)
1986 John Ngugi (Kenya)
1987 John Ngugi (Kenya)
1988 John Ngugi (Kenya)
1989 John Ngugi (Kenya)
1990 Khalid Skah (Morocco)
1991 Khalid Skah (Morocco)
1992 John Ngugi (Kenya)

Recent winners (Team)

1980 England
1981 Ethiopia
1982 Ethiopia
1983 Ethiopia
1984 Ethiopia
1985 Ethiopia
1986 Kenya
1987 Kenya
1988 Kenya
1989 Kenya
1990 Kenya
1991 Kenya
1992 Kenya

Most wins: Individual (5), John Ngugi, as above. Team (44), England, between 1903 and 1980

Recent winners
Individual (Women)

1980 Greta Waitz (Norway)
1981 Greta Waitz (Norway)
1982 Maricica Puica (Romania)
1983 Greta Waitz (Norway)
1984 Maricica Puica (Romania)
1985 Zola Budd (England)
1986 Zola Budd (England)
1987 Annette Sergent (France)
1988 Ingrid Kristiansen (Norway)
1989 Annette Sergent (France)
1990 Lynn Jennings (USA)
1991 Lynn Jennings (USA)
1992 Lynn Jennings (USA)

Recent winners
Team (Women)

1980 USSR
1981 USSR
1982 USSR
1983 USA
1984 USA
1985 USA
1986 England
1987 USA
1988 USSR
1989 USSR
1990 USSR
1991 Ethiopia and Kenya (shared)
1992 Kenya

Most wins: Individual (5), Doris Brown (USA), 1967–71; Greta Waitz (Norway), 1978–81, 1983. Team (8), USA, 1968–9, 1975, 1979, 1983–5, 1987.

CURLING

World Championships

First men's championship held in 1959; first women's championship in 1979; takes place annually.

Recent winners (Men)

1979 Norway
1980 Canada
1981 Switzerland
1982 Canada
1983 Canada
1984 Norway
1985 Canada
1986 Canada
1987 Canada
1988 Norway
1989 Canada
1990 Canada
1991 Scotland
1992 Switzerland

Recent winners (Women)

1979 Switzerland
1980 Canada
1981 Sweden
1982 Denmark
1983 Switzerland
1984 Canada
1985 Canada
1986 Canada
1987 Canada
1988 West Germany
1989 Canada
1990 Norway
1991 Norway
1992 Sweden

Most wins: Men (20), Canada, 1959–64, 1966, 1968–72, 1980, 1982–3, 1985–7, 1989–90. Women (6), Canada, as above.

CYCLING

Tour de France

World's premier cycling event; first held in 1903.

Recent winners

1979 Bernard Hinault (France)
1980 Joop Zoetemelk (Holland)
1981 Bernard Hinault (France)
1982 Bernard Hinault (France)
1983 Laurent Fignon (France)
1984 Laurent Fignon (France)
1985 Bernard Hinault (France)
1986 Greg LeMond (USA)
1987 Stephen Roche (Ireland)
1988 Pedro Delgado (Spain)
1989 Greg Le Mond (USA)
1990 Greg Le Mond (USA)
1991 Miguel Indurain (Spain)
1992 Miguel Indurain (Spain)

Most wins: (5), Jacques Anquetil (France), 1957, 1961–4; Eddy Merckx (Belgium), 1969–72, 1974; Bernard Hinault (France), 1978–9, 1981–2, 1985.

World Road Race Championships

Men's race first held in 1927; first women's race in 1958; takes place annually.

Recent winners (Professional Men)

1979 Jan Raas (Holland)
1980 Bernard Hinault (France)
1981 Freddy Maertens (Belgium)
1982 Giuseppe Saroni (Italy)
1983 Greg LeMond (USA)
1984 Claude Criquielion (Belgium)
1985 Joop Zoetemelk (Holland)
1986 Moreno Argentin (Italy)
1987 Stephen Roche (Ireland)
1988 Maurizio Fondriest (Italy)
1989 Greg Le Mond (USA)
1990 Rudy Dhaenens (Belgium)
1991 Gianni Bugno (Italy)

Recent winners (Women)

1979 Petra de Bruin (Holland)
1980 Beth Heiden (USA)
1981 Ute Enzenauer (West Germany)
1982 Mandy Jones (Great Britain)
1983 Marianne Berglund (Sweden)
1984 *not held*
1985 Jeannie Longo (France)
1986 Jeannie Longo (France)
1987 Jeannie Longo (France)
1988 Jeannie Longo (France)
1989 Jeannie Longo (France)
1990 Catherine Marsal (France)
1991 Leontien van Moorsel (Holland)

Most wins: Men (3), Alfredo Binda (Italy), 1927, 1930, 1932; Rik Van Steenbergen (Belgium), 1949, 1956–7; Eddy Merckx (Belgium), 1967, 1971, 1974. Women (5), Jeannie Longo, as above.

CYCLO-CROSS

World Championships

First held in 1950 as an open event; separate professional and amateur events since 1967.

Cyclo-Cross (cont.)

Recent winners (Professional)

1980 Roland Liboton (Belgium)
1981 Johannes Stamsnijder (Holland)
1982 Roland Liboton (Belgium)
1983 Roland Liboton (Belgium)
1984 Roland Liboton (Belgium)
1985 Klaus-Peter Thaler (West Germany)
1986 Albert Zweifel (Switzerland)
1987 Klaus-Peter Thaler (West Germany)
1988 Pascal Richard (Switzerland)
1989 Danny De Bie (Belgium)
1990 Hank Baars (Holland)
1991 Radomin Simunek (Czechoslovakia)
1992 Mike Kluge (Germany)

Recent winners (Amateur)

1980 Fritz Saladin (Switzerland)
1981 Milos Fisera (Czechoslovakia)
1982 Milos Fisera (Czechoslovakia)
1983 Radomir Simunek (Czechoslovakia)
1984 Radomir Simunek (Czechoslovakia)
1985 Mike Kluge (West Germany)
1986 Vito di Tano (Italy)
1987 Mike Kluge (West Germany)
1988 Karol Camrola (Czechoslovakia)
1989 Ondrej Glaja (Czechoslovakia)
1990 Andreas Buesser (Switzerland)
1991 Thomas Frischknecht (Switzerland)
1992 Daniele Pontoni (Italy)

Most wins: Professional (7), Eric de Vlaeminck (Belgium), 1966, 1968–73. Amateur (5), Robert Vermiere (Belgium), 1970–1, 1974–5, 1977.

DARTS

World Professional Championship
First held at Nottingham in 1978.

Winners

1978 Leighton Rees (Wales)
1979 John Lowe (England)
1980 Eric Bristow (England)
1981 Eric Bristow (England)
1982 Jocky Wilson (Scotland)
1983 Keith Deller (England)
1984 Eric Bristow (England)
1985 Eric Bristow (England)
1986 Eric Bristow (England)
1987 John Lowe (England)
1988 Bob Anderson (England)
1989 Jocky Wilson (Scotland)
1990 Phil Taylor (England)
1991 Denis Priestley (England)

Most wins: (5), Eric Bristow, as above.

World Cup
A team competition first held at Wembley in 1977; takes place every two years.

Winners (Team)

1977 Wales
1979 England
1981 England
1983 England
1985 England
1987 England
1989 England
1991 England

Winners (Individual)

1977 Leighton Rees (Wales)
1979 Nicky Virachkul (USA)
1981 John Lowe (England)
1983 Eric Bristow (England)
1985 Eric Bristow (England)
1987 Eric Bristow (England)
1989 Eric Bristow (England)
1991 John Lowe (England)

Most wins: Team (7), England, as above. Individual (4), Eric Bristow (England), as above.

DRAUGHTS

World Championship
Held on a challenge basis; the champion since 1979 has been Dr M Tinsley (USA); he has defended the title five times.

British Open Championship
The leading championship in Britain; first held in 1926; now takes place every two years.

Recent winners

1970 I Edwards (Great Britain)
1972 G Davies (Great Britain)
1974 J McGill (Great Britain)
1976 A Huggins (Great Britain)
1978 J McGill (Great Britain)
1980 T Watson (Great Britain)
1982 T Watson (Great Britain)
1984 A Long (USA)
1986 H Delvin (Great Britain)
1988 DE Oldbury (Great Britain)
1990 T Watson (Great Britain)

EQUESTRIAN EVENTS

World Championships

Show Jumping championships first held in 1953 (for men) and 1965 (for women); since 1978 they have competed together and on equal terms; team competition introduced in 1978; Three Day Event and Dressage championships introduced in 1966; all three now held every four years. Renamed the World Equestrian Games in 1990.

Winners
Show Jumping (Men)

1953 Francisco Goyoago (Spain)
1954 Hans-Günter Winkler (West Germany)
1955 Hans-Günter Winkler (West Germany)
1956 Raimondo D'Inzeo (Italy)
1960 Raimondo D'Inzeo (Italy)
1966 Pierre d'Oriola (France)
1970 David Broome (Great Britain)
1974 Hartwig Steenken (West Germany)

Winners
Show Jumping (Women)

1965 Marion Coakes (Great Britain)
1970 Janou Lefèbvre (France)
1974 Janou Tissot (*née* Lefèbvre) (France)

Winners (Individual)

1978 Gerd Wiltfang (West Germany)
1982 Norbert Koof (West Germany)
1986 Gail Greenough (Canada)
1990 Eric Navet (France)

Winners (Team)

1978 Great Britain
1982 France
1986 USA
1990 France

Winners
Three Day Event (Individual)

1966 Carlos Moratorio (Argentina)
1970 Mary Gordon-Watson (Great Britain)
1974 Bruce Davidson (USA)
1978 Bruce Davidson (USA)
1982 Lucinda Green (Great Britain)
1986 Virginia Leng (Great Britain)
1990 Blyth Tait (New Zealand)

Winners (Team)

1966 Ireland
1970 Great Britain
1974 USA
1978 Canada
1982 Great Britain
1986 Great Britain
1990 New Zealand

Winners
Dressage (Individual)

1966 Josef Neckermann (West Germany)
1970 Yelene Petouchkova (USSR)
1974 Reiner Klimke (West Germany)
1978 Christine Stückelberger (Switzerland)
1982 Reiner Klimke (West Germany)
1986 Anne Grethe Jensen (Denmark)
1990 Nicole Uphoff (West Germany)

Winners
Dressage (Team)

1966 West Germany
1970 USSR
1974 West Germany
1978 West Germany
1982 West Germany
1986 West Germany
1990 West Germany

FENCING

World Championships

Held annually since 1921 (between 1921–35, known as European Championships); not held in Olympic years.

Recent winners
Foil (Men) Individual

1975 Christian Noel (France)
1977 Alexander Romankov (USSR)
1978 Didier Flament (France)
1979 Alexander Romankov (USSR)
1981 Vladimir Smirnov (USSR)
1982 Alexander Romankov (USSR)
1983 Alexander Romankov (USSR)
1985 Mauro Numa (Italy)
1986 Andrea Borella (Italy)
1987 Mathias Gey (West Germany)
1989 Alexandr Koch (West Germany)
1990 Philippe Omnes (France)
1991 Ingo Weissenborn (Germany)

Recent winners
Foil (Men) Team

1975 France
1977 West Germany
1978 Poland
1979 USSR
1981 USSR
1982 USSR

Fencing (cont.)

1983 West Germany
1985 Italy
1986 Italy
1987 USSR
1989 USSR
1990 Italy
1991 Cuba

Most wins: Individual (5), Alexander Romankov (USSR), 1974, 1977, 1979, 1982–3. Team (15), USSR (between 1959–89).

Recent winners
Foil (Women) Individual

1975 Ecaterina Stahl (Romania)
1977 Valentina Sidorova (USSR)
1978 Valentina Sidorova (USSR)
1979 Cornelia Hanisch (West Germany)
1981 Cornelia Hanisch (West Germany)
1982 Naila Giliazova (USSR)
1983 Dorina Vaccaroni (Italy)
1985 Cornelia Hanisch (West Germany)
1986 Anja Fichtel (West Germany)
1987 Elisabeta Tufan (Romania)
1989 Olga Velitchko (USSR)
1990 Anja Fichtel (West Germany)
1991 Giovann Trillini (Italy)

Recent winners
Foil (Women) Team

1975 USSR
1977 USSR
1978 USSR
1979 USSR
1981 USSR
1982 Italy
1983 Italy
1985 West Germany
1986 USSR
1987 Hungary
1989 West Germany
1990 Italy
1991 Italy

Most wins: Individual (3), Helène Mayer (Germany), 1929, 1931, 1937; Ilona Elek (Hungary, 1934–5, 1951; Ellen Müller-Preiss (Austria), 1947, 1949, 1950; Cornelia Hanisch, as above. Team (15), USSR (between 1956–86).

Recent winners
Epee (Men) Individual

1975 Alexander Pusch (West Germany)
1977 Johan Harmenberg (Sweden)
1978 Alexander Pusch (West Germany)
1979 Philippe Riboud (France)
1981 Zoltan Szekely (Hungary)
1982 Jenö Pap (Hungary)
1983 Ellmar Bormann (West Germany)
1985 Philippe Boisse (France)
1986 Philippe Riboud (France)
1987 Volker Fischer (West Germany)
1989 Manuel Pereira (Spain)
1990 Thomas Gerull (West Germany)
1991 Andrei Chouvalov (USSR)

Recent winners
Epee (Men) Team

1975 Sweden
1977 Sweden
1978 Hungary
1979 USSR
1981 USSR
1982 France
1983 France
1985 West Germany
1986 West Germany
1987 West Germany
1989 Italy
1990 Italy
1991 USSR

Most wins: Individual (3), Georges Buchard (France), 1927, 1931, 1933; Alexei Nikanchikov (USSR), 1966–7, 1970. Team (13), Italy (between 1931–58, 1989–90).

Recent winners
Epee (Women) Individual

1989 Anja Straub (Switzerland)
1990 Taime Chappe (Cuba)
1991 Mariann Horvath (Hungary)

Recent winners
Epee (Women) Team

1989 Hungary
1990 West Germany
1991 Hungary

Recent winners
Sabre (Individual)

1975 Vladimir Nazlimov (USSR)
1977 Pal Gerevich (Hungary)
1978 Viktor Krovopuskov (USSR)
1979 Vladimir Nazlimov (USSR)
1981 Mariusz Wodke (Poland)
1982 Viktor Krovopuskov (USSR)
1983 Vasiliy Etropolski (Bulgaria)
1985 György Nebald (Hungary)
1986 Sergey Mindirgassov (USSR)

Fencing (cont.)

1987 Jean-François Lamour (France)
1989 Grigory Kirienko (USSR)
1990 György Nebald (Hungary)
1991 Grigory Kirienko (USSR)

Recent winners
Sabre (Team)

1975 USSR
1977 USSR
1978 Hungary
1979 USSR
1981 Hungary
1982 Hungary
1983 USSR
1985 USSR
1986 USSR
1987 USSR
1989 USSR
1990 USSR
1991 Hungary

Most wins: Individual (3), Aladar Gerevich (Hungary), 1935, 1951, 1955; Jerzy Pawlowski (Poland) 1957, 1965–6; Yakov Rylsky (USSR), 1958, 1961, 1963. Team (18), Hungary (between 1930–82, 1991).

GAELIC FOOTBALL

All-Ireland Championship
First held 1887; takes place in Dublin on the third Sunday in September each year.

Recent winners

1979 Kerry
1980 Kerry
1981 Kerry
1982 Offaly
1983 Dublin
1984 Kerry
1985 Kerry
1986 Kerry
1987 Meath
1988 Meath
1989 Cork
1990 Cork
1991 Down

Most wins: (30), Kerry, 1903–4, 1909, 1913–14, 1924, 1926, 1929–32, 1937, 1939–41, 1946, 1953, 1955, 1959, 1962, 1969–70, 1975, 1978–81, 1984–6.

GLIDING

World Championships
First held in 1937; current classes are Open, Standard and 15 metres; the Open class is the principal event, held every two years until 1978 and again since 1981.

Recent winners

1968 Harro Wödl (Austria)
1970 George Moffat (USA)
1972 Göran Ax (Sweden)
1974 George Moffat (USA)
1976 George Lee (Great Britain)
1978 George Lee (Great Britain)
1981 George Lee (Great Britain)
1983 Ingo Renner (Australia)
1985 Ingo Renner (Australia)
1987 Ingo Renner (Australia)
1989 Robin May (Great Britain)
1991 J Centka (Poland)

Most wins: (3), George Lee, as above; Ingo Renner, as above.

GOLF

British Open
First held at Prestwick in 1860, and won by Willie Park; takes place annually; regarded as the world's leading golf tournament.

Recent winners

1979 Severiano Ballesteros (Spain)
1980 Tom Watson (USA)
1981 Bill Rogers (USA)
1982 Tom Watson (USA)
1983 Tom Watson (USA)
1984 Severiano Ballesteros (Spain)
1985 Sandy Lyle (Great Britain)
1986 Greg Norman (Australia)
1987 Nick Faldo (Great Britain)
1988 Severiano Ballesteros (Spain)
1989 Mark Calcavecchia (USA)
1990 Nick Faldo (Great Britain)
1991 Ian Baker-Finch (Australia)
1992 Nick Faldo (Great Britain)

Most wins: (6), Harry Vardon (Great Britain), 1896, 1898–9, 1903, 1911, 1914.

United States Open
First held at Newport, Rhode Island in 1895, and won by Horace Rawlins; takes place annually.

Recent winners

1979 Hale Irwin (USA)

Golf (cont.)

1980 Jack Nicklaus (USA)
1981 David Graham (Australia)
1982 Tom Watson (USA)
1983 Larry Nelson (USA)
1984 Fuzzy Zoeller (USA)
1985 Andy North (USA)
1986 Ray Floyd (USA)
1987 Scott Simpson (USA)
1988 Curtis Strange (USA)
1989 Curtis Strange (USA)
1990 Hale Irwin (USA)
1991 Payne Stewart (USA)
1992 Tom Kite (USA)

Most wins: (4), Willie Anderson (USA), 1901, 1903–5; Bobby Jones (USA), 1923, 1926, 1929–30; Ben Hogan (USA), 1948, 1950–1, 1953; Jack Nicklaus (USA), 1962, 1967, 1972, 1980.

US Masters

First held in 1934; takes place at the Augusta National course in Georgia every April.

Recent winners

1980 Severiano Ballesteros (Spain)
1981 Tom Watson (USA)
1982 Craig Stadler (USA)
1983 Severiano Ballesteros (Spain)
1984 Ben Crenshaw (USA)
1985 Bernhard Langer (West Germany)
1986 Jack Nicklaus (USA)
1987 Larry Mize (USA)
1988 Sandy Lyle (Great Britain)
1989 Nick Faldo (Great Britain)
1990 Nick Faldo (Great Britain)
1991 Ian Woosnam (Great Britain)
1992 Fred Couples (USA)

Most wins: (6), Jack Nicklaus (USA), 1963, 1965–6, 1972, 1975, 1986.

United States PGA Championship

The last of the season's four 'Majors'; first held in 1916, and a match-play event until 1958; takes place annually.

Recent winners

1979 David Graham (Australia)
1980 Jack Nicklaus (USA)
1981 Larry Nelson (USA)
1982 Ray Floyd (USA)
1983 Hal Sutton (USA)
1984 Lee Trevino (USA)
1985 Hubert Green (USA)
1986 Bob Tway (USA)
1987 Larry Nelson (USA)
1988 Jeff Sluman (USA)
1989 Payne Stewart (USA)
1990 Wayne Grady (Australia)
1991 John Daly (USA)

Most wins: (5), Walter Hagen (USA), 1921, 1924–7; Jack Nicklaus (USA), 1963, 1971, 1973, 1975, 1980.

Ryder Cup

The leading international team tournament; first held at Worcester, Massachusetts in 1927; takes place every two years between teams from the USA and Europe (Great Britain 1927–71; Great Britain and Ireland 1973–7).

Recent winners

1969	Drawn	16–16
1971	USA	18½–13½
1973	USA	19–13
1975	USA	21–11
1977	USA	12½–7½
1979	USA	17–11
1981	USA	18½–9½
1983	USA	14½–13½
1985	Europe	16½–11½
1987	Europe	15–13
1989	Drawn	14–14
1991	USA	14½–13½

Wins: (22), USA, 1927, 1931, 1935–7, 1947–55, 1959–67, 1971–83, 1991. (3), Great Britain, 1929, 1933, 1957. (2), Europe, 1985, 1987. (2), Drawn, 1969, 1989.

GREYHOUND RACING

Greyhound Derby

The top race of the British season, first held in 1927; run at the White City every year (except 1940) until its closure in 1985; since then all races run at Wimbledon.

Recent winners

1979 Sarah's Bunny
1980 Indian Joe
1981 Parkdown Jet
1982 Laurie's Panther
1983 I'm Slippy
1984 Whisper Wishes
1985 Pagan Swallow
1986 Tico
1987 Signal Spark
1988 Hit the Lid

Greyhound Racing (cont.)

1989 Lartigue Note
1990 Slippy Blue
1991 Ballinderry Ash

Most wins: (2), Mick the Miller, 1929–30; Patricia's Hope, 1972–3.

GYMNASTICS

World Championships
First held in 1903; took place every four years, 1922–78; since 1979, every two years.

Recent winners
Individual (Men)

1962 Yuriy Titov (USSR)
1966 Mikhail Voronin (USSR)
1970 Eizo Kenmotsu (Japan)
1974 Shigeru Kasamatsu (Japan)
1978 Nikolai Adrianov (USSR)
1979 Aleksandr Ditiatin (USSR)
1981 Yuri Korolev (USSR)
1983 Dmitri Belozerchev (USSR)
1985 Yuri Korolev (USSR)
1987 Dmitri Belozerchev (USSR)
1989 Igor Korobichensky (USSR)
1991 Vitaly Scherbo (USSR)

Recent winners
Team (Men)

1962 Japan
1966 Japan
1970 Japan
1974 Japan
1978 Japan
1979 USSR
1981 USSR
1983 China
1985 USSR
1987 USSR
1989 USSR
1991 USSR

Most wins: Individual (2), Marco Torrès (France), 1909, 1913; Peter Sumi (Yugoslavia), 1922, 1926; Yuri Korolev and Dmitri Belozerchev, as above. Team (7), Czechoslovakia, 1907, 1911, 1913, 1922, 1926, 1930, 1938.

Recent winners
Individual (Women)

1962 Larissa Latynina (USSR)
1966 Vera Caslavska (Czechoslovakia)
1970 Ludmila Tourischeva (USSR)
1974 Ludmila Tourischeva (USSR)
1978 Yelena Mukhina (USSR)
1979 Nelli Kim (USSR)
1981 Olga Bitcherova (USSR)
1983 Natalia Yurchenko (USSR)
1985 Yelena Shoushounova (USSR) and Oksana Omeliantchuk (USSR)
1987 Aurelia Dobre (Romania)
1989 Svetlana Boginskaya
1991 Kim Zmeskal (USA)

Recent winners
Team (Women)

1962 USSR
1966 Czechoslovakia
1970 USSR
1974 USSR
1978 USSR
1979 Romania
1981 USSR
1983 USSR
1985 USSR
1987 Romania
1989 USSR
1991 USSR

Most wins: Individual (2), Vlasta Dekanová (Czechoslovakia), 1934, 1938; Larissa Latynina (USSR), 1958, 1962, Vera Caslavska and Ludmila Tourischeva, as above. Team (11), USSR, as above plus 1954, 1958.

HANDBALL

World Championships
First men's championships held in 1938, both indoors and outdoors (latter discontinued in 1966); first women's outdoor championships in 1949, (discontinued in 1960); first women's indoor championships in 1957.

Winners Indoors (Men)

1938 Germany
1954 Sweden
1958 Sweden
1961 Romania
1964 Romania
1967 Czechoslovakia
1970 Romania
1974 Romania
1978 West Germany
1982 USSR
1986 Yugoslavia
1990 Sweden

Handball (cont.)

Winners Outdoors (Men)

1938 Germany
1948 Sweden
1952 West Germany
1955 West Germany
1959 East/West Germany (*combined*)
1963 East Germany
1966 West Germany

Most wins: Indoors (5), Romania. Outdoors (5), West Germany (including 1 as combined East/West German team).

Winners Indoors (Women)

1957 Czechoslovakia
1962 Romania
1965 Hungary
1971 East Germany
1973 Yugoslavia
1975 East Germany
1979 East Germany
1982 USSR
1986 USSR
1990 USSR

Winners Outdoors (Women)

1949 Hungary
1956 Romania
1960 Romania

Most wins: Indoors (3), East Germany, USSR, as above. Outdoors (2), Romania, as above.

HANG GLIDING

World Championships
First held officially in 1976; since 1979, take place every two years.

Winners
Individual (Class 1)

1976 Christian Steinbach (Austria)
1979 Josef Guggenmose (West Germany)
1981 Pepe Lopez (Brazil)
1983 Steve Moyes (Australia)
1985 John Pendry (Great Britain)
1987 Rich Duncan (Australia)
1989 Robert Whittall (Great Britain)

Winners (Team)

1976 Austria
1979 France
1981 Great Britain
1983 Australia
1985 Great Britain
1987 Australia
1989 Great Britain

Most wins: Individual, no person has won more than one title. Team (3), Great Britain, as above.

HOCKEY

World Cup
Men's tournament first held in 1971, and every four years since 1978; women's tournament first held in 1974, and now takes place every three years.

Winners (Men)

1971 Pakistan
1973 Holland
1975 India
1978 Pakistan
1982 Pakistan
1986 Australia
1990 Holland

Most wins: (3), Pakistan, as above.

Winners (Women)

1974 Holland
1976 West Germany
1978 Holland
1981 West Germany
1983 Holland
1986 Holland
1990 Holland

Most wins: (5), Holland, as above.

Olympic Games
Regarded as hockey's leading competition; first held in 1908; included at every celebration since 1928; women's competition first held in 1980.

Post-war winners (Men)

1948 India
1952 India
1956 India
1960 Pakistan
1964 India
1968 Pakistan
1972 West Germany
1976 New Zealand
1980 India
1984 Pakistan
1988 Great Britain
1992 Germany

Hockey (cont.)

Winners (Women)

1980 Zimbabwe
1984 Holland
1988 Australia
1992 Spain

Most wins: Men (8), India, 1928, 1932, 1936, 1948, 1952, 1956, 1964, 1980. Women, no nation has won the title more than once.

HORSE RACING

The Derby

The 'Blue Riband' of the Turf; run at Epsom over 1½ miles; first run in 1780.

Recent winners

Horse (Jockey)
1979 Troy (Willie Carson)
1980 Henbit (Willie Carson)
1981 Shergar (Walter Swinburn)
1982 Golden Fleece (Pat Eddery)
1983 Teenoso (Lester Piggott)
1984 Secreto (Christy Roche)
1985 Slip Anchor (Steve Cauthen)
1986 Shahrastani (Walter Swinburn)
1987 Reference Point (Steve Cauthen)
1988 Kahyasi (Ray Cochrane)
1989 Nashwan (Willie Carson)
1990 Quest For Fame (Pat Eddery)
1991 Generous (Alan Munro)

Most wins: Jockey (9), Lester Piggott, 1954, 1957, 1960, 1968, 1970, 1972, 1976–7, 1983.

The Oaks

Raced at Epsom over 1½ miles; for fillies only; first run in 1779.

Recent winners

Horse (Jockey)
1979 Scintillate (Pat Eddery)
1980 Bireme (Willie Carson)
1981 Blue Wind (Lester Piggott)
1982 Time Charter (Billy Newnes)
1983 Sun Princess (Willy Carson)
1984 Circus Plume (Lester Piggott)
1985 Oh So Sharp (Steve Cauthen)
1986 Midway Lady (Ray Cochrane)
1987 Unite (Walter Swinburn)
1988 Diminuendo (Steve Cauthen)
1989 Aliysa (Walter Swinburn)
1990 Salsabil (Willie Carson)
1991 Jet Ski Lady (Christy Roche)

Most wins: Jockey (9), Frank Buckle, 1797–9, 1802–3, 1805, 1817–18, 1823.

One Thousand Guineas

Run over 1 mile at Newmarket; for fillies only; first run in 1814.

Recent winners

Horse (Jockey)
1979 One in a Million (Joe Mercer)
1980 Quick as Lightning (Brian Rouse)
1981 Fairy Footsteps (Lester Piggott)
1982 On The House (John Reid)
1983 Ma Biche (Freddy Head)
1984 Pebbles (Philip Robinson)
1985 Oh So Sharp (Steve Cauthen)
1986 Midway Lady (Ray Cochrane)
1987 Miesque (Freddy Head)
1988 Ravinella (Gary Moore)
1989 Musical Bliss (Walter Swinburn)
1990 Salsabil (Willie Carson)
1991 Shadayid (Willie Carson)

Most wins: Jockey (7), George Fordham, 1859, 1861, 1865, 1868–9, 1881, 1883.

Two Thousand Guineas

Run at Newmarket over 1 mile; first run in 1809.

Recent winners

Horse (Jockey)
1979 Tap on Wood (Steve Cauthen)
1980 Known Fact (Willie Carson)
1981 To-Agori-Mou (Greville Starkey)
1982 Zino (Freddy Head)
1983 Lomond (Pat Eddery)
1984 El Gran Senor (Pat Eddery)
1985 Shadeed (Lester Piggott)
1986 Dancing Brave (Greville Starkey)
1987 Don't Forget Me (Willie Carson)
1988 Doyoun (Walter Swinburn)
1989 Nashwan (Willie Carson)
1990 Tirol (Michael Kinane)
1991 Mystiko (Michael Roberts)

Most wins: Jockey (9), Jem Robinson, 1825, 1828, 1831, 1833–6, 1847–8.

St Leger

The oldest of the five English classics; first run in 1776; raced at Doncaster annually over 1 mile 6 furlongs 127 yards.

Horse Racing (cont.)

Recent winners

Horse (Jockey)
1979 Son of Love (Alain Lequeux)
1980 Light Cavalry (Joe Mercer)
1981 Cut Above (Joe Mercer)
1982 Touching Wood (Paul Cook)
1983 Sun Princess (Willie Carson)
1984 Commanche Run (Lester Piggott)
1985 Oh So Sharp (Steve Cauthen)
1986 Moon Madness (Pat Eddery)
1987 Reference Point (Steve Cauthen)
1988 Minster Son (Willie Carson)
1989 Michelozzo (Steve Cauthen)
1990 Snurge (Richard Quinn)
1991 Toulon (Pat Eddery)

Most wins: Jockey (9), Bill Scott, 1821, 1825, 1828–9, 1838–41, 1846.

Grand National
Steeplechasing's most famous race; first run at Maghull in 1836; at Aintree since 1839; war-time races at Gatwick 1916–18.

Recent winners

Horse (Jockey)
1979 Rubstic (Maurice Barnes)
1980 Ben Nevis (Mr Charles Fenwick)[1]
1981 Aldaniti (Bob Champion)
1982 Grittar (Mr Dick Saunders)[1]
1983 Corbiere (Ben De Haan)
1984 Hallo Dandy (Neale Doughty)
1985 Last Suspect (Hywel Davies)
1986 West Tip (Richard Dunwoody)
1987 Maori Venture (Steve Knight)
1988 Rhyme 'N' Reason (Brendan Powell)
1989 Little Polveir (Jimmy Frost)
1990 Mr Frisk (Marcus Armytage)
1991 Seagram (Nigel Hawke)
1992 Party Politics (Carl Llewellyn)

[1] 'Mr' denotes that the jockey is an amateur rider.

Most wins: Jockey (5), George Stevens, 1856, 1863–4, 1869–70. Horse (3), Red Rum 1973–4, 1977.

Prix de l'Arc de Triomphe
The leading end of season race in Europe; raced over 2400 metres at Longchamp; first run in 1920.

Recent winners

Horse (Jockey)
1979 Three Troikas (Freddy Head)
1980 Detroit (Pat Eddery)
1981 Gold River (Gary Moore)
1982 Akiyda (Yves Saint-Martin)
1983 All Along (Walter Swinburn)
1984 Sagace (Yves Saint-Martin)
1985 Rainbow Quest (Pat Eddery)
1986 Dancing Brave (Pat Eddery)
1987 Trempolino (Pat Eddery)
1988 Tony Bin (John Reid)
1989 Caroll House (Michael Kinane)
1990 Suamarez (Gerard Mosse)
1991 Suave Dancer (Cash Asmussen)

Most wins: Jockey (4), Jacko Doyasbère, 1942, 1944, 1950–1; Freddy Head, 1966, 1972, 1976, 1979; Yves Saint-Martin, 1970, 1974, 1982, 1984; Pat Eddery, as above. Horse (2), Ksar, 1921–2; Motrico, 1930, 1932; Corrida, 1936–7; Tantième, 1950–1; Ribot, 1955–6; Alleged 1977–8.

HURLING

All-Ireland Championship
First contested in 1887; played on the first Sunday in September each year.

Recent winners

1979 Kilkenny
1980 Galway
1981 Offaly
1982 Kilkenny
1983 Kilkenny
1984 Cork
1985 Offaly
1986 Cork
1987 Galway
1988 Galway
1989 Tipperary
1990 Cork
1991 Tipperary

Most wins: (27), Cork, 1890, 1892–4, 1902–3, 1919, 1926, 1928–9, 1931, 1941–4, 1946, 1952–4, 1966, 1970, 1976–8, 1984, 1986, 1990.

ICE HOCKEY

World Championship
First held in 1930; takes place annually (except 1980); up to 1968 Olympic champions also regarded as world champions.

Recent winners

1978 USSR
1979 USSR
1981 USSR
1982 USSR

Ice Hockey (cont.)

1983 USSR
1984 USSR
1985 Czechoslovakia
1986 USSR
1987 Sweden
1988 USSR
1989 USSR
1990 USSR
1991 Sweden

Most wins: (24), USSR, 1954, 1956, 1963–71, 1973–5, 1978–9, 1981–4, 1986, 1988–90.

Stanley Cup

The most sought-after trophy at club level; the end-of-season meeting between the winners of the two conferences in the National Hockey League in the USA and Canada.

Recent winners

1979 Montreal Canadiens
1980 New York Islanders
1981 New York Islanders
1982 New York Islanders
1983 New York Islanders
1984 Edmonton Oilers
1985 Edmonton Oilers
1986 Montreal Canadiens
1987 Edmonton Oilers
1988 Edmonton Oilers
1989 Calgary Flames
1990 Edmonton Oilers
1991 Pittsburgh Penguins

Most wins: (23), Montreal Canadiens, 1916, 1924, 1930–1, 1944, 1946, 1953, 1956–60, 1965–6, 1968–9, 1971, 1973, 1976–9, 1986.

ICE SKATING

World Championships

First men's championships in 1896; first women's event in 1906; pairs first contested in 1908; Ice Dance officially recognized in 1952.

Recent winners (Men)

1980 Jan Hoffman (East Germany)
1981 Scott Hamilton (USA)
1982 Scott Hamilton (USA)
1983 Scott Hamilton (USA)
1984 Scott Hamilton (USA)
1985 Alexander Fadeyev (USSR)
1986 Brian Boitano (USA)
1987 Brian Orser (Canada)
1988 Brian Boitano (USA)
1989 Kurt Browning (Canada)
1990 Kurt Browning (Canada)
1991 Kurt Browning (Canada)
1992 Viktor Petrenko (CIS)

Most wins: (10), Ulrich Salchow (Sweden), 1901–5, 1907–11.

Recent winners (Women)

1980 Anett Potzsch (East Germany)
1981 Denise Beillmann (Switzerland)
1982 Elaine Zayak (USA)
1983 Rosalynn Sumners (USA)
1984 Katarina Witt (East Germany)
1985 Katarina Witt (East Germany)
1986 Debbie Thomas (USA)
1987 Katarina Witt (East Germany)
1988 Katarina Witt (East Germany)
1989 Midori Ito (Japan)
1990 Jill Trenary (USA)
1991 Kristi Yamaguchi (USA)
1992 Kristi Yamaguchi (USA)

Most wins: (10), Sonja Henie (Norway), 1927–36.

Recent winners (Pairs)

1980 Sergei Shakrai/Marina Tcherkassova (USSR)
1981 Igor Lissovsky/Irina Vorobyeva (USSR)
1982 Tassilo Thierbach/Sabine Baess (East Germany)
1983 Oleg Vasiliev/Yelena Valova (USSR)
1984 Paul Martini/Barbara Underhill (Canada)
1985 Oleg Vasiliev/Yelena Valova (USSR)
1986 Sergey Grinkov/Yekaterina Gordeeva (USSR)
1987 Sergey Grinkov/Yekaterina Gordeeva (USSR)
1988 Oleg Vasiliev/Yelena Valorva (USSR)
1989 Sergey Grinkov/Yekaterina Gordeeva (USSR)
1990 Sergey Grinkov/Yekaterina Gordeeva (USSR)
1991 Arthur Dmtriev/Natalya Mishkutienok (USSR)
1992 Arthur Dmtriev/Natalya Mishkutienok (CIS)

Most wins: (10), Irina Rodnina (USSR), 1969–72 (with Aleksey Ulanov), 1973–8 (with Aleksander Zaitsev).

Recent winners (Ice Dance)

1980 Andras Sallay/Krisztina Regoczy (Hungary)
1981 Christopher Dean/Jayne Torvill (Great Britain)
1982 Christopher Dean/Jayne Torvill (Great Britain)
1983 Christopher Dean/Jayne Torvill (Great Britain)
1984 Christopher Dean/Jayne Torvill (Great Britain)
1985 Andrey Bukin/Natalya Bestemianova (USSR)
1986 Andrey Bukin/Natalya Bestemianova (USSR)
1987 Andrey Bukin/Natalya Bestemianova (USSR)
1988 Andrey Bukin/Natalya Bestemianova (USSR)

Ice Skating (cont.)

1989 Sergey Ponomarenko/Marina Klimova (USSR)
1990 Sergey Ponomarenko/Marina Klimova (USSR)
1991 Alexandra Zhulin/Maia Usova (USSR)
1992 Sergey Ponomarenko/Marina Klimova (CIS)

Most wins: (6), Aleksander Gorshkov and Lyudmila Pakhomova (USSR), 1970–4, 1976.

JUDO

World Championships

First held in 1956, now contested every two years; current weight categories established in 1979; women's championship instituted in 1980.

Recent winners
Open Class (Men)

1979 Sumio Endo (Japan)
1981 Yasuhiro Yamashita (Japan)
1983 Hitoshi Saito (Japan)
1985 Yoshimi Masaki (Japan)
1987 Noayo Ogawa (Japan)
1989 Noayo Ogawa (Japan)
1991 Noayo Ogawa (Japan)

Recent winners
Over 95 kg (Men)

1979 Yasuhiro Yamashita (Japan)
1981 Yasuhiro Yamashita (Japan)
1983 Yasuhiro Yamashita (Japan)
1985 Yung-Chul Cho (Korea)
1987 Grigori Vertichev (USSR)
1989 Noayo Ogawa (Japan)
1991 Sergey Kosorotov (USSR)

Recent winners
Under 95 kg (Men)

1979 Tengiz Khubuluri (USSR)
1981 Tenzig Khubuluri (USSR)
1983 Valeriy Divisenko (USSR)
1985 Hitoshi Sugai (Japan)
1987 Hitoshi Sugai (Japan)
1989 Koba Kurtanidze (Japan)
1991 Stephane Traineau (France)

Recent winners
Under 86 kg (Men)

1979 Detlef Ultsch (East Germany)
1981 Bernard Tchoullouyan (France)
1983 Detlef Ultsch (East Germany)
1985 Peter Seisenbacher (Austria)
1987 Fabien Canu (France)
1989 Fabien Canu (France)
1991 Hirotaka Okada (Japan)

Recent winners
Under 78 kg (Men)

1979 Shozo Fujii (Japan)
1981 Neil Adams (Great Britain)
1983 Nobutoshi Hikage (Japan)
1985 Nobutoshi Hikage (Japan)
1987 Hirotaka Okada (Japan)
1989 Byung-ju Kim (South Korea)
1991 Daniel Lascau (Germany)

Recent winners
Under 71 kg (Men)

1979 Kyoto Katsuki (Japan)
1981 Chon-Hak Park (Korea)
1983 Kidetoshi Nakanishi (Japan)
1985 Byeong-Keun Ahn (Korea)
1987 Mike Swain (USA)
1989 Toshihiko Koga (Japan)
1991 Toshihiko Koga (Japan)

Recent winners
Under 65 kg (Men)

1979 Nikolai Soludkhin (USSR)
1981 Katsuhiko Kashiwazaki (Japan)
1983 Nikolai Soludkhin (USSR)
1985 Yuriy Sokolov (USSR)
1987 Yosuke Yamamoto (Japan)
1989 Drago Becanovic (Yugoslavia)
1991 Udo Quellmolz (Germany)

Recent winners
Under 60 kg (Men)

1979 Thierry Ray (France)
1981 Yasuhiko Moriwaki (Japan)
1983 Khazret Tletseri (USSR)
1985 Shinji Hosokawa (Japan)
1987 Kim Jae-Yup (South Korea)
1989 Amiran Totikashvili (USSR)
1991 Tadanor Koshino (Japan)

Most titles: (4), Yashiro Yamashita (Japan), 1981 (Open), 1979, 1981, 1983 (over 95 kg); Shozo Fujii (Japan), 1971, 1973, 1975 (under 80 kg), 1979 (under 78 kg).

Recent winners
Open (Women)

1980 Ingrid Berghmans (Belgium)
1982 Ingrid Berghmans (Belgium)
1984 Ingrid Berghmans (Belgium)
1986 Ingrid Berghmans (Belgium)
1987 Fenglian Gao (China)
1989 Estela Rodriguez (Cuba)
1991 Yiaoyan Zhuang (China)

Judo (cont.)

Recent winners
Over 72 kg (Women)

1980 Margarita de Cal (Italy)
1982 Natalina Lupino (France)
1984 Maria-Teresa Motta (Italy)
1986 Fenglian Gao (China)
1987 Fenglian Gao (China)
1989 Fenglian Gao (China)
1991 Moon Ji-Yoon (South Korea)

Recent winners
Under 72 kg (Women)

1980 Jocelyne Triadou (France)
1982 Barbara Classen (West Germany)
1984 Ingrid Berghmans (Belgium)
1986 Irene de Kok (Holland)
1987 Irene de Kok (Holland)
1989 Ingrid Berghmans (Belgium)
1991 Kim Mi-Jeong (South Korea)

Recent winners
Under 66 kg (Women)

1980 Edith Simon (Austria)
1982 Brigitte Deydier (France)
1986 Brigitte Deydier (France)
1987 Alexandra Schreiber (West Germany)
1989 Emanuela Pierantozzi (Italy)
1991 Emanuela Pierantozzi (Italy)

Recent winners
Under 61 kg (Women)

1980 Anita Staps (Holland)
1982 Martine Rothier (France)
1984 Natasha Hernandez (Venezuela)
1986 Diane Bell (Great Britain)
1987 Diane Bell (Great Britain)
1989 Catherina Fleury (France)
1991 Frauke Eickhoff (Germany)

Recent winners
Under 56 kg (Women)

1980 Gerda Winklbauer (Austria)
1982 Béatrice Rodriguez (France)
1984 Ann-Maria Burns (USA)
1986 Ann Hughes (Great Britain)
1987 Catherine Arnaud (France)
1989 Catherine Arnaud (France)
1991 Miriam Blasco (Spain)

Recent winners
Under 52 kg (Women)

1980 Edith Hrovat (Austria)
1982 Loretta Doyle (Great Britain)
1984 Kaori Yamaguchi (Japan)
1986 Dominique Brun (France)
1987 Sharon Rendle (Great Britain)
1989 Sharon Rendle (Great Britain)
1991 Alessandra Giungi (Italy)

Recent winners
Under 48 kg (Women)

1980 Jane Bridge (Great Britain)
1982 Karen Briggs (Great Britain)
1984 Karen Briggs (Great Britain)
1986 Karen Briggs (Great Britain)
1987 Z Li (China)
1989 Karen Briggs (Great Britain)
1991 Cecille Nowak (France)

Most titles: (6), Ingrid Berghmans (Belgium), 1980, 1982, 1984, 1986 (Open), 1984, 1989 (both under 72 kg).

KARATE

World Championships

First held in Tokyo 1970; taken place every two years since 1980, when women first competed; there is a team competition plus individual competitions at Kumite (seven weight categories for men and three for women) and Kata.

Team winners

1970 Japan
1972 France
1975 Great Britain
1977 Holland
1980 Spain
1982 Great Britain
1984 Great Britain
1986 Great Britain
1988 Great Britain
1990 Great Britain

Most wins: (5), Great Britain, as above.

LACROSSE

World Championships
First held for men in 1967; for women in 1969; taken place every four years since 1974; since 1982 the women's event has been called the World Cup.

Winners (Men)

1967 USA
1974 USA
1978 Canada
1982 USA
1986 USA
1990 USA

Most wins: (5), USA, as above.

Winners (Women)

1969 Great Britain
1974 USA
1978 Canada
1982 USA
1986 Australia
1989 USA

Most wins: (3), USA, as above.

Iroquois Cup
The sport's best known trophy; contested by English club sides annually since 1890.

Recent winners

1979 Cheadle
1980 South Manchester
1981 Cheadle
1982 Sheffield University
1983 Sheffield University
1984 Cheadle
1985 Cheadle
1986 Heaton Mersey
1987 Stockport
1988 Mellor
1989 Stockport
1990 Cheadle
1991 Cheadle

Most wins: (17), Stockport, 1897–1901, 1903, 1905, 1911–13, 1923–4, 1926, 1928, 1934, 1987, 1989.

MODERN PENTATHLON

World Championships
Held annually since 1949 with the exception of Olympic years, when the Olympic champions automatically become world champions.

Recent winners (Individual)

1979 Robert Nieman (USA)
1980 Anatoliy Starostin (USSR)
1981 Janusz Pyciak-Peciak (Poland)
1982 Daniele Masala (Italy)
1983 Anatoliy Starostin (USSR)
1984 Daniele Masala (Italy)
1985 Attila Mizser (Hungary)
1986 Carlo Massullo (Italy)
1987 Joel Bouzou (France)
1988 Janos Martinek (Hungary)
1989 Laszlo Fabien (Hungary)
1990 Gianluca Tiberti (Italy)
1991 Arkad Skrzypaszek (Poland)
1992 Arkad Skrzypaszek (Poland)

Recent winners (Team)

1979 USA
1980 USSR
1981 Poland
1982 USSR
1983 USSR
1984 Italy
1985 USSR
1986 Italy
1987 Hungary
1988 Hungary
1989 Hungary
1990 USSR
1991 USSR
1992 Poland

Most wins: Individual (6), Andras Balczo (Hungary), 1963, 1965–9, 1972. Team (18), USSR, 1956–9, 1961–2, 1964, 1969, 1971–4, 1980, 1982–3, 1985, 1990–1.

MOTOR CYCLING

World Championships
First organized in 1949; current titles for 500 cc, 250 cc, 125 cc, 80 cc and Sidecar; Formula One and Endurance world championships also held annually; the most prestigious title is the 500 cc category.

Recent winners (500 cc)

1979 Kenny Roberts (USA)
1980 Kenny Roberts (USA)
1981 Marco Lucchinelli (Italy)
1982 Franco Uncini (Italy)
1983 Freddie Spencer (USA)
1984 Eddie Lawson (USA)
1985 Freddie Spencer (USA)
1986 Eddie Lawson (USA)
1987 Wayne Gardner (Australia)

Motor Cycling (cont.)

1988 Eddie Lawson (USA)
1989 Eddie Lawson (USA)
1990 Wayne Rainey (USA)
1991 Wayne Rainey (USA)

Most wins: (8), Giacomo Agostini (Italy), 1966–72, 1975.

Most world titles: (15), Giacomo Agostini, 500cc as above, 350cc 1968–74.

Isle of Man TT Races

The most famous of all motor cycle races; take place each June; first held 1907; principal race is the Senior TT.

Recent winners (Senior TT)

1979 Mike Hailwood (Great Britain)
1980 Graeme Crosby (New Zealand)
1981 Mick Grant (Great Britain)
1982 Norman Brown (Great Britain)
1983 Rob McElnea (Great Britain)
1984 Rob McElnea (Great Britain)
1985 Joey Dunlop (Ireland)
1986 Roger Burnett (Great Britain)
1987 Joey Dunlop (Ireland)
1988 Joey Dunlop (Ireland)
1989 Steve Hislop (Great Britain)
1990 Carl Fogarty (Great Britain)
1991 Steve Hislop (Great Britain)

Most Senior TT wins: (7), Mike Hailwood (Great Britain), 1961, 1963–7, 1979.

MOTOR RACING

World Championship

A Formula One drivers' world championship instituted in 1950; constructor's championship instituted in 1958.

Recent winners

1979 Jody Scheckter (South Africa) *Ferrari*
1980 Alan Jones (Australia) *Williams*
1981 Nelson Piquet (Brazil) *Williams*
1982 Keke Rosberg (Finland) *Ferrari*
1983 Nelson Piquet (Brazil) *Ferrari*
1984 Niki Lauda (Austria) *McLaren*
1985 Alain Prost (France) *McLaren*
1986 Alain Prost (France) *Williams*
1987 Nelson Piquet (Brazil) *Williams*
1988 Ayrton Senna (Brazil) *McLaren*
1989 Alain Prost (France) *McLaren*
1990 Ayrton Senna (Brazil) *McLaren*
1991 Ayrton Senna (Brazil) *McLaren*

Most wins: Driver (5), Juan Manuel Fangio (Argentina), 1951, 1954–7. Constructor (8), Ferrari, 1964, 1975–7, 1979, 1982–3.

Le Mans 24-Hour Race

The greatest of all endurance races; first held in 1923.

Recent winners

1979 Klaus Ludwig (West Germany)
Bill Whittington (USA)
Don Whittington (USA)
1980 Jean-Pierre Jaussaud (France)
Jean Rondeau (France)
1981 Jacky Ickx (Belgium)
Derek Bell (Great Britain)
1982 Jacky Ickx (Belgium)
Derek Bell (Great Britain)
1983 Vern Schuppan (Austria)
Al Holbert (USA)
Hurley Haywood (USA)
1984 Klaus Ludwig (West Germany)
Henri Pescarolo (France)
1985 Klaus Ludwig (West Germany)
'John Winter'[1] (West Germany)
Paolo Barilla (Italy)
1986 Hans Stück (West Germany)
Derek Bell (Great Britain)
Al Holbert (USA)
1987 Hans Stück (West Germany)
Derek Bell (Great Britain)
Al Holbert (USA)
1988 Jan Lammers (Holland)
Johnny Dumfries (Great Britain)
Andy Wallace (Great Britain)
1989 Jochen Mass (West Germany)
Manuel Reuter (West Germany)
Stanley Dickens (Sweden)
1990 John Nielsen (Denmark)
Price Cobb (USA)
Martin Brundle (Great Britain)
1991 Volker Weidler (Germany)
Johnny Herbert (Great Britain)
Bertrand Gachot (Belgium)
1992 Derek Warwick (Great Britain)
Mark Blundell (Great Britain)
Yannick Dalmas (France)

[1]pseudonym

Most wins: (6), Jacky Ickx (Belgium), 1969, 1975–7, 1981–2.

Motor Racing (cont.)

Indianapolis 500
First held in 1911; raced over the Indianapolis Raceway as part of the Memorial Day celebrations at the end of May each year.

Recent winners

1979 Rick Mears (USA)
1980 Johnny Rutherford (USA)
1981 Bobby Unser (USA)
1982 Gordon Johncock (USA)
1983 Tom Sneva (USA)
1984 Rick Mears (USA)
1985 Danny Sullivan (USA)
1986 Bobby Rahal (USA)
1987 Al Unser (USA)
1988 Rick Mears (USA)
1989 Emerson Fittipaldi (Brazil)
1990 Arie Luyendyk (Holland)
1991 Ric Mears (USA)
1992 Al Unser (USA)

Most wins: (5), Al Unser (USA), 1970–1, 1978, 1987, 1992.

Monte Carlo Rally
The world's leading rally; first held in 1911.

Recent winners

1980 Walter Röhrl (West Germany)
Christian Geistdörfer (West Germany)
1981 Jean Ragnotti (France)
Jean-Marc André (France)
1982 Walter Röhrl (West Germany)
Christian Geistdörfer (West Germany)
1983 Walter Röhrl (West Germany)
Christian Geistdörfer (West Germany)
1984 Walter Röhrl (West Germany)
Christian Geistdörfer (West Germany)
1985 Ari Vatanen (Finland)
Terry Harryman (Great Britain)
1986 Henri Toivonen (Finland)
Sergio Cresto (Italy)
1987 Miki Biasion (Italy)
Tiziano Siviero (Italy)
1988 Bruno Saby (France)
Jean-François Fauchille (France)
1989 Miki Biasion (Italy)
Tiziano Siviero (Italy)
1990 Didier Auriol (France)
Bernard Occelli (France)
1991 Carlos Sainz (Spain)
Luis Moya (Spain)
1992 Didier Auriol (France)
co-driver not known

Most wins: (4), Sandro Munari (Italy), 1972, 1975–7; Walter Röhrl/Christian Geistrdörfer (West Germany), as above.

NETBALL

World Championships
First held in 1963, then every four years.

Winners

1963 Australia
1967 New Zealand
1971 Australia
1975 Australia
1979 Australia, New Zealand, Trinidad & Tobago (*shared*)
1983 Australia
1987 New Zealand
1991 Australia

Most wins: (6), Australia, as above.

ORIENTEERING

World Championships
First held in 1966; takes place every two years (to 1978, and since 1979).

Winners Individual (Men)

1966 Age Hadler (Norway)
1968 Karl Johansson (Sweden)
1970 Stig Berge (Norway)
1972 Age Hadler (Norway)
1974 Bernt Frilen (Sweden)
1976 Egil Johansen (Norway)
1978 Egil Johansen (Norway)
1979 Oyvin Thon (Norway)
1981 Oyvin Thon (Norway)
1983 Morten Berglia (Norway)
1985 Kari Sallinen (Finland)
1987 Kent Olsson (Sweden)
1989 Peter Thoresen (Norway)
1991 Jorgen Martensson (Sweden)

Winners Individual (Women)

1966 Ulla Lindqvist (Sweden)
1968 Ulla Lindqvist (Sweden)
1970 Ingrid Hadler (Norway)
1972 Sarolta Monspart (Finland)
1974 Mona Norgaard (Denmark)
1976 Lia Veijalainen (Finland)
1978 Anne Berit Eid (Norway)
1979 Outi Bergonstrom (Finland)

Orienteering (cont.)

1981 Annichen Kringstad (Norway)
1983 Annichen Kringstad Svensson (Norway)
1985 Annichen Kringstad Svensson (Norway)
1987 Arja Hannus (Sweden)
1989 Marita Skogum (Sweden)
1991 Katarina Olch (Hungary)

Most wins: Men (2), Age Hadler (Norway), Egil Johansen (Norway), Oyvin Thon (Norway), as above. Women (3), Annichen Kringstad (Norway), as above.

Winners Relay (Men)

1966 Sweden
1968 Sweden
1970 Norway
1972 Sweden
1974 Sweden
1976 Sweden
1978 Norway
1979 Sweden
1981 Norway
1983 Norway
1985 Norway
1987 Norway
1989 Norway
1991 Switzerland

Winners Relay (Women)

1966 Sweden
1968 Norway
1970 Sweden
1972 Finland
1974 Sweden
1976 Sweden
1978 Finland
1979 Finland
1981 Sweden
1983 Sweden
1985 Sweden
1987 Norway
1989 Sweden
1991 Sweden

Most wins: Men (7), Norway, as above. Women (9), Sweden, as above.

POLO

Cowdray Park Gold Cup
First held in 1956, replacing the Champion Cup; the British Open Championship for club sides; so named because played at Cowdray Park, Sussex.

Recent winners

1979 Songhai
1980 Stowell Park
1981 Falcons
1982 Southfield
1983 Falcons
1984 Southfield
1985 Maple Leafs
1986 Tramontona
1987 Tramontona
1988 Tramontona
1989 Tramontona
1990 Tramontona
1991 Tramontona

Most wins: (6), Tramontona, 1986–91.

POWERBOAT RACING

World Championships
Instituted in 1982; held in many categories, with Formula One and Formula Two being the principal competitions; Formula One discontinued in 1986; Formula Two became known as Formula Grand Prix.

Winners
Formula One

1982 Roger Jenkins (Great Britain)
1983 Renato Molinari (Italy)
1984 Renato Molinari (Italy)
1985 Bob Spalding (Great Britain)
1986 Gene Thibodaux (USA)
Discontinued

Most wins: (2), Renato Molinari (Italy), as above.

Winners
Formula Two/Formula Grand Prix

1982 Michael Werner (West Germany)
1983 Michael Werner (West Germany)
1984 John Hill (Great Britain)
1985 John Hill (Great Britain)
1986 Jonathan Jones (Great Britain) and Buck Thornton (USA) (*shared*)
1987 Bill Seebold (USA)
1988 Chris Bush (USA)
1989 Jonathan Jones (Great Britain)
1990 John Hill (Great Britain)

Most wins: (3), John Hill (Great Britain), as above.

RACKETS

World Championship
Organized on a challenge basis, the first champion in 1820 was Robert Mackay (Great Britain).

Recent winners

1929–37 Charles Williams (Great Britain)
1937–47 Donald Milford (Great Britain)
1947–54 James Dear (Great Britain)
1954–72 Geoffrey Atkins (Great Britain)
1972–73 William Surtees (USA)
1973–74 Howard Angus (Great Britain)
1975–81 William Surtees (USA)
1981–84 John Prenn (Great Britain)
1984–86 William Boone (Great Britain)
1986–88 John Prenn (Great Britain)
1988– James Male (Great Britain)

Longest reigning champion: 18 years, Geoffrey Atkins, as above.

REAL TENNIS

World Championship
Organized on a challenge basis; the first world champion was M Clerge (France) c.1740, regarded as the first world champion of any sport.

Recent winners

1916–28 Fred Covey (Great Britain)
1928–55 Pierre Etchebaster (France)
1955–57 James Dear (Great Britain)
1957–59 Albert Johnson (Great Britain)
1959–69 Northrup Knox (USA)
1969–72 Pete Bostwick (USA)
1972–75 Jimmy Bostwick (USA)
1976–81 Howard Angus (Great Britain)
1981–87 Chris Ronaldson (Great Britain)
1987– Wayne Davies (Australia)

Longest reigning champion: 33 years, Edmond Barre (France), 1829–62.

ROLLER SKATING

World Championships
Figure skating world championships were first organized in 1947.

Recent winners (Men Combined)

1979 Michael Butzke (East Germany)
1980 Michael Butzke (East Germany)
1981 Michael Butzke (East Germany)
1982 Michael Butzke (East Germany)
1983 Joachim Helmle (West Germany)
1984 Michele Biserni (Italy)
1985 Michele Biserni (Italy)
1986 Michele Tolomini (Italy)
1987 Kevin Carroll (USA)
1988 Sandro Guerra (Italy)
1989 Sandro Guerra (Italy)
1990 Justin Bates (USA)
1991 Sandro Guerra (Italy)

Most wins: (5), Karl-Heinz Losch (West Germany), 1958–9, 1961–2, 1966.

Recent winners (Women Combined)

1979 Petre Schneider (West Germany)
1980 Petre Schneider (West Germany)
1981 Petre Schneider (West Germany)
1982 Claudia Bruppacher (West Germany)
1983 Claudia Bruppacher (West Germany)
1984 Claudia Bruppacher (West Germany)
1985 Chiara Sartori (Italy)
1986 Chiara Sartori (Italy)
1987 Chiara Sartori (Italy)
1988 Rafaela De Vinaccio (Italy)
1989 Rafaela De Vinaccio (Italy)
1990 Rafaela De Vinaccio (Italy)
1991 Rafaela De Vinaccio (Italy)

Most wins: (4), Astrid Bader (West Germany), 1965–8; Rafaela De Vinaccio (Italy), as above.

Recent winners (Pairs)

1979 Ray Chapatta/Karen Mejia (USA)
1980 Paul Price/Tina Kniesley (USA)
1981 Paul Price/Tina Kniesley (USA)
1982 Paul Price/Tina Kniesley (USA)
1983 John Arishita/Tammy Jeru (USA)
1984 John Arishita/Tammy Jeru (USA)
1985 John Arishita/Tammy Jeru (USA)
1986 John Arishita/Tammy Jeru (USA)
1987 Fabio Trevisani/Monica Mezzardi (Italy)
1988 Fabio Trevisani/Monica Mezzardi (Italy)
1989 David De Motte/Nicky Armstrong (USA)
1990 Larry McGrew/Tina Jerue (USA)
1991 Larry McGrew/Tina Jerue (USA)

Most wins: (4), Dieter Fingerle (West Germany), 1959, 1965–7; John Arishita and Tammy Jeru (USA), as above.

Recent winners (Dance)

1979 Dan Littel/Florence Arsenault (USA)
1980 Torsten Carels/Gabriele Achenback (East Germany)
1981 Mark Howard/Cindy Smith (USA)
1982 Mark Howard/Cindy Smith (USA)

Roller Skating (cont.)

1983 David Golub/Angela Famiano (USA)
1984 David Golub/Angela Famiano (USA)
1985 Martin Hauss/Andrea Steudte (West Germany)
1986 Scott Myers/Anna Danks (USA)
1987 Rob Ferendo/Lori Walsh (USA)
1988 Peter Wulf/Michela Mitzlaf (West Germany)
1989 Greg Goody/Jodee Viola (USA)
1990 Greg Goody/Jodee Viola (USA)
1991 Greg Goody/Jodee Viola (USA)

Most wins: (3), Jane Puracchio (USA), 1973, 1975–6; Dan Littel and Florence Arsenault (USA), 1977–9; Greg Goody and Jodee Viola (USA), as above.

ROWING

World Championships

First held for men in 1962 and for women in 1974; Olympic champions assume the role of world champion in Olympic years; principal events are the single sculls.

Recent winners Single Sculls (Men)

1979 Perrti Karppinen (Finland)
1980 Perrti Karppinen (Finland)
1981 Peter-Michael Kolbe (West Germany)
1982 Rudiger Reiche (East Germany)
1983 Peter-Michael Kolbe (West Germany)
1984 Perrti Karppinen (Finland)
1985 Perrti Karppinen (Finland)
1986 Peter-Michael Kolbe (West Germany)
1987 Thomas Lange (East Germany)
1988 Thomas Lange (East Germany)
1989 Thomas Lange (East Germany)
1990 Yuri Janson (USSR)
1991 Thomas Lange (Germany)
1992 Thomas Lange (Germany)

Most wins: (4), Peter-Michael Kolbe (West Germany), 1975, 1978, 1981, 1983; Perrti Karppinen (Finland), as above.

Recent winners Single Sculls (Women)

1979 Sanda Toma (Romania)
1980 Sanda Toma (Romania)
1981 Sanda Toma (Romania)
1982 Irina Fetissova (USSR)
1983 Jutta Hampe (East Germany)
1984 Valeria Racila (Romania)
1985 Cornelia Linse (East Germany)
1986 Jutta Hampe (East Germany)
1987 Magdelena Georgieva (Bulgaria)
1988 Jutta Behrendt (East Germany)
1989 Elisabeta Lipa (Romania)
1990 Brigit Peter (East Germany)
1991 Silke Laumann (Canada)
1992 Elisabeta Lipa (Romania)

Most wins: (5), Christine Hahn (*née* Scheiblich) (East Germany), 1974–8.

The Boat Race

An annual contest between the crews from the Oxford and Cambridge University rowing clubs; first contested in 1829; the current course is from Putney to Mortlake.

Recent winners

1980 Oxford
1981 Oxford
1982 Oxford
1983 Oxford
1984 Oxford
1985 Oxford
1986 Cambridge
1987 Oxford
1988 Oxford
1989 Oxford
1990 Oxford
1991 Oxford
1992 Oxford

Wins: 69, Cambridge; 68, Oxford; 1 dead-heat (1877).

Diamond Sculls

Highlight of Henley Royal Regatta held every July; first contested in 1884.

Recent winners

1979 Hugh Matheson (Great Britain)
1980 Riccardo Ibarra (Argentina)
1981 Chris Baillieu (Great Britain)
1982 Chris Baillieu (Great Britain)
1983 Steve Redgrave (Great Britain)
1984 Chris Baillieu (Great Britain)
1985 Steve Redgrave (Great Britain)
1986 Bjarne Eltang (Denmark)
1987 Peter-Michael Kolbe (West Germany)
1988 Hamish McGlashan (Australia)
1989 Vaclav Chalupa (Czechoslovakia)
1990 Erik Verdonk (New Zealand)
1991 Wim van Belleghem (Belgium)
1992 Rorie Henderson (Great Britain)

Most wins: (6), Stuart Mackenzie (Great Britain), 1957–62. Guy Nickalls (Great Britain), 1881–91, 1983–4.

RUGBY LEAGUE

Challenge Cup Final

First contested in 1897 and won by Batley; first final at Wembley Stadium in 1929.

Recent winners

1979 Widnes
1980 Hull Kingston Rovers
1981 Widnes
1982 Hull
1983 Featherstone Rovers
1984 Widnes
1985 Wigan
1986 Castleford
1987 Halifax
1988 Wigan
1989 Wigan
1990 Wigan
1991 Wigan

Most wins: (12), Wigan, 1924, 1929, 1948, 1951, 1958–59, 1965, 1985, 1988–91.

Premiership Trophy

End-of-season knockout competition involving the top eight teams in the first division; first contested at the end of the 1974–5 season.

Recent winners

1979 Leeds
1980 Widnes
1981 Hull Kingston Rovers
1982 Widnes
1983 Widnes
1984 Hull Kingston Rovers
1985 St Helens
1986 Warrington
1987 Wigan
1988 Widnes
1989 Widnes
1990 Widnes
1991 Hull

Most wins: (6), Widnes, as above.

Regal Trophy

A knockout competition, first held in 1971–2. Formerly known as the John Player Special Trophy, it adopted its current style in 1989–90.

Recent winners

1980 Bradford Northern
1981 Warrington
1982 Hull
1983 Wigan
1984 Leeds
1985 Hull Kingston Rovers
1986 Wigan
1987 Wigan
1988 St Helens
1989 Wigan
1990 Wigan
1991 Warrington
1992 Widnes

Most wins: (5), Wigan, as above.

RUGBY UNION

World Cup

The first Rugby Union World Cup was staged in 1987; New Zealand were crowned the first champions after beating France in the final. Australia won the second World Cup in 1991, defeating England in the final.

International Championship

A round robin competition involving England, Ireland, Scotland, Wales and France; first contested in 1884.

Recent winners

1980 England
1981 France
1982 Ireland
1983 France and Ireland
1984 Scotland
1985 Ireland
1986 France and Scotland
1987 France
1988 France and Wales
1989 France
1990 Scotland
1991 England
1992 England

Most outright wins: (21), Wales, 1893, 1900, 1902, 1905, 1908–9, 1911, 1922, 1931, 1936, 1950, 1952, 1956, 1965–6, 1969, 1971, 1975–6, 1978–9.

County Championship

First held in 1889.

Recent winners

1980 Lancashire
1981 Northumberland
1982 Lancashire
1983 Gloucestershire
1984 Gloucestershire
1985 Middlesex
1986 Warwickshire
1987 Yorkshire

Rugby Union (cont.)

1988 Lancashire
1989 Durham
1990 Lancashire
1991 Cornwall

Most wins: (15), Gloucestershire, 1910, 1913, 1920–2, 1930–2, 1937, 1972, 1974–6, 1983–4.

Pilkington Cup

An annual knockout competition for English Club sides; first held in the 1971–2 season. Known as the John Player Special Cup until 1988.

Recent winners

1980 Leicester
1981 Leicester
1982 Gloucester and Moseley (*shared*)
1983 Bristol
1984 Bath
1985 Bath
1986 Bath
1987 Bath
1988 Harlequins
1989 Bath
1990 Bath
1991 Harlequins

Most wins: (6), Bath, as above.

Schweppes Welsh Cup

The knockout tournament for Welsh clubs; first held in 1971–2.

Recent winners

1980 Bridgend
1981 Cardiff
1982 Cardiff
1983 Pontypool
1984 Cardiff
1985 Llanelli
1986 Cardiff
1987 Cardiff
1988 Llanelli
1989 Neath
1990 Neath
1991 Llanelli

Most wins: (7), Llanelli, 1973–6, 1985, 1988, 1991.

SHINTY

Camanachd Cup

The sport's principal trophy, it was first held in 1896 and won by Kingussie. Shinty is the popular name for the original game of Camanachd.

Recent winners

1980 Kyles Athletic
1981 Newtonmore
1982 Newtonmore
1983 Kyles Athletic
1984 Kingussie
1985 Newtonmore
1986 Newtonmore
1987 Kingussie
1988 Kingussie
1989 Kingussie
1990 Skye
1991 Kingussie

Most wins: (28), Newtonmore, 1907–86.

SHOOTING

Olympic Games

The Olympic competition is the highlight of the shooting calendar; winners in all categories since 1984 are given below.

Free Pistol (Men)

1984 Xu Haifeng (China)
1988 Sorin Babil (Romania)
1992 Konstantine Loukachik (UT)

Rapid Fire Pistol (Men)

1984 Takeo Kamachi (Japan)
1988 Afanasi Kouzmine (USSR)
1992 Ralf Schumann (Germany)

Small Bore Rifle (Three Position) (Men)

1984 Malcolm Cooper (Great Britain)
1988 Malcolm Cooper (Great Britain)
1992 Grachya Petikiane (UT)

Running Game Target (Men)

1984 Li Yuwei (China)
1988 Tor Heiestad (Norway)
1992 Michael Jakosits (Germany)

Shooting (cont.)

Trap (Men)

1984 Luciano Giovanetti (Italy)
1988 Dmitri Monakov (USSR)
1992 Petr Hrdlicka (Czechoslovakia)

Skeet (Men)

1984 Matthew Dryke (USA)
1988 Axel Wegner (East Germany)
1992 Zhang Shan (China)

Small Bore Rifle (Prone) (Men)

1984 Edward Etzel (USA)
1988 Miroslav Varga (Czechoslovakia)
1992 Lee Eun-chul (South Korea)

Air Rifle (Men)

1984 Philippe Heberle (France)
1988 Goran Maksimovic (Yugoslavia)
1992 Yuri Fedkin (UT)

Air Pistol (Men)

1988 Tariou Kiriakov (USSR)
1992 Wang Yifu (China)

Sport Pistol (Women)

1984 Linda Thom (Canada)
1988 Nino Saloukvadze (USSR)
1992 Marina Logvinenko (UT)

Air Rifle (Women)

1984 Pat Spurgin (USA)
1988 Irina Chilova (USSR)
1992 Yeo Kab Soon (South Korea)

Small Bore Rifle (Women)

1984 Wu Xiaoxuan (China)
1988 Silvia Sperber (West Germany)
1992 Launa Meili (USA)

Air Pistol (Women)

1988 Jasna Sekuric (Yugoslavia)
1992 Marino Logvinenko (UT)

SKIING

World Cup
A season-long competition first organized in 1967; champions are declared in downhill, slalom, giant slalom and super-giant slalom, as well as the overall champion; points are obtained for performances in each category.

Recent overall winners (Men)

1980 Andreas Wenzel (Liechtenstein)
1981 Phil Mahre (USA)
1982 Phil Mahre (USA)
1983 Phil Mahre (USA)
1984 Pirmin Zurbriggen (Switzerland)
1985 Marc Girardelli (Luxembourg)
1986 Marc Girardelli (Luxembourg)
1987 Pirmin Zurbriggen (Switzerland)
1988 Pirmin Zurbriggen (Switzerland)
1989 Marc Girardelli (Luxembourg)
1990 Pirmin Zurbriggen (Switzerland)
1991 Marc Girardelli (Luxembourg)
1992 Paul Accola (Switzerland)

Recent overall winners (Women)

1980 Hanni Wenzel (Liechtenstein)
1981 Marie-Therese Nadig (Switzerland)
1982 Erika Hess (Switzerland)
1983 Tamara McKinney (USA)
1984 Erika Hess (Switzerland)
1985 Michela Figini (Switzerland)
1986 Maria Walliser (Switzerland)
1987 Maria Walliser (Switzerland)
1988 Michela Figini (Switzerland)
1989 Vreni Schneider (Switzerland)
1990 Petra Kronberger (Austria)
1991 Petra Kronberger (Austria)
1992 Petra Kronberger (Austria)

Most wins: Men (4), Gustavo Thoeni (Italy), 1971–3, 1975, Pirmin Zurbriggen, Marc Girardelli, as above. Women (6), Annemarie Moser-Pröll (Austria), 1971–5, 1979.

SNOOKER

World Professional Championship
Instituted in the 1926–7 season; a knockout competition open to professional players who are members of the World Professional Billiards and Snooker Association; played at the Crucible Theatre, Sheffield.

Recent winners

1979 Terry Griffiths (Wales)
1980 Cliff Thorburn (Canada)
1981 Steve Davis (England)
1982 Alex Higgins (Ireland)
1983 Steve Davis (England)
1984 Steve Davis (England)
1985 Dennis Taylor (Ireland)
1986 Joe Johnson (England)
1987 Steve Davis (England)
1988 Steve Davis (England)
1989 Steve Davis (England)
1990 Stephen Hendry (Scotland)
1991 John Parrott (England)
1992 Stephen Hendry (Scotland)

Most wins: (15), Joe Davis (England), 1927–40, 1946.

Snooker (cont.)

World Doubles
First played in 1982.

Winners

1982 Steve Davis (England)
Tony Meo (England)
1983 Steve Davis (England)
Tony Meo (England)
1984 Alex Higgins (Ireland)
Jimmy White (England)
1985 Steve Davis (England)
Tony Meo (England)
1986 Steve Davis (England)
Tony Meo (England)
1987 Mike Hallett (England)
Stephen Hendry (Scotland)
Discontinued

Most wins: (4), Steve Davis and Tony Meo (England), as above.

World Team Championship
Also known as the World Cup; first held in 1979.

Winners

1979 Wales
1980 Wales
1981 England
1982 Canada
1983 England
1984 *not held*
1985 Ireland
1986 Ireland 'A'
1987 Ireland 'A'
1988 England
1989 England
1990 Canada
1991 *not held*
1992 *not held*

Most wins: (4), England, as above.

World Amateur Championship
First held in 1963; originally took place every two years, but annual since 1984.

Recent winners

1974 Ray Edmonds (England)
1976 Doug Mountjoy (Wales)
1978 Cliff Wilson (Wales)
1980 Jimmy White (England)
1982 Terry Parson (Wales)
1984 O. B. Agrawal (India)
1985 Paul Mifsud (Malta)
1986 Paul Mifsud (Malta)
1987 Darren, Morgan (Wales)
1988 James Wattana (Thailand)
1989 Ken Doherty (Republic of Ireland)
1990 Stephen O'Connor (Republic of Ireland)
1991 Noppodol Noppajorn (Thailand)

Most wins: (2), Gary Owen (England), 1963, 1966; Ray Edmonds (England), 1972, 1974; Paul Mifsud, as above.

SOFTBALL

World Championships
First held for women in 1965 and for men the following year; now held every four years.

Winners (Men)

1966 USA
1968 USA
1972 Canada
1976 Canada, New Zealand & USA (*shared*)
1980 USA
1984 New Zealand
1988 USA

Most wins: (5), USA, as above.

Winners (Women)

1965 Australia
1970 Japan
1974 USA
1978 USA
1982 New Zealand
1986 USA
1990 USA

Most wins: (4), USA, as above.

SPEEDWAY

World Championships
Individual championships inaugurated in 1936; team championship instituted in 1960; first official pairs world championship in 1970.

Recent winners

1979 Ivan Mauger (New Zealand)
1980 Mike Lee (England)
1981 Bruce Penhall (USA)
1982 Bruce Penhall (USA)
1983 Egon Muller (West Germany)
1984 Erik Gundersen (Denmark)
1985 Erik Gundersen (Denmark)

Speedway (cont.)

1986 Hans Nielsen (Denmark)
1987 Hans Nielsen (Denmark)
1988 Erik Gundersen (Denmark)
1989 Hans Nielsen (Denmark)
1990 Per Jonsson (Sweden)
1991 Jan Pedersen (Denmark)

Most wins: (6), Ivan Mauger (New Zealand), 1968–70, 1972, 1977, 1979.

Recent winners (Pairs) (Three in 1991)

1979 Ole Olsen/Hans Nielsen (Denmark)
1980 Dave Jessup/Peter Collins (England)
1981 Bruce Penhall/Bobby Schwartz (USA)
1982 Dennis Sigalos/Bobby Schwartz (USA)
1983 Kenny Carter/Peter Collins (England)
1984 Peter Collins/Chris Morton (England)
1985 Erik Gunderson/Tommy Knudsen (Denmark)
1986 Erik Gundersen/Hans Nielsen (Denmark)
1987 Erik Gundersen/Hans Nielsen (Denmark)
1988 Erik Gundersen/Hans Nielsen (Denmark)
1989 Erik Gundersen/Hans Nielsen (Denmark)
1990 Hans Nielsen/Jan Pedersen (Denmark)
1991 Hans Nielsen/Jan Pedersen/Tommy Knudsen (Denmark)

Most wins: (7), Hans Nielsen, as above.

Recent winners (Team)

1979 New Zealand
1980 England
1981 Denmark
1982 USA
1983 Denmark
1984 Denmark
1985 Denmark
1986 Denmark
1987 Denmark
1988 Denmark
1989 England
1990 USA
1991 Denmark

Most wins: (9), Great Britain/England, 1968, 1971–5, 1977, 1980, 1989.

SQUASH

World Open Championship

First held in 1976; takes place annually for men, every two years for women.

Winners (Men)

1979 Geoff Hunt (Australia)
1980 Geoff Hunt (Australia)
1981 Jahangir Khan (Pakistan)
1982 Jahangir Khan (Pakistan)
1983 Jahangir Khan (Pakistan)
1984 Jahangir Khan (Pakistan)
1985 Jahangir Khan (Pakistan)
1986 Ross Norman (New Zealand)
1987 Jansher Khan (Pakistan)
1988 Jahangir Khan (Pakistan)
1989 Jansher Khan (Pakistan)
1990 Jansher Khan (Pakistan)
1991 Rodney Martin (Australia)

Most wins: (6), Jahangir Khan (Pakistan), as above.

Winners (Women)

1976 Heather McKay (Australia)
1979 Heather McKay (Australia)
1981 Rhonda Thorne (Australia)
1983 Vicky Cardwell (Australia)
1985 Sue Devoy (New Zealand)
1987 Sue Devoy (New Zealand)
1989 Martine Le Moignan (Great Britain)
1990 Sue Devoy (New Zealand)

Most wins: (2), Heather McKay (Australia), as above; Sue Devoy (New Zealand), as above.

SURFING

World Professional Championship

A season-long series of Grand Prix events; first held in 1970.

Recent winners (Men)

1979 Mark Richards (Australia)
1980 Mark Richards (Australia)
1981 Mark Richards (Australia)
1982 *Season changed to encompass 1982–3*
1983 Mark Richards (Australia)
1984 Tom Carroll (Australia)
1985 Tom Carroll (Australia)
1986 Tommy Curren (USA)
1987 Damien Hardman (Australia)
1988 Barton Lynch (Australia)
1989 Martin Potter (Great Britain)
1990 Heifara Tahutini (Tahiti)

Surfing (cont.)

Recent winners (Women)

1979 Margo Oberg (Hawaii)
1980 Lyne Boyer (Hawaii)
1981 Margo Oberg (Hawaii)
1982 *not held*
1983 Margo Oberg (Hawaii)
1984 Kim Mearig (USA)
1985 Frieda Zamba (USA)
1986 Frieda Zamba (USA)
1987 Wendy Botha (South Africa)
1988 Freida Zamba (USA)
1989 Wendy Botha (South Africa)
1990 Kathy Newman (Australia)

Most wins: Men (5), Mark Richards (Australia), 1975, 1979–83. Women (3), Margo Oberg (Hawaii), Freida Zamba (USA), as above.

SWIMMING AND DIVING

World Championships
First held in 1973 and again in 1975; since 1978 take place every four years; 1990 championships postponed; the complete list of 1991 champions is given below.

1986 World Champions (Men)

50 metres freestyle	Tom Jager (USA)
100 metres freestyle	Matt Biondi (USA)
200 metres freestyle	Georgio Lamberti (Italy)
400 metres freestyle	Joerg Hoffman (Germany)
1500 metres freestyle	Joerg Hoffman (Germany)
100 metres backstroke	Jeff Rouse (USA)
200 metres backstroke	Martin Lopez Zubero (Spain)
100 metres breaststroke	Norbert Rozsa (Hungary)
200 metres breaststroke	Mike Barrowman (USA)
100 metres butterfly	Anthony Nesty (Suriname)
200 metres butterfly	Melvin Stewart (USA)
200 metres individual medley	Tamas Darnyi (Hungary)
400 metres individual medley	Tamas Darnyi (Hungary)
4 × 100 metres freestyle medley	USA
4 × 200 metres freestyle medley	East Germany
4 × 100 metres medley relay	USA
Springboard diving	Edwin Jongejans (Holland)
Highboard diving	Shuwei Sun (China)

1991 World Champions (Women)

50 metres freestyle	Yong Zhuang (China)
100 metres freestyle	Nicole Haislett (USA)
200 metres freestyle	Hayley Lewis (Australia)
400 metres freestyle	Janet Evans (USA)
800 metres freestyle	Janet Evans (USA)
100 metres backstroke	Kriszrina Egerszegi (Hungary)
200 metres backstroke	Kriszrina Egerszegi (Hungary)
100 metres breaststroke	Linley Frame (Australia)
200 metres breaststroke	Elena Volkova (USSR)
100 metres butterfly	Hong Qian (China)
200 metres butterfly	Summer Sanders (USA)
200 metres individual medley	Li Lin (China)
400 metres individual medley	Li Lin (China)
4 × 100 metres freestyle relay	USA
4 × 200 metres freestyle relay	Germany
4 × 100 metres medley relay	USA
Springboard diving	Min Gao (China)
Highboard diving	Mingxia Fu (China)
Synchronized swimming	
Solo	Sylvie Frechette (Canada)
Duet	USA
Team	USA

TABLE TENNIS

World Championships
First held in 1926 and every two years since 1957.

Recent winners
Swaythling Cup (Men's Team)

1969 Japan
1971 China
1973 Sweden
1975 China
1977 China
1979 Hungary
1981 China
1983 China
1985 China
1987 China
1989 Sweden
1991 Sweden

Recent winners
Corbillon Cup (Women's Team)

1969 USSR
1971 Japan
1973 South Korea
1975 China
1977 China
1979 China
1981 China
1983 China
1985 China
1987 China
1989 China
1991 United Korea

Most wins: Swaythling Cup (12), Hungary, 1926, 1928–31, 1933 (twice), 1935, 1938, 1949, 1952, 1979. Corbillon Cup (9), China, 1965, 1975, 1977, 1979, 1981, 1983, 1985, 1987, 1989.

Recent winners
Men's Singles

1969 Shigeo Ito (Japan)
1971 Stellan Bengtsson (Sweden)
1973 Hsi En-Ting (China)
1975 Istvan Jonyer (Hungary)
1977 Mitsuru Kohno (Japan)
1979 Seiji Ono (Japan)
1981 Guo Yuehua (China)
1983 Guo Yuehua (China)
1985 Jiang Jialiang (China)
1987 Jiang Jialiang (China)
1989 Jan-Ove Waldner (Sweden)
1991 Jorgen Persson (Sweden)

Most wins: (5), Viktor Barna (Hungary), 1930, 1932–5.

Recent winners
Women's singles

1969 Toshiko Kowada (Japan)
1971 Lin Hui-Ching (China)
1973 Hu Yu-Lan (China)
1975 Pak Yung-Sun (North Korea)
1977 Pak Yung-Sun (North Korea)
1979 Ge Xinai (China)
1981 Ting Ling (China)
1983 Cao Yanhua (China)
1985 Cao Yanhua (China)
1987 He Zhili (China)
1989 Qiao Hong (China)
1991 Deng Yaping (China)

Most wins: (6), Angelica Rozeanu (Romania), 1950–55.

Recent winners
Men's Doubles

1969 Hans Alser/Kjell Johansson (Sweden)
1971 Istvan Jonyer/Tiber Klampar (Hungary)
1973 Stellan Bengtsson/Kjell Johansson (Sweden)
1975 Gabor Gergely/Istvan Jonyer (Hungary)
1977 Li Zhenshi/Liang Geliang (China)
1979 Dragutin Surbek/Anton Stipancic (Yugoslavia)
1981 Cai Zhenhua/Li Zhenshi (China)
1983 Dragutin Surbek/Zoran Kalinic (Yugoslavia)
1985 Mikael Applegren/Ulf Carlsson (Sweden)
1987 Chen Longcan/Wei Quinguang (China)
1989 Jaerg Rosskopf/Stefen Fetzner (West Germany)
1991 Peter Karlsson/Tomas von Scheele (Sweden)

Most wins: (8), Viktor Barna (Hungary/England), 1929–33 (won two titles 1933), 1935, 1939.

Recent winners
Women's Doubles

1969 Svetlana Grinberg/Zoya Rudnova (USSR)
1971 Cheng Min-Chih/Lin Hui-Ching (China)
1973 Maria Alexandru (Romania)/Miho Hamada (Japan)
1975 Maria Alexandru (Romania)/ Shoko Takashima (Japan)
1977 Pak Yong Ok (North Korea)/Yang Yin (China)

Table Tennis (cont.)

1979 Zhang Li/Zhang Deying (China)
1981 Zhang Deying/Cao Yanhua (China)
1983 Shen Jianping/Dai Lili (China)
1985 Dai Lili/Geng Lijuan (China)
1987 Yang Young-Ja/Hyun Jung-Hwa (Korea)
1989 Quio Hong/Deng Yaping (China)
1991 Chen Zhie/Liu Wei (China)

Most wins: (7), Maria Mednyanszky (Hungary), 1928, 1930–5.

Recent winners
Mixed Doubles

1969 Nobuhiko Hasegawa/Yasuka Konno (Japan)
1971 Chang Shih-Ling/Lin Hui-Ching (China)
1973 Liang Geliang/Li Li (China)
1975 Stanislav Gomozkov/Anna Ferdman (USSR)
1977 Jacques Secretin/Claude Bergeret (France)
1979 Liang Geliang/Ge Xinai (China)
1981 Xie Saike/Huang Junqun (China)
1983 Guo Yuehua/Ni Xialian (China)
1985 Cai Zhenua/Cao Yanhua (China)
1987 Hui Jun/Geng Lijuan (China)
1989 Yoo Nam-Kyu/Hyun Jung-Hwa (South Korea)
1991 Wang Tao/Liu Wei (China)

Most wins: (6), Maria Mednyanszky (Hungary), 1927–8, 1930–1, 1933 (two titles).

TENNIS (LAWN)

Wimbledon Championships
The All-England Championships at Wimbledon are Lawn Tennis's most prestigious championships; first held in 1877.

Recent winners
Men's Singles

1979 Bjorn Borg (Sweden)
1980 Bjorn Borg (Sweden)
1981 John McEnroe (USA)
1982 Jimmy Connors (USA)
1983 John McEnroe (USA)
1984 John McEnroe (USA)
1985 Boris Becker (West Germany)
1986 Boris Becker (West Germany)
1987 Pat Cash (Australia)
1988 Stefan Edberg (Sweden)
1989 Boris Becker (West Germany)
1990 Stefan Edberg (Sweden)
1991 Michael Stich (Germany)
1992 André Agassi (USA)

Most wins: (7), William Renshaw (Great Britain), 1881–6, 1889.

Recent winners
Women's Singles

1979 Martina Navratilova (Czechoslovakia)
1980 Evonne Goolagong-Cawley (Australia)
1981 Chris Evert-Lloyd (USA)
1982 Martina Navratilova (USA)
1983 Martina Navratilova (USA)
1984 Martina Navratilova (USA)
1985 Martina Navratilova (USA)
1986 Martina Navratilova (USA)
1987 Martina Navratilova (USA)
1988 Steffi Graf (West Germany)
1989 Steffi Graf (West Germany)
1990 Martina Navratilova (USA)
1991 Steffi Graf (Germany)
1992 Steffi Graf (Germany)

Most wins: (9), Martina Navratilova (Czechoslovakia/USA), as above plus 1978.

Recent winners
Men's Doubles

1979 Peter Fleming/John McEnroe (USA)
1980 Peter McNamara/Paul McNamee (Australia)
1981 Peter Fleming/John McEnroe (USA)
1982 Peter McNamara/Paul McNamee (Australia)
1983 Peter Fleming/John McEnroe (USA)
1984 Peter Fleming/John McEnroe (USA)
1985 Heinz Gunthardt (Switzerland)/Balazs Taroczy (Hungary)
1986 Joakim Nystrom/Mats Wilander (Sweden)
1987 Ken Flach/Robert Seguso (USA)
1988 Ken Flach/Robert Seguso (USA)
1989 John Fitzgerald (Australia)/Anders Jarryd (Sweden)
1990 Rick Leach/Jim Pugh (USA)
1991 John Fitzgerald (Australia)/Anders Jarryd (Sweden)
1992 John McEnroe (USA)/Michael Stich (Germany)

Most wins: (8), Lawrence Doherty/Reg Doherty (Great Britain), 1897–1901, 1903–5.

Recent winners
Women's Doubles

1979 Billie Jean King (USA)/Martina Navratilova (Czechoslovakia)
1980 Kathy Jordan/Anne Smith (USA)
1981 Martina Navratilova/Pam Shriver (USA)
1982 Martina Navratilova/Pam Shriver (USA)
1983 Martina Navratilova/Pam Shriver (USA)
1984 Martina Navratilova/Pam Shriver (USA)
1985 Kathy Jordan/Elizabeth Smylie (Aus)
1986 Martina Navratilova/Pam Shriver (USA)

Tennis (Lawn) (cont.)

1987 Claudia Kohde-Kilsch (West Germany)/ Helena Sukova (Czechoslovakia)
1988 Steffi Graf (West Germany)/Gabriela Sabatini (Argentina)
1989 Jana Novotna/Helena Sukova (Czechoslovakia)
1990 Jana Novotna/Helena Sukova (Czechoslovakia)
1991 Natalya Zvereva/Larisa Savchenko (USSR)
1992 G Fernandez (USA)/Natalya Zvereva (CIS)

Most wins: (12), Elizabeth Ryan (USA), 1914, 1919–23, 1925–7, 1930, 1933–4.

Recent winners
Mixed Doubles

1979 Greer Stevens/Bob Hewitt (South Africa)
1980 Tracy Austin/John Austin (USA)
1981 Betty Stove (Holland)/Frew McMillan (South Africa)
1982 Anne Smith (USA)/Kevin Curren (South Africa)
1983 Wendy Turnbull (Australia)/John Lloyd (Great Britain)
1984 Wendy Turnbull (Australia)/John Lloyd (Great Britain)
1985 Martina Navratilova (USA) Paul McNamee (Australia)
1986 Kathy Jordan/Ken Flach (USA)
1987 Jo Durie/Jeremy Bates (Great Britain)
1988 Sherwood Stewart/Zina Garrison (USA)
1989 Jim Pugh (USA)/Jan Novotna (Czechoslovakia)
1990 Rick Leach/Zina Garrison (USA)
1991 John Fitzgerald/Elizabeth Smylie (Australia)
1992 Cyril Suk (Czechoslovakia)/Larisa Savchenko-Neiland (Latvia)

Most wins: (7), Elizabeth Ryan (USA), 1919, 1921, 1923, 1927–8, 1930, 1932.

United States Open

First held in 1891 as the United States Championship; became the United States Open in 1968.

Recent winners
Men's Singles

1979 John McEnroe (USA)
1980 John McEnroe (USA)
1981 John McEnroe (USA)
1982 Jimmy Connors (USA)
1983 Jimmy Connors (USA)
1984 John McEnroe (USA)
1985 Ivan Lendl (Czechoslovakia)
1986 Ivan Lendl (Czechoslovakia)
1987 Ivan Lendl (Czechoslovakia)
1988 Mats Wilander (Sweden)
1989 Boris Becker (West Germany)
1990 Pete Sampras (USA)
1991 Stefan Edberg (Sweden)

Recent winners
Women's Singles

1979 Tracy Austin (USA)
1980 Chris Evert-Lloyd (USA)
1981 Tracy Austin (USA)
1982 Chris Evert-Lloyd (USA)
1983 Martina Navratilova (USA)
1984 Martina Navratilova (USA)
1985 Hana Mandlikova (Czechoslovakia)
1986 Martina Navratilova (USA)
1987 Martina Navratilova (USA)
1988 Steffi Graf (West Germany)
1989 Steffi Graf (West Germany)
1990 Gabriela Sabatini (Argentina)
1991 Monica Seles (Yugoslavia)

Most wins: Men (7), Richard Sears (USA), 1881–7; Bill Larned (USA), 1901–2, 1907–11; Bill Tilden (USA), 1920–5, 1929. Women (7), Molla Mallory (*née* Bjurstedt) (USA), 1915–16, 1918, 1920–2, 1926; Helen Wills-Moody (USA), 1923–5, 1927–9, 1931.

Davis Cup

International team competition organized on a knockout basis; first held in 1900; contested on a challenge basis until 1972.

Recent winners

1979 USA
1980 Czechoslovakia
1981 USA
1982 USA
1983 Australia
1984 Sweden
1985 Sweden
1986 Australia
1987 Sweden
1988 West Germany
1989 West Germany
1990 USA
1991 France

Most wins: (29), USA, 1900, 1902, 1913, 1920–6, 1937–8, 1946–9, 1954, 1958, 1963, 1968–72, 1978–9, 1981–2, 1990.

TENPIN BOWLING

World Championships
First held in 1923 by the International Bowling Association; since 1954 organized by the Fédération Internationale des Quillieurs (FIQ); since 1963, when women first competed, held every four years.

Recent winners
Individual (Men)

1954 Göska Algeskog (Sweden)
1955 Nils Bäckström (Sweden)
1958 Kaarlo Asukas (Finland)
1960 Tito Reynolds (Mexico)
1963 Les Zikes (USA)
1967 David Pond (Great Britain)
1971 Ed Luther (USA)
1975 Bud Staudt (USA)
1979 Ollie Ongtawco (Philippines)
1983 Armando Marino (Colombia)
1987 Rolland Patrick (France)
1991 Jon Juneau (USA)

Recent winners
Individual (Women)

1963 Helen Shablis (USA)
1967 Helen Weston (USA)
1971 Ashie Gonzales (Puerto Rico)
1975 Annedore Haefker (West Germany)
1979 Lita de la Roas (Philippines)
1983 Lena Sulkanen (Sweden)
1987 Edda Piccini (Italy)
1991 Asa Larsson (Sweden)

Most wins: No one has won more than one title.

TRAMPOLINING

World Championships
First held in 1964 and annually until 1968; since then, every two years.

Recent winners
Individual (Men)

1970 Wayne Miller (USA)
1972 Paul Luxon (Great Britain)
1974 Richard Tison (France)
1976 Richard Tison (France)/Yevgeni Yanes (USSR) (*shared*)
1978 Yevgeni Yanes (USSR)
1980 Stewart Matthews (Great Britain)
1982 Carl Furrer (Great Britain)
1984 Lionel Pioline (France)
1986 Lionel Pioline (France)
1988 Vadim Krasnoshapka (USSR)
1990 Alexandr Moskalenko (USSR)

Most wins: (2), David Jacobs (USA), 1967–8; Wayne Miller (USA), 1966, 1970; Richard Tison (France) as above; Yevgeni Yanes (USSR) as above; Lionel Pioline (France) as above.

Recent winners
Individual (Women)

1970 Renee Ransom (USA)
1972 Alexandra Nicholson (USA)
1974 Alexandra Nicholson (USA)
1976 Svetlana Levina (USSR)
1978 Tatyana Anisimova (USSR)
1980 Ruth Keller (Switzerland)
1982 Ruth Keller (Switzerland)
1984 Sue Shotton (Great Britain)
1986 Tatyana Lushina (USSR)
1988 Khoperia Roussoudan (USSR)
1990 Elena Merkulova (USSR)

Most wins: (5), Judy Wills (USA), 1964–8.

TUG OF WAR

World Championships
Instituted in 1975, held yearly apart from 1979–84; contested at 560 kg from 1982.

Winners

	720 kg	640 kg	560 kg
1975	England	England	—
1976	England	England	—
1977	England	Wales	—
1978	England	England	—
1980	England	England	—
1982	England	Ireland	Switzerland
1984	Ireland	Ireland	England
1985	Switzerland	Switzerland	Switzerland
1986	Ireland	Ireland	England
1988	Republic of Ireland	England	England
1990	Republic of Ireland	Republic of Ireland	Switzerland

Catchweight
1984 England

Most titles: (16), England, as above.

VOLLEYBALL

World Championships

Inaugurated in 1949; first women's championships in 1952; now held every four years, but Olympic champions are also world champions in Olympic years.

Recent winners (Men)

1970 East Germany
1972 Japan
1974 Poland
1976 Poland
1978 USSR
1980 USSR
1982 USSR
1984 USA
1986 USA
1988 USA
1990 Italy
1992 Brazil

Recent winners (Women)

1970 USSR
1972 USSR
1974 Japan
1976 Japan
1978 Cuba
1980 USSR
1982 China
1984 China
1986 China
1988 USSR
1992 Cuba

Most wins: Men (9), USSR, 1949, 1952, 1960, 1962, 1964, 1968, 1978, 1980, 1982. Women (8), USSR, 1952, 1956, 1960, 1968, 1970, 1972, 1980, 1988.

WALKING

Lugano Trophy

The principal Road Walking trophy; contested every two years by men's national teams; first held in 1961.

Recent winners

1970 East Germany
1973 East Germany
1975 USSR
1977 Mexico
1979 Mexico
1981 Italy
1983 USSR
1985 East Germany
1987 USSR
1989 USSR
1991 Italy

Most wins: (5), East Germany, 1965, 1967, 1970, 1973, 1985.

Eschborn Cup

The women's equivalent of the Lugano Trophy; first held in 1979; takes place every two years.

Winners

1979 Great Britain
1981 USSR
1983 China
1985 China
1987 USSR
1989 USSR
1991 USSR

Most wins: (4), USSR, as above.

WATER POLO

World Championship

First held in 1973, and every four years since 1978; included in the World Swimming Championships; first women's event in 1986.

Winners (Men)

1973 Hungary
1975 USSR
1978 Italy
1982 USSR
1986 Yugoslavia
1990 Italy

Winners (Women)

1986 Australia
1990 USSR

Most wins: Men (2), USSR, Italy, as above.

World Cup

Inaugurated in 1979 and held every two years.

Winners

1979 Hungary
1981 USSR
1983 USSR
1985 West Germany
1987 Yugoslavia
1989 Yugoslavia
1991 Yugoslavia

Most wins: (3), Yugoslavia, as above.

WATER SKIING

World Championships
First held in 1949; take place every two years; competitions for Slalom, Tricks, Jumps, and the Overall Individual title.

Recent winners
Overall (Men)

1969 Mike Suyderhoud (USA)
1971 George Athans (Canada)
1973 George Athans (Canada)
1975 Carlos Suarez (Venezuela)
1977 Mike Hazelwood (Great Britain)
1979 Joel McClintock (Canada)
1981 Sammy Duvall (USA)
1983 Sammy Duvall (USA)
1985 Sammy Duvall (USA)
1987 Sammy Duvall (USA)
1989 Patrice Martin (France)
1991 Patrice Martin (France)

Most wins: (4), Sammy Duvall (USA), as above.

Recent winners
Overall (Women)

1969 Liz Allen (USA)
1971 Christy Weir (USA)
1973 Lisa St John (USA)
1975 Liz Allan-Shetter (USA)
1977 Cindy Todd (USA)
1979 Cindy Todd (USA)
1981 Karin Roberge (USA)
1983 Ana-Maria Carrasco (Venezuela)
1985 Karen Neville (Australia)
1987 Deena Brush (USA)
1989 Deena Mapple (née Brush) (USA)
1991 Karen Neville (Australia)

Most wins: (3), Willa McGuire (*née* Worthington) (USA), 1949–50, 1955; Liz Allan-Shetter (USA), 1965 and as above.

WEIGHTLIFTING

World Championships
First held in 1898; 11 weight divisions; the most prestigious is the 110 kg-plus category (formerly known as Super Heavyweight); Olympic champions are automatically world champions in Olympic years.

Recent champions (110 kg)

1979 Sultan Rakhmanov (USSR)
1980 Sultan Rakhmanov (USSR)
1981 Anatoliy Pisarenko (USSR)
1982 Anatoliy Pisarenko (USSR)
1983 Anatoliy Pisarenko (USSR)
1984 Dean Lukin (Australia)
1985 Antonio Krastev (Bulgaria)
1986 Antonio Krastev (Bulgaria)
1987 Aleksander Kurlovich (USSR)
1988 Aleksander Kurlorich (USSR)
1989 Stefan Botev (Bulgaria)
1990 Stefan Botev (Bulgaria)
1991 Aleksander Kurlovich (USSR)
1992 Aleksander Kurlovich (UT)

Most titles (all categories): (8), John Davies (USA), 82.5 kg 1938; 82.5+ kg 1946–50; 90+ kg 1951–2; Tommy Kono (USA), 67.5 kg 1952; 75 kg 1953, 1957–9; 82.5 kg 1954–6; Vasiliy Alexseyev (USSR), 110+ kg 1970–7.

WRESTLING

World Championships
Graeco-Roman world championships first held in 1921; first freestyle championships in 1951; each style contests 10 weight divisions, the heaviest being the 130 kg (formerly over 100 kg) category; Olympic champions become world champions in Olympic years.

Recent winners (Super-heavyweight/over 100 kg)
Freestyle

1979 Salman Khasimikov (USSR)
1980 Soslan Andiyev (USSR)
1981 Salman Khasimikov (USSR)
1982 Salman Khasimikov (USSR)
1983 Salman Khasimikov (USSR)
1984 Bruce Baumgartner (USA)
1985 David Gobedichviliy (USSR)
1986 Bruce Baumgartner (USA)
1987 Khadartsv Aslam (USSR)
1988 David Gobedzhishvilli (USSR)
1989 Ali Reiza Soleimani (Iran)
1990 David Gobedzhisvilli (USSR)
1991 Andreas Schroder (Germany)
1992 Bruce Baumgartner (USA)

Graeco-Roman

1979 Aleksander Tomov (USSR)
1980 Aleksander Kolchinsky (USSR)
1981 Refik Memisevic (Yugoslavia)
1982 Nikolai Denev (Bulgaria)
1983 Jevgeniy Artiochin (USSR)
1984 Jeffrey Blatnick (USA)

Wrestling (cont.)

1985 Igor Rostozotskiy (USSR)
1986 Thomas Johansson (Sweden)
1987 Igor Rostozotskiy (USSR)
1988 Alexsander Karoline (USSR)
1989 Alexsander Karoline (USSR)
1990 Alexsander Karoline (USSR)
1991 Alexsander Karoline (USSR)
1992 Alexsander Karoline (UT)

Most titles (all weight divisions): Freestyle (10), Aleksander Medved (USSR), 90 kg 1962–4, 1966; 100 kg 1967–8, Over 100 kg 1969–72. Greco-Roman (7), Nikolai Balboshin (USSR), 100 kg 1973–4, 1976, 1978–9; Over 100 kg 1971, 1977; Valeriy Rezantsev (USSR), 90 kg 1970–6.

YACHTING

America's Cup

One of sport's famous trophies; first won by the schooner Magic in 1870; now held approximately every four years, when challengers compete in a series of races to find which of them races against the holder; all 25 winners up to 1983 were from the United States.

Post-war winners

Winning Yacht (Skipper)
1958 Columbia (USA) (Briggs Cunningham)
1962 Weatherly (USA) (Emil Mosbacher)
1964 Constellation (USA) (Bob Bavier)
1967 Intrepid (USA) (Emil Mosbacher)
1970 Intrepid (USA) (Bill Ficker)
1974 Courageous (USA) (Ted Hood)
1977 Courageous (USA) (Ted Turner)
1980 Freedom (USA) (Dennis Conner)
1983 Australia II (Australia) (John Bertrand)
1987 Stars & Stripes (USA) (Dennis Conner)
1988 Stars & Stripes (Dennis Conner)[1]
1992 America[3] (USA) (Bill Koch)

[1] Stars and Stripes (USA) skippered by Dennis Conner won a special challenge match but on appeal the race was awarded to the New Zealand boat. However the decision was reversed by the New York Appeals court in 1989.

Most wins: (Skipper) (3), Charlie Barr (USA), 1899, 1901, 1903; Harold Vanderbilt (USA), 1930, 1934, 1937; Dennis Conner, as above.

Admiral's Cup

A two-yearly series of races in the English Channel, around Fastnet rock and at Cowes; four national teams of three boats per team; first held in 1957.

Recent winners

1969 USA
1971 Great Britain
1973 West Germany
1975 Great Britain
1977 Great Britain
1979 Australia
1981 Great Britain
1983 West Germany
1985 West Germany
1987 New Zealand
1989 Great Britain
1991 France

Most wins: (9), Great Britain, 1957, 1959, 1963, 1965, 1971, 1975, 1977, 1981, 1989.

CARD, BOARD AND OTHER INDOOR GAMES

baccarat Casino card game; most popular version **baccarat banque**, in which bank plays against players; in another, **chemin de fer**, all players take turns to hold the bank; object is to assemble, either with two or three cards, a points value of nine: picture cards and the 10 = 0; ace = one; other cards face value; if total is a double figure then the first figure is ignored, eg 18 would count as 8. Of 15th-century derivation, thought to have been introduced into France from Italy during reign of Charles VIII.

backgammon Board game for two players; each has 15 round counters which are moved around the *outer* and *inner tables* on the throw of two dice; aim is to be first to return one's pieces home to inner table and remove them from the board. Equipment similar to backgammon was found in Tutankhamen's tomb; introduced to Britain by the Crusaders; known as backgammon from c.1750.

bézique Card game played with at least two players; each has a pack but with 2s, 3s, 4s, 5s and 6s taken out; object is to win tricks (rounds of play) and score points on the basis of the cards won. Believed to have originated in Spain and brought to England in 1861; first rules drawn up 1861; a variation is **rubicon bézique**.

blackjack Casino card game with object of

CARD, BOARD AND OTHER INDOOR GAMES (cont.)

accumulating score of 21 (with two cards this is a *blackjack*). Ace = one or 11; picture cards = 10; others according to face value. Normally four packs of cards are shuffled together and dealt from a wooden 'shoe' by a banker; bets placed before first card is dealt; all cards dealt face up.

bridge Card game developed from whist, using full set of 52 playing cards, played by two pairs of players; thought to have originated in either Greece or India, introduced into Britain in 1880. Most popular forms: **auction bridge** and **contract bridge**. In the former, trumps are decided by preliminary bid or auction. In contract bridge, the most widely played form, trumps are nominated by the highest bidder. Scoring uses chart designed by US inventor, Harold Stirling Vanderbilt, based on tricks (rounds of play) contracted for and won.

canasta Card game similar to rummy, where cards are picked up and discarded; uses two packs, including four jokers; object is to collect as many of same denomination as possible. All have points value, but jokers and deuces (2s) are 'wild' (can take any value). Originated in Uruguay in the 1940s, the name deriving from the Spanish word *canasta* ('basket'), probably referring to tray where cards were discarded.

chemin de fer or **'chemmy'** Casino card game; variant of **baccarat banque**, played by up to nine players; object is to obtain total near as possible to nine with two or three cards; if total is a double figure then the first figure is ignored: 16 would count as 6. Ace = 1; picture cards = 10; others face value.

chess Game of strategy for two players using chequered board of 64 squares. Each player has 16 pieces: eight pawns, two castles or rooks, two knights, two bishops, queen and king; object is to capture or *checkmate* opponent's king; all pieces have set moves, queen is most versatile. Played in ancient India as *chaturanga*; earliest reference c.600AD; current pieces have existed in standard form for over 500 years.

Cluedo® Board game where board is divided into 'rooms' and the players, who are each dealt a few person, place, and implement cards, are characters who must find out the facts concerning a murder (ie murderer, implement used and scene of the crime), which are on cards seen by no-one and hidden in an envelope at the start. Detective work is done by deduction, arranging meetings in the rooms and asking the other character involved to reveal his or her relevant cards.

contract bridge *see* **bridge**

craps Casino dice game of American origin, adapted from game 'hazard' in 1813. Using two dice, a player loses throwing 2, 3, and 12, but wins with 7 or 11.

cribbage Card game played with two, three or four people with pack of 52 cards and a holed board, the *peg board*, used for scoring. Number of cards dealt to each player is five, six or seven, depending on number of players; cards are discarded into a dummy hand, which each player has in turn; points are scored according to cards dropped (ie for playing a card that makes a pair, a run of three or more, etc); cards are discarded in each round until total of 31 is reached; play continues until the players have discarded all their cards; value of hand then calculated.

dominoes Indoor game, various forms, played by two or more players; dominoes are either wooden or plastic rectangular blocks, with the face of each divided into two halves, each half containing a number of spots, no two identical. In a double-six set of dominoes, every combination between 6–6 and 0–0 is marked on the 27 dominoes. Object of basic game is to lay out sequence or 'line' of dominoes, each player in turn having to put down a domino of the same value as the one at either end of the line.

draughts or **checkers** (US) Game played on chess board by two players, each with 12 small, flat, round counters or *pieces*, which are lined up on alternate squares on the first three rows at either side of the board; object is to remove opponent's pieces from board by jumping over them into a vacant diagonal square, having got in a position to do so by moving only forward (until a piece reaches back row of opponent's 'territory', thus becoming a two-piece *king* and permitted to move backwards and forwards) and always on squares of the same colour; believed to have been played in ancient Egypt; first book about draughts published Spain 1547.

gin rummy *see* **rummy**

go National game of Japan; first played China c.1500BC; tactical game, played on board divided into 361 (18a x 19) squares; each player has supply of rounded counters similar to draughts pieces; players take turns to fill up board with the intention of surrounding opponent's pieces

CARD, BOARD AND OTHER INDOOR GAMES (cont.)

(army) and capturing them; far more complex than chess; handicapping system exists.

hazard Card game for four players in pairs; similar to **solo**, but to make 25 cards, all cards with face value of two to eight are discarded, and joker is added.

mah-jong Chinese game, originally played with cards, introduced to the West under its present name after World War I; usually played by four people using 144 small tiles divided into six suits. (Sets containing 136 tiles and five suits are also used.) Aim is to collect sequences of tiles. Name means 'sparrow', a bird of mythical great intelligence, which appears on one tile.

Monopoly® Board game for two or more players; aim is acquisition of property; players move a counter each around a board which has some of a capital city's streets, stations and public utility companies on it, which can be bought, built upon, mortgaged etc and for which rent must be paid (using Monopoly money) when landed on as a non-owner. Game ends when all but one player are bankrupt.

pinochle Card game derived from **bézique**; uses two packs of 24 cards, all cards from two to eight having been discarded; object is to win tricks, as in whist, and to score points according to cards won: ace = 11; ten = 10; king = 4; queen = 3; jack = 2; nine = 0.

poker Gambling card game for two to eight players; object is to get a better hand than opponents (or convince them that you have one). Hands are ranked: best hand is *Royal Flush* ie 10, Jack, Queen, King, Ace, all of the same suit. Most popular varieties: five-card draw, five-card stud and seven-card stud. Poker started in 19th-century USA.

pontoon or **vingt-et-un** Card game; a variation of **blackjack**, played by any number of players, but ideally six. Object is to try to obtain a total of 21. A *royal pontoon* consists of a picture card and an ace (ace = 11 or 1). Bets are placed and bank held by any player (usually latest *Royal Pontoon* winner).

roulette Casino game played with ball and spinning wheel, which is divided into 37 alternately either red or black segments numbered 0 to 36, but not in numerical order. Bets are placed (before the wheel is spun) on where ball will come to rest, and can take several forms – on a single number, any two numbers, or any three numbers etc, and on whether winning one will be odd or even.

rummy Domestic card game; possibly derived from **mah-jong**; cards picked up and discarded with object of forming two *hands* of three and four cards, or one of seven; hand obtained must consist of cards of same denomination, or sequence in same suit. A variation is **gin rummy**, where hands are laid face upwards and can be added to by any player during the game. Points are obtained for each card dropped according to its face value, and deducted according to cards remaining in hand when one player wins game by disposing of all his or her cards.

Scrabble® Word game on special board for two to four players; points scored by placing letter tiles of different values crossword-fashion to form interlocking words; each player has choice of seven tiles until none remain. Scores can be doubled or trebled by making use of premium squares on the board.

shogi Japanese form of **chess**, believed to have originated in India; played on square board with pieces (of which each player has 20) of different powers; object is to checkmate king.

solo Card game; a form of **whist**, and similar to **bridge**; players must declare how many tricks they will win before each game; tricks won as in whist.

Trivial Pursuit® Board game in which players make progress by giving correct answers to general knowledge questions on eg art and literature, entertainment, geography, history, science, and sport, which are written on special cards. Coloured wedges corresponding to all topics have to be won and the middle space reached to win the game.

whist Non-gambling card game; normally played with four people in pairs; each player receives 13 cards; object is to win more *tricks*, or rounds of play, than the opposing pair; trumps (suit of which cards can win against any card of any other suit) are decided before each game; at *whist drives* trumps are normally played in the following order: hearts, clubs, diamonds, spades; a round of 'no trumps' (where all suits have equal power) is also common.

HOBBIES AND PASTIMES

abseiling Descending a steep slope or mountainside; used in mountaineering but now recognized as pursuit in itself. A rope is attached either around the body or through *karabiners* (steel links with spring clips in one side) and is secured from above so that speed of downwards climb can be safely controlled.

aerobics System of exercises which are designed to increase oxygen consumption and speed blood circulation, thereby increasing fitness.

ballooning *see* **hot-air ballooning**

batik Ancient folk art of fabric design using a basic wax-resist technique; warm wax is painted onto light-coloured fabric, according to a chosen design, and then dipped into a solution of dye and water – only unwaxed fabric takes dye so when wax is removed design appears against coloured background.

bell-ringing or **campanology** Ringing church bells; two popular forms: *change ringing* (hand-pulled method) and *carillon* (uses keyboard connected to the clapper of the bells).

birdwatching or **ornithology** Study and observation of birds in their natural habitat; may involve recording details concerning bird anatomy, behaviour, song and flight patterns.

brass-rubbing Duplicating designs on ornamental brass plate, such as is found in churches; brass is covered with paper and then rubbed over with coloured crayons or chalk until copy is produced.

bungee-jumping Leaping from river-crossing bridges; practised most commonly in USA, Australia and New Zealand; person's legs are tied together, covered with protective material, and then clipped with a strong elastic (bungee) rope (adapted to their weight and height), and secured firmly to the bridge; the jumper 'dives for the horizon' from a platform on top of the bridge and freefalls on average for one second before hanging suspended by the elastic rope, experiencing a series of bouncing movements.

butterfly-collecting or **lepidoptery** Obtaining butterflies either by catching them in their natural environment or purchasing them already preserved; insects are identified and mounted, usually in a glass display unit.

calligraphy Penmanship, or writing at its most formal; a major art form in many countries of E Asia and in Arabic-speaking countries; revival of interest in Europe and America since the 19th century; special pen nibs, brushes, ink and paper usually required.

campanology *see* **bell-ringing**

candle-making Producing candles by repeatedly dipping a prepared wick into wax, pouring wax over a wick or pouring wax into moulds; paraffin wax is most often used; candles can be created in any colour, shape, size or fragrance.

climbing Generally refers to scaling anything from a 15m/50ft wall to an assault on the Himalayas, although there should be some level of difficulty in reaching highest point; as well as the physical aspect, climbing also involves psychological thrills of discovery, exploration and avoidance of danger.

coin-collecting *see* **numismatics**

cookery Preparing and cooking food; may involve production of exotic and speciality dishes and creation of new recipes.

crochet Making a variety of textile items; uses a special hook to loop yarn in a number of different stitches according to pattern requirements.

dancing The following are just a few of the many forms that dancing takes:

1 ballroom Social dance form; developed early 20th century, revealing strong influence of American ragtime, syncopated rhythms producing the foxtrot, quickstep and tango; also popular were animal dances (eg Turkey Trot, Bunny Hug) and Latin-American dances (cha-cha-cha and samba).

2 country Historic social dances began to spread across Europe in the 17th century, taught by travelling dancing masters, adding 19th-century forms such as the waltz, quadrille and polka; emphasis on spatial design, with couples in long or circular sets, using simple walking steps. **Traditional dance** in *England* began 16th century; lines, circles, and square sets are common patterns; steps based on simple walking and skipping. In *Ireland*, early forms share the European history of country and court dance; jigs and reels typical, resembling English and Scottish stepping; competitive high stepping form is a 20th-century creation; arms are held stiffly to the sides; body is erect; there is rapid, complex rhythmic use of the feet; and the knees are sharply lifted. In *Scotland* some country dances are commonly known as **Scottish reels**, but strictly, the reel is an indigenous form of stepping dance performed to bagpipes and showing French aristocratic connections; originally performed in circles as in 'round reels' (threesome, foursome, eightsome etc) and later in lines, 'longwise forms'do; feet are in balletic positions with the weight on the balls of the feet; typical steps include slip step,

HOBBIES AND PASTIMES (cont.)

pas de basque, strathspey, and schottische; men's costume is the kilt; women wear dresses with a tartan sash. Other country dances in Scotland also progress in two long lines of male/female couples, and there are square dances (eg quadrille), and circle dances (eg Circassian circle); dances take place to traditional tunes, formerly played on the fiddle, and now also on the accordion; nowadays reels danced to these instruments too. In *Wales*, due to former religious disapproval, there are few traces of traditional dance, but there are some reels and country dances similar to those in England.

3 disco Popular form of dance mainly for young people, originating 1960s; accompanying music is usually contemporary, often loud, with a rhythmic beat. Definite fashions eg new romantic style, soul, punk, break dancing, robotics, and gothic style. It takes account of Black music, particularly rapping, and heavy rock.

4 jazz N American form of vernacular dancing performed to jazz rhythms; a style that swings, owing its origins to African and Caribbean forms of dance, blended with European influences; also used in musical shows on Broadway and in the UK (eg *Cats*).

5 Morris Ceremonial form of traditional dance found in England. Distinctive features: stamping and hopping; files of performers usually dressed in white and always carrying a stick, handkerchief or garland; some wear bells; accordion or concertina with bass drum accompaniment. Originally exclusively a male domain, women can now take part.

6 step Social and often competitive form of dance relying on rhythmically complex footwork using parts of the foot, heel, and toe beats, often performed in clogs; maintained through folk festivals both as social and exhibition dance; structure in performance is part fixed and part improvised.

dressmaking Pastime usually undertaken to make low-cost clothes, using a bought tissue-paper pattern and a length of material, but also a creative hobby lending itself to sophisticated fashion design.

electronic games Games programmed and controlled by a small microprocessor; most connected to visual display unit and known as **video games**; many have war themes, others simulate sports; some board games (eg Monopoly®, Scrabble®, Trivial Pursuit®) are available in electronic form; all operated either by using a computer keyboard or a joystick plugged into home computer. Larger versions are produced for use in eg amusement arcades.

embroidery Ornamentation of fabric with decorative stitching; dates from very early times, when designs were sewn on to a base fabric by hand; became highly developed eg for rich garments and furnishings, and church vestments in the Middle East, India and Europe; famous example is 11th-century Bayeux tapestry. Hand embroidery still exists as a craft, but today computer-controlled sewing machines are also used.

fell-walking Trekking on hills or moorland, wearing specialized walking boots and using map and compass to find direction in otherwise desolate tracts of land.

gardening Laying out and cultivating plants on a piece of ground for ornamental purposes, rather than for economic gain; type of garden depends not only on gardener's tastes and space available, but also on soil type and fertility, climate, air pollution, and shelter from wind and sun, provided by eg existing trees and rocks. Some special garden types and techniques are:

1 espalier Technique involving the training of trees on a lattice-work of wood flat against a wall; tree is carefully tied to the trellis and pruned to control its shape, often creating a decorative effect in limited space.

2 herb garden Usually includes shrubs as well as herbs, all mostly perennial. The herbs are used primarily for cooking, either fresh or dried (see pp 52–4).

3 Japanese style garden Maximum use is made of evergreen plants, the only colour being eg spring-flowering azaleas, and autumn berries; features include stone lanterns, walkways, natural or simulated streams and waterfalls, and occasional stones; **bonsai** technique is associated with Japanese style, though it originated in China; involves dwarfing plants by shallow planting in containers, starvation, root and soil pruning, and the twisting of new shoots with wire to give plants gnarled, aged appearance; pine, fir and maple trees often used.

4 rock garden or **rockery** Man-made or natural heap of soil and rock fragments in a garden for growing rock plants, usually flowering, hardy perennials, and dwarf trees; rock gardens are often terraced to prevent the topsoil being washed away by rain.

5 water garden Plants arranged in and around

HOBBIES AND PASTIMES (cont.)

natural or artificial pools and streams, eg water lilies and marsh marigolds.

6 wild-flower garden Often includes native marsh or bog plants as well as forest-floor wild flowers; usually requires a rich, acid soil.

go-kart racing Driving and racing small, single-seated, motorized vehicles around outdoor tracks; originated USA; has gained a popular following in the UK.

horse-riding Involves acquirement of specialized skills learned in order to control the horse from a seated position on its back. Commands are signalled by hand, leg and voice instruction, sometimes reinforced by the use of whip and spurs.

hot-air ballooning Being carried as a passenger through the air by hot-air balloon; may involve navigating the balloon, the mechanics of getting the balloon airborne, and following the balloon in road vehicles.

ikebana Formal Japanese style of flower arrangement; a few blooms or leaves are selected and placed in very careful relationship to one another; popular 1950s and 1960s pastime in W Europe.

kite-flying Flying a light frame covered with paper, cloth or plastic at the end of a length of string, usually requiring windy conditions. Kites can be brightly coloured and of various different shapes; simplest form has only one string, but with two strings, one attached to each side, it can be more easily controlled from the ground and made to do complicated loops and dives in the air.

knitting Ancient craft used for making fabric; loops of yarn are linked together using two or three hand-held needles; machines are now used to produce complex knitted garments and fabrics of many kinds, but they cannot create all the intricate designs commonly produced by skilled hand knitters.

lace-making Most popular method (especially in Europe) of lace production is *bobbin* or *pillow* lace. As many as 1 000 bobbins are wound with thread and hung on pins which are inserted, according to the design required, into the small holes on a piece of stiff paper attached to a pillow, cushion or polystyrene base; bobbins then looped, plaited and twisted following pattern instructions until the desired item is produced.

lepidoptery *see* **butterfly-collecting**

macramé Making a type of coarse lace by knotting and plaiting; widespread revival in mid-19th century; used to make decorative fringed borders for costumes as well as furnishings eg window blinds, antimacassars, and cushions.

model-making Mainly the construction of cars, ships, trains and aeroplanes by gluing together preshaped plastic or wooden parts from specialized kits. Some enthusiasts design and produce the parts for their own models.

numismatics Studying and collecting coins, notes and other similar objects, eg medals; dates from Italian Renaissance; 17th-century collectors were first to catalogue their collections.

origami Making models of animals or other objects by folding sheets of paper into shapes, with minimum use of scissors or other implements; often used as an educational aid for young children; originated 10th-century Japan.

paintball Simulation of military combat; involves firing paint pellets which splatter on contact with clothing to indicate a hit; played by two or more teams; popular in the USA, UK and parts of Europe; believed to be beneficial in the reduction of stress.

panelology Carving thin, wooden panels which may be either framed or lodged between other upright and cross pieces normally stretching across the surface of a wall; pictures are often painted onto these panels; most effective results achieved on panels made from chestnut, oak or white poplar.

paragliding Being towed through the air by a plane whilst wearing an adapted parachute and then being separated in order to glide to the ground.

philately Collecting stamps; one of the world's most popular hobbies; often involves documentation in special books or albums; stamps issued and stamped by the post office on their first day of issue (*first-day covers*) increasingly popular; first philatelist said to have been John Tomlinson, who started collecting the day after the issue of the first postage stamp (the *penny black*) in 1840.

pigeon-fancying Breeding pigeons to exhibit or race, popular in the USA, UK and France.

pigeon racing Pigeons are taken from their loft and released at a starting point that may be hundreds of miles away; their homing instinct takes them back to their loft where a special clock times their arrival, thus establishing the fastest pigeon.

pottery or **potting** Forming clay objects; moist clay is shaped and then dried, usually by *firing* in

HOBBIES AND PASTIMES (cont.)

a *kiln* or oven. Shaping by hand may be aided by using a *potter's wheel*, on which a lump of clay is rotated so it can be *thrown* by the potter's hands; moulding may involve either pressing soft clay into a mould and allowing it to dry, or *slip moulding*, where liquid clay or *slip* is poured into a mould that absorbs the moisture; shaped or moulded objects can be decorated by etching and painted with a colour *glaze*. Pottery tends to be porous and so is protected by a second glaze, which may be transparent or opaque and also gives shiny decorative appearance. Glaze is applied after first firing (when the pottery is called *biscuit*); then object is placed in kiln a second time at a lower temperature.

scuba diving Underwater swimming with the aid of *scuba* (self-contained underwater breathing apparatus) or *aqualung*, first developed in 1942 by Jacques Cousteau and Émil Gagnan; equipment consists of air tank(s), face mask, air regulator, depth guage, weight belt and buoyancy compensator; diver propels himself with his legs, wearing large *fins* or *flippers*.

shuffleboard or **shovelboard** Deck game played aboard ship; a larger version of the popular shove-halfpenny; wooden discs, usually c.15cm/6in in diameter, are pushed along deck with long-handled drivers into scoring area.

skateboarding Riding on a single flexible board, longer and wider than the foot, fixed with four small wheels on the underside; speeds of over 100kph/60mph are possible and difficult jumps performed; developed as a way of experiencing surfing thrills on land; became popular in 1960s USA and in UK in 1970s and again in late 1980s.

skin-diving Underwater swimming, popularized in the 1930s. Skin-divers use only goggles, face mask, flippers, and short breathing tube or *snorkel*.

skipping Making jumps over a rope, the ends of which are held in each hand so that it can be twirled over the head and under the feet; often thought of as a child's pastime; recognized as good form of exercise and keep-fit.

skittles Game played in several different forms; object is to knock down nine pins with a ball. **Alley skittles** is played in long alleys and **table skittles** is played indoors on a specially constructed table with a swivelled ball attached to a mast by means of a chain; pins are much smaller than those used in tenpin bowling, and are replaced manually, rather than mechanically.

spinning Converting fibres into yarns, originally using distaff and later the spinning wheel, and now often using methods such as friction and rotor spinning; two types of yarn traditionally produced were *woollen* (fibres are randomly arranged), and *worsted* (fibres lie parallel to the length of the yarn).

stamp-collecting *see* **philately**

tapestry Creation of decorative textiles, originally hand woven, with multi-colour pictorial designs, made by passing coloured threads among fixed warp threads; Oriental in origin, used for wall hangings, furniture and floor coverings.

taxidermy Preparation and practice of creating lifelike replicas of animals and birds from their treated skins and the careful use of celluloids and other plastics.

train-spotting Identifying locomotives by their numbers or names and ticking them off in special, collectable notebooks.

video games *see* **electronic games**

weaving Ancient fabric-producing craft; warp (lengthwise) and weft (crosswise) threads are interlaced on machines called *looms*; hand looms known from very early times; modern industry uses modern weaving looms which have dispensed with shuttles – 'bullets', 'rapiers', water jets and air jets now carry the weft across the warp, with 1 000 picks per minute being possible on some machines.

yoga In Indian religious tradition, any of various physical and contemplative techniques designed to free the superior, conscious element in a person from involvement with the inferior material world. **Hatha yoga** most common form in W Hemisphere; importance of physical exercises and positions and breathing-control is stressed in promoting physical and mental well-being.

THOUGHT AND BELIEF

GREEK GODS OF MYTHOLOGY

Adonis God of vegetation and re-birth
Aeolus God of the winds
Alphito Barley goddess of Argos
Aphrodite Goddess of love and beauty
Apollo God of prophecy, music, youth, archery and healing
Ares God of war
Arethusa Goddess of springs and fountains
Artemis Goddess of fertility
Asclepius God of healing
Athene Goddess of prudence and wise council; protectress of Athens
Atlas A Titan who bears up the earth
Attis God of vegetation
Boreas God of the north wind
Cronus Father of Zeus
Cybele Goddess of the earth
Demeter Goddess of the harvest
Dionysus God of wine and vegetation
Eos Goddess of the dawn
Eros God of love
Gaia Goddess of the earth
Ganymede God of rain
Hades God of the underworld
Hebe Goddess of youth
Hecate Goddess of the moon
Helios God of the sun
Hephaestus God of fire
Hera Goddess of marriage and childbirth; queen of heaven
Hermes Messenger god
Hestia Goddess of the hearth
Hypnos God of sleep
Iris Goddess of the rainbow
Morpheus God of dreams
Nemesis God of destiny
Nereus God of the sea
Nike Goddess of victory
Oceanus God of the river Oceanus
Pan God of male sexuality and of herds
Persephone Goddess of the underworld and of corn
Poseidon God of the sea
Rhea The original mother goddess; wife of Cronus
Selene Goddess of the moon
Thanatos God of death
Zeus Overlord of the Olympian gods and goddesses; god of the sky and all its properties

ROMAN GODS OF MYTHOLOGY

Apollo God of the sun
Bacchus God of wine and ecstasy
Bellona Goddess of wine
Ceres Goddess of corn
Consus God of seed sowing
Cupid God of love
Diana Goddess of fertility and hunting
Egreria Goddess of fountains and childbirth
Epona Goddess of horses
Fauna Goddess of fertility
Faunus God of crops and herds
Feronia Goddess of spring flowers
Fides God of honesty
Flora Goddess of fruitfulness and flowers
Fortuna Goddess of chance and fate
Genius Protective god of individuals, groups and the state
Janus God of entrances, travel, the dawn
Juno Goddess of marriage, childbirth, light
Jupiter God of the sky and its attributes (sun, moon, thunder, rain, etc)
Lares Gods of the house
Liber Pater God of agricultural and human fertility
Libitina Goddess of funeral rites
Maia Goddess of fertility
Mars God of war
Mercury Messenger god; also god of merchants
Minerva Goddess of war, craftsmen, education and the arts
Mithras The sun god; god of regeneration
Neptune God of the sea
Ops Goddess of the harvest
Orcus God of death

ROMAN GODS OF MYTHOLOGY (cont.)

Pales Goddess of flocks
Penates Gods of food and drink
Picus God of woods
Pluto God of the underworld
Pomona Goddess of fruit trees
Portunus God of husbands
Prosperina Goddess of the underworld
Rumina Goddess of nursing mothers
Saturn God of fertility and agriculture
Silvanus God of trees and forests
Venus Goddess of spring, gardens and love
Vertumnus God of fertility
Vesta Goddess of the hearth
Victoria Goddess of victory
Vulcan God of fire

NORSE GODS OF MYTHOLOGY

Aegir God of the sea
Aesir Race of warlike gods, including Odin, Thor, Tyr
Alcis Twin gods of the sky
Balder Son of Odin and favourite of the gods
Bor Father of Odin
Bragi God of poetry
Fafnir Dragon god
Fjorgynn Mother of Thor
Freyja Goddess of libido
Frey God of fertility
Frigg Goddess of fertility; wife of Odin
Gefion Goddess who received virgins after death
Heimdall Guardian of the bridge Bifrost
Hel Goddess of death; Queen of Niflheim, the land of mists
Hermod Son of Odin
Hoenir Companion to Odin and Loki
Hoder Blind god who killed Baldur
Idunn Guardian goddess of the golden apples of youth; wife of Bragi
Kvasir God of wise utterances
Logi Fire god
Loki God of mischief
Mimir God of wisdom
Nanna Goddess wife of Balder
Nehallenia Goddess of plenty
Nerthus Goddess of earth
Njord God of ships and the sea
Norns Goddesses of destiny
Odin (Woden, Wotan) Chief of the Aesir family of gods, the 'father' god; the god of battle, death, inspiration
Otr Otter god
Ran Goddess of the sea
Sif Goddess wife of Thor
Sigyn Goddess wife of Loki
Thor (Donar) God of thunder and sky; good crops
Tyr God of battle
Ull Stepson of Thor, an enchanter
Valkyries Female helpers of the gods of war
Vanir Race of benevolent gods, including Njörd, Frey, Freyja
Vidar Slayer of the wolf, Fenvir
Weland (Volundr, Weiland, Wayland) Craftsman god

EGYPTIAN GODS

Amun-Re Universal god
Anubis God of funerals
Apis God of fertility
Aten Unique god
Geb God of the earth
Hathor Goddess of love
Horus God of light
Isis Goddess of magic
Khnum Goddess of creation
Khonsou Son of Amun-Re
Maat Goddess of sterility
Nephthys Goddess of funerals
Nut God of the sky
Osiris God of vegetation
Ptah God of creation
Sekmet Goddess of might
Set God of evil
Thoth Supreme scribe

FIGURES OF MYTH AND LEGEND

Bold type indicates that a figure of mythology is described elsewhere in the list.

Achilles Greek hero; son of **Peleus** and the goddess **Thetis**; his body invulnerable to injury, except his ankle, due to being held by the ankles when he was dipped in the River Styx (in another version **Cheiron** replaced his ankle bone with one taken from the fast-running giant Damysos); killed with an arrow in the heel by **Paris** or **Apollo**.

Actaeon Greek hero; a hunter who came upon **Artemis**, the goddess of chastity, while she was bathing and therefore naked; she threw water at him, changing him into a stag, so that he was pursued and then killed by his own hounds.

Adad Mesopotamian god of storms; known throughout the area of Babylonian influence; the Syrians called him Hadad, and in the Bible he is Rimmon, the god of thunder; helped to cause the Great Flood in Gilgamesh; his symbol was the lightning held in his hand and his animal the bull.

Adapa Akkadian hero; one of the seven Apkallu, beings of great brilliance and genius, and envoy of the god Ea (*see* **Enki**), the divine creator of Man, who lost the opportunity of immortality due to disagreements between Ea and **Anu**, the god of heaven.

Aditi Indian goddess; mother of the gods and all beings, and the guardian of childbirth; outwith the divine world, she represented *everything* at the same time, being the total, the beginning, the end and the opposites; adopted by Buddhist tradition.

Adonis God of Phoenician origin; son of Myrrha, the daughter of the king of Syria who had been turned into a tree; spent one third of the year with **Persephone**, goddess of hell, and two thirds with **Aphrodite** after a decision by **Zeus**; mortally wounded by a wild boar in a battle.

Aegir Norse god of the sea; a giant, who collected dead sailors in his hall on the island of Hlesey; here also he sometimes gave banquets to the gods.

Aegisthus Greek hero; son of **Thyestes**; while **Agamemnon** was absent at Troy he became the lover of **Clytemnestra**; together they killed Agamemnon on his return to Argo; later killed by **Orestes**.

Aeneas Greek hero; son of **Aphrodite**, and bravest of the Trojans after **Hector** whose command he replaced in the fight against the Greeks; sailed to coast of Italy and is said to have given Rome its divine origin; subject of the *Aeneid* by Virgil.

Aeolus Greek god of the winds; in the *Odyssey*, Aeolus lived on an island, and gave **Odysseus** the winds tied in a bag so that his ship would not be blown off course; the ship had nearly reached Ithaca when Odysseus's men opened the bag, thinking it contained treasure; as a result, the ship was blown far away.

Aesculapius *see* **Asclepius**

Agamemnon Greek king of Argos; commander of the Greek army in the Trojan War; Homer calls him 'king of men'; on his return he was murdered by his wife **Clytemnestra**.

Agni Indian god of fire; immortal god, regarded as the guide and protector of men; had two faces, one calm, one terrible, and gave both life and death.

Ahura Mazda Indo-Iranian god; had the form of the sun and nine wives; creator of other living beings and formed the world by his thought; his powers made plants grow and allowed fire to give its heat, water to quench thirst, animals to reproduce and armies to be victorious.

Ajax Two Greek heroes of the Trojan War; one was the son of Telamon, king of Salamis, therefore known as Telamonian Ajax and was proverbial for his size and strength; in all the worst situations he 'stood like a tower'; when the armour of the dead **Achilles** was not given to him, he went mad and killed himself. The second was the son of Oileus, king of Locris; returning from Troy, he provoked the anger of the gods, and was killed by **Poseidon** as he reached the shore of Greece.

Alastor Greek **demon**; the name was used by Shelley as the title of a poem outlining a myth of his own making, in which a young poet is led through various symbolic states and ultimately to destruction.

Alcestis Greek heroine; she saved her husband, Admetus, who was doomed to die, by offering to die in his place; the action so impressed **Heracles** that he wrestled with the messenger of death and brought her back to life.

Alcmaeon Greek hero; to avenge the death of his father, Amphiaros, he killed his mother, and was pursued by the **Erinnyes** until he came to a land which had not seen the sun at the time of his mother's death; he found this recently emerged land at the mouth of the R Achelous; **Apollo** commanded him to lead the expedition of the **Epigoni** against Thebes.

Alcyone *see* **Halcyone**

FIGURES OF MYTH AND LEGEND (cont.)

Alexander *see* **Paris**

Amaterasu Japanese goddess of the sun and light; considered to be the divine origin of the imperial dynasty; shut herself in a cave after a conflict with her brother Susa-no-o, plunging the world into darkness; returned light to the world when the gods managed to tempt her out.

Amazons Warrior-women of Greek myth; people of the Amazon state, where men were only tolerated for work of a servile nature; removed one breast so that they would not be restricted in the practice of archery and spear-throwing; said to be descendants of the god of war, **Ares**, and the **Nymph**, Harmony; crushed the Atlantians, occupied Gorgon and the greater part of Libya, fought with **Priam** during the Trojan war and invaded Attica; their leader, Hippolyta, married **Theseus**.

Amen *see* **Amun-Re**

Amitabha The divine buddha; one of five 'meditation buddhas' sent by Adi buddha, the original buddha; wished to gather together all those who would pray to him with faith, to enjoy perfect happiness until they entered nirvana.

Amma Dogon god; origin of all creation; with the earth gave birth to twins who were sacrificed to make the earth fertile, then brought back to life in the form of a human couple; created the sun and divided the world into two domains; his myth led to the practice of male circumcision.

Ammon *see* **Amun-Re**

Amon *see* **Amun-Re**

Amphitrite Greek goddess of the sea; married to **Poseidon**; the mother of **Triton** and other minor deities.

Amphitryon In Greek mythology, the husband of **Alcmene**; in his absence, **Zeus** took his shape and so became the father of **Heracles**.

Amun-Re (Amen, Ammon, Amon) Egyptian god; Amun was the local god of Thebes, considered as the god of air or fertility, who had the form of a man, but sometimes also the head of a ram; was likened to the sun-god Re, thus becoming Amun-Re; the pharaohs developed his cult.

Anahita Persian goddess of dawn and fertility; became a spirit of prosperity, collaborating in the work of creation, fighting for justice and initiating men into religious rites.

Anchises In Roman mythology, the Trojan father of **Aeneas**; the *Aeneid* gives an account of Aeneas's piety in carrying Anchises on his shoulders out of the blazing city of Troy.

Androcles Roman slave; escaped from his master, met a lion, and extracted a thorn from its paw; when recaptured, he was made to confront a lion in the arena, and found it was the same animal, so that his life was spared.

Andromache In Greek mythology, the wife of **Hector**, the hero of Troy; after the fall of the city she became the slave of **Neoptolemus**.

Andromeda In Greek mythology, the daughter of Cepheus, king of the Ethiopians; to appease **Poseidon**, she was fastened to a rock by the seashore as an offering to a sea-monster; rescued by **Perseus**, who used the **Gorgon's** head to change the monster to stone; the persons named in the story were all turned into constellations.

Angels Messengers of God; nine choirs were divided into three ranks: the seraphim, cherubin and thrones; the dominions, powers and virtues; and the principalities, archangels and angels. The first class was to praise and worship God, and the last was to assist the course of the stars, nations and people; angels or lesser gods would pass on messages, give orders or bring help to men.

Angra Mainyu Persian **demon**; creator of darkness and of evil things; belonged to death, filth and rottenness, inspiring disgust.

Anna Perenna Roman goddess; represented as an old woman, and worshipped in a sacred wood situated north of Rome; named Perenna, meaning eternity, when she became a **Nymph**; approached by Mars (see **Ares**) when she was old and asked to be an intermediary between himself and Minerva (see **Athena**); realizing this was impossible, she substituted herself for the chaste goddess and made fun of Mars.

Antigone Greek heroine; the guardian of the family; defied the dictator **Creon** to follow the wishes of the gods to fulfil the rite of burial for warriors considered as traitors, and for this was buried alive by Creon in the family tomb, where she hanged herself.

Anu Sumerian god of heaven; earthly royalty was descended from him, and as the god of Uruk, he gave back the city to Rim-Sin of the Larsa dynasty, who later conquered the neighbouring cities by Anu's strength.

Anubis Egyptian god; guide of souls to the world beyond; often represented with a human body and the head of a jackal or dog.

Aphrodite (Venus) Greek goddess of love, who reigned over the hearts and senses of men; a proud and cruel goddess who punished all those who would not succumb to her; as a bribe, offered

FIGURES OF MYTH AND LEGEND (cont.)

Paris the most beautiful mortal, **Helen**, causing the Trojan war; her worship was assimilated by the Romans with that of Venus, a goddess of ancient Italy.

Apis Egyptian god of strength and fecundity; represented as a bull for whom divine honours were reserved; Menes, the first Egyptian pharaoh, was said to have started the cult of Apis about 3 000BC.

Apollo Greek and Roman god; son of **Zeus**; young and handsome, seer, poet and musician, he was said to be the most powerful of the gods; often identified with the sun, his nature also had a terrifying side and even his friends were afraid of him; said to have been responsible for the death of **Achilles**.

Arachne In Greek mythology, a weaver from Lydia; challenged **Athena** to a contest; when Arachne's work was seen to be superior, Athena destroyed the web and Arachne hanged herself; Athena saved her, but changed her into a spider.

Ares (Mars) Greek god of war; a supreme fighter who cared little for the interests he defended, and delighted in bloody massacres; fought with **Athena**, the sons of **Poseidon** and **Heracles**; identified with the Roman god Mars (*see* **Ares**), said to be the father of **Romulus**, the founder of Rome.

Arethusa Greek **Nymph**; pursued by the river-god Alpheus from Arcadia in Greece to Ortygia in Sicily; the myth attempts to account for the freshwater fountain which appears in the harbour of Syracuse and is believed to have flowed under the Ionian Sea.

Argonauts Greek heroes; sailed in the *Argo* to find the Golden Fleece; under **Jason**'s leadership they sailed through the Symplegades (presumably the Dardanelles) and along the Black Sea coast to Colchis; their return is variously described, and may have included a river-passage to the North Sea.

Argus Greek watchman with a hundred eyes, appointed by **Hera** to watch over **Io**; after Argus was killed by **Hermes**, the eyes were placed in the tail of the peacock; also the name of **Odysseus**'s dog.

Ariadne In Greek mythology, the daughter of King **Minos** of Crete; enabled **Theseus** to escape from the labyrinth by giving him a ball of thread; he fled with her, but deserted her on the island of Naxos; there she eventually became the wife of **Dionysus**.

Aristaeus Greek god of the countryside; a minor deity who introduced bee-keeping, vines, and olives; pursued **Eurydice**, the wife of **Orpheus**, who trod on a snake and died; in revenge her sister **dryads** killed his bees; **Proteus** told him to sacrifice cattle to appease the dryads, and in nine days he found bees generated in the carcasses.

Arjuna Indian hero; in the *Bhagavadgita*, a poem in the *Mahabharata*, he hesitates before entering the battle, knowing the killing which will ensue; his charioteer, Krishna, urges him to fulfil the action which is his duty as a warrior, explaining that the whole universe needs the fulfilment of actions which advance God's will.

Artemis (Diana) Greek goddess; daughter of **Zeus** and sister of **Apollo**; defender of virginity and modesty, and warrior who turned against anyone who attempted to force her against her will; also the protectress of women in labour and newborn children; identified with the Roman goddess Diana, a huntress.

Arthur Celtic medieval hero; brought up by Merlin and crowned king of Britain, King Arthur; armed with his magical sword Excalibur, he rid his country of monsters and giants, drove out the invaders, conquered the continent to reach Rome and in some stories as far as Palestine, from where he brought back the Cross of Christ.

Asclepius (Aesculapius) Greek and Roman god of the earth; son of **Apollo**, he acquired the magic powers to cure and revitalize from **Cheiron** the **Centaur**; used his powers to serve mortals, curing the sick and bringing the dead back to life; became a god when killed by **Zeus**, who was enraged that Asclepius had upset the natural order by restoring **Hippolytus** to life.

Astarte *see* **Ishtar**

Atalanta Greek heroine; nurtured by a she-bear and grew up to be a strong huntress; refused to marry any man who would not take part in a foot-race with her; those who lost were killed; eventually Hippomenes (or Milanion) threw three golden apples of the **Hesperides** at her feet, so that her attention was diverted and she lost.

Aten Egyptian god; showed himself to mankind in the form of the solar disc, gave life, was the creator of all things, and all things depended on him; had no connection with the other, numerous gods.

Athena (Minerva) Greek goddess of restraint and forethought; daughter of **Zeus**, virgin and war-

FIGURES OF MYTH AND LEGEND (cont.)

rior, whose protégés were **Odysseus**, **Heracles** and **Achilles**; fought with the Achaeans in the Trojan war, and enemy of **Ares**; in competition with **Poseidon**, won the possession of Attica, beginning the era of civilization for the city of Athens; identified with the Roman god Minerva.

Atlas Greek **Titan**; made to hold up the heavens with his hands, as a punishment for taking part in the revolt against the Olympians; when books of maps came to be published, he was often portrayed as a frontispiece, hence the term atlas.

Atreus Greek king of Argos; quarrelled with his brother **Thyestes**, and placed the flesh of Thyestes' children before him at a banquet; the father of **Agamemnon** and **Menelaus**.

Atropos *see* **Moerae**

Attis (Atys) Greek god of vegetation; connected with the Asiatic cult of **Cybele**; died after castrating himself, and was resurrected; the story was later associated with the spring festival.

Atys *see* **Attis**

Aurora *see* **Eos**

Autolycus In Greek mythology, the maternal grandfather of **Odysseus**, who surpassed all men in thieving; he was said to be a son of **Hermes**.

Baal Phoenician god of fertility and fecundity; known as king of the gods, and with his sister Anat was responsible for the universal prosperity of people and animals; his victory over the god of the sea gave sailors the courage to set their boats on water.

Bacchus *see* **Dionysus**

Balder Norse god of sovereignty and power; son of **Odin** and **Frigg**; unlike the other power gods, he was kind and pleasant; a jealous god **Loki** conspired to kill him, and on death he went to the home of Hel, the terrible; the goddess of hell agreed to free him on condition that every creature would weep for him; all did, except an old woman (Loki in disguise), so that Balder would have to remain in hell until the battle (*Ragnarok*) which will bring about the end of the world.

Basilisk (Cockatrice) Greek monster; a small dragon-like creature combining features of the snake and the cockerel; its eye could freeze and kill, hence the expression: 'If looks could kill'; equivalent to the Cockatrice, which was hatched by a serpent from the egg of a cock.

Bellerophon Greek hero; sent to Lycia with a letter telling the king to put him to death; the king set him impossible adventures, notably the killing of the **Chimera**; in later accounts it is said that **Athena** helped him to tame **Pegasus**.

Berserker Norse warrior; fought in a 'bear-shirt' in such a frenzy that he was impervious to wounds; the name is the origin of the phrase 'to go beserk'.

Bes Egyptian god; depicted as a bandy-legged dwarf who was horrific in appearance, but congenial in temperament; the protector in child-birth, and guardian of the family.

Bladud Legendary king of Britain; discovered the hot spring at Bath and founded the city; one story is that he was a leper who found that the mud cured him.

Brahma Indian god; the creator; divided himself into two to make a couple bringing **Sarasvati**, feminine energy, into existence; he then developed four heads so that he could always see Sarasvati as she constantly circled him; he was also given four arms to show his power; organized the world, and laid down the rules of *karma*, the standard of reward for one's actions.

Bran Celtic hero; known as Bendigeid Vran, the son of Llyr; invaded Ireland to help his sister, and died there; his seven followers cut off his head and buried it on the site of the Tower of London, from where it protects the whole island of Britain. In another legend, he was an Irish voyager who set out to find the Other World with 27 companions; on their return, as they approached the shore, people asked who they were, and said that the only Bran they knew was the hero of the ancient tale of *The Voyages of Bran*, so Bran wandered away forever.

Brighid *see* **Brigit**

Brigit (Brighid) Irish goddess of fire and the hearth; also of poetry and handicrafts; in the Christian era a number of her attributes were taken over by St Brigid.

Brunhild (Brunhilde, Brynhild) Norse **Valkyrie** who has assumed human form; **Odin** places her behind a wall of flame where she lies in an enchanted sleep; she is woken by **Sigurd**, who is able to leap the barrier on his horse Grani; tricked into marrying Gunnar, she finally kills herself on Sigurd's funeral pyre; in the similar Nibelungen legend, she is the wife of Gunther.

Brunhilde *see* **Brunhild**

Brynhild *see* **Brunhild**

Buddha Founder of Buddhism; in legend, Siddharta Gautama was born around 560BC into a noble family, and spent his childhood in a palace of

FIGURES OF MYTH AND LEGEND (cont.)

luxury, protected from the sorrow and suffering outside; one day he discovered this and decided to save humanity from its evils; became the Buddha when he discovered the four 'great truths', attaining awakening and enlightenment; taught this to his disciples, and died at the age of 24 after a long meditation.

Bunyip In Australian aboriginal mythology, the source of evil; not to be thought of as a spirit or as a human; the **Rainbow Snake**, the mother of life, confined Bunyip to a waterhole; it haunts dark and gloomy places.

Cadmus Greek hero; son of Agenor, king of Tyre; set off in pursuit of his sister **Europa**, arrived in Greece, and founded the city of Thebes, teaching the natives to write; sowed dragon's teeth, from which armed men sprang up.

Calchas Greek seer; advised that **Iphigeneia** should be sacrificed at Aulis; at Troy he told **Agamemnon** to return Chryseis, the daughter of the priest of **Apollo**, to stop the plague; died in a combat of 'seeing'.

Calliope Greek **Muse** of epic poetry; sometimes said to be the mother of **Orpheus**.

Callisto Arcadian **Nymph**; attendant upon **Artemis**; loved by **Zeus**, she became pregnant, and was sent away from the virgin band; **Hera** changed her into a she-bear and after 15 years had passed, her son tried to spear her; taking pity on them, Zeus changed her into the constellation Ursa Major.

Cassandra Greek heroine; daughter of **Priam**, king of Troy; favoured by **Apollo**, who gave her the gift of prophecy; because she did not return his love, he decreed that while she would always tell the truth, she would never be believed; at the fall of Troy she was allotted to **Agamemnon**, and murdered on her arrival in Argos.

Castor and **Pollux** Greek heroes; twin sons of **Leda**; Pollux the son of **Zeus** and Castor the son of Tyndareus, king of Sparta, but both born at the same time; Castor was a good fighter and Pollux a skilled boxer, and the twins were inseparable; during their search for the Golden Fleece with the **Argonauts**, they saved the ship, the *Argos*, from a storm; when Castor was killed in a fight, Zeus agreed to the Pollux's pleas for Castor to share his immortality so that he would not be separated from his brother.

Cecrops (Kekrops) Greek ancestor and first king of the Athenians; born from the earth, and formed with snakelike appendages instead of legs; during his reign, **Athena** and **Poseidon** fought for the possession of Athens; buried in the Erechtheum.

Cecrops *see* **Kekrops**

Centaurs Mythical Greek monsters; half man, half horse, aggressive and unintelligent with reputations for raping and kidnapping, with two exceptions: **Cheiron**, tutor of **Apollo**, **Jason** and **Achilles**, and Pholus, friend of **Heracles**, who were kindly Centaurs.

Cerberus Greek dog; guards the entrance to the underworld; originally fifty-headed, later with three heads; any living souls visiting hell gave 'a sop to Cerberus', ie a honey-cake, to quieten him; **Heracles** carried him off as one of his labours.

Ceres *see* **Demeter**

Cernunnos Celtic god of plenty; represented with the ears and antlers of a stag, often accompanied by a serpent with the head of a ram; master of wild, earthly and aquatic animals.

Chac Mayan rain-god; characterized by two wide eyes, a long turned-up nose and two curved fangs; in the East he was red, in the North, white, in the West, black and in the South, yellow; made thunder and rain and was regarded as beneficent and friend of man.

Charon Greek ferryman of the underworld; carried the shades or souls of the dead across the R Styx; sometimes other rivers are substituted in literature, such as Acheron and Lethe; the Greeks placed a small coin in the mouth of a corpse as Charon's fee.

Chimaera *see* **Chimera**

Chimera (Chimaera) Greek monster; had the head of a lion, the body of a goat (the name means 'she-goat'), and the tail of a serpent, which breathed fire.

Cheiron Greek **Centaur**; son of **Cronus** and Philyra the **Oceanid**, who kept a school for princes in Thessaly; educated Asclepius in the art of medicine and music, **Jason** the **Argonaut**, **Odysseus** and **Achilles**; wounded by one of **Heracles**'s poisoned arrows, he gladly gave up his immortality to be rid of pain.

Circe Greek enchantress; in the *Odyssey*, detained **Odysseus** and his followers on the island of Aeaea; her house was full of wild beasts; transformed Odysseus's men into swine with a magic drink, but he was able to defeat her charms through the protection of the herb moly.

Clio Greek **Muse** of history and lyre-playing.

Clotho *see* **Moerae**

Clytemestra *see* **Clytemnestra**

FIGURES OF MYTH AND LEGEND (cont.)

Clytemnestra (Clytemestra) In Greek mythology, the twin sister of **Helen** and the wife of **Agamemnon**; murdered her husband on his return from Troy, assisted by her lover, **Aegisthus**; killed in revenge by her son, **Orestes**.

Cockatrice *see* **Basilisk**

Consentes Dii (Di) Twelve Roman gods; their statues, grouped in male/female pairs, stood in the Forum; probably Jupiter/Juno, Neptune/Minerva, Mars/Venus, Apollo/Diana, Volcanus/Vesta and Mercury/Ceres (*see* **Zeus/Hera, Poseidon/Athena, Ares/Aphrodite, Apollo/Artemis, Hephaestus/Vesta** and **Hermes/Demeter**).

Creon (Kreon) Greek kings; the name (meaning 'ruler') is applied especially to the brother of **Jocasta**, regent of Thebes, who awarded the throne to **Oedipus**; later, after the siege of the city by the seven Champions, he commanded that **Polynices** should not be buried, and condemned **Antigone** for disobedience.

Cressida In medieval accounts of the Trojan War, the daughter of Calchas, a Trojan priest; beloved by **Troilus**, a Trojan prince, she deserted him for **Diomedes** when transferred to the Greek camp.

Cronus (Kronos) Greek ruler of the universe (the second ruler); a **Titan**, the youngest son of **Uranus**, who rebelled against his father; during his rule people lived in the Golden Age; probably a pre-Greek deity, he is incorrectly, but popularly, confused with Chronos 'Time', because he too devoured his children.

Cú Chulainn Irish hero and supreme warrior; halted the progress of enemies united against his country; finally killed by Lugaid, the son of one of his victims.

Cupid *see* **Eros**

Cybele Phrygian goddess of the earth; made through the mutilation of a hermaphrodite monster by the gods, she lived in forests and mountains.

Cyclopes Greek mythological monsters; one-eyed giants who worked as smiths and were associated with volcanic activity; the Cyclops **Polyphemus** was outwitted and blinded by **Odysseus**.

Daedalus Athenian inventor; worked for King **Minos** in Crete and constructed the labyrinth; later he escaped to Sicily with wings he had made for himself and **Icarus**; there he made the golden honeycomb kept at Mt Eryx; any archaic work of skill was ascribed to him, and he was a patron saint of craftsmen in Ancient Greece.

Danaans (Danaoi) Collectively, the Greeks who joined together in the expedition to Troy.

Danae Greek heroine; daughter of King Acrisius of Argos; when an oracle prophesied that her son would kill his grandfather, Acrisius imprisoned her in a bronze tower, where **Zeus** visited her in the form of a golden shower; gave birth to a son, **Perseus**, who accidentally killed Acrisius with a discus.

Danaoi *see* **Danaans**

Danu Celtic mother-goddess; associated with hills and the earth.

Daphne Greek heroine; daughter of a river-god, Ladon (or, in another story, Peneios); pursued by the god **Apollo**, she was saved by being turned into a laurel, which became Apollo's sacred tree.

Daphnis Sicilian shepherd; half-brother of **Pan**, who was loved by a **Nymph**; he did not return her love, so she blinded him; became the inventor of pastoral poetry; in another story he would love nobody; when he died, all the beings of the island mourned him.

Deirdre In Irish legends, a girl destined to cause evil; grew up to be the most beautiful girl in Ireland; although intended for King Conchobhar, she was abducted by Naoise, a young king, and lived with him for seven years; when Naoise was killed by treachery, she was forced to marry Conchobhar, and killed herself.

Demeter (Ceres) Greek goddess of corn; presided over the interplay between life and death, and provided food; forced a compromise after **Hades** imprisoned her daughter **Persephone** in the underworld allowing her to return to the world above between spring and autumn; identified with the Roman goddess Ceres.

Demons Evil celestial beings who force men to do evil and also do harm to men themselves, taking on the appearance of foreign gods, led by Satan; invisible and innumerable, they originally preferred to live in isolated and unclean places like deserts and ruins, and were greatly feared, especially at night; exorcisms are religious rites to remove demonic influences when a demon is thought to inhabit the body of a man, stripping him of his willpower and moral awareness.

Deucalion Greek hero; son of **Prometheus**; when **Zeus** flooded the world, Deucalion and his wife Pyrrha built an 'ark' which grounded on the top of Parnassus; as the only survivors, they asked how the human race was to be restored; an oracle told them 'to throw the bones of their mother over their shoulders'; they correctly interpreted this oracle, and threw stones (the bones

FIGURES OF MYTH AND LEGEND (cont.)

of their mother Earth) which turned into human beings.

Diana *see* **Artemis**

Dido Greek heroine; in the *Aeneid*, the daughter of the king of Tyre, who founded Carthage; **Aeneas** was diverted to Africa by storms, and told her his story; they fell in love, but when Aeneas deserted her she committed suicide by throwing herself upon a pyre.

Diomede *see* **Diomedes**

Diomedes (Diomede) Greek hero; fought in the Trojan War, even taking on the gods in battle; also a wise counsellor, the partner of **Odysseus** in various schemes; in the medieval version of the story, he became the lover of **Cressida**.

Dionysus (Bacchus) Greek god of wine and the vine; lord of exuberance and drunkenness, he upset everything that got in his way, did not respect laws or customs and wandered about in caves; said to have made his followers coarse and vulgar, taught them to drink wine and caused madness.

Dragons Legendary animals presented in Chinese art, Greek and Indian mythology and medieval Christian legends; had the claws of a lion, the wings of an eagle, a powerful serpent's tail and breathed fire; sometimes represented as the guardian of treasure, eg guarding the Golden Fleece, as an incarnation of Satan, as a primordial principle and as the symbol of power of the emperor of China.

Dryad Greek mythological **Nymph**; originally connected with oak-trees, but more usually referring to a wood-nymph, living in or among the trees; were usually friendly, but could frighten travellers.

Durga Indian goddess; wife of **Shiva** and his feminine part, and both the creator and destroyer of the world; a force for leading astray as well as for salvation, and a warrior who enjoyed battle and bloodshed.

Ea *see* **Enki**

Echidna Greek monster; half-woman and half-snake, and the mother of various other monsters, eg **Hydra**.

Echo Greek **Nymph**; in one legend, beloved by **Pan**, and torn to pieces, only her voice surviving; in another story, punished by **Hera** so that she could only repeat the last words of another speaker; loved **Narcissus**, who rejected her, so that she wasted away to a voice.

Electra Heroine of Greek tragedies (but not in Homer); daughter of **Agamemnon** and **Clytemnestra**, who assisted her brother **Orestes** when he came to Argos to avenge his father, and who later married his friend Pylades; her personality is developed in different ways by the playwrights.

Endymion Greek shepherd of Mt Latmos; loved by the moon-goddess **Selene**; **Zeus** put him to sleep, while Selene looked after his flocks, and visited him every night; one of the mythological figures who was said to have founded the Olympic Games, as king of Elis.

Enki (Ea) Sumerian god who organized life on earth and developed the world; invented man and made a mould from him so that he could be reproduced, and created plants and livestock.

Enlil Sumerian god and keeper of sovereign power who maintained the order of the world; originally ruled over proletarian gods who became exhausted by their work and rebelled; it was agreed that man should be created to take over a part of the labours necessary for the maintenance of the world; later the prosperity and din of mankind, whose number was steadily increasing, irritated Enlil, who sent epidemics, suffering, death and worldwide flood.

Eos (Aurora) Greek goddess of the dawn; daughter of **Helios**, mother of **Memnon**; abducted various mortals; when she took the mortal Tithonus, **Zeus** granted her request that he should be made immortal, but she forgot to ask for perpetual youth, so he grew older and older, finally shrinking to no more than a voice or, possibly, the cicada insect.

Epigoni Greek heroes; collectively, the 'next generation'; after the failure of the **Seven against Thebes**, their sons made another expedition and succeeded; this was shortly before the Trojan War.

Epona Gallic goddess and guardian of horses; patron of civil and military horsemen, travellers and those on their way to the Great Beyond; sometimes seen as a goddess of fertility and also identified with **Rhiannon**.

Erato Greek **Muse** of lyric poetry and hymns.

Erechtheus Greek king of Athens; born from the earth and nurtured by **Athena**; sacrificed his daughter Chthonia to secure victory over the Eleusinians, but was killed by **Poseidon**; the Erechtheum, a temple on the Acropolis, is probably on the site of his palace.

Erinnyes (Furies) Greek goddesses; inhabitants of hell who were responsible for punishing bloody crimes; named Alecto, Tisiphone and Megara,

FIGURES OF MYTH AND LEGEND (cont.)

they were represented as winged spirits who had long hair entwined with snakes, and carried whips and torches; tortured their victims and drove them mad.

Eris Greek heroine; daughter of Night and the sister of **Ares**; a late story tells how she was present at the wedding of **Peleus** and **Thetis** and threw a golden apple 'for the fairest'; this brought **Hera**, **Athene**, and **Aphrodite** into contention, and was the first cause of the Trojan War; the name means 'strife' in Greek.

Eros (Cupid) Greek god, responsible for keeping the world together and for the continuation of the species; his power to inspire sexual desires could make people lose their reason and paralyse their willpower; became Cupid for the Romans.

Eteocles Greek hero; elder of **Oedipus**'s two sons, whom he cursed; became king of Thebes after his father's death, and refused to share power with his brother **Polynices**; the **Seven against Thebes** attacked the city, and Eteocles was killed by Polynices.

Eumenides A euphemistic name given to the **Erinnyes** after being domesticated at Athens in Aeschylus' play of the same name; the name means 'the kindly ones'.

Europa (Europe) Greek heroine; daughter of Agenor, king of Tyre, who was abducted by **Zeus** in the shape of a bull, and swam with her on his back to Crete; her children were **Minos** and **Rhadamanthus**.

Europe *see* **Europa**

Eurydice Greek **Dryad**; wife of **Orpheus**; after her death, Orpheus went down to the underworld and persuaded **Hades** to let her go by the power of his music; the condition was that she should follow him, and that he should not look at her until they reached the light; not hearing her footsteps, he looked back, and she disappeared back into the underworld.

Euterpe Greek **Muse**; usually associated with flute-playing.

Fates *see* **Moerae**

Faunus Roman god of agriculture; responsible for the fertility of plants and the energy of living nature; reproduced himself in fauns, **satyrs** who were half man, half goat.

Finn mac Cumhal Irish hero; warrior and magician who avenged his father who was killed in battle and reorganized his elite troops, whose qualities were intelligence, cunning, faithfulness, a hatred of money and respect for women; possessed the gift of receiving visions when he bit his thumb.

Flora Roman goddess of flowers and flowering plants; appears with the spring; given a temple in 238BC; her games were celebrated on 28 April.

Fortuna Roman goddess of fortune; introduced by King Servius Tullius (578–534BC); in the Middle Ages was highly revered as a divine and moral figure, redressing human pride; her wheel is frequently referred to and depicted, as at St Etienne in Beauvais, where figures can be seen climbing and falling off.

Freyja Norse goddess of love, fertility, fecundity, victory and peace, and sister of **Freyr**; took on the form of a falcon to travel between one world and the other.

Freyr (Frey) Norse god of fertility and fecundity and brother of **Freyja**; presided over love, wealth and orgies, brought sun and rain to make crops grow; mainly worshipped by women.

Freyr *see* **Frey**

Frigg (Frigga) Norse goddess of married love; wife of **Odin** (often confused with **Freyja**).

Frigga *see* **Frigg**

Furies *see* **Erinnyes**

Gaea (Gaia, Ge, Tellus) Greek goddess; 'the earth' personified, and later the goddess of the whole earth (not a particular piece of land); came into being after Chaos, and was the wife of **Uranus**, producing numerous children; the Romans identified her with Tellus.

Galahad, Sir One of King **Arthur's** knights; son of **Lancelot** and Elaine; distinguished for his purity, he alone was able to succeed in the adventures of the Siege Perilous and the Holy Grail.

Galatea Greek **Nymph**; a sea-nymph, wooed by **Polyphemus** the **Cyclops** with uncouth love-songs; in some versions Polyphemus destroys his rival Acis with a rock; in other versions he happily marrries Galatea; probably a Sicilian story.

Ganesha Indian god; master of intelligence and the patron of artists and writers who was given by **Brahma** the task of copying the *Mahabharata*; represented with the head of an elephant; a popular god, he put obstacles in the way of those who neglected him, and spared others.

Ganymede In Greek mythology, the son of Tros, a Trojan prince; **Zeus** sent a storm-wind, or (later and more usually) an eagle, who carried Ganymede up to Olympus, where he became the cupbearer; in return his father was given a stud of exceptional horses.

FIGURES OF MYTH AND LEGEND (cont.)

Gawain (Gawayne) One of King **Arthur**'s knights; son of King Lot of Orkney, whose character varies in different accounts; in the medieval *Sir Gawayn and the Grene Knight*, he is a noble hero undergoing a test of faith; in other stories he is a jeering attacker of reputations, especially that of **Lancelot**.

Gawayne *see* **Gawain**

Genii Spirits of mythology throughout the world; their forces were less beneficent than those of **angels**, but less wicked than those of **demons**; regarded as the doubles of objects, beings and events.

Giants Large, strong and often stupid beings from mythology throughout the world; in the Bible, the product of an unnatural union between fallen angels and the daughters of men; taught men the rudiments of the knowledge they had from being able to see from high up; for the Greeks, sons of the earth representing youth, strength and virility, who could only be killed by a god and a man together.

Gigantes Greek giants; sons of earth and Tartaros, with snake-like legs; made war on the Olympian gods, were defeated, and are buried under various volcanic islands; the Gigantomachy ('war of the giants') was the subject of large-scale sculpture, as at Pergamum; a sub-group, the Aloadi, piled Mt Pelion upon Mt Ossa.

Gilgamesh Sumerian hero; tyrannical king of Uruk and intrepid adventurer; began an adventure to search for immortality, but failed, and returned to Uruk to accept his fate and resume his former life.

Gorboduc Legendary king of Britain; first heard about in Geoffrey of Monmouth's *History*; when he grew senile, his two sons Ferrex and Porrex quarrelled over the inheritance; he was the subject of an early Elizabethan tragedy in the Senecan style, written by Norton and Sackville (1561).

Gorgons Three mythical Greek monsters; represented with hair made of angry serpents, tusks like a boar's, hands of bronze and golden wings; anyone who looked at them was turned to stone; Euryale represented sexual excess, Stheno, social perversion, and **Medusa**, vanity; Medusa's head was cut off by **Perseus**, and the children of **Poseidon** emerged from the wound.

Graces In Greek mythology, three daughters of **Zeus** and **Hera**; embodied beauty and social accomplishments; sometimes called Aglaia, Euphrosyne, and Thalia.

Graiae In Greek mythology, three sisters with the characteristics of extreme old age; had one eye and one tooth between them; **Perseus** took the eye and made them tell the route to the **Gorgons**, who were their sisters.

Griffin (Gryphon) Greek monster; originated in tales of the Arimaspians, who hunted the creature for its gold; had a lion's body, and an eagle's head, wings, and claws; collected fragments of gold to build its nest, and, instead of an egg, laid an agate.

Gryphon *see* **Griffin**

Guan Di (Kuan Ti) Chinese god of war; based on a historical person who died in the 3rd-c AD; made a god in 1594, and greatly revered.

Gudrun Norse heroine; wife of **Sigurd** the Volsung; after his death she married Atli (the legendary Attila) who put her brothers to death; in revenge she served up his sons in a dish, and then destroyed him by fire; in the similar German story she is known as Kriemhild.

Guinevere King **Arthur's** queen; originally Guanhamara in Geoffrey of Monmouth's *History*, and there are other spellings; in later romances, much is made of her affair with Sir **Lancelot** (an example of courtly love); in Malory's epic poem she survives Arthur's death and enters a nunnery.

Hadad Assyrian god of storms; invoked in curses when begged to send torrential rain to the lands of enemies, but also brought agricultural fertility.

Hades (Pluto) Greek god of hell; brother of **Zeus** and **Poseidon**; invisible god who ruled the dead, assisted by **demons**; forbade his subjects to leave his domain and became enraged when anyone tried to steal his prey; the most hated of the gods among mortals; identified by the Romans as Pluto.

Halcyone (Alcyone) In Greek mythology, daughter of **Aeolus**, who married Ceyx, son of the morning star; either for impiety, or because she mourned his death at sea, both were changed into seabirds (halcyons, or kingfishers, who are fabled to calm the sea); sometimes described instead as one of the Pleiades.

Hamadryads Greek **Nymphs**; tree-nymphs who were offended or died when the trees containing them were harmed.

Hanuman Indian god, son of the god of the winds, Vayu; as soon as he was born, rushed towards the sun believing it to be a ripe fruit, crashing into all the planets on the way; as protector, he destroyed the death rays emitted by the planets

FIGURES OF MYTH AND LEGEND (cont.)

and was known as the god of athletes and gymnasts.

Harpies Greek genii/spirits; represented as three women with wings or birds with the heads of women; seized children and souls and tortured their victims.

Harpocrates *see* **Horus**

Hathor Egyptian goddess; portrayed as a woman bearing the sun between two cow's horns representing the intoxication of pleasure, love and fertility; identified by the Greeks with **Aphrodite**.

Hebe Greek goddess of youth and youthful beauty; daughter of **Zeus** and **Hera**; became cup-bearer to the Olympians, and was married to **Heracles** after he was deified.

Hecabe *see* **Hecuba**

Hecate Greek goddess of witchcraft, spooks, and magic; not in Homer, she appears in Hesiod, and seems to represent the powerful mother-goddess of Asia Minor; worshipped with offerings at places where three roads cross, and so given three bodies in sculpture.

Hector Hero of Greek mythology; the bravest Trojan, who led out their army to battle; the son of **Priam**, and married to **Andromache**; **Achilles** killed him and dragged his body behind his chariot; Priam ransomed it at the end of the *Iliad*.

Hecuba (Hecabe) Greek heroine; wife of **Priam**, king of Troy, and mother of 18 children, including **Hector** and **Cassandra**; after the Greeks took Troy, she saw her sons and her husband killed, and was sent into slavery.

Heimdallr Norse god; born of nine mothers, he could see everything and never closed his eyes; the guardian of the gods' abode; at the moment of the end of the world, it was said that he would blow his trumpet to call all the gods to hold a council.

Hel (Hela) In Norse mythology, the youngest child of **Loki**; half her body was living human flesh, the other half decayed; assigned by **Odin** to rule Helheim (the underworld) and to receive the spirits of the dead who do not die in battle.

Hela *see* **Hel**

Helen Greek heroine; daughter of **Zeus** and **Leda**, sister to **Clytemnestra**, **Castor** and **Pollux**; the most beautiful of women who captivated all men, and as a result was the cause of the Trojan War when she was abducted by **Paris**; granted immortality by Zeus and **Apollo**.

Helios Greek god of the sun; represented as a charioteer with four horses; in early times Helios was not worshipped, except at Rhodes; in the late classical period, there was an Imperial cult of the sun, Sol Invictus.

Hellen In ancient Greek genealogies, the eldest son of **Deucalion**; father of Doros, Xuthos, and Aiolos, who were the progenitors of the Dorian, Ionian, and Aeolic branches of the Greek race; the Greeks (or Hellenes) were named after him.

Hephaestus (Volcanus, Vulcan) Greek god of fire; son of **Zeus** and **Hera**; lame (either because his mother dropped him from Olympus when she realized how ugly he was, or because Zeus threw him down onto the island when he took his mother's side in a marital dispute); volcanoes were his workshops and the **Cyclopes** his assistants in his work as a blacksmith and jeweller; identified by the Romans as Vulcan.

Hera (Juno) Greek goddess; married her brother **Zeus**; conceived some of her sons without any male assistance by hitting the ground with her hand or eating a lettuce; pursued with a vengeance Zeus's mistresses and their children, putting enormous snakes into **Heracles**'s cradle forcing Zeus to hide his illegitimate children by transforming them into animals or enclosing them in the earth; identified by the Romans as Juno; her name means 'lady'.

Heracles (Hercules) Greek hero; demonstrated amazing strength from birth, choking the serpents sent to him by the jealous **Hera**; many achievements are attributed to him including the 12 labours of Eurystheus; he delivered Troy from a monster but came back to wreak havoc on the city because it did not pay his salary; succeeded in injuring **Hades** and **Hera** with his arrows and won immortality; identified by the Romans as Hercules.

Hercules *see* **Heracles**

Hermaphroditus Greek god; a minor god with bisexual characteristics, the son of **Hermes** and **Aphrodite**; the **Nymph** Salmacis, unloved by him, prayed to be united with him; this was granted by combining them in one body.

Hermes (Mercury) Greek god of the spoken word and son of **Zeus**; intermediary who went from men to Olympus and Olympus to **Hades**; as the god of commerce, the only person to achieve immortality as a result of a contract; identified by the Romans as Mercury.

Hero and **Leander** Greek lovers; lived on opposite sides of the Hellespont; Hero was the priestess

FIGURES OF MYTH AND LEGEND (cont.)

of **Aphrodite** at Sestos, and Leander, who lived at Abydos, swam across each night guided by her light; when this was extinguished in a storm, he was drowned, and Hero committed suicide by throwing herself into the sea.

Hesperides In Greek mythology, the daughters of the evening star (Hesper); guarded the Golden Apples together with the dragon, Ladon; sang as they circled the tree, which was given by **Gaia** to **Hera** as a wedding-present; when **Heracles** had to fetch the apples, he either killed the dragon, or sent it to sleep, or, more usually, persuaded **Atlas** to get them for him while he took over Atlas' function of holding up the sky.

Hestia (Vesta) Greek goddess of hearth and home; sister of **Zeus** and **Hera**; never intervened in the stormy history of the gods and became the central point, the meeting place; identified by the Romans as Vesta.

Hiawatha Indian hero; appeared in *The Song of Hiawatha*, which retells Indian legends in the manner and metre of the Finnish *Kalevala*; Hiawatha is educated by his grandmother Nokomis, and marries Minnehaha.

Hippolytus Greek hero; son of **Theseus** and Hippolyta, leader of the Amazons; Theseus' new wife, **Phaedra**, made advances to Hippolytus, which were refused, so she falsely accused Hippolytus of rape; Theseus invoked a curse, **Poseidon** sent a frightening sea-monster, and Hippolytus was thrown from his chariot and killed.

Horae In Greek mythology, 'the seasons'; implied the right or fitting time for something to happen; given various names either connected with fertility or peace.

Horatti and **Curiatii** Early Roman legend used to justify appeals; under Tullus Hostilius there was war between Rome and Alba; two groups of three brothers were selected from Rome (the Horatii) and Alba (the Curiatii) to fight, the winners to decide the battle; all were killed except one, Horatius; when his sister, who was betrothed to a Curiatius, abused him, he murdered her, but was acquitted after appealing to the Roman people.

Horus (Harpocrates) Egyptian god; husband of **Hathor**, brother of **Seth** and ancestor of the dynasties of the pharaohs; had a falcon's head and ruled the air, his eyes being the sun and the moon; became universal king of the earth after defeating Seth, who had seized power after murdering Horus's father.

Huang-ti Chinese cultural hero; legendary emperor, patron of alchemists, doctors and seers, and one of the fathers of Taoism; born miraculously after his mother was made pregnant by lightning from the Great Bear; invented chariots, ships and houses, and understood that every activity in the world had to be preceded by putting the individual body in order; discovered the way of the Tao in a dream and searched for ways of attaining immortality.

Huitzilopochtli Aztec god of war and protector of the city; symbolized in the midday sun and represented with hummingbird feathers on his head and left leg, a black face and brandishing a serpent of turquoise or fire; massacred all his brothers and sisters immediately after he was born, as they planned to kill his mother; as a soothsayer he communed with the priests at night and as a cruel god, tore out the hearts of those who disobeyed him.

Hydra Greek monster; many-headed child of **Typhon** and **Echnida**, which lived in a swamp at Lerna; since the heads grew again when struck off, **Heracles** could kill it only with the assistance of Iolaos, who cauterized the places where the heads grew; the name means 'water-snake'.

Hygeia Greek goddess; the daughter of **Asclepius**; a minor deity, her name was a personification of the word for 'health'.

Hymen Greek god of marriage; in Ancient Greece and Rome, the cry of 'O Hymen Hymenaie' at weddings (later a marriage song) led to the invention of a being called Hymen of Hymenaeus, who was assumed to have been happily married, and therefore suitable for invocation as a god of marriage; depicted as a youth with a torch.

Hyperboreans Greek unvisited people of fabled virtue and prosperity; lived in the land 'beyond the North Wind'; in Herodotus they worshipped **Apollo** and sent offerings to Delos; could refer to a lost Greek colony in what is now Romania, or even to the Swedes at the end of the trans-European amber route.

Hyperion Greek **Titan**; son of **Uranus** and **Gaia**, and father of **Eos** (the Dawn), **Helios** (the sun), and **Selene** (the moon); later, as in Shakespeare and Keats, identified with the sun.

Iapetus Greek **Titan**; father of **Prometheus** and **Atlas**; grandfather of **Deucalion**; the close resemblance to Japhet may indicate borrowing from near Eastern sources.

Icarus In Greek mythology, the son of **Daedalus**; his father made him wings to escape from Crete,

FIGURES OF MYTH AND LEGEND (cont.)

but he flew too near the sun; the wax holding the wings melted and he fell into the Aegean at a point now known as the Icarian Sea.

Idomeneus Leader of the Cretans; a descendant of **Minos** who assisted the Greeks at Troy; caught in a storm at sea, he vowed to sacrifice the first thing he met on his safe return; this was his own son; after carrying out the sacrifice he was driven into exile.

Inanna Sumerian goddess of love and war; stole the *me* (meaning everything that makes up civilization) from **Enki** to give to her city, Uruk; attempted to seize power of the underworld from her sister but failed; in rage at her husbands lack of sympathy for her resulting predicament, she ordered the **demons** to torture him and imprison him in hell.

Indra Indian god; an athlete and exemplary warrior who gave life and light, created the ox and the horse, gave the cow milk and made all women fertile; crushed the evil **demon** Vrtra, allowing the dawn and the sunrise to be created.

Io Greek heroine; beloved by **Zeus**, who turned her into a heifer to save her from **Hera's** jealousy; Hera kept her under the gaze of the **Argus**; but she escaped with **Hermes**'s help; was then punished with a gad-fly which drove her through the world until she arrived in Egypt; there Zeus changed her back into human shape, and she gave birth to Epaphos, ancestor of many peoples.

Iphigeneia Greek priestess; daughter of **Agamemnon** and **Clytemnestra**; was about to be sacrificed at Aulis as the fleet could not sail to Troy, because the winds were against it, but at the last moment was saved by **Artemis**, who made her a priestess in the country of the Tauri (the Crimea); finally her brother **Orestes** saved her.

Irene In Greek mythology, a personification of 'peace'; one of the **Horae**.

Iris Greek goddess of the rainbow; became the messenger of the gods, especially of **Zeus** in Homer, and of **Hera** in later writers; depicted sitting under Hera's throne.

Ishtar (Astarte) Mesopotamian goddess; as the star of the morning, personified war, and as the star of the evening, personified love; came to the aid of the sexually impotent and was cruel and determined as a hostile warrior; established the fame of Assyria and was responsible for the cruelty of its kings.

Isis Egyptian goddess; mother of **Horus**; wore a solar disc and the horns of a cow, and was known as the protectress of love and mistress of destiny; obtained her powers by trickery and as a magician, cured her son who had been bitten by a snake.

Isolde *see* **Tristan** and **Isolde**

Itzamma Mayan god of heaven; the creator and civilizer of mankind, with the appearance of an old toothless man with sunken cheeks and a prominent nose, he gave places their names and distributed land between the different tribes; sometimes depicted as an enormous serpent which represented the sky.

Iuppiter *see* **Zeus**

Ixion Greek king of Thessaly; the first murderer; also the father of the **Centaurs**; for attempting to rape **Hera** he was bound to a wheel of fire, usually located in the underworld.

Izanagi no Mikoto and **Izanami no Mikoto** Japanese male and female gods; in the creation myth these were the first beings who created islands in the water and the other gods; Izanami died when she gave birth to fire; Izanagi followed her to the land of the dead (Yomi), but she turned against him and pursued him; finally he had to block the exit from Yomi with a large rock and Izanami then became the goddess of the underworld.

Janus Roman god of beginnings; a two-faced god who personified clearsightedness; protected **Saturn** when he was being hunted by Jupiter (see **Zeus**); invented money, the cultivation of soil and legislation.

Jason Greek hero; son of the king of Iolcus, who was deposed by his half-brother, Pelias; Jason claimed the power from Pelias, who challenged him to demonstrate his worthiness of the crown by bringing back the Golden Fleece, guarded by an ever-wakeful dragon, hoping that Jason would never return from such an impossible mission; a ship, the *Argo*, was built for the mission, and Jason overcame many obstacles to return with the Golden Fleece; the king did not keep his promise, and weary of war, Jason stole the fleece and left.

Jimmu Tenno First emperor of Japan in the Shinto religion; said to be descended from Amaterasu, and to have reigned between 660 and 585BC, dying at he age of 127; probably a real person, subsequently deified.

Jocasta In Greek legend, the wife of King Laius of Thebes and mother of **Oedipus**; later unwittingly became the wife of her son; she is called Epikaste

FIGURES OF MYTH AND LEGEND (cont.)

in Homer; bore Oedipus four children: **Eteocles**, **Polynices**, **Antigone**, and Ismene; killed herself when she discovered her incest.

Julunggul *see* **Rainbow Snake**

Juno *see* **Hera**

Jupiter *see* **Zeus**

Kama Indian god of love; represented with a bow and arrow; as soon as he was born, looked around him and asked who he was going to set on fire; always ready to initiate love in men or in the gods.

Kami Japanese spirits; manifestations of natural forces and superior to men; there were 80 million kami, to personify anything big or inexplicable at a time when animals, rivers, lakes and seas were objects of veneration; the drink saké was the offering preferred by the kami.

Kane *see* **Tane**

Kreon *see* **Creon**

Krishna Indian god; a lovable child and merciless warrior; endowed with exceptional strength and intelligence, he killed the monster Baku who had taken the form of a crane, and fought with Kaliya, the king of serpents; his life with 16 000 wives and 180 000 children was interspersed with numerous battles against **demons**; has become the only god in many Hindu sects.

Kronos *see* **Cronus**

Kuan Ti *see* **Guan Di**

Kumarbi Hurrian god; deposed from the divine throne by the storm-god, **Teshub**; became the father of an enormous stone man in the hope that this son could overthrow the storm-god, but this was prevented by the other gods.

Lachesis *see* **Moerae**

Laius Greek king of Thebes; father of **Oedipus**; he married **Jocasta**, and was warned by an oracle that their son would destroy him; this happened when Oedipus, assumed to be dead, returned from Corinth and accidentally killed Laius during a quarrel on the road.

Lakhsmi Indian goddess of happiness, beauty and prosperity; the wife of **Vishnu**, she was the incarnation of the great god's power.

Lancelot, Sir (Launcelot du Lac) The most famous of King **Arthur**'s knights, though he is a relatively late addition to the legend; the son of King Ban of Benwick, the courtly lover of Guinevere, and the father of **Galahad** by Elaine; in spite of his near-perfection as a knight, he was unable to achieve the Grail adventure; he arrived too late to help Arthur in the last battle.

Laocoon Trojan prince; a priest of **Apollo**, who objected to the plan to bring the Wooden Horse into Troy; two serpents came out of the sea and killed him, together with his two sons.

Lapiths In Greek mythology, a people of Thessaly; Perithous, king of the Lapiths, invited the **Centaurs** to his wedding with Hippodameia; a terrible fight took place between the two groups, in which the Centaurs were defeated.

Lares Roman gods; protectors of inhabited places; depicted as two boys accompanied by a dog; divided into two groups: *lares compitales* were found in the country, at crossroads and in meeting places; *lares familiares* were guardians of the family home.

Latinus Roman ancestor and eponymous king of the Latins; descended from **Circe** (according to Hesiod) or from **Faunus** (according to Virgil); in the *Aeneid*, Latinus gives his daughter Lavinia to **Aeneas**.

Latona *see* **Leto**

Launcelot du Lac *see* **Lancelot, Sir**

Leander *see* **Hero** and **Leander**

Lear Legendary king of Britain; son of **Bladud**, who reigned for 60 years; in his old age two of his daughters, Goneril and Regan, conspired against him, but the third daughter, Cordelia, saved him and became queen after his death (the story is changed by Shakespeare, so that she died before his eyes); Leicester is named after him.

Leda In Greek mythology, the wife of Tyndareus, king of Sparta, and mother, either by him or **Zeus**, of **Castor** and **Pollux**, **Helen**, and **Clytemnestra**; a frequent subject in art is Zeus courting Leda in the form of a swan; Helen was believed to have been hatched from an egg, preserved at Sparta into historic times.

Lemminkäinen Finnish hero; in the *Kalevala*, has to undertake impossible tasks, such as shooting the swan of Tuonela; this causes his death, and his mother has to reanimate him; his ride through a land of horrors inspired Sibelius.

Lemures Roman ghosts; wandered about outside the house on 9, 11, and 13 May (the Lemuria).

Leto (Latona) Greek **Titan**; mother by **Zeus** of the twins **Apollo** and **Artemis**; they were born at Delos, because in her jealousy **Hera** would allow no land to harbour Leto; luckily, at that time Delos was a floating island.

Leviathan Phoenician monster; personification of evil, believed to have come out of the primal chaos; sparks of fire shot from his mouth and

FIGURES OF MYTH AND LEGEND (cont.)

smoke poured from his nostrils; always present, hidden in each individual.

Lif and **Lifthrasir** In Norse mythology, the mother and father of the new race of human beings after Ragnarok (the last battle); the names presumably mean 'life' and 'strong life'.

Lilith In Jewish legend, the first wife of Adam; or, more generally, a **demon** woman.

Lohengrin In Germanic legend, the son of Parsifal (*see* **Percival, Sir**); left the temple of the Grail and was carried to Antwerp in a boat drawn by swans; there he saved Princess Elsa of Brabant, and intended to marry her; however, she asked forbidden questions about his origin, and he was forced to leave her, the swan-boat taking him back to the Grail temple.

Loki Norse god; represented deceit, disorder, malevolence and perversity; fathered horrible monsters and put obstacles in the way of happiness; as a magician, had the power to transform himself into different animals and insulted and offended the other gods.

Lotophagi *see* **Lotus-eaters**

Lotus-eaters (Lotophagi) People encountered by **Odysseus**; lived on 'a flowery food' which makes those who eat it forget their own country, and wish to live always in a dreamy state; Odysseus had to force his men to move on.

Lucrece *see* **Lucretia**

Lucretia (Lucrece) Roman wife of Collatinus; raped by Sextus, son of **Tarquinius Superbus**; after telling her story, she committed suicide; the incident led to the expulsion of the Tarquins from Rome.

Lud Legendary king of Britain; first walled the principal city, from that time called Kaerlud after him, and eventually London; buried near Ludgate, which preserves his name.

Lug Irish god; skilled in many arts and fulfilled the office of all gods; proclaimed by the king to be the wisest of the wise and given the task of organizing the battle which conquered the Fomoiri, evil beings who occupied Ireland and oppressed its inhabitants.

Lycurgus Greek king of Thrace; opposed **Dionysus** and was blinded; his name is shared by the founder of the Spartan constitution, with its military caste-system (the date when this originated has been much disputed, and is now thought to be c.600BC, much too late for the legendary Lycurgus to have participated).

Maat Egyptian goddess; represented the social and cosmic order and the guardian of ethics and rites; there at the beginning of the universe, she maintained order in heaven as on earth, and was responsible for the seasons, night and day, the movement of the stars and rainfall.

Maenads Greek 'mad women'; followed Dionysus (Bacchus) on his journeys; dressed in animal-skins, and so strong that they could uproot trees and kill wild animals, eating the flesh raw; also known as Bacchae or Bacchantes.

Manes In Roman religion, 'the dead'; the concept developed from the spirits of the dead in general, to the gods of the underworld, Di Manes, the ancestors of the family, and the spirits of individuals in grave-stone inscriptions.

Marduk Babylonian god; represented life, civilization and progress; created the winds and raised the tempest, distressing the first-born gods who declared war on him but were defeated; Marduk created heaven, earth and man; when the god of death succeeded by a ruse in making him rise from his seat, the sun stopped shining, the roads became infested with brigands, and man ate man until Marduk took his place again.

Mars *see* **Ares**

Marsyas Greek Satyr; challenged **Apollo** to a flute-contest; defeated and flayed alive by the god, his blood or tears formed a river of the same name.

Medea Greek witch; daughter of Aeetes, the king of Colchis, who assisted **Jason** in obtaining the Golden Fleece; on their return to Iolcos, she renewed the youth of Aeson, and tricked the daughters of Pelias into performing a similar ritual, so that they destroyed their own father; when deserted by Jason at Corinth, she fled in her aerial chariot after killing her children.

Medusa Greek **Gorgon**; depicted with staring eyes and snakes for hair.

Meleager Greek hero; at his birth the **Moerae** appeared and prophesied that he would die when the brand then on the fire had burnt away; his mother, Althaea, removed it and kept it; when the quarrel over the Calydonian boar took place and her brothers were killed, she threw the brand onto the fire, so that he died.

Melias *see* **Nymphs**

Melpomene Greek **Muse** of tragedy.

Memnon In Greek mythology, a prince from Ethiopia; son of **Eos**; killed at Troy by **Achilles**; the Greeks thought that one of the gigantic statues at Thebes represented him; it gave out a musical sound at sunrise.

FIGURES OF MYTH AND LEGEND (cont.)

Menelaus King of Sparta; younger brother of **Agamemnon**, who married **Helen**; took part in the Trojan War and was delayed in Egypt on his return; finally settled down at Sparta with Helen again.

Mercury *see* **Hermes**

Merlin Good wizard or sage whose magic was used to help King **Arthur**; son of an incubus and a mortal woman, and therefore indestructible, but was finally entrapped by Vivien, the Lady of the Lake, and bound under a rock for ever; famous for his prophecies.

Mermaid Legendary sea-creature; had the body of a woman and the tail of a fish, a fiction possibly based on early encounters with seals or sea-cows; in stories their singing attracts mortal men to love them; their male counterparts were Mermen.

Midas King of Phrygia; as a reward for helping the Satyr, Silenus, **Dionysus** gave Midas a wish, and he asked that anything he touched should turn to gold; however, this caused so many difficulties (eg in eating and drinking) that he asked to be released; he was told to bathe in the River Pactolus, which thereafter had golden sands.

Minerva *see* **Athena**

Minos Greek hero; son of **Zeus**, who took the form of a bull in order to impregnate Europe; claimed power as king of Crete and took part in military expeditions to avenge the murder of his son and to force Athens to provide men and women to feed to the **Minotaur**, the monster born from a bull given to Minos by **Poseidon**; became a judge in hell after being drowned in his bath.

Minotaur Greek monster; son of **Pasiphae** and a bull from the sea, half bull and half human; the name means **Minos**'s bull; kept in a labyrinth made by **Daedalus**, and killed by **Theseus** with the help of **Ariadne**.

Mithra Indo-European god; represented friendship, benevolence, non-hostility and compromise; depicted as a 'killer of the bull', plunging a sword into a dying bull's body, from which all herbs and beneficial plants were born; closely associated with the sun.

Mnemosyne Greek **Titan**; daughter of earth and heaven, and mother of all the **Muses**; her name means 'Memory'.

Modimo African god; originally from Zimbabwe, and considered to be the creator; when appearing in the east, he distributed good things and belonged to the element water; appearing in the west, he was a destroyer, responsible for drought, cyclones and earthquakes, and represented the element fire; his name was taboo and spoken only by priests or seers, and he could only be reached by imperfect beings.

Moerae (Parcae) Three Greek goddesses; named Atropos, Clotho and Lachesis, daughters of **Zeus**; the first spun a thread which signified birth, the second unravelled the thread, symbolizing the unravelling of life, and the third cut the thread, signifying death; they were the personification of inflexible law, representing destiny and the limits which could not be overstepped; in Rome assimilated to the Parcae, who were originally birth **demons**.

Moloch Biblical god of the Canaanites and other peoples; in his cult children were sacrificed by fire; a rebel angel in Milton's *Paradise Lost*; his name is used for any excessive and cruel religion.

Monsters Wild, unmanageable forces which appear as enemies in all mythologies; in general, a mixture of living creatures (eg horse and man for **Centaurs** and fish and woman for **Sirens**); signified irrational forces, the death necessary for new life and the anarchical energy which preceded and produced creation and order.

Morgan le Fay Legendary enchantress; 'Morgan the Fairy', King **Arthur**'s sister, and generally hostile towards him; one of the three queens who received him at his death.

Morpheus Roman god of sleep; one of the sons of Somnus ('sleep') who sent or impersonated images of people in the dreamer's mind; later, as in Spenser, the god of sleep.

Muses Nine Greek goddesses; daughters of **Zeus**, each with the vocation to promote an area of the arts: epic poetry, mime, history, the flute, dance, lyric art, tragedy, comedy, astronomy; they favoured communication, delighted the gods and inspired poets.

Myrmidons Greek band of warriors from Thessaly; went to the Trojan War with **Achilles**.

Naiad Greek **Nymphs**; inhabited springs, rivers, and lakes.

Narcissus Greek hero; the symbol of self-love, he was told by a seer that he would live to a ripe old age as long as he never looked at himself; caring for no one but himself, he drove his friends and those who fell in love with him to despair; the goddess **Nemesis** decided to avenge his victims by leading him to a spring in which he saw his own reflection, which he immediately fell in love with, and moving towards it, he fell into the

FIGURES OF MYTH AND LEGEND (cont.)

spring and drowned; from his body was born the flower which bears his name.

Nausicaa Greek heroine; in Homer's *Odyssey*, the daughter of King Alcinous; when **Odysseus** landed in Phaeacia, alone and naked, she was doing the laundry by the sea-shore; she took him home to her father's palace.

Nemesis Greek goddess of moderation; ruled over the distribution of wealth, taking revenge on arrogance and punishing excess; said to have prevented the Persians from seizing the city of Athens.

Neoptolemus Greek warrior; son of **Achilles**, his original name being Pyrrhus; went with **Odysseus** to persuade **Philoctetes** to come to Troy; at the end of the war he killed **Priam** and enslaved **Andromache**; for this, **Apollo** prevented him from reaching his home, and he was killed in a dispute at Delphi.

Nephthys Egyptian goddess; wife of **Seth**; cared for and protected the dead; took sides with her husband's enemies and when he was vanquished, killed and torn to pieces, helped to find the fragments of his body and put them back together, bringing him to life; Nephthys and her sister were the guardians of the tomb.

Neptune *see* **Poseidon**

Nereid Greek **Nymphs**; 50 or (in some accounts) 100 daughters of **Nereus**; lived with their father in the depths of the sea.

Nereus Greek god of the sea; the wise old man of the sea who always told the truth; **Heracles** had to wrestle with him to find the location of the Golden Apples.

Nergal Babylonian god of death; son of the god of heaven, he loved catastrophes, epidemics and war, and made death his personal territory; later acquired the power of the ruler of the underworld; tricked **Marduk** into rising up from his seat, resulting in chaos throughout the world, until Marduk regained his position.

Nessus Greek **Centaur**; attacked **Heracles**'s wife, Deinir; Heracles shot him, and the dying Centaur told Deinira that his blood would be a cure for infidelity; later, through jealousy, she put the blood on a shirt, or made Heracles wear Nessus' shirt; this coated him with poison, so that he died.

Nestor A Greek leader in the Trojan War; in the *Iliad*, Homer portrays him as a long-winded sage, whose advice is often not taken; in the *Odyssey*, he is still living at Pylos, where a Mycenaean palace was discovered in the 1930s.

Nibelungen Medieval German race of dwarfs; lived in Norway and possessed a famous treasure; the *Nibelungenlied* recounts how Siegfried obtained the treasure and his later misfortunes; Wagner conflated this with other legends for his opera cycle.

Nike Greek goddess of victory, either in war or in an athletic contest; the frequent subject of sculpture, often shown as a winged figure; identified by the Romans as Victoria.

Ninurta Sumerian god of war; chosen by the gods to fight against Anzu, who had stoled the tablets of destiny; on victory, he became champion of the gods.

Niobe Greek heroine; proud of having seven sons and seven daughters, she insulted mothers who had few children; her insults to **Leto** earned the revenge of Leto's son and daughter, **Apollo** and **Artemis**, and their father, **Zeus**, who murdered Niobe's children, left them without burial for nine days and turned her to stone on Mount Sipylus.

Nix (Nixie) European water-sprite; occasionally entrapped people in her pool; not to be confused with the deity **Nyx** in Greek mythology.

Nixie *see* **Nix**

Njord Norse god; father of **Freyr** and **Freyja**; succeeded **Odin** as sovereign and maintained peace and prosperity.

Norns Three Norse goddesses; Urdr represented the past, Verdandi, the present, and Skuld, the future; decided the fates of men and gods without reason or interest, dealing out as much good as evil.

Nox *see* **Nyx**

Nux *see* **Nyx**

Nymphs Greek goddesses; symbolized the beauty and charm of nature; for the most part, Nymphs were daughters of **Zeus** with lives lasting several centuries; dark formidable powers, whose beauty could lead to madness, and provoked sudden terror at midday; grouped into Melias, Naiads, Nereids, Oreads, Dryads and Oceanids.

Nyx (Nox, Nux) Greek goddess; a very ancient deity ('Night'), born of Chaos, and mother of Aither and Day, the **Hesperides**, and the **Moerae**; in the Orphic religion, Night was the original first principle; she laid an egg from which sprang other gods.

Oberon European king of the fairies; appears in European literature such as Shakespeare's *A Midsummer Night's Dream* and Wieland's *Oberon*.

Oceanids Greek **Nymphs**; inhabited the ocean and other watery places; daughters of **Oceanus** and **Tethys**.

FIGURES OF MYTH AND LEGEND (cont.)

Oceanus Greek **Titan**; son of **Uranus** and **Gaia**; a benign god who personified the stream of Ocean which was assumed to surround the world, as known to the Greeks.

Odin (Woden, Wotan) Norse god; keeper of all knowledge, represented as an old one-eyed bearded man wearing a multicoloured robe and a wide-brimmed hat; his horse had eight legs and galloped through the air and on the ocean as well as on ground; a cruel sovereign, he inspired deceit and was fond of human sacrifices; preserved the head of the decapitated giant Mimir, who was famous for his knowledge, and consulted it whenever he had some mystery to unravel.

Odysseus (Ulysses) Greek hero; a leader of the Achaeans in the Trojan War; returning to Greece, he became separated by a windstorm from his companions and overcame **Cyclopes**, **Sirens**, gods and magicians to return; his adventures are described in Homer's *Odyssey*.

Oedipus Greek hero; afflicted from birth by the curse that he would kill his father, marry his mother and be at the root of an endless series of misfortunes which would lead to the ruin of his family; because of this, his father abandoned him, and he was adopted by King Polybus; when the child was older and learned of the curse, he became frightened for the king, whom he believed to be his father and went into voluntary exile; he later killed his father in a fight when they met coincidentally; after being crowned king, he unknowingly married his mother, widowed by the death of his father.

Ogmios Celtic god; an old wrinkled man who wore a lion's skin and carried a club, a bow and a quiver; could draw or tow men attached by their ears to a gold chain, the end of which passed through the god's pierced tongue; attracted his followers by magic.

Olympians Greek gods and goddesses; collectively, the major gods and godesses who were thought to live on Mt Olympus, the highest mountain in Ancient Greece, situated in a range between Macedonia and Thessaly.

Ops Roman goddess of plenty, the consort of Saturn, identified with **Rhea**.

Oreads *see* **Nymphs**

Orestes In Greek legend, the son of **Agamemnon** and **Clytemnestra**; after his father's murder he went into exile, but returned to kill **Aegisthus** and his mother, for which he was pursued by the **Erinyes**.

Orion Greek gigantic hunter; beloved by **Eos** and killed by **Artemis**; changed into a constellation, and this generated further astronomical stories, for example, that he pursues the **Pleiades**.

Orpheus Greek hero; a musician and poet, he had the power to enchant gods, men, animals and inanimate objects who followed him under his spell; married the **Nymph Euridice** who was taken to hell after dying from the bite of a serpent; Orpheus charmed the rulers of hell who agreed to release Euridice on the condition that Orpheus did not turn round to look at her as she followed him out of hell; his doubts that she was not following him made him eventually turn round, to see Euridice disappear into the underworld forever.

Osiris Egyptian god of vegetation; provided laws and customs and gave the fruits of the earth; his jealous brother **Seth** conspired to kill him by trapping him in a wooden chest and sinking it in a river; his wife **Isis** recovered the body and managed to make Osiris father a son, to take vengeance on her enemies.

Ouranus *see* **Uranus**

Pan Gu Chinese first being of creation; broke open the primal egg from within, held up the sky, and prevented it from bearing down upon the earth; the world was then made from parts of him, so that his body become the mountains, his hair the stars, and his eyes the sun and moon.

Pan Greek god of animal instinct; half man, half goat with a long wrinkled face and two horns on his head; son of **Hermes** he lived in hills and woods; constantly pursued **Nymphs** and those who became possessed by him took on his characteristics.

Pandarus Trojan prince; in Homer's *Iliad*, was killed by **Diomedes**; in later developments of the story of **Troilus** and **Cressida**, he became her uncle and their 'go-between' (hence 'pander').

Pandora Greek heroine; the first woman on earth, who led men to their downfall by seduction and entrapment; a gift from **Zeus** to man, made in the form of the immortal goddesses, Pandora was divine in appearance but human in reality; with her she brought a box which she had been forbidden to open; overcome with curiosity, she opened the box and let out all the evils of the world, such as disease, death, lies and theft, which spread throughout nature.

Parasurama Indian hero; united the religious purity of a Brahman with the impurity of a warrior; cut

FIGURES OF MYTH AND LEGEND (cont.)

off his mother's head as requested by his father, who believed her to have produced the racial impurity; in 21 battles, freed the world of the ksatriya warriors.

Parcae *see* **Moerae**

Paris (Alexander) Greek hero; a prince of Troy, the son of **Priam**; because of a prophecy, he was exposed at birth on Mt Ida, where he was loved by Oenone, a **Nymph**; there he also chose **Aphrodite** as the fairest of three goddesses; she offered him the most beautiful woman in the world; he abducted **Helen**, causing the Trojan war; wounded by **Philoctetes**, and in his death-agony asked Oenone for help, which she refused.

Parsifal *see* **Perceval, Sir**

Pasiphae In Greek mythology, the daughter of **Helios**; wife of **Minos**, king of Crete; loved a bull sent by **Poseidon**, and became the mother of the **Minotaur**.

Patroclus Greek warrior; faithful follower of **Achilles** at Troy; went into battle wearing Achilles's armour, but was cut down by **Hector**; his death made Achilles return to the battle.

Pegasus Greek winged horse; sprang from the body of the **Medusa** after her death; **Bellerophon** caught it with **Athene**'s assistance; various fountains sprang from the touch of its foot, such as Hippocrene on Mt Helicon; finally it was placed in the sky as a constellation.

Peleus Greek king of Phythia in Thessaly; had to capture Thetis, a **Nereid**, before he could marry her; the gods attended the wedding feast; the father of **Achilles**.

Pelops Greek hero; protégé of **Poseidon**; eaten unknowingly by **Demeter** at birth as a result of his father's attempt to test the keenness of the gods; the other gods resurrected him to restore their reputation; protected by Poseidon on Olympus until his father led him to steal the nectar and ambrosia of the gods to give to mortals, for which he was forced to return to earth; drove his chariot drawn by winged horses to win the chance to marry Hippodameia; one of the mythological figures said to have founded the Olympic Games, in memory of his victory.

Penates Roman guardians of the storeroom; '**Lares** and Penates' were the household gods; the *penates publici* were the 'luck' of the Roman state, originally brought by **Aeneas** from Troy and kept at Lavinium.

Penelope In Greek legend, the wife of **Odysseus**; faithfully waited 20 years for his return from Troy; tricked her insistent suitors by weaving her web (a shroud for Odysseus' father, **Laertes**, which had to be finished before she could marry), and undoing her work every night.

Pentheus In Greek mythology, the king of Thebes; did not welcome **Dionysus**; disguising himself as a woman, he tried to spy on the orgiastic rites of the **Maenads**, who tore him to pieces, his mother leading them on.

Perceval, Sir (Parsifal) One of King **Arthur**'s knights; went in quest of the Holy Grail; in the German version (Parzival) his bashfulness prevented him from asking the right questions of the warden of the Grail castle, so that the Fisher King was not healed.

Peri Persian good fairy or genie; Peri-Banou, for example, was the name of a beautiful fairy in the *Arabian Nights*.

Persephone (Proserpine) Greek goddess of the underworld; daughter of **Demeter** and **Zeus**, originally called Kore ('maiden'); while gathering flowers at Enna in Sicily was abducted by **Hades** and made queen of the underworld; there she ate the seeds of the pomegranate, which meant (in fairy lore) that she was bound to stay; however, a compromise was arranged so that could return for half of every year (an allegory of the return of spring).

Perseus Greek hero; shut in a chest and thrown into the sea by his grandfather; washed up on the island of Seriphos; after he grew up, the island's tyrant demanded that he bring him the gift of the head of a **Gorgon**; with the help of **Hermes** and the **Nymphs**, he slayed **Medusa** and returned with her head; married **Andromeda** after freeing her from the sea-monster to whom she was promised; unknowingly killed his grandfather, fulfilling an oracle which predicted this.

Perun Slavic god of rain and fertility; represented as a human being with a silver head and golden moustache; controlled the seasons and destroyed the countries of wicked men with hail.

Phaedra Greek heroine; daughter of **Minos** and the second wife of **Theseus**; while he was away she fell in love with her step-son **Hippolytus**; he rejected her, so she killed herself, but left a note accusing him of trying to rape her; Theseus called on **Poseidon** to grant a promised favour, and punish Hippolytus with death.

Phaethon Greek hero; son of Helios; challenged to prove his ancestry by his friends, he asked to

FIGURES OF MYTH AND LEGEND (cont.)

drive his father's chariot for a day; as he was inexperienced in this, the horses bolted, the chariot veered off its route and everything in their path was set on fire; the earth complained to the king of Olympus, and **Zeus** struck down the charioteer.

Phenix *see* **Phoenix**

Philemon and **Baucis** Greek old man and wife; the only ones to entertain the Greek gods **Zeus** and **Hermes** when they visited the earth to test people's hospitality; in return they were saved from a flood, made priest and priestess, and allowed to die at the same time, when they were changed into trees.

Philoctetes Greek hero; son of Poeas, who inherited the bow of **Heracles** and its poisoned arrows; on the way to Troy was bitten by a snake, and the wound stank, so that he was left behind on the island of Lemnos; it was prophesied that only with the arrows of Heracles could Troy be taken, so **Diomedes** and **Odysseus** came to find Philoctetes; his wound was healed and he entered the battle, killing **Paris**.

Philomela (Philomel) and **Procne (Progne)**. In Greek mythology, daughters of Pandion, king of Athens; Procne married Tereus, king of Thrace, who raped Philomela and removed her tongue; but she was able to tell Procne by a message in her embroidery; Procne served up her son Itys, or Itylos, in a meal to his father; while pursuing the sisters, the gods changed Tereus into the hoopoe, Philomela into the swallow, and Procne into the nightingale; in Latin legend, the birds of the sisters are reversed.

Phoebe Greek **Titan**, identified with the moon; later she was confused with **Artemis**.

Phoenix (Phenix) Legendary bird; lived for a long time; killed itself on a funeral pyre, but was then reborn from the ashes.

Pleiades In Greek mythology, the seven daughters of **Atlas** and **Pleione**: Maia, Taygete, Elektra, Alkyone, Asterope, Kelaino, and Merope; after their deaths they were transformed into the star-cluster of the same name.

Pluto *see* **Hades**

Pollux *see* **Castor** and **Pollux**

Polyhymnia Greek **Muse** of dance and mime.

Polyneices *see* **Polynices**

Polynices (Polyneices) Greek hero; second son of **Oedipus**, who led the **Seven against Thebes**; **Creon**'s refusal to bury him led eventually to the death of **Antigone**.

Polyphemus Greek **Cyclops**; imprisoned **Odysseus** and some of his companions in his cave; Odysseus blinded Polyphemus's one eye, and told him that 'No one' had hurt him; as a result, when he called on the other Cyclopes for help, and they asked who had attacked him, they did not understand his answer; Odysseus's band escaped by hiding under the sheep when they were let out of the cave to graze.

Pomona Roman goddess of fruit-trees and their fruit, especially apples and pears.

Poseidon (Neptune) Greek god of the sea; represented wielding a trident and being pulled by monsters in a chariot; could evoke storms and set fire to rocks; took part in the construction of the walls of Troy, then called up a monster to devastate the area when he did not receive payment; Neptune was a Roman water god who was later associated with Poseidon.

Prajapati Indian god; master of creatures and posterity, he was born aged a thousand years from a primordial egg; created the gods, the evil spirits, man, melodies and the sun, then wasted away, exhausted by his tasks.

Priam In Greek legend, the king of Troy; son of Laomedon, and husband of **Hecuba**; presented in the *Iliad* as an old man; when **Hector** was killed, went secretly to **Achilles** to beg his son's body for burial; at the sack of Troy, he was killed by **Neoptolemus**.

Priapus Greek god; represented as a small bearded man with an oversized penis; in some traditions, the son of **Zeus** and **Aphrodite**; Zeus's jealous wife **Hera** made sure that the child was born with the extraordinary deformity to which he owes his name; Aphrodite abandoned him in the mountains; the guard of the orchard, he scared off thieves and threatened females with sexual violence.

Procrustes Thief of Attica; in the legend of **Theseus**, made travellers lie on his bed, and either cut or lengthened them to fit it; his name means 'the stretcher'; Theseus gave him the same treatment, and killed him.

Prometheus Greek hero; symbolized the revolt of man against the gods and brought to humanity all the good things refused it by the gods; punished for this when **Zeus** sent mankind the gift of **Pandora**, who spread evils throughout the world; became immortal after exchanging death for immortality with **Cheiron** the **Centaur**.

Proserpine *see* **Persephone**

Proteus Greek god of the sea; associated with seals,

FIGURES OF MYTH AND LEGEND (cont.)

and a shape-changer; he gave answers to questions after a wrestling match; was sometimes to be found on the island of Pharos, in Egypt, where **Menelaus** wrestled with him.

Psyche Greek personification of 'the soul'; usually represented by a butterfly; in the story told by Apuleius, was beloved by Cupid (*see* **Eros**), who hid her in an enchanted palace, and visited her at night, forbidding her to look at him; her sisters persuaded her to light a lamp; she saw Cupid, but was separated from him, and given impossible tasks by Venus (*see* **Aphrodite**), who impeded her search for him.

Ptah Egyptian god; principal god of the city of Memphis, known as the creator and master of craftsmen; subsequently regarded as a healing god in the form of a flat-headed dwarf and as a protective spirit.

Purusha Primordial being of India; thought to be a gigantic man who covered the earth and went beyond it; heaven made up three-quarters of his being, and the fourth quarter consisted of all mortal creatures.

Pwyll Celtic hero; wise prince of Dyfed who as a service to the king of Annwn killed the king's permanent enemy; courteous and powerful, he emerged victorious from a thousand trials.

Pygmalion In Greek mythology, a king of Cyprus; made a statue of a beautiful woman; he prayed to **Aphrodite**, and the sculptured figure came to life.

Pyramus and **Thisbe** Two lovers; kept apart by their parents, they conversed through a crack in the wall between their houses, and agreed to meet at Ninus's tomb outside the city of Babylon; finding Thisbe's blood-stained cloak, Pyramus thought she had been killed by a lion, and committed suicide; when she found him, Thisbe killed herself on his sword; incorporated into Shakespeare's *A Midsummer Night's Dream.*

Python Greek monster; lived at Delphi and was killed by **Apollo** when he took over the shrine; the name Pythia continued in use, and the Pythian games were celebrated there.

Qat Hero of Oceania; born from a rock which had been hollowed out in the centre to allow his birth; organizer of life, he created man and then death to allow renewal; initiated day and night; canoed away to a far country, taking with him the hopes of mankind.

Querinus Roman god; initially a god of the city who watched over the material well-being of the community; also likened to **Ares** by the Greeks, and to **Romulus**, founder of Rome.

Quetzalcoatl Aztec god of vegetation and wind; depicted as a bearded man wearing a mask, earrings and a conical hat; son of the sun-god and one of the five goddesses of the moon; created mankind from the bones of the ancient dead; taught measurement of time and how to discover the movement of the stars.

Ra *see* **Re**

Rainbow Snake (Julunggul) Australian Aboriginal fertility spirit; both male and female, creator and destroyer, known as Julunggul; associated with streams and waterholes, from which it emerges in the creation-story and leaves special markings on the ground.

Rama Indian hero; incarnation of the god **Vishnu** on earth; was taught magic spells to allow him to conquer the raksasa, the **demons**; saved his wife from abduction and was made king; after his wife had been swallowed up by the earth, gave up his royal status, and went to the river Sarayu to be carried off to heaven.

Re (Ra) Egyptian god; the ancient sun-god of Heliopolis; as the creator, he emerged from the primaeval waters at the beginning of time; depicted as a falcon with the sun's disc on his head: at night he appears as a ram-headed god who sails through the underworld.

Rhadamanthus (Rhadamanthys) In Greek mythology, a Cretan, son of **Zeus** and **Europa**; did not die but was taken to Elisium, where he became the just judge of the dead.

Rhadamanthys *see* **Rhadamanthus**

Rhea (Rheia) Greek **Titan**; sister and wife of **Cronus**, and mother of **Zeus** and other Olympian gods; when Cronus consumed his children, Rhea gave him a stone instead of Zeus, who was saved and later rebelled against his father.

Rheia *see* **Rhea**

Rhiannon Celtic heroine; mistress of horses and horsemen; refused all her suitors out of love for **Pwyll**, who prepared to marry her; Pwyll, however, agreed to grant a supplicant, Gnawl, any wish, and he claimed Rhiannon; Pwyll later set her free from Gnawl through trickery and became her husband; accused of infanticide after her son mysteriously disappeared, but the child later reappeared.

Roc Arabian mythical creature; an enormous bird encountered by travellers in the Indian ocean, capable of carrying off an elephant.

FIGURES OF MYTH AND LEGEND (cont.)

Rod Slavic god; initially the god of husbandmen but also a universal god, the god of heaven, the thunderbolt and rain; responsible for the nation's increase and closely linked with the worship of ancestors; later dethroned by **Perun**.

Romulus and **Remus** In Roman legend, the twin sons of Mars (*see* **Ares**) and the Vestal Virgin Rhea Silvia; an example of an invented myth, to explain the name of the city; thrown into the Tiber, which carried them to the Palatine, where they were suckled by a she-wolf; in building the wall of Rome, Remus made fun of the work and was killed by Romulus or one of his followers; having founded Rome, Romulus was later carried off in a thunder-storm.

Rosmerta Gallo-Roman goddess; represented as a woman standing draped in a long robe, holding a cornucopia and a patera; invoked to obtain fertility, fruitfulness and everything essential for a better life.

Rudra Indian god; a being with a thousand eyes and a thousand feet, with plaited hair, a black belly, a red back and armed with a bow and arrows; the great destroyer, he cast evil spells over men and beasts, and spread terror and illness.

Sakhmet (Sekmet) Egyptian goddess of Memphis; depicted with the head of a lioness; her name means 'powerful'; associated with savage cruelty, in particular towards the enemies of the Pharaoh.

Sarapis *see* **Serapis**

Sarasvati Indian goddess; wife of **Brahma**; personification of the word of the god Veda; carried the book of Veda, a musical instrument and a rosary composed of the letters of the alphabet; mother of the scriptures, the sciences and the arts; also associated with water.

Sarpedon Warrior of Greek mythology; in the *Iliad*, a son of **Zeus**, who led the Lycian troops on the Trojan side, and made an important speech on the duties of a warrior; killed by **Patroclus**, and carried off by Sleep and Death to Lycia.

Saturn Roman god; master of agriculture who invented the dressing of the vine, taught man agricultural methods and provided the first laws; depicted as being armed with a scythe; associated with the Golden Age, synonymous with religious festivals and feasts.

Satyr Greek god; a minor deity associated with **Dionysus**; usually depicted with goat-like ears, tail, and legs; rural, wild and lustful, the satyrs were said to be the brothers of the **Nymphs**.

Scylla Greek sea-monster; usually located in the Straits of Messina opposite to Charybdis; originally a woman, she was changed by **Circe** or **Amphitrite** into a snake with six heads; in the *Odyssey* she snatched six men from **Odysseus**'s ships.

Sekhmet Egyptian goddess; wife of the god **Ptah**; depicted with the head of a lioness and the body of a woman; a terrible bloodthirsty goddess, responsible for epidemics, death, carnage and war; also had the power of healing.

Sekmet *see* **Sakhmet**

Selene Greek goddess of the moon; depicted as a charioteer (the head of one of her horses may be seen among the Elgin Marbles).

Semele In Greek mythology, the daughter of Cadmus, and mother by **Zeus** of **Dionysus**; asked Zeus to appear in his glory before her, and was consumed in fire, but it made her son immortal.

Semiramis In Greek mythology, a queen of Assyria; founded many cities, including Nineveh and Babylon.

Serapis (Sarapis) Egyptian god; a compound deity, combining the names and aspects of two Egyptian gods, **Osiris** and **Apis**, to which were further added features of major Greek gods, such as **Zeus** and **Dionysus**; introduced to Alexandria by Ptolemy I in an attempt to unite Greeks and Egyptians in common worship.

Sesostris Egyptian king; alleged to have conquered vast areas of Europe, Asia, and N Africa; probably a compound of the three Egyptian pharaohs (c.20th–19th-c BC) and Rameses II (13th-c BC).

Seth Egyptian god; depicted as a strange being with a forked tail, a long gaunt body, huge ears and protruding eyes; represented all evils and caused all disasters; fought the **demon** Apopis every morning and every evening and as a result of this permanent conflict, the equilibrium of forces and universal harmony were born.

Seven against Thebes Seven Greek Champions; attacked Thebes to deprive **Eteocles** of his kingship; led by his brother **Polynices**; the names of the other six were Tydeus, Adrastus (or Eteoklos), Capaneus, Hippomedon, Parthenopaeus, and Amphiarus; defeated by another seven champions at the seven gates of Thebes; all were killed in battle, except for Amphiarus, whom the earth swallowed alive, and Adrastus, who escaped; later the sons of the Seven, the **Epigoni**, led by Adrastus, succeeded in destroying the city.

FIGURES OF MYTH AND LEGEND (cont.)

Seven Sleepers of Ephesus In medieval legend, seven persecuted Christians who fled into a cave at the time of the Emperor Decius (AD250); slept for 200 years, emerging in 447 at the time of Theodosius II; the story was thought to confirm the resurrection of Christ.

Shamash Babylonian god; depicted bearing a headdress with four rows of horns and a large beard, wearing a long robe and holding a staff and a hoop; symbolized by a solar disc rising between two mountains or by a spoked wheel; god of light and justice, he gave light to the world and distributed punishment and reward.

Shango African god of thunder; dispensed justice using the thunderbolt which was regarded as the god's punishment; the victim of his punishment was compelled to pay heavy fines and to appease him by means of sacrifices; originally a cruel king whose subjects drove him away; he hanged himself from a tree leaving a hole from which emerged an iron chain; finding the tree without the body, his supporters concluded that he had become a god.

Shiva Indian god; representing darkness, his three eyes were filled with snakes; had four arms and a girdle made of skulls; danced amid devils on cremation sites, representing the world's constructive and destructive periods; withdrew to the mountains after the suicide of his wife but later came back to produce a son to kill a **demon** which threatened the world; carried out many heroic deeds and was regarded as a beneficent force.

Sibyl (Sibylla) Roman prophetess; uttered mysterious wisdom; **Aeneas** met the Cumaean Sibyl, who was inspired by **Apollo** and whose prophecies were written on leaves; she had been given 1 000 years of life, and eventually shrank to a tiny creature hung up in a bottle; later there were said to be 10 Sibyls; the Sybilline Books were nine books of prophecy offered by the Sybil to Tarquinus Priscus, who refused to pay her price; she destroyed three, and came again, with the same result; she destroyed three more, and then Tarquin bought the remainder for the price originally asked.

Sibylla *see* **Sibyl**

Sigurd In Norse mythology, the son of Sigmund the Volsung; killed Fafnir the dragon and won Brunhild; married Gudrun, having forgotten Brunhild, and was killed by Gudrun's brother Gutthorn; virtually the same story is told of Siegfried in German legends.

Sileni Greek followers of **Dionysus**; depicted with horse ears, tail, and legs, or as old men in need of support (Papposileni); could give good advice to humans if captured; plural form of **Silenus**.

Silenus Greek demi-god; fostered and educated **Dionysus**; represented as a festive old man, usually quite drunk.

Silvanus (Sylvanus) Roman god of uncultivated land, especially woodland; he was therefore strange, and dangerous, like Pan.

Sin Sumerian god; represented the moon; depicted seated on a throne, with a long beard, holding an axe, a sceptre and a staff; his predictions were binding on the gods and man, and an eclipse was his most formidable sign, announcing catastrophe.

Sirens Three Greek demonesses; became half woman, half bird when they asked the gods for wings, to look for **Persephone** who had been taken to the underworld by **Hades**; one held a lyre, the second sang and the third played the flute; devoured sailors lured to their island by their enchanting sounds.

Sisyphus In Greek mythology, a Corinthian king who was a famous trickster; in one story he caught and bound Thanatos (Death); in the underworld was condemned to roll a large stone up a hill from which it always rolled down again.

Sita Indian heroine; emerged from a furrow in a ploughed field; married **Rama** and was abducted by Ravana; on reunion with her husband, was tested by fire and exiled as he believed she had been unfaithful; requested the earth to open up and swallow her forever.

Skanda Indian hero; son of **Shiva** and chief of the divine armies; killed the **demon** Taraka who threatened the world.

Skyamsen *see* **Thunderbird**

Soma Indian moon-god; marked the rhythm of the days and months and was the nectar of immortality, a divine drink essential to the gods.

Sucellus Gallic god; depicted with a tunic, cowl and boots, holding a club or sceptre and a vase, indicating that he was a sovereign and the dispenser of food; married to the river goddess.

Svarog Slavic god of fire; dispenser of all wealth, and judge and protector of monogamy; also a magician and soothsayer.

Sventovit Slavic god of war; depicted holding a trumpet and a bow; also the god of fertility, fruitfulness and destiny; his horse had the gift of divination, and its movement could reveal the meaning of oracles it wished to communicate.

FIGURES OF MYTH AND LEGEND (cont.)

Sylvanus *see* **Silvanus**

Syrinx Greek **Nymph**;pursued by Pan, she called on the earth to help, and so sank down into it and became a reed-bed; Pan cut some of the reeds, and made the panpipes.

Tammuz (Thammuz) Babylonian god of vegetation; beloved by Ishtar (in Syria by Astarte); returned from the dead and died again each year.

Tane (Kane) Divinity from the Pacific Islands; kept heaven and earth apart, permitting the world to exist; misfortune and death were born from his destructive war with his enemy, the god Tangaroa.

Tantalus In Greek mythology, a king of Sisyphos in Lydia; committed terrible crimes; stole the food of the gods, so becoming immortal, and served them his son **Pelops** in a dish; for this he was punished in the underworld; he sits in a pool which recedes when he bends to drink, and the grapes over his head elude his grasp.

Taranis Gallic god; master of the universe, who inspired fear by sending thunder and lightning; at the same time, brought the gentle rain which fed the earth and made crops grow; demanded human sacrifices; his victims were shut in wooden cages which were set alight, and severed heads were offered to him.

Tarpeia Roman woman who betrayed the Capitol to the Sabines, in return for 'what they wore on their left arms' (meaning gold rings); in their disgust, they threw their shields on her and crushed her to death.

Telemachus Greek hero; in the *Odyssey*, the son of **Odysseus** and **Penelope**; set out to find his father, visiting **Nestor** and **Menelaus**; later helped Odysseus fight Penelope's suitors.

Tellus *see* **Gaea**

Tengri Mongol god of heaven; imposed the order of the natural world, the organization and movements of the stars and the government of the Mongol empire; distributed good luck and wealth and showed his anger by sending thunderstorms.

Terminus Roman god of boundary marks; his statue or bust was sometimes placed there; his stone on the Capitol was within the temple of Jupiter Optimus Maximus, but was not allowed to be covered in.

Terpsichore Greek **Muse** of dance and lyric poetry.

Teshub Hurrian god of the thunderstorm; depicted holding an axe and thunderclouds; dethroned the king of heaven to become the supreme god and battled victoriously against the deposed king who sought his revenge.

Teutates Gallic god; a warrior god, sometimes compared to Mars (*see* **Ares**) and Mercury (*see* **Hermes**); depicted beside a serpent with a ram's head; a cruel god who demanded human sacrifices; the victims were drowned in a vat of water.

Tezcatlipoca Aztec god; depicted in human form with a stripe of black paint across his face and a mirror replacing one of his feet; said to have been mutilated by the mythical crocodile on which the earth was supposed to rest; reigned over the four worlds destroyed prior to the creation of the present one; with his mirror could see everything and was aware of both human actions and thoughts; a malevolent wizard who brought the custom of human sacrifice to Mexico.

Thaleia *see* **Thalia**

Thalia (Thaleia) Greek **Muse** of comedy and idyllic poetry.

Thammuz *see* **Tammuz**

Themis Greek goddess of established law and justice; a consort of **Zeus**, she was the mother of the **Horae** and the **Moerae**.

Theseus Greek hero; set out for Athens to find his father, the king, and slayed many monsters on the way; fought those who tried to depose his father and killed the **Minotaur**; assumed power and defended Attica against the **Amazons** who almost won but in the end were forced to sign a peace treaty (he married their leader, Hippolyta); later became powerless and was forced into exile before being killed when thrown into a ravine.

Thetis Greek goddess; mother of **Achilles**; saved **Zeus** from a conspiracy to remove his power; an oracle predicted that her son would be more powerful than his father, and fearing this, Zeus forced her to marry a mortal; an unhappy goddess, she failed in her determined attempts to make her children immortal.

Thor Nordic god; son of **Odin**; armed with a hammer which returned automatically to the hand of the one who hurled it, and doubled his strength by wearing a magic belt; fond of tricks and practical jokes; killed the serpent of Midgard, but was himself killed by its venom.

Thoth (Hermes) Egyptian god; skilled at calculation, secretary to the gods and master of effective speech; also a magician and capable of providing cures; identified by the Greeks as Hermes.

Thunderbird (Skyamsen) Totem figure of NW American Indian religion; lightning flashed from its eye and it fed on killer whales; the chief of the Thunderbirds was Golden Eagle (Keneun).

FIGURES OF MYTH AND LEGEND (cont.)

Thyestes In Greek mythology, a son of **Pelops**; inherited the curse upon that house; his brother **Atreus** set before him a dish made of the flesh of Thyestes's children; later became the father of **Aegisthus**.

Tiamat Akkadian goddess; a primordial divinity who represented salt water; became angry after an old god was murdered by a younger one; decided to create monsters as gods, and in the resulting confrontation was killed by **Marduk**; from one half of her corpse, heaven was created, and from the other half, Marduk formed dry land.

Tiresias In Greek mythology, a blind Theban prophet; takes a prominent part in Sophocles's plays about **Oedipus** and **Antigone**; later legends account for his wisdom by saying that he had experienced the life of both sexes.

Titania Greek female Titan; identified with the moon; in Shakespeare's *A Midsummer Night's Dream* she is the queen of the fairies, who is tricked into falling in love with Bottom the Weaver.

Titans Greek gods; members of the older generation of gods, the children of **Uranus** and **Gaia**; after **Zeus** and the Olympians took power, the Titans made war on them; but they were defeated and imprisoned in Tartarus; one or two, notably **Prometheus**, helped Zeus; may represent memories of pre-Greek Mediterranean gods.

Tlaloc Aztec god of mountains, rain and springs; represented as a man painted black with huge round eyes with circles or serpents around them, and long fangs; ordered the distribution of rain and hurricanes; sometimes killed by means of a thunderbolt; his victims were buried with a piece of dry wood which would come back to life in Tlaloc's paradise.

Tlazolteotl Aztec goddess of lust; represented as a young girl wearing a rubber mask and a crescent-shaped ornament in her nose; responsible for conjugal infidelities and at the same time the granter of pardon; also the goddess of renewal.

Triglav Slavic god; had three heads and a golden veil which covered his eyes and mouth, signifying his desire to disregard human faults; a soothsayer, priest, warrior and nourisher.

Tristan and **Isolde** Celtic heroes; Tristan was a master harp-player and huntsman; Isolde was the daughter of the king of Ireland, who was to marry Mark the king of Cornwall, and become queen; through a misunderstanding, Tristan and Isolde drank from the same love potion and became bound by an indissoluble love; discovered to be meeting secretly, Tristan and the queen were condemned to be burned alive, and both fled; King Mark searched for them, and finding them asleep, became seized with pity, leaving his sword between them and replacing a ring on Isolde's finger; moved by his generosity, the lovers returned to the court, where Isolde was accepted, but Tristan was sent into exile.

Triton In Greek mythology, the son of **Poseidon** and **Amphitrite**; depicted in art as a fish from the waist down, and blowing a conch-shell; beings of similar form (mermen) who serve Poseidon are often referred to as Tritons.

Troilus In Greek legend, a prince of Troy; son of **Priam** and **Hecuba**, who was killed by **Achilles**; in medieval stories, the lover of **Cressida**.

Tuatha de Danann Irish race of wise beings; came to Ireland in c.1500BC, and became the ancient gods of the Irish; the name means 'the people of the goddess Danu'; conquered by the Milesians, and retreated into tumuli near the R Boyne.

Tyche Greek goddess of chance or luck; prominent in the Hellenistic period; depicted as blind, or, with a wall, as the luck of a city.

Typhoeus *see* **Typhon**

Typhon (Typhoeus) Greek monster; had 100 heads and was brought forth by **Gaia**; a serious challenge to **Zeus**, who hurled his thunderbolts and thrust him down into Tartarus; in another story, said to be buried under Etna.

Tyr Nordic god; courageous and bold, he guaranteed right and justice; lost one arm in the courageous act of restraining the horrible wolf Fenrir.

Ulysses *see* **Odysseus**

Unicorn Creature of medieval legend; a horse with a single horn on its forehead; probably based on stories of the rhinoceros; could be captured only by a virgin putting its head in her lap.

Urania Greek **Muse** of astronomy.

Uranus (Ouranus) Greek god of the sky; father of the Titans; a very abstract figure, not the subject of worship or of art, he was displaced by Cronus; equivalent to Roman Caelus, 'the heavens'.

Uther Pendragon Legendary king of Britain; father of King **Arthur** by Ygerna, the wife of Duke Gorlois of Cornwall.

Vahagn Armenian deity; born of water and fire, and married to the goddess of the stars; god of victory and destroyer of obstacles; created the Milky way when he stole some straw one night and fled in

FIGURES OF MYTH AND LEGEND (cont.)

haste across the sky, leaving wisps of straw across his path.

Väinämöinen Finnish sage, shaman and bard; dominates the epic *Kalevala*; sought the sampo, the magic cauldron of plenty, and invented the kantele or harp.

Valkyries Nordic goddesses; godesses of fertility and the angels of battle; 40 are recorded as magicians and combat godesses who selected those who were doomed to die, apportioning death not as a punishment, but as a reward.

Varuna Indian god and guardian of world order; ordered nature and supervised sacrificial rites; his domain consisted of darkness and the waters, and the stars were his thousand eyes; also producing evil, he caused earthquakes and sent disease, but possessed and provided the remedies.

Venus *see* **Aphrodite**

Vesta *see* **Hestia**

Vesta Roman goddess of the hearth; particularly known for the cult dedicated to her; her temple in the Roman Forum was served by virgins who were walled up alive at the Colline Gate if they failed to remain chaste; a fire was kept lit in her honour all year round.

Viracocha Incan god; the creator and civilizer, he created the first men, but disappointed by them, he changed some into stone statues and destroyed the others by fire; recreated humanity, accompanied by the sun and moon, then provided mountains, rivers and farmland to permit them to live in a civilized way; after this mission, disappeared over the horizon, and his return is still awaited; protector of the emperor of the Incas.

Vishnu Indian god; originally a dwarf who wanted to secure dominion over the world, he became the god of space, who gave the world its stability; the origin of the fertility of both nature and man; appeared in the form of heroes and animals each time the world needed him.

Visvamitra Indian hero; tried to equal the Brahman Vasistha by leading a life of increasing rigid asceticism; finally achieved his aim by stopping eating and breathing for a number of years.

Volcanus *see* **Hephaestus**

Vulcan *see* **Hephaestus**

Wak Ethiopian god; kept heaven at a distance from the earth and covered it with stars; created man on the flat earth, then buried him for seven years while he made fire rain down to create the mountains; when after this, man sprang back to life, he said that he had slept only for a brief moment; this was said to be why man is awake for most of the day; later created woman.

Wayland Norse, German, and Old English legendary inventor; known as Wayland the Smith; lame, having been maimed by King Nidud; many heroes carry swords made by him; his 'Smithy', is a dolmen on the Berkshire Downs, UK.

Woden *see* **Odin**

Wotan *see* **Odin**

Xipe Totec Aztec god of springtime, renewal and nocturnal rain; inspired Mexican ceremonies with human sacrifices and mock battles; during the ceremonies the priests flayed the sacrifices and wore their skins.

Xiuhtecuhtli Aztec god of the hearth, fire, the sun and volcanoes; also associated with peppers and the pine, the tree from which torches were made.

Yama The first Indian man; the first mortal who on death became king of the dead; came to look for those who had used up their lifetimes; produced excessive increases of the human population when one day he became distracted and did not make a single man die.

Yggdrasil In Norse mythology, a giant ash; the World-Tree, which supported the sky, held the different realms of gods and men in its branches, and had its roots in the underworld.

Yu the Great Chinese hero; a thin, ill man who hopped about on one foot; dug out the mountains and allowed waters to flow from a catastrophic flood, working for 13 years without returning home; became a god and travelled the world to plan it; first emperor of the Hsia Dynasty.

Zanahary Madagacan god; creator god and father of heaven; terrifying, and spoke in thunder and lightning; a double god, the Zanahary from below created man and Zanahary from above gave him life; the two gods disagreed over women and became enemies, separating the worlds above and below forever.

Zeus (Jupiter, Iuppiter) Greek god of all gods; god of light and weather, and arbiter among gods and among men; had many wives and affairs with mortal women to whom he appeared in various guises, eg as a shower of gold, a bull or a swan; hanged his jealous wife **Hera** from Olympus with anvils fastened to her ankles.

RELIGIOUS SYMBOLS

The Trinity

Equilateral triangle | Triangle in circle | Circle within triangle

God the Father

All-seeing eye | Fish | Sevenfold flame

Seven branch candlestick The Menorah | Abraham

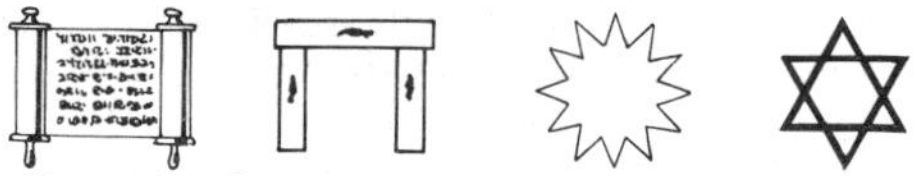

Pentateuch (The Law) | Doorposts and lintel (Passover) | Twelve tribes of Israel | Star of David

Crosses

Barbée | Trefly | Canterbury | Celtic | Cercelée | Cross crosslet

Crux ansata | Globical | Graded (Calvary) | Greek | Iona | Jerusalem

Latin | Maltese | Millvine | Papal | Patée | Patée formée | Patriarchal (or Lorraine)

Potent | Raguly or Ragulée | Russian Orthodox | St Andrews (Saltire) | St Peters | Tau (St Anthony's)

Ankh (Egyptian) | Yin-yang (Taoism) symbol of harmony | torii (shinto) | Om (Hinduism, Buddhism, Jainism; sacred syllable) | Ik-onkar (Sikhism; symbol of God) | Swastika | Yantra: Sri Cakra (wheel of fortune)

BAHA'ISM

Founded 1863 in Persia.
Founder Mirza Husayn Ali (1817–92), known as Baha Ullah (Glory of God). He declared himself the prophet foretold by Mirza ali Mohammed (1819-50), a direct descendant of Mohammed, who proclaimed himself to be the bab ('gate' or 'door').
Sacred texts Kitab al-Aqdas, Haft Wadi, al-Kalimat al-Maknnah and the Bayan.
Beliefs Baha'ism teaches the oneness of God, the unity of all faiths, the inevitable unification of humankind, the harmony of all people, universal education, and obedience to government. It does not predict an end to this world or any intervention by God but believes there will be a change within man and society.
Organization There is virtually no organization and Baha'ism has no clergy or sacraments. Although there is little formal ritual (most assemblies are simply gatherings of the faithful), there are ceremonies for marriage, funerals and naming babies and there are shrines and temples.

BUDDHISM

Founded c. 500 BC in India.
Founder Prince Siddharta Gautama (c.563–c.483 BC) who became Buddha ('the enlightened') through meditation.
Sacred texts The Pali Canon or Tripitaka made up of the Vinaya Pitaka (Discourses of the Buddha) and the Abhidhamma Pitaka (higher subtleties of law), the Mahayana Sutras, the Milindapanha and Bardo Thodol (the Tibetan Book of the Dead).
Beliefs Buddha's teaching is summarized in the Four Noble Truths: suffering is always present in life; desire is the cause of suffering; freedom from life can be achieved by nirvana (perfect peace and bliss); the Eightfold Path leads to nirvana. Karma, by which good and evil deeds result in appropriate reward or punishment, and the cycle of rebirth can be broken by taking the Eightfold Path. All Buddhas are revered but particularly Gautama.
Organization There is a monastic system which aims to create favourable conditions for spiritual development. This involves meditation, personal discipline and spiritual exercises in the hope of liberation from self. Buddhism has proved very flexible in adapting its organization, ceremony and pattern of belief to different cultural and social conditions. There are numerous festivals and ceremonies and pilgrimage is of great spiritual value.
Divisions There are two main traditions in Buddhism. Theravada Buddhism is closest to Buddha's teaching: salvation can be attained only by the few who accept the severe discipline and effort necessary to achieve it. Mahayana Buddhism developed later and is more flexible and creative, embracing popular piety. It teaches that salvation is possible for everyone and introduced the doctrine of the bodhisattva (a personal saviour). As Buddhism spread other schools sprang up including Zen, Lamaism, Tendai, Nichiven and Soka Gakkai.

MAJOR BUDDHIST FESTIVALS

Weekly Uposatha Days
Buddha's Birth Enlightenment, First Sermon and Death are observed in the different countries where Buddhism is practised but often on different dates. In some of these countries there are additional festivals in honour of Buddha.

CHRISTIANITY

Founded 1st-c AD.
Founder Jesus Christ 'the Son of God' (c.4 BC–c.30 AD).
Sacred texts The Bible consisting of the Old and New Testaments. The New Testament written between AD 30 and 150 consists of the Gospels, the Acts of the Apostles, the Epistles, and the Apocalypse.
Beliefs A world religion, centred on the life and works of Jesus of Nazareth in Judaea; he proclaimed the most important rule of life to be love of God and love of one's neighbour. Unselfishness and compassion are central themes in Christianity. Belief in Jesus's divinity and his resurrection from the dead after his crucifixion promises victory over death. The earliest followers of Jesus were Jews who believed him to be the messiah 'Saviour' promised by the prophets in the Old Testament. Christians believe he will come again to inaugurate the 'Kingdom of God'.
Organization Jesus Christ appointed 12 men to be his disciples:

1 Peter (brother of Andrew)
2 Andrew (brother of Peter)
3 James, son of Zebedee (brother of John)
4 John (brother of James)
5 Philip
6 Bartholomew
7 Thomas
8 Matthew
9 James of Alphaeus
10 Simon the Canaanite (in Matthew and Mark)
    or Simon 'the Zealot' (in Luke and the Acts)
11 Judas Iscariot

(Thaddeus in the book of Matthew and Mark is the twelfth disciple, while in Luke and the Acts the twelfth is Judas or James. Matthias succeeded to Judas's place.) Soon after the resurrection the disciples gathered for the festival of Pentecost and received special signs of the power of God, the Holy Spirit. The disciples became a defined new body, the Church. Through the witness of the Apostles and their successors, the Christian faith quickly spread and in AD 315 became the official religion of the Roman Empire. It survived the 'Dark Ages' to become the basis of civilization in the Middle Ages in Europe.
Divisions Major divisions separated as a result of differences of doctrine and practice are the Orthodox or Eastern Church, the Roman Catholic Church, acknowledging the Bishop of Rome as head, and the Protestant Churches stemming from the split with the Roman Church in the sixteenth century. All Christians recognize the authority of the Bible, read at public worship, which takes place at least every Sunday, to celebrate the resurrection of Jesus Christ. Most Churches recognize at least two sacraments (Baptism and the Eucharist, Mass, or Lord's Supper) as essential.

Major Christian Denominations

Denomination	Origins
Baptists	In radical Reformation objections to infant baptism, demands for church-state separation; John Smyth, English Separatist in 1609; Roger Williams, 1638, Providence, Rhode Island
Church of England	Henry VIII separated the English Catholic Church from Rome, 1534, for political reasons.
Lutherans	Martin Luther in Wittenberg, Germany, 1517, objected to Catholic doctrine of salvation by merit and sale of indulgences; break complete by 1519.
Methodists	John Wesley began movement, 1738, within Church of England.
Mormons	In visions of the Angel Moroni by Joseph Smith, 1827, in New York, in which he received a new revelation on golden tablets: *The Book of Mormon.*
Orthodox	Original Christian proselytizing in 1st-c; broke with Rome, 1054, after centuries of doctrinal disputes and diverging traditions.
Pentecostal	In Topeka, Kansas (1901), and Los Angeles (1906), in reaction to loss of evangelical fervour among Methodists and other denominations.

CHRISTIANITY (cont.)

Presbyterians	In Calvinist Reformation in 1500s; differed with Lutherans over sacraments, and church government. John Knox founded Scottish Presbyterian Church about 1560
Roman Catholic	Traditionally in the naming of St Peter as the 1st vicar by Jesus; historically, in early Christian proselytizing and the conversion of imperial Rome in the 4th-c.
United Church of Christ	Union of the Congregational and Christian Churches with the Evangelical and Reformed Church. An ecumenical Protestant Church, it allows for variation in organization and interpretation of doctrine but reflects its Reformed theological background.

The Ten Commandments

I	I am the Lord your God, who brought you out of the land of Egypt, out of the house of bondage. You shall have no other gods before me.
II	You shall not make for yourself a graven image. You shall not bow down to them or serve them.
III	You shall not take the name of the Lord your God in vain.
IV	Remember the sabbath day, to keep it holy.
V	Honour your father and your mother.
VI	You shall not kill.
VII	You shall not commit adultery.
VIII	You shall not steal.
IX	You shall not bear false witness against your neighbour.
X	You shall not covet.

The Ten Commandments appear in two different places in the Bible – Exodus 20:17 and Deuteronomy 5:6-21. Most Protestant, Anglican and Orthodox Christians enumerate the Commandments differently from Roman Catholics and Lutherans.

MAJOR IMMOVABLE CHRISTIAN FEASTS

For Saints' Days, *see* p 704.

Jan 1	Solemnity of Mary, Mother of God
Jan 6	Epiphany
Jan 7	Christmas Day (*Eastern Orthodox*)[1]
Jan 11	Baptism of Jesus
Jan 25	Conversion of Apostle Paul
Feb 2	Presentation of Jesus (*Candlemas Day*)
Feb 22	The Chair of Peter, Apostle
Mar 25	Annunciation of the Virgin Mary
Jun 24	Birth of John the Baptist
Aug 6	Transfiguration
Aug 15	Assumption of the Virgin Mary
Aug 22	Queenship of Mary
Sep 8	Birthday of the Virgin Mary
Sep 14	Exaltation of the Holy Cross
Oct 2	Guardian Angels
Nov 1	All Saints
Nov 2	All Souls
Nov 9	Dedication of the Lateran Basilica
Nov 21	Presentation of the Virgin Mary
Dec 8	Immaculate Conception
Dec 25	Christmas Day
Dec 28	Holy Innocents

[1] Fixed feasts in the Julian Calendar fall 13 days later than the Gregorian Calendar date.

MOVABLE CHRISTIAN FEASTS, 1990–2000

Year	Ash Wednesday	Easter	Ascension	Whit Sunday	Sundays after Trinity	Advent	Trinity Sunday	Corpus Christi
1990	28 Feb	15 Apr	24 May	3 Jun	24	2 Dec	10 Jun	14 Jun
1991	13 Feb	31 Mar	9 May	19 May	26	1 Dec	26 May	30 May
1992	4 Mar	19 Apr	28 May	7 Jun	23	29 Nov	14 Jun	18 Jun
1993	24 Feb	11 Apr	20 May	30 May	24	28 Nov	6 Jun	10 Jun
1994	16 Feb	3 Apr	12 May	22 May	25	27 Nov	29 May	2 Jun
1995	1 Mar	16 Apr	25 May	4 Jun	24	3 Dec	11 Jun	15 Jun
1996	21 Feb	7 Apr	16 May	26 May	25	1 Dec	2 Jun	6 Jun
1997	12 Feb	30 Mar	8 May	18 May	26	30 Nov	25 May	29 May
1998	25 Feb	12 Apr	21 May	31 May	24	29 Nov	7 Jun	11 Jun
1999	17 Feb	4 Apr	13 May	23 May	25	28 Nov	30 May	3 Jun
2000	8 Mar	23 Apr	1 Jun	11 Jun	23	3 Dec	18 Jun	22 Jun

Ash Wednesday, the first day of Lent, can fall at the earliest on 4 February and at the latest on 10 March.

Palm (Passion) Sunday is the Sunday before Easter; Good Friday is the Friday before Easter; Holy Saturday (often referred to as Easter Saturday) is the Saturday before Easter; Easter Saturday, in traditional usage, is the Saturday following Easter.

Easter Day can fall at the earliest on 22 March and at the latest on 25 April. Ascension Day can fall at the earliest on 30 April and at the latest on 3 June. Whit Sunday can fall at the earliest on 10 May and at the latest on 13 June. There are not less than 22 and not more than 27 Sundays after Trinity. The first Sunday of Advent is the Sunday nearest to 30 November.

SAINTS' DAYS

The official recognition of Saints, and the choice of a Saint's Day, varies greatly between different branches of Christianity, calendars and localities. Only major variations are included below, using the following abbreviations:

C Coptic *G* Greek
E Eastern *W* Western

January

1 Basil (*E*), Fulgentius, Telemachus
2 Basil and Gregory of Nazianzus (*W*), Macarius of Alexandria, Seraphim of Sarov
3 Geneviève
4 Angela of Foligno
5 Simeon Stylites (*W*)
7 Cedda, Lucian of Antioch (*W*), Raymond of Penyafort
8 Atticus (*E*), Gudule, Severinus
9 Hadrian the African
10 Agatho, Marcian
12 Ailred, Benedict Biscop
13 Hilary of Poitiers
14 Kentigern
15 Macarius of Egypt, Maurus, Paul of Thebes
16 Honoratus
17 Antony of Egypt
19 Wulfstan
20 Euthymius, Fabian, Sebastian
21 Agnes, Fructuosus, Maximus (*E*), Meinrad
22 Timothy (*G*), Vincent
23 Ildefonsus
24 Babylas (*W*), Francis de Sales
25 Gregory of Nazianzus (*E*)
26 Paula, Timothy and Titus, Xenophon (*E*)
27 Angela Merici
28 Ephraem Syrus (*E*), Paulinus of Nola, Thomas Aquinas
29 Gildas
31 John Bosco, Marcella

February

1 Bride, Pionius
3 Anskar, Blaise (*W*), Werburga, Simeon (*E*)
4 Gilbert of Sempringham, Isidore of Pelusium, Phileas
5 Agatha, Avitus
6 Dorothy, Paul Miki and companions, Vedast
8 Theodore (*G*), Jerome Emiliani

SAINTS' DAYS (cont.)

9 Teilo
10 Scholastica
11 Benedict of Aniane, Blaise (*E*), Caedmon, Gregory II
12 Meletius
13 Agabus (*W*), Catherine dei Ricci, Priscilla (*E*)
14 Cyril and Methodius (*W*), Valentine (*W*)
16 Flavian (*E*), Pamphilus (*E*), Valentine (*G*)
18 Bernadette (*France*), Colman, Flavian (*W*), Leo I (*E*)
20 Wulfric
21 Peter Damian
23 Polycarp
25 Ethelbert, Tarasius, Walburga
26 Alexander (*W*), Porphyrius
27 Leander
28 Oswald of York

March
1 David
2 Chad, Simplicius
3 Ailred
4 Casimir
6 Chrodegang
7 Perpetua and Felicity
8 Felix, John of God, Pontius
9 Frances of Rome, Gregory of Nyssa, Pacian
10 John Ogilvie, Macarius of Jerusalem, Simplicius
11 Constantine, Oengus, Sophronius
12 Gregory (the Great)
13 Nicephorus
14 Benedict (*E*)
15 Clement Hofbauer
17 Gertrude, Joseph of Arimathea (*W*), Patrick
18 Anselm of Lucca, Cyril of Jerusalem, Edward
19 Joseph
20 Cuthbert, John of Parma, Martin of Braga
21 Serapion of Thmuis
22 Catherine of Sweden, Nicholas of Fluë
23 Turibius de Mongrovejo
30 John Climacus

April
1 Hugh of Grenoble, Mary of Egypt (*E*), Melito
2 Francis of Paola, Mary of Egypt (*W*)
3 Richard of Chichester
4 Isidore of Seville
5 Juliana of Liège, Vincent Ferrer
7 Hegesippus, John Baptist de la Salle
8 Agabus (*E*)
10 Fulbert
11 Gemma Galgani, Guthlac, Stanislaus
12 Julius I, Zeno
13 Martin I
15 Aristarchus, Pudus (*E*), Trophimus of Ephesus
17 Agapetus (*E*), Stephen Harding
18 Mme Acarie
19 Alphege, Leo IX
21 Anastasius (*E*), Anselm, Beuno, Januarius (*E*)
22 Alexander (*C*)
23 George
24 Egbert, Fidelis of Sigmaringen, Mellitus
25 Mark, Phaebadius
27 Zita
28 Peter Chanel, Vitalis and Valeria
29 Catherine of Siena, Hugh of Cluny, Peter Martyr, Robert
30 James (the Great) (*E*), Pius V

May
1 Asaph, Joseph the Worker, Walburga
2 Athanasius
3 Philip and James (the Less) (*W*)
4 Gotthard
5 Hilary of Arles
7 John of Beverley
8 John (*E*), Peter of Tarantaise
10 Antoninus, Comgall, John of Avila, Simon (*E*)
11 Cyril and Methodius (*E*), Mamertus
12 Epiphanius, Nereus and Achilleus, Pancras
14 Matthias (*W*)
16 Brendan, John of Nepomuk, Simon Stock
17 Robert Bellarmine, Paschal Baylon
18 John I
19 Dunstan, Ivo, Pudens (*W*), Pudentiana (*W*)
20 Bernardino of Siena
21 Helena (*E*)
22 Rita of Cascia
23 Ivo of Chartres
24 Vincent of Lérins
25 Aldhelm, Bede, Gregory VII, Mary Magdalene de Pazzi
26 Philip Neri, Quadratus
27 Augustine of Canterbury
30 Joan of Arc

June
1 Justin Martyr, Pamphilus
2 Erasmus, Marcellinus and Peter, Nicephorus (*G*), Pothinus
3 Charles Lwanga and companions, Clotilde, Kevin
4 Optatus, Petrock
5 Boniface

SAINTS' DAYS (cont.)

6 Martha (*E*), Norbert
7 Paul of Constantinople (*W*), Willibald
8 William of York
9 Columba, Cyril of Alexandria (*E*), Ephraem (*W*)
11 Barnabas, Bartholomew (*E*)
12 Leo III
13 Anthony of Padua
15 Orsisius, Vitus
17 Alban, Botulph
19 Gervasius and Protasius, Jude (*E*), Romuald
20 Alban
21 Alban of Mainz, Aloysius Gonzaga
22 John Fisher and Thomas More, Niceta, Pantaenus (*C*), Paulinus of Nola
23 Etheldreda
24 Birth of John the Baptist
25 Prosper of Aquitaine
27 Cyril of Alexandria (*W*), Ladislaus
28 Irenaeus
29 Peter and Paul
30 First Martyrs of the Church of Rome

July

1 Cosmas and Damian (*E*), Oliver Plunket
3 Anatolius, Thomas
4 Andrew of Crete (*E*), Elizabeth of Portugal, Ulrich
5 Anthony Zaccaria
6 Maria Goretti
7 Palladius, Pantaenus
8 Kilian, Aquila and Prisca (*W*)
11 Benedict (*W*), Pius I
12 John Gualbert, Veronica
13 Henry II, Mildred, Silas
14 Camillus of Lellis, Deusdedit, Nicholas of the Holy Mountain (*E*)
15 Bonaventure, Jacob of Nisibis, Swithin, Vladimir
16 Eustathius, Our Lady of Mt Carmel
17 Ennodius, Leo IV, Marcellina, Margaret (*E*), Scillitan Martyrs
18 Arnulf, Philastrius
19 Macrina, Symmachus
20 Aurelius, Margaret (*W*)
21 Lawrence of Brindisi, Praxedes
22 Mary Magdalene
23 Apollinaris, Bridget of Sweden
25 Anne and Joachim (*E*), Christopher, James (the Great) (*W*)
26 Anne and Joachim (*W*)
27 Pantaleon
28 Innocent I, Samson, Victor I
29 Lupus, Martha (*W*), Olave
30 Peter Chrysologus, Silas (*G*)
31 Giovanni Colombini, Germanus, Joseph of Arimathea (*E*), Ignatius of Loyola

August

1 Alphonsus Liguori, Ethelwold
2 Eusebius of Vercelli, Stephen I
4 Jean-Baptiste Vianney
6 Hormisdas
7 Cajetan, Sixtus II and companions
8 Dominic
9 Matthias (*G*)
10 Laurence, Oswald of Northumbria
11 Clare, Susanna
13 Maximus (*W*), Pontian and Hippolytus, Radegunde
14 Maximilian Kolbe
15 Arnulf, Tarsicius
16 Roch, Simplicianus, Stephen of Hungary
17 Hyacinth
19 John Eudes, Sebaldus
20 Bernard, Oswin, Philibert
21 Jane Frances de Chantal, Pius X
23 Rose of Lima, Sidonius Apollinaris
24 Bartholomew (*W*), Ouen
25 Joseph Calasanctius, Louis IX, Menas of Constantinople
26 Blessed Dominic of the Mother of God, Zephyrinus
27 Caesarius, Monica
28 Augustine of Hippo
29 Beheading of John the Baptist, Sabina
30 Pammachius
31 Aidan, Paulinus of Trier

September

1 Giles, Simeon Stylites (*E*)
2 John the Faster (*E*)
3 Gregory (the Great)
4 Babylas (*E*), Boniface I
5 Zacharias (*E*)
9 Peter Claver, Sergius of Antioch
10 Finnian, Nicholas of Tolentino, Pulcheria
11 Deiniol, Ethelburga, Paphnutius
13 John Chrysostom (*W*)
15 Catherine of Genoa, Our Lady of Sorrows
16 Cornelius, Cyprian of Carthage, Euphemia, Ninian
17 Robert Bellarmine, Hildegard, Lambert, Satyrus
19 Januarius (*W*), Theodore of Tarsus
20 Agapetus or Eustace (*W*)

SAINTS' DAYS (cont.)

21 Matthew (*W*)
23 Adamnan, Linus
25 Sergius of Rostov
26 Cosmas and Damian (*W*), Cyprian of Carthage, John (*E*)
27 Frumentius (*W*), Vincent de Paul
28 Exuperius, Wenceslaus
29 Michael (*Michaelmas Day*), Gabriel and Raphael
30 Jerome, Otto

October
1 Remigius, Romanos, Teresa of the Child Jesus
2 Leodegar (Leger)
3 Teresa of Lisieux, Thomas de Cantilupe
4 Ammon, Francis of Assisi, Petronius
6 Bruno, Thomas (*G*)
9 Demetrius (*W*), Denis and companions, Dionysius of Paris, James (the Less) (*E*), John Leonardi
10 Francis Borgia, Paulinus of York
11 Atticus (*E*), Bruno (*d. 965*), Nectarius
12 Wilfrid
13 Edward the Confessor
14 Callistus I, Cosmas Melodus (*E*)
15 Lucian of Antioch (*E*), Teresa of Avila
16 Gall, Hedwig, Lullus, Margaret Mary Alacoque
17 Ignatius of Antioch, Victor
18 Luke
19 John de Bréboeuf and Isaac Jogues and companions, Paul of the Cross, Peter of Alcántara
21 Hilarion, Ursula
22 Abercius
23 John of Capistrano, James
24 Anthony Claret
25 Crispin and Crispinian, Forty Martyrs of England and Wales, Gaudentius
26 Demetrius (*E*)
28 Firmilian (*E*), Simon and Jude
30 Serapion of Antioch
31 Wolfgang

November
1 All Saints, Cosmas and Damian (*E*)
2 Eustace (*E*), Victorinus
3 Hubert, Malachy, Martin de Porres, Pirminius, Winifred
4 Charles Borromeo, Vitalis and Agricola
5 Elizabeth (*W*)
6 Illtyd, Leonard, Paul of Constantinople (*E*)
7 Willibrord
8 Elizabeth (*E*), Willehad
9 Simeon Metaphrastes (*E*)
10 Justus, Leo I (*W*)
11 Martin of Tours (*W*), Menas of Egypt, Theodore of Studios
12 Josaphat, Martin of Tours (*E*), Nilus the Ascetic
13 Abbo, John Chrysostom (*E*), Nicholas I
14 Dubricius, Gregory Palamas (*E*)
15 Albert the Great, Machutus
16 Edmund of Abingdon, Eucherius, Gertrude (the Great), Margaret of Scotland, Matthew (*E*)
17 Elizabeth of Hungary, Gregory Thaumaturgus, Gregory of Tours, Hugh of Lincoln
18 Odo, Romanus
19 Mechthild, Nerses
20 Edmund the Martyr
21 Gelasius
22 Cecilia
23 Amphilochius, Clement I (*W*), Columban, Felicity, Gregory of Agrigentum
25 Clement I (*E*), Mercurius, Mesrob
26 Siricius
27 Barlam and Josaphat
28 Simeon Metaphrastes
29 Cuthbert Mayne
30 Andrew, Frumentius (*G*)

December
1 Eligius
2 Chromatius
3 Francis Xavier
4 Barbara, John Damascene, Osmund
5 Clement of Alexandria, Sabas
6 Nicholas
7 Ambrose
10 Miltiades
11 Damasus, Daniel
12 Jane Frances de Chantal, Spyridon (*E*), Vicelin
13 Lucy, Odilia
14 John of the Cross, Spyridon (*W*)
16 Eusebius
18 Frumentius (*C*)
20 Ignatius of Antioch (*G*)
21 Peter Canisius, Thomas
22 Anastasia (*E*), Chrysogonus (*E*)
23 John of Kanty
26 Stephen (*W*)
27 John (*W*), Fabiola, Stephen (*E*)
29 Thomas à Becket, Trophimus of Arles
31 Sylvester

CONFUCIANISM

Founded 6th-c BC in China.
Founder K'ung Fu-tse (Confucius) (c.551–479 BC).
Sacred texts Shih Ching, Li Ching, Chu'un Ch'iu, I Ching.
Beliefs The oldest school of Chinese thought, Confucianism did not begin as a religion. Confucius was concerned with the best way to behave and live in this world and was not concerned with the afterlife. He emerges as a great moral teacher who tried to replace the old religious observances with moral values as the basis of social and political order. He laid particular emphasis on the family as the basic unit in society and the foundation of the whole community. He believed that government was a matter of moral responsibility, not just manipulation of power.
Organization Confucianism is not an institution and has no church or clergy. However ancestor-worship and veneration of the sky have their sources in Confucian texts. Weddings and funerals follow a tradition handed down by Confucian scholars. Social life is ritualized and colour and patterns of clothes have a sacred meaning.
Divisions There are two ethical strands in Confucianism. One, associated with Confucious and Hsun Tzu (c.298–238 BC), is conventionalistic: we ought to follow the traditional codes of behaviour for their own sake. The other, associated with Mencius and medieval neo-Confucians, is intuitionistic: we ought to do as our moral natures dictate.

MAJOR CHINESE FESTIVALS

January/February	Chinese New Year
February/March	Lantern Festival
March/April	Festival of Pure Brightness
May/June	Dragon Boat Festival
July/August	Herd Boy and Weaving Maid
August	All Souls' Festival
September	Mid-Autumn Festival
September/October	Double Ninth Festival
November/December	Winter Solstice

HINDUISM

Founded c.1500 BC by Aryan invaders of India with their Vedic religion.
Sacred texts Vedas ('knowledge'), including the Upanishads which are spiritual truths and the epic poems the Ramayana and the Mahabharata. Best known of all is the Bhagavadgita, part of the Mahabharata.
Beliefs Hinduism emphasizes the right way of living (dharma) and embraces many diverse religious beliefs and practices rather than a set of doctrines. It acknowledges many gods who are seen as manifestations of an underlying reality. Devout Hindus aim to become one with the 'absolute reality' or Brahman. Only after a completely pure life will the soul be released from the cycle of rebirth. Until then the soul will be repeatedly reborn. Samsara refers to the cycle of birth and rebirth. Karma is the law by which consequences of actions within one life are carried over into the next.
Organization There is very little formal structure. Hinduism is concerned with the realization of religious values in every part of life yet there is a great emphasis on the performance of complex demanding rituals under the supervision of a Brahman priest and teacher. There are three categories of worship: temple,

HINDUISM (cont.)

domestic and congregational. The most common ceremony is prayer (puja). Many pilgrimages take place and there is an annual cycle of festivals.

Divisions As there is no concept of orthodoxy in Hinduism there are many different sects worshipping different gods. The three most important gods are Brahman, the primeval god, Vishnu, the preserver, and Shiva, both destroyer and creator of life. The three major living traditions are those devoted to Vishnu, Shiva and the goddess Shakti. Folk beliefs and practices exist together with sophisticated philsophical schools.

MAJOR HINDU FESTIVALS

S = Sukla 'waxing fortnight'.
K = Krishna 'waning fortnight'.

Chaitra S 9	Ramanavami (Birthday of Lord Rama)
Asadha S 2	Rathayatra (Pilgrimage of the Chariot at Jagannath)
Sravana S 11–15	Jhulanayatra ('Swinging the Lord Krishna')
Sravana S 15	Rakshabandhana ('Tying on lucky threads')
Bhadrapada K 8	Janamashtami (Birthday of Lord Krishna)
Asvina S 7–10	Durga-puja (Homage to Goddess Durga) (*Bengal*)
Asvina S 1–10	Navaratri (Festival of 'nine nights')
Asvina S 15	Lakshmi-puja (Homage to Goddess Lakshmi)
Asvina K 15	Diwali, Dipavali ('String of Lights')
Kartikka S 15	Guru Nanak Jananti (Birthday of Guru Nanak)
Magha K 5	Sarasvati-puja (Homage to Goddess Sarasvati)
Magha K 13	Maha-sivaratri (Great Night of Lord Shiva)
Phalguna S 14	Holi (Festival of Fire)
Phalguna S 15	Dolayatra (Swing Festival) (*Bengal*)

ISLAM

Founded 7th-c AD.

Founder Mohammed (c.570–c.632).

Sacred texts The Koran, the word of God as revealed to Mohammed and the Hadith, a collection of the prophet's sayings.

Beliefs A monotheistic religion, God is the creator of all things and holds absolute power over man. All persons should devote themselves to lives of grateful and praise-giving obedience to God as they will be judged on the Day of Resurrection. It is acknowledged that Satan often misleads humankind but those who have obeyed God or have repented of their sins will dwell in paradise. Those sinners who are unrepentant will go to hell. Muslims accept the Old Testament and acknowledge Jesus Christ as an important prophet, but they believe the perfect word of God was revealed to Mohammed. Islam imposes five pillars of faith on its followers: belief in one God and his prophet, Mohammed; salat, formal prayer preceded by ritual cleansing five times a day, facing Mecca; saum, fasting during the month of Ramadan; Hajj, pilgrimage to Mecca at least once; zakat, a religious tax on the rich to provide for the poor.

Organization There is no organized priesthood but great respect is accorded to descendants of Mohammed and holymen, scholars and teachers such as mullahs and ayatollahs. The Shari'a is the Islamic law and applies to all aspects of life, not just religious practices.

Divisions There are two main groups within Islam. The Sunni are the majority and the more orthodox. They recognize the succession from Mohammed to Abu Bahkr, his father-in-law, and to the next three caliphs. The Shiites are followers of Ali, Mohammed's nephew and son-in-law. They believe in 12 imams, perfect teachers, who still guide the faithful from paradise. Shi'ah practice tends towards the ecstatic. There are many other subsects including the Sufis, the Ismailis and the Wahhabis.

MAJOR ISLAMIC FESTIVALS

1 Muharram	New Year's Day; starts on the day which celebrates Mohammed's departure from Mecca to Medina in AD 622.
12 Rabi I	Birthday of Mohammed (Mawlid al-Nabi) AD 572; celebrated throughout month of Rabi I.
27 Rajab	'Night of Ascent' (Laylat al-Mi̊raj) of Mohammed to Heaven.
1 Ramadan	Beginning of month of fasting during daylight hours.
27 Ramadan	'Night of Power' (Laylat al-Qadr); sending down of the Koran to Mohammed.
1 Shawwal	'Feast of breaking the Fast' (˘Id al-Fitr); marks the end of Ramadan.
8–13 Dhu-l-Hijja	Annual pilgrimage ceremonies at and around Mecca; month during which the great pilgrimage (Hajj) should be made.
10 Dhu-l-Hijja	Feast of the Sacrifice (˘Id al-Adha).

JAINISM

Founded 6th-c BC in India.
Founder Vardhamana Mahavira (599–527 BC).
Sacred Texts Svetambara canon of scripture and Digambara texts.
Beliefs Jainism is derived from the ancient jinas ('those who overcome'). They believe that salvation consists in conquering material existence through adhering to a strict ascetic discipline, thus freeing the 'soul' from the working of karma for eternal, all-knowing bliss. Liberation requires detachment from worldly existence, an essential part of which is Ahimsa, non-injury to living beings. Jains are also strict vegetarians.
Organization Like Buddhists, the Jains are dedicated to the quest for liberation and the life of the ascetic. However rather than congregating in monastic centres, Jainist monks and nuns have developed a strong relationship with lay people. There are temple rituals resembling Hindu puja. There is also a series of lesser vows and specific religious practices that give the lay person an identifiable religious career.
Divisions There are two categories of religious and philosophical literature. The Svetambara have a canon of scripture consisting of 45 texts, including a group of 11 texts in which the sermons and dialogues of Mahavira himself are collected. The Digambara hold that the original teachings of Mahavira have been lost but that their texts preserve accurately the substance of the original message. This disagreement over scriptures has not led to fundamental doctrinal differences.

JUDAISM

Founded c.2000 BC.
Founder Abraham (c.2000–1650 BC) with whom God made a covenant and Moses (15th–13th-c BC) who gave the Israelites the law.
Sacred texts The Hebrew bible consisting of 24 books, the most important of which are the Torah or Pentateuch – the first five books. Also the Talmud made up of the Mishna, the oral law, and the Gemara, an extensive commentary.
Beliefs A monotheistic religion, the Jews believe God is the creator of the world who delivered the Israelites out of bondage in Egypt, revealed his law to them, and chose them to be a light to all humankind. However varied their communities, Jews see themselves as members of a community whose origins lie in the patriarchal period. Ritual is very important and the family is the basic unit of ritual.
Organization Originally a theocracy, the basic institution is now the synagogue, operated by the congregation and led by a rabbi of their choice. The chief rabbis in France and Britain have authority over those who accept it; in Israel the two chief rabbis have civil authority in family law. The synagogue is the

JUDAISM (cont.)

centre for community worship and study. Its main feature is the 'ark' (a cupboard) containing the hand-written scrolls of the Pentateuch. Daily life is governed by a number of practices and observances: male children are circumcised, the Sabbath is observed, and food has to be correctly prepared. The most important festival is the Passover which celebrates the liberation of the Israelites from Egypt.

Divisions Today most Jews are descendants of either the Ashkenazim or the Sephardim, each with marked cultural differences. There are also several religious branches of Judaism from ultra liberal to ultra conservative, reflecting different points of view regarding the binding character of the prohibitions and duties prescribed for Jews.

MAJOR JEWISH FESTIVALS

For Gregorian calendar equivalents, *see* p 37.

1–2	Tishri	Rosh Hashana (New Year)
3	Tishri	Tzom Gedaliahu (Fast of Gedaliah)
10	Tishri	Yom Kippur (Day of Atonement)
15–21	Tishri	Sukkot (Feast of Tabernacles)
22	Tishri	Shemini Atzeret (8th Day of the Solemn Assembly
23	Tishri	Simchat Torah (Rejoicing of the Law)
25 Kislev– 2–3	Tevet	Hanukkah (Feast of Dedication)
10	Tevet	Asara be-Tevet (Fast of 10th Tevet)
13	Adar	Taanit Esther (Fast of Esther)
14–15	Adar	Purim (Feast of Lots)
15–22	Nisan	Pesach (Passover)
5	Iyar	Israel Independence Day
6–7	Sivan	Shavuot (Feast of Weeks)
17	Tammuz	Shiva Asar be-Tammuz (Fast of 17th Tammuz)
9	Av	Tisha be-Av (Fast of 9th Av)

SHINTOISM

Founded 8th-c AD in Japan.

Sacred texts Kojiki and Nihon Shoki.

Beliefs Shinto 'the teaching' or 'way of the gods', came into existence independently from Buddhism which was coming to the mainland of Japan at that time. It subsequently incorporated many features of Buddhism. Founded on the nature-worship of Japanese folk religions, it is made up of many elements: animism, veneration of nature and ancestor-worship. Its gods are known as kami and there are many ceremonies appealing to these kami for benevolent treatment and protection. Great stress is laid on the harmony between humans, their kami and nature. Moral and physical purity is a basic law. Death and other pollutions are to be avoided. Shinto is primarily concerned with life and this world and the good of the group. Followers must show devotion and sincerity but aberrations can be erased by purification procedures.

Organization As a set of prehistoric agricultural ceremonies Shinto was never supported by a body of philosophical or moralistic literature. Shamans originally performed the ceremonies and tended the shrines, then gradually a particular tribe took over the ceremonies. In the 8th-c Shinto became political with the imperial family ascribed divine origins and state Shintoism was established.

Divisions In the 19th-c Shinto was divided into Shrine (jinga) Shinto and Sectarian (kyoko) Shinto. Jinga became a state cult and it remained the national religion until 1945.

MAJOR JAPANESE FESTIVALS

Public holidays in Japan are listed on p 268. In addition, the following festivals should be noted:

1–3 Jan	Oshogatsu (New Year)
3 Mar	Ohinamatsuri (Doll's *or* Girls' Festival)
5 May	Tango no Sekku (Boys' Festival)
7 Jul	Hoshi matsuri *or* Tanabata (Star Festival)
13–31 Jul	Obon (Buddhist All Souls)

SIKHISM

Founded 15th-c in India.
Founder Guru Nanak (1469–1539).
Sacred text Adi Granth.
Beliefs Nanak preached tolerance and devotion to one God before whom everyone is equal. Sikh is the Sanskrit word for disciple. Nanak's doctrine sought a fusion of Brahmanism and Islam on the grounds that both were monotheistic. God is the true Guru and his divine word has come to humanity through the ten historical gurus. The line ended in 1708 since when the Sikh community is called guru.
Organization There is no priestly caste and all Sikhs are empowered to perform rituals connected with births, marriages, and deaths. Sikhs worship in their own temples but they evolved distinct features like the langar, 'kitchen', a communal meal where people of any religion or caste could eat. Rest houses for travellers were also provided. The tenth guru instituted an initiation ceremony, the Khalsa. Initiates wear the Five Ks (uncut hair, steel bangle, comb, shorts, ceremonial sword) and a turban. Members of the Khalsa add the name singh (lion) to their name and have to lead pure lives and follow a code of discipline. Sikhs generally rise before dawn, bathe and recite the japji, a morning prayer. Hindu festivals from northern India are observed.
Divisions There are several religious orders of Sikhs based either on disputes over the succession of gurus or points of ritual and tradition. The most important current issue is the number of Khalsa Sikhs cutting off their hair and beards and relapsing into Hinduism.

TAOISM

Founded 600 BC in China.
Founder Lao-tzu (6th-c BC).
Sacred texts Chuang-tzu, Lao-tzu (Tao-te-ching).
Beliefs Taoism is Chinese for 'the school of the tao' and the 'Taoist religion'. Tao ('the way') is central in both Confucianism and Taoism. The former stresses the tao of humanity, the latter the tao of nature, harmony with which ensures appropriate conduct. Taoist religion developed later and was probably influenced by Buddhist beliefs. The doctrine emphasizes that good and evil action decide the fate of the soul. The Taoists believe that the sky, the earth and water are deities; that Lao-tzu is supreme master; that the disciple masters his body and puts evil spirits to flight with charms; that body and spirit are purified through meditation and by taking the pill of immortality to gain eternal life; and that the way is handed down from master to disciple. Religious Taoism incorporated ideas and images from philosophical Taoist texts, especially the Tao-te-ching but also the theory of Yin-yang, the quest for immortality, mental and physical discipline, interior hygiene, internal alchemy, healing and exorcism, a pantheon of gods and spirits, and ideals of theocratic states. The Immortals are meant to live in the mountains far from the tumult of the world.
Organization This is similar to Buddhism in the matter of clergy and temple. The jiao is a ceremony to purify the ground. Zhon-gyual is the only important religious festival, when the hungry dead appear to the living and Taoist priests free the souls of the dead from suffering.
Divisions Religious Taoism emerged from many sects. These sects proliferated between 618 and 1126 AD and were described collectively as Spirit Cloud Taoists. They form the majority of Taoist priests in Taiwan, where they are called 'Masters of Methods' or Red-headed Taoists. The more orthodox priests are called 'Tao Masters' or Black-headed Taoists.

SACRED TEXTS OF WORLD RELIGIONS

Religion	Texts
Baha'ism	Kitab al-Aqdas, Haft Wadi, al-Kalimat al-Maknnah, Bayan
Buddhism	Tripitaka, Mahayana Sutra, Milindapanha, Bardo Thodol
Christianity	Old Testament: Genesis, Exodus, Leviticus, Numbers, Deuteronomy, Joshua,-Judges, Ruth, 1 Samuel, 2 Samuel, 1 Kings, 2 Kings, 1 Chronicles, 2 Chronicles, Ezra, Nehemiah, Esther, Job, Psalms, Proverbs, Ecclesiastes, Song of Solomon, Isaiah, Jeremiah, Lamentations, Ezekiel, Daniel, Hosea, Joel, Amos, Obadiah, Jonah, Micah, Nahum, Habakkuk, Zephaniah, Haggai, Zechariah, Malachi. New Testament: Matthew, Mark, Luke, John, Acts of the Apostles, Romans, 1 Corinthians, 2 Corinthians, Galatians, Ephesians, Philippians, Colossians, 1 Thessalonians, 2 Thessalonians, 1 Timothy, 2 Timothy, Titus, Philemon, ,Hebrews, James, 1 Peter, 2 Peter, 1 John, 2 John, 3 John, Jude, Revelation. Apocrypha: 1 Esdras, 2 Esdras, Tobit, Judith, Additions to Esther, Wisdom of Solomon, Ecclesiasticus, Epistle of Jeremiah, Baruch, Prayer of Azariah, Song of the Three Young Men, (History of) Susanna, Bel and the Dragon, Prayer of Manasses, 1 Maccabees, 2 Maccabbees. (The Roman Catholic Church includes Tobit, Judith, all of Esther, Maccabbees 1 and 2, Wisdom of Solomon, Ecclesiasticus, and Baruch in its canon.)
Confucianism	Shih ching, Li ching, Shu ching, Chu'un Ch'iu, I Ching
Hinduism	Vedas (Upanishads), Ramayana, Mahabharata and the Bhagavad Gita
Islam	The Koran, the Hadith
Jainism	Svetambara canon, Digambara texts
Judaism	The Hebrew Bible: Torah (Pentateuch): Genesis, Exodus, Leviticus, Numbers, Deuteronomy. Also the books of the Prophets, Psalms, Chronicles and Proverbs. The Talmud including the Mishna and Gemara. The Zohar (Book of Splendour) is a famous Cabalistic book.
Mormons	Book of Mormon
Mandeans	Ginza, Book of John
Shintoism	Kojiki, Nohon Shoki
Sikhism	Adi Granth
Taoism	Chuang-tzu, Lao-tzu (Tao-te-ching)

POPULATION DISTRIBUTION OF MAJOR BELIEFS

Figures have been compiled from the most accurate recent available information and are in most cases correct to the nearest 1%.

Where possible within Islam the relative proportion of Sunnis and Shiites is indicated.

No precise information was available for the following: Cyprus, Hong Kong, Lebanon, Micronesia, Mongolia.

Afro-Cuban syncretism
Cuba 2%

Animism
Cameroon 25%
Côte d'Ivoire 60%
Zimbabwe 40%

Bahaism
Bolivia 3%
French Guiana 1%
Kiribati 2%
Panama 1%
Papua New Guinea 1%
Tuvalu 1%
Virgin Islands (USA) 1%

Buddhism
Australia 1%
Bangladesh 1%
Bhutan 70%
Brunei 12%
Burma 89%
Cambodia 88%
China 6%
India 1%
Indonesia 1%
Japan 38%
Korea, North 2%
Korea, South 18%
Laos 58%
Macau 45%
Malaysia 17%
Nepal 5%
Singapore 28%
Sri Lanka 69%
Taiwan 43%
Thailand 95%
Vietnam 55%

Chinese folk religion
China 20%
Laos 1%
Malaysia 12%
Taiwan 49%

Chondogyo
Korea, North 14%

Christianity

1 Protestantism (includes all non-Roman Catholic denominations)
Andorra 1%
Angola 21%
Antigua and Barbuda 86%
Aruba 9%
Australia 47%
Austria 8%
Bahamas 75%
Barbados 65%
Belize 31%
Benin 3%
Bermuda 73%
Botswana 41%
Brazil 6%
Bulgaria 27%
Burkina Faso 2%
Burundi 7%
Cameroon 18%
Canada 42%
Central African Republic 50%
Chad 12%
Chile 6%
Côte d'Ivoire 5%
Commonwealth of Independent States 35%
Congo 39%
Cuba 3%
Czechoslovakia 26%
Denmark 91%
Djibouti 2%
Dominica 16%
Ethiopia 53%
Faeroe Islands 94%
Finland 90%
France 4%
French Guiana 4%
French Polynesia 55%
Gabon 31%
German Democratic Republic (East Germany) 47%
Germany, Federal Republic of (West Germany) 42%
Ghana 44%
Greece 98%
Greenland 98%
Grenada 35%
Guam 17%
Guatemala c.25%
Guyana 31%
Haiti 16%
Honduras 10%
Hungary 24%
Iceland 97%
Indonesia 7%
Ireland 3%
Jamaica 56%
Kenya 47%
Kiribati 42%
Korea, South 41%
Laos 1%
Lesotho 49%
Liechtenstein 8%
Luxembourg 1%
Macau 1%
Madagascar 25%
Malawi 37%
Malta 1%
Martinique 12%
Mauritius 4%
Mexico 3%
Mozambique 8%
Namibia 62%
Netherlands Antilles 10%
Netherlands, The 27%
New Zealand 47%
Nigeria 37%
Norway 88%
Panama 5%
Papua New Guinea 64%
Paraguay 2%
Philippines 10%
Portugal 1%
Puerto Rico 5%

DISTRIBUTION OF MAJOR BELIEFS (cont.)

Romania 80%
Rwanda 9%
Saint Kitts and Nevis 83%
Saint Lucia 11%
Saint Vincent and the Grenadines 77%
Seychelles 8%
Sierra Leone 6%
Solomon Islands 78%
South Africa 68%
Sudan, The 2%
Suriname 19%
Swaziland 66%
Sweden 90%
Switzerland 44%
Togo 7%
Tonga 73%
Trinidad and Tobago 28%
Tuvalu 98%
Uganda 29%
UK 74%
Uruguay 3%
USA 58%
Vanuatu 67%
Virgin Islands (USA) 64%
Western Samoa 72%
Yugoslavia 46%
Zaire 46%
Zambia 46%
Zimbabwe 33%

2 Roman Catholicism
Algeria 1%
Andorra 94%
Angola 69%
Antigua and Barbuda 10%
Argentina 93%
Aruba 89%
Australia 26%
Austria 84%
Bahamas 19%
Barbados 4%
Belgium 90%
Belize 62%
Benin 19%
Bermuda 14%
Bolivia 93%
Botswana 9%
Brazil 88%
Bulgaria 1%
Burkina Faso 10%
Burundi 78%
Cameroon 35%
Canada 47%
Cape Verde 98%
Central African Republic 33%
Chad 21%
Chile 81%
Côte d'Ivoire 15%
Colombia 95%
Commonwealth of Independent States 2%
Congo 54%
Costa Rica 89%
Cuba 40%
Czechoslovakia 66%
Denmark 1%
Djibouti 4%
Dominica 77%
Dominican Republic 92%
Ecuador 94%
El Salvador 93%
France 76%
French Guiana 87%
French Polynesia 39%
Gabon 65%
German Democratic Republic (East Germany) 7%
Germany, Federal Republic of (West Germany) 43%
Ghana 19%
Grenada 59%
Guadeloupe 91%
Guam 80%
Guatemala c.75%
Guyana 11%
Haiti 80%
Honduras 85%
Hungary 62%
Iceland 1%
Indonesia 3%
Ireland 93%
Italy 83%
Jamaica 5%
Kenya 26%
Kiribati 53%
Korea, South 3%
Laos 1%
Lesotho 44%
Liechtenstein 87%
Luxembourg 93%
Macau 7%
Madagascar 26%
Malawi 28%
Malta 97%
Martinique 88%
Mauritius 26%
Mexico 93%
Monaco 90%
Mozambique 31%
Namibia 20%
Netherlands Antilles 84%
Netherlands, The 36%
New Caledonia 63%
New Zealand 15%
Nicaragua 88%
Nigeria 12%
Panama 84%
Papua New Guinea 33%
Paraguay 96%
Peru 92%
Philippines 84%
Poland 95%
Portugal 95%
Puerto Rico 85%
Réunion 90%
Rwanda 65%
São Tomé and Príncipe c.84%
Saint Kitts and Nevis 7%
Saint Lucia 86%
Saint Vincent and the Grenadines 19%
San Marino 95%
Senegal 6%
Seychelles 91%
Sierra Leone 2%
Solomon Islands 19%
South Africa 10%
Spain 97%
Sudan, The 6%
Suriname 23%
Swaziland 11%
Sweden 2%
Switzerland 48%
Togo 22%
Tonga 16%
Trinidad and Tobago 32%
Uganda 50%
UK 13%
Uruguay 60%
USA 30%
Vanuatu 15%
Venezuela 92%
Vietnam 7%
Virgin Islands (USA) 34%
Western Samoa 22%

DISTRIBUTION OF MAJOR BELIEFS (cont.)

Yugoslavia 26%
Zaire 48%
Zambia 26%
Zimbabwe 12%

3 Unspecified
Albania 5%
Bahrain 7%
Brunei 9%
Burma 5%
Egypt c.10%
Equatorial Guinea 89%
Ethiopia 5%
Fiji 53%
Gambia, The 4%
Guinea 2%
Guinea-Bissau 5%
India 2%
Iran 1%
Iraq 4%
Israel 2%
Japan 4%
Jordan 5%
Korea, North 1%
Kuwait 8%
Liberia 68%
Malaysia 6%
Mali 1%
Mayotte 3%
Morocco 1%
Pakistan 2%
Qatar 6%
Saudi Arabia 1%
Singapore 19%
Sri Lanka 8%
Syria 9%
Taiwan 7%
Tanzania 34%
Thailand 1%
United Arab Emirates 4%

Druze
Israel 2%

Hinduism
Bangladesh 12%
Bhutan 25%
Burma 1%
Fiji 38%
Guyana 37%
India 83%
Indonesia 2%
Kuwait 2%
Malaysia 7%
Mauritius 53%
Nepal 90%
Oman 13%
Pakistan 2%
Qatar 1%
Seychelles 1%
Singapore 5%
South Africa 2%
Sri Lanka 16%
Suriname 27%
Trinidad and Tobago 24%
UK 1%

Islam
Afghanistan 99%
(Shiite 25%, Sunni 74%)
Albania 21%
Algeria 99% (Sunni)
Australia 1%
Austria 1%
Bahrain 85%
(Shiite 51%, Sunni 34%)
Bangladesh 87%
Belgium 1%
Benin 15%
Bhutan 5%
Brunei 67%
Bulgaria 8%
Burkina Faso 43%
Burma 4%
Burundi 1%
Cambodia 2%
Cameroon 22%
Central African Republic 3%
Chad 44%
China 2%
Côte D'Ivoire 20%
Commonwealth of Independent States 12%
Comoros 100% (Sunni)
Djibouti 94% (Sunni)
Egypt c.90% (Sunni)
Equatorial Guinea 1%
Ethiopia 31%
Fiji 8%
France 3%
French Guiana 1%
Gabon 1%
Gambia, The 95%
Germany, Federal Republic of (West Germany) 3%
Ghana 16%
Greece 2%
Guinea 85%
Guinea-Bissau 30%
Guyana 9%
India 11%
Indonesia 87%
Iran 99%
(Shiite 91%, Sunni 8%)
Iraq 96%
(Shiite 54%, Sunni 42%)
Israel 14%
Jordan 93% (Sunni)
Kenya 6%
Kuwait 90%
(Shiite 27%, Sunni 63%)
Laos 1%
Liberia 14%
Libya 97% (Sunni)
Madagascar 2%
Malawi 16%
Malaysia 53%
Maldives 100% (Sunni)
Mali 90%
Mauritania 99%
Mauritius 13%
Mayotte 97% (Sunni)
Morocco 99% (mostly Sunni)
Mozambique 13%
Nepal 3%
New Caledonia 4% (Sunni)
Niger 80% (Sunni)
Nigeria 45%
Oman 86%
Pakistan 97%
Panama 5%
Philippines 4%
Qatar 92% (mostly Sunni)
Réunion 1%
Romania 1%
Rwanda 9%
Saudi Arabia 99% (mostly Sunni)
Senegal 91% (Sunni)
Sierra Leone 39% (Sunni)
Singapore 16%
Somalia 100% (Sunni)
South Africa 1%
Sri Lanka 8%
Sudan, The 73%
Suriname 20%
Syria 90% (mostly Sunni)

DISTRIBUTION OF MAJOR BELIEFS (cont.)

Taiwan 1%
Tanzania 33%
Thailand 4%
Togo 12%
Trinidad and Tobago 6%
Tunisia 99% (Sunni)
Turkey 99% (Sunni)
Uganda 7%
UK 1%
United Arab Emirates 95% (Shiite 20%, Sunni 80%)
USA 2%
Vietnam 1%
Yemen, Republic of 100% (Shiite 47%, Sunni 43%)
Yugoslavia 10%
Zaire 1%

Jainism
India 1%

Judaism
Canada 1%
Commonwealth of Independent States 1%
Hungary 1%
Israel 82%
UK 1%
Uruguay 2%
USA 3%

Non-religious belief
Albania 74%
Aruba 2%
Australia 13%
Austria 6%
Barbados 18%
Belgium 8%
Belize 1%
Bermuda 8%
Brazil 1%
Brunei 9%
Bulgaria 65%
Canada 7%
Chile 13%
China 71%
Commonwealth of Independent States 50%
Cuba 55%
Equatorial Guinea 6%
Finland 9%
France 3%
French Guiana 3%
French Polynesia 5%
Guyana 4%
Haiti 1%
Hungary 13%
Iceland 1%
Italy 16%
Jamaica 18%
Korea, North 68%
Korea, South 36%
Laos 5%
Mexico 3%
Netherlands Antilles 3%
Netherlands, The 33%
New Zealand 16%
Norway 3%
Portugal 4%
Romania 16%
San Marino 3%
Singapore 18%
Solomon Islands 3%
Spain 3%
Trinidad and Tobago 1%
UK 9%
Uruguay 35%
USA 7%
Vanuatu 1%
Virgin Islands (USA) 1%

Rastafarianism
Antigua and Barbuda 1%
Jamaica c.5%

Shintoism
Japan 40%

Sikhism
Fiji 1%
India 2%

Spiritism
Brazil 4%
French Guiana 2%

Taoism
Singapore 13%

Traditional beliefs
Angola 10%
Benin 61%
Botswana 49%
Burkina Faso 45%
Burma 1%
Burundi 14%
Central African Republic 12%
Chad 23%
Congo 5%
Equatorial Guinea 5%
Ethiopia 11%
French Guiana 2%
Gabon 3%
Ghana 21%
Guinea 5%
Guinea-Bissau 65%
Kenya 19%
Korea, North 16%
Laos 34%
Lesotho 6%
Madagascar 47%
Malawi 19%
Mali 9%
Mozambique 48%
Niger 20%
Nigeria 6%
Papua New Guinea 3%
Rwanda 17%
Senegal 3%
Sierra Leone 52%
Sudan, The 17%
Swaziland 21%
Togo 59%
Vanuatu 8%
Zaire 3%
Zambia 27%

SIGNS OF THE ZODIAC

Signs of the Zodiac